Becoming A Teacher

Forrest W. Parkay
Washington State University

Director and Publisher: Kevin Davis
Portfolio Manager: Rebecca Fox-Gieg
Managing Content Producer: Megan Moffo
Content Producer: Yagnesh Jani
Managing Digital Producer: Autumn Benson
Media Project Manager: Daniel Dwyer
Portfolio Management Assistant: Maria Feliberty
Digital Development Editor: Christina Robb, Revampire LLC.
Executive Field Marketing Manager: Krista Clark
Procurement Specialist: Deidra Headlee
Cover and Interior Design: Pearson CSC
Cover Art: Steve Debenport/gettyimages, Monkey Business Images/Shutterstock, and SolStock/gettyimages
Full Service Vendor: Pearson CSC
Full Service Project Management: Pearson CSC, Emily Tamburri
Printer/Binder: LSC Communications, Inc.
Cover Printer: LSC Communications, Inc.
Text Font: PalatinoLTPro-Roman

Credits and acknowledgments for material borrowed from other sources and reproduced, with permission, in this textbook appear on the appropriate pages within the text.

Library of Congress Cataloging-in-Publication Data

Names: Parkay, Forrest W., author.
Title: Becoming A teacher / Forrest W. Parkay.
Description: Eleventh edition. | Boston, MA : Pearson Education, [2018] | Includes bibliographical references and indexes.
Identifiers: LCCN 2018041781 | ISBN 9780134990552 | ISBN 0134990552
Subjects: LCSH: Teaching--Vocational guidance. | Education--Study and teaching--United States.
Classification: LCC LB1775 .P28 2018 | DDC 370.71/1--dc23
LC record available at https://lccn.loc.gov/2018041781

ISBN 10: 0-134-99055-2
ISBN 13: 978-0-134-99055-2

Preface

Teaching is the world's most important profession. As you know from your own experience, teachers make a difference in students' lives. Teaching is immensely satisfying and exciting. In today's climate of accountability, high-stakes testing, and legislation such as the Every Student Succeeds Act (ESSA), however, becoming a successful teacher is challenging and requires professionalism and commitment.

The 11th edition of *Becoming a Teacher* continues to listen to the voices of those who care deeply about teaching—professionals and expert teachers, beginning teachers just learning the ropes, students in America's classrooms, and teacher education students deciding if teaching is their best career path—to help readers discover the answer to the question, "Is teaching for me?"

With the help of these stakeholders, the 11th edition focuses on teacher quality and provides in-depth coverage of critical issues such as the following:

- Every Student Succeeds Act (ESSA)
- Diversity and culturally competent teaching
- Social justice and democracy
- Students of undocumented immigrant parents
- Teacher leadership, political activism, and change facilitation
- Adverse Childhood Experiences (ACE) Study and trauma-sensitive schools
- Federal education agenda

Becoming a Teacher embraces and articulates the changing field of education, outlining ways to be an agent of change in the profession, pinpointing meaningful uses of technology in education, clarifying realities of diversity in the classroom, and clearly outlining past, present, and future thoughts on curriculum, instruction, assessment, management, philosophy, and issues in education. This down-to-earth and straightforward approach provides students with the tools and information necessary to answer the questions, "What does it take to become a high-quality teacher?" and "Do I want to teach?"

A Thoroughly Revised New Edition

The 11th edition is thoroughly revised and draws attention to the rapidly changing climate in education. I approached this revision of *Becoming a Teacher* with an eye toward providing readers with cutting-edge information impacting the teaching profession. I've also revised the text to present this information in clear, reader-friendly language. In response to reviewers' feedback, new research, and emerging trends, the 11th edition reflects the following important changes and additions.

Revel: A New Interactive Format

One of the many enhancements in this highly revised edition of *Becoming a Teacher* is the new format of the digital version, REVEL. Fully digital and highly engaging, REVEL can completely replace the print textbook and gives you everything you need to efficiently master course concepts. REVEL is an interactive learning environment that seamlessly blends *Becoming a Teacher's* narrative, media, assessments, and grading, enabling you to read, practice, and study in one continuous experience. Informed by extensive research on how people read, think, and learn, REVEL is designed to measurably boost your understanding, retention, and preparedness.

The REVEL version of *Becoming a Teacher* presents content in manageable pieces that makes it easier for you to locate, process, and remember key material. Videos and interactive exercises are interspersed regularly within the text to foster your active engagement with the content, helping you to remember it better—and more importantly—to use and apply it. The unique presentation of media as an intrinsic part of course content brings the hallmark features of Pearson's bestselling titles to life. The media interactives in REVEL have been designed to be completed quickly, and its videos are brief, so you stay focused and on task.

Dynamic content designed for the way today's students read, think, and learn brings concepts to life.

- Interactive **Application Exercises** are interspersed frequently and foster a more active role in learning. These take a variety of forms. At times, you will be presented with a video and an open-ended question that requires you to examine the video critically and respond using evidence from the video and your understanding of chapter concepts. At other times, questions require analysis of a written case. Feedback is provided for support.
- **Check Your Understanding quizzes**, located at the ends of each major section of text, present you with opportunities to check your understanding of text concepts at regular intervals via a multiple-choice quiz before moving on.
- A chapter-ending **Shared Writing** assignment allows all the students in your class to read and respond to the same prompt. You and your classmates have the opportunity to see each other's postings, creating a space for asynchronous discussion of the text.

- Case-based surveys called **Poll Your Peers** occur at the beginning of each major section of the book. These surveys present a real-life scenario relevant to the topics covered in the book section and ask you how you would respond. This activates your prior knowledge and opinions, a teaching strategy that promotes interest and effectively sets the stage for learning. After responding, you will get to see how your fellow students responded, which can prompt meaningful class discussions.
- Integrated within the narrative, **videos** empower you to engage with concepts and view a variety of teachers and classrooms, which otherwise wouldn't be available to you at this stage in your education.
- The REVEL **mobile app** lets you read, practice, and study—anywhere, anytime, on any device. Content is available both online and offline, and the app syncs work across all registered devices automatically, giving you great flexibility to toggle between phone, tablet, and laptop as you move through your day. The app also lets you set assignment notifications to stay on top of all due dates.
- A detailed Standards Mapping document that shows how each REVEL activity aligns with the subcategories of the 10 InTASC Standards and the edTPA content addressing planning, instruction, and assessment.
- **Highlighting, note taking, and a glossary** let you read and study however you like. Educators can add notes for you, too, including reminders or study tips.

Superior assignability and tracking tools help educators make sure students are completing their reading and understanding core concepts.

- The **assignment calendar** allows educators to indicate precisely which readings must be completed on which dates. This clear, detailed schedule helps students stay on task by eliminating any ambiguity as to which material will be covered during each class. When they understand exactly what is expected of them, students are better motivated to keep up.
- The **performance dashboard** empowers educators to monitor class assignment completion as well as individual student achievement. Actionable information, such as points earned on quizzes and tests and time on task, helps educators intersect with their students in meaningful ways. For example, the trending column reveals whether students' grades are improving or declining, helping educators to identify students who might need help to stay on track.
- **Blackboard Learn™ integration** provides institutions, instructors, and students easy access to their REVEL courses. With single sign-on, students can be ready to access an interactive blend of authors' narrative, media, and assessment on their first day. Flexible, on-demand grade synchronization capabilities allow educators to control exactly which REVEL grades should be transferred to the Blackboard Gradebook.

Important Content Changes In The New Edition

New Chapters

- CHAPTER 11, Curriculum, Standards, Assessment, and Student Learning, focuses on what students should know and be able to do to be successful in today's competitive world. Factors influencing the development of educational standards, curriculum, and assessments are included.
- CHAPTER 13, Becoming a Professional Teacher, provides information on the transition between student and teacher to ensure that the induction to teaching is positive and effective. The development of leadership roles is also discussed.

An Emphasis on Standards to Prepare Prospective Teachers to Meet Key Performance Standards

- The 11th edition of *Becoming a Teacher* provides prospective teachers with guidelines for acquiring the knowledge and skills necessary to meet the performance standards developed by the Interstate Teacher Assessment and Support Consortium (InTASC), the Council for the Accreditation of Educator Preparation (CAEP), the Praxis Series: Professional Assessments for Beginning Teachers, and the National Board for Professional Teaching Standards (NBPTS). The book also prepares readers to meet the accountability criteria contained in the Every Student Succeeds Act (ESSA).

An Emphasis on the Diversity of Students and their Teachers

- **Focus on Diversity** These sections in each chapter address cultural and ethnic diversity, student ability, the impact of socioeconomic status, as well as linguistic diversity in today's classrooms. The sections introduce readers to culturally competent teaching and help them learn how to meet students' diverse needs in every classroom. Throughout, special attention is paid to the education of children of undocumented immigrant parents, students protected from deportation by the Deferred Action for Childhood Arrivals (DACA) program, and students from vulnerable groups.

- **Comprehensive State Coverage** To ensure that students and teachers from all over the country see themselves mirrored in the content, the 11th edition specifically highlights master teachers, instructional issues, and curriculum initiatives from across the United States. An index of highlighted states is presented at the end of the Preface.

New Sections Highlight the Importance of STEM

- **Focus on STEM** Throughout the 11th edition, Focus on STEM sections highlight the importance of science, technology, engineering, and mathematics (STEM) at all levels of the school curriculum. These sections show how STEM activities develop students' critical thinking, creativity, design thinking, and problem-solving skills.

Latest Trends in Technology and Teaching

A thoroughly revised technology chapter explains how teachers can integrate technology into teaching in order to engage today's tech-savvy students fully and to adjust to the reality that technology has transformed how, when, and where students can learn. From blogs and wikis, to podcasting and 3-D virtual worlds, the 11th edition is filled with case examples of how teachers are integrating technology and transforming their teaching to foster collaboration, discovery, and understanding of the "big ideas" in the curriculum.

New and Expanded Chapter Coverage to Address the Most Current Trends and Issues

CHAPTER 1, Teaching: Your Chosen Profession

- Reasons why teachers join the profession (NEW)
- Qualities principals look for in a new teacher (NEW)
- Key provisions of Every Student Succeeds Act (ESSA) (NEW)
- Teachers' views on time to prepare students for tests (NEW)
- Latest data on school enrollments, race/ethnicity of students and teachers, school staffing, and teacher salaries

CHAPTER 2, Today's Teachers

- Revised chapter now covers the unique benefits of teaching in urban, suburban, and rural settings and the role of "pedagogical expertise" in teaching.
- Focus on Diversity: Black Teachers as Role Models for Black Students (NEW)
- Updated demographic information on U.S. public school teachers

CHAPTER 3, Today's Schools

- Revised chapter now covers the Adverse Childhood Experiences (ACE) Study, the impact of trauma on students' learning, and school-based wraparound services,
- Trauma-sensitive schools and trauma-sensitive school checklist (NEW)
- Expanded analysis of America's continuing dropout problem, homeless children and youth, and child maltreatment in the United States
- Updated data on child well-being in the United States, drug use among students, crime in public schools, cyberbullying, discipline problems, and dropout rates

CHAPTER 4, Philosophical Foundations of U.S. Education

- Focus on STEM: Science, Technology, Engineering, and Mathematics for the 21st Century (NEW)
- Matrix for comparing the underlying belief systems of five philosophical orientations to teaching (NEW)
- Matrix for comparing the underlying belief systems of three psychological orientations to teaching (NEW)

CHAPTER 5, Historical Foundations of U.S. Education

- Revised chapter now covers key role of teachers in preserving U.S. democracy, textbooks and American values, and the push for voucher and charter school programs under the Trump Administration.
- Every Student Succeeds Act (ESSA) and expanded role of states in educational reform (NEW)
- Updated historical timeline for U.S. education
- A new federal education agenda—diminishing support for public schools (NEW)

CHAPTER 6, Governance and Finance of U.S. Schools

- Revised chapter includes updated, expanded coverage of: state takeover of the School District of Philadelphia; state-level high school exit exams; implementation of the Every Student Succeeds Act (ESSA) under the Trump administration; and state-level voucher systems.
- Summary of five "major themes" of the Trump administration's 2018 Education Budget (New)
- Focus on STEM: A Memo from the President (NEW)
- Updated figures and tables for data on the 10 largest U.S. school districts, school expenditures, distribution

of expenditures, sources of school revenues, state education revenues, and funding priorities for education philanthropy

CHAPTER 7, Ethical and Legal Issues in U.S. Education

- Revised chapter includes updated, expanded coverage of court cases involving teachers and online social networking, student expression on social networking sites, dress codes, cyberbullying, and homeschooling.
- Updated references throughout the chapter reflect the most recent court rulings on legal issues in U.S. education
- Section on education of students protected by the Deferred Action for Childhood Arrivals (DACA) program
- Focus on Diversity: Education of Students of Undocumented Immigrant Parents (NEW)
- Focus on STEM: Design for STEM Lab Triggers Complaint to U.S. Office of Civil Rights (NEW)
- Focus on Diversity: Schoolchildren Denied Right to Literacy (NEW)

CHAPTER 8, Today's Students

- Revised chapter includes updated, expanded coverage of minority groups and academic achievement and Afrocentric schools.
- Focus on Diversity: Students of Undocumented Immigrant Parents (NEW)
- Section on the achievement gap (NEW)
- Focus on STEM: Female Students Outperform Male Students in Technology and Engineering Literacy (NEW)
- Focus on STEM: Integrating Tribal Knowledge with STEM (NEW)
- Addressing the Learning Needs of Native American and Alaskan Natives (NEW)
- How Are Schools Meeting the Needs of English Language Learners? (NEW)
- Revised and updated section, Advice for Monolingual Teachers
- Revised and updated section, What Is Multicultural Education and Culturally Responsive Teaching?
- Updated figures and tables for data on children of immigrant families, English language learners (ELLs), children living in poverty, and low-income families in the United States

CHAPTER 9, Addressing Learners' Individual Needs

- Revised chapter includes updated research on multiple intelligences.
- Focus on Diversity: National Policy Rhetoric and Stress among Vulnerable Students (NEW)
- Section on Adverse Childhood Experiences (ACEs) and their influence on health and well-being (NEW)
- Focus on STEM: Students with Special Needs Benefit from STEM (NEW)
- Focus on STEM: Vanderbilt University Offers STEM Program for Gifted and Talented (NEW)
- IDEA and Every Student Succeeds Act (ESSA) (NEW)
- New example of an Individualized Education Plan (IEP)
- Updated figures and tables for data on children with disabilities

CHAPTER 10, Creating a Community of Learners

- Revised chapter includes updated, expanded coverage of cooperative learning and cross-cultural interaction, successful classroom management, and assertive discipline.
- Graphic for Top 10 Qualities of an Effective Teacher (NEW)
- Focus on STEM: Collaboration and Teamwork Promote STEM Learning for Girls (NEW)
- Explanation of Restorative Justice (NEW)
- Graphic comparing punitive and restorative justice responses in schools (NEW)
- Updated figures and tables for data on discipline problems at school and assertive discipline policy

CHAPTER 11, Curriculum, Standards, Assessment, and Student Learning (NEW)

- Focus on Diversity: Using Curriculum to Address Racism (NEW)
- Updated sections on grit, tenacity, and perseverance; academic mindset; mindfulness/meditation skills; and curricula to enhance noncognitive strengths
- Section on the Trump administration's position regarding the Common Core State Standards Initiative (CCSSI) (NEW)
- Latest data on students' mathematics, reading, and science performance on the Program for International Student Assessment (PISA) (NEW)
- Graphic for factors in school quality (NEW)
- Focus on STEM: Future City Competition Provides Authentic Learning Experiences (NEW)

CHAPTER 12, Integrating Technology into Teaching

- Thoroughly revised chapter (with contributions by Joan Hughes, co-author of the 8th edition of *Integrating Educational Technology into Teaching* (Pearson,

2018), includes updated, expanded coverage of how technology is transforming teaching, virtual schools, availability and use of technology in schools, and the latest research studies on the use of educational technology.

- Figure to illustrate latest data on media use by children and youth (NEW)
- Explanation of four models to blend traditional face-to-face instruction and online learning (NEW)
- Reference to the International Society for Technology in Education's (ISTE) Standards for Students (NEW)
- Focus on DIVERSITY: Closing the Digital Use Divide (NEW)
- Explanation of the RAT (*Replacement, Amplification*, and *Transformation*) Matrix to analyze the degree to which technology is integrated into teaching (NEW)
- Figure to illustrate data on enrollment trends in full-time virtual schools (NEW)
- Focus on STEM; VHS (Virtual High School) Students Develop Scientific Inquiry Skills (NEW)
- Updated research on flipped classrooms and flipped teaching
- Section on digital resources needed to integrate technology into teaching and accompanying figure (NEW)
- Discussion of productivity software, instructional software, and web-based educational content with accompanying figures and classroom examples (NEW)
- Discussion of digital resources for communication, collaboration, design, creation, and making (NEW)
- Updated section on digital resources for subject areas
- Latest findings from research on technology integration and student learning
- Explanation of a school infrastructure for transformational learning and accompanying figure (NEW)

CHAPTER 13, Becoming a Professional Teacher (New)

- This new chapter covers virtual classroom simulations, professional dispositions for field experiences, U.S. Department of Education's School Ambassador Fellowship Program, and data on parent participation in school activities.
- Dear Mentor/Dear Student letter (NEW)
- Section on video observations of "real" classrooms
- Examples of classroom walkthrough observation instruments
- Graphic, "A Window on the Classroom: What Can a Camera Capture"
- Section on developing a teaching portfolio
- Graphic, "Key Components of Effective Induction Programs"
- Teaching on Your Feet, "I Now Believe I Can Fly!"
- Graphic, "Individual and Collective Dimensions of a Collaborative Community of Teachers"
- Focus on STEM: PBS Collaborative Disseminates STEM Practices Nationwide
- Graphic, "Co-teaching Approaches"

Popular Features to Engage Readers

Voices from the Field

Throughout the 11th edition, the voices of pre-service, new, and master teachers are presented.

- **"Dear Mentor" Feature** Success during the first years of teaching is a challenge for new teachers. Ask any experienced teacher to identify the key to success and most, if not all, will stress the importance of mentors. To facilitate your students' journey to becoming high-quality teachers, the popular Dear Mentor feature that opens each part of the book continues, enlisting the help of four novice teachers who pose important questions to four highly accomplished mentor teachers.
- **Readers' Voices** This feature at the beginning of each chapter provides comments by undergraduate teacher education majors about the importance of chapter content and helps readers feel confident about joining the wider community of those preparing to teach.
- **Teachers' Voices: Being an Agent of Change** This feature brings in the voices of experienced teachers—many of them National Teacher of the Year award winners—to focus on how teachers can effect change in the classroom and the community for the benefit of their students.
- **Teaching on Your Feet** This feature presents examples of how successful teachers have turned potential problem situations in the classroom into "teachable moments." Written by real teachers, this feature illustrates how professional reflection and inquiry enable teachers to meet the numerous, unpredictable challenges that are part of teaching in today's schools.

An Emphasis on Today's Technologies

- **Technology in Action** These features in each chapter highlight how teachers are integrating cutting-edge technologies—such as screen recorder software and web conferencing—into their teaching. A practical section in each feature gives readers hands-on directions for learning more about integrating the highlighted technology into their own teaching.

Instructor Supplements

The following supplements to the textbook are available for download. Visit www.pearsonhighered.com; enter the author, title, or ISBN; and then select this textbook, *Becoming a Teacher,* 11th edition. Click on the "Resources" button to view and download the supplements detailed below.

Online Instructor's Manual with Test Items

An expanded and improved online Instructor's Resource Manual (0135174341) includes numerous recommendations for presenting and extending text content. The manual consists of chapter overviews, focus questions, outlines, suggested teaching strategies, and Web resources that cover the essential concepts addressed in each chapter. You'll also find a complete chapter-by-chapter bank of test items. This new edition's Instructor's Manual also includes a detailed mapping of each REVEL activity to the subcategories of the 10 InTASC Standards and the edTPA content addressing planning instruction and assessment, all in one comprehensive table.

Digital Test Generator

The computerized test bank software, Test Gen (0134898389), allows instructors to create and customize exams for classroom testing and for other specialized delivery options, such as over a local area network or on the Web. A test bank typically contains a large set of test items, organized by chapter, and ready for your use in creating a test based on the associated textbook material. The tests can be downloaded in the following formats:

- **TestGen** Testbank file—PC
- **TestGen** Testbank file—MAC
- **TestGen** Testbank—**Blackboard 9**
- **TestGen** Testbank—**Blackboard CE/Vista (WebCT)**
- **Angel** Test Bank
- **D2L** Test Bank
- **Moodle** Test Bank
- **Sakai** Test Bank

PowerPoint Slides

These lecture slides (0135185289) highlight key concepts and summarize key content from each chapter of the text.

Acknowledgments

I would like to thank the many members of the Pearson Education team who provided expert guidance and support during the preparation of the 11th edition of *Becoming a Teacher*. Clearly, Portfolio Manager Rebecca Fox-Gieg and Development Editor Christina Robb head the list. From skillfully coordinating all phases of the revision process to providing thoughtful, substantive feedback on each chapter, their expertise and hard work are deeply appreciated. I also wish to acknowledge Joan Hughes, Associate Professor in the Department of Curriculum and Instruction at the University of Texas-Austin, and co-author of the 8th edition of *Integrating Educational Technology into Teaching* (Pearson, 2018), for her contributions to the revision of Chapter 12.

I extend a very special thanks to Kevin Davis, Vice President and Editorial Director; Megan Moffo, Managing Content Producer; Yagnesh Jani, Content Producer; and Emily Tamburri, Editorial Project Manager—all of whom were steadfast in their support of the 11th edition. I also extend a special thanks to Joyce E. Myers for writing the Test Bank and preparing the Instructor's Resource Manual and PowerPoints for this edition.

For their patience, encouragement, and understanding while their dad has worked on revisions of this book since its first edition in 1990, I give warm thanks and a hug to each of my wonderful daughters: Anna, Catherine, Rebecca, and Anchitta. And for her friendship, spiritual support, and encouragement during the revision process, I thank my wife, Phensri. Her ability to maintain a positive outlook while meeting life's inevitable challenges is remarkable; each day, she brings sunshine and joy into my life.

In addition, the faculty, teaching assistants, and research assistants at Washington State University (WSU) provided much-appreciated suggestions, encouragement, and support. Among those colleagues are Paul E. Pitre, Chancellor, WSU North Puget Sound at Everett; Michael Trevisan, Dean of the College of Education; Sola Adesope, Boeing Distinguished Professor of STEM Education; and Tariq Akmal, Chair, Department of Teaching and Learning. I also greatly appreciate the assistance provided by Seyed Abdollah Shahrokini, Ph.D. Candidate in Language Literacy and Technology Education at WSU, and Mona Janbozorgi, a student in WSU's Doctor of Pharmacy Program.

Supportive colleagues at other institutions include Walter H. Gmelch, Professor, Leadership Studies, University of San Francisco; Qi Li, Professor and Director, Higher Education & Student Affairs Program, Beijing Normal University; and Eric J. Anctil, Associate Professor of Education and Director of the Center for Innovation at the University of Portland.

I give a sincere thanks to students (many of them now teachers and school administrators) in the classes I have taught at WSU. Conversations with them over the years have been thought provoking and professionally rewarding. I extend warm thanks to Ingrid Spence, Clinical Assistant Professor, University of Idaho, and her students for their excellent suggestions for this edition. And for demonstrating the power of professional inquiry, I owe a profound debt to a great teacher, mentor, and friend, the late Herbert A. Thelen, Professor of Education at the University of Chicago.

I am also grateful to the many people throughout the United States who have used the previous edition and provided suggestions and materials for this edition, including my students at Washington State University. I also wish to thank the following reviewers, who provided concise, helpful suggestions during the developmental stages of this book: Tina Allen, University of Louisiana at Monroe; Robert A. Schultz, University of Toledo; and Curtis Visca, Saddleback College; as well as the following reviewers of earlier editions: Tami Baker, East Tennessee State University; Kara Dawson, University of Florida; Larry Froehlich, Kent State University; Lynne Hamer, University of Toledo; Judy Jackson May, Bowling Green State University; Sandi McCann, Columbus State University; Lois Paretti, University of Nevada, Las Vegas; Sarah Swicegood, Sam Houston State University; and Barbara Taylor, Western New Mexico University.

State Coverage

The 11th edition of *Becoming a Teacher* considers educational issues and contributions as they apply to teaching across the country. You'll see specific state coverage throughout the chapters.

CHAPTER 1: TEACHING: YOUR CHOSEN PROFESSION

California
Colorado
Delaware
Florida
Georgia
Hawaii
Illinois
Kansas
Maryland
Massachusetts
New York
North Carolina
Ohio
Pennsylvania
Rhode Island
Tennessee
Texas
Washington
Washington, DC

CHAPTER 2: TODAY'S TEACHERS

California
Connecticut
Idaho
Louisiana
Maryland
Massachusetts
Pennsylvania
Texas

CHAPTER 3: TODAY'S SCHOOLS

Alabama
California
Florida
Hawaii
Illinois
Massachusetts
Minnesota
Mississippi
New Jersey
New York
Ohio
Oklahoma
Pennsylvania
Texas
Washington
Washington, DC

CHAPTER 4: PHILOSOPHICAL FOUNDATIONS OF U.S. EDUCATION

Arkansas
California
Indiana
Ohio
Texas
Washington

CHAPTER 5: HISTORICAL FOUNDATIONS OF U.S. EDUCATION

California
New Hampshire
Virginia
West Virginia

CHAPTER 6: GOVERNANCE AND FINANCE OF U.S. SCHOOLS

Arkansas
California
Colorado
Florida
Illinois
Kentucky
Michigan
Minnesota
Missouri
Nebraska
New Mexico
New York
North Carolina
Ohio
Pennsylvania
South Carolina
Texas
Virginia
Washington
West Virginia

CHAPTER 7: ETHICAL AND LEGAL ISSUES IN U.S. EDUCATION

California
Florida
Louisiana
Missouri
New Hampshire
Pennsylvania
Virginia

CHAPTER 8: TODAY'S STUDENTS

Alaska
Arizona
California
Colorado
Florida
Illinois
Indiana
Minnesota
New Mexico
New York
Oklahoma
Texas
Utah
Washington

CHAPTER 9: ADDRESSING LEARNERS' INDIVIDUAL NEEDS

California
Connecticut
Florida
Illinois
Indiana
Maine
Nevada
Oregon
Texas

CHAPTER 10: CREATING A COMMUNITY OF LEARNERS

Kansas
Texas
Virginia
Washington

CHAPTER 11: CURRICULUM, STANDARDS, ASSESSMENT, AND STUDENT LEARNING

Alabama
Alaska
Arizona
California
Colorado
Connecticut
Florida
Hawaii
Maine
Massachusetts
Nevada
New Jersey
New York
North Dakota
Ohio
Oklahoma
Oregon
Rhode Island
South Carolina
South Dakota
Texas
Virginia
Washington
Wyoming

CHAPTER 12: INTEGRATING TECHNOLOGY INTO TEACHING

Alabama
California
Connecticut
Florida
Georgia
Hawaii
Idaho
Illinois
Maine
Michigan
North Carolina
Vermont
Washington
West Virginia
Wisconsin

CHAPTER 13: BECOMING A PROFESSIONAL TEACHER

Alabama
California
Colorado
Connecticut
Delaware
Florida
Georgia
Indiana
Kansas
Nebraska
New Mexico
New York
North Carolina
Ohio
Oregon
South Dakota
Tennessee
Texas
Vermont
Virginia
Washington
West Virginia
Wisconsin

Brief Contents

Part I The Teaching Profession 1

1 Teaching: Your Chosen Profession 1

2 Today's Teachers 28

3 Today's Schools 63

Part II Foundations of Teaching 99

4 Philosophical Foundations of U.S. Education 99

5 Historical Foundations of U.S. Education 137

6 Governance and Finance of U.S. Schools 174

7 Ethical and Legal Issues in U.S. Education 214

Part III The Art of Teaching 258

8 Today's Students 258

9 Addressing Learners' Individual Needs 294

10 Creating a Community of Learners 331

11 Curriculum, Standards, Assessment, and Student Learning 363

12 Integrating Technology into Teaching 413

Part IV Your Teaching Future 446

13 Becoming a Professional Teacher 446

Contents

Preface iii
About the Author xxi

Part I The Teaching Profession 1

1 Teaching: Your Chosen Profession 1

Dear Mentor 2
Dear Kourtni 2
READERS' VOICES: Why do I want to teach? 3
Why do I Want to Teach? 3
Desire to Make a Difference in Students' Lives 3
A Passion for Teaching 5
PASSION FOR THE SUBJECT • A PASSION FOR THE TEACHING LIFE • A PASSION FOR THE TEACHING–LEARNING PROCESS
Influence of Teachers 7
Desire to Serve 8
What are the Benefits of Teaching? 9
Salaries and Benefits 9
What are the Challenges of Teaching? 12
Long Working Hours 12
High-Stakes Testing and Increased Accountability 12
Today's Tech-Savvy Students 14
What Will Society Expect of Me as a Teacher? 16
The Public Trust 16
Teacher Competency and Effectiveness 17
Teacher Accountability 17
What is the Job Outlook for Teachers? 17
Continuing Need for Teachers 18
Focus on Diversity: Demand for Teachers of Color 19
Demand for Teachers by Geographic Region and Specialty Area 20
How Will I Become an Effective Teacher? 20
Professional Standards 22
Certification and Licensure 22
The Praxis Tests 22
State Licensure Certification Requirements 24
Alternative Certification 25
Summary • Professional Reflections and Activities • Professional Portfolio

2 Today's Teachers 28

READERS' VOICES: Who are today's teachers? 29
Who are Today's Teachers? 29
Grade-Level Designations 30
PRE-K TEACHERS • ELEMENTARY TEACHERS • MIDDLE SCHOOL TEACHERS • HIGH SCHOOL TEACHERS
Teachers in Urban, Suburban, and Rural Settings 32
Teachers in Nontraditional School Settings 34
PRIVATE SCHOOL TEACHERS • CHARTER SCHOOL TEACHERS • ALTERNATIVE SCHOOL TEACHERS • MAGNET SCHOOL TEACHERS
Teachers in Specialized Areas 35
SPECIAL EDUCATION TEACHERS
Focus on Diversity: Teachers of English Language Learners (ELLs) 37
ART TEACHERS • MUSIC TEACHERS • VOCATIONAL EDUCATION TEACHERS • PHYSICAL EDUCATION TEACHERS
What Do Teachers *Do* in the Classroom? 39
Teacher as a Role Model for Students 40
Focus on Diversity: Black Teachers as Role Models for Black Students 40
Focus on Diversity: Teacher as a Model of Cross-Cultural Competence 41
Teacher as a Spontaneous Problem Solver 42
Teacher as a Reflective Thinker 43
What Knowledge and Skills Do Today's Teachers Need? 45
Self-Knowledge 45
Knowledge of Students 45
Knowledge of Subject and Pedagogical Expertise 46
Knowledge of How to Use Educational Theory and Research 46
Knowledge of How to Integrate Technology into Teaching 47
A Problem-Solving Orientation 48
To What Extent is Teaching a Full Profession? 50
Institutional Monopoly of Services 50
Professional Autonomy 51
Years of Education and Training 52
Provision of Essential Service 53
Degree of Self-Governance 53
Professional Knowledge and Skills 54
Trust in the Profession 55
Prestige, Benefits, and Pay 55
Accepting the Challenge of a Profession 56
Professional Associations 56
To What Professional Organizations do Teachers Belong? 57
The National Education Association 57
The American Federation of Teachers 58
Other Professional Organizations 58
How are Teacher Leaders Transforming the Profession of Teaching? 59
Summary • Professional Reflections and Activities

3 Today's Schools 63

READERS VOICES: What is the role of schools in today's society? 64

What is the Role of the School and What Makes a School Successful? 64
Diverse Views on the Purpose of Schools 64
SCHOOLS AND PROSOCIAL VALUES • SCHOOLS AND SOCIALIZATION OF THE YOUNG • SCHOOLS AND SOCIAL CHANGE
Focus on Diversity: Schools and Equal Educational Opportunity 66
The Characteristics of Successful Schools 67
RESEARCH ON SCHOOL EFFECTIVENESS AND SCHOOL IMPROVEMENT
How Can Schools Be Described? 68
Focus on Diversity: Schools and Social Class 69
Four Types Of Schools 69
School Settings 70
RURAL SCHOOL SETTINGS • URBAN AND SUBURBAN SCHOOL ENVIRONMENTS
Focus on Diversity: Overcoming the Effects of Poverty 71
School Culture 72
THE PHYSICAL ENVIRONMENT • FORMAL PRACTICES OF SCHOOLS • SCHOOL TRADITIONS • CULTURE OF THE CLASSROOM
What Social Problems Affect Schools And Place Students At Risk? 74
Identifying Students at Risk 74
Focus on Diversity: America's Dropout Problem 75
Children and Poverty 77
Childhood Stress and Trauma 78
Substance Abuse 81
Violence and Crime 82
CYBERBULLYING
Teen Pregnancy 84
Suicide Among Children and Youth 86
How Are Schools Addressing Societal Problems? 86
Trauma-Sensitive Schools 87
Peer Counseling/Mentoring 88
Focus on Diversity: Peer Mediation to Promote Tolerance 89
Community Schools 89
Compensatory Education 90
Alternative Schools and Curricula 91
OUT-OF-SCHOOL-TIME (OST) ACTIVITIES
Expanded Learning Time (ELT) Schools 93
How Can Community-Based Partnerships Help Students Learn? 94
The Community as a Resource for Schools 94
CIVIC ORGANIZATIONS • VOLUNTEER MENTOR PROGRAMS • CORPORATE–EDUCATION PARTNERSHIPS • 21ST CENTURY COMMUNITY LEARNING CENTERS (CCLCS)
Summary • Professional Reflections And Activities

Part II Foundations of Teaching 99

4 Philosophical Foundations of U.S. Education 99

Dear Mentor 100
Dear Alison 100
READERS' VOICES: Why is philosophy important to teachers? 101
Why is Philosophy Important to Teachers? 101
The Nature of Philosophy 102
Your Educational Philosophy 103
Beliefs About Teaching and Learning 103
Beliefs About Students 105
Focus on Diversity: Accepting all Students 105
Beliefs About Knowledge 106
Beliefs About What Is Worth Knowing 106
What Are The Branches Of Philosophy? 108
Metaphysics 108
Epistemology 109
Axiology 110
Ethics 110
Aesthetics 111
Logic 111
What Are Five Modern Philosophical Orientations To Teaching? 113
Perennialism 113
PERENNIALIST EDUCATIONAL PHILOSOPHERS • PORTRAIT OF A PERENNIALIST TEACHER
Essentialism 116
Focus on STEM: Science, Technology, Engineering, and Mathematics for the 21St Century 117
PORTRAIT OF AN ESSENTIALIST TEACHER
Progressivism 118
PROGRESSIVE STRATEGIES • PORTRAIT OF A PROGRESSIVE TEACHER
Existentialism 120
EXISTENTIALISM AND POSTMODERNISM • PORTRAIT OF AN EXISTENTIALIST TEACHER
Social Reconstructionism 122
SOCIAL RECONSTRUCTIONISM AND PROGRESSIVISM • PORTRAIT OF A SOCIAL RECONSTRUCTIONIST TEACHER
Focus on Diversity: Critical Pedagogy 124
Focus on Diversity: Feminist Pedagogy 125
COMPARING PHILOSOPHICAL ORIENTATIONS TO TEACHING
What Psychological Orientations Have Influenced Teaching Philosophies? 127
Humanistic Psychology 127
PORTRAIT OF A HUMANIST TEACHER
Behaviorism 128
FOUNDERS OF BEHAVIORISTIC PSYCHOLOGY • PORTRAIT OF A BEHAVIORIST TEACHER
Constructivism 129
PORTRAIT OF A CONSTRUCTIVIST TEACHER • COMPARING PSYCHOLOGICAL ORIENTATIONS TO TEACHING
How Can You Develop Your Educational Philosophy? 131
Summary • Professional Reflections And Activities

5 Historical Foundations of U.S. Education 137

READERS' VOICES: Why is educational history important? 138

How Did European Education Influence Teaching and Schools in the American Colonies (1620–1750)? 138

Education in Ancient Greece 139

SOCRATES • PLATO AND ARISTOTLE

Education in Ancient Rome 140

From the Middle Ages to the Renaissance 140

Educational Thought in 18th-Century Europe 141

Teaching and Schools in the American Colonies (1620–1750) 142

THE STATUS OF TEACHERS • COLONIAL SCHOOLS • THE DAME SCHOOLS • READING AND WRITING SCHOOLS • LATIN GRAMMAR SCHOOLS • SCHOOLS FOR AFRICAN AMERICANS AND NATIVE AMERICANS • THE ORIGINS OF MANDATED EDUCATION

What Were the Goals of Education During the Revolutionary Period (1750–1820)? 147

Benjamin Franklin's Academy 147

Education for Girls 147

Thomas Jefferson's Philosophy 148

Textbooks and American Values 149

Education for African Americans and Native Americans 149

How Did State-Supported Common Schools Emerge (1820–1865), and How Did Compulsory Education Change Schools and Teaching (1865–1920)? 150

Horace Mann's Contributions 150

IMPROVING SCHOOLS • THE NORMAL SCHOOL

Reverend W. H. McGuffey's Readers 151

Justin Morrill's Land-Grant Schools 152

Segregation of Schools 152

Compulsory Education 152

THE KINDERGARTEN • SCHOOLING FOR AFRICAN AMERICANS • HIGHER EDUCATION FOR AFRICAN AMERICANS • THE PROFESSIONALIZATION OF TEACHING • COMMITTEE OF TEN • COMMITTEE OF FIFTEEN • REORGANIZATION OF SECONDARY EDUCATION • WOMEN'S INFLUENCE ON TEACHING

What Were the Aims of Education During the Progressive Era (1920–1945) and the Modern Postwar Era (1945–2000)? 155

John Dewey's Laboratory School 155

Maria Montessori's Method 157

The Decline of Progressive Education 157

Focus on Diversity: Education of Immigrants and Minorities 157

World War II and Increasing Federal Involvement in Education 159

The Modern Postwar Era (1945–2000) 160

THE 1950s: DEFENSE EDUCATION AND SCHOOL DESEGREGATION • THE 1960s: THE WAR ON POVERTY AND THE GREAT SOCIETY • THE 1970s: ACCOUNTABILITY AND EQUAL OPPORTUNITY • THE 1980s: A GREAT DEBATE • THE 1990s: TEACHER LEADERSHIP

What Are the Educational Issues and Priorities of the 21st Century (2000–the Present)? 165

Focus on Diversity: Equity for all Students 166

Excellence 166

EVERY STUDENT SUCCEEDS ACT (ESSA)

Accountability 169

A NEW FEDERAL EDUCATION AGENDA—DIMINISHING SUPPORT FOR PUBLIC SCHOOLS

Continuing the Quest for Excellence and Equity 170

Summary • Professional Reflections and Activities

6 Governance and Finance of U.S. Schools 174

READERS' VOICES: Why do you need to understand educational politics? 175

Why do You Need to Understand Educational Politics and How Local Communities Influence Schools? 175

Five Dimensions of Educational Politics 176

How Local Communities Influence Schools 178

LOCAL SCHOOL DISTRICT • LOCAL SCHOOL BOARD • SUPERINTENDENT OF SCHOOLS • THE ROLE OF PARENTS • SCHOOL RESTRUCTURING • SCHOOL-BASED MANAGEMENT • INNOVATIVE APPROACHES TO SCHOOL GOVERNANCE

How do States and Regional Education Agencies Influence Education? 186

The Roles of State Government in Education 187

THE LEGISLATURE • THE STATE COURTS • THE GOVERNOR • STATE TAKEOVER OF SCHOOLS

State Board of Education 191

State Department of Education 191

Chief State School Officer 192

Regional Education Agencies and Assistance to Schools 192

How does the Federal Government Influence Education? 193

Federal Initiatives 193

THE IMPACT OF PRESIDENTIAL POLICIES

Focus on STEM: a Memo from the President 194

U.S. Department of Education 195

How are Schools Financed in the United States? 195

Education Funding and the Nation's Economy 196

The Challenge of Equitable Funding 197

Sources of Funding 197

Local Funding 198

State Funding 199

Federal Funding 201

What are Some Trends in Funding for Equity and Excellence? 201

Focus on Diversity: Inequitable Funding of Schools in Poor Communities 202

Tax Reform and Redistricting 203

Vertical Equity 203

School Choice 204

Voucher Systems 204

EVALUATION OF VOUCHER PROGRAMS
Education–Business Coalitions 206
How is the Privatization Movement Affecting Equity and Excellence in Education? 208
Charter Schools 208
RESEARCH ON CHARTER SCHOOLS
For-Profit Schools 209
K12 INC. • TEACHER-OWNED SCHOOLS?
Summary • Professional Reflections and Activities

7 Ethical and Legal Issues in U.S. Education 214
READERS' VOICES: Why do teachers need to know about education and the law? 215
Why Do you Need to Know about Education and the Law and Have a Code of Ethics? 215
Professional Code of Ethics 215
Ethical Dilemmas in the Classroom and School 217
What are Your Legal Rights as a Teacher? 218
Certification 219
Teachers' Rights to Nondiscrimination 219
Teaching Contracts 220
Due Process in Tenure and Dismissal 221
Academic Freedom 223
FAMOUS CASES • STATES' RIGHTS AND ACADEMIC FREEDOM
Do Student Teachers Have the Same Rights as Teachers? 225
What are Your Legal Responsibilities as a Teacher? 226
Avoiding Tort Liability 227
NEGLIGENCE • PROFESSIONAL MALPRACTICE
Reporting Child Abuse 229
Observing Copyright Laws 231
PHOTOCOPIES • OFF-AIR RECORDINGS • SOFTWARE • EMAIL AND THE INTERNET • POSTING ON THE INTERNET
Teachers and Social Networking 234
What are the Legal Rights of Students and Parents? 235
Right to an Education 236
Focus on Diversity: Education of Students of Undocumented Immigrant Parents 236
Focus on STEM: Design for STEM Lab Triggers Complaint to U.S. Office for Civil Rights 237
Freedom of Expression 237
CENSORSHIP • STUDENT EXPRESSION ON SOCIAL NETWORKING SITES • DRESS CODES
Due Process in Suspension and Expulsion 240
Reasonable Search and Seizure 242
Privacy 244
EXCEPTIONS • VIDEO CAMERAS IN CLASSROOMS
Students' Rights to Nondiscrimination 245
What are Some Issues in the Legal Rights of School Districts? 247
Corporal Punishment 247
Sexual Harassment 248
Cyberbullying and the Law 249
Religious Expression 250
EVOLUTION VERSUS CREATIONISM AND INTELLIGENT DESIGN • LEGAL RULINGS • GUIDELINES FOR RELIGIOUS ACTIVITIES IN SCHOOLS
Educational Malpractice 253
Focus on Diversity: School Children Denied Right to Literacy 253
Homeschooling 254
Summary • Professional Reflections and Activities

Part III The Art of Teaching 258

8 Today's Students 258
Dear Mentor 259
Dear Richard 259
READERS' VOICES: How is culture important in today's schools? 260
What Contributes to the Cultural Diversity In U.S. Classrooms? 260
Focus on Diversity: Rising Number of Students of Undocumented Immigrant Parents 261
Defining *Culture* 262
Stereotyping and Racism 263
Contributors to Cultural Identity 263
LANGUAGE AND CULTURE • ETHNICITY, RACE, AND CULTURE • SOCIOECONOMIC STATUS AND CULTURE • THE ACHIEVEMENT GAP
Religion and Culture 268
How Can Teachers Strive to Provide Equal Educational Opportunity for All Students? 269
Education and Gender 271
GENDER-FAIR CLASSROOMS AND CURRICULA
Focus on STEM: Female Students Outperform Male Students in Technology and Engineering Literacy 273
Lesbian, Gay, Bisexual, Transgender, and Questioning (LGBTQ) Students 274
Education and African Americans 275
THE DESEGREGATION ERA • RESEGREGATION OF SCHOOLS IN THE UNITED STATES • ADDRESSING THE LEARNING NEEDS OF AFRICAN AMERICAN STUDENTS
Education and Latino and Hispanic Americans 277
SOCIOECONOMIC FACTORS • ADDRESSING THE LEARNING NEEDS OF SPANISH-SPEAKING STUDENTS
Education and Asian Americans and Pacific Islanders 278
HISTORICAL, CULTURAL, AND SOCIOECONOMIC FACTORS • ADDRESSING THE LEARNING NEEDS OF ASIAN AMERICAN STUDENTS
Education and Native Americans and Alaskan Natives 280
HISTORICAL, CULTURAL, AND SOCIOECONOMIC FACTORS • ADDRESSING THE LEARNING NEEDS OF NATIVE AMERICANS AND ALASKAN NATIVES
Focus on STEM: Integrating Tribal Knowledge with STEM 282

How are Schools Meeting the Needs of English Language Learners (ELLs)? 283
Research and Debate on Teaching ELL Students 284
Advice for Monolingual Teachers 284
What is Multicultural Education and Culturally Responsive Teaching? 287
Dimensions of Multicultural Education 288
Culturally Responsive Teaching 289
Multicultural Curricula 289
Summary • Professional Reflections and Activities

9 Addressing Learners' Individual Needs 294
READERS' VOICES: Why should teachers address students' individual needs? 295
How Do Students' Needs Change as they Develop? 295
Piaget's Model of Cognitive Development 295
Erikson's Model of Psychosocial Development 297
Kohlberg's Model of Moral Development 298
Maslow's Model of a Hierarchy of Needs 301
Developmental Stresses and Tasks of Childhood 302
ADVERSE CHILDHOOD EXPERIENCES
Developmental Stresses and Tasks of Adolescence 303
Focus on Diversity: National Policy Rhetoric and Stress Among Vulnerable Students **305**
How do Students Vary in Intelligence? 306
Intelligence Testing 306
Multiple Intelligences 307
Learning Style Preferences 308
How do Students Vary in Ability and Disability? 309
Students with Special Needs 309
Focus on Diversity: Students with Special Needs **310**
Focus on STEM: Students with Special Needs Benefit from STEM **314**
Focus on Diversity: Students who are Gifted and Talented **315**
ACCELERATION • SELF-DIRECTED OR INDEPENDENT STUDY • INDIVIDUAL EDUCATION PROGRAMS (IEPS) • ALTERNATIVE OR MAGNET SCHOOLS
Focus on STEM: University Offers STEM Program for Gifted Students **316**
What are Special Education and Inclusion? 317
Special Education Laws 317
RESPONSE TO INTERVENTION (RTI) • INDIVIDUAL EDUCATION PROGRAM • RELATED SERVICES • CONFIDENTIALITY OF RECORDS • DUE PROCESS • IDEA AND EVERY STUDENT SUCCEEDS ACT (ESSA)
Meeting the Inclusion Challenge 321
The Debate over Inclusion 322
Focus on Diversity: Equal Opportunity for Exceptional Learners **324**
How can You Teach all Learners in Your Inclusive Classroom? 325
Collaborative Consultation with Other Professionals 326
Partnerships with Parents 326
Assistive Technology for Special Learners 327
Summary • Professional Reflections and Activities

10 Creating a Community of Learners 331
READERS' VOICES: What determines the culture of a classroom? 332
What Determines the Culture of the Classroom? 332
Classroom Climate 332
Classroom Dynamics 334
COMMUNICATION SKILLS • INTERACTIONS AMONG STUDENTS
How Can You Create a Positive Learning Environment? 336
The Caring Classroom 336
Focus on Diversity: Caring and Multicultural Classrooms **336**
The Physical Environment of the Classroom 339
Classroom Organization 340
GROUPING STUDENTS BY ABILITY • GROUPING STUDENTS FOR COOPERATIVE LEARNING
Focus on Diversity: Cooperative Learning and Cross-Cultural Interaction **343**
Focus on STEM: Collaberation and Teamwork Promote STEM Learning for Girls **343**
DELIVERING INSTRUCTION • HOW TIME IS USED
What are the Keys to Successful Classroom Management? 346
The Democratic Classroom 347
Preventive Planning 347
ESTABLISHING RULES AND PROCEDURES • ORGANIZING AND PLANNING FOR INSTRUCTION
Effective Responses to Student Behavior 349
SEVERITY OF MISBEHAVIOR
Focus on Diversity: Analysis Reveals Discipline Disparities for Black Students, Boys, and Students with Disabilities **351**
ZERO TOLERANCE • CONSTRUCTIVE ASSERTIVENESS • RESTORATIVE JUSTICE • TEACHER PROBLEM SOLVING • DEVELOPING YOUR OWN APPROACH TO CLASSROOM MANAGEMENT
What Teaching Methods do Effective Teachers Use? 356
Methods Based on Learning New Behaviors 357
Methods Based on Child Development 357
Methods Based on the Thinking Process 358
Methods Based on Peer-Mediated Instruction 360
Summary • Professional Reflections and Activities

11 Curriculum, Standards, Assessment, and Student Learning 363
READERS' VOICES: What do students learn from the curriculum? 364
What do Students Learn from the Curriculum? 364
Kinds of Curricula 364
EXPLICIT CURRICULUM • HIDDEN CURRICULUM • NULL CURRICULUM

Focus on Diversity: Using Curriculum to Address Racism **367**
EXTRACURRICULAR/COCURRICULAR PROGRAMS
Curriculum Content and Student Success 368
GRIT, TENACITY, AND PERSEVERANCE • ACADEMIC MINDSET • MINDFULNESS/MEDITIATION SKILLS • CURRICULA TO ENHANCE NONCOGNITIVE STRENGTHS
How is the School Curriculum Developed and What Factors Influence It? 373
The Focus of Curriculum Planning 374
Student-Centered Versus Subject-Centered Curricula 374
The Integrated Curriculum 375
Influences on Curriculum Development 375
SOCIAL ISSUES AND CHANGING VALUES • TEXTBOOK PUBLISHING
What are Curriculum Standards and what Role will they Play in Your Classroom? 377
Standards-Based Education and Its Influence on Teaching 378
CONTENT AND PERFORMANCE STANDARDS • STANDARDS DEVELOPED BY PROFESSIONAL ASSOCIATIONS • ALIGNING CURRICULUA AND TEXTBOOKS WITH STANDARDS AND CURRICULUM FRAMEWORKS
What is the Common Core State Standards Initiative and How does It Influence Teaching? 381
The Common Core State Standards Initiative (CCSSI) 381
Early Reactions to the Common Core 382
Continuing Controversy about the Common Core 383
Arguments in Support of Raising Standards 383
Arguments against Raising Standards 384
What is the Role of Assessment in Teaching? 385
Challenges of Assessing Students' Learning 386
Standardized Assessments 387
INTERNATIONAL ASSESSMENTS • NORM-REFERENCED ASSESSMENTS • CRITERION-REFERENCED ASSESSMENTS
Accountability 392
High-Stakes Testing 392
HIGH-STAKES TESTS AND EDUCATOR ACCOUNTABILITY
Focus on Diversity: Unintended Consequences of High-Stakes Tests **394**
How Will You Assess Student Learning and Develop High-Quality Assessments? 395
Formal and Informal Assessments 395
Quantitative and Qualitative Assessment 396
Measurement and Evaluation 396
Formative and Summative Evaluation 397
Emerging Trends in Classroom Assessment 397
AUTHENTIC ASSESSMENT
Focus on STEM: Future City Competition Provides Authentic Learning Experiences **398**
PORTFOLIO ASSESSMENT • PEER ASSESSMENT • SELF-ASSESSMENT • PERFORMANCE-BASED ASSESSMENT • ALTERNATE ASSESSMENTS • PROJECT-BASED LEARNING (PBL)
Developing High-Quality Classroom Assessments 404
VALIDITY AND RELIABILITY
Scoring Rubrics 406
Multiple Measures of Student Learning 409
Summary • Professional Reflections and Activities

12 Integrating Technology into Teaching 413
READERS' VOICES: How is technology transforming teaching and learning? 414
How is Technology Transforming Teaching and Learning? 415
Focus on Diversity: Closing the Digital Use Divide **419**
Realizing the Full Transformative Impact of Technology on Learning 420
Virtual Schools and Online Learning 421
Focus on STEM: VHS Students Develop Scientific Inquiry Skills **423**
CONCERNS ABOUT VIRTUAL SCHOOLS AND ONLINE LEARNING • FLIPPED CLASSROOMS
What Digital Resources are Needed to Integrate Technology Into Teaching? 425
Connectivity 426
Devices 426
Accessibility 427
Resources 427
PRODUCTIVITY SOFTWARE • INSTRUCTIONAL SOFTWARE • WEB-BASED EDUCATIONAL CONTENT • RESOURCES FOR COMMUNICATION, COLLABORATION, DESIGN, CREATION, AND MAKING
Digital Resources for Subject Areas 433
THE FINE ARTS • LANGUAGE ARTS • MATHEMATICS • SCIENCE • SOCIAL STUDIES
What Does Research Say About Technology Integration And Student Learning? 436
Technology's Negative Effects on Students 436
Findings from Multiple Research Studies 437
What are the Challenges of Integrating Technology Into Teaching? 439
Technology Training for Teachers 440
Infrastructure for Transformational Learning 442
Summary • Professional Reflections and Activities

Part IV Your Teaching Future 446

13 Becoming a Professional Teacher 446
Dear Mentor 447
Dear Monica 447
READERS' VOICES: What are the concerns of a beginning teacher? 448
How Can You Learn from Observing in Classrooms? 448
Video Observations of "Real" Classrooms 448
Focused Observations 449
Observation Instruments 450
How Can You Gain Practical Experience for Becoming a Teacher? 451

Classroom Experiences 452
MICROTEACHING • SIMULATIONS • PRACTICA • CLASSROOM AIDES
Student Teaching 454
STUDENT TEACHING JOURNAL • REFLECTIVE TEACHING LOGS
Teaching Portfolio 457
PORTFOLIO CONTENTS • USING A PORTFOLIO
Substitute Teaching 458
How Can You Obtain Support As a Teacher? 459
Problems and Concerns of Beginning Teachers 460
Induction into the Profession 460
The Benefits of Having a Mentor 461
What Leadership Opportunities Will You Have Beyond the Classroom? 462
Teacher Involvement in Teacher Education, Certification, and Staff Development 463
Teacher Leaders 463
Teacher Leadership Beyond the Classroom 465
HYBRID TEACHERS AND TEACHERPRENEURS
How Will You Help to Build a Learning Community and Collaborate With Teachers? 466
RELATIONSHIPS WITH STUDENTS • RELATIONSHIPS WITH COLLEAGUES AND STAFF • RELATIONSHIPS WITH ADMINISTRATORS • RELATIONSHIPS WITH PARENTS OR GUARDIANS
Teacher Collaboration 469
Focus on STEM: PBS Collaborative Disseminates STEM Strategies Nationwide 473
PEER COACHING • PROFESSIONAL DEVELOPMENT
Focus on Diversity: Professional Development by Learning Another Language 475
TEAM TEACHING • CO-TEACHING
Summary • Professional Reflections and Activities
Glossary 479
References, 11th Edition 488
Name Index 505
Subject Index 512

Special Features

Teaching on Your Feet

The Abolishment of "I Can't" 6
Opening the Gates to Empower Students 43
Lies Our Students Tell Themselves 75
Reluctant Readers 114
Worth the Struggle 146
"We Are All Responsible for One Another . . . " 185
Respect in the Classroom Is a Two-Way Street 216
¡Sí Se Puede! (It Can Be Done!) 291
Connecting with a Hard-to-Reach Student 313
I See a Story in Every Learner 337
The Benefits of Peer Assessment 400
Half of Teaching Is Learning 441
"I Now Believe I Can Fly!" 467

Technology in Action

Wikis in High School U.S. History 16
E-Portfolios in 12th-Grade Industrial Arts 48
Video Editing to Teach Study Skills and Responsibility in Sixth Grade 65
Web Conferencing Leads to Better Understanding of Another Culture and Oneself 107
Screen-Recorder Software in 12th-Grade Calculus 167
Virtual Worlds and an Interdisciplinary Curriculum 183
Virtual Labs in a Ninth-Grade Biology Classroom 233
Using Text-to-Speech in a Third-Grade Reading Class 285
Word-Prediction Software in the Classroom 314
Podcasting in Fifth-Grade Social Studies 342
Autograded Quizzes and Exams in Eighth-Grade Social Studies 405
Teacher Earns Online Master's Degree 474

Teachers' Voices ➔ Being an Agent of Change

Necessity and the Art of Differentiation 21
Preparing "Citizens of the World" Who Respect Cultural Differences 42
Students Cope With Stress Through Writing 78
Every Day Is Filled With Deep Thinking And Contemplation 109
Native American Teachers Need Support 158
Using Technology to Increase Teachers' Voices 177
Teaching for Social Justice 245
Dollars and Points 270
"Creating an Inclusive Environment . . . Has Always Been my Mission" 324
Encouraging Global Citizenship in the Classroom 338
Project-Based Learning: Building Houses 386
Is Blended Learning Worth the Hype? 416
A "Techno-Librarian" Shares New Ideas across the Globe 471

About the Author

Forrest W. Parkay is Professor Emeritus, Educational Leadership and Higher Education, at Washington State University (WSU). He was Professor of Educational Leadership at the University of Florida for eight years and at Texas State University for five years. Forrest is also Adjunct Professor of Higher Education at Beijing Normal University.

Forrest received his B.A. and M.A. degrees in English education from the University of Illinois–Urbana. He earned his Ph.D. in education at the University of Chicago, and he is a graduate of Harvard University's Management Development Program (MDP). He was Chair of the Department of Teaching and Learning at WSU for three years. For eight years, Forrest taught at DuSable High School on Chicago's South Side, and he served as Chairman of DuSable's English Department for four years. He also taught rhetoric in the English Department at the University of Illinois–Urbana for two years.

Forrest is the author or coauthor of more than 60 refereed journal articles and several books, including *Becoming a Teacher, Fifth Canadian Edition* (Pearson Canada, 2018) and *Curriculum Leadership: Readings for Developing Quality Educational Programs* (Pearson, 2014). The 8th edition of *Becoming a Teacher* was translated into Mandarin, and the 7th and 8th editions into Indonesian. His research has appeared in the field's leading peer-reviewed journals, including *Phi Delta Kappan, American Journal of Education,* and *Educational Administration Quarterly*.

Forrest's honors include a Fulbright Scholar Award, Fulbright Specialist's Award, Faculty Excellence Award for Research (WSU), and Presidential Seminar Award (Texas State University). He is past president of the North Central Florida Chapter of Phi Delta Kappa.

From 2010–2015, Forrest directed WSU's International School Leadership Program (ISLP), a collaborative program with the University of San Francisco. The ISLP is designed for school administrators, teachers, and educational staff at international schools in Southeast Asia who are interested in professional development, graduate education, and principal certification.

A former Fulbright Scholar at Kasetsart University's Center for Research on Teaching and Teacher Education, in Thailand, Forrest has facilitated educational reform programs and conducted cross-national research in China, Thailand, Korea, Japan, Pakistan, India, and Singapore. He has been a Visiting Professor at Beijing Normal University and at Assumption University in Thailand. Forrest also serves as Advantage Education's vice president of teaching and learning. Advantage Education is a group of leading educators in China and the United States focused on helping Chinese students fulfill their dream of studying at U.S. high schools, colleges, and universities.

His hobbies include classic cars, camping, kayaking, and photography. Forrest is the proud father of four daughters: Anna, Catherine, Rebecca, and Anchitta.

PART I

The Teaching Profession

Chapter 1

Teaching: Your Chosen Profession

Cathy Yeulet/123RF

Learning Outcomes

After reading this chapter, you will be able to do the following:

1.1 Explain why you want to teach.

1.2 Identify and explain the benefits of teaching.

1.3 Identify and explain the challenges of teaching.

1.4 Explain what society will expect of you as a teacher.

1.5 Describe the job outlook for teachers.

1.6 Explain how you will become an effective teacher.

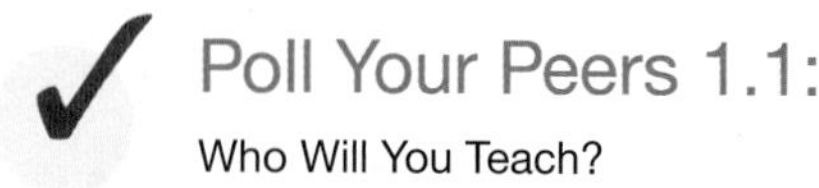

Poll Your Peers 1.1:
Who Will You Teach?

Dear Mentor

In two years, I will graduate with a bachelor's degree in elementary education; then, I will continue on to a fifth-year master's program in special education. I hope to work in the western half of the United States. At this point, I do not have a particular town or state in mind.

While teaching, I would like to work on my Media Specialist Endorsement. This will enable me to work in a school library. While working in a library, my master's in special education will allow me to be on an IEP (Individual Education Program) team.

The current economic climate and education reforms have left me with many questions concerning teaching. Have I chosen the right profession? Do you anticipate more or less job availability for teachers in the future? Do you see teaching as a lifetime career choice?

SINCERELY, KOURTNI MCHUGH
Missoula, MONTANA

Dear Kourtni

Education is an exciting field and, yes, there is reform taking place, some of which is long overdue. Don't fear the word "reform." Teachers who are dynamic and experts in their field know that reform or change is another opportunity to take on a new challenge. No one has a crystal ball to see into the future; however, rest assured that there are, and will continue to be, jobs in education—especially in harder-to-fill specialties such as special education, math, and science.

You are making some excellent decisions about your future as an educator, and they will serve you well once you start trying to land your first teaching position. Having a master's of education degree plus your library and special education endorsements makes you a more marketable job applicant. Multiple endorsements will also serve you well further down the road in your teaching career since, once you are teaching full-time, you may find it challenging and costly to go back to school to add additional endorsements. By entering the teaching profession with a master's degree and two endorsements, you will have more freedom in making decisions about what and where you would like to teach.

Personally, I see teaching as a fantastic career. You know many of the pluses of the job already: summers off; after several years of teaching, you make a decent wage; and, for the most part, the benefits are decent, too. Teaching is like no other profession—you will make a difference in the lives of children, their families, and your community. Once you establish yourself at a school, you will be both surprised and delighted to see that the positive relationships you build with students in your classroom also carry over into your community.

While you are finishing up your certification, I urge you to talk to as many educators as you can, especially those who have been in the profession awhile. Ask them what they love about teaching; every one of them will have a different reason for staying in the profession. Yes, teaching has huge challenges, but it has huge rewards as well. You have most certainly heard this before, but it is worth saying again: "Education is a rewarding field that is unlike any other." Best of luck to you!

SINCERELY, ADRIENNE LEHMAN, M.ED.
English Language Learner Specialist,
Puyallup School District
Puyallup, WASHINGTON

READERS' VOICES

Why do I want to teach?

I want to teach because I was taught. Throughout my childhood and into my adult life, I have had important teachers who inspired me to accomplish my dreams. These wonderful people in my life inspired me to become a teacher.

— **DENISEA,**
Teacher Education program, first year

Congratulations on deciding to become a teacher! Teaching can be exciting, rewarding, and uplifting. Teachers receive great satisfaction from knowing that they often make a difference in their students' lives. I hope you share my belief that teaching is the world's most important profession and is vitally important to our nation's future.

I also hope your commitment to teaching will become deeper and stronger as you move through your teacher education program. Perhaps your experience will be similar to the many students who have told me that, after considering other majors, they were glad they decided to become a teacher. At a deep level, they knew that they were meant to become a teacher.

Teaching is a challenging but rewarding profession—one that is not for everyone, however. This book will orient you to the world of teaching and help you answer your own questions about the career you have chosen. What is teaching really like? What rewards do teachers experience? What are the trends and issues in the profession? What problems can you expect to encounter in the classroom? What will you need to know and be able to do to become an effective teacher?

Video Example 1.1

Welcome: Your author, Forrest W. Parkay, welcomes you to the exciting, dynamic profession of teaching.

I believe that successful teachers know why they want to teach. They examine their motives carefully, and they understand why, at first, they might have been uncertain about choosing to become a teacher. The first chapter of this book, then, addresses the six learning outcomes listed on the previous page, which will help you decide if teaching is the right profession for you.

The learning outcomes in each chapter of this book address *your future* as a teacher. Achieving these learning outcomes will provide you with a reality-based look at the world of teachers, students, classrooms, and schools and their surrounding communities. After reading this book, you will have a broad understanding of one of the world's most exciting, satisfying, and honorable professions. And you will know if teaching is the right profession for you.

Why do I Want to Teach?

You may want to teach for many reasons. Your desire to teach may be the result of positive experiences with teachers when you were a child. You may be attracted to teaching because the life of a teacher is exciting, varied, and stimulating. Or you may see teaching as a way of making a significant contribution to the world and experiencing the joy of helping children grow and develop. Figure 1.1 shows the most significant reasons more than 3,300 public school teachers gave for entering the profession. How do your reasons compare with those of the teachers surveyed?

Desire to Make a Difference in Students' Lives

Although teaching may be challenging and teachers' salaries modest, most teach simply because they care about students. Teachers derive great satisfaction when their students learn—when they make a difference in students' lives. In fact, 88 percent of K–12 teachers in a national survey reported they were "satisfied" with their decision to become a teacher, and 68 percent would recommend the profession to others (Harris Poll, 2015).

Figure 1.1 Most significant reasons why teachers joined the profession

To make a difference in students' lives	68%
To help students reach their full potential	45%
A teacher inspired me when I was young	37%
To be a part of those "aha" moments when things just click for a student	32%
To share my enthusiasm for the subject I teach	31%
To make a difference in the larger community	24%
To have a good work/family balance	15%
To have a nontraditional work schedule (e.g., summers off)	7%

Note: Teachers could select up to three responses from a set of 12 reasons.

SOURCE: Used with permission from Listen to Us: Teacher Views and Voices. Center on Education Policy, Courtesy of The George Washington University.

As a teacher, your day-to-day interactions with students will build strong bonds between you and them. Daily contact will enable you to become familiar with your students' personal and academic needs. Concern for their welfare will help you cope with the difficulties and frustrations of teaching. The teacher's potential to make a difference in students' lives can be profound; for example, John King, former Secretary of Education under President Obama and now president and CEO of the Education Trust, explains how teachers influenced him:

> I lost my parents at a very young age. But in my New York City public schools, I was fortunate to have great teachers who made school engaging, challenging, and nurturing. Amazing teachers at P.S. 276 in Canarsie and Mark Twain Junior High School in Coney Island gave me a sense of hope and possibility. If I had not had those teachers, I wouldn't be alive today. They literally saved my life. (The Education Trust, 2017)

Like most teachers, you appreciate the unique qualities of youth. You enjoy the liveliness, curiosity, freshness, openness, and trust of young children or the abilities, wit, spirit, independence, and idealism of adolescents. As one teacher told me, "I know I make a difference in my students' lives, especially those who may not see themselves as 'good' students. It is so rewarding when they tell me that they *can learn*, that they can 'change the world.'"

As a teacher, you will also derive significant rewards from meeting the needs of diverse learners. Students from our nation's more than 100 racial and ethnic groups and students with special needs are increasing in number, so your classroom will be enriched by the varied backgrounds of your students. To ensure that you can experience the satisfaction of helping all students learn, significant portions of this book are devoted to **student variability** (differences among students in regard to their developmental needs, interests, abilities, and disabilities) and **student diversity** (differences among students in regard to gender, race, ethnicity, culture, language, religion, sexual orientation, and socioeconomic status). Your appreciation for diversity will help you to experience the rewards that come from enabling each student to make his or her unique contribution to classroom life. In addition, you can be proud of your role in promoting social justice and helping our nation realize its democratic ideals.

Like the following two teachers who responded to a nationwide survey of 207 teachers, you may be drawn to teaching because you know that teachers can have a powerful influence on children and youth, regardless of their stages of development or their life circumstances:

> With teaching, every day is different. You are constantly in motion, engaged and working toward something that is more important than you. Your work is critical,

life-changing, and ultimately the most empowering gift you can give to your students. It is an expression of not only the love you have for your students but the bone-deep belief that they will achieve. (The New Teacher Project, 2013, p. 21)

I love being with kids every day and hearing them say, "I get it now, miss." I enjoy figuring out and applying strategies that will help my kids think and learn, using life-changing texts. I like making daily decisions for myself. (The New Teacher Project, 2013, p. 21)

A Passion for Teaching

Figure 1.2 shows that a "passion for teaching" is among the most important qualities principals look for when hiring teachers. What does it mean to be *passionate* about teaching?

Figure 1.2 What qualities do principals look for in a new teacher?

"I look for an individual with a *passion* to receive and impart knowledge, someone who can relay the information they receive to students with diverse abilities . . . . A person who knows beyond the shadow of a doubt that teaching is the greatest of all professions."

---Principal, alternative school, Georgia

"Passion . . . in body language, the eyes, gestures, chosen words of speech, and speech inflection. I look for those things when words are mentioned regarding *children, teaching*, and *learning.*"

--Assistant principal, K–8 school, Ohio

" . . . someone who will create a positive, exciting atmosphere for learning. A candidate who shows enthusiasm for teaching during the interview."

---Principal, elementary school, Illinois

"I try to find a teacher who will be a 'Kid magnet.' Once a student really connects emotionally to the teacher, then the rest will follow!"

--Principal, middle school, New York

"The single most important characteristic [in a teacher is] their compassion for children, as that is the essence of the profession."

--Vice principal, 7–12 private school, California

"When empathy and compassion are present along with intelligence, training, knowledge of subject, creativity, the learning environment is enhanced. To determine if a teacher has empathy, I ask 'How would you handle a situation where one child is always chosen last?' Or, 'What would you do for a child who always sits alone at lunch?'"

-Principal, elementary school, Texas

"I am interested in discerning what interpersonal skills a candidate possesses that will 'connect' with the student. This connection—this caring attitude—motivates learners to learn. I ask, 'What do you do to make students successful?'"

--Principal, elementary school, Oklahoma

Used with permission from Hopkins, G. (2017). What qualities do principals look for in a new teacher? Education World. Retrieved from http://www.educationworld.com/a_admin/admin/admin071.shtml. Copyright Education World, Inc. All Rights Reserved.

PASSION FOR THE SUBJECT You may be passionate about teaching because you are passionate about teaching in your discipline. Teaching can give you an opportunity to share with students your passion for science, computers, sports, or the outdoors, for example. When students see that you *really do love* a subject, they will respond—their interest will be aroused, and they will appreciate that you have shared an important part of your life with them. As evidence of this, recall how your own interest has been piqued whenever your teachers shared their passion for the subject. What you experienced during those moments was a special "invitation" to share a teacher's excitement about an important part of his or her life.

A PASSION FOR THE TEACHING LIFE Perhaps you are eager to experience the "joy" of teaching that motivates the following teacher: "I see [teaching] as a career

Rawpixel/Shutterstock

Teachers can play a critical role in shaping the future of young people. What positive effects might this teacher have on these students?

where I can sing a little, dance a little, do math, study history and science, and teach from the heart" (Center for Education Policy, 2016, p. 13). The life of a teacher appeals to you—to be in an environment that encourages a high regard for education and the life of the mind, and to have daily opportunities to see students become excited about learning. Albert Einstein, for example, regretted that he did not devote his career to the teaching life, commenting on children's openness to knowledge and how much he enjoyed being with them (Bucky, 1992).

A PASSION FOR THE TEACHING–LEARNING PROCESS You may be passionate about teaching because you are excited about helping students learn. The prospect of thinking on your feet and capitalizing on teachable moments is appealing. Perhaps you had expert teachers who made you appreciate the "artistic" dimensions of teaching, and you marveled at their ability to maintain students' interest in learning from moment to moment and to improvise on the spot.

The great educator and philosopher John Dewey explains how skilled teachers improvise. Teachers, he said, are sensitive to the inner lives of children and therefore aware of what students are learning (or not learning) as a result of their teaching. He explains:

> As every teacher knows, children have an inner and an outer attention. The inner attention is the giving of the mind without reserve or qualification to the subject at hand. . . .
>
> To be able to keep track of this mental play, to recognize the signs of its presence or absence, to know how it is initiated and maintained, how to test it by results attained, and to test apparent results by it, is the supreme mark and criterion of a teacher. (Dewey, 1904, pp. 13–14)

Philip Jackson describes the unpredictability of teaching in his well-known book *Life in Classrooms*: "[As] typically conducted, teaching is an opportunistic process. . . . Neither teacher nor students can predict with any certainty exactly what will happen next. Plans are forever going awry and unexpected opportunities for the attainment of educational goals are constantly emerging" (Jackson, 1990, p. 166).

Research tells us that teachers may make up to 3,000 low-level decisions in a single school day (Jackson, 1990). Most decisions are easy and natural, but some require critical thinking. Stepping into the minds of teachers to see how they turned a negative situation into a positive learning experience for students is the purpose of the Teaching on Your Feet feature in each chapter of this book. For example, students at risk need teachers who can recognize opportunities in the classroom to build up their confidence as learners, as Jennifer Michele Diaz illustrates in the Teaching on Your Feet feature for this chapter.

Teaching on Your Feet:

The Abolishment of "I Can't"

Thirty-two little hands burst into the air as I reached into a jar of student numbers to randomly select a student to read aloud. It was the second week of school for my fourth graders, and the second week of my first year of teaching. The students were excited and enthusiastic about the possibility of being selected to read aloud from the new brightly colored social studies textbook.

"Congratulations, student number three! Let's follow along as we listen to Anthony read aloud," I said, when I pulled Anthony's number from the jar. Several students dropped their hands back down to their desks in disappointment. (My students seemed to think that if they raised their hands while rising slightly out of their seats their number would magically be selected. Their sense of naïveté melted my heart.)

Silence fell over the classroom, and Anthony gazed at the book. He squirmed in his chair and began to rock back and forth gently. He began to stumble through the words "The state of California is. . . ." Then he blurted out, "I can't read, Miss Diaz," and began to giggle, perhaps hoping to give the impression that a fit of laughter was the cause of his inability to read aloud.

Anthony's laughter sparked giggles among his classmates but caused me to feel panic. I knew that Anthony had been retained a year. The fact that he was a year older than his classmates yet several years behind them in terms of reading ability alarmed me. How should I, as a first-year teacher, respond to his near-illiteracy?

Quickly bringing myself back to the immediacy of a classroom of 32 students, I praised Anthony for being courageous enough to read aloud and helped him read the rest of the short paragraph. Setting the social studies lesson aside, I took the opportunity provided by Anthony's comment to insert a mini-lesson on the need to eliminate the phrase "I can't" from my students' vocabulary. I noted that even though Anthony may have felt that he could not read aloud, he did in fact read (albeit, with my guidance).

During my mini-lesson, one student suggested that we ban the phrase "I can't" from our classroom. As a class, we then collectively created a list of phrases that could be used instead of "I can't" when we become frustrated with a challenging task. These phrases included "I do not understand . . . "; "I am confused about . . . "; *and* "I need some extra help/extra time with . . . ." *Our time quickly ran out, and it was time to go to lunch. As my long line of fourth graders made its way to the cafeteria, I could hear the voices of several students echoing in the halls as they chanted, "There's no such thing as 'I can't'!" Although our social studies lesson was delayed, it was well worth the boost in confidence and understanding that filled our classroom because Anthony was now encouraged rather than embarrassed.*

JENNIFER MICHELE DIAZ
Fourth-Grade Teacher, Westmont Elementary School
Anaheim, **CALIFORNIA**

Analyze

I was taken aback by Anthony's comment about what he saw as his inability to read. I don't think he was trying to be humorous or disruptive; he actually believed he could not read. My goal was to show not only Anthony but also his classmates that he could read, and that the phrase "I can't" had no place in my class. By abolishing "I can't" from my classroom, my students could see that knowledge is power and that their inquisitiveness, resilience, and diligence could help them learn and be successful. Anthony's use of "I can't" also served as a green light for me to become an advocate for a student who needed help to think positively. That lesson was not about "sinking or swimming" as a teacher but also reflecting on how an unforeseen event in the classroom could be used to help a student see himself as successful.

Reflect

1. What resources would you use to help a student with reading difficulties similar to Anthony's?
2. How would you handle a student's embarrassment at not being able to perform in front of the class?
3. What strategies can teachers use to enhance students' self-esteem?

Influence of Teachers

The journey toward becoming a teacher often begins early in life. Although few people are born teachers, their early life experiences often encourage them to become teachers. With the exception of parents or guardians, the adults who have the greatest influence on children are often their teachers. A positive relationship with a teacher may have been the catalyst for your decision to become a teacher. Perhaps you were influenced by teachers similar to those the following students have described to me as "great" teachers:

> *A great teacher really likes kids. You can tell that they really want to help us learn. I love all of my teachers; they are great.* — Elementary student

> *Great teachers make it fun to be in their class. We laugh and have fun, but we also learn a lot.* — Elementary student

> *A great teacher cares for his or her students. A teacher like that understands that it can be hard sometimes to be a middle-school student. He or she listens to us and is always willing to help us.* — Middle-level student

> *Someone who explains things clearly—that's a great teacher. Someone who knows how to relate to kids and make things interesting.* — Middle-level student

> *A great teacher knows how to help us understand difficult stuff. If we have trouble learning one way, they try another way. It's like they really believe in you—they know you can be successful. They make you believe in yourself.* — High school student

> *Someone who understands what it's like to be in high school and helps us plan for the future; I think that's a great teacher. They have creative and fun ways to get us interested in the subject. They can manage a class without being mean or sarcastic. They are patient and really want to help us learn; they make us feel like we are on the same team.* — High school student

> *A great teacher respects his or her students. A teacher like that really listens to students and is open to what we think and feel. With a teacher like that, a student just naturally wants to cooperate and be a good student.* — High school student

Similar to most people who become teachers, you may have been more influenced by your teachers as people than as subject-matter experts. Often, the process of becoming a teacher begins early in life. For example, a teacher's influence during your formative years may have been the catalyst that started you thinking about the possibility of, one day, becoming like that teacher. Over time, the inspirational memory of that teacher led you to the teaching profession.

Desire to Serve

You may have chosen teaching because you want to serve others. You want your life's work to have meaning, to be more than just a job. As Arnie Duncan, former U.S. Secretary of Education, put it, "No other profession carries a greater burden for securing our economic future. No other profession holds out more promise of opportunity to children and young people from disadvantaged backgrounds. And no other profession deserves more respect" (U.S. Department of Education, February 15, 2012).

Your decision to serve through teaching may have been influenced by your experiences as a volunteer. One such teacher is Noah Zeichner, a former volunteer teacher in Ecuador who now teaches at Chief Sealth International High School in Seattle, **WASHINGTON**. His Ecuadorian students, he says, "had the desire to learn, in spite of overwhelming economic hardships. I figured if I could be successful there—with 12 students ages 12 to 18—I could do it in the United States" (Berry et al., 2011).

After the 9/11 terrorist attacks, many people reported that the uncertainty caused by the attacks led them to consider teaching as a career. According to school officials, the national wave of soul-searching after the attacks swelled the number of people seeking jobs as teachers. Clearly, they saw teaching as a way to serve.

Explore more deeply your reasons for becoming a teacher by completing the activity presented in Figure 1.3. The figure presents several characteristics that may indicate your probable satisfaction with teaching as a career.

Figure 1.3 Why do I want to teach?

Explore your reasons for becoming a teacher. Rate each of the following characteristics and experiences in relation to how each describes your motivation for choosing teaching as a career. Rate each item on a scale from 1–5 (1 = "very applicable"; 5 = "not at all applicable"). Which factors are most applicable to you? What is your strongest reason for becoming a teacher?

	Very applicable			Not at all applicable			Very applicable			Not at all applicable	
1. A passion for learning	1	2	3	4	5	**7.** Good verbal and writing skills	1	2	3	4	5
2. Success as a student	1	2	3	4	5	**8.** Appreciation for the arts	1	2	3	4	5
3. Good sense of humor	1	2	3	4	5	**9.** Experiences working with children (camp, church, tutoring, etc.)	1	2	3	4	5
4. Positive attitude toward students	1	2	3	4	5	**10.** Other teachers in family	1	2	3	4	5
5. Tolerance toward others	1	2	3	4	5	**11.** Encouragement from family to enter teaching	1	2	3	4	5
6. Patience	1	2	3	4	5	**12.** Desire to serve	1	2	3	4	5

What are the Benefits of Teaching?

Perhaps you are drawn to teaching by its practical advantages. Teachers' hours and vacations are well-known advantages. Although the hours most teachers devote to their jobs go far beyond the number of hours they actually spend at school, their schedules are more flexible than those of other professionals. Teachers who have young children can often be at home when their children are not in school, and nearly all teachers, regardless of years of experience, have numerous holidays and a long summer vacation. On the other hand, teachers at the nation's nearly 3,200 public year-round schools in 46 states have three or four mini-vacations throughout the year (NICHE, 2016). Teachers at year-round schools welcome the flexibility of being able to take vacations during off-peak seasons.

Salaries and Benefits

Although intangible rewards are a significant attraction to teaching, teachers want the public to acknowledge the value and status of teaching by supporting higher salaries. Support for higher teacher salaries was evident in the responses adults gave to a question on a 2016 nationwide survey: "If taxes are raised to try to improve your local public schools, what's the number one thing the money should be spent on?" Thirty-four percent said the money should be spent on teachers; 17 percent on supplies; 17 percent on classes/extracurriculars; 8 percent on infrastructure improvements and new schools; and 6 percent on learning specialists/counselors (Phi Delta Kappa, 2016, p. K16). Public support for higher teacher salaries has contributed to steady salary increases since 2000. The average salary of all teachers in 1999–2000 was $41,807; as Table 1.1 shows, for 2018, the average salary was $ 60,483 (National Education Association, 2018).

Although the general consensus is still that teachers are underpaid, teacher salaries are becoming more competitive with those of other occupations. Teachers in high-paying districts in states like California, Michigan, New York, and Pennsylvania with about 25 years of experience, advanced degrees, and additional school responsibilities could make more than $100,000 in 2017 (American Federation of Teachers, 2016).

Salaries could become an attraction of the profession if schools like the Equity Project (TEP) Charter School in New York City become more common. All TEP teachers earn $125,000 per year and are eligible for a $25,000 annual bonus based on schoolwide performance (TEP, 2017). The school was designed on the basis of research showing

Table 1.1 Teacher salaries, 2017; estimated average salaries, 2018; and percent change

	2017	2018	2017–18
	Salary ($)	Salary ($)	Change (%)
Alabama	50,391	50,239	–0.3
Alaska	68,138	69,474	2.0
Arizona	47,403	47,746	0.7
Arkansas	48,304	49,017	1.5
California	79,128	81,126	2.5
Colorado	51,808	52,389	1.1
Connecticut	73,147	73,113	0.0
Delaware	60,214	60,484	0.4
District of Columbia	75,692	76,486	1.0
Florida	47,267	47,721	1.0
Georgia	55,532	56,329	1.4
Hawaii	56,651	57,866	2.1
Idaho	47,504	49,225	3.6
Illinois	64,933	65,776	1.3
Indiana	54,308	54,846	1.0
Iowa	55,647	56,790	2.1
Kansas	49,422	50,403	2.0
Kentucky	52,338	52,952	1.2
Louisiana	50,000	50,256	0.5
Maine	51,077	51,663	1.1
Maryland	68,357	69,761	2.1
Massachusetts	78,100	79,710	2.1
Michigan	62,287	62,702	0.7
Minnesota	57,346	57,782	0.8
Mississippi	42,925	43,107	0.4
Missouri	48,618	49,208	1.2
Monatana	51,422	52,776	2.6
Nebraska	52,338	53,473	2.2
Nevada	57,376	57,812	0.8
New Hampshire	57,522	57,833	0.5
New Jersey	69,623	69,917	0.4
New Mexico	47,122	47,839	1.5
New York	81,902	83,585	2.1
North Carolina	49,970	50,861	1.8
North Dakota	52,968	54,421	2.7
Ohio	58,202	58,000	–0.3
Oklahoma	45,292	45,678	0.9
Oregon	61,862	63,143	2.1
Pennsylvania	66,265	67,398	1.7
Rhode Island	66,477	66,758	0.4
South Carolina	50,000	51,027	2.1
South Dakota	46,979	47,944	2.1
Tennessee	50,099	50,900	1.6
Texas	52,575	53,167	1.1
Utah	47,244	47,604	0.8
Vermont	57,349	58,527	2.1
Virginia	51,049	51,265	0.4

(continued)

Table 1.1 (continued)

	2017	2018	2017–18
	Salary ($)	Salary ($)	Change (%)
Washington	54,433	55,175	1.4
West Virginia	45,555	45,642	0.2
Wisconsin	54,988	55,895	1.6
Wyoming	58,187	58,578	0.7
United States	59,660	60,483	1.4

Adapted from *Rankings of the States 2017 and Estimates of School Statistics 2018.* Washington, DC: National Education Association, April 2018, p. 49. Data used with permission of the National Education Association © 2018. All rights reserved.

that teacher quality is the most important school-based factor in the academic success of students, particularly those from low-income families (Goldhaber & Anthony, 2003). The school uses what it calls the "3 Rs" to recruit master teachers: Rigorous Qualifications, Redefined Expectations, and Revolutionary Compensation. The school does not fundraise to support its investment in teachers' salaries; instead, "TEP's mission is to demonstrate that schools can make a radical investment in teacher equity by reallocating existing public funding" (TEP, 2017).

A teaching career at TEP involves weekly peer observations and co-teaching, an annual six-week Summer Development Institute, and a mandatory sabbatical once every five or six years. These Redefined Expectations are based on the realization that student achievement is increased when teachers have the time and support to improve their craft.

The Every Student Succeeds Act (ESSA) signed into law by the Obama administration in 2015, requires states to develop "equity plans" to improve the quality of teaching for all students. Most state plans include strategies for significantly increasing teacher salaries. The Teacher Salary Project analyzed state plans and identified the following strategies:

- Increasing salaries overall
- Increasing starting salaries
- Increasing long-term salary potential
- Ensuring salaries are competitive to recruit and retain teachers
- Salary increases for hard-to-staff schools
- Salary increases for hard-to-staff subjects
- Salary increases based on teacher effectiveness
- Bonuses based on teacher effectiveness
- Changing the teacher salary scale or system
- Tiered certification process, increased salaries at higher certification phases (Kraus, Sherratt, and Calegari, 2017, p. 8)

When comparing teachers' salaries state by state, remember that higher salaries are frequently linked to a higher cost of living, a more experienced teaching force, and a more desirable location. In addition, many districts have salary policies that attract the best graduates of teacher education programs, encourage quality teachers to remain in the classroom, or draw teachers into subjects and geographic areas in which there are shortages. These policies can increase a teacher's salary by thousands of dollars.

Teachers' salaries are typically determined by years of experience and advanced training, as evidenced by graduate credit hours or advanced degrees. When you become a teacher, you may be able to increase your salary by taking on additional duties, such as coaching an athletic team, producing the yearbook and school newspaper, or sponsoring clubs. In addition, your district may offer limited summer employment for teachers who wish to teach summer school or develop curriculum materials. Additionally, about one fourth of the nation's approximately 3.2 million public school teachers moonlight (i.e., hold a second job) to increase their earnings.

Teachers also receive various **fringe benefits**, such as medical insurance and retirement plans, which are usually given in addition to base salary. These benefits vary from district to district and are determined during collective bargaining sessions. When considering a school district for your first position, carefully examine the fringe benefits package as well as the salary schedule and opportunities for extra pay.

What are the Challenges of Teaching?

Like all professions, teaching has undesirable or difficult aspects. Frank McCourt, a teacher at four New York City high schools over a 30-year period and a noted author after his retirement from teaching, said a teacher needs to be "a drill sergeant, a rabbi, a disciplinarian, a low-level scholar, a clerk, a referee, a clown, a counselor, and therapist" (McCourt, 2005).

As a prospective teacher, you should consider the challenges as well as the satisfactions you are likely to encounter. You can make the most of your teacher education program if you are informed. Awareness of the realities of teaching will enable you to develop your personal philosophy of education, build a repertoire of teaching strategies, strengthen your leadership skills, and acquire a knowledge base of research and theory to guide your actions. In this manner, you can become a true professional—free to enjoy the many satisfactions of teaching and confident of your ability to deal with its challenges. The following sections discuss three challenges that are part of teachers' daily lives: long working hours, accountability for student learning in a high-stakes-testing environment, and motivating today's tech-savvy students.

Long Working Hours

The length of a teacher's workday may appear attractive, but teachers' actual working hours are another matter. Teachers' contracts do not include additional hours for lesson planning and evaluating students' work, nor do they include noninstructional assignments found at all levels of teaching—from recess duty to club sponsorship and coaching. Teachers spend an average of 50 hours a week on instructional duties, including an average of 12 hours a week devoted to noncompensated activities such as grading papers, bus duty, and advising clubs (National Education Association, 2017).

The need to keep accurate, detailed records of students' academic progress, absences, and lateness, as well as other forms of paperwork, is one of the teacher's most time-consuming tasks. Other nonteaching tasks include supervising students on the playground, at extracurricular events, and in the hallways, study halls, and lunchrooms; attending faculty meetings, parent conferences, and open houses; and taking tickets or selling concessions for athletic events. Nonteaching responsibilities often are enjoyable and provide opportunities to interact informally with students; however, they can lessen the amount of time and energy teachers have available for teaching-related tasks.

High-Stakes Testing and Increased Accountability

A significant challenge for today's teachers is the continuing emphasis on **high-stakes tests**. Since the mid-1960s, each state has mandated a standardized test to assess students' mastery of academic standards. For example, students in **WASHINGTON** State must take the Smarter Balanced Assessment based on the Common Core State Standards. Students in grades 3 through 8 and 11 take tests in English language arts and math; students in grades 5 and 8 take the Measurement of Student Progress (MSP) for Science; and students in grade 10 take a math and a biology end-of-course test. Students with significant cognitive challenges take the Washington Access to Instruction & Measurement (WA-AIM) tests for English language arts, math, and science. In **TEXAS**, students must take the State of Texas Assessments of Academic Readiness (STAAR), which assesses how well they have mastered the Texas Essential Knowledge and Skills (TEKS) in English language arts, mathematics, science, and social studies.

Some districts use high-stakes tests to determine whether a student can participate in extracurricular activities. In addition, 13 states require students to pass an "exit exam" before they can graduate from high school (FairTest, 2017).

Students' performance on tests can also determine whether teachers and administrators receive merit pay increases. For example, **FLORIDA** uses **value-added modeling** and requires that 50 percent of a teacher's evaluation is based on students' test scores. Value-added modeling measures the teacher's contribution in a given year by comparing test scores of their current students to the scores of those same students in previous school years, as well as to the scores of other students in the same grade. In this manner, the contribution, or "value added," each teacher provides in a given year is determined, and this "value" can be compared to the "value added" measures of other teachers.

In 2002, President George W. Bush, to fulfill his pledge to "leave no child behind," signed into legislation the **No Child Left Behind (NCLB) Act**, reauthorizing the Elementary and Secondary Education Act (ESEA) launched in 1965 as part of President Johnson's Great Society program. NCLB mandated statewide testing in reading and mathematics each year in grades 3–8. Also, NCLB required that, by the end of the academic year 2013–2014, public schools guarantee that all students were prepared to pass state proficiency tests. An additional key provision of NCLB was for schools to provide evidence each year that students were making **adequate yearly progress (AYP)**. Schools that failed to make AYP could be identified as "in need of improvement." The first year a school did not make AYP, it had to provide transportation for pupils who wanted to enroll in another public school. If the school failed to make AYP again, it had to pay for supplemental services, including tutoring.

Though NCLB was scheduled for revision in 2007, Congress did not approve the Obama administration's revision until 2015. The new law, the **Every Student Succeeds Act (ESSA)**, was intended to "fix" NCLB. More than 1,000 pages long, ESSA increased the authority of states and school districts for educational reform and improvement, while it reduced federal government authority in those areas.

ESSA, fully implemented in 2017–2018, requires that states set high curriculum standards in reading or language arts, math and science, and any other subject(s) identified by the state. Each state must demonstrate that its standards are aligned with higher education entrance requirements and state career and technical education standards.

Unlike NCLB, states are not required to submit their standards to the U.S. Department of Education. Moreover, the Department cannot influence or direct the states as they decide what standards to adopt and implement.

Similar to NCLB, ESSA requires that states have annual assessments in reading or language arts and math for grades 3–8 and once in high school. ESSA also requires science assessments—once in each of the following grade spans: 3–5, 6–9, and 10–12. ESSA allows states to use an alternative assessment to assess up to 1% of students with cognitive disabilities. To improve state assessment systems for English learners and students with disabilities, ESSA allows states to apply for additional federal funding. Instead of using a required statewide assessment, ESSA also allows local school districts to select a nationally recognized high school academic assessment (the ACT or SAT, for example) if the state has reviewed and approved that assessment.

ESSA replaces the Adequate Yearly Progress (AYP) requirement of NCLB with a requirement that states create their own accountability systems to determine student performance and school quality. States and school districts are required to assess the effectiveness of schools each year and, at least once every three years, to identify schools in need of comprehensive support and improvement.

With the continuing emphasis on high-stakes testing and teacher accountability for student learning, many districts and schools place great emphasis on preparing students for tests. Critics even suggest that curriculum goals are shifting from academic content to test preparation. In this environment, many teachers feel compelled to "teach to the test"; however, they point out that they have no control over many of the variables that influence student learning, such as poverty and underfunded schools. Figure 1.4 shows that 62% of more than 3,300 public school teachers surveyed believe they spend too much time preparing students for state-mandated tests, and 51% believe they spend too much time preparing students for district-mandated tests. Two teachers who responded to the survey explain why they believe too much time is devoted to testing:

> **Teacher 1:** Between screening tests, monitoring tests, and state testing, kids stop caring. They don't really see the impact of these scores, as they do not affect grades, and some of them don't care, especially students in high-poverty schools. All it does is reduce the amount of instructional time available to teachers.
>
> **Teacher 2:** Every year my students are given the Iowa Tests of Basic Skills, on the pretense that we are to use the results to plan for student achievement. By the time we get the results it is second semester and just about time for kids to take [the] state mandated test. It is a waste of time. . . . (Center on Education Policy, 2016, pp. 57–58)

Figure 1.4 Teacher views on whether the time spent preparing students for tests is appropriate

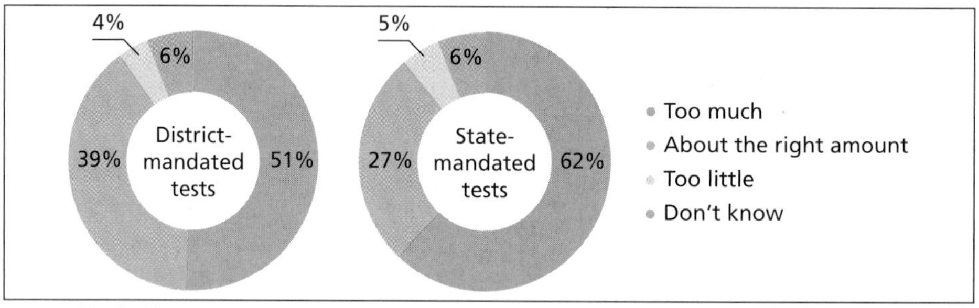

SOURCE: Used with permission from Listen to Us: Teacher Views and Voices. Center on Education Policy, Courtesy of The George Washington University.

Today's Tech-Savvy Students

Understanding how technology affects students and schools and integrating technology into teaching come easy for some teachers; for other teachers, however, it can be a challenge. Students in your classroom can be viewed as "digital natives"—that is, they were born *after* digital technologies were introduced on a wide scale. Much of their time each day is spent using technology. For example, American teenagers (13- to 18-year-olds) spend almost nine hours (8:56) each day using entertainment media (watching TV, movies, and online videos; playing video, computer, and mobile games; using social media; using the Internet; reading; and listening to music). Tweens (8- to 12-year-olds) spend almost six hours (5:55) each day using entertainment media daily (Rideout, 2015, p. 13).

Many schools have not kept up with the rapid changes in technology. Today's students have iPods, smartphones, video cameras, laptops, and digital cameras. Websites like Facebook, WhatsApp, Twitter, Instagram, Tumblr, Snapchat, and Pinterest are changing the way students communicate, socialize, and network. Sites like YouTube and iTunes bring media to students seamlessly, whether at home, school, or on the move. Media content comes into schools through smartphones, the Internet, email, text messages, and general entertainment (music, video, and blogs, for example). No longer are they merely passive receivers of information disseminated by media giants; today's young people can reach worldwide audiences on their own, at any time.

Vlue/Shutterstock

For these students, using advanced technology is an everyday part of their lives. How can teachers remain up to date regarding the role that technology plays in their students' lives?

To keep up with the media and technology environment today's students inhabit outside school, teachers must integrate technology into their teaching. For example, Marissa King, a fifth-grade teacher in Tulsa, **OKLAHOMA**, uses text messages and Instagram captions to teach her students about writing conventions and levels of formality. As she explains, "Our students spend a lot of time tweeting, composing Instagram captions, and text messaging. In the process, they are carefully observing and decoding the subtleties of social media text. They know when it's cool to replace 'yes' with 'yas' and how to turn a common courtesy into a sarcastic 'thanksss' with just a few extra letters" (King, 2017).

Application Exercise 1.2:

Integrating Technology

Another teacher who has integrated technology into teaching is Loveland, **COLORADO**, high school French teacher Toni Theisen. Her students use wikis, VoiceThreads, and Voki avatars; they comment on class films in real time using a free chat room site called TodaysMeet; and they answer questions using their cell phones and the Poll Everywhere site. In addition, they learn French by creating videos with Animoto.com and comic strips with Toon-Doo.

Theisen uses technology to connect her classes with people around the world. For instance, when her students were reading *Le Petit Prince*, Theisen came across a Twitter post from a New Zealand teacher who mentioned that her class was reading it, too. Within days, Theisen set up a wiki for the two classes to share, and students began posting audio podcasts describing the character they most identified with and creative videos interpreting the text. Today, Theisen's students manage a wiki with a partner school in La Réole, France, and through videos, podcasts, and VoiceThreads, Loveland students practice French and La Réole students practice English. Theisen's students even created a Flip cam tour of Loveland High for their French peers (George Lucas Educational Foundation, 2010).

Effective teachers recognize that technology can be a powerful tool for enhancing students' inquiry, reflection, and problem solving. They also realize that technology cannot be grafted onto existing teaching strategies; it must be integrated into those strategies. Chapter 12 of this book is designed to help you become a tech-savvy teacher. In addition, the Technology in Action feature in each chapter demonstrates practical applications of technology in real classrooms, by real teachers. These features also include technology-based learning activities designed to give you hands-on experience at integrating technology into teaching. The following Technology in Action feature explains how to create a wiki and provides an example of how a wiki could be used to discuss issues and content presented in *Becoming a Teacher*.

TECHNOLOGY in ACTION

Wikis in High School U.S. History

Maria Valquez has asked her high school U.S. History students to track and report on 2016 national election activities. She has organized her four U.S. History classes into 28 groups of 3 students each. Each group is assigned an aspect of the election to cover, such as specific political parties, an individual candidate, hot topic issues, media campaign messages, and so on. Maria wants her students to share the information they find with the rest of the school and the community. In addition to researching election activities, she hopes that students will find common ground and form a consensus on controversial issues. To facilitate this communication and sharing of information, Maria needs a technology tool that is not controlled by a single group or individual. She needs a tool that allows all students in her social studies classes to have an equal say. She decides to create a wiki.

As part of the social networking movement on the Internet, wikis follow the logic that many voices are better than one. A wiki is a website that allows collaborative work by various authors. A wiki website allows anyone or designated members of a group to create, delete, or edit the content on the website.

By using a wiki, students can explore a book, an events calendar, a field trip, and so on. A wiki can be a long-term exploration, such as the results of a newly formed conservation club, or a short-term event, like your high school basketball team going to the state tournament. In addition, many school districts use wikis for staff professional development. For example, the Avon Grove School District in **PENNSYLVANIA** uses a wiki for curriculum development, new teacher induction, and peer coaching.

VISIT: Several free wiki services are available to educators; among these are TeachersFirst, WikiWorks, Wikia, PBworks, and Wikispaces.

Check Your Understanding 1.3

What Will Society Expect of Me as a Teacher?

The prevailing view within our society is that teachers are public servants accountable to the people. As a result, society has high expectations of teachers—some would say too high. Entrusted with our nation's most precious resource—its children and youth—today's teachers are expected to have advanced knowledge and skills and high academic and ethical standards. Although promoting students' academic progress has always been their primary responsibility, teachers are also expected to further students' social, emotional, and moral development and to safeguard students' safety, health, and well-being. Increasingly, the public calls on teachers and schools to address the social problems and risk factors that affect student success.

The Public Trust

Teaching is subject to a high degree of public scrutiny and control. Because of its faith in the teaching profession, the public invests teachers with considerable power over its children. For the most part, parents willingly allow their children to be influenced by teachers and expect their children to obey and respect teachers. The public appears to have great confidence in local schools; however, attitudes toward schools elsewhere in the nation are significantly lower. For example, the 2017 annual Phi Delta Kappa Poll of the Public's Attitudes Toward the Public Schools revealed that 49 percent of citizens gave public schools in their community a grade of "A" or "B," whereas only 24 percent gave the same grades to the nation's schools (Phi Delta Kappa, 2017).

Teacher Competency and Effectiveness

Society believes that competent, effective teachers are important keys to a strong system of education. As U.S. Secretary of Education, Betsy DeVos, said at a White House reception honoring 2017 State Teachers of the Year: "Teachers shape our nation's future directly. [They] are educating the rising generations of leaders, thinkers, inventors, entrepreneurs and artists. [They] are helping to launch the problem-solvers and innovators of the future" (U.S. Department of Education, 2017).

As a teacher, you will be expected to be proficient in the use of instructional strategies, curriculum materials, advanced educational technologies, and classroom management techniques. You will also be expected to have a thorough understanding of the developmental levels of students and a solid grasp of the content you teach. To maintain and extend this high level of skill, you will be expected to keep informed of exemplary practices and to demonstrate a desire for professional development.

Teacher competency and effectiveness include the responsibility to help all learners succeed. Although today's students come from diverse backgrounds, society will expect you to believe in the potential of *all* children. Regardless of your students' ethnicity, language, gender, socioeconomic status, sexual orientation, religion, family backgrounds and living conditions, abilities, and disabilities, you will have a responsibility to ensure that all students develop to their fullest potential. To accomplish this, you will be expected to have a repertoire of instructional strategies and resources to create meaningful learning experiences that promote students' growth and development.

Teacher Accountability

Teachers must also be mindful of what society expects of its teachers—the duties and obligations that come with being a teacher. Society agrees that teachers are primarily responsible for promoting students' learning, although different members of society are not always in agreement about what students should learn. As a teacher, you will be expected to understand how factors such as student backgrounds, attitudes, and learning styles can affect achievement. You will be expected to create a safe and effective learning environment for your students, and you will be accountable for equalizing educational opportunity, promoting social justice, and maintaining high professional standards.

What is the Job Outlook for Teachers?

When you think ahead to a career in teaching, a question you are likely to ask yourself is, What is the job outlook for teachers? From time to time, figures reflecting **teacher supply and demand** have painted a rather bleak picture for those entering the teaching profession. At other times, finding a position has not been difficult. Even during times of teacher surplus, talented, qualified teachers are able to find jobs. Teaching is one of the largest professions in the United States; out of a national population of more than 326 million, more than 50 million attended public elementary and secondary schools during 2017–2018, where they were taught by more than 3 million teachers (National Center for Education Statistics, 2017). Figure 1.5 shows that public elementary and secondary school enrollment is projected to increase from 50.3 million students in 2014 to 51.7 million by 2026, an increase of 3 percent. Within such a large profession, annual openings resulting from retirements and career changes alone are numerous.

Employment of K–12 teachers in public and private schools is expected to increase from more than 3.5 million in 2016 to more than 3.8 million by 2023, more than an 8 percent increase (Hussar & Bailey, 2016, p. 48). The job outlook is brightest for teachers in high-demand fields such as science, technology, engineering, and mathematics (STEM); bilingual and special education; and in less desirable urban or rural school districts. In addition, the number of teachers retiring will continue to increase for the foreseeable future, and this will create many job openings (Bureau of Labor Statistics, 2017).

Figure 1.5 Actual and projected public school enrollment, by level: Fall 2000 through fall 2026

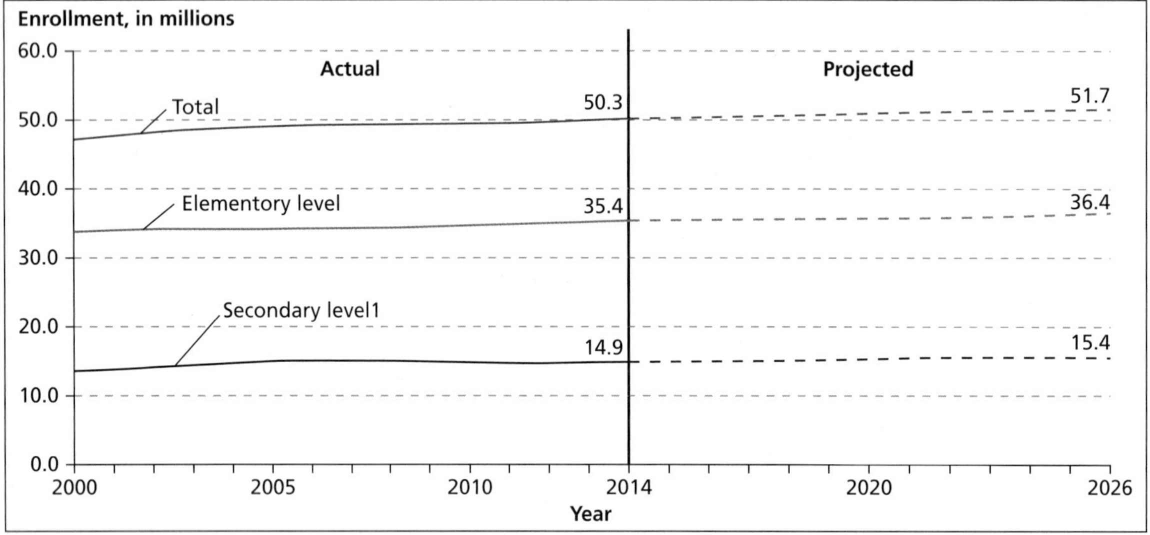

Note: The total ungraded counts of students were prorated to the elementary level (prekindergarten through grade 8) and the secondary level (grades 9 through 12).

[1]Includes students reported as being enrolled in grade 13.

SOURCE: McFarland, J., Hussar, B., de Brey, C., Snyder, T., Wang, X., Wilkinson-Flicker, S., Gebrekristos, S., Zhang, J., Rathbun, A., Barmer, A., Bullock Mann, F., and Hinz, S. (2017). *The Condition of Education 2017* (NCES 2017-144). U.S. Department of Education. Washington, DC: National Center for Education Statistics. Retrieved from https://nces.ed.gov/pubsearch/pubsinfo.asp?pubid=2017144.

Continuing Need for Teachers

Though the nation's economy may have its ups and downs, teachers will have many job opportunities in the near future. Currently, many school districts are luring teachers from other states and districts with bonuses and higher pay. In addition, increasing enrollments of students from minority groups and a shortage of teachers from minority groups are leading to increased efforts to recruit minority teachers. Also, the number of non-English-speaking students has grown dramatically, especially in **CALIFORNIA** and **FLORIDA**, creating a demand for bilingual teachers and teachers of English as a second language.

In response to a current shortage of teachers in some locations and anticipated teacher retirements, many states are implementing policies that will encourage more college students to become teachers. Some states give large signing bonuses distributed over the teacher's first few years of teaching. Some are increasing state scholarships, issuing loans for moving expenses, and implementing loan-forgiveness programs (U.S. Department of Labor, 2017).

For the foreseeable future, there will be exceptional job opportunities for teachers from diverse racial and ethnic backgrounds and for teachers with disabilities. Students from diverse racial, ethnic, and cultural backgrounds and students with disabilities benefit from having role models with whom they can easily identify. In addition, teachers from diverse groups and teachers with disabilities may have, in some instances, an enhanced understanding of student diversity and student variability that they can share with other teachers.

FOCUS ON **DIVERSITY**: DEMAND FOR TEACHERS OF COLOR

Video Example 1.2

Diversity in Schools: A middle school teacher discusses the importance of having teachers of diverse backgrounds in schools.

Approximately 50 percent of public school students were part of a minority group during 2017. By 2026, the percentage will be approximately 55 percent (National Center for Education Statistics, 2017). In the nation's 25 largest cities, students of color represent half or more of the student population (National Center for Education Statistics, July 2012).

When contrasted with the diverse mosaic of student enrollments, the backgrounds of today's teachers reveal less diversity. This issue, is due, in part, to the fact that minority students frequently attend our nation's most impoverished schools. At such schools, students receive little motivation to become teachers; and, if their school experiences are negative, they have little incentive to pursue a career in teaching.

The typical undergraduate candidate preparing to teach is a young, White female who recently graduated from high school and is attending college full-time. Postbaccalaureate-level individuals preparing to teach tend to be older, to include slightly more people of color and more males, to be transitioning into teaching from an occupation outside the field of education, to have prior teaching-related experience, and to be attending college part-time.

Figure 1.6 illustrates the differences between the racial and ethnic composition of students enrolled in U.S. public schools and that of teachers at those schools. The figure shows that the population of public school teachers has gradually become more diverse over time. During the 1987–88 school year, 87 percent of public school teachers were White compared to 82 percent during 2011–12 school year.

Figure 1.6 (a) Percentage distribution of U.S. public school students enrolled in prekindergarten through 12th grade, by race/ethnicity: Selected years, fall 2002, fall 2012, and fall 2024. (b) Percentage distribution of teachers in public elementary and secondary schools, by race/ethnicity: Selected years, 1987–88 through 2011–12.

(a)

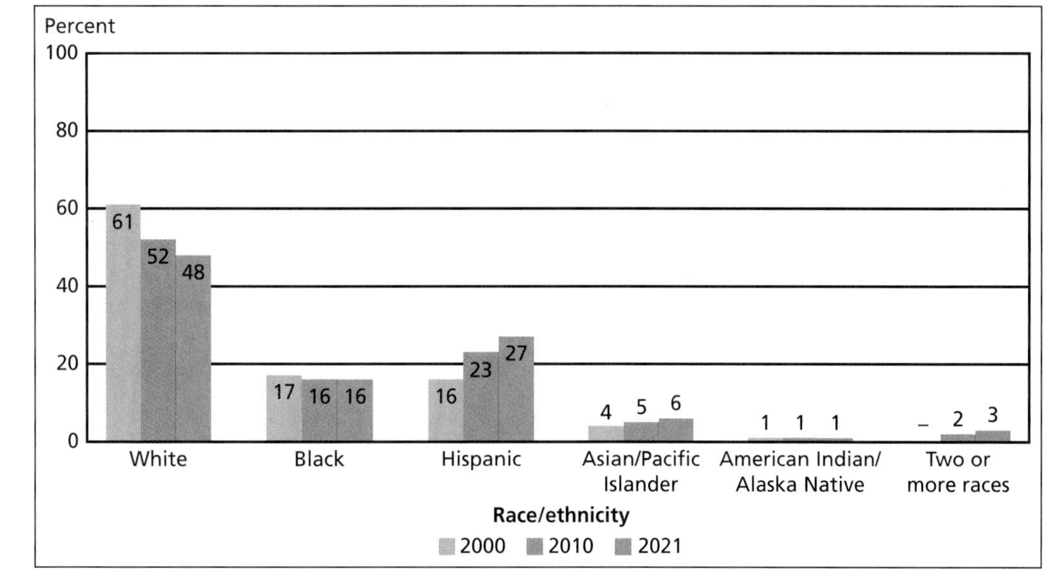

† Not applicable.

Note: Prior to 2008, separate data on students of two or more races were not collected. Detail may not sum to totals because of rounding. Data for 2024 are projected.

(continued)

Figure 1.6 Continued

(b)

School type and selected school characteristic	Total number of teachers	Percent of teachers by race/ethnicity						
		Hispanic, regardless of race	White, non-Hispanic	Black, non-Hispanic	Asian, non-Hispanic	Native Hawaiian/ Pacific Islander, non-Hispanic	American Indian/ Alaska Native, non-Hispanic	Two or more races, non-Hispanic
All public schools	3,385,200	7.8	81.9	6.8	1.8	0.1	0.5	1.0
School classification								
Traditional public	3,269,500	7.6	82.3	6.6	1.8	0.1	0.5	1.0
Charter school	115,600	13.1	69.9	11.8!	2.8	‡	0.6!	1.7!
Community type								
City	‡	‡	‡	‡	‡	‡	‡	‡
Suburban	1,096,400	7.6	83.6	5.7	1.5	‡	0.3!	1.2
Town	411,00	5.6	87.7	3.6	1.6!	0.1!	0.6	0.8
Rural	916,600	4.7	88.7	4.2	0.7	‡	0.8	0.8
School level								
Primary	1,626,800	8.7	81.2	7.1	1.7	‡	0.4	0.8
Middle	592,100	7.0	81.6	7.7	1.7	0.2!	0.4	1.3
High	961,300	6.8	83.6	5.6	2.1	0.2!	0.5!	1.2
Combined	206,000	7.4	80.9	7.9!	1.2!	‡	1.1	1.3

*Data for years 1987–88 through 1999–2000 are only roughly comparable to data for later years, because the new category of two or more races was introduced in 2003–04.

Note: Excludes prekindergarten teachers. Data are based on a head count of full-time and part-time teachers rather than on the number of full-time-equivalent teachers reported in other tables. The detail may not sum to totals because of rounding, missing data, and cell suppression. Race categories exclude persons of Hispanic ethnicity. The Other category represents the sum of Asian, Pacific Islander, American Indian or Alaska Native, and two or more races.

SOURCE: *The State of Racial Diversity in the Educator Workforce*. Policy and Program Studies Service Office of Planning, Evaluation and Policy Development, Washington, DC: U.S. Department of Education, May 2016, pp. 5–6.

Demand for Teachers by Geographic Region and Specialty Area

Through 2023, elementary and secondary school enrollments are projected to rise more slowly than in the past, as children of the baby boom generation will leave the school system. Enrollments will vary widely across the nation, however. The West and South will experience the largest increases, whereas enrollments in the Midwest will remain about the same, and those in the Northeast will decline (Hussar & Bailey, 2016). The ease with which you will find your first teaching position is also related to your area of specialization. In 2019, for example, job seekers able to teach bilingual education, special education, English as a second language (ESL), mathematics, chemistry, or physics were in an especially favorable position.

Wavebreak Media Ltd\123RF

Teachers with disabilities can be highly effective at teaching students in "regular" classrooms. In what ways can teachers with disabilities be role models for students without disabilities?

How Will I Become an Effective Teacher?

NCLB required that all students be taught by **highly qualified teachers (HQTs)**. "Highly qualified" teachers would have (1) a bachelor's degree, (2) full state certification, and (3) knowledge of each subject they teach. Though ESSA no longer continues NCLB's "highly qualified teacher" requirement, the law requires that teachers at schools with high percentages of students have full state certification. States must also submit a definition of an "ineffective teacher" and a plan to ensure that "ineffective" teachers aren't disproportionately teaching in schools primarily serving poor and minority students.

How will you make the transition from being a teacher education student to being an effective, highly qualified teacher? At this point in your journey to become a teacher, you can do a great deal to make your entry into teaching professionally rewarding and to ensure that you will become an effective teacher. During your journey toward becoming an effective teacher, you will become immersed in the world of professional standards.

TEACHERS' VOICES  BEING AN AGENT OF CHANGE

CARLA HUDSON

Necessity and the Art of Differentiation

Some may say that necessity is the mother of invention, but in my classroom, necessity is the mother of *differentiation.*

Three years ago, my school district assigned me to the Beaver Valley School in Plain, **WASHINGTON**. Beaver Valley is one of only 8 "remote and necessary" schools in Washington, and one of less than 400 in the United States. *Remote and necessary* is the current term for what was formerly known as a *one-room schoolhouse*. I approached my new assignment with trepidation. At various times, I had taught kindergarten, first grade, and third grade. Now I was being asked to teach grades 1–4 all at the same time and in the same classroom.

Differentiation is a word regularly utilized in education circles. In general, it refers to modulating instruction so that all students learn at a pace and on a level suitable for their academic abilities. Most teachers agree with the goal of differentiation but find it hard to implement in practice. Faced with four grades and 22 beaming faces, I realized very quickly that differentiation was not optional in this classroom.

To set up my classroom for success, I differentiated my classroom in three ways: (1) by establishing flexible groupings across grades; (2) by organizing reading and math into grade-level rotations; and (3) by utilizing paraprofessional, parent, and community support.

Flexible Groupings

Flexible grouping enables me to place students at certain times of day according to their ability level. The advantage to a multigrade classroom is that I have all of the curricula for each of the grades available at my fingertips. In the early morning, my children enter the class and begin work on a short math and reading review. Children work independently and on their own level. For instance, I have a third grader who works on fourth-grade math during this time, but does his reading review on the second-grade level. The combinations vary widely, but the activity is independent and the shared learning spontaneous. For some children, this is a time of enrichment; for others, it is a time of review.

Grade-Level Rotations

To ensure that each student is exposed to the grade-level expectations, I keep my reading groups in grade-level bands. I've organized the reading and math times into rotation centers. During the one and a half-hour reading block, I meet with each grade level for 30 minutes (grades 3–4 combined). While I am with a reading group, the other grade levels rotate between the computer center and the silent reading/workbook center. Focused instruction on the learning standards is provided during this time. Math is organized similarly so that each grade is taught independently even though the class remains intact. Timed fast-fact drills, however, are naturally differentiated. I have a first grader who is working on multiplication facts, while some older children are still mastering addition and subtraction.

Paraprofessional, Parent, and Community Support

Successful differentiation requires that a support system be in place. I utilize my paraprofessional teacher with parents and community volunteers. While I am working with one grade level, they are supervising the work of the other children in their various centers. In addition, because we don't have any specialized services available to our students, the support team also helps with progress monitoring and provides extra assistance to those students who need a bit more instruction in order to be successful.

Conclusion

My colleagues from other schools often shake their heads in amazement when I tell them that I teach four grades in one classroom. They wonder how it is possible to meet the needs of such a wide range of children at multiple grade levels. A deliberate focus on differentiation has been the key to making my multigrade classroom function efficiently. However, now that I have navigated the differentiation waters successfully, I see no reason why the same system would not work at a single grade level. Success requires developing a well-organized curriculum, putting learning systems into place, and efficiently utilizing school and volunteer personnel. Necessity is truly the mother of differentiation.

PERSONAL REFLECTION

1. Hudson says her approach to differentiation (i.e., teaching four grades in one classroom) could "work at a single grade level." To what extent do you agree with her? Disagree?
2. According to Hudson, one key to her success is "efficiently utilizing" volunteers. How might volunteers help you be successful during your first year of teaching?

Carla Hudson, formerly a multigrade teacher at Beaver Valley School in Plain, **WASHINGTON**, is now K–12 Principal, Wilbur School District, Wilbur, **WASHINGTON**.

Professional Standards

To ensure that all students are taught by highly qualified teachers, several professional associations and state departments of education have developed standards that reflect what teachers should know and be able to do. Most likely, the teacher education program in which you are enrolled will use one or more of these sets of standards to evaluate your progress toward becoming an effective teacher. During your training, you are sure to hear repeatedly about plans instituted by state departments of education to assess teachers and students alike on an ongoing basis. After you become a teacher, you may learn even more about state standards if you have a mentor like Carla Hudson, author of this chapter's Teachers' Voices: Being an Agent of Change. Hudson represents her school on **WASHINGTON** State's Teacher/Principal Evaluation Pilot (TPEP), a statewide program launched in 2011 to evaluate teachers and principals.

The professional standards that have had the greatest impact on teacher education programs nationally (as well as on teachers' ongoing professional growth and development) are those developed by the **Interstate Teacher Assessment and Support Consortium (InTASC)**, the **Council for the Accreditation of Educator Preparation (CAEP)**, the **Praxis Series: Professional Assessments for Beginning Teachers**, and the **National Board for Professional Teaching Standards (NBPTS)**. Figure 1.7 provides an overview of their standards. How have these standards influenced the teacher education program in which you are enrolled? Does your state have a set of professional standards that also applies to your teacher education program?

Certification and Licensure

Successful completion of a college or university teacher preparation program will not automatically enable you to teach. State certification or licensure is required for teaching in the public schools and in many private schools as well. The terms *certification* and *licensure* are essentially synonymous in the teaching profession; some states issue teaching certificates, whereas others issue licenses. States also differ in the types of certificates offered; teachers can be granted provisional certificates, professional or permanent certificates, or emergency certificates. In some cases, large cities (e.g., Chicago, New York, Buffalo) have their own certification requirements that must be met. And certain local school districts have additional requirements, such as a written examination, before one can teach in those districts.

A **teaching certificate** is actually a license to teach. The department of education for each of the 50 states and the District of Columbia sets the requirements for certification or licensure. A certificate usually indicates at what level and in what content areas one may teach. One might be certified, for example, for all-level (K–12) physical education or art, secondary English, elementary education, or middle-level education. Currently, about two-thirds of the states offer certification for teaching at the middle school or junior high level—an increase from 1987 when about half of the states offered such certification. In addition, a certificate may list other areas of specialization, such as driver's training, coaching, or journalism. If you plan to go into nonteaching areas such as counseling, librarianship, or administration, special certificates are usually required.

The Praxis Tests

Nationwide, 47 states require completion of the *Praxis Tests* developed by Educational Testing Service (ETS) in consultation with teachers, educational researchers, the National Education Association, and the American Federation of Teachers. The Praxis Tests (*praxis* means "putting theory into practice") enable states to create a system of tests that meet their specific licensing requirements.

The Praxis Series, which replaced the National Teacher Examination in the mid-1990s, consists of three components:

Praxis Core Academic Skills for Educators (Core)—Praxis Core covers the reading, writing, and mathematics skills that all teachers need, regardless of grade or subject taught. The Praxis Core, a computer-based assessment administered through an ETS test center, is given early in a student's teacher education program. Programs may use Core tests to evaluate students for entry into a teacher education program, and many states require Praxis Core scores for licensure. To help students pass Praxis Core, ETS offers Study Companions and other study tools, as well as practice tests.

Praxis Subject Assessments—Praxis Subject Assessments measure teacher education students' knowledge of the subjects they will teach and general and

Figure 1.7 Professional standards for teachers: What should teachers know and be able to do?

InTASC Core Teaching Standards

InTASC is a consortium of states that has developed standards used by 38 states for initial teaching licensing. InTASC "Model Core Teaching Standards that outline what teachers should know and be able to do to ensure every P-12 student reaches the goal of being ready to enter college or the workforce in today's world. This "common core" outlines the principles and foundations of teaching practice that cut across all subject areas and grade levels and that all teachers share" (InTASC, p. 3)

CAEP Standards

CAEP Advances equity and excellence in educator preparation through evidence-based accreditation that assures quality and supports continuous improvement to strengthen P-12. student learning. [CAEP ensures that] educator programs prepare new teachers to know their subjects, their students, and have the clinical training that allows them to enter the classroom ready to teach effectively.

Standard 1. Content and Pedagogical Knowledge

Candidates develop a deep understanding of the critical concepts and principles of their discipline and, by completion, are able to use discipline-specific practices flexibly to advance the learning of all students toward attainment of college and career-readiness standards. Candidates demonstrate an understanding of the 10 InTASC standards...in the following categories: the learner and learning; content; instructional practice, and professional responsibility.

Standard 2. Clinical Partnerships and Practice

Effective partnerships and high-quality clinical practice are central to preparation so that candidates develop the knowledge, skills, and professional dispositions necessary to demonstrate positive impact on all P-12. students' learning and development.

Standard 3. Candidate Quality, Recruitment, and Selectivity

[The Teacher preparation program] demonstrates that the quality of candidates is a continuing and purposeful part of its responsibility from recruitment, at admission, through the progression of courses and clinical experiences, and to decisions that completers are prepared to teach effectively and are recommended for certification.

Standard 4. Program Impact

[The teacher preparation program] demonstrates the impact of its completers on P-12 student learning and development, classroom instruction, and schools, and the satisfaction of its completers with the relevance and effectiveness of their preparation.

Standard 5. [Program Quality Assurance and Continuous Improvement]

[The teacher preparation program] maintains a quality assurance system comprised of valid data from multiple measures, including evidence of candidates' and completers' positive impact on P-12 student learning and development (CAEP, June 2016)

Praxis Tests

The *Praxis* tests measure teacher candidates' knowledge and skills. The tests are used for licensing and certification processes and include:

- ***Praxis* Core Academic Skills for Educators (Core)**

  These tests measure academic skills in reading, writing, and mathematics. They were designed to provide comprehensive assessments that measure the skills and content knowledge of candidates entering teacher preparation programs.

- ***Praxis* Subject Assessments**

  These tests measure subject-specific content knowledge, as well as general and subject-specific teaching skills, that you need for beginning teaching.

- ***Praxis* Content Knowledge for Teaching Assessments (CKT)**

  These tests measure subject-specific content knowledge, with a focus on specialized content knowledge used in elementary school teaching. (Educational Testing Service, 2018. Retrieved from https://www.ets.org/praxis/about)

NBPTS Standards

This board issues professional certificates to teachers who possess extensive professional knowledge and the ability to perform at a high level. Certification candidates submit a portfolio including video of classroom instruction and samples of student work plus the teacher's reflective comments. NBPTS evaluators, who teach in the same field as the candidate, judge all elements of assessments. NBPTS has developed the "core propositions" on which voluntary national teacher certification is based. (NBPTS, 2017)

1. Teachers are committed to students and their learning.
2. Teachers know the subjects they teach and how to teach those subjects to students.
3. Teachers are responsible for managing and monitoring student learning.
4. Teachers think systematically about their practice and learn from experience.
5. Teachers are members of learning communities.

subject-specific teaching skills and knowledge. In most cases, Subject Assessment tests are taken after completion of an undergraduate program. The tests, available in more than 70 subject areas, have a core content module required by every state, with the remaining modules selected on an individual basis by the states. Each state can base its assessment on multiple-choice items or on candidate-constructed response modules. In addition, Praxis Subject Assessments includes the Principles of Learning and Teaching (PLT) test, designed to assess teachers' professional knowledge. The PLT is available in three versions: K–6, 5–9, and 7–12.

Praxis Content Knowledge for Teaching Assessments (CKT)—Praxis Content Knowledge for Teaching Assessments is designed for those seeking licensure as elementary teachers. CKT tests assess whether prospective elementary teachers have the reading and language arts, mathematics, science, and social studies content knowledge needed at the time of entry to the profession. The tests measure subject-specific content knowledge and specialized content knowledge used in elementary-level teaching. The Praxis Elementary Education: Content Knowledge for Teaching (CKT) and Elementary Education: Applied Content Knowledge for Teaching tests measure both types of knowledge. CKT assessment tasks focus on how well one can recognize, understand, and respond to the content problems teachers encounter in day-to-day teaching and apply content knowledge to solve those problems.

State Licensure Certification Requirements

For a person to receive a license to teach, all states require successful completion of an approved teacher education program that culminates with at least a bachelor's degree. To be approved, programs must pass a review by the state department of education approximately every five years. In addition to approval at the state level, most of the nearly 1,300 programs in the nation have regional accreditation, and about half voluntarily seek accreditation by the Council for the Accreditation of Educator Preparation (CAEP). Currently, all states require an average of six to eight semester credits of supervised student teaching. Alabama, Colorado, Idaho, Indiana, Nevada, New York, and Virginia require a master's degree for advanced certification; and Arizona, Maryland, Montana, Oregon, and Washington require either a master's degree or a specified number of semester credits after certification (Kaye, 2016). Additional requirements may also include U.S. citizenship, an oath of loyalty, fingerprinting, a background check, or a health examination.

A few states, including Iowa, New Mexico, North Carolina, and Oklahoma, waive state licensing requirements for teachers certified by the National Board for Professional Teaching Standards (NBPTS). About half of the states issue a license to a person from another state who holds a valid NBPTS certificate. For a current listing of state and local action supporting NBPTS certification, visit the website for NBPTS.

Nearly all states now require testing of teachers for initial licensure. States use either a standardized test (usually the Praxis Tests) or a test developed by outside consultants. Areas covered by the states' tests usually include basic skills, professional knowledge, and general knowledge. Many states also require an on-the-job performance evaluation for licensure.

Today, most states do not grant a teaching license for life. Some states issue three- to five-year licenses, which may be renewed only with proof of coursework completed beyond the bachelor's degree. And, amid considerable controversy, several states, including Connecticut, Maryland, Massachusetts, New Hampshire, Rhode Island, South Carolina, and Wisconsin, have enacted testing for **recertification** of experienced teachers.

Licensure requirements differ from state to state, and they are frequently modified. To remain up to date on the requirements for the state in which you plan to teach, it is important that you keep in touch with your teacher placement office or the certification officer at your college or university. You may also wish to refer to *Requirements for Certification of Teachers, Counselors, Librarians, Administrators for Elementary and Secondary Schools* (University of Chicago Press), an annual publication that lists state-by-state certification requirements. Or you may contact the teacher certification office in the state where you plan to teach. Currently, 47 states and the District of Columbia are members of the **National Association of State Directors of Teacher Education and Certification's (NASDTEC) Interstate Agreement**, a reciprocity agreement whereby a certificate obtained in one state will be honored in another. If you plan to teach in a state other than the one in which you are currently studying, you should find out whether both states are members of the NASDTEC Interstate Agreement.

More than 424,000 teachers, many of whom are noncertified, teach in the growing system of private, parochial, for-profit, and charter schools in the United States (Snyder, de Brey, and Dillow, 2016, p. 149). Private and parochial schools supported largely by tuition and gifts, and for-profit schools operated by private educational corporations, usually have no certification requirements for teachers. Also, charter schools, although most are publicly funded, are often free of state certification requirements. A school's charter (an agreement between the school's founders and its sponsor—usually a local school board) may waive certification requirements if the school guarantees that students will attain a specified level of achievement.

Alternative Certification

Despite the national movement to make certification requirements more stringent, concern about meeting the demand for new public school teachers and attracting minority-group members into the teaching profession has resulted in increasing use of **alternative teacher certification** programs. In 2012, nearly 15 percent of public school teachers and 25 percent of charter school teachers entered the teaching profession through alternative routes (National Center for Education Statistics, 2012).

Alternative certification programs are designed for people who already have at least a bachelor's degree in a field other than education and want to become licensed to teach. Most alternative certification programs are collaborative efforts among state departments of education, teacher education programs in colleges and universities, and school districts. For example, Washington State University, in collaboration with area school districts, has a federally funded program to prepare paraprofessional educators (teachers' aides, for example) in southwest Washington to become bilingual/ESL teachers. Also, many school districts offer teaching fellows programs that provide provisional certification and tuition for graduate-level study in education. Compared with recent college graduates who enter teaching directly from a traditional college-based teacher preparation program, those who enter teaching through alternate routes tend to be "older, more diverse, and more willing to teach wherever the jobs are and in high-demand subjects than are traditionally trained teachers" (Feistritzer & Haar, 2008, p. 126).

Summary

What Do I Want to Teach?

- Individual reasons for becoming a teacher may be intrinsic (desire to work with young people, passion for the subject, influence of teachers, a desire to serve others and society) as well as extrinsic (work hours, vacations).

What Are the Benefits of Teaching?

- Practical benefits of teaching include on-the-job hours at school, vacations, increasing salaries, and benefits.

What Are the Challenges of Teaching?

- The challenges of teaching include long working hours, meeting the accountability demands of high-stakes testing and federal legislation that emphasizes closing the achievement gap and the need for "great" teachers in every classroom, and understanding the pervasive influence of technology on today's children and youth.

What Will Society Expect of Me as a Teacher?

- Society expects teachers to be competent and effective, and it holds teachers accountable for student achievement, for helping all learners succeed, for promoting social justice, and for maintaining high standards of conduct.

What Is the Job Outlook for Teachers?

- The job outlook for teachers is positive, especially for teachers in high-demand fields and in less desirable urban or rural school districts.
- In contrast to the diversity of student enrollments, the backgrounds of today's teachers are less diverse; thus, teachers from diverse racial and ethnic backgrounds and teachers with disabilities will experience exceptional employment opportunities for the foreseeable future.
- Teacher supply and demand in content areas and geographic regions influences finding a teaching position.

How Will I Become an Effective Teacher?

- Four sets of professional standards have a great impact on teacher education programs nationally (as well as on teachers' ongoing professional growth and development): standards developed by the Interstate Teacher Assessment and Support Consortium (InTASC), the Council for the Accreditation of Educator Preparation (CAEP), the Praxis Tests, and the National Board for Professional Teaching Standards (NBPTS).
- State certification is required for teaching in public schools and in many private schools. Some large cities and local school districts have additional criteria for certification. Certification requirements for teachers vary from state to state and are frequently modified. Some states waive licensing requirements for teachers certified by the National Board for Professional Teaching Standards (NBPTS).
- Most states require testing of teachers for initial certification, and some require recertification after a three- to five-year period.
- States that are members of the Interstate Certification Agreement Contract honor teaching certificates granted by certain other states.

Professional Reflections and Activities

Teacher's Journal

1. Think about a time when a teacher truly motivated you to learn. What did that teacher do to motivate you? Do you believe other students in the class had the same reaction to this teacher? Why or why not?
2. Consider your reasons for deciding to become a teacher. How do they compare with those described in this chapter?

Teacher's Research

1. Locate three or more articles in newspapers, magazines, and on the Internet that discuss the Every Student Succeeds Act (ESSA). Synthesize the information presented in those articles and share your findings with the rest of your class.
2. Formulate a research question concerning demographic aspects of teachers in the United States. Your question might relate to one or more of the following topics:
   - Teachers' attitudes
   - Characteristics of the teaching force
   - Teacher recruitment
   - Teacher supply and demand
   - Teaching salaries and benefits

Begin your data search at the website for the U.S. Department of Education's National Center for Education Statistics. Present a brief oral report to the rest of your class that summarizes the results of your data search.

Observations and Interviews

1. In a small group of three or four of your classmates, visit a local school and interview teachers to learn about their perceptions of the rewards and challenges of teaching. Share your findings with other members of your class.
2. Interview one or more teachers at a local elementary, middle, junior, or senior high school. Ask the teacher(s) to identify the characteristics of "great," highly qualified teachers.

Professional Portfolio

To help you in your journey toward becoming a teacher, each chapter in this textbook includes suggestions for developing your professional portfolio—a collection of evidence documenting your growth and development while learning to become a teacher. At the end of this course, you will be well on your way toward a portfolio that documents your knowledge, skills, and attitudes for teaching and contains valuable resources for your first teaching position.

For your first portfolio entry, identify significant experiences in your life that have contributed to your decision to become a teacher. In your entry (or videotaped version), discuss your reasons for becoming a teacher and the rewards teaching will hold for you. Before developing your portfolio entry, you might wish to visit the website for the National Teacher of the Year Program, co-sponsored by the Council of Chief State School Officers (CCSSO) and the Pearson Foundation. Here, you can watch short videos in which Teachers of the Year from 2007 to the present explain "Why I teach."

Chapter 2
Today's Teachers

Tyler Olson/Shutterstock

Learning Outcomes

After reading this chapter, you will be able to do the following:

2.1 Describe the work of teachers in different types of schools and in different subject areas.

2.2 Explain how teachers are role models for students, spontaneous problem solvers, and reflective thinkers.

2.3 Explain the four types of essential knowledge that today's teachers must have.

2.4 Explain the extent to which teaching meets the commonly agreed-upon characteristics of a full profession.

2.5 Describe the major professional organizations to which teachers belong.

2.6 Explain how teacher leaders are transforming the profession of teaching.

READERS' VOICES

Who are today's teachers?

I decided to become a teacher because I want to have a huge, positive influence on my students' lives—just like my own teachers influenced me.

—**HERB,**
Teacher Education program, first year

Who are Today's Teachers?

Teaching is the largest profession in the United States. Kindergarten, elementary school, middle school, secondary school, and special education teachers total about 3.76 million. Of those teachers, about 179,200 are kindergarten teachers, 1.48 million are elementary school teachers, 641,700 are middle school teachers, 1.01 million are secondary school teachers, and 450,700 are special education teachers (U.S. Department of Labor, 2017).

Table 2.1 shows that today's public school teachers are well educated—almost half have a master's degree, compared to 27 percent who had that degree in 1971 (National Education Association, 2010); and 40 percent of teachers have 15 or more years of classroom experience.

Today's teachers teach in schools with different grade configurations; they teach in different subject-matter and specialized areas; and they teach students with different types of learning needs.

Table 2.1 Public School Teachers in the United States

Sex	
Male	23.7%
Female	76.3%
Race/Ethnicity	
Hispanic, regardless of race	7.8%
White, non-Hispanic	81.9%
Black, non-Hispanic	6.8%
Asian, non-Hispanic	1.8%
Native Hawaiian/Pacific Islander, non-Hispanic	0.1%
American Indian/Alaska Native, non-Hispanic	0.5%
Two or more races, non-Hispanic	1.0%
Highest Degree Earned	
No bachelor's degree	3.8%
Bachelor's degree	39.9%
Master's degree	47.7%
Higher than master's degree	8.7%
Years of Teaching Experience	
Less than 4 years	11.3%
4–9 years	28.6%
10–14 years	20.9%
15 or more years	39.3%

Adapted from Goldring, R., Gray, L., and Bitterman, A. (2013). *Characteristics of Public and Private Elementary and Secondary School Teachers in the United States: Results from the 2011–12 Schools and Staffing Survey* (NCES 2013-314). U.S. Department of Education. Washington, DC: National Center for Education Statistics, pp. 6, 8, 10, 12, 14, 16, and 18–19. Retrieved July 24, 2017, from https://nces.ed.gov/pubs2013/2013314.pdf.

Grade-Level Designations

Teachers in U.S. schools teach students who are approximately 3 through 17 years of age and attend schools from the pre-kindergarten (pre-K) through high school levels. Figure 2.1 shows the most common grade-level designations for education in the United States. Some school districts have slightly different grade-level designations—for example, districts that include middle schools at the 6th- through 8th-grade levels, or junior high schools that include 6th- through 9th-grade levels and senior high schools that include 10th- through 12th-grade levels.

Figure 2.1 The most common grade-level designations for education in the United States

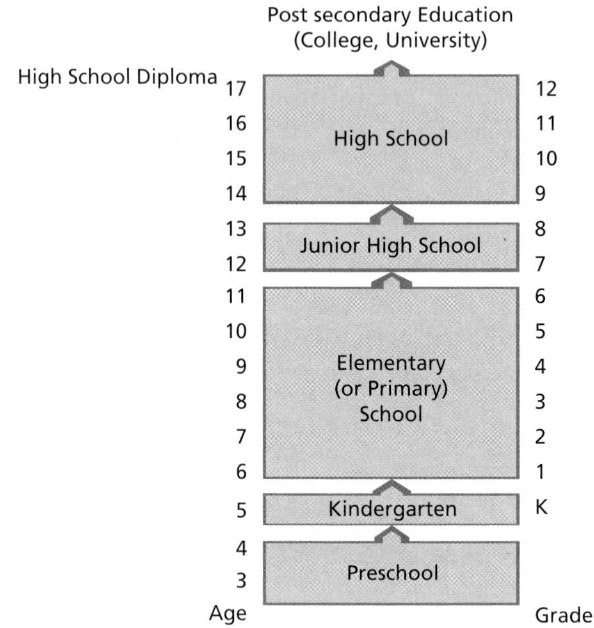

PRE-K TEACHERS Teachers involved in **pre-K education** (also termed **early childhood education** and, less frequently, nursery school education) teach children ranging from birth to age 8. Pre-K teachers play a critical role in the development of children. What children learn and experience during their early years shapes their views of themselves and the world and influences their later success in school, work, and their personal lives.

Pre-K teachers use a less structured approach than teachers of older students. Children at the pre-K level are involved in small-group lessons; one-on-one instruction; and learning through creative activities such as art, dance, and music. Kindergarten teachers use play and hands-on activities also; however, academic learning becomes more important in kindergarten classrooms. Letter recognition, phonics, numbers, and basic understanding of nature and science are introduced at the kindergarten level.

If you had a pre-K educational experience, you probably remember learning through play and interactive activities. Your pre-K teacher(s) most likely used play to further your language and vocabulary development (storytelling, rhyming games, and play acting, for example), improve your social skills (cooperating with other children to build a small town in a sandbox), and introduce scientific and mathematical concepts (learning to balance and count blocks when building a skyscraper or mixing colors for fingerpainting).

ELEMENTARY TEACHERS Elementary school teachers usually teach one class, from grades 1 through 6, of about 25 children in several subjects. In some elementary schools, two or more teachers work as a team with a group of students in at least one subject. In other elementary schools, a teacher may teach one subject—often music, art, reading, science, arithmetic, or physical education—to a number of classes. Increasing numbers of teachers teach in **multiage**, or multigrade, **classrooms**, with students from different grade levels. Elementary school teachers introduce children to mathematics, language, science, and social studies. They use games, music, artwork, films, books, computers, and other tools to teach basic skills.

Elementary school teachers write daily lesson plans based on school or state requirements, and they record student attendance each day. They assign homework, grade papers, and record grades on tests and homework. At regular intervals, they evaluate each child's academic progress and write progress reports for parents. On the progress report, they note any behavioral or social problems and disciplinary actions. Elementary teachers also supervise activities on playgrounds, in cafeterias, and in other areas of the school.

Elementary teachers also meet with parents or guardians to discuss student progress or problems. If a child is not adjusting well to school, teachers work with the child; administrators; and parents, guardians, or other family members to find solutions.

Some elementary school teachers teach subjects such as art or music. Art teachers develop art projects, maintain art supplies, and help children develop art skills. Music teachers teach music and lead singing groups, and sometimes they direct the school band. Other teachers teach physical education to help children develop physical coordination. Often, these teachers work at several schools during a week. Some elementary teachers coordinate volunteer groups and/or oversee special projects in addition to their regular duties.

Elementary teachers frequently work with parent volunteers in the classroom. They also attend in-service workshops to learn about new instructional methods and materials. Typically, elementary teachers meet regularly with other staff members to discuss school issues.

MIDDLE SCHOOL TEACHERS Middle school teachers help students learn more about the subjects studied in elementary school. Most middle school teachers specialize in a specific subject, such as English, mathematics, or science, and they teach several classes a day in that subject area. However, some middle school teachers work in self-contained classrooms and teach all major subjects to one group of students.

Monkey Business/Fotolia

Middle-level students are at a unique stage of life and have different developmental needs. Why is it important that teachers understand their students' developmental needs?

During the middle school years, young adolescents are dealing with an array of physical, intellectual, emotional, and social challenges. Some mature rapidly, whereas others mature more slowly. Some may be physically mature yet socially immature. Middle school students have very different developmental needs. Middle school teachers understand these needs and are skilled at providing students with developmentally appropriate learning activities. They also understand that students must believe that teachers really care about their lives. Teachers convey genuine caring when they actively listen to students' concerns and show interest in the important events in students' lives. An event that may seem trivial to an adult—a minor disagreement with a friend, for example—can have huge importance to a middle school student.

HIGH SCHOOL TEACHERS Most high school teachers teach four or five courses within a single content area. For example, a high school math teacher might teach two classes of Algebra I, a trigonometry class, and two geometry classes. An English teacher might teach two classes of sophomore English, one advanced-placement (AP) English literature class for which students receive college credit, one honors English class, and one journalism class.

In addition to teaching, some high school teachers monitor study halls and homerooms or supervise extracurricular activities. On occasion, they may supervise events such as school dances or athletic contests or accompany students on field trips. They may also counsel students regarding classes to take at the high school and/or plans for college, training, or employment after high school.

High school teachers also participate in faculty meetings, professional development workshops, and educational conferences. If they have students with behavioral or academic problems, they may meet with those students, their parents or guardians, and administrators to resolve the problems. They may also identify students with physical or mental difficulties and refer them to the school counselor, special education teacher(s), or other professionals.

Cathy Yeulet/123RF

High school students are at a unique stage of life. What are some of the rewards and challenges of teaching high school-age students?

Teachers in Urban, Suburban, and Rural Settings

Schools in rural, suburban, and urban settings tend to have different cultures. Each type of setting has its "pluses and minuses." Some teachers prefer rural settings; others prefer suburban settings; while still others prefer urban settings. What's important is to find the *right setting for you*—whether it's a rural, suburban, or urban school.

Approximately 7.1 million students attended rural schools during 2015–16 (Showalter, Klein, Johnson, & Hartman, 2017). Montana has the highest percentage of rural students (74.0%) and Massachusetts has the lowest (5.5%). Rural schools are typically smaller than suburban and urban schools. In fact, in 2007, 327 one-room schools remained in rural areas of our country (Brimley, Verstegen, & Garfield, 2012).

Students in rural districts tend to be less culturally diverse than those in urban and suburban districts, although this varies from state to state. For example, cultural minorities make up more than 85.6 percent of the student population in New Mexico, compared to less than 3.7 percent in Rhode Island (Showalter, et al., 2017). During 2013–2014, 72.4 percent of rural students were White, 9.3 percent were Black, 12.2 percent were Hispanic, 1.6 percent were Asian/Pacific Islander, 2.1 percent were American Indian/Alaska Native, and 2.4 percent were of two or more races. Approximately 248,000 students, or 3.5 percent of the total rural enrollment, were English language learners (ELLs) (Snyder, de Brey, & Dillow, 2016).

Poverty is also a growing issue in rural districts, particularly in the Southeast, Southwest, and Appalachia. For example, during 2015–16, more than half of the rural students in 23 states were eligible for free or reduced lunch. During 2011–12, only 9 states had that proportion of eligible students (Showalter, et al., 2017).

Teaching in rural schools has advantages and disadvantages. Rural districts often lack resources to provide students with the latest learning materials and educational technology. On the other hand, teachers at rural schools may find it easier to develop close relationships with students, families, and the community: As Yvonne Butterfield, a science teacher at Mauston High School in rural Wisconsin says, "You can develop a personal relationship with students and families. You see them on the streets, at the gas station or in sports activities you are involved in with your own kids. It's a good thing" (Armitage, 2017).

Approximately 19.7 million students attended the nation's 30,922 public suburban schools during 2013–2014 (Snyder, et al., 2016). That school year, 51.5 percent of suburban students were White, 13.7 percent were Black, 24.6 percent were Hispanic, 6.4 percent were Asian/Pacific Islander, 0.5 percent were American Indian/Alaska Native, and 3.2 percent were of two or more races. Approximately 1.7 million students, or 8.5 percent of the total suburban enrollment, were English language learners (ELLs).

Suburban schools are larger and may lack the cohesiveness of rural schools. On the other hand, suburban schools often have more resources such as laboratories, sports facilities, educational technology, and library materials to enhance students' learning. A teacher describes her experiences at a large suburban high school: "We have a lot more programs, materials, clubs, and after-school activities. Parents are really involved—which can be a good thing or not. Parents have high expectations of teachers and don't hesitate to complain."

More than 15.1 million students attended the nation's 26,545 public urban schools during 2013–2014 (Snyder, et al., 2016). That school year, 30.0 percent of urban students were White, 23.9 percent were Black, 35.1 percent were Hispanic, 7.1 percent were Asian/Pacific Islander, 0.7 percent were American Indian/Alaska Native, and 3.2 percent were of two or more races. Approximately 2.1 million students, or 8.5 percent of the total urban enrollment, were English language learners (ELLs).

The cultures of urban schools vary considerably. Some are academically oriented and serve parents who are as involved in the education of their children as parents in surrounding, often more affluent, suburbs. Other urban schools, unfortunately, are in the lowest percentiles of academic achievement. Urban schools found in or near low-income areas often reflect the social problems of the surrounding area, such as poverty, drug abuse, and crime. Though challenging, the rewards of teaching at an urban school can be significant, as Lincoln Johnson, a special education mathematics teacher at Locke Launch to College Academy in Los Angeles, California, makes clear:

> My students have given me reason, purpose, and triumph that no money could buy. I teach for students who have no fathers or male role models. I teach for children who know neither who they are nor what they want to be. I teach for students who have gaps in their skills and abilities that need filling. I teach for students who feel they are failures . . . (Johnson, 2010, p. 9)

Teachers in Nontraditional School Settings

In addition to teachers who work in pre-K, elementary, middle, and high school programs, some teachers teach in nontraditional school settings, such as private schools, charter schools, alternative schools, and magnet schools.

PRIVATE SCHOOL TEACHERS Private schools are not administered by local school districts and are funded by tuition instead of through public taxation. More than 441,000 teachers teach full-time at 33,600 private schools (Broughman & Swaim, 2016). Most private schools do not require a state-issued teaching certificate. If a private school requires certification, it may hire a noncertified teacher provisionally if the teacher can meet state certification requirements within a reasonable period of time.

Many private schools are religiously affiliated. Religious sects operate about 70 percent of private schools, and the remainder are nonsectarian (Broughman & Swaim, 2016). There are schools founded on the Christian, Jewish, and Muslim faiths, to name a few. The Catholic Church has one of the largest networks of religious schools in the country—6,429 schools—comprised of 5,224 elementary schools and 1,205 secondary schools (National Catholic Education Association, 2017). Nearly 139,000 teachers teach full-time at Catholic schools (Broughman & Swaim, 2016).

Teachers in private schools often have smaller class sizes and more control over determining the curriculum and standards for performance and discipline. Their students also tend to be more motivated because private schools can be selective in their admissions processes. Essentially, private schools can deny enrollment to students that they believe lack the necessary academic drive. Although private school teachers may earn less than public school teachers, they may have other benefits, such as free or subsidized housing. Table 2.2 presents average salaries for teachers at public and private schools.

Table 2.2 Median Pay for Teachers at Public and Private Schools, 2016

Kindergarten and elementary teachers	$55,490
Middle school teachers	$56,720
High school teachers	$58,030
Special education teachers	$57,910
Private school teachers	$47,471

SOURCE: Bureau of Labor Statistics, U.S. Department of Labor, *Occupational Outlook Handbook, 2016-17 Edition*.

CHARTER SCHOOL TEACHERS **Charter schools** are independent public schools that are given a charter to operate by a school district, state, or national government. They are funded with taxpayer money but administered privately, often with the goal of making a profit. For a charter school to be approved, the school must agree to document students' mastery of predetermined outcomes. To some extent, teachers at charter schools have freedom from many of the regulations that apply to traditional public school teachers. However, charter school teachers must account—usually to a state or local school board—for producing positive academic results and adhering to the charter contract. A teacher at Somerset Prep Public Charter School in **WASHINGTON, D.C.** explains why she decided to teach at a charter school:

> The smaller class sizes allow for more personalization of instruction and the flexibility of the curriculum allows me to be creative in my teachings. However, the main reason I chose a charter school . . . was the sense of family you find in a charter school that I knew would be hard to find in a typical school setting. The relationships made between educators and students at my current school . . . [do] not end at the graduation stage. (Garcia, 2016)

The number of charter schools is growing. The first charter school opened in Minnesota in 1992. From 1999 to 2016, the number of charter schools increased from 1,542 to 6,939. During that same period, the number of students enrolled in public charter schools increased from 0.35 million to 3.2 million students. In 2016, 129,000 teachers taught at charter schools (National Alliance of Public Charter Schools, 2016). Charter schools may grow even more rapidly under the administration of President Donald Trump. As Betsy DeVos, U.S. Secretary of Education appointed by President Trump in 2017, pointed out:

> The president is proposing the most ambitious expansion of education choice in our nation's history. The proposal's aim is to empower states and give leaders . . . the flexibility and opportunity to enhance the choices [for students]. Our nation's students deserve to have their individual educations supported through state and local programs that provide parents with the most freedom and flexibility. (DeVos, 2017)

ALTERNATIVE SCHOOL TEACHERS Alternative schools are designed to meet the needs of students at risk of failure and dropping out. Students are referred to alternative schools because of low grades, truancy, disruptive behavior, suspension, pregnancy, or similar factors associated with early withdrawal from school. There is no single commonly accepted definition for an **alternative school** or program (Lange & Sletten, 2002); however, an alternative school is usually a small, highly individualized school separate from the regular school. Most public school districts have at least one alternative school or program for at-risk students. Approximately 7,700 teachers teach at the more than 900 alternative schools around the country (Broughman & Swaim, 2016).

Because they often have small class sizes and the freedom to be creative in meeting students' needs, alternative school teachers usually find their work very satisfying. As a teacher at one alternative school said, "Here, you finally have a sense of ownership as a teacher. You have to come in the morning and create something and keep working at it, and it's a tremendous experience" (Firestone, 2008).

MAGNET SCHOOL TEACHERS Magnet schools are free public schools of choice operated by school districts or a consortium of districts. A **magnet school** offers a curriculum that focuses on a specific area such as science, technology, engineering, and mathematics (STEM), fine and performing arts, International Baccalaureate, international studies, MicroSociety, career and technical education (CTE), and world languages. Magnet schools, which often draw students from a larger attendance area than regular schools, are frequently used to promote voluntary desegregation. In 2017, teachers taught 2.6 million students at over 3,800 magnet schools in the United States (Magnet Schools of America, 2017).

Teachers at magnet schools may experience greater levels of autonomy, influence on school policies, and professional development than teachers at traditional schools. One example of a professional magnet school teacher is Tere Pujol-Burns, who teaches kindergarten through fifth grade at Sunset Elementary School in Miami, **FLORIDA**. Selected as Magnet Schools of America's 2013 National Teacher of the Year, Pujol-Burns is the Lead Teacher of the International Studies Magnet Program at her school. She developed the Change for Change program and brought together teachers, students, and parents to identify areas of need in the local and international community and to provide service-learning opportunities for students. Her students have raised funds for kangaroo adoption, rainforest preservation, Save the Waves Coalition, and UNICEF (Magnet Schools of America, 2013; Miami-Dade County Public Schools, 2013).

Teachers in Specialized Areas

Some teachers, regardless of level, teach in areas differentiated according to the learning needs of students in various groups, for example, special education teachers who specialize in teaching students with special needs. Other teachers specialize in teaching students whose first language is not English (often called English language learners [ELLs]) while still others teach specialized areas such as art, vocational education, music, or physical education.

Table 2.3 shows how the number of teachers in different teaching fields has changed between 1987 and 2012. Note that ESL, a small field, had a 1,088-percent increase in the number of teachers reporting it as their main field! Special education, the second-largest field in teaching, increased by 92 percent.

Table 2.3 Number and Percent of Teachers by Teaching Field, 1987–2012

	1987–88		2011–12		Change from 1987–88 to 2011–12	
Teacher characteristics	Number of teachers	Percent of teachers	Number of teachers	Percent of teachers	Change in the number of teachers	Percent change in the number of teachers
Field						
General elementary	974,400	37.0	1,231,700	32.0	257,200	26.4
Math	140,900	5.4	326,000	8.5	185,100	131.4
Natural science	124,700	4.7	259,900	6.8	135,200	108.4
Social science	126,200	4.8	239,700	6.2	113,500	89.9
English/language arts	169,800	6.5	435,800	11.3	266,000	156.7
Foreign language	56,900	2.2	130,900	3.4	74,000	130.1
Vocational-technical	125,900	4.8	159,200	4.1	33,300	26.5
Art and music	164,400	6.3	225,600	5.9	61,200	37.2
Drama or dance[1]	—	—	19,600	0.5	—	—
Health and P.E.	127,400	4.8	202,000	5.2	74,600	58.6
English as a second language (ESL)	6,000	0.2	71,600	1.9	65,600	1,088.3
Special education	235,200	8.9	450,500	11.7	215,300	91.6
Other	378,400	14.4	97,500	2.5	−281,000	−74.3

–Not available

NOTE: The 1987–88 survey did not include measures of the teaching fields of drama and dance.

SOURCE: Adapted from Ingersoll, R., and Merrill, L. (2017). *A Quarter Century of Changes in the Elementary and Secondary Teaching Force: From 1987 to 2012*. Statistical Analysis Report (NCES 2017-092). U.S. Department of Education. Washington, DC: National Center for Education Statistics, p. 17. Retrieved July 24, 2017, from http://nces.ed.gov/pubsearch.

SPECIAL EDUCATION TEACHERS Special education teachers work with children and youth who have a variety of disabilities. Special education teachers held a total of about 491,100 jobs in 2014. About 25,500 worked at the preschool level; 198,100 worked at the kindergarten and elementary level; 93,000 worked at the middle school level; and 134,000 worked at the high school level (Bureau of Labor Statistics, 2017). Most special education teachers work in public and private educational institutions. A few work for individual and social assistance agencies or residential facilities, or in homebound or hospital environments.

Often, special education teachers specialize in working with students who have specific disabilities—learning disabilities, autism, and brain injuries, for example. Special education teachers must develop an **individualized education program (IEP)** for students and work collaboratively with regular classroom teachers, parents, social workers, school psychologists, and other school staff. Special education teachers are trained to use advanced educational technologies—for example, word-prediction software, voice-recognition computers, and speech synthesizers—to help students with special needs learn.

As schools become more inclusive, special education teachers and general education teachers increasingly work together in general education classrooms. Special education teachers help general educators adapt curriculum materials and teaching techniques to meet the needs of students with disabilities. They coordinate the work of teachers, teacher assistants, and related personnel, such as therapists and social workers, to meet the individualized needs of the student within inclusive special education programs. A large part

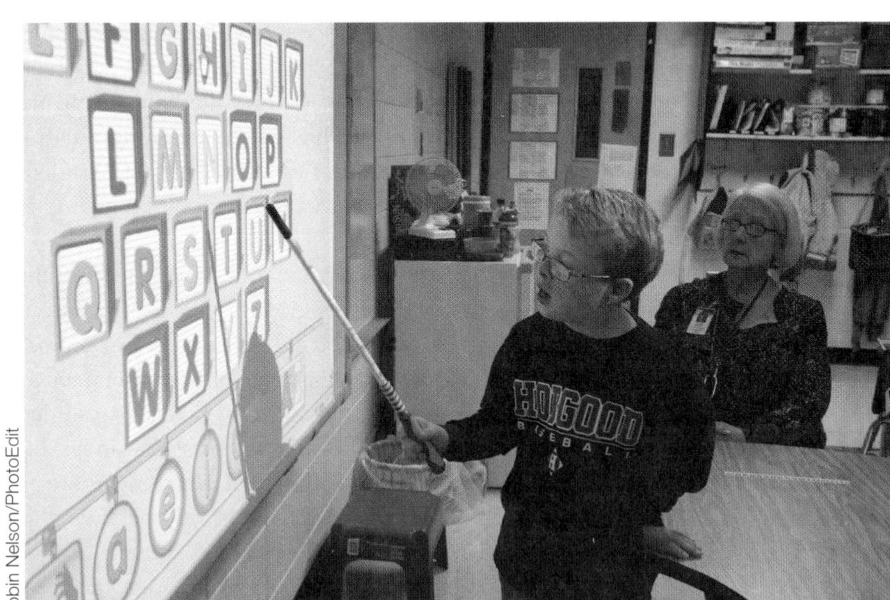

The Individualized Education Program (IEP) for this student with multiple disabilities provides for educational technology to help him learn.

of a special education teacher's job involves communicating and coordinating with others involved in the child's well-being, including parents, social workers, school psychologists, occupational and physical therapists, school administrators, and other teachers.

Special education teachers work in a variety of settings. Some have their own classrooms and teach only special education students; others work as special education resource teachers and offer individualized help to students in general education classrooms; and others teach alongside general education teachers in classes that have both general and special education students. Some teachers work with special education students for several hours a day in a resource room, separate from their general education classroom.

In schools that use the **response to intervention (RTI) model**, special education teachers work with general education teachers on schoolwide screenings and progress monitoring to ensure that students are "responsive" to instruction they receive in the classroom. According to the response to intervention (RTI) model, students who do not make adequate academic progress and who are at risk for reading and other learning disabilities receive increasingly intensive instructional services. The RTI model is designed to determine, as early as possible, if a student's low achievement is due to instructional or behavioral factors or whether the student has a possible learning disability. The goal is to provide the student with appropriate instruction and educational assistance *before* he or she experiences years of low achievement.

FOCUS ON **DIVERSITY**: TEACHERS OF ENGLISH LANGUAGE LEARNERS (ELLs)

Many teachers, whether they have specialized training or not, teach **English language learners (ELLs)**, students whose first language is not English. About 21.8 percent of children ages 5–14 speak a language other than English at home (U.S. Census Bureau, August 2013). Ten percent or more of public school students in the following states are ELLs: Oregon, Hawaii, Alaska, Colorado, Texas, New Mexico, Nevada, and California (Aud, Wilkinson-Flicker, Kristapovich, Rathbun, Wang, and Zhang, 2013). Among the population five years and older who spoke a language other than English at home during 2011, more than 15 percent spoke English "not well," and 7 percent spoke English "not at all" (U.S. Census Bureau, August 2013).

Only 30 percent of teachers who instruct ELL students have received training to teach ELL students, and fewer than 3 percent have earned a degree in English as a second language (ESL) or bilingual education (Aud, Fox, & KewalRamani, 2010). Nevertheless, as comments by the following teacher who has no ELL training illustrate, professional teachers are committed to teaching *all* their students: "They [ELL students] need to be in the classroom . . . . My job is to teach the kids. If they don't know English, that's my job" (Valli & Buese, 2007, p. 532).

Seeing ELL students develop as learners can be very rewarding. Most teachers find their ELL students eager to learn. Once they realize that their teachers want them to succeed, ELL students, in turn, will want to please their teachers by being successful in the classroom. As a result, they are willing to work hard to adjust to an English-language environment. For example, one ELL teacher told the author how much "fun" she now has teaching students from three different language backgrounds—Spanish, Somali, and Russian—in her high school classroom. Now, two months after the start of the school year, her students are participating actively in class activities, and she takes tremendous satisfaction knowing that she is "making a difference in students' lives." According to her, "My ELL students are good kids—I can tell that they really want to learn. They are so cooperative. Also, they really appreciate it when they know that I am interested in learning about their cultures. In a way, I learn as much from my students as they learn from me."

Application Exercise 2.1
Making English Relevant for ELL Students

ART TEACHERS From elementary school through high school, art teachers teach students the visual arts—painting, sketching, designing, and sculpting, for instance. Art teachers may specialize in teaching one or more areas of art, such as illustration, art history, or commercial art, and at times they may organize student art contests or arrange for student artwork to be exhibited. In some cases, art teachers travel from school to school.

More than other areas of the curriculum, art and music (discussed in the following subsection) have had an insecure position. When schools face budget cutbacks or increased pressure to prepare students for high-stakes tests, eliminating art and music is often considered.

MUSIC TEACHERS Music teachers instruct students in vocal or instrumental music and foster music appreciation. Elementary and secondary school music teachers often direct the school chorus, choir, orchestra, or marching band, as well as give group and private lessons. They instruct students in the technical aspects of music, conduct rehearsals, and evaluate student performances. School music teachers sometimes take students on field trips to musical presentations, or the students may perform off campus under the direction of the teacher.

VOCATIONAL EDUCATION TEACHERS Vocational education teachers (sometimes called vocational/technical education [votech] teachers) train students to work in fields such as healthcare, business, auto repair, communications, and technology. About 12,730 teachers taught vocational education at the middle school level in 2016, and 80,100 taught at the high school level (U.S. Department of Labor, 2017). They often teach courses that are in high demand by area employers, who may provide input into the curriculum and offer internships to students. Many vocational teachers play an active role in developing and overseeing these internships. To prepare students for the real world of specific vocational or technical careers, vocational education teachers use a hands-on approach to teach academic and vocational skills.

PHYSICAL EDUCATION TEACHERS Physical education teachers teach students from the elementary through high school levels. The ultimate aim of their teaching is to introduce students to physical activities that develop within them a desire to maintain physical fitness throughout life.

At the high school level, physical education teachers often teach one or two classes of health, coach one or more sports, or teach driver education. Physical education teachers teach individual and team sports that promote the development of students' physical abilities. They organize and referee indoor and outdoor sports, such as volleyball, football, baseball, and basketball. They teach students beginning or advanced calisthenics, gymnastics, or corrective exercises. They teach and demonstrate the use of gymnastic and training equipment such as trampolines and weight-lifting equipment.

At one time, physical education teachers placed greater emphasis on highly competitive team sports. Many students, however, did not do well at such sports and may have experienced a lowered sense of self-esteem as a result. Today's physical education teachers offer activities to meet the needs and abilities of all students, not just the athletically talented. In addition to traditional team sports such as football, basketball, and baseball, and individual sports such as swimming and wrestling, students participate in activities such as aerobics, badminton, gymnastics, volleyball, golf, soccer, and yoga.

What Do Teachers *Do* in the Classroom?

At first, this question may appear easy to answer. From your own experiences as a student, you know that teachers assign learning tasks. They ask questions and evaluate students' responses. They lecture and, on occasion, demonstrate what students are to do. They assign chapters to read in the text and then conduct recitations or give quizzes on that material. They praise some students for right answers or good work, and they prod and chastise others in the hope that their work will improve. And near the end of the term or semester, they decide who has passed and who has failed.

More specifically, you also know what effective teachers do. They develop interesting, engaging curriculum materials and learning activities. They write lesson plans and implement those plans using different teaching strategies to meet the learning needs of students. They carefully monitor students' efforts to learn new material. They assess students' learning using a variety of formal and informal assessments. They create a positive, well-managed classroom environment. They know how to prevent student misbehavior; and when discipline problems arise, they respond quickly and effectively. In Part 3 of this book, The Art of Teaching, and throughout the remainder of your teacher preparation program, you will learn how to develop these and additional professional skills.

However, teaching is more than the sum of the behaviors that you have observed in your own teachers. As you move ahead in your journey toward becoming a teacher, you will discover that teaching involves more than performing certain behaviors in front of a group of students. A significant portion of the teacher's work is mental and involves problem solving in response to unforeseen events that emerge in the classroom.

Teaching is a creative act in which teachers continually shape and reshape lessons, events, and the experiences of their students. A former teacher and now head of an organization that creates small, personalized, public high schools in collaboration with their communities describes the creative dimensions of teaching this way: "The act of being a teacher is the act of . . . using your skills and love for kids to figure out how to create the best environment to help your students [learn]" (Littky, 2004, p. 12).

Although your teachers reflected different personalities and methods, your experiences as a student are similar to the experiences of other students. Our recollections about teachers who were good or bad, easy or hard, interesting or dull are drawn from a commonly shared set of experiences. The universality of these experiences leads us to conclude that we know "the way teaching is" and what teachers do. However, in a seminal article aptly titled "The Way Teaching Is," noted educational researcher Philip Jackson points out that teaching is "fleeting and ephemeral" because of the "fragile quality of the psychological condition that is created by the teacher" (Jackson, 1965, p. 62).

The following sections examine three dimensions of teaching that illustrate how, on the one hand, teaching involves "enduring puzzlements, persistent dilemmas, complex conundrums, [and] enigmatic paradoxes" (Eisner, 2006, p. 44) while, on the other, it offers opportunities for "saving lives, rescuing a child from despair, restoring a sense of hope, soothing discomfort" (p. 46). Effective teachers understand that they are role models for students, spontaneous problem solvers, and reflective thinkers.

Teacher as a Role Model for Students

Clearly, teachers are role models for their students. In the elementary grades, teachers are idolized by their young students. At the high school level, teachers have the potential to inspire students' admiration if they model positive attitudes and behaviors. Teachers teach not only through what they *say* and *do* in the classroom—they teach through who they *are* as people. They have the power to influence their students' lives in the present; and, often, this influence endures into the future and has a profound effect on students' development throughout life.

In *Listening to Urban Kids: School Reform and the Teachers They Want* (Wilson & Corbett, 2001), students express the following expectations about their teachers' attitudes and behaviors:

> I heard teachers talking about people, saying "Those kids can't do nothing." Kids want teachers who believe in them. (p. 86)
>
> A good teacher to me is a teacher who is patient, willing to accept the fact that she might be dealing with students who have problems. (p. 87)
>
> Since this is one of his first year's teaching, I give him credit. He relates, but he also teaches . . . . He advises us. He not only tries to teach but gets involved with us. (p. 88)

Developing positive relationships with students is important, particularly in today's culturally diverse classrooms. To develop learning activities that are interesting and relevant to their students, teachers must learn about their backgrounds and experiences. Teachers use this knowledge to make decisions about the curriculum, teaching methods, classroom management, and assessment of students' learning.

Teachers also model attitudes toward the subjects they teach and show students through their example that learning is an ongoing, life-enriching process that does not end with diplomas and graduations. Their example confirms the timeless message of Rabindranath Tagore that is inscribed above the doorway of a public building in India: "A teacher can never truly teach unless he is still learning himself. A lamp can never light another lamp unless it continues to burn its own flame."

FOCUS ON **DIVERSITY**: BLACK TEACHERS AS ROLE MODELS FOR BLACK STUDENTS

Black teachers can be significant role models for black male students. An Institute of Labor Economics study found that having at least one black teacher in grades 3 through 5 reduced students' probability of dropping out by 29 percent. Having a

Figure 2.2 Influence of having a black teacher in 3rd-5th grade on persistently poor black male students' probability of dropping out and interest in college.

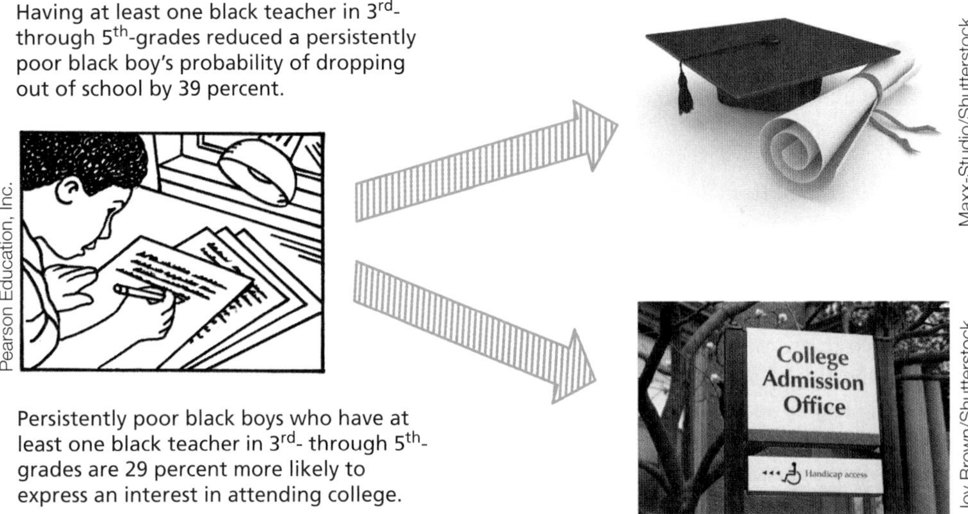

Having at least one black teacher in 3rd- through 5th-grades reduced a persistently poor black boy's probability of dropping out of school by 39 percent.
Persistently poor black boys who have at least one black teacher in 3rd- through 5th-grades are 29 percent more likely to express an interest in attending college.
College Admission Office
Pearson Education, Inc.
Maxx-Studio/Shutterstock
Joy Brown/Shutterstock

Note: "Persistently poor" indicates that the student was persistently eligible for free or reduced price lunch in each of grades 3–8.

SOURCE: Based on data from Seth, G., Hart, C. M. D., Lindsay, C. C., & Papageorge, N. W. (2017). *The long-run impacts of same-race teachers*. Discussion Paper. Bonn, Germany: Institute of Labor Economics.

black teacher also made them 18 percent more likely to express an interest in attending college after graduation. For low-income black students (those who received free or reduced-price lunches throughout elementary school), the impact was even greater. Figure 2.2 shows that their chance of dropping out was 39 percent less, and they were 29 percent more likely to say they were considering college (Seth, Hart, Lindsay, & Papageorge, 2017).

FOCUS ON **DIVERSITY**: TEACHER AS A MODEL OF CROSS-CULTURAL COMPETENCE

In this chapter's Teachers' Voices: Being an Agent of Change, George Watson discusses the role of teachers in a dynamic, global world. Teachers have a responsibility to prepare students to be successful in a global, interdependent economy, according to Watson. Toward that end, he and his colleagues are developing a global issues program at his school that would bring together a variety of high school courses organized around an international theme. In addition, Watson believes that teachers should develop students' appreciation for diverse cultures and the ability to communicate cross-culturally. For more than a decade, he has been "working/fighting" to have more foreign languages offered at the middle and elementary school levels. Watson models to students his own love of learning and the importance of cross-cultural competence—in addition to Spanish, he speaks French and has studied Italian and German. He is also studying Chinese and hopes to start an exchange program with China, in addition to the school's exchange programs with Costa Rica and France.

TEACHERS' VOICES  BEING AN AGENT OF CHANGE

GEORGE WATSON

Preparing "Citizens of the World" Who Respect Cultural Differences

Buenos dias. I teach Spanish at Walpole High School in Walpole, **MASSACHUSETTS**. I am also the department head of foreign languages for grades 6 through 12. When I was a student many years ago, I really looked up to my teachers. I saw them as people who had devoted themselves to a very noble profession, and that belief has not changed. Teaching, along with parenting, is probably the most important job that any one individual can do in any society, in any culture, on any continent.

I teach because I believe that every child wants to learn, is able to learn, and must learn. Furthermore, I teach because I believe that every child should have access to foreign language education. And every child should have access no matter what their reading level, no matter what their learning style and, really, no matter what grade they are in.

Over the course of my career, I have had the privilege to give my students the skills to communicate effectively in a second language and to give them confidence to navigate in a foreign culture. And I've seen students who have had very difficult middle school years come to my ninth-grade freshman Spanish class and achieve success. I've seen students from both Walpole, Massachusetts and Palmares, Costa Rica participate in our exchange program and establish friendships and bonds that last for years and years. I've seen students who over the course of their four years in high school achieve incredible linguistic success and progress, so by the time that they are seniors in my AP class I know that they're going to be successful in college; I know that they are going to eventually participate in a global economy, which is more than just rewarding for me personally—it's nationally critical.

And last, it's wonderful for me, as a teacher and a department head, to celebrate the achievement of students—this is so very important; we just don't do this enough, I think, in public education. In Walpole, we have a very special foreign language awards night where we do just that, and we highlight not just what students have learned, but what students can do with the skills that we've provided them.

Yes, I am a teacher. I want to do my part to prepare my students to be citizens of the world, to be lifelong, self-confident learners, to be students who appreciate and respect cultural differences—those cultural differences that make our society and our world so fascinating and so very, very rich.

PERSONAL REFLECTION

1. With respect to the subject area and grade level for which you are preparing to teach, how can you help students become "citizens of the world"?
2. After you become a teacher, what are some ways that you can demonstrate to students your own love of learning?

George Watson was **MASSACHUSETTS** Teacher of the Year for 2009.

Teacher as a Spontaneous Problem Solver

When teachers are preparing to teach or reflecting on previous teaching, they can afford to be consistently deliberate and rational. Planning for lessons, grading papers, reflecting on the misbehavior of a student—such activities are usually done alone and with a generous amount of time allotted to the task. But in the classroom, teachers must respond to unpredictable events that are rapidly changing, multidimensional, and fragmented. Events happen immediately and with a sense of urgency.

Video Example 2.1

Water Table Center (Part 1): A teacher asks questions to build student understanding of STEM concepts while teaching prosocial skills like turn taking.

While working face to face with students, you must be able to think on your feet and respond appropriately to complex, ever-changing situations. You must be flexible and ready to deal with the unexpected. During a discussion, for example, you must operate on at least two levels. On one level, you respond appropriately to students' comments, monitor other students for signs of confusion or comprehension, formulate the next comment or question, and remain alert for signs of misbehavior. On another level, you ensure that participation is evenly distributed among students, evaluate the content and quality of students' contributions, keep the discussion focused and moving ahead, and emphasize major content areas.

In the Teaching on Your Feet feature for this chapter, you can see how one teacher responded to several unpredictable events in the classroom.

Teaching on Your Feet:

Opening the Gates to Empower Students

It is said that mathematics, and especially algebra, is the greatest of gatekeepers. Indeed, it is the subject that prevents most students from aspiring to higher education. I teach mathematics at a school that is mostly comprised of students of color (75 percent Hispanic, 8 percent African American). Here, roughly 50 to 60 percent of the students will manage to graduate within their four years. Furthermore, less than 20 percent of those who do graduate go on to pursue a 4-year college degree. Needless to say, as a teacher of Mexican descent, my teaching and the learning of mathematics is a personal endeavor.

A few years ago, I took my geometry class on an excursion throughout our campus. We were studying shapes and their angles. Students sketched and described the geometrical relationships of the school's buildings and their features. My objective for my students was to allow them to discover not only the usefulness of mathematics but its liberating power to those who can maneuver through it and make it their own. I wanted to empower them to move past academic barriers to a life with more choices. As my students scattered to explore and investigate the architectural geometry that is our school, two boys asked me if they could simply go back to the classroom. They saw no point in the activity. They were bored.

Rather than have them meander back to our classroom and cause any disruptions, I asked them what it was that they saw besides a cluster of impersonal and inanimate objects such as buildings. They looked dumbfounded by my odd question. "What do you mean?" they asked me. "Look around you. Who is always cleaning the trash and filth that the students carelessly leave behind after lunch? And now think who is in the office making decisions about your education?" I did not have to say much after that. The point of my questions was clear to the boys as they saw men who looked like them cleaning the campus.

SERGIO MORA
Montclair High School, Montclair, **CALIFORNIA**

Analyze

As teachers, we have difficulty seeing whether we have made a difference in the young minds that are entrusted to us. We may plant seeds that never flower but we may also one day, in the distant future, see the blossom of that seed. One of my students from many years ago who had seen no point in school came back to visit me. He was a freshman at Cal Poly University in Pomona. As we talked, our conversation traveled back to that one day when the class was exploring the geometry of the school. He asked me if I remembered what I had told him. I recounted the basic story but I was surprised when he quoted me: "There are two kinds of people in this world: those who own the building and those who clean it. Your education will determine who you become." Even though I had forgotten I had said those specific words to him, he had obviously internalized them. As he left, a wide grin on his face, he said: "I want to use my body from the neck up rather than from the neck down."

I guess those seeds we plant can sometimes take root and eventually build the foundation of our students' characters. It is that tender hope in this truth that gives life to our teacher's heart . . . our spirit. As we come to believe in this, we become the guardians or our students' hopes and dreams.

Reflect

1. What are some other gatekeeping academic subjects that may limit students' life choices if they do not master them?
2. How could a teacher who is not of Mexican decent handle a similar situation without offending the students?
3. What guest speakers could a teacher invite to motivate students to persist through studies that currently seem meaningless to them?

Teacher as a Reflective Thinker

Teachers must be reflective thinkers. They must be able to think carefully and deliberately about the outcomes of their teaching. Reflection guides them as they make decisions about how to improve their teaching.

Teachers' thought processes (including professional reflection and decision making) cannot be observed directly. Reflection and decision making are influenced by the teacher's classroom experiences, curricular and instructional goals, and theories and beliefs about students and how they learn. A teacher's thought processes and actions can be constrained by the physical setting of the classroom or external factors such as the curriculum, the principal, or the community. On the other hand, teachers' thought processes and actions may be influenced by unique opportunities, such as the chance to engage in curriculum reform or school governance. Figure 2.3 shows how personal characteristics influence a teacher's thought processes while teaching.

Figure 2.3 Influences on teachers' thought processes while teaching

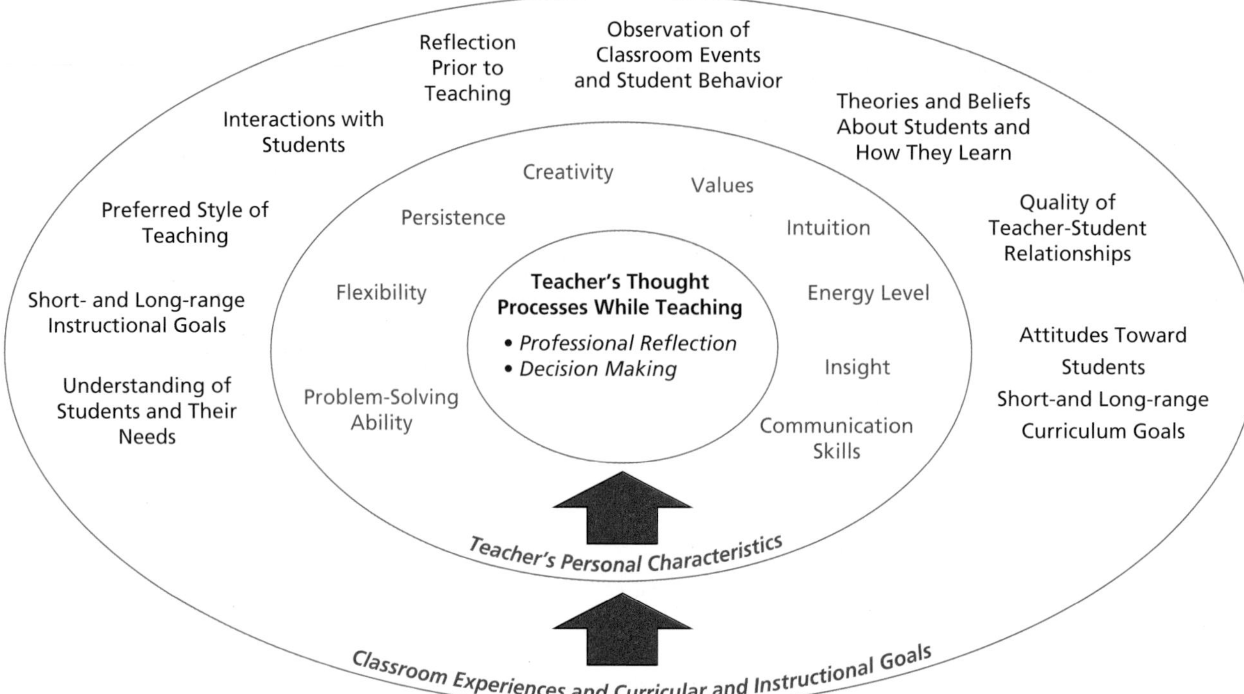

The relationships among teacher behavior, student behavior, and student achievement are reciprocal. What teachers do is influenced not only by their thought processes before, during, and after teaching but also by student behavior and student achievement. This complexity contributes to the uniqueness of the teaching experience and the importance of allowing time for reflection.

In Internet blogs many teachers maintain, they frequently comment on how reflection has helped them become successful in the classroom. For example, Nicholas Provenzano, a high school English teacher and technology curriculum specialist for Grosse Pointe Public Schools in **MICHIGAN**, explained in a blog post how **reflection** helped him become a better teacher (Provenzano, 2013). In particular, reflection helped him identify changes he needed to make in his classroom practice.

Now a successful teacher and leader for his profession, Provenzano recognized early in his career that the hallmark of professionalism is the ability to reflect on one's experiences in the classroom. He learned that teaching is a complex act—one that requires thoughtfulness, insight into the motivations of others, and good judgment. Interviewed several times by the *New York Times* about his innovative use of technology in the classroom, Provenzano is also co-host of a talk show on the BAM! Radio Network that features leading education experts and advocates for quality education. He received the 2013 Technology Using Teacher of the Year Award from his state.

Check Your Understanding 2.2

What Knowledge and Skills Do Today's Teachers Need?

To respond effectively to the complexities of teaching, you must have four kinds of knowledge: knowledge of yourself and your students, knowledge of subject, knowledge of educational theory and research, and knowledge of how to integrate technology into teaching.

Self-Knowledge

Effective teachers understand themselves. What is the connection between self-knowledge and the ability to promote student learning? If you understand your own needs (and can satisfy those needs), you are in a better position to help students learn. A teacher's self-understanding and self-acceptance help students to know and accept themselves. In addition, a willingness to examine your own cultural attitudes, values, and beliefs will enhance your ability to "connect" with students from diverse cultural, ethnic, and religious backgrounds.

Your self-evaluations as a teacher are influenced by the feelings you may experience while teaching—feelings that may range from great joy and satisfaction to anxiety or loneliness. For example, teachers can experience anxiety when starting to use a new, more complex teaching strategy. Or their mood at school may be influenced by factors unrelated to teaching—lack of sleep, personal problems, or national politics, for example. To improve her mood and manage stress while at school, Rhonda Stewart, a 6th- through 8th-grade teacher, uses a meditation app on her phone:

> I am working on keeping myself motivated, upbeat, and staving off the winter blues. There is a free app that you can download to your phone . . . .It coaches you through a brief meditation. I use this app at home and decided to use it at work as well, especially during times of dealing with stress. It is definitely *five minutes of peace*! It helps to keep my mind clear and focused so that I do not feel like I have the weight of the world on my shoulders. (Stewart, 2016)

As a teacher, you will experience feelings of happiness, excitement, and wonder as a result of the time you spend with students. You may also experience occasional feelings of loneliness or isolation because most of your time will be spent with children and youth, not adults. Although teachers are behind the classroom door most of the day, today's teachers have more opportunities to collaborate with their colleagues, whether it be serving on a school improvement committee, developing new curricula, or mentoring new teachers.

Video Example 2.2

A Teacher's Self-Reflection: A teacher who knows himself and thinks deeply discusses the connection between self-knowledge and the ability to promote student learning.

Knowledge of Students

Without a doubt, knowledge of your students and their lives is important. The value of this knowledge is evident in comments made by an intern at a middle school:

> To teach a kid well you have to know a kid well. . . . Teaching middle school takes a special breed of teachers who understand the unique abilities and inabilities . . . [of] those undergoing their own metamorphosis into teenagers (Henry et al., 1995, pp. 124–125).

Student characteristics such as aptitudes, talents, learning styles, stages of development, and readiness to learn new material are also among the essential knowledge you must have. In Chapter 8, you will learn about the diverse groups of students who comprise today's school population, and in Chapter 9, you will learn about learners' individual needs. In addition, after you become a teacher, you will expand your knowledge of students through additional study, observation, and interactions with students.

Parents or guardians can be a teacher's greatest partners in determining the success of his or her students. What are some ways you can reach out to know your students' parents or guardians and gain their support?

Africa Studio/Shutterstock

Knowledge of Subject and Pedagogical Expertise

Teachers are assumed to have extensive knowledge of their subjects. However, knowledge of subject matter does not translate into an understanding of how to impart that knowledge to students—a point illustrated in a case study conducted by the National Center for Research on Teacher Learning. The case focused on "Mary," an undergraduate literature major enrolled in a teacher education program at a major university. By any standards, Mary was a subject-matter expert—she was valedictorian of a large, urban high school; had straight A's in the literature courses she had taken; and had a sophisticated understanding of literature, especially poetry. The case study revealed that Mary had little understanding of classroom activities that would show her students how to read with sophistication and concluded that "Some prospective teachers may come to teacher education unaware of how they have learned the processes they use and that render them experts. Unaided by their disciplines in locating the underpinnings of their expertise, these skilled, talented, and desirable recruits may easily become, ironically, those who can do but who cannot teach" (Holt-Reynolds, 1999, p. 43).

In addition to extensive knowledge of subject matter, teachers must have **pedagogical expertise**—an understanding of how best to present subject matter to students. As the National Board for Professional Teaching Standards explains: "Pedagogical expertise incorporates wisdom related to the teaching and learning processes, as well as the dynamic between student needs and content demands. Accomplished teachers use their knowledge of the most appropriate ways to present subject matter through strategies and techniques such as demonstrations, experiments, analogies and metaphors, interactive learning, and appropriate uses of technology" (2016, p. 20).

Video Example 2.3

Warm Up—Language strand review: Learn about how an energetic approach to building language skills engages more students than the traditional sentence diagramming task.

Knowledge of How to Use Educational Theory and Research

A theory is an explanation of a complex phenomenon or process. The explanation is based on research that involves careful observation, analysis, and testing.

Theories about learners and learning will guide your decision making as a teacher. The following are two examples of educational theories—the first might help a teacher decide how to teach 1st-grade students to add and subtract. The second might encourage a high school general science teacher to have high-achieving students tutor students who are having trouble understanding the objects in our solar system.

- Children in early grades learn mathematics more effectively if they use physical objects in their lessons.
- Students tutoring other students can lead to improved learning for both student and tutor, as well as improved attitudes toward learning.

With an understanding of educational theories, not only will you know that a certain strategy works, you will also know why it works. Because you realize the importance of theories, you will have a greater range of available options for problem solving than teachers who do not have a repertoire of theories. Your ultimate goal as a professional is to learn how to apply theoretical knowledge to the practical problems of teaching. An example of a teacher who applies such knowledge to her teaching is Desiree Daring, a 6th-grade math teacher at Spark Academy in Lawrence, **MASSACHUSETTS**. After learning about research showing that physical movement is important for brain development, she changed what she does in the classroom. Almost every day, she breaks up 70-minute math blocks with 3- to 5-minute "brain boosts." Some days, kids do boot camp exercises; other days, Zumba. "When they have an opportunity to let that excess energy out, they're able to come back and focus" (Hennick, 2017).

Research on students' learning does not set forth, in cookbook fashion, exactly what you should do to increase students' learning. Instead, it may be helpful to think of educational research as providing you with "rules of thumb" to guide your practice, or, to recall a comment by noted educational psychologist Lee Cronbach (quoted in Eisner, 1998, p. 112), "[educational research] is to help practitioners use their heads."

Educational researchers are still learning *what* good teachers know and *how* they use that knowledge. As a result, many people believe that a knowledge base for teaching should consist of not only what educational researchers have learned about teaching but also what teachers themselves know about teaching—often called teachers' craft knowledge or practitioner knowledge (Burney, 2004; Hiebert, Gallimore, & Stigler, 2002; Kennedy, 1999; Leinhardt, 1990). **Teachers' craft knowledge** is developed by teachers in response to specific problems of practice. For example, while teaching a complex topic, teachers with a high degree of craft knowledge know which parts of the lesson will be most difficult for students and, therefore, require more time. They know what kind of help particular students will need, and they are able to provide that help in a way that students understand.

Knowledge of How to Integrate Technology into Teaching

As a teacher, you will be expected to know how to integrate technology into your teaching. And, throughout your teaching career, you will be expected to be familiar with newly emerging technologies and how they can be used in the classroom. Chapter 12 of this book explains how digital technologies can be integrated into teaching.

Using technology to enhance students' learning requires more than knowing how to use the latest hardware and software. Conducting classroom demonstrations augmented with multimedia, using presentation graphics to address students' varied learning styles, and designing lessons that require students to use technology as a tool for inquiry should be second nature for teachers.

One teacher who uses technology to promote student learning is Tracy J. Tarasuik, an English teacher at Park Campus School in Round Lake, **ILLINOIS**. In "Combining Traditional and Contemporary Texts: Moving My English Class to the Computer Lab,"

Video Example 2.4

Educational Technology: A teacher, Judy McDonald, uses technology in her 1st grade classroom.

an article she wrote for the *Journal of Adolescent & Adult Literacy*, Tarasuik explains why she decided to make greater use of technology:

> I discovered that most of my students were reading and writing on the Internet regularly . . . . I began to understand that my adolescent students, including struggling readers, were capable Internet and technology users and enjoyed reading. As they read traditional materials, there were also online creating websites, downloading information, and communicating . . . . (Tarasuik, 2010)

To increase your skills in using advanced technologies to enhance student learning, this chapter's Technology in Action feature focuses on e-portfolios. E-portfolios not only show the finished product, which could be a paper, artwork, project, musical score, and so on; they also highlight the process that the student engaged in and the stages the work went through to achieve the finished product.

TECHNOLOGY in ACTION

E-Portfolios in 12th-Grade Industrial Arts

Bill Thompson has taught in the industrial arts automotive technology program for over a year. His students are diverse in terms of interest, gender, and ethnicity. However, they share pride in the work they do in Mr. Thompson's classes. He knows the importance of having his students do more than rebuild engines. They learn to problem solve; work in teams; and think critically about the possible effects of the decisions they make on safety, the environment, and personal finances. However, Mr. Thompson is bothered by the fact that the school and even some of his own students see his classes as being for "gear-heads" only. Mr. Thompson wants to show the school and his students that the outcomes of his program go beyond just building a neat car.

At lunch one day, he is talking with Mrs. Watson, the technology coordinator for the school, and she suggests that his students might enjoy creating an e-portfolio to share with others. She explains that an e-portfolio is an electronic portfolio of a student's work. Students could upload text, video, audio, and graphics of individual projects they work on and then share that site with other students in their class, the school at large, or even the community.

The next day, Mr. Thompson explains to his students that they will be required to develop an e-portfolio of their work during the school year. Students are to use the e-portfolio to document work, explain processes and decisions, show and discuss stages of work for each project, and provide a personal reflection statement about their group work. Outside his office, he sets up a computer workstation that uses a free e-portfolio website as a home page. He also provides a digital camera, a video camera, and a microphone.

During the school year, students develop their e-portfolios. Mr. Thompson shares some of the e-portfolios with his principal, who shares them with the school board. Some of his students even get summer jobs because they shared e-portfolios with prospective employers.

VISIT: Visit one of the free e-portfolio services available on the Internet for features, options, and samples.

A Problem-Solving Orientation

The preceding discussion of essential knowledge and skills for teaching highlights the fact that teaching is complex and demanding. As you use your knowledge and skills to meet the challenges of teaching, a **problem-solving orientation** should guide you.

Application Exercise 2.2

Applying a Problem-Solving Orientation

SpeedKingz/Shutterstock

With a teacher's guidance, students can use a free e-portfolio service to upload text, video, audio, and graphics to a website that features examples of their work.

Figure 2.4 shows how problem solving will enable you to determine how to use knowledge of self and students (including cultural differences), knowledge of subject matter, knowledge of educational theory and research, and knowledge of how to integrate technology into teaching to create optimum conditions for student learning. The figure also shows that you can use problem solving to decide which essential skills to use and how to use them.

Figure 2.4 A problem-solving orientation for the professional teacher

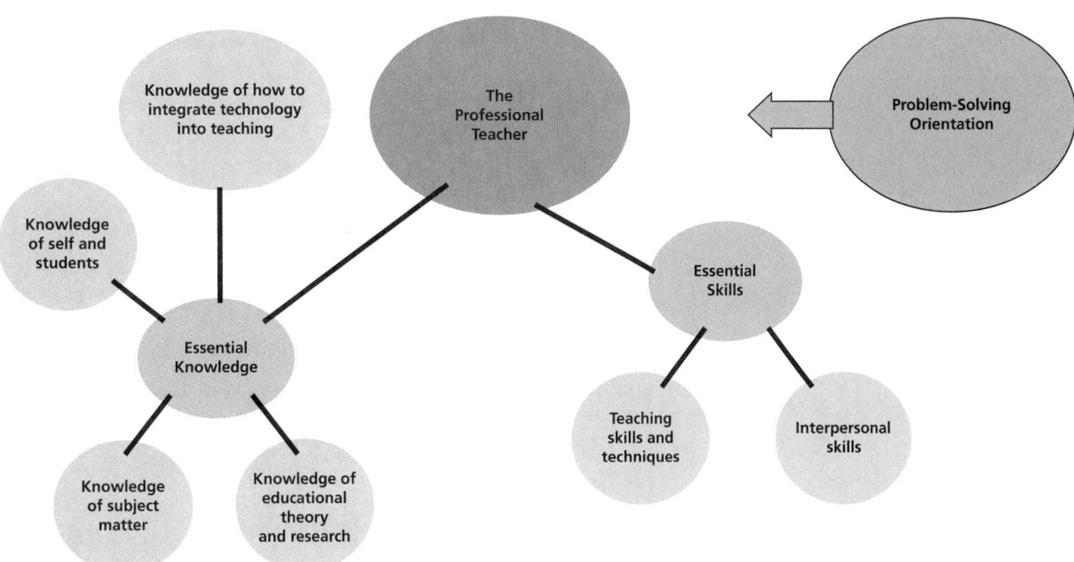

To What Extent is Teaching a Full Profession?

There is some debate about whether teaching can be considered a profession comparable to medicine and law. In general, members of more "elite" professions—chief executive officers, physicians, and lawyers, for example—are paid more, receive more respect, and have greater autonomy.

It is human nature to want high status in one's social circle, profession, and society in general. In addition, researchers at the University of California–Berkeley's School of Business found that "people's subjective well-being, self-esteem, and mental and physical health appear to depend on the level of status they are accorded by others" (Anderson, Hildreth, & Howland, 2015, p. 574).

Characteristics of highly professionalized occupations are summarized in Figure 2.5. Before reading further, reflect on each characteristic and decide whether it applies to teaching. Then continue reading about the extent to which teaching satisfies each of these commonly agreed-upon characteristics of a full **profession**. Do the following discussions of the characteristics agree with your perceptions of teaching as a profession?

Figure 2.5 Does teaching meet the criteria for a profession?

Yes	Uncertain	No	
❍	❍	❍	1. Professionals are allowed to institutionalize a monopoly of essential knowledge and services. For example, only lawyers may practice law; only physicians may practice medicine.
❍	❍	❍	2. Professionals are able to practice their occupation with a high degree of autonomy. They are not closely supervised, and they have frequent opportunities to make their own decisions about important aspects of their work. Professional autonomy also implies an obligation to perform responsibly, to self-supervise, and to be dedicated to providing a service rather than meeting minimum requirements of the job.
❍	❍	❍	3. Professionals must typically undergo a lengthy period of education and/or training before they may enter professional practice. Furthermore, professionals usually must undergo a lengthy induction period following their formal education or training.
❍	❍	❍	4. Professionals perform an essential service for their clients and are devoted to continuous development of their ability to deliver this service. This service emphasizes intellectual rather than physical techniques.
❍	❍	❍	5. Professionals have control over their governance, their socialization into the occupation, and research connected with their occupation.
❍	❍	❍	6. The knowledge and skills held by professionals are not usually available to nonprofessionals.
❍	❍	❍	7. Professionals enjoy a high level of public trust and can deliver services that are clearly superior to those available elsewhere.
❍	❍	❍	8. Professionals are granted a high level of prestige and higher-than-average financial rewards.
❍	❍	❍	9. Members of a profession form their own vocational associations, which have control over admissions to the profession, educational standards, examinations and licensing, career development, ethical and performance standards, and professional discipline.

Institutional Monopoly of Services

On one hand, teachers do have a monopoly of services. As a rule, only those who are certified members of the profession may teach in public schools. On the other hand, varied requirements for certification and for teaching in private schools weaken this monopoly. (Although state certification and teacher education courses are generally not required to teach in private schools, a college degree is a minimum requirement.)

Any claim teachers might have as exclusive providers of a service is further eroded by the practice of many state systems to approve temporary or **emergency certification** measures (or waivers) to deal with teacher shortages. Emergency certification is strongly resisted by professional teacher organizations and several state departments of education. A U.S. Department of Education report, *Certification Status and Experience of U.S. Public School Teachers*, found that 94 percent of K–12 students in urban and suburban schools and 95 percent of students in town and rural schools were taught by teachers with full state certification (Rahman, Fox, Ikoma, & Gray, 2017, p. 8). While the goal of No Child Left Behind (NCLB) was to have a fully certified teacher in every classroom, the Every Student Succeeds Act (ESSA) allows each state to set certification requirements. Most states allow emergency certification in all subject areas, except special education.

The widespread practice of out-of-field teaching also weakens teachers' monopoly of services. The U.S. Department of Education report on certification found that almost 39 percent of middle school students studying mathematics and 31 percent studying science were taught by teachers with neither certification nor a major in those areas. At the high school level, almost 11 percent of students studying mathematics and 9 percent of students studying science were taught by teachers with neither certification nor a major in those areas (Rahman, Fox, Ikoma, & Gray, 2017, p. 10). Thus teaching is the only profession that allows individuals certified in one area to teach in other areas for which they are not certified. This is comparable to a lawyer who passed the bar exam in New York being allowed, because of a lawyer shortage in California, to practice in that state without taking the California bar exam. Or a pediatrician "filling in" as a neurologist because of a neurologist shortage.

Perhaps the most significant argument against teachers claiming to be the exclusive providers of a service, however, is the fact that a great deal of teaching occurs in informal, nonschool settings and is done by people who are not state-certified teachers. Every day, thousands of people teach various kinds of how-to-do-it skills: how to water-ski, how to make dogs more obedient, how to make pasta from scratch, how to tune a car's engine, and how to meditate.

In the final analysis, teachers may not have a narrowly conceived monopoly of services comparable to the practice of law or medicine. However, teaching is the only profession that has as its primary aim promoting the education, growth, and development of others. Teaching is the only profession that aspires to achieve the aim of education as described by two of the world's most preeminent individuals: "Education develops in the body and soul of the pupil all the beauty and all the perfection he [or she] is capable of" (Plato). "By education I mean an all-round drawing out of the best in child and man's body, mind, and spirit" (Mahatma Gandhi).

Professional Autonomy

There are obvious constraints placed on teachers and their autonomy. Public school teachers, unlike doctors and lawyers, must accept all the "clients" who are sent to them. Only infrequently does a teacher actually reject a student assigned to him or her.

Teachers must also agree to teach what state and local officials say they must. And the work of teachers is subject to a higher level of public scrutiny than that found in other professions. Because the public provides "clients" (students) and pays for schools, it has a significant say regarding the work of teachers.

On the other hand, teachers have extensive freedom regarding how they structure the classroom environment. They may emphasize discussions as opposed to lectures. They may set certain requirements for some students and not for others. They may delegate responsibilities to one class and not another. And, within the guidelines set by local and state authorities, teachers may determine much of the content they teach.

Overall, teachers have considerable autonomy. Teachers usually work behind a closed classroom door, and seldom does another adult observe their work. In fact, one of the norms among teachers is that the classroom is a castle of sorts, and teacher privacy a closely guarded right. Although the performance of new teachers may be observed and evaluated on a regular basis by supervisors, veteran teachers are observed much less frequently, and they usually enjoy a high degree of autonomy.

Years of Education and Training

To practice law, future lawyers earn a bachelor's degree and then study for another 3 years in a postgraduate program. The average American physician spends 14 years training for the job. The preparation of teachers is comparatively short. In many instances, teachers are only required to obtain a bachelor's degree, and in some cases only 15 percent of the average bachelor's degree program is devoted to courses specifically training the candidate to *teach*.

However, several colleges and universities have begun 5-year teacher education programs. Similarly, the National Commission on Teaching and America's Future recommended that teacher education be moved to the graduate level. Similar to a law degree, in this model, the teacher candidate would earn a bachelor's degree and then receive specialized education on how to teach in a postgraduate program. If the trend toward 5-year and graduate-level teacher education programs continues, the professional status of teaching will definitely be enhanced.

In most professions, new members must undergo a prescribed induction period. Physicians, for example, must serve an internship or a residency before beginning practice, and most lawyers begin as clerks in law firms. In contrast, teachers usually do not go through an extended induction period before assuming full responsibility for their work. Student teaching comes closest to serving as an induction period. Student teaching is a college-supervised instructional experience, usually the culminating course in a teacher education program in which the teacher candidate gets a chance to teach in a real classroom, mentored by an experienced teacher. However, this experience is often relatively short (one term), informal, and lacking in uniformity.

Today, however, increasing numbers of veteran teachers are helping new teachers "learn the ropes." Veteran teachers are helping new teachers identify with the profession, contribute to school-based learning communities, and assume leadership responsibilities.

Drawing from the career structure of other professions, the U.S. Department of Education has suggested a multistage career ladder for teaching (see Figure 2.5). The first stage would be that of a *Resident* teacher. For one year, a *Resident* teacher would work under a *Master* teacher's supervision. After a one-year residency and demonstrating a

Figure 2.6 A multistage career ladder for teachers

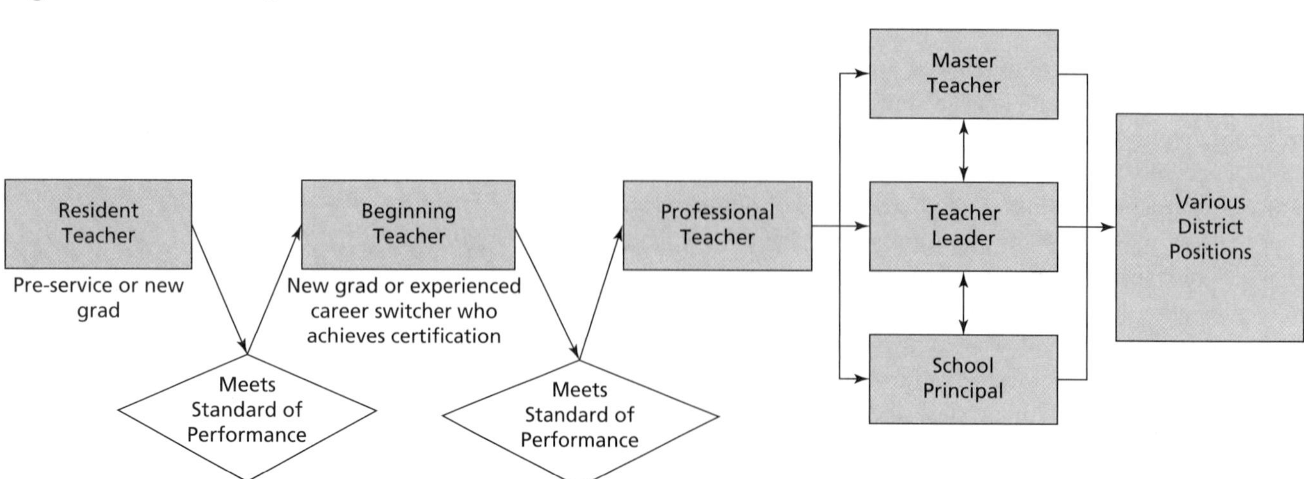

SOURCE: U.S. Department of Education. (2013, April). *Blueprint for Recognizing Educational Success, Professional Excellence and Collaborative Teaching (RESPECT)*. Washington, DC, p. 24.

minimum level of knowledge and skills for teaching, the *Resident* would be certified as a *Beginning* teacher. The *Beginning* teacher would have full teaching responsibilities and receive careful mentoring, nurturing, and evaluation by a *Master* teacher. After 2 to 5 years of successful teaching, a *Beginning* teacher might apply for promotion to *Professional* teacher. Promotion to *Professional* teacher would require consistent evidence of teaching effectiveness and might include the granting of tenure. *Beginning* teachers who do not meet the criteria for promotion to *Professional* teacher would not continue in the profession. *Professional* teachers might remain in this role for their entire careers, or they might choose to pursue various leadership roles.

A *Master* teacher is a "teacher of adults" and provides constructive feedback to *Resident* and *Beginning* teachers, while also serving as a key member of a school's leadership team. A *Master* teacher might spend half of each day teaching and the other half supporting his or her colleagues. Similarly, a *Teacher Leader* might teach part-time and devote the remaining time to various leadership activities—for example, working with the principal and other members of the leadership team, directing a school-based research project, or developing an evaluation system for *Resident* and *Beginning* teachers.

Perhaps an overlooked benefit of teaching is that it encourages the professional to continue learning far beyond the required formal years of education and training. As Heather Wolpert-Gawron, a middle-school English language arts teacher, says:

> Teaching is one of those rare professions that keeps your brain young, allowing you to continue your own journey as a student and a lifelong learner. We as educators speak often about creating lifelong learners, but if we aren't buying into it ourselves, then our students don't stand a chance.
>
> Michelle Pfeiffer once said that being an actor allows her, with every new character, to learn something new, immersing herself in a distinct universe with each project. Being a teacher is that and so much more. (Wolpert-Gawron, 2009)

Provision of Essential Service

In the United States, children are required to receive a public education from ages 5 through 16. Most get this education from public school teachers. Although it is generally acknowledged that teachers provide a service that is vital to the well-being of individuals and groups, the public does need to be reminded of this fact from time to time. This importance was driven home on a large scale during the early 1980s when reports such as *A Nation at Risk* linked the strength of our country to the quality of its schools, or more than 30 years later when NBC News hosted its 4th-annual weeklong "Education Nation Summit" during October 2013. The Summit stressed the connection between education and America's future and the need "to provide information to Americans so they can make decisions about how best to improve our education system both in the near and long terms, and to shine a spotlight on one of the most urgent national issues of our time" (NBC News, Education Nation, 2013).

In the final analysis, there is no doubt that teachers provide an essential service. Perhaps, our nation most appreciates this during each presidential election. The hard-fought, tumultuous election of 2016 was no exception. Both sides agreed that teachers are vital to our nation's future. The 2016 Republican Platform made it clear that "maintaining American preeminence requires a world-class system of education in which all students can reach their potential" (p. 33). And the Democratic Platform stated that "we must have the best-educated population and workforce in the world" (p. 32).

Degree of Self-Governance

Without a doubt, if members of a profession feel empowered, they have higher morale. If they participate in decisions about job-related policies, and if their expertise is acknowledged, they are more invested in their work. The limited freedom of teachers to govern themselves, however, has detracted from the overall status of the profession. In many states, licensing guidelines are set by government officials who may or may not be educators, and at the local level, decision-making power usually resides with local boards of education, largely made up of people who have not taught. As a result, teachers have had little say over what they teach, when they teach, whom they teach, and—in extreme instances—how they teach.

However, efforts to empower teachers and to professionalize teaching are creating new roles for teachers and expanded opportunities to govern important aspects of their work. At schools throughout the country, teachers are developing leadership skills and playing a greater role in decisions related to curriculum development, staffing, budget, and the day-to-day operation of schools. For example, Figure 2.7 shows that teachers play a significant role in selecting and hiring new teachers at their schools.

Figure 2.7 Influence of different groups on hiring process in schools (percentage)

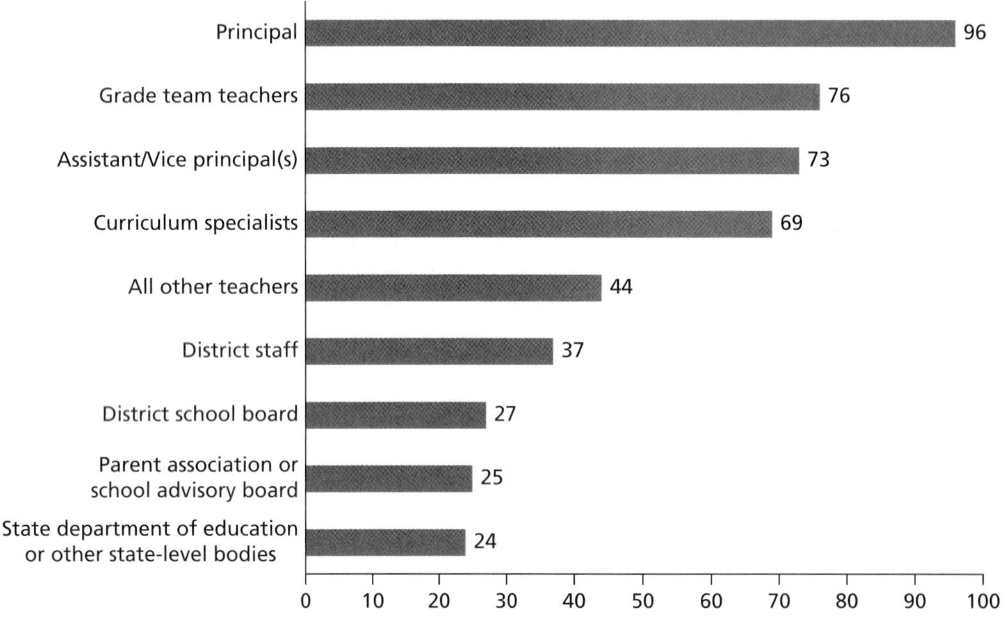

Note: The survey item was worded as follows: "How much influence does each of the groups or individuals listed below have on the process of selecting and hiring new full-time classroom teachers at your school?" For each group or individual, principals could choose "Major Influence," "Moderate Influence," "Minor Influence," or "No Influence/NA." Groups or individuals were considered to influence the hiring process if the principal indicated that they had moderate or major influence. Responses are from both elementary and middle school principals.

SOURCE: Based on Glazerman, S. A. Protik, B. Teh, J. Bruch, N. Seftor, N. (2012). Moving High-Performing Teachers: Implementation of Transfer Incentives in Seven Districts (NCEE 2012-4051). Washington, DC: National Center for Education Evaluation and Regional Assistance, Institute of Education Sciences, U.S. Department of Education, p. 39.

Although teachers differ significantly in their opinions about the amount of influence they believe teachers have, it is clear that teachers will experience greater self-governance as principals respond to increasing pressure to become more effective at facilitating collaborative, emergent approaches to leadership. Increasingly, principals realize that "leadership in instructional matters should emerge freely from both principals and teachers. After all, teachers deliver the instruction in the classroom; they have expertise in curriculum and teaching, and they have mastered a substantive body of knowledge" (Hoy & Hoy, 2013, p. 2).

Professional Knowledge and Skills

Professionals are granted a certain status because they possess knowledge and skills not normally held by the general public. For example, in order to practice law in a specific jurisdiction, a candidate must pass a bar examination assessing the candidate's knowledge of law in that location. There is no such universally accepted assessment of a teacher's knowledge and skills. In spite of the ongoing efforts of educational researchers, there is no agreement on the knowledge and skills considered necessary to teach. This lack of agreement is reflected in the varied programs at the 1,300 or so colleges and universities that train teachers.

However, since it was established in 1987, the National Board for Professional Teaching Standards (NBPTS) has made significant progress toward clarifying the knowledge base for teaching and enhancing the status of the profession. The NBPTS (the majority of whose members are teachers) offers national board certification to teachers who possess a high level of NBPTS-identified knowledge and skills. Similar to board-certified physicians and accountants, NBPTS-certified teachers have demonstrated mastery of rigorous standards through intensive study, self-assessment, peer review, and evaluation by panels of experts. By 2017, the NBPTS had granted national certification to more than 112,000 individuals (NBPTS, 2017).

Notwithstanding the difficulty of specifying precisely the knowledge and skills teachers must have, there is no doubt that accomplished teaching requires a sophisticated knowledge and skills set. As the 205 school of education deans who signed a National Education Policy Center position paper submitted to the White House in 2017 asserted, "Teaching is an exceedingly complicated process that demands the highest caliber of professionals" (Education Deans for Justice and Equity, 2017).

Trust in the Profession

Although all professions have some members who might be described as unprofessional and not worthy of the public's trust, teaching is especially vulnerable to such charges. The sheer size of the teaching force makes it difficult to maintain consistently high professional standards. Moreover, teaching is subject to a level of public scrutiny and control that other, more established professions traditionally have not tolerated.

At present, the teaching profession does not have a uniform **code of ethics** similar to the Hippocratic oath, which all doctors are legally required to take when they begin practice. However, the largest professional organization for teachers, the National Education Association (NEA), has a code of ethics for members that includes the following statement: "The educator accepts the responsibility to adhere to the highest ethical standards" (NEA, 2017). Table 2.4 shows that the public considers elementary and high school teachers to be highly trustworthy.

Prestige, Benefits, and Pay

Although "many teachers and school administrators . . . are thought to be of a more elite social class than the majority of the population in the United States" (Parker & Shapiro, 1993, p. 42), this higher status is based on level of education attained rather than wealth. Teachers have not received salaries in keeping with other professions requiring approximately the same amount of schooling. Nevertheless, there is significant support for reducing the salary gap. For example, the U.S. Department of Education (2013) proposed the following salary structure for teachers:

> . . . starting salaries for fully licensed professional teachers should be $60,000–65,000, adjusted as appropriate to the cost of living in different regions. Additionally, salaries would increase faster than they do today, and maximum salaries would be higher, so that Master teachers and other teacher-leaders would have the ability to earn as much as $120,000–150,000 after about 7–10 years. Principals would earn comparable salaries. Whereas today's compensation tends to be linked solely to years of service or professional credentials, under this new vision, salary would reflect the quality of a teacher's work, his or her effectiveness helping students to grow academically, and the scope of the teacher's responsibility. (p. 23)

Table 2.4 Honesty/ethics in professions

Please tell me how you would rate the honesty and ethical standards of people in these different fields—very high, high, average, low, or very low?

	Very High %	High %	Average %	Low %	Very Low %	No Opinion %	Very High/ High %
Nurses	29	55	13	2	1	*	84
Grade School Teachers	25	45	23	5	1	1	70
Pharmacists	15	52	26	6	2	*	67
Medical Doctors	15	50	29	5	2	*	65
High School Teachers	16	44	29	7	2	2	60
Dentists	10	49	34	5	2	1	59
Police Officers	16	42	29	10	3	*	58
Funeral Directors	12	32	41	8	1	5	55
College Teachers	10	37	32	12	16	2	47
Day Care Providers	11	35	43	6	1	4	46
Judges	10	35	37	12	4	2	45
Clergy	12	32	39	9	4	5	44
Accountants	6	33	51	7	*	3	39
Chiropractors	5	33	45	10	3	4	38
Psychiatrists	6	32	45	9	3	4	38
Auto Mechanics	5	14	53	12	4	1	29
Bankers	2	22	46	22	8	*	24
Real Estate Agents	2	18	53	20	5	2	20
Lawyers	3	15	45	25	11	1	18
State Governors	2	16	45	27	8	1	18
Business Executives	2	15	50	23	9	1	17
Stockbrokers	2	10	46	28	11	3	12
Advertising Practitioners	1	10	46	29	11	3	11
Insurance Salespeople	1	10	51	28	10	1	11
Car Salespeople	1	8	45	31	15	*	9
Members of Congress	1	7	31	39	20	1	8

SOURCE: Based on Honesty/Ethics in Professions, The Harris Poll. Based on telephone interviews of U.S. adults conducted 2013-2016. Retrieved August 29, 2017, from http://www.gallup.com/poll/1654/honesty-ethics-professions.aspx#1.

Accepting the Challenge of a Profession

In sum, the preceding discussions of the criteria of a full profession suggest that teaching meets some of the criteria more fully than others. All professions have challenges and drawbacks. However, the drawbacks to teaching—modest salaries and a high level of public scrutiny, for example—are more than offset by the benefits, the greatest of which is the satisfaction that comes from helping students grow and develop.

Recall my statement in the first paragraph of this book: " Teaching is the world's most important profession." Can the first word of that sentence, *teaching*, be replaced with the name of another profession? I don't believe so. Moreover, virtually all members of other professions have teachers to thank for providing them with the education that enabled them to enter their chosen profession. Nothing could be more important than helping others realize their dreams and fulfill their potential!

Professional Associations

Like other professionals, teachers have formed vocational associations that focus on issues such as admission to the profession, educational standards, examinations and licensing, career development, ethical and performance standards, and professional discipline. Collectively, these associations provide ways for teachers to become empowered, to demonstrate to the public and policy makers that "We know things about this enterprise that researchers and policy makers can never know. We have engaged in this intimate experience [teaching], and we have things to tell you" (Moyers, 1989, p. 161).

As teachers become more empowered through professional associations, their morale and self-esteem improve. They participate more in decisions about job-related policies. Their expertise is acknowledged, and they become more invested in their work.

To What Professional Organizations do Teachers Belong?

The expanding leadership role of teachers has been supported through the activities of more than 500 national teacher organizations (*National Trade and Professional Associations of the United States*, 2017). These organizations and the scores of hardworking teachers who run them support a variety of activities to improve teaching and schools. Through lobbying in **WASHINGTON, D.C.** and at state capitols, for example, teacher associations acquaint legislators, policymakers, and politicians with critical issues and problems in the teaching profession. Many associations have staffs of teachers, researchers, and consultants who produce professional publications, hold conferences, prepare grant proposals, engage in school improvement activities, and promote a positive image of teaching to the public. Two unions have led the quest to improve the professional lives of all teachers: the National Education Association (NEA) and the American Federation of Teachers (AFT). These two groups have had a long history of competition for the allegiance of teachers.

The National Education Association

Membership in the **National Education Association (NEA)**, the oldest and largest organization, includes both teachers and administrators. Originally called the National Teachers Association when it was founded in 1857, the group was started by 43 educators from a dozen states and the District of Columbia (Laurence, 2000).

The NEA has affiliates in every state plus Puerto Rico and the District of Columbia, and its local affiliates number more than 14,000. About two-thirds of the teachers in this country belong to the NEA. More than 78 percent of NEA's 3 million members are teachers; about 12 percent are guidance counselors, librarians, and administrators; almost 3 percent are university professors; about 2 percent are college and university students; about 3 percent are support staff (teacher aides, secretaries, cafeteria workers, bus drivers, and custodians); and about 2 percent are retired members (NEA, 2017). NEA membership has tended to be suburban and rural.

To improve education in this country, the NEA has standing committees in the following areas: affiliate relationships, higher education, human relations, political action, teacher benefits, and teacher rights. These committees engage in a wide range of activities, among them preparing reports on important educational issues, disseminating the results of educational research, conducting conferences, working with federal agencies on behalf of children, pressing for more rigorous standards for the teaching profession, helping school districts resolve salary disputes, developing ways to improve personnel practices, and enhancing the relationship between the profession and the public.

Currently, more than two-thirds of states have passed some type of collective bargaining laws that apply to teachers. There is little uniformity among these laws, with most of the 31 states permitting strikes only if certain conditions have been met.

The NEA has gone on record as supporting a federal statute that would set up uniform procedures for teachers to bargain with their employers.

The NEA continues today to focus on issues of concern to teachers, primarily in the area of professional governance. Efforts are being made to broaden teachers' decision-making powers related to curriculum, extracurricular responsibilities, staff development, and supervision. To promote the status of the profession, the NEA conducts annual research studies and opinion surveys in various areas, and publishes *NEA Today* and *Tomorrow's Teachers* for NEA student members.

The American Federation of Teachers

The **American Federation of Teachers (AFT)** was founded in 1916. Three teachers' unions in Chicago issued a call for teachers to form a national organization affiliated with organized labor. Teacher unions in Gary, Indiana; New York City; the state of Oklahoma; Scranton, Pennsylvania; and Washington, D.C., joined the three Chicago unions to form the AFT.

The AFT has more than 1.6 million members who are organized through 43 state affiliates and more than 3,000 local affiliates (AFT, 2017). The AFT is affiliated with the American Federation of Labor–Congress of Industrial Organizations (AFL-CIO), which has over 13 million members. Traditionally, the AFT has been strongest in urban areas. Today, the AFT represents teachers not only in Chicago and New York but in Philadelphia; Washington, D.C.; Kansas City; Detroit; Boston; Cleveland; and Pittsburgh.

The AFT differs from the NEA because it is open only to teachers and nonsupervisory school personnel. To promote the idea that teachers should have the right to speak for themselves on important issues, the AFT does not allow superintendents, principals, and other administrators to join. The AFT is active today in organizing teachers, bargaining collectively, fostering public relations, and developing policies related to various educational issues. In addition, the organization conducts research in areas such as educational reform, bilingual education, teacher certification, and evaluation, and also represents members' concerns through legislative action and technical assistance.

Unlike the NEA, the AFT has been steadfastly involved throughout its history in securing economic gains and improving working conditions for teachers. None other than the great educator and philosopher John Dewey took out the first AFT membership card in 1916. After 12 years as a union member, Dewey (1955) made his stance on economic issues clear:

> It is said that the Teachers Union, as distinct from the more academic organizations, overemphasizes the economic aspect of teaching. Well, I never had that contempt for the economic aspect of teaching, especially not on the first of the month when I get my salary check. I find that teachers have to pay their grocery and meat bills and house rent just the same as everybody else. (pp. 60–61)

Other Professional Organizations

In addition to the NEA and AFT, more than 500 other national organizations represent teachers' professional interests. Several of these are concerned with improving the quality of education at all levels and in all subject areas. **Phi Delta Kappa (PDK)**, for example, is an international professional and honorary fraternity of educators concerned with enhancing quality education through research and leadership activities. Founded in 1906, Phi Delta Kappa has a membership of about 35,000. Members, who are graduate students, teachers, and administrators, belong to one of 250 chapters. To be initiated into Phi Delta Kappa, one must have demonstrated high academic achievement, have completed at least 15 semester hours of graduate work in education, and have made a commitment to a career of educational service. Phi Delta Kappa members receive *Phi Delta Kappan*, a journal of education published 10 times a year.

Another example is **ASCD** (formerly the Association for Supervision and Curriculum Development), a professional organization of teachers, supervisors, curriculum coordinators, education professors, administrators, and others. ASCD is interested in school improvement at all levels of education. Founded in 1943, the association has a membership of about 115,000. ASCD provides professional development experiences in curriculum and supervision; disseminates information on educational issues; and encourages research, evaluation, and theory development. ASCD also conducts several National Curriculum Study Institutes around the country each year and provides a free research information service to members. Members receive *Educational Leadership*, a well-respected journal published eight times a year. ASCD also publishes a yearbook, with each edition devoted to a particular educational issue, and occasional books in the area of curriculum and supervision.

Many professional associations exist for teachers of specific subject areas, such as mathematics, English, social studies, music, physical education, and so on, as well as for teachers of specific student populations, such as exceptional learners, young children, and students with limited English proficiency.

How are Teacher Leaders Transforming the Profession of Teaching?

Teaching is changing in dramatic and exciting ways. Steadily, the **professionalization of teaching** is occurring in the United States. National board certification, state-sponsored teacher networks, shared decision making, peer review, teacher-mentor programs, and the growing influence of teacher researchers are among the changes that are providing unprecedented opportunities for teachers to assume leadership roles beyond the classroom. Along with these new opportunities for leadership, teaching as a profession is developing greater political influence and acquiring higher status in the public's eye. As a **NORTH CAROLINA** teacher told *The RESPECT Project: A National Conversation About the Teaching Profession*: "It is time for sweeping changes to education" (U.S. Department of Education, 2013, p. 1). Similarly, a **NEW MEXICO** teacher told the Project, "The time is ripe for teachers to reclaim our ideas and change our profession" (p. IV).

Perhaps the most dramatic change in teaching is how school administration is becoming more collaborative and participatory. Throughout the nation, teachers are playing a key role in school governance. For example, the U.S. Department of Education identified shared, distributed leadership as a key element for the transformation of teaching:

> A culture of shared responsibility requires principals who bring together coalitions of teacher-leaders who have the skills to meet the school's objectives and create a culture of continuous learning and shared decision-making. Teams of teacher-leaders and principals work in partnerships to identify challenges, propose solutions, and share in distributed leadership and decision-making at all levels, including hiring, structuring the school day and school year, and designing professional learning. (U.S. Department of Education, 2013, p. 21)

Today's professional teachers willingly respond to the call to leadership, and they become involved at the local, state, and federal levels in the quest to improve our nation's schools. They understand that teachers must play a vital role in school governance and that their roles will continue to change in fundamental and positive ways during the future.

Among the nation's thousands of teacher leaders are the seven teachers selected by the U.S. Department of Education to be Teaching Ambassador Fellows for 2016–2017. The following three provided leadership for the profession through an array of leadership activities:

- Anna E. Baldwin, an English and history teacher at Arlee High School on the Flathead Indian Reservation in **MONTANA**, was an adjunct assistant professor of education at the University of Montana–Missoula. She is the author of education-related articles and multimedia presentations about indigenous education. At her school, she served as an instructional coach, college prep program instructor, freshman academy guide, and National Honor Society adviser. She founded the Reservation Ambassadors Club, which strives to break down stereotypes about reservation life by building relationships with students at off-reservation schools. She received the Excellence in Culturally Responsive Teaching Award from the Southern Poverty Law Center.
- Arthur Everett is a social studies teacher and a special education teacher support service provider at the High School of Telecommunication Arts and Technology in Brooklyn, **NEW YORK**. He served on his state's ELA (English Language Arts) Standards Review Committee to adopt ELA standards as outlined by the Every Student Succeeds Act (ESSA). He also served on the New York State Education Department's Social Studies Content Advisory Panel. The U.S. Department of Education's blog, *The Teacher's Edition*, featured Everett as an African American teacher of excellence.
- Sean McComb, an English teacher at Patapsco High School and Center for the Arts in Baltimore, **MARYLAND**, is an adjunct instructor at Towson University and a Teacher Laureate on the Teaching Channel. He has delivered over one hundred keynote presentations around the world, including keynotes for the Council of Chief State School Officers, the National Association of State Boards of Education, the National Education Association, the Education Commission of the States, and the National School Boards Association. He has worked with the Maryland State Department of Education on the distribution of high-quality teachers.

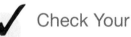

Check Your Understanding 2.6

Summary

Who Are Today's Teachers?

- Teachers teach in schools with different grade configurations, they teach in different subject-matter and specialized areas, and they teach students with different types of learning needs.
- Today's teachers are better educated and more qualified than ever.
- In addition to teachers who work in pre-K, elementary, middle, and high school programs, some teachers teach in nontraditional school settings, such as private schools, charter schools, alternative schools, and magnet schools.
- Some teachers teach in specialized areas such as art, vocational education, music, or physical education. Special education teachers specialize in teaching students with disabilities and/or special needs. Many teachers, whether they have specialized training or not, teach students whose first language is not English (often called English language learners [ELLs]).

What Do Teachers *Do* in the Classroom?

- What teachers do goes beyond observable behaviors; the effective teacher understands that, simultaneously, he or she must be a role model for students, a spontaneous problem solver, and a reflective thinker.

What Knowledge and Skills Do Today's Teachers Need?

- Teachers need four kinds of knowledge: knowledge of self and students, knowledge of subject, knowledge of educational theory and research, and knowledge of how to integrate technology into teaching.
- Self-knowledge influences your ability to understand your students; ongoing reflection and a problem-solving orientation continue to guide your instruction.
- Teachers must know their students' aptitudes, talents, learning styles, stages of development, and readiness to learn new material so they can modify instructional strategies based on students' needs.
- Knowledge of educational theory and research enables teachers to know why certain strategies work and offers general guidelines for practice.
- Teachers also use craft knowledge, what they know about teaching as a result of reflecting on their classroom experiences.

To What Extent Is Teaching a Full Profession?

- Of the following nine criteria for a profession, teaching meets some more fully than others: (1) institutional monopoly of services; (2) teacher autonomy; (3) years of education and training; (4) provision of essential service; (5) degree of self-governance; (6) professional associations; (7) professional knowledge and skills; (8) level of public trust; and (9) prestige, benefits, and pay.
- A multistage career ladder for teaching proposed by the U.S. Department of Education consists of the following roles: *Resident* teacher, *Beginning* teacher, *Professional* teacher, *Master* teacher, and *Teacher Leader*.

To What Professional Organizations Do Teachers Belong?

- As the oldest and largest professional organization for educators, the National Education Association (NEA) has played a key role in addressing issues of concern to the 78 percent of its members who are teachers.
- Affiliated with organized labor and open only to teachers and nonsupervisory personnel, the American Federation of Teachers (AFT) has done much to secure greater financial rewards and improved working conditions for teachers.
- Teachers are members of professional associations for specific subject areas and student populations.

How Are Teacher Leaders Transforming the Profession of Teaching?

- School governance is becoming more collaborative, and today's teachers have unprecedented opportunities to assume leadership roles beyond the classroom.
- The U.S. Department of Education's Teaching Ambassador Fellows program is one example of how teachers are providing leadership to improve our nation's schools.

Professional Reflections and Activities

Teacher's Journal

1. Do you plan to join a professional organization for teachers, such as the NEA, AFT, Phi Delta Kappa, or ASCD? What are your reasons? What advantages and disadvantages of joining are most important to you?
2. Regarding the grade level and subject area for which you are preparing to teach, what do you find most appealing, and why? What do you find least appealing, and why?

Teacher's Research

1. On the Internet, use your favorite search engine to search for information by keywords or topics such as *teachers' working conditions, teacher accountability*, and *teacher professional development*. Report your findings to the rest of your class.
2. Review several recent issues of the NEA publication *NEA Today* and the AFT publication *American Teacher*. Compare and contrast concerns or issues that each publication addresses. What overall differences do you find between the NEA and AFT publications?

Observations and Interviews

1. Interview a few adults who are not involved in education to get their views on teaching as a profession. What image do these adults have of teaching? What are their suggestions for improving the profession?
2. Interview a teacher about the knowledge and skills he or she thinks teachers must have. Which of the knowledge and skills discussed in this chapter does the teacher mention? Does he or she mention knowledge and skills not discussed in this chapter? If so, explain.

Professional Portfolio

Get on the Internet and begin to gather materials from teacher organizations that are relevant to the grade level and subject area for which you are preparing to teach. The following is a partial list of professional organizations. For information about these and other professional associations, see the *Encyclopedia of Associations: National Organizations of the U.S.*, 56th Edition (Gale, 2017).

- American Alliance for Health, Physical Education, Recreation and Dance (AAHPERD)
- American Alliance of Teachers of French (AATF)
- American Association of Teachers of German (AATG)
- American Association of Teachers of Spanish and Portuguese (Hispanic) (AATSP)
- American Classical League (Language) (ACL)
- American Council on the Teaching of Foreign Languages (ACTFL)
- Council for Exceptional Children (CEC)
- Foundation for Exceptional Children (FEC)
- International Reading Association (IRA)
- Music Teachers National Association (MTNA)
- National Art Education Association (NAEA)
- National Association for Bilingual Education (Bilingualism) (NABE)
- National Association of Biology Teachers (NABT)
- National Association for the Education of Young Children (NAEYC)
- National Association for Gifted Children (NAGC)
- National Association for Trade and Industrial Education (NATIE)
- National Business Education Association (NBEA)
- National Council for the Social Studies (NCSS)
- National Council of Teachers of English (NCTE)
- National Council of Teachers of Mathematics (NCTM)
- National Middle School Association (NMSA)
- National Science Teachers Association (NSTA)
- Speech Communication Association (SCA)
- Teachers of English to Speakers of Other Languages (TESOL)

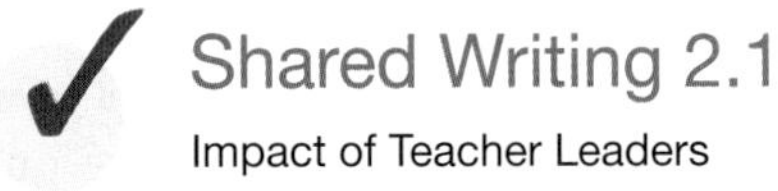

Chapter 3
Today's Schools

antoniodiaz\Shutterstock

Learning Outcomes

After reading this chapter, you will be able to do the following:

3.1 Explain the role of schools in today's society and describe the characteristics of successful schools.

3.2 Explain different ways to describe schools.

3.3 Identify and discuss social problems that affect schools and place students at risk.

3.4 Describe how schools are addressing societal problems.

3.5 Explain how community-based partnerships can help students learn.

READERS VOICES

What is the role of schools in today's society?

The role of today's schools is to prepare students for life in the 21st century. At their schools, students acquire the knowledge and skills needed to live in an increasingly complex and competitive world.

—**SHAWNDRA,**
Teacher Education program, first year

Schools do not exist in a vacuum. Schools must respond to the changing expectations of students, parents, teachers, communities, and the public at large. As the following section shows, today's schools have a complex, multifaceted role in today's society.

What is the Role of the School and What Makes a School Successful?

Philosophical, political, religious, and cultural beliefs and ideologies aside, people believe that schools should teach academic content; however, disagreement exists regarding the overall *purpose* for learning academic content.

Diverse Views on the Purpose of Schools

Some people believe that the primary purpose of learning should be to promote the personal growth and development of students. Others believe that the primary purpose of schooling is to ensure the success of the United States in a global economy and to prepare students for jobs of the future. For example, the mission of the U.S. Department of Education is "to promote student achievement and *preparation for global competitiveness* by fostering educational excellence and ensuring equal access" (italics added) (U.S. Department of Education, 2017).

SCHOOLS AND PROSOCIAL VALUES Although debate continues about the primary purpose of schooling in the United States, the public does agree that schools should teach **prosocial values** such as responsibility, honesty, fairness, and civility. The well-being of any society requires support of such values; they enable people from diverse backgrounds to live together peacefully. For example, the U.S. Department of Education (2013, December 3) makes the following comments about the importance of values to the individual and to our society:

> We want our children to develop respect and compassion for others. We want them to be honest, decent and thoughtful—to stand up for their principles, to cooperate with others and to act responsibly. We want them to make sound moral choices. The payoffs for encouraging a child's values are enormous: those who grow up with strong, consistent and positive values are happier, do better in school and are more likely to contribute to society. (U.S. Department of Education, 2013)

The Technology in Action feature for this chapter explains how teachers can use video editing to teach students the importance of study skills and responsibility, a prosocial value.

SCHOOLS AND SOCIALIZATION OF THE YOUNG Emile Durkheim (1858–1917), the great French sociologist and philosopher, stated in *Education and Sociology* that "Society can survive only if there exists among its members a significant degree of homogeneity; education perpetuates and reinforces this homogeneity by fixing in the child, from the beginning, the essential similarities collective life demands" (Durkheim, 1956, p. 70). One of the roles of the school is to provide the common foundational experiences that

TECHNOLOGY in ACTION

Video Editing to Teach Study Skills and Responsibility in Sixth Grade

A study skills unit has been a mainstay of Rachael Yelmin's sixth-grade language arts class for years. When her students enter middle school from elementary school, they seem to struggle to keep up with the pace of middle school. Two years ago, she experimented with a new way to teach study skills and responsibility. Instead of telling her students about the things they need to do to be successful in middle school—like taking responsibility, time management, reading for comprehension, and so on—she decided to let them tell her.

Ms. Yelmin now divides her students into groups of four and asks each group to create a high-definition video for fifth-grade students that highlights the study skills necessary to be successful in middle school. Each group checks out a video camera and accesses a free video-editing software program online. Also, they are given a DVD on which to burn their video.

The project begins with each group writing a storyboard for their video. At this point, students conduct research, select topics, and decide on their video sequence. This stage allows students to make important development decisions (with Ms. Yelmin's help) prior to the actual shooting and editing of their videos. After the storyboard is written, students perform in front of the camera, take video of important locations in the school, interview students and staff, develop graphics, select music, and write text. Then they edit the raw footage using the video-editing software program.

When the project is complete, Ms. Yelmin sends DVDs of the completed videos to fifth-grade classrooms at schools in the community. Ms. Yelmin has found that students who create a study skills video retain the study skills information much better than students to whom she merely lectures about study skills. She has also found that her incoming students (the fifth-graders who watch the videos created by "upperclassmen") have a good foundation from which to begin their middle school years.

VISIT: Several free and open-source video-editing software programs are available on the Internet. A few sites allow you to compare video-editing options and features. You need a computer, a video source (such as a camera or already-captured video), enough hard drive space on which to store the raw video, video-editing software, and creativity.

promote enlightened citizens. Without such a citizenry to hold it together, a society, especially a democratic society, is at risk.

Through their common experiences in schools, children and youth become socialized. Students from diverse ethnic, racial, linguistic, and cultural backgrounds come together in U.S. schools to learn the values and customs of the country. For example, 9.4 percent of public school students, or 4.6 million students, were English language learners (ELLs) during the 2014–15 school year. The percentage of ELLs ranged from 1 percent in West Virginia to 22.4 percent in California (McFarland, et al., 2017). Through the schools, children and youth from such diverse backgrounds learn English and learn about the importance of U.S. holidays such as the Fourth of July and Memorial Day; the contributions of Thomas Jefferson, Abraham Lincoln, and Dr. Martin Luther King Jr.; and the importance of citizenship in a democracy.

The goal of socializing students is evident in countless local schools whose mission statements focus on preparing students for responsible citizenship, further learning, and productive employment in our nation's economy. For example, the mission of Westport Public Schools in Westport, Connecticut is "to prepare all students to reach their full potential as life-long learners and socially responsible contributors to our global community" (Westport Public Schools, 2017). In effect, schools reflect, or mirror, society; they reproduce the knowledge, skills, values, and attitudes that society has identified as essential.

SCHOOLS AND SOCIAL CHANGE Schools also provide students with the knowledge and skills to improve society. However, "Schools find it difficult to accomplish [social change] because of influences outside their control, such as family, wealth, peer group activities, neighborhood conditions, and gender and racial discrimination" (Spring, 2018, pp. 62–63).

In addition, not everyone agrees that schools *should* attempt to improve society; instead, politicians often blame schools for social problems like crime, poverty, and drug abuse. Rather than change society to reduce those problems, politicians claim that schools are failing to teach young people to become honest, contributing members of society.

A less controversial approach to social change involves service-learning activities that require students to help improve their local communities. Some high schools require that every student complete a service requirement to help students understand that they are members of a larger community to which they are accountable. The Chicago Public Schools require that each high school choose one of the following options as a requirement for the graduating classes of 2017 through 2019:

- One classroom-integrated service-learning project + 25 individual service hours
- Two classroom-integrated service-learning projects + 15 individual service hours
- Three classroom-integrated service-learning projects

For the graduating classes of 2020 and beyond, schools can choose among the following:

- One service-learning project related to a civics or Advanced Placement (AP) government course, plus a service-learning project related to another course area
- One service-learning project related to a civics or AP government course, plus a service-learning project developed independently by students in an area of interest (Chicago Public Schools, 2017)

Service learning provides students with opportunities to deliver service to their communities while engaging in reflection and study on the meaning of those experiences. Service learning brings young people into contact with people who are older, ill, of a lower income level, and homeless, and it acquaints them with neighborhood and governmental issues.

FOCUS ON **DIVERSITY**: SCHOOLS AND EQUAL EDUCATIONAL OPPORTUNITY

Ample evidence exists that certain groups in U.S. society do not have equality of opportunity economically, socially, and educationally. For example, if we look at the percentage of children three to four years old who participate in early childhood programs such as Head Start, nursery school, and prekindergarten—experiences that help children from less advantaged backgrounds start elementary school on an equal footing with other children—we find that children from lower-income families are less likely to have such opportunities (McFarland et al., 2017). In addition, there is a positive relationship between parents' educational attainment and their children's enrollment in early childhood programs; also, Latino children are less likely to be enrolled than White or African American children (McFarland et. al., 2017).

The United States has always derived strength from the diversity of its people, and all students should receive a quality education so that they may make their unique contributions to society. To reach this goal, extensive programs at the federal, state, and local levels provide equity for students—regardless of race, ethnicity, language, gender, sexual orientation, or religion. Equity is a key provision of the Every Student Succeeds Act (ESSA), signed into law by President Obama in 2015. ESSA has several provisions designed to "advance equity and excellence throughout our nation's schools for students of color, low-income students, English learners, students with disabilities, and those who are homeless or in foster care" (Cook-Harvey, C.M., Darling-Hammond, L., Lam, L., Mercer, C., & Roc, M. (2016).). A focus on equity is one way that schools attempt to positively implement social change.

The goal of providing equal educational opportunity for all has long distinguished education in the United States from that found in most other countries. Since the 1850s, schools in the United States have been particularly concerned with providing children from diverse backgrounds with the education they need to succeed in our society. As James Banks (2014, p. 6) suggests, "Education within a pluralistic society should affirm and help students understand their home and community cultures. [To] create and maintain a civic community that works for the common good, education in a democratic society should help students acquire the knowledge, attitudes, and skills needed to participate in civic action to make society more equitable and just."

The Characteristics of Successful Schools

Many schools in all settings and with all kinds of students are highly successful. One measure of success, naturally, is that students at these schools achieve at a high level and complete requirements for graduation. Whether reflected in scores on standardized tests or other documentation of academic learning gains, students at these schools are learning. They are achieving literacy in reading, writing, computation, and computer skills. They are learning to solve problems, think creatively and analytically, and, most important, they are learning to learn.

Another valid measure of success for a school is that it achieves results that surpass those expected from comparable schools in comparable settings. The achievement of students goes beyond what one would expect. In spite of surrounding social, economic, and political forces that impede the educative process at other schools, these schools are achieving results.

Finally, successful schools are those that are improving, rather than getting worse. School improvement is a slow process, and schools that are improving—moving in the right direction rather than declining—are also successful.

RESEARCH ON SCHOOL EFFECTIVENESS AND SCHOOL IMPROVEMENT Since the early 1990s, researchers have studied schools to identify the characteristics of successful (or effective) schools. The characteristics of successful schools were described in different ways in several research projects. The following is a synthesis of those findings.

- **Strong leadership**—Successful schools have strong leaders—individuals who value education and see themselves as educational leaders, not just as managers or bureaucrats. They monitor the performance of everyone at the school—teachers, staff, students, and themselves. These leaders have a vision of the school as a more effective learning environment, and they take decisive steps to bring that about.
- **High expectations**—Teachers at successful schools have high expectations of students. These teachers believe that all students—rich or poor—can learn, and they communicate this to students through realistic yet high expectations.
- **Emphasis on basic skills**—Teachers at successful schools emphasize student achievement in the basic skills of reading, writing, and mathematical computation.
- **Orderly school environment**—The environments of successful schools are orderly, safe, and conducive to learning. Discipline problems are at a minimum, and teachers can devote greater amounts of time to teaching.

- **Frequent, systematic evaluation of student learning**—The learning of students in successful schools is monitored closely. When difficulties crop up, appropriate remediation is provided quickly.
- **Sense of purpose**—Those who teach and those who learn at successful schools have a strong sense of purpose. From the principal to the students, everyone at the school is guided by a vision of excellence.
- **Collegiality and a sense of community**—Teachers, administrators, and staff at successful schools work well together. They are dedicated to creating an environment that promotes not only student learning but also their own professional growth and development.

Since the 1990s, researchers have focused, increasingly, on the characteristics of schools that improve over time. A key finding of **school improvement research** is that teachers must play a significant role in providing leadership for the improvement process. In other words, "If real reform is to occur, classroom teachers must be active in defining its objectives, design, implementation, and assessment. Reform as a product handed down to teachers must be redesigned to be a process in which teachers are vital contributors" (Armstrong, 2008, p. 142).

Schools that are improving are made up of collaborative teams of teachers, school administrators, and other stakeholders who are committed to working together to increase student learning. Teacher leadership teams; parent and community representation on school councils; and open, two-way communication with all stakeholders are examples of shared leadership. In short, the culture of a school that is improving encourages teachers to grow and to develop in the practice of their profession. It encourages them to develop knowledge and skills to respond to social problems such as those described in the following sections.

How Can Schools Be Described?

Given the wide variation in schools and their cultures, different approaches can be used to describe the distinguishing characteristics of schools. Schools can be described according to the focus of their curricula; for example, high schools may be college prep, vocational, or general. The curricula at some private schools include content based on various religious beliefs, in addition to traditional subjects. Some private schools emphasize an interdisciplinary, applied approach to STEM (science, technology, engineering, and mathematics) education. Others focus on the performing and visual arts, health professions, information technology, or international studies and languages. Some private schools teach curricula based on an approach to teaching and learning (e.g., experiential, project-based learning) or the ideas of a well-known educational philosopher (e.g., John Dewey or Maria Montessori).

Another way to describe schools is according to their organizational structure, for example, alternative schools, charter schools, online schools, or magnet schools. A few schools are even organized as schools "without walls." For example, the School Without Walls Senior High School in **WASHINGTON, D.C.**, a public magnet school, has the following motto: "The City as a Classroom."

FOCUS ON **DIVERSITY**: SCHOOLS AND SOCIAL CLASS

In spite of a general consensus that schools should promote social change and equal opportunity, some individuals believe that schools "reproduce" the existing society by presenting different curricula and educational experiences to students from different socioeconomic classes. Students at a school in an affluent suburb, for example, may study chemistry in a well-equipped lab and take a field trip to a high-tech industry to see the latest application of chemical research, whereas students at a school in an impoverished inner-city neighborhood learn chemistry from out-of-date texts, have no lab in which to conduct experiments, and take no field trips because the school district has no funds.

In effect, schools preserve the stratification within society and maintain the differences between the haves and the have-nots. As Joel Spring (2018, pp. 87–88) explains: "[T]he economic level of the family determines educational attainment. Children from low-income families do not attain so high a level of education as children from rich families. From this standpoint the school reinforces social stratification and contributes to intergenerational immobility." Moreover, rich families can afford to live in affluent school districts or send their children to private schools. This, in turn, increases the chances that their children will attend the "best" colleges and universities and ultimately maintain or increase the family's social-class status.

In addition, children from lower-income families tend to develop "restricted" language patterns with their use of English, whereas children from more affluent backgrounds tend to develop more "elaborated" language patterns (Bernstein, 2000; Heath, 1983). In many cases, children from lower-income families encounter a mismatch between the language patterns used in the home and those they are expected to use in school. This mismatch can be "a serious stumbling block for working class and non-white pupils" (MacLeod, 2008, p. 18). Therefore, it is important for teachers to understand the different types of knowledge students bring with them into the classroom and how this knowledge can conflict with the norms and values of schools and teachers.

Four Types Of Schools

A useful way to talk about the relationship between schooling and social class in the United States is suggested by the four categories of schools that Jean Anyon (1996) described in her study of several elementary schools in urban and suburban **NEW JERSEY**. Anyon maintains that schools "reproduce" the existing society by presenting different curricula and educational experiences to students from different socioeconomic classes. As a result of their experiences at school, students are prepared for particular roles in the dominant society.

The first kind of school she calls the *working-class school*. In this school, the primary emphasis is on having students follow directions as they work at rote, mechanical activities such as completing photocopied worksheets. Students have little opportunity to exercise their initiative or to make choices. Teachers may make negative, disparaging comments about students' abilities and, through subtle and not-so-subtle means, convey low expectations to students. Additionally, teachers at working-class schools may spend much of their time focusing on classroom management, dealing with absenteeism, and keeping extensive records.

The *middle-class school* is the second type identified by Anyon. Here, teachers emphasize to students the importance of getting right answers, usually in the form of words, sentences, numbers, or facts and dates. Students have slightly more opportunity to make decisions, but not much. Most lessons are textbook based. Anyon points out that "while the teachers spend a lot of time explaining and expanding on what the textbooks say, there is little attempt to analyze how or why things happen . . . . On the occasions when creativity or self-expression is requested, it is peripheral to the main activity or it is 'enrichment' or 'for fun'" (Anyon, 1996, p. 191).

Unlike the previous two types of schools, the *affluent professional school* gives students the opportunity to express their individuality and to make a variety of choices. Fewer rules govern the behavior of students in affluent professional schools, and teacher and students are likely to negotiate about the work the students will do.

Anyon provides the following definition of the fourth type of school she identified, the *executive elite school*:

> In the executive elite school, work is developing one's analytical intellectual powers. Children are continually asked to reason through a problem, to produce intellectual products that are both logically sound and of top academic quality. (Anyon, 1996, p. 196)

In the affluent professional and executive elite schools, teacher–student relationships are more positive than those in the working-class and middle-class schools. Teachers are polite to their students, seldom give direct orders, and almost never make sarcastic or nasty remarks.

In applying Anyon's categories to schools in the United States, keep in mind that few schools are one type exclusively and that few schools actually fit the categories in all ways. Instead, most schools probably contain individual classrooms that represent all four types. Also, it is possible for one type of school to exist within a school of another type—for example, an advanced-placement program (essentially an affluent professional or executive elite school) within an urban working-class school.

Also keep in mind that Anyon studied a small group of schools in one metropolitan area, and her criteria are linked almost exclusively to socioeconomic status. There are many schools in poor urban areas, for example, whose culture is more like the affluent professional school Anyon describes than the working-class school, and vice versa. Nevertheless, regardless of how schools in the United States are categorized, it seems they do reflect the socioeconomic status of the communities they serve.

School Settings

RURAL SCHOOL SETTINGS Rural schools are often the focal point for community life and reflect values and beliefs that tend to be more conservative than those associated with urban and suburban schools. While the small size of a rural school may contribute to the development of a family-like culture, its small size may also make it difficult to provide students with an array of curricular experiences equal to that found at larger schools in more populated areas. In contrast, large suburban or urban schools may provide students with more varied learning experiences, but these schools may lack the cohesiveness and community focus of rural schools.

URBAN AND SUBURBAN SCHOOL ENVIRONMENTS The differences among the environments that surround schools can be enormous. Urban schools found in or near decaying centers of large cities often reflect the social problems of the surrounding area, such as drug abuse, crime, and poverty. One of the most serious problems confronting education in the United States is the quality of such schools. Across the country—in Chicago, New York, Los Angeles, St. Louis, Detroit, and Cleveland—middle-class families who can afford to do so move away from urban centers or place their children in private schools. As a result, students in urban school districts are increasingly from low-income backgrounds.

In *Shame of the Nation*, Jonathan Kozol (2005) documents the startling contrast between the neighborhoods that surround impoverished inner-city schools and those that surround affluent suburban schools. He also examines the significant discrepancy between per-pupil spending for students at the two types of schools. For example, at the time, per-pupil funding for the Highland Park/Deerfield, **ILLINOIS**, School District—an affluent suburb north of Chicago—was $17,291. Ninety percent of students in the district were White or "other," and 10 percent were Black and Hispanic. On the other hand, per-pupil funding for Chicago Public Schools was $8,482. In Chicago, 87 percent of students were Black and Hispanic, and 18 percent were White or "other" (Kozol, 2005, p. 321).

Peter Byron/PhotoEdit, inc

In what ways do schools reflect their communities and the wider U.S. society? How might the surrounding neighborhood influence this school? The students who attend it? The teachers who work there?

In Kozol's earlier book, *Savage Inequalities* (1991), he compares New Trier High School in affluent Winnetka, Illinois, and Chicago's DuSable High School, an inner-city school at which I taught for 8 years. He points out that New Trier is in a neighborhood of "circular driveways, chirping birds and white-columned homes" (p. 62). In contrast, DuSable's surroundings are "almost indescribably despairing"; across the street from the school is "a line of uniform and ugly 16-story buildings, the Robert Taylor Homes, which constitute . . . the city's second-poorest neighborhood" (pp. 68, 71).

FOCUS ON **DIVERSITY**: OVERCOMING THE EFFECTS OF POVERTY

As my description of DuSable in *White Teacher, Black School* suggests, the extreme poverty found in some communities can affect schools in undesirable ways:

> The largest housing project in the world, Robert Taylor Homes overshadowed DuSable High School both physically and spiritually . . . . In many buildings of the project, children outnumbered adults three to one. Gang violence was a way of life . . . (1983, p. 4)

In spite of grim conditions surrounding the school, many DuSable teachers made students feel "rich" in ways that went beyond material wealth. Two teachers share how they saw students not as living in poverty but as young people whom they could help to realize their full potential.

> We get along very well. I don't have any discipline problems . . . . I don't really pat them on the back too much, but underneath I'm really proud of them, and I think they feel this. (pp. 102–103)
>
> I have confidence in my students, and I feel that the students have confidence in me. I have, I don't know why, a certain kind of idealistic view toward the young generation. (p. 111)

And three DuSable students comment on how caring, supportive teachers help them learn:

> I feel that this teacher has helped me a lot. He is not as impersonal as some of the teachers in our school, and he makes learning very enjoyable. (p. 107)
>
> I feel very relaxed in class. She doesn't front you off or get smart with you like other teachers often do. She tries to help you with your problems if there's some reason why you can't make it on time. (p. 108)

> She is a really nice and down-to-earth person, and I like her a lot. She is my favorite teacher this year and is very nice to talk to. She is also very warm, understanding, and considerate toward her students. I like her method of teaching very much. I also have to say I learn a lot out of her class the short time I've been there. (p. 108)

School Culture

Much like a community, a school has a distinctive culture—a collective way of life. Terms that have been used to describe **school culture** include *climate*, *ethos*, *atmosphere*, and *character*. Some schools may be characterized as community-like places where there is a shared sense of purpose and commitment to providing the best education possible for all students. Other schools lack a unified sense of purpose or direction and drift, rudderless, from year to year. Still others are characterized by internal conflict and divisiveness and may even reflect what Deal and Peterson (2009) term a "toxic" school culture; students, teachers, administrators, and parents may feel that the school is not sufficiently meeting their needs.

Schools with a community-like culture are characterized by open, two-way communication between teachers and administrators. Teachers feel free to make suggestions to the school's leadership team; and, in turn, teachers welcome feedback from members of the leadership team. In contrast, schools that have a negative or "toxic" culture are often characterized by low teacher morale and high teacher turnover. Such schools frequently have a succession of new principals.

The following sections discuss three dimensions of schools that have a significant influence on a school's culture: the physical environment, formal practices, and traditions.

THE PHYSICAL ENVIRONMENT The physical environment of the school both reflects and helps to create the school's overall culture. Some schools are located on attractive campuses in quiet, upscale neighborhoods; others are located in congested areas of large cities. Some schools are dreary places or, at best, aesthetically bland. The tile floors; concrete block walls; long, straight corridors; and rows of fluorescent lights often found in these schools contribute little to their inhabitants' sense of beauty, concern for others, or personal comfort.

Other schools are much more attractive. They are clean, pleasant, and inviting, and teachers and students take pride in their building. Overall, the physical environment has a positive impact on those who spend time in the school; it encourages learning and a spirit of cohesiveness.

FORMAL PRACTICES OF SCHOOLS The formal practices of schools are well known to anyone who has been educated in U.S. schools. With few exceptions, students attend school from 5 or 6 years of age through 16 at least—and usually to 18—Monday through Friday, September through May, for 12 years. For the most part, students are assigned to a grade level on the basis of age rather than ability or interest. Assignment to individual classes or teachers at a given grade level, however, may be made on the basis of ability or interest.

The **self-contained classroom** is the most traditional and prevalent arrangement in elementary through secondary schools. In open-space schools, however, students are free to move among various activities and learning centers. Instead of self-contained classrooms, **open-space schools** have large instructional areas with movable walls and furniture that can be rearranged easily. Grouping for instruction is much more fluid and varied. Students do much of their work independently, with a number of teachers providing individual guidance as needed.

In middle schools and junior and senior high schools, students typically study four or five academic subjects taught by teachers who specialize in them. In this organizational arrangement, called **departmentalization**, students move from classroom to classroom for their lessons. High school teachers often share their classrooms with other teachers and use their rooms only during scheduled class periods.

SCHOOL TRADITIONS **School traditions** are those elements of a school's culture that are handed down from year to year. The traditions of a school reflect what students, teachers, administrators, parents, and the surrounding community members believe is important and valuable about the school. One school, for example, may have developed a tradition of excellence in academic programs; another school's traditions may emphasize the performing arts; and yet another may focus on athletic programs. Whatever a school's traditions, they are usually a source of pride for members of the school community.

Ideally, traditions are the glue that holds together the diverse elements of a school's culture. They combine to create a sense of community, identity, and trust among people affiliated with a school. Traditions are maintained through stories that are handed down, rituals and ceremonial activities, student productions, and trophies and artifacts that have been collected over the years. For example, Joan Vydra, formerly principal of Briar Glen Elementary School in Wheaton, **ILLINOIS**, initiated Care Week as part of the fall tradition at her former school, Hawthorne Elementary. Vydra believed that a tradition of care would nurture student success. On the first day of Care Week, students learn the importance of caring for themselves; on Tuesdays, caring for their families; on Wednesdays, caring for each other; on Thursdays, caring for the school; and on Fridays, caring for those served by local charities (Deal & Peterson, 2009, p. 139).

CULTURE OF THE CLASSROOM Just as schools develop their unique cultures, each classroom develops its own culture or way of life. **Classroom culture** is determined in large measure by the manner in which teachers and students interact and participate in common activities.

The quality of teacher–student interactions is influenced by the physical characteristics of the setting (classroom, use of space, materials, resources, etc.) and the social dimensions of the group (norms, rules, expectations, cohesiveness, distribution of power and influence). These elements interact to shape classroom culture. Teachers who appreciate the importance of these salient elements of classroom culture are more likely to create environments that they and their students find satisfying and growth promoting.

Students believe that effective teachers develop positive, task-oriented classroom cultures, whereas ineffective teachers develop negative cultures. One inner-city school, for example, provides an illustration of these two very different classroom cultures:

> [Sixth-grade] students saw their social studies/language arts teacher as someone they could learn from and relate to well, while they seemed to constantly do battle with their math and science teacher. Students portrayed [the math and science teacher] as overdemanding, impatient, and insensitive; [the social studies/language arts teacher] seemed to be just the opposite. [The math and science teacher], according to one student, "has an attitude problem. She wants us to be so good the first time. She wants us to always be perfect. She has us walk in a line in the hallway. We are the only class in the school to do that . . . . She is the only [teacher] who won't go over things. She never comes in with a smile; she is always evil. By not going over it, we got a bad attitude. I haven't learned nothing in her class." (Wilson & Corbett, 2001, pp. 54–55)

Monkey Business Images\Shutterstock

These students are participating in the culture of their school. What other behaviors, formal practices, and school traditions are probably part of their school culture?

Video Example 3.1

Informal Cooperative Learning: One teacher builds relationships through her use of instructional strategies.

Clearly, the math and science teacher has developed an adversarial, counterproductive relationship with students. The social studies/language arts teacher, on the other hand, recognizes the importance of developing positive relationships with students and understands how such relationships pave the way for student learning.

Good teachers know how to recognize the strengths of their students and build relationships that foster learning while also building a positive classroom culture.

Check Your Understanding 3.2

What Social Problems Affect Schools And Place Students At Risk?

A complex and varied array of social issues affects schools. These problems often detract from the ability of schools to educate students. Furthermore, schools are often charged with the difficult (if not impossible) task of providing a frontline defense against such problems. Nevertheless, effective teachers understand how social issues influence student learning, and they are able to reduce the negative impact of those issues.

Identifying Students at Risk

An alarming number of young people live under conditions characterized by extreme stress, chronic poverty, crime, and lack of adult guidance. For example, a few days after a gunman fatally shot 20 children and 6 adults at Sandy Hook Elementary School in Newtown, Connecticut, on December 14, 2012, James Garbarino, author of *Lost Boys: Why Our Sons Turn Violent and How We Can Save Them* (1999) suggested that some youth have developed a "war zone mentality." This view, according to Garbarino, can lead a disturbed young person to imagine that their world is filled with "enemies" who ultimately must be destroyed. In addition, Garbarino believes that American culture desensitizes some youth to violence. The easy availability of guns and the popularity of video games in which the player shoots and kills others, he maintains, can lead some youth to think that violence is a justified way of achieving their version of justice in a dangerous world (Garbarino, 2012).

Frustrated, lonely, and feeling powerless, many youth escape into music with violence-oriented and/or obscene lyrics, violent video games, cults, movies and television programs that celebrate gratuitous violence and sex, and cruising shopping malls or hanging out on the street. Others turn also to crime, gang violence, promiscuous sex, or substance abuse. Not surprisingly, these activities place many young people at risk of academic failure and eventually dropping out of school.

Many children in the United States live in families that help them grow up healthy, confident, and skilled, but many do not. Instead, their life settings are characterized by problems of alcoholism or other substance abuse, family or gang violence, unemployment, poverty, poor nutrition, teenage parenthood, and a history of school failure. Such children live in communities and families that have many problems and frequently become dysfunctional, unable to provide their children with the support and guidance they need. When young children grow up in such settings, they are more likely to experience difficulties later in life—poor health, unemployment, and drug and alcohol abuse, for example.

It is important to remember that at-risk factors are only an indication of *potential* academic problems. The majority of children and youth who live in environments affected by poverty, crime, and other social problems are academically successful.

FOCUS ON **DIVERSITY**: AMERICA'S DROPOUT PROBLEM

Every school day, about 7,000 students decide to drop out of school—a total of more than 1.2 million students each year—and only about 70 percent of entering high school freshmen graduate every year (White House Press Release, 2010). Male and female students drop out at approximately the same rate. Figure 3.1 shows that the dropout rate decreased from 10.9 percent in 2000 to 5.9 percent in 2015. During this time, the Hispanic dropout rate decreased by 18.6 percent, while the Black and White dropout rates decreased by 6.6 and 2.4 percentage points, respectively. Nevertheless, in 2015 the Hispanic status dropout rate (9.2 percent) remained higher than the Black (6.5 percent) and White (4.6 percent) dropout rates. Students at risk of dropping out tend to get low grades, perform below grade level academically, are older than the average student at their grade level because of previous retention, and have behavior problems in school. **Students at risk** need teachers who can recognize opportunities in the classroom to build up their confidence as learners, as Cynthia Gibson illustrates in the Teaching on Your Feet feature for this chapter.

Figure 3.1 Status dropout rates of 16- to 24-year-olds by race/ethnicity: 2000 through 2015

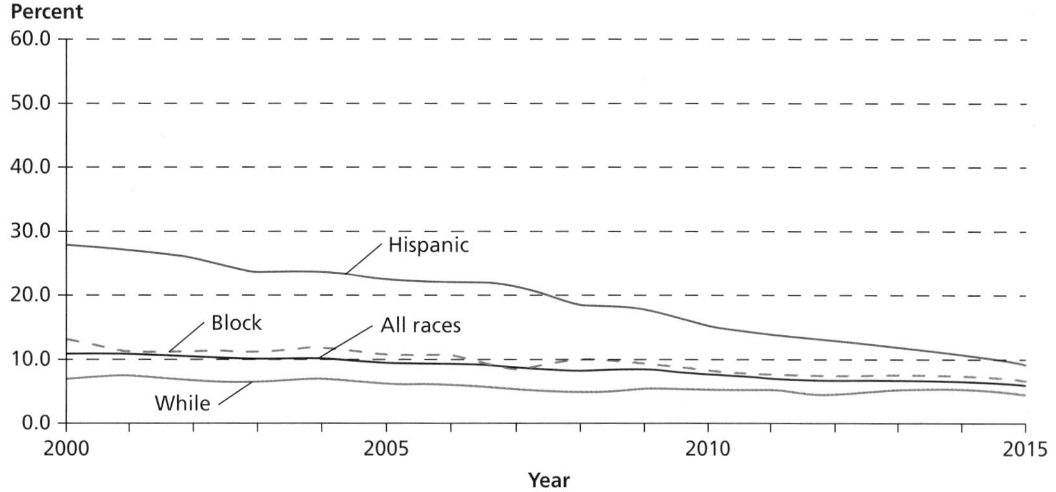

Note: The "status dropout rate" is the percentage of 16- to 24-year-olds who are not enrolled in school and have not earned a high school credential (either a diploma or an equivalency credential such as a GED certificate). Data are based on sample surveys of the civilian noninstitutionalized population, which excludes persons in prisons, persons in the military, and other persons not living in households. Data for all races include other racial/ethnic categories not separately shown. Race categories exclude persons of Hispanic ethnicity.

SOURCE: *The Condition of Education 2017*. U.S. Department of Education. Washington, DC: National Center for Education Statistics, p. 221.

Teaching on Your Feet

Lies Our Students Tell Themselves

"I'm too poor and too black."

That's what one student told me not long after I started teaching here in Selma, Alabama. He didn't beat around the bush, and I wasn't just reading some subtle message into his behavior. He said it plainly—that he was "too poor and too black" to make it in this world.

I hear statements like that from my students far too often. They have opened my eyes to the battle I face every day. As teachers, each time we step into the classroom we vow to fight the lies that hold our students down.

I've been immersed in the culture of Selma for the past 15 months. The world knows Selma as a focal point of the civil rights movement. Presidents and presidents-to-be have come here to commemorate the city's role in the struggle for equal voting rights.

Despite the city's prominence in the public eye, progress in Selma is slow. This racially and economically divided town

(continued)

exemplifies the need for change, the need for social justice, and the need for healing.

I teach in a rural, all-Black school just outside of town. My students are hopeful yet disillusioned, free yet held down, youthful yet already grown. Many live at or below the national poverty line, have faced racial struggles, and can relate to at least one of Langston Hughes's deferred dreams. On the way to work I pass a golf course—one that even in the year 2008 is closed to Blacks, and therefore to all of my students.

Yet it's not so much the racist minority in the community that disturbs me. What disturbs me is the mindset I see in many of my students who—subtly—seem to believe that they are inferior, that their life options are limited, that they are unworthy of their own hopes and dreams. Statements like "too poor and too black" hint at a belief in the lie.

Here, the enemy comes in the form of that mindset. In your neighborhood, students may suffer from other toxic lies, ones no less damaging—lies of sexism, economic power, religious bigotry or intolerance toward anyone or anything different. No matter what their form, there's only one way to counter these lies: by changing lives, one mindset at a time.

On a recent field trip to the Civil Rights Memorial Center in Montgomery, I saw an immediate change in the mindset of many of my students.

Take "Jack," for example. Just a few days earlier, Jack had made a derogatory comment about gays. As we walked the hall dedicated to contemporary issues, however, he was the first to announce, "We have to treat everyone right, no matter what!" This unexpected remark came as a response to a story about a hate crime directed at a gay man.

Then there's "Alfred," a student with a sweet smile who tries to put on a rough exterior. On the ride home, I looked at him and stated, "You are *not* the thug you pretend to be." We talked candidly, and he said he realized that he is a better person than the tough-guy act he had created. I saw that spark in him and a big, soft heart. Since the trip, Alfred has been one of the best-behaved and most motivated students in class.

There's also "Daneka," who talked about her commitment to being different, to going to college, and to helping others.

But the deepest change I feel personally is in me. I have grown to love the kids as family. Sharing a piece of their lives has renewed my commitment to breaking down barriers and challenging misguided mindsets. Teaching is about creating change and giving hope. When you give hope, I've found, you receive hope. I can't think of a better reason to teach.

CYNTHIA GIBSON
Selma, **ALABAMA**

Analyze

What changed and inspired these kids? It was simply information—information about their own history, information that led to a greater understanding of those who are different from themselves, and information that sorted the truth from the lie. It wasn't just data in a textbook. It was real information my students could relate to like information about social justice. If you aren't teaching social justice and tolerance, you aren't really teaching at all.

A little education can change a mindset, and when mindsets change, futures change. That student who, a year ago, was "too poor and too black" to go to college has just been admitted to Samford University—his dream school. By learning the truth about himself, he has overcome a childhood of abuse, poverty, and lack of parenting. This young man stands as an example of how dramatically a life can change when we are willing to stand together to fight against injustice.

Reflect

1. What strategies can teachers use to counteract the "lies" students tell themselves about their abilities and future potential?
2. How would you handle a student's embarrassment over not being able to perform in front of the class?

Note: Reprinted with permission of Teaching Tolerance, a project of the Southern Poverty Law Center. www.tolerance.org. Gibson is currently Writing Center Coordinator at Wallace Community College in Selma, **ALABAMA**.

Many youth take more than the typical 4 years to complete high school, or they eventually earn a high school graduate equivalency diploma (GED). If these alternative routes to high school completion are considered, however, there are still significant differences among racial/ethnic groups. For example, U.S. Census Bureau data indicate that 88.9 percent of Asians 25 years and over have completed high school, compared to 88.1 percent of Whites, 85.0 percent of African Americans, and 65.0 percent of Hispanics (U.S. Census Bureau, 2013, December).

The life experiences of students who are at risk of dropping out can be difficult for teachers to imagine. Encountering the realities of poverty for the first time can be upsetting. For students living in poverty, lunch at school may be the main meal of the day. For several days in a row, they may wear the same clothes to school. At home, they may not have paper, pencils, crayons, or scissors to complete homework assignments. Day in and day out, it may be hard for teachers to witness how poverty can prevent a child from living up to his or her potential.

Children and Poverty

Although the United States is one of the wealthiest countries in the world, by no means has it achieved an enviable record with regard to poverty among children (see Figure 3.2). In 2017, 21 percent of children (15 million) lived in families below the poverty level ($24,600 for a family of two adults and two children). Growing up

Figure 3.2 Child well-being, by race and Hispanic origin

		National Average	African American	American Indian	Asian and Pacific Islander	Hispanic	Non-Hispanic White	Two or More Races
ECONOMIC WELL-BEING								
Children in Poverty	2015	21%	36%	34%	13%	31%	12%	21%
Children Whose Parents Lack Secure Employment	2015	29%	45%	47%	21%	34%	23%	33%
Children Living in Households With a High Housing Cost Burden	2015	33%	47%	32%	32%	45%	24%	35%
Teens Not in School and Not Working	2015	7%	10%	13%	3%	9%	6%	7%
EDUCATION								
Young Children Not in School#	2011–15	53%	49%	56%	46%	60%	51%	52%
Fourth Graders Not Proficient in Reading	2015	65%	82%*	78%*	47%*	79%	54%	62%*
Eighth Graders Not Proficient in Math	2015	68%	88%*	81%*	42%*	81%	58%	65%*
High School Students Not Graduating on Time	2014/15	17%	25%*	28%*	10%*	22%	12%	N.A.
HEALTH								
Low-Birthweight Babies	2015	8.1%	13.0%	7.5%	8.4%	7.2%	6.9%	N.A.
Children Without Health Insurance	2015	5%	4%	13%	4%	8%	4%	4%
Child and Teen Deaths per 100,000	2015	25	36	28	15	20	24	N.A.
Teens Who Abuse Alcohol or Drugs	2014^	5%	4%*	5%*	2%**	6%	5%	3%*
FAMILY AND COMMUNITY								
Children in Single-Parent Families	2015	35%	66%	52%	16%	42%	25%	41%
Children in Families Where the Household Head Lacks a High School Diploma	2015	14%	12%	19%	10%	33%	6%	9%
Children Living in High-Poverty Areas	2011–15	14%	32%	31%	7%	23%	5%	12%
Teen Births per 1,000	2015	22	32	26	7	35	16	N.A.

#Data are from 5-year American Community Survey (ACS) data and are not comparable to the national average using 3 years of pooled 1-year ACS data.
*Data are for non-Hispanics.
^These are single-year race data for 2014. Data in index are 2013–14 multiyear estimates.
Data results do not include Native Hawaiians/Pacific Islanders.
N.A. = Data not available.

SOURCE: 2017 *Kids Count Data Book: State Trends in Child Well-Being*. Baltimore: Annie E. Casey Foundation, 2017, p. 16. Used with Permission.

in poverty can negatively impact a child's developing brain and lead to problems in school and poor health and academic outcomes. It also can lead to higher rates of risky health-related behaviors among adolescents.

Despite the overall high standard of living, homelessness in the United States is a major social problem. Prior to the 1980s, homelessness was largely confined to the poorest areas of the nation's largest cities. Since then, changes in social policies such as welfare, minimum wages, and affordable housing—coupled with economic upheavals and continued unequal distributions of wealth—have swelled the number of homeless people. In addition, homelessness is moving beyond cities to rural areas where single mothers (often migrant farm workers) and their children make up the largest percentage of the homeless population (National Coalition for the Homeless, 2013a).

About 75 percent of homeless or runaway children have dropped out or will drop out of school (National Coalition for the Homeless, 2013b). A host of barriers can make it difficult for them to attend school. First is the need to overcome health problems, hunger, and the difficulty of obtaining clothing and school supplies. Second, providing documentation for school enrollment is often almost impossible for homeless guardians. School districts are often reluctant to eliminate requirements for birth certificates, immunization records, and documentation of legal guardianship. Third, homeless shelters and other temporary housing may not be on regular school district bus routes, making it difficult for homeless children to get to and from school. And homeless children can be difficult to identify because they are often highly mobile and may not wish to be identified.

The nation's first law to provide assistance to homeless persons, particularly children, was passed in 1987. The McKinney Act (renamed the **McKinney-Vento Homeless Assistance Act** in 2000) requires states to provide homeless children with free public education. According to the McKinney-Vento Act, schools must remove obstacles to school registration for homeless students—requirements for residency, guardianship, immunization, and previous school records—as well as provide transportation to and from school. In addition, the law requires that each school district have a liaison whose responsibility is to help identify homeless students and to ensure their success in school.

Childhood Stress and Trauma

Children can experience stress in their lives that negatively impacts their development and well-being. If their families are coping with financial problems, drug addiction, domestic violence, neighborhood crime, or mental illness, children may experience levels of stress that are overwhelming, even traumatic. In this chapter's Teachers' Voices: Being an Agent of Change, I describe how a literary magazine I started gave my students opportunities to write about the stress in their lives.

TEACHERS VOICES  BEING AN AGENT OF CHANGE

FORREST W. PARKAY

Students Cope With Stress Through Writing

I began my teaching career as a member of the English Department at DuSable High School on Chicago's South Side. The school, located at 4934 S. Wabash, was designed for an enrollment of just over 2,000 students; however, during my first three years at the school, enrollment peaked at more than 3,000 students.

Severe overcrowding contributed to an environment that was, on occasion, stressful and chaotic. For example, while monitoring the first-floor lunchroom (part of my assignment as a beginning teacher) that first year, I was shocked on a few occasions when riots erupted and chairs went flying through the air.

All of the students at DuSable were African American, and most were from poor families. Many students lived just across the street in the Robert Taylor Homes, the largest housing project in the U.S. Gang violence occurred frequently in the surrounding neighborhood; on occasion, it spilled over into the school's long hallways.

In my Remedial English classes, I quickly realized that the curriculum developed by the Chicago Board of Education was not that relevant to many of my students. After school and on the weekends, I wondered, how can I teach my students the content of English in a way that will be meaningful and relevant to them?

Early on, I observed that students would often express themselves in writing not only on crumpled sheets of notebook paper, but on restroom walls and lockers. Perhaps, I thought, these personal expressions could be channeled in a more formal way. At that moment, I decided to launch *Write On: A Magazine of Student Writing*.

Write On was an immediate success! One hundred copies of the first edition sold out in a day. Two students and I photocopied the first two editions; after that, the magazine was offset printed by students in the school's print shop.

Word about the magazine spread quickly, and students began to stop me in the hallway to give me their stories and poems. Their writing focused on topics such as drugs, racism, violence, and the meaning of "true love." The following excerpts from *Write On* illustrate how students coped with stress through writing.

Top Secret, by Walter: "The Hater Gun is the key to all wars. There will not be another war with the Hater Gun. It knocks out all the hate in people. This gun works on a lever. In reverse, it will bring hate; forward, it brings on love."

Dialogue by a Locker, by Barbara: "*Debra*: Hey, girl, did you hear what happened? *Marchell*: Naw, girl. What happened? *Debra*: A girl got shot over by Beethoven School yesterday. She was coming out of the building and someone shot her in the head. *Marchell*: It is a pity people get shot for doing nothing. *Debra*: The police came and the ambulance took the girl away. *Marchell*: Did the police find who did it? *Debra*: Naw, girl. I'll see you tomorrow."

Hunger, by Cedric: "Hunger! Will change a man, brain a man, and sometimes even hang a man. Hunger! Will put a man to his last dime. Will make a man leave dreams behind. Hunger! Will make a man who cannot hide turn up committing suicide. Hunger! Will make a man a man no more."

PERSONAL REFLECTION

1. What are the characteristics of teachers who help students from stressful home environments be successful, engaged learners while at school? Which of those characteristics do you possess?
2. Reflecting on your own experiences as a K–12 student, do you recall learning activities that helped you cope with stress in your life? Explain your answer.

Forrest W. Parkay taught English at DuSable High School for 8 years and served as chairman of the English Department for 4 years.

The U.S. Department of Health and Human Services reported that Child Protective Services (CPS) agencies investigated 3.4 million reports of alleged child maltreatment in 2015. Of these children, CPS determined that about 683,000 were victims of child maltreatment—three-quarters (75.3%) were neglected, 17.2 percent were physically abused, and 8.4 percent were sexually abused (U.S. Department of Health & Human Services, 2017). Clearly, the burden of having to cope with such abuse in the home environment does not prepare a child to come to school to learn. Such stress is often associated with health and emotional problems, failure to achieve, behavioral problems at school, and dropping out of school.

Since the mid-1990s, the **Adverse Childhood Experiences (ACE) Study** has surveyed thousands of people regarding the prevalence of 10 categories of stressful, traumatic experiences they had prior to reaching age 18. ACE researchers developed an ACE "score" to reflect the number of categories (not incidents or events) a person experienced during childhood. Thus, a person's ACE score can range between 0 and 10. Approximately 36 percent of the U.S. population have ACE scores of 0. Twenty-six percent have a score of 1; 16 percent a score of 2; 10 percent a score of 3; and 13 percent a score of 4 or more (Centers for Disease Control and Prevention, Kaiser Permanente, 2016). Table 3.1 shows the percentage of adults who reported experiences in each category.

The ACE Study results show that more than half of the students enrolled in public schools have dealt with adverse experiences, and one in six struggles with complex trauma (Felitti & Anda, 2009). **Complex trauma** occurs if a child experiences repeated adverse experiences from which he or she cannot escape. Complex trauma can result from physical, sexual, or emotional neglect and abuse; witnessing repeated acts of domestic violence; experiencing severe poverty, deprivation, or homelessness; or experiencing prejudice or bullying. "Over time, such chronic stress produces neurobiological changes in the brain, which researchers have linked to poor physical health and to poor cognitive performance" (Terrasi & De Galarce, 2017, p. 37).

Table 3.1 Categories of Adverse Childhood Experiences

Abuse, by Category	Prevalence (%)
Psychological (by parents; recurrent threats, humiliation)	11%
Physical (by parents; beating, not spanking)	28%
Sexual (anyone)	22%
Neglect, by Category	
Emotional	15%
Physical	10%
Household Dysfunction, by Category	
Alcoholism or drug use in home	27%
Divorce or loss of biological parent (before age 18)	23%
Depression or mental illness in home	17%
Mother treated violently	13%
Imprisoned household member	5%

NOTE: Percentages based on data gathered from 17,337 "middle-class" adults—average age 57 years; almost equally divided among men and women; approximately 80% White including Hispanic, 10% Black, 10% Asian; and 74% had attended college.
SOURCE: Felitti, V.J. & Anda, R.F. (2014). The lifelong effects of adverse childhood experiences. In Chadwick, D.L., et al. Eds. *Chadwick's child maltreatment, Vol 2: Sexual abuse and psychological maltreatment 4th Edition*. Florissant, MO: STM Learning, Inc., p. 205.

If children view the home environment as not safe, they can become anxious and hypervigilant and view others as a potential threat to their safety. Coping strategies a child naturally and understandably develops to survive in a dysfunctional environment may, however, contribute to behavioral and academic problems in school. Research from Washington State University's Area Health Education Center found that children who have an ACE score of 3 are more than twice as likely to be suspended from school, 6 times more likely to experience behavioral problems, and 5 times more likely to have attendance issues. Students with higher ACE scores are also more likely to have problems with reading and lower grade point averages.

Figure 3.3 Percent of Students with One or More Academic Concerns by ACE Exposure

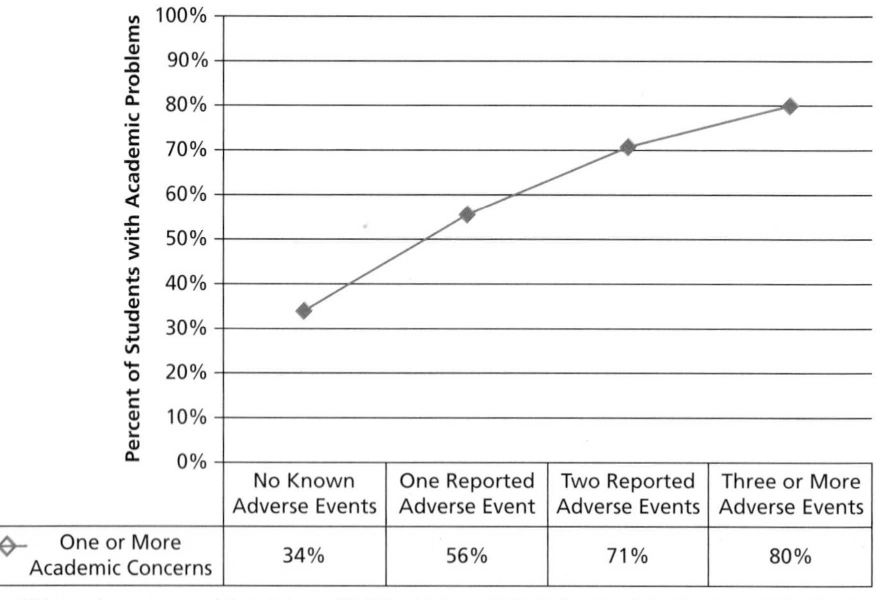

Note: 179 teachers reported the status of 2,101 children at 10 K–6 schools in Spokane, Washington. "Academic problems" were defined as (1) not meeting grade level expectations in one or more core subject areas, (2) attendance problems that interfere with academic progress, and (3) behavior problems that interfere with academic progress.

SOURCE: Blodgett, C., et al. (2017). *Research Brief: Adverse Childhood Experience and Developmental Risk in Elementary Schoolchildren*, Washington State University, Child and Family Research Unit, p. 3. Retrieved from http://ext100.wsu.edu/cafru/wp-content/uploads/sites/65/2015/02/Adverse-Childhood-Experience-and-Developmental-Risk-in-Elementary-Schoolchildren-Research-Briefx.pdf

For example, Figure 3.3 shows that higher ACE scores among elementary-age students increase the likelihood that they will have "academic problems" in school.

The trauma students can experience is illustrated in a blog post written by Tiana Silvas, a 5th-grade public school teacher in New York City:

> I will never forget an incident that happened when I taught in the South Bronx. One of our students was caught in gang crossfire and his mother was killed trying to shield him. The next day, students looked stunned and asked me many questions. I knew that this was not my students' first experience with adversity, nor their last. Students that day said, "This happens. It's sad, but it happens." (Silvas, May 1, 2018)

Substance Abuse

A 2016 study by the National Institute on Drug Abuse (NIDA) showed a continuing decline since the 1990s in the use of illicit drugs among students in grades 8, 10, and 12. However, the NIDA data displayed in Figure 3.4 indicate that substance abuse continues to be a significant concern for today's schools. In addition, the NIDA reported that the following percentages of eighth graders said it would be "fairly easily" or "very easy" to get the following drugs: marijuana (34.6 percent), crack (11.1 percent), cocaine powder (11.0 percent), and crystal methamphetamine (ice; 6.6 percent). For 10th graders, the percentages were marijuana (64.0 percent), crack (13.9 percent), cocaine powder (14.9 percent) and crystal methamphetamine (ice; 8.2 percent); and, for 12th graders, the percentages were marijuana (81.0 percent), crack (19.8 percent), cocaine powder (22.9 percent), and crystal methamphetamine (ice; 14.5 percent) (Miech, et al., 2017, pp. 492, 494, 497).

Figure 3.4 Incidence of use of various drugs: A comparison of responses from 8th, 10th, and 12th graders, 2016

Grade level of respondents:	Marijuana	Inhalants	Hallucinogens[a]	LSD	Hallucinogens other than LSD	Ecstasy (MDMA)	Cocaine	Crack	Cocaine other than Crack	Heroin	Amphetamines[b]	Tranquilizers	Alcohol	Been Drunk	Cigarettes	Cigarettes (Daily)[c]	Smokeless Tobacco	E-Cigarettes
Percentage who used by end of 6th grade																		
8th	4.1	4.4	0.6	0.4	0.4	0.4	0.4	0.3	0.4	0.3	2.1	0.9	9.6	2.1	5.3	0.6	3.3	4.4
10th	2.9	2.8	0.4	0.2	0.2	0.3	0.1	0.1	0.1	0.2	0.9	0.4	6.3	1.7	4.2	0.3	1.9	1.5
12th	2.0	1.0	0.2	0.1	0.2	0.6	0.3	0.2	0.1	0.1	0.8	0.3	4.0	1.1	4.7	0.3	1.5	0.4
Percentage who used by end of 8th grade																		
8th	12.8	7.7	1.9	1.2	1.3	1.7	1.4	0.9	1.1	0.5	5.7	3.0	22.8	8.6	9.8	1.4	6.9	17.1
10th	13.0	5.0	1.4	0.9	1.0	1.1	0.7	0.4	0.7	0.4	2.9	1.4	22.0	8.3	10.5	1.2	5.4	12.6
12th	10.7	2.3	0.8	0.5	0.5	0.9	0.5	0.4	0.3	0.3	1.7	0.9	14.9	6.5	10.9	1.3	4.1	2.4
Percentage who used by end of 10th grade																		
10th	29.7	6.6	4.4	3.2	2.1	2.8	2.1	0.8	1.9	0.6	8.8	6.1	43.4	26.0	17.5	2.7	10.2	28.6
12th	28.9	3.1	3.3	2.3	2.3	2.5	1.4	0.8	1.6	0.6	4.9	3.0	41.1	27.4	20.8	3.6	10.2	16.3

Notes: For 8th and 10th graders, all drugs were asked about in all four forms except for the following: hallucinogens, LSD, hallucinogens other than LSD, heroin, amphetamines, tranquilizers, and smokeless tobacco, which were asked about in only two forms. The approximate *N* for all forms was 16,900 for 8th graders and 14,700 for 10th graders. For 12th graders, percentages are based on two of six forms (*N* = approximately 3,900) except for cocaine, crack, and cigarettes, for which percentages are based on three of six forms (*N* = approximately 5,900); and inhalants, MDMA, other forms of cocaine, and e-cigarettes for which percentages are based on one of six forms (N = approximately 2,000).

a. Unadjusted for underreporting of certain drugs.

b. Based on data from the revised question, which attempts to exclude the inappropriate reporting of nonprescription amphetamines.

c. Data based on the percentage of regular smokers (ever).

SOURCE: Miech, R. A., Johnston, L. D., O'Malley, P. M., Bachman, J. G., Schulenberg, J. E., & Patrick, M. E. (2017). *Monitoring the Future: National survey results on drug use, 1975–2016: Volume I, Secondary school students*. Ann Arbor: Institute for Social Research, University of Michigan, p. 329.

The use of drugs among young people varies from community to community and from year to year, but overall it is disturbingly high. Mind-altering substances used by young people include not only illicit drugs and some prescription medications, but also new synthetics that continually flood the illegal drug marketplace. The abuse of drugs not only poses the risks of addiction and overdosing but also is related to problems such as HIV/AIDS, teenage pregnancy, depression, suicide, automobile accidents, criminal activity, and dropping out of school. For an alarming number of young people, drugs are seen as a way of coping with life's problems.

Violence and Crime

The *Indicators of School Crime and Safety, 2017* reported a decrease between 1995 and 2015 in the percentage of students reporting victimization at school. About 10 percent of public school students reported being victims at school in 1995, compared to 3 percent in 2015. However, 7 percent of fourth-grade students and 13 percent of eighth-grade students attended schools in 2015 that were less than safe and orderly, according to data reported by their teachers. *Indicators* also reported that, during 2013–14, 65 percent of public schools had one or more incidents of violence—an estimated 757,000 crimes. This figure translates to approximately 15 crimes per 1,000 students enrolled that year (Musu-Gillette, Zhang, Wang, Zhang, & Oudekerk, 2017).

According to *Indicators*, the percentage of students ages 12–18 that reported the presence of gangs at their school decreased from 20 percent in 2001 to 11 percent in 2015. Figure 3.5 shows that, in 2015, 15 percent of schools in urban areas reported gang activity, whereas the percentage for schools in suburban and rural communities was much less—10 and 4 percent, respectively.

Many youth see gang membership as providing them with several advantages: a sense of belonging and identity, protection from other gangs, opportunities for excitement, or a chance to make money through selling drugs or participating in other illegal activities. Still others are forced to join gangs by threats and/or violent beatings. Although few students are gang members, a small number of gang-affiliated students can disrupt the learning process, create disorder in a school, and cause others to fear for their physical safety. Strategies for reducing the effect of gang activities on schools include identifying gang members, implementing dress codes that ban styles of dress identified with gangs, and quickly removing gang graffiti from the school.

Figure 3.5 Percentage of students ages 12–18 who reported that gangs were present at school during the school year, by urbanicity: Selected years, 2001 through 2015

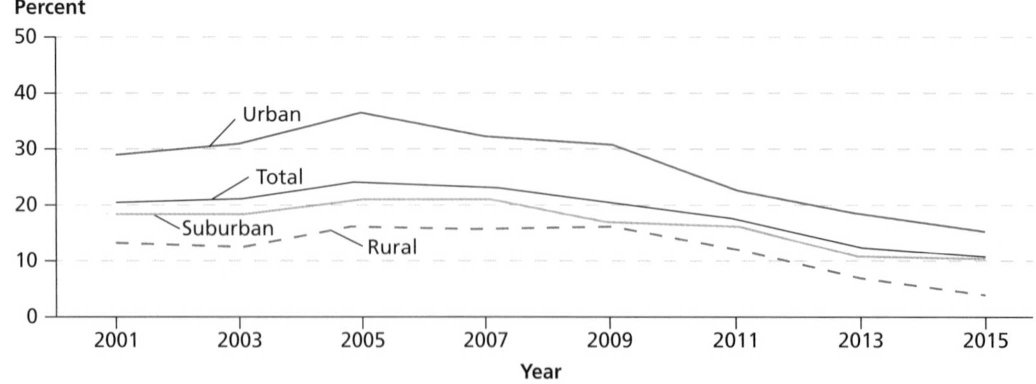

Note: "Urbanicity" refers to the Standard Metropolitan Statistical Area (MSA) status of the respondent's household as defined by the U.S. Census Bureau. Categories include "central city of an MSA (Urban)," "in MSA but not in central city (Suburban)," and "not MSA (Rural)." All gangs, whether or not they are involved in violent or illegal activity, are included. "At school" includes in the school building, on school property, on a school bus, and going to and from school.

SOURCE: Musu-Gillette, L., Zhang, A., Wang, K., Zhang, J., and Oudekerk, B.A. (2017). *Indicators of School Crime and Safety: 2016* (NCES 2017-064/NCJ 250650). National Center for Education Statistics, U.S. Department of Education, and Bureau of Justice Statistics, Office of Justice Programs, U.S. Department of Justice. Washington, DC, p. 65.

Periodically, the nation's attention is riveted by a school shooting such as the one that took the lives of 20 children and 6 adults at Sandy Hook Elementary School in 2012. With each instance of horrific school violence, the recurring question is Why? and there is a renewed effort to understand the origins of youth violence. After each shooting, the nation debates gun control measures; the influence of violence in television, movies, and point-and-shoot video games; and steps that parents, schools, and communities can take to curb school crime and violence. The belief that shooters are loners who "just snap" was contradicted by a U.S. Secret Service and U.S. Department of Education study of 37 school shootings that identified the following patterns:

- Incidents of targeted violence at school rarely were sudden, impulsive acts.
- Prior to most incidents, other people knew about the attacker's idea and/or plan to attack.
- Most attackers did not threaten their targets directly prior to advancing the attack.
- There is no accurate or useful "profile" of students who engaged in targeted school violence.
- Most attackers engaged in some behavior prior to the incident that caused others concern or indicated a need for help.
- Most attackers had difficulty coping with significant losses or personal failures. Moreover, many had considered or attempted suicide.
- Many attackers felt bullied, persecuted, or injured by others prior to the attack.
- Most attackers had access to and had used weapons prior to the attack.
- In many cases, other students were involved in some capacity.
- Despite prompt law enforcement responses, most shooting incidents were stopped by means other than law enforcement intervention. (Vossekuil, Fein, Reddy, Borum, & Modzeleski, 2002, pp. 11–12)

Based on the results of their study, the two departments then issued *Threat Assessment in Schools: A Guide to Managing Threatening Situations and to Creating Safe School Climates* and recommended that schools take the following steps:

- Assess the school's emotional climate.
- Emphasize the importance of listening in schools.
- Adopt a strong but caring stance against the code of silence.
- Prevent, and intervene in, cases of bullying.
- Involve all members of the school community in planning, creating, and sustaining a school culture of safety and respect.
- Develop trusting relationships between each student and at least one adult at school.
- Create mechanisms for developing and sustaining safe school climates. (Fein et al., 2004)

As a result of school shootings and the public's concern with school crime and violence, most schools have developed crisis management plans to cope with violent incidents on campus. Many schools use the "School Safety Checklist" (see Table 3.2), which is excerpted from the National School Safety Center's *School Safety Check Book*.

CYBERBULLYING With the popularity of social media platforms such as Facebook, Twitter, LinkedIn, Pinterest, Snapchat, Google+, Instagram, and dozens of others, bullying has gone online. About one out of every four teens has experienced cyberbullying, and about one out of every six has done it to others (Patchin & Hinduja, 2017). **Cyberbullying** involves the use of social media and communication technologies to

Table 3.2 School Safety Checklist

Give your school a thorough crime prevention inspection now. Use this checklist as a guideline to determine your school's strengths and weaknesses.

	Yes	No
1. Is there a policy for dealing with violence and vandalism in your school? (The reporting policy must be realistic and strictly adhered to.)	______	______
2. Is there an incident-reporting system?	______	______
3. Is the incident-reporting system available to all staff?	______	______
4. Is statistical information about the scope of the problems at your school and in the community available?	______	______
5. Have the school, school board, and administrators taken steps or anticipated any problems through dialogue?	______	______
6. Does security fit into the organization of the school? (Security must be designed to fit the needs of the administration and made part of the site.)	______	______
7. Are the teachers and administrators aware of laws that pertain to them? To their rights? To students' rights? Of their responsibility as to enforcement of and respect for rules, regulations, policies, and the law?	______	______
8. Is there a working relationship with your local law enforcement agency?	______	______
9. Are students and parents aware of expectations and school discipline codes?	______	______
10. Are there any actual or contingency action plans developed to deal with student disruptions and vandalism?	______	______
11. Is there a policy for restitution or prosecution of perpetrators of violence and vandalism?	______	______
12. Is there any in-service training available for teachers and staff in the areas of violence and vandalism and other required reporting procedures?	______	______
13. Is there a policy for consistent monitoring and evaluation of incident reports?	______	______
14. Is the staff trained in standard crime-prevention behavior?	______	______

SOURCE: Excerpted from *The School Safety Check Book* by the National School Safety Center, Dr. Ronald D. Stephens, 141 Duesenberg Dr., Suite 11, Westlake Village, CA, 91362, http://www.nssc1.org. Used with Permission.

harass or threaten an individual or group. Cyberbullies send harassing emails or instant messages; post obscene, insulting, and slanderous messages to online bulletin boards; or develop websites to promote and disseminate defamatory content. As Figure 3.6 shows, a 2016 survey of 5,700 middle and high school students revealed that almost 34 percent of students had experienced cyberbullying during their lifetime, with almost 17 percent experiencing it within the previous 30 days. And female students were more likely than males to have experienced cyberbullying during their lifetime (36.7 percent to 30.5 percent, respectively).

Bullying and cyberbullying can manifest in many ways and trust and communication between teacher and student is key in combatting bullying.

Video Example 3.2

Eliminating Bullying in Schools: A teacher leads students through a discussion about what bullying is and how students can respond to bullying.

Teen Pregnancy

Most teachers of adolescents today may expect to have at least some students who are or have been pregnant. Since peaking in 1990, the teenage pregnancy, birth, and abortion rates have declined, largely the result of more effective contraceptive practices among sexually active teenagers. However, the U.S. teen birth rate is higher than that of many other similar countries, including Canada and the United Kingdom, and teen pregnancies remain a serious problem in U.S. society. Approximately one in four girls will be pregnant at least once before age 20, and about one in five teen moms will have a second child during her teen years (National Council of State Legislatures, 2016).

Because the physical development of girls in adolescence may not be complete, complications can occur during pregnancy and in the birthing process. Also, adolescents are less likely to receive prenatal care in the crucial first trimester; they tend not to eat well-balanced diets; and they are not free of harmful substances such as alcohol, tobacco, and drugs, which are detrimental to a baby's development. "Children born to teen moms often do not perform as well as children of older

Figure 3.6 Cyberbullying

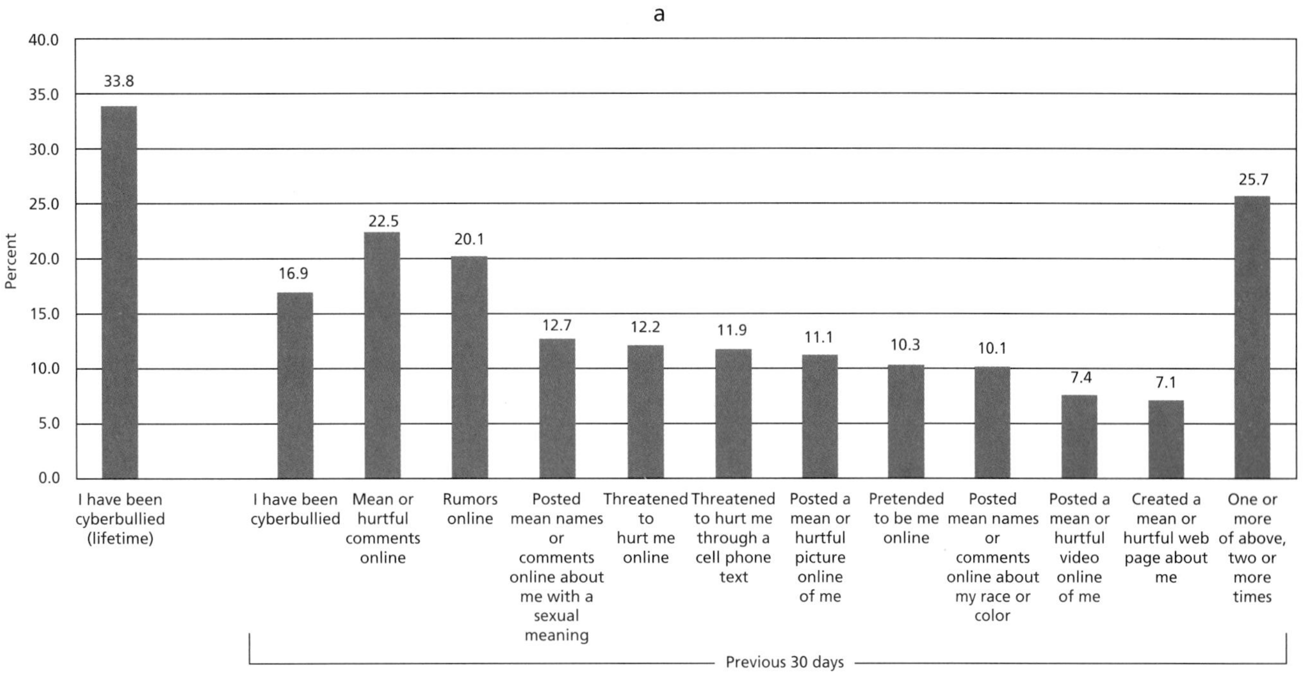

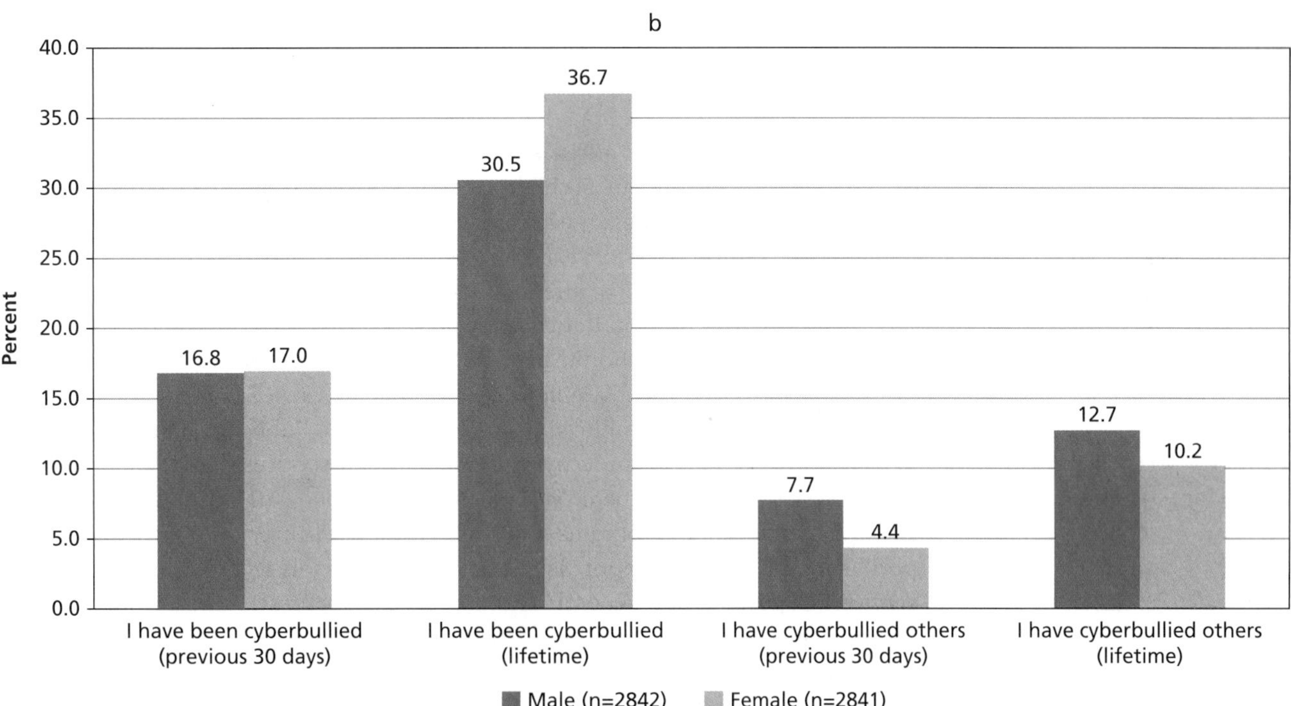

SOURCE: Hinduja, S., and Patchin, J. W. "2016 Cyberbullying Data." Cyberbullying Research Center. Retrieved August 9, 2017, from https://cyberbullying.org/2016-cyberbullying-data

mothers on early childhood development indicators and school readiness measures, such as communication, cognition, and social skills. [They] have lower educational performance, score lower on standardized tests, and are twice as likely to repeat a grade" (National Council of State Legislatures, 2016). Because most teen mothers drop out of school, forfeiting their high school diplomas and limiting their access to decent, higher-paying job opportunities, they and their children stay at the bottom of the economic ladder.

Suicide Among Children and Youth

The increase in individual and multiple suicides is alarming. After "unintentional injuries," suicide is the second leading cause of death for young people 10 to 24 years of age and accounts for approximately 5,500 lives lost each year. A survey of youth in grades 9–12 in public and private schools found that 1 out of 6 reported seriously considering suicide during the past year (Centers for Disease Control and Prevention, 2016, July 19).

Although female students are more likely than male students to have seriously considered attempting suicide during the preceding 12 months, about four times as many male students as females actually commit suicide. Latino students are about two times more likely than White students to attempt suicide, and students in grade 9 are about four times more likely than students in grade 12 to make a suicide attempt that requires medical attention (Centers for Disease Control and Prevention, 2009). Also, nearly one third (29 percent) of lesbian and gay youth had attempted suicide at least once during the prior year compared to 6 percent of heterosexual youth (Kann, et al., 2016).

How Are Schools Addressing Societal Problems?

Responding to the needs of at-risk students is a crucial challenge for schools, families, and communities. Because most children attend school, it is logical that this preexisting system be used for reaching large numbers of at-risk children (and, through them, their families). During the last decade, many school districts have taken innovative steps to address societal problems that affect students' lives.

Although programs that address social problems are costly, most of the public believes that schools should be used for the delivery of health and social services to students and their families. For example, Figure 3.7, based on the 2017 Phi Delta Kappa Pool of the Public's Attitudes toward the Public Schools, shows strong agreement that schools should provide wraparound services to students who don't have access to them elsewhere. More than 9 in 10 Americans support public schools providing after-school programs, with 77 percent reporting that they "strongly support" such programs. Support is also strong for schools to provide mental health services (87 percent) and general health services (79 percent). In addition, 76 percent of Americans agree that schools are justified in seeking additional public funds for these services (Phi Delta Kappa, 2017).

Under pressure to find solutions to increasing social problems among children and adolescents, educators have developed an array of intervention programs. In general, the aim of these programs is to address the behavioral, social, and academic adjustment of at-risk children and adolescents so they can receive maximum benefit from their school experiences.

The following sections describe seven strategies that have proven effective in addressing academic, social, and behavioral problems among children and adolescents: trauma-sensitive schools, peer counseling/mentoring, peer mediation, community schools, compensatory education, alternative schools and curricula, and expanded learning time (ELT) schools.

Figure 3.7 Support for wraparound services

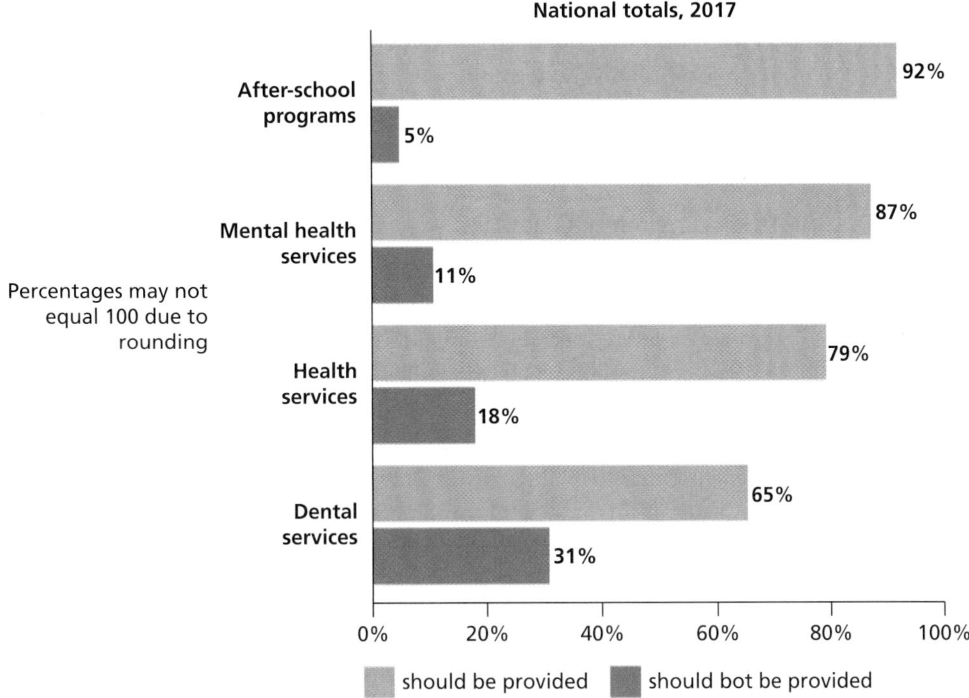

SOURCE: Phi Delta Kappa. (2017). The 49th annual PDK poll of the public's attitudes toward the public schools. *Phi Delta Kappan*, Vol. 99, No. 1, p. K21.

Trauma-Sensitive Schools

To address the trauma that many students have experienced, some states and school districts have developed **trauma-sensitive schools**. "Trauma-sensitive schools emphasize safety, empowerment, and collaborative partnership between children and adults. Within this model, children's negative behaviors are [understood as] the direct or indirect result of an 'injury' caused by physical, emotional, or social maltreatment" (Craig, 2016, p. 5).

In 2011, Washington became the first state to pass legislation in support of trauma-sensitive schools. The law identifies and promotes strategies to reduce the effects of adverse childhood experiences (ACEs) on children's wellbeing and learning. Pennsylvania and Massachusetts have also passed similar legislation.

All staff at a trauma-sensitive school—teachers, administrators, counselors, school nurses, cafeteria workers, custodians, and teacher aides—understand how childhood trauma can affect learning, behavior, and interpersonal relationships. The environment of a trauma-sensitive school supports students and makes them feel safe—physically, emotionally, and socially. Adults at the school understand how unresolved trauma can lead to behavior and learning problems at school. They understand that traumatized children may not trust their school environment and the people in it, and they may have difficulty forming positive relationships with others. An article titled "The Trauma-Sensitive Teacher" further explains the perspective of teachers at trauma-sensitive schools:

> Fostering positive relationships with traumatized children starts with recognizing that early adversity has played a role in their neural development. Behaviors that now threaten these children's academic and social mastery were originally adaptions they made to the uncontrollable stress in their lives. With this knowledge, teachers can approach students whom they previously viewed as oppositional or defiant with a better understanding of what's behind their trauma-related behaviors (Craig, 2016, p. 32)

Figure 3.8 presents a trauma-sensitive school checklist that schools can use to evaluate whether schoolwide policies and practices, classroom strategies and techniques, collaboration and linkages with mental health, family partnerships, and community linkages are effectively meeting the needs of students who have experienced trauma. Chapter 10 of this book explains how trauma-sensitive teachers respond to the misbehavior of students who have experienced trauma in their lives and create classroom environments in which students feel safe, understood, and accepted.

Peer Counseling/Mentoring

To address the social problems that affect students, some schools have initiated student-to-student **peer-counseling** or **peer-mentoring programs**—usually monitored by a school counselor or other specially trained adult. In peer-counseling/mentoring programs, students can address problems and issues such as low academic achievement, interpersonal problems at home and at school, substance abuse, and career planning. Evidence indicates that both peer counselor/mentors and students experience increased self-esteem and greater ability to deal with problems (Garringer & MacRae, 2008).

When peer counseling/mentoring is combined with cross-age tutoring, younger students can learn about drugs, alcohol, premarital pregnancy, delinquency, dropping

Figure 3.8 Trauma-sensitive school checklist

A trauma-sensitive school is a safe and respectful environment that enables students to build caring relationship with adults and peers, self-regulate their emotions and behaviors, and succeed academically, while supporting their physical health and well-being.
This checklist is organized by five components involved in creating a trauma-sensitive school. Each component consists of several elements. Please assess your school on each element according to following scale:
1 = Not in place 2 = Partially in place 3 = Mostly in place 4 = Fully in place

Schoolwide policies and practices

School contains predictable and safe environments (including classrooms, halfways, playgrounds, and school bus) that are attentive to transitions and sensory needs.
1 ________ 2 ________ 3 ________ 4 ________

Leadership (including) principal and/or superintendent) develops and implements a trauma-sensitive action plan, identifies barriers to progress, and ealuates success.
1 ________ 2 ________ 3 ________ 4 ________

General and special educators consider the role that trauma may be playing in learning difficulties at school.
1 ________ 2 ________ 3 ________ 4 ________

Discipline policies balance accountability with an understanding of trauma.
1 ________ 2 ________ 3 ________ 4 ________

Support for staff is available on a regular basis, including supervision and/or consultation with a trauma expert, classroom observations, and opportunities for team work.
1 ________ 2 ________ 3 ________ 4 ________

Opportunities exist for confidential discussion about students.
1 ________ 2 ________ 3 ________ 4 ________

School participates in safety planning, including enforcement of court orders, transferring records safely, restricting access to student-record information, and sensitive handling of reports of suspected incidents of abuse or neglect.
1 ________ 2 ________ 3 ________ 4 ________

Ongoing professional development opportunities occur as determined by staff needs assessments.
1 ________ 2 ________ 3 ________ 4 ________

Classroom strategies and techniques

Expectations are communicated in dear, concise, and positive ways, and goals for achievement of students affected by traumatic experiences are consistent with the rest of the class.
1 ________ 2 ________ 3 ________ 4 ________

Students' strengths and interests are encouraged and incorporated.
1 ________ 2 ________ 3 ________ 4 ________

Activities are structured in predictable and emotionally safe ways.
1 ________ 2 ________ 3 ________ 4 ________

Opportunities exist for students to learn and practice regulation of emotions and modulation of behaviors.
1 ________ 2 ________ 3 ________ 4 ________

Classrooms employ positive supports for behavior.
1 ________ 2 ________ 3 ________ 4 ________

Information is presented and learning is assessed using multiple modes.
1 ________ 2 ________ 3 ________ 4 ________

Opportunities exist for learning how to interact effectively with others.
1 ________ 2 ________ 3 ________ 4 ________

Opportunities exist for learning how to plan and follow through on assignments.
1 ________ 2 ________ 3 ________ 4 ________

Collaborations and linkages with mental health

Policies describe how, when, and where to refer families for mental health supports; and staff actively facilitate and follow through in supporting families' access to trauma-competent mental health services.
1 ________ 2 ________ 3 ________ 4 ________

Access exists to trauma-competent services for prevention, early intervention, treatment, and crisis intervention.
1 ________ 2 ________ 3 ________ 4 ________

Protocols exist for helping students transition back to school from other placements.
1 ________ 2 ________ 3 ________ 4 ________

Mental health services are linguistically appropriate and culturally competent.
1 ________ 2 ________ 3 ________ 4 ________

Staff has regular opportunities for assistance from mental health providers in responding appropriately and confidentiaily to families.
1 ________ 2 ________ 3 ________ 4 ________

Family partnerships

Staff uses a repertoire of skills to actively engage and build positive relationships with families.
1 ________ 2 ________ 3 ________ 4 ________

Strategies to involve parents are tailored to meet individual family needs, and include flexibility in selecting times and places for meetings, availability of interpreters, and translated materials.
1 ________ 2 ________ 3 ________ 4 ________

All communiations with and regarding families respect the bounds of confidentiality.
1 ________ 2 ________ 3 ________ 4 ________

Community linkages

School develops and maintains ongoing partnerships with state human service agencies and with community-based agencies and with community-based agencies to facilitate access to resources.
1 ________ 2 ________ 3 ________ 4 ________

When possible, school and community agencies leverage funding to increase the array of supports available.
1 ________ 2 ________ 3 ________ 4 ________

SOURCE: Lesley University Center for Special Education; Trauma and Learning Policy Initiative of Massachusetts Advocates for Children; and the Legal Services Center of Harvard Law School. (2012). Used with Permission.

out, HIV/AIDS, suicide, and other relevant issues. Here, the groups are often college-age students meeting with those in high school, or high school students meeting with those in junior high school or middle school. In these preventive programs, older students sometimes perform dramatic episodes that portray students confronting problems and model strategies for handling the situations presented.

Approximately 250 schools around the country have implemented Peer Group Connection (PGC). PGC trains older students (11th and 12th graders in high school and eighth graders in middle schools) during a daily, 45-minute leadership development class. The class prepares students to become positive role models and discussion leaders for ninth-grade or sixth-grade students. Working in pairs, peer mentors co-lead groups of 10 to 14 younger students during weekly sessions.

The effectiveness of peer mentoring is confirmed by Doris Lee, principal at Village Academy Middle School in Queens, New York City: "Students are not able to focus in the classroom if they don't feel emotionally secure. What [peer mentoring] has helped me do with my school community is create kind of a positive peer pressure where the leaders are working with younger students and using their relationships to help them do the right thing" (Ross, 2016).

FOCUS ON **DIVERSITY**: PEER MEDIATION TO PROMOTE TOLERANCE

Peer-mediation programs are similar to peer-counseling programs. The focus of **peer mediation** is on cultivating a classroom climate in which students influence one another to be more accepting of differences, not of solving problems per se. In some peer-mediation programs, students participate in role-plays and simulations to help them develop empathy, social skills, and awareness of prejudice.

An example of peer mediation can be found at John Marshall Middle School, in Long Beach, **CALIFORNIA**, where students increase their understanding of cultural differences by learning about peer mediation. Students become "diversity ambassadors" by attending workshops on peer mediation, cultural diversity, tolerance, and conflict resolution. The workshops focus on issues of racial and ethnic barriers for fellow students. The diversity ambassadors host a school assembly on school violence in partnership with the Long Beach Police Department's Gang Unit. Marshall School teachers and students report that the diversity ambassadors have improved the school climate (Learning in Deed, 2004).

Another approach to peer mediation is used by Highlands Elementary School in Edina, **MINNESOTA**. Students are taught to be "peacemakers" during 30 minutes of training each day for 30 days. After the training, teachers select two students to serve as mediators each day. Conflicts students cannot resolve on their own are referred to the class mediators. Mediators wear official T-shirts, patrol the playground and lunchroom, and are available to mediate all conflicts. The role of class mediator rotates, allowing each student to serve as a class mediator an equal amount of time (Edina Schools, 2017).

Community Schools

In response to the increasing number of at-risk students, approximately 7,500 schools around the country are serving their communities by creating **community schools** that integrate educational, medical, social, and/or human services (Institute for Educational Leadership, 2017, p. 4). These schools are often located in low-income urban areas to meet the needs of children and their families.

The Institute for Educational Leadership's Coalition for Community Schools explains how community schools serve their communities:

> Community schools are the kind of public schools that families want and children deserve. Where students are safe, loved, and challenged. Where families and educators partner with doctors, nurses, social workers, community agencies, businesses, higher education, and others to provide the comprehensive academic and non-academic supports that meet each student's unique needs and taps his/her unique talents. Counseling and health care for some. Food and shelter for others. GED and job training for community residents. Quality instruction, enrichment, and extracurriculars for all. Where schools are open 24/7: early mornings, late afternoons, nights, weekends, and during the summer. (Institute for Educational Leadership, 2017, p. 3)

Evaluations of community school programs indicate that they contribute to improved student achievement. They are also linked to increased attendance and reduced levels of high-risk behaviors (e.g., drug use and sexual activity). In addition, because community schools support families, family involvement in school programs increases and family functioning improves. Parents are more likely to support the school in maintaining high expectations for learning and behavior (Coalition for Community Schools, 2017).

Enrico Toni Elementary School, a pre-K through fifth-grade school of 1,200 students on Chicago's Southwest Side, is an example of how a community school can be transformative for the school and its community. When the school became part of the Chicago Public Schools' Community Schools Initiative (CSI) in 2012, the school was on academic probation. The school was at the lowest level in the district's school quality rating system—in need of "intensive intervention." By 2017, however, the school had earned the district's second highest rating and achieved an average daily attendance of more than 96 percent. The school is now a neighborhood hub for parents and community members. "Parents feel that they are not just dropping off their children," according to the school's vice principal (Institute for Educational Leadership, 2017, p. 16).

Community schools can also help communities deal with adversity. For example, right after Hurricane Harvey struck Houston in 2017, Richard Carranza, superintendent of the Houston Independent School District (ISD), announced that the city would increase the number of community schools: "Wraparound services is absolutely part of our strategic plan. Community schools are going to become an increasingly vital part of what we do" (Kamenetz, 2017). All ISD students were eligible to receive three free meals at school for the entire school year. The district also gave out free school uniforms and held a "Parent Summit" to connect parents to information, transportation, clothing, and school supplies.

Compensatory Education

To meet the learning needs of at-risk students, several federally funded **compensatory education programs** for elementary and secondary students have been developed, the largest of which is Title I. Title I provides all children with the opportunity to receive a fair, equitable, high-quality education, and to close the achievement gap. In 2010, more than 56,000 public schools across the country used Title I funds for programs that served more than 21 million children (U.S. Department of Education, Office of Elementary and Secondary Education, 2015).

Launched in 1965 as part of the Elementary and Secondary Education Act (ESEA) and President Lyndon Johnson's Great Society education program, Title I (called Chapter I between 1981 and 1994) was designed to improve the basic skills (reading, writing, and mathematics) of low-ability students from low-income families.

In December 2015, President Obama signed the Every Student Succeeds Act (ESSA) into law, replacing No Child Left Behind (NCLB). According to ESSA's Title I guidelines, public schools receive federal funding from their Local Education Agencies (LEAs) based on the number of students from low-income households that attend district schools. Each year, states must identify schools that have a consistently underperforming subgroup of students and provide them with compensatory programs.

Students who participate in Title I programs are usually taught through pullout programs, in which they leave the regular classroom to receive additional instruction individually or in small groups. Title I teachers, sometimes assisted by an aide, often have curriculum materials and equipment not available to regular classroom teachers.

Research on the effectiveness of Title I programs has been inconclusive, with some studies reporting achievement gains not found in other studies. Research has found positive effects on students' achievement in the early grades, but these gains tend to dissipate during the middle grades. However, *Title I Implementation—Update on Recent Evaluation Findings* (U.S. Department of Education, 2009, January), reported that, across a sample of seven Title I school districts, students in supplemental educational services experienced gains in reading and mathematics achievement that were greater than the gains for nonparticipating students.

Some critics of Title I and other compensatory education programs argue that they are stopgap measures at best. Instead, they call for reducing social problems—poverty, the breakdown of families, drug abuse, and crime, for example—that contribute to poor school performance. However, the testimony Megan Allen, a fifth-grade Title 1 teacher at Shaw Elementary School in Tampa, **FLORIDA**, gave before the U.S. House of Representatives is a compelling example of how Title 1 programs can transform the lives of children:

> Of my 36 students, I have 10 with special needs, who work with the support of an exceptional education teacher. They have disabilities ranging from Emotional Behavioral Disorder to Schizophrenia. I have two students who are Haitian, whose families show up to every school event dressed in their best, for their dreams and hopes are placed in their children.
>
> I have five students who are English Language Learners, receiving daily support from a translator so they can better understand their academics and so I can communicate with their families.
>
> I have two students with arrest records, one who is in a live-in program for troubled youth.
>
> I have four 10 and 11 year-old boys in a special program for our most troubled boys, where they learn manners, wear coats and ties, and learn what it means to be a man.
>
> I have five girls who receive extra support in a lunch group for girls with low self-esteem.
>
> I have two young ladies who receive intense counseling at school, one because she is a rape victim, one because she is a ten-year-old with an ulcer due to anxiety about taking care of her siblings now that her mom has been deported.
>
> I have one student who is checked out of school every Thursday to visit her mother, who is in jail.
>
> I have students who go to bed afraid because of violence in their neighborhood, who look to school as their place to call home. Who go home hungry on the weekends and look forward to two solid meals a day during the school week.
>
> But most of all, I have 36 students who dream. Who have beautiful goals. Who see school as the lever to break the chains of poverty and achieve something amazing in life for themselves and their families. And our school is working to make that happen. Our students are winning county science fairs, making great gains in their student learning, and shining in and out of the classroom. Our students are moving towards greatness. (Allen, 2013)

Alternative Schools and Curricula

To meet the needs of students at risk of education failure because of various social problems, many school districts have developed alternative schools and curricula. These programs are designed to minimize students' high-risk behavior and address concerns about violence, weapons, and drugs in schools. During 2014–2015, approximately 5,500 public alternative schools enrolled nearly 6.2 million students (Glander, 2016).

An **alternative school** is usually a small, highly individualized school separate from the regular school; in other cases, the alternative school is organized as a **school-within-a-school**. Alternative school programs usually provide remedial instruction, some vocational training, and individualized counseling. Because they usually have much smaller class sizes, alternative school teachers can monitor students' progress more closely and, when problems do arise, respond more quickly and with greater understanding of student needs.

One exemplary alternative school is the Union Alternative School in Tulsa, **OKLAHOMA**, serving 9th- through 12th-grade students. The atmosphere at Union is supportive. To increase students' success, the school provides extensive counseling services, and teachers use innovative teaching methods. Students can pursue an individualized course of study based on a flexible schedule, and the teacher–student ratio in classrooms is 1 to 15 or less.

During two class periods of each school day, students may attend elective classes at the regular high school, participate in a work/study program, perform school or community service projects, attend classes at Tulsa Technology Center, or receive tutorial or enrichment assignments (Union Alternative School, 2017).

In a blog post titled "A Day in the Life of an Alternative High School Teacher," Shanna Bowden explains the benefits of teaching at an alternative school near Denver, **COLORADO**:

> We offer a place for students to learn in a non-judgmental and caring environment. Students do not have letter grades but have points they earn for each class every day. If they do not demonstrate their learning, they do not get their point. Teachers have a group of students called a 'family' that they are with until they graduate. Teachers act as counselors for their students, advocating for them in all stages of their high school career.
>
> This flexibility allows teachers to create curriculum that is relevant, essential, and engaging to our students, as long as it is connected to Common Core standards. Classes that have been taught in the past include: Designing a LEED-certified greenhouse (STEM), Serial Podcast (Am. Lit/Elective), Yoga (Health/PE), and The History of Terrorism (World History). Imagine a school where nearly each student has choice and is excited about what they are learning.
>
> The flexibility and authenticity of our schedule is something that drew me to teaching here . . . . I wouldn't be anywhere else. (Bowden, 2016)

Although they don't work in alternative school settings, many highly effective regular teachers have developed alternative curricula to meet the unique learning needs of students at risk. Many teachers, for example, link students' learning to the business, civic, cultural, and political segments of their communities. The rationale is that connecting at-risk students to the world beyond their schools will enable them to see the relevance of education.

Application Exercise 3.3

Benefits of Alternative School for Students

OUT-OF-SCHOOL-TIME (OST) ACTIVITIES One approach to reducing high-risk behaviors among youth is to involve them in **out-of-school-time (OST) activities** (often called *extracurricular activities*). OST activities support and promote youth's development because they (a) place youth in safe environments; (b) prevent youth from engaging in delinquent activities; (c) teach youth general and specific skills, beliefs, and behaviors; and (d) provide opportunities for youth to develop relationships with peers and mentors (Simpkins, 2003). OST programs provide opportunities for growth and development at times when youth are unsupervised and might be tempted to engage in risky behaviors.

Frequently, children living in poverty don't have the same opportunities as other children to participate in music and dance, sports programs, and other OST activities. Students who spend 1 to 4 hours in OST activities each week are 49 percent less likely to use drugs and 37 percent less likely to become teen parents than students who do not participate in such activities (Little & Harris, 2003).

An exemplary OST program is the 4-H Job Experience and Training Program (JET) located in a 4-H education center in Dayton, **OHIO**. JET is a work-based learning program at Adventure Central, an urban education center in Dayton. Extension educators from Ohio State University run the JET program. The program runs for 6 months and culminates in an 8-week summer work experience in collaboration with a local park district (Ferrari, Arnett, & Cochran, 2007; Job Experience and Training [JET] Program, 2010).

For several years, the After-School Plus (A+) Program in **HAWAII** has operated afternoon enrichment programs from 2:00 to 5:00 for children in kindergarten through sixth grade. The children, who are free to do art, sports, drama, or homework, develop a sense of *ohana*, or "feeling of belonging." More than 59,000 K–12 students participate in after-school programs in Hawaii (Afterschool Alliance, 2010).

Expanded Learning Time (ELT) Schools

Increasingly, educational policymakers recognize that the traditional school year of approximately 180 days is not the best arrangement to meet students' learning needs. As President Obama explained in his first major education address in March of 2009, "We can no longer afford an academic calendar designed when America was a nation of farmers who needed their children at home plowing the land at the end of each day. That calendar may have once made sense, but today, it puts us at a competitive disadvantage" (White House Press Release, 2009).

One approach to addressing the educational and developmental needs of students affected by social problems is year-round schooling. Approximately 3,181 year-round schools enrolled about 10 percent of the nation's K–12 students during 2016–2017. The dropout rate at year-round schools is approximately 2 percent, compared to 5 percent at non-year-round schools (Statistic Brain Research Institute, 2017). When Iroquois Community School in suburban Chicago celebrated 20 years of being on a year-round schedule, Manuel Bustos, a social studies and science teacher, offered the following perspective:

> Having experienced both sides—the traditional calendar when I taught in Chicago and the year-round, balanced calendar—I really am a strong proponent of [the year-round schedule]. This format is a very strong way for education to be. (Placek, 2016)

Another approach to increasing time for teaching and learning is to add time to the school day. Schools in **TEXAS**, for example, can participate in an optional flexible year program (OFYP) that allows them to provide additional instruction in reading and mathematics to students at risk of being retained a grade (Texas Education Agency, 2018).

Similarly, **MASSACHUSETTS** implemented the Expanded Learning Time (ELT) Initiative to increase student achievement, opportunities for enrichment, and partnerships with community organizations. In 2014–2015, 135 **expanded learning time (ELT) schools** served 67,159 students in the state and provided an average of 278 additional hours of instruction. Approximately 70.5 percent of the students at each school were from low-income families, and 19.2 percent were English language learners (ELLs) (Massachusetts Department of Elementary & Secondary Education, 2017).

Kuss Middle School in Fall River, **MASSACHUSETTS**, is an ELT success story. The school was the first school to be declared "chronically under-performing" by the Commonwealth of Massachusetts. Student proficiency on the Massachusetts Comprehensive Assessment System (MCAS) was persistently among the lowest in the state.

A team of teachers, administrators, parents, community partners, and representatives of the local teachers' union developed an ELT schedule and launched it in 2006. The ELT program provides the school's nearly 800 students with a customized balance of academic courses and enrichment. Students choose among science electives options like DesignLab, Project Go-Green, and Astronomy. Other electives include video production, martial arts, and an award-winning theater arts program. The program also provides more time for teachers to collaborate to improve instruction and meet student needs.

Since the ELT program began, the school has achieved the state's highest accountability rating—Level 1. Among the 74 middle schools in Massachusetts with a student population at least 60 percent low income, the school is one of only seven to achieve Level 1 status. Marc Charest, a Kuss Middle School teacher, explains the benefits of ELT: "More learning time has significantly increased student engagement and allowed students and staff to establish more meaningful relationships that create credibility in the classroom" (Farbman, 2016, p. 3).

How Can Community-Based Partnerships Help Students Learn?

The previous section looked at intervention programs that schools have developed to ensure the optimum behavioral, social, and academic adjustment of at-risk children and adolescents to their school experiences. This section describes innovative, community-based partnerships that some schools have developed recently to prevent social problems from hindering students' learning.

The Community as a Resource for Schools

To assist schools in addressing the social problems that affect students, many communities are acting in the spirit of a recommendation made by the late Ernest Boyer (1928–1995): "Perhaps the time has come to organize, in every community, not just a *school* board, but a *children's* board. The goal would be to integrate children's services and build, in every community, a friendly, supportive environment for children" (Boyer, 1995, p. 169).

In partnerships between communities and schools, individuals, civic organizations, or businesses select a school or are selected by a school to work together for the good of students. The ultimate goals of such projects are to provide students with better school experiences and to assist students at risk. For example, in Seattle, **WASHINGTON**, a referendum required that a percentage of taxes be set aside to provide services to elementary-age children. In **FLORIDA**, Palm Beach County officials created the Children's Services Council to address 16 areas, from reducing the dropout rate to better child care. From parent support groups, to infant nurseries, to programs for students with special needs, the council has initiated scores of projects to benefit the community and its children.

CIVIC ORGANIZATIONS To develop additional sources of funding, many local school districts have established partnerships with community groups interested in improving educational opportunities in the schools. Some groups raise money for schools. The American Jewish Committee and the Urban League raised funds for schools in Pittsburgh, **PENNSYLVANIA**, for example. Other partners adopt or sponsor schools and enrich their educational programs by providing funding, resources, or services.

One example of partnerships with community groups involved the Phenix City (**ALABAMA**) schools. Students worked with civic organizations to raise awareness among students and community members about important health issues. The Healthcare Science and Technology (HST) Department and the Western District medical/dental associations taught preventive health skills—including hand washing and oral hygiene—to all kindergarten, first-grade, and special education students in the Phenix City school system. Working with the civic organizations, the students developed and prepared all materials used in the training programs. In addition, students collaborated with the organizations to provide the community with educational programs on diabetes, and they offered blood sugar screenings to the community.

VOLUNTEER MENTOR PROGRAMS Mentorship is a trend in community-based partnerships today, especially with students at risk. Parents, business leaders, professionals, and peers volunteer to work with students in neighborhood schools. Goals might include dropout prevention, high achievement, improved self-esteem, and healthy decision making. Troubleshooting on lifestyle issues often plays a role, especially in communities plagued by drug dealing, gang rivalry, casual violence, and crime. Mentors also model success.

Some mentor programs target particular groups. For instance, Concerned Black Men (CBM), a **WASHINGTON, D.C.**–based organization with 31 chapters around the country, targets inner-city African American male youth. African American men in diverse fields and from all walks of life participate as CBM mentors to students in area schools. Their goal is to serve as positive adult male role models for youth, many of whom live only with their mothers or grandmothers and lack male teachers in school. To date, CBM has given cash awards and scholarships to several thousand youth selected on the basis of high academic achievement, motivation, leadership in academic and nonacademic settings, and community involvement (Concerned Black Men, 2017).

CBM volunteer mentors receive training and attend class every day, working as teachers' aides, contributing materials, arranging field trips, and running an after-school program for latchkey children. Many volunteers started working with first and second graders and saw these same children all the way through their elementary school years. The program's good results have made it a model for mentorship programs in other schools.

CORPORATE–EDUCATION PARTNERSHIPS Business involvement in schools has taken many forms, including, for example, contributions of funds or materials needed by a school, release time for employees to visit classrooms, adopt-a-school programs, cash grants for pilot projects and teacher development, educational use of corporate facilities and expertise, employee participation, student scholarship programs, and political lobbying for school reform. Extending beyond advocacy, private-sector efforts include job initiatives for disadvantaged youth, in-service programs for teachers, management training for school administrators, minority education and faculty development, and even construction of school buildings.

Business-sponsored school experiments focus on creating model schools, laboratory schools, or alternative schools that address particular local needs. In Minneapolis, **MINNESOTA**, for example, the General Mills Foundation provided major funding to create the Metropolitan Federation of Alternative Schools (MFAS), an alliance of 10 community-based organizations that operates 12 alternative schools. MFAS is designed to serve students who have not been successful in regular school programs.

Tracy Whiteside/Shutterstock

What risk factors might affect these youth? What are some effective approaches for helping students succeed in school?

The goals for students who attend MFAS schools include returning to regular school when appropriate, graduating from high school, and/or preparing for postsecondary education or employment. MFAS schools have small class sizes, increased individual academic help, enhanced supplemental services, and strong parental involvement (MFAS, 2010).

In addition to contributing more resources to education, chief executive officers and their employees are donating more time; 83 percent of the top managers surveyed by a recent *Fortune* poll said they "participate actively" in educational reform, versus 70 percent in 1990. For example, IBM MentorPlace enables more than 6,000 IBM employees in more than 35 countries to provide students with online academic assistance and career counseling and to volunteer in schools. IBM mentors work with teachers to identify online activities they would like students to work on with their mentors. Online activities cover all core academic areas, including science and math (IBM MentorPlace, 2017).

21ST CENTURY COMMUNITY LEARNING CENTERS (CCLCS) The 21st Century Community Learning Center (CCLC) program provides federal funding for community learning centers that provide academic enrichment opportunities during nonschool hours for children, particularly those who attend high-poverty and low-performing schools. CCLCs are located in schools, community facilities, and/or faith-based facilities and provide services to support student learning and development. These services include tutoring and mentoring, homework assistance, academic enrichment (such as hands-on science or technology programs), community service opportunities, music, art, sports, and cultural activities. Centers also provide safe environments for students during non-school hours.

According to a U.S. Department of Education evaluation report, student participation in Community Learning Centers led to improvements in achievement and behavior. Half of students improved their homework completion and in-class participation. More than a third of the participants also improved their grades and achievement in math and English (U.S. Department of Education, 2016).

✓ Check Your Understanding 3.5

Summary

What Is the Role of Schools in Today's Society, and What Are the Characteristics of Successful Schools?

- Although the debate about the role of schools continues, many people in the United States believe that schools have a responsibility to socialize students to participate intelligently and constructively in society.
- Research has identified seven characteristics of effective schools: strong leadership, high expectations, emphasis on basic skills, orderly school environment, frequent and systematic evaluation of student learning, sense of purpose, and collegiality and a sense of community.
- Three views of successful schools have been suggested: (1) their students manifest a high level of learning, (2) their results surpass those for comparable schools, and (3) they are improving rather than getting worse.

How Can Schools Be Described?

- Schools can be categorized according to the focus of their curricula and according to their organizational structures.

What Social Problems Affect Schools and Place Students at Risk?

- In response to life experiences characterized by extreme family stress, poverty, crime, and lack of adult guidance, growing numbers of youth are at risk of dropping out of school. Minority at-risk students may also have to contend with intangible obstacles such as language barriers, conflicts with fellow students and teachers, and racism and discrimination. The Adverse Childhood Experiences (ACE) Study has revealed that an alarming number of children and youth have had traumatic experiences that negatively affect brain development and lead to behavior and learning problems at school.

How Are Schools Addressing Societal Problems?

- Seven effective intervention and prevention programs that schools have developed to address social problems are trauma-sensitive schools, peer counseling/mentoring, peer mediation, community schools, compensatory education, alternative schools and curricula, and expanded learning time (ELT) schools.
- Since 1965, an array of federally funded compensatory education programs has provided educational services to improve the basic skills of low-ability students from low-income families.
- Many school districts have developed alternative schools or schools within a school that provide highly individualized instructional and support services for students who have not been successful in regular schools. Also, highly effective teachers modify their techniques and develop alternative curricula to meet the needs of students at risk.

How Can Community-Based Partnerships Help Students Learn?

- Community and corporate partnerships can help schools address social problems that hinder students' learning by providing various forms of support.

Professional Reflections And Activities

Teacher's Journal

1. Write a short paper based on your own high school experience, addressing the following:
   - Who comprised the at-risk population?
   - What percentage of the school population would you have considered at risk? How did this affect the overall school program?
   - What special considerations were made for at-risk students?
   - Describe the personalities or actions of any teachers or counselors who were dedicated to helping this population succeed.
   - Describe one success story involving an at-risk student from your school experience.
   - Describe one failure. What might have changed that failure to success?
2. What are the characteristics of teachers who effectively meet the needs of students placed at risk? Which of those characteristics do you possess? How can you develop those characteristics more fully as you progress through your teacher education program?

Teacher's Research

1. Gather data on the Internet about children and/or adolescents that reflect issues of health, safety, and welfare in your state. State government databases are good places to start. Narrow your search to one of the following areas:

- Childhood poverty and homelessness
- Student nutrition and health
- Teen pregnancy
- Bullying in school
- Child abuse and neglect
- Student drug, alcohol, and tobacco abuse
- School violence and crime
- Truancy
- Juvenile delinquency
- Suicide among children and youth

2. Go to the home page for the National Education Association (NEA). From there, click on the link to NEA's Legislative Action Center. At that site, gather information about federal or state legislation that addresses meeting the educational needs of students at risk. Send an email message to Congress or one of your state's legislators explaining your position regarding that legislation.

Observations and Interviews

1. Reflect on your experiences relating to social problems at the elementary, middle, or high school level. Then, visit a school to gather statistics and information about how the school is responding to the social problems you identified. Interview several teachers. How have the teachers responded to these social issues? From their point of view, what resources would enable them to respond more effectively to these issues?
2. Interview a social worker in your community. According to him or her, what kind of relationship should exist between the schools and social service agencies?

Professional Portfolio

Develop a case study of a school's culture. Visit a local school or base your study on a school you have attended. Organize your case in terms of the following categories of information:

- **Environment**—How would you describe the school facility or physical plant and its material and human resources? How is space organized? What is the climate of the school?
- **Formal Practices**—What grades are included at the school? How is the school year organized? How is time structured? How are students and teachers grouped for instruction?
- **Traditions**—What events and activities and products seem important to students, teachers, and administrators? What symbols, slogans, and ceremonies identify membership in the school? How do community members view and relate to the school?

Draw conclusions from your case study: What aspects of the school culture seem to support learning and academic achievement? On the basis of your case study, draft a position statement on the kind of culture you would like to create or promote in your classroom.

PART II

Foundations of Teaching

Chapter 4

Philosophical Foundations of U.S. Education

dotshock/Shutterstock

Learning Outcomes

After reading this chapter, you will be able to do the following:

4.1 Explain why philosophy is important to teachers.

4.2 Explain six branches of philosophy that are important to teachers.

4.3 Describe five modern philosophical orientations to teaching.

4.4 Explain three schools of psychological thought that can influence a teacher's philosophy.

4.5 Explain how you will develop an eclectic educational philosophy to guide your own teaching.

Dear Mentor

I am in my final quarter of my freshman year at Otterbein University. I plan to major in early childhood education (ECE). I'll graduate in three years and begin my search for a teaching position in Columbus, **OHIO**, or the surrounding area.

I have chosen the ECE program because I am comfortable in an early childhood environment. Such an environment is constantly changing, so being prepared and organized is key. When comparing careers that best fit my personality, I decided that this area of concentration suits me because of my ability to develop relationships with children; my organizational skills; and my caring nature as a peer, mentor, and teacher.

During this final freshman quarter at Otterbein, I student taught at various schools in Westerville, Ohio. During that time, I acquired knowledge about the constantly changing classroom and the individuality of each student.

Today, in these changing times, students are faced with many challenges. As a teacher, I must have a knowledgeable perspective on ethnic, cultural, and linguistic diversity among students. What guidance do you have for preparing to meet these challenges in today's diverse classrooms?

SINCERELY, ALISON THOMPSON

Dear Alison

Start with your own self-exploration. Be cognizant that diversity has many faces, and it does not just include ethnicity, gender, or socioeconomic levels. You must understand your own values, style of speaking and interacting, and response to the various forms of diversity. It is imperative that you are able to articulate your mores and traditions, as your values may be in conflict with some children's family cultures. Developing sensitivity to differences will help you to provide a richer social and learning environment for your students.

Furthermore, start researching the cultures and other forms of diversity presently represented in your area. Seek out people, experiences, and other resources that will help you understand the customs and way of life of other populations. Attend some community functions, ask questions, and be alert to classroom implications. Have discussions with classroom teachers as to the impact diversity has had on their teaching.

When you begin teaching, remember to always be respectful of the various types of families that are represented in your community. Also, be constantly aware that those parents may have different values and beliefs surrounding education that could be markedly different than your own. Include *all* families in the education-related decisions about their children. And lastly, it is important to always rely on school and district professional guidelines, standards, and ethics to inform decision making concerning your students.

EDUCATIONALLY YOURS, LYNN HINES
NBCT (National Board Certified Teacher) 1995, 2005
Western Kentucky University,
NBPTS (National Board for Professional Teaching Standards)
Program Faculty, NBPTS

READERS' VOICES

Why is philosophy important to teachers?

Philosophy is important to teachers because it helps them understand how their beliefs and values influence the curriculum they present to students. Educational philosophy helps teachers focus on the true purpose of education—providing students with knowledge that is worthwhile and useful to them.

—ÁNGELITA,
Teacher Education program, first year

If you think about your own teachers in elementary through high school, you no doubt recall that each of them had a different approach to teaching. Each had a different set of responses to the vital questions that all teachers must answer: What should the purpose(s) of education be? What knowledge is of most worth? What values should teachers encourage their students to develop? How should learning be evaluated? As difficult as these questions might be, teachers must answer them. To answer these and similar questions, teachers use philosophy.

Why is Philosophy Important to Teachers?

Today's schools reflect the philosophical foundations and the aspirations and values brought to this country by its founders and generations of settlers. Understanding the philosophical ideas that have shaped education in the United States is an important part of your education as a professional. This understanding will enable you "to think clearly about what [you] are doing, and to see what [you] are doing in the larger context of individual and social development" (Ozmon & Craver, 2012).

An example of a teacher who has thought carefully and clearly about how her teaching relates to "the larger context of individual and social development" is Ashley McCall, a third-grade bilingual teacher at Cesar E. Chavez Multicultural Academic Center in Chicago. The enrollment at Chavez is 95.5 percent Latino and 99.2 percent low-income.

> My commitment to teaching is explicitly a commitment to social justice, racial justice, and teaching truth to power. I teach where I teach because students of color deserve to be validated and celebrated. I've taught in three different neighborhoods, each with their own demographics, economic challenges, and cultural distinctiveness. Each neighborhood is also home to creative young minds eager to make their mark on the world. Every day in the classroom is an opportunity for acknowledgement, affirmation, and evolution. (McCall, 2017)

Still, you may wonder, what is the value of knowing about the philosophy of education? Will that knowledge help you become a better teacher? An understanding of the philosophy of education will enhance your professionalism in three important ways. First, knowledge of philosophy of education will help you understand the complex political forces that influence schools. When people act politically to influence schools, their actions reflect their educational philosophies. Second, knowledge of how philosophy has influenced our schools will help you evaluate more effectively current proposals for change. You will be in a better position to evaluate changes if you understand how schools have developed and how current proposals might relate to previous change efforts. Last, awareness of how philosophy has influenced teaching is a hallmark of professionalism in education.

In addition, philosophy can reveal principles to guide professional action. (Some teachers disagree and believe philosophical reflections have nothing to contribute to the actual act of teaching; this stance, of course, is itself a philosophy of education.) For example, when deciding how to present new information to students, a teacher with a well-thought-out philosophy of education might realize "that a particular approach to teaching is better to adopt than its alternative because it treats subject matter intellectually rather than as solely a store of facts, which means regarding students as human beings capable of thought rather than merely of absorption" (Hansen, 2007, p. 7). Without the benefit of an educational philosophy, the teacher might have focused exclusively on students merely "absorbing" the new information. Similarly, educational philosophy can help teachers make appropriate decisions in the middle of a lesson—for example, deciding to "ask a thoughtful question about the novel at hand when students are restless rather than automatically piling on more information about it" (Hansen, 2007, p. 7).

Philosophy is also important to schools. As the great educational philosopher John Dewey (1916, p. 383) put it, to be concerned with education is to be concerned with philosophy: "If we are willing to conceive education as the process of forming fundamental dispositions, intellectual and emotional, toward nature and fellow men, philosophy may even be defined as *the general theory of education*."

Most schools have a statement of philosophy that serves to focus the efforts of teachers, administrators, students, and parents in a desired direction. A school's philosophy is actually a public statement of school values, a description of the educational goals it seeks to attain. So important is a school's philosophy that school accrediting agencies evaluate schools partially on the basis of whether they achieve the goals set forth in their statements of philosophy. The following is an excerpt from the philosophy that guides a high school I recently visited in the Midwest:

> The purpose of our school is to educate, empower, and enable all students to become caring, contributing citizens who can succeed in an always-changing, complex world. Our school conveys high expectations for all students, and we are committed to helping *all students* be successful at meeting those expectations. Students will experience challenging learning opportunities within a supportive, caring community based on respect and responsibility. The ultimate goal of our curriculum is for students to acquire the *knowledge, skills*, and *attitudes* to become lifelong learners who have a positive, productive influence on our world.)

The Nature of Philosophy

Philosophy is concerned with identifying the basic truths about being, knowledge, and conduct. Whereas the religions of the world arrive at these truths based on supernatural revelations, philosophers use their reasoning powers to search for answers to the fundamental questions of life. Philosophers use a careful, step-by-step, question-and-answer technique to extend their understanding of the world. Through very exacting use of language and techniques of linguistic and conceptual analysis, philosophers attempt to describe the world in which we live.

The word *philosophy* may be literally translated from the original Greek as "love of wisdom." In particular, a philosophy is a set of ideas formulated to comprehend the world. Among the giants of Western philosophy have been Socrates, Plato, Aristotle, St. Thomas Aquinas, René Descartes, John Locke, David Hume, Jean-Jacques Rousseau, Immanuel Kant, Georg Hegel, John Stuart Mill, Karl Marx, John Dewey, Jean-Paul Sartre, and Mortimer Adler. They devoted their lives to pondering the significant questions of life: What is truth? What is reality? What life is worth living?

Your Educational Philosophy

In simplest terms, your **educational philosophy** consists of what you believe about education—the set of principles that guides your professional action. Every teacher, whether he or she recognizes it, has a philosophy of education—a set of beliefs about how human beings learn and grow and what one should learn in order to live a good life. Professional teachers recognize that teaching, because it is concerned with *what ought to be*, is basically a philosophical enterprise.

Your behavior as a teacher is strongly connected to your beliefs about teaching and learning, students, knowledge, and what is worth knowing (see Figure 4.1). Regardless of where you stand in regard to these dimensions of teaching, you should be aware of the need to reflect continually on *what* you do believe and *why* you believe it. Taken together, your beliefs about different dimensions of teaching are the foundation of your educational philosophy and will determine *how* you interact with students.

Figure 4.1 Educational beliefs and teaching behavior

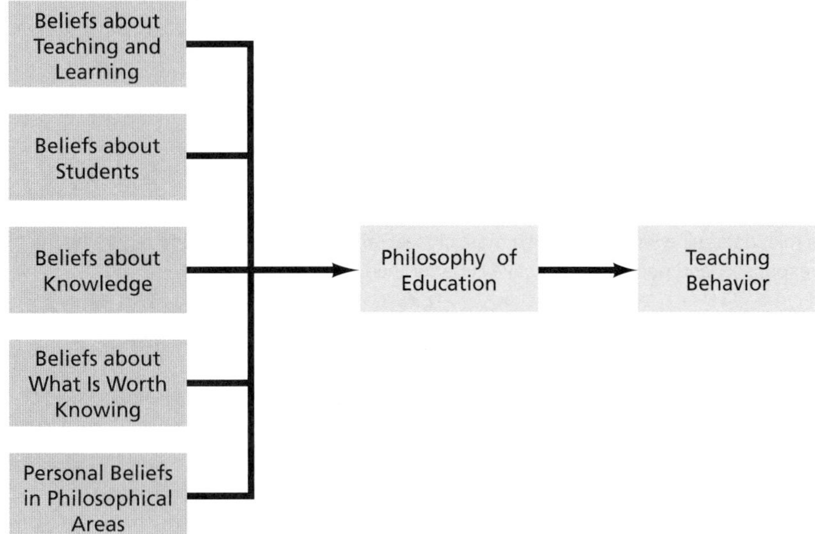

The worth of knowledge in a subject area is reflected in the educational philosophy of Paul Gray, who teaches social studies and AP (Advanced Placement) Human Geography at Russellville High School in Russellville, **ARKANSAS.** His philosophy emphasizes the critical importance of learning geography in today's world:

> There is no more important course a student can take in a post-9/11 world than geography. Students today have to live in an ever-changing global environment. Students must be able to understand and deal with other cultures, religions, and worldviews. Geography is the only discipline that can teach students how to connect politics to religion, urban issues to cultural issues, history to politics, and so on. (Gray, 2008)

Beliefs About Teaching and Learning

One of the most important components of your educational philosophy is your set of beliefs about teaching and learning. In other words, what will be your primary role as a teacher? Will it be to transmit knowledge to students and then to guide their practice as they develop skills in using that knowledge? Or will it be to develop self-directed learners by building on students' interests, prior experiences, and current understandings? The first view emphasizes *transmission* of knowledge to students, whereas the second view emphasizes students' *construction* of knowledge.

The transmission view emphasizes changes in students' behavior. Learning involves making associations between various stimuli and responses. In other words, learning results from forces that are *external* to the individual. Noted Brazilian educator Paulo Freire (1921–1997) compared the transmission view to a form of "banking" in which teacher and students do not engage in authentic, two-way communication:

> Education thus becomes an act of depositing, in which the students are the depositories and the teacher is the depositor. Instead of communicating, the teacher issues communiques and makes deposits which the students patiently receive, memorize, and repeat. This is the "banking" concept of education, in which the scope of action allowed to the students extends only as far as receiving, filing, and storing the deposits. (Freire, 2000, p. 72)

The constructivist view, on the other hand, emphasizes the individual student's experiences and cognitions. Learning occurs when personal experiences lead to changes in thoughts or actions. That is, learning is largely the result of *internal* forces within the individual. To assess your current beliefs about teaching and learning, complete the activity presented in Figure 4.2.

Figure 4.2 Where do you stand?

For each pair of statements about the teacher's role, determine which response most closely reflects where you stand regarding the two perspectives. Remember, there are no correct responses, and neither perspective is better than the other.

Constructivist Perspective				***Transmission Perspective***
"I mainly see my role as a facilitator. I try to provide opportunities and resources for my students to discover or construct concepts for themselves."		***VS.***		"That's all nice, but students really won't learn the subject unless you go over the material in a structured way. It's my job to explain, to show students how to do the work, and to assign specific practice."
Definitely Prefer	Tend to Prefer	Cannot Decide	Tend to Prefer	Definitely Prefer
"It is a good idea to have all sorts of activities going on in the classroom. Some students might produce a scene from a play they read. Others might create a miniature version of the set. It's hard to get the logistics right, but the successes are so much more important than the failures."		***VS.***		"It's more practical to give the whole class the same assignment, one that has clear directions, and one that can be done in short intervals that match students' attention spans and the daily class schedule."
Definitely Prefer	Tend to Prefer	Cannot Decide	Tend to Prefer	Definitely Prefer
"The most important part of instruction is that it encourage 'sense-making' or thinking among students. Content is secondary."		***VS.***		"The most important part of instruction is the content of the curriculum. That content is the community's judgment about what children need to be able to know and do."
Definitely Prefer	Tend to Prefer	Cannot Decide	Tend to Prefer	Definitely Prefer
"It is critical for students to become interested in doing academic work—interest and effort are more important than the particular subject-matter they are working on."		***VS.***		"While student motivation is certainly useful, it should not drive what students study. It is more important that students learn the history, science, math, and language skills in their textbooks."
Definitely Prefer	Tend to Prefer	Cannot Decide	Tend to Prefer	Definitely Prefer

SOURCE: Adapted from Jason L. Ravitz, Henry Jay Becker, and Yan Tien Wong. *Constructivist-Compatible Beliefs and Practices Among U.S. Teachers*. Center for Research on Information Technology and Organizations, University of California, Irvine; and University of Minnesota, July 2000.

Beliefs About Students

Your beliefs about students will have a great influence on how you teach. Every teacher formulates an image in his or her mind about what students are like—their dispositions, skills, motivation levels, and expectations. What you believe students are like is based on your unique life experiences, particularly your observations of young people and your knowledge of human growth and development.

As a teacher, it is important that your beliefs about students are not based on "deficit thinking." **Deficit thinking** can lead a teacher to have lower expectations for students from cultural backgrounds that differ from the more affluent dominant culture. If such students are not successful in school, it is because they lack readiness to learn and their parents are not interested in education. Teachers may even view these students as less intelligent, less capable, and unmotivated.

Teachers who use deficit thinking do not value the **cultural capital** students possess—the knowledge, behaviors, and skills that enable them to be successful in their own cultures. Nor do these teachers understand that their students' families have **funds of knowledge**—"the historically accumulated and culturally developed bodies of knowledge and skills essential for household or individual functioning and well-being" (Moll, Amanti, Neff, & Gonzalez, 2001, p. 133).

For a teacher, the antidote to deficit thinking is a desire to learn about students and their families. The following comments by a White female teacher at a predominantly African American urban K–5 public school illustrate the value of learning about students and their cultures:

> The most important way to reach children is to develop an interpersonal connection with them. I'm pretty well knit into the community here. I go to volleyball games. I go to basketball games. I go to my kids' soccer games. I go to parties that parents throw. I think it's really important to try to immerse yourself in the community in which you work. (Walker, 2011, p. 587)

Similarly, I explain in the following, how knowledge of my students when I taught at DuSable High School on Chicago's South Side enriched my English classes:

> My primary goal while teaching came to be the creation of a group climate in which listening, sharing, and thinking would occur. I would listen to my students; they would listen to me and to each other; and, as much as possible, we would think together on commonly perceived tasks or problems. I measured the success of my classes by whether or not a meaningful student-teacher dialogue had occurred. Often this dialogue amounted to a cultural tradeoff—my students had a lot that they were able to teach me, and I, of course, had a lot that I was able to teach them. (Parkay, 1983, p. 122)

Negative views of students may promote teacher–student relationships based on fear and coercion rather than on trust and helpfulness. Extremely positive views may risk not providing students with sufficient structure and direction and not communicating sufficiently high expectations. In the final analysis, the truly professional teacher—the one who has a carefully thought-out educational philosophy—recognizes that, although children differ in their predispositions to learn and grow, they all *can* learn. In regard to beliefs about students, it is important that teachers convey positive attitudes toward their students and a belief that they *can* learn.

FOCUS ON **DIVERSITY**: ACCEPTING ALL STUDENTS

As a teacher, you should guard against negative attitudes toward individual students or groups of students. Although you cannot eliminate the prejudice, inter-group hostility, and racism that are found in society at large, you will have an obligation to see that your actions in the classroom do not convey negative attitudes about students on the basis of factors such as gender, race, ethnicity, religion, sexual orientation, family lifestyle, manner of dress, language, or socioeconomic status. A teacher who models positive attitudes toward all students is Cathleen Cadigan, who teaches at Thomas Jefferson High School in Dallas, **TEXAS**. Although her school has surveillance cameras in the hallways, a police officer assigned to the school, and a metal detector at the main entrance, Cadigan reports that "There is not a thug in this building. We have some who *think* they are. [There is no one] who wouldn't say, 'Miss Cadigan, can I carry that box for you? Can I hold the door for you?' They are just as sweet as sweet can be . . . they are probably the most polite kids I have ever met" (College Board and Phi Delta Kappa, 2009, p. 7).

Application Exercise 4.1
The Importance of a Personal Philosophy of Education

Beliefs About Knowledge

How teachers view knowledge is directly related to how they go about teaching. If teachers view knowledge as the sum total of small bits of subject matter or discrete facts, students will most likely spend a great deal of time learning that information in a straightforward, rote manner. Recall your own school days; perhaps you had to memorize the capitals of the 50 states, definitions for the eight parts of speech, the periodic table in chemistry, and so on.

Other teachers view knowledge more conceptually, that is, as consisting of the big ideas that enable us to understand and influence our environment. Such a teacher would want students to be able to explain how legislative decisions are made in the state capital, how an understanding of the eight parts of speech can empower the writer and enliven one's writing, and how chemical elements are grouped according to their atomic numbers.

Finally, teachers differ in their beliefs about whether students' increased understanding of their own experiences is a legitimate form of knowledge. Knowledge of self and one's experiences in the world is not the same as knowledge about a particular subject, yet personal knowledge is essential for a full, satisfying life. In addition, as Steven Crawford, a Spanish teacher at a Bellevue, **WASHINGTON**, high school points out, self-understanding is essential for teachers: "[Good teaching] is just having a center of yourself and an understanding of who you are in front of the kids and who they need you to be" (College Board and Phi Delta Kappa, 2009, p. 25). The Technology in Action feature for this chapter profiles a teacher who believes that study of a foreign language should go beyond knowledge of correct grammatical structures and rote memorization of vocabulary words. For this teacher, the personal knowledge a student gains from cross-national communication is a valid goal for foreign language study. Through conversations with their peers in another country, U.S. students have an opportunity to reflect on how their own values, beliefs, and attitudes are different from or similar to those of students in the other country.

Beliefs About What Is Worth Knowing

Teachers have different ideas about what should be taught. One teacher, who tends to prefer a transmission view of teaching, believes it is most important that students learn the basic skills of reading, writing, computation, and oral communication. These are the skills they will need to be successful in their chosen occupations, and it is the school's responsibility to prepare students for the world of work. Another teacher believes that the most worthwhile content is to be found in the classics, or the Great Books. Through mastering the great ideas from the sciences, mathematics, literature, and history, students will be well prepared to deal with the world of the future. Still another teacher—one who tends toward a constructivist view of teaching—is most concerned with students learning how to reason, communicate effectively, and solve problems. Students who master these cognitive processes will have learned how to learn—and this is the most realistic preparation for an unknown future. And finally, another teacher is concerned with developing the whole child, teaching students to become self-actualizing persons. Thus the content of the curriculum should be meaningful to the student, contributing as much as possible to the student's efforts to become a mature, well-integrated person. As you can see, there are no easy answers to the question: What knowledge is of most worth?

Check Your Understanding 4.1

TECHNOLOGY in ACTION

Web Conferencing Leads to Better Understanding of Another Culture and Oneself

Louise Zhao has taught Advanced Chinese at Lincoln High School for the past five years. Her approach is part presentation of grammar and vocabulary—and lots and lots of practice. Whenever possible, she tries to bring in native Chinese speakers to speak to her class, but this usually takes the form of a presentation. However, these presentations don't give her students what she is really after—to have her students engage in extensive one-on-one conversations with Chinese speakers.

Mrs. Zhao was born in Shanghai and still has family living there. She communicates with them often using various online communication tools, but it was not until she walked in on her 13-year-old son carrying on a video phone call with his cousin in Shanghai that she realized she had the solution to her classroom dilemma. The next day she went to her principal and presented her idea. He agreed and she began to develop her lesson plan.

Through her family connections, she contacted Mr. Lee, who teaches English to students at a high school in Shanghai. The two teachers agreed that they would have their students meet once each week, for 1 hour, via Blackboard Collaborate. Blackboard Collaborate is web conferencing software that allows individuals or groups to conference via text, audio, and/or graphics online. The local community college had just purchased an Elluminate web conferencing license. As part of its community outreach, the community college allowed the local school district in its service area to use the tool. Each student in Mrs. Zhao's class would be paired with a student in Mr. Lee's class. During their 1-hour Elluminate session, they would speak Chinese for the first 30 minutes and then speak English for the next 30 minutes. The session would also be recorded so Mr. Lee and Mrs. Zhao could review the individual conversations at a later time and provide feedback to their students.

To make this happen, however, Mrs. Zhao realized she had a lot to do. She had to schedule the weekly events—adjusting for time-zone differences. She had to pair the students, ensure that they stayed on task, and create a setting conducive for one-on-one conversation.

Luckily for Mrs. Zhao, the school's computer lab was up to date, and each computer in the lab had been fitted with microphone headsets. The headset speakers would keep out external noise so that her 20-plus students seated in the computer lab could chat away and not disturb their neighbors. With the setting and technology taken care of, the next thing she had to deal with was timing. There was no way that she could make the timing of this event coincide within the hours of the standard school day. What she decided to do was make these events voluntary. To her surprise, all of her students agreed to attend the first session. At 4:00 p.m. each Thursday, her students would meet in the computer lab, click on their Elluminate session proposal, and connect with their counterparts in Shanghai, who were seated at their computers at 7:00 a.m. the next day, their time. This novelty was the first thing the students discussed. Although they are only halfway through the semester, the students appear each week for their conversations with their friends on the other side of the world.

(continued)

Web conferencing allows individuals or groups to connect on the web via video and/or audio. This is usually a synchronous or live session in which individuals are seated at their computers and interact with others. Participants can be in the same building or in another country. To participate in a web video conference, you will need a USB video input, a microphone, appropriate computer sound and video cards, the video conferencing software or plugin, and an Internet connection robust enough to handle a web conference.

Teachers have used web conferencing for tutoring sessions, meeting with parents, bringing outside speakers into their classrooms, pursuing professional development opportunities, and connecting with colleagues around the country.

VISIT:

There are many options to choose from if you would like your students to participate in a web video conference. A few websites offer thorough reviews of free or inexpensive software options for web conferencing, such as ClickMeeting, Zoho Meeting, eVoice, Amazon Chime, Google+ Hangouts, Skype, iChat (for Macintosh), Zoom, Windows Live Messenger, Cisco WebEx, and GoToMeeting. Reviews cover topics such as real-time web conferencing, desktop video conferencing, screen sharing, online meetings, web seminars, and host sites.

You can try many of these options on a temporary basis for free. One easy web conferencing solution is Windows Messenger. Just open Messenger and click on Start Video Conversation. Type in the email address of the person you want to conference with, and you are connected.

What Are The Branches Of Philosophy?

To provide you with additional tools to use in formulating and clarifying your educational philosophy, this section presents brief overviews of six areas of philosophy that are of central concern to teachers: metaphysics, epistemology, axiology, ethics, aesthetics, and logic. Each of these areas focuses on one of the questions that have concerned the world's greatest philosophers for centuries: What is the nature of reality? What is the nature of knowledge, and is truth ever attainable? According to what values should one live life? What is good and what is evil? What is the nature of beauty and excellence? And finally: What processes of reasoning will yield consistently valid results?

Metaphysics

Metaphysics is concerned with explaining, as rationally and as comprehensively as possible, the nature of reality (in contrast to how reality *appears*). What is reality? What is the world made of? These are metaphysical questions. Metaphysics is also concerned with the nature of being and explores questions such as, What does it mean to exist? What is humankind's place in the scheme of things? Metaphysical questions such as these are at the very heart of educational philosophy. As one educational philosopher put it, "Nothing short of the fullest awareness possible of 'man's place in the cosmos' is the constant problem of the philosopher of education" (Bertocci, 1960, p. 158). Or as two educational philosophers put it: "Our ultimate preoccupation in educational theory is with the most primary of all philosophic problems: metaphysics, the study of ultimate reality" (Morris & Pai, 1994, p. 28).

Metaphysics has important implications for education because the school curriculum is based on what we know about reality. And what we know about reality is driven by the kinds of questions we ask about the world. In fact, any position regarding what the schools should teach has behind it a particular view of reality, a particular set of responses to metaphysical questions. This chapter's Teachers' Voices: Being an Agent of Change feature profiles a teacher who encourages her students to grapple with metaphysical questions.

TEACHERS VOICES  BEING AN AGENT OF CHANGE

KAREN TOAVS

Every Day Is Filled With Deep Thinking And Contemplation

I teach because I want to help students figure out what they are going to do in the world. I want students to realize that they have the power and the imagination to help change where we're going to go.

The students I see every day in my classroom are very different from students of the past. Their world is full of technology and full of insights, and they need to have direction with where they want to go with that.

When I have students in my room, one of the most important things we do is engage in conversation. So I share with them what I know about human knowledge and where we've been. Part of my challenge to them is: Where do you want to take this? Where is our future going to go? Because it's that future that's so important.

For me, teaching is a gift because every day is filled with laughter and filled with deep thinking and contemplation—sometimes arguments, sometimes debates—but that's all part of the magic of helping kids understand the world and helping kids develop their own opinions about where we should go in the future.

In my classroom, part of helping students record that is a technique called visual mapping. When students walk in my classroom every day, they create one page per day as a visual map, a graphic organizer. We use all sorts of colors, images, texts, key words, and deep reflections. Students record the entire time that we are talking or learning everything that goes on in the classroom that hour.

As a result of that, we have a database, a place to start the next day. Every day we move forward, and our discussions get deeper and deeper, and the kids realize great things about the world. I love watching them grow in that depth.

As a Teacher of the Year, one of the things that I've enjoyed the most is the deep discussions that we have as colleagues about where we come from in education, what we hope for our students; and, universally, it's all the same . . . we teach because we want students to believe that they *can* change the world. We teach inspiration, and, unfortunately, that's not something that's easily tested; that's not something that's easily measured.

Yes, I believe what students learn in my classroom for content and the things that they do on their visual maps are so important to help them understand the world, but it's not nearly as important as what they do when they walk out of my classroom. I want students to know that they have the power to go out there and do all the great things that they want to accomplish. I teach because I want to help students change the world.

PERSONAL REFLECTION

1. Toavs uses "visual mapping" to stimulate her students' "deep thinking and contemplation." With reference to the subject area and grade level for which you are preparing to teach, how might you use visual mapping with your students? What are some examples of possible "deep thinking" by your students?
2. Based on Toavs's comments, what do you think are her beliefs about teaching and learning? Beliefs about students? Beliefs about knowledge? Beliefs about what is worth knowing?
3. Toavs says that teachers "teach inspiration." Reflecting on your own teachers, have any of them "taught" you inspiration? How did they do that? How might you "teach" inspiration to your future students?

Karen Toavs was the 2011 **NORTH DAKOTA** State Teacher of the Year. This feature is adapted from her Council of Chief State School Officers Teacher of the Year video retrieved February 2, 2014, from http://www.pearsonfoundation.org/ccsso-toy/2011/nd/autoplay

Epistemology

The next major set of philosophical questions that concerns teachers is called **epistemology**. These questions all focus on knowledge: What knowledge is true? How does knowing take place? How do we know what we know? How do we decide between opposing views of knowledge? Is truth constant, or does it change from situation to situation? And finally: What knowledge is of most worth?

How you answer the epistemological questions that confront all teachers will have significant implications for your teaching. First, you will need to determine what is true about the content you will teach, then you must decide on the most appropriate means of teaching this content to students. Even a casual consideration of epistemological questions reveals that there are many ways of knowing about the world, at least five of which are of interest to teachers.

1. **Knowing based on authority**—for example, knowledge from the sage, the poet, the priest, or the ruler. In schools, the textbook, the teacher, and the administrator are the sources of authority for students. In everyday conversations, we refer to unnamed experts as sources of authoritative knowledge: "*They* say we'll have a manned flight to Mars by the middle of the century."
2. **Knowing based on divine revelation**—for example, knowledge in the form of supernatural revelations from the sun god of early peoples, the many gods of the ancient Greeks, or the Judeo-Christian god.
3. **Knowing based on empiricism (experience)**—for example, knowledge acquired through the senses, the informally gathered empirical data that direct most of our daily behavior. When we state that "experience is the best teacher," we refer to this mode of knowing.
4. **Knowing based on reason and logical analysis**—for example, knowledge inferred from the process of thinking logically. In schools, students learn to apply rational thought to tasks such as solving mathematical problems, distinguishing facts from opinions, or defending or refuting a particular argument. Many students also learn a method of reasoning and analyzing empirical data known as the scientific method. Through this method, a problem is identified, relevant data are gathered, a hypothesis is formulated based on these data, and the hypothesis is empirically tested.
5. **Knowing based on intuition**—for example, knowledge arrived at without the use of rational thought. Intuition draws from our prior knowledge and experience and gives us an immediate understanding of the situation at hand. Our intuition convinces us that we know something, but we don't know how we know.

Axiology

The next set of philosophical problems concerns values. Teachers are concerned with values "because school is not a neutral activity. The very idea of school expresses a set of values" (Nelson, Carlson, & Palonsky, 2000, p. 304).

Among the axiological questions teachers must answer for themselves are: What values should teachers encourage students to adopt? What values raise humanity to our highest expressions of humaneness? What values does a truly educated person hold? And most importantly, perhaps, "*Whose* social values or morality should form the basis of instruction in public schools?" (italics added) (Spring, 2018, p. 4).

Axiology highlights the fact that the teacher has an interest not only in the *quantity* of knowledge that students acquire but also in the *quality* of life that becomes possible because of that knowledge. Extensive knowledge may not benefit the individual if he or she is unable to put that knowledge to good use. This point raises additional questions: How do we define quality of life? What curricular experiences contribute most to that quality of life? All teachers must deal with the issues raised by these questions.

Ethics

Whereas axiology addresses the question, What is valuable?, **ethics** focuses on, What is good and evil, right and wrong, just and unjust?

Knowledge of ethics can help the teacher solve many of the dilemmas that arise in the classroom. Frequently, teachers must take action in situations where they are unable to gather all the relevant facts and where no single course of action is totally right or wrong. For example, a student whose previous work was above average plagiarizes a term paper: Should the teacher fail the student for the course if the example of swift, decisive punishment will likely prevent other students from plagiarizing? Or should the teacher, following her hunches about what would be in the student's long-term interest, have the student redo the term paper and risk the possibility that other students might get the mistaken notion that plagiarism has no negative consequences? Another ethical dilemma: Is an elementary mathematics teacher justified in trying to increase achievement for the whole class by separating two disruptive girls and placing one in a mathematics group beneath her level of ability?

Ethics can provide the teacher with ways of thinking about problems for those situations where it is difficult to determine the right course of action. Ethics also helps teachers to understand that "ethical thinking and decision making are not just following the rules" (Strike & Soltis, 1985, p. 3).

Aesthetics

The branch of axiology known as **aesthetics** is concerned with values related to beauty and art. Although we expect that teachers of music, art, drama, literature, and writing regularly have students make judgments about the quality of works of art, we can easily overlook the contributions that the arts can make to *all* areas of the curriculum. For example, "Participating in plays, songs, and dances fills children with joy, and this joy carries over into the rest of their education" (Nussbaum, 2009, p. 58). Clearly, educational philosopher Harry Broudy (1979) was correct when he made his often-quoted statement that "The arts are necessary, not 'just nice'" (pp. 347–350).

Aesthetics can also help the teacher increase his or her effectiveness. Because it may be viewed as a form of artistic expression, teaching can be judged according to artistic standards of beauty and quality. In this regard, the teacher is an artist whose medium of expression is the spontaneous, unrehearsed, and creative encounter between teacher and student.

Logic

Logic is the area of philosophy that deals with the process of reasoning and identifies rules that will enable the thinker to reach valid conclusions. The public is nearly unanimous in its belief that a key goal of education is to teach students how to think. The two kinds of logical thinking processes that teachers most frequently have students master are *deductive* and *inductive* thinking. The deductive approach requires the thinker to move from a general principle or proposition to a specific conclusion that is valid. By contrast, inductive reasoning moves from the specific to the general. Here, the student begins by examining particular examples that eventually lead to the acceptance of a general proposition. Inductive teaching is often referred to as discovery teaching—by which students discover, or create, their own knowledge of a topic.

Perhaps the best-known teacher to use the inductive approach to teaching was the Greek philosopher Socrates (ca. 470–399 B.C.). His method of teaching, known today as the Socratic method, consisted of holding philosophical conversations (dialectics) with his pupils. **Socratic questioning** is a discussion that is characterized by the following:

- The discussion leader only asks questions.
- The discussion is systematic (not a free-for-all).
- The leader's questions direct the discussion.
- Everyone participates in an effort to "go beneath the surface" and to explore the complexities of the topic or issue under discussion.

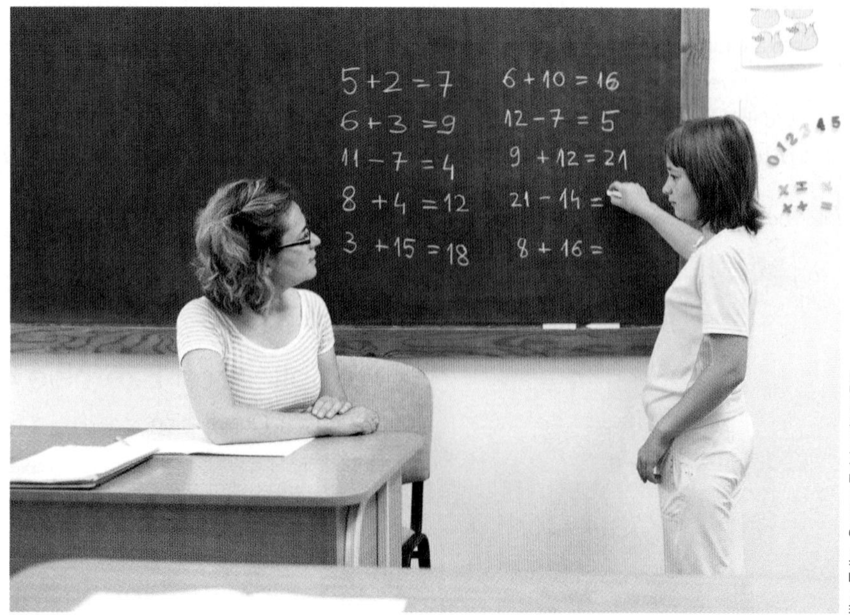

Ilka Erika Szasz-Fabian/123RF

How might this teacher be helping her students develop their logical thinking skills? With reference to the level and subject area for which you are preparing to teach, what activities can help students develop their ability to think logically?

An example of a teacher who understands the importance of Socratic questioning is Alyssa Hucaro, a sixth-grade special education teacher at Wooddale Middle School in Memphis, **TENNESEE**. Her plans for the new school year include strategies for students to become independent thinkers:

> As the turn of a new school year approaches . . . I ask myself, will I teach my students to think for themselves? Are my students able to express themselves freely in the classroom, so that they can advocate for themselves better and become self-sufficient members of the community? To make my classroom more meaningful, I'll need to incorporate strategies that increase the opportunities for my students to think on their own and formulate new ideas. (Nucaro, August 15, 2017)

The legacy of Socrates lives on in all teachers who use Socratic questioning to encourage students to think for themselves. Figure 4.3 presents "Eight Guidelines for Facilitating a Socratic Discussion."

Figure 4.3 Eight guidelines for facilitating a Socratic discussion

The following guidelines can be used to facilitate a Socratic discussion with students. After some experience with the approach, students could even take turns leading a Socratic discussion in small groups of 5–6 students. In addition to a student who acts as discussion leader, one student should be an observer and provide feedback to the group about how well it followed the guidelines. After each guideline, suggested comments for the discussion leader are presented in italics. Each student should have a copy of the guidelines to use during the discussion.

1. At the beginning of the discussion, did the discussion leader clarify the goal(s) of the discussion?
   (The goal(s) of this discussion is(are) . . .)
2. Each time a student answered a question, did the discussion leader respond with another question?
   (Based on your comment, I'd like you to respond to the following question . . .)
3. As the discussion proceeded, did the discussion leader ask for additional relevant information, evidence, or data?
   (On what information, evidence, or data is your comment based?)
4. As appropriate, did the discussion leader question the conclusions, interpretations, and/or inferences made by participants in the discussion?
   (What evidence led you to draw that conclusion? Can you explain your thinking? Might there be another possible explanation?)
5. Did the discussion leader keep the discussion focused on topics related to the goal(s) of the discussion?
   (Can you explain how your comment is related to the goal(s) of our discussion?)
6. Did the discussion leader ask participants to explain unwarranted assumptions?
   (What leads you to make that assumption?)
7. As appropriate, did the discussion leader ask for the implications and/or consequences of statements made by participants?
   (What are the implications of your statement? What might be the consequences if people did as you are suggesting?)
8. Did the discussion leader ask participants to consider the point(s) of view reflected in comments?
   (What would someone who has a different point of view think about your comment? What would you say to that person?)

Based on Richard Paul and Linda L. Elder. (2006). *The Thinker's Guide to the Art of Socratic Questioning*. Dillon Beach, CA: Foundation for Critical Thinking, p. 10.

What Are Five Modern Philosophical Orientations To Teaching?

Five major philosophical orientations to teaching address the branches of philosophy examined in the previous sections. These orientations can guide teachers as they grapple with questions about metaphysics, epistemology, axiology, ethics, aesthetics, and logic. The five orientations, or schools of thought, are perennialism, essentialism, progressivism, existentialism, and social reconstructionism. The following sections present a brief description of each orientation, moving from those that are teacher centered to those that are student centered (see Figure 4.4). Each description concludes with a sample portrait of a teacher whose behavior, to a considerable extent, illustrates that philosophical orientation in action. Remember, though, that most teachers develop an approach to teaching that reflects an *eclectic blend* of two or more orientations to teaching.

Figure 4.4 Five philosophical orientations to teaching

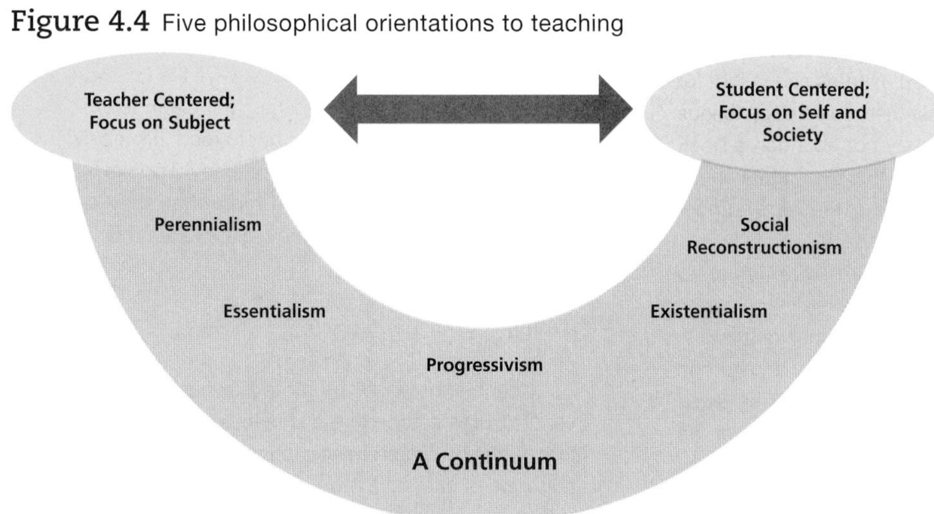

Perennialism

As the term implies, **perennialism** views truth as constant, or perennial. The aim of education, according to perennialist thinking, is to ensure that students acquire knowledge of these unchanging principles or great ideas, and "The function of the school is to educate the intellect" (Leahy, 2009, p. 44). Perennialists also believe that the natural world and human nature have remained basically unchanged over the centuries; thus, the great ideas continue to have the most potential for solving the problems of any era. Furthermore, the perennialist philosophy emphasizes the rational thinking abilities of human beings; the cultivation of the intellect makes human beings truly human and differentiates them from other animals.

The curriculum, according to perennialists, should stress students' intellectual growth in the arts and sciences. To become culturally literate, students should encounter in these areas the best, most significant works that humans have created. In regard to any area of the curriculum, only one question needs to be asked: Are students acquiring content that represents humankind's most lofty accomplishments in that area? Thus, a high school English teacher would require students to read Melville's *Moby Dick* or any of Shakespeare's plays rather than a novel on the current best-seller list. Similarly, science students would learn about the three laws of motion or the three laws of thermodynamics rather than build a model of the space shuttle. The Teaching on Your Feet feature for this chapter profiles a teacher who understands that a perennialist curriculum requires that students become readers—"I let them know that the most important thing they can do for me is read."

Teaching on Your Feet:

Reluctant Readers

I have over 400 book titles in my classroom library. There is a wide range of genres and reading levels. I've read nearly all of them. Within our literacy block I make sure there is time for my students to read their self-selected books. We confer and I note their progress. I've implemented ideas based on books I've read and workshop sessions I've attended. There is a 40-book goal each year for the students. Student as well as teacher book chats take place frequently. Students have a "someday list" in their reading and writing logs, and add books to this list during book chats if the book interests them. I let them know that the most important thing they can do for me is read. They are to read at least 20 minutes each night for homework, and I let them know I trust them to do this; no logs are used. As a class rule, students may not abandon a book until they have read at least 50 pages minus their age. I check in with them and note what they are reading, the page number and their insights. This all builds accountability.

Sometimes a read aloud can help. *Indian in the Cupboard* by Lynn Reid Banks is a favorite, and I find even my reluctant readers want me to read more. This book touches on history, fantasy, and realistic fiction with beautiful imagery and humor. *Flying Solo* by Ralph Fletcher is another book that engages even my most reluctant readers. Once they connect with an author or genre, having them read on their own is a risk they are willing to step into.

As a teacher, students need to know you are a reader, too. They need to understand that you will support them, that you have high expectations, and that you won't give up on them. I find books that relate to their interests and suggest them to students. Providing this scaffolding can move them from reluctant to more engaged.

I have a student this year who has already made great progress. He now asks me for book recommendations and is reading. He may have only read three books so far eight weeks into the year, but that's two more than he did over the same period last year. I consider that success. Giving up on reluctant readers is not an option.

"DANDRE"

Analyze

Not all students come through the door with a love of reading. Some have done their best to avoid reading on their own. I have parents tell me early on that their child doesn't like to read. Since students fill out interest surveys the first week, and I confer with each of them, I use this as I begin to work on a way to find a book that they will want to read. It's a challenge. It takes time. These students may not read 40 books this year, but my goal is to have them read more than they read last year. I hope to find a book that they relate to and help to build a purpose for reading.

Reflect

1. As a teacher, how will you motivate your "reluctant readers?" With reference to the subject area and grade level for which you are preparing to teach, what book titles might be of interest to your students?
2. Dandre says, "As a teacher, you need to let your students know you are a reader, too." Why is this important? What books have you read during the last year that you would like to tell your students about?

Note: From October 19, 2013, blog post by "dandre" at the Pearson Education, Inc. Teachability website. Retrieved February 3, 2014, from http://www.teachability.com/thread/3159.

PERENNIALIST EDUCATIONAL PHILOSOPHERS Two of the best-known advocates of the perennialist philosophy are Robert Maynard Hutchins (1899–1977) and Mortimer Adler (1902–2001). As president of the University of Chicago, Hutchins developed an undergraduate curriculum based on the study of the Great Books and discussions of these classics in small seminars (Hutchins & Adler, 1963). Hutchins's perennialist curriculum was based on three assumptions about education:

1. Education must promote humankind's continuing search for truth. Whatever is true will always, and everywhere, be true; in short, truth is universal and timeless.
2. Because the mind's work is intellectual and focuses on ideas, education must also focus on ideas. The cultivation of human rationality is the essential function of education.
3. Education should stimulate students to think thoughtfully about significant ideas. Teachers should use correct and critical thinking as their primary method, and they should require the same of students.

Noted educational philosopher Mortimer Adler, along with Hutchins, was instrumental in organizing the Great Books of the Western World curriculum. Through the study of over 100 enduring classics, from Plato to Einstein, the Great Books approach aims at the major perennialist goal of teaching students to become independent and critical thinkers. It is a demanding curriculum, and it focuses on the enduring disciplines of knowledge rather than on current events or student interests. The value of careful study of the Great Books is evident in Tamara Mann's description of teaching Socrates' *The Apology* to low-income, mostly minority high school students during a summer program at Columbia University:

> "I'll tell you," Quanisha offered, "but don't laugh. I wonder what this guy Socrates is saying. I just don't understand him. I have been up all night. I read this three times and I don't know what he is saying and I wonder about it."
>
> So our seminar really began, with that familiar little phrase, "Let's turn to the text."
>
> It was Socrates' description of wisdom that caused the most collective confusion. "I don't get it," Lanique piped, "he is wise and not wise, but wiser than other people and still ignorant. That doesn't seem very wise to me."
>
> I smiled knowing that my students cared and were close to understanding something of great value. "Let's look closely at what he says when he is off investigating those who might have a claim to wisdom," I said.
>
> The class found its rhythm and my students, drawing deeply from their reading of the *Apology*, debated the contours of wisdom, knowledge, and learning for the greater part of an hour. The morning ended with our own working definition of wisdom that we would try to apply to our future seminars, "Wisdom is being upfront about what you don't know and then carefully, ploddingly, figuring out how you would learn more about it." (Mann, 2015)

PORTRAIT OF A PERENNIALIST TEACHER Mrs. Bernstein has been teaching English at the high school level since the late 1990s. Among students and teachers as well, she has a reputation for demanding a lot. As one student put it, "You don't waste time in Mrs. Bernstein's classes. Turn off your cell phone, no texting, no multitasking—you pay attention to what she says."

From time to time, she encounters students who insist on being taught subjects that they call "relevant." A graduate of a top-notch university in the East, where she received a classical, liberal education, Mrs. Bernstein refuses to lessen the emphasis in her classes on great works of literature that she believes students need to know—*Beowulf* and the works of Chaucer, Dickens, and Shakespeare, for example.

Kablonk/Golden Pixels LLC/Alamy Stock Photo

Perennialist teachers often inspire students to seek truth, discover universalities in human experience, and celebrate the achievements of human civilization. How might this art lesson reflect perennialist ideas? How might the lesson be different if it were based on the essentialist educational philosophy?

As far as her approach to classroom management is concerned, another student sums it up this way: "She doesn't let you get by with a thing; she never slacks off on the pressure. She lets you know that she's there to teach and you're there to learn." Mrs. Bernstein believes that hard work and effort are necessary if one is to get a good education. As a result, she gives students very few opportunities to misbehave, and she appears to be immune to the grumbling of students who do complain openly about the workload.

She becomes very animated when she talks about the value of the classics to students who are preparing to live as adults in the 21st century:

> The classics are unequaled in terms of the insights they can give students into the major problems that they will have to deal with during their lifetimes. Though our civilization has made impressive technological advances during the last two centuries, we have not really progressed that much in terms of improving the quality of our lives as human beings. The observations of a Shakespeare or a Dickens on the human condition are just as relevant today as they were when they were alive.

Essentialism

Essentialism, which has some similarities to perennialism, is a conservative philosophy of education originally formulated as a criticism of progressive trends in schools by William C. Bagley (1874–1946), a professor of education at Teachers College, Columbia University. Bagley founded the Essentialistic Education Society and, to promote the society's views, the educational journal *School and Society*.

Essentialism was later advanced by E.D. Hirsch's book, *Cultural Literacy: What Every American Needs to Know* (1987). In the book, Hirsch maintains that U.S. students lack basic knowledge needed to function in today's world. They lack "cultural literacy"—background information that great writers and speakers assume their audience possesses. The book includes 5,000 facts that Hirsch believes every American should know. Hirsch also launched the Core Knowledge Foundation that provides curriculum materials to more than 1,200 Core Knowledge schools around the nation.

Essentialism holds that our culture has a core of common knowledge that the schools are obligated to transmit to students in a systematic, disciplined way. Unlike perennialists, who emphasize a set of external truths, essentialists stress what they believe to be the essential knowledge and skills (often termed "the basics") that productive members of our society need to know.

According to essentialist philosophy, schooling should be practical and provide children with sound instruction that prepares them for life; schools should not try to influence or set social policies. Critics of essentialism, however, charge that such a tradition-bound orientation to schooling will indoctrinate students and rule out the possibility of change. Essentialists respond that, without an essentialist approach, students will be indoctrinated in humanistic and/or behavioral curricula that run counter to society's accepted standards and need for order.

An example of the essentialist approach to teaching is a three-week lesson on ancient Rome that Bridgit McCarthy taught her third-grade students at New Dimensions, a public charter school in Morganton, **NORTH CAROLINA**, that teaches the Core Knowledge curriculum. Her reflections on the unit illustrate the importance of students' background knowledge:

> While I always have high expectations in my classroom, I was a bit nervous when we started the ancient Rome unit. The objectives are complex, the vocabulary is challenging. The content itself includes a great deal of geography and culture, plenty of politics, and an assumption that . . . kids already knew quite a bit about ancient Greece.
>
> [However], my third graders had no problems here. Building on their existing knowledge of other cultures' gods and goddesses made the new material easier to access. I also didn't have to "teach" polytheism because the very idea that people had separate deities for different aspects of their lives was old hat to them, having explored it in first grade with Mesopotamia and Egypt and again in second with ancient Greece. (McCarthy, 2015)

FOCUS ON **STEM**: SCIENCE, TECHNOLOGY, ENGINEERING, AND MATHEMATICS FOR THE 21ST CENTURY

A current example of essentialist philosophy is the emphasis on STEM education in K–12 schools. **STEM education** refers to student learning in the broad areas of science, technology, engineering, and math. STEM should also include "Art + Design," according to the Rhode Island School of Design and proponents around the nation. They maintain that "Art + Design" should be at the center of STEM and that innovation requires artists and designers. Thus, STEM + Art = STEAM (STEM to STEAM, 2017).

Business leaders, policymakers, and others point out that our nation's future depends, increasingly, on STEM. Economic growth and development, national security, innovation, and global competitiveness require a workforce knowledgeable in STEM. However, few U.S. students pursue advanced study in STEM fields, and there is a shortage of teachers in those subjects.

Jobs of the future will be increasingly STEM based. Figure 4.5 shows the projected job openings and growth rates in percentages for types of STEM occupations from 2014 to 2024. The computer occupations group will have more than 1 million job openings, a growth rate of 12.5 percent. The STEM group projected to grow the fastest from 2014 to 2024 is the mathematical sciences group at 28.2 percent. This group includes occupations such as mathematicians and statisticians.

Figure 4.5 Projected job openings and growth rates for types of STEM occupations, 2014 to 2024

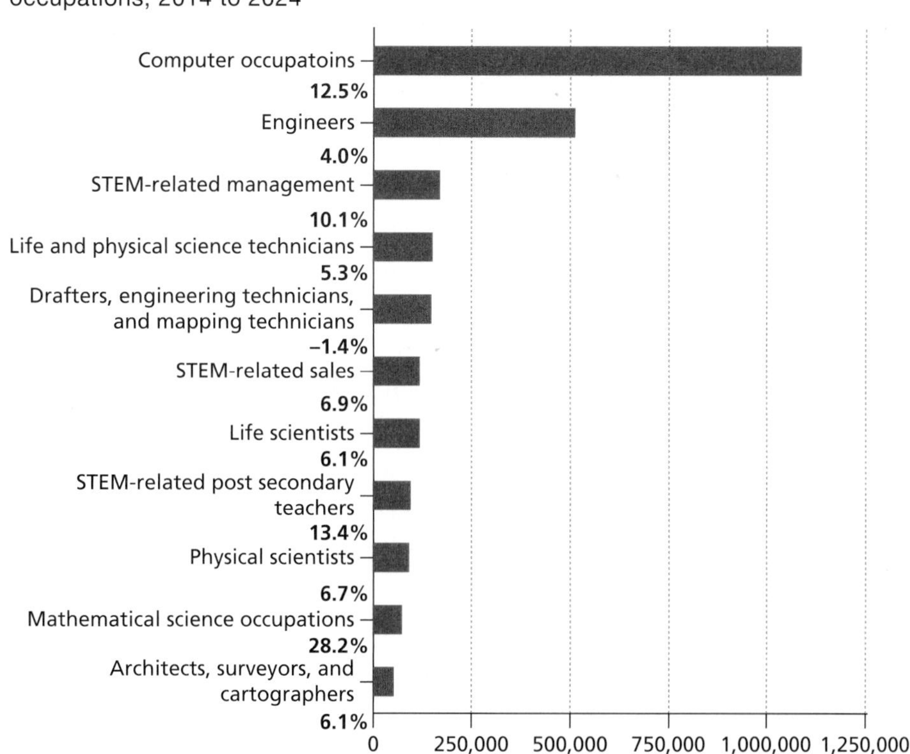

Source: Adapted from United States Department of Labor, Bureau of Labor Statistics. *STEM Occupations: Past, Present, and future*, January 2017, pp. 10 and 12; and online figures at https://www.bls.gov/spotlight/2017/science-technology-engineering-and-mathematics-stem-occupations-past-present-and-future/home.htm

PORTRAIT OF AN ESSENTIALIST TEACHER Mr. Samuels teaches mathematics at a junior high school in a poor section of a major urban area. Prior to coming to this school six years ago, he taught at a rural elementary school.

Middle-aged and highly energetic, Mr. Samuels is known around the school as a hardworking, dedicated teacher. His commitment to children is especially evident when he talks about preparing "his" children for life in high school and beyond. "A lot of teachers nowadays have given up on kids," he says with a touch of sadness to his voice. "They don't demand much of them. If we don't push kids now to get the knowledge and skills they're going to need later in life, we've failed them. My main purpose here is to see that my kids get the basics they're going to need."

Mr. Samuels has made it known that he does not approve of the methods used by some of the younger, more humanistic-oriented teachers in the school. At a recent faculty meeting, for example, he was openly critical of some teachers' tendency to "let students do their own thing" and spend time "expressing their feelings." He called for all teachers to focus their energies on getting students to master subject-matter content, "the things kids will need to know," rather than on helping students adjust to the interpersonal aspects of school life. He also reminded everyone that "kids come to school to learn." All students would learn, he pointed out, if "teachers based their methods on good, sound approaches that have always worked—not on the so-called innovative approaches that are based on fads and frills."

Mr. Samuels's students have accepted his no-nonsense approach to teaching. With few exceptions, his classes are orderly and businesslike. Each class period follows a standard routine. Students enter the room quietly and take their seats with a minimum of the foolishness and horseplay that mark the start of many other classes in the school. As the first order of business, the previous day's homework is returned and reviewed. Following this, Mr. Samuels presents the day's lesson, usually a 15- to 20-minute explanation of how to solve a particular kind of math problem. His mini-lectures are lively, and his wide-ranging tone of voice and animated, spontaneous delivery convey his excitement about the material and his belief that students can learn. During large-group instruction, Mr. Samuels also makes ample use of a whiteboard, software such as Geometer's Sketchpad, and manipulatives such as a large abacus and colored blocks of different sizes and shapes.

Progressivism

Progressivism is based on the belief that education should be child-centered rather than focused on the teacher or the content area. The writing of John Dewey (1859–1952) in the 1920s and 1930s contributed a great deal to the spread of progressive ideas. Briefly, Deweyan progressivism is based on the following three central assumptions:

1. The content of the curriculum ought to be derived from students' interests rather than from the academic disciplines.
2. Effective teaching takes into account the whole child and his or her interests and needs in relation to cognitive, affective, and psychomotor areas.
3. Learning is essentially active rather than passive.

In addition, progressive teachers understand that meaningful teaching and learning requires positive, caring relationships between teacher and students. Progressive teachers, therefore, make it a point to nurture close relationships with their students. They understand that students must feel valued in the classroom—accepted for who they are. Progressive teachers are guided by a maxim attributed to former President Theodore Roosevelt: "Nobody cares how much you know until they know how much you care."

PROGRESSIVE STRATEGIES The progressive philosophy also contends that knowledge that is true in the present may not be true in the future. Hence, the best way to prepare students for an unknown future is to equip them with problem-solving strategies that will enable them to discover meaningful knowledge at various stages of their lives. Teachers with a progressive orientation give students considerable freedom to determine their school experiences. "They guide students in various projects and discoveries, relying in part, on the child's natural curiosity" (Leahy, 2009, p. 34). Contrary to the perceptions of many, however, progressive education does not mean that teachers do not provide structure or that students are free to do whatever they wish. Progressive teachers begin with where students are and, through the daily give-and-take of the classroom, lead students to see that the subject to be learned can enhance their lives.

In a progressively oriented classroom, the teacher serves as a guide or resource person whose primary responsibility is to facilitate student learning. The teacher helps students learn what is important to them rather than passing on a set of so-called enduring truths. Toward this end, the progressive teacher tries to provide students with experiences that replicate everyday life as much as possible. Students have many opportunities to work cooperatively in groups, often solving problems that the group, not the teacher, has identified as important.

PORTRAIT OF A PROGRESSIVE TEACHER Mr. Barkan teaches social studies at a middle school in a well-to-do part of the city. Boyishly handsome and in his mid-30s, Mr. Barkan usually works in casual attire—khaki pants, soft-soled shoes, and a sports shirt. He seems to get along well with students. Mr. Barkan likes to give students as much freedom of choice in the classroom as possible. Accordingly, his room is divided into interest and activity centers, and much of the time students are free to choose where they want to spend their time. One corner at the back of the room has a library collection of paperback and hardcover books, an easy chair, and an area rug; the other back corner of the room is set up as a project area and has a worktable on which are several globes, maps, large sheets of newsprint, and assorted drawing materials. At the front of the room in one corner is a small media center with a computer and flat-screen monitor, laser printer, and DVD/VCR.

Mr. Barkan makes it a point to establish warm, supportive relationships with his students. He is proud of the fact that he is a friend to his students. "I really like the kids I teach," he says in a soft, gentle voice. "They're basically good kids, and they really want to learn if we teachers, I mean, can just keep their curiosity alive and not try to force them to learn. It's up to us as teachers to capitalize on their interests."

The visitor to Mr. Barkan's class today can sense his obvious regard for students. He is genuinely concerned about the growth and nurturance of each one. As his students spend most of their time working in small groups at the various activity centers in the room, Mr. Barkan divides his time among the groups. He moves from group to group and seems to immerse himself as an equal participant in each group's task. One group, for example, has been working on making a papier-mâché globe. Several students are explaining animatedly to him how they plan to transfer the flat map of the world they have drawn to the smooth sphere they have fashioned out of papier-mâché. Mr. Barkan listens carefully to what his students have to say and then congratulates the group on how cleverly they have engineered the project. When he speaks to his students, he does so in a matter-of-fact, conversational tone, as though speaking to other adults.

As much as possible, he likes to bring textbook knowledge to life by providing his students with appropriate experiences—field trips, small-group projects, simulation activities, role-playing, Internet explorations, and so on. Mr. Barkan believes that his primary function as a teacher is to prepare his students for an unknown future. Learning to solve problems at an early age is the best preparation for this future, he feels.

> The increase in the amount of knowledge each decade is absolutely astounding. What we teach students as true today will most likely not be true tomorrow.

Video Example 4.1

Progressivism in Preschool: A preschool teacher describes opportunities she gives her students to discover learning and share interests. She also conveys that her philosophy of education is not always strictly a reflection of one model. Often you need to pull in beliefs from the different philosophies to create one that is personally yours.

> Therefore, students have to learn how to learn and become active problem-solvers. In addition, students need to learn how to identify problems that are meaningful to them. It doesn't make much sense to learn to solve problems that belong to someone else. To accomplish these things in the classroom, teachers have to be willing to take the lead from the students themselves—to use their lives as a point of departure for learning about the subject. What this requires of the teacher is that he or she be willing to set up the classroom along the lines of a democracy, a close community of learners whose major purpose for being there is to learn. You can't create that kind of classroom atmosphere by being a taskmaster and trying to force kids to learn. If you trust them and let them set their own directions, they'll respond.

Existentialism

Existential philosophy is unique because it focuses on the experiences of the individual. In general, existentialism emphasizes creative choice, the subjectivity of human experiences, and concrete acts of human existence over any rational scheme for human nature or reality. Other philosophies are concerned with developing systems of thought for identifying and understanding what is common to *all* reality, human existence, and values. **Existentialism**, on the other hand, offers the individual a way of thinking about *my* life, what has meaning for *me*, what is true for *me*. "The purpose of life, for the existentialists, is to define oneself" (Leahy, 2009, p. 38).

The writings of Jean-Paul Sartre (1905–1980), a well-known French philosopher, novelist, and playwright, have been most responsible for the widespread dissemination of existential ideas. According to Sartre (1972), every individual first exists, and then he or she must decide what that existence is to mean. The task of assigning meaning to that existence is the individual's alone; no preformulated philosophical belief system can tell one who one is. It is up to each of us to decide who we are. According to Sartre (1972), "Existence precedes essence . . . . First of all, man exists, turns up, appears on the scene, and, only afterwards, defines himself" (p. 98).

Life, according to existential thought, has no meaning, and the universe is indifferent to the situation humankind finds itself in. Moreover, "Existentialists [believe] that too many people wrongly emphasize the optimistic, the good, and the beautiful—all of which create a false impression of existence" (Ozmon & Craver, 2007). With the freedom that we have, however, we must commit ourselves to assign meaning to our *own* lives. As Maxine Greene, who has been described as "the preeminent American philosopher of education today" (Ayers & Miller, 1998, p. 4), stated: "We have to know about our lives, clarify our situations if we are to understand the world from our shared standpoints" (Greene, 1995a, p. 21). The human enterprise that can be most helpful in promoting this personal quest for meaning is the educative process. Therefore, teachers must allow students freedom of choice and provide them with experiences that will help them find the meaning of their lives. This approach, contrary to the belief of many, does not mean that students may do whatever they please; logic indicates that freedom has rules, and respect for the freedom of others is essential.

Existentialists judge the curriculum according to whether it contributes to the individual's quest for meaning and results in a level of personal awareness that Greene terms "wide-awakeness." As Greene (1995b, pp. 149–150) suggests, the ideal curriculum is one that provides students with extensive individual freedom and requires them to ask their own questions, conduct their own inquiries, and draw their own conclusions: "To feel oneself en route, to feel oneself in a place where there are always possibilities of clearings, of new openings, this is what we must communicate to the young if we want to awaken them to their situation and enable them to make sense of and to name their worlds."

EXISTENTIALISM AND POSTMODERNISM A philosophical orientation that has received increased attention since the 1980s, **postmodernism** has many similarities with existentialism. Postmodern thinking influences the curriculum content and instructional strategies some teachers use.

Postmodernists challenge the metaphysical views—or explanations of "reality"—presented in many textbooks. These books, they claim, present a "historically constructed" view of reality that gives advantages to some persons and groups in our society (White males, for example), whereas it marginalizes others (people of color, women, and unskilled workers, for example).

Postmodernist educators are critical of school curricula that advance the perspectives of dominant groups and ignore other "voices." They point out, for example, that some history books, written from a Eurocentric perspective, state that Columbus "discovered" a "New World." The people who lived in what is now the United States centuries before the arrival of Columbus, of course, have a very different perspective because their native cultures endured disease, genocide, and forced assimilation at the hands of the Europeans.

Similarly, English teachers with a postmodern orientation point out that most of the literature students are required to read has been written by "dead White men" (Shakespeare, Melville, and Hawthorne, for example). Students seldom have opportunities to read the "voices" of authors who represent women, people of color, and writers from developing countries.

In general, postmodernists believe there are no absolute truths. Postmodernism disputes the certainty of scientific, or objective, explanations of reality. In addition, postmodernism is skeptical of explanations that claim to be true for all groups, cultures, traditions, or races. Similar to existentialists, postmodernists emphasize what is true for the individual. Reality is based on our interpretations of what the world means to us individually. Postmodernism emphasizes concrete experience over abstract principles.

Postmodernism is "post" because it rejects the "modern" belief that there are scientific, philosophical, and religious truths. Postmodernists believe there are many truths, and many different voices that need to be heard.

Postmodernists maintain that knowledge is invented or constructed in the minds of people, not discovered as modernists claim. Thus the knowledge that teachers teach and students learn does not necessarily correspond to reality. Instead, that knowledge is a human construction. Knowledge, ideas, and language are created by people, not because they are true but because they are useful.

According to postmodernists, reality is a "story." Reality exists only in the minds of those who perceive it. As a result, no version of reality can claim to be the truth because versions of reality are merely human creations. An example of a postmodern teacher who wants students to understand that history is based on "stories" told from particular points of view is David Knight, a teacher at Boston Arts Academy, a public school for the visual and performing arts. An excerpt from his blog post, "Teaching Courage in a Postmodern World," explains his approach to teaching students about the civil rights movement:

> "You do know that children and teenagers played a huge role in the civil rights movement?" I asked [my students].
>
> Come to find out, they did not. Students thought of history and social change in terms of iconic figures, heroes and heroines, instead of common folk. They didn't know about the leaders behind the scenes, such as Ella Baker, Fannie Lou Hamer, Septima Poinsette Clark, Bayard Rustin, or the hundreds of child activists in the Children's Crusade in Birmingham, Alabama, in 1963.
>
> The coming weeks in my class included more reading and discussion of young, unacknowledged change agents. I used Ellen Levine's *Freedom's Children* and Elizabeth Partridge's *Marching for Freedom*, both nonfiction books about

> young people's involvement in the civil rights movement. Students read the story of Claudette Colvin, the 15-year-old girl who refused to give up her seat in Montgomery, Alabama., nine months before Rosa Parks did the same thing.
>
> My goal was to explode conventional ideas about who makes history and why. I wanted my students to know that we all make history, even if our names don't make it into history books. And that these activists were people who made mistakes, had doubts, worried about skin color and their looks and had other experiences to which my students could relate . . . . [My students] all learned that studying history is difficult, complicated and dependent on the storyteller's point of view. (Knight, 2013)

PORTRAIT OF AN EXISTENTIALIST TEACHER After he started teaching English eight years ago at a suburban high school, Algernon Gates began to have doubts about the value of what he was teaching students. Although he could see a limited, practical use for the knowledge and skills he was teaching, he felt he was doing little to help his students answer the most pressing questions of their lives. Also, Algernon had to admit to himself that he had grown somewhat bored with following the narrow, unimaginative Board of Education curriculum guides.

During the next eight years, Algernon gradually developed a style of teaching that placed emphasis on students finding out who they are. He continued to teach the knowledge covered on the achievement test mandated by his state, but he made it clear that what students learned from him, they should use to answer questions that were important to them. Now, for example, he often gives writing assignments that encourage students to look within in order to develop greater self-knowledge. He often uses assigned literature as a springboard for values clarification discussions. And whenever possible, he gives his students the freedom to pursue individual reading and writing projects. His only requirement is that students be meaningfully involved in whatever they do.

Algernon is also keenly aware of how the questions his students are just beginning to grapple with are questions that he is still, even in his mid-30s, trying to answer for himself. Thoughtfully and with obvious care for selecting the correct words, he sums up the goals that he has for his students:

> I think kids should realize that the really important questions in life are beyond definitive answers, and they should be very suspicious of anyone—teacher, philosopher, or member of organized religion—who purports to have the answers. As human beings, each of us faces the central task of finding *our own* answers to such questions. My students know that I'm wrestling with the same questions they're working on. But I think I've taught them well enough so that they know that my answers can't be their answers.

Algernon's approach to teaching is perhaps summed up by the bumper sticker on the car he drives: "Question authority." Unlike many of his fellow teachers, he wants his students to react critically and skeptically to what he teaches them. He also presses them to think thoughtfully and courageously about the meaning of life, beauty, love, and death. He judges his effectiveness by the extent to which students are able and willing to become more aware of the choices that are open to them.

Social Reconstructionism

As the term implies, **social reconstructionism** holds that schools should take the lead in changing or reconstructing the current social order. Theodore Brameld (1904–1987), acknowledged as the founder of social reconstructionism, based his philosophy on two fundamental premises about the post–World War II era: (1) We live in a period of great crisis, most evident in the fact that humans now have the capability of destroying civilization overnight, and (2) humankind also has the intellectual, technological, and moral potential to create a world civilization of "abundance, health, and humane capacity" (Brameld, 1956, p. 19). In this time of great need, then, the schools should become the primary agent for planning and directing social change. In short, schools should not only *transmit* knowledge about the existing social order; they should seek to *reconstruct* it as well.

SOCIAL RECONSTRUCTIONISM AND PROGRESSIVISM Social reconstructionism has clear ties to progressive educational philosophy. Both provide opportunities for extensive interaction between teacher and students and among students themselves. Furthermore, both place a premium on bringing the community, if not the entire world, into the classroom. Student experiences often include field trips, community-based projects of various sorts, and opportunities to interact with persons beyond the four walls of the classroom.

A social reconstructionist curriculum highlights the need for various reforms and, whenever possible, allows students to have firsthand experiences in reform activities. Teachers realize that they and their students can play a significant role in helping to resolve the challenges that confront humanity. An example of a teacher with a social reconstructionist educational philosophy is Jim Trogdon, a middle school science teacher in Coventry, **OHIO.** His students work on project-based learning units that are part of the EarthEcho Water Challenge. The Challenge involves the public in protecting water resources around the world. Trogdon's students monitor water quality in local rivers and raise trout in their classroom to stock the rivers. Recently, they helped to "daylight" a stream—i.e., brought a trapped tributary back from underground. His students are part of a local team that includes civil engineers, tree planting experts, an ecologist, landscape designers, and hydrologists (EarthEcho International, 2017).

According to Brameld and social reconstructionists such as George Counts, who wrote *Dare the School Build a New Social Order?* (1932), schools should provide students with methods for dealing with the significant crises that confront the world: war, climate change, international terrorism, hunger, natural disasters, and ever-accelerating technological advances. The logical outcome of such education would be the eventual realization of a worldwide democracy (Brameld, 1956). Unless we actively seek to create this kind of world through the intelligent application of present knowledge, we run the risk that the destructive forces of the world will determine the conditions under which humans will live in the future.

Application Exercise 4.3
To Change the Social Order

PORTRAIT OF A SOCIAL RECONSTRUCTIONIST TEACHER At the urban high school where she teaches social studies and history, Martha Hernandez has the reputation for being a social activist. On first meeting her, she presents a casual and laid-back demeanor. Her soft voice and warm smile belie the intensity of her convictions about pressing world issues, from international terrorism and hunger to peaceful uses of space and the need for all humans to work toward a global community.

Martha feels strongly about the importance of having students learn about social problems as well as discovering what they can do about them. "It's really almost immoral if I confront my students with a social problem and then we fail to do anything about it," she says. "Part of my responsibility as a teacher is to raise the consciousness level of my students in regard to the problems that confront all human beings. I want them to leave my class with the realization that they can make a difference when it comes to making the world a more humane place."

For Martha to achieve her goals as a teacher, she frequently has to tackle controversial issues—issues that many of her colleagues avoid in the classroom. She feels that students would not learn how to cope with problems or controversy if she were to avoid them.

> I'm not afraid of controversy. When confronted with controversy, some teachers do retreat to the safety of the more "neutral" academic discipline. However, I try to get my students to see how they can use the knowledge of the discipline to work for social justice. So far, I've gotten good support from the principal. She's backed me up on several controversial issues that we've looked at in class: the nuclear energy plant that was to be built here in this county, the right to die, and absentee landlords who own property in the poorer sections of the city.

Two additional philosophical orientations may be placed under the broad umbrella of social reconstructionism—critical pedagogy and feminist pedagogy. These orientations have a significant influence on the curriculum content some teachers emphasize and the instructional strategies they use. The following sections provide brief descriptions of these orientations.

FOCUS ON **DIVERSITY**: CRITICAL PEDAGOGY

Much like social reconstructionism, **critical pedagogy** focuses on how education can promote **social justice**, especially for underrepresented groups that often do not enjoy positions of power and influence in society. Critical pedagogy teaches students how to identify and to understand the complexities of social injustice. It gives them "the tools to better themselves and strengthen democracy, to create a more egalitarian and just society, and thus to deploy education in a process of progressive social change" (Kellner, 2000).

An example of how critical pedagogy and social justice can provide a focus for teaching is evident in Mansur Buffins's explanation of why he decided to become a teacher.

> I would like to teach in a secondary school serving predominantly low-income, African American students. And I am entering the profession as an intentional form of activism. My goal is to actively break down inequities that negatively impact my students, in schools and in life . . . .
>
> My classroom will be a space of critical thinking that uses history lessons to instill within students a sense of agency to positively impact the world today. My students will engage in projects and assignments that prepare them for civic engagement and active resistance to social injustices and inequities, planting a seed for future activism . . . As a Black male teacher, I will be a role model, mentor, and father figure to my students. (Buffins, 2017)

One educator who advocated critical pedagogy was Paulo Freire (1921–1997). He spent his childhood in the comfort of the Brazilian middle class. However, he encountered poverty when his father lost his job as a military officer during the economic crisis of 1929 (Smith & Smith, 1994). That experience "led him to make a vow, at age eleven, to dedicate his life to the struggle against hunger, so that other children would not have to know the agony he was then experiencing." It also led him to understand what he described as "'the culture of silence' of the dispossessed" (Freire, 2000, p. 10). The difficulty poor people encountered when they tried to improve the quality of their lives he attributed to the physical conditions of poverty and to a deep sense that they were not entitled to move beyond their plight. Freire also believed that paternalism embedded in the political and educational systems led to inequality of opportunity. "Rather than being encouraged and equipped to know and respond to the concrete realities of their world, they [poor students] were kept 'submerged' in a situation in which such critical awareness and response were practically impossible" (Freire, 2000, p. 11).

Freire regarded education, and particularly literacy, as the best way to improve the quality of one's life. Influenced by numerous philosophers, psychologists, and political thinkers, including Sartre, Mahatma Gandhi, and Martin Luther King, Jr., he developed a philosophy of education for his doctoral dissertation in 1959. His dissertation provided the basis for his now internationally famous book *Pedagogy of the Oppressed.* The key premise of his book is that "human interaction rarely escapes oppression of one kind or another; by reason of class, race, or gender, people tend to be victims and/or perpetrators of oppression" (Torres, 1994, p. 181). His approach to education "calls for dialogue and ultimately conscientization—critical consciousness or awareness—as a way to overcome relationships of domination and oppression" (Torres, 1994, p. 187).

Freire's success in working with poor, illiterate adults in northern Brazil was so great that he was regarded as a threat to the existing political order. He was imprisoned and eventually exiled.

FOCUS ON **DIVERSITY**: FEMINIST PEDAGOGY

According to an advocate of **feminist pedagogy** and a teacher at an elementary school in **INDIANA**, schools "serve the power of dominant ideologies and beliefs" (Scering, 1997, p. 62). To ensure the growth and well-being of *all* students in a society dominated by the beliefs and perspectives of White men, then, "Feminist pedagogy challenges the emphasis on efficiency and objectivity that perpetuate the domination of masculine rationality . . . . The role of schools in perpetuating unequal social, cultural, political, and economic realities is a central theme of [feminist pedagogy]" (Scering, 1997, p. 62). Thus, the goal of feminist pedagogy is to create caring communities of engaged learners who respect differences and work collaboratively to make democracy a reality for all classes of people.

Feminist pedagogy is particularly applicable to today's calls to increase the number of girls who enroll in STEM (science, technology, engineering, and mathematics) classes. An example a teacher committed to this goal is Ashley Lauren Samsa, a high school English teacher in a South Chicago, **ILLINOIS** suburb:

> Teachers play a key role in helping girls realize that entering STEM careers is not only possible but necessary. At my school, elective STEM classes are often full of boys; teachers are lucky to have one or two girls sign up. And those girls tend to drop out or look for other electives, either because the class doesn't offer the academic and emotional support they need or because they just feel too isolated to continue. This phenomenon funnels girls who might be interested in STEM into other fields where women are more widely represented. (Samsa, 2015)

A leading advocate for feminist pedagogy is bell hooks (she does not use capital letters in her name). According to hooks,

> Feminist education—the feminist classroom—is and should be a place where there is a sense of struggle, where there is a visible acknowledgment of the union of theory and practice, where we work together as teachers and students to overcome the estrangement and alienation that have become so much the norm . . . . Most importantly, feminist pedagogy should engage students in a learning process that makes the world "more real than less real." (hooks, 1989, p. 51)

In *Teaching to Transgress: Education as the Practice of Freedom,* hooks (1994, p. 12) states that education should be viewed as "the practice of freedom, [and] more than ever before . . . educators are compelled to confront the biases that have shaped teaching practices in our society and to create new ways of knowing, different strategies for the sharing of knowledge." hooks (2003, p. xv) also maintains that the classroom should be "a place that is life-sustaining and mind-expanding, a place of liberating mutuality where teacher and student together work in partnership."

Advocates of feminist pedagogy point out that different voices and different ways of knowing tend not to be acknowledged in classrooms dominated by Eurocentric, patriarchal curricula. hooks (2003, p. 3), for example, calls for the "decolonisation of ways of knowing."

Another well-known advocate of feminist pedagogy and a scholar instrumental in developing the legal definition of sexual harassment, Catharine MacKinnon (1989), explains how what is viewed as *the truth* in our society is determined by those in positions of power: "Having power means, among other things, that when someone says, 'this is how it is,' it is taken as being that way . . . . Powerlessness means that when you say, 'this is how it is,' it is not taken as being that way. This makes articulating silence, perceiving the presence of absence, believing those who have been socially stripped of credibility, critically contextualizing what passes for simple fact, necessary to the epistemology of a politics of the powerless."

COMPARING PHILOSOPHICAL ORIENTATIONS TO TEACHING Figure 4.6 presents a matrix that compares the underlying belief systems of the five philosophical orientations to teaching. After reading the description of each teacher, try to think of additional words or phrases for each cell that would describe that teacher's beliefs.

Figure 4.6 A matrix for comparing the underlying belief systems of five philosophical orientations to teaching

	Philosophical Orientations to Teaching				
Educational Beliefs	Perennialist Teacher	Essentialist Teacher	Progressive Teacher	Existentialist Teacher	Social Reconstructionist Teacher
Beliefs About Teaching and Learning	Teaching is transmission of knowledge and concepts through lecture, rigorous discussion, and analysis. Learning is acquisition of knowledge and concepts through rigorous study of organized disciplines of knowledge.	Teaching is effective, efficient transmission of knowledge and skills. Learning involves mastering knowledge and skills through repetition and practice.	Teachers are trusted guides and coaches who create educative experiences based on students' interests and concerns. Learning is natural and springs from students' genuine interests and concerns.	Teachers help students develop deeper understanding of their experiences and the meaning of their lives. Meaningful learning occurs when students have the courage to ask important questions about the meaning of their lives.	Teachers organize inquiry-oriented, problem-solving groups of students that learn how to improve society and the quality of people's lives. Meaningful learning involves accepting one's responsibility to become a contributing member of a group that is committed to improving society and the quality of people's lives.
Beliefs About Students	Students' primary role is to develop rigorous intellectual discipline to study organized bodies of knowledge.	Students' primary role is to memorize and master facts and information.	Students are internally motivated to learn how to solve personally meaningful problems.	Students' primary role is to become "wide awake" and begin to ask important questions about the meaning of their lives.	Students' primary role is to become involved in social change and develop a commitment to improving society and the quality of people's lives.
Beliefs About Knowledge	Knowledge consists of concepts and big ideas developed by outstanding, preeminent individuals throughout history.	Knowledge is units of subject matter, discrete facts.	Knowledge results from the experience of learning how to solve personally meaningful problems.	Knowledge is awareness that leads to greater and deeper understanding of one's unique experience and the meaning of life.	Knowledge emerges from active involvement in the change process required to improve society and the quality of people's lives.
Beliefs About What Is Worth Knowing	Eminent accomplishments by humankind and time-honored "great ideas" and concepts are most worth knowing.	Common core of essential knowledge and skills is most worth knowing.	How to solve personally meaningful problems and thus live a productive, satisfying life is most worth knowing.	The meaning of one's experience and purpose in life is most worth knowing.	Knowledge of the process of social change and how to improve society and the quality of people's lives is most worth knowing.

What Psychological Orientations Have Influenced Teaching Philosophies?

In addition to the five philosophical orientations to teaching described in previous sections of this chapter, several schools of psychological thought have formed the basis for teaching philosophies. These psychological theories are comprehensive worldviews that serve as the basis for the way many teachers approach their teaching. Psychological orientations to teaching are concerned primarily with understanding the conditions that are associated with effective learning. In other words, what motivates students to learn? What environments are most conducive to learning?

Chief among the psychological orientations that have influenced teaching philosophies are humanistic psychology, behaviorism, and constructivism. The following sections present a brief description of each orientation. Following each description is a sample portrait of a teacher whose behavior, to a considerable extent, illustrates that psychological orientation in action.

Humanistic Psychology

Humanistic psychology emphasizes personal freedom, choice, awareness, and personal responsibility. As the term implies, it also focuses on the achievements, motivation, feelings, actions, and needs of human beings. The goal of education, according to this orientation, is individual self-actualization.

Humanistic psychology is derived from the philosophy of **humanism**, which developed during the European Renaissance and Protestant Reformation and is based on the belief that individuals control their own destinies through the application of their intelligence and learning. People "make themselves." The term *secular humanism* refers to the closely related belief that the conditions of human existence relate to human nature and human actions rather than to predestination or divine intervention.

Video Example 4.2

Humanism in Action: A teacher who is influenced by humanistic psychology focuses on nurturing personal responsibility and awareness in students. This video conversation among teachers focuses on how they build relationships with students and empower them to make positive choices.

In the 1950s and 1960s, humanistic psychology became the basis of educational reforms that sought to enhance students' achievement of their full potential through self-actualization (Maslow, 1954, 1962; Rogers, 1961). According to this psychological orientation, teachers should not force students to learn; instead, they should create a climate of trust and respect that allows students to decide what and how they learn, to question authority, and to take initiative in "making themselves." Teachers should be what noted psychologist Carl Rogers (1982) calls facilitators, and the classroom should be a place "in which curiosity and the natural desire to learn can be nourished and enhanced" (p. 31). Through their nonjudgmental understanding of students, humanist teachers encourage students to learn and grow.

PORTRAIT OF A HUMANIST TEACHER Ten years ago, Ramerra Alexander began teaching at a small rural middle school—a position she enjoys because the school's small size enables her to develop close relationships with her students and their families. Her teaching style is based on humane, open interpersonal relationships with her students, and she takes pride in the fact that students trust her and frequently ask her advice on problems common to children in early adolescence. The positive rapport

Ramerra has developed with her students is reflected in the regularity with which former students return to visit or to seek her advice.

Ramerra is also committed to empowering her students, to giving them opportunities to shape their learning experiences. As she puts it: "I encourage students to give me feedback about how they feel in my classroom. They have to feel good about themselves before they can learn. Also, I've come to realize that students should help us [teachers] plan. I've learned to ask them what they're interested in. 'What do you want to do?' 'How do you want to do it?'"

Much of Ramerra's teaching is based on classroom discussions in which she encourages students to share openly their ideas and feelings about the subject at hand. Ramerra's interactions with students reveal her skill at creating a conversational environment that makes students feel safe and willing to contribute. During discussions, Ramerra listens attentively to students and frequently paraphrases their ideas in a way that acknowledges their contributions. She frequently responds with short phrases that indicate support and encourage the student to continue the discussion, such as the following: "I see. Would you say more about that?" "That is an interesting idea; tell us more."

When Ramerra is not facilitating a whole-group discussion, she is more than likely moving among the small cooperative-learning groups she has set up. Each group decided how to organize itself to accomplish a particular learning task—developing a strategy for responding to a threat to the environment or analyzing a poem about brotherhood, for example. "I think it's important for students to learn to work together, to help one another, and to accept different points of view," says Ramerra.

Behaviorism

Behaviorism is based on the principle that desirable human behavior can be the product of design rather than accident. According to behaviorists, it is an illusion to say that humans have a free will. Although we may act as if we are free, our behavior is really determined by forces in the environment that shape our behavior. "We are what we are and we do what we do, not because of any mysterious power of human volition, but because outside forces over which we lack any semblance of control have us caught in an inflexible web. Whatever else we may be, we are not the captains of our fate or the masters of our soul" (Power, 1982, p. 168).

FOUNDERS OF BEHAVIORISTIC PSYCHOLOGY John B. Watson (1878–1958) was the principal originator of behavioristic psychology and B. F. Skinner (1904–1990) its best-known promoter. Watson first claimed that human behavior consisted of specific stimuli that resulted in certain responses. In part, he based this new conception of learning on the classic experiment conducted by Russian psychologist Ivan Pavlov (1849–1936). Pavlov had noticed that a dog he was working with would salivate when it was about to be given food. By introducing the sound of a bell when food was offered and repeating this several times, Pavlov discovered that the sound of the bell alone (a conditioned stimulus) would make the dog salivate (a conditioned response). Watson was so confident that all learning conformed to this basic stimulus–response model (now termed classical or type S conditioning) that he once boasted, "Give me a dozen healthy infants, well-formed, and my own specified world to bring them up in, and I'll guarantee to take any one at random and train him to become any type of specialist I might select—doctor, lawyer, artist, merchant-chief and, yes, even beggarman and thief, regardless of his talents, penchants, tendencies, abilities, vocations, and race of his ancestors" (Watson, 1925, p. 82).

Skinner went beyond Watson's basic stimulus–response model and developed a more comprehensive view of conditioning known as operant (or type R) conditioning. Operant conditioning is based on the idea that satisfying responses are conditioned; unsatisfying ones are not. In other words, "The things we call pleasant have an energizing or strengthening effect on our behaviour" (Skinner, 1972, p. 74). Thus the teacher can create learners who exhibit desired behaviors by following four steps:

1. Identify desired behaviors in concrete (observable and measurable) terms.
2. Establish a procedure for recording specific behaviors and counting their frequencies.
3. For each behavior, identify an appropriate reinforcer.
4. Ensure that students receive the reinforcer as soon as possible after displaying a desired behavior.

PORTRAIT OF A BEHAVIORIST TEACHER Ramona Day teaches fourth grade at a school with an enrollment of about 500 in a small Midwestern town. Now in her fifth year at the school, Ramona has spent the last three years developing and refining a systematic approach to teaching. Last year, the success of her methods was confirmed when her students received the highest scores on the state's annual basic skills test.

Her primary method is individualized instruction, wherein students proceed at their own pace through modules she has put together. The modules cover five major areas: reading, writing, mathematics, general science, and spelling. She is working on a sixth module, geography, but it won't be ready until next year. She has developed a complex point system to keep track of students' progress and to motivate them to higher levels of achievement. The points students accumulate entitle them to participate in various in-class activities: free reading, playing with the many games and puzzles in the room, drawing or painting in the art corner, or playing video games on one of the two personal computers in the room.

Ramona has tried to convert several other teachers at the school to her behavioristic approach, and she is eager to talk to anyone who will listen about the effectiveness of her systematic approach to instruction. When addressing this topic, her exuberance is truly exceptional: "It's really quite simple. Students just do much better if you tell them exactly what you want them to know and then reward them for learning it."

In regard to the methods employed by some of her colleagues, Ramona can be rather critical. She knows some teachers in the school who teach by a trial-and-error method and "aren't clear about where they're going." She is also impatient with those who talk about the "art" of teaching; in contrast, everything that she does as a teacher is done with precision and a clear sense of purpose. "Through careful design and management of the learning environment," she says, "a teacher can get the results that he or she wants."

Constructivism

In contrast to behaviorism, constructivism focuses on processes of learning rather than on learning behavior. According to **constructivism**, students use cognitive processes to *construct* understanding of the material to be learned—in contrast to the view that they *receive* information transmitted by the teacher. Constructivist approaches support student-centered rather than teacher-centered curriculum and instruction. The student is the key to learning.

Unlike behaviorists who concentrate on directly observable behavior, constructivists focus on the mental processes and strategies that students use to learn. Our understanding of learning has been extended as a result of advances in **cognitive science**—the study of the mental processes students use in thinking and remembering. By drawing from research in linguistics, psychology, anthropology, neurophysiology, and computer science, cognitive scientists are developing new models for how people think and learn.

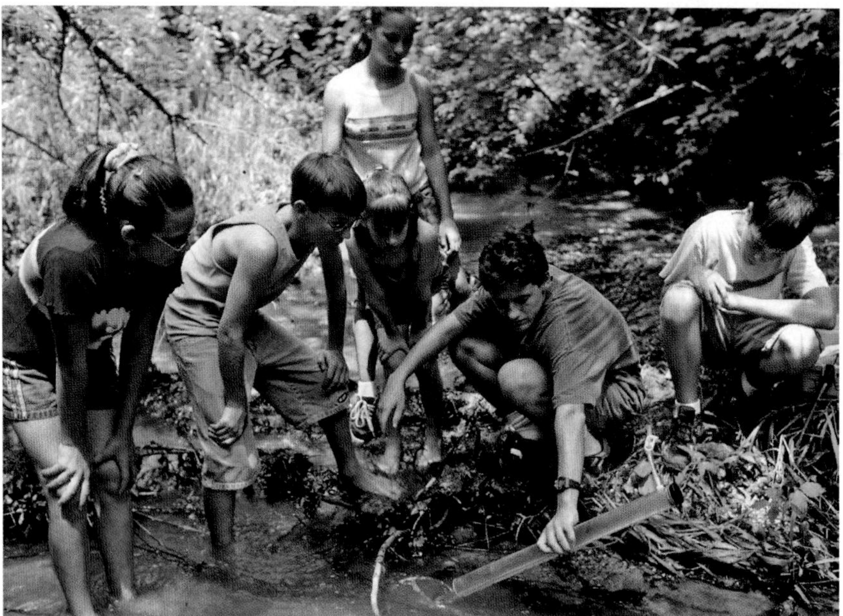

USDA/NRCS

These children are active learners in a real or relevant context, and they are constructing their own meanings through direct experience. How might this lesson be seen as an eclectic blend of progressive, existential, and constructivist ideals?

Teachers who base classroom activities on constructivism know that learning is an active, meaning-making process, that learners are not passive recipients of information. In fact, students are continually involved in making sense out of activities around them. Thus, the teacher must *understand students' understanding* and realize that students' learning is influenced by prior knowledge, experience, attitudes, and social interactions.

PORTRAIT OF A CONSTRUCTIVIST TEACHER Lisa Sanchez teaches English at a middle school in a large city on the East Coast. The walls of her classroom are decorated with students' work—poetry, drawings, and students' writing reflecting various stages of the writing process: prewriting, revising, and final drafts.

Working in five groups, four students in each group, Lisa's eighth-grade students are translating *Romeo and Juliet* into modern English. Each group is translating a different act. Later, each group of students will choose a scene to enact, after designing a set and contemporary costumes. Lisa points out that her students will have to make decisions regarding the most appropriate costumes for each character based on their understanding of Shakespeare's play. "I want them to understand how *Romeo and Juliet* is relevant even today."

As students discuss the most appropriate translation line by line, Lisa moves from group to group. She asks clarifying questions and provides encouragement as students work to understand the meaning of Shakespeare's words.

At the end of class, Lisa explains her approach to teaching: "My teaching is definitely student centered. I try to create a democratic classroom environment. My students are actively involved in creating meaning and knowledge for themselves. They do a lot of work in small groups, and they learn to question, investigate, hypothesize, and invent. They have to make connections between what they already know and new knowledge."

COMPARING PSYCHOLOGICAL ORIENTATIONS TO TEACHING Figure 4.7 presents a matrix that compares the underlying belief systems of the three psychological orientations. After reading the description of each teacher, try to think of additional words or phrases for each cell that would describe that teacher's beliefs.

Figure 4.7 A matrix for comparing the underlying belief systems of three psychological orientations to teaching

	Psychological Orientations to Teaching		
Educational Beliefs	**Humanist Teacher**	**Behaviorist Teacher**	**Constructivist Teacher**
Beliefs About Teaching and Learning	Teachers are facilitators who create supportive, nurturing environments that help students become self-actualized and realize their full potential. Learning is natural and springs from the human being's innate drive to grow and develop.	Teachers identify desired observable behaviors students should demonstrate and then reinforce those behaviors when they occur. Learning occurs when conditioning and reinforcement lead to desired observable and measurable behaviors.	Teachers guide the mental processes and strategies students use to construct their understanding of new material; teachers respond to students' learning efforts. Learning involves the mental process of using what one already knows to construct understanding of new material to be learned.
Beliefs About Students	Students are internally motivated, able to take responsibility for their learning, and want to become self-actualized.	Students are conditioned by their environment, and their primary role is to memorize facts and demonstrate mastery of desired skills.	Students' primary role is to actively make sense and ***construct*** understanding of subject matter rather than to ***receive*** information transmitted by the teacher.
Beliefs About Knowledge	Knowledge is personal and fosters growth and development within the individual.	Knowledge is units of subject matter, discrete facts.	Knowledge is constructed from a base of prior knowledge.
Beliefs About What Is Worth Knowing	Knowledge that promotes the individual's growth, development, and self-actualization is most worth knowing.	Knowledge, skills, values, and attitudes required by society are most worth knowing.	How to use prior knowledge to construct understanding of new material is most worth knowing.

How Can You Develop Your Educational Philosophy?

As you read the preceding brief descriptions of five educational philosophies and three psychological orientations to teaching, perhaps you felt that no single philosophy fit perfectly with your idea of the kind of teacher you want to become. Or there may have been some element of each approach that seemed compatible with your own emerging philosophy of education. In either case, don't feel that you need to identify a single educational philosophy around which you will build your teaching career. In reality, few teachers follow only one educational philosophy, and as Figure 4.8 shows, educational philosophy is only one determinant of a teacher's behavior in the classroom. A teacher's behavior is also influenced by factors such as student's needs and interests, economic conditions, the culture of the school, political dynamics, family expectations, social forces, and community expectations.

Most teachers develop an *eclectic* philosophy of education, which means they develop their own unique blending of two or more philosophies. To help you identify the philosophies most consistent with your beliefs and values about educational goals, curriculum, and teachers' and students' roles in learning, complete the philosophic inventory in Figure 4.9. The self-knowledge you glean from completing the inventory and the philosophical constructs presented in this chapter provide a useful framework for understanding various periods of our nation's educational history. For example, philosophical orientations to education waxed and waned during different periods—whether it was the perennialism and essentialism that characterized colonial schools, the progressivism of the 1920s and 1930s, the essentialism of the 1950s and 1980s, the humanism and social reconstructionism of the 1960s, or the constructivism of the 1990s and the first decade of the new century.

Figure 4.8 Factors that shape an eclectic philosophy of education and teaching behaviors

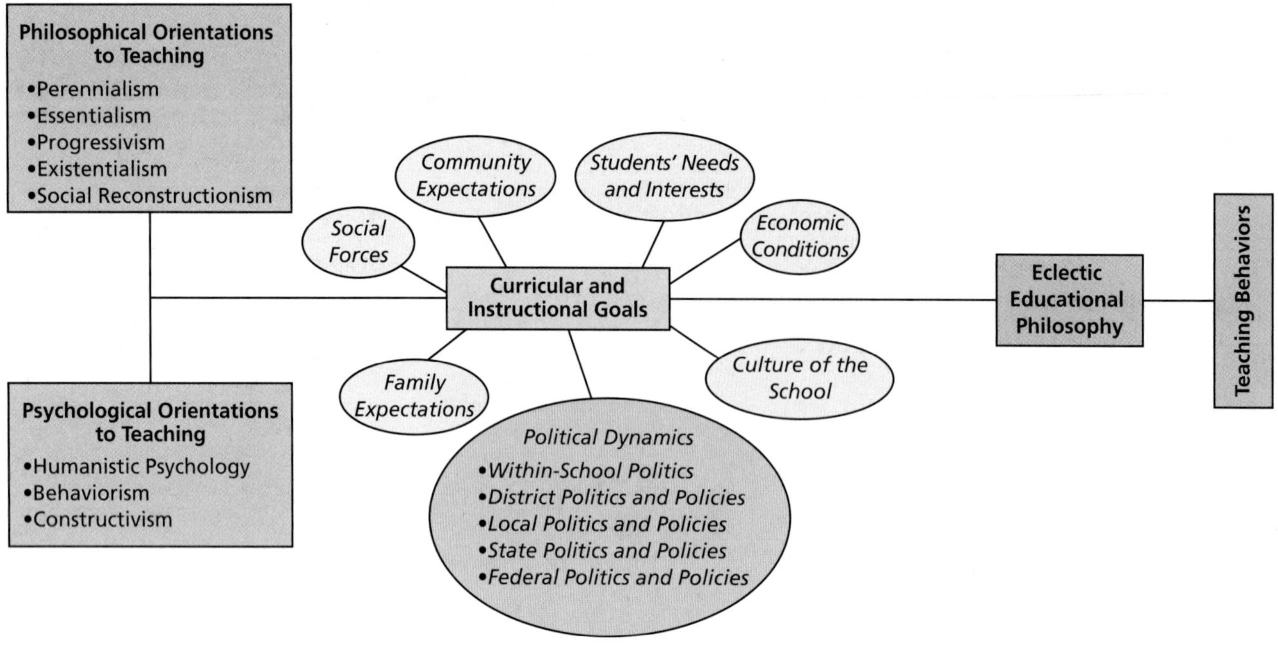

Figure 4.9 Philosophic inventory

The following inventory is to help identify your educational philosophy. Respond to the statements on the scale from 5, "Strongly Agree," to 1, "Strongly Disagree," by circling the number that most closely fits your perspective.

	Strongly Agree				Strongly Disagree
1. The curriculum should emphasize essential knowledge, *not* students' personal interests.	5	4	3	2	1
2. All learning results from rewards controlled by the external environment.	5	4	3	2	1
3. Teachers should emphasize interdisciplinary subject matter that encourages project-oriented, democratic classrooms.	5	4	3	2	1
4. Education should emphasize the search for personal meaning, *not* a fixed body of knowledge.	5	4	3	2	1
5. The ultimate aim of education is constant, absolute, and universal: to develop the rational person and cultivate the intellect.	5	4	3	2	1
6. Schools should actively involve students in social change to reform society.	5	4	3	2	1
7. Schools should teach basic skills, *not* humanistic ideals.	5	4	3	2	1
8. Eventually, human behavior will be explained by scientific laws, proving there is no free will.	5	4	3	2	1
9. Teachers should be facilitators and resources who guide student inquiry, *not* be managers of behavior.	5	4	3	2	1
10. The best teachers encourage personal responses and develop self-awareness in their students.	5	4	3	2	1
11. The curriculum should be the same for everyone: the collective wisdom of Western culture delivered through lecture and discussion.	5	4	3	2	1
12. Schools should lead society toward radical social change, *not* transmit traditional values.	5	4	3	2	1
13. The purpose of schools is to ensure practical preparation for life and work, *not* to encourage personal choice.	5	4	3	2	1
14. The best teachers manage student behavior and accurately measure learning of prescribed objectives.	5	4	3	2	1
15. Curriculum should emerge from students' needs and interests: therefore, it *should not* be prescribed in advance.	5	4	3	2	1
16. Helping students develop personal values is more important than transmitting traditional values.	5	4	3	2	1
17. The best education consists primarily of exposure to great works in the humanities.	5	4	3	2	1
18. It is more important for teachers to involve students in activities to criticize and transform society than to teach the "Great Books."	5	4	3	2	1

Statement	Strongly Agree				Strongly Disagree
19. Schools should emphasize discipline, hard work, and respect for authority, *not* reform society.	5	4	3	2	1
20. Human learning can be controlled: Anyone can be taught to be a scientist or a thief; therefore, personal choice is a myth.	5	4	3	2	1
21. Education should enhance personal growth through problem solving in the present, *not* emphasize preparation for a distant future.	5	4	3	2	1
22. Because we are born with an unformed personality, personal growth should be the focus of education.	5	4	3	2	1
23. The universal constant in human nature is the ability to reason; therefore, the sole focus of education should be to develop reasoning ability.	5	4	3	2	1
24. Schools perpetuate racism and sexism camouflaged as traditional values.	5	4	3	2	1
25. Teachers should efficiently transmit a set fixed body of knowledge, *not* experiment with curriculum.	5	4	3	2	1
26. Teaching is primarily management of student behavior to achieve the teacher's objectives.	5	4	3	2	1
27. Education should involve students in democratic activities and reflective thinking.	5	4	3	2	1
28. Students should have significant involvement in choosing what and how they learn.	5	4	3	2	1
29. Teachers should promote the permanency of the "classics," *not* practical preparation for life.	5	4	3	2	1
30. Learning should lead students to involvement in social reform.	5	4	3	2	1
31. On the whole, school should and must indoctrinate students with traditional values.	5	4	3	2	1
32. If ideas cannot be proved by science, they should be ignored as superstition and nonsense.	5	4	3	2	1
33. The major goal for teachers is to create an environment where students can learn on their own by guided reflection on their experiences.	5	4	3	2	1
34. Teachers should create opportunities for students to make personal choices, *not* shape their behavior.	5	4	3	2	1
35. The aim of education should be the same in every age and society, *not* differ from teacher to teacher.	5	4	3	2	1
36. Education should lead society toward social betterment, *not* confine itself to essential skills.	5	4	3	2	1

Philosophic Inventory Score Sheet

Record the number you circled for each statement (1–36). Total the number horizontally and record it in the space on the far right of the score sheet. The highest total indicates your educational philosophy.

Essentialism

Essentialism was a response to progressivism. It advocates a conservative philosophic perspective. The emphasis is on intellectual and moral standards that should be transmitted by the schools. The core of the curriculum should be essential knowledge and skills. Schooling should be practical and not influence social policy. It is a "back-to-basics" movement that emphasizes facts. Students should be taught discipline, hard work, and respect for authority. Influential essentialists: William C. Bagley, H. G. Rickover, Arthur Bestor, and William Bennett; E. D. Hirsch's *Cultural Literacy* could fit this category.

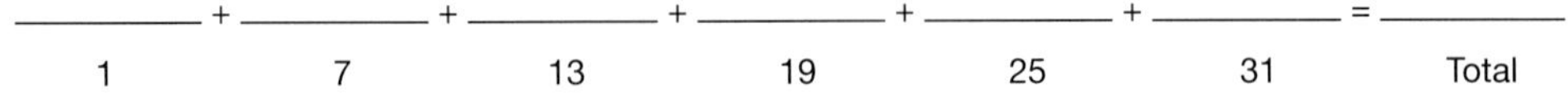

1 7 13 19 25 31 Total

Behaviorism

Behaviorism denies free will and maintains that behavior is the result of external forces, which cause humans to behave in predictable ways. Behaviorism is linked with empiricism, which stresses scientific experiment and observation. Behaviorists are skeptical about metaphysical claims. Behaviorists look for laws governing human behavior the way natural scientists look for empirical laws governing natural events. The role of the teacher is to identify behavioral goals and establish a reward system to achieve goals. Influential behaviorists: B. F. Skinner, Ivan Pavlov, J. B. Watson, and Benjamin Bloom.

2 8 14 20 26 32 Total

Progressivism

Progressivism focuses more on the child than the subject matter. The students' interests and personal growth are important. Learners should be active and learn to solve problems by reflecting on their experiences. The school should help students develop democratic personal and social values. Because society is always changing, new ideas are important to make the future better than the past. Influential progressivists: John Dewey, William Kilpatrick, and Francis Parker.

_________ + _________ + _________ + _________ + _________ + _________ = _________

3 9 15 21 27 33 Total

Existentialism

Existentialism is a highly subjective philosophy that stresses the importance of the individual and emotional commitment to living authentically. It emphasizes individual choice over the importance of rational theories, history, and social institutions. Jean-Paul Sartre, the French philosopher, claimed "Existence precedes essence." Sartre meant that people are born and must define themselves through personal choices. Influential existentialists: Jean-Paul Sartre, Soren Kierkegaard, Martin Buber, Martin Heidegger, Gabriel Marcel, Friedrich Nietzsche, Albert Camus, Carl Rogers, A. S. Neill, and Maxine Greene.

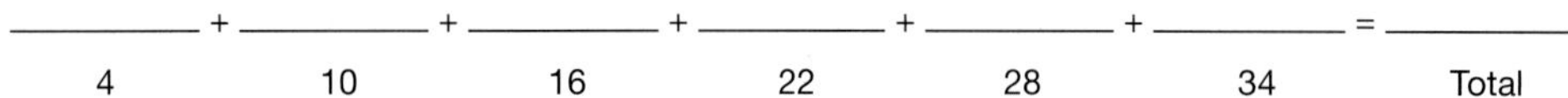

4 10 16 22 28 34 Total

Perennialism

Perennialists advocate that the aim of education is to ensure that students acquire knowledge about the great ideas of Western culture. Human beings are rational, and it is this capacity that needs to be developed. Cultivation of the intellect is the highest priority of an education worth having. The highest level of knowledge in each field should be the focus of curriculum. Influential perennialists: Robert Maynard Hutchins, Mortimer Adler, and Allan Bloom.

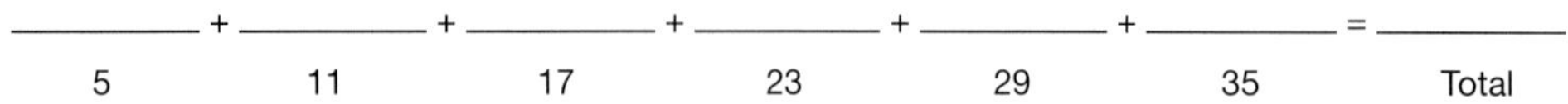

5 11 17 23 29 35 Total

Reconstructionism

Reconstructionists advocate that schools should take the lead to reconstruct society. Schools have more than a responsibility to transmit knowledge; they have the mission to transform society as well. Reconstructionists go beyond progressivists in advocating social activism. Influential reconstructionists: Theodore Brameld, George Counts, Paulo Freire, and Henry Giroux.

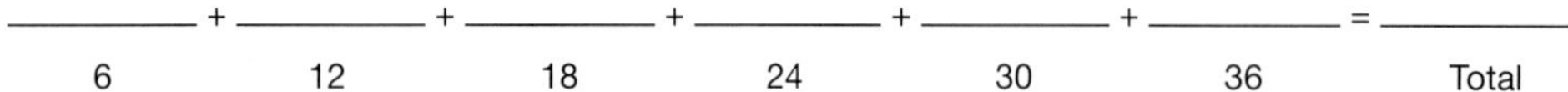

6 12 18 24 30 36 Total

SOURCE: Originally prepared by Robert Leahy for *Becoming a Teacher: Accepting the Challenge of a Profession*, 3d ed., 1995. Revised by the author for inclusion in *Authentic Educating*, 2009, Lanham, MD: University Press of America, Inc., pp. 17–21. Used by permission of the author.

Summary

What Is Philosophy Important to Teachers?

- Knowledge of educational philosophy enables teachers to understand the complex political forces that influence schools, to evaluate more effectively current proposals for change, and to grow professionally. Professional teachers continually strive for a clearer, more comprehensive answer to basic philosophical questions.
- Most schools have a statement of philosophy that describes educational values and goals.
- Philosophy, which means "love of wisdom," is concerned with pondering the fundamental questions of life: What is truth? What is reality? What life is worth living?
- An educational philosophy is a set of beliefs about education, a set of principles to guide professional action.
- A teacher's educational philosophy is made up of personal beliefs about teaching and learning, students, knowledge, and what is worth knowing.

What Are the Branches of Philosophy?

- The branches of philosophy and the questions they address are (1) metaphysics (What is the nature of reality?), (2) epistemology (What is the nature of knowledge and is truth attainable?), (3) axiology (What values should one live by?), (4) ethics (What is good and evil, right and wrong?), (5) aesthetics (What is beautiful?), and (6) logic (What reasoning processes yield valid conclusions?).

What Are Five Modern Philosophical Orientations to Teaching?

- **Perennialism**—Students should acquire knowledge of enduring great ideas.
- **Essentialism**—Schools should teach students, in a disciplined and systematic way, a core of "essential" knowledge and skills.
- **Progressivism**—The aim of education should be based on the needs and interests of students.
- **Existentialism**—In the face of an indifferent universe, students should acquire an education that will enable them to assign meaning to their lives. Postmodernism, which is similar to existentialism, maintains that there are no absolute truths and disputes the certainty of scientific, or objective, explanations of reality.

- **Social reconstructionism**—In response to the significant social problems of the day, schools should take the lead in creating a new social order. Critical pedagogy, much like social reconstructionism, focuses on how education can promote social justice, especially for those who do not enjoy positions of power and influence in society. Feminist pedagogy, also similar to social reconstructionism, maintains that different voices and different ways of knowing tend not to be acknowledged in classrooms that are dominated by Eurocentric, patriarchal curricula.

What Psychological Orientations Have Influenced Teaching Philosophies?

- **Humanism**—Children are innately good, and education should focus on individual needs, personal freedom, and self-actualization.
- **Behaviorism**—By careful control of the educational environment and with appropriate reinforcement techniques, teachers can cause students to exhibit desired behaviors.
- **Constructivism**—Teachers should "understand students' understanding" and view learning as an active process in which learners construct meaning.

How Can You Develop Your Educational Philosophy?

- Instead of basing their teaching on only one educational philosophy, most teachers develop an eclectic educational philosophy.
- Professional teachers continually strive for a clearer, more comprehensive answer to basic philosophical questions.

Professional Reflections And Activities

Teacher's Journal

1. To illustrate educational philosophies in action, this chapter presents "portraits" of eight different teachers. Imagine that you are a colleague of one of these teachers—a teacher whose educational philosophy is very different from your own. Write that teacher a letter in which you react to his or her philosophical orientation to teaching. Your letter might include questions or concerns about the teacher's educational philosophy, as well as an explanation of why your educational philosophy is more appropriate for today's students.
2. Review the six philosophical and five psychological orientations discussed in this chapter. With reference to today's schools, what is the current status of each—that is, is it widespread or not? Which orientation do you think is most popular among teachers? Least popular?
3. Recall one of your favorite teachers at the elementary, middle, or high school levels. Which of the educational philosophies or psychological orientations to teaching described in this chapter best capture that teacher's approach to teaching? Write a descriptive sketch of that teacher in action. How has this teacher influenced your educational philosophy?

Teacher's Research

1. Numerous organizations influence educational policy and practice in the United States. Visit the websites of two or more of the following organizations and compare the educational philosophies that are reflected in their goals, position statements, and political activities with regard to education:
   - Alternative Public Schools Inc. (APS)
   - American Federation of Teachers (AFT)
   - National Education Association (NEA)
   - Chicago Teachers Union (or other municipal teachers' organization)
   - National Congress of Parents and Teachers (PTA)
   - Parents as Teachers (PAT)
   - Texas State Teachers Association (or other state teachers' organization)
2. Explore encyclopedias, bibliographies, periodicals, news sources, and other online reference works to research in greater detail the contributions of one of the educational philosophers included in this chapter. In a brief oral report, present your findings to the rest of your class.

Observations and Interviews

1. Interview a teacher for the purpose of understanding his or her educational philosophy. Formulate your interview questions in light of the philosophical concepts discussed in this chapter and the questions posed at the beginning of this chapter. What should the purpose(s) of education be? What knowledge is of most worth? What values should teachers encourage their students to develop? How should learning be evaluated? Discuss your findings with classmates.
2. Observe the class of a teacher at the level at which you plan to teach. Which of the six philosophies or five psychological orientations to teaching discussed in this chapter most characterizes this teacher? Describe the teacher–student interactions that result in your response.

Professional Portfolio

Each month, prepare a written (or videotaped) statement in which you explain one of the following key elements of your educational philosophy (see Figure 4.1, on page 103). At the end of 5 months, you should have a statement for each set of beliefs.

- Beliefs about teaching and learning
- Beliefs about students
- Beliefs about knowledge
- Beliefs about what is worth knowing
- Personal beliefs in philosophical areas

As appropriate, revise your belief statements throughout the course and during the remainder of your teacher education program. On completion of your teacher education program, review your portfolio entry and make any appropriate revisions. The ability to provide a full explanation of your philosophy of education will be a definite advantage when you begin to look for your first job as a teacher.

Shared Writing 4.1
Philosophical Foundations of U.S. Education

Chapter 5

Historical Foundations of U.S. Education

Susan Montgomery/Shutterstock

Learning Outcomes

After reading this chapter, you will be able to do the following:

5.1 Explain how European education influenced teaching and schools in the American colonies (1620–1750).

5.2 Explain approaches to education during the Revolutionary period (1750–1820).

5.3 Explain how state-supported common schools emerged (1820–1865) and describe how compulsory education changed schools and teaching (1865–1920).

5.4 Explain how education changed during the progressive era (1920–1945) and the modern postwar era (1945–2000).

5.5 Explain the educational issues and priorities of the 21st century (2000 to the present).

READERS' VOICES

Why is educational history important?

Educational history helps us understand how schools have evolved—how our country has continuously sought to improve schools. Also, educational history serves as a guide for what we must do today to continue that improvement and to provide a quality education for all students.

—ALIANNA,
Teacher Education program, first year

In *The Life of Reason*, George Santayana said, "Those who cannot remember the past are condemned to repeat it." For teachers, the implication of this statement is clear—the past has an impact on teaching and schools today. Accomplished teachers learn from our nation's educational past. They know that educational practices from the past have not disappeared—they continue to evolve, and they shape the present, as well as the future.

We cannot understand schools today without a look at what they were yesterday. Today's teachers must be students of our educational past so they can provide leadership to improve our educational future. For example, the history of education in the United States reveals countless examples of how political forces, social class, special-interest groups, religion, and cultural and ethnic diversity have influenced schools; and professional teachers understand these influences.

The current system of public and private education in the United States is an ongoing reflection of its historical foundations and of the aspirations and values brought to this country by its founders and generations of settlers. Thus it is impossible to understand schools today without a look at what they were yesterday. Becoming familiar with events that have shaped the quest for educational quality and equity in the United States is an important part of your education as a professional.

Still, you may wonder, what is the value of knowing about the history of U.S. education? Will that knowledge help you to be a better teacher? First, knowledge of the events that have influenced our schools will help you evaluate more effectively current proposals for change. You will understand how schools have developed and how current proposals might relate to previous change efforts.

Second, awareness of events that have influenced teaching is a hallmark of professionalism in education. Just as an effective democracy demands enlightened, aware citizens, so, too, does a profession require knowledgeable professionals. The critical role teachers play in preserving our democracy was highlighted by the president of the American Federation of Teachers during the politically tumultuous first six months of 2017: "If the next generation is to defend democratic institutions, our students must learn from the past. Who better to teach them than America's educators?" (Weingarten, 2017).

This chapter begins with a brief description of some of the European influences on U.S. education. Next, the chapter presents brief overviews of seven periods of education in the United States. Each section examines the individuals, social forces, and events that, in the author's judgment, have had the greatest impact on schools in our country.

How Did European Education Influence Teaching and Schools in the American Colonies (1620–1750)?

Many practices in today's schools originated in much earlier societies throughout the world. Non-Western civilizations in ancient Egypt, China, and India, for example, emphasized the need for practical education in mathematics, astronomy, medicine, engineering, agriculture, and geography. Similarly, early Western civilizations emphasized the role of education in preparing children and youth for their roles as adults in society. The timeline in Figure 5.1 shows major events and individuals in Europe that had an impact on the development of education in 17th-century colonial America. This section presents (1) an overview of education in Greece and Rome, (2) a brief glimpse of the kaleidoscope of European history from the fall of Rome to the start of the 18th century, and (3) a review of how four 18th-century European thinkers influenced education in colonial America.

Figure 5.1 European influences on American education, 5000 B.C.–1900 A.D.

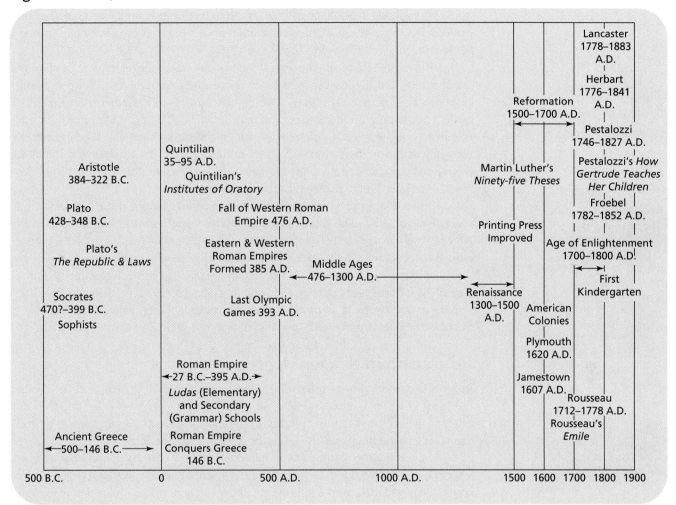

Aristotle 384–322 B.C.
Plato 428–348 B.C.
Plato's *The Republic & Laws*
Socrates 470?–399 B.C.
Sophists
Ancient Greece ←500–146 B.C.→
Quintilian 35–95 A.D.
Quintilian's *Institutes of Oratory*
Fall of Western Roman Empire 476 A.D.
Eastern & Western Roman Empires Formed 385 A.D.
Middle Ages ←476–1300 A.D.→
Last Olympic Games 393 A.D.
Roman Empire ←27 B.C.–395 A.D.→
Ludas (Elementary) and Secondary (Grammar) Schools
Roman Empire Conquers Greece 146 B.C.
Reformation 1500–1700 A.D.
Martin Luther's *Ninety-five Theses*
Printing Press Improved
Renaissance 1300–1500 A.D.
American Colonies
Plymouth 1620 A.D.
Jamestown 1607 A.D.
Lancaster 1778–1883 A.D.
Herbart 1776–1841 A.D.
Pestalozzi 1746–1827 A.D.
Pestalozzi's *How Gertrude Teaches Her Children*
Froebel 1782–1852 A.D.
Age of Enlightenment 1700–1800 A.D.
First Kindergarten
Rousseau 1712–1778 A.D.
Rousseau's *Emile*
500 B.C. | 0 | 500 A.D. | 1000 A.D. | 1500 | 1600 | 1700 | 1800 | 1900

Education in Ancient Greece

Education in ancient Greece (500–146 B.C.) has had an enduring impact on today's schools. The Greeks believed that people should use leisure time to reflect on the practical and aesthetic values of life. Based on principles of moderation and balance, the goal of Greek education was the well-rounded development of mind and body.

Although the pursuit of knowledge by the ancient Greeks is worthy of imitation, other facets of this ancient civilization conflict with the values and goals of today's society. For example, the leisure enjoyed by the small middle and upper classes in ancient Greece was made possible by a vast population of slaves, and women were not eligible to become citizens.

Several philosophers in ancient Greece shaped ideas about the relationship between education and life. Perhaps the greatest contributions were made by Socrates (ca. 470–399 B.C.), Plato (428–348 B.C.), and Aristotle (384–322 B.C.).

SOCRATES What little we know about Socrates comes to us from his portrayal in the *Dialogues* written by his student, Plato. Socrates' questioning strategies, his emphasis on discussion to promote inquiry, and his quest for virtue are reflected in today's teaching practices. Socrates questioned his students in a manner that led them to see errors and inconsistencies in their thinking. By using an inductive approach, Socrates believed that the truth could be discovered. **Socratic questioning**, according to contemporary educational philosopher Mortimer Adler (1982), is essential for the study of six great ideas: truth, beauty, goodness, liberty, equality, and justice. By questioning students repeatedly, Socrates led his students to these eternal truths.

PLATO AND ARISTOTLE A student and disciple of Socrates, Plato believed that the individual's abilities should be developed through education for the good of society. To promote his views among Athenians, Plato founded the free, coeducational Academy, often referred to as the world's first university.

Plato believed that boys and girls should be educated from age 6 to 18, with music, mathematics, and gymnastics the main areas of study. Music was a source of "noble" emotions and included the study of literature and history. Mathematics linked the powers of reason with the processes of nature and enabled one to influence the environment. And gymnastics, which emphasized physical and mental well-being, included the study of dance, rhythm, athletics, and military arts. Taken together, the aim of this three-part curriculum was to improve the soul and enable the individual to achieve moral excellence and to realize the ultimate good.

Aristotle, Plato's most famous student, studied and taught at the Academy for 20 years. Whereas Plato was an idealist and believed that ideas are the ultimate reality, Aristotle was a realist and believed that reality, knowledge, and value exist in the physical world independent of the mind. Goodness and virtue depend on deeds, not knowledge.

Like Plato, Aristotle believed that society needed a strong system of education. Aristotle supported education for all Athenian citizens; however, the majority of Athens' inhabitants were not citizens. Women, for example, were ineligible for citizenship because it was felt they lacked the rational capacities for citizenship and wisdom.

Education in Ancient Rome

In 146 B.C., Greece was conquered by a Roman army. In 27 B.C., Augustus established the Roman Empire, which continued until A.D. 395, when it was divided into the Western Roman Empire, with the capital at Rome, and the Eastern Roman Empire, with the capital at Constantinople. In A.D. 476, the Roman Empire fell.

Roman education was heavily influenced by Greek education. The Roman school system consisted of the *ludus,* or elementary school, and a secondary or grammar school. Boys and girls aged 7 to 12 attended the *ludi*, where they learned to read, write, and compute. The education of girls seldom went beyond the *ludus*. Upper-class boys aged 12 to 16 attended grammar schools, where they studied Greek or Latin grammar and literature. Boys aged 16 to 20 attended a school of rhetoric, where they studied grammar, rhetoric, dialectic, music, arithmetic, geometry, and astronomy.

From the Middle Ages to the Renaissance

The period from the fall of the Roman Empire to the 14th century is known as the Middle Ages, or medieval times. During the medieval period, the Roman Catholic Church came to have the greatest influence on education in Europe. For the most part, the prevailing class structure based on feudalism was not fertile ground for the growth of schools during the Middle Ages. However, the clergy received instruction in the monasteries and at cathedral schools, and medieval universities were established in Spain, France, and England.

A rebirth of interest in Greco-Roman traditions of art, literature, and learning began in the 14th century and reached a peak in the 15th century. This period, known as the Renaissance, began in northern Europe and Italy and spread throughout Europe.

The key to improving the human condition, according to Renaissance humanists, was to transfer wealth and power from the Church to the people. In addition, humanists believed that an educational system similar to ancient Rome's should be created. They also believed that instruction should consist of the study of ancient classical literature, particularly the work of Plato and Aristotle. The ideal curriculum of the time was based on the seven liberal arts: the *trivium* of grammar, logic, and rhetoric, and the *quadrivium* of arithmetic, geometry, astronomy, and music. Figure 5.2 illustrates the seven liberal arts, with Socrates and Plato in the inner circle.

Figure 5.2 The Seven Liberal Arts

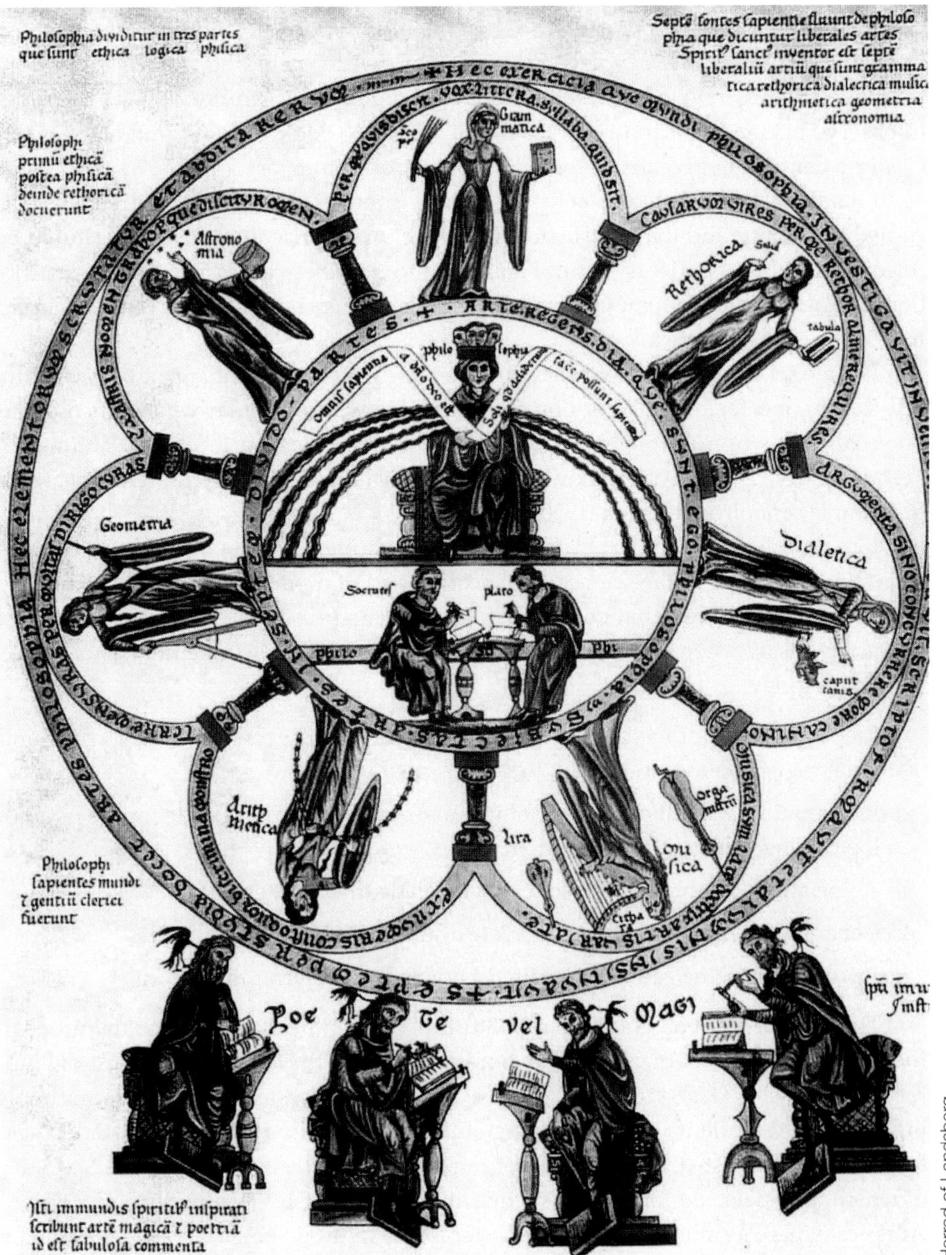

Herrad of Landsberg

SOURCE: https://upload.wikimedia.org/wikipedia/commons/7/71/Septem-artes-liberales_Herrad-von-Landsberg_Hortus-deliciarum_1180.jpg

Educational Thought in 18th-Century Europe

The Reformation, with its questioning of religious doctrines, revived interest in the scientific understanding of nature. The 18th century came to be known as the Age of Enlightenment or the Age of Reason because reasoning and scientific inquiry were being used to improve society. European thinkers of the 1700s have had a lasting impact on education in the United States.

Jean-Jacques Rousseau (1712–1778), considered by some to be the "father of modern child psychology" (Mayer, 1973), believed that children progressed through stages of growth and development. According to Rousseau, knowledge of these stages should guide the development of instructional strategies. Rousseau also believed in the innate goodness of children—a natural goodness that society corrupts. Rousseau's child-centered educational theories influenced many educators in France and beyond. For example, John Dewey, whose educational philosophy shaped the progressive education movement in the United States from 1920–1945, was influenced by Rousseau.

Johann Heinrich Pestalozzi (1746–1827) was a Swiss educator who implemented many of Rousseau's ideas. Noted educators worldwide, including Horace Mann from the United States, traveled to Pestalozzi's experimental school in Yverdon, Switzerland, to observe his methods and learn from him. His 1826 book, *How Gertrude Teaches Her Children,* contributed greatly to the development of elementary schools.

Like Rousseau, Pestalozzi believed that the innate goodness of children was corrupted by society, and that instructional practices and curriculum materials should be selected in light of students' natural abilities and readiness to learn. Effective instruction, Pestalozzi believed, moved from concrete experiences to abstract concepts, from the simple to the complex.

Pestalozzi also recognized that children's learning was enhanced by a healthy self-esteem and feelings of emotional security. He was particularly concerned about poor children whom he believed needed to feel loved by their teachers. Paintings of Pestalozzi from that era often showed him lovingly embracing the children of peasants in a simple schoolroom (Ulich, 1950).

Johann Friedrich Herbart (1776–1841) was a student of Pestalozzi's and became known as the father of the science of education and of modern psychology (Schubert, 1986). Herbart believed that education should focus primarily on developing moral character. His five-step systematic approach for presenting new material to students is still in use today:

1. Preparation: helping students make connections between what they know and what they are about to learn.
2. Presentation: introducing material in a manner that is appropriate for the psychological development of the student.
3. Association: combining new and previously learned material.
4. Generalization: moving from concrete examples to abstract principles.
5. Application: using recently acquired knowledge to learn more.

The development of schools in the 18th and 19th centuries was related to European industrialization, urbanization, and population growth. For example, in England, Joseph Lancaster (1778–1838) developed a **monitorial system** for crowded schools in which older students taught younger students. According to the Lancasterian system, one teacher instructed hundreds of pupils through the use of student monitors—older students selected for their academic abilities. Lancaster eventually emigrated to America, where monitorial schools spread rapidly in urban areas after the first school opened in New York City in 1806.

Teaching and Schools in the American Colonies (1620–1750)

Education in colonial America had its primary roots in English culture. The settlers of our country initially tried to develop a system of schooling that paralleled the British two-track system. If students from the lower classes attended school at all, it was at the elementary level for the purpose of acquiring practical skills in reading, writing, and computation and receiving religious instruction. Students from the upper classes had the opportunity to attend Latin grammar schools, where they were given a college-preparatory education that focused on subjects such as Latin and Greek classics.

Above all, the colonial curriculum stressed religious objectives. Generally, no distinction was made between secular and religious life in the colonies. The religious motives that impelled the Puritans to endure the hardships of settling in a new land were reflected in the schools' curricula. The primary objective of elementary schooling was to learn to read so that one might read the Bible and religious catechisms and thereby receive salvation and spend eternity in heaven.

THE STATUS OF TEACHERS Because those who taught in colonial schools could do so with minimal qualifications—and for little pay—their status was relatively low. Respect increased with grade level and the amount of education required for the position. Elementary school teachers, the majority of whom had no more than an elementary education themselves, were given the least respect, and teachers in the few secondary schools were accorded the highest status.

Colonial teachers were "special but shadowed," according to Dan Lortie (1975). Because teachers, and members of the clergy, were educated, they were "special" and expected to have high moral character. On the other hand, teachers were "shadowed" because they were subordinate to the clergy, the power elite in the community. Teachers' extra duties reflected their marginal status: For example, teachers had to ring church bells, sweep classrooms, teach Bible lessons, and even fill in for a sick pastor (Lortie, 1975).

North Wind Picture Archives/Alamy Stock Photo

What textbooks might students have used in this early classroom? What educational beliefs and values were reflected in the curriculum and instruction of this period?

Teaching was also shadowed by what was seen as the "real" work of the community—farming. Farming was vital to the community. Though male teachers were preferred by the community, men were needed to work on the farms during the warmer months. Thus, women were recruited as teachers (Lightfoot, 1978).

COLONIAL SCHOOLS In the New England colonies (Massachusetts Bay, New Hampshire, and Connecticut), there was a general consensus that church, state, and schools were interrelated. As a result, town schools were created throughout these colonies to teach children the basics of reading and writing so they could learn the scriptures. These schools were heavily influenced by the Puritans, a group of Protestants who believed in strict religious discipline and simplified religious ceremonies.

The Puritan view of the child included the belief that people are inherently sinful. Even natural childhood play was seen as devil-inspired idleness. The path to redemption lay in learning to curb one's natural instincts and behave like an adult as quickly as possible.

To bring about this premature growth, the teacher had to correct the child constantly and try to curb his or her natural instincts. Colonial schoolmasters viewed children as miniature adults who were morally corrupt. School lessons, therefore, were harsh and dogmatic. Poorly trained, ill-tempered teachers meted out strict discipline. Students who broke rules were physically punished with whips, canes, paddles, and rods.

The middle colonies (New York, New Jersey, Pennsylvania, and Delaware) were more diverse, and groups such as the Irish, Scots, Swedes, Danes, Dutch, and Germans established **parochial schools** based on their religious beliefs. Anglicans, Lutherans, Quakers, Jews, Catholics, Presbyterians, and Mennonites in the middle colonies tended to establish their own schools. In the largely Protestant southern colonies (Virginia, Maryland, Georgia, and North and South Carolina), wealthy plantation owners believed the primary purpose of education was to promote religion and to prepare their children to attend colleges and universities in Europe. The vast majority of small farmers received no formal schooling, and the children of African slaves received only the training they needed to serve their masters.

No one type of schooling was common to all the colonies. The most common types, however, were the dame schools, the reading and writing schools, and the Latin grammar schools.

THE DAME SCHOOLS Dame schools provided initial instruction for boys and often the only schooling for girls. These schools were run by widows or housewives in their homes and supported by modest fees from parents. At **dame schools**, classes were usually held in the kitchen, where children learned only the barest essentials of reading, writing, and arithmetic during instruction lasting for a few weeks to one year. Girls might also be taught sewing and basic homemaking skills.

Students often began by learning the alphabet from a hornbook. Developed in medieval Europe, the **hornbook** was a copy of the alphabet written on parchment and covered by a thin transparent sheet made from a cow's horn. This sheet of horn protected the parchment from damage by students' hands. The alphabet and the horn covering were attached to a paddle-shaped piece of wood. Students often hung their hornbooks around their necks with a leather cord threaded through a hole in the paddle.

READING AND WRITING SCHOOLS At **reading and writing schools**, boys received an education that went beyond what their parents could teach them at home or what they could learn at a dame school. Reading lessons were based on the Bible, various religious catechisms, and the *New England Primer*, first printed in 1690. The *Primer* introduced children to the letters of the alphabet through the use of illustrative woodcuts and rhymed couplets. The first couplet began with the pronouncement that

> *In Adam's fall*
> *We sinned all.*

And the final one noted that

> *Zaccheus he*
> *Did climb the Tree*
> *His Lord to see.*

The *Primer* also presented children with large doses of stern religious warnings about the proper conduct of life.

LATIN GRAMMAR SCHOOLS The Boston Latin School was founded in 1635 to provide a pre-college education for the new country's future leaders. At a mass meeting that April, the residents of Boston decided to open the school in the home of Philemon Pormont, who served as schoolmaster. The **Latin grammar school**, comparable to today's secondary school, was patterned after the classical schools of Europe. Boys enrolled in the Latin grammar schools at the age of seven or eight, whereupon they began to prepare to enter Harvard College (established in 1636). Following graduation from Harvard, they would assume leadership roles in the church.

At first, grammar schools were seven-year schools; later, they were made into four-year schools. The quality of teaching in the Latin grammar schools was higher than that found in the dame schools or reading and writing schools. In addition, grammar school teachers assumed that students had learned to read and write, either at home or in dame schools.

Latin and Greek were the principal studies in these schools, although arithmetic was introduced in 1745. Students were required to read Latin authors and to speak Latin in poetry and prose as well as conjugate Greek verbs. Both the curriculum and the mode of instruction in Latin schools were rigorous. The course of study was seven years, and school was in session six days a week, winter through summer. The school day ran from 6:00 to 11:00 in the morning and 1:00 to 4:00 or 5:00 in the afternoon, and boys sat on hard wooden benches (Rippa, 1984).

Teachers relied on the *memoriter* method of drill and rote learning. Through repeated recitations, students learned to respond with definite answers to specific questions. The schoolmaster would often hit a student for a poor recitation. Class discussions were not allowed, and school rules specified the type and amount of corporal punishment for fighting, lying, cursing, and playing cards or throwing dice (Rippa, 1984).

SCHOOLS FOR AFRICAN AMERICANS AND NATIVE AMERICANS One of the first schools for African Americans and Native Americans was started by Elias Neau in New York City in 1704. Neau spoke out against slavery and the lack of education for the children of the slaves. When he asked the Church of England to provide a teacher, church leaders appointed him to teach African Americans and Native Americans how to read as part of the church's efforts to convert students (Pierre, 1916).

THE ORIGINS OF MANDATED EDUCATION As today's citizens know, compulsory education laws require that parents, or those who have custody of children between certain ages, send their children to school. During the colonial era, however, this was not the case.

Universal compulsory education had its origins in the **Massachusetts Act of 1642**, viewed by some as the first school law in the colonies (Urban & Wagoner, 2013). Prior to this date, parents could decide whether they wished their children to be educated at home or at a school. Church and civic leaders in the colonies, however, decided that education could no longer remain voluntary. They saw that many children were receiving inadequate occupational training. Moreover, they realized that organized schools would serve to strengthen and preserve Puritan religious beliefs.

The Puritans decided to make education a civil responsibility of the state. The Massachusetts General Court passed a law in 1642 that required each town to determine whether young people could read and write. Parents and apprentices' masters whose children were unable to read and understand basic religious doctrines and the laws of the country could be fined and possibly lose custody of their children.

Although the Massachusetts Act of 1642 did not mandate the establishment of schools, it did make it clear that the education of children was a direct concern of the local citizenry. In 1648, the court revised the 1642 law, reminding town leaders that "the good education of children is of singular behoof and benefit to any commonwealth" and that some parents and masters were still "too indulgent and negligent of their duty" (Cohen, 1974, pp. 394–395). As the first educational law in this country, the Massachusetts Act of 1642 was a landmark.

The **Massachusetts Act of 1647**, often referred to as the Old Deluder Satan Act (because education was seen as the best protection against the wiles of the devil), mandated the establishment and support of schools. In particular, towns of 50 households or more were to appoint a person to instruct all children to read and write. Teachers were to be paid by parents or guardians of children, or by the townspeople (Rippa, 1997). This act also required towns of 100 households or more to establish a Latin grammar school to prepare students for Harvard College. A town that failed to satisfy this law could be assessed a fine of five pounds.

Support for mandated education was later expanded by passage of the Northwest Ordinance in 1785, which gave federal land to the states for educational purposes. The Ordinance divided the Northwest Territories (now Illinois, Indiana, Michigan, Ohio, Wisconsin, and part of Minnesota) into 36-square-mile sections, with the 16th square mile designated for public schools.

Teaching on Your Feet

Worth the Struggle

"If there is no struggle, there is no progress." Frederick Douglass's words apply not only to history but also to teaching. When I first became a teacher, I thought I would enter the classroom and instantly inspire all of my students to fall in love with American history. Although I have taught many students who eventually come to appreciate history, I have also struggled with student issues that transcend academic subject matter; indeed, the biggest challenge most teachers encounter is unmotivated students.

I remember one unmotivated student especially well. Frank (not his real name) arrived in the middle of the year, when my classroom was running smoothly and all of my students were accustomed to my classroom policies and procedures. Frank had long hair that nearly covered his face, kept his head down, and rarely looked me in the eye. I quickly realized that Frank was not just unmotivated; he was also emotionally troubled. He was moody and frequently missed school, and when I asked him a question, he would usually shrug his shoulders and whisper, "I don't care." He was falling behind in his schoolwork and was unresponsive to the motivational speeches I often gave when students failed to turn in a homework assignment. Despite his behavior, I wanted to help Frank. I offered him individual attention through after-school tutoring.

To ensure that Frank received proper help, I shared my concerns with the school psychologist. She met with Frank and suggested that I could best help Frank by listening to him and showing a genuine interest in him and his life. I decided to ignore his antisocial behavior and treat him as if he were the most interesting student in class.

The tutoring sessions turned out to be the perfect environment to get to know Frank well. Initially, Frank was very quiet and withdrawn. The first few tutoring sessions were very mechanical: I reviewed a lesson with him, then he would work on the homework. During lessons, I tried to relate the material to his life. I tried to connect history with his life in the here and now. Although it took some time, he slowly began to open up and to talk to me about his life and family. I took the time to listen and to relate his experiences to a lesson.

After two months of tutoring sessions, I began to see an improvement in Frank's mood. He was still shy, but he started answering questions in class and showing an interest in American history. At the end of the school year, Frank participated in the eighth-grade promotion ceremony. Afterward, to my surprise, he handed me a card. I read the card later that evening. It was a simple message thanking me for being kind to him.

Analyze

I originally thought I had helped Frank academically, but I came to realize that I had helped him personally, too. What meant more to Frank than any mere history lesson was the attention and kindness shown to him by a teacher. As teachers, we must always remember that students are people first and that personal kindness can make kids want to succeed. Having an unmotivated student is a challenge, but the progress you can make in a student's life by caring is worth it.

Reflect

1. Was contacting the school psychologist an appropriate step? Why or why not?
2. What other strategies can teachers use to connect with discouraged or withdrawn students?
3. How can middle and high school teachers compliment their students without causing them to be made fun of or even ridiculed by their peers?

ELIZABETH GUBBINS
Las Palmas Middle School Covina, **CALIFORNIA**
Used with Permission.

What Were the Goals of Education During the Revolutionary Period (1750–1820)?

Education in the United States during the Revolutionary period was characterized by a general decline of European influences on schools. Religious traditions that had their origins in Europe continued to affect the curriculum; however, the young country's need to develop agriculture, shipping, and commerce also exerted an influence on the curriculum. By this time, the original settlers who had emigrated from Europe had been replaced by a new generation whose most immediate roots were in the new soil of the United States. This new, exclusively American identity was enhanced by the rise of civil town governments, the great increase in books and newspapers that addressed life in the new country, and a turning away from Europe toward the unsettled West. The colonies' break with Europe was most potently demonstrated in the American Revolution of 1776.

Following independence, many leaders were concerned that new disturbances from within could threaten the well-being of the new nation. Among these leaders were Benjamin Franklin, Sarah Pierce, Thomas Jefferson, and Noah Webster. To preserve the freedoms that had been fought for, a system of education became essential. Through education, people would become intelligent, participating citizens of a constitutional democracy.

Benjamin Franklin's Academy

Benjamin Franklin (1706–1790) designed and promoted the Philadelphia Academy, a private secondary school, which opened in 1751. This school, which replaced the old Latin grammar school, had a curriculum that was broader and more practical and also focused on the English language rather than Latin. The academy was also a more democratically run institution than previous schools had been. Although **academies** were largely privately controlled and privately financed, they were secular and often supported by public funds. Most academies were public because anyone who could pay tuition could attend, regardless of church affiliation (Rippa, 1997).

In his *Proposals Relating to the Education of Youth in Pennsylvania*, written in 1749, Franklin noted that "the good Education of youth has been esteemed by wise men in all ages, as the surest foundation of the happiness both of private families and of commonwealths" (Franklin, 1931, p. 151).

Franklin's proposals for educating youth called for a wide range of subjects that emphasized the classics as well as practical knowledge and skills: English grammar, composition, and literature; classical and modern foreign languages; science; writing and drawing; rhetoric and oratory; geography; various kinds of history; agriculture and gardening; arithmetic and accounting; and mechanics.

Education for Girls

English academies, often called people's colleges, multiplied across the country, reaching a peak of 6,185 in 1855, with an enrollment of 263,096 (Spring, 2013). Usually, these academies served boys only; a notable exception was Sarah Pierce's Litchfield Female Academy in Litchfield, Connecticut. Pierce (1767–1852) began her academy in the dining room of her home with two students; eventually, the academy grew to 140 girls from nearly every state and from Canada (Button & Provenzo, 1989).

For the most part, however, girls received little formal education in the 17th and 18th centuries and were educated for entirely different purposes than were boys. As the following mission statement for Pierce's Academy suggests, a curriculum that emphasized practical knowledge and skills, rather than the classics, was appropriate for girls:

> Our object has been, not to make learned ladies, or skillful metaphysical reasoners, or deep read scholars in physical science: there is a more useful, tho' less exalted and less brilliant station that woman must occupy, there are duties of incalculable importance that she must perform: that station is home; these duties are the alleviation of the trials of her parents; the soothing of the labours & fatigues of her partner; & the education for time and eternity of the next generation of immortal beings. (Button & Provenzo, 1989, p. 88)

Some women enrolled in **female seminaries**, first established in the early 19th century to train women for higher education and public service outside the home. Educational opportunities for women expanded in conjunction with social reform movements that gradually led to greater political equality for women, including the right to vote in the 20th century. For example, Troy Seminary, founded in 1821 by educator and poet Emma Willard (1787–1870), became one of the first women's colleges in the country.

Thomas Jefferson's Philosophy

Thomas Jefferson (1743–1826), author of the Declaration of Independence, viewed the education of common people as the most effective means of preserving liberty. Providing basic education to citizens, he believed, was necessary in order "to raise the mass of the people to the high ground of moral respectability necessary to their own safety, and to orderly government" (Urban & Wagoner, 2009, p. 83).

Jefferson was born at Shadwell, Virginia, to a father who was a member of Virginia's landed gentry. Educated at the College of William and Mary, the second college to open in America, Jefferson went on to become one of this country's most influential leaders. Author of the Declaration of Independence at age 33, he also served the public as a member of the Virginia legislature, governor of Virginia, minister to France, secretary of state, vice president, and two-term president of the United States. His life demonstrated his wholehearted dedication to education. He was fluent in Latin, Greek, and many modern languages. He was strongly influenced by the work of the English philosopher John Locke, various British ideas on constitutional law, and the writings of French educators.

Jefferson was dedicated to human freedom and repulsed by any form of tyranny or absolutism. "I have sworn," he once said, "eternal hostility against every form of tyranny over the mind of man" (Rippa, 1984, p. 68). Toward this end, Jefferson was decidedly influential in the intellectual and educational circles of his day. He was a member of the American Academy of Arts and Sciences and president of the American Philosophical Society.

For a society to remain free, Jefferson felt, it must support a continuous system of public education. He proposed to the Virginia legislature in 1779 his Bill for the More General Diffusion of Knowledge. This plan called for state-controlled elementary schools that would teach, with no cost to parents, three years of reading, writing, and arithmetic to all White children. In addition, 20 state grammar schools would be created in which selected poor students would be taught free for a maximum period of six years. Jefferson's plan departed somewhat from the practical orientation of Franklin because the grammar schools would teach boys a more academic curriculum: English grammar, Greek, Latin, geography, and advanced arithmetic.

Jefferson was unsuccessful in his attempt to convince the Virginia House of Burgesses of the need for a uniform system of public schools as outlined in his bill. Jefferson was able to implement many of his educational ideas, however, through his efforts to found the University of Virginia. He devoted the last years of his life to developing the university, and he lived to see the university open with 40 students in March 1824, a month before his 81st birthday.

Application Exercise 5.1
Franklin and Jefferson's Legacy for United States Education

Textbooks and American Values

In the years following the Revolution, several textbooks were printed in the United States. Writers and publishers saw the textbook as an appropriate vehicle for promoting democratic ideals and cultural independence from England. Toward this end, U.S. textbooks were filled with patriotic and moralistic maxims. Among the most widely circulated books of this type were Noah Webster's *Elementary Spelling Book* and *The American Dictionary*.

Born in Connecticut, Noah Webster (1758–1843) had successful careers as a lawyer, writer, politician, and schoolmaster. He first introduced his speller in 1783 under the cumbersome title *A Grammatical Institute of the English Language*. Later versions were titled the *American Spelling Book* and the *Elementary Spelling Book*. Webster's speller earned the nickname "the old blue-back" because early copies of the book were covered in light blue paper and later editions were covered with bright blue paper.

In the introduction to his speller, Webster declared that its purpose was to help teachers instill in students "the first rudiments of the language, some just ideas of religion, morals and domestic economy" (Button & Provenzo, 1989, p. 65). Throughout, the little book emphasized patriotic and moralistic virtues. Short, easy-to-remember maxims taught pupils to be content with their lot in life, to work hard, and to respect the property of others. Readers were cautioned to "prefer solid sense to vain wit" and to "let no jest intrude to violate good manners." Webster also gave readers extensive instructions on how to behave in school:

> He that speaks loud in school will not learn his own book well, nor let the rest learn theirs; but those that make no noise will soon be wise, and gain much love and good will.
>
> Shun the boy that tells lies, or speaks bad words; for he would soon bring thee to shame. (Commager, 1962, pp. 61–63)

Webster's speller was so popular that it eventually sold over 24 million copies. Historian Henry Steele Commager (1958) said of the book, "The demand was insatiable.... No other secular book had ever spread so wide, penetrated so deep, lasted so long" (p. 12). It has been estimated that more than 1 billion people have read Webster's book.

Webster's speller addressed so many topics that it has been called one of the first curriculum guides for the elementary grades (Johanningmeier, 1980). Webster was a post-Revolutionary educational leader who had a profound impact on the American language and culture, and he "did much to help define the new nation" (Urban & Wagoner, 2004, p. 79).

Education for African Americans and Native Americans

At the close of the American Revolution, nearly all of the half million African Americans were slaves who could neither read nor write (Button & Provenzo, 1989). In most cases, those who were literate had been taught by their masters or through small, church-affiliated programs. Literate Native Americans and Mexican Americans usually had received their training at the hands of missionaries.

Other schools for African and Native Americans were started by the Quakers, who regarded slavery as a moral evil. One of the best known schools for African Americans was founded in Philadelphia in 1770 by Anthony Benezet, who believed that African Americans were "generously sensible, humane, and sociable, and that their capacity is as good, and as capable of improvement as that of White people" (Button & Provenzo, 1989, p. 45). Schools modeled on the Philadelphia African School opened elsewhere in the Northeast, and so-called Indian schools were also founded as philanthropic enterprises.

The Quakers also founded Indian schools as philanthropic enterprises. In 1819, federal funds for reservation schools were first granted through the newly created Office of Indian Affairs. Federal involvement brought little improvement in programs and enrollments, however. In 1901, for instance, only 300 of the 4,000 to 5,000 school-age Navajos attended school (Button & Provenzo, 1989).

How Did State-Supported Common Schools Emerge (1820–1865), and How Did Compulsory Education Change Schools and Teaching (1865–1920)?

The first state-supported high school in the United States was the Boston English Classical School, established in 1821. The opening of this school, renamed English High School in 1824, marked the beginning of a long, slow struggle for state-supported **common schools** in this country. Those in favor of free common schools tended to be city residents and nontaxpayers, democratic leaders, philanthropists and humanitarians, members of various school societies, and working people. Those opposed were rural residents and taxpayers, members of old aristocratic and conservative groups, owners of private schools, members of conservative religious sects, Southerners, and non-English-speaking residents. By far, the most eloquent and effective spokesperson for the common school was Horace Mann.

Horace Mann's Contributions

Horace Mann (1796–1859) was a lawyer, Massachusetts senator, and the first secretary of a state board of education. He is best known as the champion of the common school movement, which has led to the free, public, locally controlled elementary schools we know today. Mann worked tirelessly to convince people that their interests would be well served by a system of universal free schools for all:

> [A free school system] knows no distinction of rich and poor, of bond and free, or between those, who, in the imperfect light of this world, are seeking, through different avenues, to reach the gate of heaven. Without money and without price, it throws open its doors, and spreads the table of its bounty, for all the children of the State. (Mann, 1868, p. 754)

IMPROVING SCHOOLS In 1837, Mann accepted the position of secretary of the Massachusetts State Board of Education. At the time, conditions in Massachusetts schools were deplorable, and Mann immediately began to use his new post to improve the quality of schools. Through the 12 annual reports he submitted while secretary and through *The Common School Journal*, which he founded and edited, Mann's educational ideas became widely known in this country and abroad.

In his widely publicized *Fifth Report* (published in 1841), Mann told the moneyed conservative classes that support of common public schools would provide them "the cheapest means of self-protection and insurance." Where could they find, Mann asked, "any police so vigilant and effective, for the protection of all the rights of person, property and character, as such a sound and comprehensive education and training, as our system of Common Schools could be made to impart?" (Rippa, 1997, p. 95).

In his *Seventh Report* (published in 1843), Mann extolled the virtues of schools he had visited in Prussia that implemented the humanistic approaches of noted Swiss educator Johann Heinrich Pestalozzi (1746–1827). He was impressed by "the harmonious relationship that existed between the Pestalozzian teachers and their charges, [and he] advocated a similar approach in Massachusetts' schools, one that valued children and their interests" (Urban & Wagoner, 2009, p. 125).

THE NORMAL SCHOOL During the late 1830s, Mann put forth a proposal that today we take for granted. Teachers, he felt, needed more than a high school education to teach; they should be trained in professional programs. The French had established the *école normale* for preparing teachers, and Mann and other influential educators of the period, such as Catherine Beecher (1800–1878), whose sister, Harriet Beecher Stowe (1811–1896), wrote *Uncle Tom's Cabin*, believed that a similar program was needed in the United States. Through her campaign to ensure that women had access to an education equal to that of men and her drive to recruit women into the teaching profession, Beecher contributed significantly to the development of publicly funded schools for training teachers (Holmes & Weiss, 1995).

The first public **normal school** in the United States opened in Lexington, Massachusetts, on July 3, 1839. The curriculum consisted of general-knowledge courses plus courses in pedagogy (or teaching) and practice teaching in a model school affiliated with the normal school. In 1849, Electa Lincoln Walton (1824–1908), an 1843 graduate of the normal school, became acting head administrator and the first woman to administer a state normal school. Walton was energetic and determined to succeed, as her journal reveals:

> Many people think women can't do much. I'd like to show them that they can keep a Normal School and keep it well too . . . . I will succeed . . . . I will never be pointed at as an example of the incompetency of woman to conduct a large establishment well. (Holmes & Weiss, 1995, p. 42)

When Mann resigned as secretary in 1848, his imprint on education in the United States was broad and deep. As a result of his unflagging belief that education was the "great equalizer of the conditions of men—the balance wheel of the social machinery" (Mann, 1957, p. 87), Massachusetts had a firmly established system of common schools and led the way for other states to establish free public schools.

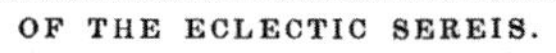
OF THE ECLECTIC SEREIS. 15

LESSON VIII.

his	this	bite	keep	wants
can	four	play	moon	watch
hog	cow	kind	sheep	stands
how	dark	most	chase	shines

See how this dog stands on his feet. He wants to play with John.

A dog has four feet. A dog and a cat can see in the dark.

Dogs keep watch at night, and bark. They bark most when the moon shines.

A dog will chase a sheep, or a hog, or a cow, and bite it. If you are kind to the dog, he will not bite you.

What did children learn from typical lessons in 19th-century textbooks like this one, the story of "The Boy and Dog" from McGuffey's *The Eclectic First Reader?*

Reverend W. H. McGuffey's Readers

Reverend William Holmes McGuffey (1800–1873) had perhaps the greatest impact on what children learned in the new school. Far exceeding Noah Webster's speller in sales were the famous **McGuffey readers**. Between 1836, when the book first appeared, and 1860, approximately 120 million copies of the six-volume series were sold (Urban & Wagoner, 2009). The six readers ranged in difficulty from the first-grade level to the sixth-grade level. Through such stories as "The Wolf," "Meddlesome Matty," and "A Kind Brother," the readers emphasized virtues such as hard work, honesty, truth, charity, and obedience.

Absent from the McGuffey readers were the dour, pessimistic views of childhood so characteristic of earlier primers. Nevertheless, they had a religious, moral, and ethical influence over millions of American readers. Through their reading of the "Dignity of Labor," "The Village Blacksmith," and "The Rich Man's Son," for example, readers learned that contentment outweighs riches in this world. In addition to providing explicit instructions on right living, the McGuffey readers also taught countless children and adults how to read and study.

Justin Morrill's Land-Grant Schools

The common school movement and the continuing settlement of the West stimulated the development of public higher education. In 1862, the **Morrill Land-Grant Act**, sponsored by Congressman Justin S. Morrill (1810–1898) of Vermont, provided federal land for states either to sell or to rent in order to raise funds for the establishment of colleges of agriculture and mechanical arts. Each state was given a land subsidy of 30,000 acres for each representative and senator in its congressional delegation.

Eventually, $7.5 million from the sale of over 17 million acres was given to land-grant colleges and state universities. The Morrill Act of 1862 set a precedent for the federal government to take an active role in shaping higher education in the United States. A second Morrill Act in 1890 provided even more federal funds for land-grant colleges.

Segregation of Schools

From the 17th to the late 20th centuries, schools were segregated by race. The first recorded official ground for school segregation dates back to a decision of the Massachusetts Supreme Court in 1850. When the Roberts family sought to send their daughter Sarah to a White school in Boston, the court ruled that "equal, but separate" schools were being provided and that the Robertses therefore could not claim an injustice (*Roberts v. City of Boston*, 1850). From the beginning, however, schools were not equal, and students did not have equal educational opportunity.

As the nation moved toward civil war, positions on the institution of slavery and the education of slaves hardened. While abolitionists established schools for free and escaped blacks, some Southern states made the teaching of reading and writing to slaves a crime.

Compulsory Education

From the end of the Civil War to the end of World War I, publicly supported common schools steadily spread westward and southward from New England and the Middle Atlantic states. Beginning with Massachusetts in 1852, compulsory education laws were passed in 32 states by 1900 and in all states by 1930.

Because of compulsory attendance laws, an ever-increasing proportion of children attended school. In 1869–1870, only 64.7 percent of 5- to 17-year-olds attended public school. By 1919–1920, this proportion had risen to 78.3 percent; and in 2006–2007, it was 92.8 percent (Snyder & Dillow, 2010). The growth in enrollment on the high school level was exceptional. Historical data from the National Center for Education Statistics (Snyder & Dillow, 2010) show that the population in the United States increased 108 percent between 1880 and 1920, whereas high school enrollment increased 1,900 percent!

As common schools spread, school systems began to take on organizational features associated with today's schools: centralized control; increasing authority for state, county, and city superintendencies; and a division of labor among teachers and administrators at the individual school site. Influenced by the work of Frederick W. Taylor (1856–1915), an engineer and the founder of **scientific management**, school officials undertook reforms based on management principles and techniques from big business. For example, they believed that top-down management techniques should be applied to schools as well as factories.

THE KINDERGARTEN Early childhood education also spread following the Civil War. Patterned after the progressive, humanistic theories of the German educator Friedrich Froebel (1782–1852), the **kindergarten**, or "garden where children grow," stressed the motor development and self-directed activity of children before they began formal schooling at the elementary level. Through play, games, stories, music, and language activities, a foundation beneficial to the child's later educational and social development would be laid. After founding the first kindergarten in 1837, Froebel developed child-centered curriculum materials that were used in kindergartens in the United States and throughout the world.

Margarethe Schurz (1832–1876), a student of Froebel, opened the first U.S. kindergarten in her home at Watertown, Wisconsin, in 1855. Her small neighborhood class was conducted in German. In 1860, Elizabeth Palmer Peabody (1804–1891), sister-in-law of Horace Mann and the American writer Nathaniel Hawthorne, opened the first private English-speaking kindergarten in this country in Boston.

Initially, kindergartens were privately supported, but in St. Louis in 1873, Susan Blow (1843–1916) established what is commonly recognized as the first successful public kindergarten in the United States. She patterned her kindergarten after one she visited while in Germany. She was a fierce advocate for public kindergartens, and in 1873 she stated that "We shall see the day when [the kindergarten] will have grown into a mighty tree, and I am more than ever anxious to see the system introduced into our Public schools." So successful was her program that by 1879, a total of 131 teachers were working in 53 kindergarten classes (Button & Provenzo, 1989, p. 169).

The U.S. Bureau of Education recorded a total of 12 kindergartens in the country in 1873, with 72 teachers and 1,252 students. By 2012, enrollments had mushroomed to 2,681,000 in public kindergartens and 289,000 in private kindergartens (Snyder & Dillow, 2014).

SCHOOLING FOR AFRICAN AMERICANS After the Civil War and emancipation, schools for former slaves were opened throughout the South by African American communities. Approximately 500 of these schools operated in the South shortly after the war ended (Urban & Wagoner, 2013). In 1865, African American leaders in Georgia formed an education association to raise money and to supervise their own schools. That same year, an editorial in the *New Orleans Black Republican* stated that "Freedom and school books and newspapers go hand in hand. Let us secure the freedom we have received by the intelligence that can maintain it" (Urban & Wagoner, 2009, p. 164).

In addition to schools operated by African Americans, Congress established the **Freedmen's Bureau** to provide the "foundations for education" for former slaves. Throughout the South, the Freedmen's Bureau operated "a vast network of reading, writing, and industrial schools that operated by day, night, and on Sundays" (Urban & Wagoner, 2009, p. 161). By 1869, more than 9,500 teachers taught both girls and women and boys and men at freedmen's schools. In 1870, when the Bureau ended, 4,329 freedmen's schools had been established, with a total enrollment of more than 247,000 students (Franklin, 1947).

HIGHER EDUCATION FOR AFRICAN AMERICANS In *Up from Slavery*, Booker T. Washington (1856–1915) recounts how he walked part of the 500 miles from his home in West Virginia to attend the Hampton Normal and Agricultural Institute of Virginia, one of the country's first institutions of higher education for African Americans. Four years after graduating from Hampton, Washington returned to be the school's first African American instructor.

Washington had a steadfast belief that education could improve the lives of African Americans, just as it had for White people: "Poverty and ignorance have affected the black man just as they affect the white man. But the day is breaking, and education will bring the complete light" (Rippa, 1997, p. 122). In 1880, Washington helped to found the Tuskegee Institute, an industrial school for African American men and women in rural Alabama. According to Washington, the institute would play a key role in bringing about racial equality:

> The Tuskegee idea is that correct education begins at the bottom, and expands naturally as the necessities of the people expand. As the race grows in knowledge, experience, culture, taste, and wealth, its wants are bound to become more and more diverse; and to satisfy these wants there will be gradually developed within our ranks—as already has been true of the whites—a constantly increasing variety of professional and business men and women. (Button & Provenzo, 1989, p. 274)

Not all African Americans shared Washington's philosophy and goals. William E. Burghardt DuBois (1868–1963), the first African American to be awarded a Ph.D. and one of the founders of the National Association for the Advancement of Colored People (NAACP), challenged Booker T. Washington's views on education. In his book *The Souls of Black Folks*, DuBois criticized educational programs that seemed to imply that African Americans should accept inferior status and develop manual skills. DuBois called for the education of the most "talented tenth" of the African American population to equip them for leadership positions in society as a whole.

THE PROFESSIONALIZATION OF TEACHING During the later 1800s, professional teacher organizations began to have a great influence on the development of schools in America. The National Education Association (NEA), founded in 1857, and the American Federation of Teachers (AFT), founded in 1916, labored diligently to professionalize teaching and to increase teachers' salaries and benefits. The NEA also appointed its Committee of Ten in 1892 and its Committee of Fifteen in 1893 to make recommendations for secondary and elementary curricula, respectively. In 1913, the NEA appointed the Commission on the Reorganization of Secondary Education to reexamine the secondary curriculum in regard to students' individual differences.

COMMITTEE OF TEN During 1892–1893, the directors of the National Education Association appropriated $2,500 for a **Committee of Ten** to hold nine conferences that focused on the following subjects in the high school curriculum: (1) Latin; (2) Greek; (3) English; (4) other modern languages; (5) mathematics; (6) physics, astronomy, and chemistry; (7) natural history (biology, botany, and zoology); (8) history, civil government, and political science; and (9) geography (physical geography, geology, and meteorology). The group's members decided that the primary function of high schools was to take intellectually elite students and prepare them for life. Their recommendations stressed mental discipline in the humanities, languages, and science.

COMMITTEE OF FIFTEEN The report of the Committee of Ten sparked such discussion that in 1893 the National Education Association appointed the **Committee of Fifteen** to examine the elementary curriculum. In keeping with the view that high schools were college preparatory institutions, the committee's report, published in 1895, called for the introduction of Latin, the modern languages, and algebra into the elementary curriculum. In addition, the curriculum was to be organized around five basic subjects: grammar, literature, arithmetic, geography, and history.

REORGANIZATION OF SECONDARY EDUCATION In 1913, the National Education Association appointed the **Commission on the Reorganization of Secondary Education**. The commission's report, *Cardinal Principles of Secondary Education*, was released in 1918 and called for a high school curriculum designed to accommodate individual differences in scholastic ability. Seven educational goals, or "cardinal principles," were to provide the focus for schooling at all levels: health, command of fundamental processes (reading, writing, and computation), worthy home membership, vocation, citizenship, worthy use of leisure time, and ethical character.

WOMEN'S INFLUENCE ON TEACHING By the early 1900s, the demand for teachers had grown dramatically. Because of greater demand for teachers, greater job mobility, and more and more women becoming teachers, the character of teaching changed. Both respected and regarded with suspicion, teachers became distanced from the communities they served. In his classic book *The Sociology of Teaching*, Willard Waller (1932) refers to this distancing as an "impenetrable veil" between the teacher and the rest of the community. Nevertheless, women were viewed as virtuous and thus ideal teachers for schools that emphasized students' moral development.

In spite of their diminished status in society, women became influential in shaping educational policies during the early 1900s, in part through the women's suffrage movement that led to the right to vote. Women such as Ella Flagg Young (1845–1918), superintendent of Chicago schools from 1909 to 1915, and Catherine Goggin and Margaret Haley, leaders of the Chicago Teachers Federation, played important roles in the governance of Chicago schools (Spring, 2013). Another Chicagoan and visionary educational leader, Jane Addams (1860–1935), founded Hull House, a social and educational center for poor immigrants. In *Democracy and Social Ethics* (published in 1902), Addams drew from her training as a social worker and developed a philosophy of socialized education that linked schools with other social service agencies and institutions in the city. At the ceremony to present her the Nobel Peace Prize in 1931, Addams was described as "the foremost woman of her nation" (Rippa, 1997, p. 142).

 Check Your Understanding 5.3

What Were the Aims of Education During the Progressive Era (1920–1945) and the Modern Postwar Era (1945–2000)?

From the end of World War I to the end of World War II, education in the United States was influenced significantly by the philosophy of progressivism. **Progressivism** is a philosophical orientation based on the belief that life is evolving in a positive direction, that people may be trusted to act in their own best interest, and that education should focus on children's interests and practical needs.

During the late 19th and early 20th centuries, supporters of the **progressive movement** were intent on social reform to improve the quality of American life. In 1919, the Progressive Education Association was founded and went on to devote the next two decades to implementing progressive theories in the classroom that they believed would lead to the improvement of society.

Progressives were not united by a single educational philosophy. For the most part, they were opposed to autocratic teaching methods; teaching styles that relied almost exclusively on textbooks, recitations, and rote memorization; the relative isolation of the classroom from the real world; and classroom discipline based on fear or physical punishment.

Teachers in progressive schools functioned as guides rather than taskmasters. They first engaged students through providing activities related to their natural interests, and then they moved students to higher levels of understanding. To teach in this manner was demanding and required exceptional talent: Teachers in progressive schools had to have broad and deep knowledge of the disciplines; the ability to design meaningful, authentic learning experiences; and a keen appreciation of students' thinking while learning new material.

John Dewey's Laboratory School

Progressive educational theories were synthesized most effectively and eloquently by John Dewey (1859–1952). Born in the year that Darwin's *Origin of Species* was published, Dewey graduated from the University of Vermont when he was 20. He later earned a doctorate at Johns Hopkins University, where his thinking was strongly influenced by the psychologist William James.

From 1894 to 1904, Dewey served as head of the departments of philosophy, psychology, and pedagogy at the University of Chicago. From 1904 until he retired in 1930, Dewey was a professor of philosophy at Columbia University. Dewey's numerous writings have had a profound impact on U.S. schools. In his best-known works, *The School and Society* (1900) and *The Child and the Curriculum* (1902), Dewey states that school and society are connected and that teachers must begin with an understanding of the child's world, the psychological dimension, and then progress to the logical dimension represented by the accumulated knowledge of the human race.

While at the University of Chicago, Dewey and his wife, Alice, established the Laboratory School for testing progressive principles in the classroom. The school opened in 1896 with two instructors and 16 students and, by 1902, had grown to 140 students with 23 teachers and 10 university graduate students as assistants. The children, 4 to 14 years old, learned traditional subjects by working cooperatively in small groups of 8 to 10 on projects such as cooking, weaving, carpentry, sewing, and metalwork (Rippa, 1997).

With Dewey as director and his wife as principal, the school became a virtual laboratory for testing Dewey's ideas. The school was so unique that historian Lawrence Cremin (1961) referred to it as "the most interesting experimental venture in American education" (p. 136). In addition to giving students a meaningful, relevant education, Dewey's school was designed to demonstrate, test, and refine Dewey's theoretical principles.

What made Dewey's Laboratory School unique was that it was thoroughly child centered. The curriculum was a natural outgrowth of the children's interests. The faculty was committed to following the lead set by students. For example, "A student or students might express an interest in milk. The teacher would guide the students to sources of the production, chemistry, and distribution of milk. Groups of students might visit the local dairy and develop a group project on milk for the classroom. During this group study of milk, students might learn chemistry, economics, arithmetic, social history, and cooperation" (Spring, 2008, pp. 300–301).

What hallmarks of progressive education are evident in this photograph of one of the first classrooms in the country operated according to Dewey's philosophy? How would a progressive classroom look today?

Maria Montessori's Method

While Dewey's ideas provided the basis for the development of progressive education in the United States, progressive educators in Europe were similarly developing new approaches that would also affect U.S. education. Chief among these was Maria Montessori (1870–1952), an Italian physician who was influenced by Rousseau and believed that children's mental, physical, and spiritual development could be enhanced by providing them with developmentally appropriate educational activities.

At Montessori's school for poor preschool-age children in Rome, teachers created learning environments based on students' levels of development and readiness to learn new material. According to the **Montessori method**,

> [C]hildren pass through "sensitive periods" for particular intellectual, social, and moral awakenings. These are sensitive periods for language, movement, music, order, and so on. The central role of the adult . . . is to recognize these sensitive periods and direct the child to work designed to foster those awakenings. (Cossentino & Whitcomb, 2007, p. 117)

Montessori teachers use prescribed sets of materials and physical exercises to develop students' knowledge and skills, and students are allowed to use or not use the materials as they see fit. The materials arouse students' interest, and the interest motivates them to learn. Through highly individualized instruction, students develop self-discipline and self-confidence. Montessori's ideas spread throughout the world; by 1915, almost 100 Montessori schools were operating in the United States (Webb, Metha, & Jordan, 2017). Today, thousands of Montessori schools operate around the world, and Montessorian materials and activities are a standard part of the early childhood and elementary curricula in public schools throughout the nation.

The Decline of Progressive Education

By the start of World War II, the progressive education movement, faced with rising public criticism, began a rapid decline. An angry public believed that progressive education was not meeting the needs of the nation. Many of the schools' deficiencies were blamed on progressive approaches that were seen as soft and lacking the structure and discipline children needed. In 1955, the Progressive Education Association ceased operation. According to one historian, when the association began in 1919, "progressive education meant all that was good in education; 35 years later nearly all the ills in American education were blamed on it" (Graham, 1967, p. 145).

In spite of its short life, the progressive education movement had an unmistakable impact on American education. Many current practices in schools have their origins in the experimentation of the progressive era: inquiry or discovery learning, self-paced instructional approaches, field trips, flexible scheduling, open-concept classrooms, non-graded schools, small-group activities, and school-based counseling programs, to name a few.

FOCUS ON **DIVERSITY**: EDUCATION OF IMMIGRANTS AND MINORITIES

The diversity of America's school population increased dramatically during the late 19th and early 20th centuries. Latin Americans, eastern Europeans, and southern Europeans followed earlier waves of western and northern European immigrants such as the Irish and Germans. As with Native American education, the goal of immigrant education was rapid assimilation into an English-speaking Anglo-European society that did not welcome racially or ethnically different newcomers.

Also at stake was the preservation or loss of traditional culture. In some areas, school policies included the punishment of Cuban and Puerto Rican children, for example, for speaking Spanish in school, and children learned to mock their unassimilated parents. In other areas, efforts were made to exclude certain groups, such as Asians, and ethnic enclaves established separate schools for the purpose of preserving, for example, traditional Chinese culture.

By the time Native Americans were granted U.S. citizenship in 1924, confinement on reservations and decades of forced assimilation had devastated Native American cultures and provided few successful educational programs. The federal government mandated that tribal children attend boarding schools in an effort to assimilate them into the dominant culture. Boarding school children who spoke their native language were beaten with a strap, while other children were forced to watch. By the early 1930s, an estimated two thirds of Native Americans had attended boarding schools. The emotional scars from the boarding school experience continue into the present, and the national Boarding School Healing Project was launched in South Dakota in 2002 by Native Americans from various states (King, 2008).

In 1928, a landmark report titled *The Problem of Indian Administration* recommended that Native American education be restructured. Recommendations included building day schools in Native American communities and the reform of boarding schools for Native American children. In addition, the report recommended that school curricula be revised to reflect tribal cultures and the needs of local tribal communities. In the Teachers' Voices feature for this chapter, a Native American teacher stresses the importance of curricula that affirm the identity of Native American students.

TEACHERS' VOICES  BEING AN AGENT OF CHANGE

KRISTINE SHOTLEY

Native American Teachers Need Support

When I was studying to be a teacher, a White female student in the same program asked me what I thought my chances were of finding a job after graduation. I replied that, because I am Native American, and a woman, I thought I would have excellent opportunities for immediate employment. "How nice," she said, "to turn two negatives into two positives!" I was taken aback. It had not occurred to me that, in this day and age, I would still have to defend my identity.

In the United States, most Native American children are still taught by non-Native teachers. There are fewer than 18,000 Native American teachers working today.

To recruit more teachers, we need to develop curricula that affirm our Native American identity. For example, elementary school kids need to learn an accurate and truthful account of American history. How many times do we have to reiterate that Christopher Columbus did not "discover" America?

When I was growing up, Native American history was not taught. I endured the appalled looks of my White classmates when our teachers presented a one-sided account of American history. I felt apologetic for my ancestors who tried to defend their lands from White settlers.

The United States [must address] the lack of Native American teachers. I want my son and other Native American sons and daughters to realize they can become anything they choose because they have the educational background they need.

PERSONAL REFLECTION

1. Shotley says teachers should develop curricula that "affirm" Native American identity. What are the characteristics of curricula that "affirm" the diverse identities of today's students?
2. What should a teacher do if the only instructional materials available present outdated, perhaps even distorted, interpretations of American history?

Kristine Shotley is a member of the Fond Du Lac Tribe of Ojibwe in Minnesota, and she writes for *The Circle*, a Native American news and arts paper published in **MINNEAPOLIS**. This article is from Progressive Media Project, January 12, 2000.

An early champion of the educational rights of African Americans was Mary McLeod Bethune (1875–1955). The 15th child of former slaves in South Carolina, Bethune attended a school operated by the Presbyterian Board of Missions for Freedmen and Barber-Scotia College in Concord, North Carolina. She then went on to study at the Moody Bible Institute in Chicago. She went to Daytona Beach in 1904 where, with only $1.50 in savings, she founded the Daytona Normal and Industrial School for Training Negro Girls.

The school was in a rundown building Bethune rented. At first, she had only six students, including her son. To keep the school open, Bethune and her students sold sweet potato pies and fried fish and gave concerts in nearby resort hotels. In 1923, the school merged with a boys' school in Jacksonville, Florida, and became Bethune-Cookman College a year later.

Native American children who attended boarding schools were not allowed to speak their native languages. Why is it important for school curricula to reflect and honor students' cultural backgrounds?

Library of Congress Prints and Photographs Division Washington, D.C. 20540 USA [LC-USZ62-72450]

Bethune was an eloquent spokesperson for the educational rights of African American youth. During the Great Depression of the 1930s, she was appointed to the Advisory Board of the National Youth Administration (NYA). That year, almost 24 percent of the 21 million youth between 16 and 24 years of age were out of school and jobless. When Bethune spoke eloquently about the needs of African American youth, President Franklin Roosevelt added an office of minority affairs to the NYA and asked Bethune to direct it.

The level of Bethune's commitment to education is reflected in a comment she made in the *Journal of Negro Education* (Collier-Thomas, 1982): "I cannot rest while there is a single Negro boy or girl lacking a chance to prove his worth." As director of the NYA, she made it possible for 150,000 African American young people to attend high school and for 60,000 to graduate from college.

World War II and Increasing Federal Involvement in Education

World War II created conditions in this country that led the federal government to fund several educational programs. One of these, the **Lanham Act** (1941), provided funding for (1) the training of workers in war plants by U.S. Office of Education personnel, (2) the construction of schools in areas where military personnel and workers on federal projects resided, and (3) the provision of child care for the children of working parents.

Another influential and extensive federal program in support of education was the Servicemen's Readjustment Act, popularly known as the **G.I. Bill of Rights**. Signed into law by President Franklin D. Roosevelt in 1944, the G.I. bill has provided millions of veterans with payments for tuition and room and board at colleges and universities and at special schools. Similar legislation was later passed to grant educational benefits to veterans of the Korean and Vietnam conflicts. Not only did the G.I. bill stimulate the growth of American colleges and universities, it also changed the character of the higher education student population. Generally, the returning veterans were older and more serious than students who had not served in the military.

The Modern Postwar Era (1945–2000)

Throughout the 20th century, many long-standing trends in U.S. education continued. These trends may be grouped and summarized in terms of three general patterns, shown in Figure 5.3. At the same time, the decades since the end of World War II have seen a series of profound changes in U.S. education. These changes have addressed three as-yet unanswered questions: (1) How can full and equal educational opportunity be extended to all groups in our culturally pluralistic society? (2) What knowledge and skills should be taught in our nation's schools? (3) How should knowledge and skills be taught?

THE 1950s: DEFENSE EDUCATION AND SCHOOL DESEGREGATION Teachers and education were put in the spotlight in 1957 when the Soviet Union launched the first satellite, *Sputnik*, into space. Stunned U.S. leaders immediately claimed that the U.S. was second in the "space race" because of a weak education system. The Soviet Union was first into space, they maintained, because schools had embraced progressive education and de-emphasized science and mathematics. U.S. students, for example, were taught less science and mathematics, and fewer foreign languages, than their European counterparts.

From our perspective today, the 1950s was an era of intense competition between U.S. and Soviet school systems—each trying to produce the best scientists and engineers needed to develop a strong military. In the public's mind, the ability of America to defend itself was directly related to the quality of its schools. As the title of the first chapter of Vice Admiral H. G. Rickover's (1959) book *Education and Freedom* put it: "Education is our first line of defense."

The federal government appropriated millions of dollars over the next decade for educational reforms that reflected the importance of teaching knowledge and skills viewed as essential for adult life. Through provisions of the **National Defense Education Act of 1958**, the U.S. Office of Education sponsored research and innovation in science, mathematics, modern foreign languages, and

Figure 5.3 Three general patterns of trends in U.S. education

Americanization

- Americanizing of European educational institutions and instructional models
- Americanizing of English language textbooks and curriculum
- Cultural assimilation of immigrants and others through education
- Aims of education based on moral didacticism and pragmatism
- Aims of education relating to child development and child welfare
- Aims of education relating to success in a society based on capitalism
- Aims of education relating to citizenship in a democracy

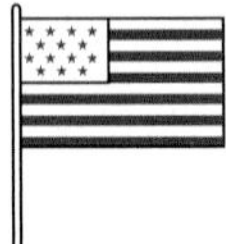

Democratization

- Steady growth of compulsory, free, secular, publicly funded education
- Preservation of state, local, and parental control of schooling and schools
- Protection of teachers' and students' rights under the U.S. Constitution
- Shifts in educational reform initiatives that reflect a two-party electoral system
- Continual expansion of early childhood education
- Continual expansion of opportunities for higher education and adult education
- Traumatic periodic extensions of educational opportunity to "other" Americans (women; racial, ethnic, and language minorities; people with disabilities)

Professionalization

- Professionalizing of teaching as an occupation
- Professionalizing of teacher organizations and associations
- Growth in scientific and bureaucratic models for the management of schools
- Rising standards for qualifications to teach
- Continual development of institutions and programs for teacher education
- Greater application of theory and research on teaching and learning
- Generally rising status and salaries for teachers as members of a profession

guidance. Out of their work came the "new math"; new science programs; an integration of anthropology, economics, political science, and sociology into new social studies programs; and renewed interest and innovations in foreign language instruction. Teachers were trained in the use of new methods and materials at summer workshops, schools were given funds for new equipment, and research centers were established. In 1964, Congress extended the act for three years and expanded Title III of the act to include money for improving instruction in reading, English, geography, history, and civics.

When African American students desegregated Little Rock Central High School in 1957, they were protected by the National Guard. What is the legacy of school desegregation today?

Library of Congress Prints and Photographs Division Washington [LC-USZ62-72450]

The end of World War II also saw the beginning of school **desegregation**. On May 17, 1954, the U.S. Supreme Court rejected the "separate but equal" doctrine used since 1850 as a justification for excluding African Americans from attending school with Whites. In response to a suit filed by the NAACP on behalf of a Kansas family, Chief Justice Earl Warren declared that to segregate school children "from others of similar age and qualifications solely because of their race generates a feeling of inferiority as to their status in the community that may affect their hearts and minds in a way unlikely ever to be undone" ***(Brown v. Board of Education of Topeka*, 1954)**.

The Supreme Court's decision did not bring an immediate end to segregated schools. Although the court, one year later, ordered that desegregation proceed with "all deliberate speed," opposition to school integration arose in school districts across the country. Some districts, whose leaders modeled restraint and a spirit of cooperation, desegregated peacefully. Other districts became battlegrounds, characterized by boycotts, rallies, and violence.

Video Example 5.1

Public Reaction to Integration of Laws: This video uses newscast footage from the 1950's and 1960's. Try to imagine the commitment it took from individuals to make desegregation happen in the United States.

THE 1960s: THE WAR ON POVERTY AND THE GREAT SOCIETY The 1960s, hallmarked by the Kennedy administration's spirit of action and high hopes, provided a climate that supported change. Classrooms were often places of pedagogical experimentation and creativity reminiscent of the progressive era. The open-education movement, team teaching, individualized instruction, the integrated-day concept, flexible scheduling, and non-graded schools were some of the innovations that teachers were asked to implement. These structural, methodological, and curricular changes implied the belief that teachers were capable professionals.

During the reform activity of the 1960s, public school enrollments rose dramatically. In 1950, about 25 million children were enrolled; in 1960, about 36 million; and in 1970, about 50 million. As a result of a decline in births, however, this trend stopped abruptly in the late 1970s. In the fall of 1979, for example, 41.5 million students were enrolled in K–12 classes, a decrease of 1,069,000, or 2.5 percent, from the year before (Rippa, 1984).

The curriculum reform movement of the 1960s did not bear the positive results that its supporters hoped for. The benefits of the new federally funded programs reached only a small percentage of teachers. In regard to some of the new materials—those related to the "new math," for example—teachers complained that the recommended approaches failed to take into account the realities of classroom life. Many of the materials, it turned out, were developed by persons who had little or no classroom experience. Thus, many teachers of the 1960s ignored the innovations and continued teaching as they had always done. With each new curriculum reform, a common expression among teachers during the 1960s was "This too shall pass."

The image of teachers in the 1960s was enhanced by the publication of several books by educators who were influenced by the progressivist educational philosophy and humanistic psychology. A. S. Neill's *Summerhill* (1960), Sylvia Ashton-Warner's *Teacher* (1963), John Holt's *How Children Fail* (1964), Herbert Kohl's *36 Children* (1967), James Herndon's *The Way It Spozed to Be* (1969), and Jonathan Kozol's *Death at an Early Age* (1967)—a few of the books that appeared at the time—gave readers inside views of teachers at work and teachers' perceptions of how students learn.

The administrations of Presidents Kennedy and Johnson funneled massive amounts of money into a War on Poverty. Education was seen as the key to breaking the transmission of poverty from generation to generation. The War on Poverty developed methods, materials, and programs such as subsidized breakfast and lunch programs, Head Start, Upward Bound, and the Job Corps that would be appropriate to children who had been disadvantaged due to poverty.

The War on Poverty President Johnson announced during his State of the Union address on January 8, 1964, has proved much more difficult to win than imagined, and the results of such programs 55 years later have been mixed. The 3- to 6-year-olds who participated in Head Start did much better when they entered public schools; however, academic gains appeared to dissolve over time. Although the Job Corps enabled scores of youth to avoid a lifetime of unemployment, many graduates returned to the streets, where they eventually became statistics in unemployment and crime records. The education of low-income children received a boost in April 1965 when Congress passed the **Elementary and Secondary Education Act**. As part of President Johnson's Great Society program, the act allocated funds on the basis of the number of poor children in school districts. Thus, schools in poverty areas that frequently had to cope with problems such as low achievement, poor discipline, truancy, and high teacher turnover rates received much-needed assistance in addressing their problems.

In 1968, the Elementary and Secondary Education Act was amended with Title VII, the Bilingual Education Act. This act provided federal aid to low-income children "of limited English-speaking ability." The act did not spell out clearly what bilingual education might mean other than to say that it provided money for local school districts to "develop and carry out new and imaginative elementary and secondary school programs" to meet the needs of non-English-speaking children. Since the passing of Title VII, debate over the ultimate goal of bilingual education has been intense: Should it help students make the transition to regular English-speaking classrooms, or should it help such students maintain their non-English language and culture?

THE 1970s: ACCOUNTABILITY AND EQUAL OPPORTUNITY The 1970s saw drops in enrollment, test scores, and public confidence in our nation's schools. At the same time, new educational policies called for equality of education for all in the United States. Troubled by the continued low academic performance of many U.S. students, parents, citizens groups, and policymakers initiated a back-to-basics movement and called for increased teacher accountability.

Many school systems had to cope with financial crises during the 1970s. Public and private elementary school enrollments, instead of increasing as they had since 1940, declined by nearly five million during the 1970s (National Center for Education Statistics, 2008). As a result of declining enrollments, schools received less state aid. Moreover, voters frequently failed to support referendums to increase school funding because they lacked confidence in the schools.

Many parents responded to the crisis by becoming education activists, seeking or establishing alternative schools, or joining the home education movement led by John Holt, who by then had given up on reforming schools. These parents believed they could provide a better education for their children than public school teachers. Those who kept their children in the public schools demanded teacher **accountability**, which limited teachers' instructional flexibility and extended their evaluation paperwork. Basal readers and teacher-proof curricular packages descended on teachers, spelling out with their cookbook directions the deeper message that teachers were not to be trusted to teach on their own. Confidence in teachers reached a low point.

In addition, during the late 1960s and early 1970s, increasing numbers of young people questioned what the schools were teaching and how they were teaching it. Thousands of them mobilized in protest against an establishment that, in their view, supported an immoral, undeclared war in Vietnam and was unconcerned with the oppression of minorities at home. In their search for reasons why these and other social injustices were allowed to exist, many militant youth groups singled out the schools' curricula. From their perspective, the schools taught subjects irrelevant to finding solutions to pressing problems.

Responding in good faith to their critics' accusations, schools greatly expanded their curricular offerings and instituted a wide variety of instructional strategies. In making these changes, however, school personnel gradually realized that they were alienating other groups: taxpayers who accused schools of extravagant spending; religious sects that questioned the values that children were being taught; **back-to-basics** advocates who charged that students were not learning how to read, write, and compute; and citizens who were alarmed at steadily rising school crime, drugs, and violence.

Despite the siege on teachers and schools, however, the reforms of the 1960s and 1970s did result in a number of improvements that have lasted into the present. More young people graduate from high school now than in previous decades, more teachers have advanced training, school buildings are better equipped, and instructional methods and materials are both more relevant to learners and more diverse.

Video Example 5.2

What Does LRE Look Like?: Learn about the evolution of special education within our schools and how it has affected our implementation of least restrictive environment (LRE) today."

For those people who had been marginalized by the educational system, the federal acts that were passed in the 1970s brought success and encouragement: the Title IX Education Amendment prohibiting sex discrimination (1972), the Indian Education Act (1972), the Education for All Handicapped Children Act (1975), and the Indochina Migration and Refugee Assistance Act (1975).

Title IX of the Education Amendments Act, which took effect in 1975, stated that "no person in the United States shall, on the basis of sex, be excluded from participation in, be denied the benefits of, or be subjected to discrimination under any education program or activity receiving Federal financial assistance."

The **Education for All Handicapped Children Act (Public Law 94–142)**, passed by Congress in 1975, extended greater educational opportunities to children with disabilities. This act (often referred to as the **mainstreaming** law) specifies extensive due process procedures to guarantee that children with special needs will receive a free, appropriate education in the least restrictive educational environment. Through the act's provisions, parents are involved in planning educational programs for their children. Chapter 9 explains in detail the provisions of Public Law 94-142, as well as additional special education laws and amendments enacted since 1975.

THE 1980s: A GREAT DEBATE The first half of the 1980s saw a continuation, perhaps even an escalation, of the criticisms aimed at the schools during the two previous decades. In fact, Lee Shulman (1987) characterized much of the 1980s as an era of "teacher bashing." With the

Dennis MacDonald/Alamy Stock Photo

What impact has Title IX had on the education of girls? What does equal educational opportunity for girls and boys really mean?

publication in 1983 of the report by the National Commission on Excellence in Education, ***A Nation at Risk: The Imperative for Educational Reform***, a great national debate began on how to improve the quality of schools. *A Nation at Risk* and dozens of other national reports on U.S. schools gave evidence to some that the schools were failing miserably to achieve their goals. The following excerpt from the first paragraph of *A Nation at Risk* exemplifies the tone of the **educational reform movement**:

> Our Nation is at risk. Our once unchallenged preeminence in commerce, industry, science, and technological innovation is being overtaken by competitors throughout the world . . . the educational foundations of our society are presently being eroded by a rising tide of mediocrity that threatens our very future as a Nation and a people. (National Commission on Excellence in Education, 1983)

Responses included more proposals for curriculum reform. Mortimer Adler's **Paideia Proposal** (1982) called for a perennialist core curriculum based on the Great Books. **High School: A Report on Secondary Education in America** (1983), written by Ernest Boyer (1928–1995) for the Carnegie Foundation for the Advancement of Teaching, suggested strengthening the academic core curriculum in high schools, a recommendation that was widely adopted. In 1986, former secretary of the U.S. Department of Education William Bennett advocated an intellectually rigorous high school curriculum that he described in *James Madison High School* (1987). Educators at the middle school level began to create small learning communities, eliminate tracking, and develop new ways to enhance student self-esteem as a result of the Carnegie Council on Adolescent Development report *Turning Points: Preparing American Youth for the 21st Century* (1989). These and other reform reports that swept the nation during the 1980s made a lasting imprint on education in the United States.

THE 1990s: TEACHER LEADERSHIP The push to reform schools begun in the 1980s continued throughout the 1990s, and teaching was transformed in dramatic ways. In response to challenges such as greater diversity, greater international competition, less support for public education, and decentralization and deregulation of schools, innovative approaches to teaching and learning were developed throughout the United States (see Figure 5.4). Teachers went beyond the classroom and assumed leadership roles in school restructuring and educational reform. Through collaborative relationships with students, principals, parents, and the private sector, teachers changed the nature of their profession.

Figure 5.4 The 1990s: A sample of trends in education

CHALLENGES	RESPONSES
Greater Diversity	Multicultural Curriculum Reform Bilingual Education Debate Mainstreaming and Inclusion
Greater International Competition	Greater Accountability National Goals and Standards School-to-Work Programs
Less Support for Public Education	School Vouchers and School Choice Privatization of Education Business-School Partnerships
Decentralization and Deregulation of Schools	School-Based Management School Restructuring Charter Schools

✓ Check Your Understanding 5.4

What Are the Educational Issues and Priorities of the 21st Century (2000–the Present)?

Without a doubt, the world of teaching between now and the middle of the century will be characterized by rapid, complex changes. Among the major trends that will continue to influence teaching are increasing ethnic and cultural diversity, new leadership roles for teachers, and the continuing influence of new technologies on education.

When you become a teacher, your influence on the profession will be enhanced if you understand and appreciate the historical context for U.S. education. Figure 5.5

Figure 5.5 Historical timeline for U.S. education, 1920 to present

Movement	Decade	Year	Event
	1920	1930s & 1940s	Progressive education movement stresses curriculum based on student's needs and interests. Home economics, health, family living, citizenship, and woodshop added to the curriculum.
	1940	1957	Soviet *Sputnik* sparks emphasis on science, mathematics, and languages.
The Excellence Movement	1960	1960s	Calls for relevancy result in expanded course offerings and electives.
		Mid-1970s	Back-to-basics movement emphasizes reading, writing, mathematics, and oral communication.
	1980	1983	*Nation at Risk* report calls for "five new basics"—English, mathematics, science, social studies, and computer science.
		1985	Rigorous core curricula advocated at all levels in an effort to increase standards and to ensure quality.
		1989	The Carnegie Council on Adolescent Development report, *Turning Points*, recommends the creation of learning communities and a core academic program for middle-level students. President George H. W. Bush convenes education summit meeting for 50 state governors.
		1990	President George H.W. Bush unveils Goals 2000, identifying six educational goals: readiness for school; high school completion; student achievement and citizenship: science and mathematics; adult literacy and life-lonfg learning; and safe, disciplined, and drug-free schools.
Equity for all Students		1994	President Bill Clinton signs into law Goals 2000: Educate America Act.
		1995	President Bill Clinton creates the National Information Infrastructure (NII) to encourage schools to become connected to the "information superhighway."
		1996	President Bill Clinton launches the President's Educational Technology Initiative.
		1999	President Bill Clinton signs into law the Educational Excellence for All Children Act, reauthorizing the Elementary and Secondary Education act (ESEA).
	2000		
High-Stakes Testing; School and Teacher Accountability		2002	President George W. Bush signs into law the No Child Left Behind (NCLB) Act of 2001, reauthorizing ESEA and calling for all students to make "adequate yearly progress" (AYP).
		2009	National Governors Association (NGA) and Council of Chief State School Officers (CCSSO) organize the Common Core State Standards Initiative (CCSSI). Forty-eight states participate in developing the Standards.
	2010	2010	President Barack Obama proposes broad changes to NCLB and releases *A Blueprint for Reform*, calling for the reauthorization of ESA. Schools will no longer be singled out for not making "adequate yearly progress." Race to the Top and the Teacher and Leader Innovation Fund are key elements of *A Blueprint*. Common Core State Standards for K-12 English-language arts and mathematics released.
		2011	Congress fails to act on the call to reauthorize ESEA; the Obama administration announces that states can voluntarily seek "ESEA flexibility" and be exempt from certain requirements of NCLB by submitting comprehensive plans to improve education for all students.
		2012	Race to the Top expanded to include competition for school districts; 55 districts receive a total of $400 million.
		2013	Forty-five states submit plans for ESEA flexibility, and 42 are approved. More than $4 billion in Race to the Top funds are awarded to 19 states. Forty-five states adopt Common Core Standards; a few states pass legislation to delay or withdraw from using the Common Core Standards.
		2014	Common Core Standards come under attack; conservatives claim the Standards are a national curriculum and violate tradition of state and local control of education; several states repeal the Standards and replace with state-developed standards.
		2015	President Barack Obama signs into law the Every Student Succeeds Act (ESSA).
		2016	President Donald Trump nominates Betsy DeVos as U.S. Secretary of Education.
		2017	U.S. Senate confirms nomination of DeVos for Secretary of Education by a 51-50 margiin; Devos advocates expanded school choice and unregulated free market competition among charter schools.
		2018	Federal Court temporarily blocks the Trump administration's 2017 repeal of the Deferred Action for Childhood Arrivals (DACA) which allowed those brought to the U.S. illegally as children to receive a two-year period of "deferred action" from deportation. Trump administration's "zero tolerance" policy for illegal entry to the U.S. separates hundreds of immigrant children from their parents at the U.S. border.
		2019	The U.S. Department of Education's National Center for Education Statistics gathers data for the 2019-2020 National Teacher and Principal Survey (NTPS); Survey topics include characteristics of teachers, principals, and schools; teacher training opportunities; retention; retirement; and hiring.
		2020	A sample of teachers who completed the 2019-2020 NTPS complete the 2020-2021 Teacher Follow-Up Survey (TFS) to determine how many teachers remained at the same school, moved to another school, or left the profession.

presents a timeline for U.S. education from 1920 to the present. The left-hand column of the timeline identifies three trends that began nearly a century ago and will continue to be educational priorities during the decades ahead: *equity* for all students, *excellence* and high standards, and *accountability* for schools and teachers.

FOCUS ON **DIVERSITY**: EQUITY FOR ALL STUDENTS

Although reform efforts during the 1950s through the 1990s resulted in significant improvements in education, data gathered during the first two decades of the new century indicate that an **achievement gap** continues to exist between Hispanic, Black, and American Indian/Alaska Native students and other groups on many measures of educational achievement. For example, Table 5.1 shows the 2015 National Assessment of Educational Progress (NAEP) mathematics and reading scale scores of 12th-grade students by race/ethnicity.

Table 5.1 Average National Assessment of Educational Progress (NAEP) reading and mathematics scale scores of 12th-grade students, by race/ethnicity: 2015

Mathematics Scale Scores		Reading Scale Scores	
Asian	174	White	297
White	157	Asian	296
Two or more races	155	Two or more races	291
Pacific Islander	151	Pacific Islander	289
American Indian/Alaska Native	134	Hispanic	279
Hispanic	133	American Indian/Alaska Native	277
Black	127	Black	273

NOTE: Mathematics scale scores ranged from 0 to 300; reading scale scores ranged from 0 to 500.

SOURCE: Musu-Gillette, L., de Brey, C., McFarland, J., Hussar, W., Sonnenberg, W., and Wilkinson-Flicker, S. (2017). *Status and trends in the education of racial and ethnic groups 2017* (NCES 2017-051). U.S. Department of Education, National Center for Education Statistics. Washington, DC, pp. 52, 48.

Promoting the achievement of students from diverse racial, cultural, and social-class groups continues to be a challenge for U.S. education. Rod Paige, former U.S. Secretary of Education (2001–2005) and his sister, Elaine Witty, former education dean at Norfolk State University, make this point very clear in the title of their book *The Black-White Achievement Gap: Why Closing It Is the Greatest Civil Rights Issue of Our Time* (Paige & Witty, 2010).

Excellence

In spite of the historic nationwide recession that began in 2008, states continued to develop new, cost-effective ways to promote excellence during the new century. They implemented comprehensive strategies to ensure that teachers have the skills, knowledge, and support required to raise achievement for all students.

Approximately half of the states have enacted laws to promote excellence. For example, **WEST VIRGINIA** created a process for designating schools as "innovation zones." This ensures that, in exchange for greater accountability, schools approved by the State Board of Education would have greater control over curriculum, personnel, organization of the school day and year, technology use, and delivery of educational services to improve student learning. Innovation in Education designations are awarded to public schools in the following priority areas: science, technology, engineering, and math (STEM), community-school partnerships, entrepreneurship, career pathways, and the arts. In 2017, West Virginia approved Innovation in Education designations for nine schools (West Virginia Department of Education, 2017). The Technology in Action feature for this chapter illustrates how one teacher used screen recorder software to help all of his students achieve excellence in their study of calculus.

TECHNOLOGY in ACTION

Screen-Recorder Software in 12th-Grade Calculus

Some students struggle in Mr. DeWilt's 12th-grade calculus class. The textbook, his teaching, and the text's website are good, but he needs something more. He needs to supplement his in-class explanations of calculus with something that is flexible and personal. Most of his students understand the material most of the time. However, when he "does the math" over the course of a school year, Mr. DeWilt realizes that a number of students don't "get it."

The textbook he uses has a supplemental DVD that allows students to view video examples of solutions to calculus problems—in his opinion, these are very effective. During a web search for additional similar support for his teaching, Mr. DeWilt located a free web-based calculus tool. The tool allows students to plug in a problem and complete the equation. However, this free tool was not user-friendly and had little technical help and documentation. When he used it with his students, he spent more time explaining how to use the tool than how to understand the calculus concepts he wanted his students to learn. He needed something that students could access any time they ran into trouble, something they could return to again and again.

At first, he tried videotaping his work on the computer screen, but that did not work. The audio was poor, and the image quality was worse. Also, it was extremely time-consuming to set up the video equipment for each concept in which he wished to provide students with additional support for their learning.

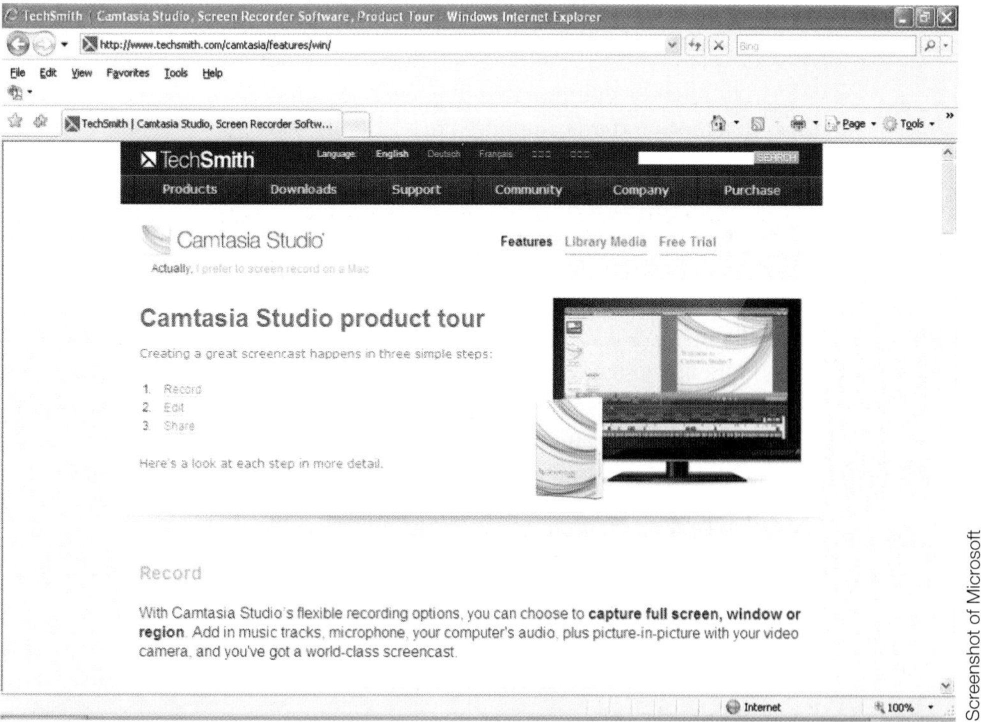

Screenshot of Microsoft

Source: © 1995–2011, Techsmith Corporation. All right reserved. Retrieved March 6, 2011, from http://www.techsmith.com/camtasia/features/win. Used by permission.

(continued)

Frustrated, Mr. DeWilt sent an email to the textbook's publisher asking how the computer screen recordings on the DVD were made so clear. He learned that the publisher used a screen-recorder software program called Camtasia Studio.

A screen recorder is a tool that allows you to record your movements on a computer screen while adding voice, text, and graphics. This is an easy-to-use, cost-effective way to create custom, just-in-time tutorials, examples, and navigation on your computer screen. To use this tool, you will need at least 1 GB of RAM, a sound card, a video card, microphone, and speakers.

Screen-recorder software can be used to record website navigation, software tutorials, or any other computer-based activity that you want to demonstrate to an audience. Teachers have used screen-recorder software to help students understand how to navigate a complex website. Teachers have also used screen recorder software to develop tutorials to help their students use a specific piece of software.

After a brief conversation with Jenny Seasam, the building instructional technology (IT) person, Mr. DeWilt had a copy loaded onto his office computer. Now, when a student comes to him with a calculus problem, he opens the free web-based calculus tool, puts on his headset microphone, launches Camtasia, and walks the student through the application. When he finishes, he saves the file as a web file and publishes it on his class website. Students can access it anytime, anywhere. This solution not only helps his students with their technical issues, it also helps reinforce the calculus concepts he wants students to learn.

VISIT: As a teacher, you have several screen-recorder options available. The tool highlighted in this feature is just one example you can use. If you want to demo Camtasia, you can download a free trial version (Windows or Mac) from the Internet. Once you have downloaded the software and installed it, merely click on the Camtasia icon on your desktop or the Camtasia link in your Start menu. Next, you will be prompted to open an existing project or start a new one.

States also promoted excellence by participating in the **Common Core State Standards Initiative (CCSSI)**. To bring uniformity to a "patchwork quilt" of state standards, the Council of Chief State School Officers (CCSSO) and the National Governors Association Center for Best Practices (NGA Center) organized the CCSSI during 2009. 48 states, not including Texas and Alaska, participated in developing K–12 standards in English language arts and mathematics that were released the following year.

By 2013, 45 states had formally adopted the Standards, whereas a few states passed legislation to delay or withdraw from using the Standards. States also collaborated to develop common assessments aligned to the Common Core Standards, and assessments were to begin during the 2014–2015 school year.

At first, reactions to the Standards were largely positive; however, a heated national debate over the Standards emerged. Although the CCSSI made it clear that the standards were "voluntary"—they *were not* a federal initiative—many observers claimed that the Standards amounted to a federal "takeover" of school curricula and implementation of a national curriculum. Several states repealed the Standards and replaced them with state-developed standards.

The U.S. Department of Education also promoted excellence on many fronts. The Obama administration released *A Blueprint for Reform* in 2010, calling for the reauthorization of the Elementary and Secondary Education Act (ESEA) and proposing broad changes to No Child Left Behind (NCLB). According to the *Blueprint,* schools would no longer be singled out for not making "adequate yearly progress" (AYP), and by 2014, all students would leave high school "college or career ready." To promote excellence and innovation at the state level, the Blueprint included a competitive $4 billion Race to the Top program and the Teacher and Leader Innovation Fund. Race to the Top was expanded in 2012 to include competition for school districts, and 55 districts subsequently received $400 million.

By 2011, Congress had failed to act on the call to reauthorize ESEA, which led the Obama administration to announce that states could voluntarily seek "ESEA flexibility" and be exempt from certain requirements of NCLB by submitting comprehensive plans to improve education for all students. 45 states submitted such plans by 2013, and 42 were approved.

Congress did not approve a reauthorization of the Elementary and Secondary Education Act (ESEA) until 2015. The new law, the Every Student Succeeds Act (ESSA), was designed to "fix" NCLB.

EVERY STUDENT SUCCEEDS ACT (ESSA) More than 1,000 pages long, ESSA increased the authority of states and school districts for educational reform and improvement, while it reduced federal government authority in important areas such as testing, teacher quality, and low-performing schools. ESSA is to be fully implemented during 2017–2018; however, it will take some time to fully understand the impact this complex educational legislation will have on our nation's schools.

ESSA requires that states set high curriculum standards in reading or language arts, math and science, and any other subject(s) identified by the state. Each state must demonstrate that its standards are aligned with higher education entrance requirements and state career and technical education standards.

Unlike NCLB, states are not required to submit their standards to the U.S. Department of Education. Moreover, the Department cannot influence or direct the states as they decide what standards to adopt and implement.

Like NCLB, ESSA requires that each state has annual assessments in reading or language arts and math for grades 3-8 and once in high school. ESSA also requires three science assessments—once in each of the following grade spans: 3-5, 6-9, and 10-12. ESSA also allows states to use an alternative assessment to assess up to 1% of students with cognitive disabilities. ESSA also allows states to apply for additional federal funding to improve state assessment systems for English learners and students with disabilities.

Instead of using a required statewide assessment, ESSA allows local school districts to select a nationally recognized high school academic assessment (the ACT or SAT, for example) if the state has reviewed and approved that assessment. Chapter 6 explains the provisions of ESSA in greater detail.

Accountability

Politicians, business leaders, and citizens continued to hold schools, teachers, and administrators accountable for student learning during the first two decades of the new century. To hold educators accountable for student learning, some states linked test results to merit rewards, increased funding, or sanctions; others provided additional funds for high-performing schools or bonuses for educators at those schools. For example, **CALIFORNIA** implemented several merit-based incentive programs for teachers, schools, and administrators, including the "Governor's Performance Awards" that gave money to schools based on their "academic performance index." Similarly, in New York City, **NEW YORK**, the school system gave bonuses to principals and other administrators whose schools showed significant gains on test scores. School system administrators grouped schools into three performance categories—low, middle, and high—taking into account students' economic circumstances. For high schools, factors such as dropout rates were also used.

ESSA replaced the Adequate Yearly Progress (AYP) requirement of NCLB with a requirement that states create their own accountability systems to determine student performance and school quality. These accountability plans must still be submitted to the U.S. Department of Education. Though states can develop their own goals for accountability, these goals must address proficiency on tests, English-language proficiency, and graduation rates. In addition, state goals must include steps to close achievement gaps and graduation rates for groups of students who are furthest behind. States and school districts are required to assess the effectiveness of schools each year and, at least once every three years, to identify schools in need of comprehensive support and improvement.

A NEW FEDERAL EDUCATION AGENDA—DIMINISHING SUPPORT FOR PUBLIC SCHOOLS The beginning of Donald Trump's presidency in 2017 saw the emergence of widespread, vigorous debate in the country about the role of public schools in a democracy. The Trump administration, citing what it labeled "failing government schools" (Stewart, 2017), vowed to push for unregulated free market competition among charter schools, expanded school choice, and a reallocation of resources from traditional public schools to private charter schools and voucher programs. In response, teacher unions, teacher leaders, educational researchers and policymakers, and a majority of the public responded with a renewed call to strengthen public schools. Strong public schools, they asserted, promote democracy, guard against emerging authoritarian trends in society, increase social justice, and ensure educational excellence and equity for all students.

In November 2016, President-elect Donald Trump announced that he would nominate Betsy DeVos as U.S. Secretary of Education. Her nomination was strongly opposed during the next few months. The president of the American Federation of Teachers called DeVos "the most ideological, anti-public education nominee" since President Jimmy Carter appointed the first Secretary of Education in 1979. In spite of widespread opposition to her nomination, the U.S. Senate eventually confirmed her nomination by a 51–50 margin.

During a May, 2017 speech, DeVos stated that the Trump administration would provide "the most ambitious expansion" of school choice within American history. She went on to say that "We stand on the verge of the most significant opportunity we have ever had to drag American education out of the Stone Age and into the future" (Danilova, 2017).

The voucher and charter school programs advocated by DeVos faced intense opposition from teachers unions. They claimed the programs would drain resources from already underfunded public schools while failing to increase student achievement. An independent national survey of public school parents conducted for the American Federation of Teachers found that respondents strongly favored investing in traditional public schools rather than investing in more charter and voucher programs (see Table 5.2).

Continuing the Quest for Excellence and Equity

In spite of the challenges and uncertainties that confront the U.S. system of education, ours is one of the few countries in the world to offer a free public education to *all* of its children. When we look to the future and consider ways to make our educational system even stronger, we must acknowledge the debt we owe to those who have shaped the history of U.S. education up to the present moment. We must be students of our past if we are to improve education in the future.

Table 5.2 Preferred Approach for Improving Education, Key Subgroups

	Invest in Neighborhood Schools	More Charters/ Vouchers		Invest in Neighborhood Schools	More Charters/ Vouchers
Mothers	84%	16%	Major city	72%	28%
Fathers	76%	24%	Urban	76%	24%
Age 18 to 34	83%	17%	Suburban	81%	19%
Age 35 to 49	79%	21%	Small town/rural	82%	18%
Age 50/older	79%	21%	2016 Clinton voters	84%	16%
Whites	82%	18%	2016 Trump voters	82%	18%
Age 50/older	79%	21%	2016 Clinton voters	84%	16%
African Americans	76%	24%	2016 nonvoters	82%	18%
Hispancis	78%	22%	Reg. public school parents	81%	19%
Income under $45K	81%	19%	Charter school parents	57%	43%
Income $45K to $75K	79%	21%	Very/fairty satisfied w/schools	81%	19%
Income over $75K	80%	20%	Less/not satisfied w/schools	78%	22%
Democrats	84%	16%			
Independents	79%	21%			
Republicans	76%	24%			

SOURCE: *Public school parents on the value of public education: Findings from a national survey of public school parents conducted for the AFT.* Washington, DC: Hart Research Associates, September 2017, p. 6.

The United States has set for itself an education mission of truly ambitious proportions. To realize fully this mission during the decades to come will be difficult, but an examination of our history shows that it is not impossible. In less than 400 years, our education system has grown from one that provided only a minimal education to an advantaged minority to one that now provides maximal educational opportunity to the majority. Clearly, the first two decades of the new century provide ample evidence that our nation will not waver from its long-standing commitment to ensuring that all children have equal access to educational excellence.

Check Your Understanding 5.5

Summary

How Did European Education Influence Teaching and Schools in the American Colonies (1620–1750)?

- Many practices in today's schools had their origins in Europe, where the role of education was to prepare children and youth for adulthood.
- Ancient Greeks believed that leisure should be used to reflect on practical and aesthetic values and to develop a well-rounded mind and body.
- Socrates questioned pupils to reveal errors in their thinking and to lead them to eternal truths.
- Plato, a student of Socrates, founded the Academy, often called the world's first university.
- Aristotle, a student of Plato, was a realist who believed that reality, knowledge, and value exist independent of the mind.
- Roman education, patterned after Greek education, consisted of the *ludus,* or elementary school, and a secondary or grammar school.
- Education in the European Middle Ages was mediated through the Roman Catholic Church. The Renaissance marked a rebirth of interest in Greco-Roman art, literature, secular learning, and humanism.
- Four 18th-century European thinkers who influenced American education are Rousseau, Pestalozzi, Herbart, and Lancaster.
- Colonial education was patterned after the British two-track system, and its primary objective was to promote religion.
- Colonial teachers had low status, although respect increased with the grade level taught.
- Puritans believed children were naturally corrupt and sinful and should be disciplined sternly at the dame schools, reading and writing schools, and Latin grammar schools common to the colonies.
- One of the first schools for African Americans and Native Americans was started in 1704.
- Mandated education in the United States had its origins in two colonial laws: the Massachusetts Acts of 1642 and 1647.

What Were the Goals of Education During the Revolutionary Period (1750–1820)?

- During the Revolutionary period, characterized by a declining European influence on American education, education in the new democracy was shaped by the ideas of Benjamin Franklin, Sarah Pierce, Thomas Jefferson, and Noah Webster.
- At the end of the American Revolution, the few African and Native Americans who were literate were taught at church-sponsored schools that were segregated by race.
- Educational opportunities for women were often limited to preparing them for family life.

How Did State-Supported Common Schools Emerge (1820–1865), and How Did Compulsory Education Influence Schools and Teaching (1865–1920)?

- Horace Mann, a strong advocate for state-supported, free common schools, believed that teachers should receive postsecondary training in normal schools.
- The six-volume McGuffey reader, with its moral lessons and emphasis on virtue, formed the basis of what children learned at school.
- The Morrill Land-Grant Act, passed in 1862, provided federal land for colleges and set a precedent for federal involvement in education.
- A Massachusetts Supreme Court ruling in 1850 supported "equal, but separate" schools for African Americans.

- The spread of common schools and dramatic increases in their enrollments led to the use of scientific management techniques for their operation.
- Booker T. Washington, founder of the Tuskegee Institute, believed education could prepare African Americans to live peaceably with Whites, whereas W. E. B. DuBois believed African Americans should educate themselves for leadership positions and not accept inferior status.
- Kindergartens became common and used child-centered curricula patterned after German educator Friedrich Froebel's ideas.
- After the Civil War and emancipation, schools for former slaves were opened throughout the South by African American communities; the Freedmen's Bureau also operated schools for former slaves and their children.
- The National Education Association (NEA) and the American Federation of Teachers (AFT) were founded to professionalize teaching and increase teachers' salaries and benefits.
- The NEA appointed the Committee of Ten and the Committee of Fifteen to make recommendations for the secondary and elementary school curricula, respectively.
- The Commission on the Reorganization of Secondary Education, appointed by the NEA to reexamine the secondary curriculum in regard to students' individual differences, developed "seven cardinal principles" for schooling at all levels: health, command of fundamental processes (reading, writing, and computation), worthy home membership, vocation, citizenship, worthy use of leisure time, and ethical character.

How Did Education Change During the Progressive Era (1920–1945) and the Modern Postwar Era (1945–2000)?

- John Dewey's Laboratory School at the University of Chicago, a model of progressive education, offered a curriculum based on children's interests and needs.
- Progressive educator Maria Montessori developed age-appropriate materials and teaching strategies that were implemented in the United States and throughout the world.
- Public criticism of progressive education led to its decline at the start of World War II.
- School enrollments became increasingly diverse as a result of immigration, and a goal of education was the rapid assimilation of all groups into an English-speaking Anglo-European culture.
- The Soviet Union's launching of *Sputnik* in 1957 sparked educational reform, particularly in science, mathematics, and foreign language education. Schools were ordered to desegregate with "all deliberate speed" as a result of a 1954 decision by the Supreme Court in *Brown v. Board of Education of Topeka.*
- Innovative curricula and instructional strategies were used in many classrooms of the 1960s. The Elementary and Secondary Education Act of 1965, part of President Johnson's Great Society and War on Poverty programs, provided federal money to improve the education of poor children.
- Alarmed by declining test scores, the public became critical of schools during the 1970s and demanded accountability. An array of federal legislation was passed to provide equal educational opportunity for all students.
- *A Nation at Risk* and other reports during the 1980s addressed weaknesses in U.S. schools and sparked debate on how to improve U.S. education.
- In response to continuing challenges to education today, teachers are taking leadership roles in school restructuring, school governance, curriculum change, and other aspects of educational reform.

What Are the Educational Issues and Priorities of the 21st Century (2000–the Present)?

- The Every Student Succeeds Act (ESSA) increased the authority of states and school districts for educational reform and improvement, while it reduced federal government authority in important areas such as testing, teacher quality, and low-performing schools.
- The administration of President Donald Trump began a push for unregulated free market competition among charter schools, expanded school choice, and a reallocation of resources from traditional public schools to private charter schools and voucher programs. An independent national survey for the American Federation of Teachers found that public school parents strongly favor investing in traditional public schools rather than investing in more charter and voucher programs.
- Three trends will continue to be educational priorities during the 21st century: *equity* for all students, *excellence* and high standards, and *accountability* for schools and teachers.

Professional Reflections and Activities

Teacher's Journal

1. Benjamin Franklin suggested that education is "the surest foundation" for happiness. To what extent do you agree or disagree with Franklin's statement?
2. What remnants remain of the Puritan influence on American education? Of the progressive influence?
3. Reflect on the "daily school routine" you experienced as an elementary school child. How does that routine differ from that experienced by children in colonial schools? Recall how your teachers handled classroom discipline; how do those approaches differ from those used by colonial teachers?

Teacher's Research

1. Examine several textbooks currently in use at the level of education that interests you the most. Then, visit one of many online digital collections and locate a few texts that were used at that level during the 1700s or 1800s. For example, the Library of Congress' "Books that Shaped America" exhibition has textbooks in digital form from the 1700s through the 1800s. Similarly, the University of Pittsburgh maintains the Nietz Old Textbook Collection of more than 16,000 volumes. What differences do you notice? Report your findings to your classmates.
2. Use online references to research in greater detail the contributions of a pioneer in education whose work is summarized in this chapter.

Observations and Interviews

1. Interview veteran teachers and administrators at a local school and ask them to comment on the changes in education that they have observed and experienced during their careers. In particular, compare their remarks to this chapter's discussion of education during the post–World War II era, using this chapter's descriptions of the era to guide your questions. What events do respondents identify as having had the greatest impact on their teaching?
2. Visit a museum in your area for the purpose of examining artifacts from early U.S. educational history. Take notes on what you find and describe several of the artifacts to the rest of your class.
3. Interview several elderly people, at a nursing home perhaps, about their school experiences. Do any of their recollections coincide with the descriptions of the time periods discussed in this chapter?

Professional Portfolio

Prepare a videotaped oral history that focuses on the changes that have occurred over the years in local schools or an interest of local concern. You may decide to interview experienced teachers, administrators, or school board members, or you may decide to interview older members of the community.

Prior to conducting your interviews, prepare several interview questions that focus on your area of interest. At the conclusion of each interview, invite the interviewee to provide any other relevant information he or she might have.

Shared Writing 5.1
The Future of Public Education

Chapter 6

Governance and Finance of U.S. Schools

Maciej Maksymowicz/123RF

Learning Outcomes

After reading this chapter, you will be able to do the following:

6.1 Explain why teachers must understand educational politics and how local communities influence schools.

6.2 Explain how states and regional education agencies influence schools.

6.3 Explain how the federal government influences education.

6.4 Explain how schools are financed in the United States.

6.5 Describe trends in funding for educational equity and excellence.

6.6 Explain how the privatization movement is affecting equity and excellence in education.

READERS' VOICES

Why do you need to understand educational politics?

An understanding of national, state, and local educational politics enables teacher leaders to help set the direction of educational reform in our country. From influencing policies about school funding, to what and how teachers teach, to how teachers are evaluated—teachers must become politically involved in their profession.

—NATHAN,
Teacher Education program, first year

Why do You Need to Understand Educational Politics and How Local Communities Influence Schools?

At this point in your teacher education program, you are probably most concerned about the challenges of teaching—creating a positive classroom climate; ensuring that all students learn; and learning to work with teachers, administrators, and parents, for example. Compared to meeting these challenges, understanding how educational politics influences school governance may not seem important. However, it is important for teachers to understand that America's schools are subjected to pressures from special interest groups—professional teacher and administrator organizations, teachers' unions, religious groups, business interests, think tanks and educational foundations, and parents, for example.

Perhaps you think that politics and teaching should remain separate. However, education is not (and never will be) apolitical. It is a fact of life that school policies are developed in a political milieu, and operating and improving schools is a political process, not merely a technical, rational process.

Many complex political forces currently influence school governance in the United States (see Figure 6.1).

Figure 6.1 Political influences on schools

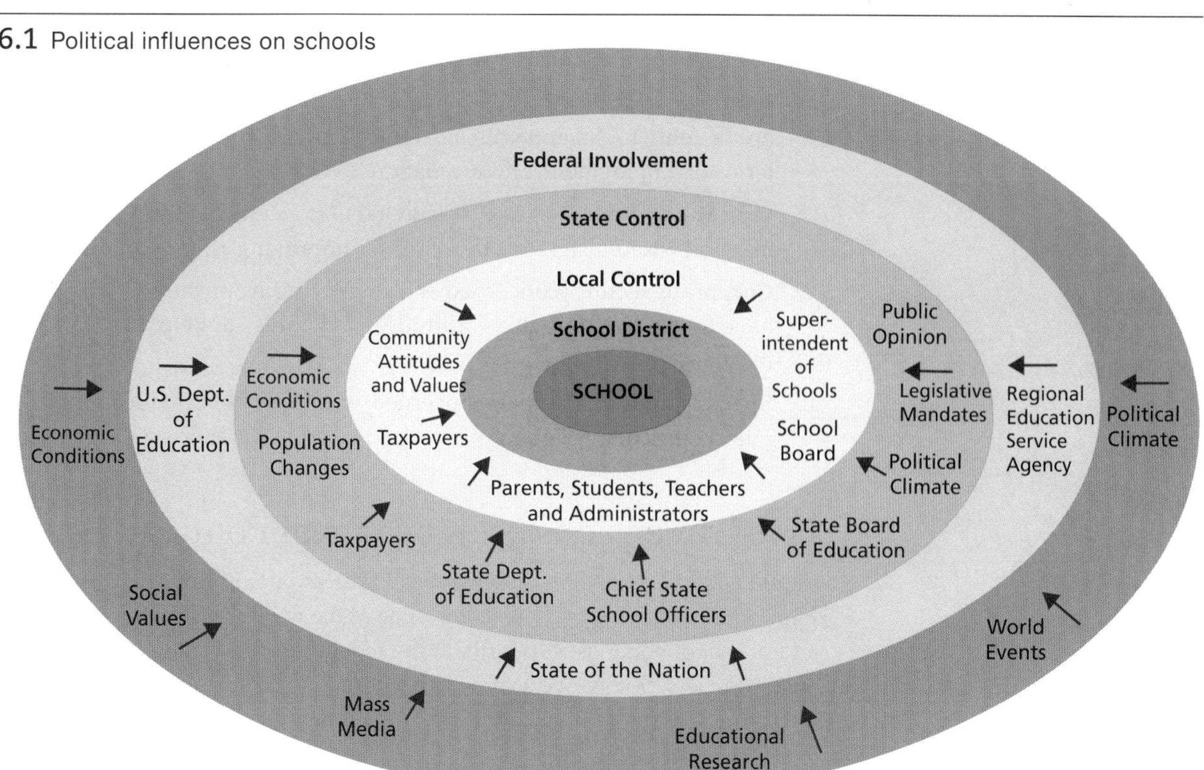

In general, *politics* refers to how people use power, influence, and authority within an organization to persuade others to act in desired ways. **Educational politics** refers to how people use power, influence, and authority to affect instructional and curricular practices within a school or school system. Clearly, you will have much to gain from becoming politically astute and involved. For instance, the following examples illustrate how several teachers benefited from their knowledge of educational politics:

- Two teachers, members of the local school council (LSC) for a school in a poor urban area, organized a group of parent volunteers who eventually helped reduce student truancy and improve students' attitudes toward school.
- Three high school English teachers received a state grant to develop a humanities program—their grant application included letters of support from the president of the board of education and the superintendent.
- A group of teachers went door to door passing out information about a much-needed remodeling and expansion project at their school; two months later, voters approved funding for the project.

Among the groups who will compete to shape educational policies during your teaching career, at least 10 can be identified:

1. **Parents**—concerned with controlling local schools so that quality educational programs are available to their children.
2. **Students**—concerned with policies related to freedom of expression, dress, behavior, and curricular offerings.
3. **Teachers**—concerned with their role in school reform, improving working conditions, terms of employment, and other professional issues.
4. **Administrators**—concerned with providing leadership so that various interest groups, including teachers, participate in the shared governance of schools and the development of quality educational programs.
5. **Taxpayers**—concerned with maintaining an appropriate formula for determining local, state, and federal financial support of schools.
6. **Federal, state, and local authorities**—concerned with the implementation of court orders, guidelines, and legislative mandates related to the operation of schools.
7. **Ethnic and racial groups**—concerned with the availability of equal educational opportunity for all and with legal issues surrounding administrative certification, terms of employment, and evaluation.
8. **Educational theorists and researchers**—concerned with using theoretical and research-based insights as the bases for improving schools at all levels.
9. **Corporate sector**—concerned with receiving from the schools graduates who have the knowledge, skills, attitudes, and values to help an organization realize its goals.
10. **Special-interest groups**—concerned with advancing educational reforms that reflect particular religious, philosophical, and economic points of view.

Five Dimensions of Educational Politics

Figure 6.2 illustrates five dimensions of educational politics that influence teachers. First, whether it is federal legislation such as the Every Student Succeeds Act (ESSA) or a local school bond issue, politics at the federal, regional, state, and local levels influences teachers. Second, educators, citizens, and policymakers use politics to lobby for the development of educational programs that reflect their beliefs about *what* should

Figure 6.2 Five dimensions of educational politics that influence teachers

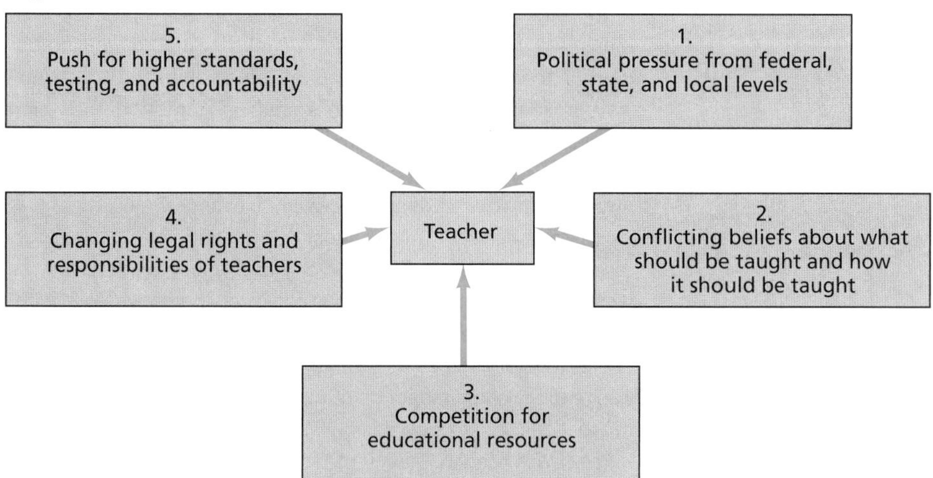

be taught and *how* it should be taught. Third, the allocation of resources to schools can easily become a political issue in a community, as anyone who has voted on a school bond issue knows. Fourth, the legal rights and responsibilities of teachers and students are continuously changing, often as a result of conflicting political views about education. And fifth, one of the "hottest" politically charged issues in education today involves the push for higher standards; mandated testing to ensure that students have mastered those standards; and calls for accountability to ensure that schools, teachers, and administrators produce results.

Indeed, it is no exaggeration to say that educational politics can place a teacher "in the line of fire." For example, the following statement by a teacher illustrates how teachers can come into "the line of fire" if they publicly express their ideas about what should be taught and how it should be taught.

> *I have to be very careful about what I say about* ____________ *[a commercial reading program adopted by my school]* because it's almost heresy to suggest that something else might work as well or even better. *I don't know why these teachers won't say what they believe.* They are frustrated with it but they won't say anything against it. If they do, it's reported to the principal and he reprimands them for "being against [the reading program]." (Garan, 2004, p. 84)

In this chapter's Teachers' Voices: Being an Agent of Change feature, Melody Arabo explains how she uses technology to connect with other teachers and to influence educational policy markers at the federal level.

TEACHERS' VOICES  BEING AN AGENT OF CHANGE

Melody Arabo

Using Technology to Increase Teachers' Voices

It took me a while to feel comfortable with Twitter. I opened a personal account years ago, but I just didn't see what all the buzz was about.

Once my district started encouraging teachers to build their Professional Learning Networks, however, I reluctantly created a professional account. I was a little skeptical that it would be more of a distraction and less of a genuine resource, but it didn't take long to convince me otherwise. I only spend an average of five minutes a day on Twitter, and in that short time, I find new ideas, get the most recent news in education, research the latest best practices, discover the most

(continued)

cutting-edge apps and read inspirational quotes that remind me why our job is so important.

As it turns out, Twitter is a place for teachers to share, to learn, to grow and to connect, which is exactly what we encourage our students to do. I read a great article on teachthought.com called, "What if Every Teacher Tweeteed?" and it got me thinking about the people I'm representing this year as a Teacher Ambassador Fellow with the U.S. Department of Education.

The 2017-18 cohort of School Ambassador Fellow are always looking for ways to connect and collaborate with other educators to bring practitioner perspective to leaders at the federal level, and social media makes it easier than ever. As a way to reach those beyond our own networks, we will be hosting #FellowsAtEd chats through @usedgov the first Wednesday of each month.

Highlighting STEM

We kicked off the series in December with a STEM focus in honor of Computer Education Week. We wanted to know how people are innovating STEM education in their schools and classrooms and communities so we could highlight those practices at the Department.

Without the Twitter chat, we never would have known that Sarah Gross's (@thereadingzone) students from High Tech Technology High School in Lincroft, **NEW JERSEY**, have a camera trap project. They wrote a grant, set up cameras on campus as a biology research project and blog about the fascinating wildlife. Or that a group of girls from the same school started a STEMinist club.

We also learned about some incredible tools Audra Damron (@audra_damron) uses to introduce coding to preschoolers. These are successes we should be celebrating and finding inspiration from, and we are grateful to find them through the power of a hashtag.

#FellowsAtED

If you have something to share or want to be inspired by new ideas, we invite you to engage in #FellowsAtED by joining our next chat on Wednesday, January 3rd through the @usedgov Twitter account. The topic is social and emotional learning because we know, as educators, how important it is to focus on the whole child, and we want to hear how you and your schools are meeting your students' needs in innovative ways.

I don't consider myself a techie, but I understand the importance and value of using technology to connect to the rest of the world. If we expect our students to challenge themselves with technology, we should embrace that for ourselves and our colleagues.

Educators across the country are already connected by our desire to make an impact on our students and their futures. Let's make it official. Let's do this TOGETHER. Learn from each other. Inspire each other. Lift each other up when we are feeling down. Push each other. Make each other better. #FellowsAtED can make us one colossal classroom. Let's get connected.

PERSONAL REFLECTION

1. Thinking ahead to your future as a teacher, how can you use technology to promote your professional learning and to assume a leadership role in the teaching profession?
2. Join the conversation at #FellowsAtED. Respond to a few tweets, explaining why you agree, or disagree, with the authors' ideas.

The preceding is Melody Arabo's January 3, 2018, blog post, "ED's School Ambassador Fellows Connect with #FellowsAtED Twitter Chats," retrieved from https://blog.ed.gov/2018/01/eds-school-ambassador-fellows-connect-with-fellowsated-twitter-chats/. Melody Arabo was a 2017 Teaching Ambassador Fellow with the U.S. Department of Education and served as the 2015 Michigan Teacher of the Year. She is a third-grade teacher at Keith Elementary in Walled Lake, **MICHIGAN.**

The next four sections of this chapter examine how educational politics at the local, state, regional, and national levels influence schools and teachers.

How Local Communities Influence Schools

Although the Constitution does not address public education, the 10th Amendment is used as the basis for giving states the legal authority to create and manage school systems. In addition, as illustrated in Figure 6.1, various individuals and groups, although not legally empowered, compete vigorously to influence those legally entitled to operate the schools.

The 10th Amendment gives to the states all powers not reserved for the federal government and not prohibited to the states. The states, in turn, have created local school districts, giving them responsibility for the daily operation of public schools. As a result of efforts to consolidate districts, the number of local public school districts declined from 117,108 in 1939–1940 to 13,601 in 2014–2015 (National Center for Education Statistics, 2017b).

LOCAL SCHOOL DISTRICT **Local school districts** vary greatly in regard to demographics such as number of school-age children; educational, occupational, and income levels of parents; operating budget; number of teachers; economic resources; and number of school buildings. Some serve extremely wealthy communities; others serve impoverished ghetto neighborhoods or rural areas. Their operations include approximately 300 one-teacher elementary schools in this country (Snyder & Dillow, 2014) as well as scores of modern, multibuilding campuses in heavily populated areas.

The largest school districts are exceedingly complex operations. The largest—the New York City school system—has 32 community school districts, each with its own superintendent, and a total budget of $30.8 billion for the 2017-18 school year. The New York system, overseen by a schools chancellor, has more than 67,000 teachers (a number that exceeds the number of students in San Francisco; Boston; Detroit; Portland, Oregon; and Seattle) (New York City Department of Education, 2017). Table 6.1 shows selected statistics for the 10 largest school districts in the United States for the 2014–2015 school year.

The organizational structures of school districts also differ. Large urban systems, which may contain several districts, tend to have a more complex distribution of roles and responsibilities than do smaller districts. Figure 6.3 shows the organizational chart for a school district of about 20,000 pupils.

LOCAL SCHOOL BOARD A local **school board**, acting as a state agent, is responsible for the following: approving the teachers, administrators, and other school personnel hired by the superintendent; developing organizational and educational policies; and determining procedures for evaluating programs and personnel. More than 90,000 men and women are members of 13,809 local school boards in the U.S. (National School Boards Association, 2017).

Table 6.1 Selected statistics for the 10 largest public school districts, 2014–2015

Name of district	Enrollment, fall 2014	Number of English language learners, 2014	Percent eligible for free or reduced-price lunch, 2014	Number of FTE classroom teachers, 2014	Public high school 4-year adjusted cohort graduation rate (ACGR) 2014[1]	Number of schools, fall 2014
New York City	995,192	114,849	71.7	67,482	68%	1,636
Los Angeles Unified	646,683	164,349	75.8	27,669	72%	999
City of Chicago	392,558	69,091	86.9	22,559	77%	594
Dade County, FL	356,964	65,163	73.4	20,837	78%	527
Clark County, NV	324,093	59,400	56.4	15,423	72%	367
Broward County, FL	266,265	28,139	61.5	15,211	77%	353
Houston Independent School District	215,225	51,277	75.4	11,422	79%	283
Hillsborough, FL	207,469	24,784	60.1	16,788	76%	310
Orange County, FL	191,648	26,508	59.3	12,069	78%	250
Palm Beach, FL	186,605	21,153	56.7	12,683	79%	274

[1] The ACGR is the percentage of public high school freshmen who graduate with a regular diploma within 4 years of starting ninth grade. Students who are entering ninth grade for the first time form a cohort for the graduating class. This cohort is "adjusted" by adding any students who subsequently transfer into the cohort and subtracting any students who subsequently transfer out, emigrate to another country, or die.

SOURCE: Adapted from *Digest of Education Statistics 2016.* National Center for Education Statistics, Institute of Education Sciences, U.S. Department of Education. Washington, DC. Table 215.10, retrieved October 1, 2017, from https://nces.ed.gov/programs/digest/d16/tables/dt16_215.10.asp?current=yes, and Table 215.30, retrieved October 1, 2017, from https://nces.ed.gov/programs/digest/d16/tables/dt16_215.30.asp?current=yes.

Figure 6.3 Typical organizational structure for a medium-size school district (20,000 pupils)

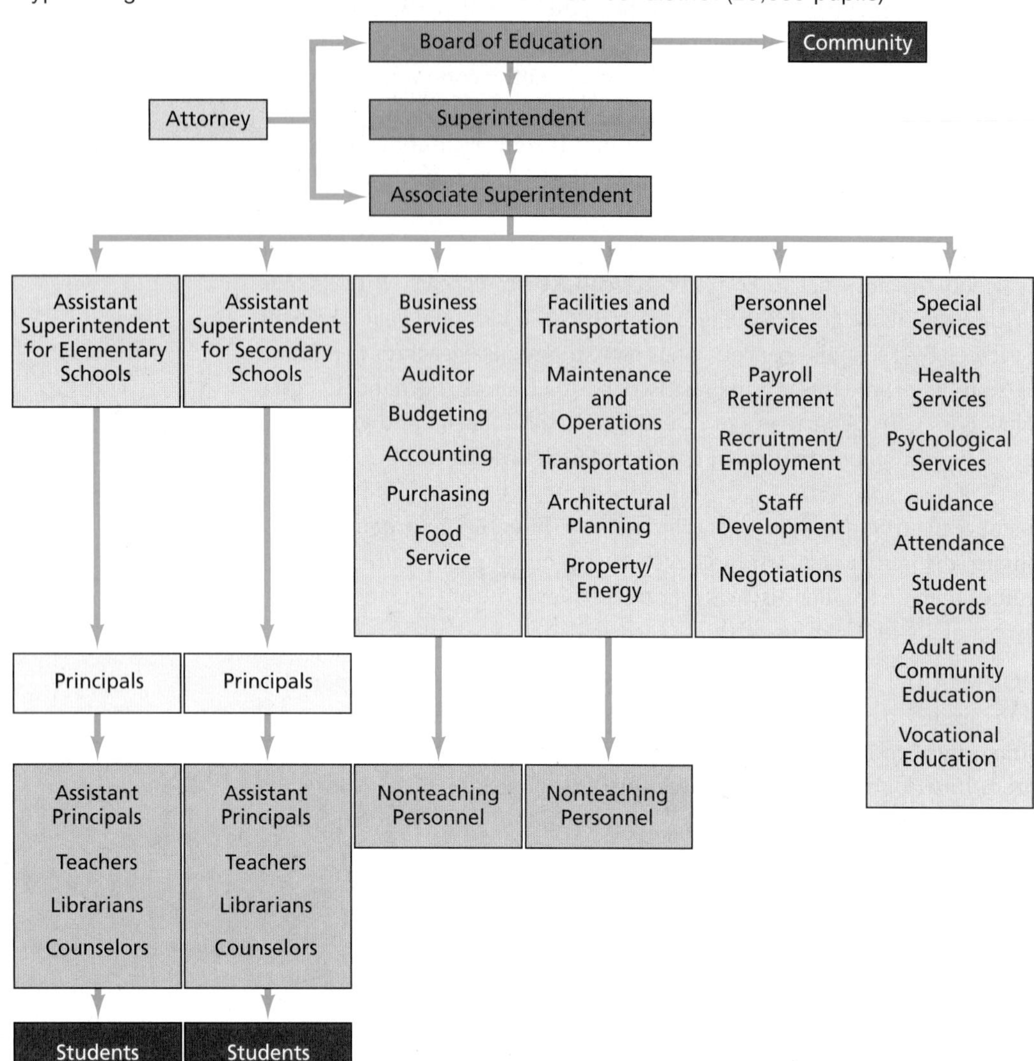

In most communities, school board members are elected in general elections. In some urban areas, however, board members are selected by the mayor. Board members typically serve a minimum of 3 to 5 years, and their terms of office are usually staggered. School boards usually range from 5 to 15 members, with 5 or 7 frequently suggested as the optimum size. Board members in urban areas usually are paid, but in most other areas they are not.

Nearly all school board meetings are open to the public; in fact, many communities even provide radio and television coverage. Open meetings allow parents and interested citizens an opportunity to express their concerns and to get more information about problems in the district.

A national survey of school board members (Hess & Meeks, 2010) revealed the following characteristics of board members:

- White, 80.7 percent; African American, 12.3 percent; and Hispanic, 3.1 percent. Large districts (15,000 or more students), however, have more minority-group board members: African American, 21.8 percent, and Latinos, 6 percent.
- Nearly three fourths of board members have at least a bachelor's degree, far exceeding the 29 percent of American adults over age 25 who hold at least a B.A.

In large districts, 85 percent of board members have at least a B.A., and more than half report that they have earned an advanced degree.

- Politically, 47.3 percent view themselves as moderates, 32.3 percent as conservatives, and 20.4 percent as liberals.
- Fifty-six percent are men, and 44 percent are women. Nearly two thirds of board members in small districts (1,000–2,499 students) are male, whereas less than half are male in large and medium-sized (2,500–14,999 students) districts.
- The most common occupations for board members are education (27.1 percent), business or commerce (18.1 percent), nonprofit organizations and government (14.4 percent), and professional services like law and medicine (14 percent).

School boards play a critical role in the U.S. education system. However, school boards have been criticized for not educating themselves about educational issues, being reluctant to seek input from their communities, not communicating a vision of educational excellence to their communities, and not developing positive relationships with superintendents. Some critics have suggested that public schools would be better served if school districts were led by visionary leaders rather than members of the local community (Spring, 2018; Ballantine, Hammack, & Stuber, 2017; Hess & Meeks, 2010).

Some states have taken steps to reform school boards. For example, **ARKANSAS** provides board members with training in developing partnerships with their communities, creating a vision of educational excellence, and team building. **WEST VIRGINIA** restructured school boards, and board members must complete training that focuses on "boardmanship and governing effectiveness." The National School Boards Association found that "effective" school boards have the eight characteristics summarized in the following:

1. High expectations for student achievement and quality instruction
2. Strong beliefs and values about students' ability to learn and the school system's ability to teach all children
3. Accountability driven—spend less time on operational issues, more time on policies to improve student achievement
4. Collaborative relationship with staff and the community
5. Data savvy; they use data to drive continuous improvement
6. Align and sustain resources to meet district goals
7. United team with the superintendent; and
8. Engage in team development and training (National School Boards Association & Center for Public Education, 2011)

SUPERINTENDENT OF SCHOOLS Although school boards operate very differently, the **superintendent** is the key figure in determining a district's educational policy. The board of education delegates broad powers to the superintendent, but his or her policies require board approval. The specific responsibilities of the superintendent are many. Among the most important are the following:

- To serve as professional adviser to the board of education and to make policy recommendations for improving curricular and instructional programs
- To act as employer and supervisor of professional and nonteaching personnel (janitors, cafeteria workers, etc.)
- To represent the schools in their relations with the community and to explain board of education policies to the community
- To develop policies for the placement and transportation of students within the district

- To prepare an annual school budget and adhere to the budget adopted by the school board

How the superintendent and his or her board work together is related to the size of the school district, with superintendents and school boards in larger districts more likely to be in conflict. School boards in smaller districts are more effective, however, when they do oppose the superintendent. In large districts, the board's own divisiveness makes it less likely that the board will successfully oppose the superintendent (Wirt & Kirst, 2009).

Superintendents must have great skill to respond appropriately to the many external political forces that demand their attention, and conflict is inevitable. Effective superintendents demonstrate that they are able to play three roles simultaneously: politician, manager, and teacher. It is a demanding position, and turnover is high; for example, the average tenure for superintendents during 2014 was 3.18 years (Council of the Great City Schools, 2014). Between 2000 and 2018, the New York City school system had 5 chancellors (New York City Department of Education, 2017).

Video Example 6.1

Building Parent Relationships: This teacher explains how she builds relationships with parents by sharing how their children will be learning in the classroom.

THE ROLE OF PARENTS Parents may not be involved legally in the governance of schools, but they do play an important role in education. One characteristic of successful schools is that they have developed close working relationships with parents. Children whose parents or guardians support and encourage school activities have a definite advantage in school.

Through participation on school advisory and site-based councils, parents are making an important contribution to restructuring and school reform efforts around the country. In addition, groups such as the parent-teacher association (PTA), parent-teacher organization (PTO), or parent advisory council (PAC) give parents the opportunity to communicate with teachers on matters of interest and importance to them. Through these groups, parents can become involved in the life of the school in a variety of ways—from making recommendations regarding school policies to providing much-needed volunteer services, or to initiating school-improvement activities such as fundraising drives.

One example of how parents can serve as advocates for their children's education is Zakiyah Ansari, a parent activist with the New York City Coalition for Educational Justice (CEJ)—a parent-led collaborative whose mission is to address education inequities—and the **NEW YORK** state chapter of the Alliance for Educational Justice (AEJ). The mother of eight children who graduated from or now attend New York City public schools, Ansari has organized parents, teachers, and community members to work for increased school funding, more support services for students, and coaching and mentoring programs to promote teachers' professional growth (Ansari, 2011).

Many parents are also influencing the character of education through their involvement with the growing number of private, parochial, for-profit, and charter schools. In addition, many parents are activists in promoting school choice, voucher systems, and the home schooling movement.

Some parents even join well-funded conservative think tanks that launch sophisticated national campaigns to remove from public schools practices and materials that they find objectionable. In 2016, the American Library Association's Office for Intellectual Freedom reported 323 attempts to remove books from schools and libraries. Approximately 49 percent of challenged books were held by public libraries; 30 percent by schools; 20 percent by school libraries; and 1 percent by special libraries. Objections to the books' content included allegations of offensive language, sexually explicit content, LGBT content, and religious viewpoint. Out of the hundreds of book challenges each year, about 10 percent of those books are eventually removed (American Library Association, 2017).

SCHOOL RESTRUCTURING During the 1990s, many school districts began to make exciting changes in how schools were controlled locally. To improve the performance of schools, to decentralize the system of governance, and to enhance the professional status of teachers, some districts began **restructuring** their school systems. Restructuring goes by several names: shared governance, administrative decentralization, teacher empowerment, professionalization, bottom-up policymaking, school-based planning, school-based management, distributed leadership, and shared decision making. What all these approaches have in common is allowing those who know students best—teachers, principals, aides, custodians, librarians, secretaries, and parents—greater freedom in deciding how to meet students' learning needs.

The Technology in Action feature for this chapter describes how a leadership team of teachers increased students' access to the latest technology by working with their principal to purchase a Second Life "island," a 3D virtual world where students can interact with other students and build virtual environments.

The purpose of restructuring changed when the No Child Left Behind (NCLB) Act was signed into law in 2001. Restructuring became a series of steps a state could take

TECHNOLOGY in ACTION

Virtual Worlds and an Interdisciplinary Curriculum

Candis Randall knew her students loved video games. In fact, she had incorporated a few video games into her 11th-grade history classroom, and her students really enjoyed them. However, the free or less expensive video games she could access were quite prescriptive. That is, the variables programmed into the games only allowed for specific actions and reactions. This was fine for basic lessons, but she wanted applications that emphasized more in-depth concepts and critical thinking. After research on the Internet, she found an alternative approach, something different than video games--virtual worlds. Virtual worlds allow students to explore interesting places alone or in groups; to interact with other students; and to build structures, environments, and/or organisms.

Virtual worlds are online, three-dimensional spaces in which participants can explore, interact, and create. In addition to their stunning visual effects, the social interactions fostered in these worlds can have a great impact on students' learning. Unlike video games like those for Xbox or PlayStation, virtual worlds have no preprogrammed variables—no objectives, no action/reactions programmed into them. Instead, students create the rules and objectives, and they create some of the buildings. They determine what they look like and how they will communicate.

Teachers have used virtual worlds to have students visit active volcanoes, experience schizophrenia, walk through the scene of a Van Gogh painting, and explore the solar system. Students have experienced life in a post–Civil War Western town, responded to a natural disaster as a medical provider, seen artificial intelligence at work, and been granted citizenship in Athens.

Ms. Randall began to explore Second Life, ActiveWorlds, and There, three of several 3D virtual worlds available on the Internet. Eventually, she decided to set up her avatar (a 3D representation of herself) at Second Life (SL). She found several islands that she could use in her lessons, but the real benefit occurred after she demonstrated Second Life to her fellow teachers. After the demo and a series of in-depth conversations, the teachers convinced their principal to purchase an island for the school. They also decided that the English teacher, Mr. Lee; the math teacher, Mrs. Sanchez; the art teacher, Mr. Hummer; the technology teacher, Ms. Sushak; and Ms. Randall would participate in a pilot activity.

They agreed that they would spend the next month using SL as their virtual classroom. They and their students would participate in SL activities that would cover the concepts and learning outcomes normally addressed for that month in each of their classes. They created a new form of combined or blended classroom, which allows individual teachers to address specific academic disciplines using connected subject matter or a common theme.

(continued)

The teachers agreed that the first activity would be a lesson on medieval England. The students in Mrs. Sanchez's math class were asked to build a castle on the school's SL island. Mr. Hummer's students created thematic graphics, such as family crests, portraits, and landscapes. Mr. Lee's students set prose requirements on the island; that is, students could not speak to one another unless they "speaketh correctly." And Ms. Randall's students researched the type of activities that might take place around a medieval castle.

Then they set up a series of roles that individual students would assume. There were a lord and his lady, groomsmen, knights, a constable, and more. Each student was assigned a role to play and was required to interact appropriately.

The activity was a tremendous success. As word got out about the fun these students were having in math, history, English, and art, other students and teachers in the school began visiting the school's medieval community. A rumor started that a student from a neighboring high school heard about the activities taking place and was trying to raise an army to storm the castle.

VISIT: Currently, the most popular virtual world is Second Life. To try it out, visit the Second Life website and download the software. You will create a user account that will eventually become a 3D representation of yourself, known as an avatar. Choose your name carefully because it will remain with you for all time in SL. Once you have your name, decide what you will look like—your gender, race, body type, hair (or no), clothing, and gestures. Once your avatar is complete, you will walk through a tutorial, where you learn how to walk, shop, fly, and talk. Once the tutorial is completed, you are free to live your second life.

for schools consistently unable to show that students were making adequate yearly progress (AYP) as required by NCLB. Schools were required to develop restructuring plans to improve student achievement. These plans required reorganizing a school's governance structure. Available options included adopting a charter and becoming a charter school; replacing some or all school staff, including the principal; or contracting with an outside private entity to operate the school.

SCHOOL-BASED MANAGEMENT A frequently used approach to restructuring schools is **school-based management (SBM)**. Most SBM programs have three components in common:

1. Power and decisions formerly made by the superintendent and school board are delegated to teachers, principals, parents, community members, and students at local schools. At SBM schools, teachers can become involved directly in decisions about curriculum, textbooks, standards for student behavior, staff development, promotion and retention policies, teacher evaluation, school budgets, and the selection of teachers and administrators.
2. At each school, a decision-making body (known as a board, cabinet, site-based team, or council)—made up of teachers, the principal, and parents—implements the SBM plan.
3. SBM programs operate with the full support of the superintendent of schools.

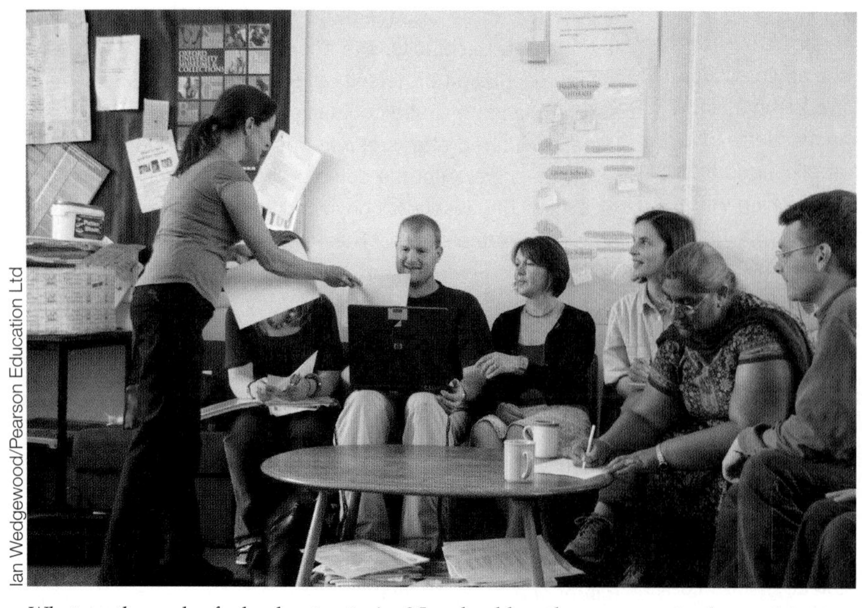

Ian Wedgewood/Pearson Education Ltd

What are the goals of school restructuring? In school-based management, who participates in the governance and management of schools? How is school-based management different from the school board model of local governance?

INNOVATIVE APPROACHES TO SCHOOL GOVERNANCE Although traditionally organized school districts govern most schools in the United States, several districts are using innovative approaches in response to academic, financial, and political challenges to educating students. Among the large-city school districts experimenting with innovative approaches to school governance are New York City; Washington, D.C.; Memphis; and New Orleans.

Schools in New York, **NEW YORK** switched to a mayoral control system of governance when Mayor Michael Bloomberg won the right in 2002 to replace an elected school board with a board he appointed. Mayor Bloomberg also appointed a chancellor to head the city's school system. Similarly, in 2007, Mayor Adrian Fenty won the right to appoint the chancellor of **WASHINGTON, D.C.** schools.

After decades of financial strife and low academic performance, the Memphis, **TENNESSEE** school system changed from a traditional district of 205 schools to a system comprised of different approaches to governance. In 2010, the state created the Achievement School District, which took over 15 low-performing schools, with plans to take over more than 50 schools during subsequent years. In addition, the former 104,000-student Memphis district, which served a high-poverty, majority African American student body, merged during summer 2013 with the neighboring, wealthier Shelby County school system. The merged district also authorized more than 40 charter schools that would be governed under a "charter-management organization." However, by the end of the year, six suburban municipalities began the process of withdrawing from the merged district to form their own school districts for the 2014–2015 school year. Shelby County and the Memphis City Council filed a lawsuit against the suburban districts, claiming that the new districts would resegregate the county's schools and violate the equal protection clause of the 14th Amendment. In response, the suburbs said they wanted a system with more local control (Zubrzycki, 2014).

New Orleans, **LOUISIANA** provides a final example of innovative approaches to school governance. After Hurricane Katrina in 2005, most schools in New Orleans became charter schools operated by the privately run Recovery School District (RSD). The RSD empowers teachers, principals, and parents by providing them the following roles in school governance:

- Teachers, rather than the district, select the methods and materials they use to teach students.
- Principals, rather than the district office, hire teachers and manage a school's budget.
- Parents choose the schools their children attend; previously, children's home addresses determined the schools they attended (Recovery School District, 2014).

Teaching on Your Feet

"We Are All Responsible for One Another. . . ."

LISA M. WEINBAUM was awarded a $2,000 grant for a "Homeless but Not Hopeless" project for her students at a Las Cruces, **NEW MEXICO** middle school. She applied for the grant after her students made fun of the homeless. According to Weinbaum, they thought homeless people were lazy and might be "faking it."

"We are all responsible for one another and not just ourselves," Weinbaum wrote in her grant application. "The dispossessed still starve, and no one knows or cares to know."

She used the grant money to buy reading material about the homeless, take her students to a homeless shelter, and print a student-written anthology of oral histories, essays, poems, and stories honoring the homeless of Las Cruces.

In the following, Weinbaum describes how a field trip to a pauper's cemetery increased her students' understanding of how homelessness and poverty affect death as well as life. Her students also "learned they have political power, the ability to help eradicate injustice."

A no-name cemetery containing about 100 unmarked graves was located about five blocks from our school, but few of my students knew it existed . . . .

Even for Las Cruces, it was an unseasonably warm late September day and perhaps too hot for a walking field trip. I decided to escort my students anyway, but not all were enthused about making an uphill trek to an abandoned paupers'

(continued)

graveyard in the blistering sun. "What could this cemetery possibly have to do with us?" they demanded.

About 70 percent of my school's students receive free or reduced-price lunch, and many families are relegated to low-paying jobs. Because we were studying the societal causes of homelessness within a unit titled "Homeless but Not Hopeless," I wanted to illustrate that poverty affects life as well as death. In short, this cemetery had everything to do with them. Moreover, I knew that middle school students possess a profound regard for justice.

Once in sight of the cemetery, the students' complaining ceased, replaced with a sudden flurry of note-taking. They stared at the small earthen mounds, at the unkempt, overgrown gravesites. Single cinderblock headstones adorned some graves, while others sprouted misshapen mesquite shrubs or prickly pear cacti. Rough, weather-worn crosses lay haphazardly on the ground, nails protruding. Remnants of windblown Wal-Mart bags, broken Budweiser bottles, and faded pink plastic roses littered the landscape. But the final disgrace was the presence of tiny American flags, obviously planted decades ago, perhaps to honor fallen veterans. Tattered and torn, they were threadbare and colorless. Clearly, the souls buried within the cemetery had long since been abandoned by our community.

Totally disgusted, my students vowed to clean the graveyard. They were willing to return on their own, beyond school hours, to complete the job if necessary. But upon contacting a government official, I was told that because the cemetery was located on Doña Ana County property, approval must first be granted from government attorneys, which could take months.

Incensed by the county's bureaucratic run-around and the apparent indifference toward the plight of the cemetery and those interred there, my students wrote protest letters to our local newspapers. Intrigued by the students' concerns, the Las Cruces Sun-News *featured a front-page exposé about the cemetery, followed the next day by an editorial chastising the county for abandoning the dead. Later, the cemetery story aired on the TV news in El Paso, 45 miles to our south, and Albuquerque, 250 miles to our north.*

Embarrassed by the unflattering publicity initiated by my students, the county quickly sponsored a community cleanup at the cemetery. Early on a November Saturday morning, led by my students and their parents with help from other teachers from our school, county employees and local residents, we cleaned the graveyard. Doña Ana County provided heavy machinery, water bottles, gloves, shovels, rakes, and trash bags, while a local restaurateur supplied breakfast burritos. In addition, a recreational vehicle dealership made available an RV rest station. One gentleman, so moved by my students' letters, donated a granite monument engraved not only with the names of the departed, but also with the inscription, "For the Forgotten of Doña Ana County, Both Living and Deceased."

My students were so proud of themselves. Through the strength of their collective speech, they learned their voices are valued. They learned they have political power, the ability to help eradicate injustice. Through their passion, perseverance, and eloquence, they captured our attention. And perhaps for the first time in their educational lives, they were taken seriously. No longer were they labeled as "at-risk" kids relegated to remedial reading; they were the kids who forced our community to look. *They were the kids who forced our community to* act.

They are writers. They are activists. They are heroes. They are my students.

LISA M. WEINBAUM
Seventh-Grade Literature, Lynn Middle School Las Cruces, **NEW MEXICO**

Analyze

Weinbaum finds that her students are more engaged and motivated if she integrates social justice into her teaching. "The kids buy into it, this sense of fairness, what's right and what's wrong," she says. "They know what's 'messed up,' to put it in their words."

Reflect

1. Do you agree with Weinbaum that it is a good idea for teachers to integrate social justice issues into their teaching? Explain your response.
2. Should teachers encourage their students to become politically involved?
3. What might be some negative consequences if students become politically involved?

Weinbaum's article that appeared in Teaching Tolerance, "'At Risk' of Greatness," Spring 2007. Retrieved February 20, 2011, from http://www.tolerance.org/magazine/number-31-spring-2007/risk-greatness.

How do States and Regional Education Agencies Influence Education?

Above the level of local control, states have a great influence on schools. Since the 1990s, the influence of the state on educational policy has increased steadily. For example, every state has statewide academic standards, and every state has mandated a standardized test to assess students' mastery of academic standards. Currently, 13 states require students to attain minimum scores on state assessments to graduate from high school, down from a high of 26 states during 2011 (FairTest, 2017). In addition, more than 20 states give state boards of education the authority to intervene in academically "bankrupt" schools whose students score too low as a group.

In response to criticisms of U.S. education, many states launched extensive initiatives to improve education, such as the following:

- Increased academic standards
- Greater accountability for teachers
- Testing students in teacher education programs prior to graduation
- Frequent assessments of students' mastery of basic skills
- Professional development as a criterion for continued employment of teachers
- Recertification of experienced teachers

As mentioned previously, the 10th Amendment to the Constitution allows the states to organize and to administer education within their boundaries. To meet the responsibility of maintaining and supporting schools, the states have assumed several powers:

- The power to levy taxes for the support of schools and to determine state aid to local school districts
- The power to set the curriculum and, in some states, to identify approved textbooks
- The power to determine minimum standards for teacher certification
- The power to establish standards for accrediting schools
- The power to pass legislation necessary for the proper maintenance and support of schools

To carry out the tasks implied by these powers, the states have adopted a number of different organizational structures. Most states, however, have adopted a hierarchical structure similar to that presented in Figure 6.4.

The Roles of State Government in Education

Various people and agencies play a role in operating the educational system within each state. Although state governments differ, the state legislature, the state courts, and the governor have a direct, critical impact on education in each state.

THE LEGISLATURE In nearly every state, the legislature is responsible for establishing and maintaining public schools and for determining basic educational policies within the state. Among the policies that the state legislature may determine are the following:

- How the state boards of education will be selected and what their responsibilities will be
- How the chief state school officer will be selected and what his or her duties will be
- How the state department of education will function
- How the state will be divided into local and regional districts
- How higher education will be organized and financed
- How local school boards will be selected and what their powers will be

In addition, the legislature may determine how taxes will be used to support schools, what will or will not be taught, the length of the school day and school year, how many years of compulsory education will be required, and whether or not the state will have community colleges and/or vocational/technical schools. Legislatures may also make policies that apply to matters such as pupil attendance, admission, promotion, teacher certification, teacher tenure and retirement, and collective bargaining.

Figure 6.4 Organizational structure of a typical state school system

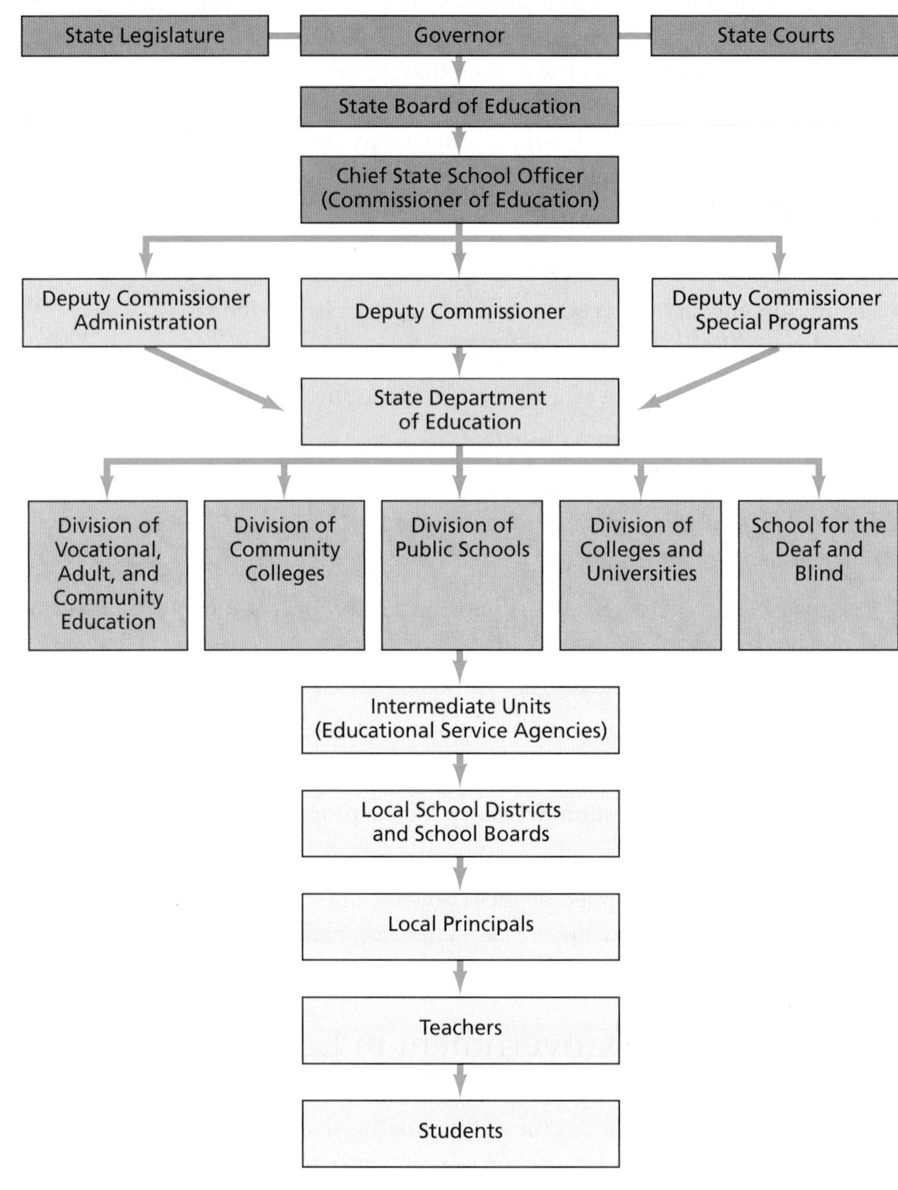

Other policies developed by the state legislature may also apply to nonpublic schools in the state—policies related to health services, building construction, safety, school lunch services, textbooks, and testing of pupils, for example. In general, state legislatures may pass laws that provide for the reasonable supervision of nonpublic educational institutions.

THE STATE COURTS From time to time, state courts are called on to uphold the power of the legislature to develop laws that apply to schools. The state courts must determine, however, that this power does not conflict with the state constitution or the U.S. Constitution. It is important to remember, too, that the role of state courts is not to develop laws but to rule on the reasonableness of laws that apply to specific educational situations.

Perhaps no state court has had a greater impact on education than the Kentucky Supreme Court. In 1989, the court ruled that the state's entire school system was "inadequate." Naming the state superintendent and the state education agency as part of the problem and pointing out that **KENTUCKY** schools were ineffective and inequitable, the court labeled the school system "unconstitutional." The court called on the governor and the legislature to develop an entirely new system of education for the state. A 22-member task force, appointed by the governor and the legislature, then developed the 906-page **Kentucky Education Reform Act (KERA)** passed in 1990. KERA required each school to form a school-based management council by 1996 with authority to set policy in eight areas: curriculum, staff time, student assignment, schedule, school space, instructional issues, discipline, and extracurricular activities. Each council comprised three teachers, two parents (elected by their peers), and the principal. In addition, KERA included the following major changes to the state's education system:

- More rigorous assessment of academic goals and accountability measures for reaching those goals
- Reforms in school governance
- More equitable school funding
- A corps of trained educators to assist or take over underperforming schools and/or districts
- Changes in the training and certification of teachers and administrators
- Expanded inclusion of children with special needs in regular classrooms
- A comprehensive program of tutorial/remedial services for students
- Family Resource/Youth Service Centers to serve preschool and K–12 students and their families
- Multiage environments for K–3 students

KERA dramatically equalized funding across the state, and some school districts made substantial gains in funding for students. School districts with low property value per student had educational spending rates similar to districts in wealthy areas. In addition, teacher salaries and student/teacher ratios improved compared to national averages.

Evidence suggests that KERA led to significant improvements in Kentucky's system of education. For example, from 1992 to 2002, Kentucky increased six points in reading on the 4th Grade National Assessment of Educational Progress (NAEP); only five other states showed larger gains. From 1998 to 2002, Kentucky increased three points on eighth-grade NAEP reading, which exceeded the national average increase. Furthermore, results from Kentucky's 2002 Comprehensive Test of Basic Skills Test (CTBS) assessment showed sustained progress in reading, language arts, and mathematics, with Kentucky above the national average at all three testing stages: grades 3, 6, and 9. Last, in 2000, Kentucky *led* the nation in the percentage increase in the high school completion rate for 25- to 34-year-olds (Haselton & Davis, 2004).

KERA also resulted in positive changes that were beyond numerical measurement. For example, two Kentucky educators noted that "We [have seen] a potent, though hard to quantify, change in the culture of our schools. This is visible in the strong record of local revenue efforts since the reform began, in the clear decline in hiring based on family and political ties, and in the strong achievement emphasis now heard among the rising leadership among school boards, superintendents, and other educators" (Weston & Sexton, 2009, p. 32).

Many other observers, such as the following, came to a different conclusion about the impact of KERA: "In its 20 years of existence, a large number of KERA's major efforts have proven unsuccessful. This despite the fact that educators assured citizens time and again—often using terms like 'the research shows'—that their fad ideas were succeeding" (Innes, 2010, p. 2).

The debate about the impact of KERA notwithstanding, there is a mutually agreed-upon lesson from KERA. Improving a statewide system of education is a complex, political process. As Kentucky, like most other states, continues its efforts to improve education by implementing more rigorous standards, developing better approaches to assessing students' learning, and considering innovative approaches to governance such as charter schools, these efforts must be driven by a strong desire to improve education for all students.

THE GOVERNOR Although the powers of governors vary greatly from state to state, a governor can, if he or she chooses, have a great impact on education within the state. The governor may appoint and/or remove educators at the state level, and in some states the governor may even appoint the chief state school officer. Furthermore, in every state except North Carolina, the governor may use his or her veto power to influence the legislature to pass certain laws related to education.

Governors are also extremely influential because they make educational budget recommendations to legislatures and, in many states, they may elect to use any accumulated balances in the state treasury for education. Governors can also have a significant impact on matters related to curriculum and instruction within the state and, indeed, across the nation. For example, Roy Romer, former governor of **COLORADO**, was instrumental in organizing ACHIEVE, an effort by U.S. governors and corporate leaders to raise academic standards and develop accountability systems for schools. In addition, the **National Governors' Association (NGA)** is active in teacher education and school reforms.

STATE TAKEOVER OF SCHOOLS Since passage of the No Child Left Behind Act of 2001, **state takeover** is an intervention that can be applied to chronically low-achieving schools and districts. The School District of Philadelphia, **PENNSYLVANIA** has been the site of the nation's largest takeover of schools. In 2002, the state of Pennsylvania, frustrated by years of low achievement and a decade of budget crises in the School District of Philadelphia, took charge of the city's 200,000-pupil system. The state replaced Philadelphia's nine-member school board with an appointed school reform commission (SRC) composed of three members appointed by the governor and two appointed by the city's mayor. The SRC then hired a new CEO who immediately instituted sweeping changes, including the implementation of districtwide common curricula and a system of frequent benchmark assessments to be used for diagnostic purposes.

More controversially, the SRC adopted a "diverse provider" model as it turned over management of 45 of the district's lowest-performing elementary and middle schools to seven for-profit and nonprofit organizations, including two local universities. The private managers were given additional per-pupil funding to support their work.

During 2002–2006, achievement gains at Philadelphia schools managed privately did not exceed achievement gains at schools in the rest of the district. "With respect to state takeover, results are ambiguous: Subsequent to the state's takeover of the district, proficiency percentages increased district-wide, but the total increase over four years was not substantially greater than the increase of other low-achieving schools in the state, in most cases" (Gill, Zimmer, Christman, & Blanc, 2007).

By 2013, the nation had recovered somewhat from the Great Recession of 2008; however, Philadelphia schools faced a financial crisis. In response to the district's $304 million shortfall, the U.S. Secretary of Education stated: "There's no excuse for a public school system anywhere in the U.S. to be in this situation in the 21st century, and it's even worse to see it in Philadelphia, the cornerstone of this great country and the cradle for our founding principles" (U.S. Department of Education, 2013).

More than 15 years after Pennsylvania took control of Philadelphia schools, the arrangement remains controversial, and the governor and other critics continue to call for a return to local control. While there is no agreement among researchers about which form of school governance—state takeover, elected local board, or mayoral control—leads to greater student learning, researchers agree that uncertainty and instability have made it difficult for Philadelphia schools to improve (Pew Charitable Trust, 2016).

State Board of Education

The **state board of education**, acting under the authority of the state legislature, is the highest educational agency in a state. Every state, with the exception of Wisconsin, has a state board of education. Most states have two separate boards, one responsible for elementary through secondary education, the other for higher education.

The method of determining board members varies from state to state. In some states, the governor appoints members of the state board; in other states, members are selected through general elections. People disagree on which is better: electing or appointing board members. Some believe that election to the state board may cause members to be more concerned with politics than with education. Others argue that elected board members are more aware of the wishes of the public, whom the schools are supposed to serve. People in favor of appointing members to the state board suggest that appointment increases the likelihood that individuals will be chosen on the basis of merit rather than politics.

The regulatory and advisory functions generally held by state boards are as follows:

- Ensuring that local school districts adhere to legislated educational policies, rules, and regulations
- Setting standards for issuing and revoking teaching and administrative certificates
- Establishing standards for accrediting schools
- Managing state monies appropriated for education
- Developing and implementing a system for collecting educational data needed for reporting and program evaluation
- Advising the governor and/or the state legislature on educational issues
- Identifying both short- and long-range educational needs in the state and developing plans to meet those needs
- Hearing all disputes arising from the implementation of its educational policies

In addition, a few state boards of education have instituted a statewide textbook adoption system. In the adoption system, boards choose a small number of titles for each subject area and grade level for all the state's schools. Individual schools and teachers then select their textbooks from this list. **NORTH CAROLINA**, for example, has created a 23-member textbook commission made up of teachers, principals, parents, and a local superintendent. Textbooks are evaluated using criteria based on the North Carolina Standard Course of Study, and adopted textbooks are placed on the statewide textbook list for five years.

State Department of Education

The educational program of each state is implemented by the state's department of education, under the leadership of the chief state school officer. State departments of education have a broad set of responsibilities, and they affect literally every school, school district, and teacher education program in a state. In general, the state board of education is concerned with policymaking, the **state department of education** with the day-to-day implementation of those policies.

A great boost for the development of state departments of education came with the federal government's Elementary and Secondary Education Act of 1965. This act and its subsequent amendments required that local applications for federal funds be used for innovative programs and for the education of disadvantaged, disabled, bilingual, and migrant students.

Today, the responsibilities of state departments of education include (1) certifying teachers, (2) distributing state and federal funds to school districts, (3) reporting to the public the condition of education within the state, (4) ensuring that school districts adhere to state and federal guidelines, (5) accrediting schools, (6) monitoring student transportation and safety, and (7) sponsoring research and evaluation projects to improve education within the state.

Perhaps the most significant index of the steady increase in state control since the 1980s is the fact that the states now supply the majority of funding for schools. Clearly, the power and influence of state departments of education will continue to be extensive.

Chief State School Officer

The **chief state school officer** (known as the commissioner of education or superintendent of public instruction in many states) is the chief administrator of the state department of education and the head of the state board of education. In 23 states, the state board of education appoints the chief state school officer; in 13 states, the office is filled through a general election; and in the remaining 14, the governor appoints an individual to that position (Education Commission of the States, 2016).

Although the specific responsibilities of the chief state school officer vary from state to state, most individuals in this position hold several responsibilities in common:

1. Serving as chief administrator of the state department of education and state board of education
2. Selecting state department of education personnel
3. Recommending educational policies and budgets to the state board
4. Interpreting state school laws and state board of education policies
5. Ensuring compliance with state school laws and policies
6. Mediating controversies involving the operation of schools within the state
7. Arranging for studies, committees, and task forces to address educational problems and recommend solutions
8. Reporting on the status of education to the governor, legislature, state board, and public

Regional Education Agencies and Assistance to Schools

When you think about how schools are governed and the sources of political pressure applied to them, you probably think of influences originating at three levels: local, state, and federal. There is, however, an additional source of control—the regional, or intermediate, unit. The intermediate unit of educational administration, or the **regional educational service agency (RESA)**, is the least understood branch of the state public school system. Through the intermediate unit, local school districts can receive supportive services that, economically and logistically, they could not provide for themselves.

Today, about half of the states have some form of intermediate or regional unit. The average unit is made up of 20 to 30 local school districts and covers a 50-square-mile area. The intermediate or regional unit has many different names: educational service district (in **WASHINGTON**), county education office (in **CALIFORNIA**), education service center (in **TEXAS**), intermediate school district (in **MICHIGAN**), multicounty educational service unit (in **NEBRASKA**), and board of cooperative educational services (in **NEW YORK**).

The primary role of the intermediate unit is to provide assistance directly to districts in the areas of staff development, curriculum development, instructional media, and program evaluation. Intermediate or regional units also help school districts with their school improvement efforts in targeted areas such as bilingual education, vocational education, educational technology, and the education of gifted and talented students and students with disabilities. Although intermediate units monitor local school districts to see that they follow state educational guidelines, local districts, in fact, exert great influence over RESAs by identifying district-level needs that can be met by the intermediate unit.

Application Exercise 6.1
Benefits of a Regional Educational Service Agency

How does the Federal Government Influence Education?

Since the birth of the United States, the federal government has played a major role in shaping the character of schools. This branch of government has always recognized that the strength and well-being of the country are directly related to the quality of its schools. The importance of a quality education, for example, has been highlighted by many U.S. Supreme Court rulings supporting the free speech rights of teachers and students under the 1st Amendment and the right of all citizens to equal educational opportunity under the 14th Amendment.

Federal Initiatives

The federal government has taken aggressive initiatives to influence education at several points in U.S. history, such as the allocation of federal money to improve science, mathematics, and foreign language education after the former Soviet Union launched *Sputnik*, the world's first satellite. During World War II, the federal government funded several new educational programs. One of these, the Lanham Act (1941), provided funding for (1) the training of workers in war plants by U.S. Office of Education personnel, (2) the construction of schools in areas where military personnel and workers on federal projects resided, and (3) the provision of child care for the children of working parents.

Another influential and extensive federal program in support of education was the Servicemen's Readjustment Act, popularly known as the **G.I. Bill of Rights**. Signed into law by President Franklin D. Roosevelt in 1944, the G.I. bill has provided millions of veterans with payments for tuition and room and board at colleges, universities, and technical schools. Similar legislation was later passed to grant educational benefits to veterans of the Korean and Vietnam conflicts. Not only did the G.I. bill stimulate the growth of colleges and universities in the United States, but it also opened higher education to an older and nontraditional student population.

The executive, legislative, and judicial branches of the federal government influence education in four ways:

1. **Exert moral suasion**—develop a vision and promote educational goals for the nation; for example, U.S. Secretary of Education Betsy DeVos launched a six-state "Rethink School" tour in September 2017, showcasing creative ways in which education leaders are meeting the needs of students in K–12 education.
2. **Provide categorical aid**—assist school systems with funding if they adopt federally endorsed programs, methods, or curricula.
3. **Regulate**—withhold federal funds if a school system fails to follow legal statutes related to equal educational opportunity.
4. **Fund educational research**—identify and then fund research projects related to federal goals for education.

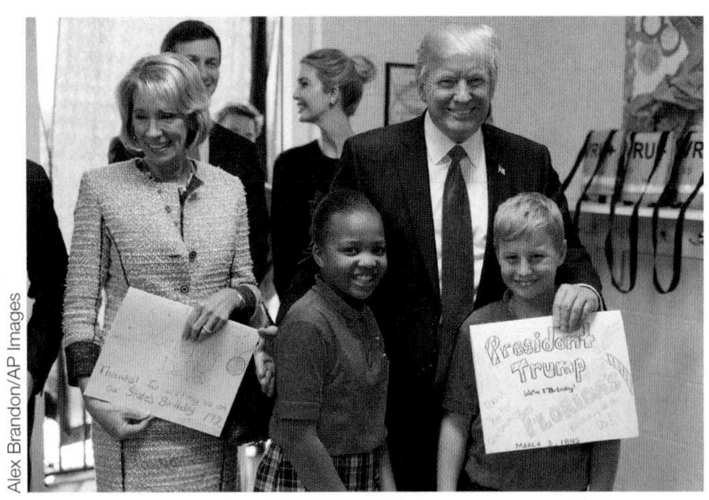

Alex Brandon/AP Images

How do federal education initiatives influence schools at the local level? How does federal funding help reduce inequities among schools?

THE IMPACT OF PRESIDENTIAL POLICIES Presidential platforms on education can have a profound effect on education. Presidents Reagan and George H.W. Bush, for example, scaled back federal involvement in education. President Clinton's administration, on the other hand, assumed a more active role in ensuring equal educational opportunity. And the No Child Left Behind (NCLB) Act developed and implemented during President George W. Bush's two terms had a significant impact on our nation's schools.

In 2010, President Barack Obama's administration released **A Blueprint for Reform**, calling for the reauthorization of ESEA and significant changes to NCLB. However, Congress did not reauthorize ESEA until five years later.

In December 2015, President Obama signed into law the Every Student Succeeds Act (ESSA) that reauthorized ESEA and replaced the NCLB Act. Overall, ESSA expands the states' role in education and reduces federal involvement. For example, each state sets its own curriculum standards, and these standards no longer must be submitted to the U.S. Department of Education. In addition, schools no longer must demonstrate that students have made adequate yearly progress (AYP) as required by NCLB. Instead, states can create their own systems for assessing students' learning and determining the performance of schools.

Full implementation of ESSA did not begin until 2017–2018. At the start of President Donald Trump's administration, newly appointed U.S. Secretary of Education Betsy DeVos assured chief state school officers in a personal letter "I fully intend to implement and enforce the statutory requirements of the ESSA" (U.S. Department of Education, 2017, February 10). However, the Trump administration would have an opportunity to determine how the complex law would be interpreted and applied during the years ahead.

President Trump began to advance his educational platform with his $59 billion education budget request for Fiscal Year 2018. The request addressed five "major themes":

- Expanding school choice, ensuring more children have an equal opportunity to receive a great education
- Maintaining strong support for the Nation's most vulnerable students
- Simplifying funding for postsecondary education
- Continuing to build evidence around educational innovation
- Eliminating or reducing Department programs consistent with the limited Federal role in education (U.S. Department of Education, 2017, October 7)

FOCUS ON **STEM**: A MEMO FROM THE PRESIDENT

In September 2017, President Trump issued a presidential memorandum with the following subject line: "Increasing Access to High-Quality Science, Technology, Engineering, and Mathematics (STEM) Education." The following excerpts from that memo illustrate how a president can influence education in the U.S.

> A key priority of my Administration is to better equip America's young people with the relevant knowledge and skills that will enable them to secure high-paying, stable jobs throughout their careers. With the growing role of technology in driving the American economy, many jobs increasingly require skills in science, technology, engineering, and mathematics (STEM)—including, in

> particular, Computer Science. These skills open the door to jobs, strengthening the backbone of American ingenuity, driving solutions to complex problems across industries, and improving lives around the world.
>
> Today, too many of our Nation's K-12 and post-secondary students lack access to high-quality STEM education, and thus are at risk of being shut out from some of the most attractive job options in the growing United States economy.
>
> The Department of Education, therefore, should prioritize helping districts recruit and train teachers capable of providing students with a rigorous education in STEM fields, focusing in particular on Computer Science.

Source: U.S. Department of Education, Press Release, September 25, 2017

U.S. Department of Education

In 1979, President Carter signed a law creating the Department of Education. This new Cabinet-level department assumed the responsibilities of the U.S. Office of Education, which had been formed in 1953 as a branch of the Department of Health, Education, and Welfare. Shirley Hufstedler, a state Supreme Court judge, became the first Secretary of Education when the new department opened in mid-1980. In 1983, President Reagan suggested that the Department of Education be dismantled and replaced with a Foundation for Education Assistance. However, public response to the reform report *A Nation at Risk* convinced the President that education was too important an issue not to be represented at the Cabinet level.

A proposal to eliminate the Department of Education was soundly defeated at the 1984 Republican National Convention. So solid was the rejection of the proposal to eliminate the Department that former Secretary of Education Terrel H. Bell was moved to comment that "dissolution of the department will not, in my opinion, ever again be a serious issue. The Education Department is here to stay" (Bell, 1986, p. 492).

Today, the Department of Education employs about 4,400 people and had an annual budget of approximately $69 billion for Fiscal Year 2017. The mission of the Department is to "promote student achievement and preparation for global competitiveness by fostering educational excellence and ensuring equal access." The Department is dedicated to:

- establishing policies on federal financial aid for education, and distributing as well as monitoring those funds.
- collecting data on America's schools and disseminating research.
- focusing national attention on key educational issues.
- prohibiting discrimination and ensuring equal access to education (U.S. Department of Education, 2017, August 31).

How are Schools Financed in the United States?

To provide free public education to all school-age children in the United States is a costly, complex undertaking. Today's school districts are big-business enterprises and must provide services and facilities to students from many ethnic, racial, social, cultural, linguistic, and individual backgrounds.

Education Funding and the Nation's Economy

In 2008, the nation entered the worst financial crisis since the Great Depression of the 1930s. Nationwide, the unemployment rate rose from less than 5 percent at the end of 2007 to about 10 percent by the end of 2009, before dropping to about 4.8 percent by January 2017. State funding for education dropped dramatically, and many school districts, facing large budget deficits, had to lay off teachers and close schools. To keep layoffs to a minimum, school districts trimmed their budgets in other areas—eliminating summer school programs, after-school programs, bus routes, and days from the school calendar, for example.

In response to the Great Recession, the American Recovery and Reinvestment Act of 2009 included $100 billion for education. That stimulus money enabled school districts to avoid thousands of scheduled teacher layoffs and to rehire teachers previously laid off. At the beginning of the 2010–2011 school year, the federal government provided another $10 billion for school districts to retain or rehire teachers and other educational staff. However, the real estate meltdown, high unemployment, and severe shortfalls in state and federal budgets during that time have had a long-lasting impact on school funding. Today, a common expression among educators is "We have to do more with less."

The Great Recession resulted in a decline in total expenditures for public elementary and secondary education of nearly $75 billion between fiscal years 2008 and 2011. However, total expenditures are expected to rise through 2025–2026 (see Figure 6.5). Total expenditures for public elementary and secondary schools during the 2017–2018 school year were approximately $623.5 billion, and the total **per-pupil expenditure** was $12,300 (National Center for Education Statistics, 2017b). Figure 6.6 shows expenditures per student by function for school years 2003–04, 2008–09, and 2013–14.

Figure 6.5 Actual and projected current expenditures for public elementary and secondary schools (in constant 2014–15 dollars): School years 2000—2001 through 2025–2026

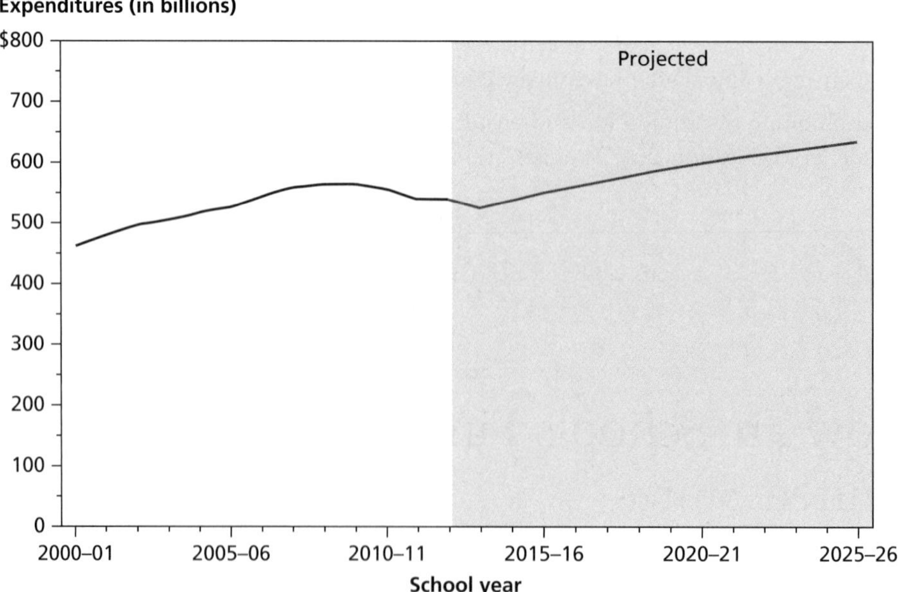

Note: Numbers were placed in constant dollars using the Consumer Price Index (CPI) for all urban consumers, Bureau of Labor Statistics, U.S. Department of Labor.

SOURCE: Hussar, W.J., and Bailey, T.M. (2017). *Projections of Education Statistics to 2025* (NCES 2017-019). U.S. Department of Education, Washington, DC: National Center for Education Statistics, p. 20.

Figure 6.6 Current expenditures per student in fall enrollment in public elementary and secondary schools, by function of expenditure: 2003–04, 2008–09, and 2013–14

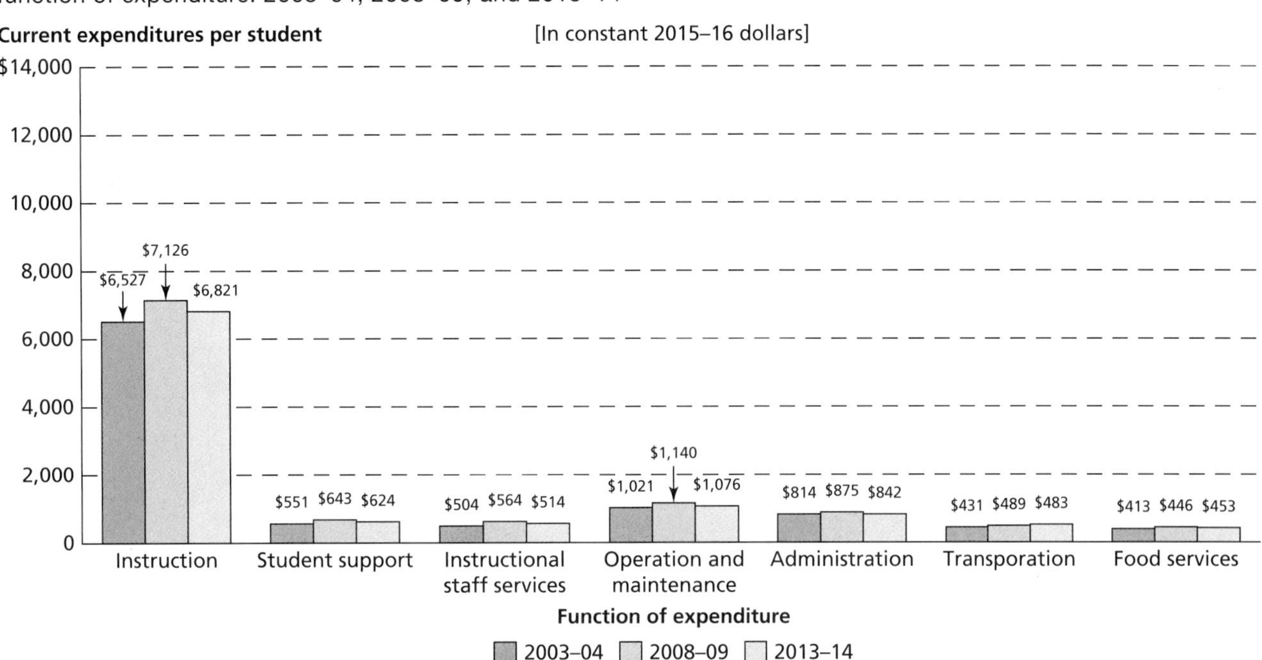

Note: "Instruction," "Student support," "Instructional staff services," "Operation and maintenance," "Administration," "Transportation," and "Food services" are subcategories of current expenditures. "Student support" includes expenditures for guidance, health, attendance, and speech pathology services. "Instructional staff services" include expenditures for curriculum development, staff training, libraries, and media and computer centers. "Administration" includes both general administration and school administration. "Transportation" refers to student transportation. The two smallest subcategories in 2013–14 dollars, enterprise operations and other support services, are not included in this figure. Expenditures are reported in constant 2015–16 dollars, based on the Consumer Price Index (CPI).

SOURCE: McFarland, J., Hussar, B., de Brey, C., Snyder, T., Wang, X., Wilkinson-Flicker, S., Gebrekristos, S., Zhang, J., Rathbun, A., Barmer, A., Bullock Mann, F., and Hinz, S. (2017). *The Condition of Education 2017* (NCES 2017-144). U.S. Department of Education. Washington, DC: National Center for Education Statistics, p. 150.

The Challenge of Equitable Funding

Financing an enterprise as vast and ambitious as the U.S. system of free public schools has not been easy. It has proved difficult both to devise a system that equitably distributes the tax burden for supporting schools and to provide equal educational services and facilities for all students.

An additional funding challenge is that, rather than one national education system, there are 50 state systems that receive revenues from local, state, and federal sources. Dollars are distributed quite unequally across the states, districts, and schools.

Moreover, financial support of schools tends to be outpaced by factors that continually increase the cost of operating schools—inflation, rising enrollments, and the need to update aging facilities, for example. Not surprisingly, "lack of funding" has been the number one problem confronting local schools from 2002 to 2017, according to Gallup polls of the public's attitudes toward public schools (Phi Delta Kappa, 2017).

Sources of Funding

A combination of revenues from local, state, and federal sources is used to finance public elementary and secondary schools in the United States. As Figure 6.7 shows, schools received 46.2 percent of 2013–14 funding from the state, 45.0 percent from local sources, and 8.7 percent from the federal government. Since 1980, schools have received almost equal funding from local and state sources. Prior to that date, however, schools received most of their revenues from local sources, and early in the 20th century, most school revenues were generated from local property taxes. In 1919–20, for example, 83.2 percent of revenues were from local sources, 16.5 percent from state sources, and 0.3 percent from federal sources (National Center for Education Statistics, 2017b).

Figure 6.7 Percentage distribution of revenues for public elementary and secondary schools, by source of funds: 2013–14

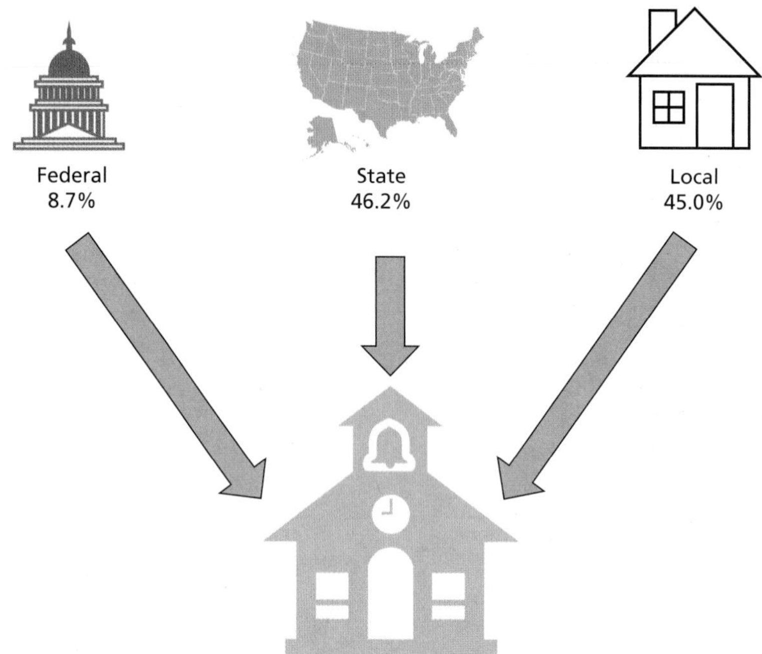

Note: Excludes revenues for state education agencies. Detail may not sum to totals because of rounding.

SOURCE: Based on data from *Digest of Education Statistics 2016.* National Center for Education Statistics, Institute of Education Sciences, U.S. Department of Education. Washington, DC, Table 235.20. Retrieved October 2, 2017, from https://nces.ed.gov/programs/digest/d16/tables/dt16_235.20.asp?current=yes

Many factors influence revenues for education, including the apportionment of taxes among the local, state, and federal levels; the size of the tax base at each level; and competing demands for allocating funds at each level. In addition, the following factors influence funding for education:

- The rate of inflation
- The health of the national economy
- The size of the national budget deficit
- Taxpayer revolts to limit the use of property taxes to raise money, such as Proposition 13 in California and Oregon's property tax limitation
- Changes in the size and distribution of the population
- School-financed lawsuits to equalize funding and ensure educational opportunity

Local Funding

At the local level, most funding for schools comes from **property taxes**, which are determined by the value of property in the school district. Property taxes are assessed against real estate and, in some districts, also against personal property such as cars, household furniture and appliances, and stocks and bonds. Increasing taxes to meet the rising costs of operating local schools or to fund needed improvements is often a heated issue in many communities.

Although property taxes provide a steady source of revenue for local school districts, there are inequities in how taxes are determined. By locating in areas where taxes are lowest, for example, businesses and industries often avoid paying higher taxes while continuing to draw on local resources and services. In addition, the fair market value of property is often difficult to assess, and groups within a community sometimes pressure assessors to keep taxes on their property as low as possible. Most states specify by law the minimum property tax rate for local school districts to set. In many districts, an increase in the tax rate must have the approval of voters. Some states place no cap, or upper limit, on tax rates, and other states set a maximum limit.

State Funding

Most state revenues for education come from sales taxes and income taxes. Sales taxes are added to the cost of items such as general goods, gasoline, amusements, alcohol, and insurance. Income taxes are placed on individuals (in many states) and on business and industry.

As mentioned previously, states contribute 46.2 percent of the resources needed to operate the public schools. The money that a state gives to its cities and towns is known as **state aid**. Table 6.2 compares selected states on the percentage of education funds received from local, state, and federal sources in relation to total revenues for 2013–14. The table also shows that the greatest percentage of local funds comes from property taxes, whereas a small percentage come from private sources such as gifts and tuition and fees.

States also differ from each other in terms of their per-pupil expenditures. For example, Figure 6.8 shows that per-pupil spending during fiscal year 2015 varied from a high of $16,000 or more to a low of less than $8,000.

Figure 6.8 Public elementary–secondary school system per pupil current spending by state: Fiscal year 2015

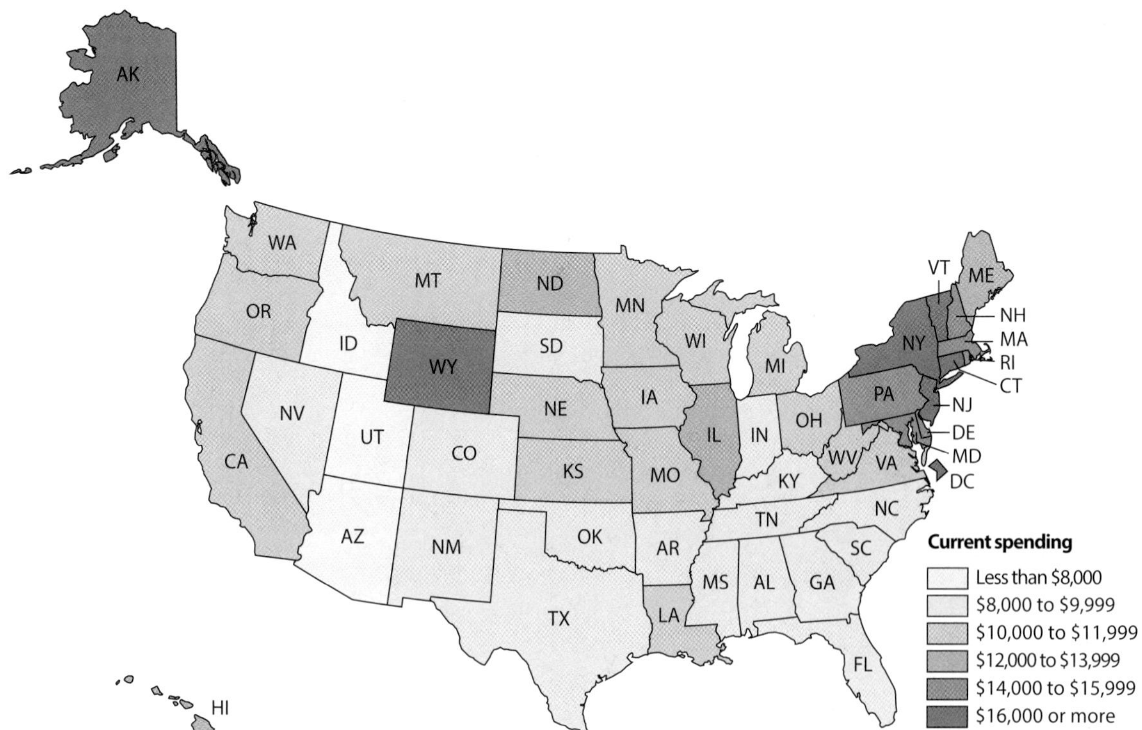

Note: Annual Survey of School System Finances statistics include the finances of charter schools whose charters are held directly by a government or a government agency. Charter schools whose charters are held by nongovernmental entities are deemed to be out of scope for the Annual Survey of School System Finances.

SOURCE: U.S. Census Bureau. (June 2017). *Public Education Finances: 2015.* G15-ASPEF, U.S. Government Printing Office, Washington, DC, 2017, p. 10.

Table 6.2 Revenues for public elementary and secondary schools, by source of funds and state or jurisdiction: 2013–14

[In current dollars]

		Federal			State		Local (including intermediate sources below the state level)					
									Property taxes		Private[2]	
State or jurisdiction	Total (in thousands)	Amount (in thousands)	Per pupil	Percent of total	Amount (in thousands)	Percent of total	Amount (in thousands)[1]	Percent of total	Amount (in thousands)	Percent of total	Amount (in thousands)	Percent of total
1	2	3	4	5	6	7	8	9	10	11	12	13
United States	**$623,208,803**	**$54,505,424**	**$1,090**	**8.7**	**$288,196,281**	**46.2**	**$280,507,097**	**45.0**	**$227,019,185**	**36.4**	**$11,544,893**	**1.9**
Alabama	7,396,933	838,650	1,124	11.3	4,065,546	55.0	2,492,738	33.7	1,128,860	15.3	330,578	4.5
California	69,342,921	6,942,640	1,100	10.0	39,293,076	56.7	23,107,205	33.3	18,407,321	26.5	396,235	0.6
District of Columbia	2,169,360	207,177	2,651	9.6	†	†	1,962,183	90.4	636,590	29.3	11,839	0.5
Florida	25,897,090	3,182,434	1,170	12.3	10,460,926	40.4	12,253,729	47.3	10,198,865	39.4	945,552	3.7
Illinois	27,240,148	2,302,774	1,115	8.5	7,088,669	26.0	17,848,704	65.5	15,789,880	58.0	472,805	1.7
Massachusetts	16,812,408	905,629	948	5.4	6,597,170	39.2	9,309,609	55.4	8,657,853	51.5	244,145	1.5
Minnesota	11,590,204	695,414	817	6.0	8,090,950	69.8	2,803,840	24.2	1,576,469	13.6	336,468	2.9
Mississippi	4,430,399	665,244	1,351	15.0	2,244,101	50.7	1,521,054	34.3	1,246,581	28.1	109,308	2.5
New York	60,861,023	3,323,852	1,216	5.5	24,927,367	41.0	32,609,804	53.6	29,665,944	48.7	325,251	0.5
North Carolina	13,123,423	1,595,793	1,042	12.2	8,153,922	62.1	3,373,708	25.7	2,823,684	21.5	206,017	1.6
Pennsylvania	28,105,857	1,934,312	1,102	6.9	10,381,524	36.9	15,790,021	56.2	12,476,886	44.4	408,407	1.5
Rhode Island	2,387,115	197,333	1,390	8.3	947,049	39.7	1,242,733	52.1	1,201,465	50.3	24,784	1.0
Tennessee	9,323,601	1,099,765	1,107	11.8	4,320,820	46.3	3,903,016	41.9	1,881,977	20.2	431,109	4.6
Texas	53,377,147	5,872,783	1,140	11.0	22,127,610	41.5	25,376,754	47.5	23,197,992	43.5	1,008,133	1.9
Utah	4,905,540	433,639	693	8.8	2,673,267	54.5	1,798,634	36.7	1,367,586	27.9	215,472	4.4
Vermont	1,706,096	103,889	1,171	6.1	1,532,612	89.8	69,596	4.1	1,132	0.1	23,648	1.4
Virginia	15,049,477	1,008,658	792	6.7	5,984,788	39.8	8,056,031	53.5	4,887,311	32.5	249,569	1.7
Washington	12,932,336	1,030,232	973	8.0	7,833,028	60.6	4,069,076	31.5	3,451,346	26.7	318,925	2.5
Wisconsin	10,980,723	855,893	979	7.8	4,981,241	45.4	5,143,588	46.8	4,714,091	42.9	216,430	2.0

† Not applicable.
[1] Includes other categories of revenue not separately shown.
[2] Includes revenues from gifts, and tuition and fees from patrons.
Note: Excludes revenues for state education agencies. Detail may not sum to totals because of rounding.

SOURCE: Adapted from *Digest of Education Statistics 2016*. National Center for Education Statistics, Institute of Education Sciences, U.S. Department of Education. Washington, DC, Table 235.20. Retrieved October 1, 2017, from https://nces.ed.gov/programs/digest/d16/tables/dt16_235.20.asp?current=yes.

Federal Funding

The role of the federal government in providing resources for education has been limited. The federal share of funding for public elementary and secondary schools peaked in 1979–1980 at 9.8 percent, and as Figure 6.7 shows, it was 8.7 percent during 2013–14. Prior to 1980, the federal government had, in effect, bypassed the states and provided funding for local programs that were administered through various federal agencies, such as the Office of Economic Opportunity (Head Start, migrant education, and Follow Through) and the Department of Labor (Job Corps and the Comprehensive Employment Training Act [CETA]).

Since the Reagan administration (1980–1988), federal aid has been given increasingly directly to the states in the form of **block grants**, which a state or local education agency may spend as it wishes, with few limitations. The 1981 **Education Consolidation and Improvement Act (ECIA)** gave the states a broad range of choices in spending federal money. The ECIA significantly reduced federal aid to education, however, thus making state aid to education even more critical.

Although a small proportion of the funds for schools comes from the federal level, the federal government has enacted supplemental programs to help meet the educational needs of special student populations. Such programs are often referred to collectively as **entitlements**. The most significant entitlement is the Elementary and Secondary Education (ESEA) Act of 1965, which President George W. Bush reauthorized in 2002 as the No Child Left Behind Act. In December 2015, ESEA was again reauthorized when President Barack Obama signed into law the Every Student Succeeds Act (ESSA).

The largest entitlement of ESEA is Title I, which allocates funds to school districts with large numbers of students from low-income families. President Trump's Title I Budget Request for Fiscal Year 2018 was $14.9 billion (U.S. Department of Education, 2017). Among the other funded entitlement programs are the Vocational Education Act (1963), the Manpower Development and Training Act (1963), the Economic Opportunity Act (1964), the Bilingual Education Act (1968), the Indian Education Act (1972), and the Education for All Handicapped Children Act (1975).

The federal government also provides funding for preschool programs such as Project Head Start. **Head Start** promotes the school readiness of children ages birth to five from low-income families by enhancing their cognitive, social, physical, and emotional development. The Early Head Start program serves children from birth to 3 years of age. The Head Start program includes children ages 3 to 5 years. And the Migrant and Seasonal Head Start includes those children from birth to 5 years old whose families earn their income primarily from agricultural work.

Since the program began in 1965, Head Start has served almost 30 million children, and more than 1 million children are served each year. President Trump's Head Start Budget Request for Fiscal Year 2018 was $9.17 billion.

What are Some Trends in Funding for Equity and Excellence?

The fact that schools rely heavily on property taxes for support has resulted in fiscal inequities for schools. Districts with higher property wealth can generate more money per pupil than can districts with lower property values. The degree of inequity between the wealthiest and the poorest districts, therefore, can be quite large. In some states, the ability of one district to generate local property tax revenues may be several times greater than another district's.

ESSA will provide greater transparency regarding resource allocation across the states with its requirement that states and school districts report per-pupil expenditures of federal, state, and local funds. Thus, it will be possible to compare student learning outcomes in a state with that state's per-pupil expenditures. In addition, ESSA requires that school districts identify resource inequities in the plans they must submit to the state.

FOCUS ON **DIVERSITY**: INEQUITABLE FUNDING OF SCHOOLS IN POOR COMMUNITIES

The degree of inequity between the wealthiest and the poorest school districts in the United States can be quite large. In addition, wealthy families can choose to live in school districts with funding to support outstanding schools, whereas poor families do not have that option. Therefore, students from poor families are less likely to have access to educational opportunities and resources such as the following:

- Preschool programs
- Outstanding teachers
- Rigorous curricula
- High standards
- Cutting-edge technology
- Up-to-date facilities
- After-school enrichment programs

In *The Shame of the Nation: The Restoration of Apartheid Schooling in America*, Jonathan Kozol (2005) presented a compelling analysis of differences between per-pupil expenditures in major U.S. cities and their wealthy nearby suburbs. More than a decade later, my analysis of data from the U.S. Census Bureau and *Education Week's* Research Center reveals that such inequities are still common. For example, the following list compares per-pupil spending and minority enrollments between five major U.S. cities and wealthy nearby suburbs for 2017.

New York City ($20,295; 85 percent minority) > Syosset, NY ($28,444; 32 percent minority

Chicago ($11,615; 85 percent minority) > Lake Forest, IL ($16,817; 9 percent minority)

Detroit ($13,369; 98 percent minority) > Bloomfield Hills, MI ($15,910; 30 percent minority)

Los Angeles ($10,667; 86 percent minority) > Laguna Beach, CA ($13,513; 15 percent minority)

Milwaukee ($11,992; 98 percent minority) > Maple Dale-Indian Hill, WI ($14,864; 32 percent minority)

Such discrepancies in per-pupil funding are an example of **institutional racism**—institutional policies and practices that result in racial inequalities.

Politics also contribute to funding inequities among schools. The following political factors have made it difficult for school reform efforts to reach students in resource-poor schools:

- Local school boards are political and have many agendas, some of which detract from a sharp focus on improved learning for all students.

- School districts allocate funds and other resources based on political influences from the community; often, schools that serve poor students receive lower per-pupil allocations and have the oldest facilities and equipment.
- Teachers with seniority, degrees from more prestigious institutions, and other qualities that make them attractive to "better" schools in the district can usually avoid teaching at schools considered "less desirable."

Tax Reform and Redistricting

To correct funding inequities, several court suits were initiated during the 1970s. In the 1971 *Serrano v. Priest* case in California, it was successfully argued that the relationship between spending and property wealth violated the state's obligation to provide equal protection and education. The California Supreme Court ruled that the quality of a child's education should not depend on the "wealth of his parents and neighbors." The court also recognized that communities with a poor tax base could not be expected to generate the revenues of more affluent districts. Nevertheless, the court did not forbid the use of property taxes to fund education.

Then, in 1973, the U.S. Supreme Court decided in *San Antonio Independent School District v. Rodriguez* that fiscal inequities stemming from unequal tax bases did not violate the Constitution. That Court's decision reversed a lower court's ruling claiming that school financing on the basis of local property taxes was unconstitutional.

Regardless of the mixed outcomes of court challenges, many state legislatures have enacted school finance equity reforms during the last 15 years. Some states (**CALIFORNIA**, **HAWAII**, **NEW MEXICO**, **WASHINGTON**, and **WEST VIRGINIA**, for example) have **full-funding programs** in which the state sets the same per-pupil expenditure level for all schools and districts.

Other states have adopted new funding formulas to broaden their revenue base. Level funding augmented by sales taxes, cigarette taxes, state lottery revenues, property taxes on second homes, and school-choice plans are among the solutions tried. One of the most dramatic changes in educational funding occurred in **MICHIGAN** in 1993 with the passage of Proposal A, a plan that greatly reduced school funding from local property taxes and increased funding from the state's sales tax.

Because each state has been free to determine the number of districts within its boundaries, a common approach to achieving equal funding is **redistricting**, redrawing school district boundaries to reduce the range of variation in the ability of school districts to finance education. Redistricting not only equalizes funding; it can also reduce the cost of maintaining and operating schools if smaller districts are combined. The per-pupil cost of instruction, supplies, and equipment is usually lower in large districts. In addition, greater resources often allow larger districts to offer a broader curriculum and higher salaries to attract more qualified teachers.

Vertical Equity

Other states have developed various mechanisms to provide **vertical equity**, that is, allocating funds according to legitimate educational needs. Thus, additional support is given to programs that serve students from low-income backgrounds; those with limited English proficiency; those with special gifts and talents; and those who need special education or vocational programs. Vertical equity is based on the assumption that students with greater learning needs should have access to greater resources.

Additional state-appropriated funds to cover the costs of educating students with special needs are known as **categorical aid**. Funding adjustments are also made to compensate for differences in costs within a state—higher expenses due to rural isolation or the higher cost of living in urban areas, for example. Some states even conduct periodic regional cost of living analyses, which are then used to determine adjustments in per-pupil funding.

School Choice

One of the most bitter struggles for control of schools in the United States is centered around **school choice**, the practice of allowing parents to choose the schools their children attend. The issue is especially heated for choice programs that would allow parents to choose a private school, with the public paying all or part of the tuition. According to the 2017 Phi Delta Kappa/Gallup poll of the public's attitudes toward the public schools, 52 percent opposed and 39 percent favored such school choice programs if the government paid the tuition (Phi Delta Kappa, 2017).

Debate continues about whether school choice programs will, in fact, promote equity and excellence. Advocates of school choice believe that giving parents more options will force public schools to adjust to free-market pressures—low-performing schools would have to improve or shut down. They also contend that parents whose children must now attend inferior, and sometimes dangerous, inner-city schools would be able to send their children elsewhere. In addition, some supporters see choice as a way to reduce the influence of top-heavy school bureaucracies and teachers' unions.

On the other hand, opponents believe that school choice would have disastrous consequences for public schools and lead to students being sorted by race, income, and religion. School choice, they argue, would subsidize the wealthy by siphoning money away from the public schools and further widen the gap between rich and poor districts. School choice could also lead to the creation of segregated schools and schools that would be more committed to competing for education dollars and the most able, manageable students.

Opponents also point out that many public schools, especially high schools, offer greater choice of academic and extracurricular options than private schools. For example, public high schools are far more likely to offer Advanced Placement, gifted/honors, and distance learning courses than private schools. And almost all public high schools (98 percent) offer career preparation through dual credit opportunities, career and technical education, internships, or a career academy. In addition, public schools have more counselors to help students develop a course of study and plan for their future—while 20 percent of public schools have no counselor, 68 percent of private schools have no counselor (National Association of School Boards, 2017).

Voucher Systems

One approach to providing educational equity that has generated considerable controversy is the **voucher system** of distributing educational funds. According to voucher plans, parents would be given government-funded vouchers to purchase educational services at the schools of their choice. Currently, 14 states and the District of Columbia have voucher programs (Education Commission of the States, 2017, March 6).

Voucher systems were first suggested more than 50 years ago by Milton Friedman, a well-known conservative economist and Nobel laureate. Friedman believed that schools would be much better if they were operated by private businesses rather than the government. "If we had a system of free choice we would also have a system of competition, innovation, which would change the character of education. . . . Reform has to come through competition from the outside, and the only way you can get competition is by making it possible for parents to have the ability to choose" (Friedman, 2003).

The most controversial voucher proposals would allow parents to choose from among public as well as private (secular, parochial, for-profit, and charter) schools; others would limit parents' choice to public schools. Voucher programs require that parents and guardians reflect on the kind of educational experiences they want for their children.

Debates about vouchers regularly make the national news. In 1999, **FLORIDA** became the first state to offer state-paid tuition to children in failing public schools to attend a public, private, or religious school of choice; however, a Florida judge ruled in 2006 that the program violated the Florida Constitution because it gave tax money to religious schools (*Bush v. Holmes*, 2006). However, in 2002, the Supreme Court ruled that a school voucher program in Cleveland did not infringe on the constitutional separation of church and state (*Zelman v. Simmons-Harris*, 2002). The Court majority said that the parents had a sufficient range of choices among secular and religious schools, and that the voucher plan did not violate the 1st Amendment prohibition against the establishment of religion and was "religiously neutral."

EVALUATION OF VOUCHER PROGRAMS Approximately 25 different voucher programs exist in the 14 states and the District of Columbia that have voucher programs (Education Commission of the States, 2017, March 6). Each program has different rules and regulations controlling its size and scope and the terms of participation. Because complex state regulations make it difficult to distinguish voucher programs that are large and inclusive from those that are restrictive and less inclusive, the Center for Education Reform released *School Choice Today: Voucher Laws across the States* in 2014.

The report evaluates and ranks the nation's school voucher programs on several criteria, including degree of restrictions on students who can apply, number of vouchers that can be awarded, the value of the voucher, and at what type of private schools parents may use the voucher. According to the Center's grading system, state voucher programs can receive a total of 50 points.

School Choice Today reported that the best voucher programs—those that received a grade of "A"—are in Indiana (32 points), Ohio (30 points), and Wisconsin (30 points). The following programs received a grade of "B": Washington, DC (27 points), North Carolina (27 points), and Arizona (27 points). These state programs received a grade of "C": Louisiana (23 points), Florida (23 points), Georgia (23 points), Oklahoma (22 points), Colorado (20 points), Utah (19 points) and Mississippi (19 points). In last place, Vermont (18 points) and Maine (17 points) received a grade of "D" (Center for Education Reform, 2014).

Another study evaluated the District of Columbia School Choice Incentive Act—the first federally funded, private school voucher program in the United States. This study evaluated the long-term effects of the program, renamed the DC Opportunity Scholarship Program (OSP), on families who were given the option to move from a public school to a participating private school of their choice. The OSP provided low-income residents, particularly those whose children attended "schools in need of improvement" or "corrective action" under the Elementary and Secondary Education Act, with "expanded opportunities to attend higher performing schools in the District of Columbia." The OSP scholarship, worth up to $7,500, could be used to cover the costs of tuition, school fees, and transportation to a participating private school.

The study compared the outcomes of 2,300 eligible applicants randomly assigned to receive a voucher (treatment group) or not receive a voucher (control group) of an OSP scholarship through a series of lotteries. Test scores, high school graduation rates, and perceptions of school safety and satisfaction were collected annually during a 4- to 5-year period. Some students offered scholarships never used them, whereas others used their scholarships to attend a participating private school at some point during the 4- to 5-year period. Study results revealed the following:

- ***There [was] no conclusive evidence that the OSP affected student achievement.*** On average, after at least four years students who were offered (or used) scholarships had reading and math test scores that were statistically similar to those who were not offered scholarships. The same pattern of results holds for students who applied from schools in need of improvement (SINI), the group Congress designated as the highest priority for the OSP.
- ***The OSP significantly improved students' chances of graduating from high school.*** Although students may not have raised their test scores in reading and math as a result of the OSP, they graduated at higher rates. The offer of an OSP scholarship raised students' probability of completing high school by 12 percentage points overall. The graduation rate based on parent-provided information was 82 percent for the treatment group compared to 70 percent for the control group. The offer of a scholarship improved the graduation prospects by 13 percentage points for the high-priority group of students from schools designated SINI in 2003–2005 (79 percent graduation rate for the treatment group versus 66 percent for the control group).
- ***The OSP raised parents', but not students', ratings of school safety and satisfaction.*** Parents were more satisfied and felt school was safer if their child was offered or used an OSP scholarship. The OSP had no effect on students' reports on school conditions (Wolf et al., 2010, pp. v–vi).

In addition to the federal study of OSP, the *Washington Post* found a lack of quality controls for schools involved in the program. For example, hundreds of students used their vouchers to attend nonaccredited schools or schools in "unconventional" settings—a family-run K–12 school operating out of a storefront, a Nation of Islam school based in a converted home, and a school built around the philosophy of a Bulgarian psychotherapist. Furthermore, the District of Columbia had no say over the quality of school curricula or school leadership. Parents selected schools based on marketing from the schools, not performance data for the schools. Unlike public schools, DC voucher program schools were not accountable for students' learning. The schools had to give a standardized test; however, the schools could choose the test. Test scores were not made public, and schools could continue in the voucher program regardless of students' performance (Layton & Brown, 2012).

Wisconsin's statewide voucher program provides an example of how providing private school tuition may have a negative impact on funding for a state's public schools. A University of Wisconsin study found that, unless Wisconsin increases the amount of per-pupil funding provided by the state, continued expansion of the voucher program will result in a reduction of state financial support for each student (Bruecker, 2017).

It is clear that the debate over school choice will continue for the foreseeable future. Gradually, support for school choice appears to be increasing—currently, almost half of the states allow some form of "interdistrict" transfer, which allows students to attend public schools outside their home district.

Education–Business Coalitions

To develop additional sources of funding for equity and excellence, many local school districts have established coalitions with the private sector. Businesses may contribute funds or materials needed by a school; sponsor sports teams; award scholarships; provide cash grants for pilot projects and teacher development; provide mentors, volunteers, or expertise; and even construct school buildings. Among the types of education–business coalitions are Grantmakers for Education (GFE), the nation's largest network of education funders; the National Alliance of State Science and Mathematics Coalitions (NASSMC); the Business Roundtable, a group of CEOs of leading U.S. companies; and partnerships with chambers of commerce.

One example of an education–business partnership is the GE Foundation's Developing Futures in Education program. Since 2005, the program has provided $200 million to improve student achievement in seven U.S. school districts: Louisville, **KENTUCKY**; Stamford, **CONNECTICUT**; Cincinnati, **OHIO**; Erie, **PENNSYLVANIA**; Atlanta, **GEORGIA**; New York, **NEW YORK**; and Milwaukee, **WISCONSIN**. The Foundation "recognizes the urgent need to improve student achievement and college and career readiness in the K–12 public education system" (GE Foundation, 2014, March 10).

With assistance from the Developing Futures in Education program, the targeted districts accomplished the following:

- Jefferson County Public Schools, **KENTUCKY**, achieved a 14-point gain on students' mathematics scores, compared with an overall state gain of 6 points.
- Cincinnati Public Schools, **OHIO**, was 13th out of 609 school districts in student achievement.
- Stamford Public Schools, **CONNECTICUT**, cut the achievement gap in mathematics almost in half.

The GE Foundation also provided a 4-year, $18 million grant to help states and school districts implement the Common Core State Standards (CCSS). The grant was used to develop exemplary sample lessons aligned to the CCSS and to provide CCSS professional development Immersion Institutes for more than 1,500 teachers and principals.

The largest amount of private support for education in the United States comes from the Bill and Melinda Gates Foundation. The Foundation has spent more than $1 billion on more than 1,500 partnerships with our nation's schools. Chicago has opened 100 new schools with the help of Gates Foundation money, and New York City has opened 200. A priority for the Foundation is the reform of high schools in urban areas and helping schools develop more academically rigorous curricula. The Foundation awarded the Chicago Public Schools $21 million to develop new curricula and to make classes more rigorous.

As mentioned previously, some businesses contribute funds to build new schools. A weak economy since the 2008 recession has made the public less likely to support the construction of new schools; as a result, school districts often seek support from the business community. The need to improve school buildings goes beyond a desire for more attractive buildings. Inadequate, badly maintained, or poorly designed facilities can hinder students' learning and reduce teachers' effectiveness.

Typically, the burden of paying for school construction and renovation has fallen on local districts and their constituents. But with the needs so large and widespread, it is evident that local communities cannot carry the weight by themselves—the help of the business community is often needed.

At least five factors have contributed to the current need to improve the condition of U.S. school buildings: (1) gradual deterioration as buildings age, (2) increasing enrollments, (3) mounting evidence that poor facilities diminish student learning, (4) increased use of technology in schools, and (5) the continuing quest to equalize the distributions of resources for schools. If local districts are to respond effectively to these factors, it is clear that they will definitely need more assistance from the business community. In addition, school buildings constructed during the 1950s to cope with the "baby boom" generation are reaching a critical age. Many of those buildings were built quickly and cheaply, and their flaws are becoming more evident as they become older. In addition, years of deferred maintenance have worsened the substandard conditions of many of these buildings.

If schools in the United States are to succeed in meeting the challenges of the future, they will need to be funded at a level that provides quality educational experiences to students from a diverse array of backgrounds. Although innovative approaches to school funding have been developed, much remains to be done before both excellence and equity characterize all schools in the United States.

How is the Privatization Movement Affecting Equity and Excellence in Education?

One of the most dramatic reforms in U.S. education during the last decade has been the development of charter schools and for-profit schools, both of which provide an alternative to the perceived inadequacies of the public schools. On many different levels—governance, staffing, curricula, funding, and accountability—the **privatization movement** is a radical departure from schools as most people have known them.

Since 1995, the number of for-profit private companies operating public schools increased from 5 to 97, and the number of schools operating has increased from 6 to 840. Enrollment at these schools has grown from approximately 1,000 students in 1995–1996 to 462,926 in 2011–2012 (Miron & Gulosino, 2013).

Charter Schools

In 1991, **MINNESOTA** passed the nation's first charter school legislation calling for up to eight teacher-created and teacher-operated, outcome-based schools that would be free of most state and local rules and regulations. When the St. Paul City Academy opened its doors in September 1992, it became the nation's first charter school. Since then, the charter school movement has grown to more than 6,900 charter schools, enrolling an estimated 3.1 million students (National Alliance of Public Charter Schools, 2017). By 2016, 43 states and the District of Columbia had legislation authorizing charter schools (Education Commission of the States, 2016).

Charter schools are independent, innovative, outcome-based public schools that provide diverse educational programs from which parents and students may choose. To open a charter school, an original charter (or agreement) is signed by the school's founders and a sponsor (usually the local school board). The **charter** specifies the learning outcomes that students will master before they continue their studies.

Charter schools, which usually operate in the manner of autonomous school districts (a feature that distinguishes them from the alternative schools that many school districts operate), are public schools and must teach all students. If admission requests for a charter school exceed the number of available openings, students are selected by drawing.

Charter schools contribute to the improvement of public education in the following ways:

- Increasing access to quality education for all students
- Providing opportunities for parents and students to choose among public schools in the local community
- Developing more accurate and rigorous measures of accountability for public education
- Encouraging new approaches to teaching
- Creating opportunities for teachers to assume leadership roles in educational reform
- Increasing the involvement of parents and community in public education
- Serving as a catalyst for the broader reform of public education

Video Example 6.2

Charter School Mission: A teacher at Charlotte Lab School, a charter school, explains the mission of the school and how his teaching strategies reflect that mission.

Because charter schools are designed to promote the development of new teaching strategies that can be used at other public schools, they can prove to be an effective tool for promoting educational reform and the professionalization of teaching in the future. Charter schools also give teachers unprecedented leadership opportunities and the ability to respond quickly to students' needs.

RESEARCH ON CHARTER SCHOOLS The *National Charter School Study 2013,* conducted by Stanford University's Center for Research on Education Outcomes, analyzed charter school effectiveness in 27 of the 43 states (including the District of Columbia) that allowed charter schools. The researchers compared academic growth during a school year for students at charter schools and at traditional public schools. The study reported that "The analysis of the pooled 27 states shows that charter schools now advance the learning gains of their students more than traditional public schools in reading" (Center for Research on Education Outcomes, 2013, p. 3).

A critique of the Stanford study by the National Education Policy Center at the University of Colorado–Boulder, however, pointed out that "The [Stanford] study overall shows that less than one hundredth of one percent of the variation in test performance is explainable by charter school enrollment. . . . in practical terms these effects are so small as to be regarded, without hyperbole, as trivial. The bottom line appears to be that, once again, it has been found that, in aggregate, charter schools are basically indistinguishable from traditional public schools in terms of their impact on academic test performance" (Maul & McClelland, 2013, p. 4).

Regardless of the mixed results on the effectiveness of charter schools, few charter schools have been closed because of failure to meet academic outcomes. Instead, charter school closings have been the result of low enrollments, problems with facilities, financial problems, or mismanagement.

In the final analysis, it is important to remember that there are "good" and "not so good" charter schools, just as there are traditional public schools that meet those descriptions. Regardless of their shortcomings, charter schools do hold out the promise of developing new approaches to teaching and school governance that can benefit the entire system of public education in the U.S.

For-Profit Schools

One of the hottest educational issues today is the practice of turning the operation of public schools over to private, for-profit companies. Advocates of privatization believe privately operated schools are more efficient, and they reduce costs and maximize "production"—that is, student achievement. For-profit schools also create a healthy competitive environment for public education—schools will have to improve, or they will be forced to close. Opponents, however, are concerned that profit, rather than increasing student achievement, is the real driving force behind **for-profit schools**. Critics of for-profit schools are also concerned that school districts may not be vigilant enough in monitoring the performance of private education companies and that limited resources for schools are used for another "layer" of administration, service fees, and profits.

For-profit companies operated 840 schools in 35 states during 2011–2012. With 79 percent of its charter schools operated by for-profit companies, **MICHIGAN** leads the nation in for-profit involvement in charter schools. The states with the greatest number of schools managed by for-profit companies are **MICHIGAN** (204), **FLORIDA** (177), **OHIO** (110), and **ARIZONA** (108). The largest for-profit company, Imagine Schools, manages 89 schools. The next largest companies are Academica (76 schools), National Heritage Academies (68 schools), K^{12} Inc. (57 schools), and Edison Learning (53 schools). Among the for-profit companies, K^{12} Inc. had in 2013 the largest total enrollment (87,091 students) (Miron & Gulosino, 2013, pp. ii–iii).

K^{12} INC. One of the largest for-profit managers of schools, K^{12} Inc., states that its mission is to focus on "each child's potential," and the company is committed to "putting students first." Through its online private school, the company offers individualized learning programs to both public and private schools worldwide. The company also provides courses directly to students based on their needs and interests and to those involved in homeschooling.

Although K^{12}'s CEO states that the company "operates schools with high integrity and a focus on strong academic performance for all students," the company has been the target of multiple class-action suits related to academic performance and educational quality in K^{12}-managed public schools. In 2013, the company's insurance carriers paid $6.75 million to settle a class-action suit based on the following:

- Concealment of K^{12}'s academic performance and annual growth measures
- Excessive and burdensome student-to-teacher ratios
- Improper grading and attendance policies at K^{12}-managed schools
- Hiring of unqualified teachers who were not properly certified
- Failure of special education programs to meet government standards
- Misleading high parent satisfaction scores

Another class-action lawsuit was filed during February 2014 in Virginia on behalf of those who purchased stock in K^{12}. The lawsuit alleged that the company misrepresented or failed to disclose various "operational failures in the enrollment process" (Reuters, 2014).

The inability of for-profit companies like K^{12} to operate schools that truly provide quality education to all students is aptly explained by Larry Cuban, a Stanford University education professor:

> CEOs and investors learned the hard way that what worked in companies to make silicon chips, crank out case after case of soda, and create brand-new cereals flopped when managers tried to turn low-performing students around and get higher test scores. . . . And then there is K^{12}, Inc., a for-profit company, that pulled in over $800 million in 2013 through selling online courses and curriculum, software, and blended programs to private and public schools. . . . Recently, investigations have shown how K^{12} Inc. squeezed money out of each of their operations to give investors a high rate of return on their shares.
>
> Sure, there is money to be made in the education market. After all, for decades big and small companies selling textbooks, classroom furniture, transportation, low- and high-tech equipment from blackboards (oops! green and whiteboards) to smartboards have profited from providing basic products and services to this stable market. These profit-driven companies, however, do not take over schools or districts. They provide services and products for already existing agencies running schools, not the tough business of turning failing ones around. That is a sinkhole that many companies eager to turn a profit have slipped into in the past and are primed to do so now. (Cuban, 2013)

TEACHER-OWNED SCHOOLS? An innovative approach to for-profit schools has been suggested by Richard K. Vedder (2003) in his book *Can Teachers Own Their Own*

Schools? New Strategies for Educational Excellence. Vedder believes that for-profit public schools would benefit from competition and develop cost-effective ways to achieve educational quality. In addition, such schools would attract the additional funding and expertise needed to revolutionize school systems.

Vedder's approach is patterned after Margaret Thatcher's privatization of government council housing in England, privatization reforms in Latin America, and the employee stock ownership plan (ESOP) movement in the United States. He suggests that teachers, administrators, and other educational stakeholders become the owners of schools, thus acquiring an attractive financial stake in the process. Such privatization reforms could pave the way for new, cost-effective means of improving education for all students. Vedder believes that schools in which teachers, administrators, and parents have a significant financial stake would foster vibrant school communities with increased parental involvement and the innovation and efficiency essential to produce educational excellence.

One example of a teacher-owned school is Avalon, a public charter school in St. Paul, **MINNESOTA**, run by a 15-teacher cooperative. The school's 200 7th- to 12th-grade students take traditional classes and work on individual projects they design with their teachers. The school has no principal; instead, patterning their practice after doctors and lawyers, teachers decide everything, from salaries to the curriculum. As Carrie Bakken, a teacher at the school, says, "The job is more appealing when you own your school" (Hawkins, 2010).

Another example of a teacher-owned school is the GW Community School, a college-prep high school serving 9th- to 12th-grade students in Springfield, **VIRGINIA**. The school is "operated by teachers who understand the learning process, students' needs, and who genuinely enjoy teaching adolescents" (GW Community School, 2017). The mission of the school is to develop students to their full potential and to provide them with a rigorous college-prep curriculum that emphasizes not just the acquisition of subject matter, but how to apply that knowledge to solve authentic, real-world problems. Teachers at the school have flexibility over the curriculum and teaching methods. As a result, classes like "Conspiracy Theories," "Political Geography," and "Sea Adventures" are offered in addition to traditional courses.

Summary

Why Do You Need to Understand Educational Politics and How Local Communities Influence Schools?

- Understanding educational politics is an important form of professional knowledge.
- *Politics* refers to how people use power, influence, and authority within an organization to persuade others to act in desired ways.
- Parents; students; teachers; administrators; taxpayers; federal, state, and local authorities; ethnic and racial groups; educational theorists and researchers; the corporate sector; and special-interest groups exert political influence on education.
- Teachers can use within-school politics to influence instructional and curricular practices within a school.
- Five dimensions of educational politics influence teachers: (1) political pressure from federal, state, and local levels; (2) conflicting ideas about what to teach and how to teach it; (3) competition for educational resources; (4) changing legal rights and responsibilities of teachers; and (5) the push for higher standards, testing, and accountability.
- Local school districts, which vary greatly in size, locale, organizational structure, demographics, and wealth, are responsible for the management and operation of schools.

- Local school boards, whose members are usually elected, set educational policies for a district; however, many people believe that boards should be reformed to be better informed and more responsive.
- The superintendent, the chief administrator of a local district, has a complex array of responsibilities and must work cooperatively with the school board and others in an environment that is often politically turbulent.
- Through groups like the PTA or PTO, some parents are involved in local school activities and reform efforts; others are involved with private schools; and some actively promote alternative approaches to education such as school choice, voucher systems, and home schooling.

How Do States and Regional Education Agencies Influence Schools?

- The state legislature, state courts, and the governor significantly influence education by setting policies related to the management and operation of schools within a state; many states have even passed legislation allowing them to take over academically failing school districts or individual schools.
- The state board of education, the highest educational agency in a state, regulates education and advises the governor and others on important educational policies.
- The state department of education implements policies related to teacher certification, allocation of state and federal funds, enforcement of state and federal guidelines, school accreditation, and research and evaluation projects to improve education.
- The chief state school officer oversees education within a state and, in collaboration with the governor, legislature, state board of education, and the public, provides leadership to improve education.
- The regional educational service agency (RESA), an intermediate unit of educational administration in about half of the states, provides assistance to two or more school districts for staff development, curriculum development, instructional media, and program evaluation.

How Does the Federal Government Influence Education?

- The federal government influences education at the state level through funding general and categorical programs, establishing and enforcing standards and regulations, conducting and disseminating educational research, providing technical assistance to improve education, and encouraging equity and excellence for the nation's schools.
- The national legislature, federal and state supreme courts, and the president significantly influence education by exerting moral suasion for the improvement of schools, providing categorical aid for federal programs, ensuring that school systems follow legal statutes, and funding educational research.
- The U.S. Department of Education supports and disseminates educational research, administers federal grants in education, and assists the president in developing and promoting a national agenda for education.
- At times, the roles of the federal, state, and local governments in education are in conflict.

How Are Schools Financed in the United States?

- The Great Recession that began in 2008 resulted in severe shortfalls in local, state, and federal budgets, and these shortfalls are continuing to have a great impact on school funding.
- Schools are supported with revenues from the local, state, and federal levels, with most funding now coming from the state level. Local funding is provided through property taxes, which in many instances results in inequitable funding for schools located in areas with an insufficient tax base.
- One challenge to financing schools has been the development of an equitable means of taxation for the support of education.

What Are Some Trends in Funding for Equity and Excellence?

- Inequities among school districts often reflect differences in the value of property that can be taxed for the support of schools.
- Many state legislatures have enacted tax reforms, including full-funding programs, that set the same per-pupil expenditures for all schools and districts. Some states have achieved greater equity through redistricting—redrawing district boundaries to reduce funding inequities.
- Some states achieve vertical equity by providing additional funding, or categorical aid, to educate students with special needs. Also, many local districts and schools receive additional funding through partnerships with the private sector and/or community groups.
- School choice and voucher programs are two controversial approaches to providing parents the freedom to select the schools their children attend.

How Will the Privatization Movement Affect Equity and Excellence in Education?

- Charter schools and for-profit schools, both part of the privatization movement, were developed in response to perceived inadequacies of the public schools.
- Charter schools are independent, innovative, outcome-based public schools started by a group of teachers,

parents, or others who obtain a charter from a local school district, a state, or the federal government.

- Research on charter schools is mixed—some studies show that charter school students outperform students at other schools, whereas other studies show the opposite.
- K^{12}, Inc. is an example of for-profit schools operated by private corporations.
- For-profit schools owned by teachers, administrators, and other stakeholders have been suggested as one way to improve the quality of schools.

Professional Reflections and Activities

Teacher's Journal

1. As this chapter points out, many individuals and groups believe that they should play an important role in school governance. Rank order (from *greatest influence* to *least influence*) the extent to which you think each of the following individuals or groups *should* control schools: students, teachers, administrators, parents, the school board, the local school district, the state government, and the federal government. Are there certain areas of schooling that should be controlled by these individuals and groups? Compare your rankings with those of your classmates. What differences do you note?
2. Imagine that you are going to open a charter school. How would this school differ from the schools in your community? What would you say to parents to convince them to send their children to your school?

Teacher's Research

1. Use your favorite search engine to visit the websites for several charter schools. What do these schools have in common? How are they different?
2. Visit the U.S. Department of Education's charter school website and click on the State Policies for Charter Schools link. How do the states' charter school policies differ? How are they similar?

Observations and Interviews

1. Visit a private (secular, parochial, for-profit, or charter) school. Find out how teachers and other staff members are hired and how the school is organized and governed. How does the management and operation of this school differ from that of public schools?
2. Using Figure 6.2 on page 177 as a guide, interview a teacher in a local school about his or her perceptions of the political influences on teachers. Ask the teacher to select one influence and describe how it currently affects the school where the teacher works.
3. Interview a teacher and ask him or her to rank order (from *greatest influence* to *least influence*) the extent to which each of the following individuals or groups *should* control schools: students, teachers, administrators, parents, the school board, the local school district, the state government, and the federal government. How do the teacher's beliefs compare with your own?

Shared Writing 6.1

Influence of Politics on Education

Professional Portfolio

Prepare a profile of a school district. The district may be in your hometown, your college or university community, or a community in which you would like to teach. Information on the district may be obtained on the Internet or from your university library, public library, school district office, state board of education, or professional teacher associations.

Keeping in mind that school district statistics are more readily available in some cases than in others, your profile might include the following types of information:

- Organizational chart showing (if possible) personnel currently assigned to each position
- Tables showing numbers of school buildings, students, teachers, administrators, support personnel, and so forth
- Graduation/dropout rate
- Scores on standardized achievement tests
- Total annual budget
- Expenditures per pupil
- Entitlement programs
- Demographic characteristics of population living in the area served by the district—age, race or ethnicity, socioeconomic status, unemployment rate, and so forth
- Volunteer groups serving schools in the district
- Pupil-to-teacher ratio
- Percent of ethnic minority students, students with disabilities, students eligible for free or reduced-fee lunch, and so forth
- Percentage of students going on to college

Chapter 7
Ethical and Legal Issues in U.S. Education

Monkey Business Images/Shutterstock

Learning Outcomes

After reading this chapter, you will be able to do the following:

7.1 Explain why teachers need to know about education and the law and why they need a professional code of ethics.

7.2 Explain the legal rights of teachers.

7.3 Explain the legal responsibilities of teachers.

7.4 Explain the legal rights of students and parents.

7.5 Discuss current issues in the legal rights of school districts.

READERS' VOICES

Why do teachers need to know about education and the law?

Teachers should be aware of the ethical and legal dimensions of their work—from knowing how to solve ethical dilemmas in the classroom to understanding the rights and responsibilities of teachers. Failure to follow the laws that apply to teachers, schools, and students can place a teacher in legal jeopardy.

—VINCENT,
Teacher Education program, first year

Our country has a long history of protecting human rights through the enactment of specific laws. From the early colonists who sought religious freedom to African Americans involved in the civil rights movement, Americans have sought protection under the law. During the last several decades, the legal aspects of education have received increased attention. For example, the number of education cases that reached state and federal courts increased from an average of about 1,500 a year during the 1940s to more than 6,500 by 2009 (Dunn & West, 2009).

Why Do you Need to Know about Education and the Law and Have a Code of Ethics?

At this point in your teacher education program, understanding how the law influences schools and teachers may not seem important. However, federal and state legislation and court decisions will affect your life as a teacher. What are your legal responsibilities when you take students on a field trip? Are you responsible if a student is injured during your class? Can a parent prevent you from using curriculum materials that the parent finds offensive? What guidelines must you follow when photocopying instructional materials from books and magazines? How can you copyright-protect materials you and your students upload to the Internet? How can social networking and technologies like smartphones that empower students also place teachers and schools at risk? These are just a few legal issues you might encounter as a teacher. Without knowledge of the legal dimensions of such issues, you will be ill equipped to protect your rights and the rights of your students. This chapter examines ethical and legal issues that affect the rights and responsibilities of teachers, administrators, students, and parents.

Professional Code of Ethics

At present, the teaching profession does not have a uniform **code of ethics** similar to the Hippocratic Oath, which all doctors are legally required to take when they begin practice. However, the largest professional organization for teachers, the National Education Association (NEA), has a code of ethics for its members that includes the following statement: "The educator accepts the responsibility to adhere to the highest ethical standards." You can review the entire code of ethics at the NEA website.

Your actions as a teacher will be determined not only by what is legally required of you but also by what you know you *ought* to do. You must do what is *legally right*, and you must *do the right thing*. In many cases, doing the right thing and doing what is required by law are the same. As Figure 7.1 shows, you would have an ethical and legal responsibility to ensure the safety of students during a field trip to a museum in a nearby city. The figure also shows that doing the right thing may not be required by law. For example, you should use the same criteria to grade students—giving girls higher grades than boys, or

Figure 7.1 The relationship of ethics and law to three examples of professional practice as a teacher

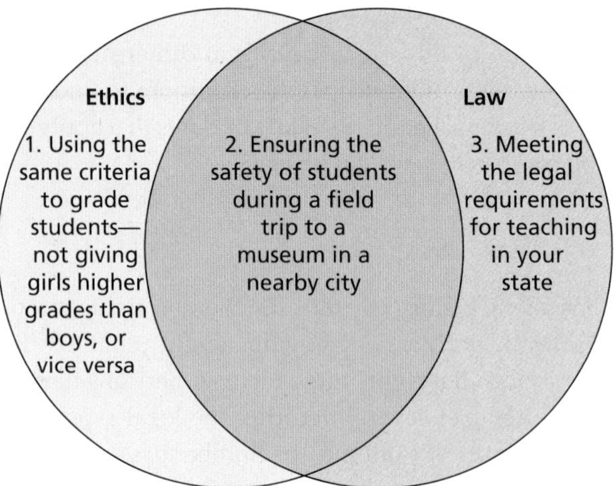

vice versa, would be unethical, but it would not be illegal. Last, meeting the legal requirements to become a teacher in your state is a legal matter, not an ethical matter.

A specific set of values will guide you as a teacher. A deep and lasting commitment to professional practice should characterize your role as a teacher. You will need to adopt a high standard of professional ethics and model behaviors that are in accordance with that code of ethics. Teachers are responsible for setting a good example; their actions should reflect good moral character.

Teaching is an ethical enterprise; that is, a teacher has an obligation to act ethically, to follow what he or she knows to be the most appropriate professional action to take. The best interests of students, not the teacher, provide the rule of thumb for determining what is ethical and what is not. Behaving ethically is more than a matter of following the rules or not breaking the law—it means acting in a way that promotes the learning and growth of students and helps them realize their potential. The Teaching on Your Feet feature for this chapter illustrates how one teacher modified his behavior to promote the learning and growth of a "problem" student.

Teaching on Your Feet

Respect in the Classroom Is a Two-Way Street

MARK TWAIN once said, "I could live two months on one good compliment." That statement also applies to today's students. When confronted with challenging situations in the classroom, ask yourself, "Do my students feel that I respect them?" Answering that question honestly might make your day-to-day life in the classroom much more productive, as Julius Dichosa illustrates in the following excerpt.

When I was a beginning teacher, I asked several veteran teachers at my school for advice before my first day of teaching. To my surprise, they all said the same thing: "Don't smile until Christmas!" That advice was not very reassuring, since it does not fit my personality. Although they didn't mean it literally, they felt strongly about being strict and not becoming "friends" with students. After my first few weeks of teaching, I understood exactly what they meant, even if I did not totally agree with their philosophy.

I started off the first week by making sure that my students understood the rules and expectations for my class. Typical for many junior high classes, I was met with rolling eyes and witty remarks from a select few in each class. So, I put on my strictest face and made sure that those students knew that I meant business. After that, there was only one who continued to fight me on it. I'll call him Johnny.

During the next couple of months, Johnny and I disagreed on several occasions. Johnny demanded attention; he had a comment for everything that occurred in class. He would not take "no" for an answer. Each time we had a disagreement, I sent him to the guidance office, called his parents, and hoped for the best. But the next day, I would be met with even more resistance and negativity. After repeating this process several times, I decided to change my strategy. Why was Johnny giving me such a hard time? What was I doing wrong? I thought being strict and firm was the way to start off the school year, but to be honest, it consumed all of my energy in and out of class. It was time to find a better way to reach Johnny.

After speaking to the administration and some of Johnny's other teachers, I realized that I was not alone. With one exception, they all had problems with him. To my surprise, the exception was a beginning teacher like myself. I had to know her secret. When I asked her how she "handled" Johnny, she simply said, "Some students deserve a break." She explained that there are some students who respond to consequences and others who don't. Johnny was one who did not. He needed a "break" to be successful.

The next day, I called Johnny out of class to speak to him one-on-one. I reassured him that he wasn't in trouble—all I wanted to do was talk to him. I asked him what it was about me that he didn't like, and he responded, "You treat me like all the other teachers do." When I asked him how he wanted to be treated, he said, "I don't know . . . with respect." I proceeded to tell him that in order to get respect, you have to give it. Then he said something that surprised me. "You need to take some of your own advice." In that moment, my two-month career as a schoolteacher flashed before my eyes. I was speechless. After an awkward silence, I sent him back to class. I thought long and hard about how I was coming across to my students and came to the conclusion that, while being strict and firm (without cracking a smile) worked for the majority of my students, I was at times being disrespectful to a select few—Johnny, in particular.

Following class the next day, I thanked Johnny for our conversation. He seemed surprised by my reaction. I joked with him, telling him that he could make big money as an advisor to teachers. I apologized for the way I had been treating him in front of the class. I told him that students in the class looked up to him and saw him as a leader. I assured him that he could use his influence with students in a positive way and persuade them to act appropriately. I could tell that those words meant a lot to him. From that day forward, Johnny and I had a mutually respectful relationship. And, most important, I had an influential student who supported my approach to classroom management.

JULIUS DICHOSA
Eighth-Grade Physical Science, Department Chair,
Las Palmas Middle School, Covina, **CALIFORNIA**

ANALYZE

Classroom management cannot be learned entirely from a textbook. It must also be learned through experience, and it must fit the teacher's personality. No single approach to classroom management works for all students in a classroom. Each class has students who respond differently to a teacher's approach. Regardless of the approach used, effective classroom management requires that students respect their teachers and, in turn, teachers respect their students. Respect in the classroom is a two-way street.

REFLECT

1. What are the pros and cons of taking the advice of other teachers regarding classroom management?
2. What are other strategies a teacher can use to have a positive influence on students who chronically misbehave?
3. Why is there no universally effective approach to classroom management? Explain.

Unethical acts break the trust and respect on which good teacher–student relationships are based. Examples of unethical conduct would be to use grades as a form of punishment, express rage in the classroom, or intentionally trick students on tests. Perhaps you can think of other examples from your own experience as a student.

Ethical Dilemmas in the Classroom and School

As a teacher, you will probably encounter **ethical dilemmas** in the classroom and in the school. You will have to take action in situations in which all the facts are not known or for which no single course of action can be called right or wrong. At these times, it can be quite difficult to decide what an ethical response might be. Dealing satisfactorily with ethical dilemmas in teaching often requires the ability to see beyond short-range consequences to consider long-range consequences.

An important part of responding to an ethical dilemma is identifying possible consequences of one's actions. Consider, for example, the following three questions based on actual case studies. On the basis of the information given, how would you respond to each situation? What might be the consequences of your actions?

1. Should the sponsor of the high school literary magazine refuse to print a well-written story by a budding writer if the piece appears to satirize a teacher and a student?
2. Is a reading teacher justified in trying to increase achievement for an entire class by separating two disruptive students and placing one in a reading group beneath his reading level?
3. Should a chemistry teacher punish a student (on the basis of circumstantial, inconclusive evidence) for a laboratory explosion if the example of decisive, swift punishment will likely prevent the recurrence of a similar event and thereby ensure the safety of all students?

There are no "right" answers to these questions. To the extent possible, you want to make the "best" decision in each case. A noted scholar of professional ethics, Kenneth A. Strike, suggests the following characteristics of a "good," ethical decision:

1. The decision is supported by evidence. This evidence supports the claim that acting on this decision is more likely to achieve desired ends at an appropriate cost than other courses of action that might be taken.
2. The ends aimed at by the decision are the ends that ought to be aimed at.
3. The decision can be implemented morally.
4. The decision has been legitimately achieved. (Strike, 2007, p. 113)

What are Your Legal Rights as a Teacher?

With each freedom that we have comes a corresponding responsibility to others and to the community in which we live. As long as there is more than one individual on this planet, there is a need for laws to clarify individual rights and responsibilities. This necessary balance between rights and responsibilities is perhaps more critical to teaching than to any other profession. Teachers have the same rights as other citizens; however, teachers must carry out their professional responsibilities within the guidelines of statutory law, state and federal education case law, and school district policies. The primary legal rights of teachers are illustrated in Figure 7.2.

Figure 7.2 Teachers' legal rights

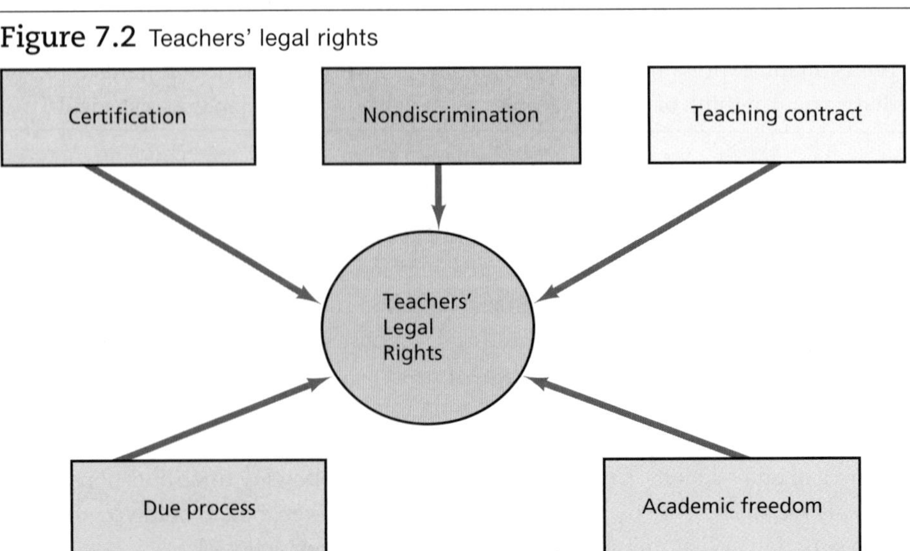

Although schools do have limited power over teachers, teachers' rights to **due process** cannot be violated. Like all citizens, teachers are protected from being treated arbitrarily by those in authority. A principal who disagrees with a teacher's methods cannot suddenly fire that teacher. A school board cannot ask a teacher to resign merely by claiming that the teacher's political activities outside school are "disruptive" to the educational process. A teacher cannot be dismissed for "poor" performance without ample documentation that the performance was, in fact, poor and without sufficient time to meet clearly stated performance evaluation criteria.

Certification

No teacher who meets all of a state's requirements for initial certification can arbitrarily be denied a certificate. However, receiving a certificate does not guarantee the right to keep it.

> Suppose, for example, that Peggy Hernandez is a junior high school English teacher and lives in a state with a law specifying that a teacher must show proof of five years of successful teaching experience for a teaching certificate to be renewed. Last year was Peggy's fifth year of teaching, and her principal gave her an unsatisfactory performance rating. Peggy's principal told her that her teaching certificate cannot be renewed. Is the principal correct?

Peggy's principal is mistaken about the grounds for nonrenewal of a teaching certificate. According to the state's law, failure to complete the school year is grounds for nonrenewal of a certificate—not performance that is judged to be unsatisfactory. Because state laws vary and unsatisfactory performance is defined differently in different states, however, Peggy's principal might have been correct if she taught in another state.

For a certificate to be revoked, the reason must be job related and demonstrably impair the teacher's ability to perform satisfactorily. In this regard, the case of a **CALIFORNIA** teacher whose certificate was revoked because someone admitted to having a homosexual relationship with the teacher is often cited. The court determined that the teacher's homosexual conduct was not an impairment to the teacher's performance and ordered the certificate restored (*Morrison v. State Board of Education*, 1969).

In addition, it is almost impossible for a school system to deny employment or dismiss a teacher based on his or her sexual orientation. Twenty states and the **DISTRICT OF COLUMBIA** prohibit discrimination based on sexual orientation and gender identity (Human Rights Campaign, 2017). In the few instances in which courts have upheld the refusal to hire and the right to terminate lesbian, gay, bisexual, or transgender (LGBT) teachers, these decisions have been influenced by factors such as sexual involvement with students or public acts of indecency.

Teachers' Rights to Nondiscrimination

The right to **nondiscrimination** in regard to employment is protected by Title VII of the Civil Rights Act of 1964, which states:

> It shall be an unlawful employment practice for an employer (1) to fail or refuse to hire or to discharge any individual, or otherwise to discriminate against any individual with respect to his compensation, terms, conditions, or privileges of employment, because of such individual's race, color, religion, sex, or national origin; or (2) to limit, segregate, or classify his employees or applicants for employment in any way which would deprive or tend to deprive any individual of employment opportunities or otherwise adversely affect his status as an employee, because of such individual's race, color, religion, sex, or national origin (U.S. Equal Employment Opportunity Commission, 1964).

States may impose certain limitations on initial certification as long as those limitations are not discriminatory with regard to race, religion, ethnic origin, sex, or age. Nearly all the states, for example, require that applicants for a teaching certificate pass a test that covers basic skills, professional knowledge, or academic subject areas. Qualifications for initial certification may also legally include certain personal qualities.

> Suppose George, who pled guilty to possession of marijuana and cocaine in a criminal trial, was not reinstated in his teaching position after his criminal record was expunged. George claims that he is being discriminated against because of his past. Is he right?

George's case is based on a Louisiana case involving a man who was not reinstated in his teaching position, even though his criminal record had been expunged. The court maintained that he had committed the act, and that expunging the record did not erase that fact, nor did it erase the "moral turpitude" of the teacher's conduct (*Dubuclet v. Home Insurance Company*, 1995).

Note that there is currently no federal law that protects lesbian, gay, bisexual, and transgender (LGBT) individuals from employment discrimination. The Employment Non-Discrimination Act (ENDA), first introduced to Congress in 1994, would prohibit workplace discrimination based on sexual orientation or gender identity. ENDA is modeled after Title VII of the Civil Rights Act and the Americans with Disabilities Act. The bill has yet to pass both houses of Congress. Most recently, it passed the Senate in 2013; however, it died in the House.

Teaching Contracts

A **teaching contract** represents an agreement between the teacher and a board of education. For a contract to be valid, it must contain these five basic elements:

1. **Offer and acceptance**—The school board has made a formal offer, and the employee has accepted the contract terms.
2. **Competent parties**—The school board is not exceeding the authority granted to it by the state, and the teacher meets the criteria for employment.
3. **Consideration**—Remuneration is promised to the teacher.
4. **Legal subject matter**—The contract terms are neither illegal nor against public policy.
5. **Proper form**—The contract adheres to state contract laws.

Before signing a teaching contract, read it carefully and be certain that it is signed by the appropriate member(s) of the board of education or board of trustees. Ask for clarification of any sections you don't understand. Any additional nonteaching duties should be spelled out in writing rather than left to an oral agreement. Because all board of education policies and regulations will be part of your contract, you should also read any available teacher handbook or school policy handbook.

The importance of carefully reading a contract and asking for clarification is illustrated in the following case:

> Victor Ming had just begun his first year as an English teacher at a high school in a city of about 300,000. Victor became quite upset when he learned that he had been assigned by his principal to sponsor the poetry club. The club was to meet once a week after school. Victor refused to sponsor the club, saying that the contract he had signed referred only to his teaching duties during regular school hours. Could Victor be compelled to sponsor the club?

Certain assignments, although not specified in a contract, may be required of teachers in addition to their regular teaching load, as long as there is a reasonable relationship between the teacher's classroom duties and the additional assignment. Such assignments can also include supervision of school events on weekends. Although Victor's contract did not make specific reference to club sponsorship, such a duty would be a reasonable addition to his regular teaching assignment.

When school authorities have assigned teachers to additional duties not reasonably related to their teaching, the courts have tended to rule in favor of teachers who file suit. For example, a school's directive to a tenured teacher of American history to assume the additional role of basketball coach was not upheld by a court of appeals (*Unified School District No. 241 v. Swanson*, 1986).

Due Process in Tenure and Dismissal

Tenure is a policy that provides the individual teacher with job security by (1) preventing his or her dismissal on insufficient grounds and (2) providing him or her with due process in the event of dismissal. Tenure is granted to teachers by the local school district after a period of satisfactory teaching, usually two to five years. In most cases, tenure may not be transferred from one school district to another.

The following case highlights the importance of tenure to a teacher's professional career:

> A teacher was dismissed from his teaching position by the school board after it learned that the teacher was a homosexual. The teacher filed suit in court, claiming that his firing was arbitrary and violated the provisions of tenure that he had been granted. The school board, on the other hand, maintained that his conduct was inappropriate for a teacher. Was the school board justified in dismissing the teacher?

The events in this case were actually heard by a court, which ruled that the teacher was unfairly dismissed (*Burton v. Cascade School District Union High School No. 5*, 1975). The court said that the board violated the teacher's rights as a tenured employee by failing to show "good and just cause" for dismissal. The teacher was awarded the balance due under his contract and an additional one-half year's salary. In a similar case, however, a court upheld the dismissal of a teacher whose sexual orientation was the target of parents' complaints and students' comments. The court ruled that the teacher could no longer effectively carry out his teaching duties (*Gaylord v. Tacoma School District No. 10*, 1977).

The practice of providing teachers with tenure is not without controversy. Some critics point out that tenure policies make it too difficult to dismiss incompetent teachers and that performance standards are high in many other fields that do not provide employees with job security. Generally, however, the courts have held the position that tenure enables teachers to perform their professional duties without interference from special-interest groups or political factions.

Just about every state today has a tenure law that specifies that a teacher may be dismissed with good cause. What counts as a good cause varies from state to state, however. The courts have ruled on a variety of reasons for **dismissal**: (1) insubordination, (2) incompetence or inefficiency, (3) neglect of duty, (4) conduct unbecoming a teacher, (5) subversive activities, (6) retrenchment or decreased need for services, (7) physical and/or mental health, (8) age, (9) causing or encouraging disruption, (10) engaging in illegal activities, (11) using offensive language, (12) personal appearance, (13) sex-related activities, (14) political activities, and (15) use of drugs or intoxicants.

For a tenured teacher to be dismissed, a systematic series of steps must be followed so that the teacher receives due process and his or her constitutionally guaranteed rights are not violated. Due process involves a careful, step-by-step examination of the charges brought against a teacher. Most states have outlined procedures that adhere to the following nine steps:

1. The teacher must be notified of the list of charges.
2. Adequate time must be provided for the teacher to prepare a rebuttal to the charges.
3. The teacher must be given the names of witnesses and access to evidence.
4. The hearing must be conducted before an impartial tribunal.
5. The teacher has the right to representation by legal counsel.
6. The teacher (or legal counsel) can introduce evidence and cross-examine adverse witnesses.
7. The school board's decision must be based on the evidence and findings of the hearing.
8. A transcript or record must be maintained of the hearing.
9. The teacher has the right to appeal an adverse decision.

These steps notwithstanding, it should be noted that due process is "a dynamic concept . . . [and] depends largely on a combination of the specific facts in a situation, the law governing the situation, the particular time in history in which judgment is being rendered, and the predilections of the individual judge(s) rendering the decision" (LaMorte, 2012, p. 5). The following case illustrates these points:

> Near the start of his fifth year of teaching at an elementary school in a small city, and two years after earning tenure, Mr. Mitchell went through a sudden and painful divorce. A few months later, a woman whom he had met around the time of his divorce moved into the house he was renting.
>
> For the remainder of the school year, he and the woman lived together. During this time, he received no indication that his lifestyle was professionally unacceptable, and his teaching performance remained satisfactory.
>
> At the end of the year, however, Mr. Mitchell was notified that he was being dismissed because of immoral conduct; that is, he was living with a woman he was not married to. The school board called for a hearing and Mr. Mitchell presented his side of the case. The board, nevertheless, decided to follow through with its decision to dismiss him.
>
> Was the school board justified in dismissing Mr. Mitchell?

At one time, teachers could readily be dismissed for living, unmarried, with a member of the opposite sex. However, in today's environment, the courts rarely hear a case for dismissal of an adulterous teacher, an unmarried pregnant teacher, or an unmarried teacher living with a person of the opposite sex. Because the board had not shown that Mr. Mitchell's alleged immoral conduct had a negative effect on his teaching, his dismissal would probably not hold up in court unless the community as a whole was upset by his behavior. Moreover, Mr. Mitchell could charge that his right to privacy, as guaranteed by the 9th Amendment to the Constitution, had been violated. Overall, it appears that the decision to dismiss Mr. Mitchell was arbitrary and based on the collective bias of the board. Nevertheless, teachers should be aware that courts frequently hold that teachers are role models, and the local community determines "acceptable" behavior both in school and out of school.

Teachers also have the right to organize and to join teacher organizations without fear of dismissal. In addition, most states have passed **collective bargaining** laws that require school boards to negotiate contracts with teacher organizations. Usually, the teacher organization with the most members in a district is given the right to represent teachers in the collective bargaining process.

An important part of most collective bargaining agreements is the right of a teacher to file a **grievance**, a formal complaint against his or her employer. A teacher may not be dismissed for filing a grievance, and he or she is entitled to have the grievance heard by a neutral third party. Often, the teachers' union or professional association that negotiated the collective bargaining agreement will provide free legal counsel for a teacher who has filed a grievance.

One right that teachers are not granted by collective bargaining agreements is the right to strike. Like other public employees, teachers do not have the legal right to strike in most states. Teachers who do strike run the risk of dismissal (*Hortonville Joint School District No. 1 v. Hortonville Education Association,* 1976); however, when teacher strikes occur, a school board cannot possibly replace all the striking teachers.

Academic Freedom

Although the courts have held that teachers have the right to academic freedom, it is not absolute and must be balanced against the interests of society. For a court to uphold a teacher's right to academic freedom, "It must be shown that the teacher did not defy legitimate state and local curriculum directives; followed accepted professional norms for that grade level and subject matter; discussed matters which were of public concern; and acted professionally and in good faith when there was no precedent or policy" (LaMorte, 2012, p. 176).

The following case illustrates the limits that may apply to a teacher's right to academic freedom:

> A teacher of at-risk students at an alternative high school used a classroom management/motivational technique called Learnball. The teacher divided the class into teams, allowed students to elect team leaders and determine class rules and grading exercises, and developed a system of rewards that included listening to the radio and shooting baskets with a foam ball in the classroom. The school board ordered the teacher not to use the Learnball approach. Did the teacher have the right to continue using this teaching method?

This case is based on actual events involving a teacher in Pittsburgh, **PENNSYLVANIA**. The teacher brought suit against the board to prevent it from imposing a policy that banned Learnball in the classroom. The teacher cited the principle of **academic freedom** and claimed that teachers have a right to use teaching methods and materials to which school officials might object. A U.S. District Court, however, upheld the school board policy against Learnball (*Murray v. Pittsburgh Board of Public Education,* 1996).

FAMOUS CASES A landmark case involving academic freedom focused on John Scopes, a biology teacher who challenged a Tennessee law in 1925 that made it illegal to teach in a public school "any theory which denies the story of the Divine Creation of man as taught in the Bible, and to teach instead that man is descended from a lower order of animals." Scopes maintained that Darwin's theory about human origins had scientific merit and that the state's requirement that he teach the biblical account of creation violated his academic freedom.

Scopes's trial, which came to be known as the monkey trial, attracted national attention. Prosecuting Scopes was the "silver-tongued" William Jennings Bryan, a famous lawyer, politician, and presidential candidate. The defending attorney was Clarence Darrow.

Scopes believed strongly in academic freedom and his students' right to know about scientific theories. He expressed his views in his memoir, *Center of the Storm*:

> Especially repulsive are laws restricting the constitutional freedom of teachers. The mere presence of such a law is a club held over the heads of the timid. Legislation that tampers with academic freedom is not protecting society, as its authors piously proclaim. By limiting freedom they are helping to make robot factories out of schools; ultimately, this produces non-thinking robots rather than the individualistic citizens we desperately need—now more than ever before. (Scopes, 1966, p. 277)

The monkey trial ended after 11 days of heated, eloquent testimony. Scopes was found guilty of violating the Butler Act and was fined $100. The decision was later reversed by the Tennessee Supreme Court on a technicality.

Since the Scopes trial, controversy has continued to surround the teaching of evolution. In many states during the 1980s, for example, religious fundamentalists won rulings that required science teachers to give equal time to both creationism and evolution in the classroom. The Supreme Court, however, in *Edwards v. Aguillard* (1987) ruled that such "balanced treatment" laws were unconstitutional. In the words of the court: "Because the primary purpose of the [Louisiana] Creationism Act is to advance a particular religious belief, the Act endorses religion in violation of the First Amendment."

In 1999, controversy over evolution again emerged when the Kansas State Board of Education removed the teaching of evolution and discussion of the origin of the universe from state science standards. A newly elected Kansas Board of Education voted to restore evolution to state science standards in 2001, however. Similarly, evolution became a topic of public debate in Ohio during 2006, when the Ohio State Board of Education voted to eliminate from state science curriculum standards a statement that encouraged students to "critically analyze" evolution.

Another case suggesting that a teacher's right to academic freedom is narrow and limited is *Krizek v. Cicero-Stickney Township High School District No. 201* (1989). In this instance, a district court ruled against a teacher whose contract was not renewed because she showed her students an R-rated film (*About Last Night*) as an example of a modern-day parallel to Thornton Wilder's play *Our Town*. Although the teacher told her students that they would be excused from viewing the film if they or their parents objected, she did not communicate directly with their parents. The teacher's attempt to consider the objections of students and parents notwithstanding, the court concluded that the length of the film indicates that its showing was more than an inadvertent mistake or a mere slip of the tongue, but rather was a planned event, and thus indicated that the teacher's approach to teaching was problematic.

Although concerned more with the right of a school to establish a curriculum than with the academic freedom of teachers per se, other cases have focused on the teacher's use of instructional materials. In *Mozert v. Hawkins County Board of Education* (1987, 1988), for example, a group of Tennessee parents objected to "secular humanist" materials used by their children's teachers. In *Smith v. Board of School Commissioners of Mobile County* (1987), 624 parents and teachers initiated a court suit alleging that 44 history, social studies, and home economics texts used in the Mobile County, Alabama, public schools encouraged immorality, undermined parental authority, and were imbued with the "humanist" faith. In both cases, the courts supported the right of schools to establish a curriculum even in the face of parental disapproval. In *Smith v. Board of School Commissioners of Mobile County* (1987), the Eleventh Circuit Court stated that "[i]ndeed, given the diversity of religious views in this country, if the standard were merely inconsistency with the beliefs of a particular religion there would be very little that could be taught in the public schools."

STATES' RIGHTS AND ACADEMIC FREEDOM The previously described cases notwithstanding, the courts have not set guidelines for situations when the teacher's freedom conflicts with the state's right to require teachers to follow certain curriculum guidelines. The same federal court, for example, heard a similar case regarding a high school teacher who wrote a vulgar word for sexual intercourse on the blackboard during a discussion of socially taboo words. The court sidestepped the issue of academic freedom and ruled instead that the regulations authorizing teacher discipline were unconstitutionally vague, and therefore the teacher could not be dismissed. The court did observe, however, that a public school teacher's right to traditional academic freedom is "qualified," at best, and the "teacher's right must yield to compelling public interests of greater constitutional significance."

In reviewing its decision, the court also said, "Nothing herein suggests that school authorities are not free after they have learned that the teacher is using a teaching method of which they disapprove, and which is not appropriate to the proper teaching of the subject, to suspend him [or her] until he [or she] agrees to cease using the method" (*Mailloux v. Kiley*, 1971).

Although some teachers have been successful in citing academic freedom as the basis for teaching controversial subjects, others have not. Teachers have been dismissed for ignoring directives regarding the teaching of controversial topics related to sex, polygamy, race, and religion. Although the courts have not been able to clarify just where academic freedom begins and ends, they have made it clear that the state does have a legitimate interest in what is taught to impressionable children.

Do Student Teachers Have the Same Rights as Teachers?

It has been observed that a student teacher "is a special hybrid, being partially a student in higher education but not with the typical full load of campus classes and partially a teacher in K–12 education but not with the compensation and benefits of a full-fledged employee" (Zirkel & Karanxha, 2009, p. xi). Fewer than half of the states have statutes that apply specifically to student teachers (Zirkel & Karanxha, 2009). In addition, no state has a statutory provision regulating the dismissal of a student teacher, the assignment of a student teacher, or the denial of the right to student-teach (Morris & Curtis, 1983). Nevertheless, student teachers should be aware that a potential for liability exists with them just as it does with certified teachers.

The following case illustrates the difference between the legal status of a certified teacher and a student teacher:

> Meg Grant looked forward to the eight weeks she would spend as a student teacher in Mrs. Walker's high school English classes. Meg knew that Mrs. Walker was one of the best supervising teachers she might have been paired with, and she was anxious to do her best.
>
> In Mrs. Walker's senior class, Meg planned to teach *Brave New World*. Mrs. Walker pointed out to Meg that this book was controversial and some parents might object. She asked Meg to think about selecting an additional title that students could read if their parents objected to *Brave New World*. Meg felt that Mrs. Walker was bowing to pressure from conservative parents, so she decided to go ahead and teach the book.
>
> Two weeks later, Meg was called down to the principal's office where she was confronted by an angry father who said, "You have no right to be teaching my daughter this communist trash; you're just a student teacher."
>
> What should Meg do? Does she have the same rights as a fully certified teacher?

In some states, a student teacher such as Meg might have the same rights and responsibilities as a fully certified teacher; in others, her legal status might be that of an unlicensed visitor. The most prudent action for Meg to take would be to apologize to the father and assure him that if any controversial books are assigned in the future, alternative titles would be provided. In addition, Meg should learn how important it is for a student teacher to take the advice of his or her supervising teacher.

One area of debate regarding student teachers is whether they can act as substitutes for their cooperating teachers or even other teachers in a school building. Unfortunately, many school districts have no policy regarding this practice. Depending on statutes in a particular state, however, a student teacher may substitute under the following conditions:

- A substitute teacher is not immediately available.
- The student teacher has been in that student-teaching assignment for a specified minimum number of school days.
- The supervising teacher, the principal of the school, and the university supervisor agree that the student teacher is capable of successfully handling the teaching responsibilities.
- A certified classroom teacher in an adjacent room or a member of the same teaching team as the student teacher is aware of the absence and agrees to assist the student teacher if needed.
- The principal of the school or the principal's representative is readily available in the building.
- The student teacher is not paid for any substitute service. (This matter is negotiable in some jurisdictions.) (Dunklee & Shoop, 2006, pp. 114–115)

Given the ambiguous status of student teachers, it is important that you begin your student-teaching assignment with knowledge of the legal aspects of teaching and a clear idea of your rights and responsibilities. During your student teaching experience, you should follow the six recommendations in Figure 7.3.

Figure 7.3 Legal advice for your student teaching experience

1. If the school has a faculty handbook, become familiar with its contents, particularly the roles and responsibilities that apply to teachers. If you have questions about the handbook, ask your cooperating teacher.
2. Become familiar with district guidelines that might apply to the curriculum you will teach. For example, does the district require (or prohibit) the use of certain books and/or teaching methods?
3. Understand the potential risks associated with the learning activities you plan to use during your student teaching experience. Discuss any concerns with your cooperating teacher.
4. Review with your cooperating teacher the school's rules for safety and the procedures to follow in the event of an emergency.
5. Remember that students' records are confidential. School records should be used to improve your teaching and/or to increase students' learning.
6. If you have problems with certain students or with a particular class, document your concerns and seek advice from your cooperating teacher.

What are Your Legal Responsibilities as a Teacher?

Teachers are responsible, of course, for meeting the terms of their teaching contracts. As noted previously, teachers are responsible for duties not covered in the contract if they are reasonably related to teaching. Among these duties may be club sponsorship; lunchroom, study hall, or playground duty; academic counseling of students; and record keeping. Figure 7.4 illustrates three primary additional legal responsibilities of teachers.

Figure 7.4 Teachers' legal responsibilities

Avoid Tort Liability
- *Neglience*
- *Professional Malpractice*

Observe Copyright Laws
- *Photocopies*
- *Videotapes*
- *Software*
- *E-mail and the Internet*
- *Internet Posts*

Teacher's Legal Responsibilities

Report Child Abuse

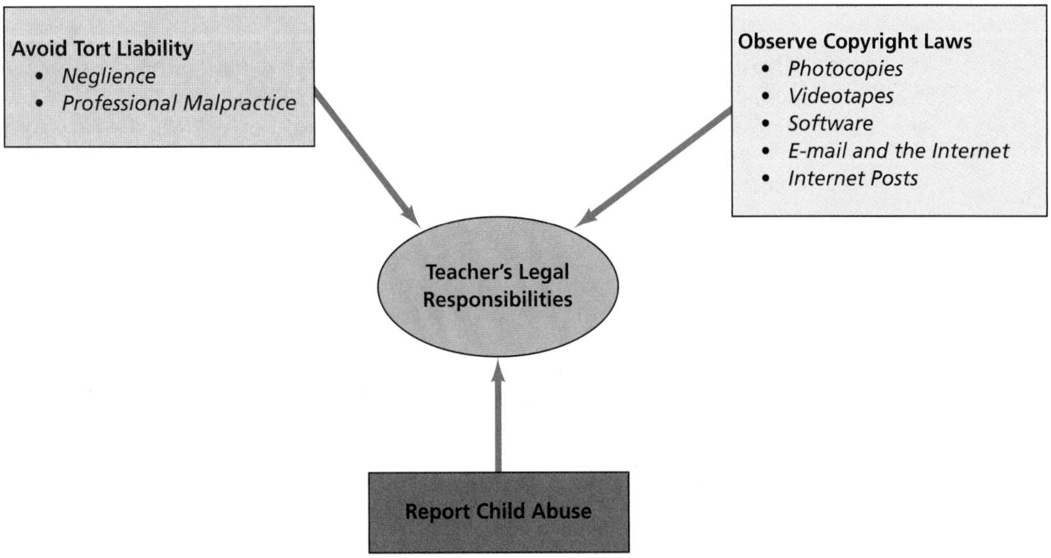

Avoiding Tort Liability

Teachers are legally responsible for the safety and well-being of students assigned to them. Although it is not expected that a teacher be able to control completely the behavior of young, energetic students, a teacher can be held liable for any injury to a student if it is shown that the teacher's negligence contributed to the injury. Read the following short case—do you think the teacher should be liable for the student's injuries?

> An eighth-grade science teacher in Louisiana left her class for a few moments to go to the school office to pick up some forms. While she was gone, her students continued to do some laboratory work that involved the use of alcohol-burning devices. Unfortunately, one girl was injured when she tried to relight a defective burner.

These events actually occurred (*Station v. Travelers Insurance Co.,* 1974). The court that heard the case determined that the teacher failed to provide adequate supervision while the students were exposed to dangerous conditions. Considerable care is required, the court observed, when students handle inherently dangerous objects, and the need for this care is magnified when students are exposed to dangers they don't appreciate.

At times, teachers may have concerns about their liability for damages as a result of their actions. The branch of law concerned with compensating an individual who suffers losses resulting from another's negligence is known as tort law. "Tort law deals with a variety of matters including negligent or intentional behavior causing harm, defamation, and injuries resulting from defects in buildings or land" (Imber et al., 2014, p. 4).

According to **tort liability** law, an individual who is negligent and at fault in the exercise of his or her legal duty may be required to pay monetary damages to an injured party. Generally, the standard of behavior applied by the courts is "the care that a reasonable and prudent person would take in the circumstances" (Imber et al., 2014, p. 287). However, teachers are held to a higher standard than ordinary citizens, and certain teachers (e.g., physical education, chemistry, and shop teachers) are held to an even higher standard because of the increased risk of injury involved in the classes they teach. Figure 7.5 presents several examples of cases in which students were injured and educators were found to have breached their duty of care.

Figure 7.5 Selected court decisions in which school personnel were found negligent for failure to meet a "standard of care"

1. A woodworking instructor allowed a student to operate a table saw without the use of a safeguard, which resulted in serious damage to his proximal interphalangeal joint. *Borbin v. State,* 506 So, 2d 888 (La. App. 1987).
2. A student dislocated his shoulder during an intramural football game, when the school provided no protective equipment and improper supervision of the game. *Locilento v. John A. Coleman Catholic High School,* 525 N.Y.S.2d 198 (A.D.3d Dept. 1987).
3. An 11-year-old student suffered serious head injuries from a blow to the head during a kickball game and was without medical attention for more than an hour. The one-hour delay caused a hematoma to grow from the size of a walnut to that of an orange. *Barth v. Board of Education,* 490 N.E.2d 77 (Ill. App. 1st Dist. 1986).
4. An 8-year-old girl was seriously burned when her costume caught fire from a lighted candle on her teacher's desk. *Smith v. Archbishop of St. Louis*, 632 S.W.2d 516 (Mo. App. 1982).
5. A 12-year-old boy was killed when he fell through a skylight at school while retrieving a ball. *Stabl v. Cocolico School District,* 534 A.2d 1141 (Pa. Cmwlth. 1987).
6. A boy was seriously injured while playing on school grounds when he fell into a hole filled with glass, trash, and other debris, due to the absence of school officials to warn him of the dangerous condition. *Dean v. Board of Education,* 523 A.2d 1059 (Md. App. 1987).
7. A female student was en route to class when she pushed her hand through a glass panel in a smoke-colored door, causing severe and permanent damage. *Bielaska v. Town of Waterford,* 491 A.2d 1071 (Conn. 1985).
8. A high school student was seriously injured when he was tackled and thrown to the ground during a touch football game in gym class that was inadequately supervised and the players began to use excessive force. *Hyman v. Green,* 403 N.W.2d 597 (Mich. App. 1987).

Adapted from Nathan L. Essex. *School Law and the Public Schools: A Practical Guide for Educational Leaders*, 5th edition. Boston: Allyn & Bacon, 2012, pp. 175–188. Copyright © by Allyn & Bacon. Reprinted by permission.

NEGLIGENCE In contrast to the decision reached by the Louisiana court mentioned earlier, the courts have made it clear that there are many accidents that teachers cannot reasonably foresee that do result in student injuries. For example, a teacher on playground duty was found not to be negligent when a student threw a rock that struck another student in the eye. After the teacher walked past a group of boys, one boy threw a small rock that hit a larger rock on the ground and then bounced up to hit the other boy in the eye. The court ruled that "[w]here the time between an act of a student and injury to a fellow student is so short that the teacher had no opportunity to prevent injury, it cannot be said that negligence of the teacher is a proximate cause of the injury" (*Fagen v. Summers,* 1972). In another case, the court ruled that a New York teacher could not have anticipated that the paper bag she asked a student to pick up contained a broken bottle that cut the student (*West v. Board of Education of City of New York,* 1959). In two almost identical cases, the courts ruled that a teacher of a class with a good behavior record could not reasonably be expected to anticipate that a student would be injured by a pencil thrown by a classmate while the teacher was momentarily out of the room attending to her usual duties (*Ohman v. Board of Education,* 1950; *Simonetti v. School District of Philadelphia,* 1982).

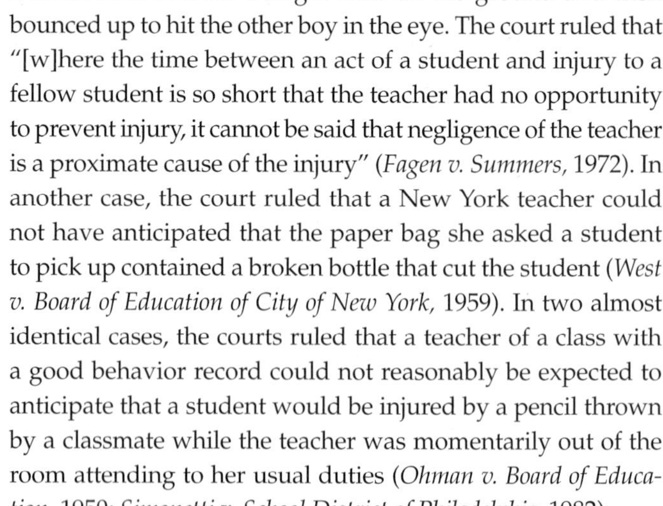

Cathy Yeulet/123RF

What legal responsibilities did a teacher consider when designing this laboratory experiment for students?

When a court considers a case involving tort liability, evidence is examined to determine whether the responsible party (the school district, the administrator, or the teacher) acted negligently. For a school official to be considered liable, the following must be shown to be present: "(1) a legal duty, (2) a breach of duty, (3) a causal connection often referred to as 'proximate cause' between the conduct and the resultant injury, and (4) actual loss or damage" (LaMorte, 2012, p. 327).

As a teacher, you should be alert to conditions that might lead to accidental injury of one or more students. You will have a duty to your pupils, and you could be held liable for injuries that students incur as a result of your **negligence**. However, your liability extends only to injuries your students might suffer if you fail to provide the degree of care for pupils that a reasonable person would. A review of court cases involving the tort liability of teachers suggests that most cases involve at least one of the following:

- Inadequate supervision
- Inadequate instruction
- Lack of or improper medical treatment of pupils
- Improper disclosure of defamatory information concerning pupils—for example, release of school records that contain negative statements about a student

Teachers' concern about their potential liability for failing to prevent injury to students has been lessened by the availability of liability insurance. Many professional teacher organizations offer liability coverage as part of their membership benefits. Teachers may also purchase individual liability insurance policies. In addition, school districts in approximately half of the states have immunity from liability for torts committed by district employees (LaMorte, 2012, p. 328).

Application Exercise 7.1
Indoor Recess

PROFESSIONAL MALPRACTICE Malpractice suits are well known within the field of medicine. Patients can sue physicians for incorrect diagnoses and incompetent surgery. **Professional malpractice** within the field of teaching occurs if a teacher lacks the skill to provide competent instruction or advice. Students can experience psychological, emotional, or educational damage as a result of poor teaching, improper placement, inappropriate testing, or lack of feedback to parents about a lack of progress.

With few exceptions, however, students have not been successful in their malpractice suits against specific teachers. In one case, for example, an Ohio high school student sued her psychology teacher after she failed the teacher's course and was unable to graduate on time. The student argued that the teacher recorded only three grades during the semester, until the last day of classes when the teacher gave a final exam and three quizzes in a 25-minute period. The student also argued that the teacher failed to notify her that she was in danger of failing the course. The Ohio Court of Appeals dismissed the student's lawsuit. The court noted that the teacher had not acted "with malicious purpose, in bad faith, or in a wanton or reckless manner." The court also noted "factors such as the student's attitude, motivation, temperament, past experience and home environment may all play an essential and immeasurable role in learning" (*Poe v. Hamilton,* 1990).

Video Example 7.1

Being Proactive to Prevent Bullying: Notice the actions this elementary teacher takes to identify and address bullying behavior before it causes the student psychological, emotional, or educational damage.

Reporting Child Abuse

Teachers are required by law to report suspected child abuse. Local, state, and federal child welfare agencies encourage teachers to be observant of children's appearance and behavior that might indicate symptoms of physical, emotional, or sexual abuse. Figure 7.6 presents a list of physical and behavioral indicators of potential child abuse. Many communities, through their police departments or other public and private agencies, provide programs adapted for children to educate them about child abuse and to show them how to obtain help.

The Fourth Amendment guarantees protection against unlawful search and seizure, and on occasion, parents and guardians have alleged a Fourth Amendment violation, claiming that school personnel should not have questioned or examined a student to determine if child abuse had occurred. In a **PENNSYLVANIA** case, the court concluded that the Fourth Amendment had not been violated as a result of school personnel questioning a student about suspected abuse. According to the court, Pennsylvania's Child Protective Services Law required teachers and administrators to determine if there was "reason to believe" that a student had been abused (*Picarella v. Terrizzi,* 1995).

Schools usually have a process for dealing with suspected abuse cases that involves the school principal, a nurse, and the reporting teacher. Because a child's welfare may be further endangered when abuse is reported, caution and sensitivity are required.

Figure 7.6 Physical and behavioral indicators of child abuse and neglect

Signs of physical abuse

Physical Indicators

- Unexplained bruises and welts on the face, throat, upper arms, buttocks, thighs, or lower back in unusual patterns or shapes that suggest the use of an instrument (belt buckle, electrical cord) on an infant in various stages of healing and that regularly appear after an absence, the weekend, or a vacation
- Unexplained burns or cigarette burns, especially found on the palms, the soles of feet, abdomen, buttocks; immersion burns producing "stocking" or "glove" demarcations on hands and feet; doughnut-shaped burns on buttocks or genital area
- Rope burns
- Infected burns indicating delay in treatment; burns in the shape of common household utensils or appliances

Behavioral Indicators

- Behavioral extremes (withdrawal, aggression, regression, depression)
- Inappropriate or excessive fear of parent or caretaker
- Antisocial behavior such as substance abuse, truancy, running away, fear of going home
- Unbelievable or inconsistent explanation for injuries
- Lies unusually still while surveying surroundings (for infants)
- Unusual shyness; wariness of physical contact

Signs of sexual abuse

Physical Indicators

- Torn, stained, or bloody underclothes
- Frequent, unexplained sore throats; yeast or urinary infections
- Somatic complaints, including pain and irritation of the genitals
- Sexually transmitted diseases
- Bruises or bleeding from external genitalia, vagina, or anal region
- Pregnancy

Behavioral Indicators

- The victim's disclosure of sexual abuse
- Regressive behaviors (thumb sucking, bed-wetting, fear of the dark)
- Promiscuity or seductive behaviors
- Disturbed sleep patterns (recurring nightmares)
- Unusual and age-inappropriate interest in sexual matters
- Avoidance of undressing or wearing extra layers of clothes
- Sudden decline in school performance; truancy
- Difficulty in walking or sitting

Signs of emotional abuse

Physical Indicators

- Eating disorders, including obesity or anorexia
- Speech disorders (stuttering, stammering)
- Developmental delays in the acquisition of speech or motor skills
- Weight or height substantially below norm
- Flat or bald spots on head (infants)
- Nervous disorders (rashes, hives, facial tics, stomachaches)

Behavioral Indicators

- Habit disorders (biting, rocking, head banging)
- Cruel behavior; seeming to get pleasure from hurting children, adults, or animals; seeming to get pleasure from being mistreated
- Age-inappropriate behaviors (bed-wetting, wetting, soiling)
- Behavioral extremes: overly compliant–demanding; withdrawn–aggressive; listless–excitable

Figure 7.6 *(Continued)*

Signs of neglect

Physical Indicators

- Poor hygiene, including lice, scabies, severe or untreated diaper rash, bedsores, body odor
- Squinting
- Unsuitable clothing; missing key articles of clothing (underwear, socks, shoes); overdressed or underdressed for climate conditions
- Untreated injury or illness
- Lack of immunizations
- Indicators of prolonged exposure to elements (excessive sunburn, insect bites, colds)
- Height and weight significantly below age level

Behavioral Indicators

- Unusual school attendance
- Chronic absenteeism
- Chronic hunger, tiredness, or lethargy
- Begging or collecting leftovers
- Assuming adult responsibilities
- Reporting no caretaker at home

Adapted from Childabuse.com. (2017). Anchorage, AK. Retrieved from http://www.childabuse.com/help.htm

Observing Copyright Laws

The continuing development of information technology has resulted in a new set of responsibilities for teachers regarding **copyright laws** pertaining to the use of photocopies, videotapes, and computer software. Congress revised the Copyright Act in 1976 by adding the doctrine of fair use. Although the fair-use doctrine cannot be precisely defined, it is generally interpreted as it was in *Marcus v. Rowley* (1983)—that is, one may "use the copyrighted material in a reasonable manner without [the copyright holder's] consent" as long as that use does not reduce the demand for the work or the author's income.

To "move the nation's copyright law into the digital age," the **Digital Millennium Copyright Act (DMCA)** amended the Copyright Act in 1998. The DMCA makes it illegal to circumvent copy-blocking measures (encryption and encoding, for example) that control access to copyrighted works. However, according to the statute, educational institutions may circumvent access control measures "solely for the purpose of making a good faith determination as to whether they wish to obtain authorized access to the work."

With the vast amount of material (in text, audio, video, and graphic formats) available over the Internet, teachers must consider copyright laws and restrictions that apply to this material. Unfortunately, the Copyright Act does not provide guidelines for the use of intellectual property found on the Internet. In any case, teachers should understand that content they view on the Internet is published material, and the doctrine of fair use applies to the use of such materials.

PHOTOCOPIES To clarify the fair-use doctrine as it pertained to teachers photocopying instructional materials from books and magazines, Congress endorsed a set of guidelines developed by educators, authors, and publishers. These guidelines allow teachers to make single copies of copyrighted material for teaching or research, but they are more restrictive regarding the use of multiple copies. The use of multiple copies of a work must meet the tests of brevity, spontaneity, and cumulative effect.

- Brevity means that short works can be copied. Poems or excerpts cannot be longer than 250 words, and copies of longer works cannot exceed 1,000 words or 10 percent of the work (whichever is less). Only one chart or drawing can be reproduced from a book or an article.
- The criterion of spontaneity means that the teacher doing the copying would not have time to request permission from the copyright holder.

- The criterion of cumulative effect limits the use of copies to one course and limits the material copied from the same author, book, or magazine during the semester. Also, no more than nine instances of multiple copying per class are allowed during a semester.

OFF-AIR RECORDINGS Guidelines for the use of off-air recordings made by teachers of television broadcasts were issued by Congress in 1981. Recorded material may be used in the classroom only once by the teacher within the first 10 days of recording. Additional use is limited to reinforcing instruction or evaluation of student learning, and the recording must be erased within 45 days.

SOFTWARE With the explosion of computers in schools, teachers face a new ethical and legal issue—adhering to copyright laws as they relate to software. Making an illegal copy of software on a hard drive—in effect, stealing another person's intellectual property—is quite easy. It is important therefore that, as a teacher, you be an exemplar of ethical behavior regarding copyrighted software. Just as you would not allow students to plagiarize written material or submit work that was not their own, you should follow the same standard of behavior regarding the use of software.

Software publishers have become concerned about the abuse of their copyrighted material. Limited school budgets and the high cost of software have led to the unauthorized reproduction of software. To address the problem, the Copyright Act was amended in 1980 to apply the fair-use doctrine to software. Accordingly, as a teacher, you may now make one backup copy of a program. If you were to make multiple copies of software, the fair-use doctrine would be violated because the software is readily accessible for purchase and making multiple copies would substantially reduce the market for the software. Software publishers have several different options for licensing their software to schools, and you should be aware of the type of license that has been purchased with each software program you use.

Video Example 7.2

Internet Safety and Saying Thank You: This teacher shares how to teach third graders about responsible use of other's digital property.

The increased practice of networking computer programs—that is, storing a copy of a computer program on a network file server and serving the program to a computer on the network—is also of concern to software publishers. The practice has not yet been tested in the courts. As more public schools develop computer networks, however, the issue of networked software will most likely be debated in the courts.

Currently, the Copyright Act is being revised to reflect how the doctrine of fair use should be applied to digital data. Two questions currently not answered by copyright law as it pertains to the educational use of computer software are the legality of (1) installing a single program on several computers in a laboratory and (2) modifying the program for use in a computer network. The Copyright Act specifies four factors for determining whether use of copyrighted material constitutes **fair use** or an infringement: (1) the purpose and character of the use, including whether such use is of a commercial nature or is for nonprofit educational purposes; (2) the nature of the copyrighted work; (3) the amount and substantiality of the portion used in relation to the copyrighted work as a whole; and (4) the effect of the use on the potential market for or value of the copyrighted work.

EMAIL AND THE INTERNET With the huge increase in the transmission of documents via email, copyright laws have been extended to cyberspace. Material published online may include a statement by the author(s) that the material is copyright-protected and may not be duplicated without permission. In other cases, the material may include a statement such as the following: "Permission is granted to distribute this material freely through electronic or by other means, provided it remains completely intact and unaltered, the source is acknowledged, and no fee is charged for it." If the material is published without restrictions on the Internet, one may assume that the author waives copyright privileges; however, proper credit and a citation should accompany the material if it is reproduced. The Technology in Action feature in this chapter explains how **virtual labs** can help students understand academic areas such as biology, astronomy, chemistry, and physics. If students use material from such sites in written papers and reports, they should be sure to cite the source of their information.

The following are guidelines for determining how much of a certain medium is considered fair to use without obtaining permission from the copyright holder:

- **Motion media**—Up to 10 percent or three minutes, whichever is less
- **Text**—10 percent or 1,000 words, whichever is less.
- **Poems**—An entire poem up to 250 words may be used, but no more than three poems by one poet or five poems by different poets from any anthology. For longer poems, 250 words may be used.
- **Music, lyrics, and music video**—Up to 10 percent but no more than 30 seconds. Any alterations shall not change the basic melody or the character of the work.
- **Illustrations and photography**—No more than five images by an artist or a photographer.
- **Numerical data sets**—Up to 10 percent or 2,500 cell entries, whichever is less. (Green, Brown, & Robinson, 2008, p. 120)

POSTING ON THE INTERNET Thousands of teachers and their students around the globe are posting material on their home pages on the Internet. Teacher- and

TECHNOLOGY in ACTION

Virtual Labs in a Ninth-Grade Biology Classroom

At this time each year, Mrs. Rajid's students start to squirm. She teaches introductory ninth-grade science, and the class will be dissecting frogs during the coming weeks. Many of her students will bring notes from their parents excusing them from the lesson. Mrs. Rajid has evidence of a direct correlation between those students who do not participate in the frog-dissecting activity and their gradual poor performance in high school science classes. She needs something to help her students understand the concepts of the lesson, rather than fixate on how "gross" it is to cut open a frog.

So, Mrs. Rajid goes on a frog-dissection webquest and finds several options; one is quite user-friendly, accessible on the web, and free. She decides to use the virtual lab (a software program that replicates the activities in a physical lab) in her next lesson, before the permission slips are sent home. Virtual labs deliver basic desired learning outcomes without the need for equipment, supplies, and dangerous materials. Although the effectiveness of virtual labs is debated among practitioners, there is no doubt that their growing popularity, combined with the technology enhancements of the industry, is a promising development for teachers. These labs usually take the form of interactive animation in which students make decisions, select tools, and perform actions, while the animation program responds appropriately. Some virtual labs use video, graphics, and audio to supplement the learning materials.

Teachers have successfully used virtual labs to help students understand biology, physics, astronomy, and chemistry. For example, virtual labs can allow students to practice appropriate stream restoration techniques, explore a human cadaver and perform an autopsy, and mix complex combinations of elements to see how those elements interact with one another.

The next day, Mrs. Rajid takes her students into the computer lab, has them open a web browser, and instructs them to navigate to the frog-dissection website. She then asks them to dissect their virtual frogs. A few students make comments like "Yuck" and "Gross," but the students perform quite well. They each have a frog preserved in formaldehyde; they dissect it and are able to identify the appropriate organs and structure.

Next week, when it is time to send home the permission slips for dissecting the real frog, she finds that a much higher percentage of her students are planning to participate. She also finds that her students are much better prepared to perform the real activity. They know what to do, how to do it, and what the goals of the activity are. Mrs. Rajid thinks that someday this virtual lab might indeed replace the need for the actual experience—at much less cost and with no formaldehyde smell.

VISIT: Open a web browser and search for the Directory of Science website. Click on the Biology link. Then enter "virtual frog" in the internal search engine. Several options will come up; pick the one that looks most appealing. Or you can click on other areas of science that interest you—aeronautics and aerospace, astronomy, chemistry, earth sciences, or medical science, for example.

student-produced materials can be copyright-protected by including a statement that the materials may not be duplicated without permission. In addition, teachers should be careful not to include information that would enable someone to identify children in a class. Children's last names should never be posted, nor should photos of children be posted with any identifying information.

Teachers and Social Networking

The rapid growth of social networking sites like Facebook, Instagram, Reddit, Pinterest, Tumblr, Google+, YouTube, Flickr, Snapchat, WhatsApp, and Twitter, each of which has more than 100 million users, has introduced new legal and ethical concerns for teachers. Educators who use such virtual communities should realize that their postings can be seen by the public and school officials. Increasingly, the media are reporting cases of teachers being fired or disciplined because of "inappropriate" profiles on Facebook or tweets on Twitter—teachers posting personal opinions about students or uploading inappropriate pictures of themselves, for example—or inappropriate communication with students.

A **PENNSYLVANIA** teacher was suspended after students saw photos of her on Facebook posing with a stripper. A Florida teacher was suspended after posting a note saying he "hated" his students and his school. A Washington, D.C. special education teacher faced scrutiny after school officials found this phrase about a student on her personal page: "You're a retard, but I love you." A math and science department supervisor was fired after she called her students "germ bags" on Facebook and described parents as "snobby" and "arrogant" (Sullivan, 2010).

In some cases, teachers have encountered problems with Facebook postings made by others. Another **PENNSYLVANIA** teacher was suspended for 30 days in 2010 after a friend posted a picture of her on Facebook with a stripper at a bachelorette party attended by a group of teachers. The teacher asked that the photo be removed within days, but not before it was brought to the attention of school officials. With the help of the American Civil Liberties Union (ACLU), the teacher sued her school district and won back pay (Sullivan, 2010).

Three New York City (NYC) high school teachers were fired in 2010 for having inappropriate interactions with students on Facebook—one of which culminated in a sexual relationship. One of the fired teachers, a male, "friended" several female students and wrote inappropriate comments under their Facebook photos. A female paraprofessional at an NYC high school was fired for posting a photo of her kissing an 18-year-old male former student. A male substitute teacher was barred from working in NYC schools after investigators learned that he had sent inappropriate messages to female students. Another male high school teacher, found to be giving extra credit to students who "friended" him, was not disciplined. To address teacher–student social networking issues, the New York City Department of Education eventually issued a 14-page document titled "Social Media Guidelines" in 2013.

Some school districts in **WISCONSIN**, **NEW HAMPSHIRE**, **OHIO**, and **FLORIDA** have advised teachers not to "friend" students on social networking sites. For example, the Lee County School District in **FLORIDA** issued the following guidelines for teacher use of social networking sites: "It could be viewed as inappropriate for District employees to communicate with current students enrolled in the District on any public social networking site (Facebook, Twitter, etc.). This includes becoming 'friends' or allowing students to access your personal page to communicate" (Lee County School District, 2017).

The governor of **LOUISIANA** signed a law making it illegal for teachers to contact students on Facebook (Murphy, 2010). According to the governor, "It's wonderful that our teachers and administrators can now directly email our kids and work on assignments quickly over the Internet, but we cannot allow these same devices to be used as an avenue to prey on our children, out of sight of parental supervision. This new law is an important step to help protect our children from abusive and plainly inappropriate communications from educators" (Sullivan, 2010).

Schools should consider developing policies for employees' use of social networking sites, according to the director of the Center for Safe and Responsible Internet Use: "It's safer for teachers and students to be interacting on the educational plane—not a friendship plane. Socializing on Facebook can cross over into areas that are potentially dangerous" (Chiaramonte & Gonen, 2010). Similarly, an attorney for the National School Boards Association says, "If it were me, and I were a teacher, I'd say just don't do it. Don't engage in social networking with students at all. The name says it all. It's about *social* networking. Social. Those are not the kinds of relationships that teachers are supposed to have with students. . . . A wise district says to teachers that they should never engage in peer-like activity with students—ever. Every interaction between students and teacher should be professional" (Sullivan, 2010).

A 79-year-old **NEW HAMPSHIRE** teacher terminated because she had about 250 "friends" on Facebook has a different opinion, however. Upon refusing to follow school policy and "unfriend" students, the teacher said, "There's a paranoia about the Internet, and I think that we're not realizing how valuable Facebook can be [if] used properly" (Rosenfield, 2014).

What are the Legal Rights of Students and Parents?

As a prospective teacher, you have an obligation to become familiar with the rights of students. Since the 1960s, students have confronted teachers and school districts more often with what they perceive to be illegal restrictions on their behavior. The following sections present brief summaries of selected major court decisions that clarify students' legal rights as illustrated in Figure 7.7.

Figure 7.7 Students' legal rights

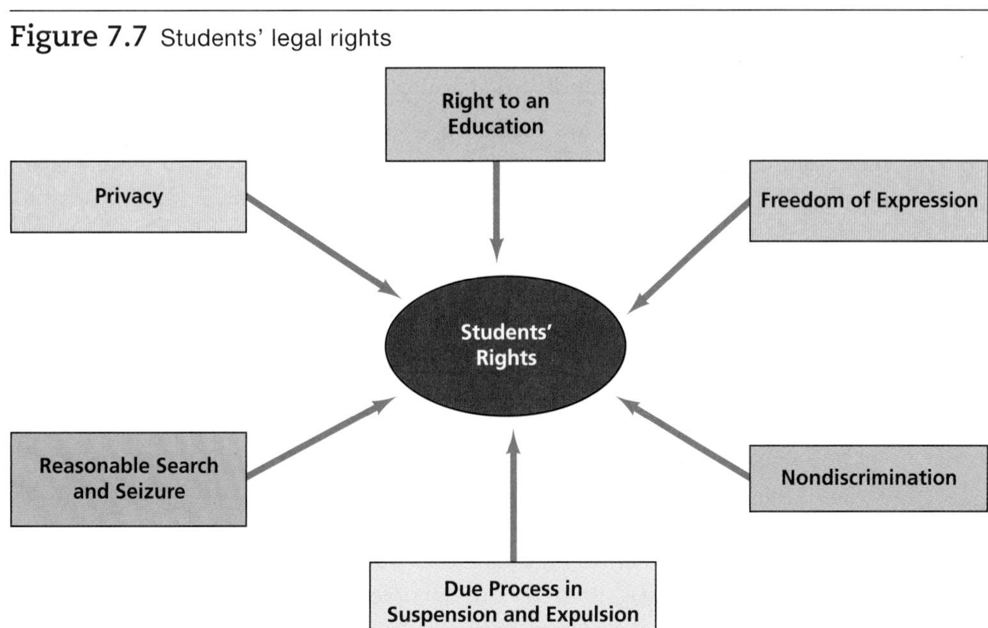

Right to an Education

In *San Antonio Independent School District v. Rodriguez* (1973), the Supreme Court ruled on a lawsuit alleging that school financing in Texas discriminated against students in poor communities. According to the suit, the state's system of financing denied students their fundamental right to education and violated the Equal Protection Clause of the Fourteenth Amendment. The Court ruled, however, that there is no fundamental right to education in the U.S. Constitution, and Texas school financing did not violate the Equal Protection Clause.

Though education is not a right under the U.S. Constitution, each state constitution mandates a system of public education that is available to all students. In addition, nine state constitutions require public education for students with disabilities (Education Commission of the States, 2016). Interestingly, since Washington, D.C. is not a state and uses the U.S. Constitution, there is actually no constitutional foundation for public education in Washington, D.C.

FOCUS ON **DIVERSITY**: EDUCATION OF STUDENTS OF UNDOCUMENTED IMMIGRANT PARENTS

In 1982, the Supreme Court ruled in *Plyler v. Doe* that states cannot constitutionally deny students a free public education because of their immigration status. With a 5-4 vote, the Court struck down a Texas law that denied education to children of undocumented parents.

Since the *Plyler v. Doe* ruling, the courts have upheld the Equal Protection Clause, which states that no person shall be denied "the equal protection of the laws." Nevertheless, some states and local communities have implemented measures and policies not in keeping with *Plyler v. Doe,* as the following examples illustrate.

- In 1994, California voters enacted Proposition 187, which prohibited public schools from admitting students not lawfully present in the U.S. The Proposition also required that schools notify federal immigration authorities within 45 days of any student in violation of federal immigration laws. Citing *Plyler v. Doe*, however, a federal court eventually struck down the Proposition.
- In 2006, the Elmwood Park Community Unit School District in Elmwood Park, Illinois denied enrollment to a student who had overstayed the tourist visa on which he had originally entered the U.S. The district eventually allowed the student to enroll, after the Illinois State Board of Education threatened to withhold funding.
- In 2011, Alabama passed a law requiring school administrators to determine the immigration status of newly enrolled students and submit data to the state board of education. After passage of the law, absence rates for Latino students increased. Eventually, however, a federal court blocked the law (American Immigration Council, 2016).

In addition to measures such as the preceding, some local school districts have adopted unofficial policies counter to the ruling in *Plyler v. Doe*. For example, a few districts have required immigrant students or parents to submit Social Security numbers or provide additional documents prior to enrolling. However, a 2014 "Dear Colleague" letter sent by the Department of Education and the Department of Justice reminded school administrators that they may not deny enrollment to students who are unwilling or unable to provide a Social Security number, or who provide a foreign birth certificate at the time of enrollment (U.S. Department of Education & Department of Justice, 2014).

Debate about educating children of undocumented parents intensified with the election of President Donald Trump. In September 2017, the Trump administration announced plans to eliminate the Deferred Action for Childhood Arrivals (DACA) program. Initiated by President Obama, DACA protects undocumented immigrants brought to the U.S. as children from deportation. Those in favor of eliminating DACA pointed out that educating children of undocumented immigrants reduces resources for students who are U.S. citizens.

In response to tightening immigration enforcement, some school districts joined a national "resistance movement" and identified their schools as "sanctuaries" for students of undocumented parents. School districts in Miami, Milwaukee, Chicago, New York City, Des Moines, and Portland, Oregon, for example, promised to shield students' personal data from Immigration and Customs Enforcement (ICE) and to block their access to school property unless they presented a warrant. In spite of such assurances, some schools reported increased absences of students fearful of an ICE "raid" at their school. For example, a Las Cruces, New Mexico, public school reported a 60 percent increase in student absences one Thursday compared to the week before. Approximately 2,100 of the district's 25,000 students missed school that day. That same day, the district's superintendent sent a letter to parents, in English and Spanish, informing them that "We do not anticipate any ICE activity occurring on school campuses" (Blitzer, 2017).

FOCUS ON **STEM**: DESIGN FOR STEM LAB TRIGGERS COMPLAINT TO U.S. OFFICE FOR CIVIL RIGHTS

A community advocacy group filed a complaint with the U.S. Department of Education's Office for Civil Rights alleging that the STEM lab included in a Portland, **OREGON** high school remodel plan would violate students' civil rights. The complaint against Portland Public Schools claimed that the STEM lab for Roosevelt High School—a school with 70 percent minority enrollment—was poorly designed and inequitable. The complaint further alleged that the remodel design for the STEM lab at Franklin High School—a majority-white school—had no design flaws. Both schools had enrollments of about 1,700 students.

The STEM workspace at Roosevelt High would be two areas (2,000 sq. ft. and 3,500 sq. ft.) in different parts of the school building. In contrast, the STEM workspace at Franklin High would be one space (9,000 sq. ft.). The complaint pointed out that STEM programs require a large workspace where resources to design and build innovative projects are located in the same area.

To no avail, the advocacy group "spent months" outlining to the school district the expertise required to design a STEM workspace and provided school board members with research on best practices in STEM. The group eventually submitted a complaint to the U.S. Office for Civil Rights, calling the Roosevelt plan "a fatally flawed design that runs counter to the fundamentals of STEM—connectedness and collaboration" (Cohen & Purkey, 2014).

Freedom of Expression

The case of *Tinker v. Des Moines Independent Community School District* (1969) is perhaps the most frequently cited case concerning students' **freedom of expression**. The Supreme Court ruled in *Tinker* that three students, ages 13, 15, and 16, had been denied their First Amendment freedom of expression when they were suspended from school for wearing black armbands to protest the Vietnam War. The Court ruled that neither teachers nor students "shed their rights to freedom of speech or expression at the schoolhouse gate." In addition, the Court found no evidence that the exercise of such a right interfered with the school's operation.

CENSORSHIP One area of student expression that has generated frequent controversy is that of student publications. Prior to 1988, the courts generally made it clear that student literature enjoyed constitutional protection and that it could be regulated only if it posed a substantial threat of school disruption, if it was libelous, or if it was judged vulgar or obscene after publication. However, school officials could use "prior **censorship**" and require students to submit literature before publication if such controls were necessary to maintain order in the school.

Within these guidelines, students frequently defended successfully their right to freedom of expression. For example, the right of high school students to place in the school newspaper an advertisement against the war in Vietnam was upheld (*Zucker v. Panitz,* 1969). Students' right to distribute information on birth control and on laws regarding marijuana was also upheld in *Shanley v. Northeast Independent School District* (1972). And other cases upheld the right of students to publish literature that was critical of teachers, administrators, and other school personnel (*Scoville v. Board of Education of Joliet Township High School District 204,* 1970, 1971; *Sullivan v. Houston Independent School District*, 1969).

In January 1988, however, the Supreme Court, in a 5–3 ruling in *Hazelwood School District v. Kuhlmeier*, departed from the earlier *Tinker* decision and gave public school officials considerable authority to censor school-sponsored student publications. The case involved a Missouri high school principal's censorship of articles in the school newspaper, the *Spectrum*, on teenage pregnancy and the impact of divorce on students. The principal believed the articles were inappropriate because they might identify pregnant students and because references to sexual activity and birth control were inappropriate for younger students. Several students on the newspaper staff distributed copies of the articles on their own and later sued the school district, claiming that their First Amendment rights had been violated.

Writing for the majority in *Hazelwood School District v. Kuhlmeier*, Justice Byron White (who had voted with the majority in *Tinker*) said school officials could bar "speech that is ungrammatical, poorly written, inadequately researched, biased or prejudiced, vulgar or profane, or unsuitable for immature audiences." White also pointed out that *Tinker* focused on a student's right of "personal expression," and the Missouri case dealt with school-sponsored publications that were part of the curriculum and bore the "imprimatur of the school." According to White, "Educators do not offend the First Amendment by exercising editorial control over the style and content of student speech in school-sponsored expressive activities so long as their actions are reasonably related to legitimate pedagogical concerns."

A case involving an attempt to regulate an underground student newspaper entitled *Bad Astra*, however, had a different outcome. Five high school students in Renton, **WASHINGTON** produced a four-page newspaper at their expense, off school property, and without the knowledge of school authorities. *Bad Astra* contained articles that criticized school policies, a mock poll evaluating teachers, and several poetry selections. The students distributed 350 copies of the paper at a senior class barbecue held on school grounds.

After the paper was distributed, the principal placed letters of reprimand in the five students' files, and the district established a new policy whereby student-written, non-school-sponsored materials with an intended distribution of more than 10 were subject to pre-distribution review. The students filed suit in federal district court, claiming a violation of their First Amendment rights. The court ruled, however, that the new policy was "substantially constitutional." Maintaining that the policy was unconstitutional, the students filed an appeal in 1988 in the Ninth Circuit Court and won. The court ruled that *Bad Astra* was not "within the purview of the school's exercise of reasonable editorial control" (*Burch v. Barker,* 1987, 1988).

STUDENT EXPRESSION ON SOCIAL NETWORKING SITES Whereas teachers are increasingly advised not to communicate with students via social networking sites, students have few constraints to their online expression. The law is still evolving regarding what students may and may not say online about their teachers and school administrators. School districts generally have no right to control student expression off campus, unless their speech could lead to a serious disruption on campus—a riot, for example. In addition, the law is unclear about students using school computers or mobile devices while on campus to access Facebook pages that are critical of teachers and administrators (Willard, 2010).

In **FLORIDA**, a student was suspended and faced other punishments for creating a Facebook fan page devoted to calling her English teacher "The worst teacher I've ever met," and inviting others to join. With help from the ACLU, the student sued, and in 2010 a U.S. District Court in Florida sided with her, forcing the school district to clear her record.

Two **PENNSYLVANIA** cases similar to the Florida case resulted in different conclusions by two circuit courts. In one case, involving a middle school student who created a MySpace page insinuating that his principal was a pedophile, the court found in favor of the school, citing potential disruption. In the second case, another middle school student created a profile indicating that his principal used marijuana, and encouraged other students to do the same. Despite the fact that some of the sites were accessed on school grounds, the court found in favor of the student, saying no serious disruption of school activities occurred (Sullivan, 2010).

DRESS CODES Few issues related to the rights of students have generated as many court cases as have dress codes and hairstyles. The demand on the courts to hear such cases prompted Supreme Court Justice Hugo L. Black to observe that he did not believe "the federal Constitution imposed on the United States Courts the burden of supervising the length of hair that public school students should wear" (*Karr v. Schmidt*, 1972). In line with Justice Black's observation, the Supreme Court has repeatedly refused to review the decisions reached by the lower courts.

In general, the courts have suggested that schools may have dress codes as long as such codes are clear and reasonable, and students are notified. However, when the legality of such codes has been challenged, the rulings have largely indicated that schools may not control what students wear unless it is immodest or is disruptive of the educational process.

Students in private schools, however, do not have First Amendment protections provided by *Tinker v. Des Moines Independent Community School District* because private schools are not state affiliated. As a result, students at private schools can be required to wear uniforms, and "[d]isagreements over 'student rights' . . . are generally resolved by applying contract law to the agreement governing the student's attendance" (LaMorte, 2008, p. 117).

At one time, educators' concerns about student appearance may have been limited to hairstyles and immodest dress; however, today's educators, as Michael LaMorte (2012, p. 141) points out, may be concerned about "[t]-shirts depicting violence, drugs (e.g., marijuana [leaves]), racial epithets, or characters such as Bart Simpson; ripped, baggy, or saggy pants or jeans; sneakers with lights; colored bandanas; baseball or other hats; words shaved into scalps, brightly colored hair, distinctive haircuts or hairstyles, or ponytails for males; exposed underwear; Malcolm X symbols; Walkmans, cellular phones, or beepers; backpacks; tattoos, unusual-colored lipsticks, pierced noses, or earrings; and decorative dental caps."

Because gangs, hate groups, and violence in and around public schools have become more prevalent during the last decade, rulings that favor schools are becoming more common when the courts "balance the First Amendment rights of students to express themselves against the legitimate right of school authorities to maintain a safe and disruption-free environment" (LaMorte, 2012, p. 141). This balance is clearly illustrated in *Jeglin v. San Jacinto Unified School District* (1993). In this instance, a school's dress code prohibiting the wearing of clothing with writing, pictures, or insignia of professional or college athletic teams was challenged on the grounds that it violated students' freedom of expression. The court acknowledged that the code violated the rights of elementary and middle school students, but not those of high school students. Gangs known to be present at the high school had intimidated students and faculty in connection with the sports-oriented clothing. The court ruled that the curtailment of students' rights did not "demand a certainty that disruption will occur, but only the existence of facts which might reasonably lead school officials to forecast substantial disruption."

After the 1999 Columbine High School shootings in Littleton, Colorado, which left 14 students and a teacher dead—including the two gunmen, who were members of a clique called the Trench Coat Mafia—many school districts made their rules for student dress more restrictive. Ten days after the shootings, a federal judge who upheld a school's decision to suspend a student for wearing a T-shirt that said "Vegan" (a vegetarian who doesn't eat animal products), said "Gang attire has become particularly troubling since two students wore trench coats in the Colorado shooting." And in Jonesboro, Arkansas, where four students and a teacher were shot and killed the previous year, a group of boys and girls identifying themselves as the Blazer Mafia were suspended for 10 days (Portner, 1999).

To reduce disruption and violence in schools, some school districts now require younger students to wear uniforms. In 1994, the 90,000-student Long Beach, California school system became the first in the nation to require K–8 students to wear uniforms. Currently, the Birmingham, Alabama; Chicago; Dayton, Ohio; Oakland, California; and San Antonio public schools require elementary-age students to wear uniforms. At the beginning of the 2002–2003 school year, Memphis took steps to become the nation's first large urban district to require all students to wear uniforms when school commissioners voted 8–1 to implement a school uniform policy for the district's 175 schools (Richard, 2002).

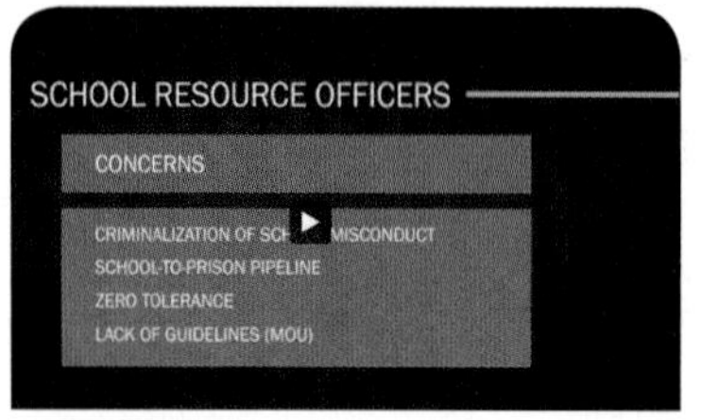

Video Example 7.3

School Resource Officer: Learn more about how some school policies have changed in the wake of the shootings at Columbine.

Between 2000 and 2010, the percentage of public schools requiring that students wear uniforms increased from 12 to 19 percent with 10 percent of high schools requiring uniforms, 19 percent of middle schools, and 22 percent of primary schools (Robers, Kemp, & Truman, 2013). School uniform policies usually "apply to students in grades K–8 and may be either voluntary or mandatory with opt-out provisions for exemptions based on philosophical or religious objections or medical reasons" (LaMorte, 2012, p. 143). Courts have upheld mandatory school uniform policies. For example, a court ruled against a parent who challenged New York City's school uniform policy for pre-K through eighth-grade students. The parent claimed that the opt-out provision would make his daughter stick out, while the New York City Board of Education stated that the policy would "promote a more effective learning climate; foster school unity and pride; improve student performance; foster self-esteem; eliminate label competition; simplify dressing and minimize costs to parents; teach children appropriate dress and decorum in the 'workplace'; and help to improve student conduct and discipline" (*Lipsman v. New York City Board of Education*, 1999).

Due Process in Suspension and Expulsion

In February and March 1971, a total of nine students received 10-day suspensions from the Columbus, **OHIO** public school system during a period of citywide unrest. One student, in the presence of his principal, physically attacked a police officer who was trying to remove a disruptive student from a high school auditorium. Four others were suspended for similar conduct. Another student was suspended for his involvement in a lunchroom disturbance that resulted in damage to school property. All nine students were suspended in accordance with Ohio law. Some of the students and their parents were offered the opportunity to attend conferences prior to the start of the suspensions, but none of the nine was given a hearing. Asserting that their constitutional rights had been denied, all nine students brought suit against the school system.

In a sharply divided 5–4 decision, the Supreme Court ruled that the students had a legal right to an education, and that this "property right" could be removed only through the application of procedural due process. The Court maintained that suspension is a "serious event" in the life of a suspended child and may not be imposed by the school in an arbitrary manner (*Goss v. Lopez*, 1975).

As a result of cases such as *Goss v. Lopez*, every state has outlined procedures for school officials to follow in the suspension and expulsion of students. In cases of short-term suspension (defined by the courts as exclusion from school for 10 days or less), the due process steps are somewhat flexible and determined by the nature of the infraction and the length of the suspension. As Figure 7.8 shows, however, long-term suspension (more than 10 days) and expulsion require a more extensive due process procedure. The disciplinary transfer of a disruptive student to an alternative school, designed to meet his or her needs, is not considered an expulsion (Alexander & Alexander, 2012; LaMorte, 2012).

Figure 7.8 Due process in suspension and expulsion

Suspension

1. Adequate notice must be provided to students and parents regarding the existence of rules governing student behavior. These should be clearly communicated to all affected by their implementation.
2. A record should be compiled that includes the following information:
   a. The infraction allegedly committed
   b. The time of the alleged infraction
   c. The place the alleged infraction occurred
   d. Those person(s) who witnessed the alleged act
   e. Previous efforts made to remedy the alleged misbehavior
3. Students facing suspension should, at minimum, be provided some type of notice followed by a brief informal hearing.
4. Students should be provided either oral or written notice of charges against them, the evidence school authorities have to support the charges, and an opportunity to refute the charges.
5. Because permanent removal is not intended, no delay is necessary between the time notice is given and the time of the actual hearing. In most instances, school officials may informally discuss alleged misconduct with students immediately after it is reported.
6. During the hearing, the school official should listen to all sides of the issue. There should be adequate time provided for students to present their side of the issue without interruption.
7. Parents or guardians should be informed of the hearing and provided written notification of the action that results from the hearing. At a minimum, the written notice should include:
   a. The charge(s) brought against the student
   b. A description of the evidence used to support the charge(s)
   c. The number of days suspended
   d. A determination of whether suspension is an in-school or out-of-school suspension
   e. A list of other conditions that must be met before the student returns to school (e.g., a conference with parent or guardian)
   f. A statement that informs parents or guardians that the suspension can be appealed to the district's pupil personnel director or a designee
8. Parents or guardians should be informed by phone of the suspension, followed by written notification, which should be promptly mailed, preferably by registered mail on the day of the hearing.

Expulsion

1. Students, parents, or legal guardians should be informed based on school or district policy of specific infractions that may result in expulsion. They should also be informed of their Fourteenth Amendment rights regarding substantive and procedural due process.
2. In cases of serious misconduct for which serious disciplinary measures may be imposed, the student is entitled to written notice of the charges and has the right to a fair hearing. Written notice must be furnished to the students and parent or guardian well in advance of the actual hearing.
3. At a minimum, the following procedural steps should be considered:
   a. Written notice of charges
   b. Right to a fair hearing
   c. Right to inspect evidence
   d. Right to present evidence on student's behalf
   e. Right to legal counsel
   f. Right to call witnesses
   g. Right to cross-examination and to confrontation
   h. Right against self-incrimination
   i. Right to appeal

Adapted from Nathan L. Essex. *School Law and the Public Schools: A Practical Guide for Educational Leaders*. Boston: Pearson, pp. 87, 90.

In response to an increase of unruly students who disrupt the learning of others, a few districts and states have granted teachers the authority to suspend students for up to 10 days. Teachers in Cincinnati, **OHIO** and Dade County, **FLORIDA**, for example, have negotiated contracts that give them authority to remove disruptive students from their classrooms; however, district administrators decide how the students will be disciplined. In 1995, Indiana became the first state to grant teachers the power to suspend students, and the following year, **NEW YORK**'s governor proposed legislation to allow teachers to remove students from their classrooms for up to 10 days for "committing an act of violence against a student, teacher, or school district employee; possessing or threatening to use a gun, knife, or other dangerous weapon; damaging or destroying school district property; damaging the personal property of teachers or other employees; or defying an order from a teacher or administrator to stop disruptive behavior" (Lindsay, 1996, p. 24).

Reasonable Search and Seizure

According to the Fourth Amendment, citizens are protected from search and seizure conducted without a search warrant. With the escalation of drug use in schools and school-related violence, however, cases involving the legality of **search and seizure** in schools have increased. For example, you have reason to believe that a student has drugs, and possibly a dangerous weapon, in his locker. Do you, as a teacher, have the right to search the student's locker and seize any illegal or dangerous items? The following cases suggest guidelines that you can follow if confronted with a similar situation.

The case of *New Jersey v. T.L.O.* (1985) involved a 14-year-old student (T.L.O.) whom a teacher found smoking a cigarette in a restroom. The teacher took the student to the principal's office, whereupon the principal asked to see the contents of her purse. On opening the purse, the principal found a pack of cigarettes and what appeared to be drug paraphernalia and a list titled "People who owe me money." T.L.O. was arrested and later found guilty of delinquency charges.

After being sentenced to one year's probation, T.L.O. appealed, claiming that the evidence found in her purse was obtained in violation of the Fourth Amendment and that her confession to selling marijuana was tainted by an illegal search. The U.S. Supreme Court found that the search had been reasonable. The Court also developed a two-pronged test of "reasonableness" for searches: (1) a school official must have a reasonable suspicion that a student has violated a law or school policy, and (2) the search must be conducted using methods that are reasonable in scope.

Another case focused on the use of trained dogs to conduct searches of 2,780 junior and senior high school students in Highland, **INDIANA**. During a 2½- to 3-hour period, six teams with trained German shepherds sniffed the students. The dogs alerted their handlers a total of 50 times. Seventeen of the searches initiated by the dogs turned up beer, drug paraphernalia, or marijuana. Another 11 students, including 13-year-old Diane Doe, singled out by the dogs were strip-searched in the nurse's office. It turned out that Diane had played with her dog, who was in heat, that morning and that the police dog had responded to the smell of the other dog on Diane's clothing.

Diane's parents later filed suit, charging that their daughter was searched illegally. The court ruled that the use of dogs did not constitute an unreasonable search, nor did holding students in their homerooms constitute a mass detention in violation of the Fourth Amendment. The court did hold, however, that the strip searches of the students were unreasonable. The court pointed out that the school personnel did not have any evidence to suggest that Diane possessed contraband because she had emptied her pockets as requested prior to the strip search. Diane was awarded $7,500 in damages (*Doe v. Renfrow,* 1980, 1981).

Court cases involving search and seizure in school settings have maintained that school lockers are the property of the schools, not students, and may be searched by school authorities if reasonable cause exists. In addition, students may be sniffed by police dogs if school authorities have a reasonable suspicion that illegal or dangerous items may be found. Last, educators on occasion use intrusive searches, or "strip searches," when looking for drugs or weapons. Courts determine the reasonableness of such searches by considering "the student's age, the student's record and disciplinary history, the seriousness and the prevalence of the problem, and the exigency requiring an immediate warrantless search" (LaMorte, 2012, p. 137).

In general, the courts have tried to balance the school's need to obtain information and the student's right to privacy. To protect themselves from legal challenges related to searches, educators should follow guidelines that have been suggested by school law experts:

- Inform students and parents at the start of the school year of the procedures for conducting locker and personal searches.
- Base any search on "reasonable suspicion."
- Conduct any search with another staff member present.
- Avoid strip searches or mass searches of groups of students.
- Require that police obtain a search warrant before conducting a search in the school.

Some schools use drug testing as a requirement for either attendance or interscholastic participation, including sports competition, or as a means of discipline. A 1988 court case upheld a urinalysis drug test for randomly selected student athletes because those whose tests were positive were suspended only from participating in sports for a period of time and no disciplinary or academic penalties were imposed (*Schaill v. Tippecanoe School Corp.*, 1988). Similarly, the U.S. Supreme Court reversed a lower court's ruling and stated that a school district's desire to reduce drug use justified the degree of intrusion required by random tests of student athletes' urine (*Acton v. Vernonia School District*, 1995). A few school districts have attempted to implement mandatory drug testing of teachers. So far, the courts have upheld the decision rendered in *Patchogue-Medford Congress of Teachers v. Board of Education of Patchogue-Medford Union Free School District* (1987) that drug testing of teachers violates the Fourth Amendment's prohibition of unreasonable searches.

What are students' rights with regard to their persons, personal property, and records in school and on school grounds? How are school districts' rights of search and seizure decided? In what ways have students' rights to privacy been upheld?

Privacy

Prior to 1974, students and parents were not allowed to examine school records. On November 19, 1974, Congress passed the Family Educational Rights and Privacy Act (FERPA), which gave parents of students under 18 and students 18 and older the right to examine their school records. Every public or private educational institution must adhere to the law, known as the **Buckley Amendment**, or lose federal money.

Under the Buckley Amendment, schools must do the following:

1. Inform parents and students of their rights
2. Provide information to parents and students about the type of educational records available and how to obtain access to them
3. Allow parents or students to review records; request changes; request a hearing if changes are not allowed; and, if necessary, add their own explanation about the records
4. Not give out personally identifiable information without prior written, informed consent of a parent or students
5. Allow parents and students to see the school's record of disclosures

The Buckley Amendment actually sets forth the minimum requirements that schools must adhere to, and many states and school districts have gone beyond these minimum guidelines in granting students access to their records. Most high schools, for example, now grant students under age 18 access to their educational records, and all students in **VIRGINIA**, elementary through secondary, are guaranteed access to their records.

Facebook's announcement in April 2018 that user data for as many as 87 million people may have been "improperly shared" with Cambridge Analytica raised new issues about students' privacy. Educators pointed out that, often, students must maintain Facebook accounts to participate in school activities, thus allowing Facebook to collect data about students and their Facebook friends. Data mining practices by Facebook and other digital marketing corporations violate students' privacy and have a negative influence on their development, according to the National Education Policy Center:

> Every day, student data are vulnerable to the same kind of abuses revealed by the Cambridge Analytica scandal . . . the U.S economy is now a surveillance economy constructed by corporations that relentlessly, invisibly, and very profitably, gather information and create profiles on hundreds of millions of people. In particular, digital platforms in schools feed children into this surveillance economy.
>
> Facebook's "engagement" algorithms nudge users to become ever more extreme in their views and behaviors. This manipulation is especially problematic and potent for children, whose worldviews are still developing. Children in and outside of school are now routinely subjected to all the marketing firepower that money can buy. They are without recourse as their personal data are gathered and sold on. Using these data, advertisers attempt to shape their attitudes about how they should think about their families, friendships, romantic relationships, environment, society, and themselves (Molnar & Boninger, 2018, pp. 3, 6).

EXCEPTIONS Several exceptions are allowed by the Buckley Amendment. The teacher's gradebook, psychiatric or treatment records, notes or records written by the teacher for his or her exclusive use or to be shared with a substitute teacher, or the private notes of school law enforcement units, for example, are not normally subject to examination.

The provisions of FERPA came to the nation's attention in 2000 when Kristja Falvo challenged the practice of having students grade one another's papers (peer grading) on the grounds that it was embarrassing to her three children and resulted in grading errors. A district court disagreed and ruled in favor of the school district, maintaining that peer grading is a common school practice. However, the Tenth Circuit Court of Appeals reversed that decision and ruled that the practice of peer grading violated students' privacy because grades are entered into teachers' gradebooks and thus fit the definition of "educational records" (*Falvo v. Owasso Independent School District,* 2000). Eventually, however, the case reached the Supreme Court, which ruled 9–0 that the privacy law was not intended to protect grades on day-to-day classroom assignments and that students could grade one another's work (*Owasso Independent School District v. Falvo,* 2002).

VIDEO CAMERAS IN CLASSROOMS Another privacy-related issue emerged in 2003 when schools in Biloxi, **MISSISSIPPI** became the first in the nation to use video cameras to monitor activities in classrooms. Previously, some schools used cameras to monitor hallways, cafeterias, auditoriums, and parking lots.

Some observers worry that cameras in classrooms will interfere with learning activities and could be misused. Others contend that teachers' and students' privacy is violated by the use of cameras. Nevertheless, regarding the presence of 500 cameras in classrooms at the start of the school year, a Biloxi School District official pointed out: "Students, parents and teachers don't mind them at all" (Lewis, 2003).

Students' Rights to Nondiscrimination

Schools are legally bound to avoid discriminating against students on the basis of race, sex, religion, disability, sexual orientation, marital status, or infection with a disease such as HIV/AIDS that poses no threat to students. The Teachers' Voices: Being an Agent of Change feature for this chapter profiles a teacher who has developed classroom activities to promote social justice and to increase students' understanding of diversity, prejudice, and discrimination.

TEACHERS VOICES ➔ BEING AN AGENT OF CHANGE

SUSIE RENNER

Teaching for Social Justice

I am an eighth-grade language arts teacher in Durham, New Hampshire. My students have grown up in an environment where there is very little exposure to ethnic, racial, or LGBT (lesbian, gay, bisexual, and transgender) communities. They are ripe for learning, and are in a unique position to "be" the change.

To foster a better understanding of diversity, prejudice, and discrimination, I created a social justice unit based on readings in varied genres of literature. We begin with an overview and discussions based on segments of various videos such as *If You Cried You Died, The Long Walk Home,* and *Come See the Paradise.* Each student chooses a topic that focuses on one particular group of people who have suffered prejudice and discrimination. Last year, student choices included American Indians, African Americans, American Muslims, Japanese Americans during World War II, LGBT issues, Latinos, and European Jews during the Holocaust.

Once students choose a topic, they are required to read nonfiction overviews, primary sources such as diaries and letters, a book (historical fiction, a biography, or an autobiography) as well as poetry written by survivors of prejudice. As they read independently in class, students share excerpts that powerfully reflect what it feels like to experience

(continued)

prejudice and discrimination. They also copy these excerpts into their notes, in preparation for their writing piece.

When students finish their readings, they write a three- to five-page story based on the literature. These stories must be told from the first-person perspective and must reflect what it is like to experience prejudice. Stories can be in the form of a narrative, journal, letters, or poetry. Students weave excerpts from the literature into their writing, and cite their sources. They then share their writing with one another, to teach or learn about other topics. Some years, younger students at our middle school are invited into our classroom, so that my eighth graders can share their knowledge with them.

As a culminating activity, I partner with the Office of Multicultural Affairs at the University of New Hampshire, and invite a panel of college students to spend the day in my classroom. The students are of varied ethnicities, sexual orientations, and races. The panel presents its own stories, invites questions, and fosters powerful discussions. At the end of this study, I ask my students to write reflections of the entire unit for their portfolios. Their thoughts and feelings show the enormous impact that this study can have on young peoples' perspectives. In fact, former students who come back to visit years later comment on the impact that this study had on their approach to tolerance and intolerance.

PERSONAL REFLECTION

1. What personal experiences have helped you develop a better understanding of diversity, prejudice, and discrimination?
2. Regarding the grade level and subject area for which you are preparing to teach, what classroom activities can you use to teach for social justice?
3. What action(s) should a teacher take if he or she observes in the school an instance of discrimination or prejudice toward others on the basis of race, gender, religion, disability, or sexual orientation?

Susie Renner teaches at Oyster River Middle School in Durham, **NEW HAMPSHIRE.**

Susie Renner, Teaching Tolerance, Fall 2010, p. 15

One trend that has confronted schools with the need to develop more policies that are fair and free of discrimination has been the epidemic in teenage pregnancies. Regarding students who are married, pregnant, or parents, the courts have been quite clear: Students in these categories may not be treated differently. A 1966 case in Texas involving a 16-year-old mother established that schools may provide separate classes or alternative schools on a voluntary basis for married and/or pregnant students. However, the district may not require such students to attend separate schools, nor may they be required to attend adult or evening schools (*Alvin Independent School District v. Cooper,* 1966).

The courts have made an about-face in their positions on whether students who are married, pregnant, or parents can participate in extracurricular activities. Prior to 1972, participation in these activities was considered a privilege rather than a right, and restrictions on those who could participate were upheld. In 1972, however, cases in **TENNESSEE**, **OHIO**, **MONTANA**, and **TEXAS** established the right of married students (and, in one case, a divorced student) to participate (*Holt v. Sheldon,* 1972; *Davis v. Meek,* 1972; *Moran v. School District No. 7,* 1972; and *Romans v. Crenshaw,* 1972). Since then, restrictions applicable to extracurricular activities have been universally struck down.

During the 1980s, many school districts became embroiled in controversy over the issue of how to provide for the schooling of young people with HIV/AIDS and whether school employees with HIV/AIDS should be allowed to continue working. In rulings on HIV/AIDS-related cases since then, the courts have sided with the overwhelming medical evidence that students with AIDS pose no "significant risk" of spreading the disease. "To date, courts have revealed a high degree of sensitivity to students with HIV or AIDS and to their being included in the public school mainstream" (LaMorte, 2012, p. 277). In 1987, for example, a judge prevented a **FLORIDA** school district from requiring that three hemophiliac brothers who were exposed to HIV/AIDS through transfusions be restricted to homebound instruction (*Ray v. School District of DeSoto County,* 1987).

To stem the spread of HIV/AIDS, school systems in many large cities—New York, Los Angeles, San Francisco, and Seattle, to name a few—have initiated programs to distribute condoms to high school students. New York's condom-distribution program, which initially did not require parental consent, was challenged in 1993 (*Alfonso v. Fernandez*). The court ruled that the program was a "health issue" and that the district could not dispense condoms without prior parental approval. The court maintained that the program violated parents' due process rights under the Fourteenth Amendment to raise their children as they see fit; however, the program did not violate parents' or students' freedom of religion. Three years later, however, the U.S. Supreme Court declined to review a **MASSACHUSETTS** high court ruling that upheld a school board's decision to place condom machines in high school restrooms and allow junior- and senior-level students to request condoms from the school nurse (*Curtis v. School Committee of Falmouth*, 1995, 1996).

What are Some Issues in the Legal Rights of School Districts?

Clearly, the law touches just about every aspect of education in the United States today. The media remind us daily that ours is an age of litigation; no longer are school districts as protected as they once were from legal problems. Corporal punishment, sexual harassment, cyberbullying, religious expression, educational malpractice, and homeschooling are among the issues in the legal rights of school districts.

Corporal Punishment

The practice of **corporal punishment** has had a long and controversial history in education in the United States. Currently, policies regarding the use of corporal punishment vary widely from state to state, and even from district to district.

Critics believe that corporal punishment "is neither a necessary nor an effective response to misbehavior" (Slavin, 2015, p. 287), and some believe that the practice is "archaic, cruel, and inhuman and an unjustifiable act on the part of the state" (LaMorte, 2012, p. 124). In spite of such arguments against its effectiveness, corporal punishment continues to be widespread. Nevertheless, almost half of the states and many school districts currently ban corporal punishment, and many others restrict its use (Alexander & Alexander, 2012; LaMorte, 2012).

The most influential Supreme Court case involving corporal punishment is *Ingraham v. Wright*, decided in 1977. In Dade County, **FLORIDA** in October 1970, junior high school students James Ingraham and Roosevelt Andrews were paddled with a wooden paddle. Both students received injuries as a result of the paddlings, with Ingraham's being the more severe. Ingraham, who was being punished for being slow to respond to a teacher's directions, refused to assume the "paddling position" and had to be held over a desk by two assistant principals while the principal administered 20 "licks." As a result, Ingraham "suffered a hematoma requiring medical attention and keeping him out of school for several days."

The Court had two significant questions to rule on in *Ingraham*: Does the Eighth Amendment's prohibition of cruel and unusual punishment apply to corporal punishment in the schools? Second, if it does not, should the due process clause of the Fourteenth Amendment provide any protection to students before punishment is administered? In regard to the first question, the Court, in a sharply divided 5–4 decision, ruled that the Eighth Amendment was not applicable to students being disciplined in school, only to persons convicted of crimes. On the question of due process, the Court said, "We conclude that the Due Process clause does not require notice and a hearing prior to the imposition of corporal punishment in the public schools, as that practice is authorized and limited by the common law." The Court also commented on the severity of the paddlings in *Ingraham* and said that, in such cases, school personnel "may be held liable in damages to the child and, if malice is shown, they may be subject to criminal penalties."

Although the Supreme Court has upheld the constitutionality of corporal punishment, many districts around the country have instituted policies banning its use. Where corporal punishment is used, school personnel are careful to see that it meets minimum criteria that have emerged from other court cases involving corporal punishment:

- Specific warning is given about what behavior may result in corporal punishment.
- Evidence exists that other measures attempted failed to bring about the desired change in behavior.
- Administration of corporal punishment takes place in the presence of a second school official.
- On request, a written statement is provided to parents explaining the reasons for the punishment and the names of all witnesses. (Dunklee & Shoop, 2006, p. 154)

Sexual Harassment

Although few victims report it, 80 percent of students in a national survey reported that they had been sexually harassed, and one in three said they experienced it "often" (American Association of University Women, 2002, p. III-2). Another survey found that 64 percent of lesbian, gay, bisexual, or transgender (LGBT) students fear for their safety while at school, and about two thirds were sexually harassed (Kosciw & Diaz, 2006). By 2008, nine states had anti-bullying policies that specifically mention sexual orientation (Robinson, 2008).

In addition to harassment by the opposite sex, same-sex harassment, usually against **lesbian, gay, bisexual, and transgender (LGBT) students**, is a problem at some schools. Since the mid-1990s, several school districts have faced lawsuits filed by gay and lesbian students who claimed that school officials failed to protect them from verbal and physical anti-gay harassment.

In *Flores v. Morgan Hill Unified School District* (2003), several students claimed their school did not respond adequately to a seven-year period of anti-homosexual harassment they endured. In its ruling that teachers and administrators failed to enforce the school district's anti-harassment and anti-discrimination policies, the Court stated, "The record contains sufficient evidence for a jury to conclude that the defendants intentionally discriminated against the plaintiffs in violation of the Equal Protection Clause." The school district eventually agreed to pay $1.1 million to six of the students.

On the other hand, the courts have been reluctant to hold school districts liable unless the harassment was foreseeable and preventable, and they deliberately failed to intervene. School districts were not found liable for damages in the following cases: Student aides videotaped the girls' locker room and bathrooms over a two-year period (*Harry A. v. Duncan*, 2005); a student received a punch intended for another student (*Mohammed ex rel. Mohammed v. School District of Philadelphia*, 2005); and a student was verbally harassed due to ancestry and race (*Yap v. Oceanside Union Free School District*, 2004).

Regarding **sexual harassment** of students by educators, the courts have generally ruled that school districts may be held liable if the district knew or should have known of the harassment. In one case, *Franklin v. Gwinnett County Public Schools* (1992), the Supreme Court found a school district liable because district administrators knew that a teacher had repeatedly sexually abused a student and took no steps to stop the harassment. The Court ruled that the student could collect damages for sexual harassment under Title IX of the Education Act of 1972. In *Gebser v. Lago Vista Independent School District* (1998), however, the Supreme Court ruled that a school district was not liable for damages resulting from teacher-to-student harassment, unless a school official with "authority to institute corrective measures on the district's behalf has actual notice of, and is deliberately indifferent to, the teacher's misconduct."

Increased reports of sexual harassment of students by educators and the Supreme Court ruling in *Franklin v. Gwinett County Public Schools* are causing some teachers to be apprehensive about working closely with students and, particularly, touching them. In a few instances, teachers have even reported that they fear being falsely accused of sexual harassment by angry, disgruntled students. To address the problem, many school districts have suggested guidelines that teachers can follow to show concern for students, offer them encouragement, and congratulate them for their successes. Frequently, these guidelines also advise teachers to avoid behaviors such as touching or hugging that a student may experience as sexual harassment.

Cyberbullying and the Law

Cyberbullies, unlike traditional face-to-face bullies, make use of social networking sites, cell phones, instant messaging, camera phones, email, and various sites on the Internet. They can bully their victims any time, from anywhere; and their user name, screen name, or stolen identity allows them to remain anonymous.

They bully their victims via text messages, postings on social networking sites like Facebook (or the more vitriolic Enemybook, or Hatebook), and discussions in online chat rooms. They forward email messages to huge groups of friends and post embarrassing, sometimes altered, photographs and video clips of their victims to the Internet. In some instances, students hack into other students' email accounts or social networking sites and create havoc by sending hateful messages or posting inflammatory content that appears to have been authored by their victims (Bissonette, 2009). Figure 7.9 presents several forms of cyberbullying and examples.

By early 2012, 46 states had anti-bullying laws; 36 of these specifically prohibited cyberbullying, and "13 grant schools the authority to address off-campus behavior that creates a hostile school environment" (*Deskbook Encyclopedia of American School Law*, 2013, p. 1). An example of anti-bullying legislation is the Anti-Bullying Bill of Rights Act in **NEW JERSEY**, which requires each school to appoint an anti-bullying specialist and anti-bullying coordinator, as well as form a school safety team.

Figure 7.9 Forms of cyberbullying and examples

Flaming. Online fights using electronic messages with angry and vulgar language. *Joe and Alec's online exchange got angrier and angrier. Insults were flying. Joe warned Alec to watch his back in school the next day.*

Harassment. Repeatedly sending nasty, mean, and insulting messages. *Sara reported to the principal that Kayla was bullying another student. When Sara got home, she had 35 angry messages on her social networking profile. Some from complete strangers.*

Denigration. "Dissing" someone online. Sending or posting gossip or rumors about a person to damage his or her reputation or friendships. *Some students created a "We Hate Joe" group where they posted jokes, cartoons, gossip, and rumors, all dissing Joe.*

Impersonation. Pretending to be someone else and sending or posting material to get that person in trouble or danger or to damage that person's reputation or friendships. *Laura watched closely as Emma logged on to her account and discovered her password. Later, Laura logged on to Emma's account and sent a hurtful message to Emma's boyfriend, Adam.*

Outing. Sharing someone's secrets or embarrassing information or images online. *Greg, an obese high school student, was changing in the locker room after gym class. Matt took a picture of him with his cell phone camera. Within seconds, the picture was flying around the phones at school.*

Trickery. Talking someone into revealing secrets or embarrassing information, then sharing it online. *John sent a message to Jessica pretending to be interested in her. Over a few days, Jessica responded, ultimately sharing intimate personal information and a very provocative image. John then sent this image to many other people.*

Exclusion. Intentionally and cruelly excluding someone from an online group. *Millie tries hard to fit in with a group of girls at school. She recently got on the "outs" with a leader in this group. All of the girls have now deleted their friendship links to her social networking profile.*

Cyberstalking. Repeated, intense harassment and denigration that includes threats or creates significant fear. *When Annie broke up with Sam, he sent her many angry, threatening, pleading messages. He spread nasty rumors about her to her friends and posted a sexually suggestive picture she had given him in a sex-oriented discussion group, along with her email address and cell phone number.*

Sexting. Sending nude sexy images and messages electronically. *Jessica was with a couple of friends. They all took nude sexy images of each other. Jessica sent some to her boy friend. Then they broke up. He was angry and sent her images to other students.*

Adapted from Willard, N. (2011). *Educator's Guide to Cyberbullying, Cyberthreat and Sexting*. Center for Safe and Responsible Use of the Internet. Retrieved February 9, 2011, from http://www.csriu.org/documents/documents/educatorsguide.pdf

In a "Dear Colleague" letter sent to the nation's schools, the U.S. Department of Education stressed the need for schools to address bullying:

> Bullying of any student by another student, for any reason, cannot be tolerated in our schools. Bullying is no longer dismissed as an ordinary part of growing up, and every effort should be made to structure environments and provide supports to students and staff so that bullying does not occur. Teachers and adults should respond quickly and consistently to bullying behavior and send a message that bullying is not acceptable. Intervening immediately to stop bullying on the spot can help ensure a safer school environment. . . .
>
> Addressing and reporting bullying is critical. Students who are targets of bullying behavior are more likely to experience lower academic achievement and aspirations, higher truancy rates, feelings of alienation from school, poor relationships with peers, loneliness, or depression. Bystanders, or those who only see or hear about bullying, also may be negatively affected as bullying tends to have harmful effects on overall school climate. Bullying can foster fear and disrespect and negatively affect the school experience, norms, and relationships of all students, families, and school personnel. (U.S. Department of Education, Office of Special Education and Rehabilitative Services, 2013)

Existing case law on free speech and sexual harassment does not readily apply to cyberbullying, and the limited court rulings to date have been inconsistent. As two school law experts note, "In the face of modern technology, school officials have daunting difficulties in protecting the students and the decorum of the schools. As with school officials, the judges who sit in [cyberbullying] cases find themselves largely applying 'horse and buggy laws' to modern technology" (Alexander & Alexander, 2012, p. 443).

Increasingly, though, students who are cyberbullied and their parents are filing lawsuits that name schools as defendants (Bissonette, 2009). Schools are "in a legal quandary. If they punish a student for something they did off school grounds, they could get hit with a freedom of speech claim. If they do nothing, they could get hit with failure to act litigation" (Baldas, 2007).

One case of cyberbullying was *J.C. v. Beverly Hills Unified School Distric*t (2009). In this case, J.C. created a video of several other students disparaging C.C. and posted this video on YouTube. C.C. and her mother brought the video to the attention of the school, and J.C. was suspended.

In response to the suspension, J.C. filed suit. Eventually, the district court decided to apply the *Tinker* standard and upheld J.C.'s freedom of expression. The court decided that substantial disruption of school activities did not occur, nor was it foreseeable. The results of *J.C.* indicate that when districts sanction students for cyberbullying, they must be prepared to present reasonable evidence of interference with the education of the bullied student.

Religious Expression

Conflicts over the proper role of religion in schools are among the most heated in the continuing debate about the character and purposes of education in the United States. Numerous school districts have found themselves embroiled in legal issues related to school prayer, Bible reading, textbooks, creationism, intelligent design, singing of Christmas carols, distribution of religious literature, New Age beliefs, secular humanism, religious holidays, use of school buildings for religious meetings, and the role of religion in moral education, to name a few. On the one hand, conservative religious groups wish to restore prayer and Christian religious practices in the public schools; on the other hand, secular liberals see religion as irrelevant to school curricula and maintain that public schools should not promote religion. In addition, somewhere between these two positions are those who believe that although schools should not be involved in the *teaching of* religion, they should *teach about* religion.

EVOLUTION VERSUS CREATIONISM AND INTELLIGENT DESIGN Issues related to religious expression in the schools have been most heated in regard to the teaching of evolution in science classes. School law experts Kern Alexander and M. David Alexander (2012, p. 381) explain how efforts to diminish the teaching of evolution and advance the teaching of creationism in schools have changed over the years:

> The efforts of Christian Fundamentalists to insert the biblical Book of Genesis' explanation into the teaching of science in the public school classrooms evolved in stages from direct state prohibitions to teaching Darwinian evolution, to teaching creation as a science, to balanced treatment of both creationism and evolution, and finally to the latest intelligent design movement (IDM).

LEGAL RULINGS Scores of court cases have addressed school activities related to the First Amendment principle of separation of church and state. As two education law experts put it: "By far the most common constitutional objection raised against a school program is that it fails to respect the wall of separation between church and state" (Imber & van Geel, 2010, p. 16). In one of these landmark cases (*Engel v. Vitale*, 1962), the U.S. Supreme Court ruled that recitation of a prayer said in the presence of a teacher at the beginning of each school day was unconstitutional and violated the First Amendment, which states: "Congress shall make no law respecting an establishment of religion, or prohibiting the free exercise thereof." Justice Hugo Black, who delivered the opinion of the Court, stated, "[I]t is no part of the business of government to compose official prayers for any group of the American people to recite as a part of a religious program carried on by government."

The following year, the U.S. Supreme Court ruled that Bible reading and reciting the Lord's Prayer in school were unconstitutional (*School District of Abington Township v. Schempp,* 1963). In response to the district's claim that unless these religious activities were permitted, a "religion of secularism" would be established, the Court stated, "[W]e agree of course that the State may not establish a 'religion of secularism' in the sense of affirmatively opposing or showing hostility to religion, thus 'preferring those who believe in no religion over those who do believe.' We do not agree, however, that this decision in any sense has that effect."

To determine whether a state has violated the separation of church and state principle, the courts refer to the decision rendered in *Lemon v. Kurtzman* (1971). In this instance, the U.S. Supreme Court struck down an attempt by the **RHODE ISLAND** legislature to provide a 15 percent salary supplement to teachers of secular subjects in nonpublic schools and **PENNSYLVANIA** legislation to provide financial supplements to nonpublic schools through reimbursement for teachers' salaries, texts, and instructional materials in certain secular subjects. According to the three-part test enunciated in *Lemon v. Kurtzman*, governmental practices "must (1) have a secular legislative purpose; (2) have a principal or primary effect that neither advances nor inhibits religion; and (3) not foster an excessive entanglement with religion" (LaMorte, 2012, p. 33). Although criticized vigorously by several Supreme Court justices since 1971, the so-called **Lemon test** has not been overruled. Figure 7.10 presents additional selected U.S. Supreme Court cases related to religion and schools.

Since the mid-1990s, lower courts have heard several cases addressing the question of whether parents' right to direct their children's upbringing meant they could demand curricula and learning activities that were compatible with their religious beliefs. Without exception, the courts have rejected parent-rights cases against the schools. Those rights, according to a U.S. Court of Appeals ruling in support of a schoolwide assembly on HIV/AIDS, "do not encompass a broad-based right to restrict the flow of information in the public schools" (*Brown v. Hot, Sexy and Safer Productions, Inc.,* 1996). In a similar case, parents objected to a **MASSACHUSETTS** school district's policy of distributing condoms to junior and senior high school students who requested them. The state's Supreme Judicial Court rejected the parent-rights argument and their argument that the

Figure 7.10 Selected U.S. Supreme Court cases related to religion and schools (listed in chronological order)

Epperson v. Arkansas (1968): Court overturned the state's anti-evolution statute on the grounds that a state may not deny students access to scientific information because of religious convictions.

Wisconsin v. Yoder (1972): Court decision exempted Amish children from mandatory school attendance beyond the eighth grade if the Amish provided a structured vocational training program for their children.

Stone v. Graham (1980): Court ruled that a Kentucky law mandating the posting of the Ten Commandments in public school classrooms was designed to advance a particular faith, thus violating the First Amendment's establishment of religion clause.

Mueller v. Allen (1983): Court upheld Minnesota's tax deductions for expenses incurred while sending children to secular elementary or secondary schools.

Wallace v. Jaffree (1985): Court invalidated Alabama's school-sponsored moment of silence in Mobile, Alabama.

Edwards v. Aguillard (1987): Court overturned Louisiana's requirement that equal time be devoted to evolution and creationism.

Board of Education of Westside Community Schools v. Mergens (1990): Court upheld the legality of the Equal Access Act (1984), which allowed student religious groups to meet in public secondary schools during noninstructional time.

Zobrest v. Catalina Foothills School District (1993): Court ruled that parochial school sign-language interpreters paid with public funds did not violate the First Amendment.

Agostini v. Felton (1997): Decision overturned the *Aguilar v. Felton* (1985) ruling that prohibited public school employees from providing remedial instruction in sectarian institutions. The *Agostini* ruling focused on Title I of the Elementary and Secondary Education Act of 1965, which required that comparable services be offered to parochial school pupils.

Mitchell v. Helms (2000): Court allowed the use of government funds to provide instructional materials to religious schools.

Santa Fe Independent School District v. Jane Doe (2000): Court ruled that a Texas school district's policy of allowing voluntary student-initiated and student-led invocations before football games violated the establishment clause of the First Amendment.

Good News Club v. Milford Central School (2001): Court ruled that a public school could not deny a Christian group from meeting in the school after hours; if a district allows community groups to use the school, it cannot deny use to religious groups.

program infringed on their First Amendment right to free exercise of religion: "Parents have no right to tailor public school programs to meet their individual religious or moral preferences" (*Curtis v. School Committee of Falmouth*, 1995).

Efforts to replace teaching of creationism in science classrooms with intelligent design (ID) theory have been similarly rejected by the courts. In a case that received nationwide attention, *Kitzmiller v. Dover Area School District* (2005), a federal court struck down an attempt by the Dover, **PENNSYLVANIA** School Board to insert the teaching of intelligent design in the classroom. The court concluded that ID is not science:

> We find that ID fails on three different levels, any one of which is sufficient to preclude a determination that ID is science. They are (1) ID violates centuries-old ground rules of science by invoking and permitting supernatural causation; (2) the argument of irreducible complexity, central to ID, employs the same flawed and illogical contrived dualism that doomed creation science in the 1980s; and (3) ID's negative attacks on evolution have been refuted by the scientific community.

GUIDELINES FOR RELIGIOUS ACTIVITIES IN SCHOOLS In 2003, the U.S. Department of Education issued federal guidelines requiring school districts to allow students and teachers to engage in religious activities, including prayer, at school. Districts that violate the rules—or fail to promise in writing that they will comply with the guidelines—risk the loss of federal education funds. The following points are included in the guidelines:

- Students may "read their Bibles or other scriptures, say grace before meals, and pray or study religious materials with fellow students during recess, the lunch hour or other non-instructional time."

- Teachers should not discriminate against students who "express their beliefs about religion in homework, artwork, and other written and oral assignments."
- In certain circumstances, schools may have to grant parental requests to "excus[e] students from class" for religious reasons.
- Teachers and other school employees, "when acting in their official capacities as representatives of the state," cannot encourage or participate in prayer activities with students. Before school or during lunch, however, school employees are free to meet with other employees for prayer or Bible study (*NEA Today*, 2003, p. 13).

szeyuen/Fotolia

Today's students come from families with diverse religious backgrounds. What challenges do schools face in educating students from diverse religious backgrounds? How can teachers be sure they do not discriminate against students from religious backgrounds that differ from their own?

Educational Malpractice

Since the mid-1970s, several plaintiffs have charged in their **educational malpractice** suits that schools should be responsible for a pupil whose failure to achieve is significant. In the first of such cases, the parents of Peter W. Doe charged that the San Francisco Unified School District was negligent because it allowed him to graduate from high school with a fifth-grade reading level and this handicap would not enable him to function in adult society. In particular, they charged that the "defendant school district, its agents and employees, negligently and carelessly failed to provide the plaintiff with adequate instruction, guidance, counseling and/or supervision in basic academic skills such as reading and writing, although said school district had the authority, responsibility, and ability [to do so]." They sought $500,000 for the negligent work of the teachers who taught Peter.

In evaluating the claim of Peter and his parents, the court pointed out that the alleged injury was not within the realm of tort law and that many factors beyond a school's responsibility or control can account for lack of achievement. The court did not hold the school responsible for Peter's lack of achievement and made it clear that to do so would be to set a precedent with potentially drastic consequences: "To hold [schools] to an actionable duty of care, in the discharge of their academic functions, would expose them to the tort claims—real or imagined—of disaffected students and parents in countless numbers. . . . The ultimate consequences, in terms of public time and money, would burden them—and society—beyond calculation" (*Peter Doe v. San Francisco Unified School District*, 1976).

FOCUS ON **DIVERSITY**: SCHOOL CHILDREN DENIED RIGHT TO LITERACY

A class action suit (*Gary B. v. Snyder*, 2016) filed in a Michigan District Court claims that the state is denying Detroit public school students their Constitutional right to learn to read and excluding them from the state's educational system. The suit is on behalf of all children who attend Detroit schools. The suit aims to secure students' legal right to literacy under the Fourteenth Amendment. It also aims to build on the 1954 U.S. Supreme Court ruling in *Brown v. Board of Education* that an educated citizenry is critical to a well-functioning society.

The lawsuit asks the Court to order the state to provide relief that includes "appropriate, evidence-based literacy" instruction at all grade levels and to address physical school conditions that impair access to literacy. According to the lawyers who filed the suit, "students (who attend five of Detroit's lowest-performing schools) are receiving an education so inferior and underfunded that it's as if they're not attending school at all" (Wong, 2018).

A federal judge in Detroit concluded that the Constitution does not require schools to promote students' literacy and dismissed the suit in late June 2018. Immediately after the dismissal, however, lawyers for the plaintiffs filed an appeal with the federal appeals court in Cincinnati. The appeal argues that the Constitution does guarantee the right to become literate because other rights in the Constitution require the ability to read.

In a similar case, disability rights lawyers filed a class action suit in a California U.S. District Court in 2017 against Berkeley Unified School District (BUSD) for systemically failing to educate students with reading disorders, and students who are suspected to have reading disorders. The district is being sued for failure to comply with federal and state laws that ensure all students receive a free appropriate public education. The suit charges that "Despite being aware for years of needed changes to its policies and practices, BUSD has systemically failed to identify, evaluate, and provide appropriate reading intervention services and accommodations to students with reading disorders that are necessary for them to learn to read and advance academically from grade to grade" (*Student A et al v. Berkeley Unified School District et al,* 2017).

An attorney for the plaintiffs stated that "This is a civil rights class action that challenges a school district's failure to teach children with reading disorders such as dyslexia to learn to read. Without appropriate reading intervention services, these students fall further and further behind academically. Students with reading disorders in BUSD and every public school in this country have the fundamental right to learn to read and participate fully with their peers" (Disability Rights Education & Defense Fund, 2017).

Homeschooling

One spin-off of the public's heightened awareness of the problems that schools face has been the decision by some parents to educate their children in the home. Although most homeschoolers view homeschooling as an opportunity to provide their children with a curriculum based on religious values, many homeschoolers are motivated not by religious doctrine but by concern about issues such as school violence, poor academic quality, or peer pressure.

As of 2015–2016, around 1,690,000 children, or 3.3 percent of all school-aged children, were being homeschooled in the U.S. 59 percent of homeschooled students are White, 26 percent are Hispanic, 8 percent are Black, 3 percent are Asian or Pacific Islander, and 4 percent are American Indian and Alaska Native or a race/ethnicity not included in the U.S. Department of Education survey (McQuiggan & Megra, 2017).

Homeschooling is legal in all states and the District of Columbia; however, how it is regulated, and whether resources are allocated, vary greatly. In most states, homeschoolers must demonstrate that their instruction is "equivalent" to that offered in the public schools, a standard set in *New Jersey v. Massa* (1967). Additional requirements may include participation in standardized testing, a minimum number of hours of instruction, submission of attendance records and lesson plans, adherence to a minimum curriculum, and minimum academic credentials for parents or guardians (LaMorte, 2012).

Legal support for homeschooling has been mixed. In 1998, a **MASSACHUSETTS** court ruled that home visits by a local superintendent were not a valid requirement for approval by school officials of a homeschooling program (*Brunelle v. Lynn Public Schools,* 1998). In 1993 and 1994, legislation to require homeschool teachers to be state certified was defeated in South Dakota and Kansas, and similar laws were overturned in Iowa and North Dakota. However, a federal district court upheld a West Virginia statute making children ineligible for homeschooling if their standardized test scores fell below the 40th percentile (*Null v. Board of Education,* 1993). In Iowa, mandatory homeschooling reports to the state were upheld in *State v. Rivera* (1993); homeschoolers in that state must submit course outlines and weekly lesson plans, and provide the amount of time spent on areas of the curriculum. A **MARYLAND** law requiring the state's monitoring of homeschooling was upheld despite a parent's claim that the state's curriculum promoted atheism, paganism, and evolution (*Battles v. Anne Arundel County Board of Education,* 1996). And courts have not been sympathetic to homeschoolers who would like to have their children participate in extracurricular activities or other after-school activities (for example, *Swanson v. Guthrie Independent School District No. 1,* 1998).

As the preceding cases related to homeschooling show, school law is not static—instead, it is continually evolving and changing. The legal issues examined in this chapter make it clear that the law touches just about every aspect of the teacher's professional life. Ours is an age of litigation, and the teacher is no longer quite as free as in the past to determine what happens behind the closed classroom door.

Although the review of school law in this chapter has answered some of the more common questions teacher education students have about their rights and responsibilities as a teacher, it may have made you aware of other questions for which you need answers. Because school law is constantly changing and laws pertaining to education vary from state to state, you may wish to consult current publications on school law in your state.

Summary

What Do You Need to Know About Education and the Law and Have a Professional Code of Ethics?

- Federal and state legislation and court decisions affect the daily lives of teachers, and teachers must have knowledge of school law to protect their rights and the rights of students.
- A professional code of ethics guides teachers' actions, helps them see beyond the short-range consequences of their actions to the long-range consequences, and helps them respond appropriately to ethical dilemmas in the classroom.
- Ethical decisions (1) are supported by evidence, (2) aim at ends that ought to be aimed at, (3) can be implemented morally, and (4) are legitimately achieved.

What Are Your Legal Rights as a Teacher?

- The right to due process protects teachers from arbitrary treatment by school districts and education officials regarding certification, nondiscrimination, contracts, tenure, dismissal, and academic freedom.
- The constitutional rights of teachers must be balanced against a school's need to promote its educational goals.
- Student teachers should be aware that a potential for liability exists for them just as it does with certified teachers, and they should clarify their rights and responsibilities prior to beginning student teaching.

What Are Your Legal Responsibilities as a Teacher?

- Teachers are responsible for meeting the terms of their teaching contracts, including providing for their students' safety and well-being.
- Three legal responsibilities that concern teachers are avoiding tort liability, recognizing the physical and behavioral indicators of child abuse and then reporting suspected instances of such abuse, and observing copyright laws for instructional materials used in the classroom.
- Teachers' use of online social networking sites like Facebook, Myspace, and Twitter has introduced new legal and ethical concerns for teachers. Increasingly, school districts are advising teachers not to "friend" students on social networking sites and reminding them that their postings can be seen by the public and school officials.

What Are the Legal Rights of Students and Parents?

- Generally, students' freedom of expression can be limited if it is disruptive of the educational process or incongruent with the school's mission.
- The courts have indicated that students have few constraints to their online expression. School districts generally have no right to control student expression off campus and on social networking sites, unless their speech could lead to a serious disruption on campus.
- Students can be neither suspended nor expelled without due process.
- Courts have developed a two-pronged test for search and seizure actions involving students: (1) School officials must have "reasonable" suspicion that a student has violated a law or school policy, and (2) the search must be done using methods that are reasonable and appropriate given the nature of the infraction.
- Under the Buckley Amendment, students have the right to examine their school records, and schools may not give third parties information about students without the students' prior written consent.
- Schools may not discriminate against students on the basis of race, sex, religion, disability, marital status, or infection with a noncommunicable disease such as HIV/AIDS.

What Are Some Issues in the Legal Rights of School Districts?

- Some states and school districts allow the use of corporal punishment if it meets criteria that have emerged from other court cases involving corporal punishment.
- School officials can be held responsible if they fail to act on reports of sexual harassment of students by their peers or by professional staff. School officials also can be held responsible if they fail to take steps to protect gay and lesbian students from anti-gay harassment.
- To bully others, cyberbullies use social networking sites, cell phones, instant messaging, camera phones, email, and various sites on the Internet. Existing case law on free speech and sexual harassment does not readily apply to cyberbullying; however, there is a trend for students who are cyberbullied to file lawsuits that name schools as defendants.
- The First Amendment principle of separation of church and state has been applied to numerous court cases involving religious expression in the public schools. In 2003, the U.S. Department of Education issued guidelines outlining religious activities that are allowed at school.
- Recently, a few class action suits have claimed that school districts have denied students their constitutional right to learn.
- Homeschooling is legal in all states, although most require homeschoolers to demonstrate that their instruction is equivalent to that in public schools.

Professional Reflections and Activities

Teacher's Journal

1. Read the National Education Association's Code of Ethics for Teachers, which is available on the Internet. Regarding Principle I, a teacher's commitment to students, describe a situation you have observed or experienced in which you think a teacher may have violated this principle. Regarding Principle II, a teacher's commitment to the profession, describe a situation in which a teacher might have violated that principle. What are your goals for ethical conduct as a teacher?
2. How can you accommodate students in your classroom who may come from backgrounds with worldviews that differ from Christianity—for example, Islam, Judaism, Buddhism, or a naturalistic worldview that is free of supernatural and mystical elements?
3. What limits do you believe should be placed on *what* teachers teach? On *how* they teach? Which of the legal cases on academic freedom discussed in this chapter support your views?

Teacher's Research

1. Go to the American Bar Association's website, where you can access its journal, a database of court decisions, and analyses of many of those decisions. Read the complete court decision for one or more legal cases mentioned in this chapter. After reading the case, do you agree with the court's decision? Why or why not?
2. Go to the websites for the National Education Association and the American Federation of Teachers. What legal information related to the legal issues discussed in this chapter do these sites provide for teachers?

Observations and Interviews

1. Interview an experienced teacher about the legal rights of teachers. Ask this teacher for examples of situations for which it was important that he or she (or another teacher) was familiar with the legal rights of teachers.
2. Interview another experienced teacher about the legal responsibilities of teachers. Ask this teacher for

examples of situations in which it was important that he or she (or another teacher) was familiar with the legal responsibilities of teachers.

3. During an observation of a teacher's day, identify an ethical dilemma that the teacher confronts. Describe the dilemma and the teacher's response in a journal entry.

Professional Portfolio

Survey a group of students, teachers, and/or parents regarding a legal issue in education.

Among the legal issues and questions you might address are the following:

- Should tenure for teachers be abolished? Does tenure improve the quality of the education that students receive?
- Under what circumstances should restrictions be placed on what teachers teach and how they teach?
- Should parents be allowed to provide homeschooling for their children?
- Are parents justified in filing educational malpractice suits if their children fail to achieve in school?
- Under what circumstances should restrictions be placed on students' freedom of expression?
- Should schools have the right to implement dress codes? Guidelines for students' hairstyles? School uniforms?
- Should corporal punishment be banned? If not, under what circumstances should it be used?
- How should schools combat the problem of sexual harassment?
- To combat drug abuse, should schools implement mandatory drug testing of students? Of teachers?
- Should students have access to their educational records? Should their parents or guardians?
- As part of an HIV/AIDS prevention program, should condoms be distributed to high school students? Should parental approval be required for participation?

The report summarizing the results of your survey should include demographic information such as the following for your sample of respondents: gender, age, whether they have children in school, level of education, and so on. When you analyze the results, look for differences related to these variables.

Shared Writing 7.1
The Reality of Law for Teachers

PART III
The Art of Teaching

Chapter 8
Today's Students

michaeljung/shutterstock

Learning Outcomes

After reading this chapter, you will be able to do the following:

8.1 Explain aspects of identity that contribute to the cultural diversity of U.S. classrooms.

8.2 Explain how teachers strive to provide equal educational opportunity for all students.

8.3 Explain how schools are meeting the needs of English language learners (ELLs).

8.4 Discuss the key elements of multicultural education and culturally responsive teaching.

Dear Mentor

This summer I will be starting my college career at Ohio State University. I hope to stay in the Columbus area to teach after I graduate with my bachelor's degree in middle childhood education. Throughout my high school career, I had a few teaching experiences. As a result of these experiences, I have a few questions that you may help me answer and thus increase my success as a teacher.

- How do teachers develop effective classroom management techniques and learn to respond effectively to students' misbehavior when it occurs?
- What should be considered when developing a lesson plan?
- How do teachers develop a community of learners?
- How do teachers set an efficient pace for learning when the classroom is a mix of advanced students and those who are behind in their learning?
- How will I keep up with newly emerging technologies that teachers are expected to master?

I realize that you may not be able to answer all my questions; however, anything you have learned from your teaching experiences will be greatly appreciated. I look forward to your response.

THANK YOU, RICHARD PATTERSON
Used with Permission of Patterson, Richard

Dear Richard

You ask many good questions. I agree; reflecting on these questions now will increase your success as a teacher.

Developing effective classroom management techniques and responding effectively really begins when your students walk through your door the first day. You need to immediately lay the foundation for mutual respect. Engaging your students in helping to develop classroom expectations and consequences, and making sure they understand these, establishes the groundwork for classroom management.

Getting to know your students—where they come from and their values and beliefs—will be invaluable in gaining their respect and developing a community of learners. Once they know they can trust you to be fair and a good listener, you will find that there are more positive behaviors than negative. Through building trust, you are building a community of learners.

I also recommend that you engage parent volunteers. This provides an opportunity to let parents be involved in their children's education, and it provides you with extra help for one-on-one or small-group intervention.

Establishing clear expectations and then making sure students are aware of the learning targets will create an atmosphere of ownership and achievement. When I develop my lesson plans, I collaborate with my colleagues on the yearlong plan. Big units are developed from our state standards and essential learning skills, from which weekly learning targets are established. Using quality pre-assessments before new skills are introduced gives me the information needed to provide enrichments and interventions for students who need additional help. Having enrichment and intervention techniques built into my lesson plans each week provides me with the tools I need to address each student at his or her appropriate learning level.

Your last question concerning keeping up with new technology is a tough one. Your district should have technology experts available for in-service training. If not, there are many online training resources available, and collaborative efforts to integrate technology within your building and district should be at the top of your list.

In closing, becoming a teacher will be one of the most rewarding experiences you could ever have. I wish you well as you pursue this honorable profession!

SINCERELY, LAURIE GRAVES
Used with permission of Laurie Graves
NBCT (National Board Certified Teacher) Middle Childhood Generalist
2011 WYOMING Teacher of the Year

READERS' VOICES

How is culture important in today's schools?

In many classrooms in America today, students' cultural backgrounds differ from the cultural background of the teacher. Effective teachers understand how to incorporate these differences into their lessons, so that students—regardless of race, ethnicity, religion, or language spoken at home—realize their maximum potential in school.

—AALIMAH,
Teacher Education student, first year

Teachers must be sensitive to the needs of all students regardless of background. This chapter looks at cultural diversity in the United States and the challenges of equalizing educational opportunity for all students. A goal for your professional development as a teacher, then, is to see cultural diversity as an asset to be preserved and valued. The United States has always derived strength from the diversity of its people, and all students should receive a high-quality education so that they may make their unique contributions to society.

It would be impossible to develop a different curriculum for each group of students in your multicultural classroom—that would place undue emphasis on differences among students. Instead, you can develop a curriculum that affirms all students' cultures and increases their awareness and appreciation of the rich diversity in U.S. culture.

What Contributes to the Cultural Diversity In U.S. Classrooms?

The percentage of ethnic minorities in the United States has been growing steadily since the end of World War II. Minorities made up 38.7 percent of the U.S. population in 2016. By 2044, more than half of all Americans are projected to belong to a minority group, and by 2060, nearly one in five of the nation's total population is projected to be foreign born. The Hispanic population is projected to increase from 55.4 million in 2014 to 119.0 million in 2060; similarly, the Asian population is projected to more than double, from 20.0 million in 2014 to 48.6 million in 2060 (U.S. Census Bureau, 2015).

Increasing **diversity** in the United States as a whole is reflected, of course, in the nation's schools. Approximately 50.5 percent of public school students were considered part of a minority group during 2014, an increase of 8.5 percent from 2004 (McFarland et al., 2017). In the nation's 25 largest cities, students of color represent half or more of the student population (National Center for Education Statistics, 2017a).

Approximately 13.5 percent of the total U.S. population was foreign-born as of 2016 (43.7 million people). More than half (53 percent) were born in Latin America and more than one fourth (29 percent) in Asia. More than half (56 percent) lived in just four states: California, New York, Texas, and Florida. Less than half (45 percent) were naturalized citizens (U.S. Census Bureau, 2016). Each year, more than 1 million immigrants obtain legal permanent resident status in the United States (U.S. Department of Homeland Security, 2016).

Figure 8.1 shows that more than 17.7 million U.S. children under age 18 had at least one foreign-born parent during 2015. The figure also shows that, nationally, more than half of immigrant children have parents from Latin American countries—Mexico, Central America and Spanish-speaking Caribbean, and South America.

Figure 8.1 Children in immigrant families by parents' region of origin, 2015

Note: The share of children under age 18 either foreign-born or who have at least one foreign-born parent with at least one parent from Latin America, Europe, Asia, or Africa.

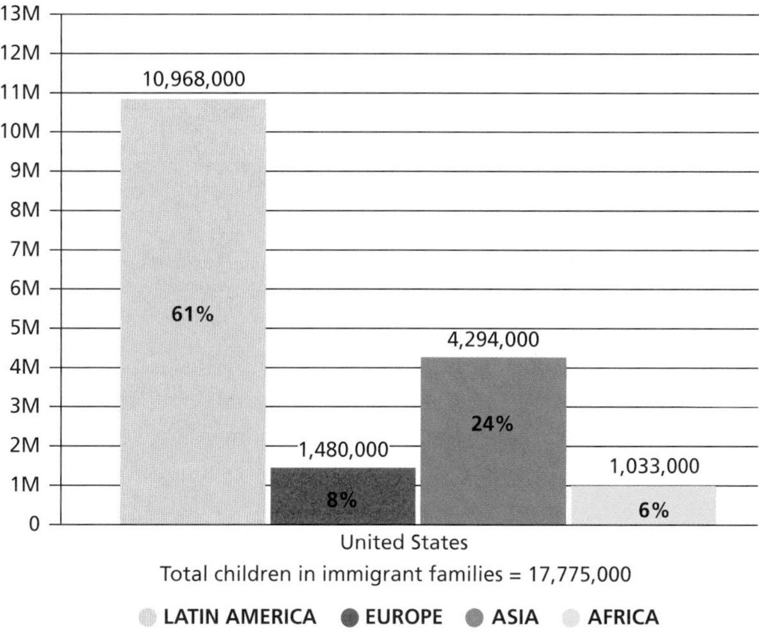

SOURCE: Based on data from the U.S. Census Bureau. (2016). *American Community Survey 2015*. Washington, DC.

FOCUS ON **DIVERSITY**: RISING NUMBER OF STUDENTS OF UNDOCUMENTED IMMIGRANT PARENTS

Figure 8.2 shows that the percentage of K–12 students with undocumented immigrant parents has risen significantly since the end of the Great Recession in 2009. About 3.9 million K–12 students in U.S. public and private schools in 2014, or 7.3 percent of the total, were children of unauthorized immigrants. However, 81 percent of those children were U.S.-born children and thus citizens of the U.S. The highest percentages of K–12 students with at least one undocumented parent are in the West and Southwest; Nevada has the highest percentage (17.6 percent); Texas (13.4 percent); California (12.3 percent); Arizona (12.2 percent); Colorado (10.2 percent); and New Mexico (10.1 percent) (Pew Research Center, 2016, November 17). In a study by UCLA researchers, 58 percent of teachers surveyed reported that students have expressed concerns about the deportation of undocumented immigrants (Rogers, J., et al., 2017). Chapter 9 discusses stress among potentially vulnerable students in more detail and the steps teachers can take to support their students.

Figure 8.2 Share of K–12 students with unauthorized immigrant parents has risen since 2009 in the U.S.

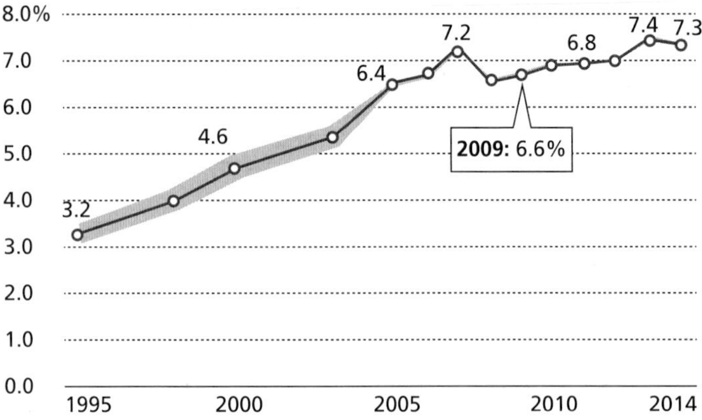

Note: Shading surrounding line indicates low and high points of the estimated 90% confidence interval. Data labels are for 1995, 2000, 2005, 2007, 2009, 2011, 2013, and 2014. Change for 2009 to 2014 is statistically significant at 90% confidence interval.

SOURCE: Based on Pew Research Center. Passel, J. S. & Cohn, D. (November 17, 2016). Children of unauthorized immigrants represent rising share of K-12 students. Retrieved from http://www.pewresearch.org/fact-tank/2016/11/17/children-of-unauthorized-immigrants-represent-rising-share-of-k-12-students/

Differences in student backgrounds offer opportunities to enhance the learning environment; however, these differences also raise challenges for schools. Changes in the racial and ethnic composition of student enrollments are expanding the array of languages and cultures found in the nation's public schools. For example, there is an increased demand for English as a second language (ESL) programs and teachers of English language learners (ELLs) in many parts of the country. All but a few school districts face a critical shortage of minority teachers. And there is a need to develop curricula and strategies that address the needs and backgrounds of all students—regardless of their social class; gender; sexual orientation; or ethnic, racial, or cultural identity.

Defining *Culture*

Simply put, **culture** is the way of life common to a group of people. It consists of the values, attitudes, and beliefs that influence their traditions and behavior. It is also a way of interacting with and looking at the world. At one time, it was believed that the United States was like a melting pot in which ethnic cultures would melt into one common U.S. culture; however, ethnic and cultural differences have remained very much a part of life in the United States. A salad-bowl analogy captures more accurately the **cultural pluralism** of U.S. society. That is, the distinguishing characteristics of cultures are to be preserved rather than blended into a single culture.

Indeed, the intersections of many factors combine to form a person's **cultural identity**, an overall sense of who one is. These factors might include language, religion, age, racial identity, **ethnic group**, exceptionality, gender, sexual orientation, socioeconomic status, and geographic region. The regional culture of New England, for example, is quite different from that of the Southeast. Similarly, Californians are culturally different from Iowans.

Subcultures come with their own customs and beliefs. The importance of these subcultures differs among people. For some, their cultural identity is most strongly determined by their occupations; for others, it is determined by their ethnicity; and for others, by their religious beliefs.

Stereotyping and Racism

Although teachers should expand their knowledge of and appreciation for the diverse cultural backgrounds of their students, they should also guard against forming stereotypes or overgeneralizations about those cultures. **Stereotyping** is the process of attributing behavioral characteristics to all members of a group. In some cases, stereotypes are formed on the basis of limited experiences with and information about the group being stereotyped, and the validity of these stereotypes is not questioned.

Within any cultural group that shares a broad cultural heritage, however, considerable diversity exists. For example, two Puerto Rican children who live in the same community and attend the same school may appear alike to their teachers when, in reality, they are very different. One may come from a home where Spanish is spoken and Puerto Rican holidays are observed; the other child may know only a few words of Spanish and observe only the holidays of the majority culture.

In addition to being alert for stereotypes they and others may hold, teachers should learn to recognize **individual racism**, the prejudicial belief that one's ethnic or racial group is superior to others. An obvious feature of racism in the United States "is that many whites see themselves as better than persons and groups of color, and as a result exercise their power to prevent people of color from securing the prestige, power, and privilege held by them" (Gollnick & Chinn, 2009, p. 63). Teachers should also be able to recognize **institutional racism**, which occurs when institutions "behave in ways that are overtly racist (i.e., specifically excluding people-of-color from services) or inherently racist (i.e., adopting policies that while not specifically directed at excluding people-of- color, nevertheless result in their exclusion)" (Randall, 2001).

In light of the arbitrariness of the concept of race, James A. Banks (2009) points out, "[i]n most societies, *the social significance of race is much more important than the presumed physical differences among groups*" (p. 71). Unfortunately, many people attach great importance to the concept of race. If you believe "that human groups can be validly grouped on the basis of their biological traits and that these identifiable groups inherit certain mental, personality, and cultural characteristics that determine their behavior" (Banks, 2009, p. 72) then you hold racist beliefs. When people use such beliefs as a rationale for oppressing other groups, they are practicing racism.

As a teacher, you will not be able to eliminate stereotypic thinking or racism in society. However, you have an obligation to all your students to see that your curriculum and instruction are free of any forms of stereotyping or racism. You need to assess your own cultural attitudes and values and determine whether you have stereotypes about other cultural groups.

Contributors to Cultural Identity

LANGUAGE AND CULTURE About 4.6 million **English language learners (ELLs)** attended public schools in 2014–2015, or about 9.4 percent of the total enrollment (McFarland et al., 2017). ELL students have limited ability to understand, read, or speak English, and they have a first language other than English. Ten percent or more of public school students were ELL in the **DISTRICT OF COLUMBIA** and the following states during 2015: **ALASKA, CALIFORNIA, COLORADO, ILLINOIS, NEVADA, NEW MEXICO,** and **TEXAS**. Among the states, California enrolled the greatest percentage of ELL students—22.4 percent (McFarland et al., 2017).

ELL students in the United States speak more than 150 languages, with about 77.1 percent claiming Spanish as their native language. Next in frequency of use is Arabic, spoken by approximately 2.8 percent; Chinese, spoken by 2.2 percent; and Vietnamese, spoken by 1.8 percent (McFarland et al., 2017). Although states in the West report particularly high numbers of ELL students, Figure 8.3 indicates that the continued increase in the number of ELL students is being felt throughout the United States.

Figure 8.3 Percentage of public school students who were English language learners, by state: School year 2014–15

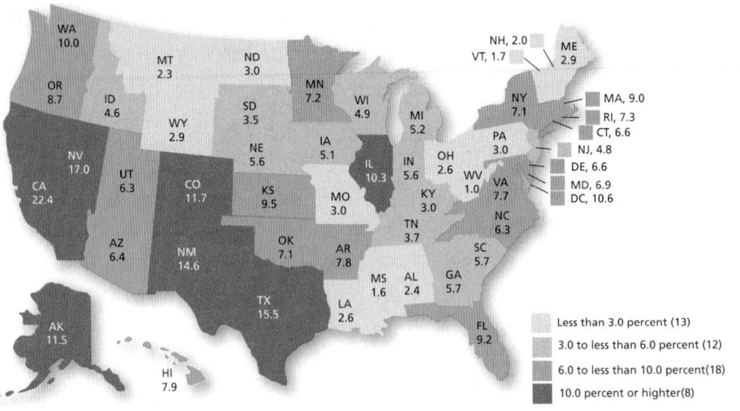

Note: Categorizations are based on unrounded percentages.

SOURCE: McFarland, J., Hussar, B., de Brey, C., Snyder, T., Wang, X., Wilkinson-Flicker, S., Gebrekristos, S., Zhang, J., Rathbun, A., Barmer, A., Bullock Mann, F., and Hinz, S. (2017). *The Condition of Education 2017* (NCES 2017-144). U.S. Department of Education. Washington, DC: National Center for Education Statistics, p. 106.

Students' language patterns became a topic of national debate in late 1996 when the Oakland, **CALIFORNIA** school district passed a resolution on Ebonics (a blend of the words *ebony* and *phonics*), also known as African American Vernacular English (AAVE). The resolution, which recognized Ebonics as the primary language of many of the district's 28,000 African American students, called for them to be taught in their primary language and suggested that some students might be eligible for state and federal bilingual education or ESL money.

Critics of the resolution pointed out that Black English is a nonstandard form of English or a dialect of English—not a foreign language. Other critics were concerned that students and teachers would be taught Ebonics. In the midst of intense national debate, the district revised the resolution so that it no longer called for students to be taught in their primary language (or dialect of English). Instead, the district would implement new programs to move students from the language patterns they bring to school toward proficiency in Standard English.

Teachers should remember that "African Americans as a group include the entire spectrum of speakers from fluent native speakers of AAVE to eloquent speakers of standard English. It would therefore be a mistake to equate an African American racial heritage with Ebonics or any specific linguistic behavior" (Baugh, 2012, p. 53). In *Through Ebony Eyes: What Teachers Need to Know But Are Afraid to Ask About African American Students*, Gail Thompson (2004, p. 148) suggests that teaching African American students to speak Standard English requires:

> . . . a respect for the home language that students bring to school . . . [then] these teachers can help students understand why they need to learn to speak Standard English, and to realize that the ability and willingness to use Standard English when necessary can empower them. Moreover, they can convince students they do not have to give up their home language to become empowered.

In addition, some educators maintain that teachers can use Black English, hip hop, and rap to enhance the learning of Black students, and that students naturally learn to "code switch" from Black English to standard English as appropriate (Emdin, 2017). Similarly, research shows that Black children using technology to learn math and science learn more if the computer instructs them in Black English (Chiles, 2015).

Other dialects of English and their use in the classroom have been debated from time to time—for example, Chicano English, Cajun English, or Hawaiian Creole English (more popularly known as pidgin English).

ETHNICITY, RACE, AND CULTURE **Ethnicity** refers to a "shared sense of peoplehood, culture, identity, and shared language and dialects" (Banks, 2009, p. 16). On the other hand, **race** is a subjective concept that distinguishes among human beings on the basis of biological traits. Anthropologist John Hartigan (2013) points out that "[r]ace is a *biosocial fact*. This assertion purposefully stands in contrast to the position that race is a social construction" (p. 4).

As a result of the diversity among humans and the mixing of genes that has taken place over time, no single set of racial categories is universally accepted. Because many genetic factors are invisible to the naked eye (DNA, for example), noted anthropologist Ashley Montagu has suggested that there could be as few as three "races" (Negroid, Caucasoid, and Mongoloid) or as many as 300, depending on the kind and number of genetic features chosen for measurement. In his classic book, *Man's Most Dangerous Myth: The Fallacy of Race*, Montagu (1974) pointed out:

> It is impossible to make the sort of racial classification which some anthropologists and others have attempted. The fact is that all human beings are so . . . mixed with regard to origin that between different groups of individuals . . . "overlapping" of physical traits is the rule. (p. 7)

In the U.S., the questionnaire for the 2010 Census was changed so that people could select from among 15 racial categories for their racial identity, including a place to write in races not listed on the form. In addition, the "Spanish/Hispanic/Latino" category allowed respondents to choose among the following: Mexican, Mexican American, and Chicano; Puerto Rican; Cuban; and "other" Hispanic/Latino/Spanish. Similarly, respondents who self-identified as "Asian or Pacific Islander" had the following choices: Asian Indian, Chinese, Filipino, Japanese, Korean, Vietnamese, "other" Asian, Native Hawaiian, Guamanian or Chamorro, Samoan, and "other" Pacific Islander.

According to the 2010 U.S. Census, about 8 percent of marriages are mixed race. A 2015 Pew Research Center survey found that almost 7 percent of the population identified themselves as being two or more races. In addition, the number of multiracial babies born in the U.S. is growing three times faster than the country as a whole (Pew Research Center, 2015, June). For people of mixed race, decisions about how to identify themselves are influenced by how and where they were raised, how others perceive them, what they look like, and the cultural identity with which they most strongly identify.

People with a mixed-race identity received more attention when Barack Obama, who has a White mother from Kansas and a Black father from Kenya, was elected president in 2008. As an educator who identifies herself as African American, American Indian, and White said, "I think Barack Obama [brought] these deeply American stories to the forefront. Maybe we'll get a little bit further in the dialogue on race" (Navarro, 2008). Her optimism was borne out by a November 2008 survey showing that 52 percent of the public believed Obama's election resulted in "better" race relations and only 9 percent "worse" relations. However, the same survey after the election of Donald Trump in 2016 saw much different results: 25 percent believed Trump's election resulted in "better" race relations and 46 percent "worse" relations. Moreover, after Trump's first year in office, 8 percent believed his election resulted in "better" race relations and 60 percent "worse" race relations (Pew Research Center, 2017, December 19).

Video Example 8.1

Using Parents as Cultural Resources: This teacher explains how her teachers learn about the culture of their diverse students by communicating with parents.

SOCIOECONOMIC STATUS AND CULTURE "One of the most critical issues that educators routinely face is that of social class and poverty" (Gollnick & Chinn, 2009, p. 339). In 2016, the federal poverty level was $24,300 a year for a family of four. As Figure 8.4 shows, the poverty rate for children under age 18 that year was 18.0 percent, higher than the rates for people aged 18 to 64 and those aged 65 and older. Additionally, in 2016, children represented 23.0 percent of the U.S. population (about 74.3 million); however, they accounted for 32.6 percent of people in poverty (Semega, Fontenot, & Kollar, 2017).

Figure 8.4 Poverty rates by age: 1959 to 2016

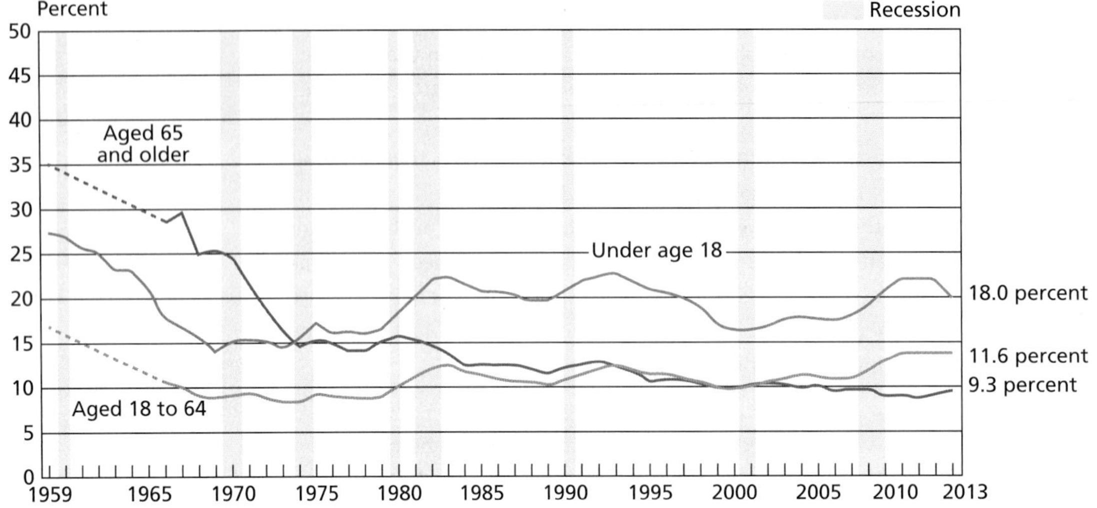

Note: The data for 2013 and beyond reflect the implementation of the redesigned income questions. The data points are placed at the midpoints of the respective years. Data for people aged 18 to 64 and aged 65 and older are not available from 1960 to 1965.

SOURCE: Semega, J. L., Fontenot, K.R., and Kollar, M.A. U.S. Census Bureau, Current Population Reports, P60-259, *Income and Poverty in the United States: 2016*, U.S. Government Printing Office, Washington, DC, 2017, p. 14.

The percentage of children in poverty also varies by race/ethnicity. For example, Figure 8.5 shows that, among different racial groups, Asian households had the highest median income in 2016 ($81,431). The median income for non-Hispanic White households was $65,041; for Hispanic households, $47,675; and for Black households, $39,490. Figure 8.5 also shows that the real median household income for each of the race and Hispanic-origin groups has not yet recovered to its pre-2001–recession median household income peak.

Figure 8.5 Real median household income by race and Hispanic origin: 1967 to 2016

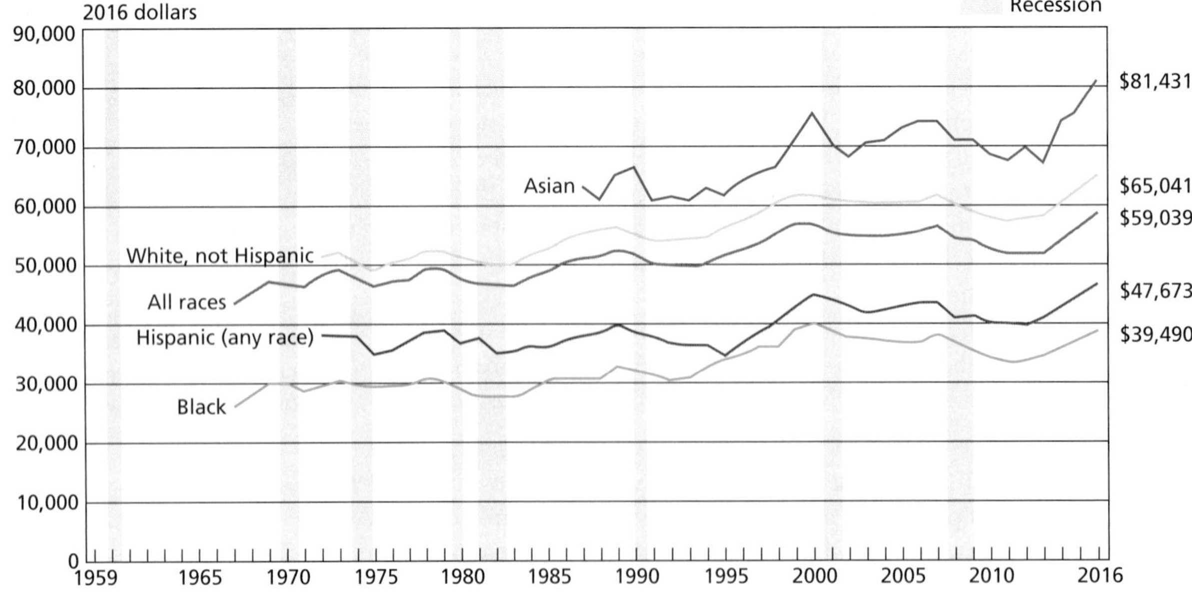

Note: The data for 2013 and beyond reflect the implementation of the redesigned income questions. The data points are placed at the midpoints of the respective years. Median household income data are not available prior to 1967.

SOURCE: Semega, Jessica L., Kayla R. Fontenot, and Melissa A. Kollar, U.S. Census Bureau, Current Population Reports, P60-259, *Income and Poverty in the United States: 2016*, U.S. Government Printing Office, Washington, DC, 2017, p. 5.

Teachers in inner-city schools or schools in poor rural communities may find that nearly all their students are from families who live in poverty. For children, poverty can contribute to depression, lower levels of sociability and/or initiative, problematic peer relations, and disruptive classroom behavior (Eamon, July 2001). Poverty can impede children's ability to learn and contribute to social, emotional, and behavioral problems.

THE ACHIEVEMENT GAP From 1990 to 2015, the high school completion rates for students in all minority groups increased. For example, the rate for Hispanic students increased from 59 to 88 percent; and for Black students, 83 to 92 percent (Musu-Gillette et al., 2017b). Despite these gains, progress is uneven, and an **achievement gap** exists between White students and Hispanic, Black, and American Indian/Alaska Native students on many measures of educational achievement. For example, Figure 8.6 shows, by race/ethnicity, the percentage of fourth- and eighth-grade students who reached *proficient* on the 2015 National Assessment of Educational Progress (NAEP) in reading and mathematics.

Figure 8.6 Percentage at or above *Proficient* in NAEP for selected student groups in 2015

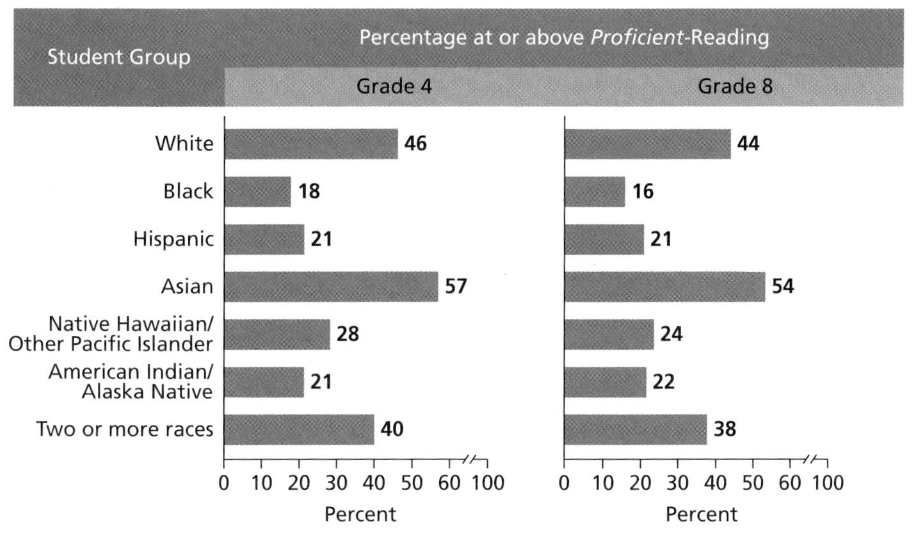

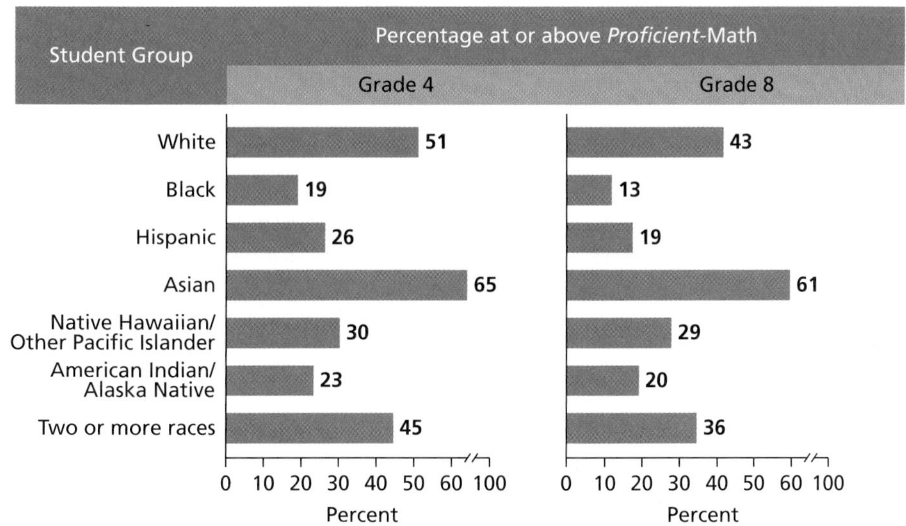

SOURCE: Adapted from The Nation's Report Card: 2015 Mathematics and Reading Assessments. U.S. Department of Education, Institute of Education Sciences, National Center for Education Statistics. Retrieved from https://www.nationsreportcard.gov/reading_math_2015/#?grade=4

When we consider the lower achievement levels of minority students, it is important to note the much higher incidence of poverty among minority families and the research showing that socioeconomic status—not race, language, or culture—contributes most strongly to students' achievement in school (Coleman et al., 1966; Jencks et al., 1972; Jencks & Phillips, 1998; National Center for Education Statistics, 1980). It is understandably difficult for poor children to learn well if they endure the stress of living in crime-ridden neighborhoods, dwelling in dilapidated homes, or going to school hungry.

In addition, it is important to remember that test scores are but a narrow measure of educational quality. A report from the National Education Policy Center suggests that paying attention only to comparisons of test scores among different racial and ethnic groups may lead to the mistaken notion that "[o]nly those schools that are predominantly White, or Asian, or both are considered 'good'" (Wells, 2014, p. 13). Moreover, placing undue emphasis on test scores reduces the likelihood that *all students* receive an education that prepares them for a culturally complex, diverse society:

> the current approach to accountability not only leads to more negative perceptions of racially diverse schools, but also limits educators' ability to tap into the educational benefits of the cultural diversity within those schools to help all students thrive intellectually. The more narrow the measures used to judge schools, teachers, and students, the less likely the educational system as a whole can envision racial, ethnic, and cultural diversity as an asset in preparing all children for the 21st Century. (Wells, 2014, p. 12)

Religion and Culture

Among more than a dozen major religious traditions in the U.S., there are hundreds of distinct religious groups. Overall, about 7 in 10 (70.6 percent) adults report belonging to various forms of Christianity, about 5.9 percent belong to non-Christian faiths, and almost 1 in 6 (22.8 percent) are not affiliated with any particular religion (Pew Research Center, 2015, May 12).

In addition, religious pluralism in the U.S. is changing. Comparing the results of its survey, *America's Changing Religious Landscape,* with its *U.S. Religious Landscape Survey* seven years earlier, the Pew Research Center noted that

> the percentage of adults (ages 18 and older) who describe themselves as Christians has dropped by nearly eight percentage points in just seven years, from 78.4% in 2007 to 70.6% in 2014. Over the same period, the percentage of Americans who are religiously unaffiliated—describing themselves as atheist, agnostic or "nothing in particular"—has jumped more than six points, from 16.1% to 22.8%. And the share of Americans who identify with non-Christian faiths also has inched up, rising 1.2 percentage points, from 4.7% in 2007 to 5.9% in 2014. (Pew Research Center, 2015, May 12, p. 3)

Table 8.1 shows that the racial and ethnic profiles of many religious groups in the U.S. have become more diverse. Between 2007 and 2014, for example, the percentage of White Evangelicals, mainline Protestants, Catholics, and religiously unaffiliated has declined, while Hispanic members of these groups have increased.

Different religious groups in America can have different expectations of the schools. Depending on the religious makeup of a local community, areas such as the following can emerge as points of conflict between the community and the school: sex education, teaching of evolution and/or intelligent design, and liberal points of view in textbooks. In a religiously pluralistic society such as the United States, teachers should know which religious groups are represented in their communities and schools. That knowledge is necessary to respect the religious rights of all students.

Table 8.1 Racial and Ethnic Composition of Religious Groups

	2007					2014				
	White, non-Hispanic	Black, non-Hispanic	Asian, non-Hispanic	Other, non-Hispanic	Hispanic	White, non-Hispanic	Black, non-Hispanic	Asian, non-Hispanic	Other, non-Hispanic	Hispanic
	%	%	%	%	%	%	%	%	%	%
Full sample[1]	**71**	**11**	**3**	**3**	**12=100**	**66**	**12**	**4**	**4**	**15=100**
Christian	**71**	**12**	**1**	**3**	**13**	**66**	**13**	**2**	**3**	**16**
Protestant	74	16	1	3	5	69	18	1	4	8
Evangelical	*81*	*6*	*2*	*4*	*7*	*76*	*6*	*2*	*5*	*11*
Mainline	*91*	*2*	*1*	*3*	*3*	*86*	*3*	*1*	*3*	*6*
Historically back	*2*	*92*	*	*1*	*4*	*2*	*94*	*0*	*1*	*3*
Catholic	65	2	2	2	29	59	3	3	2	34
Orthodox Christian	87	6	2	3	1	81	8	3	2	6
Mormon	86	3	1	3	7	85	1	1	5	8
Jehovah's Witness	48	22	*	5	24	36	27	*	6	32
Non-Christian faiths	**69**	**5**	**16**	**6**	**4**	**61**	**6**	**21**	**5**	**6**
Jewish	95	1	*	2	3	90	2	2	2	4
Muslim	33	32	20	7	7	38	28	28	3	4
Buddhist	53	4	32	5	6	44	3	33	8	12
Hindu	5	1	88	4	2	4	2	91	2	1
Unaffiliated	**73**	**8**	**4**	**4**	**11**	**68**	**9**	**5**	**4**	**13**
Atheist	86	3	4	2	5	78	3	7	2	10
Agnostic	84	2	4	4	6	79	3	4	4	9
Nothing in particular	70	10	3	4	12	64	12	5	5	15
Religion not important[2]	79	5	4	4	8	72	7	6	4	12
Religion important[2]	60	16	2	5	17	53	18	3	6	19

Note: 2014 Religious Landscape Study, conducted June 4–Sept. 30, 2014. Figures may not add to 100% due to rounding. Results recalculated to exclude nonresponse. The 2007 Religious Landscape Study used slightly different question wording to measure race and ethnicity.

[1]The demographic characteristics of the 2014 Religious Landscape Study's overall sample were weighted to known parameters from the Census Bureau's 2012 American Community Survey (ACS), which helps to ensure that the demographic characteristics of the sample closely match those of the U.S. adult population.

[2]Those who describe their religion as "nothing in particular" are subdivided into two groups. The "religion not important" group includes those who say (in Q.F2) religion is "not too" or "not at all" important in their lives as well as those who decline to answer the question about religion's importance. The "religion important" category includes those who say religion is "very" or "somewhat" important in their lives.

SOURCE: Based on Pew Research Center, May 12, 2015, *America's Changing Religious Landscape*, p. 52.

How Can Teachers Strive to Provide Equal Educational Opportunity for All Students?

Teachers must appreciate how many groups of people have continuously struggled to obtain full educational, economic, political, and social opportunities in society. Along with minority racial and ethnic groups, others who have traditionally lacked power in U.S. public life are immigrants; the poor; children and the elderly; non-English speakers;

members of minority religions; people who have no religion; women; and people who are gay, lesbian, bisexual, or transgender. Groups who have been most frequently discriminated against in terms of the quality of education they have received include African Americans, Spanish-speaking Americans, Native Americans, Asian Americans, exceptional learners, and women. There is mounting evidence that many students from these groups continue to receive a substandard education that does not meet their needs or empower them to participate fully and equally in life in the United States.

Providing an equal educational opportunity to all students means that teachers and schools promote the full development of students as individuals, without regard for race, ethnicity, gender, sexual orientation, socioeconomic status, religion, abilities, or disabilities. More specifically, educators fulfill this important mission by continually evaluating the appropriateness of the curricular and instructional experiences they provide to each student. The Teachers' Voices: Being an Agent of Change feature in this chapter, by Marcus Goodyear, describes how he learned that the primary goal of a teacher should be to promote the full development of students—that a teacher should "always err on the side of the student."

TEACHERS' VOICES  BEING AN AGENT OF CHANGE

MARCUS GOODYEAR

Dollars and Points

Teacher Marcus Goodyear faced a dilemma after giving a student a grade of 50 for her final research paper because half of it was plagiarized. The research paper grade gave the student a six-weeks' grade of 69 (one point short of a passing grade of 70). The failing grade made the girl ineligible to compete in athletics. However, the teacher reflects on whether he made the "right" decision after meeting with the girl's upset parents and learning that the father has serious health problems.

After almost a week, I asked my principal for advice. What would he do? I asked my department head. Miraculously neither of them had ever become cynical, and so I trusted them. "Give her the point," they said. "It isn't worth it to hold the line. They'll drag you to the school board. They'll make you look like the villain. They'll examine every minor grade under a microscope. Just give her the point and let her have a seventy."

On the grade change form I checked "teacher error." The student became eligible. She went on to the state competition that year. "What will you say to the people you beat?" I wanted to ask her. "What will you say to the students who had enough honor not to plagiarize their research papers?" But I swallowed my pride. I swallowed some of my moral self-righteousness. I even swallowed my anger at parents who will bully their way through teachers and administrators and anyone else standing between them and their entitlements. Because I hadn't known about her dad's health problems. If the girl had just told me that she thought her father might die, I would have given her extra time on the paper. I would have allowed more makeup work. I would have helped her. I should have helped her.

Part of me still felt like I was compromising academics for athletics. Part of me wanted to punish the student for the actions of her parents. But I learned an important lesson: Always err on the side of the student.

Because I do make mistakes, of course. I made a big mistake with that plagiarized paper—I assumed the worst of my student. I should have given the girl a chance to confess and rewrite the paper. Now I know to reward students for what they do well, rather than punish students for what they do poorly. Some students will need to face consequences for their mistakes, but that can never become my focus as a teacher. It would destroy me. It would make me shrivel up into bitterness and indignation that the students, the teachers, the whole educational system was just going to hell. Everyone makes mistakes in the classroom, even me. That is what the classroom is for. And those mistakes will only make me worthless and vindictive if I remain proud and absolute. Like some one-room schoolhouse tyrant. Or like the cynics down the hall.

During that conference [with the girl's parents] I also realized that no amount of points brings value to a student's education. Passing my class, passing the state achievement test, even passing the Advanced Placement test were all based on an economic view of the world. These things reduce human actions and feelings to a few numbers—either test scores or the price of a college class. These things work as external rewards, but the biggest rewards are always internal. In addition to points, I can give my students respect and trust and confidence and faith. They need to become adults; they need me to treat them like adults.

Why would I treat them any other way?

Above all, I finally realized that I teach for the students. Not their parents. Not my peers. Not even for myself or the paycheck at the end of every month. I teach for my students to rise above their mistakes.

And the mistakes of their teachers.

Some of them will. I know it.

PERSONAL REFLECTION

1. Based on his account of the plagiarism incident, what do you think *equal educational opportunity* means to Goodyear?
2. Why does Goodyear decide to change his student's grade? Do you agree or disagree with his decision? Why?
3. When you begin to teach, what steps can you take to ensure that all your students have equal educational opportunity?

Based on Marcus Goodyear formerly taught at O'Connor High School in San Antonio, **TEXAS.** The preceding is excerpted from his chapter that appears in Molly Hoekstra (ed.), *Am I Teaching Yet? Stories from the Teacher-Training Trenches* (Portsmouth, NH: Heinemann, 2002), pp. 70–75.

The following sections review the progress that has been made to provide students from diverse groups with equal educational opportunity and present strategies for teaching in diverse classrooms. Anglo-European Americans are omitted from the review, not because students from this very diverse group have always had equal educational opportunities, or because "Anglo-European Americans" is a single, monolithic culture. However, this group represents the historically dominant culture. To a great extent, it has determined the curricular and instructional practices found in schools.

Education and Gender

Cultural differences between males and females are partially shaped by society's traditional expectations of them. Through **sex role stereotyping**, families, the media, the schools, and other powerful social forces condition boys and girls to act in certain ways regardless of abilities or interests. One dimension of the **sex role socialization** process conveys to students certain expectations about the way boys and girls are "supposed" to act. Girls are "supposed" to play with dolls, boys to play with trucks. Girls are "supposed" to be passive; boys are "supposed" to be active. Girls are "supposed" to express their feelings and emotions when in pain; boys are "supposed" to repress their feelings and deny pain.

Students may be socialized into particular gender-specific roles as a result of the curriculum materials they use at school. By portraying males in more dominant, assertive ways and portraying females in ways that suggest that they are passive and helpless, textbooks can subtly reinforce expectations about the way girls and boys "should" behave. Within the last few decades, however, publishers of curriculum materials have become more vigilant about avoiding these stereotypes.

It was not until Title IX of the Education Amendments Act was passed in 1972 that women were guaranteed equality of educational opportunity in educational programs receiving federal assistance. Title IX has had the greatest impact on athletic programs in schools. The law requires that both sexes have equal opportunities to participate in and benefit from the availability of coaches, sports equipment, resources, and facilities. For contact sports such as football, wrestling, and boxing, sports that were not open to women, separate teams are allowed.

The right of females to equal educational opportunity was further enhanced with the passage of the **Women's Educational Equity Act (WEEA)** of 1974. This act provides the following opportunities:

- Expanded math, science, and technology programs for females
- Programs to reduce sex role stereotyping in curriculum materials
- Programs to increase the number of female educational administrators
- Special programs to extend educational and career opportunities to minority, disabled, and rural women
- Programs to help school personnel increase educational opportunities and career aspirations for females
- Encouragement for more females to participate in athletics

Despite reforms stemming from WEEA, several reports in the early 1990s criticized schools for subtly discriminating against girls in tests, textbooks, and teaching methods. Research on teacher interactions in the classroom seemed to point to widespread unintentional gender bias against girls. Two of these studies, *Shortchanging Girls, Shortchanging America* (1991) and *How Schools Shortchange Girls* (1992), both commissioned by the American Association of University Women (AAUW), claimed that girls were not encouraged in math and science and that teachers favored boys' intellectual growth over that of girls.

In the mid-1990s, however, some gender equity studies had more mixed findings. In their analysis of data on achievement and engagement of 9,000 eighth-grade boys and girls, University of Michigan researchers Valerie Lee, Xianglei Chen, and Becky A. Smerdon (1996) concluded that "the pattern of gender differences is inconsistent. In some cases, females are favored; in others males are favored." Similarly, University of Chicago researchers Larry Hedges and Amy Nowell found in their study of 32 years of mental tests given to boys and girls that, while boys do better than girls in science and mathematics, they were "at a rather profound disadvantage" in writing and scored below girls in reading comprehension (Hedges, 1996, p. 3).

Additional research and closer analyses of earlier reports on gender bias in education were beginning to suggest that boys, not girls, were most shortchanged by the schools (Gurian & Stevens, 2007; Sommers, 1996, 2000). Numerous articles, as well as a PBS series that began with a program titled "The War on Boys," challenged the conclusions of the earlier AAUW report, *How Schools Shortchange Girls*. Other commentary discounted gender bias in the schools as a fabrication of radical feminism; among the first to put forth this view was Christina Hoff Sommers's (1994) controversial book, *Who Stole Feminism? How Women Have Betrayed Women*; Judith Kleinfeld (1998) followed with *The Myth That Schools Shortchange Girls: Social Science in the Service of Deception*, as did Cathy Young (1999) with *Ceasefire! Why Women and Men Must Join Forces to Achieve True Equality*.

What some people had come to call the "gender wars" took another turn when the AAUW released *Where the Girls Are: The Facts About Gender Equity in Education* in 2008. The report, which examined trends in standardized test scores by gender, race, ethnicity, and family income during the past 35 years, found that family income, not gender, is most closely associated with academic success. The analysis of scores on tests such as the SAT and ACT college entrance exams led the AAUW to conclude:

> The overarching message of this report is one of good news. Overall and within racial/ethnic groups and family income levels, girls and boys are improving by most measures of educational achievement, and most achievement gaps are narrowing. The past few decades have seen remarkable gains for girls and boys in education, and no evidence indicates a crisis for boys in particular. If a crisis exists, it is a crisis for African American and Hispanic students and students from lower-income families—both girls and boys. (American Association of University Women, 2008, p. 68)

GENDER-FAIR CLASSROOMS AND CURRICULA Although research and debate about the bias boys and girls encounter in school will no doubt continue, it is clear that teachers must encourage girls and boys to develop to the full extent of their capabilities and provide them an education that is free from **gender bias**—subtle favoritism or discrimination on the basis of gender. Following is a list of basic guidelines for creating a **gender-fair classroom**.

- Become aware of differences in interactions with girls and boys.
- Promote boys' achievement in reading and writing and girls' achievement in mathematics and science.
- Reduce young children's self-imposed sexism.
- Teach about sexism and sex role stereotyping.
- Foster an atmosphere of collaboration between girls and boys.

For example, the following comments by a first-year high school science teacher stress what teachers can do to promote a gender-fair classroom.

> I have high expectations for all of my students, not just the boys. If I challenge a boy to figure out the answer to a scientifically engaging problem for himself, and then go and give the answer to a girl, I send an unconscious message that I do not think my female student can figure it out by herself. I encourage the girls' active participation when it is easy for them to be drowned out by the louder and more aggressive boys. I encourage girls to ask questions and help them use scientific methodology to find answers. I challenge them to think about why there are more men who do science than women. (Oakes & Lipton, 2007, p. 278)

FOCUS ON **STEM**: FEMALE STUDENTS OUTPERFORM MALE STUDENTS IN TECHNOLOGY AND ENGINEERING LITERACY

The 2014 National Assessment of Educational Progress (NAEP) included the first-ever nationwide assessment of students' technology and engineering literacy (TEL). TEL refers to the ability to use, understand, and evaluate technology, as well as to understand technological principles and strategies needed to develop solutions and achieve goals.

Figure 8.7 Average scores and score differences for eighth-grade students assessed in technology and engineering literacy (TEL) *content areas* and *practice areas*, by gender: 2014

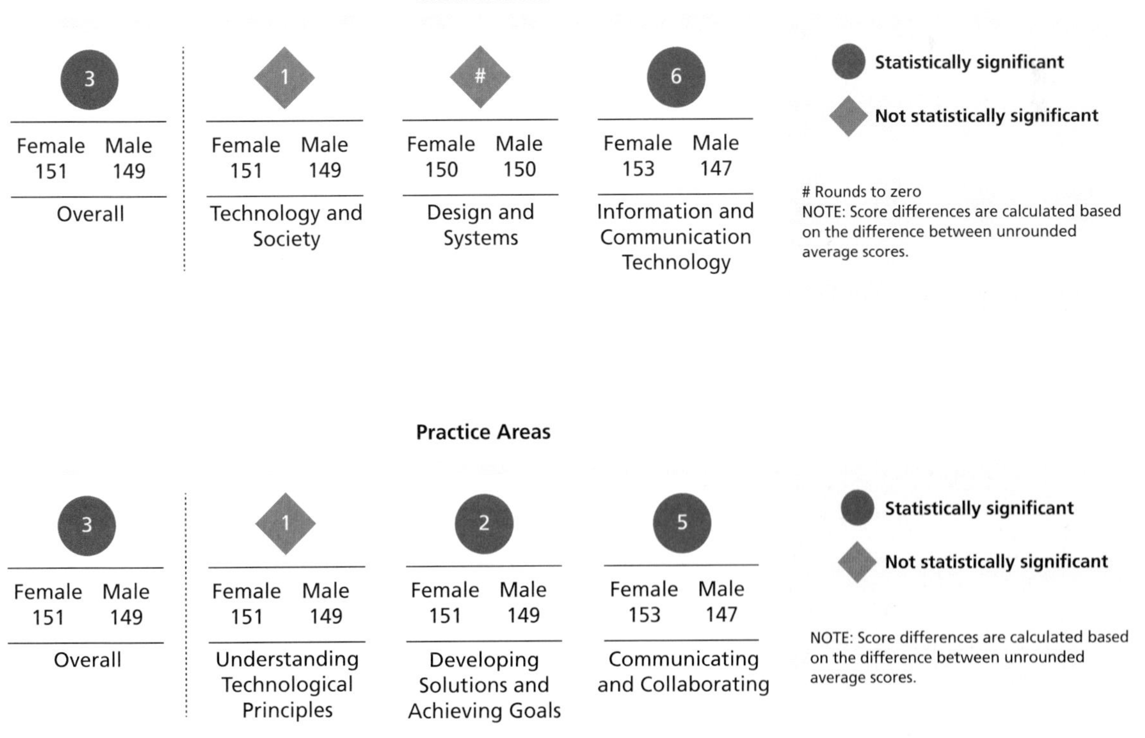

SOURCE: Adapted from the Nation's Report Card: 2014 Technology & Engineering Literacy (TEL). U.S. Department of Education, Institute of Education Sciences, National Center for Education Statistics, National Assessment of Educational Progress (NAEP). Retrieved from https://www.nationsreportcard.gov/tel_2014/#results/overall

Approximately 21,500 eighth-grade students from 840 schools across the nation responded to interactive scenario-based tasks involving technology and engineering challenges. *Content-related* questions covered technology and society, design and systems, and information and communication technology. *Practice-related* questions covered understanding technological principles, developing solutions and achieving goals, and communicating and collaborating.

Figure 8.7 shows that eighth-grade female students scored higher on average than male students in TEL overall, in both content-related and practice-related areas. The figure also shows that these differences were statistically significant—that is, not likely due to chance.

Lesbian, Gay, Bisexual, Transgender, and Questioning (LGBTQ) Students

In addition to gender bias, some students experience discrimination on the basis of their gender identity and/or sexual orientation. According to Gallup, about 4.1 percent of U.S. adults, or more than 10 million people, identify as lesbian, gay, bisexual, or transgender (Gallup, 2017). To help all students realize their full potential, teachers should acknowledge the special needs of gay, lesbian, bisexual, transgender, and questioning students.

Based on estimates that 4 percent of U.S. society is LGBTQ, a high school with an enrollment of 1,500 might have as many as 60 gay, lesbian, bisexual, transgender, or questioning students. The National Education Association, the American Federation of Teachers, and several professional organizations have passed resolutions urging members and school districts to acknowledge the special needs of these students.

The nation's first dropout prevention program targeting gay, lesbian, and bisexual students was implemented in the Los Angeles school system. Known as Project 10, the program focuses on education, suicide prevention, dropout prevention, creating a safe environment for homosexual students, and HIV/AIDS education (Uribe & Harbeck, 1991). In 1993, **MASSACHUSETTS** became the first state to adopt an educational policy prohibiting discrimination against gay and lesbian students and teachers. At many high schools today, LGBTQ students have created school-sanctioned student organizations that give students a safe place to discuss sexual orientation issues.

In 2003, about 100 students enrolled in the Harvey Milk School, the nation's first public high school for gay, lesbian, bisexual, and transgender students. Housed in an office building in New York City, the school is named after California's first elected gay official—a member of the board of supervisors in San Francisco—who was assassinated after less than a year in office. New York City also cosponsors after-school programs, such as art and music, and counseling and support services for as many as 2,000 gay and lesbian students (Ferguson, 2003).

Homosexual students can experience school-related problems and safety risks. The hostility that gay, lesbian, and bisexual youth can encounter may cause them to feel confused, isolated, and self-destructive. This reality came to the nation's attention during fall 2010 when several homosexual students committed suicide as a result of school-based bullying they experienced. Teachers and other school personnel can provide much-needed support. Informed, sensitive, and caring teachers can play an important role in helping all students develop to their full potential. Such teachers realize the importance of recognizing diverse perspectives, and they create inclusive classroom environments that encourage students to respect differences among themselves and others and to see the contributions that persons from all groups have made to society.

Education and African Americans

Of the more than 325.7 million persons living in the United States, approximately 45.8 million are African Americans (U.S. Census Bureau, 2018). According to U.S. Census Bureau projections, the African American population is expected to increase to 59.7 million (14.3 percent of the total) in 2060. The struggle of African Americans to improve their quality of life after the end of slavery has been hampered for generations by persistent racism, discrimination, poverty, crime, unemployment, and underemployment. Subsequently, the incidence of social problems such as unemployment, crime, drug abuse, poverty, inadequate housing, and dropping out of school is proportionally greater for African Americans than for Whites.

The civil rights movement of the 1960s and 1970s made it clear that African Americans had been denied full access to many aspects of U.S. life, including the right to a good education. A 1976 report by the United States Commission on Civil Rights, for example, revealed that a Southern school district in the 1930s spent nearly 18 times as much for the education of White pupils as it did for the education of African Americans.

THE DESEGREGATION ERA Perhaps the most blatant form of discrimination against African Americans has been school segregation and unequal educational opportunity. Prior to the 1950s, an attempt was made to justify segregation with the idea of separate but equal schools. It was not until the National Association for the Advancement of Colored People (NAACP) brought suit on behalf of a Kansas family (*Brown v. Board of Education of Topeka, Kansas*) in 1954 that the concept of separate but equal schools was decidedly struck down.

The parents of Linda Brown felt that the education their fourth grader was receiving in the segregated Topeka schools was inferior. When their request that she be transferred to a White school was turned down, they filed suit. In a landmark decision, the U.S. Supreme Court ruled that segregated schools are "inherently unequal" and violate the equal protection clause of the Fourteenth Amendment. U.S. citizens, the justices asserted, have a right to receive an equal opportunity for education.

As a result of opportunities created during the civil rights movement, a substantial number of African Americans are now members of the middle class. Affirmative action programs have enabled many African Americans to attain high-ranking positions in the business, medical, legal, and educational professions. For example, there were 55,770 African American physicians and surgeons, 76,799 postsecondary teachers, 64,524 lawyers, and 48,090 chief executives in the United States during 2014 (U.S. Bureau of Labor Statistics, 2015). And in 2014, Census Bureau data included the following:

- Of African Americans 25 and older, 1.6 million held advanced degrees (i.e., master's, doctorate, medical, or law); in 1996, 683,000 African Americans had this level of education.
- In the fall of 2012, 3.7 million African Americans attended college, a 28 percent increase over the 2.9 million who attended college in 2007. (U.S. Census Bureau, 2014)

RESEGREGATION OF SCHOOLS IN THE UNITED STATES As the United States continues to become more ethnically and racially diverse, there is evidence that schools are resegregating (Orfield & Yun, 1999; Orfield & Ee, 2017). For example, studies by Harvard University and the University of California include the following findings:

- As African Americans and Latinos move to the suburbs, they are attending segregated schools, especially in urban areas.

- States with a high proportion of African American students made progress toward desegregation in the 1970s; however, all have shown increases in school segregation since the 1990s.
- Segregated schools, with the exception of those for White students, tend to have a high concentration of poverty, which has a negative influence on student achievement.

More specifically, a U.S. Government Accountability Office (GAO) report found that the percentage of K–12 public schools with 75 to 100 percent Black or Hispanic student enrollments increased from 9 to 16 percent between 2001 and 2014 (Government Accountability Office, 2016). In addition, the GAO analysis found that, compared with other schools, these schools offered disproportionately fewer math, science, and college preparatory courses and had disproportionately higher rates of students who were held back in ninth grade, suspended, or expelled.

One reason for the trend back to resegregation has been Supreme Court rulings that removed judicial supervision of school districts' efforts to desegregate—for example, *Board of Education of Oklahoma City Public Schools v. Dowell* (1991), *Freeman v. Pitts* (1992), and *Brown v. Unified School District No. 501* (1999). In addition, the Supreme Court ruled in *Missouri v. Jenkins* (1995) that Kansas City schools did not have to maintain desegregation through a magnet school approach until actual benefits for African American students were shown. Such rulings by the Supreme Court prompted the filing of many lawsuits to end desegregation in several large school districts.

ADDRESSING THE LEARNING NEEDS OF AFRICAN AMERICAN STUDENTS Research on factors related to students' success in school suggests that schools are monoethnic and do not take into account the diverse needs of ethnic minority-group students (Banks, 2009; Bennett, 2015). In the case of African American students, the failure of the school curriculum to address their learning needs may contribute to high dropout rates and below-average achievement.

To address the educational inequities that African American and other minority-group students may experience as a result of segregation, many communities have tried to create more ethnically and racially diverse classrooms through the controversial practice of busing students to attend schools in other neighborhoods. Also, some African Americans have recently begun to call for **Afrocentric schools**—schools that focus on African American history and cultures for African American pupils. Proponents believe that the educational needs of African American students can be met more effectively in schools that offer Afrocentric curricula and build on the strengths of the African American community.

Private Afrocentric schools, or Black academies, have sprung up across the country in recent years, many supported by the growing number of African Americans who practice Islam. Curricula in these schools emphasize the people and cultures of Africa and the history and achievements of African Americans. Teaching methods are often designed for culture-based learning styles, such as choral response, learning through movement, and sociability. One Afrocentric school is the Betty Shabazz International Charter School (Shabazz School) in Chicago, **ILLINOIS**. Shabazz School is comprised of three Chicago campuses: Betty Shabazz Academy (grades K–8), Barbara A. Sizemore Academy (grades K–8), and the DuSable Leadership Academy (grades 9–12), located at the former DuSable High School where the author taught for eight years. Students at the school, the majority of whom are from families in poverty, have higher scores on state tests and higher college acceptance rates than students at other schools in the district (Ahmed-Ullah, 2013). The Shabazz School curriculum instills pride and a community-like spirit in students as they learn how African culture has influenced countries around the world. Teaching methods and displays throughout the school emphasize African history, values, languages, arts, traditions, and ceremonies (Betty Shabazz International Charter School, 2014).

Another Afrocentric school, the Young Geniuses Academy in Seattle, **WASHINGTON**, is collaborating with the Africatown Center for Education and Innovation to deliver programs that develop children's talents in science, technology, engineering, and mathematics (STEM). Students at the Academy experience a culturally relevant curriculum that introduces students to the contributions African people have made in STEM fields and the arts (Africatown Center for Education and Innovation, 2014).

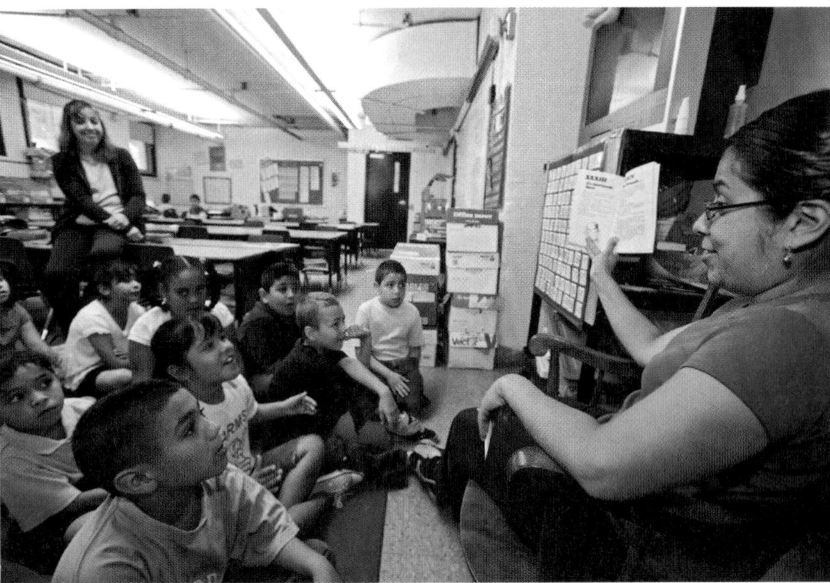

Jim West/Alamy Stock Photo

What effects has the growing Hispanic population in the U.S. had on schools both throughout the country as well as in some states in particular? Why might some Hispanic Americans prefer assimilation over bilingual education for their children?

Education and Latino and Hispanic Americans

Hispanic Americans, people whose ancestors were Spanish speaking, are the fastest growing minority group in the United States. This group accounts for about 17 percent of the nation's population, and it has been estimated that an additional 5 million illegal aliens who speak Spanish may be in the country. By 2060, the Hispanic population is expected to more than double, from 55.4 million in 2014 to 119.0 million in 2060. Consequently, by the end of the period, nearly one in three U.S. residents would be Hispanic, up from about one in six today (U.S. Census Bureau, 2015). Included in the category of Hispanic Americans are people who call themselves Latinos (people whose ancestors are from Latin America) and Chicanos (people whose ancestors are from Mexico).

Seven states have populations that are more than 20 percent Hispanic: **NEW MEXICO, CALIFORNIA**, **TEXAS**, **ARIZONA, NEVADA, FLORIDA**, and **COLORADO** (Pew Research Center, 2016, September 8). Many states have passed English-only laws and made efforts to restrict Hispanic immigrants' access to education. Prior to 1983, six states had English-language laws; however, efforts by political action groups such as U.S. English, founded by the late Senator S.I. Hayakawa of California in 1983, and ProEnglish were instrumental in getting English-only laws passed in 31 states by 2017 (ProEnglish, 2017). U.S. English and ProEnglish have lobbied periodically the U.S. Congress to pass legislation to make English the official language of the United States. Most recently, the English Language Unity Act of 2017 was introduced to the House of Representatives.

SOCIOECONOMIC FACTORS Although some Spanish-speaking immigrants come to the United States hoping to escape a life of poverty in their home country, many others come because they have relatives in the United States or they wish to take advantage of business opportunities in this country. For those Spanish-speaking immigrants who lack job skills and have little education, however, adjusting to the complexities and demands of life in the United States may be difficult.

Socioeconomic factors affect the education of some Hispanics, such as the children of migrant farm workers. Among the estimated 1 million or so migrant farm workers in this country, more than 70 percent are Spanish speaking. The dropout rate among all migrant workers is 90 percent, and 50 percent leave school before finishing the ninth grade (Bennett, 2015). Migrant children are handicapped by the language barrier, deprivation resulting from poverty, and irregular school attendance. Some states have educational intervention programs in place for reaching this group.

ADDRESSING THE LEARNING NEEDS OF SPANISH-SPEAKING STUDENTS What can easily happen to Spanish-speaking learners if they are taught by teachers who are not sensitive to their learning needs is illustrated in Christine I. Bennett's (2015) portrait of Jesús, an ELL student:

> Jesús Martinez was a bright, fine-looking six-year-old when he migrated with his family from Puerto Rico to New York City. At a time when he was ready to learn to read and write his mother tongue, Jesús was instead suddenly thrust into an English-only classroom where the only tool he possessed for oral communication (the Spanish language) was completely useless to him. Jesús and his teacher could not communicate with each other because each spoke a different language, and neither spoke the language of the other. Jesús felt stupid, or retarded; his teacher perceived him to be culturally disadvantaged and beyond her help. However, she and the school officials agreed to allow him to "sit there" because the law required that he be in school. (p. 6)

Bennett (2003) also captures well the dilemma that many Spanish-speaking ELL students find themselves in: "Students with limited English proficiency are often caught up in conflicts between personal language needs—for example, the need to consolidate cognitive skills in the native language—and a sociopolitical climate that views standard English as most desirable and prestigious" (p. 271).

The degree to which students from Spanish-speaking backgrounds are motivated to learn English varies from group to group. Mexican American students who live in the Southwest may retain the Spanish language to maintain ties with family and friends in Mexico. Recently arrived Cubans, on the other hand, may have a stronger motivation to learn the language of their new country. In regard to what they wish to learn, children take their cues from the adults around them. If their parents or guardians, friends, and relatives have learned English and are bilingual, then they will be similarly motivated. Many Hispanic Americans who value assimilation over their traditional culture favor English-only education.

However, the limited English proficiencies of many children raised in native Spanish-speaking families contribute significantly to the difficulties they have in school. To address the needs of these students, federally funded structured English immersion (SEI) programs encourage teachers to view bicultural knowledge as a bridge to the school's curriculum. English as a second language (ESL) programs are examined in detail later in this chapter.

Education and Asian Americans and Pacific Islanders

Asian Americans and Pacific Islanders, the fastest growing racial group in the U.S., represent about 6.8 percent, or 21.4 million, of the total population (U.S. Census Bureau, March 2015). The U.S. Census Bureau estimates that the Asian and Pacific Islander population in the United States will increase to 51.5 million (12.4 percent of the total) in 2060 (U.S. Census Bureau, 2015).

This group, comprising at least 34 ethnic groups speaking more than 300 languages and dialects (Asian Americans/Pacific Islanders in Philanthropy, 1997), is tremendously diverse and includes people from South Asia, primarily Bangladesh, India, and Pakistan; Southeast Asia, including Indochina (Laos, Thailand, Indonesia, Malaysia, and Vietnam) and the Philippines; East Asia, including China, Hong Kong, Japan, Korea, and Taiwan; and the Pacific Islands, including Hawaii, Guam, and Samoa. About half of the total Asian American and Pacific Islander population lives in the western United States (U.S. Census Bureau, 2015).

HISTORICAL, CULTURAL, AND SOCIOECONOMIC FACTORS The six largest Asian American groups in 2016 were Chinese (4.95 million), Indian (3.98 million), Filipinos (3.89 million), Vietnamese (1.98 million), Koreans (1.82 million), and Japanese

(1.41 million) (U.S. Census Bureau, 2016). Although these groups differ significantly, each "came to the United States seeking the American dream, satisfied important labor needs, and became victims of an anti-Asian movement designed to prevent their further immigration to the United States. [They] also experienced tremendous economic, educational, and social mobility and success in U.S. society" (Banks, 2009, p. 398).

The California gold rush of 1849 brought the first immigrants from Asia—Chinese men who worked in mines, on railroads, and on farms, and who planned to return to their families and homeland. Early Chinese immigrants encountered widespread discrimination in their new country, with anti-Chinese riots occurring in San Francisco, Los Angeles, and Denver between 1869 and 1880. In 1882, Congress passed the Immigration Act, which ended Chinese immigration until 1902. The Chinese were oriented toward maintaining their traditional language and religion and established tight-knit urban communities, or Chinatowns. Recently, many upwardly mobile, professional Chinese Americans have been assimilated into suburban communities, while newly arrived, working-class immigrants from China and Hong Kong are settling in redeveloped Chinatowns.

Japanese immigrants began to arrive in Hawaii and the U.S. mainland in the late 1800s; most worked in agriculture, fisheries, the railroads, or industry and assimilated rapidly despite racial discrimination. The San Francisco Board of Education, for example, began to segregate all Japanese students in 1906, and the Immigration Act of 1924 ended Japanese immigration until 1952. During World War II, the United States was at war with Japan. In response to war hysteria over the "yellow peril," the U.S. government interned 110,000 Japanese Americans, most of them American born, in 10 detention camps from 1942 to 1946. Since World War II, Japan has developed into one of the world's leading economic and technological powers—an accomplishment that has contributed, no doubt, to a recent decline in Japanese immigration to the United States.

Filipinos began to immigrate to Hawaii and the mainland as field laborers during the 1920s. They, too, encountered racism; in 1934, Congress passed the Tydings-McDuffie Act, which limited Filipino immigration to the United States to 50 persons annually. The following year, President Franklin Roosevelt signed the Repatriation Act, which provided free transportation to Filipinos willing to return to the Philippines. Whereas most early Filipino immigrants had little education and low income, recent immigrants have tended to be professional, technical workers who hope to obtain employment in the United States more suitable for their education and training than they could in the Philippines (Banks, 2009).

ADDRESSING THE LEARNING NEEDS OF ASIAN AMERICAN STUDENTS Asian Americans are frequently stereotyped as hard-working, conscientious, and respectful of authority, what many people view as a so-called "model minority." In fact, 51 percent of Asian Americans aged 25 years and over have a bachelor's degree or more, compared to 30 percent for all Americans 25 and older (Pew Research Center, 2017, September 8). The unreliability of such stereotypes notwithstanding, Asian American parents do tend to require their children to respect authority and value education. However, the model-minority view overlooks the economic, racial, cultural, and linguistic diversity among Asian Americans. Moreover, "[i]t hides the fact that a substantial number of Asian Americans live in poverty [and] causes Asian immigrants and Asian Americans to feel pressure to be super human, exceptional students and career people" (Bennett, 2015, p. 259).

Families may pressure children to be successful academically through sacrifice and hard work. At the same time, there has been an increase in the number of Asian American youth who are in conflict with their parents' way of life. Leaders in Asian American communities have expressed concern about increases in dropout rates, school violence, and declining achievement. Some Indochinese Americans, for example, face deep cultural conflict in schools. Values and practices that are accepted in U.S. culture, such as dating and glorification of the individual, can be sources of conflict between many Indochinese students and their parents (Fong, 2007).

Teachers need to be sensitive to cultural conflicts that may contribute to problems in school adjustment and achievement for Asian American students and realize that:

> [s]tereotypes about Asian "whiz kids" and jealousy over the relatively high percentages of Asian Americans in the nation's colleges and universities may blind some non-Asian parents, fellow students, and teachers to the deep cultural conflict many Southeast Asian Americans face in our schools. (Bennett, 2015, p. 258)

To help Asian American students adjust to the U.S. culture, Qiu Liang offers teachers the following advice based on his school experiences as a Chinese immigrant:

> They [teachers] should be more patient [with an immigrant child] because it is very difficult for a person to be in a new country and learn a new language. Have patience. If the teacher feels there is no hope in an immigrant child, then the child will think, "Well, if the teacher who's helping me thinks that I can't go anywhere, then I might as well give up myself." (Igoa, 1995, pp. 99–100)

Similarly, Dung Yoong offers these recommendations based on her educational experiences as a Vietnamese immigrant:

> Try to get them to talk to you. Not just everyday conversation, but what they feel inside. Try to get them to get that out, because it's hard for kids. They don't trust—I had a hard time trusting and I was really insecure because of that.
>
> [P]utting an immigrant child who doesn't speak English into a classroom, a regular classroom with American students, is not very good. It scares [them] because it is so different. [Teachers] should start [them] slowly and have special classes where the child could adapt and learn a little bit about American society and customs. (Igoa, 1995, p. 103)

Education and Native Americans and Alaskan Natives

Native Americans and Alaskan Natives peopled the Western Hemisphere more than 12,000 years ago. They represent about 2 percent of the total U.S. population, or about 6.6 million people. The Native American and Alaska Native population is expected to increase to 10.2 million, or 2.4 percent of the population, by 2060 (U.S. Census Bureau, 2016, November 2).

This group consists of 567 federally recognized and 365 state-recognized tribes, each with its own language, religious beliefs, and way of life. The six largest federally recognized tribes are the Navajo Nation, with over 308,000 members enrolled in the tribe; the Cherokee Nation, 285,000; the Sioux Nation, 131,000; the Chippewa Nation, 115,000; the Choctaw Nation, 89,000; and the Apache Nation, 65,000 (U.S. Census Bureau, 2010).

More than one-half million Native Americans live on 275 reservations located primarily in the West. In rank order, the five states with the largest proportion of Native Americans and Alaskan Natives are **ALASKA** (19.5 percent), **OKLAHOMA** (13.6 percent), **NEW MEXICO** (11.8 percent), **SOUTH DAKOTA** (10.3 percent), and **MONTANA** (8.3 percent) (U.S. Census Bureau, 2016, November 2). Although most Native Americans live in cities, many are establishing connections with reservation Native Americans as a means of strengthening their cultural identities.

Native Americans are an example of the increasing ambiguity of racial and ethnic identities in the United States. For example, controversy exists over who is Native American. "Some full-blooded native people do not regard a person with one-quarter native heritage as qualifying, while others accept 1/128" (Bennett, 2015, p. 184). Whereas most Native Americans consider a person with one-quarter or more tribal heritage to be a member, the U.S. Census Bureau considers anyone who claims native identity to be a member. An expert on Native Americans and Alaskan Natives, Arlene Hirschfelder (1986), points out that 52 legal definitions of Native Americans have been identified. Native Americans were declared U.S. citizens in 1924, and Native

American nations have been recognized as independent, self-governing territories since the 1930s.

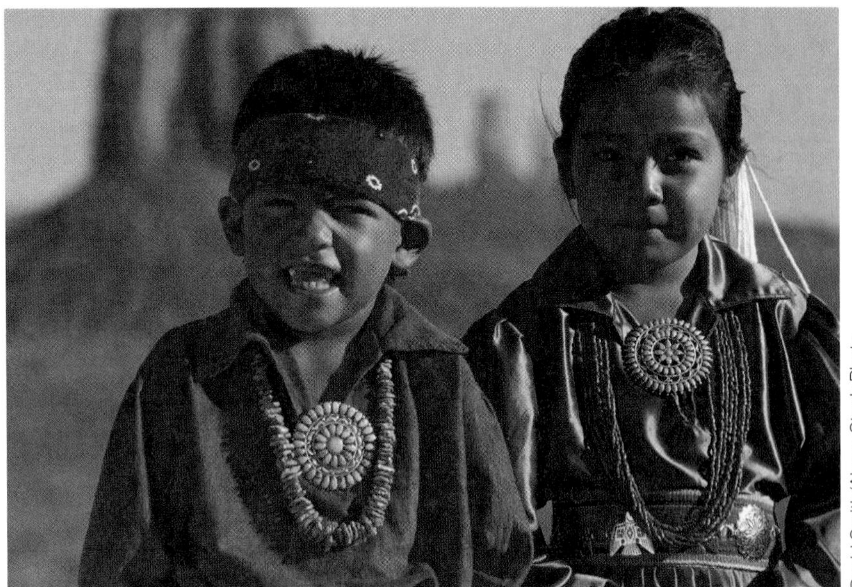
David Smith/Alamy Stock Photo

What factors contribute to below-average achievement levels of Native American children? How do forces toward assimilation and cultural preservation coexist in the Native American experience?

HISTORICAL, CULTURAL, AND SOCIOECONOMIC FACTORS Perhaps more than any other minority group, Native Americans have endured systematic long-term attempts to eradicate their languages and cultures. Disease, genocide, confinement on reservations, and decades of forced assimilation have devastated Native American cultures. A member of the Muscogee (Creek) Nation explains the impact of these forces on the education of Native Americans:

> For centuries, American Indian, Alaska Native, and Native Hawaiian families and communities have exercised their sovereign rights to educate their children according to their own values, goals, and circumstances. Sovereign self-education *by* Native communities has for much of the past 5 centuries been at odds with, forcibly suppressed by, or actively criminalized by colonial systems of schooling that provided an education for American Indians dedicated to "erasing and replacing" assimilationist policies and practices. (Lomawaima, 2012, p. 104)

It was not until 2000 that the U.S. government officially apologized for the Bureau of Indian Affairs' "legacy of racism and inhumanity that included massacres, forced relocation of tribes and attempts to wipe out Indian languages and cultures" (Kelly, 2000, p. 1).

In 1492, Native American people used 2 billion acres of land; currently, they own about 94 million acres of land, or about 5 percent of U.S. territory (Bennett, 2015). Today, the rates of unemployment, poverty, and lack of educational attainment among Native Americans are among the nation's highest. Since the 1970s, however, there has been a resurgence of interest in preserving or restoring traditional languages, skills, and land claims.

There are hundreds of Native American languages, which anthropologists have attempted to categorize into six major language families (Banks, 2014). Older tribal members fluent in the original tribal language and younger members often speak a form of so-called reservation English. The challenge of educating Native Americans from diverse language backgrounds is further complicated by the difference in size of various Native American populations. These range from the more than 285,000 people enrolled in the federally recognized Cherokee Nation to the 650 or so Havasupai of **ARIZONA**. As a result of the extreme diversity among Native Americans, it has even been suggested that "There is no such thing as an 'Indian' heritage, culture, or value system. [N]avajo, Cherokee, Sioux, and Aleut children are as different from each other in geographic and cultural backgrounds as they are from children growing up in New York City or Los Angeles" (Gipp, 1979, p. 19).

Education for Native American children living on reservations is currently administered by the federal government's Bureau of Indian Affairs (BIA). The **Indian Education Act of 1972 and 19°74 Amendments** supplement the BIA's educational programs and provide direct educational assistance to tribes. The act seeks to improve Native American education by providing funds to school districts to meet the special needs of Native American youth, to Indian tribes and state and local education agencies to improve education for youth and adults, to colleges and universities for the purpose of training teachers for Indian schools, and to Native American students to attend college.

ADDRESSING THE LEARNING NEEDS OF NATIVE AMERICANS AND ALASKAN NATIVES Considerable debate has occurred over the best approaches for educating Native Americans and Alaskan Natives. For example, Banks (2016) points out that "since the 1920s, educational policy for Native Americans has vacillated between strong assimilationism to self-determination and cultural pluralism" (p. 45). The number of Native American and Alaskan Native students who leave school before completion remains high. Their dropout rate is 12.5 percent, almost twice the rate of all groups combined (McFarland et. al., 2017, p. 221).

Increasingly, Native Americans and Alaskan Natives are designing multicultural programs to preserve their traditional cultures and ways of knowing. Although these programs are sometimes characterized as emphasizing separatism over assimilation, for many Native Americans and Alaskan Natives they are a matter of survival. For example, the Native American Community Academy in Albuquerque, **NEW MEXICO**, was created to preserve the languages and cultures of 37 different tribes. The school offers classes in the Navajo and Lakota languages and a high school class in Dine (Navaho) government (Native American Community Academy, 2018).

Cultural preservation is also the primary concern at Alaskan Native schools in remote parts of western **ALASKA**. At the Alaska Native Cultural Charter School, for example, elders come into the classroom to teach children how to skin a seal, an education that few Alaskan Native children receive today at home. The school also organizes occasional field trips to the Anchorage Museum. At the museum, students are able to work with artists who show them moose hide tanning, sewing in the Dene tribal way, and traditional drum making (Alaska Native Cultural Charter School, 2018).

FOCUS ON **STEM**: INTEGRATING TRIBAL KNOWLEDGE WITH STEM

Washington State University (WSU) received a four-year, $2.5 million grant in 2017 from the National Science Foundation (NSF) to increase Native American students' learning in STEM. The project is called ISTEM, since it focuses on Indigenous STEM learning. Five WSU faculty members will coordinate the project with three Pacific Northwest Plateau Tribes: the Warm Springs Tribe, the Colville Tribe, and the Coeur D'Alene Tribe.

More than 500 Native American students in grades 4–9 will participate in ISTEM learning opportunities at their respective tribal schools during the academic year. In addition, approximately 80 middle school students will participate annually in enrichment programs on the WSU campus, including field trips during the academic year and residential ISTEM summer camps.

The project will integrate tribal knowledge with STEM. As the Project Director points out: "ISTEM is more than just implementing technology, it's a philosophy that approaches teaching, learning, and assessment from Indigenous knowledge systems. That means we entwine tribal knowledge with Western science by utilizing existing Indigenous knowledge systems, land education, and digital tools to connect their culture, language, and land with science" (Chapman, 2017).

Since many teachers at tribal schools are not tribal members, the ISTEM project will include professional development for teachers to become more effective teachers of Native American students.

How are Schools Meeting the Needs of English Language Learners (ELLs)?

Various types of **English as a second language (ESL)** programs meet the needs of **English language learners (ELLs)**. Bilingual education programs provide instruction in English and a student's native language. Other programs immerse English language learners in English-only classrooms. Still other programs provide a bridge between the two programs. Regardless of the instructional approach used, the goal is for ELL students to become proficient in English. Students are also encouraged to become **bicultural**, that is, able to function effectively in two or more linguistic and cultural groups.

In 1968, Congress passed the Bilingual Education Act, which required that language-minority students be taught in both their native language and English. In response to the act, school districts implemented an array of **bilingual education programs** that varied greatly in quality and effectiveness. As a result, many parents filed lawsuits, claiming that bilingual programs were not meeting their children's needs.

In 1974, the Supreme Court heard a class action suit (*Lau v. Nichols*) filed by 1,800 Chinese students in San Francisco who charged that they were failing to learn because they could not understand English. The students were enrolled in all-English classes and received no special assistance in learning English. In a unanimous ruling, the Court asserted that federally funded schools must "rectify the language deficiency" of students who "are certain to find their classroom experiences wholly incomprehensible." That same year, Congress adopted the Equal Educational Opportunity Act (EEOA), which stated in part that a school district must "take appropriate action to overcome language barriers that impede equal participation by its students in its instructional programs."

The Every Student Succeeds Act (ESSA) passed in 2015 states that ELLs are to become proficient in English and meet state-mandated standards for English proficiency. ESSA requires that all schools demonstrate that they are improving the English language proficiency of ELLs. In addition, improving English language proficiency is a required indicator in the school accountability system that each state must develop.

Although most ESL programs serve Latino and Hispanic American students, there is an increasing need for ESL teachers who are proficient in a variety of second languages. In fact, many school districts are offering salary bonuses for ESL teachers.

ESL programs are tremendously varied. There is no single "right" method for teaching ELL students. For example, four types of bilingual programs are currently available to provide special assistance to the 4.6 million ELL students in the United States (see Figure 8.8).

Figure 8.8 Four types of bilingual education programs

Immersion programs: Students learn English and other subjects in classrooms where only English is spoken. Aides who speak the first language of students are sometimes available, or students may also listen to equivalent audiotape lessons in their first language.

Transition programs: Students receive reading lessons in their first language and lessons in English as a second language (ESL). Once they sufficiently master English, students are placed in classrooms where English is spoken and their first language is discontinued.

Pullout programs: On a regular basis, students are separated from English-speaking students so that they may receive lessons in English or reading lessons in their first language. These are sometimes called sheltered English programs.

Maintenance programs: To maintain the student's native language and culture, instruction in English and instruction in the native language are provided from kindergarten through 12th grade. Students become literate in both languages.

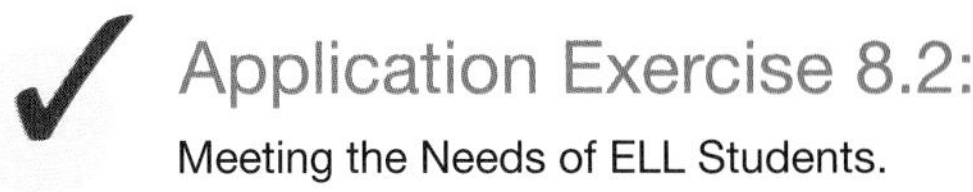

Application Exercise 8.2:
Meeting the Needs of ELL Students.

Research and Debate on Teaching ELL Students

Research on strategies for teaching ELL students is inconclusive (Bennett, 2015; Gollnick & Chinn, 2009). For example, some who have examined the research on bilingual programs conclude that they have little effect on achievement (American Institutes of Research, 2003; Hakuta, 2001a, 2001b). In fact, the U.S. Supreme Court ruled in *Horne v. Flores* (2009) that "[r]esearch on ELL instruction indicates there is documented, academic support for the view that SEI (Structured English Immersion) is significantly more effective than bilingual education." Others have found that well-designed bilingual programs do increase students' achievement and are superior to monolingual programs (Crawford, 2004, 2007; Krashen & McField, 2005; Nieto, 2002).

Considerable debate surrounds bilingual programs in the United States. Those in favor of bilingual education make the following points:

- Students are better able to learn English if they are taught to read and write in their native language.
- Bilingual programs allow students to learn content in their native language rather than delaying that learning until they master English.
- Further developing competencies in students' native languages provides important cognitive foundations for learning English and academic content.
- Second-language learning is a positive value and should be as valid for a Spanish speaker learning English as for an English speaker learning Spanish.
- Bilingual programs support students' cultural identity, social context, and self-esteem.

Video Example 8.2

Maintaining a Child's Native Language: This teacher shares her philosophy of how she feels a maintenance program approach to teaching ELL students is the best way to teach ELL students.

On the other hand, those opposed to bilingual programs make the following points:

- Public schools should not be expected to provide instruction in all the first languages spoken by their students, nor can schools afford to pay a teacher who might teach only a few students.
- The cost of bilingual education is high. Bilingual programs divert staff and resources away from English-speaking students.
- If students spend more time exposed to English, they will learn English more quickly.
- Bilingual programs emphasize differences among and barriers between groups; they encourage separateness rather than assimilation and unity.
- Bilingual education is a threat to English as the nation's first language.

Advice for Monolingual Teachers

While the debate about ESL programs in the U.S. continues, today's teachers must meet the needs of a growing population of English language learners. These needs are best met by teachers who speak their native language as well as English (Snipes, Soga, & Uro, 2007). This is often not possible, however, and monolingual teachers will find increasing numbers of ELL students in their classrooms. The following classroom strategies are useful for both monolingual and bilingual teachers:

- Be aware of each student's language abilities.
- Make sure appropriate cultural experiences are reflected in the material.
- Document the success of selected materials.
- Experiment with the materials until you find the most appropriate for your particular student.
- Make a smooth transition into the new material.
- Be sure to become knowledgeable about the cultures and heritages of your students to ensure appropriateness and compatibility of the material. (Ariza, 2006, pp. 110–111)

Additional tips for adapting material for ELL students are:

- Develop your own supplemental materials.
- Tape-record directions for the material so students can replay them for clarity.
- Provide alternatives to responding verbally to questions (e.g., use prearranged signals—give students a card to hold up, a flag, or any indicator they can use instead of speaking).
- Rewrite sections of the text to condense the reading for those with lower proficiency levels.
- Outline the material for the students before they read.
- Teach students the meaning of using bold headings, italicized words, subheadings, and transition words (*first, last, however, although,* etc.).
- Reduce the number of pages or items to be completed by the student.
- Break tasks into smaller subtasks.
- Substitute a similar, less complex task.
- Develop study guides for all students. (Ariza, 2006, p. 110)

The Technology in Action feature in this chapter profiles a teacher who uses text-to-speech software to provide individual instruction for her ELL students.

TECHNOLOGY in ACTION

Using Text-to-Speech in a Third-Grade Reading Class

Mrs. Kelly teaches ELL students at Wilson Elementary. Although she understands the importance of one-on-one instruction, she has found that the varied English proficiency of her students makes it difficult to work with individual students for any extended period of time. She prefers to work with students individually, helping them pronounce words, reading along with them, and helping when they encounter words they do not understand. The problem with this approach is the time it requires—there are only so many hours in a day.

Mrs. Kelly knows it is important for her ELL students to hear the words they are reading. Often, she stands at the front of her classroom and reads to students as they follow along in their books. The problem with this approach is that each student has a different level of English proficiency. If students speak up when they have difficulty (which is rare due to the large class size), she finds that the more proficient speakers are impatient as she helps a student who is having difficulty.

To solve this problem, Mrs. Kelly decides to introduce a text-to-speech (TTS) program in her class. (TTS uses a synthesized computer voice to read text on a computer screen or in an electronic file). Students now sit at the computer and read along with the TTS program as it highlights the text that is being spoken. With this program, students can select an appealing voice: male or female, older or younger, softer or more authoritative.

Mrs. Kelly finds that the text-to-speech program provides the individual instruction that her students need. It has improved their reading ability, vocabulary retention, and pronunciation. For example, when she listens to her students read, she identifies words that are difficult for a particular student to pronounce, and she writes a list of these words for each student. The student then plugs those words into the TTS program and listens to the correct pronunciation of the words. Each student can listen to a word as many times as needed. Her students see the TTS program as a second teacher and now identify difficult pronunciations before they read for Mrs. Kelly.

Text-to-speech programs convert electronic text to digital audio. The TTS program reads the text and then speaks the words for the listener. There are two approaches for converting text to speech. The first is user-directed, the other author-directed. The user-directed application requires that the user of TTS identify the text to be converted. This can be done by highlighting the identified text or uploading an electronic file of the text to the TTS program. The author-directed application requires the author of the website, video game, or text file to identify the text to be spoken. Several text-to-speech programs are available today. The most popular programs use a realistic human voice.

(continued)

Teachers have used text-to-speech programs to proofread student writing, listen to term papers on their iPod during their commute to and from work, help students with reading or vision difficulties, create e-books for their students, and improve instruction for ELL students.

VISIT: Most TTS software products have demonstrations at their websites, and some allow users to download a free version of TTS software and to view an applications demonstration. There are also text-to-speech options in the Ease of Use settings for Windows and System Preferences on Mac that are included with the operating systems.

As they help ELL students become fluent in English, teachers should keep in mind the difference between *language learning* and *language acquisition*. The goal is to help ELL students *acquire* English, not necessarily just *learn* it. Language acquisition is a natural process. With few exceptions, each of us *acquired* our first language rather than *learned* it as a result of having been taught formally. The authors of *50 Strategies for Teaching English Language Learners* further explain how ELL students benefit from an emphasis on language acquisition:

> When a learner is placed in a stressful situation in which language production or performance is demanded, the student's ability to learn or produce spoken language may be impaired . . . . Language acquisition is gradual, based on receiving and understanding messages, building a listening (receptive) vocabulary, and slowly attempting verbal production of the language in a highly supportive, nonstressful setting. It is exactly these same conditions that foster the acquisition of a second language. (Herrell & Jordan, 2016, p. 2)

The authors of *50 Strategies* also suggest the following five general strategies for teaching ELL students:

1. Teachers should provide instruction in a way that ensures students are given *comprehensible input* (material presented in a manner that leads to a student's understanding of the content, i.e., visual, manipulative, scaffolded in the child's first language, etc.).
2. Teachers should provide opportunities to increase verbal interaction in classroom activities.
3. Teachers should provide instruction that contextualizes language as much as possible.
4. Teachers should use teaching strategies and grouping techniques that reduce the anxiety of students as much as possible.
5. Teachers should provide activities in the classroom that offer opportunities for active involvement of the students (Herrell & Jordan, 2016, p. 10).

Additionally, you should be aware that "[a]lthough second language learners often present challenges within the classroom, they may also bring a number of advantages" (Adesope, Lavin, Thompson, & Ungerleider, 2010, p. 231). In an analysis of 63 research studies (including more than 6,000 participants) of the cognitive outcomes associated with bilingualism, Olusola Adesope and his colleagues (2010) found that people who are bilingual tend to have several cognitive "advantages" over monolingual people. Among these advantages are:

Video Example 8.3

Teaching ELL Students How to Provide More Detail: Observe how this teacher uses a graphic organizer to help a small group of ELL students add details to a sentence.

- Greater metacognitive awareness (knowledge about one's own cognitive processes and ability to self-regulate learning strategies)
- Greater cognitive flexibility and creativity
- Enhanced skills for divergent thinking and abstract and symbolic reasoning
- Enhanced problem-solving skills
- Greater efficiency of working memory
- Enhanced ability to control attention while engaged in linguistic and nonverbal tasks

✓ Check Your Understanding 8.3

What is Multicultural Education and Culturally Responsive Teaching?

Multiculturalism stresses the importance of seeing the world from different cultural frames of reference, and recognizing and valuing the rich array of cultures within a nation and within the global community. **Multiculturalism** affirms the need to create schools where differences related to race, ethnicity, gender, sexual orientation, exceptionality, and social class are acknowledged and all students are viewed as valuable resources for enriching the teaching–learning process. Furthermore, a central purpose of multiculturalism is to prepare students to live in a culturally pluralistic world.

For teachers, multiculturalism also means actively seeking out experiences within other cultures that lead to increased understanding of and appreciation for those ways of life. To provide such cross-cultural experiences for their students, some teacher education programs have developed cultural immersion experiences that enable prospective teachers to live in their students' neighborhoods and communities while student teaching. The University of Alaska–Fairbanks Future Teachers of **ALASKA** Program, for example, enables students to live in remote Alaskan Native villages during their yearlong student teaching experience. Students at **INDIANA** University can participate in the Global Gateway for Teachers program that includes the Navajo Nation Program, the Overseas Program, and the Urban Program. These projects provide experiences for student teachers on the Navajo Indian Reservation, the nation's largest reservation, located in northeastern **ARIZONA**, southeastern **UTAH**, and northwestern **NEW MEXICO**; in 18 different countries; and in inner-city Chicago. Through student teaching on a reservation, in another country, or on the Rio Grande border, students have a life-altering cultural immersion experience, as the following comment by a Navajo Nation Program participant illustrates:

> My cultural experiences on the Navajo Reservation are ever-present in my life. When I share my experiences with others, I feel as though I am giving a gift. Not only do I reflect on my own experiences, but I use such opportunities to educate others about Navajo culture. I recently received a letter from a student who is beginning Fort Lewis College this fall. My heart melted and I can't help but think I had some small influence in her educational success. The project has affected my life in ways I am only beginning to comprehend.

Multicultural education is committed to the goal of providing all students with equal opportunities to learn in school. Multicultural education is also based on the fact that students do not learn in a vacuum—their culture predisposes them to learn in certain ways. And finally, multicultural education recognizes that current school practices have provided—and continue to provide—some students with greater opportunities for learning than students who belong to other groups. The suggestions presented in the preceding section are examples of multicultural education in practice.

As multiculturalism has become more pervasive in U.S. schools, controversy over the need for multicultural education and its purposes has emerged. "Multicultural education is sometimes criticized as focusing on differences rather than similarities among groups. On the other side, it is criticized for not adequately addressing issues of power and oppression that keep a number of groups from participating equitably in society" (Gollnick & Chinn, 2009, p. 8). Although multicultural education is being challenged by some, public dialogue and debate about how schools can address diversity more effectively is healthy—an indicator that our society is making real progress toward creating a culture that incorporates the values of diverse groups.

Dimensions of Multicultural Education

According to James A. Banks, "Multicultural education is a way of viewing reality and a way of thinking, and not just content about various ethnic, racial, and cultural groups" (Banks, 2006, p. 8). More specifically, Banks suggests that multicultural education consists of five dimensions: (1) content integration, (2) the knowledge construction process, (3) prejudice reduction, (4) an equity pedagogy, and (5) an empowering school culture and social structure (see Figure 8.9). As you progress through your teacher education program and eventually begin to prepare curriculum materials and instructional strategies for your multicultural classroom, remember that integrating content from a variety of cultural groups is just one dimension of multicultural education.

Multicultural education promotes students' positive self-identity and pride in their heritage, acceptance of people from diverse backgrounds, and critical self-assessment. In addition, multicultural education can prompt students, perhaps with guidance from their teachers, to promote social justice and to take action against prejudice and discrimination within their school. For example, students might reduce the marginalization of minority-group students in their school by inviting them to participate in extracurricular and after-school activities.

As a teacher, you will teach students who historically have not received full educational opportunity—students from the many racial and ethnic minority groups in the United States; students from low-income families or communities; students with

Figure 8.9 The dimensions of multicultural education

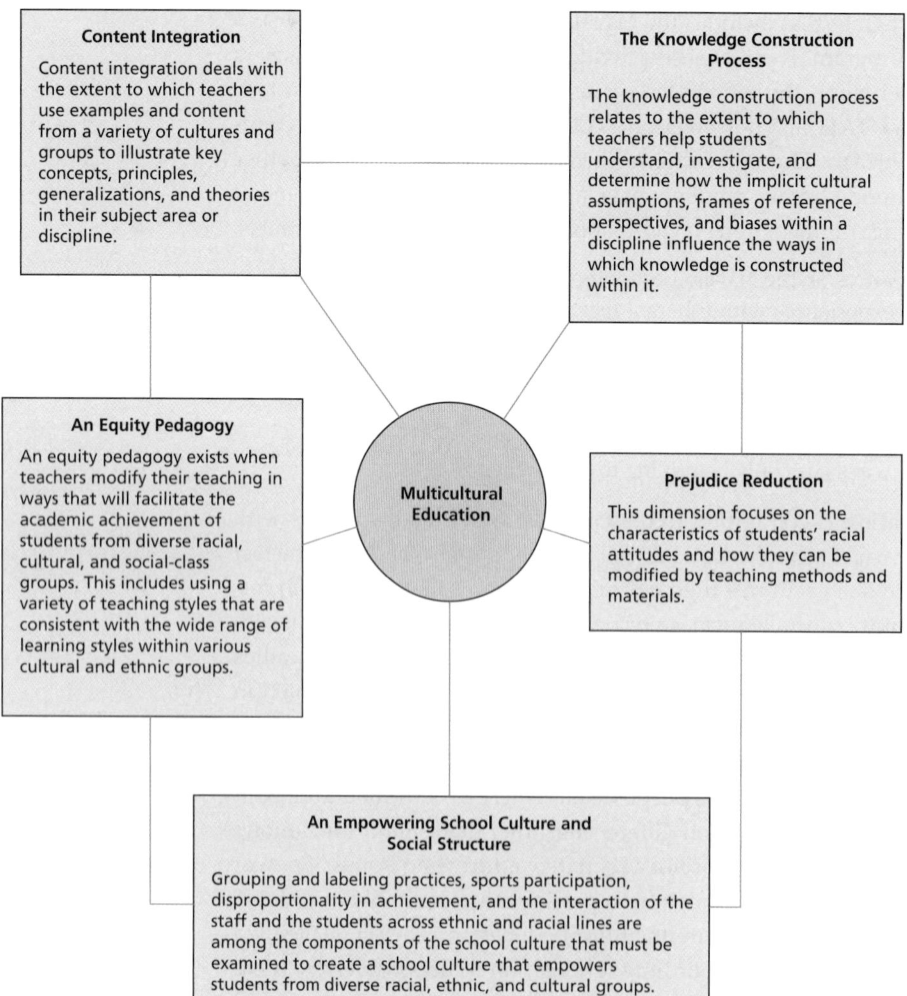

SOURCE: Reprinted with the permission of James A. Banks, from James A. Banks, *An Introduction to Multicultural Education* (Fourth Edition). Upper Saddle River, NJ: Allyn & Bacon.

exceptional abilities or disabilities; and students who are lesbian, gay, bisexual, transgender, or questioning (LGBTQ). You will face the challenge of reaching out to all students and teaching them that they are persons of worth who can learn. The following case about 12-year-old Yvette illustrates that challenge.

> Yvette is 12 years old and lives with her older brother and younger sister in an apartment in the city. Yvette and her brother were born in Puerto Rico, and her sister was born in the United States. Yvette's mother and father brought the family to the mainland two years ago.
>
> Three months ago, Yvette transferred into your class. It appears that the transition is difficult for her. Her work would improve if she got more involved, you think. However, she seems afraid to risk making mistakes, especially in reading and language arts.
>
> Yvette seems to trust you, so you've decided to talk to her after school today. She usually waits in your classroom until her brother Juan arrives to walk her home.
>
> You begin by asking, "How is school going?"
>
> As she speaks, timidly at first and then more openly and naturally, you realize that Yvette is still struggling to adjust to the challenges of living on the mainland. She misses her grandmother, who lived with the family in Puerto Rico. She also says she does not speak English well enough. She is worried that the other children will tease her if she speaks out in class. You also learn that Yvette has missed school frequently because of bad headaches and stomach problems. When you ask Yvette if her parents are coming to the next PTA meeting, Yvette tells you they probably will not come because they do not speak English.
>
> How can you get Yvette more involved in classroom activities? What strategies could you use to help her to increase her reading, speaking, and writing skills? How might you make Yvette's parents feel welcome and comfortable at the school?

Culturally Responsive Teaching

To create classrooms that are truly multicultural, teachers must practice **culturally responsive teaching**. Teachers are culturally responsive if they use instructional strategies and curriculum materials that reflect and value students' cultural backgrounds. Figure 8.10 identifies the knowledge and skills that are essential for culturally responsive teaching. By developing knowledge and skills in these eight areas, you will be well prepared to meet the educational needs of all your students.

Video Example 8.4

Being Culturally Responsive: Early childhood centers are becoming more and more diverse throughout the United States. Listen to the role respecting a child's culture plays in the child feeling safe and being successful at school.

One of the best ways to develop as a culturally responsive teacher is to learn as much as possible about students' cultural backgrounds. Also, you can seek out and participate wholeheartedly in cross-cultural experiences. A teacher's willingness to learn about other cultures is very important to students and their parents, as Yvonne Wilson, a first-grade teacher in Talmoon, **MINNESOTA**, and an Ojibwe Indian, points out,

> People in the community know if you are trying to understand their culture. Students also see it. Becoming involved—going to a powwow or participating in other cultural events—shows people that here is a teacher who is trying to learn about our culture.

Multicultural Curricula

As a culturally responsive teacher, you will develop a curriculum that increases students' awareness and appreciation of the rich diversity in U.S. culture. A **multicultural curriculum** addresses the needs and backgrounds of all students regardless of their cultural identity. As Banks (2009) suggests, the multicultural curriculum "enable[s] students to derive valid generalizations and theories about the characteristics of ethnic groups and to learn how they are alike and different, in both their past and present experiences . . . . [It] focus[es] on a range of groups that differ in their racial characteristics, cultural experiences, languages, histories, values, and current problems" (p. 16). Teachers who provide multicultural education hold the following beliefs:

Figure 8.10 Essential knowledge and skills for culturally responsive teaching

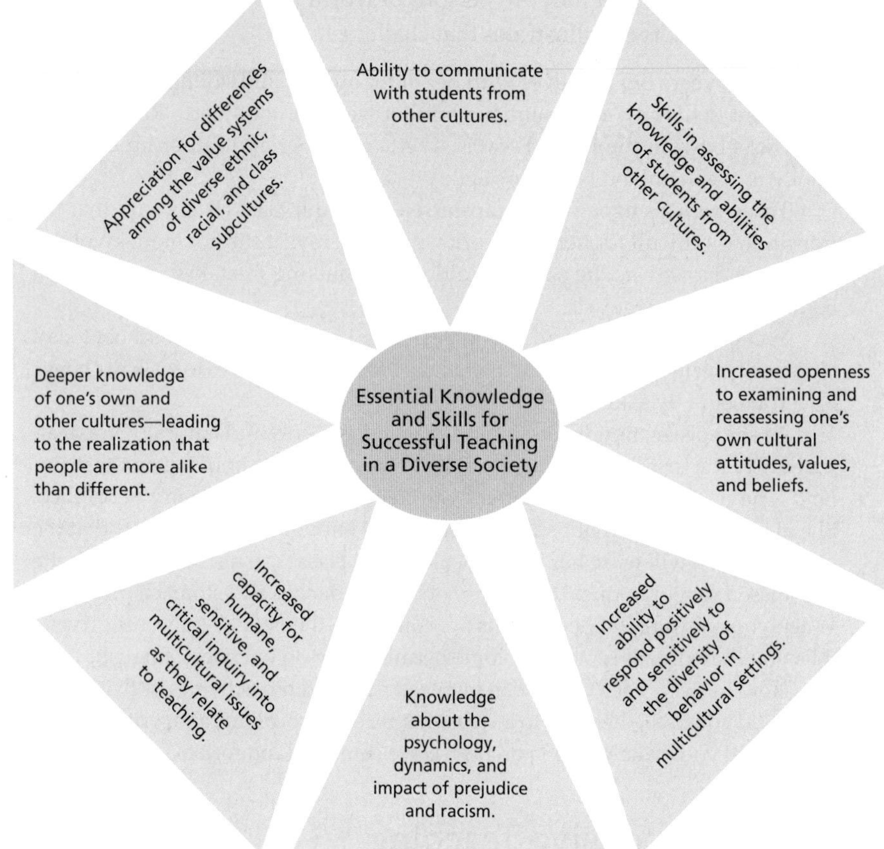
Ability to communicate with students from other cultures.
Skills in assessing the knowledge and abilities of students from other cultures.
Increased openness to examining and reassessing one's own cultural attitudes, values, and beliefs.
Increased ability to respond positively and sensitively to the diversity of behavior in multicultural settings.
Knowledge about the psychology, dynamics, and impact of prejudice and racism.
Increased capacity for humane, sensitive, and critical inquiry into multicultural issues as they relate to teaching.
Deeper knowledge of one's own and other cultures—leading to the realization that people are more alike than different.
Appreciation for differences among the value systems of diverse ethnic, racial, and class subcultures.
Essential Knowledge and Skills for Successful Teaching in a Diverse Society

SOURCE: Adapted from Forrest W. Parkay and Henry T. Fillmer, "Improving Teachers' Attitudes Toward Minority-Group Students: An Experimental Approach to Multicultural Inservice," *New Horizons Journal of Education*, November 1984, pp. 178–179.

- Cultural differences have strength and value.
- Schools should be models for the expression of human rights and respect for cultural and group differences.
- Social justice and equality for all people should be of paramount importance in the design and delivery of curriculum.
- Attitudes and values necessary for participation in a democratic society should be promoted in schools.
- Teachers are key to students' learning the knowledge, skills, and dispositions (i.e., values, attitudes, and com-mitments) they need to be productive citizens.
- Educators working with families and communities can create an environment that is supportive of multiculturalism, equality, and social justice. (Gollnick & Chinn, 2017, p. 19)

In developing a multicultural curriculum, you should be sensitive to how your instructional materials and strategies can be made more inclusive so that they reflect cultural perspectives, or "voices," that previously have been silent or marginalized in discussions about what should be taught in schools and how it should be taught. Effective teachers attend to these previously unheard voices not as an act of tokenism, but with a genuine desire to make the curriculum more inclusive. The Teaching on Your Feet feature in this chapter describes how Romaine Washington was able to relate curriculum content to her students' cultural backgrounds.

Teaching on Your Feet

¡Sí Se Puede! (It Can Be Done!)

What do you do when multiculturalism gets shaved down to biculturalism and students ask why more groups are not represented in the literature? From Puritanism to the Slave Narrative, from Transcendentalism to the Harlem Renaissance, Modernists, Beat Poets, Post-Modernists, and the Black Arts Movement, students are presented with myriad voices and views of American life. Mario asked one day, "Why is everything black and white?" Melissa followed his question with, "Where are Mexicans in these stories? Weren't they around? Why don't we read about them?"

The questions Mario and Melissa raised were on my mind as I prepared to teach the poignant, readily accessible novel Of Mice and Men. *From previous experience, I knew that students would love Lennie and hate Curly. We would identify the themes of loneliness and alienation. We would explore the concept of the American dream, as told by George. We would have a mock trial, and the jury would decide whether euthanasia is pardonable under certain circumstances. Yet when it is all said and done, we would still be left with the Mexican migrant worker waiting at the roadside for his story to be told.*

This year my English class would be half Latino, with quite a few English language learners. I longed to engage them on another level. I recalled the legacy of Cesar Chavez, which would provide the cultural, historical, and literary connection I needed. Although he was not an activist at the time in which Of Mice and Men *takes place, he was a child during that time period. He had a difficult time in school because he was the child of migrant workers who had moved more than 35 times. In addition, he spoke only Spanish. Children at his school would be hit on the knuckles when they did not speak English. I inform my students that, despite those challenges, Chavez became a great orator and activist for migrant workers.*

We speculate about the difference his presence might have made if he had been an activist during the time period of the novel. We read some of his quotes and relate them to the novel's characters and conflicts. Finally, we deconstruct a collage picture of Cesar Chavez in which his face, clothes, and the background are made up of migrant workers in the fields and holding peaceful demonstrations. All of the images in the collage symbolize important aspects of Chavez's life. I ask students to write about what they see and what they think it symbolizes. Detail by detail, they embrace the lesson. Phillip asks, "Can I have the picture we are writing about? I really like it." I respond using the slogan of the UFW (United Food Workers), "¡Sí se puede!"

ROMAINE WASHINGTON
English Teacher
Los Osos High School
Alta Loma, **CALIFORNIA**

Analyze

Because of time constraints and limited resources, what should be multicultural education often ends up being marginal and bi-cultural. It is impossible to each all about all cultures, but it is imperative that we at least try to include the cultures represented in our classrooms. Incorporating the lesson on Cesar Chavez broadened the class's cultural boundaries and validated the observation and request made by the students. This will serve to encourage them to speak up in the future when they feel underrepresented.

Reflect

1. How can teachers create a supportive environment where students feel comfortable discussing concerns about culture in the curriculum?
2. What are other ways teacher can incorporate multicultural context and content into the curriculum if resources are not readily made available?

Culturally responsive teachers also select instructional materials that are sensitive, accurately portray the contributions of ethnic groups, and reflect diverse points of view. They recognize that "[S]ome of the books and other materials on ethnic groups published each year are insensitive, inaccurate, and written from mainstream and insensitive perspectives and points of view" (Banks, 2009, p. 108). Some guidelines for selecting multicultural instructional materials follow:

- Books and other materials should accurately portray the perspectives, attitudes, and feelings of ethnic groups.
- Fictional works should have strong ethnic characters.
- Books should describe settings and experiences with which all students can identify and yet should accurately reflect ethnic cultures and lifestyles.
- The protagonists in books with ethnic themes should have ethnic characteristics but should face conflicts and problems that are universal.

- The illustrations in books should be accurate, ethnically sensitive, and technically well done.
- Ethnic materials should not contain racist concepts, clichés, phrases, or words.
- Factual materials should be historically accurate.
- Multiethnic resources and basal textbooks should discuss major events and documents related to ethnic history. (Banks, 2009, pp. 109–110)

Summary

What Contributes to the Cultural Diversity in U.S. Classrooms?

- The percentage of ethnic minorities in the United States has been growing steadily since World War II. Minorities made up 38.7 percent of the U.S. population in 2016. By 2044, more than half of all Americans are projected to belong to a minority group, and by 2060, nearly one in five of the nation's total population is projected to be foreign born. Currently, the majority of students in several states and many urban districts are from groups traditionally thought of as minority.
- Culture is defined as the way of life common to a group of people, including beliefs, attitudes, habits, values, and practices.
- Ethnicity refers to a commonly shared racial or cultural identity and a set of beliefs, values, and attitudes. The concept of race is used to distinguish among people on the basis of biological traits and characteristics. A minority group is a group of people who share certain characteristics and are fewer in number than the majority of a population.
- The increase of people who identify themselves as mixed race is one indication that racial and ethnic identities in the United States are becoming more complex.
- Stereotyping is the process of attributing certain behavioral characteristics to all members of a group, often on the basis of limited experiences with and information about the group being stereotyped. Individual racism is the prejudicial belief that one's own ethnic or racial group is superior to others, and institutional racism refers to laws, customs, and practices that lead to racial inequalities.
- The lower achievement levels of certain minority-group students compared to those of their Anglo-European American and Asian American counterparts reflect the strong connection between socioeconomic status and achievement. It is understandably difficult for poor children to do well in school if they must cope also with the stress of living in a state of chronic impoverishment.

How Can Teachers Strive to Provide Equal Educational Opportunity for All Students?

- Equal educational opportunity means that teachers promote the full development of students without regard for race, ethnicity, gender, sexual orientation, socioeconomic status, abilities, or disabilities.
- The behavior of boys and girls in our society is influenced by sexism, sex role socialization, and sex role stereotyping.
- The latest research indicates that family income, not gender, is most closely associated with academic achievement.
- Teachers can provide an education free of gender bias by creating gender-fair classrooms and curricula and providing students with safe, supportive learning environments.
- Teachers can meet the needs of minority students by becoming familiar with their cultural and linguistic backgrounds.
- In spite of increasing diversity in the United States, there has been a trend since 1990 for schools to resegregate.

How Are Schools Meeting the Needs of English Language Learners (ELLs)?

- Four approaches to meet the needs of English language learners (ELLs) are immersion, transition, pullout, and maintenance programs. Bilingual education programs provide instruction in English and a student's native language. Immersion programs provide instruction in English-only classrooms.

What Is Multicultural Education and Culturally Responsive Teaching?

- Five dimensions of multicultural education have been suggested: content integration, the knowledge construction process, prejudice reduction, an equity pedagogy, and an empowering school culture and social structure.
- Culturally responsive teachers use multicultural materials and instructional strategies that include the contributions of ethnic groups and reflect diverse points of view, or "voices," that previously may have been silenced or marginalized in society.

Professional Reflections and Activities

Teacher's Journal

1. Reflecting on your experiences in schools and the five dimensions of multicultural education (see Figure 8.9, page 288), describe the steps your teachers took to create an empowering school culture and social climate.
2. During your school years, did you ever experience discrimination as a member of a "different" group? Write about one outstanding incident that you feel affected your performance as a student.

Teacher's Research

1. Gather data from the National Center for Education Statistics regarding trends in achievement levels, educational attainment, and dropout rates for one of the following groups of which you are not a member: African Americans, Latino and Hispanic Americans, Asian Americans and Pacific Islanders, and Native Americans and Alaskan Natives. To what extent are achievement levels and educational attainment increasing? To what extent are dropout rates decreasing?
2. Go to the website for the National Assessment of Educational Progress (NAEP) and download the latest NAEP reports. The reports present achievement data by gender, race, and ethnicity. What are some implications these data have for teachers?

Observations and Interviews

1. If possible, visit a school that has an enrollment of students whose cultural or socioeconomic backgrounds differ from your own. What feelings and questions about these students emerge as a result of your observations? How might your feelings affect your teaching and teaching effectiveness? How can you research answers to your questions?
2. Interview a teacher at the school identified in the previous activity. What special satisfactions does he or she experience from teaching at the school? What significant problems relating to diversity does he or she encounter, and how are they dealt with?

Professional Portfolio

Prepare an annotated directory of local resources for teaching students about diversity, implementing multicultural curricula, and promoting harmony or equity among diverse groups. For each entry, include an annotation—that is, a brief description of the resource materials and their availability. Resources for your personalized directory should be available through local sources such as your university library, public library, community agencies, and so on. Among the types of resources you might include are the following:

- Films, videos, audiocassettes, books, and journal articles
- Simulation games designed to improve participants' attitudes toward diversity
- Motivational guest speakers from the community
- Ethnic museums and cultural centers
- Community groups and agencies dedicated to promoting understanding among diverse groups
- Training and workshops in the area of diversity

Shared Writing 8.1:
Through the Eyes of an ELL Student

Chapter 9

Addressing Learners' Individual Needs

Monkey Business Images/Shutterstock

Learning Outcomes

After reading this chapter, you will be able to do the following:

9.1 Explain how students' needs change as they develop.

9.2 Explain how students vary in intelligence.

9.3 Discuss how students vary in ability and disability.

9.4 Explain special education and inclusion.

9.5 Explain how you can teach all learners in your inclusive classroom.

READERS' VOICES

Why should teachers address students' individual needs?

Effective teachers understand that students are not the same—they have different needs, different learning styles, and different experiences. They learn best from teachers who know how to adjust their teaching methods and materials for different types of students.

—**SHAWNDRA**,
Teacher Education program, first year

As the preceding reader's comment suggests, when you become a teacher you must understand and appreciate students' unique learning and developmental needs. You must be willing to learn about students' abilities and disabilities and to explore the special issues and concerns of students at three broad developmental levels—childhood, early adolescence, and late adolescence. Learning about your students as individuals is essential. Reflect on your own experiences for a moment. You appreciate it when people treat you as an individual. You don't want to be "treated like a number." You appreciate it when others acknowledge your uniqueness. Your students will be no different.

Understanding how students' interests, questions, and problems will change throughout their school years will help you serve them in the present. This chapter examines how students' needs change as they develop and how their needs reflect various intelligences, abilities, and disabilities.

How Do Students' Needs Change as they Develop?

Development refers to the predictable changes that all human beings undergo as they progress through the life span—from conception to death. It is important to remember that students develop at different rates. Within a given classroom, for example, some students will be larger and physically more mature than others, some will be socially more sophisticated, and some will be able to think at a higher level of abstraction.

As humans progress through different **stages of development**, they mature and learn to perform the tasks that are a necessary part of daily living. There are several different types of human development. For example, as children develop physically, their bodies undergo numerous changes. As they develop cognitively, their mental capabilities expand so that they can use language and other symbol systems to solve problems. As they develop socially, they learn to interact more effectively with other people—as individuals and in groups. And as they develop morally, their actions come to reflect a greater appreciation of principles such as equity, justice, fairness, and altruism.

Because no two students progress through the stages of cognitive, social, and moral development in quite the same way, teachers need perspectives on these three types of development that are flexible, dynamic, and, above all, useful. By becoming familiar with models of cognitive, social, and moral development, teachers at all levels, from preschool through college, can better serve their students. Three such models are Piaget's theory of **cognitive development**, Erikson's stages of **psychosocial development**, and Kohlberg's stages of **moral reasoning**.

Piaget's Model of Cognitive Development

Jean Piaget (1896–1980), the noted Swiss biologist and philosopher, made extensive observational studies of children. He concluded that children reason differently from adults and even have different perceptions of the world. Piaget surmised that children learn through actively interacting with their environments, much as scientists do, and proposed that a child's thinking progresses through a sequence of four cognitive stages

Figure 9.1 Piaget's stages of cognitive growth

Vanessa Davies/Dorling Kindersley, Ltd.

1. **Sensorimotor Intelligence (birth to 2 years):** Behavior is primarily sensory and motor. The child does not yet "think" conceptually; however, "cognitive" development can be observed.

spass/Shutterstock

2. **Preoperational Thought (2–7 years):** Development of language and rapid conceptual development are evident. Children begin to use symbols to think of objects and people outside of their immediate environment. Fantasy and imaginative play are natural modes of thinking.

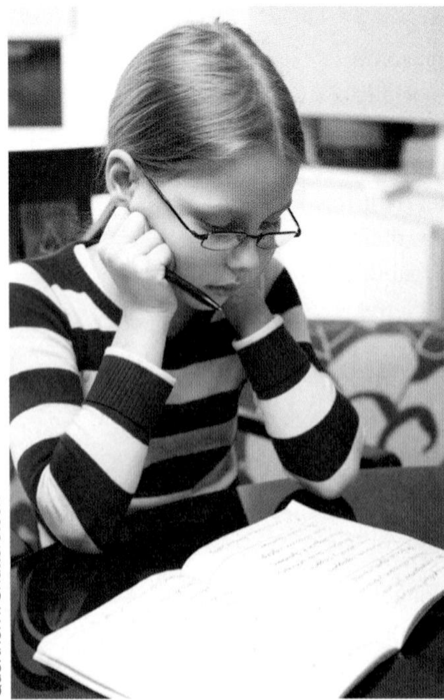

Quorthon1/Shutterstock

3. **Concrete Operations (7–11 years):** Children develop ability to use logical thought to solve concrete problems. Basic concepts of objects, number, time, space, and causality are explored and mastered. Through use of concrete objects to manipulate, children are able to draw conclusions.

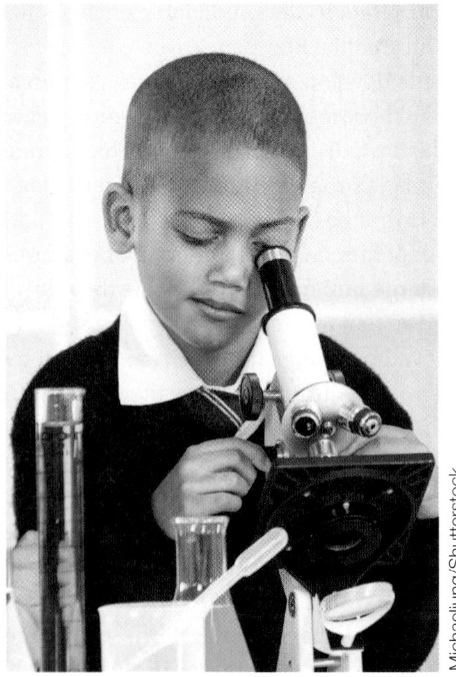

Michaeljung/Shutterstock

4. **Formal Operations (11–15 years):** Cognitive abilities reach their highest level of development. Children can make predictions, think about hypothetical situations, think about thinking, and appreciate the structure of language as well as use it to communicate. Sarcasm, puns, argumentation, and slang are aspects of adolescents' speech that reflect their ability to think abstractly about language.

(see Figure 9.1). According to Piaget's theory of cognitive development, the rate of progress through the four stages varies from individual to individual.

During the school years, students move through the **preoperational stage**, the **concrete operations stage**, and the **formal operations stage**; however, because of individual interaction with the total environment, each student's perceptions and learning will be unique. According to Piaget:

> The principal goal of education is to create [learners] who are capable of doing new things, not simply repeating what other generations have done—[learners] who are creative, inventive, and discoverers. [We] need pupils who are active, who learn early to find out by themselves, partly by their own spontaneous activity and partly through material we set up for them; who learn early to tell what is verifiable and what is simply the first idea to come to them. (quoted in Ripple & Rockcastle, 1964, p. 5)

Video Example 9.1

Using a Magnifier for Different Perspectives: A teacher works with toddlers in the preoperational stage.

Figure 9.2, based on Piaget's work and more recent research, presents strategies for teaching children as their thinking abilities develop during the preoperational stage, the concrete operations stage, and the formal operations stage.

Figure 9.2 Suggested strategies for teaching children at Piaget's stages of cognitive growth

Preoperational Stage

1. Use concrete objects and visual aids—pictures, drawings, photos, etc.
2. Provide opportunities to classify and group objects—by color, shape, size, use, etc.
3. Provide short instructions and explanations of ideas and concepts.
4. Use words and actions to instruct and explain.
5. Build skills by providing hands-on practice.
6. Teach simple skills first, then build on these to teach more complex skills.
7. Provide activities that give students a wide variety of learning experiences.

Concrete Operations Stage

1. Use concrete objects and visual aids to teach more complex material.
2. Provide explanations and readings that are short, clear, and well organized.
3. Explain more complex ideas and concepts by comparing them to familiar examples.
4. Provide opportunities to classify and group increasingly complex objects and concepts.
5. Present problems that require logical, analytical, scientific, and creative thinking.

Formal Operations Stage

1. Study topics in increasing depth.
2. Go beyond "facts" and teach increasingly complex concepts, ideas, and theories.
3. Provide increasingly sophisticated explanations for what students observe and experience.
4. Ask students to explain the meaning of proverbs—for example: "The pen is mightier than the sword," "There is no free lunch," and "Necessity is the mother of invention."
5. Discuss social, political, moral, and ethical issues that relate to subject matter.
6. Have students design experiments to test hypotheses related to subject matter.

Erikson's Model of Psychosocial Development

Erik Erikson's (1902–1994) model of psychosocial development delineates eight stages, from infancy to old age (see Table 9.1). For each stage, a **psychosocial crisis** is central in the individual's emotional and social growth. Erikson expresses these crises in polar terms; for instance, in the first stage, that of infancy, the psychosocial crisis is trust versus mistrust. Erikson explains that the major psychosocial task for the infant is to develop a sense of trust in the world but not to give up totally a sense of distrust. In the tension between the poles of trust and mistrust, a greater pull toward the more positive pole is considered healthy and is accompanied by a virtue. In this case, if trust prevails, the virtue is hope.

Table 9.1 Erikson's Eight Stages of Psychosocial Development

Stage	Approximate Age	Psychosocial "Crisis"	Description	"Basic Strength" (Positive Result if Crisis Is Adequately Resolved)
1. Infancy	Birth to 18 months	Trust versus basic mistrust	Infant needs to be nurtured and loved; if not, he or she becomes insecure and mistrustful.	Drive and hope
2. Early childhood	18 months to 3 years	Autonomy versus shame	Child focuses on developing physical skills—toilet training, walking, talking, feeding self; inadequate resolution of crisis leads to feelings of shame and doubt.	Self-control, courage, and will
3. Play age	3 to 6 years	Initiative versus guilt	Child learns to develop skills through play and cooperation; inadequate resolution of crisis leads to sense of guilt and fearfulness.	Purpose and direction
4. School age	6 to 12 years	Industry versus inferiority	Child acquires new skills, knowledge; develops sense of achievement; inadequate resolution of crisis leaves child feeling inadequate and inferior.	Competence and method
5. Adolescence	12 to 20 years	Identity versus role confusion, identity diffusion	Adolescent focuses on clarifying identity, developing social relationships with peers and others, and grappling with moral issues; inadequate resolution of crisis leads to self-doubt and self-consciousness.	Fidelity and devotion
6. Young adulthood	20 to 35 years	Intimacy versus isolation	Young adult seeks companionship and love through relationships with friends and becoming intimate with a "significant other"; inadequate resolution of crisis leads to feelings of isolation and distance from others.	Love and affiliation
7. Middle adulthood	35 to 65 years	Generativity versus self-absorption or stagnation	Adult focuses on family relationships, parenting, and creative and meaningful work; inadequate resolution of crisis leads to feelings of stagnation and alienation.	Care and production
8. Late adulthood	65 to death	Integrity versus despair	Adult focuses on meaning and purpose in one's life, lifetime accomplishments and contributions, acceptance of oneself and fulfillment; inadequate resolution of crisis leads to feelings of failure, disdain for world, and fear of death.	Wisdom and acceptance

When we examine the issues and concerns of students in childhood and early and late adolescence later in this chapter, we will return to Erikson's model of psychosocial development. For further information on this significant and useful theory of development, you may wish to read Erikson's first book, *Childhood and Society* (1963).

Kohlberg's Model of Moral Development

According to Lawrence Kohlberg (1927–1987), the reasoning process people use to decide what is right and wrong evolves through three levels of development. Within each level, Kohlberg has identified two stages. Figure 9.3 shows that at Level I, the preconventional level, the individual decides what is right on the basis of personal needs and rules developed by others. At Level II, the conventional level, moral decisions reflect a desire for the approval of others and a willingness to conform to the expectations of family, community, and country. At Level III, the postconventional level, the individual has developed values and principles that are based on rational, personal choices that can be separated from conventional values.

Kohlberg (2014) suggests that "over 50 percent of late adolescents and adults are capable of full formal reasoning [i.e., they can use their intelligence to reason abstractly, form hypotheses, and test these hypotheses against reality], but only 10 percent of these adults display principled (Stages 5 and 6) moral reasoning" (p. 184). In addition, Kohlberg found that maturity of moral judgment is not highly related to IQ or verbal intelligence.

Figure 9.3 Kohlberg's Theory of Moral Reasoning

I. Preconventional Level of Moral Reasoning

Child is responsive to cultural rules and labels of good and bad, right or wrong, but interprets these in terms of consequences of action (punishment, reward, exchanges of favors).

Stage 1:	*Punishment-and-obedience orientation* Physical consequences of action determine its goodness or badness. Avoidance of punishment and deference to power are valued.
Stage 2:	*The instrumental-relativist orientation* Right action consists of that which satisfies one's own needs and occasionally the needs of others. Reciprocity is a matter of "You scratch my back and I'll scratch yours."

II. Conventional Level of Moral Reasoning

Maintaining the expectations of the individual's family, group, or nation is perceived as valuable, regardless of consequences.

Stage 3:	*The interpersonal concordance or "good boy–nice girl" orientation* Good behavior is that which pleases or helps others and is approved by them.
Stage 4:	*The "law and order" orientation* Orientation toward fixed rules and the maintenance of the social order. Right behavior consists of doing one's duty and showing respect for authority.

III. Postconventional, Autonomous, or Principled Level of Moral Reasoning

Effort to define moral principles that have validity and application apart from the authority of groups.

Stage 5:	*The social-contract, legalistic orientation* Right action defined in terms of rights and standards that have been agreed on by the whole society. This is the "official" morality of the U.S. government and Constitution.
Stage 6:	*The universal-ethical-principle orientation* Right is defined by conscience in accord with self-chosen ethical principles appealing to logic and universality.

SOURCE: Based on Kohlberg, L. (2014). "The cognitive developmental approach to moral education." In F.W. Parkay, E.J. Anctil, & G. Hass (Eds.), *Curriculum leadership: Readings for developing quality educational programs* (10th ed., p. 182). The original version appeared in *Journal of Philosophy, 70*(18), 1973, 631–632.

Kohlberg's model has been criticized because it focuses on moral reasoning rather than actual behavior, and it tends to look at moral development from a male perspective. Carol Gilligan, for example, suggests that men's moral reasoning tends to address the rights of the individual, whereas women's moral reasoning addresses the individual's responsibility to other people. In her book *In a Different Voice: Psychological Theory and Women's Development* (1993), Gilligan refers to women's principal moral voice as the "ethics of care," which emphasizes care of others over the more male-oriented "ethics of justice." Thus, when confronted with a moral dilemma, women tend to suggest solutions based more on altruism and self-sacrifice than on rights and rules.

The question remains: Can moral reasoning be taught? Can you help students develop so that they live according to principles of equity, justice, caring, and empathy? Kohlberg suggests the following three conditions that can help children internalize moral principles:

1. Exposure to the next higher stage of reasoning
2. Exposure to situations posing problems and contradictions for the child's current moral structure, leading to dissatisfaction with his [her] current level
3. An atmosphere of interchange and dialogue combining the first two conditions, in which conflicting moral views are compared in an open manner. (Kohlberg, 2014, p. 189)

One approach to teaching values and moral reasoning is known as **character education**, a movement that "promotes the teaching of core values that can be taught directly through course curricula, especially in literature, social studies, and social science classes" (Power et al., 2008, p. xxxvi). There is no single way for teachers to develop students' character; however, in comments made shortly after the shooting deaths of 14 students and a teacher at Columbine High School in Colorado, well-known sociologist and organizer of several White House conferences on character education Amitai Etzioni (1999) said, "What schools should help youngsters develop—if schools are going to help lower the likelihood of more Columbines—are two crucial behavior characteristics: the capacity to channel impulses into prosocial outlets, and empathy with others." Figure 9.4 illustrates a 12-point strategy teachers can use to create moral classroom communities.

Figure 9.4 A 12-point comprehensive approach to character education

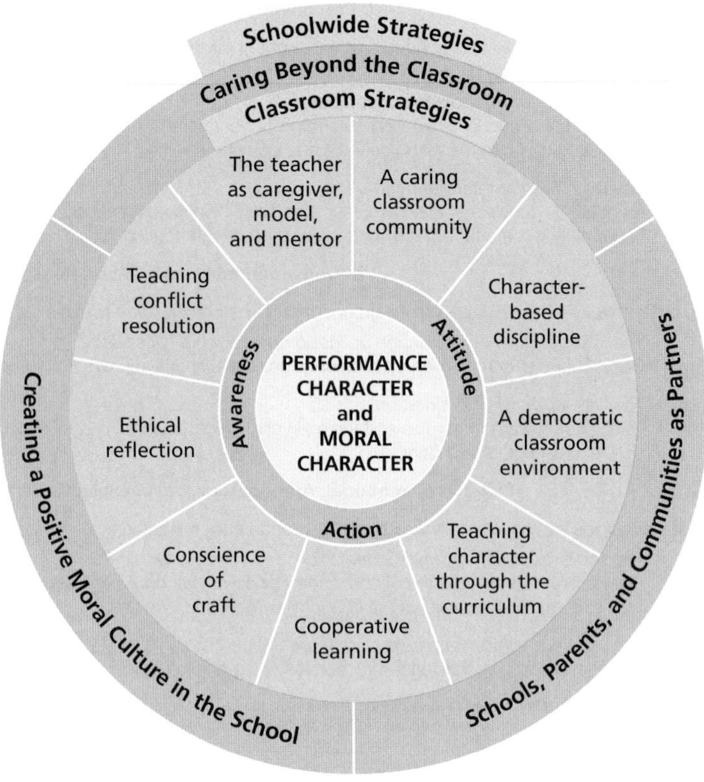

1. **The teacher as caregiver, model, and mentor:** treating students with love and respect, encouraging right behavior, and correcting wrongful actions.
2. **A caring classroom community:** teaching students to respect and care about each other.
3. **Character-based discipline:** using rules and consequences to develop moral reasoning, self-control, and a generalized respect for others.
4. **A democratic classroom environment:** using the class meeting to engage students in shared decision making and in taking responsibility for making the classroom the best it can be.
5. **Teaching character through the curriculum:** using the ethically rich content of academic subjects as vehicles for values teaching.
6. **Cooperative learning:** fostering students' ability to work with and appreciate others.
7. **Conscience of craft:** developing students' sense of academic responsibility and the habit of doing their work well.
8. **Ethical reflection:** developing the cognitive side of character through reading, research, writing, and discussion.
9. **Teaching conflict resolution:** teaching students how to solve conflicts fairly, without intimidation or violence.
10. **Caring beyond the classroom:** using role models to inspire altruistic behavior and providing opportunities for school and community service.
11. **Creating a positive moral culture in the school:** developing a caring school community that promotes the core virtues.
12. **School, parents, and communities as partners:** helping parents and the whole community join the schools in a cooperative effort to build good character.

SOURCE: Used with permission of Thomas Lickona. (2014). Center for the 4th and 5th Rs. *Cortland, NY: SUNY School of Education. Retrieved from http://www2.cortland.edu/centers/character/12-pt-comprehensive-approach.dot*

Many schools, such as the Hyde Schools in Bath, **MAINE** and Woodstock, **CONNECTICUT**, emphasize specific moral values in their curricula. The character-based educational program at the Hyde Schools focuses on five words: *Courage,*

Integrity, Leadership, Curiosity, and *Concern.* The program also emphasizes student development in the following areas: Emotional Maturity, Self-Reflection, Independence, How to Interact in a Community, Resilience, Wellness, Leadership, and Integrity (Hyde Schools, 2018).

Kennedy Middle School in Eugene, **OREGON** emphasizes character development through the PRIDE program, based on the following words: *Positive Attitude, Respect, Integrity, Discipline,* and *Excellence.* To demonstrate their commitment to these character traits, students must follow behavioral guidelines appropriate for each word. For example, students demonstrate a Positive Attitude by participating in class discussions, following directions, encouraging others to do their best, and communicating in a positive manner. They demonstrate Excellence by learning as much as they can, taking pride in their schoolwork, always doing their best, and completing assignments and turning them in on time (Kennedy Middle School, 2014).

Maslow's Model of a Hierarchy of Needs

Students' developmental levels also vary according to how well their biological and psychological needs have been satisfied. Psychologist Abraham Maslow (1908–1970) formulated a model of a **hierarchy of needs** (see Figure 9.5) suggesting that people are first motivated by basic needs for survival and safety. When these basic needs have been met sufficiently, people naturally seek to satisfy higher needs, the highest of which is self-actualization—the desire to use one's talents, abilities, and potentialities to the fullest. Students whose needs for safety have been fairly well satisfied will discover strong needs for friendship, affection, and love, for example. If efforts to satisfy the various needs are thwarted, the result can be maladjustment and interruption or delay in the individual's full and healthy development.

Students differ markedly in terms of where they are on Maslow's hierarchy of needs. Many families lack the resources to provide adequately for children's basic needs.

Figure 9.5 Maslow's Hierarchy of Needs

Note: The four lower-level needs are called *deficiency needs* because the motivation to satisfy them decreases when they are met. On the other hand, when *being (growth) needs* are met, motivation to fulfill them increases.

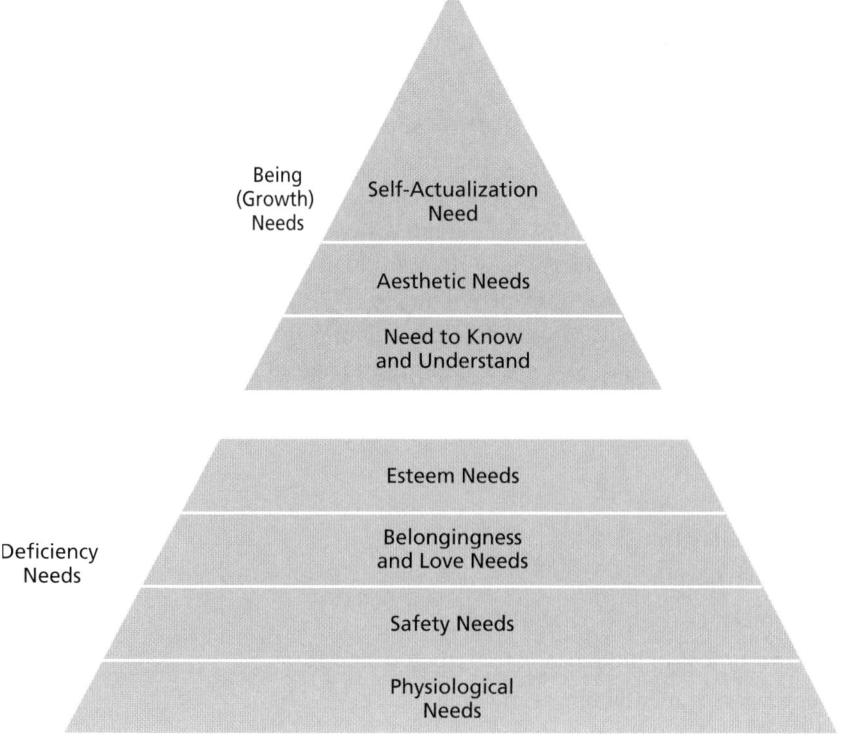

SOURCE: Based on Abraham H. Maslow, *Toward a Psychology of Being*. 3rd Edition. New York: John Wiley & Sons, 1998 and *Motivation and Personality*, 3rd Edition. Boston: Addison-Wesley, 1987.

Children from families that are concerned with day-to-day survival may not receive the support that could help them succeed in school. They come to school tired and hungry and may have trouble paying attention in class. Others may be well fed and clothed but feel unsafe, alienated, or unloved; they may seek to protect themselves by withdrawing emotionally from activities around them.

Developmental Stresses and Tasks of Childhood

During Erikson's school-age stage, children strive for a sense of industry and struggle against feelings of inferiority. If successful, they gain the virtue of competence, believing in their abilities to do things. If children find evidence that they are inferior to others, if they experience failure when they try new tasks, and if they struggle without ever gaining a sense of mastery, then they feel incompetent.

Cathy Yeulet/123rf.com

What developmental tasks do middle school students need to accomplish as part of their psychosocial development? How can their teachers help with those developmental tasks?

Children gain the sense of industry needed at this age by playing seriously, mastering new skills, producing products, and being workers. When they first go to school, they are oriented toward accomplishing new things. (Some kindergartners expect to learn to read on their first day of school and are disappointed when they don't!) For young schoolchildren, the idea of work is attractive; it means that they are doing something grown up.

Is childhood a time of carefree play or a period of stress? Certainly the answer depends on the life circumstances and personality of the individual child. In a study of stressful events in the lives of more than 1,700 children in the second through the ninth grades in six countries, Karou Yamamoto and his associates found that the most stressful events "threaten[ed] one's sense of security and occasion[ed] personal denigration and embarrassment" (Yamamoto et al., 1996, p. 139).

ADVERSE CHILDHOOD EXPERIENCES An alarming number of children in America experience levels of stress that have serious, long-lasting consequences for their development and well-being. As mentioned in Chapter 3, the **Adverse Childhood Experiences (ACE) Study** has documented how children's development can be impacted if their families are coping with financial problems, drug addiction, domestic violence, neighborhood crime, or mental illness.

The ACE Study examined the prevalence of the following 10 categories of adverse childhood experiences (ACEs) people had prior to age 18.

1. Psychological abuse
2. Physical abuse
3. Sexual abuse
4. Emotional neglect
5. Physical neglect
6. Alcoholism or drug use in home
7. Divorce or loss of biological parent (before age 18)
8. Depression or mental illness in home
9. Mother treated violently
10. Imprisoned household member

Figure 9.6 Mechanism by which adverse childhood experiences influence health and well-being throughout the lifespan

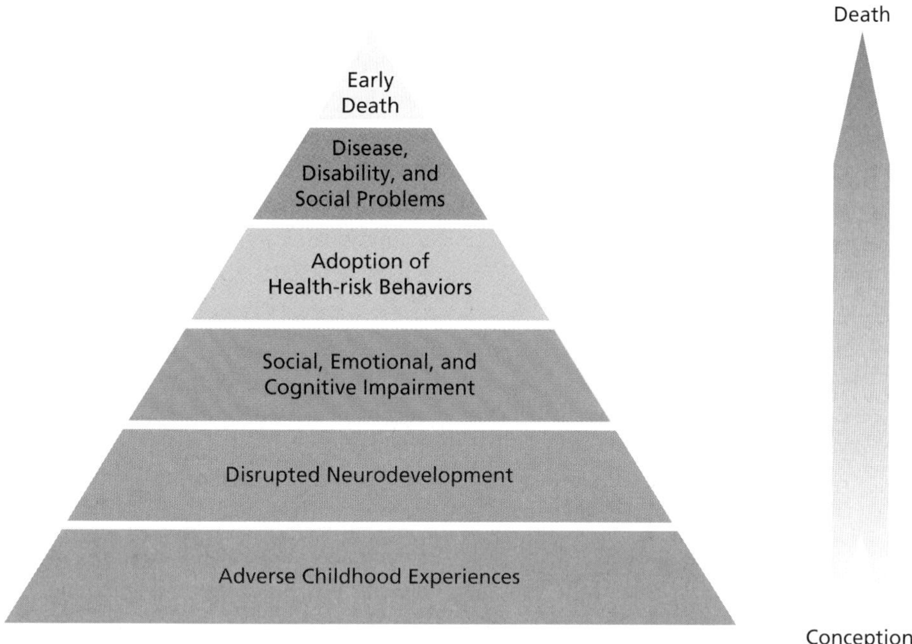

SOURCE: U.S. Department of Health & Human Services, Centers for Disease Control and Prevention, National Center for Injury Prevention and Control, Division of Violence Prevention. (June 14, 2016). Retrieved from https://www.cdc.gov/violenceprevention/acestudy/about.html

A person's ACE "score" reflects the number of categories experienced during childhood and can range between 0 and 10. People who experience more ACEs during childhood are at greater risk for disease and lack of well-being throughout the lifespan. For example, an ACE score of 4 nearly doubles the risk of heart disease and cancer. It increases the likelihood of becoming an alcoholic by 700 percent and the risk of attempted suicide by 1,200 percent (Stevens, 2017). The life expectancy for people who report 6 or more ACEs is estimated to be as much as 20 years less than people who report none (Conaboy, January 1, 2018). Figure 9.6 illustrates the link between adverse childhood experiences (ACEs) and risk factors for disease and lack of well-being throughout the lifespan.

Developmental Stresses and Tasks of Adolescence

Many psychologists believe that adolescence contains two distinct stages: an early period covering the ages of 10 to 12 through the ages of 14 to 16, and a late period from approximately 15 to 16 through 19. Although continuity exists in each individual's life, the psychosocial issues of adolescence—coping with change and seeking identity—vary in form and importance as individuals progress through the transition from childhood to adulthood.

In Erik Erikson's eight-stage model of human development, identity versus role diffusion is the psychosocial crisis for the adolescent years. Although the quest for identity is a key psychosocial issue for both early and late adolescence, many believe that Erikson's identity-versus-role-diffusion stage fits best for early adolescence. During this time, young adolescents, using their new thinking abilities, begin integrating a clearer sense of personal identity. Erikson's role diffusion refers to the variety of roles that adolescents have available to them.

According to Erikson's theory, when adolescents identify themselves with a peer group, with a school, or with a cause, their sense of fidelity—the virtue of this stage—is clear and strong. At this stage, adolescents are loyal and committed, sometimes to people or ideas that may dismay or alarm their parents, sometimes to high ideals and dreams.

In late adolescence, the quest for identity shifts from relying on others to self-reliance. Young people continue to work on strengthening their sense of identity in late adolescence, but as they do so, they draw less on the reactions of their peers and more on their own regard for what matters. Although late adolescents possess an array of interests, talents, and goals in life, they share a desire to achieve independence. More like adults than children, late adolescents are anxious to use newly acquired strengths, skills, and knowledge to achieve their own purposes, whether through marriage, parenthood, full-time employment, education beyond high school, a career, or military service.

The vulnerability of today's adolescents is evident in the results of a survey based on 40 "developmental assets" youth need to become healthy, mature adults. For optimal development, youth should have the following "external" and "internal" assets: *external assets*—support, empowerment, boundaries and expectations, and constructive use of time; *internal assets*—commitment to learning, positive values, social competencies, and positive identity. The survey of almost 150,000 sixth- to twelfth-grade youth in 202 communities revealed that:

> the average young person experiences only 18.6 of the 40 assets. In general, older youth have lower average levels of assets than younger youth. And boys experience fewer assets than girls. While there is no "magic number" of assets young people should have . . . data indicate that 31 is a worthy, though challenging, benchmark for experiencing their positive effects most strongly. Yet . . . only 8 percent of youth have 31 or more assets. More than half have 20 or fewer assets. (Search Institute, 2010)

As a teacher, what can you do to help children and adolescents develop to their full potential? To help prevent the problems that place them at risk, an energetic, creative, and multifaceted approach is necessary. Figure 9.7 presents several strategies for helping students develop competence, positive self-concepts, and high esteem and for intervening to prevent or address problems that place them at risk.

Figure 9.7 What teachers can do to help children and adolescents develop

1. **Provide opportunities and encouragement for students to develop competence.**
   - Provide a learning environment in which students can risk making mistakes.
   - Assign work that students can perform successfully and still be challenged.
   - Have realistic but high expectations for students.
   - Express belief in students' ability to succeed.
   - Encourage industry by letting students work on goals or projects of their choosing.
   - Provide opportunities for students to take special responsibility.
   - Assign older students to work with younger ones.
   - Reward industry and competence.
2. **Promote the development of positive self-concept and high self-esteem.**
   - Give praise more than criticism.
   - Take students and their work seriously.
   - Respect students' dignity.
   - Plan individual and group activities that boost morale.
   - Provide opportunities for students to interact and work cooperatively.
   - Teach and model acceptance of human diversity and individuality.
   - Develop systems for the recognition and reward of individual and group achievement.
   - Support students' efforts to achieve and appropriately express independence.
3. **Intervene to prevent or address problems that place students at risk.**
   - Provide a safe and structured learning environment where students feel secure.
   - Practice effective leadership and classroom management.
   - Provide opportunities to discuss preferences, values, morals, goals, and consequences.
   - Teach and model critical thinking, decision making, and problem solving.
   - Teach and model prosocial attitudes and behaviors and conflict resolution strategies.
   - Provide information on subjects of special concern to students and parents.
   - Cultivate family involvement.
   - Collaborate, consult, network, and refer on behalf of students.

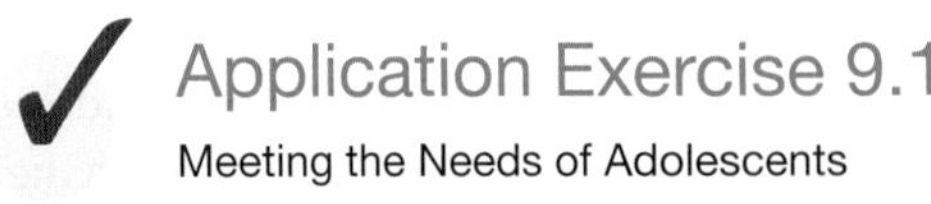

Application Exercise 9.1
Meeting the Needs of Adolescents

FOCUS ON **DIVERSITY**: NATIONAL POLICY RHETORIC AND STRESS AMONG VULNERABLE STUDENTS

In the aftermath of the tumultuous 2016 presidential election, many students from vulnerable groups reported feeling less safe while at school. For example, UCLA researchers asked 1,535 teachers at 333 public high schools how many students in a typical class had expressed concern "about their well-being or the well-being of their family due to political rhetoric or changing political conditions" on five key issues. 79 percent of all teachers said their students expressed concerns for themselves or their families in response to at least one of the issues. Figure 9.8 shows the percentage of teachers reporting that some students expressed concern about each issue.

Figure 9.8 Percentage of teachers reporting some students have expressed concern about . . .

Deportation of undocumented immigrants	58%
President's executive order restricting travel from six primarily Muslim countries	36%
Limiting rights of LGBTQ youth	38%
Reform and/or Repeal of the Affordable Care Act (or "Obamacare")	44%
Deregulation of environmental protections	45%

SOURCE: Based on Rogers, J., Franke, M., Yun, J.E., Ishimoto, M., Diera, C., Geller, R., Berryman, A., Brenes, T. (2017). *Teaching and Learning in the Age of Trump: Increasing Stress and Hostility in America's High Schools.* Los Angeles, CA: UCLA's Institute for Democracy, Education, and Access, p. 7.

In addition, the following teacher responses to the open-ended question, "How has classroom and school climate changed this past year as a result of changes in national politics?" convey the levels of stress students from vulnerable groups experienced:

> "I had students coming to me, upset, crying, talking about being targeted because [of] their brown skin, Muslim faith, and sexual orientation" (Rogers et al., 2017, p. 18). *Maryland English teacher*
>
> "I had students stand up in the middle of class and directly address their peers with racial slurs. This is not something I have seen before" (p. 17). *Ohio social studies teacher*
>
> "LGBTQ and immigrant students tried to make themselves invisible to potential assailants. They just kind of went underground . . . they didn't engage. They kind of hid" (p. 20). *Missouri social studies teacher*

While political leaders have perhaps the greatest responsibility for addressing the underlying causes of incivility in our national discourse, proactive teachers can help to create tolerant, respectful climates in their schools and classrooms. They can promote civil exchange and greater understanding among students from different groups by establishing clear norms for classroom discussions. If vulnerable students express concerns about their well-being, teachers should remind them that there is a support system of people who care about them at the school.

How do Students Vary in Intelligence?

In addition to developmental differences, students differ in terms of their intellectual capacity. Unfortunately, test scores, and sometimes intelligence quotient (IQ) scores, are treated as accurate measurements of students' intellectual ability because of their convenience and long-time use. What is intelligence, and how has it been redefined to account for the many ways in which it is expressed?

Although many definitions of **intelligence** have been proposed, the term has yet to be completely defined. One view is that intelligence is the ability to learn. As David Wechsler (1958), the developer of the most widely used intelligence scales for children and adults, said: "Intelligence, operationally defined, is the aggregate or global capacity to act purposefully, to think rationally, and to deal effectively with the environment" (p. 7). Other perspectives on intelligence include the following:

- It is *adaptive*. It can be used flexibly to respond to a variety of situations and problems.
- It is related to *learning ability*. People who are intelligent in particular domains learn new information and skills in those domains more quickly and easily than people who are less intelligent in those domains.
- It involves the *use of prior knowledge* to analyze and understand new situations effectively.
- It involves the complex interaction and coordination of *many different mental processes*.
- It is *culture-specific*. What is considered to be intelligent behavior in one culture isn't necessarily intelligent behavior in another culture. (Ormrod, Anderman, & Anderman, 2017, p. 130)

Intelligence Testing

The intelligence tests that we now use can be traced to the 1905 Metrical Scale of Intelligence designed by French psychologists Alfred Binet and Theodore Simon. They wanted a way to identify children who would need special help with their learning. Binet revised the scale in 1908, which was adapted for American children in 1916 by Lewis Terman, a psychologist at Stanford University. Terman's test was further adapted, especially by the U.S. Army, which transformed it into a paper-and-pencil test that could be administered to large groups. The use of such intelligence tests has continued throughout the years. Approximately 67 percent of the population have an IQ between 85 and 115—the range of normal intelligence.

Individual intelligence tests are presently valued by psychologists and those in the field of special education because they can be helpful in diagnosing a student's strengths and weaknesses. However, group intelligence tests given for the purpose of classifying students into like-score groups have been criticized.

Group IQ tests are criticized because test items and tasks are culturally biased, drawn mostly from White middle-class experience. Thus the tests are more assessments of how informed students are about features in a specific class or culture than of how intelligent they are in general. This complaint became a formal, legal challenge when, on the basis of their IQ test scores, a group of African American children were put into special classes for mentally retarded children. Their parents brought the complaint to the courts in 1971 and persisted with it all the way to the federal appellate court, where a decision was eventually made in their favor in 1984. In that well-known case, *Larry P. v. Riles* (1984), the court decided that IQ tests were discriminatory and culturally biased. However, in another case, *PASE v. Hannon* (1980), an Illinois district court ruled that when IQ tests were used in conjunction with other forms of assessment, such as teacher observation, they were not discriminatory for placement purposes. Although the criticism continues, psychometricians are attempting to design culture-free intelligence tests.

Multiple Intelligences

Most theorists believe that intelligence is a basic ability that enables one to perform mental operations in the following areas: logical reasoning, spatial reasoning, number ability, and verbal meaning. However, they also point out "that conventional notions of intelligence are incomplete and hence inadequate. [One's] ability to achieve success depends on capitalizing on one's strengths and correcting or compensating for one's weaknesses through a balance of analytical, creative, and practical abilities" (Sternberg, 2002, pp. 447–448).

In the absence of a full, scientific explanation of intelligence, Howard Gardner has proposed a theory of **multiple intelligences**. According to Gardner, human beings possess 7 to 10 separate forms of intelligence, each of which functions like a computer—"one . . . computes linguistic information, another spatial information, another musical information, another information about other people, and so on" (Gardner, 2013).

Drawing on the theories of others and research findings on savants, prodigies, and other exceptional individuals, Gardner originally suggested in *Frames of Mind* (1983) that human beings possess seven human intelligences: logical-mathematical, linguistic, musical, spatial, bodily-kinesthetic, interpersonal, and intrapersonal. In the mid-1990s, he identified an eighth intelligence, that of the naturalist. According to Gardner, every person possesses at least the eight intelligences (see Figure 9.9), yet each person has his or her particular blend of the intelligences.

While the idea that everyone is "smart" in some way is perhaps true, there is little research to support Gardner's theory of multiple intelligences (Allix, 2000; Brody, 1992; Roberts & Lipnevich, 2012; Waterhouse, 2006). In fact, Gardner even admitted that there is "little hard evidence for MI theory" (Gardner and Connell, 2000, p. 292). Nevertheless, Gardner's theory of multiple intelligences is a reminder that teachers "should avoid thinking about children as smart or not smart, because there are many ways to

Figure 9.9 The eight intelligences

Logical-mathematical intelligence enables individuals to use and appreciate abstract relations. Scientists, mathematicians, and philosophers all rely on this intelligence. So do the students who "live" baseball statistics or who carefully analyze the components of problems—either personal or school related—before systematically testing solutions.

Linguistic intelligence allows individuals to communicate and make sense of the world through language. Poets exemplify this intelligence in its mature form. Students who enjoy playing with rhymes, who pun, who always have a story to tell, who quickly acquire other languages—including sign language—all exhibit linguistic intelligence.

Musical intelligence allows people to create, communicate, and understand meanings made out of sound. While composers and instrumentalists clearly exhibit this intelligence, so do the students who seem particularly attracted by the birds singing outside the classroom window or who constantly tap out intricate rhythms on the desk with their pencils.

Spatial intelligence makes it possible for people to perceive visual or spatial information, to transform this information, and to re-create visual images from memory. Well-developed spatial capacities are needed for the work of architects, sculptors, and engineers. The students who turn first to the graphs, charts, and pictures in their textbooks, who like to "web" their ideas before writing a paper, and who fill the blank space around their notes with intricate patterns are also using their spatial intelligence.

Bodily-kinesthetic intelligence allows individuals to use all or part of the body to create products or solve problems. Athletes, surgeons, dancers, choreographers, and craftspeople all use bodily-kinesthetic intelligence. The capacity is also evident in students who relish gym class and school dances, who prefer to carry out class projects by making models rather than writing reports, and who toss crumpled paper with frequency and accuracy into wastebaskets across the room.

Interpersonal intelligence enables individuals to recognize and make distinctions about others' feelings and intentions. Teachers, parents, politicians, psychologists, and salespeople rely on interpersonal intelligence. Students exhibit this intelligence when they thrive on small-group work, when they notice and react to the moods of their friends and classmates, and when they tactfully convince the teacher of their need for extra time to complete the homework assignment.

Intrapersonal intelligence helps individuals to distinguish among their own feelings, to build accurate mental models of themselves, and to draw on these models to make decisions about their lives. Although it is difficult to assess who has this capacity and to what degree, evidence can be sought in students' uses of their other intelligences—how well they seem to be capitalizing on their strengths, how cognizant they are of their weaknesses, and how thoughtful they are about the decisions and choices they make.

Naturalist intelligence allows people to distinguish among, classify, and use features of the environment. Farmers, gardeners, botanists, geologists, florists, and archaeologists all exhibit this intelligence, as do students who can name and describe the features of every make of car around them.

be smart" (Slavin, 2015, p. 92). Thus, teachers should use a variety of teaching methods so that students can use their diverse abilities to learn new material.

In addition to the possibility of multiple intelligences, some students are talented in terms of their interpersonal relations and exhibit natural leadership abilities. Others seem to have a high degree of what some researchers have termed **emotional intelligence**—awareness of and ability to manage their feelings (Salovey & Feldman-Barrett, 2002; Salovey, Mayer, & Caruso, 2002; Salovey & Sluyter, 1997).

Learning Style Preferences

It has been suggested that students have particular learning styles; for example, auditory learners more quickly learn things they hear while "visual learners" learn faster when they see material in writing. Teachers have been advised to adjust instruction to meet the learning style of the individual to achieve improvements in learning. However, there is little evidence to support the validity of dozens of models for distinct learning styles and learning style inventories (e.g., Pashler, McDaniel, Rohrer, & Bjork, 2008; Brophy, 2010; Eggen & Kauchak, 2016). Moreover, "[t]he research bases encouraging learning style assessments and the differentiated curriculum and instruction based on them is virtually nonexistent" (Eggen & Kauchak, 2016, p. 178).

Students do seem to have **learning style preferences**—their preferred approaches to learning. Some like to learn via listening; others prefer to read. Some like a lot of structure; others enjoy when they can be independent and follow their desires. Some like formal settings; others prefer informal, relaxed environments. Some prefer almost total silence to concentrate; others revel in noisy, active environments.

It is important to remember, however, that "learning 'styles' are basically just preferences . . . . It is not the case that students with one preferred style cannot learn just as well when information is presented in other ways" (Ormrod, Anderman, & Anderman, 2017, p. 139).

Nevertheless, knowledge of your students' learning style preferences will help you to individualize instruction and motivate your students. As a teacher, you should keep track of information related to students' learning style preferences, as well as academic progress and individual learning needs.

Hill Street Studios/Blend Images/Alamy Stock Photo

As a teacher, you will quickly learn that no one instructional approach matches the learning style preferences and needs of every student. How can you gather information about your students' preferred approaches to learning?

How do Students Vary in Ability and Disability?

Students also differ according to their special needs and talents. Some enter the world with exceptional abilities or disabilities, others encounter life experiences that change their capabilities significantly, and still others struggle with conditions that medical scientists have yet to understand. To the fullest extent possible, all children and youth with exceptionalities are given a public education in the United States.

Students with Special Needs

General education teachers today have an increasing number of students with disabilities in their classrooms. Approximately 95 percent of 6- to 21-year-old students with disabilities attend regular schools, and more than 62 percent of these students are in general education classrooms 80 percent or more of the time (National Center for Education Statistics, 2017b). To realize their potential, **students with disabilities** are provided with special education and related services. Among the **exceptional learners** teachers may encounter in the classroom are students who have physical, mental, or emotional disabilities and students who are gifted or talented.

Students with special needs are often referred to synonymously as *handicapped* or *disabled*. However, it is important for teachers to understand the following:

> Many individuals with disabilities believe that the terms *disability* and *handicap* have very different meanings and interpretations. They are convinced that it is because of their *disabilities* (e.g., conditions and impairments) that society *handicaps* them (e.g., presents challenges and barriers).... Thus the ways in which people are treated by society and by other individuals are what present the real barriers that influence people's outcomes. Difficult situations occur not because of a condition or disability but, rather, because people with disabilities are denied full participation in society as a consequence of their minority status. (Smith, 2007, pp. 9–10)

For example, Stephen W. Hawking (1942–2018), a gifted physicist, had amyotrophic lateral sclerosis (also known as Lou Gehrig's disease), which required him to use a wheelchair for mobility and a speech synthesizer to communicate. If Hawking had to enter a building accessible only by stairs, or if a computer virus infected his speech synthesizer program, his disability then became a handicap. As Hawking pointed out in his widely read book *A Brief History of Time: From the Big Bang to Black Holes* (1988), "I was fortunate that I chose theoretical physics, because it is all in the mind. So my disability has not been a serious handicap."

In addition, as a teacher you should know that current language use emphasizes the concept of "people first." In other words, a disabling condition should not be used as an adjective to describe a person. Thus you should say "a child with a visual impairment," not a "blind child" or even a "visually impaired child."

You should also realize that the definitions for disabilities are generalized, open to change, and significantly influenced by the current cultural perception of normality. For example, the American Association on Mental Retardation (AAMR) has changed its definition of mental retardation several times since 1950 to reflect shifting views of people with cognitive disabilities. In 2010, President Obama signed "Rosa's Law," which replaced the term *mental retardation* with *intellectual disability* in federal education, health, and labor laws. The parents of Rosa Marcellino, a 9-year-old with Down syndrome, worked for two years to remove the words *mentally retarded* from the health and education code in **MARYLAND**. Upon signing the law, President Obama quoted Rosa's brother, Nick: "What you call people is how you treat them. If we change the words, maybe it will be the start of a new attitude towards people with disabilities" (White House Press Release, 2010).

Cautions about labeling should also apply to gifted and talented students. Unfortunately, people commonly have a negative view of gifted and talented youngsters.

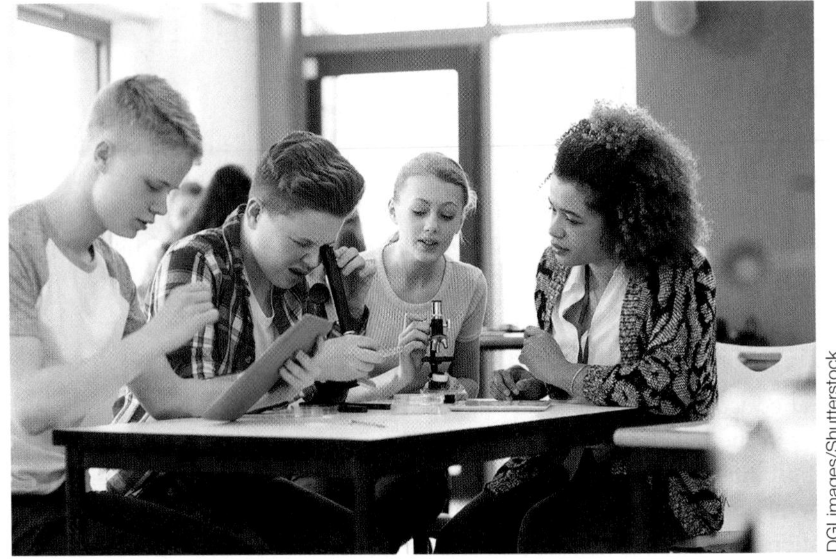

DGLimages/Shutterstock

Gifted and talented students benefit from enriched learning experiences and individualized plans that give them the opportunity to grow at an accelerated rate. What are some forms of enrichment you will offer your students?

Like many ethnic groups, gifted students are "different" and thus have been the target of many myths and stereotypes. However, a landmark study of 1,528 gifted males and females begun by Lewis Terman (Terman, Baldwin, & Bronson, 1925; Terman & Oden, 1947, 1959) in 1926 and continued until 2010 has "exploded the myth that high-IQ individuals [are] brainy but physically and socially inept. In fact, Terman found that children with outstanding IQs were larger, stronger, and better coordinated than other children and became better adjusted and more emotionally stable adults" (Slavin, 2015, p. 315).

FOCUS ON **DIVERSITY**: STUDENTS WITH SPECIAL NEEDS

Figure 9.10 shows that more than 6.4 million students, or about 13 percent of those enrolled in public schools, participated in federally supported education programs for students with special needs during 2014. Various tests and other forms of assessment are used to identify persons in different categories of disability.

The following brief definitional characteristics are based on the Individuals with Disabilities Education Act (IDEA) and definitions used by professional organizations dedicated to meeting the needs of persons in each category.

1. **Specific learning disabilities (LD)**—learning is significantly hindered by difficulty in listening, speaking, reading, writing, reasoning, or computing
2. **Speech or language impairments**—significant difficulty in communicating with others as a result of speech or language disorders
3. **Intellectual disability**—significant limitations in cognitive ability
4. **Serious emotional disturbance (SED)**—social and/or emotional maladjustment that significantly reduces the ability to learn
5. **Hearing impairments**—permanent or fluctuating mild to profound hearing loss in one or both ears
6. **Orthopedic impairments**—physically disabling conditions that affect locomotion or motor functions
7. **Other health impairments**—limited strength, vitality, or alertness caused by chronic or acute health problems
8. **Visual impairments**—vision loss that significantly inhibits learning
9. **Multiple disabilities**—two or more interrelated disabilities

10. **Deaf-blindness**—vision and hearing disability that severely limits communication
11. **Autism and other**—significantly impaired communication, learning, and reciprocal social interactions

Figure 9.10 shows that about 35 percent of the 6.4 million children and youth receiving special education services had a specific learning disability. Since the term

Figure 9.10 Children 3 to 21 years old served under Individuals with Disabilities Education Act, Part B, by type of disability: 2013–14

Type of disability	Number served (in thousands)	Number served as a percent of total enrollment[1]
All disabilities	**6,464**	**12.9**
Autism	538	1.1
Deaf-blindness	1	#
Developmental delay	410	0.8
Emotional disturbance	354	0.7
Hearing impairment	77	0.2
Intellectual disability	425	0.9
Multiple disabilities	132	0.3
Orthopedic impairment	56	0.1
Other health impairment[1]	817	1.6
Preschool disabled	†	†
Specific learning disability	2,264	4.5
Speech or language impairment	1,334	2.7
Traumatic brain injury	26	0.1
Visual impairment	28	0.1

(a) Number served and percentage of total school enrollment, by primary type of disability

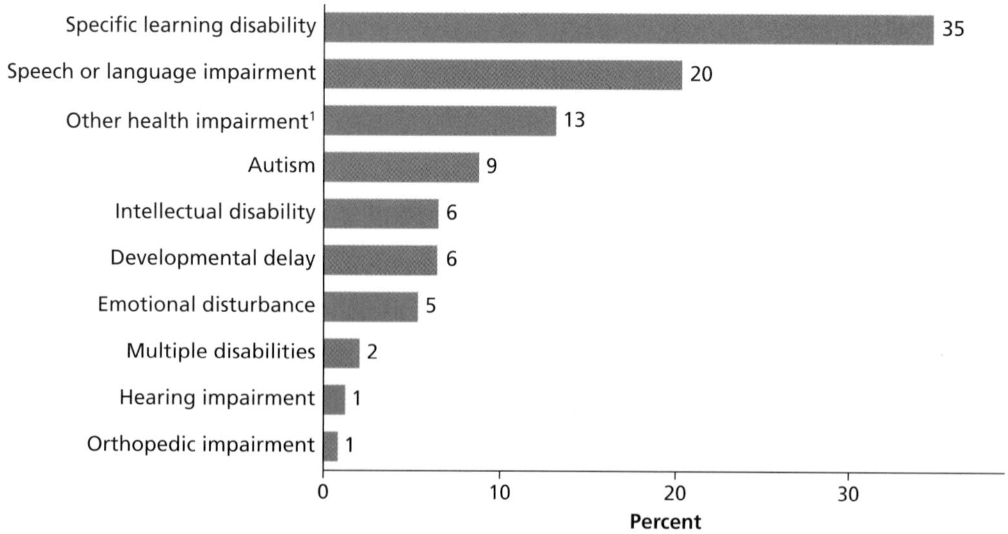

(b) Percentage distribution of 3- to 21-year-olds served, by primary type of disability

a. † Not applicable.

Rounds to zero.

[1] Other health impairments include having limited strength, vitality, or alertness due to chronic or acute health problems such as a heart condition, tuberculosis, rheumatic fever, nephritis, asthma, sickle cell anemia, hemophilia, epilepsy, lead poisoning, leukemia, or diabetes.

b. NOTE: Deaf-blindness, traumatic brain injury, and visual impairment are not shown because they each account for less than 0.5 percent of children served under IDEA. Due to categories not shown, detail does not sum to 100 percent. Although rounded numbers are displayed, the figures are based on unrounded estimates.

SOURCE: Adapted from Snyder, T.D., de Brey, C., and Dillow, S.A. (2016). *Digest of Education Statistics 2015* (NCES 2016-014). National Center for Education Statistics, Institute of Education Sciences, U.S. Department of Education. Washington, DC, p. 119, and McFarland, J., Hussar, B., de Brey, C., Snyder, T., Wang, X., Wilkinson-Flicker, S., Gebrekristos, S., Zhang, J., Rathbun, A., Barmer, A., Bullock Mann, F., and Hinz, S. (2017). *The Condition of Education 2017* (NCES 2017-144). U.S. Department of Education. Washington, DC: National Center for Education Statistics, p. 110.

learning disability (LD) was first introduced in the early 1960s, there has been no universally accepted definition. According to the National Joint Committee on Learning Disabilities (2016), a learning disability is a neurological disorder. People with a learning disability are no less intelligent than others; however, they have difficulty with cognitive processes such as reading, writing, spelling, and remembering information. Teachers should teach students with learning disabilities in ways that reduce the effects of the disability.

Imagine that you are concerned about two of your new students—Mary and Bill. Mary has an adequate vocabulary and doesn't hesitate to express herself, but her achievement in reading and mathematics doesn't add up to what you believe she can do. Often, when you give the class instructions, Mary seems to get confused about what to do. In working with her one on one, you've noticed that she often reverses letters and numbers the way much younger children do—she sees a *b* for a *d* or a *6* for a *9*. Mary may have a learning disability, causing problems in taking in, organizing, remembering, and expressing information. Like Mary, students with learning disabilities often show a significant difference between their estimated intelligence and their actual achievement in the classroom.

Bill presents you with a different set of challenges. He is obviously bright, but he frequently seems to be out of sync with classroom activities. He gets frustrated when he has to wait for his turn. He sometimes blurts out answers before you've even asked a question. He can't seem to stop wiggling his toes and tapping his pencil, and he often comes to school without his backpack and homework. Bill may have **attention deficit hyperactivity disorder (ADHD)**, one of the most commonly diagnosed disabilities among children. It is estimated that between 3 and 5 percent of children have ADHD in the United States. In a classroom of 25 to 30 students, at least one will probably have ADHD. Students with an **attention deficit disorder (ADD)** have difficulty focusing their attention long enough to learn well. Children with ADD/ADHD do not qualify for special education unless they also have another disability in a federally defined category.

Treatment for students with ADD/ADHD includes behavior modification and medication. Since the early 1980s, stimulant medications such as Ritalin and Adderall have become the most commonly prescribed drugs for ADD/ADHD. The Centers for Disease Control and Prevention estimates that an annual average of 6.1 million physician office visits are made by children aged 4-17 with a primary diagnosis of ADD/ADHD (Albert, Rui, & Ashman, 2017).

Teachers can help in the early identification of students with learning disabilities so they can receive the instructional adaptations or special education services they need by being alert for students who exhibit several of the following academic and behavioral characteristics:

- Significant discrepancy between potential and achievement
- Inability to problem-solve
- Substantial delay in academic achievement
- Lack of engagement with learning tasks
- Poor language and/or cognitive development
- Lack of basic reading and decoding skills
- Lack of attention during lectures or class discussion
- Excessive movement, hyperactivity
- Impulsivity
- Poor motor coordination and spatial relation skills
- Poor motivation

Some students have trouble remembering verbal instructions or recognizing words in print (*dyslexia*), whereas others have trouble working with numbers (*dyscalculia*). A learning disability can't be cured or fixed; it is a lifelong issue. With the right support and intervention, however, children with learning disabilities can succeed in school and go on to successful, often distinguished careers later in life. Parents can help children with learning disabilities achieve such success by encouraging their strengths, knowing their weaknesses, understanding the educational system, working with professionals, and learning about strategies for dealing with specific difficulties. The Teaching on Your Feet feature in this chapter profiles Tonia Grimes, who learned how to meet the needs of a "hard-to-reach" student with a learning disability.

Teaching on Your Feet

Connecting with a Hard-to-Reach Student

I navigated through my first year [as a fifth-grade teacher] fairly successfully, while working to form relationships with my students in an effort to keep one step ahead of them, which was no easy feat! There was one child in particular, Alexander, who I just couldn't seem to connect with. He was a student with special needs who had learning disabilities in both math and reading. He rarely bathed, his clothes were filthy, and the other children were sometimes very cruel to him. He was a difficult child to get to open up, but I was dogged in my efforts.

You can imagine my delight when finally, in late spring, Alexander raised his hand during math class. Not only did it go up, but it was accompanied by "Ooh, ooh, ooh," as he waved it frantically. Thrilled that Alexander was eager to participate in our discussion for the first time ever, I immediately called on him.

Well, you can imagine my surprise when he suddenly lunged into a story about his grandma, whom he was excited to tell us, had a hole in her head. You see, we were studying fractions that day, and I had just explained that a fraction is "a part of a whole." Alexander obviously didn't realize the difference between W-hole and H-ole. "Homophones," I told myself, "had better be tomorrow's English lesson!"

Acknowledging Alexander that day was exactly what he needed from me. We had suddenly bonded. Alexander felt such a connection to me after that, that he even went one step further.

I arrived at the school the following morning and was genuinely surprised to find Alexander and his grandma waiting for me. Grandma began by saying, "Alexander said he told you that I have a hole in my head." I smiled nervously and said, "Don't worry. You know kids! They have great imaginations!" Grandma replied, "You didn't believe him, did you?" "No, of course not," I stammered. Well, just that quick, Grandma proudly popped out her glass eye, revealing that she truly did have a hole in her head!

I will never forget that day, and the lessons that I learned from being Alexander's teacher. He taught me that:

1. *Students with learning disabilities can connect to a word or phrase, even if it is a homophone, and then just need to vocalize their thoughts.*
2. *I can connect with the hard-to-reach students if I allow them to speak when they are ready to.*
3. *The child who sits by himself, who is shunned by his peers, and who appears to be "on another planet" most days, may just be waiting for the right moment to share something with you. He is testing you to see if you really do care about him.*
4. *We need to look beyond the "package" that our students and their families come wrapped in, so that we can see inside them, and find out what motivates them.*
5. *If a child ever again tells me about a family member with a hole in his or her head . . . BELIEVE HIM!*

TONIA L. GRIMES
Tippecanoe Valley School Corporation
Akron, **INDIANA**
Reprinted with permission.

Analyze

Teaching well means being open to creative ways to connect with all students, including those with learning disabilities. It means taking the time to listen carefully to what they are saying, looking for clues about how to teach them more effectively.

Reflect

1. In what ways can teachers learn from their students?
2. What are the characteristics of teachers who are highly effective at connecting with hard-to-reach students?

Grimes was **INDIANA'S** 2009 Teacher of the Year.

The preceding is excerpted from her online article at http://www. beliefnet.com/Inspiration/Chicken-Soup-For-The-Soul/2010/03/Connecting.aspx

FOCUS ON **STEM**: STUDENTS WITH SPECIAL NEEDS BENEFIT FROM STEM

Educational researchers have found that STEM schools can benefit students with special needs (Wei et al., 2013; Chen, 2016). For example, STEM^3 Academy near Los Angeles reports that STEM subjects help students diagnosed with autism spectrum disorder, ADHD, and learning disabilities overcome difficulties in social situations.

Teachers at the Academy use a "flipped" model of teaching. Instead of lecturing or teaching during school hours, teachers use class time to help students finish homework assignments and projects. After school, students study on their own and review the next day's lesson. As the director of the Academy explains: "Our emphasis is on learning versus teaching. Our students learn by doing, experiencing, and constructing rather than just sitting in a classroom listening to a teacher" (Chen, 2016).

According to the mother of a student diagnosed with autism, STEM study has benefited her son. Before enrolling at the Academy, he struggled socially at school. "[There has] been a big change. Before he wouldn't talk much about his day. Now he comes home and has conversations with me about what he did at school" (Chen, 2016).

TECHNOLOGY in ACTION

Word-Prediction Software in the Classroom

"I don't like to write." "I don't know how to spell." Miss Hernandez often hears comments like these from her eighth-grade students with disabilities. She understands that some students with learning disabilities may not be able to retain ideas in their memories long enough to express them in writing, whereas others may have difficulty with spelling. Students with motor disabilities may be challenged when forming letters with a pen or pencil or making repetitive keystrokes on a word processor.

Recently, Miss Hernandez visited Mr. Wu's classroom to observe how one of his students with a motor disability that affects her ability to write is using word-prediction software to reduce the number of keystrokes needed to type words. As Miss Hernandez watched, the student would type the first letter of a word, and then a numbered list of words beginning with that letter would appear on the computer screen. If the desired word was on the list, the student would enter the number and the word would be typed automatically. Miss Hernandez watched as the student wrote the word *tonight* to complete the sentence "I will watch TV tonight." First, she entered a "t" and the list of common "t" words shown in screen #1 appeared. Because the word *tonight* was not on this list, she typed an "o" and screen #2 appeared. Because *tonight* was on this list, she typed a number "3" and the word was entered automatically. Thus the seven keystrokes needed to write *tonight* were reduced to three.

WORD-PREDICTION SOFTWARE: Word-prediction software can be installed on most word-processing programs. The software is even included on some versions of Microsoft Word. Word-prediction software helps students by guessing the words that they are typing into the word processor and saving keystrokes. Students can save more than 40 percent of the keystrokes they would normally enter into a traditional word processor.

Most good word-prediction software programs also work phonetically. For example, if a student puts a "k" for the first letter of the word *campus*, the software would overlook the error. Some word-prediction software programs can also correct for dyslexic spelling errors, where some characters may be transposed. The following list describes additional features of various word-prediction software programs.

- **Synthesized speech output**—To provide additional support for students while they write, some word-prediction programs also have synthesized speech output. For students with limited reading abilities, this feature helps them monitor the structure and meaning of their work.
- **Prediction methods**—Some programs predict on the basis of spelling only, while others consider the words that have come before in the sentence; for example, only nouns are listed after the word *a* or *an*.
- **List updating**—After "learning" a student's vocabulary, the word prediction program tailors the word prediction lists to the student's usage. Some programs update automatically, whereas others allow the user to decide when to update.

- **Prediction window customizing**—Some programs have prediction lists that appear with a set number of words in a fixed-size window in a specific location on the screen. Others allow users to customize the size, the screen location, and the amount of words in the window.
- **Keyboard sensitivity adjustment**—Keyboard sensitivity can be adjusted to prevent repetition if keys are not quickly released.

In addition to helping students with learning disabilities or motor disabilities, word-prediction software is helpful for general education students who are challenged by the writing process. With word-prediction software, students are better able to complete written assignments and thus experience greater success in the classroom. As an administrator at a district that makes word-prediction software available to *all* students at the district's 122 schools points out, "We're operating on the premise that adaptive technology is necessary for students with learning disabilities and good for all students. Good teaching dictates that we hit all of the learning modalities that kids need. Just because a student is doing well or moderately well doesn't mean that they couldn't benefit from adaptive technology. There are children other than our kids with learning disabilities who are stronger verbally than they are in a written context" (Kinross, 2009).

VISIT: Some word-prediction software sites on the Internet allow you to download a free demonstration version of the software. Also, some sites have links to videos that show how to install and use the software.

FOCUS ON **DIVERSITY**: STUDENTS WHO ARE GIFTED AND TALENTED

Gifted and talented students, those who have demonstrated a high level of attainment in intellectual ability, academic achievement, creativity, or visual and performing arts, are evenly distributed across all ethnic and cultural groups and socioeconomic classes. Although you might think it is easy to meet the needs of gifted and talented students, you will find that this is not always the case. "Working with students with gifts and talents can be especially challenging for classroom teachers considering the wide range of achievement levels in today's classrooms" (Hallahan, Kauffman, & Pullen, 2015, p. 392).

Variations in criteria used to identify gifted and talented students are especially evident in the reported incidence of giftedness from state to state. For example, Vermont and Massachusetts report that only 0.8 percent of students are enrolled in gifted and talented programs, whereas Oklahoma and Kentucky report 14.0 and 13.8 percent, respectively (National Center for Education Statistics, 2017b). Depending on the criteria used, estimates of the number of gifted and talented students range from 3 to 5 percent of the total population (Hallahan, Kauffman, & Pullen, 2015, p. 381). Among the cognitive characteristics of the gifted are the following:

- Ability to manipulate abstract symbol systems
- Power of concentration
- Unusually well-developed memory
- Early language interest and development
- Curiosity
- Preference for independent work
- Multiple interests
- Ability to generate original ideas (Friend, 2018, pp. 461–462)

Effective teachers of the **gifted and talented** have many of the same characteristics as their students. "Characteristics that reoccur across the studies of exemplary teachers of the gifted include: intellectualism, subject matter expertise, a personal rapport with high-ability learners, and enjoyment in teaching them" (Robinson, 2008, p. 676). Four innovative approaches for meeting the educational needs of gifted students are acceleration, self-directed or independent study, Individual Education Programs (IEPs), and alternative or magnet schools.

ACCELERATION The effectiveness of accelerated programs for intellectually precocious students is "striking" (Gross, 2008, p. 248). For example, in a review of hundreds of research findings in education, Kulik (2004) was "not able to find any educational treatment that consistently yielded higher effect size (i.e., positive results) than [acceleration]" (p. 20). The following types of **acceleration** have proven to be the most beneficial at different grade levels:

- **Elementary school**—early entrance, grade skipping, nongraded classes, and curriculum compacting (modifying the curriculum to present it at a faster pace)
- **Junior high school**—grade skipping, grade telescoping (shortening the amount of time to complete a grade level), concurrent enrollment in a high school or college, subject acceleration, and curriculum compacting
- **Senior high school**—concurrent enrollment, subject acceleration, advanced-placement (AP) classes, mentorships, credit by examination, and early admission to college

One approach to acceleration is known as "curriculum compacting," which encourages brighter students to forge ahead in the regular curriculum while all students work to their strengths, and less able students still get the time and attention they need. Also, many colleges and universities now participate in accelerated programs whereby gifted youth who have outgrown the high school curriculum may enroll in college courses.

SELF-DIRECTED OR INDEPENDENT STUDY For some time, self-directed or independent study has been recognized as an appropriate way for teachers to maintain the interest of gifted students in their classes. Gifted students usually have the academic backgrounds and motivation to do well without constant supervision and the threat or reward of grades. At their own pace, gifted students can engage in accelerative learning, which offers advanced curricula and encourages individual creativity, positive reinforcement, and relaxation.

Video Example 9.2

Gifted Students in the Classroom: A teacher explains how she uses the abilities and interests of a very bright student with autism to challenge him and include him in her class. (Note, the teacher uses the term "Aspergers" which was one of several subtypes of autism that was then folded into a single diagnosis of "autism spectrum disorder" in 2013.)

INDIVIDUAL EDUCATION PROGRAMS (IEPS) Since the passage of PL 94-142 and the mandating of IEPs for special education students, IEPs have been promoted as an appropriate means for educating gifted students. Most IEPs for gifted students involve various enrichment experiences; self-directed study; and special, concentrated instruction given to individuals or small groups in pullout programs. For example, QuestBridge, part of the Quest Scholars Program, links gifted and talented students with the nation's best colleges and universities. QuestBridge links exceptional students with colleges and universities, scholarship providers, employers, and organizations seeking gifted and talented students who have excelled despite obstacles (QuestBridge, 2016).

ALTERNATIVE OR MAGNET SCHOOLS Several large-city school systems have developed magnet schools organized around specific disciplines, such as science, mathematics, fine arts, basic skills, and so on. The excellent programs at these schools are designed to attract superior students from all parts of the district. Many of these schools offer outstanding programs for gifted and talented youth.

FOCUS ON **STEM**: UNIVERSITY OFFERS STEM PROGRAM FOR GIFTED STUDENTS

To meet the needs of gifted students attending Metropolitan Nashville Public Schools (MNPS), Vanderbilt University collaborated with MNPS and opened the School for Science and Math at Vanderbilt (SSMV). The SSMV offers public high school students a four-year, interdisciplinary, research-centered learning experience at Vanderbilt. The STEM curriculum integrates cutting-edge "real world" content through research projects collaboratively designed by students, SSMV faculty, and Vanderbilt faculty.

Students apply for the program in eighth grade through a selection process that involves teacher recommendations, essays, and interviews. Each year, about 100 students, 24 to 26 at each high school grade level, participate in the program. During the academic year, students attend SSMV classes on the Vanderbilt campus one full day per week. Each summer, 9th-, 10th-, and 11th-grade students complete one of the following research courses:

Research I—a 3-week summer course with a focus on field research that spans ecology, geology, archaeology, chemistry, and engineering.

Research II—a 3-week summer course that allows students to complete a group research project of their choosing and then communicate this research to other students through research poster presentations.

Research III—a 6-week summer internship in a Vanderbilt laboratory where students work alongside a research team to complete a project for national science competitions where they can earn prestigious recognition and scholarships. Also, much of this work is highlighted in the *Young Scientist* research journal (School for Science and Math at Vanderbilt, 2018).

During their senior year, students take the Advanced Research course, designed to "help students communicate their research not only to the scientific community but also to the broader public. A significant portion of the course concentrates on students participating in community-engaged research projects that benefit Nashville and beyond" (School for Science and Math at Vanderbilt, 2018).

What are Special Education and Inclusion?

Prior to the 20th century, children with special needs were usually segregated from regular classrooms and taught by teachers in state-run and private schools. Today, an array of programs and services in general and special education classrooms is aimed at developing the potential of exceptional students. Two critical concepts to promote the growth, talents, and productivity of exceptional students are special education and inclusion.

Special education is "the means through which children who have disabilities receive an education specifically designed to help them reach their learning potential" (Friend, 2018, p. 4). Teachers who are trained in special education become familiar with special materials, techniques, equipment, and facilities for students with special needs. For example, children with visual impairment may require reading materials in large print or Braille; students with hearing impairment may require hearing aids and/or instruction in sign language; those with physical disabilities may need special equipment; those with emotional disturbances may need smaller and more highly structured classes; children with special gifts or talents may require access to working professionals.

Special Education Laws

Until 1975, the needs of students with disabilities were primarily met through self-contained special education classes within regular schools. That year, however, Congress passed the **Education for All Handicapped Children Act (Public Law 94-142)**. This act guaranteed to all children with special needs a free and appropriate public education. The law, which applied to every teacher and every school in the country, outlined extensive procedures to ensure that exceptional students between the ages of 3 and 18 were granted due process in regard to identification, placement, and educational services received. As a result of PL 94-142, the participation of students with special needs in all classrooms and school programs became routine.

In 1990, PL 94-142 was replaced by the **Individuals with Disabilities Education Act (IDEA)**. IDEA included the major provisions of PL 94-142 and extended the availability of a free, appropriate education to youth with special needs between the ages of 3 and 21. IDEA, which is one of the most important and far-reaching pieces of educational legislation ever passed in this country, has

Figure 9.11 Educational service options for students with disabilities

Level	Educational Delivery System	Professional Responsibility
Most inclusive I	Student placed in general classroom; no additional or specialized assistance (*Greatest number of pupils*)	General education has primary responsibility for student's educational program. Special education is a support service designed to facilitate student's success in educational mainstream.
II	Student placed in general classroom; the special education teacher in a consultative role provides assistance to classroom teacher	
III	Student placed in general classroom for majority of school day; attends special education resource room for specialized instruction in areas of need	
IV	Student placed in special education class for majority of school day; attends general class in subject areas consonant with capabilities	Special education has primary responsibility for student's educational program.
V	Student placed in full-time special education class in general education school	
VI	Student placed in separate school for children with special needs	
VII	*Most restrictive* Student educated through homebound or hospital instructional program (*Least number of pupils*)	

SOURCE: From Hardman/Drew/Egan. Human Exceptionality, 11E. © 2014 South-Western, a part of Cengage Learning, Inc. Reproduced by permission. www.cengage.com/permissions

several provisions with which all teachers should be familiar. In 1997, the **Amendments to the Individuals with Disabilities Education Act (IDEA 97)** were passed. IDEA 97, and its reauthorization in 2004, went beyond IDEA's focus on public school *access* for students with special needs to emphasize educational *outcomes*, modified eligibility requirements, IEP guidelines, public and private placements, student discipline guidelines, and procedural safeguards.

IDEA requires that all children with special needs be educated in the **least restrictive environment**. In other words, a student must be "mainstreamed" into a general education classroom whenever such integration is feasible and appropriate and the child would receive educational benefit from such placement. Figure 9.11 shows the educational service options for students with disabilities, from the least restrictive to the most restrictive. Among schools with high-incidence disabilities (i.e., disabilities that are most common among school children), students with speech or language impairments and specific learning disabilities are served in the regular classroom for most of the school day. Students with emotional disturbance, intellectual disability, and multiple disabilities typically receive services outside the regular classroom for more than 60 percent of the school day (National Center for Education Statistics, 2017b).

Video Example 9.3

Jennifer's Story: A college student with a learning disability, looks back and discusses her struggle to qualify for special education services when she was a K-12 student.

RESPONSE TO INTERVENTION (RTI) Prior to IDEA 2004, the criterion of "unexpected underachievement" was used to identify students with learning disabilities. Unexpected underachievement was based on a "severe discrepancy" between a student's expected achievement level and actual achievement level. However, this approach was criticized because, often, a student needed to have a history of significant academic failure before a severe discrepancy was found to exist. According to some critics, this amounted to a "wait-to-fail" approach for identifying students with learning disabilities (Fletcher, Denton, & Francis, 2005).

After passage of IDEA 2004, however, states were required to use a systematic approach to provide *early intervention* for students having academic difficulty but not yet identified as needing special education services. A new approach was mandated because previous methods of identifying students with learning disabilities were often not reliable or valid (Friend, 2018; Hardman, Egan, & Drew, 2017; Hallahan, Kauffman, & Pullen, 2015). According to IDEA 2004, to be identified as eligible for special education services, a student's academic difficulty must be the result of a learning disability rather than a lack of good teaching.

To meet the requirements of IDEA 2004, many states adopted the **response to intervention (RTI) model**. According to RTI, general education teachers work with special education teachers on schoolwide screenings and academic progress monitoring to ensure that students are "responsive" to instruction they receive in the classroom. The RTI approach ensures that students who do not make adequate academic progress and who are at risk for reading and other learning disabilities receive increasingly intensive instructional services that include "scientific, research-based interventions." The RTI model is designed to determine, as early as possible, if a student's low achievement is due to instructional or behavioral factors or whether the student has a possible learning disability. The goal is to provide the student with appropriate instruction and educational assistance *before* he or she experiences years of low achievement.

Figure 9.12 illustrates a three-tier RTI model that many school districts follow to identify students with reading and/or learning problems. As the figure shows, a student who continues to struggle academically, even after receiving three "tiers" of increasingly intensive, individualized instruction, is then referred to a special education team that determines if the student has a learning disability.

INDIVIDUAL EDUCATION PROGRAM Every child with a disability must have a written **Individualized Education Program (IEP)** that meets the child's needs and

Figure 9.12 Response to Intervention (RTI): A three-tiered model for identifying students with learning disabilities

Special Education Services

Student does not respond as expected to previous three tiers of high-quality instruction. Student is then referred to intervention team to determine if student has a learning disability and should receive special education services.

Tier 3, Tertiary Intervention

Teachers monitor academic progress and determine that student continues to struggle academically. More intensive, individualized instruction is then provided, with weekly monitoring of academic progress.

Tier 2, Secondary Intervention

Screening measures determine that student continues to struggle academically, in spite of highly effective instructional strategies. Student receives Tier 2 intervention—e.g., more systematic, structured teaching; small-group instruction; and/or peer tutoring.

Tier 1, Primary Intervention

Student in general education class receives high-quality instruction in core areas such as reading and mathematics.

specifies educational goals, methods for achieving those goals, and the number and quality of special educational services to be provided. The IEP must be reviewed annually by five parties: (1) a parent or guardian, (2) the child, (3) a teacher, (4) a professional who has recently evaluated the child, and (5) others, usually the principal or a special education resource person from the school district.

Figure 9.13 presents portions of IEPs for Ruby, a second-grade student, and Alejandro, a 10th-grade student. The IEPs include present level of educational

Figure 9.13 Portions of IEPs for Ruby and Alejandro

Ruby

Current Grade: 2

Present Levels of Educational Performance

- Ruby is in good health with no known physical performance issues, and she socializes well with her peers.
- Ruby performs at grade level in all subjects except reading.
- Ruby can identify all letters of the alphabet and knows the sound of most consonants and short vowels.
- Her sight vocabulary is approximately 65 to 70 words, and she reads on the primer level.
- Ruby can spell most words in a first-grade textbook, but has difficulty with words in the second-grade textbook.

Annual Goals

1. By the end of the school year, Ruby will read at a beginning second-grade level with 90% accuracy in word recognition and 80% accuracy in word comprehension.

   Person Responsible: Resource Teacher
2. By the end of the school year, Ruby will increase her sight word vocabulary to 150 words.

   Person Responsible: Resource Teacher
3. By the end of the school year, Ruby will read and spell at least 75% of the second-grade spelling words.

   Person Responsible: Second-Grade Teacher

Amount of Participation in General Education

- Ruby will participate in all second-grade classes and activities except for reading.

Special Education and Related Services

- Ruby will receive individualized and/or small-group instruction in reading from the Resource Teacher for 30 minutes each day.

Alejandro

Current Grade: 10

Present Levels of Educational Performance

- Alejandro is in good health, has some fine motor skills delays, and ambulates using a wheelchair.
- Alejandro appears to have good socialization skills with his peers.
- Alejandro is passing all his courses and is enrolled in AP Calculus and AP English.

Annual Goals

1. By the end of the school year, Alejandro will successfully complete 10th-grade classes.

   Person Responsible: General Education Teacher and Adapted Physical Education Teacher
2. Alejandro will increase his writing speed with the use of a computer with word-prediction software.

   Person Responsible: Assistive Technology Specialist

Amount of Participation in General Education

- Alejandro will participate in all general education classes except for physical education.

Special Education and Related Services

- Alejandro will receive special transportation services between home and school.
- Alejandro will receive adapted physical education for one period each day.
- Alejandro will receive an assessment and ongoing support as needed from the Assistive Technology Specialist.
- The resource teacher will consult with the general education teachers as needed.

SOURCE: LEWIS, RENA B.; WHEELER, JOHN J.; CARTER, STACY L., REVEL FOR TEACHING STUDENTS WITH SPECIAL NEEDS IN GENERAL EDUCATION CLASSROOMS WITH LOOSE-LEAF VERSION, 9th Ed., ©2017. Reprinted and Electronically reproduced by permission of Pearson Education, Inc., New York, NY.

performance, annual goals, and the person responsible for helping the student achieve those goals. The examples also include amount of participation in general education and the special education and related services to be provided.

RELATED SERVICES IDEA 97 ensures that students with special needs receive any related services that will help them benefit from special education services. "These supports are not directly related to a student's instruction, but they are needed so that a student can access instruction. Related services for any single student could include a bus equipped with a wheelchair lift, individual counseling, and physical therapy" (Friend, 2018, p. 4).

CONFIDENTIALITY OF RECORDS IDEA also ensures that records on a child are kept confidential. Parental permission is required before any official may look at a child's records. Parents can amend a child's records if they feel information in it is misleading, inaccurate, or violates the child's rights.

DUE PROCESS IDEA gives parents the right to disagree with an IEP or an evaluation of their child's abilities. If a disagreement arises, it is settled through an impartial due process hearing presided over by an officer appointed by the state. At the hearing, parents may be represented by a lawyer, give evidence, and cross-examine, and are entitled to receive a transcript of the hearing and a written decision on the case. If either the parents or the school district disagrees with the outcome, the case may then be taken to the civil courts.

IDEA AND EVERY STUDENT SUCCEEDS ACT (ESSA) The Every Student Succeeds Act (ESSA), signed into law in 2015, resulted in several changes to the regulatory language of IDEA. For example, the following terms were removed from IDEA because they no longer appeared in ESSA: *core academic subjects, highly qualified special education teachers,* and *scientifically based research.* In addition, since ESSA reduced the role of the federal government and returned more accountability to the states, advocacy groups for students with disabilities began to shift their focus to the state level.

Meeting the Inclusion Challenge

To help you satisfy the provisions of IDEA, you will probably have opportunities as a teacher to participate in in-service programs designed to acquaint classroom teachers with the unique needs of students with special needs. In addition, your teacher education program may require a course on teaching students with special educational needs.

The guidelines for IDEA suggest that schools must make a significant effort to include, or mainstream, all children in the classroom. However, it is not clear how far schools must go to meet this inclusion requirement. For example, should children with severe disabilities be included in general education classrooms if they are unable to do the academic work? Recent court cases have ruled that students with severe disabilities must be included if there is a potential benefit for the child, if the class would stimulate the child's language development, or if other students could act as appropriate role models for the child. In one case, the court ordered a school district to place a child with an IQ of 44 in a regular second-grade classroom and rejected as exaggerated the district's claim that the placement would be prohibitively expensive (*Board of Education, Sacramento City Unified School District v. Holland,* 1992). In another case, the court rejected a school district's argument that inclusion of a child with a severe disability would be so disruptive as to significantly impair the learning of the other children (*Oberti v. Board of Education of the Borough of Clementon School District,* 1992).

To meet the inclusion challenge, you must have knowledge of various disabilities and the teaching methods and materials appropriate for each. Because teachers with negative attitudes toward students with special needs can convey these feelings to all students in a class and thereby reduce the effectiveness of inclusion (Friend, 2018; Hardman, Egan, & Drew, 2017; Hallahan, Kauffman, & Pullen, 2015), as a teacher you must have positive attitudes toward students receiving special education. An accepting, supportive climate can significantly enhance the self-confidence of students with special needs.

In addition, you should be prepared to participate in the education of exceptional learners. You should be willing to do the following:

1. Make maximum effort to accommodate individual students' needs
2. Evaluate academic abilities and disabilities
3. Refer [students] for evaluation [as appropriate]
4. Participate in eligibility conferences [for special education]
5. Participate in writing individualized education programs
6. Communicate with parents or guardians
7. Participate in due process hearings and negotiations
8. Collaborate with other professionals in identifying and making maximum use of exceptional students' abilities (Hallahan, Kauffman, & Pullen, 2015, pp. 35–36)

Video Example 9.4

Partnering Different Capabilities of Learners: How does the teacher take into account learners' different capabilities as she groups students for collaborative learning?

The Debate over Inclusion

Whereas "mainstreaming" refers to the application of the least restrictive environment clause of PL 94-142, **inclusion** goes beyond mainstreaming to integrate all students with disabilities into general education classes and school life with the active support of special educators and other specialists and service providers, as well as **assistive technology** and adaptive software. Advocates of inclusion have a philosophy similar to Joe Clifford, principal of West Hernando Middle School in Brooksville, **FLORIDA**:

> Our philosophy is that when a kid comes into West Hernando Middle School, our teachers and other staff engage in collaborative decision making to decide how to support the kid and help him fit in. We don't have programs for students with certain labels. We look at the individual student, and figure out what will work so the student will fit in. They're everyone's kids and part of our community. We're all responsible for making sure they're successful. This is inclusion for us. (McLeskey et al., 2010, pp. 4, 9)

Full inclusion goes even further and maintains that "all pupils with disabilities be educated in the general education classroom" (Gargiulo & Gouck, 2018, p. 603). Full inclusion is the most appropriate full-time placement not only for students with mild learning and behavior problems, but also for students with more severe disabilities. According to the full-inclusion approach, if a child needs support services, these are brought *to the child*; the child does not have to participate in a pullout program to receive support services. Advocates of full inclusion maintain that pullout programs stigmatize participating students because they are separated from their general education classmates, and pullout programs discourage collaboration between general and special education teachers. Those who oppose full inclusion maintain that classroom teachers, who may be burdened with large class sizes and be assigned to schools with inadequate support services, often lack the training and instructional materials to meet the needs of all exceptional students.

In addition, some parents of children with disabilities believe that full inclusion could mean the elimination of special education as we know it, along with the range of services currently guaranteed by federal special education laws. Full inclusion, they reason, would make them depend on individual states, not the federal government, to meet their children's needs. Some parents believe that special education classes provide their children with important benefits.

How do students in general education classrooms feel about their classmates with disabilities? Fifth-grade classmates of Jessica, a student who is nonverbal, nonambulatory, and unable to feed, dress, or care for herself, made these comments (presented in their original form):

- I feel that Jessica has changed my life. How I feel and see handicapped people has really changed. . . . I used to think about handicapped people being really weak and if I would touch her I would hurt her but now I think differently.
- I really like Jessica in my class. Before I met her I never really cared about handycapt people. Jessie is really nice and I like her a lot. Jessica is almost like a sister to me. I like to spend my recess playing with her. I thought a handycapt kid would never be part of my life, but now one and alot more are.
- I think it is great that Jessica is in our room. Jessica is very fun. She laughs and smiles a lot. Sometimes she crys but that is OK. I have learned that Handicapped people are just like the others. I used to say "ooh" look at the person but now I don't I have a big fear for handicapped because they are interesting they can do things that other people can't do. I think Jessica has changed because she is with lots of other kids. (Lewis & Doorlag, 2006, p. 12)

Lin Chang, an eighth-grade teacher, addresses the concerns that general education teachers may have about the availability of resources to help them be successful in inclusive classrooms:

> At first I was worried that it would all be my responsibility. But after meeting with the special education teacher, I realized that we would work together and I would have additional resources if I needed them. (Vaughn, Bos, & Schumm, 1997, p. 18)

In addition, the following comments by Octavio Gonzalez, a ninth-grade English teacher who has three students with disabilities in two of his five sections of English, express the satisfaction that teachers can experience in inclusive classrooms:

> At first I was nervous about having students with disabilities in my class. One of the students has a learning disability, one student has serious motor problems and is in a wheelchair, and the third student has vision problems. Now I have to say the adaptations I make to meet their special learning needs actually help all of the students in my class. I think that I am a better teacher because I think about accommodations now. (Vaughn et al., 1997, p. 18)

The attitudes of the two teachers just quoted are confirmed in research on teachers' attitudes toward inclusion. Two studies, for example, found that teachers who had experience with inclusion and opportunities for professional development had more positive attitudes toward inclusion and more confidence in their ability to fulfill students' IEPs (Avramidis, Bayliss, & Burden, 2000; Van Reusen, Shoho, & Barker, 2000). The Teachers' Voices: Being an Agent of Change feature in this chapter profiles Michelle Shearer, 2011 National Teacher of the Year. Shearer successfully includes students with a variety of special needs in her high school AP chemistry classes. Moreover, she has encouraged many of her students to continue their education beyond high school. For example, a former student at the Maryland School for the Deaf says Shearer's belief in him was the primary reason he was able to earn his bachelor's degree in mathematics (Hicks, 2011).

TEACHERS' VOICES  BEING AN AGENT OF CHANGE

MICHELLE SHEARER

"Creating an Inclusive Environment . . . Has Always Been my Mission"

Since I began teaching AP chemistry over a decade ago, I have successfully accommodated exceptional students with low vision, dyslexia, dysgraphia, attention deficit disorder, and Asperger's syndrome into my AP chemistry classroom. In 2003, after building rapport and a relationship with both profoundly deaf and hard-of-hearing students at the Maryland School for the Deaf (MSD), I taught AP chemistry, offered for the first time in the school's 135-year history. I conducted the class exclusively in American Sign Language and will always remember the unique experience of discussing complex concepts such as kinetics, electrochemistry, and chemical equilibria with students communicating solely with our hands. When I suggested that these students also study AP calculus, they looked at me with inquisitive expressions and signed, "WHY?" I signed back: "BECAUSE YOU CAN." For the next 2 years, I taught during my planning period so that these enthusiastic, academically motivated students would have the opportunity to study AP calculus and probability and statistics, which otherwise would not have been offered. I proudly share inspirational stories of MSD students who have proven that deaf and hard-of-hearing individuals can succeed in rigorous classes, pass AP exams, earn college degrees, and build successful careers as professionals in our society.

Creating an inclusive environment in which all students are able to experience the world of chemistry has always been my mission as a teacher. One of my greatest rewards is the tremendous growth of our current AP chemistry program and the diversity of the students it attracts. There were 11 students enrolled in AP chemistry when I returned to Urbana High in 2006; there are 92 students enrolled this year. This eight-fold increase is a testament to the high level of commitment and interest on behalf of our students and evidence of their confidence in my ability to provide a meaningful, relevant, rigorous, and yes "fun," chemistry program accessible to a broad range of students.

I am most proud of the fact that every student I have ever taught in AP chemistry, regardless of age, gender, race, hearing status, or learning challenge, has finished the journey with pride and completed the exam to the best of his or her ability. Many continue to keep me informed of their scientific accomplishments as professionals in the fields of health, engineering, and scientific research. Even the self-proclaimed "non-scientists" who finish my course reflect on the experience with a profound sense of pride in their personal achievements. One such student recently emailed, "Who knew that I could enjoy chemistry so much? Thank you for helping me to not dread taking science in college!" It is especially rewarding to collaborate with former students, now professional educators in STEM areas, who implement some of the teaching strategies I utilized when they were students in my classroom. I have connected with so many students whom I consider members of my ever-expanding "extended family," and I never tire hearing of the personal and professional accomplishments they have achieved beyond my classroom!

PERSONAL REFLECTION

1. Recall a teacher who helped you overcome self-doubt and believed that you could learn complex, difficult subject matter. How did the teacher do that?
2. Write a short note to the teacher referenced above, thanking him or her for helping you see yourself as a capable learner.

Michelle Shearer teaches chemistry at Urbana High School in Ijamsville, **MARYLAND**. She was the 2011 National Teacher of the Year.

The preceding is excerpted from Michelle Shearer's application for the National Teacher of the Year award at http://www.ccsso.org/Documents/2011/news/2011_NTOY_Press.pdf

FOCUS ON **DIVERSITY**: EQUAL OPPORTUNITY FOR EXCEPTIONAL LEARNERS

Like many groups in our society, exceptional learners have not often received the kind of education that most effectively meets their needs. More than 6.4 million learners in public schools, approximately 13 percent of the school-age population, are classified as exceptional (National Center for Education Statistics, 2017a).

Exceptional learners require special education because they differ significantly from most children. They may have intellectual disabilities, learning disabilities, emotional or behavioral disorders, physical disabilities, disorders of communication, autism, traumatic brain injury, impaired hearing, impaired sight, or special gifts or talents.

Just as there are no easy answers for how teachers should meet the needs of students from diverse cultural backgrounds, there is no single strategy for teachers to follow to ensure that all exceptional students receive an appropriate education. The key, however, lies in not losing sight of the fact that "the most important characteristics of exceptional children are their abilities, not their disabilities" (Hallahan & Kauffman, 2015, p. 4).

To build on students' strengths, classroom teachers must work cooperatively and collaboratively with special education teachers, and students in special education programs must not become isolated from their peers. In addition, teachers must understand how some people can be perceived as "different" and presumed to be "handicapped" because of their appearance or physical condition. Evidence suggests, for example, that people who are short, obese, or unattractive are often victims of discrimination, as are people with conditions such as AIDS, cancer, multiple sclerosis, or epilepsy. It is significant that many individuals with clinically diagnosable and classifiable impairments or disabilities do not perceive themselves as handicapped. The term itself means "permanently unable to be treated equally."

Officially labeling students has become a necessity with the passage of laws that provide education and related services for exceptional students. The classification labels help determine which students qualify for the special services, educational programs, and individualized instruction provided by the laws, and they bring to educators' attention many exceptional children and youth whose educational needs could otherwise be overlooked, neglected, or inadequately served. Detrimental aspects include the fact that classification systems are imperfect and have arbitrary cutoff points that sometimes lead to injustices. Also, labels tend to evoke negative expectations, which can cause teachers to avoid and underteach these students, and their peers to isolate or reject them, thereby stigmatizing individuals, sometimes permanently. The most serious detriment, however, is that students so labeled are taught to feel inadequate, inferior, and limited in terms of their options for growth.

How Can You Teach All Learners in Your Inclusive Classroom?

Teachers have a responsibility to address all students' developmental, individual, and exceptional learning needs. Although addressing the range of student differences in the inclusive classroom is challenging, it can also be very rewarding. Consider the comments of three teachers who reflect on their experiences teaching diverse learners:

> This is a note I wrote on the bottom of her [final] report card: "Sara is a sweet, bright child. As much as she could be a challenge, she made me a better teacher by keeping me on my toes. I will truly, truly miss her!" (teacher of a student with Turner syndrome)

> It was a gratifying year. I had no idea at the beginning that we would see the progress that we did. . . . Irina came back for a visit today. She ran right up to me and gave me a hug. A year ago, such an obvious display of emotion would have been unthinkable! (teacher of a student with an attachment disorder resulting from a lack of human contact during the years she spent in a Romanian orphanage)
>
> On complex and difficult days, it sometimes feels like it would be a lot easier not to have children with special needs in my classroom. . . . But, you know, I really mourned having to give Daniel up at the end of the school year. There was a special connection I made with that child, and I wanted to be sure that his next teacher felt the same way. (teacher of a student with Down syndrome) (Kostelnik, Onaga, Rohde, & Whiren, 2002, pp. 55, 92–93, 149)

Attention to three key areas will enable you to create a truly inclusive classroom: collaborative consultation with other professionals, partnerships with parents, and assistive technology for special learners.

Collaborative Consultation with Other Professionals

One approach to meeting the needs of all students is known as **collaborative consultation**, an approach in which a classroom teacher meets with one or more other professionals (a special educator, school psychologist, or resource teacher, for example) to focus on the learning needs of one or more students. Collaborative consultation often involves shared decision making and co-teaching relationships (Mastropieri & Scruggs, 2010), and participants assume equal responsibility for meeting students' needs. When working with a consultant, your role will include "preparing for meetings, using data to describe your concern about the student [or students], being open to the consultant's suggestions, implementing the agreed-upon strategies systematically, and documenting the effectiveness of the ideas you try" (Friend & Bursuck, 2015, p. 87).

To meet the educational goals of a student's IEP, regular education teachers are part of an IEP team that includes special educators, other support personnel, and parents. The following special education professionals are among those who consult with and/or collaborate with regular education teachers:

Consulting teacher—a special educator who provides technical assistance such as arranging the physical setting, helping to plan for instruction, or developing approaches for assessing students' learning

Resource-room teacher—a special educator who provides instruction in a resource room for students with disabilities

School psychologist—consults with the general education teacher and arranges for the administration of appropriate psychological, educational, and behavioral assessment instruments; may observe a student's behavior in the classroom

Speech and language specialist—assesses students' communication abilities and works with general education teachers to develop educational programs for students with speech and/or language disorders

Physical therapist—provides physical therapy for students with physical disabilities

Occupational therapist—instructs students with disabilities to prepare them for everyday living and work-related activities

Partnerships with Parents

In addition to working with education professionals to meet the learning needs of all students, effective teachers develop good working relationships with parents. As the following comment by the mother of a daughter with Rett syndrome makes clear, parents of children with special needs expect their teachers to be committed to meeting the learning needs of their children: "My child will never be considered a poster child. She does not give professionals the satisfaction of making great progress, nor is she terribly social. But I need the same type of investment by professionals as any other parents of children without disabilities. The most important thing any educator can do for me is to love my Mary" (Howard, Williams, Port, & Lepper, 2001, p. 123). Parents of exceptional children can be a source of valuable information about the characteristics, abilities, and needs of their children. Also, they can be helpful in securing necessary services for their children, and they can assist you by reviewing skills at home and praising their children for their learning.

Assistive Technology for Special Learners

The ability of teachers to create inclusive classrooms has increased dramatically as a result of many technological advances that make it easier for exceptional students to learn and communicate. The array of assistive technologies for students with disabilities is extensive. For example, personal digital assistants (PDAs), BlackBerrys, and iPhones enable students to access the Internet, send and receive email, and keep track of school assignments. Other examples include computer-based word-processing and math tutorials that greatly assist students with learning disabilities in acquiring literacy and computational skills. Students with hearing impairments can communicate with other students by using telecommunications equipment, and students with physical disabilities can operate computers through voice commands or with a single switch or key.

Assistive technology also allows persons with disabilities to express themselves in new ways. For example, a young autistic woman posts videos on YouTube about her condition. Using a device that enables her to communicate, she explains the thoughts and feelings behind her movements and gestures. Additional recent developments in assistive technology include the following:

- Talking word processor
- Speech synthesizer
- Touch-sensitive computer screens
- Computer screen image enlarger
- Teletypewriter (TTY) (connects to telephone and types a spoken message to another TTY)
- Customized computer keyboards
- Ultrasonic head controls for computers
- Voice-recognition computers
- Television closed captioning
- Kurzweil reading machine (scans print and reads it aloud)

Assistive technology also includes devices to enhance the mobility and everyday activities of people with special needs (wheelchairs, lifts, adaptive driving controls, scooters, laser canes, feeders). Many technology-related special education resources and curriculum materials are available on the Internet. One of these sites, the TechMatrix, is

Video Example 9.5

More Alike Than Different: This parent offers advice about accepting a child with a disability.

maintained by the National Center for Technology Innovation (NCTI), funded by the U.S. Department of Education, Office of Special Education Programs. TechMatrix is an online database to help educators and families find educational and assistive technology resources and help for students with special needs. Users can even follow TechMatrix on Twitter. The dazzling revolution in microelectronics will continue to yield new devices to enhance the learning of all students.

Summary

How Do Students' Needs Change as They Develop?

- *Development* refers to predictable changes throughout the human lifespan.
- People move through different stages of cognitive, psychosocial, and moral development throughout their lives.
- Piaget maintains that children pass through four stages of cognitive development as they mature. Effective teachers are aware of the characteristics of school-age children's thinking during three of these stages: the preoperational stage, the concrete operations stage, and the formal operations stage.
- According to Erikson's model of psychosocial development, people pass through eight stages of emotional and social development throughout their lives. Each stage is characterized by a "crisis" with a positive and negative pole. Healthy development depends on a satisfactory, positive resolution of each crisis.
- Kohlberg believes that moral development, the reasoning people use to decide between right and wrong, evolves through three levels. Evidence suggests that males and females base their moral reasoning on different factors.
- Character education emphasizes teaching values and moral reasoning.
- Maslow suggests that human growth and development depend on how well the individual's biological and psychological needs have been met.
- Adverse Childhood Experiences (ACEs) contribute to risk factors for disease and lack of well-being throughout the lifespan.

How Do Students Vary in Intelligence?

- Conflicting definitions of intelligence range from "what IQ tests measure" to "goal-directed adaptive behavior." Some theorists believe intelligence is a single, basic ability, although recent research suggests that there are many forms of intelligence.
- According to Gardner's theory of multiple intelligences, there are at least 8 (perhaps 10) human intelligences.
- Although there is conflict about the concept of learning styles, effective teachers are aware of differences among students regarding their preferences for learning activities.

How Do Students Vary in Ability and Disability?

- Some students are called "exceptional" because they have abilities or disabilities that distinguish them from other students. Students with physical, cognitive, or emotional disabilities and students who are gifted and talented have unique learning needs.
- Learning disabilities are the most common disability among students, with attention deficit hyperactivity disorder (ADHD) and attention deficit disorder (ADD) the most common learning disabilities.

What Are Special Education and Inclusion?

- Special education includes a variety of educational services to meet the needs of exceptional students. Key provisions of the Individuals with Disabilities Education Act (IDEA) include least restrictive environment, Individualized Education Program (IEP), confidentiality of records, and due process.
- Response to Intervention (RTI) is a systematic approach to identifying students with learning disabilities.
- Mainstreaming is the process of integrating students with disabilities into regular classrooms.
- Inclusion integrates all students with disabilities into regular classrooms, with the support of special education services as necessary. Full inclusion is the integration of students with disabilities in general education classrooms at all times regardless of the severity of the disability.

How Can You Teach All Learners in Your Inclusive Classroom?

- Through collaborative consultation, an arrangement whereby the regular classroom teacher collaborates with other education professionals, teachers can meet the needs of exceptional students. Collaborative consultation is based on mutuality and reciprocity, and all participants assume responsibility for meeting students' needs.
- An array of assistive technologies and resources is available to help exceptional students learn and communicate in inclusive classrooms.

Professional Reflections and Activities

Teacher's Journal

1. Relate Erikson's stages of psychosocial development to your own experiences as a child and as an adolescent. How did sources of stress, psychosocial crises, and your resolutions of them affect your learning in school?
2. Do you know your IQ or recall participating in an IQ test? How do you regard yourself in terms of intelligence, and how did you come by your beliefs about your intelligence? Do you think these beliefs influenced your motivation, choices, and achievement as a student? Do you think they influenced your school or class placements? Do you think they influenced the way your teachers and peers responded to you? What criteria would you now use to evaluate the fairness of IQ testing and the appropriate use of IQ scores?
3. Describe your preferred learning environment. Where, when, and how do you learn best? Think about how you acquire new information—are you analytical and abstract or more concrete, relying on common sense? Do you prefer to learn alone, in a small group, or in a large group? When given an assignment, do you prefer structure and details or open-ended, unstructured assignments?

Teacher's Research

1. Visit the TechMatrix website and compile a list of assistive technology resources to meet the needs of students with the disabilities listed in Figure 9.10 on page 311.
2. Select two of the major educational journals that focus on the subject area and grade level for which you are preparing to teach. Collect articles that present tips and resources for adapting teaching for students with special needs. In addition, you may wish to look at journals that focus on special education—for example, *Teaching Exceptional Children, Learning Disabilities Research and Practice, Exceptional Children, Remedial and Special Education, Focus on Exceptional Children,* and *Journal of Special Education*.

Observations and Interviews

1. Observe in a classroom that has exceptional students. What steps does the teacher take to meet the needs of these students? Interview the teacher to determine what he or she sees as the challenges and rewards of teaching exceptional students. What does the teacher think are the advantages and disadvantages of inclusion?
2. Visit a local school that provides services for exceptional students. What teams serve students with special needs, and who serves on those teams? How often do they meet, and how do they work with general education teachers? If possible, observe a team meeting. Who are members of the team? To what extent do they have similar recommendations for students' individual education plans? To what extent do they have different recommendations?

Professional Portfolio

For the grade level and content area you are preparing to teach, identify learning activities that address each of the eight multiple intelligences identified by Gardner. For example, you might plan activities such as the following. For one activity in each category, list the preparations you would need to make and/or the materials you would need to gather, and add this information to your portfolio.

Logical-Mathematical

- Design an experiment on . . .
- Describe the rules for a new board game called . . .

Linguistic

- Write a short story about . . .
- Write a biographical sketch of . . .

Musical

- Write song lyrics for . . .
- Locate music that sounds like . . .

Spatial

- Draw, paint, or sculpt a . . .
- Create an advertisement for . . .

Bodily-Kinesthetic

- Role-play a person who is . . .
- Do a dance that shows . . .

Intrapersonal

- Assess your ability to . . .
- Describe how you feel about . . .

Interpersonal

- Show one or more of your classmates how to . . .
- In a small group, construct a . . .

Naturalist

- Identify the trees found in . . .
- Classify the rocks found in . . .

Chapter 10
Creating a Community of Learners

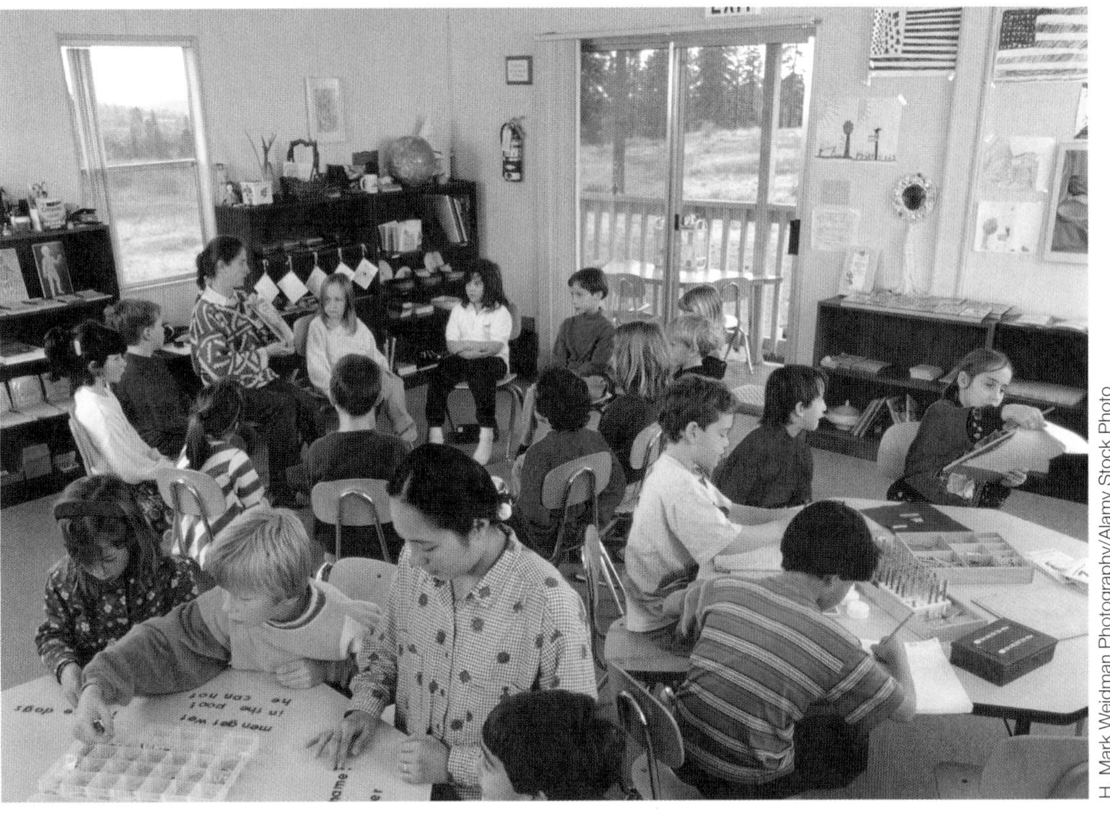

H. Mark Weidman Photography/Alamy Stock Photo

Learning Outcomes

After reading this chapter, you will be able to do the following:

10.1 Identify and describe the factors that determine the culture of a classroom.

10.2 Explain how teachers create a positive learning environment.

10.3 Identify and explain the keys to successful classroom management.

10.4 Describe the teaching methods that effective teachers use.

READERS' VOICES

What determines the culture of a classroom?

Classroom culture is determined by the ability of a teacher to develop a good, positive environment—an environment that meets each student's needs and takes into account each student's diverse cultural background.

—ALICIA,
Teacher Education student, first year

As the Readers' Voices comment points out, a teacher's primary responsibility is to create a positive learning environment—a cohesive community of learners. Successful teachers know that they must make careful decisions about curriculum goals and objectives, instructional strategies, and classroom management techniques. They understand that, to create a community of learners, they must know not only *what* to teach, but *how* to teach it.

For teacher education students like you, making the transition between the study of teaching and actual teaching can be a challenge. You will make that transition smoothly, however, if you understand that to create a cohesive community of learners, you will need to "(1) earn the respect and affection of students; (2) be consistent and, therefore, credible and dependable; (3) assume responsibility for seeing that [your] students learn; and (4) value and enjoy learning and expect students to do so, too" (Good & Lavigne, 2018, p. 125).

What Determines the Culture of the Classroom?

A community of learners has a strong positive *culture*—the way of life common to a group of people. In much the same way, each classroom develops its own culture.

As a teacher, you will make countless decisions. Your decisions about seating arrangements, classroom rules and procedures, the content and relevance of the curriculum, when to shift from one activity to another, when to use discussion rather than lecture, how to respond to misbehavior, and the quality of your interactions with students from diverse cultural and linguistic backgrounds will have a strong influence on the culture that emerges in your classroom.

Classroom Climate

One dimension of classroom culture is **classroom climate**—the atmosphere or quality of life in a classroom. The climate of your classroom will be determined by how you interact with your students and "by the manner and degree to which you connect with your students, show warmth and support, encourage cooperation, and allow for independent judgment and choice" (Borich, 2017, p. 78).

From the students' perspective, your classroom climate should convince them that you care about them and believe they can learn, are sensitive to their differing needs and abilities, are familiar with their cultural backgrounds, know the subject matter, and can maintain effective discipline. As Figure 10.1 shows, other stakeholders—teachers, principals, and parents—also have a remarkably similar view of the qualities of effective teachers. The data in Figure 10.1 are from a national survey of what each stakeholder group believes are "most important" qualities for a teacher to be effective. The most common responses across the stakeholder groups show that effective teachers are *patient* and *caring,* and they build trusting *relationships* with their students. In addition, effective teachers have extensive *knowledge of learners.*

Figure 10.1 Top 10 qualities of an effective teacher by stakeholder group

Parents	%	Principals	%	Students	%	Teachers	%
Relationships	17.6	Relationships	15.8	Relationships	23.5	Relationships	12.7
Patient, Caring	16.6	Know Learners	9.3	Patient, Caring	15.9	Patient, Caring	11.0
Dedication	7.4	Professional	6.6	Know Learners	8.6	Know Learners	7.9
Subject Knowledge	7.2	Dedication	6.4	Dedication	8.5	Dedication	7.2
Know Learners	6.9	Patient, Caring	6.2	Engaging	6.5	Subject Knowledge	6.7
Engaging	6.0	Subject Knowledge	5.4	Subject Knowledge	5.9	Professional	5.6
Professional	6.0	Creativity	5.4	Teaching Skills	5.4	Creativity	5.0
Creativity	4.5	Teaching Skills	5.0	Professional	5.1	Engaging	4.6
Make Ideas Clear	3.5	Class Mgt	4.8	Class Mgt	2.6	Teaching Skills	4.5
Teaching Skills	3.2	Always Learning	4.4	Make Ideas Clear	2.5	Always Learning	4.4

Note: Respondents were asked to list, in their own words, between 3 and 15 qualities that they feel are *most important* in making an "effective" teacher. The survey did not define "effective" for respondents, other than that it meant "good," allowing respondents to define what an effective teacher meant for themselves. Percentages indicate the frequency by which each category was endorsed by each stakeholder group.

SOURCE: Based on United States: What makes an effective teacher? 2016 Pearson Education, Inc., pp. 3, 30.

The climate of your classroom will be complex and multidimensional; its character will be determined by a wide array of variables, many of which will be beyond your control. However, many classroom variables will be within your control. You can take specific steps to create a classroom climate with the following eight characteristics:

1. A productive, task-oriented focus
2. Group cohesiveness
3. Open, warm relationships between teacher and students
4. Cooperative, respectful interactions among students
5. Low levels of tension, anxiety, and conflict
6. Humor
7. High expectations
8. Frequent opportunities for student input regarding classroom activities

The degree to which these dimensions of classroom climate are present within your classroom will be influenced by your style of communicating and treating students. As the following case illustrates, creating a classroom climate characterized by these eight dimensions is not easy. The moment-to-moment decisions teachers make about how to respond to classroom events can enhance or reduce group cohesiveness and students' motivation to learn.

> Dari feels uncomfortable as she makes the seemingly endless trip from her desk to the drinking fountain at the back of the room. If she had a choice, she wouldn't make the trip at all. She is well aware that her classmates resent her being allowed to get a drink whenever she wants to, whereas they have to wait

until recess or lunch. They know that the medicine she takes every morning makes her thirsty, but they still tease her about being "Teacher's Pet."

"Why can't the others get drinks when they want to?" she wonders. "It wouldn't be any big deal. Besides, Ms. Patterson is *always* drinking her coffee. She carries that stupid coffee mug around so much that it looks as if it's attached to her body."

"Hey, Ms. Patterson, can I get a drink?" Craig calls out. "It's a really hot day, and I'm thirsty."

"Of course not, Craig. You know my rule about that." Ms. Patterson is obviously annoyed at his question.

Craig persists. "It's not fair. *You* can drink your coffee whenever you want to."

"I never said, 'Life is fair,'" Ms. Patterson replies. "I'm the teacher, so I have certain privileges. I need to have something to drink because I do most of the talking and my mouth gets dry. Besides, my job is to make sure that you children learn, and I can't do that if you're running to the drinking fountain all the time. It won't kill you to wait until recess to get a drink."

"But we could use a water bottle," Huong suggests.

"No, that won't work. A couple of years ago, I let my students bring water bottles to school, and they used them to squirt one another all the time. When are you people going to learn that *no* means *no*?"

"But you let Dari go to the fountain whenever she wants to," Shelby points out.

"Dari has medical problems," Ms. Patterson responds. "Anyway, I know that she'll only get a drink if she really, really needs one. Right, Dari?"

Dari nods self-consciously and then tries to make herself smaller by scrunching low in her seat.

"Yeah, she's special, all right," Guy scoffs. "She's Teacher's Pet." (Ormrod & McGuire, 2007, p. 111)

How would you describe this classroom climate using the eight dimensions listed earlier? Should Ms. Patterson allow her students to get a drink during class? Is it fair that she drinks coffee in front of her students? Could Ms. Patterson help Dari feel more socially connected to her classmates?

Although how you regard and treat students influences your classroom climate, the instructional decisions you make also influence it. Your decisions can result in three types of relationships among members of the class: cooperative or positive interdependence, competitive or negative interdependence, and individualistic or no interdependence (Johnson & Johnson, 2017; Johnson, Johnson, & Holubec, 2008). A group project to measure classroom furniture would promote *cooperative interdependence*. A race to be the first student to measure the furniture would call for *competitive interdependence*. And having a student measure the furniture independently would be an example of *no interdependence*. Obviously, you should use strategies that foster all three forms of interactions, depending on your instructional goals. In most cases, though, your primary emphasis will be on furthering cooperative interdependence.

Classroom Dynamics

Interactions between teachers and students are at the very core of teaching. As a teacher, the quality of your interactions with students reveals how you feel about them. In addition, high-quality "teacher-child relationships play an important role in children's socio-emotional and behavioral development." Such relationships act as "protective factors" and "help prevent behavior problems" (O'Connor, Dearing, & Collins, 2011, pp. 120, 125).

If you empathize with students, genuinely respect them, and expect them to learn, you are more likely to develop a classroom climate free of management problems. In classrooms with positive group dynamics, teachers and students work toward a common goal—learning. In classrooms with negative interactions, the energy of teachers and students may be channeled into conflict rather than into learning.

There is no precise formula to guarantee success in the classroom; however, a classroom climate characterized by the following four qualities results in greater student motivation to learn and more positive teacher–student and student–student interactions:

1. Learning activities are well organized, progress smoothly, and are free from distractions or interruptions.
2. The teacher is caring, patient, and supportive, and never ridicules or criticizes students for their efforts to learn.
3. The curriculum is challenging but not so difficult that students become frustrated and decide not to learn.
4. Learning activities are authentic and, to the degree possible, relevant to students' interests and experiences.

COMMUNICATION SKILLS Successful teachers possess effective communication skills. They express themselves verbally and nonverbally (and in writing) in a manner that is clear, concise, and interesting. They "are able to communicate clearly and directly to their students without wandering, speaking above students' levels of comprehension, or using speech patterns that impair their presentation's clarity" (Borich, 2017, p. 7). In addition, they are good listeners. Their students feel that not only are they heard, they are understood.

Effective teachers relish the interactive, spontaneous dimensions of classroom discourse. They respond appropriately to events that could sabotage the plans of less effective teachers—a student's misbehavior, announcements on the PA system, interruptions by other teachers or parents, arguments between students, or the mood of the class at a given time.

INTERACTIONS AMONG STUDENTS In addition to engaging in positive, success-oriented interactions with their students, effective teachers foster positive, cooperative interactions among students. In culturally diverse classroom settings, students easily and regularly interact with peers from different cultural and linguistic backgrounds. As a result, students feel supported by their peers and free to devote their attention to learning. The climate of such a group is characterized by "maturity, autonomy, and productivity [and] a group identity emerges" (Johnson & Johnson, 2017, p. 30). Typically, the classroom climate has evolved through four stages of group development (see Figure 10.2).

Figure 10.2 Characteristics of groups at four stages of development

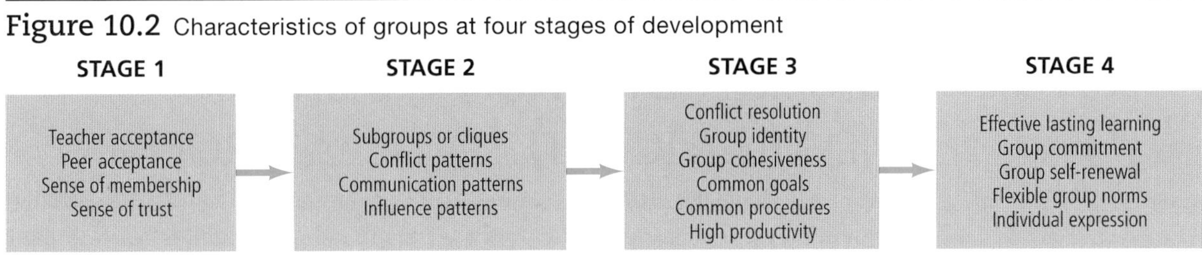

During stage 1, students are on their best behavior. Teachers can use this honeymoon period to their advantage. They can discuss classroom rules and procedures, outline learning goals, and clarify expectations. During stage 2, teachers can encourage student participation and communication, while discouraging the formation of cliques.

Groups that have reached stage 2 then move into stage 3, which may last for the remainder of the school year. In stage 3, the group sets clear goals, shares tasks, and agrees on deadlines. A fully evolved group reaches stage 4. In this stage, group members accept responsibility for the quality of life in the group, and they continuously strive to improve it.

Video Example 10.1

Creating Cooperative Interactions: The teacher encourages cooperative interactions among children.

Teachers who facilitate group processes in their classrooms recognize that students as well as teachers exert leadership in the classroom. Accomplished teachers identify student leaders and are able to influence these students to use their leadership abilities to help the entire group reach its goals.

Check Your Understanding 10.1

How Can You Create a Positive Learning Environment?

A positive classroom climate and positive classroom dynamics are essential for a good learning environment. Developing and then maintaining such an environment is a complex challenge. No single set of strategies will ensure success in all situations. However, educational researchers have identified teacher behaviors that tend to be associated with high levels of student learning. Effective teachers know how to use these behaviors and *for what purposes* they are best suited. The following sections address three important dimensions of positive learning environments: the **caring classroom**; the physical classroom environment; and classroom organization, including procedures for grouping students for instruction and managing time.

The Caring Classroom

At this point in your preparation to become a teacher, you may doubt your ability to create a positive classroom climate and to orchestrate the complex dynamics of the classroom so that you and your students become a cohesive, productive, and mutually supportive group. In your quest to develop these abilities, remember that an authentic spirit of caring is at the heart of an effective learning environment. "*[C]aring pedagogy* [italics added] can . . . create or restore self-confidence needed for participating in the positive learning opportunities in the classroom. It can also help form the moral foundation of responsible citizenship, productive community membership and leadership, and lifelong engagement in learning" (Paul & Colucci, 2000, p. 45). This chapter's Teaching on Your Feet feature profiles a teacher who cared enough about a troubled, angry student to figure out a way for the student to make his own unique contribution to a positive learning environment.

FOCUS ON **DIVERSITY**: CARING AND MULTICULTURAL CLASSROOMS

How can you establish a **caring classroom** in today's culturally diverse schools? First, you can demonstrate caring through your efforts to help all students learn to their fullest potential. You can learn as much as you can about your students' abilities, their

Teaching on Your Feet:

I See a Story in Every Learner

I see the world in stories. I [revel] in the transformative power of language that can divide and unite us. When I look in a classroom, I see a story in every learner, unique and yearning to be read. Creating a community for learning means creating more than a classroom; it means constantly intertwining our stories in a way that reveals our potential . . . .

Several years ago I taught New Start English where the 28 students who had failed Freshman English came to me, disengaged and disgruntled, each with a story that seemed to explain why. To stay positive, I ate lunch in my room so I could respond to a daily journal I had started with each student. Then, just before they would arrive, I would remind myself what I liked about each.

One particularly troubled student, Tyler, [was] troubled and angry, intelligent and formidable; lost and scared. [He] wielded an uncanny power over his peers. They knew he was smart, both in mind and experience. He was their hero, the tough and seemingly confident person they all wanted to be. In many ways, understanding Tyler meant understanding the class.

I discovered through these daily journals that Tyler loved to draw and for several weeks I invited him to bring in some of his artwork until he finally did.

One day, he came into the room, angrier than usual, but calmed by his art. At the end of class he took his sketch, complex in emotion and execution, and tacked it to the bulletin board. Later, my AP class came in and aptly noticed the new addition. They immediately recognized in it the literary archetypes we'd been studying. I quickly grabbed a pile of sticky notes, asked the students to write down their thoughts and post the notes on the illustration.

The next morning before school I had the office call Tyler into my classroom where I had a note ready for him: "The greatest measure of an artist's worth is the impact he can make on others. Look what you've done," I nodded towards his illustration.

That afternoon he put another [illustration] up and received more sticky notes. Soon after, I discovered how many artists I had in class, all wanting feedback on their work. It became routine—my at-risk learners posted their artwork, my AP learners responded to it.

This didn't magically transform my 5th hour class, but those kids, Tyler especially, came and said hello nearly every day for the next two years as they struggled time and again, just to graduate.

SARAH BROWN WESSLING
English Teacher, Johnston Community School District
Johnston, **IOWA**

Analyze

Highly effective teachers understand that building a positive relationship with a difficult-to-reach student benefits not only the individual student, but other students as well. If they encounter a student such as Tyler, who is troubled and angry and not part of the classroom community, they keep trying to figure out how the student can make a positive contribution to the culture of the classroom. Such teachers are guided by a deep conviction that each student can learn and make a positive contribution to classroom life. They understand that the teacher's primary responsibility is to discover what works for each student.

Reflect

1. Can you recall a time when one of your teachers used an imaginative, creative approach to develop a positive classroom culture? What did the teacher do? How did the teacher's approach influence you and other students in the class? Did the teacher's actions influence your motivation to learn? If so, how so?
2. What are the characteristics of teachers who can develop novel, spur of the moment strategies to develop a positive classroom culture?

Sarah Brown Wessling teaches high school English in the Johnston Community School District in Johnston, **IOWA**. She was the 2010 National Teacher of the Year.

The preceding is adapted and excerpted from Sarah Brown Wessling's application for the 2010 National Teacher of the Year award at http://www.ccsso.org/Documents/NTOY/Applications/2010NTOYAPP.pdf.

cultural and linguistic backgrounds, and what motivates them to do their best. You should actually become a *student of your students*. In addition, as the teacher profiled in the Teachers' Voices: Being an Agent of Change feature in this chapter explains, you can make your classroom a welcoming place for all students—a place where "students from 'different sides of the tracks' [intermingle] of their own accord."

You should also realize that how you speak and listen to students determines the extent to which they believe you care about them. A synthesis of research on classroom environments that enhance students' learning found that "students learn more when their classes are satisfying, challenging, and friendly and they have a voice in decision

TEACHERS' VOICES ➔ BEING AN AGENT OF CHANGE

R. ANDRE STEMM-CALDERON

Encouraging Global Citizenship in the Classroom

Schools should stop the extreme focus on testing and conceive of a broader view of education that takes into account the whole, creative child who is a citizen of the world. I do not oppose standardized testing. In an ideal world, students would simply pause for a few days at the end of the year to take tests and then return to their creative, motivating curriculum.

However, the testing culture has invaded all aspects of our school. Typically, these tests do not assess the right-brain aptitudes of our students; therefore, we stop developing it, leaving our students at a huge disadvantage when it comes to global understanding. However, many American families embrace the concept of global citizenship and desire such an education for their children.

Currently, I am teaching in a program that embraces a global perspective. This program joins two cultures, two languages, and, in some ways, two classes of people. The two-way dual language program brings Spanish-speaking, Mexican Americans from predominately lower-income communities together with English-speaking Anglo students from predominately middle-class backgrounds. In my 10 years of teaching, I have never witnessed the things I see in my classroom. I see students from "different sides of the tracks" intermingling of their own accord. I see friendships between a middle-class Anglo girl and a very poor Mexican American girl blossom. These girls do not understand how rare this is in American education. They have never visited the highly segregated schools that exist across America that separate by class and race. Our program has normalized this type of interaction. It is true that at the beginning of the year they will sit together, segregated in their "tribes" (White with White, Hispanic with Hispanic, etc.). However, by March we have students interacting in all sorts of configurations. Unfortunately, two-way dual language programs are still rare in the United States, although some reports suggest a growing trend. Programs that represent other cultures, languages, and even social classes expand the opportunities for our students and prepare them to function and thrive in a diverse and complex world.

As an immigrant to the United States, I understand the importance of global citizenry. I was raised in a bicultural, bilingual home all around California and Texas, where learning about cultures was encouraged. I also had the privilege of traveling during and after college. These opportunities have increased my curiosity about other places in the world. These experiences have broadened my thinking, challenged my values, and opened my mind to other ideas and philosophies. I am challenged to think about world problems from a human level instead of solely an American point of view. In the end, my global citizenry makes me a better teacher, equipped with the perspective and compassion to work alongside my fellow world citizens.

PERSONAL REFLECTION

1. With reference to the grade level and subject area for which you are preparing to teach, how can you foster global citizenship? How can you develop a welcoming tone for all students and their families?
2. What challenges can a teacher face when trying to foster global citizenship and develop a welcoming tone in their classroom? How can a teacher overcome these challenges?

R. Andre Stemm-Calderon is a teacher at Mission View Elementary School in Wenatchee, **WASHINGTON**. Andre taught in **TEXAS** for 8 years and was 2003–2004 Teacher of the Year at Jenard Gross Elementary School in Houston.

making. [When] classes are unfriendly, cliquish, and fragmented, they leave students feeling rejected and therefore impede learning" (Walberg & Greenberg, 1997, p. 46). Table 10.1 is based on this study; it presents 15 dimensions of classroom life and how each influences students' learning at the junior and senior high school levels.

Although students learn best in caring classrooms, students must also learn to care for others. Toward this end, Stanford University professor Nel Noddings (2002) recommends reorganizing the school curriculum around "themes of care" and suggests that "all students should be engaged in a general education that guides them in caring for self, intimate others, global others, plants, animals, the environment, objects and instruments, and ideas" (p. 99). In addition, Noddings (2007) points out that "relations of care and trust should improve (or at least not hurt) achievement, [and] they also might contribute to greater safety, stronger social ties, better citizenship, and greater satisfaction for both teachers and students" (p. 83).

Table 10.1 Fifteen dimensions of classroom environment

Dimension	Learning		Percent Positive Influence on Description
Satisfaction	100%	(17)	Students enjoy classroom work and find it satisfying.
Challenge	87	(16)	Students find the work difficult and challenging.
Cohesiveness	86	(17)	Students know one another well and are helpful and friendly toward one another.
Physical environment	85	(15)	Adequate books, equipment, space, and lighting are available.
Democracy	85	(14)	Students share equally in making decisions that affect the entire class.
Goal direction	73	(15)	Learning goals are clear.
Competition	67	(9)	Competition among students is minimized.
Formality	65	(17)	Class is informal, with few formal rules to guide behavior.
Speed	54	(14)	Students have sufficient time to finish their work.
Diversity	31	(14)	Students' interests differ and are provided for.
Apathy	14	(15)	Students don't care about what the class does.
Favoritism	10	(13)	All students do not enjoy the same privileges; the teacher has favorites.
Cliquishness	8	(13)	Certain students work only with close friends and refuse to interact with others.
Disorganization	6	(17)	Activities are disorganized and confusing, rather than well organized and efficient.
Friction	0	(17)	Tension and quarreling among students characterize the classroom.

NOTE: Percent indicates the percentage of research studies that reported a positive influence on learning for that dimension; number in parentheses indicates number of research studies that investigated that dimension.
SOURCE: Based on Herbert J. Walberg and Rebecca C. Greenberg, "Using the Learning Environment Inventory," Educational Leadership, May 1997, p. 47.

Comstock/Getty Images

This dynamic kindergarten class exhibits many of the characteristics of a caring classroom climate. Relations are open and trusting; everyone is accepted and actively engaged; a sense of order prevails even in an activity format that calls for self-expression.

The Physical Environment of the Classroom

When you become a teacher, the physical environment of your school will probably be similar to that of schools you attended. With the help of your students, however, it is possible to improve your surroundings. Fresh air; plants; clean, painted walls; displays of students' work; a comfortable reading or resource area; and a few prints or posters help to create a positive learning environment. Seating arrangements and the placement of other classroom furniture also do much to shape the classroom environment. Although seating by rows may be very appropriate for whole-group instruction or examinations, other arrangements may be more beneficial for other activities. For example, you can enhance small-group activities by moving desks into small clusters in different parts of the room. Figure 10.3 shows the arrangement of a classroom at an exemplary elementary school. The room is designed to encourage students to learn through discovery at learning centers located around the room.

Figure 10.3 Learning centers in an elementary classroom

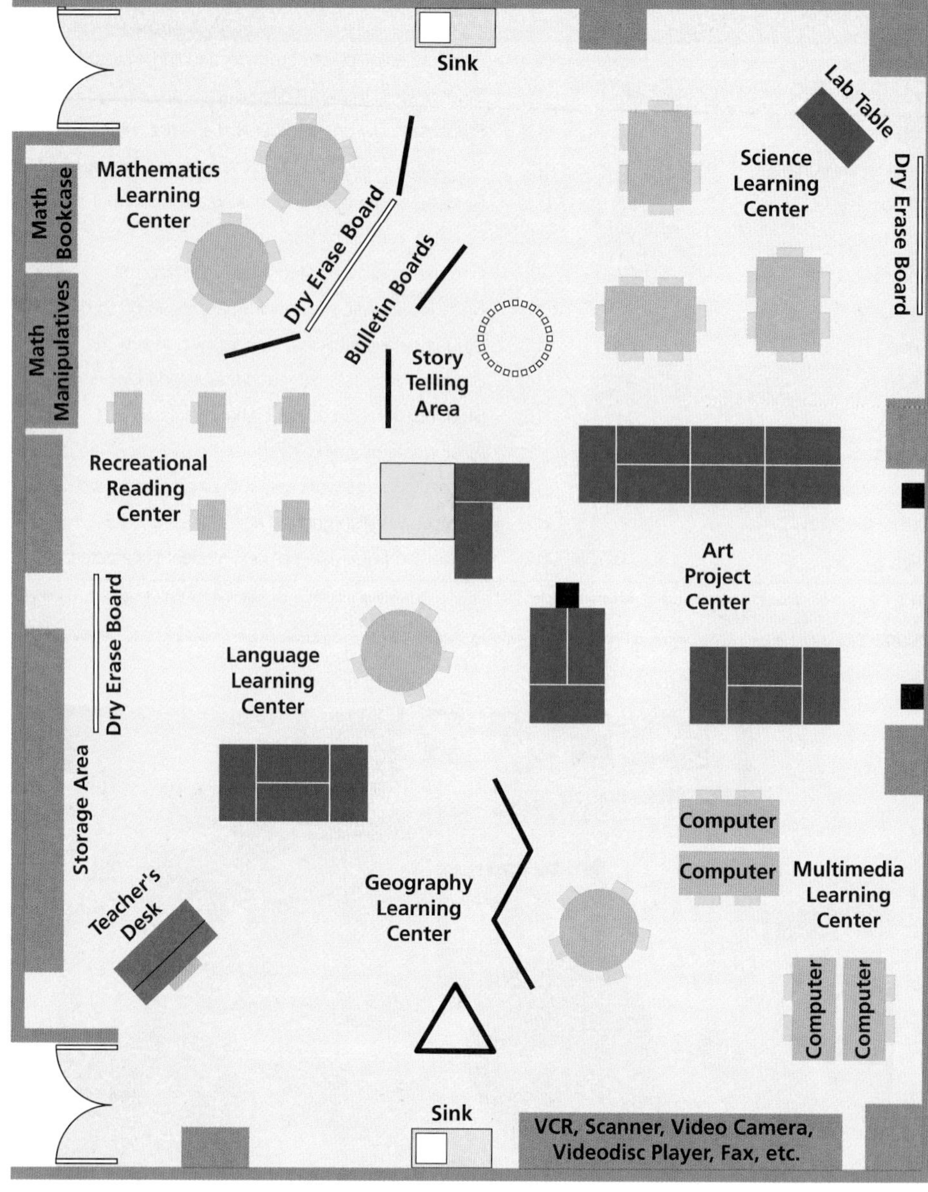

However you design your classroom, be certain that seating arrangements do not reduce the opportunity of some students to learn. For example, students in some classrooms receive more attention if they are seated in the so-called *action zone*, the middle front-row seats and seats on the middle aisle. Teachers often stand near this area and unknowingly give students seated there more opportunities to speak.

Classroom Organization

A critical factor in creating a positive learning environment is **classroom organization**—how teachers and students are grouped for instruction, how learning tasks are structured, and how other resources are used. The following sections focus on these aspects of classroom organization.

GROUPING STUDENTS BY ABILITY Two common approaches for grouping students on the basis of shared characteristics are between-class ability grouping, often called tracking, and within-class ability grouping. Students who attend schools where **between-class ability grouping** is practiced are assigned to classes on the basis of ability or achievement (usually determined by scores on standardized tests). Another form of between-class ability grouping, especially at the high school level, is based on students' goals after graduation. Many high schools, for example, have a college preparatory track, a vocational track, and a business education track.

For the most part, between-class ability grouping does not contribute to greater achievement (Good & Lavigne, 2018). Supporters nevertheless claim that teachers are better able to meet the needs of students in homogeneous groupings. Among the alternatives to between-class ability grouping are heterogeneous (or mixed-ability) grouping, regrouping by subject area, the Joplin Plan (regrouping students for reading instruction by ability across grade levels), and cooperative learning.

Within-class ability grouping is often used for instruction in reading and mathematics within a class, where a teacher instructs students in homogeneous, small groups. Within-class grouping is used widely in elementary classrooms. You may recall learning to read in a small group with a name such as the Eagles, the Redbirds, or the Mustangs. Like tracking, within-class ability grouping can heighten pre-existing differences in achievement between groups of students, especially if teachers give high-achieving groups more attention. Also, once students are grouped, they tend not to be regrouped, even when differences in achievement are reduced.

At best, evidence to support student groupings is mixed. Whether students are grouped on the basis of ability, curricular interests, or disabling condition, there is a danger that some group labels can evoke negative expectations, causing teachers to under-teach certain students, and their peers to isolate or reject them. The most serious consequence, of course, is that students so labeled are taught to feel inadequate, inferior, and limited in their options for growth.

GROUPING STUDENTS FOR COOPERATIVE LEARNING Cooperative learning is an approach to teaching in which students work in small groups, or teams, sharing the work and helping one another complete assignments. Student-Team-Learning, for example, is a cooperative approach teachers use to increase the basic skills achievement of at-risk students. In cooperative learning arrangements, students are motivated to learn in small groups through rewards that are made available to the group as a whole and to individual members of the group. **Cooperative learning** includes the following key elements:

- Small groups (four to six students) work together on learning activities.
- Assignments require that students help one another while working on a group project.
- In competitive arrangements, groups may compete against one another.
- Group members contribute to group goals according to their talents, interests, and abilities.

Cooperative learning also enables students to learn a variety of roles and responsibilities, as described in the Technology in Action feature which discusses how a fifth-grade social studies teacher combined cooperative learning and podcasting as a way for her students to study the history of the local community.

TECHNOLOGY in ACTION

Podcasting in Fifth-Grade Social Studies

Mrs. Warren teaches U.S. history at Miliken High School. She is a firm believer in connecting her students to their community. Each year, she has her students research historical and current events from their community and write up the stories they uncover. In the past, she posted these written stories on the school's website, printed them in a newspaper format, or compiled them in a hard-copy book. This year, she decides to try something different: Mrs. Warren wants to podcast her students' stories.

Podcasting is the delivery of audio files over the Internet. What makes podcasting unique is syndication. Syndication allows subscribers to receive, through a web feed, frequently updated web content. Teachers have used podcasts to deliver lecture material to students, to improve their teaching by accessing relevant professional development materials, to improve student reading comprehension, to improve learning through student-generated material, and to update parents on the daily events that transpire in their classrooms.

To start, she divided her students into groups of four. Each group was formed around a series of basic skill sets. Each group had a student who was comfortable with podcasting technologies, a student who had strong writing skills, a student who was comfortable speaking into a microphone, and a student who had research skills. The groups were asked to identify an aspect of their community that they wanted to explore. They were also asked to identify one historical event and one current event to report on.

Once Mrs. Warren approved the topics, the students started researching those topics. They developed research notes, a storyboard, and a script for narration. When they had these components, they started creating their audio files. Mrs. Warren allowed the students to either record directly on the computer or use a mobile recording device. Selection of a device depended on the needs of the group. Some groups performed in teams, with one student reading, then another. Some of the groups chose to act out historical events. Members of the group would take on the roles of historical figures from the community, like an old-time radio broadcast. Other groups delivered their podcast as a news report. Some students interviewed members of the community, some acted as news anchors, and others as roving reporters. Mrs. Warren was very impressed with the creativity and accuracy of the reports and the excitement that the activity generated among the students.

What made the activity a true success was Mrs. Warren's approach to publicizing the podcasts. After the first podcast was created, Mrs. Warren made an announcement over the school's public address (PA) system. She alerted the whole school to the availability of the podcasts and where they could get information on accessing the podcasts. Most important, she informed them of a competition. She offered free merchandise at the school store if students answered questions about the stories in the podcasts.

At any moment, walking down the hallway, in the lunchroom, or in class, Mrs. Warren would ask questions. For each correct answer, the student was entered into a drawing. Friday morning of each week, Mrs. Warren would draw a name from the pool of entries and announce the winners over the PA system.

By the second week, students in the school were downloading the podcast to their smartphones, the computers at school, and—according to parents she spoke with—computers at home. Without a doubt, students were really learning about their community.

TRY IT OUT: To create a podcast, you need access to a computer, a microphone, and a web server. The first step is to create an audio file. You can use any audio recording software to create the file—programs such as Audacity work well. Once the audio file is created, you need to convert it to an MP3 format. Once your audio file is converted to MP3, you need to upload that file, along with a Really Simple Syndication (RSS) file, to a web server. If you are familiar with basic HTML, then creating an RSS file is quite simple. If you are not familiar with basic HTML, a quick tutorial will get you ready in a short time. Once the MP3 and RSS file are uploaded to your web server, the file is ready for prime time and is accessible to your registered audience.

FOCUS ON **DIVERSITY**: COOPERATIVE LEARNING AND CROSS-CULTURAL INTERACTION

In addition, cooperative learning is an instructional method that can strengthen students' interpersonal skills. When students from different racial, ethnic, and cultural backgrounds and students with special needs all contribute to a common group goal, friendships increase and group members tend to view one another as more equal in status and worth. The contribution that cooperative learning can make to the culture of the classroom is supported by research that indicates that "students of color and White students have a greater tendency to make cross-racial friendship choices [if] they have participated in interracial learning teams. [Also], the academic achievement of students of color . . . is increased . . . while the academic achievement of White students remains about the same in both cooperative and competitive learning situations" (Banks, 2014, p. 122).

FOCUS ON **STEM**: COLLABERATION AND TEAMWORK PROMOTE STEM LEARNING FOR GIRLS

Cooperative teams are the best way to create a classroom environment that engages students in the four C's of STEM: Creativity, Communication, Critical Thinking, and Collaboration. The following three programs feature cooperative teams specifically designed for high school girls to study STEM on college campuses during the summer:

- **Restoration Ecology Summer Scholars Program**: Working in small teams, girls develop plans for a wetlands restoration during this program at Mount Holyoke College in South Hadley, **MASSACHUSETTS**. Teams monitor water quality through chemical and macroinvertebrate sampling, analyze soil, and create an herbarium that represents vegetation in an ecosystem.
- **Explore Engineering for High School Girls**: Teams work with engineering faculty and undergraduate engineering students during this program at Sweet Briar College in Sweet Briar, **VIRGINIA**. Teams progress through brainstorming and designing projects to testing and revising prototypes. Past students have designed and built computer-controlled "smart" wearables, automated musical devices, sustainable building materials, and a pet bowl that automatically refills.
- **MIT Women's Technology Program (WTP)**: Girls work on team-based projects that focus on electrical engineering, computer science, and mechanical engineering during this program on the MIT campus in Cambridge, **MASSACHUSETTS** (O'Neill, 2017).

DELIVERING INSTRUCTION The delivery of instruction is a key element in creating positive learning environments. What the teacher and the students do has a powerful influence on learning and on the quality of classroom life. A common activity format in elementary schools consists of students doing seatwork on their own or listening to their teachers and participating in whole-class recitations. In addition, students participate in reading groups, games, and discussions; take tests; check work; view films; give reports; gather information from the Internet; help clean up the classroom; and go on field trips.

As a teacher, you must answer the question: What activity will enable me to accomplish my instructional goals? You should also realize that learning activities should meet students' goals; that is, the activities must be meaningful and authentic for students. **Authentic learning tasks** enable students to see the connections between classroom learning and the world beyond the classroom—both now and in the future. For example, Figure 10.4 is an example of an authentic assignment to create a map of the route to school.

Figure 10.4 An authentic learning activity

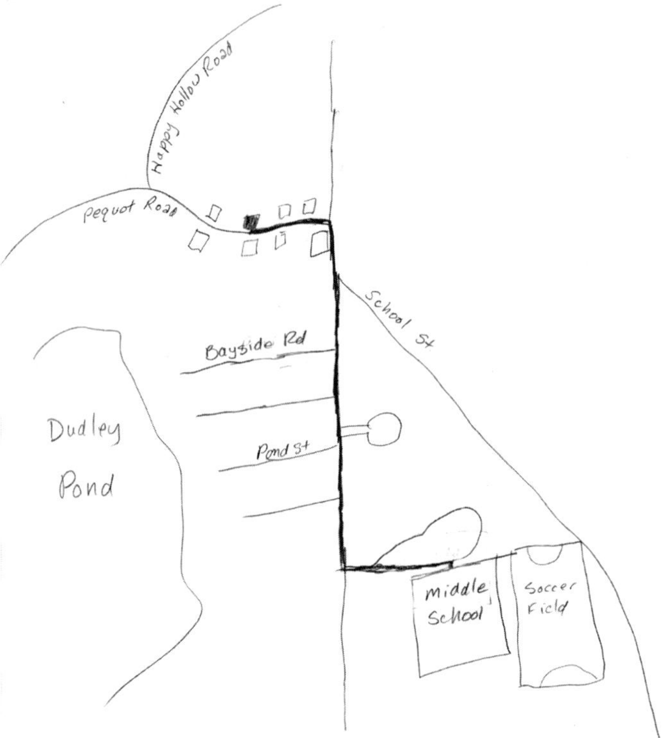

To understand how authentic learning tasks can motivate students to learn, reflect on your own school experiences. Do you recall memorizing facts only because they would appear on a test? Did you ever wonder why a teacher asked you to complete a learning task? Did you ever feel that a teacher asked you to do busywork? What kinds of learning tasks motivated you the most? How often were you involved in authentic learning activities such as the following?

- Giving oral reports based on research you conducted
- Writing an editorial for the school or local newspaper
- Representing the pro or con side in a debate
- Conducting an experiment and then writing up the results
- Creating a model to illustrate a process like photosynthesis, a solar eclipse, or combustion in a gasoline engine
- Completing an art project and then participating in an art exhibit for the community
- Tutoring younger children in reading, mathematics, or science
- Developing a website to document an in-class project
- Creating an infomercial using video-editing software and then getting reactions to the infomercial from other classes in your school
- Developing a science webquest and then posting the webquest for evaluation

A comprehensive nationwide study of successfully restructured schools reported that "authentic pedagogy" helps students to (1) "construct knowledge" through the use of higher-order thinking, (2) acquire "deep knowledge" (relatively complex understandings of subject matter), (3) engage in "substantive conversations" with teachers and peers, and (4) make connections between substantive knowledge and the world beyond the classroom (Newmann et al., 1996; Newmann & Wehlage, 1995). In addition, the study found that highly authentic pedagogy classes boost achievement for students at all grade levels.

HOW TIME IS USED How teachers use time affects student learning. **Allocated time** is the time teachers allocate for instruction in various areas of the curriculum. Teachers vary widely in their instructional use of time. Their attitudes toward a subject influence the amount of time they spend teaching that subject. For example, "Teachers who enjoyed mathematics spent 50 percent more time on the subject each week than teachers who did not enjoy it" (Good & Lavigne, 2018, p. 106).

Researchers have shown that **time on task**—the amount of time students are actively engaged in learning activities—is directly related to learning. As anyone who has ever daydreamed while appearing to pay attention can confirm, time on task is difficult to measure. In response to this difficulty, researchers have introduced the concept of **academic learning time**—the amount of time a student spends working on academic tasks with a high level of success (80 percent or higher). Not surprisingly, learning time, like allocated time, varies greatly from classroom to classroom. For example, a study of how elementary teachers actually use the more than 1,000 hours most states mandate for instruction revealed that students were truly engaged in meaningful, appropriate tasks for only about 300 hours. The other 700 hours were devoted to activities such as the following: recess, lunch, transitions, clerical and administrative tasks, "off-task" behaviors by students (Weinstein & Migano, 2010).

An additional concept that is proving useful in understanding teachers' use of time in the classroom is known as **opportunity to learn (OTL)**. OTL is based on the premise that teachers should use time to provide all students with challenging content through appropriate instruction. Many states are developing OTL standards for how teachers should use time in the classroom.

Claudia Meek, a third-grade teacher in California, points out in her *Phi Delta Kappan* article that state- and district-mandated testing and the time needed to prepare students for testing reduce the amount of instructional time available to teachers. During a 1-year period, approximately 32 hours of her class time were devoted to testing. That same year, 262 hours were devoted to fundraising, disaster preparedness, socialization, holidays, assemblies, regular interruptions, and miscellaneous time losses. Taken together, more than one third of Meek's classroom time was devoted to these activities. Her observations are based on a large-scale research study conducted by the National Center for Education Statistics and an analysis of data collected from her own classroom (Meek, 2003). To increase the time available for active learning, many high schools have implemented block scheduling arrangements. **Block scheduling** uses longer blocks of time each class period, with fewer periods each day. Longer blocks of time allow more in-depth coverage of subject matter and lead to deeper understanding and higher-level applications. Block scheduling also gives teachers more time to present complex concepts and students more time to practice applying those concepts to authentic problems.

Check Your Understanding 10.2

What are the Keys to Successful Classroom Management?

For most new teachers, classroom management is a primary concern. How can you prevent discipline problems from arising and keep students productively engaged in learning activities? Effective **classroom management** cannot be reduced to a cookbook recipe. However, you can take definite steps to create an effective learning environment in your classroom.

Consider the following scenarios of two high school classrooms—the same group of students with two different teachers. In which classroom is misbehavior more likely to emerge?

Classroom 1 is a beehive of activity as students continue to study global warming in their science class. Students are working in small groups at four multimedia centers, each with a desktop computer. Each group is developing questions they will post on the class blog for scientists participating on the Andrill Research Immersion for Science Educators (ARISE) team stationed in Antarctica. "What do you eat in Antarctica?" "How cold is it right now?" "Have you seen any polar bears, seals, penguins, or other wildlife?" The teacher circulates from group to group—listening, asking clarifying questions, and encouraging each group's effort. Some students suggest questions; others clarify the group's thinking—clearly, the students are deeply engaged in the activity.

Classroom 1 is filled with instructional materials. Student work—clay models of igloos, polar bears, and penguins, for example—is on the shelves that line the walls. On the classroom walls are maps of Antarctica drawn by students, color photos of Antarctica printed out on the printer at each learning center, and color printouts of PowerPoint presentations on Antarctica.

Science class is over, and students are now in classroom 2 studying language arts. Students are seated in rows, staring at their literature books while student after student reads two paragraphs from the book. The teacher sits on the desk at the front of the room and occasionally asks a question or makes a comment about the material just read. Several commercially printed posters are on the classroom walls—"Elements of a Novel or Short Story," "Punctuation Rules," and "What Good Readers Do." On one side of the room, beneath the windows, paperback and hardcover books are neatly lined up on the shelves of two bookcases. The room is quiet except for the sound of the student reading, the teacher's occasional comment or question, and the loud ticking of the clock above the classroom door.

These two scenarios illustrate the fact that good classroom management focuses on "establishing a productive learning environment, rather than control of misbehavior" (Good & Lavigne, 2018, p. 125). Sound classroom management techniques are based on the guidelines for creating an effective learning environment presented previously in this chapter—in other words, (1) creating a caring classroom, (2) organizing the physical classroom environment, (3) grouping students for instruction, (4) providing authentic learning tasks, and (5) structuring the use of time to maximize students' learning. Positive leadership and preventive planning thus are central to effective classroom management.

In addition, you should remember that classroom management refers to how teachers structure their learning environments to prevent, or minimize, behavior problems. *Discipline* refers to the methods teachers use *after* students misbehave. *Classroom management* is prevention oriented, while discipline is control oriented. The goal of classroom management is to structure the classroom environment to *maximize student attention* and *minimize disruptive behavior.* The following strategies will help you create a well-managed classroom environment:

- Arrange classroom furniture (desks, tables, and chairs) so that you can easily monitor students' behavior for signs of inattention, boredom, and misbehavior from any point in the room.

- Arrange classroom furniture so that students can move from place to place without disturbing their classmates.
- Keep very interesting instructional materials (for example, a replica of a human skeleton, a model of the solar system, or a large collection of insects) out of sight until you need to use them.
- Separate friends who tend to misbehave and get off-task when they are seated near one another, or separate students who dislike one another and are more likely to misbehave if they are seated close to one another.
- Assign chronically misbehaving students to seats close to your desk.

The Democratic Classroom

Teachers who allow students to participate in making decisions about the physical classroom environment, classroom rules and procedures, modifications to the curriculum, and options for learning activities also have fewer discipline problems. Students in **democratic classrooms** have more power and more responsibility than students in conventional classrooms. If students are to live in a democracy, they must learn to manage freedom responsibly; teachers model democracy by giving their students some choices and some control over classroom activities.

William Glasser, well-known psychiatrist and author of *Quality School* (1998a), *The Quality School Teacher* (1998b), *Choice Theory* (1998c), and (with Karen Dotson) *Choice Theory in the Classroom* (1998), recommends that teachers develop "quality" classrooms based on democratic principles. According to Glasser, many teachers struggle with classroom management because their actions are guided by stimulus-response theory. They try to coerce students through rewards or punishment, or what many teachers term *logical consequences.* Instead, Glasser believes that teachers should establish "quality" environments in the classroom by following choice theory. Choice theory recognizes that human beings make choices that enable them to create "quality worlds" that satisfy four needs: the need to belong, the need for power, the need for freedom, and the need for fun.

From a **choice theory** perspective, misbehavior in the classroom arises when students' learning experiences do not enable them to create quality worlds for themselves. Therefore, teachers "must give up bossing and turn to 'leading'" (Glasser, 1997, p. 600). We follow leaders, Glasser says, because we believe they are concerned about our welfare. To persuade students to do quality schoolwork, teachers must establish warm, noncoercive relationships with students; teach students meaningful skills rather than ask them to memorize information; enable them to experience satisfaction and excitement by working in small teams; and move from teacher evaluation to student self-evaluation.

Creating a democratic classroom community is not easy; however, the benefits can be significant. Teachers who create a democratic classroom environment often report that their classrooms were teacher centered at the beginning of the school year; however, as the year progressed, they were able to transition to a communal environment. In such an environment, students understood that the guiding question for the class was "*What are we going to do*?" rather than "*What does the teacher want us to do*?"

Preventive Planning

The key to preventing discipline problems is excellent planning and an understanding of life in classrooms. In addition, if you master the essential teaching skills, you will have fewer discipline problems because students will recognize that you are prepared, well organized, and have a sense of purpose. You will be confident of your ability to teach all students, and your task-oriented manner will tend to discourage misbehavior.

In a seminal study of how teachers prevent discipline problems, Jacob Kounin looked at two sets of teachers: (1) those who managed their classrooms smoothly and productively, with few disruptions, and (2) those who seemed to be plagued with discipline problems and chaotic working conditions. He found that the teachers who managed their classrooms successfully had certain teaching behaviors in common: They (1) displayed the proverbial *eyes in the back of the head,* a quality of alertness Kounin referred to as *with-it-ness*; (2) used individual students and incidences as models to communicate to the rest of the class their expectations for student conduct—Kounin's *ripple effect*; (3) supervised several situations at once effectively; and (4) were adept at handling transitions smoothly (Kounin, 1970).

In addition to the principles of effective classroom management that Kounin found, two key elements of preventive planning are (1) establishing rules and procedures and (2) organizing and planning for instruction.

ESTABLISHING RULES AND PROCEDURES Successful classroom managers have carefully planned rules and procedures, which they teach early in the year using clear explanations, examples, and practice (Emmer & Evertson, 2013; Evertson & Emmer, 2013; Good & Lavigne, 2018). Your classroom rules should be clear, concise, reasonable, and few in number. For example, four general rules for elementary-age students might include: (1) respect and be polite to all people, (2) be prompt and be prepared, (3) listen quietly while others are speaking, and (4) obey all school rules (Evertson & Emmer, 2017, pp. 54–55). Rules for the middle and secondary levels might stipulate the following: (1) respect and be polite to all people, (2) be prompt and be prepared, (3) listen and stay seated when someone is talking, (4) respect other people's property, and (5) obey all school rules (Emmer & Evertson, 2017, p. 31).

It is important to enforce classroom rules consistently and fairly. "Consistency is a key reason some rules are effective while others are not. Rules that are not enforced or not applied consistently over time result in a loss of respect for the person who created the rules and is responsible for enforcing them" (Borich, 2017, p. 84).

Video Example 10.2

A Strategy for Creating Groups: Note how this teacher proactively explains the procedures for developing teams for group work.

Procedures—the routines your students follow as they participate in learning activities—are also essential for smooth classroom functioning and minimizing opportunities for misbehavior. How will homework be collected? How will supplies be distributed? How will housekeeping chores be completed? How will attendance be taken? How do students obtain permission to leave the classroom? Part of developing classroom rules and procedures is to decide what to do when students do not follow them. Students must be made aware of the consequences for failing to follow rules or procedures. For example, consequences for rule infractions can range from an expression of teacher disapproval to penalties such as loss of privileges, detention after school, disciplinary conference with a parent or guardian, or temporary separation from the group.

ORGANIZING AND PLANNING FOR INSTRUCTION Organizing instructional time, materials, and activities so that classes run smoothly enables you to keep your students engaged in learning, thereby reducing the need for discipline. Time spent planning authentic learning activities that are appropriate for students' needs, interests, and abilities enables you to enjoy the professional satisfaction that comes from having a well-managed classroom.

The following examples illustrate how one eighth-grade teacher began the school year by carefully organizing and planning for instruction. The teacher across the hall, however, was not as well organized; as a consequence, she is more likely to experience misbehavior in her classroom as the year progresses.

> Donnell Alexander is waiting at the door for her eighth graders with prepared handouts as students come in the room. She distributes them and says, "Take your seats quickly, please. You'll find your name on the desk. The bell is going to ring in less than a minute and everyone needs to be at their desk and

quiet when it does. Please read the handout while you're waiting." She is standing at the front of the room, surveying the class as the bell rings. When it stops, she begins, "Good morning, everyone."

Vicki Williams, who also teaches eighth graders across the hall from Donnell, is organizing her handouts as the students come in the room. Some take their seats while others mill around, talking in small groups. As the bell rings, she looks up and says over the hum of the students. "Everyone take your seats, please. We'll begin in a couple minutes," and she turns back to finish organizing her materials (Kauchak & Eggen, 2012, p. 82).

Matka Wariatka/Fotolia

From this photo, what can you tell about this teacher's proficiency in planning and preparation, structuring the classroom environment, and instruction?

Application Exercise 10.2

Facilitating Classroom Management

Effective Responses to Student Behavior

When students do misbehave, effective teachers draw from a repertoire of problem-solving strategies. These strategies are based on their experience and common sense, their knowledge of students and the teaching–learning process, and their knowledge of human psychology.

There are many structured approaches to classroom management; some are based on psychological theories of human motivation and behavior, while others reflect various philosophical views regarding the purposes of education. None of these approaches, however, is appropriate for all situations, for all teachers, or for all students. The usefulness of a given method depends, in part, on the teacher's individual personality and leadership style and the ability to analyze the complex dynamics of classroom life. In addition, what works should not be the only criterion for evaluating structured or packaged approaches to discipline; what they teach students about their self-worth, ability to meet challenges, and prospects for future success is also important.

SEVERITY OF MISBEHAVIOR Your response to student misbehavior will depend, in part, on whether an infraction is mild, moderate, or severe, and whether it is occurring for the first time or is part of a pattern of chronic misbehaviors. For example, a student who throws a wad of paper at another student might receive a warning for the first infraction. Another student who repeatedly throws objects at other students might receive an after-school detention. Definitions of the severity of misbehavior vary from school to school and from state to state. Table 10.2 shows the percentage of public

Table 10.2 Percentage of public schools reporting selected types of disciplinary problems occurring at school, by frequency and selected school characteristics: School year 2015–2016

	Happens daily or at least once a week[1]						Happens at least once a month[2]		
	Student racial/ethnic tensions	Student bullying[3]	Student sexual harassment of other students[4]	Widespread disorder in classrooms	Student verbal abuse of teachers	Student acts of disrespect for teachers other than verbal abuse	Gang actitivies[5]	Student harassment of other students based on sexual orientation[6]	Student harassment of other students based on gender identity[7]
All public schools	1.7	11.9	1.0	2.3	4.8	10.3	1.2	2.2	1.0
Level[8]									
Primary	1.2!	8.1	‡	1.6!	3.6	8.8	‡	‡	‡
Middle	3.2	21.8	2.1	4.9	8.2	15.9	2.0	4.7	1.9
Higher school	2.3	14.7	2.5	2.6	7.6	12.1	4.2	5.2	3.7
Combined	‡	11.0	‡	‡	‡	4.3!	‡	3.8!	‡
Enrollment size									
Less than 300	‡	6.4	‡	‡	3.6!	6.4	‡	1.3!	‡
300–499	‡	9.6	0.7!	1.3	3.4	9.1	‡	1.2!	0.5!
500–999	2.3	14.0	1.4	3.8	6.0	12.4	0.9	2.7	0.7
1,000 or more	2.6	22.1	2.4!	3.8	7.0	14.4	4.2	5.7	4.1
Locale									
City	1.8!	12.9	0.9!	4.9	9.6	15.3	2.2	2.9	1.2
Suburb	2.3	10.3	0.9!	1.9	3.3	8.1	1.1	1.5	0.9
Town	‡	18.3	1.2!	1.5!	5.4	14.5	‡	3.2	‡
Rural	0.9!	9.7	1.2	‡	1.3!	5.9	‡	2.0	0.8!
Percent White, non-Hispanic enrollment									
More than 95 percent	‡	15.6	‡	‡	‡	‡	‡	‡	‡
More than 80 to 95 percent	1.0!	10.8	1.4!	0.8!	2.1!	6.5	‡	1.7	0.9!
More than 50 to 80 percent	1.4!	11.0	0.9	1.1	3.6	9.9	‡	1.9	1.4
50 percent or less	2.6	12.5	1.0	4.3	7.9	13.7	2.5	2.8	0.9

! Interpret data with caution. Estimate is unstable because the standard error represents more than 30 percent of the estimate.
‡ Reporting standards not met. Either there are too few cases for a reliable estimate or the standard error represents more than 50 percent of the estimate.
[1] Includes schools for which one of the following two response categories was selected: "daily" or "at least once a week."
[2] Includes schools that selected "at least once a month" as well as those that selected "daily" or "at least once a week."
[3] "Bullying" was defined for respondents as any unwanted aggressive behavior(s) by another youth or group of youths who are not siblings or current dating partners that involves an observed or perceived power imbalance and is repeated multiple times or is highly likely to be repeated.
[4] "Sexual harassment" was defined for respondents as conduct that is unwelcome, sexual in nature, and denies or limits a student's ability to participate in or benefit from a school's education program. The conduct can be carried out by school employees, other students, and non-employee third parties. Both male and female students can be victims of sexual harassment, and the harasser and the victim can be of the same sex. The conduct can be verbal, nonverbal, or physical.
[5] "Gang" was defined for respondents as an ongoing loosely organized association of three or more persons, whether formal or informal, that has a common name, signs, symbols, or colors, whose members engage, either individually or collectively, in violent or other forms of illegal behavior.
[6] "Sexual orientation" was defined for respondents as meaning one's emotional or physical attraction to the same and/or opposite sex.
[7] "Gender identity" was defined for respondents as meaning one's inner sense of one's own gender, which may or may not match the sex assigned at birth. Different people choose to express their gender identity differently. For some, gender may be expressed through, for example, dress, grooming, mannerisms, speech patterns, and social interactions. Gender expression usually ranges between masculine and feminine, and some transgender people express their gender consistent with how they identify internally, rather than in accordance with the sex they were assigned at birth.
[8] "Primary schools" are defined as schools in which the lowest grade is not higher than grade 3 and the highest grade is not higher than grade 8. "Middle schools" are defined as schools in which the lowest grade is not lower than grade 4 and the highest grade is not higher than grade 9. "High schools" are defined as schools in which the lowest grade is not lower than grade 9 and the highest grade is not higher than grade 12. "Combined schools" include all other combinations of grades, including K–12 schools.

NOTE: "At school" was defined for respondents to include activities happening in school buildings, on school grounds, on school buses, and at places that hold school-sponsored events or activities. Responses were provided by the principal or the person most knowledgeable about school crime and policies to provide a safe environment.

SOURCE: Diliberti, M., Jackson, M., and Kemp, J. (2017). *Crime, Violence, Discipline, and Safety in U.S. Public Schools: Findings From the School Survey on Crime and Safety: 2015–16* (NCES 2017-122). U.S. Department of Education, National Center for Education Statistics. Washington, DC, p. 9.

schools, categorized by level, size, locale, and minority-group enrollment, that reported different types of discipline problems during 2015–2016.

FOCUS ON **DIVERSITY**: ANALYSIS REVEALS DISCIPLINE DISPARITIES FOR BLACK STUDENTS, BOYS, AND STUDENTS WITH DISABILITIES

An analysis of discipline in nearly all K-12 public schools revealed that Black students, boys, and students with disabilities were disproportionately disciplined during 2013–2014 (United States Government Accountability Office, 2018). Six types of discipline were included in the analysis: out-of-school suspension, in-school suspension, referral to law enforcement, expulsion, corporal punishment, and school-related arrest. Disparities were widespread and present regardless of the type of disciplinary action, level of school poverty, or type of public school attended.

For example, Black students accounted for 15.5 percent of all public school students, but represented about 39 percent of students suspended from school. Boys accounted for just over half of all public school students, but were at least two thirds of students who received the six types of discipline. And students with disabilities represented approximately 12 percent of all public school students; however, they accounted for nearly 25 percent or more of students referred to law enforcement, arrested for a school-related incident, or suspended from school.

ZERO TOLERANCE In response to concerns about violence, drugs, and weapons, some schools have implemented zero tolerance policies. The purpose of **zero tolerance policies** is to communicate to students the types of misbehavior that will result in automatic suspension and/or expulsion. Zero tolerance policies are based on the assumption that awareness of automatic, severe consequences for certain types of misbehavior will deter students from those misbehaviors. Evidence indicates, however, that such policies have little effect on students who are inclined to engage in serious misbehavior, and they do not help to create conditions that deter such misbehavior (Losinski, Katsiyannis, Ryan, & Baughan, 2014; National Association of School Psychologists, 2008). In light of such evidence, the National Association of School Psychologists (2008) has concluded, "Systemic school-wide violence prevention programs, social skills curricula and positive behavioral supports lead to improved learning for all students and safer school communities" (p. 3).

CONSTRUCTIVE ASSERTIVENESS The effectiveness of your responses to students' misbehavior depends, in part, on your ability to use constructive assertiveness (Emmer & Evertson, 2017; Evertson & Emmer, 2017). Constructive assertiveness "lies on a continuum of social response between aggressive, overbearing pushiness and timid, ineffectual submissiveness. Assertiveness skills allow you to communicate to students that you are serious about teaching and about maintaining a classroom in which everyone's rights are respected. Assertiveness does not limit or hamper teachers' and students' caring for one another" (Evertson & Emmer, 2017, p. 205). Communication based on constructive assertiveness is not hostile, sarcastic, defensive, or vindictive; it is clear, firm, and concise. **Constructive assertiveness** includes three basic elements:

- A direct, clear statement of the problem
- Body language that is unambiguous (e.g., direct eye contact with students, erect posture, and facial expressions that are congruent with the content and tone of corrective statements)
- Firm, unwavering insistence on correct behavior

Lee Canter developed an approach to discipline based on teacher assertiveness. The approach calls on teachers to establish firm, clear guidelines for student behavior and to follow through with consequences for misbehavior. Canter (1989, p. 58) comments on how he arrived at the ideas behind assertive discipline: "I found that, above all, the master teachers were assertive; that is, they taught students how to behave. They established clear rules for the classroom, they communicated those rules to the students, and they taught students how to follow them." **Assertive discipline** requires teachers to do the following:

1. Make clear that they will not tolerate anyone preventing them from teaching, stopping learning, or doing anything else that is not in the best interest of the class, the individual, or the teacher.
2. Instruct students clearly and in specific terms about what behaviors are desired and what behaviors are not tolerated.
3. Plan positive and negative consequences for predetermined acceptable or unacceptable behaviors.
4. Plan positive reinforcement for compliance. Reinforcement includes verbal acknowledgment, notes, free time for talking, and tokens that can be exchanged for appropriate rewards.
5. Plan a sequence of steps to punish noncompliance. These range from writing a youngster's name on the board to sending the student to the principal's office (MacNaughton & Johns, 1991, p. 53).

Figure 10.5 presents the assertive discipline policy used by a high school teacher of accounting in Jefferson, **OHIO**.

Research on the effectiveness of assertive discipline is mixed. Some research studies suggest that rewarding students for good behavior may reduce their intrinsic motivation to learn and/or to conform to the teacher's expectations (Oakes, Lipton, Anderson, and Stilman, 2013). In such cases, students come to expect "rewards" for behaving properly. This has led some teachers to discontinue using assertive discipline.

RESTORATIVE JUSTICE Instead of responding to student misbehavior with punitive approaches such as suspensions or expulsions, **restorative justice** helps students understand how their misbehavior can be disruptive, hurtful, or harmful to others. Restorative justice focuses on "righting" these wrongs (Johnson & Johnson, 2017; Morrison & Ahmed, 2006). A well-known example of restorative justice was the National Truth and Reconciliation Commission in South Africa that allowed injured parties to describe, publicly, the injustices they experienced and sometimes confront those who harmed them.

The goal of restorative justice in schools is to resolve past conflicts and create conditions for long-term future cooperation. The process must be voluntary. Participants in the conflict meet with a facilitator (usually, the teacher) and sometimes members of their families. The victim and the offender express their views and describe their experiences, and the facilitator ensures that the discussion remains productive. If the process works well, the participants express remorse for hurting each other, forgive the perceived transgressions, and reconcile their conflict.

"Reconciliation usually includes an apology, communicates that justice has prevailed, recognizes the negativity of the acts perpetuated, restores respect for the social identity of those formerly demeaned, validates and recognizes the suffering

Figure 10.5 Assertive discipline policy

JEFFERSON AREA SR. HIGH SCHOOL ASSERTIVE DISCIPLINE PLAN

2017–2018

Room B-204 - Mr. Michael Barney

CLASS RULES

1. All school rules apply, such as no fighting, no swearing, no cheating, etc.
2. Do not talk while I am talking.
3. Food and drinks are not permitted in the lab.
4. Remain in your assigned seat unless you have permission.
5. No wheeling around in your chair. If you need to get something please get out of your chair.
6. I will dismiss you from class, not the bell. Remain in your seats until I dismiss you from class.
7. Do not touch or unplug any wires in the computer lab. This also includes the computer towers and the monitors.
8. Be respectful of yourself, others, and the property of others.
9. Be tolerant of everyone and their opinions. No ridiculing, putdowns, verbal abuse, or discriminatory remarks. No swearing or vulgar language.
10. Raise your hand to speak. No talking or interrupting without permission.
11. No working on classwork from other classes. It will be taken and thrown away.
12. Keep your hands, feet, and other objects in your own space and to yourself.
13. No sleeping.
14. Clean up your area before leaving. Check your workstation and the floor for pens, pencils, papers, etc.
15. All computer assignments and projects must be completed in class.

Negative consequences if you choose to break a rule:

1st time: Warning, verbal, or telephone call to parents

2nd time: A stronger warning (This may also include a reassigned seat, isolation, or other suitable measure.)

3rd time: Office referral

Severe clause: A student may be sent directly to the office for repeated offenses or extreme offenses (fighting, abusive language, damaging property, insubordination, etc.).

Sign and return the bottom portion to Mr. Barney. Keep the top portion in your class folder.

Students: I have read the rules, consequences, and rewards and I understand them. I agree to abide by this plan while in Room B-204.

________________________ ________________________

(Student Name Printed) **(Date)**

Parents: My son/daughter has discussed this plan with me. I understand it and will support it.

________________________ ________________________

(Parent Signature) **(Date)**

________________________ ________________________

(Parent Signature) **(Date)**

SOURCE: Jefferson Area High School, Jefferson, OH. Retrieved January 19, 2018, from https://sites.google.com/a/jalsd.org/michaelbarney/language-arts/resources. Used with permission from Janet Grout.

undergone by the victim and relevant community members, establishes trust between victim and offender, and removes the reasons for either party to use violence to 'right' the wrongs of the past" (Johnson and Johnson, 2017, p. 430).

The outcome of restorative justice is usually an agreement that includes how to re-establish cooperation and participation in the classroom community—perhaps an apology of action, restitution, and a plan for dealing positively with possible future conflicts. Figure 10.6 compares punitive and restorative justice responses to misbehavior in schools.

Hinkley High School, a Colorado school that enrolls more than 2,000 students—75 percent of whom qualify for free or reduced lunches—showed a dramatic decrease in school violence after it implemented a restorative justice program. The school had 263 physical violence incidents in 2007–2008, but only 31 in 2013–2014.

Figure 10.6 A comparison of punitive and restorative justice responses in schools

Punitive	Restorative
Misbehavior defined as breaking school rules or letting the school down.	Misbehavior defined as harm (emotional/mental/physical) done to one person/group by another.
Focus is on what happened and establishing blame or guilt.	Focus on problem-solving by expressing feelings and needs and exploring how to address problems in the future.
Adversarial relationship and process. Includes an authority figure with the power to decide on penalty. In conflict with wrongdoer.	Dialogue and negotiation, with everyone involved in the communication and cooperation with each other.
Imposition of pain or unpleasantness to punish and deter/prevent.	Restitution as a means of restoring both parties, the goal being reconciliation and acknowledging responsibility for choices.
Attention to rules and adherence to due process.	Attention to relationships and achievement of a mutually desired outcome.
Conflict/wrongdoing represented as impersonal and abstract; individual versus school.	Conflict/wrongdoing recognized as interpersonal conflicts with opportunity for learning.
One social injury compounded by another.	Focus on repair of social injury/damage.
School community as spectators, represented by member of staff dealing with the situation; those directly affected uninvolved and powerless.	School community involved in facilitating restoration; those affected taken into consideration; empowerment.
Accountability defined in terms of receiving punishment.	Accountability defined as understanding impact of actions, taking responsibility for choices, and suggesting ways to repair harm.

SOURCE: A comparison of punitive and restorative justice responses in schools", by Ashley, J. & Burke, K. (October 2009). Implementing restorative justice: A guide for schools. Chicago: Illinois Criminal Justice Information Authority, p. 7. Retrieved from http://www.icjia.state.il.us/publications/implementing-restorative-justice-a-guide-for-schools. Used with Permission from Illinois Criminal Justice Information Authority.

Suspensions at the school decreased, and absenteeism dropped nearly 50 percent and tardiness 60 percent. As Principal Matthew Willis explains: "Every single year over the last three full years that we have been doing restorative justice, you see significant declines in defiance, disobedience and use of profanity" (PBS NewsHour, February 20, 2014).

TEACHER PROBLEM SOLVING If your efforts to get a student to stop misbehaving are unsuccessful, a problem-solving conference with the student is warranted. A problem-solving conference may give you additional understanding of the situation, thus paving the way for a solution. A conference also helps you and the student understand one another's perspectives better and begin to build a more positive relationship.

The goal of a problem-solving conference is for the student to accept responsibility for their behavior and make a commitment to change it. Although there is no right way to conduct a problem-solving conference, Glasser's choice theory lends itself to a conferencing procedure that is flexible and appropriate for most situations. Students will usually make good choices (that is, behave in an acceptable manner) if they experience success and know that teachers care about them. The following steps are designed to help misbehaving students see that the choices they make may not lead to the results they want:

1. Have the misbehaving student evaluate and take responsibility for their behavior. Often, a good first step is for the teacher to ask, "What are you doing?" and then, "Is it helping you?"
2. Have the student make a plan for a more acceptable way of behaving. If necessary, the student and the teacher brainstorm solutions. Agreement is reached on how the student will behave in the future and the consequences for failure to follow through.
3. Require the student to make a commitment to follow the plan.
4. Don't accept excuses for failure to follow the plan.
5. Don't use punishment or react to a misbehaving student in a punitive manner. Instead, point out to the student that there are logical consequences for failure to follow the plan.
6. Don't give up on the student. If necessary, remind the student of their commitment to desirable behavior. Periodically ask, "How are things going?"

DEVELOPING YOUR OWN APPROACH TO CLASSROOM MANAGEMENT No approach to classroom management is effective with all students at all times. How you respond to misbehavior in your classroom depends on your personality, value system, and beliefs about children and ranges along a continuum from the minimum power of giving students nonverbal cues to the maximum power of physical intervention.

To summarize, most teachers tend to rely on one of the following three general approaches to maintaining discipline in the classroom:

1. The *humanist approach* involves the use of minimum power and requires that the teacher develop caring relationships with students and actively listen to their concern. This approach is based on the assumption that misbehavior often reflects a student's inner turmoil or lack of confidence. The teacher uses a problem-solving approach to help the student change their behavior and to become more self-disciplined. Glasser's choice theory is an example of the humanist approach (Glasser, 1998a, 1998b, 1998c).
2. The *behaviorist approach* draws from research on human behavior and emphasizes behavior modification techniques and reinforcement of desired behavior in the classroom. Constructive assertiveness is an example of this approach (Emmer & Evertson, 2017; Evertson & Emmer, 2017).
3. The *classroom management approach* emphasizes preventive planning, establishing reasonable rules and procedures, and organizing and planning for instruction. The classroom management approach focuses on preventing discipline problems from occurring.

In your journey toward becoming a professional teacher, you will draw from these three approaches and develop a repertoire of strategies for classroom management. When you encounter a discipline problem in the classroom, you can analyze the situation and respond with an effective strategy. The ability to do so will give you confidence, as the following beginning teacher told the author:

> I went into the classroom with some confidence and left with lots of confidence. I felt good about what was going on. I established a comfortable rapport with the children and was more relaxed. Each week I grew more confident. When you first go in, you are not sure how you'll do. When you know you are doing okay, your confidence improves.

Spencer Grant/PhotoEdit

What students experience at school can lead them to display negative attitudes in class. What are examples of in-school experiences that promote positive behavior among students?

✓ Check Your Understanding 10.3

What Teaching Methods do Effective Teachers Use?

Beliefs about teaching and learning, students, knowledge, and what is worth knowing influence the instructional methods a teacher uses. In addition, variables such as the teacher's style, learners' characteristics, the culture of the school and surrounding community, and the resources available all influence the methods a teacher uses. All of these components contribute to the model of teaching you use in the classroom. A model of teaching provides you with rules of thumb to follow to create a particular kind of learning environment. As the authors of *Models of Teaching* point out, "Models of teaching are really models of *learning*. As we help students acquire information, ideas, skills, values, ways of thinking, and means of expressing themselves, we are also teaching them how to learn" (Joyce, Weil, & Calhoun, 2015, p. 7). Table 10.3 presents brief descriptions of four widely used models of teaching.

Effective teachers use a repertoire of teaching models and assessment strategies, depending on their situations and the goals and objectives they wish to attain. Your teaching strategies in the classroom will most likely be eclectic—that is, a combination of several models and assessment techniques. Also, as you gain classroom experience and acquire new skills and understanding, your personal model of teaching will evolve, enabling you to respond appropriately to a wider range of teaching situations.

Table 10.3 Four instructional models

	Goals and Rationale	Methods
Cooperative learning	Students can be motivated to learn by working cooperatively in small groups if rewards are made available to the group as a whole and to individual members of the group.	• Small groups (four to six students) work together on learning activities. • Assignments require that students help one another while working on a group project. • In competitive arrangements, groups may compete against one another. • Group members contribute to group goals according to their talents, interests, and abilities.
Theory into practice	Teachers make decisions in three primary areas: content to be taught, how students will learn, and the behaviors the teacher will use in the classroom. The effectiveness of teaching is related to the quality of decisions the teacher makes in these areas.	The teacher follows seven steps in the classroom: 1. Orients students to material to be learned 2. Tells students what they will learn and why it is important 3. Presents new material that consists of knowledge, skills, or processes students are to learn 4. Models what students are expected to do 5. Checks for student understanding 6. Gives students opportunity for practice under the teacher's guidance 7. Makes assignments that give students opportunity to practice what they have learned on their own
Behavior modification	Teachers can shape student learning by using various forms of enforcement. Human behavior is learned, and behaviors that are positively reinforced (rewarded) tend to increase and those that are not reinforced tend to decrease.	• Teacher begins by presenting stimulus in the form of new material. • The behavior of students is observed by the teacher. • Appropriate behaviors are reinforced by the teacher as quickly as possible.
Nondirective teaching	Learning can be facilitated if teachers focus on personal development of students and create opportunities for students to increase their self-understanding and self-concepts. The key to effective teaching is the teacher's ability to understand students and to involve them in a teaching–learning partnership.	• Teacher acts as a facilitator of learning. • Teacher creates learning environments that support personal growth and development. • Teacher acts in the role of a counselor who helps students to understand themselves, clarify their goals, and accept responsibility for their behavior.

Methods Based on Learning New Behaviors

Many teachers use instructional methods that have emerged from our greater understanding of how people acquire or change their behaviors. **Direct instruction**, for example, is a systematic instructional method that focuses on the transmission of knowledge and skills from the teacher (and the curriculum) to the student. Direct instruction is organized on the basis of observable learning behaviors and the actual products of learning. Generally, direct instruction is most appropriate for step-by-step knowledge acquisition and basic skill development, but it is not appropriate for teaching less structured, higher-order skills such as writing, the analysis of social issues, and problem solving.

Extensive research was conducted in the 1970s and 1980s on the effectiveness of direct instruction (Gagné, 1974, 1977; Rosenshine, 1988; Rosenshine & Stevens, 1986). The following eight steps represent a synthesis of research on direct instruction and may be used with students ranging in age from elementary to senior high school:

1. Orient students to the lesson by telling them what they will learn.
2. Review previously learned skills and concepts related to the new material.
3. Present new material, using examples and demonstrations.
4. Assess students' understanding by asking questions; correct misunderstandings.
5. Allow students to practice new skills or apply new information.
6. Provide feedback and corrections as students practice.
7. Include newly learned material in homework.
8. Review material periodically.

A direct instruction method called **mastery learning** is based on two assumptions about learning: (1) Almost all students can learn material if they are given enough time and taught appropriately, and (2) students learn best when they participate in a structured, systematic program of learning that enables them to progress in small, sequenced steps (Bloom, 1981; Carroll, 1963). The following five steps present the mastery learning cycle:

1. Set objectives and standards for mastery.
2. Teach content directly to students.
3. Provide corrective feedback to students on their learning.
4. Provide additional time and help in correcting errors.
5. Follow a cycle of teaching, testing, reteaching, and retesting.

Video Example 10.3

Correcting Misunderstandings: The teacher is working with groups of students in a science class. Note how the teacher uses questioning to help students reach the correct conclusions.

In mastery learning, students take diagnostic tests and then are guided to complete corrective exercises or activities to improve their learning. These may take the form of programmed instruction, workbooks, computer drill and practice, or educational games. After the corrective lessons, students are given another test and are more likely to achieve mastery.

Methods Based on Child Development

As you know from reflecting on your own development as a human being, children move through stages of cognitive, psychosocial, and moral development. Effective instruction includes methods that are developmentally appropriate, meet students' diverse learning needs, and recognize the importance of learning that occurs in social contexts. For example, one way that students reach higher levels of development is to observe and then imitate their parents, teachers, and peers, who act as models. "In many ways, students become what we model for them, and part of our influence on them depends on our own states of growth—our own self-concepts—and how we communicate them to children" (Joyce, Weil, & Calhoun, 2015, p. 301).

Effective teachers also use **modeling** by thinking out loud and following three basic steps of mental modeling: (1) demonstrating to students the thinking involved in a task,

(2) making students aware of the thinking involved, and (3) focusing students on applying the thinking. In this way, teachers can help students become aware of their learning processes and enhance their ability to learn. "For example, as a teacher demonstrates cutting out a construction paper square to serve as a math manipulative during the next lesson, she might 'think out loud' in class, saying, 'I am cutting this square very carefully because we will be using it today to create fractional shapes. I need the sides of my square to be very neat. My smaller, fraction pieces should be accurate in size'" (Dell'Olio & Donk, 2007, p. 80).

Since the mid-1980s, several educational researchers have examined how learners construct understanding of new material. "Constructivist views of learning, therefore, focus on how learners make sense of new information—how they construct meaning based on what they already know" (Parkay, Anctil, & Hass, 2014, p. 229). Teachers with this constructivist view of learning focus on students' thinking about the material being learned and, through carefully orchestrated cues, prompts, and questions, help students arrive at a deeper understanding of the material. The common elements of **constructivist teaching** include the following:

- The teacher elicits students' prior knowledge of the material and uses this as the starting point for instruction.
- The teacher not only presents material to students but also responds to students' efforts to learn the material. While teaching, the teacher must learn about students' learning.
- Students not only absorb information but also actively use that information to construct meaning.
- The teacher creates a social milieu within the classroom—a community of learners—that allows students to reflect and talk with one another as they construct meaning and solve problems.

Constructivist teachers provide students with support, or scaffolding, as they learn new material. By observing the child and listening carefully to what he or she says, the teacher provides **scaffolding** in the form of clues, encouragement, suggestions, or other assistance to guide the student's learning efforts. The teacher varies the amount of support given on the basis of the student's understanding—if the student understands little, the teacher gives more support; conversely, the teacher gives progressively less support as the student's understanding becomes more evident. Overall, the teacher provides just enough scaffolding to enable the student to "discover" the material on their own.

Video Example 10.4

Story Writing Scaffolding: This teacher uses scaffolding to support a kindergarten student through a story-writing process. The teacher allows the student to independently do what he can in the writing process by making pictures and some letters. Then the teacher listens, providing clues and encouragement to help the student create a story.

The concept of scaffolding is based on the work of L. S. Vygotsky, a well-known Soviet psychologist. Vygotsky (1978, 1986) coined the term *zone of proximal development* to refer to the point at which students need assistance to continue learning. The effective teacher is sensitive to the student's zone of proximal development and ensures that instruction neither exceeds the student's current level of understanding nor underestimates the student's ability.

Methods Based on the Thinking Process

Some teaching methods are derived from the mental processes involved in learning, thinking, remembering, problem solving, and creativity. **Information processing**, for example, is a branch of cognitive science concerned with how people use their long- and short-term memory to access information and solve problems. The computer is often used as an analogy for information-processing views of learning:

> Like the computer, the human mind takes in information, performs operations on it to change its form and content, stores the information, retrieves it when needed, and generates responses to it . . . According to this model, stimuli from the environment (input) flow into the sensory registers, one for each sensing modality ([seeing], hearing, tasting, etc.). From there, some information is encoded and moves to short-term memory. Short-term memory holds information very briefly, combines it with information from long-term memory, and

with enough effort, moves some information into long-term memory storage. Short-term memory is also responsible for generating responses or output (Woolfolk, 2016, pp. 292–293).

Although several systematic approaches to instruction are based on information processing—teaching students how to memorize, think inductively or deductively, acquire concepts, or use the scientific method, for example—they all focus on how people acquire and use information. Psychologists have identified three types of memory stores used in information processing:

1. ***Sensory memory***—information stored briefly until it can be processed by the information-processing system; sensory memory retains information for about 1 second for vision and 2 to 4 seconds for hearing (Leahey & Harris, 2001; Pashler & Carrier, 1996).
2. ***Working memory***—holds information while a person processes it; working memory is the conscious part of our information-processing system.
3. ***Long-term memory***—a permanent store of information; working memory is limited to about seven items of information for a few seconds; however, long-term memory is vast and may remain for a lifetime (Schunk, 2012).

Table 10.4 presents general teaching guidelines based on these three types of memory stores.

Table 10.4 Capitalizing on the Characteristics of the Memory Stores to Promote Learning in Your Students

Sensory Memory

1. Sensory memory briefly holds incoming stimuli from the environment until the information can be processed. To keep students from losing important information, allow them to attend to one message before presenting a second one.
   - **Elementary**: A second-grade teacher asks one question at a time and gets an answer before asking a second question.
   - **Middle School**: A prealgebra teacher displays two similar problems on the document camera and waits until students have copied them before she starts discussing them.
   - **High School**: A geography teacher places a map on the document camera and says, "I'll give you a minute to examine the geography of the countries on this map in the front of the room. Then we'll discuss what you're noticing."

Working Memory

2. Working memory is where learners consciously process information, and its capacity is limited. To avoid overloading learners' working memories, develop lessons with questioning and avoid extended periods of lecturing.
   - **Elementary**: A third-grade teacher writes directions for seatwork on the board. He asks different students to repeat and explain the directions before they begin.
   - **Middle School**: A teacher in a woodworking class begins by saying, "The density of wood from the same kind of tree varies, depending on the amount of rainfall." He waits a moment, holds up two pieces of wood, and says, "What do you notice about the rings on these pieces?"
   - **High School**: An Algebra II teacher "walks" students through the solutions to problems by having a different student describe each step in the solution.
3. Automaticity is the ability to perform tasks with little conscious effort. To develop automaticity in your students, provide frequent practice and present information in both verbal and visual forms.
   - **Elementary**: A first-grade teacher has his students practice their writing by composing two sentences each day about an event of the previous evening. As they practice their letters, he demonstrates how they should look and describes correct procedures verbally.
   - **Middle School**: To capitalize on the distributed processing capability of working memory, an eighth-grade history teacher prepares a flowchart of the events leading to the Revolutionary War. As she questions students, she refers to the chart for each point and shows students how to use the chart to organize their notes.
   - **High School**: A physics teacher demonstrates the relationship between force and acceleration by pulling a cart along a desktop with a constant force so students can see that the cart accelerates. He then asks them to describe what they see.

Long-Term Memory

4. Information is organized into schemas in learners' long-term memories. To help your students make these schemas as meaningful as possible, encourage them to look for relationships among the ideas they study.
   - **Elementary**: During story time, a second-grade teacher uses "how," "when," and "why" questions to encourage students to explain how the events in a story are related and contribute to the conclusion.
   - **Middle School**: In developing the rules for solving equations by substitution, an algebra teacher asks, "How does this process compare to solving equations by addition?"
   - **High School**: To help his students understand cause-and-effect relationships, a world history teacher asks questions such as, "Why was shipping so important in ancient Greece?," "Why was Troy's location so important?," and "How do these questions relate to the location of today's big cities?"

SOURCE: Eggen, P., & Kauchak, D. (2016). Educational psychology: Windows on classrooms, 10th edition. Boston: Pearson. pp. 280-281. Used with Permission from Pearson Education, Inc.

In **inquiry learning** and **discovery learning**, students are given opportunities to inquire into subjects so that they discover knowledge for themselves. When teachers ask students to go beyond information in a text to make inferences, draw conclusions, or form generalizations, and when teachers do not answer students' questions, preferring instead to have students develop their own answers, they are using methods based on inquiry and discovery learning. These methods are best suited for teaching concepts, relationships, and theoretical abstractions, and for having students formulate and test hypotheses. The following example shows how inquiry and discovery learning in a first-grade classroom fostered a high level of student involvement and thinking.

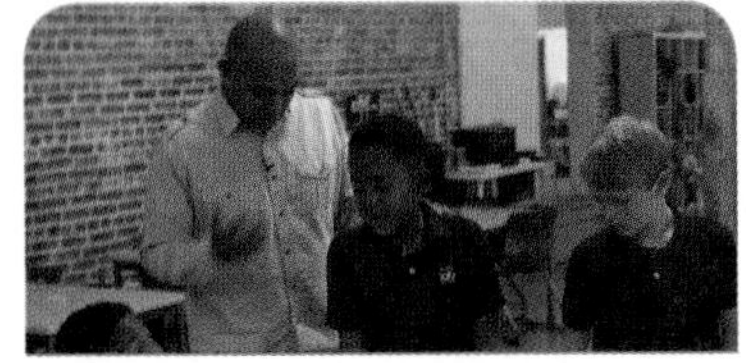

Video Example 10.5

Discovery Learning: A teacher uses discovery learning to help students problem-solve a rationale for having paper poppers in schools. Note the positive interaction between students and how the teacher gives them reminders, not answers, that act as guidelines for their presentation.

> The children are gathered around a table on which a candle and jar have been placed. The teacher, Jackie Wiseman, lights the candle and, after it has burned brightly for a minute or two, covers it carefully with the jar. The candle grows dim, flickers, and goes out. Then she produces another candle and a larger jar, and the exercise is repeated. The candle goes out, but more slowly. Jackie produces two more candles and jars of different sizes, and the children light the candles, place the jars over them, and the flames slowly go out. "Now we're going to develop some ideas about what has just happened," she says. "I want you to ask me questions about those candles and jars and what you just observed" (Joyce, Weil, & Calhoun, 2015, p. 24).

Monkey Business Images/Shutterstock

These students are building on prior knowledge and using inquiry to acquire new knowledge. What kinds of learning activities require students to use their cognitive abilities this way?

Methods Based on Peer-Mediated Instruction

Student peer groups can be a deterrent to academic performance (Sternberg, Dornbusch, & Brown, 1996), but they can also motivate students to excel. Because school learning occurs in a social setting, **peer-mediated instruction** provides teachers with options for increasing students' learning. Cooperative learning, described earlier in this chapter, is an example of peer-mediated instruction.

Another example is **group investigation**, in which the teacher's role is to create an environment that allows students to determine what they will study and how. Students are presented with a situation to which they "react and discover basic conflicts among their attitudes, ideas, and modes of perception. On the basis of this information, they identify the problem to be investigated, analyze the roles required to solve it, organize themselves to take these roles, act, report, and evaluate these results" (Thelen, 1960, p. 82).

The teacher's role in group investigation is multifaceted; they are an organizer, guide, resource person, counselor, and evaluator. The method is very effective in increasing student achievement (Sharan & Sharan, 1989/1990, pp. 17–21; Joyce, Weil, & Calhoun, 2015), positive attitudes toward learning, and the cohesiveness of the classroom group. The model also allows students to inquire into problems that interest them and enables each student to make a meaningful, authentic contribution to the group's effort based on their experiences, interests, knowledge, and skills.

Other common forms of peer-mediated instruction include peer tutoring and cross-age tutoring. In **peer-tutoring** arrangements, students are tutored by other pupils in the same class or the same grade. **Cross-age tutoring** involves, for example, sixth-grade students tutoring second-grade students in reading. With proper orientation and training, cross-age tutoring can greatly benefit both the student teaching and the learner (Henriques, 1997; Schneider & Barone, 1997; Utay & Utay, 1997; Zukowski, 1997). Pilot programs pairing students at risk of dropping out of school with younger children and with students with special needs have proved especially successful.

Check Your Understanding 10.4

Summary

What Determines the Culture of the Classroom?

- From seating arrangements to classroom rules and procedures, the content and relevance of the curriculum, and the quality of interactions with students from diverse cultural and linguistic backgrounds, teachers make many decisions that influence the culture of the classroom.
- Classroom climate refers to the atmosphere or quality of life in a classroom. An important element of a positive learning environment is a caring classroom climate.

How Can You Create a Positive Learning Environment?

- Teachers show care for students by providing support, structure, and appropriate expectations.
- The physical environment of a classroom—seating arrangements and the placement of other classroom furniture, for example—can make a positive contribution to students' learning.
- Classroom organization—how students are grouped for instruction and how time is used—is an important element of the effective learning environment.

What Are the Keys to Successful Classroom Management?

- Teachers who prevent problems before they occur foster effective, harmonious interpersonal interactions; understand how their leadership style influences students; and facilitate the development of the classroom group so that it becomes more cohesive and supportive.
- When management problems occur, effective teachers base their responses on three elements of constructive assertiveness: a clear statement of the problem or concern; unambiguous body language; and a firm, unwavering insistence on appropriate behavior.
- Most teachers tend to rely on one of three general approaches to maintaining discipline in the classroom: the humanist approach, the behaviorist approach, or the classroom management approach.

What Teaching Methods Do Effective Teachers Use?

- Direct instruction and mastery learning are based on the view that learning is the acquisition of new behaviors.
- Modeling, constructivism, and scaffolding are based primarily on an understanding of how students construct meaning as they learn new material.
- Psychologists have identified three types of memory stores used in information processing: sensory memory, working memory, and long-term memory.
- Peer-mediated instruction, which views learning as taking place in social situations, includes cooperative learning, group investigation, and peer- and cross-age tutoring.

Professional Reflections and Activities

Teacher's Journal

1. Recall the teachers and classmates you had during your school career. Select one class and analyze its group processes in terms of the stages of group development discussed in this chapter. At what stage of development was the group near the end of the school year? What conditions facilitated or impeded the development of this group?
2. Describe the "ideal" physical classroom environment for you. How would the seating arrangement facilitate the attainment of your instructional goals and objectives? How would you involve students in arranging the classroom?
3. Describe your leadership style as it relates to classroom management. In which aspects of leadership and classroom management do you feel most and least confident? What might you do, or what skills might you acquire, to strengthen your effectiveness in areas where you feel you lack confidence? Develop your ideas into a statement of professional goals.

Teacher's Research

1. Visit the homepages for a few of the following educational research publications on the Internet.
   - *American Educational Research Journal*
   - *Cognition and Instruction*
   - *Contemporary Educational Psychology*
   - *Educational Psychologist*
   - *Educational Psychology Review*
   - *Educational Researcher*
   - *Journal of Educational Psychology*
   - *Journal of Teaching and Teacher Education*
   - *Review of Educational Research*
   - *Review of Research in Education*
   - *Social Psychology of Education*

Select an article of interest related to increasing student learning. Summarize the article and present a brief oral report to your class. Based on the research findings presented in the article, what are the implications for teaching?

2. Visit several school district websites to examine their discipline policies. What similarities and differences do you note among the policies? To what extent do the policies address the following topics: democratic classrooms, choice theory, constructive assertiveness, assertive discipline, caring classrooms, zero tolerance, bullying, sexual harassment, and gangs?

Observations and Interviews

1. Observe several teachers at the level for which you are preparing to teach and try to identify the teaching methods they are using as part of their instructional repertoires.

Professional Portfolio

Prepare a poster depicting a classroom arrangement appropriate for the subject area and grade level for which you are preparing to teach. The poster should indicate the seating arrangement, location of other classroom furniture, and educational technology areas. In addition, make a list of classroom rules that will be posted in the room. You may wish to organize the rules according to the following categories.

- Rules related to academic work
- Rules related to classroom conduct
- Rules that must be communicated on your first teaching day
- Rules that can be communicated later

Chapter 11
Curriculum, Standards, Assessment, and Student Learning

Lisa F. Young/Shutterstock

Learning Outcomes

After reading this chapter, you will be able to do the following:

11.1 Explain what students learn from the different types of curricula they experience at school.

11.2 Describe the curriculum development process and factors that influence it.

11.3 Describe the key features of standards-based education and explain the role of standards in today's classrooms.

11.4 Explain the Common Core State Standards Initiative and how it has influenced teaching.

11.5 Explain the role of assessment in teaching.

11.6 Describe several approaches to assessing students' learning and developing high-quality classroom assessments.

READERS' VOICES

What do students learn from the curriculum?

The curriculum teaches students how to survive in today's competitive world. Students learn not only knowledge of content, but also people skills in order to live in today's society.

—DREW,
Teacher Education program, first year

What do Students Learn from the Curriculum?

Think back to your experiences as a student at the elementary, middle, junior, and high schools you attended. What did you learn? The curriculum you experienced certainly included reading, computation, penmanship, spelling, geography, and history. In addition to these topics, though, did you learn something about cooperation, competition, stress, football, video games, social networking, smartphones, popularity, and the opposite sex? Or did you perhaps learn to love chemistry and to hate English grammar?

The countless things you learned in school make up the curriculum that you experienced. Curriculum theorists and researchers have suggested several different definitions for **curriculum**, with no single definition that is universally accepted. Here are some definitions in current use:

1. A course of study, derived from the Latin *currere*, meaning "to run a course"
2. Course content, the information or knowledge that students are to learn
3. Planned learning experiences
4. Intended learning outcomes, the results of instruction as distinguished from the means (activities, materials, etc.) of instruction
5. All the experiences that students have while at school

None of these five is in any sense the "right" definition. The way we define the word *curriculum* depends on our purposes and the situation we find ourselves in. If, for example, we were advising a high school student on the courses they need to prepare for college, our operational definition of curriculum would most likely be "a course of study." However, if we were interviewing sixth-grade students for their views on the K–6 elementary school they just graduated from, we would probably want to view curriculum as "all the experiences that students have while at school." Let us, then, posit an additional definition of curriculum: *Curriculum refers to the experiences, both planned and unplanned, that enhance (and sometimes impede) the education and growth of students.*

Kinds of Curricula

Elliot Eisner, a noted educational researcher, has said that "schools teach much more—and much less—than they intend to teach. Although much of what is taught is explicit and public, a great deal is not" (Eisner, 2002, p. 87). For this reason, we need to look at the four curricula that all students experience: the explicit curriculum, the hidden curriculum, the null curriculum, and the extracurricular/cocurricular program. Figure 11.1 illustrates that the ultimate goal of these experiences is the learning and growth of students. The more we understand these curricula and how they influence students, the better we will be able to develop educational programs that do, in fact, promote learning and growth.

Figure 11.1 Four kinds of curricula students experience

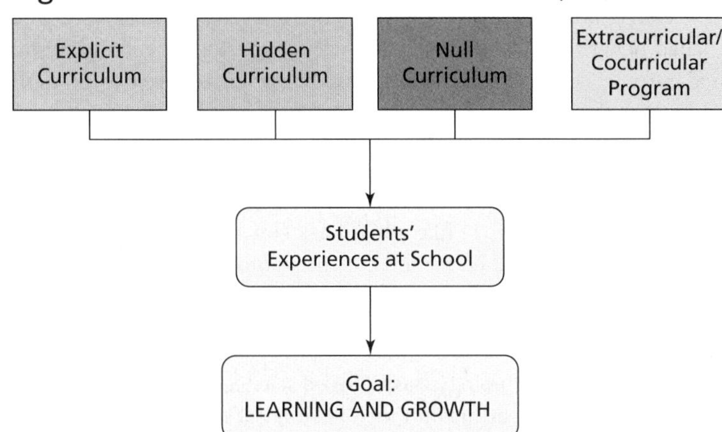

EXPLICIT CURRICULUM The explicit, or overt, curriculum refers to what a school intends to teach students. This curriculum is made up of several components: (1) the aims, goals, and learning objectives the school has for all students; (2) the courses that make up each student's program of study; and (3) the knowledge, skills, and attitudes that teachers want students to acquire. If we asked a principal to describe the educational program at their school, our question would be in reference to the explicit curriculum. Similarly, if we asked a teacher to describe what they wished to accomplish with a particular class, we would be given a description of the explicit curriculum.

In short, the **explicit curriculum** represents the publicly announced expectations the school has for its students. These expectations range from learning how to read, write, and compute to learning to appreciate music, art, and cultures other than one's own. In most instances, the explicit curriculum takes the form of written plans or guides for the education of students. Examples of such written documents are course descriptions, curriculum guides that set forth the goals and learning objectives for a school or district, texts and other commercially prepared learning materials, and teachers' lesson plans. Through the instructional program of a school, then, these curricular materials are brought to life.

Video Example 11.1

Early Childhood Curriculum: This teacher describes how she goes about aligning the preschool's explicit curriculum with the activities for children.

HIDDEN CURRICULUM The **hidden curriculum** (also called the *implicit curriculum*) refers to the behaviors, attitudes, and knowledge the culture of the school unintentionally teaches students (Parkay, Anctil, & Hass, 2014). What students learn via the hidden curriculum can be positive or negative, depending on their day-to-day experiences at school. For example, from teachers who are knowledgeable, well organized, and personable, students are likely to develop positive habits and abilities—cooperating with others, taking responsibility, planning ahead, and forgoing immediate gratification to obtain long-range goals. On the other hand, from teachers who are ill prepared, apathetic, or aloof, students are likely to acquire habits and attitudes that are negative and that discourage personal growth and development—for example, a dislike for learning, the ability to deceive or defy adult authority figures, or a tendency to procrastinate.

In the following excerpts from letters written about their teachers, four students describe the hidden curricula they experienced in school. In examples 1 and 2, the hidden curricula "taught" students to be more confident in their ability to learn. In examples 3 and 4, the hidden curricula undermined the students' confidence and desire to learn.

Example 1

I was in your grade 10 English class. I sure felt safe to take a risk in your class. I actually tried hard, knowing I might fail, but felt safe enough to do so. (Paul, Christensen, & Falk, 2000, p. 23)

Example 2

I was in your grade 9 class and you praised me for my creative writing. Until that time, I had never thought of myself as a very creative person but your faith in me spurred me on to choose English as my major at the university. (Paul et al., 2000, p. 23)

Example 3

The teacher just put [material] on the board and if you don't know how, the teacher get angry. I try to get help but when I come after school, they gotta go somewhere and can't help you . . . like when I ask somebody to help me, just because some other kid won't need help, then they think others won't either; some kids are smarter. (Wilson & Corbett, 2001, p. 38)

Example 4

I was in your 11th-grade biology class. I loved science and biology until I took your class. You gave me a great disdain for the subject. Your teaching methods bored the class to tears. We read each chapter out loud at the beginning of the week and spent the rest of the week working quietly on the questions at the end of the chapter along with the endless dittos you passed out. We never discussed anything and you never taught us anything. We were graded on how well we could come up with the answers you thought were right and heaven forbid if we did not head our paper using the "correct" format. I think the only thing I learned in your class was conformity. (Colucci, 2000, p. 38)

As a result of the hidden curriculum of schools, students learn more than their teachers imagine. As a teacher, you will not be aware of all that students are learning through the hidden curriculum of your classroom. However, you can increase the likelihood that what it teaches will be positive. By allowing students to help determine the content of the explicit curriculum, by providing them with challenges appropriate for their stage of development, and by encouraging them to put forth their best effort and to persevere when learning new material, teachers can ensure that the outcomes of the hidden curriculum will be largely positive.

NULL CURRICULUM One aspect of the hidden curriculum is the **null curriculum**. The null curriculum refers to topics students are not taught. These topics may not be taught because they are perceived as controversial or not relevant to students' future success. Or a teacher may have insufficient knowledge about certain topics or not feel comfortable including them in the curriculum.

Perhaps you have wondered why schools teach what they do. Why is so much of the K–12 curriculum devoted to language arts, mathematics, science, and history or social studies? Why are students seldom taught anthropology, sociology, psychology, law, economics, filmmaking, or architecture? The answer may be that "[w]e teach what we teach largely out of habit, and in the process neglect areas of study that could prove to be exceedingly useful to students" (Eisner, 2002, p. 103).

In addition, U.S. school curricula are largely based on manipulations of words and numbers—skills that neuroscience informs us are performed by the left hemisphere of the brain. Right-hemispheric thinking that is imaginative, subjective, and poetic is stressed only incidentally. School curricula in non-Western cultures frequently show a great integration of right- and left-hemispheric thinking. Japanese schools, for example, require considerably more art, music, and literature than most U.S. schools. In addition, all Japanese students must study handicrafts and calligraphy. It is possible that many of the well-documented successes of Japanese business and industry may be traced back to curricula that go beyond verbal and numerical thinking to include the development of aesthetic capabilities. Unlike some of their U.S. counterparts, the Japanese would be reluctant to consider eliminating art, music, or physical education (which includes dance) from the curriculum.

FOCUS ON **DIVERSITY**: USING CURRICULUM TO ADDRESS RACISM

The Black Lives Matter (BLM) movement that began in response to violence and systemic racism against black people in the U.S. has led to debate among teachers about how best to discuss race in the classroom. For example, many Philadelphia teachers elected to participate in a BLM-initiated program (not sponsored by the school system) to include BLM in their lesson plans during January 2017. Other teachers chose not to participate. Curriculum materials included coloring book pages titled "The Revolution Is Always Now" for very young students, and science lessons about the biology of skin color for high schoolers.

Teachers who supported the BLM program said it gave students an opportunity to learn about, and engage with, a critical social issue in a more thoughtful and informed way. As a high school English and history teacher pointed out, "This is a critical issue of our time—in our society, but also in our students' lives. It's important for us to dive in" (Kauffman, 2017). However, other teachers argued that including BLM in the curriculum encourages divisions in our society. As a high school English teacher said, "I don't think kids should be taught that Western society is perpetrating a war on black people" (Kauffman, 2017).

Similarly, hundreds of teachers in Seattle participated in a "Black Lives Matter at School" event and wore BLM shirts to school on October 19, 2016. The event was organized by the Seattle Education Association (SEA) after unanimously passing the following resolution: "Whereas the SEA promotes equity and supports anti-racist work in our schools . . . . Therefore be it resolved that the SEA Representative Assembly endorse and participate in an action wearing Black Lives Matter t-shirts on Wednesday, October 19, 2016, with the intent of showing solidarity, promoting anti-racist practices in our schools, and creating dialogue in our schools and communities" (I Am an Educator, 2016).

In support of "Black Lives Matter at School," teachers at Washington Middle School in Seattle pointed out that "This is a consciousness-raising event. School is part of society, students and staff are part of society, and so what is happening within our society deserves and demands our attention. This is a 'teachable moment' for the Seattle Public School community" (I Am an Educator, 2016).

EXTRACURRICULAR/COCURRICULAR PROGRAMS The curriculum includes school-sponsored activities—music, drama, special-interest clubs, sports, student government, and honor societies, to name a few—that students may pursue in addition to academic subjects. When such activities are perceived as additions to the academic curriculum, they are termed *extracurricular*. When these activities are seen as having important educational goals—and not merely as extras added to the academic curriculum—they are termed *cocurricular*. To reflect the fact that these two labels are commonly used for the same activities, I use the term *extracurricular/cocurricular activities*. Although **extracurricular/cocurricular programs** are most extensive at the secondary level, many schools at the elementary, middle, and junior high levels also provide their students with a broad assortment of extracurricular/cocurricular activities. For students who choose to participate, such activities provide an opportunity to use social and academic skills in many different contexts.

Participation in extracurricular/cocurricular activities results in several positive outcomes for students (Vandell, 2013). For example, those who participate in the arts have greater self-efficacy and achievement orientation (Li & Vandell, 2013; Vandell, Pierce, & Karsh, 2011). Students who participate in sports have better work habits, self-efficacy, school attachment, and achievement orientation (Vandell, Pierce, & Karsh, 2011).

In addition, extracurricular/cocurricular activities promote positive social skills with peers and prosocial behavior, as well as reductions in aggression, misconduct (e.g., skipping school, getting into fights), and illegal substance use (Durlak et al., 2010; Vandell, Reisner, & Pierce, 2007). Participation in extracurricular/cocurricular activities also increases student engagement, intrinsic motivation, concentrated effort, and positive states of mind (Larson, 2000; Shernoff & Vandell, 2008).

Furthermore, students themselves tend to identify extracurricular/cocurricular activities as a high point in their school careers. However, students who might benefit the most from participating in extracurricular/cocurricular activities—those below the norm in academic achievement and students at risk—tend not to participate. In addition, students from low socioeconomic backgrounds participate less often (McFarland, et al., 2017).

Curriculum Content and Student Success

Curricula in U.S. schools have changed frequently since our colonial period. Goals for schools are debated, additional needs of society emerge, and student populations become more diverse. Since our nation's founding, society has set the following goals for schools:

- Prepare students to meet religious and family responsibilities
- Provide employers with literate workers
- Desegregate society
- Reduce crime, poverty, and injustice
- Help the U.S. remain competitive in the world economy
- Provide the scientists, mathematicians, and engineers to keep our country strong
- Educate students for intelligent participation in a democracy

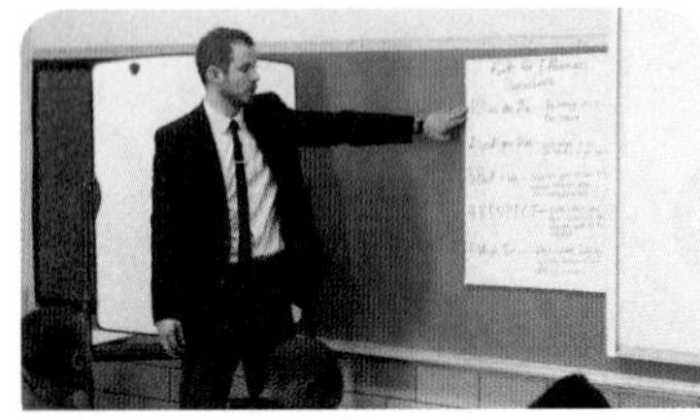

Video Example 11.2

Communicating Expectations: This teacher is setting up the next part of the class activity for his students. He shares the standards and then gives guidelines for effective discussion. Note that the guidelines incorporate some soft skills such as appropriate ways to share what you think and respect for others.

The nation's schools teach what the larger society believes young people should learn to be successful. For example, Figure 11.2 shows that the majority (36 percent) of the U.S. public believes it is most important for students to develop "soft skills" such as cooperation, respect, and persistence at problem solving in school. In contrast, only 6 percent believe student performance on standardized tests is most important. The data presented in the figure also show that one fourth of the public believes the STEM areas of technology and engineering are most important.

Although the primary aim of school curricula is to promote student success in the future, success is not easy to achieve in our increasingly complex, interdependent world. To realize their full potential, students must navigate an environment shaped by forces such as continually evolving technology, economic volatility, and climate change. This requires more than content knowledge and intellectual accomplishments. For example, we know that high-achieving individuals usually possess certain attitudes, dispositions, social skills, intrapersonal resources, and interpersonal competencies that contribute to their success. Moreover, these qualities are, to a great extent, teachable, and they should be made part of the school curriculum. Figure 11.3 illustrates three noncognitive areas that are receiving more attention in school curricula: grit, tenacity, and perseverance; academic mindset; and mindfulness/meditation skills.

Figure 11.2 Most important factor in school quality, national totals, 2017

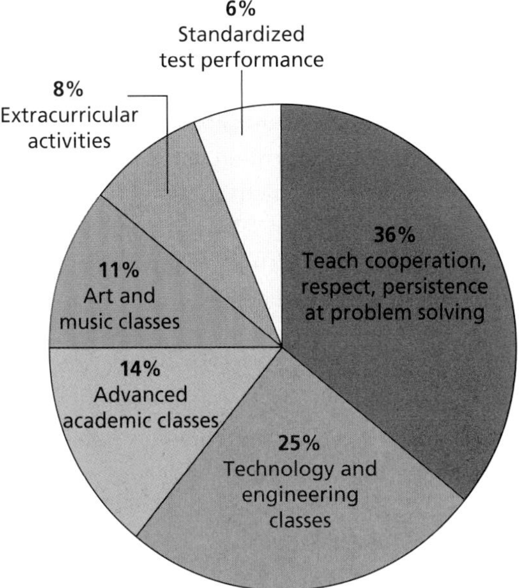

Note: Data are based on a random phone survey of 1,588 adults. Interviewees responded to the following: "For each item I name, please tell me how important it is in school quality—extremely important, very important, somewhat important, not so important, or not important at all." If a respondent chose multiple items as "extremely important," the interviewer then asked: "Which one of those is the 'single most important?'"

SOURCE: Based on Phi Delta Kappa. (2017). The 49th annual PDK poll of the public's attitudes toward the public schools. *Phi Delta Kappan*, Vol. 99, No. 1, p. K24; and About the poll. Retrieved from http://pdkpoll.org/about

Figure 11.3 Three noncognitive factors that contribute to academic achievement

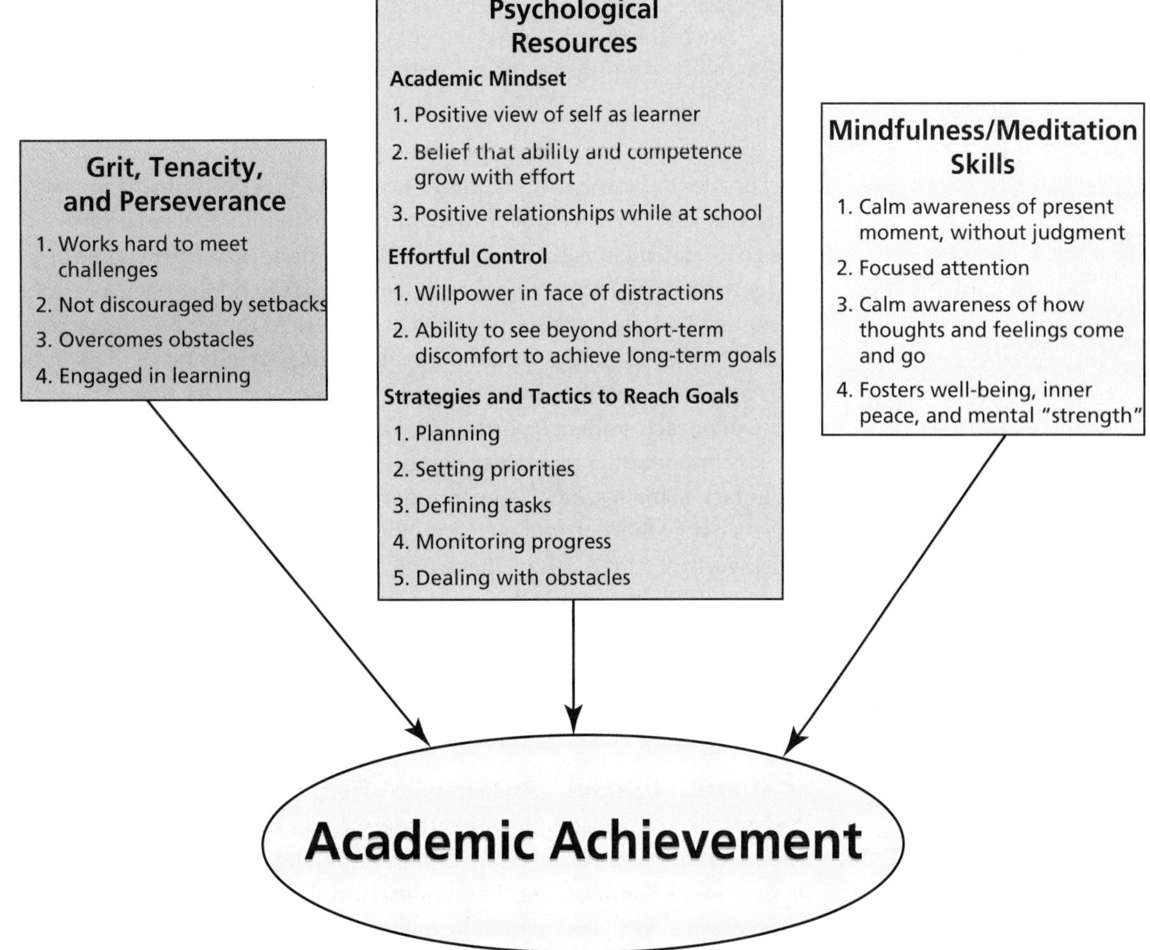

GRIT, TENACITY, AND PERSEVERANCE In your own life, grit, tenacity, and perseverance may have helped you succeed. These personal qualities helped you work toward long- and short-term goals. Today, they are helping you to follow through on your decision to become a teacher. Tomorrow, they will help you become a successful beginning teacher.

In *Promoting Grit, Tenacity, and Perseverance: Critical Factors for Success in the 21st Century*, the U.S. Department of Education stated that " . . . conventional educational approaches have tended to focus on intellectual aspects of success, such as content knowledge. However, this is not sufficient. If students are to achieve their full potential, they must have opportunities to engage and develop a much richer set of skills. Indeed, a growing body of research suggests that noncognitive factors can have just as strong an influence on academic performance and professional attainment as intellectual factors" (Shechtman et al., 2013, p. 75).

Individuals who possess a high level of grit, tenacity, and perseverance tend to characterize themselves with the following phrases: "I am diligent," "Setbacks don't discourage me," and "I have overcome setbacks to conquer an important challenge." Grit, tenacity, and perseverance enable students to work hard to meet challenges and to maintain commitment and interest over time, in spite of occasional failure, hardships, and plateaus in progress toward goals. They have a distinct "advantage" over students who lack grit, tenacity, and perseverance. Whereas disappointment, boredom, and setbacks lead some students to "cut their losses" and quit, students with grit, tenacity, and perseverance "stay the course" until they succeed. The following describes how these students view themselves as learners:

> First, they believe that they belong in school academically and socially. Second, they are engaged in learning, view effort positively, and can forgo immediate pleasures for the sake of schoolwork. Third, difficulty, be it intellectual or social, does not derail them. They see a setback as an opportunity for learning or a problem to be solved rather than as a humiliation, a condemnation of their ability or worth, a symbol of future failures, or a confirmation that they do not belong. (Dweck, Walton, & Cohen, 2011, pp. 5–6).

To foster grit, tenancy, and perseverance in his classroom, ninth-grade language arts teacher Alex Adams has his students keep a writing portfolio. At the beginning of the year, Alex guides each student to identify three to four goals to improve their writing. The goals statement is the first item in the portfolio. Over the course of the year, Alex meets with each student to give advice on what to add to their portfolio, including exemplars and pieces that illustrate challenges. At the end of the year, Alex asks his students to reflect on the growth of their writing overall and to think about how their setbacks show how they have learned and improved over time. This reflection is the last item in each student's portfolio.

It is important to remember that grit, tenacity, and perseverance are not related to IQ. In fact, some researchers even report that grit, tenacity, and perseverance predict success over other attributes like intelligence, self-control, and grade point average (Duckworth & Allred, 2012; Duckworth, Kirby, Tsukayama, Berstein, & Ericsson, 2010; Duckworth, Peterson, Matthews, & Kelly, 2007). Other researchers, however, suggest that the connection between grit and success is not that strong. For example, an analysis of 88 research studies of grit involving over 66,000 people concluded that grit is only weakly related to success and very similar to the personality trait known as *conscientiousness* (Credé, Tynan, & Harms, 2017).

ACADEMIC MINDSET Students who have grit, tenacity, and perseverance, as well as students who are conscientious, also have what might be called an "academic mindset." As Figure 11.3 illustrates, students with an **academic mindset** have positive views of themselves as learners, and they understand that effort is required to develop ability and competence related to their schoolwork. The degree to which a student possesses an academic mindset, of course, depends on having positive relationships while at school—positive relationships with teachers, classmates, and other school staff.

In addition, students with an academic mindset employ learning strategies to help themselves learn. They know how to plan, set priorities, define tasks, monitor their progress, and deal with obstacles as they learn new, challenging material. As Camille A. Farrington, a former inner-city high school teacher in Chicago, and her colleagues point out, students are much more likely to persist at academic tasks despite setbacks and to demonstrate the kinds of academic behaviors that lead to success if they possess the following four beliefs about themselves as learners:

1. I belong in this academic community.
2. My ability and competence grow with my effort.
3. I can succeed at this.
4. This work has value for me. (Farrington, et al., 2012, p. 12)

A teacher who promotes students' academic mindset is Frank Salazar, a ninth-grade basic math teacher at an urban high school. Frank read an article about academic mindset in *Child Development* (Blackwell, Trzesniewski, & Dweck, 2007). The article explained the results of a study in which one group of seventh-grade students with declining math grades participated in eight weekly 25-minute sessions during which they learned that intelligence is changeable and that the brain is like a muscle that grows "stronger" with use. Another group of seventh-grade students, also with declining math grades, did not participate in the sessions. After the sessions, the math grades of students in the first group stabilized, while the grades of students in the second group continued to decline. By the end of the school year, the math grades of students in the first group were 0.30 grade points higher than the grades of students in the second group.

Eager to put the results of the research into practice, Frank explained to his students how, with effort, they could make their "math brains" stronger. He started to encourage his students more often; he even began to tell them that he was their math "coach." He excitedly told them how famous scientists and inventors like Charles Darwin, Alexander Graham Bell, and Thomas Edison struggled with math during their school days.

Within a few weeks, Frank saw definite improvement in the math scores for most of his students. The atmosphere in his classroom also changed—students became more interested in learning math, and they seemed to be happier while in class.

MINDFULNESS/MEDITIATION SKILLS As humans, each of us experiences a more or less continuous flow of thoughts and feelings. Our minds flit from one thought to another, occasionally making it difficult to concentrate on an important task at hand. This flow of thoughts and feelings can even make us anxious and stressed, thus reducing our ability to perform. One way to become more of *an observer of*, rather than *a reactor to*, our thoughts and feelings as they come and go is to learn mindfulness/meditation skills. According to the Association of Mindfulness in Education, the following practices can enhance students' attention and well-being:

- Becoming aware of the breath
- Feeling the various physical sensations of an emotion
- Noticing thoughts as they pass through the mind
- Paying attention to all the sounds in the room
- Noticing what happens in the body when there is stress
- Watching the thoughts that arise when there is boredom
- Feeling the stomach rise and fall with each breath
- Choosing to respond rather than react to stressful situations (Association of Mindfulness in Education, 2018)

Those who have mastered complex, demanding skills and can perform at an elite level—athletes, musicians, brain surgeons, and trapeze artists, for example—provide us with everyday examples of how becoming more aware of how our minds work and developing mindfulness/meditation skills can enhance performance. Prior to performing, these individuals focus their attention, laser-like, on the forthcoming event; "tune out" surrounding external distractions; and greatly reduce their mind's tendency to flit from thought to thought. William James, the great psychologist and founder of experimental psychology, commented on the benefit of such mental concentration and the role that education ought to play in developing this skill: "The faculty of voluntarily bringing back a wandering attention, over and over again, is the very root of judgment, character, and will . . . An education which should improve this faculty would be the education par excellence" (James, 1890).

Like elite performers, students can benefit from developing mindfulness/meditation skills. Whether dealing with the stress of a forthcoming exam; responding to a bully on the playground; coping with the trauma of violence in their neighbourhoods; preparing for a musical or sports event; improving communication with peers, teachers, and parents/guardians; or reducing anxiety about their future, mindfulness/meditation skills can enhance students' ability to respond to the challenges that life brings.

Dozens of schools in major cities like Los Angeles, San Francisco, New York, Chicago, Detroit, and Washington, D.C., have started to include mindfulness/meditation skills as part of the curriculum. School-based mindfulness programs are most often found in low-income areas, where students often experience high levels of stress. For example, students at Gage Park High School on Chicago's Southwest Side participate in Quiet Time (QT), a transcendental meditation program. QT is sponsored by the David Lynch Foundation, a nonprofit organization co-founded by the movie director.

More than 98 percent of Gage Park students are considered low income. The neighborhood around Gage Park is frequently punctuated with gunfire. Most students know someone who's been shot or did the shooting. According to a Gage Park teacher of English as a second language, "In their neighborhood, they are fighting to survive, literally" (O'Connell, 2017).

Researchers at the University of Chicago are studying the effects of QT at Gage Park by collecting grades, test scores, attendance and disciplinary records, out-of-school arrests, and crime victimization. Shortly after the program began, the principal reported a decrease in suspensions and improved SAT prep scores. Moreover, students such as the following explained how QT has helped them manage stress and deal with anger issues:

> "I was a real belligerent person and a hothead before, and it's really calming and releases stress. It relaxes me, and it opens my mind up." (Rakiha)
>
> "When I first heard about it, I said, 'What is this? What are we doing?' When you really get into it, I really got some stress off my mind. I really think before I do certain things." (Breana)
>
> "It helps you to slow your mind. It helps you to slow down and focus." (James) (O'Connell, 2017).

QT at Gage Park occurs twice a day for 20 minutes. After teachers take attendance in the morning, a tinkling bell marks the beginning of QT. Most students close their eyes and meditate, and others read silently. For 20 minutes, the entire school is silent.

There are several easy-to-learn, nonreligious approaches to mindfulness/meditation. Hundreds of research studies document the educational benefits of mindfulness/meditation. The following are among these benefits:

- Increased prosocial behaviors, emotion regulation, and academic performance (Harpin, Rossi, Kim, & Swanson, 2016).
- Lower depression and anxiety, resulting in improved academic attainment (Bennett & Dorjee, 2016).

- Decreased stress, leading to greater focus on school (Costello & Lawler, 2014).
- Less stress, anxiety, and negative coping, leading to improved ability to deal with academic stress and achieve success (Sibinga, Perry-Parrish, Chung, Johnson, Smith, & Ellen, 2013).
- Less aggression and conduct problems for children with attention deficit hyperactivity disorder (ADHD) (Singh, Soamya, & Ramnath, 2016).
- Greater well-being and increased use of mindfulness in school for homeless middle school students, leading to increased quality of life and academic achievement (Viafora, Mathiesen, & Unsworth, 2015).

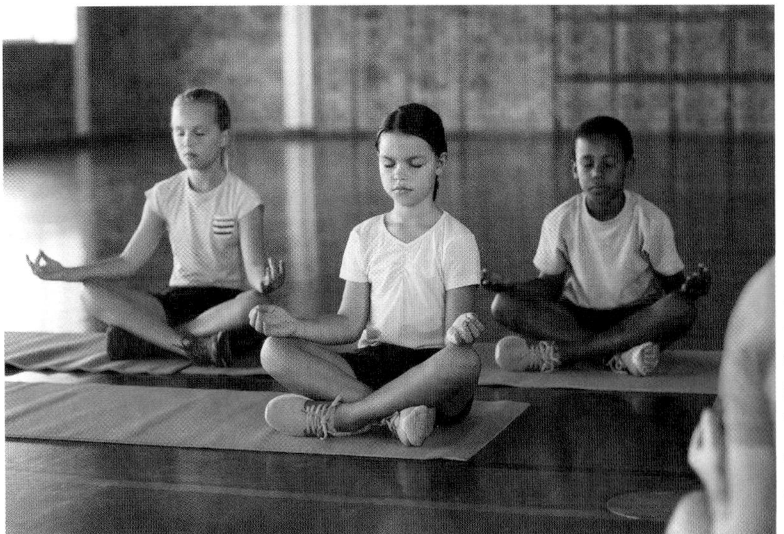

wavebreakmedia/Shutterstock

In what ways can mindfulness/meditation enhance a student's learning?

CURRICULA TO ENHANCE NONCOGNITIVE STRENGTHS To prepare students for successful lives in the future, the school curriculum should help them increase their grit, tenacity, and perseverance; academic mindset; and mindfulness/meditation skills. Although the preceding noncognitive strengths may be "teachable" to some extent, students' strengths in these areas are most likely to increase if their school experiences make them feel validated for who they are and encourage them to develop "strong, supported, and sustained relationships with adults and peers that are set within caring communities" (Nagoaka et al., 2015, p. 38). Curricula that enhance students' noncognitive strengths are characterized by the following:

- Goals are challenging and optimally meaningful to students.
- Goals require that students plan, set priorities, define tasks, monitor their progress, and overcome obstacles.
- Teachers convey the expectation that all students, with effort, can achieve these goals.
- The classroom culture emphasizes the importance of an "academic mindset," effortful control, and developing strategies and tactics to reach goals.
- Students are encouraged to develop grit, perseverance, and tenacity.
- Failure should be seen as part of learning,
- Students are given constructive feedback and encouraged to improve their work.

Check Your Understanding 11.1

How is the School Curriculum Developed and What Factors Influence It?

The title of Franklin Bobbitt's classic work *How to Make a Curriculum* (1924) might suggest that developing a curriculum is a straightforward process. According to Bobbitt, a curriculum should be developed "scientifically" by analyzing the daily activities of adult life and then creating behavioral objectives for those activities. However, curriculum development is more complicated than Bobbitt suggests. There is no single right way to develop a curriculum—there is no "cookbook" to follow.

Although there is no easy-to-follow set of procedures for developing curriculum, Ralph Tyler (1902–1994), a University of Chicago professor instrumental in shaping the Elementary and Secondary Education Act of 1965, has provided four fundamental questions that must be answered in developing any curriculum or plan of instruction. These four questions, known as the **Tyler rationale**, are as follows (Tyler, 1949, p. 1):

1. What educational purposes should the school seek to attain?
2. What educational experiences can be provided that are likely to attain these purposes?
3. How can these educational experiences be effectively organized?
4. How can we determine whether these purposes are being attained?

When first introduced, Tyler's model represented a "modern" view of curriculum design. Developing the curriculum, according to Tyler, required a mechanical, rational approach that could be followed systematically in any context, with any group of students. Today, however, some educators believe the Tyler rationale underestimates the complexities of curriculum development because it advocates a straightforward, step-by-step process that is difficult to follow in the real classroom, and it does not make allowances for diverse points of view regarding what should be taught. Nevertheless, Tyler's classic work has been used by a great number of school systems to bring some degree of order and focus to the curriculum development process.

The Focus of Curriculum Planning

In discussing curriculum development, it is helpful to clarify the focus of curriculum planning. The focus of curriculum planning may be at the macro- or the micro-level. At the macro-level, decisions about the content of the curriculum apply to large groups of students. Curriculum guidelines developed by state departments of education are examples of macro-level curricular decisions. At the micro-level, curriculum decisions are made that apply to groups of students in a particular school or classroom. To some extent, you will be a micro-level curriculum developer—that is, you will make numerous decisions about the curricular experiences students have in your classroom.

Another dimension of curriculum planning is the time orientation—does the planning focus on the present or the future? In addition to state-level curriculum guidelines, the semester-long or monthly plans or unit plans that teachers make are examples of future-oriented curriculum planning. Present-oriented curriculum planning usually occurs at the classroom level and is influenced by the unique needs of specific groups of students. The daily or weekly curriculum decisions and lesson plans that teachers make are examples of present-oriented curriculum planning.

Student-Centered Versus Subject-Centered Curricula

A key concern in curriculum development is whether greater emphasis should be given to the requirements of the subject area or to the needs of the students. It is helpful to imagine where a school curriculum might be placed on the following continuum:

Although no curriculum is entirely subject- or student-centered, curricula vary considerably in the degree to which they emphasize one or the other. The **subject-centered curriculum** places primary emphasis on the logical order of the discipline students are to study. The teacher of such a curriculum is a subject-matter expert and is primarily concerned with helping students understand the facts, laws, and principles of the discipline. Subject-centered curricula are more typical of high school education.

Some teachers develop curricula that reflect greater concern for students and their needs. Although teachers of the **student-centered curriculum** also teach content, they emphasize the growth and development of students. This emphasis is generally more typical of elementary school curricula. A major challenge of keeping students engaged in learning a curriculum is maintaining their interest, especially when the curriculum is primarily subject-centered. As a teacher, you should try to make subject-centered curricula relevant to students' lives and timely. You might accomplish this by using examples from current events, students' personal experiences, and real-world scenarios or case studies.

The Integrated Curriculum

To provide students with more meaningful learning experiences, you may decide to use an integrated approach to developing the school curriculum. Used most frequently with elementary-age students, the **integrated curriculum** draws from several different subject areas and focuses on a theme or concept rather than on a single subject. Early childhood education experts Suzanne Krogh and Pamela Morehouse (2014) suggest that an integrated approach based on thematic webs is a more natural way for children to learn:

> When children learn in a way that is most natural to themselves, they unconsciously integrate subject areas into a complex whole based on their current interests. Teachers who consciously adapt this method of learning to the classroom see the curriculum as a fully spun web that incorporates a number of components at one time. (p. 74)

Influences on Curriculum Development

Various agencies and people outside the school influence the curriculum development process. Textbook publishers, for example, influence what is taught because many teachers use textbooks as curriculum guides. The federal government contributes to curriculum development by emphasizing goals for our nation's schools, and state departments of education develop curriculum standards and specific minimum competencies for students to master.

Within a given school, the curriculum planning team and the classroom teacher plan the curriculum that students actually experience. As a teacher, you will draw from a reservoir of curriculum plans prepared by others, thus playing a vital role in the curriculum planning process. Whenever you make decisions about what material to include in your teaching, how to sequence content, and how much time to spend teaching certain material, you are planning the curriculum.

From the earliest colonial schools to schools of the 21st century, curricula have been broadly influenced by a variety of religious, political, and utilitarian agendas. Figure 11.4 illustrates the influence of community pressures, court decisions, students' life situations, testing results, national reports, teachers' professional organizations, research results, and other factors. The inner circle of the figure represents factors that have a more direct influence on curriculum development (such as students' needs and interests, and school policies). The outer circle represents factors that are more removed from the school setting or have less obvious effects on the curriculum. Individual schools respond to all these influences differently, which further affects their curricula. Let us examine some of these influences in greater detail.

SOCIAL ISSUES AND CHANGING VALUES Values that affect curriculum planning include prevailing educational theories and teachers' educational philosophies. In addition, curriculum planners respond to social issues and changing values in the wider society. As a result, current social concerns find their way into textbooks, teaching aids, and lesson plans. Often curriculum changes are made in the hope that changing what students learn will help solve social problems or achieve local, statewide, or national goals.

Figure 11.4 Influences on the school curriculum

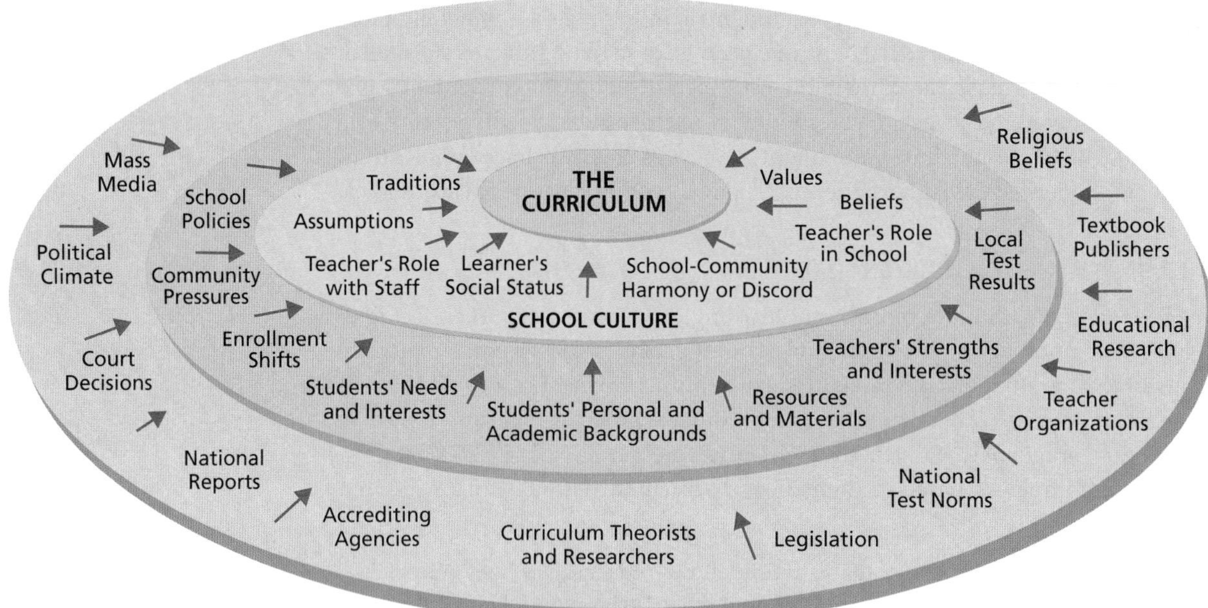

Because the United States is so culturally diverse, proposed curriculum changes also reflect divergent interests and values. This divergence then leads to controversies over curriculum content and conflicting calls for reform. For example, the courts have become involved in legal issues surrounding the demands of some groups that Christian teachings and observances be included in the public school curricula or that materials regarded as objectionable on religious grounds be censored or banned. Additionally, curriculum controversies have erupted in the 32 states that have passed English-only laws (U.S. English, 2018). Other curriculum controversies have arisen over calls for the elimination of all activities or symbols that have their origins in organized religion, including even secularized or commercialized ones such as Halloween and the Easter bunny. Curriculum changes to promote greater social integration or equity among racial or ethnic groups may draw complaints of irrelevancy or reverse discrimination. Traditionalists may object to curriculum changes that reflect feminist views.

As you can imagine, consensus on many curriculum reform issues is never achieved. Because of their public accountability, however, schools must consider how to respond to those issues. In the end, the creative and evaluative tasks of choosing and developing curriculum materials are a source of both empowerment and frustration for teachers. Budget constraints, social and legal issues, and state and local curriculum mandates often determine curriculum choices.

TEXTBOOK PUBLISHING Textbooks greatly influence the curriculum. Without a doubt, most teachers base classroom lessons and homework on textbooks. In addition, textbook publishers influence school curricula by providing teaching objectives, learning activities, tests, audiovisual aids, and other supplements to assist their customers.

Like curriculum planners, textbook authors and publishers are influenced by trends in education and by social issues. In response to criticism, for example, publishers now tend to avoid bias in terms of gender, religion, sexual orientation, class, race, and culture. However, because the goal of business is profit, publishers are most responsive to market trends and customer preferences. They are often reluctant to risk losing sales by including subjects that are controversial or that may be offensive to their bigger customers. They may also modify textbooks to appeal to decision makers in populous states that make statewide adoptions of textbooks, such as California and Texas. As an editor at a major publishing house reveals: "When it comes to setting the agenda for textbook publishing, only the 22 states that have a formal adoption process count. The other 28 are irrelevant—even though they include populous giants like New York, Pennsylvania, and Ohio—because they allow all publishers to come in and market programs directly to local school districts" (Ansary, 2010, p. 301). In addition, California and Texas are among several states that systematically review state-approved textbooks for accuracy. Texts with too many errors are dropped from state-approved lists, and publishers are levied fines for failing to correct errors. Because highly populated states influence publishers more than less populated states, it has been observed that as California and Texas go regarding the development of state-approved textbook adoption lists, so goes the rest of the nation.

Educators have criticized textbooks for inoffensiveness to the point of blandness, for artificially lowered reading levels (called "dumbing down"), and for pedagogically questionable gimmicks to hold students' attention. Although the publishing industry continually responds to such criticisms, you would be wise to follow your school district's guidelines in evaluating and selecting textbooks and other curriculum materials.

What are Curriculum Standards and what Role will they Play in Your Classroom?

As the media remind us almost daily, the public is concerned about low test scores, U.S. students' performance on international comparisons of achievement, and our nation's standing in a competitive global economy. Calls from parents, citizen groups, and politicians to hold teachers accountable for student learning have led to a push for school curricula based on higher standards. **Standards** in education (on occasion called *content standards, goals, expectations, learning results*, or *learning outcomes*) have come to be seen primarily as statements that reflect what students should know and be able to do within a particular discipline or at a particular grade level. To meet demands for higher standards, schools have undertaken numerous curriculum reforms over the years and used more sophisticated methods for measuring the educational outcomes of these reforms.

Curriculum standards are key elements in the move to hold educators more accountable for student learning. Parents and guardians want to know that schools are educating their children well, and the community wants to know that its investment in school buildings, teachers' salaries, and curricular resources is returning educational dividends. The Every Student Succeeds Act (ESSA), signed into law in 2015 and fully implemented in 2017–2018, calls for each state to develop its own curriculum standards. ESSA requires that states set high curriculum standards in reading or language arts, math and science, and any other subject(s) identified by the state. Clearly, curriculum standards will be a fact of life during your career as a teacher.

Standards can take different forms. The type of standards most important to the individual often depends on whether one is a school administrator, teacher, or student. Administrators, for example, are very concerned about standards related to *students' performance on standardized tests of achievement*. In such instances, the administrator (and their school board) might focus on a standard such as the following: "During the next five years, the percentage of students scoring above the norm will increase by at least 2 percent each year."

Teachers, of course, are also concerned about standards related to students' performance on standardized tests. In addition, teachers understand that another important standard is their expectations for *student performance and behavior at the classroom level*. Teachers demonstrate their commitment to high standards by giving students intellectually demanding reading and writing assignments; providing extensive, thoughtful feedback on students' work; and presenting intellectually stimulating lessons.

Students often have yet another perspective on standards; for them, the school curriculum should meet the *standard of being personally relevant, interesting, and meaningful*. The school curriculum should help them meet the developmental challenges of moving from childhood to adulthood. It should help them realize the goals they have set for themselves.

Application Exercise 11.1

Role of Curriculum Standards

Standards-Based Education and Its Influence on Teaching

Current efforts at educational reform in the United States emphasize **standards-based education (SBE)**—that is, basing curricula, teaching, and assessment of student learning on rigorous, world-class standards. SBE is based on the belief that all students are capable of meeting high standards. In the past, expectations for students from poor families and students who are members of minority groups were sometimes lower than for other students. Today, SBE is seen as a way of ensuring that excellence and equity become part of our nation's public school system. For example, in his 2018 State of the Union Address, President Donald Trump referenced high standards when he called for "great" schools that would enable "our future workers [to] learn a craft and realize their full potential" (White House, 2018).

To meet the demand for higher standards, each state has adopted state standards for what students should know and be able to do. For example, here are standards in geometry from three states:

Video Example 11.3

Let Your Standards do the Driving: A teacher shares how a standard drives her instruction.

> **COLORADO:** Students use geometric concepts, properties, and relationships in problem-solving situations and communicate the reasoning used in solving these problems. (Colorado Academic Standards)
>
> **NORTH DAKOTA:** Students understand and apply geometric concepts and spatial relationships to represent and solve problems in mathematical and nonmathematical situations. (North Dakota Common Core State Standards)
>
> **WYOMING:** Students apply geometric concepts, properties, and relationships in problem-solving situations. Students communicate the reasoning used in solving these problems. (Wyoming Content and Performance Standards)

As these examples show, state standards are broad statements of learning outcomes against which student achievement can be measured.

CONTENT AND PERFORMANCE STANDARDS Standards documents prepared by state education agencies, local school districts, and professional associations typically refer to two types of standards—content standards and performance standards. **Content standards**, as the term implies, refer to the content—or knowledge and skills—students should acquire in various academic disciplines. A common phrase in standards documents is that content standards represent "what students should know and be able to do."

Content standards are often subdivided into benchmarks (frequently called *indicators*). **Benchmarks** are content standards that are presented as specific statements of what students should understand and be able to do *at specific grade levels or developmental stages*. Here are three statements from the **IOWA** Core Content Benchmarks:

> **Reading, grades 3–5:** Students can draw conclusions, make inferences, and deduce meaning.
>
> **Mathematics, grades 6–9:** Students can understand and apply concepts and procedures of algebra.
>
> **Science, grades 9–12:** Students can understand and apply the processes and skills of scientific inquiry.

In addition, many standards documents refer to performance standards. A **performance standard** specifies "how good is good enough." Performance standards are used to assess the degree to which students have attained standards in an academic area. Performance standards require teacher judgment about the quality of performance or level of proficiency required. Unlike content standards, performance standards reflect levels of proficiency. For example, Iowa performance standards specify the following levels: High Performance Level (Distinguished, Accomplished), Intermediate Performance Level (Skilled, Moderate), and Low Performance Level (Marginal, Weak). Here are samples of Iowa performance standards for reading, mathematics, and science:

Grade 3 Literacy Standards

- **Distinguished:** Understands factual information and new words in context. Can make inferences and interpret either non-literal language or information in new contexts. Can determine a selection's main ideas and analyze its style and structure.
- **Moderate:** Usually understands factual information and new words in context. Often is able to make inferences and interpret either non-literal language or information in new contexts. Sometimes can determine a selection's main ideas and analyze its style and structure.
- **Weak:** Seldom understands factual information or new words in context. Rarely is able to make inferences and interpret either non-literal language or information in new contexts. Seldom can determine a selection's main ideas and analyze aspects of its style and structure.

Grade 8 Mathematics

- **Distinguished:** Understands math concepts and is able to solve word problems. Usually can use estimation methods. Is able to interpret data from graphs and tables.
- **Moderate:** Usually can understand math concepts and sometimes is able to solve word problems. Sometimes can use estimation methods and interpret data from graphs and tables.
- **Weak:** Seldom can understand math concepts or solve word problems. Rarely can use estimation methods or interpret data from graphs and tables.

Grade 11 Science

- **Distinguished:** Makes inferences or predictions from data, judges the relevance and adequacy of information, and recognizes the rationale for and limitations of scientific procedures.
- **Moderate:** Sometimes makes inferences or predictions from data, judges the relevance and adequacy of information, and usually recognizes the rationale for and limitations of scientific procedures.
- **Weak:** Seldom makes inferences or predictions from data, sometimes judges the relevance and adequacy of information, and rarely recognizes the rationale for and limitations of scientific procedures.

STANDARDS DEVELOPED BY PROFESSIONAL ASSOCIATIONS In addition to national, state, and local efforts to raise standards, professional associations are playing a key role in SBE by developing standards in the subject-matter disciplines. In many cases, professional associations have developed specific, grade-level **performance expectations**—established levels of achievement, quality of performance, or level of proficiency—for recommended standards as well as classroom activities related to standards.

Standards developed by professional associations are used in the following ways:

- State departments of education, school districts, and schools can use the standards as a guide for developing curricula and assessments of student learning.

- Teachers can use standards to (1) develop goals and objectives for units and courses, (2) evaluate their teaching, and (3) develop ideas for instructional activities and classroom assessments.
- Parents and community members can use standards to assess the quality of education in their local schools and to monitor the achievement levels of their children.

Figure 11.5 presents several professional associations that have recommended curriculum standards in various academic disciplines. You can obtain complete sets of standards from the websites these associations maintain.

Figure 11.5 Curriculum standards developed by professional associations

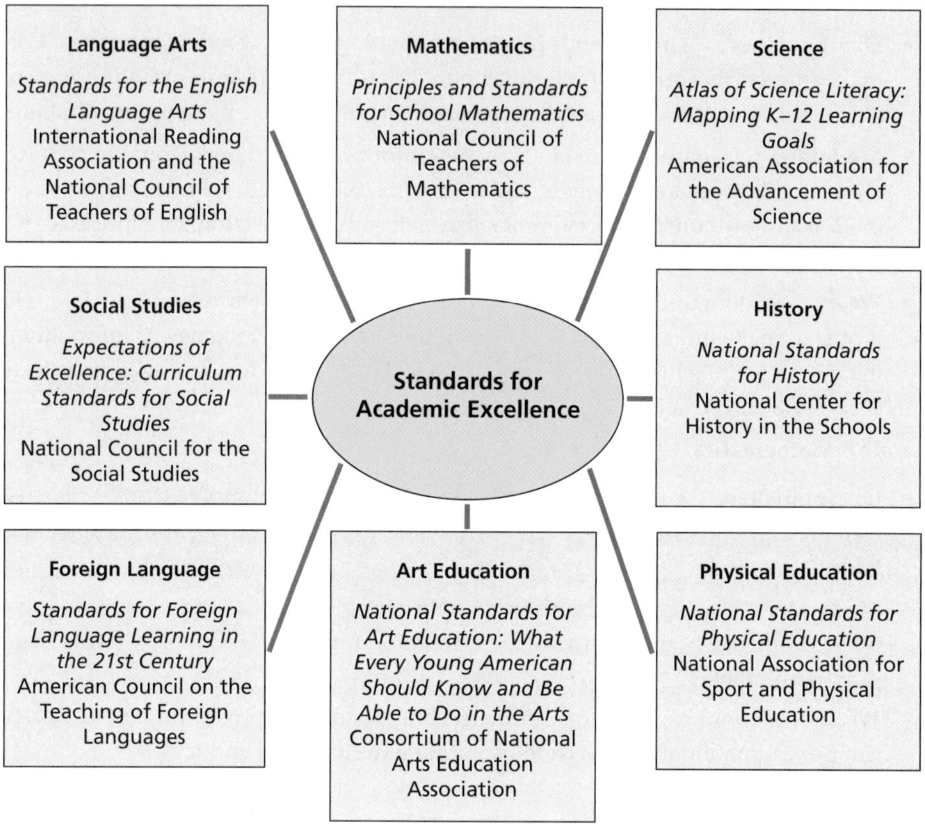

ALIGNING CURRICULUA AND TEXTBOOKS WITH STANDARDS AND CURRICULUM FRAMEWORKS An important part of SBE in the United States is aligning curricula and textbooks with national and state standards and curriculum frameworks. **Curriculum alignment** may take two forms. Horizontal alignment occurs when teachers within a specific grade level coordinate instruction across disciplines and examine their school's curriculum to ensure that course content and instruction dovetail across and/or within subject areas. Vertical alignment occurs when subjects are connected across grade levels so that students experience increasingly complex instructional programs as they move through the grades.

A **curriculum framework** is a document, usually published by a state education agency, that provides guidelines, recommended instructional and assessment strategies, suggested resources, and models for teachers to use as they develop curricula that are aligned with national and state standards. Curriculum frameworks are usually written by teams of teachers and state agency personnel, and they serve as a bridge between national and state standards and local curriculum and instructional strategies. Figure 11.6 presents a curriculum framework I have used when conducting staff development workshops for English Teachers in **ILLINOIS, TEXAS, FLORIDA,** and **WASHINGTON**. The figure illustrates a sequence of steps teachers can have their students follow when they are learning how to write a clear, well organized essay.

Figure 11.6 Steps for writing a clear, well-organized essay

Remember Aristole's advice to writers: ***tell your audience what you are going to say, say it, and then tell them what you have said.***

Like teachers, textbook authors and publishers are influenced significantly by the development of academic standards throughout the nation. Many publishers are revising their textbooks so they are in alignment with state standards and curriculum frameworks, particularly in populous states that make statewide adoptions of textbooks, such as **CALIFORNIA** and **TEXAS**. In states such as these, school districts can purchase only those textbooks that are on state textbook adoption lists.

What is the Common Core State Standards Initiative and How does It Influence Teaching?

The Common Core State Standards Initiative (CCSSI)

To bring uniformity to the "patchwork quilt" of 50 sets of state standards, the Council of Chief State School Officers (CCSSO) and the National Governors Association Center for Best Practices (NGA Center) organized the **Common Core State Standards Initiative (CCSSI)**. In March 2010, CCSSI released a draft set of K–12 standards in English/language arts and mathematics for public comment. According to the CCSSI, Common Core Standards:

- are aligned with college and work expectations;
- are clear, understandable, and consistent;

- include rigorous content and application of knowledge through higher-order skills;
- build upon strengths of and lessons learned from current state standards;
- are informed by other top-performing countries, so that all students are prepared to succeed in a global economy and society; and
- are evidence- and research-based.

With the exception of Texas and Alaska, 48 states, two territories, and the District of Columbia participated in developing the standards. The federal government had no role in developing the standards.

Early Reactions to the Common Core

Many observers responded positively to the release of the Common Core Standards. Some suggested that the standards were long overdue:

> After more than 20 years of messy thinking, mistakes, and misguided direction, policy makers have finally given teachers and students a solid set of standards in mathematics and literacy. The Common Core of Standards only begins the process of moving academic performance in these subjects to the levels we need, but it's such a relief to have them. (Philips & Wong,2010, p. 37)

However, a vigorous debate over the Standards soon emerged, and "manifestos" setting forth very different views were released within a year. First, the Albert Shanker Institute (2011), named for the late, long-time leader of the American Federation of Teachers, released *A Call for Common Content*, in which more than 100 leading educators and policymakers asserted that:

> We therefore applaud the goals of the recently released Common Core State Standards, already adopted in most states, which articulate a much clearer vision of what students should learn and be able to do as they progress through school. For our nation, this represents a major advance toward declaring that "equal educational opportunity" is a top priority—not empty rhetoric.

A "counter-manifesto" titled "Closing the Door on Innovation: Why One National Curriculum Is Bad for America" and signed by a "broad coalition of over 100 educational and other leaders" took the opposite position and made the following points:

1. There is no constitutional or statutory basis for national standards, national assessments, or national curricula.
2. There is no consistent evidence that a national curriculum leads to high academic achievement.
3. The national standards on which the administration is planning to base a national curriculum are inadequate.
4. There is no body of evidence for a "best" design for curriculum sequences in any subject.
5. There is no evidence to justify a single high school curriculum for all students. (Evers, Greene, Forster, Stotsky, & Wurman, 2011)

Upon release of the Common Core Standards, CCSSI made it clear that the standards are "voluntary"—they were *not* a federal initiative. And, three years after the standards were released, the U.S. Secretary of Education pointed out, emphatically, that the standards were *not* a federal initiative: "I believe the Common Core State Standards may prove to be the single greatest thing to happen to public education in America since *Brown versus Board of Education*—and the federal government had nothing to do with creating them. The federal government didn't write them, didn't approve them, and doesn't mandate them. And we never will. Anyone who says otherwise is either misinformed or willfully misleading" (U.S. Department of Education, 2013, June 25).

Continuing Controversy about the Common Core

The Common Core State Standards Initiative intensified an already widespread, often heated national debate about the role of standards in educational reform. The U.S. Secretary of Education pointed out that the standards had become "a topic for dueling newspaper editorials. Why? That's because a new set of standards—rigorous, high-quality learning standards, developed and led by a group of governors and state education chiefs—are under attack as a federal takeover of the schools" (U.S. Department of Education, 2013, June 25).

In 2017, President Donald Trump announced his intention to "repeal" the Common Core when he said, "I like the fact of getting rid of Common Core. Common Core . . . we have to end it" (White House Press Release, 2017). However, the Common Core cannot be repealed by the federal government, since it is not a federal initiative. It was developed and approved by the individual states, and only the states can decide to drop it.

As of 2018, seven states had officially rejected the Common Core: Oklahoma, Texas, Virginia, Alaska, Nebraska, Indiana, and South Carolina. Among the remaining 43 states, many reduced controversy by merely renaming the standards to reflect the state's identity (Illinois Common Core Standards and Hawaii Common Core Standards, for example) or slightly revising the standards. Six states opted to label their "new" standards the College- and Career-Readiness Standards. Still others created unique names for their "new" standards: Ohio introduced Ohio's New Learning Standards; Florida, the Next Generation Sunshine State Standards; and Wyoming, Content and Performance Standards.

Arguments in Support of Raising Standards

Those who advocate the use of educational standards and assessing students' mastery of those standards put forth several arguments:

- Standards define clearly what is to be taught and how students will demonstrate mastery of those standards.
- Standards promote educational growth and achievement for all students, and test results that show mastery of those standards can be reported easily to students, teachers, parents and guardians; colleges and universities; and employers.
- Standards provide a way to track the educational achievement of minority-group students and thus promote equal educational opportunity and narrowing the "achievement gap" between White and minority-group students.
- State-level standards provide a way of comparing educational programs among the 50 states and the District of Columbia.

In addition to the arguments just outlined, it is clear that the U.S.—as a society rich in ethnicities, religions, nationalities, and language groups—also needs common, rigorous standards for unity. With increasing immigration to the country, which brings diverse groups of people to its urban and suburban neighborhoods and rural areas, schools need to provide a common core of knowledge about the democratic heritage of our country and a common curriculum based on high academic standards.

As a mobile society, the U.S. needs common educational standards so that children from one area will not fall behind when they move to another. Children from a farming community in Minnesota should be able to move to the heart of Dallas without finding themselves behind or ahead of their peers in school. Children from a school in Seattle should be able to transfer to a school in Cincinnati and recognize the curricula studied there.

In addition, some people believe that the educational standards currently in use should be higher. Proponents of raising standards point out that educational goals and standards can motivate citizens to excel. Without them, people may become complacent and satisfied with mediocrity. Proponents cite studies like the Trends in International Mathematics and Science Studies that show U.S. students' achievement lagging behind that of students from other countries. They suggest raising U.S. standards to, hopefully, increase that achievement. Just as a runner will run faster when paced by another, the U.S. educational system can become more effective as a result of comparisons with educational systems in other countries.

Arguments Against Raising Standards

Opponents of raising standards point out that the failure of many schools to achieve adequate yearly progress as mandated by No Child Left Behind is evidence that a new approach to educational reform is needed. Instead, they contend, we should become more aware of the lack of uniformity in schools around the country and the needs of the children they serve. As Jonathon Kozol's books *Savage Inequalities* (1991) and *The Shame of the Nation* (2005) vividly illustrate, equal education in the United States is an illusion. To compare the performance of a student in a poor Chicago housing project with that of a student in the city's wealthy suburbs is to confront the "savage inequalities" found throughout our educational system.

Also, sanctions imposed on low-performing schools will not ensure that students in those schools are not left behind. The record of success when sanctions such as staff reassignment and school takeover have been imposed is mixed. Students in low-performing schools may not be helped by sanctions, and there is some risk that they will be harmed (Stecher & Hamilton, 2002). Thus, higher standards would further bias educational opportunities in favor of students from advantaged backgrounds, intensify the class-based structure of U.S. society, and increase differences between well-funded and poorly funded schools.

Opponents of raising standards in U.S. schools put forth numerous additional concerns. The following are among their arguments:

- Raising standards might lead to a national curriculum and an expanded role of the federal government in education.
- The push to raise standards is fueled by conservative interest groups that want to undo educational gains made by traditionally underrepresented groups.
- A focus on higher standards diverts attention from more meaningful educational reform.
- Increased emphasis on tested subjects often results in a decrease in emphasis on subjects not tested.
- "World-class" standards are often vague and not linked to valid assessments and scoring rubrics.
- Standards frequently describe learning activities, not the knowledge and skills students are expected to learn—for example, "Students will experience various forms of literature."
- Raising standards would increase educational opportunities in favor of students from advantaged backgrounds and increase the differences between "poor" and "rich" schools.

- The scope and sequence of what students should learn with reference to standards and benchmarks has been unclear; in other words, to what degree and in what order should students learn material?
- Grade-level benchmarks have been created that are unrealistic and developmentally inappropriate for some students; often students are hurried through their learning without sufficient time and instruction to acquire underlying concepts and skills.
- SBE and high-stakes tests based on those standards lead to the practice of teaching to the test, giving priority to academic content covered by the tests and deemphasizing areas of the curriculum not covered.

As a teacher, you and your colleagues will no doubt participate in an ongoing dialogue about academic standards at your school. Thus, the role that standards will play in your professional life will be significant. The following eight questions may help you decide the nature of SBE in your school:

1. Where will we get our standards?
2. Who will set the standards?
3. What types of standards should we include?
4. In what format will the standards be written?
5. At what levels will benchmarks be written?
6. How should benchmarks and standards be assessed?
7. How will student progress be reported?
8. How will we hold students accountable? (Marzano, 1997)

What is the Role of Assessment in Teaching?

Effective schools emphasize the assessment of student learning. To achieve academic excellence *for all students*, these schools conduct frequent, systematic assessments of student learning. When these assessments reveal problems in student learning, appropriate remediation is provided quickly.

Assessment has been defined as a process that "provides teachers with information to make decisions about teaching and provides students with information to make decisions about learning" (Brookhart & Nitko, 2015, p. 1). As a professional teacher, you will remain up to date regarding the latest approaches to assessing student learning. You will also understand that (1) assessment helps students learn more effectively, and (2) assessment helps teachers teach more effectively. You will use assessment to evaluate your effectiveness because you recognize that "the best assessments are those that inform instruction" (Wright, 2008, p. 243).

For most people, the term *classroom assessment* brings to mind a four-step process: (1) the teacher prepares a test (or selects a pre-existing test) to cover material that has been taught, (2) students take the test, (3) the teacher corrects the test, and (4) the teacher assigns grades based on how well students performed on the test. Classroom assessment, however, involves more—it provides information that teachers use to (1) determine how well students are learning the material being taught, (2) identify the type of feedback that will enhance student learning, (3) develop strategies for improving their effectiveness as teachers, and (4) determine if students have reached certain levels of performance.

TEACHERS' VOICES  BEING AN AGENT OF CHANGE

MARY RUSSELL

PROJECT-BASED LEARNING: BUILDING HOUSES

I just completed a unit on houses with my kindergarten class. . . . By engaging students with a project, in phases, I am able to help them understand the generalizations that frame the unit:

- Houses are built with different kinds of materials.
- Houses come in many shapes and sizes.
- Climate affects the type of house that is built.
- Building a house requires many job skills.
- Design and materials affect the quality of houses. . . . .

For the generalization "Design and materials affect the quality of houses" I had them make houses out of marshmallows and toothpicks. We had interesting designs but alas—only certain houses remained standing. We analyzed why, and tried the same theories with block houses.

The preceding activities completed phases one and two of the unit. Phase three was sharing and playing. We shared with parents and other classes. Playing in the house is the reward for all the hard work. [Regarding] insights I . . . have about helping students understand the importance of concepts . . . I think it is the connection to real life. You can find real-life applications of concepts within any theme. Connect students with the real-world applications and let them play the required roles. This is especially true for primary children. Any time a child takes on an adult role, it is important to him or her.

Making the project big in size helps also. I observed the sixth-graders looking at our house. They immediately got in and wanted to play. I began to think about the kind of house they would make and the details they could achieve. I almost wanted to move up a few grades! Teachers need to keep the learning as hands-on as possible. Children will naturally read, write, use mathematics skills, etc., if teachers demand they show their understanding of concepts and generalizations in different ways as they work on a big project.

PERSONAL REFLECTION

1. With reference to the grade level and subject area for which you are preparing to teach, what are some examples of how you might use project-based learning?
2. Project-based learning allows students to study material in greater depth; however, this leaves less time to cover a broader range of material. With respect to the amount of material that can be covered, what do you see as the advantages and disadvantages of project-based learning?

Mary Russell is a teacher at Ponderosa Elementary School, Spokane Valley, **WASHINGTON**. The preceding is excerpted from her contribution to H. Lynn Erickson, Stirring the Head, Heart, and Soul: Redefining Curriculum, Instruction, and Concept-Based Learning, 3rd ed. Thousand Oaks, CA: Corwin Press, 2008, pp. 200-201. Used with Permission. She was the 2012 National Teacher of the Year.

Challenges of Assessing Students' Learning

Assessing students' learning is not as straightforward as one might imagine. First, it is difficult to assess with 100 percent accuracy everything that students actually learn as a result of being taught. The ultimate purpose of teaching is to lead the student to a greater understanding of the things and ideas of this world. However, a moment's reflection on our own experiences reminds us that it is difficult, perhaps impossible, to determine precisely what another person does or does not understand. Moreover, "the effects of a teacher's work are still maturing a half-century or more after students' formal education is completed" (Joyce, Weil, & Calhoun, 2015, p. xix).

Second, although the outcomes of teaching may be specified with exacting detail, one of the realities of teaching is that some of what students learn may be beyond direct measurement.

A third challenge of assessing students' learning was suggested by Albert Einstein, a former member of the American Federation of Teachers, when he pointed out that: "Not everything that counts can be counted, and not everything we count, counts" (quoted in Weingarten, 2014, p. 1). Similarly, the recipient of the 2011 National Teacher of the Year Award, high school chemistry teacher Michelle Shearer, reminds us that many important learning outcomes cannot be reduced to numerical scores. As she said in her application for the Teacher of the Year Award:

What should be the basis of teacher accountability? Consider the following examples from my teaching, formatted as the multiple-choice question, "*Which of the following is the best evidence of effective teaching?*"

A. Over the past three years, Mrs. Shearer's AP chemistry students have achieved passage rates of 91%, 91%, and 88% (with 100% student participation).
B. Mrs. Shearer's former student, a 2000 graduate, recently earned his Ph.D. from Yale University in biophysical chemistry and is currently exploring options for teaching science at the high school and college levels.
C. Mrs. Shearer's 2005 class of deaf and hard-of-hearing students, identified as "below grade," frequently arrived at class before the bell and asked to begin early because they were so eager to see what awaited them in the lab.
D. Five of Mrs. Shearer's seniors asked to return *after* graduation to participate in the post-AP exam lab activities.
E. A minority student hesitant to take AP Chemistry considered her final "B" average one of her greatest personal achievements, one that gave her the confidence to attend college to pursue a scientific major.
F. All of the above.

(*Correct answer*: F!)

Numerical data [are] concrete, objective, and easily communicated, yet teacher accountability for student success cannot be tied solely to test scores. I am accountable not only for my students' AP scores, but also for fostering habits of mind such as creativity, innovation, problem-solving, and skills essential to success in college and careers. I am accountable for ensuring students' self-confidence, independence, resilience, perseverance, and traits essential to success in *life*. . . . Teaching is too complex and awesome a task for any simple measure of accountability . . . (Shearer, 2011)

Standardized Assessments

Standardized assessments (or standardized tests) are pencil-and-paper tests that are taken by large groups of students and scored in a uniform manner. The test items, conditions under which students take the test, how the tests are scored, and how the scores are interpreted are standardized for all who take the test. This standardization enables educators to compare scores for different groups of students in different schools around the country. Standardized assessments are administered at the district, state, and national levels.

The first standardized test in the United States was administered by Horace Mann (1796–1859) in the mid-1800s. Mann, who eventually came to be known as the "father of the common school," wanted to classify students by ability and gather evidence for the effectiveness of the state school system. He hoped to use the results of the state test to further his educational reform efforts. Prior to the use of this standardized test, teachers conducted their own assessments at the individual classroom level.

Current examples of standardized tests are the Iowa Test of Basic Skills, California Achievement Test, Metropolitan Achievement Tests, the Stanford Achievement Test, the Scholastic Assessment Test (SAT), and the ACT Assessment (ACT). Two consortia have developed standardized tests to align with the Common Core Standards: the Partnership for Assessment of Readiness for College and Careers (PARCC)

Art of Success/Fotolia

How can teachers best prepare students to take important standardized assessment tests?

and the Smarter Balanced Assessment Consortium (SBAC). In 2018, six states used PARCC, and nine used the Smarter Balanced Assessment (ArborBridge, 2018).

In addition, the federal government funds the National Assessment of Educational Progress (NAEP). Periodically, the NAEP is used to sample student achievement around the country. On a biannual basis, the performance of national samples of 9-, 13-, and 17-year-olds is assessed. Educational policymakers then use the results—reported by geographic region, gender, and ethnic background—to guide their decision making. First administered in 1969, the NAEP has assessed student learning in all areas of the curriculum.

INTERNATIONAL ASSESSMENTS The United States participates in several international assessments—for example, the **Trends in International Mathematics and Science Study (TIMSS)** and the **Progress in International Reading Literacy Study (PIRLS)**, both conducted by the International Association for the Evaluation of Educational Achievement (IEA).

In 2015, U.S. students participated in the **Program for International Student Assessment (PISA)**, an assessment of 15-year-olds' performance in reading, mathematics, and science. PISA measures how well students can take concepts taught in the classroom and use them to solve real-world problems. PISA is conducted every three years by the 35 member countries of the Organization for Economic Cooperation and Development (OECD). PISA 2015 results included assessments from 72 countries and economies.

PISA 2015 results (see Figure 11.7) show the mean scores of students in mathematics, reading, and science. The figure shows that U.S. students' scores were below the OECD mean in mathematics (470 compared to 490). However, U.S. students' scores were higher in science (496 compared to 493) and reading (497 compared to 493). The figure also shows that, in mathematics, the U.S. share (percentage) of "low achievers" was significantly higher than the OECD average, whereas the share of "high achievers" was significantly lower than the OECD average.

Since the publication of *A Nation at Risk* in 1983, there has been an unbroken trend for the media and some observers of U.S. education to decry the perceived poor performance of U.S. students on international comparisons of achievement. A closer examination of international comparisons, however, reveals the seldom-reported fact that the United States' position in country-by-country rankings is based on *aggregate* achievement scores—in other words, achievement scores of *all students* are used to make the comparisons. Not taken into account is the United States' commitment to educating all students—not just the academically able or those from home environments that encourage education. For example, *50 Myths and Lies That Threaten America's Public Schools: The Real Crisis in Education* points out that:

> the modest U.S. national average [on international tests] is reasonably attributed to a child poverty rate . . . that exceeds 20%—considerably higher than comparable countries. . . . In the United States, if we looked only at the students who attend schools where child poverty rates are under 10%, we would rank as the number one country in the world, outscoring countries like Finland, Japan, and Korea. (Berliner & Glass, 2014, p. 15)

50 Myths and Lies includes the following additional points, suggesting that international comparisons of achievement should be made very cautiously, if at all:

- Comparing achievement across countries is very different from comparing Olympic rankings.
- Trends in International Mathematics and Science Study (TIMMS) tests use the metric system, not the imperial system used in the United States.
- Translation issues make it unlikely that achievement tests written in different languages have the same level of cognitive difficulty.

Figure 11.7 2015 Program for international student assessment (PISA): Snapshot of performance in mathematics, reading, and science

Countries/economies with a mean performance/share of top performers **above** the OECD average Countries/economies with a share of low achievers **below** the OECD average
Countries/economies with a mean performance/share of top performers/share of low achievers not significantly different from the OECD average
Countries/economies with a mean performance/share of top performers **below** the OECD average Countries/economies with a share of low achievers **above** the OECD average

	Science		Reading		Mathematics		Science, reading and mathematics	
	Mean score in PISA 2015	Average three-year trend	Mean score in PISA 2015	Average three-year trend	Mean score in PISA 2015	Average three-year trend	Share of top performers in at least one subject (Level 5 or 6)	Share of low achievers in all three subjects (below Level 2)
	Mean	Score dif.	Mean	Score dif.	Mean	Score dif.	%	%
OECD average	493	−1	493	−1	490	−1	15.3	13.0
Singapore	556	**7**	535	**5**	564	1	39.1	4.8
Japan	538	3	516	−2	532	1	25.8	5.6
Estonia	534	2	519	**9**	520	2	20.4	4.7
Chinese Taipei	532	0	497	1	542	0	29.9	8.3
Finland	531	**−11**	526	**−5**	511	**−10**	21.4	6.3
Macao (China)	529	**6**	509	**11**	544	**5**	23.9	3.5
Canada	528	−2	527	1	516	**−4**	22.7	5.9
Viet Nam	525	−4	487	**−21**	495	**−17**	12.0	4.5
Hong Kong (China)	523	−5	527	−3	548	1	29.3	4.5
B-S-J-G (China)	518	m	494	m	531	m	27.7	10.9
Korea	516	−2	517	**−11**	524	−3	25.6	7.7
New Zealand	513	**−7**	509	**−6**	495	**−8**	20.5	10.6
Slovenia	513	−2	505	**11**	510	2	18.1	8.2
Australia	510	**−6**	503	**−6**	494	**−8**	18.4	11.1
United Kingdom	509	−1	498	2	492	−1	16.9	10.1
Germany	509	−2	509	**6**	506	2	19.2	9.8
Netherlands	509	**−5**	503	−3	512	**−6**	20.0	10.9
Switzerland	506	−2	492	−4	521	−1	22.2	10.1
Ireland	503	0	521	**13**	504	0	15.5	6.8
Belgium	502	−3	499	−4	507	**−5**	19.7	12.7
Denmark	502	2	500	3	511	−2	14.9	7.5
Poland	501	3	506	3	504	**5**	15.8	8.3
Portugal	501	**8**	498	4	492	**7**	15.6	10.7
Norway	498	3	513	**5**	502	1	17.6	8.9
United States	496	2	497	−1	470	−2	13.3	13.6
Austria	495	**−5**	485	−5	497	−2	16.2	13.5
France	495	0	499	2	493	**−4**	18.4	14.8
Sweden	493	**−4**	500	1	494	**−5**	16.7	11.4
Czech Republic	493	**−5**	487	5	492	**−6**	14.0	13.7
Spain	493	2	496	**7**	486	1	10.9	10.3
Latvia	490	1	488	2	482	0	8.3	10.5
Russia	487	3	495	**17**	494	**6**	13.0	7.7
Luxembourg	483	0	481	**5**	486	−2	14.1	17.0
Italy	481	2	485	0	490	**7**	13.5	12.2

Figure 11.7 (Continued)

	Science		Reading		Mathematics		Science, reading and mathematics	
	Mean score in PISA 2015	Average three-year trend	Mean score in PISA 2015	Average three-year trend	Mean score in PISA 2015	Average three-year trend	Share of top performers in at least one subject (Level 5 or 6)	Share of low achievers in all three subjects (below Level 2)
	Mean	Score dif.	Mean	Score dif.	Mean	Score dif.	%	%
Hungary	477	**-9**	470	**-12**	477	**-4**	10.3	18.5
Lithuania	475	-3	472	2	478	-2	9.5	15.3
Croatia	475	**-5**	487	**5**	464	0	9.3	14.5
CABA (Argentina)	475	**51**	475	**46**	456	**38**	7.5	14.5
Iceland	473	**-7**	482	**-9**	488	**-7**	13.2	13.2
Israel	467	**5**	479	2	470	**10**	13.9	20.2
Malta	465	2	447	3	479	**9**	15.3	21.9
Slovak Republic	461	**-10**	453	**-12**	475	**-6**	9.7	20.1
Greece	455	**-6**	467	**-8**	454	1	6.8	20.7
Chile	447	2	459	5	423	4	3.3	23.3
Bulgaria	446	4	432	1	441	**9**	6.9	29.6
United Arab Emirates	437	**-12**	434	-8	427	-7	5.8	31.3
Uruguay	435	1	437	**5**	418	-3	3.6	30.8
Romania	435	6	434	4	444	**10**	4.3	24.3
Cyprus1	433	-5	443	-6	437	-3	5.6	26.1
Moldova	428	**9**	416	**17**	420	**13**	2.8	30.1
Albania	427	**18**	405	**10**	413	**18**	2.0	31.1
Turkey	425	2	428	**-18**	420	2	1.6	31.2
Trinidad and Tobago	425	**7**	427	**5**	417	2	4.2	32.9
Thailand	421	2	409	**-6**	415	1	1.7	35.8
Costa Rica	420	-7	427	**-9**	400	-6	0.9	33.0
Qatar	418	**21**	402	**15**	402	**26**	3.4	42.0
Colombia	416	**8**	425	6	390	**5**	1.2	38.2
Mexico	416	2	423	-1	408	**5**	0.6	33.8
Montenegro	411	1	427	**10**	418	**6**	2.5	33.0
Georgia	411	**23**	401	**16**	404	**15**	2.6	36.3
Jordan	409	**-5**	408	2	380	-1	0.6	35.7
Indonesia	403	3	397	-2	386	**4**	0.8	42.3
Brazil	401	3	407	-2	377	**6**	2.2	44.1
Peru	397	**14**	398	**14**	387	**10**	0.6	46.7
Lebanon	386	m	347	m	396	m	2.5	50.7
Tunisia	386	0	361	**-21**	367	**4**	0.6	57.3
FYROM	384	m	352	m	371	m	1.0	52.2
Kosovo	378	m	347	m	362	m	0.0	60.4
Algeria	376	m	350	m	360	m	0.1	61.1
Dominican Republic	332	m	358	m	328	m	0.1	70.7

1. Note by Turkey: The information in this document with reference to "Cyprus" relates to the southern part of the Island. There is no single authority representing both Turkish and Greek Cypriot people on the Island. Turkey recognises the Turkish Republic of Northern Cyprus (TRNC). Until a lasting and equitable solution is found within the context of the United Nations, Turkey shall preserve its position concerning the "Cyprus issue".
Note by all the European Union Member States of the OECD and the European Union: The Republic of Cyprus is recognised by all members of the United Nations with the exception of Turkey. The information in this document relates to the area under the effective control of the Government of the Republic of Cyprus.

NOTES: Values that are statistically significant are marked in bold. The average trend is reported for the longest available period since PISA 2006 for science, PISA 2009 for reading, and PISA 2003 for mathematics. *Countries and economies are ranked in descending order of the mean science score.*

SOURCE: Adapted from OECD (Organization for Economic Cooperation and Development). (2016), *PISA 2015 Results in Focus*, Paris: OECD, p. 5. Used with permission.

- Contrary to popular belief, the United States has never led the world on international achievement tests; the relative ranking of U.S. students has changed little since international assessments began.
- International test scores do not reflect the quality of a nation's educational system, nor do they predict future national prosperity.
- During the 1970s, the United States was one of four nations that decided their students would not be allowed to use calculators on the TIMMS tests.

Lastly, using a test score to declare that American students have fallen behind their peers ignores other measures that reflect the quality of U.S. education. For example, of the top 10 universities in the world, eight are in the U.S.; of the top 100, more than half are in the U.S. (Times Higher Education World University Rankings, 2018; QS World University Rankings, 2018). Moreover, when compared to other countries on various critical dimensions, the U.S. achieved the following rankings:

- 2018 Global Entrepreneurship Index—ranked first of 137 countries
- 2017–2018 Global Competitiveness Index—ranked second among 137 countries
- 2017 Global Innovation Index—ranked fourth of 128 countries
- 2015 Global Creativity Index—ranked second of 139 countries

NORM-REFERENCED ASSESSMENTS Some standardized assessments are norm-referenced—that is, students' scores are compared with scores of other students who are similar. The comparison group of students, called the *norm group*, is usually from the same age group and grade level. An individual student's score is then compared to the average, or mean, score for the total group. Norm-referenced tests are used to determine where a student is compared to the typical performance of other students at the same age and grade level. Thus, **norm-referenced assessments** enable teachers to rank students in terms of their achievement.

To understand the meaning of scores on a norm-referenced assessment, imagine that a student received a total of 75 points on a 100-point norm-referenced assessment. If the mean, or average, score for the comparison group of students were also 75, the student would be at the 50th percentile. That is, 50 percent of the students in the comparison group scored higher, and 50 percent scored lower. However, if the mean score for the comparison group were 90, the student would be in the 30th percentile. That is, 70 percent of the students in the comparison group scored higher, and 30 percent scored lower.

The preceding example can also be used to illustrate how scores on norm-referenced tests should be interpreted carefully. Norm-referenced test scores can be misused. If the student scored in the 30th percentile, it would be a mistake to assume that the score is evidence that the student is doing poorly. The student might not have done well on the material covered by the norm-referenced assessment; however, the student might be doing quite well in other areas not included in the test. Four examples of norm-referenced interpretations of students' performance follow:

1. Alfredo won the 1-mile race.
2. On the test of basic skills, Jiling's scores were near the average.
3. On the chemistry test given district-wide, our school had the best scores.
4. On the test of physical fitness, Susan was in the 90th percentile.

CRITERION-REFERENCED ASSESSMENTS Other standardized assessments are criterion-referenced—that is, students' learning is compared with clearly defined criteria or standards rather than the performance of other students. **Criterion-referenced assessments** do not indicate what is average or typical for students from the same age group and grade level. Criterion-referenced assessments indicate what students know and can do within a specific subject area. Students' scores are not compared with the scores of other groups of students.

A teacher might use a criterion-referenced assessment to assess a student's ability to calculate the square root of a number, to write a well-organized paragraph, or to type 60 words per minute on a computer keyboard. In other words, the assessment is made with reference to an instructional objective, rather than the performance of other students on the assessment. Similarly, the student's score is interpreted without reference to how other students performed. Following are four examples of criterion-referenced interpretations of students' performance:

1. In the chemistry lab, Mary can light a Bunsen burner correctly.
2. Juan can identify each element on a periodic table.
3. Yiming can calculate the sine, cosine, and tangent of angles.
4. Using a map of the world, Lashandra can identify the countries that were involved in World War II.

Accountability

Today's schools and teachers are held accountable for students' mastery of state-mandated educational standards. As part of this push for **accountability**, some states—Florida and South Carolina, for example—rank schools on how well their students learn. In **FLORIDA**, schools are graded from A through F. A school's grade determines if the school receives supplemental funding, if a change in principals is necessary, if students can transfer out, or if the school can be closed. A school's grade is based on 11 components: four achievement components, four learning gains components, a middle school acceleration component, and components for graduation rate and college and career acceleration. Each component is worth up to 100 points (Florida Department of Education, 2018).

Some educators have criticized the Florida Standards Assessment (FSA) test—it is not an accurate measure of school performance, and it emphasizes test preparation rather than critical thinking.

SOUTH CAROLINA'S School Report Cards rate schools as either *Excellent, Good, Average, Below Average*, or *At-Risk*. An "Average" rating means a district or school meets the standard that "all students graduate with the knowledge and skills necessary to compete successfully in the global economy, participate in a democratic society, and contribute positively as members of families and communities." Report Cards also contain Growth Ratings that compare student test scores from one year to the next.

Every state has mandated a standardized test to assess students' mastery of academic standards, and most districts are assisting schools in bringing standards-based reform into classrooms. As a result of standards-based reforms at the state level, *how* and *what* teachers teach is changing, and in many cases student achievement is increasing.

High-Stakes Testing

Testing students to assess their learning is not new. However, state-mandated tests often have high-stakes consequences for students, teachers, and administrators. For example, performance on **high-stakes tests** may determine whether a student can participate in extracurricular activities or graduate, or whether teachers and administrators are given merit pay increases.

Each year, exit exams deny diplomas to thousands of U.S. high school students. In 2018, 13 states required students to pass comprehensive exit exams or end-of-course exams to receive a high school diploma: **FLORIDA, INDIANA, LOUISIANA, MARYLAND, MASSACHUSETTS, MISSISSIPPI, NEW JERSEY, NEW MEXICO, NEW YORK, OHIO, TEXAS, VIRGINIA,** and **WASHINGTON**. In addition, 8 states require a passing score on a civics exam modeled on the 100-question immigration citizenship test: **ARIZONA, ARKANSAS, IDAHO, KENTUCKY, MISSOURI, NEVADA, NORTH DAKOTA,** and **UTAH**.

Students with disabilities, English language learners, African American, Latino, American Indian, and low-income students are more likely to be denied a diploma for not passing an exit exam (Hyslop, 2014; Papay, Murnane & Willet, 2010). For example, among the Massachusetts high school class of 2015, 92 percent of White students passed all three graduation exams (English, math, and science); however, just 76 percent of Black students, 71 percent of Latino students, 61 percent of students with disabilities, and 41 percent of English language learners passed (FairTest, 2017).

In addition, exit exams have been linked to increased incarceration rates (Baker & Lang, 2013; Hyslop, 2014). High-stakes tests increase the risk that students will become part of the "school-to-prison pipeline." High-stakes exit exams are associated with a 12 percent increase in incarceration rates (Baker & Lang, 2013).

Armadillo Stock/Shutterstock

Several states require students to pass an exit or end-of-course exam before they graduate. Do you agree with this requirement? What might be some consequences of this requirement?

HIGH-STAKES TESTS AND EDUCATOR ACCOUNTABILITY For teachers and administrators, test results are frequently linked to merit rewards, increased funding, or sanctions. Some states and large school districts provide additional funds for high-performing schools or bonuses for educators at those schools. For example, **CALIFORNIA** has several merit-based incentive programs for teachers, schools, and administrators, including the Governor's Performance Awards that give money to schools based on their academic performance index. Similarly, the **NEW YORK** City school system gives bonuses of up to $15,000 to principals and other administrators whose schools show significant gains on test scores. School system administrators group schools into three performance categories—low, middle, and high—taking into account students' economic circumstances. For high schools, factors such as dropout rates are also used.

On the other hand, schools and even entire districts that do poorly on tests can be taken over by the state or, in some cases, closed. 26 states allow full state control of low-performing schools or districts (State Policy Report Card, 2014). Several of those states allow students to leave low-performing schools, taking their proportional amount of state funding aid with them. A few of these states directly punish low-performing schools by taking aid away from them. Whereas some states use test scores as one of several accountability indicators, many rely solely on scores.

Testing can also have significant consequences when schools are ranked according to how well they attain a state or district's performance goals. Usually, school rankings are reported in relation to schools of similar size and demographics because test results are closely linked to students' economic backgrounds, with the lowest scores often earned by schools that serve the neediest children (Fetler, 2001; Lindjord, 2000).

High-stakes testing and the push to hold teachers accountable for student learning has led many districts and schools to place great emphasis on preparing students for the tests. In fact, critics assert that the curricular emphasis in schools is shifting from academic content to test preparation. Many teachers feel compelled to teach to the test, or to emphasize item teaching rather than curriculum teaching.

FOCUS ON **DIVERSITY:** UNINTENDED CONSEQUENCES OF HIGH-STAKES TESTS

An unintended consequence of high-stakes tests is that they emphasize differences in achievement (often termed the "achievement gap") between White students and students who are Black, Latina/Latino, Native American, English language learners (ELLs), or from low-income families. High-stakes tests can also unfairly highlight achievement differences between students who attend "resource-rich" schools and those who attend "resource-poor" schools. Moreover, "[t]ests reinforce the social status quo, and to focus on them exclusively runs the risk of freezing the existing social order, injustices, inequities, exclusivities, and the prevailing power distribution of the here and now into the future" (English, 2010, p. 107).

Some researchers are critical of high-stakes tests and how they lead to a narrow emphasis on test score differences among students from different groups. Instead, they urge educators to move beyond "gap gazing" to emphasize effective teaching strategies for students of color and students from low-income families (Gutierrez, 2008; Matthews, 2008; Rodriguez, 2001). In an article titled "A 'Gap-Gazing' Fetish in Mathematics Education? Problematizing Research on the Achievement Gap," Gutierrez (2008, p. 362) calls for the following changes:

- Less research that documents the achievement gap
- Less research that identifies causes of the achievement gap
- Less research that focuses on single variables to predict student success
- More research on effective teaching and learning environments for Black, Latina/Latino, First Nations, English language learning, and working-class students, plus richer descriptions of those environments, including their origins and development
- More focus on making that research accessible to and usable by practitioners

Clearly, the debate over the effectiveness and consequences of high-stakes tests based on state-mandated standards will continue for some time. However, professional teachers understand that participating in these programs is only part of their assessment responsibility—they must develop high-quality classroom assessments for day-to-day use in the classroom. The ability to develop and implement high-quality assessments of students' learning is a fundamental part of professional accountability for today's teachers. Teachers must know whether their methods of assessing students' learning are, in fact, enhancing students' ability to learn.

How Will You Assess Student Learning and Develop High-Quality Assessments?

Figure 11.8 illustrates the essential elements of effective classroom assessment and the questions that will guide your decision making in this important area of teaching. Assessment-related decisions require an understanding of the following: formal and informal assessments, qualitative and quantitative assessments, measurement and evaluation, and formative and summative evaluation.

Figure 11.8 Effective classroom assessment

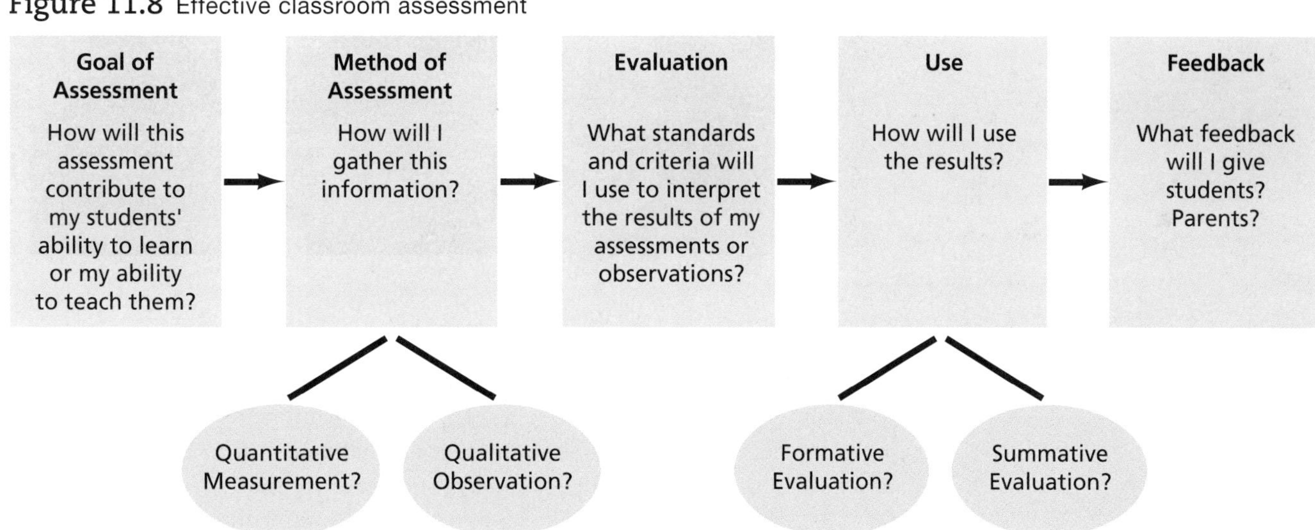

Formal and Informal Assessments

Assessment of student learning can be both formal and informal. **Formal assessments** are developed prior to having students complete the assessments. Formal assessments include final exams, tests, and quizzes on subject matter studied; in-class seatwork and homework; and critiques of performances, for example, tryouts for a school play or athletic team.

Informal assessments occur during teaching, and they are made spontaneously. You might, for example, note students' facial expressions to determine their level of understanding of the material taught, listen carefully to a student's explanation of how she solved a problem in mathematics, or ask questions to monitor students' levels of understanding during a lecture. Teachers frequently make informal assessments of their students at the beginning of each school day or class session.

Informal assessments are less obvious to the classroom observer. In other words, during a classroom observation, an observer may not know just when a teacher is making informal assessments of student learning. Actually, professional teachers continuously assess students' responses to their teaching.

Quantitative and Qualitative Assessment

To assess student learning, you can use both quantitative and qualitative approaches. Quantitative approaches make use of measurement and evaluation techniques—such as teacher-made classroom tests comprised of multiple-choice, true/false, matching, or essay items—or performance-based assessments. **Quantitative assessments** yield numerical scores that teachers use to evaluate student learning as well as the effectiveness of their teaching.

What type of assessment might this teacher be using?

Hongqi Zhang/123RF

Qualitative approaches may include formal and informal observations of students' performance on various learning tasks, the manner with which they approach those learning tasks, or students' self-reports of their interests and attitudes. For example, teachers routinely assess students' **work habits**. *Work habits*, similar to *academic mindset* discussed previously, is a term suggested by the Coalition of Essential Schools (2017) for various dispositions important for effective thinking and learning, including reading with curiosity; reflecting critically on one's own work; developing independence, clarity, and incisiveness of thought; willingness to work hard; an ability to manage time effectively; persistence; accuracy and precision; and working collaboratively. **Qualitative assessments** are more subjective than quantitative assessments. However, quantitative assessments are also subjective because teachers must interpret the meaning of the scores.

Measurement and Evaluation

To assess student learning, you will use measurement and evaluation techniques. **Measurement** is the gathering of quantitative data related to the knowledge and skills students have acquired. Measurement yields scores, rankings, or ratings that teachers can use to determine the degree to which students have attained specified standards. For example, a high school teacher might use an informal reading inventory test to identify students' strengths and weaknesses in reading expository and persuasive essays.

Evaluation is a critical teaching skill. In your role as an evaluator, you will make judgments about the performance of students and about your own effectiveness as a teacher. **Evaluation** involves making judgments about or assigning a value to measurements the teacher makes of student learning.

Formative and Summative Evaluation

When teachers measure students' attainment of knowledge and skills for the purpose of making decisions about their teaching, they are engaging in **formative evaluation**. Teachers use the results of formative evaluations to make decisions about what learning activities are appropriate for students. For example, as an aid to planning for a new unit of instruction, you may assess students' understanding of a subject by having them take a short diagnostic test or quiz, complete homework or seatwork assignments, or participate in a group project.

As a teacher, you will also conduct informal formative evaluations while you are teaching. For example, you will pay close attention to what students say, you will use probing questions to gauge students' understanding of the subject, and you will note students' facial expressions and behavior. During these informal formative evaluations, you will not only assess students' understanding; you will also assess students' attitudes toward learning the subject. For example, in the following, Amy James, a high school science teacher in **KENTUCKY**, makes some candid comments about how she learned to use informal formative evaluations while teaching:

> When I began teaching, I would teach a concept over one to two weeks assuming that my students were "getting it" along the way and then would quiz students over that concept. The quiz did very little to inform my instruction, but instead rewarded those students who "got it" and punished those who didn't. . . . Now I am probing constantly for understanding with both formal and informal styles of formative assessment. I give both verbal and written feedback, as opposed to simply grades, so that both the student and I know what they understand and where they are struggling. I have broken units of study into manageable chunks, or specific learning targets, and assess students in a progressive manner on each learning target. Remediation occurs immediately, allowing students to revisit learning targets that they struggle with. This allows for easy differentiation and grouping, focusing on what each individual student needs help with and allowing those students who have reached understanding to delve deeper into the concepts. (quoted in Chappuis & Stiggins, 2017, p. 96)

When teachers use measurements to determine grades at the end of a unit, semester, or year and to decide whether students are ready to proceed to the next phase of their education, they are engaging in **summative evaluation**. Summative evaluations usually provide the teacher with an overview of student learning across a broad range of knowledge and skills. Formative evaluations, on the other hand, are usually more focused and cover a narrower range of knowledge and skills. Teachers also use summative evaluations to make changes in their teaching that might be beneficial with the next group of students.

Video Example 11.4

Assessment with Technology: A Chief Technology Officer describes how technology has enabled teachers to differentiate instruction based on formative assessment feedback.

Emerging Trends in Classroom Assessment

As mentioned earlier, there is a trend to assess student learning with ever-increasing numbers of tests. More recently, however, new forms of assessment are being used. Innovations in assessment are partly in response to criticisms of the fairness and objectivity of standardized tests, such as the Iowa Test of Basic Skills, the Scholastic Assessment Test (SAT), and the American College Test (ACT). Educators and the public have criticized these tests not only for class and gender bias in their content but also for failing to measure accurately students' true knowledge, skills, and levels of achievement. For all these reasons, educators are increasingly going beyond traditional pencil-and-paper tests, oral questioning, and formal and informal observations. In addition, they are using an array of new assessment tools—individual and small-group projects, portfolios of work, exhibitions, recorded demonstrations of skills, and community-based activities, to name a few.

Increasingly, teachers are using **alternative assessments**—that is, assessments that "directly measure student performance through 'real-life tasks'" (Kauchak & Eggen, 2012, p. 421). Alternative assessments require that students apply knowledge and skills to solve problems rather than merely regurgitate isolated facts. The following sections examine several forms of alternative assessments: authentic assessment, portfolio assessment, peer assessment, self-assessment, performance-based assessment, alternate assessment, and project-based learning.

AUTHENTIC ASSESSMENT Authentic assessment (sometimes called *alternative assessment*) requires students to use higher-level thinking skills to perform, create, or solve a real-life problem, not just choose one of several designated responses, as on a multiple-choice test item. A teacher might use authentic assessment to evaluate the quality of individual and small-group projects, recorded demonstrations of skills, or participation in community-based activities. In science, for example, students might design and conduct an experiment to solve a problem and then explain in writing how they solved the problem.

Authentic assessments require students to solve problems or to work on tasks that approximate as much as possible those they will encounter beyond the classroom. For example, **authentic assessment** might allow students to select projects on which they will be evaluated, such as writing a brochure, making a map, creating a recipe, writing and directing a play, critiquing a performance, inventing a working machine, producing a video, creating a model, writing a children's book, and so on. In addition, authentic assessment encourages students to develop their own responses to problem situations by allowing them to decide what information is relevant and how that information should be organized and used.

When teachers use authentic assessment to determine what students have learned—and the depth to which they have learned—student achievement and attitudes toward learning improve. Real-life problem-solving situations provide students with opportunities to think deeply; develop in-depth understanding; and apply academic learning to important, realistic problems.

FOCUS ON **STEM:** FUTURE CITY COMPETITION PROVIDES AUTHENTIC LEARNING EXPERIENCES

Future City is an annual competition sponsored by the engineering community to promote technological literacy and engineering to middle school students. Through hands-on, real-world applications, students imagine, research, design, and build cities of the future.

Future City starts with a question—how can we make the world a better place? To answer it, students work in teams to create a city 100 years in the future that solves a citywide sustainability issue. Previous competitions have addressed stormwater management, urban agriculture, public spaces, and green energy. For 2017–2018, the theme was "The Age-Friendly City." Teams identified an age-related challenge that exists in today's urban environments and engineered two innovative solutions that would allow their future city's senior citizens to be as active and independent as they want to be.

Participants completed five "deliverables": a project plan; a virtual city design (using SimCity software); a 1,500-word city essay; a three-dimensional scale model built from recycled materials; and a presentation to a panel of judges at regional competitions. Regional winners represented their region at the Finals in Washington, D.C. (Future City, 2017).

PORTFOLIO ASSESSMENT Portfolio assessment is based on a collection of student work that "offers an ideal way to assess final mastery, effort, reflection, and growth in learning. In sum, it tells the learner's story of achievement" (Borich, 2017, p. 402). In short, a portfolio provides examples of important work undertaken by a student, and it represents that student's best work. For example, a high school physics student might include in a portfolio: (1) a written report of a physics lab experiment illustrating how vector principles and Newton's laws explain the motion of objects in two dimensions, (2) photographs of that experiment in progress, (3) a certificate of merit received at a local science fair, and (4) an annotated list of Internet sites related to vector principles and Newton's laws. For students, an important part of **portfolio assessment** is clarifying the criteria used to select work to be included in the portfolio, and then organizing and presenting that work for the teacher to assess.

There are three types of portfolios:

1. A *working portfolio* represents works in progress. It serves as a depository for student accomplishments that are on the way to being selected and polished for a more permanent assessment or display portfolio.
2. A student selects his or her best works from a working portfolio for a *display* or *show portfolio*. With the aid of the teacher, the student learns to critically judge the works, focusing on those qualities that make some stand out above others.
3. An *assessment portfolio* may contain all or some of the selections in a display portfolio as well as some of those that began in a working portfolio. Although the purpose of the working portfolio is to develop good products and the purpose of the display portfolio is to show off finished products, some of the contents of these collections are often used for the purpose of assessment. The teacher, therefore, is the primary audience of the assessment (Borich, 2017, p. 402).

As students prepare portfolios, four general guidelines should be followed to maximize the learning that results from their involvement in the process of portfolio development:

1. Have students individualize their portfolios—that is, portfolios should focus on the attainment of instructional goals that are important and meaningful for the students.
2. Portfolios should focus on students' accomplishments, their best work—not on their mistakes or limitations.
3. Portfolios should be collaboratively evaluated by teacher and students.
4. Use students' portfolios to discuss their progress with parents, counselors, and other teachers.

Among the states that require exit exams to graduate from high school, several also require that students present a portfolio. **OHIO** has replaced the Ohio Graduation Test (OGT) with a three-part assessment system that requires high school students to complete a senior portfolio project. Similarly, **RHODE ISLAND** has a new exit exam policy that, in addition to state assessments in reading and math and completion of required coursework, requires that students complete exhibitions and portfolios.

Several states that do not require an exit exam for high school graduation do require a portfolio. For example, **CONNECTICUT** requires a one-credit "demonstration project." In **HAWAII**, students working toward receiving an advanced Board of Education Recognition diploma must enroll in a one-credit senior project course that includes a portfolio. And **SOUTH DAKOTA**'s High School 2025 plan includes opportunities for high school students to complete a relevant and rigorous capstone experience by the end of their senior year, such as an entrepreneurship experience, youth internship, or pre-apprenticeship. Students who complete a senior experience will receive credit for creating a portfolio, product, research paper, and presentation related to the capstone experience.

PEER ASSESSMENT Peer assessment occurs when students assess one another's work. Typically, peer assessment is done informally during a class session. At times, a student may be more open to accepting critical feedback from a peer than from the teacher. Also, a peer may use a manner of speaking typical of his or her age level (word choice, for example), and it may be easier for another student to understand the feedback. The Teaching on Your Feet feature in this chapter provides an example of how feedback from their peers enabled one teacher's students to understand a concept that they had not understood previously.

Teaching on Your Feet

The Benefits of Peer Assessment

Despite my lesson plans, the suggestions I took from the text, and the numerous examples I gave during the day, nothing seemed to work—my sixth-grade class did not understand adjectives. I needed to find a new way to teach my students.

Then it hit me! Have them describe something they see in their bedrooms or on the way home from school each afternoon. So, I changed that night's homework assignment to observing their environment in preparation to write about it the next day. I didn't tell them that I was going to have them share their writing with a classmate.

The next day students came ready to share what they had observed. We did a 5-minute brainstorm before they wrote their descriptions. After 20 minutes of nonstop writing, I had the students switch papers with a neighbor. The neighbor was to draw exactly what the writing described.

I gave them 20 minutes to draw the picture, then hand it back to their neighbor. That's when I heard, "Man, you didn't put any grass in the park. I told you the sun was shining!" "Where's the color? My comforter is blue with white trim. You didn't show that."

Those were the responses I hoped to hear. Because students had not used adjectives, their peers' drawings did not portray what they thought they described. "Ms. Gore, are you saying that using adjectives helps the reader see what I am describing?" asked Melissa. "Now, I get it. Adjectives are colors and sizes. They make things come to life, right? Can we try it again, please?"

Aha! They finally understood adjectives. The assignment for that night was to rewrite their descriptions, which they would again share in class.

The next day, students came in eager to share their writing and then see their classmates' drawings. The results were wonderful—at last, my students understood the importance of using adjectives.

Used with permission of **LESLIE U. GORE**
Literacy Coach
Horace Mann Middle School
Los Angeles, **CALIFORNIA**

Analyze

Ms. Gore's lesson illustrates how it is sometimes helpful for a teacher to shift a lesson from the abstract to the concrete. When her students did not grasp the abstract concept of adjectives, Ms. Gore made the lesson more concrete—she had students describe something they saw in their bedrooms or on their way home from school. In addition, Ms. Gore made the material to be learned familiar. She personalized the lesson by having students relate it to their own experiences. And last, Ms. Gore's use of peer assessment enabled her students to get immediate feedback. They could see immediately whether their writing communicated what they intended.

Reflect

1. How might you personalize a lesson in a subject area you plan to teach?
2. What are other methods that provide immediate feedback for students?
3. What are other examples of how a teacher might use a concrete approach to teach an abstract concept?

In the following, fourth-grade language arts team teachers Jessica Barylski, Audrey Eckert, and Robyn Eidam explain how they modeled for students the process of giving quality feedback during the **peer assessment** process:

> When concluding a writing lesson, we used to have students conduct a peer review of their work with a partner. We would provide them with checklists and tell them to use these checklists, assuming that they would know what to do. While students were giving each other feedback, we would monitor their conversations. We noticed that students simply read their writing pieces to each other and gave very few suggestions to improve their writing because they believed that was what peer review was. . . .
>
> To introduce peer review now, we list the criteria for quality peer feedback. Then we show the students a videotape of ourselves modeling weak and strong examples of peer feedback. Including this component adds a visual model to help the students engage. As students watch the clips, they are looking for the criteria that will help them identify the strong example. After thoroughly discussing each video clip, the students apply the peer feedback criteria to their own writing pieces. . . .
>
> They took ownership of their peer review process, they followed the peer feedback model and criteria, and they took their time and allowed for corrections. They used constructive criticism and their conversations were more meaningful than in the past. We saw growth and improvement in our students' final writing pieces as well. (quoted in Chappuis & Stiggins, 2017, p. 36)

SELF-ASSESSMENT **Self-assessment** occurs when students assess their own work and their thought processes while completing that work. It has been suggested that "[self-assessment] is the most underused form of classroom assessment but has the most flexibility and power as a combined assessment and learning tool" (Tileston, 2004, p. 99). When students assess their own work, they become more aware of the factors that promote or hinder their learning. Students may, for example, ask assessment questions such as the following: What have I learned as a result of this activity? What problems did I encounter during my learning? How will I overcome these problems in the future?

Alexander Raths/Shutterstock

What are some of the advantages of using peer assessment in the classroom?

As a teacher, you should help your students, particularly low-achieving students, develop skills of self-assessment. As the following teacher indicates, once students develop self-assessment skills, their learning can improve dramatically:

> The kids are not skilled in what I am trying to get them to do. I think the process is more effective long term. If you invest time in it, it will pay off big dividends, this process of getting the students to be more independent in the way that they learn and to take the responsibility themselves. (Black, Harrison, Lee, Marshall, & Wiliam, 2004, p. 14)

Some teachers have taught students how to assess their work using the analogy of a common traffic light. Students label their work green, yellow, or red based on whether they have good, partial, or little understanding, respectively. The teacher then has the "greens" and the "yellows" meet in small groups to help one another, while the teacher meets with the "reds" to address their learning problems.

PERFORMANCE-BASED ASSESSMENT Put simply, **performance-based assessment** is based on observation and judgment (Chappuis & Stiggins, 2017). We observe a student perform a task or review a student-produced product, and we judge its quality. We could observe a student's science experiment and judge the quality of the thinking involved, or we could read a student's research report in history and judge the quality of argumentation and writing. Performance assessment is used to determine what students can do as well as what they know. In some cases, the teacher observes and then evaluates an actual performance or application of a skill; in others, the teacher evaluates a product created by the student.

Performance-based assessment focuses on students' ability to apply knowledge, skills, and work habits through the performance of tasks they find meaningful and engaging. Whereas traditional testing helps teachers answer the question, "Do students *know* content?" performance-based assessment helps answer the question, "How well can students *use* what they know?"

Students should find that performance tasks are interesting and relevant to the knowledge, skills, and work habits emphasized in the curriculum. If appropriate, students can help teachers construct performance-based assessments. For example, elementary-level and high school–level students helped their teachers construct the following two performance-based assessments, each of which required students to create graphs:

Example 1—Elementary Level

At various times during the school day, students observe and count, at 15-minute intervals, the number of cars and trucks that cross an unlit intersection near their school. Students also gather the same information for a lit intersection near the school. Using data for both intersections, students construct graphs to illustrate the results. If the data suggest the need for a light at the unlit intersection, the graphs will be sent to the local police department.

As students work on various parts of this performance task, the teacher would observe students and make judgments about the quality of their work. Do the counts of cars and trucks appear to be accurate? Do the graphs illustrate the results clearly? Is the students' decision about the need for a traffic light supported by the data they have gathered?

Example 2—High School Level

Students go online to find data on traffic accidents in their state. Based on the data they locate, students prepare graphs that show, by driver's age, various types of accidents, fatalities, speed at the time of accident, and so on. Exemplary graphs will be displayed in the driver education classroom.

As with the elementary-level example, the teacher would make judgments about the quality of the high school students' work. Naturally, these judgments would reflect the teacher's beliefs about the characteristics of exemplary student work at the high school level. Did students visit online sites that have extensive, accurate data on traffic accidents? Were students exhaustive in their online search? Do their graphs show a high degree of technical accuracy? Do the graphs "look professional"?

Many states have developed statewide performance-based curriculum goals. **WASHINGTON** State, for example, uses the Measurements of Student Progress (MSP) exam to assess students' performance in reading, mathematics, writing, and science. Teachers, parents, community members, and business representatives developed Performance-Level Descriptors (PDLs) for the knowledge and skills a student should demonstrate on the MSP. The PDLs are at three performance levels: Basic, Proficient, and Advanced.

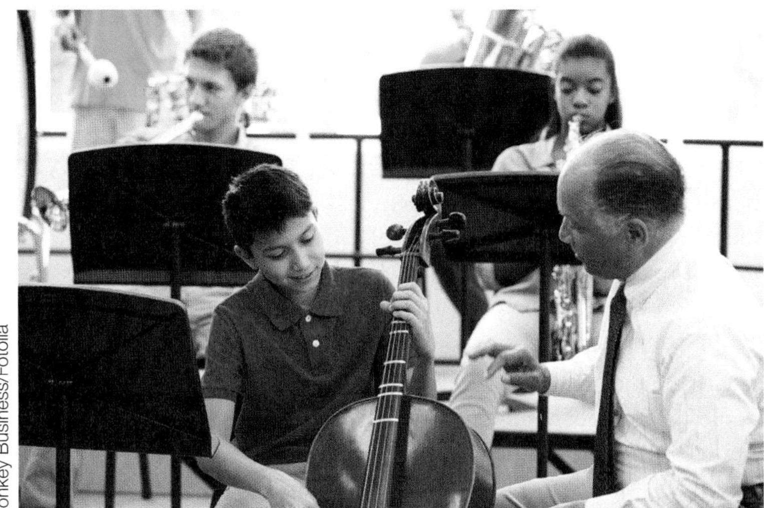
Monkey Business/Fotolia

This teacher is using performance-based assessment. What types of performance-based assessment might you use as a teacher?

ALTERNATE ASSESSMENTS **Alternate assessments** are designed to measure the performance of students who are unable to participate in the traditional large-scale assessments used by districts and states. An alternate assessment is an alternative way of gathering data about what a student, regardless of the severity of his or her disability, knows and can do. Alternate strategies for collecting data might consist of observing the student during the school day, asking the student to perform a task and noting the level of performance, or interviewing parents or guardians about the student's activities outside school.

The primary purpose for alternate assessments in state assessment systems is to provide information about how well a school, district, or state is doing in terms of enhancing the performance of *all* students. Gathering data through alternate assessments requires rethinking traditional assessment methods.

An alternate assessment is neither a traditional large-scale assessment nor an individualized diagnostic assessment. For students with special needs, alternate assessments can be administered to students who have a unique array of educational goals and experiences and who differ greatly in their ability to respond to stimuli, solve problems, and provide responses.

PROJECT-BASED LEARNING (PBL) A growing body of research supports the use of project-based learning as a way to develop students' cognitive and cooperative-learning skills, engage them, and cut absenteeism (Fogleman et al., 2011; Geier et al., 2008; Halvorsen et al., 2012; Harris et al., 2014). In **project-based learning (PBL)**, students work in teams to explore real-world problems and create presentations to share what they have learned. Compared with learning solely from textbooks, this approach has many benefits for students, including deeper knowledge of subject matter, increased self-direction and motivation, and improved research and problem-solving skills.

PBL, which transforms teaching from teachers telling to students doing, includes five key elements:

1. Engaging learning experiences that involve students in complex, real-world projects through which they develop and apply skills and knowledge
2. Recognizing that significant learning taps students' inherent drive to learn, their capability to do important work, and their need to be taken seriously

3. Learning for which general curricular outcomes can be identified up front, while specific outcomes of the students' learning are neither predetermined nor fully predictable
4. Learning that requires students to draw from many information sources and disciplines to solve problems
5. Experiences through which students learn to manage and allocate resources such as time and materials

These five key elements are reflected in the following examples of project-based learning:

- At Mountlake Terrace High School in Mountlake Terrace, **WASHINGTON**, teams of students in a high school geometry class design a state-of-the-art high school for the year 2050. The students create a site plan, make simple architectural drawings of rooms and a physical model, plan a budget, and write a narrative report. They present their work to real architects, who judge the projects and "award" the contract.
- At Newsome Park Elementary School in Newport News, **VIRGINIA**, second graders curious about the number of medicines a classmate takes and her frequent trips to the doctor investigate—with the classmate's permission—the causes of cystic fibrosis. They invite experts to tell them about the disease, write their research, use graphs and PowerPoint presentations to tell the story, sell pledges to a cystic fibrosis walkathon, and participate in the walkathon.
- At the Mott Hall School in **NEW YORK** City's Harlem, a fifth-grade project on kites involves using creative-writing skills in poems and stories with kite themes. Students design their own kites on the computer and then make them by hand. They learn about electromagnetism and the principles of ratios and proportions. A casual remark by one student leads to an in-depth study of the role of kites in various cultural celebrations.

Developing High-Quality Classroom Assessments

You should use various criteria to grade the assignments students complete and the tests they take. Among the criteria you may consider are effort, neatness, correctness, how well students did compared with other students or with their own past performance, and how long students had been studying the topic. These criteria, of course, focus on what *students* do to demonstrate their learning. To develop high-quality classroom assessments, however, you must focus on what *you* do to ensure that assessments fairly and accurately measure students' knowledge, skills, and levels of achievement. To assess student learning, you should be skilled in the following:

- Choosing and/or developing assessment methods appropriate for attaining instructional goals and objectives
- Administering, scoring, and interpreting the results of both externally-produced and teacher-produced assessment methods
- Using assessment results when making decisions about individual students, planning teaching, developing curriculum, and school improvement
- Developing valid grading procedures based on high-quality assessment of student learning
- Communicating assessment results to students, parents, other nonteaching audiences, and other educators
- Recognizing unethical, illegal, and otherwise inappropriate assessment methods and uses of assessment information

The teacher profiled in the Technology in Action feature in this chapter figured out a way to assess his students' understanding of complex concepts. As a result of his classroom-based inquiry and reflection, he began to use a quiz creator to develop autograded self-assessments for his students.

TECHNOLOGY in ACTION

Autograded Quizzes and Exams in Eighth-Grade Social Studies

Mr. Winchell has been using a quiz creator for the past year to create autograded self-assessments. (Autograded quiz-making tools allow teachers to construct their own assessments.) The quiz creator allows Mr. Winchell to create Flash-driven quizzes that include audio, animation, and text. The quizzes can be true/false, short answer, clickable maps, multiple-choice, and other auto-reply formats. The tool allows him to create assessments that review classroom discussion, group projects, and current events, and it quickly and easily puts them in a format that allows students to access the assessments and receive immediate feedback on their responses—not just with right or wrong answers, but with detailed explanations of the correct answer.

At the end of each lesson, Mr. Winchell has his students submit questions that cover the day's events. They provide the questions, the correct answers, and several not-so-correct answer choices. If Mr. Winchell uses a student's question in the daily quiz, the student receives several extra-credit points for that day. Mr. Winchell then loads the questions, the correct answers, and the incorrect choices into the quiz creator. The other students then access the questions, take the quiz, and see how they performed. They can take the quiz as many times as they want for as long as they want.

Mr. Winchell found that, as effective as the autograded quiz tool is, the exercise of having students write questions works equally well in helping students retain course-specific information. By the end of the year, Mr. Winchell has an extensive series of questions and answers covering the entire term and that students can review at any time. And, best of all, he never had to grade a single question!

Several quiz-making tools are available to teachers. Most of these tools allow teachers to import questions and answers from other sources like Excel or Word; insert screen shots, animation, music, and sound; randomize question-and-answer sets; provide automated feedback on performance and correct responses for each question; and provide detailed reporting to teachers. Some quiz creators include a management system that allows the teacher to group students and assign quizzes to that group. Teachers often post quiz-creator links to social media or their own websites so students can take quizzes for practice.

Teachers have used autograded assessments to improve student performance, save time, provide for diverse student self-assessment opportunities, and help students take control of their learning experience.

VISIT: Several quiz-making sites provide visitors with opportunities to try the quiz-creation tool, see examples of autograded assessment instruments, and obtain technical requirements for running the tool.

VALIDITY AND RELIABILITY Two important qualities of classroom assessments—whether teacher-made or commercially prepared—are validity and reliability. Because high-quality assessments are directly related to teaching effectiveness, assessments must be valid and reliable. **Validity** refers to the extent to which assessments measure what they are supposed to measure. If assessments fail to do this, they are useless. Valid assessments, however, ensure that what students are asked to do is a direct reflection of stated standards, goals, expectations, and/or targeted learning outcomes. If assessments are valid, teachers can use that information to improve their teaching, and students can use that information to improve their learning.

Surprisingly, examples of assessments that lack sufficient validity can be found among state-mandated tests of student learning. For example, the California Alliance of Researchers for Equity in Education questioned the validity of state-mandated assessments given to millions of students around the nation. The Alliance, made up of 100 researchers from Stanford, UCLA, University of California–Berkeley, and other California universities, pointed out that, "Without an understanding that the scores have not been proven to be valid or fair for determining proficiency or college readiness, students and their parents are likely to internalize failing labels with corresponding beliefs about academic potential" (California Alliance of Researchers for Equity in Education, 2016).

Reliability refers to the degree to which an assessment provides results that are consistent over time. In other words, an entire test (or individual test item) is considered to be reliable if it yields similar results at different times and under different conditions. For example, imagine that Mr. Hernandez wants to assess his students' multiplication and division skills using whole numbers by giving them a 40-point quiz (20 points for multiplication, 20 points for division). After scoring his students' quizzes, Mr. Hernandez is uncertain about whether he should begin teaching the more complex skills of multiplying and dividing using fractions. He decides to gather more information by giving another quiz three days later on the same multiplication and division skills. The following table presents the scores several students received on both quizzes:

	Multiplication		Division	
Student	**Quiz 1**	**Quiz 2**	**Quiz 1**	**Quiz 2**
Carlos	20	18	17	9
Kim	14	13	13	17
Shawn	11	11	12	17
Nong	16	17	16	12
Mary	20	19	15	14

The items that assessed students' multiplication skills, Mr. Hernandez notes, are quite consistent (or reliable). On quizzes 1 and 2, all five students received comparable scores, with Carlos and Mary receiving the highest scores on both quizzes, and Shawn and Kim receiving the lowest scores. On the other hand, the items that assessed students' division skills are less consistent (or reliable). On quiz 1, Carlos and Nong received the highest scores on the division items, while Kim and Shawn received the highest scores on the items for quiz 2.

At this point, Mr. Hernandez must make a judgment about the reliability of the information he has gathered. Because the results for the multiplication items are fairly consistent and those for the division items are fairly inconsistent, he decides to spend one more class session instructing students on division using whole numbers before he proceeds to teach multiplication and division using fractions.

Scoring Rubrics

Rubrics are an important element of quality classroom assessments. Sometimes called *scoring guides*, **scoring rubrics** are rating scales that consist of pre-established performance criteria. As a teacher, you can use rubrics to differentiate between levels of student performance on a rating scale, and students can even use them to guide their learning. Rubrics can be used to specify performance criteria for a variety of learning activities—writing an essay, conducting a science experiment, or delivering an informative speech, for example.

Students benefit from seeing examples of excellent work appropriate to their grade and ability levels. "Given clear requirements for success, students can approach learning from a more efficacious perspective; that is, they are better able to gauge the appropriateness of their own preparation and thus gain control over their own academic well-being. Students who feel in control of their own chances for success are more likely to care and to strive for excellence" (Stiggins & Chappuis, 2012, p. 43).

In addition to developing rubrics, you should collect models of exemplary performances and products by your students. Besides using a scoring rubric to learn about the specific elements that will be used to assess the quality of their work, students must see what quality looks (sounds, feels, smells, or tastes) like. Over time, you should collect sets of excellent work such as graphs, nonfiction writing, solutions to open-ended math problems, and designs for science experiments from students. Less-than-exemplary work may also be used in the process of teaching students how to use the rubrics.

Rubrics are typically used as scoring instruments when teachers evaluate student performances or products resulting from a performance task. There are two types of rubrics: holistic and analytic. A **holistic rubric** requires the teacher to score the overall process or product as a whole, without judging the component parts separately (Brookhart & Nitko, 2015; Chappuis & Stiggins, 2017). Figure 11.9 presents a generic framework for developing a holistic scoring rubric based on a 5-point scale.

As an illustration, a high school English teacher might use the framework presented in Figure 11.10 for holistic assessment of students' ability to write a clear, well-organized essay. A score of 5 would mean the essay reflected characteristics such as clear organization, accurate and precise use of words, adequately developed ideas, insightful analysis of the topic, and effective transitions from paragraph to paragraph. An essay with a score of 3 might have grammatical errors, problems with logic, confusing sentences, and a lack of transitions from paragraph to paragraph. And an essay with a score of 1 might be very confusing and contain only a few sentences that are clear and understandable.

Unlike the holistic scoring rubric, an **analytic rubric** requires that the teacher score separate, individual parts of the product or performance according to prespecified criteria, then add the individual scores to obtain a total score (Brookhart & Nitko, 2015; Chappuis & Stiggins, 2017). Figure 11.10 presents a generic framework for developing an analytic scoring rubric based on a 4-point scale.

Figure 11.9 Generic framework for a holistic scoring rubric

Score	Description
5	Performance or product reflects complete understanding of the assessment task or problem. The performance or product reflects all requirements of the task or problem.
4	Performance or product reflects considerable understanding of the assessment task or problem. The performance or product reflects all requirements of the task or problem.
3	Performance or product reflects partial understanding of the assessment task or problem. The performance or product reflects nearly all requirements of the task or problem.
2	Performance or product reflects little understanding of the assessment task or problem. Many requirements of the task or problem are missing.
1	Performance or product reflects no understanding of the assessment task or problem.
0	Task or problem not undertaken.

Figure 11.10 Generic framework for an analytic rubric

Criterion	Beginning	Developing	Accomplished	Highly Accomplished	Score
Criterion 1	Performance or product reflects beginning level of performance.	Performance or product reflects emerging performance at the mastery level.	Performance or product reflects performance at the mastery level.	Performance or product reflects performance at the highest level of mastery.	
Criterion 2	Performance or product reflects beginning level of performance.	Performance or product reflects emerging performance at the mastery level.	Performance or product reflects performance at the mastery level.	Performance or product reflects performance at the highest level of mastery.	
Criterion 3	Performance or product reflects beginning level of performance.	Performance or product reflects emerging performance at the mastery level.	Performance or product reflects performance at the mastery level.	Performance or product reflects performance at the highest level of mastery.	
Criterion 4	Performance or product reflects beginning level of performance.	Performance or product reflects emerging performance at the mastery level.	Performance or product reflects performance at the mastery level.	Performance or product reflects performance at the highest level of mastery.	

Video Example 11.5

Using Checklists as Formative Assessment: The teacher helps students use a checklist to understand the expectations of a project and how the checklist can help them determine if they are getting the grade they desire.

Let's continue with the example that focuses on teaching essay writing at the high school level. A teacher might evaluate students' essays with reference to the following four criteria, each of which would be evaluated according to the description of performances in Figure 11.10 at the "beginning," "developing," "accomplished," and "highly accomplished" levels:

- Criterion 1: The essay is organized clearly—the introduction sets the stage for what follows and the conclusion summarizes key ideas.
- Criterion 2: The essay is free of grammatical errors.
- Criterion 3: The essay has a unifying idea that is clear and easy to follow.
- Criterion 4: Effective paragraphing and transitions from one paragraph to the next provide an organizing structure and facilitate movement from one idea to the next.

To help you develop scoring rubrics for eventual use in your classroom, Figure 11.11 presents a step-by-step process for designing holistic and analytic scoring rubrics.

Checklists are one form of scoring rubrics.

Figure 11.11 Designing scoring rubrics: A step-by-step procedure

Step 1: Reexamine the learning objectives to be addressed by the task.

Step 2: Identify specific observable attributes that you want to see (as well as those you don't want to see) your students demonstrate in their product, process, or performance.

Step 3: Brainstorm characteristics that describe each attribute.

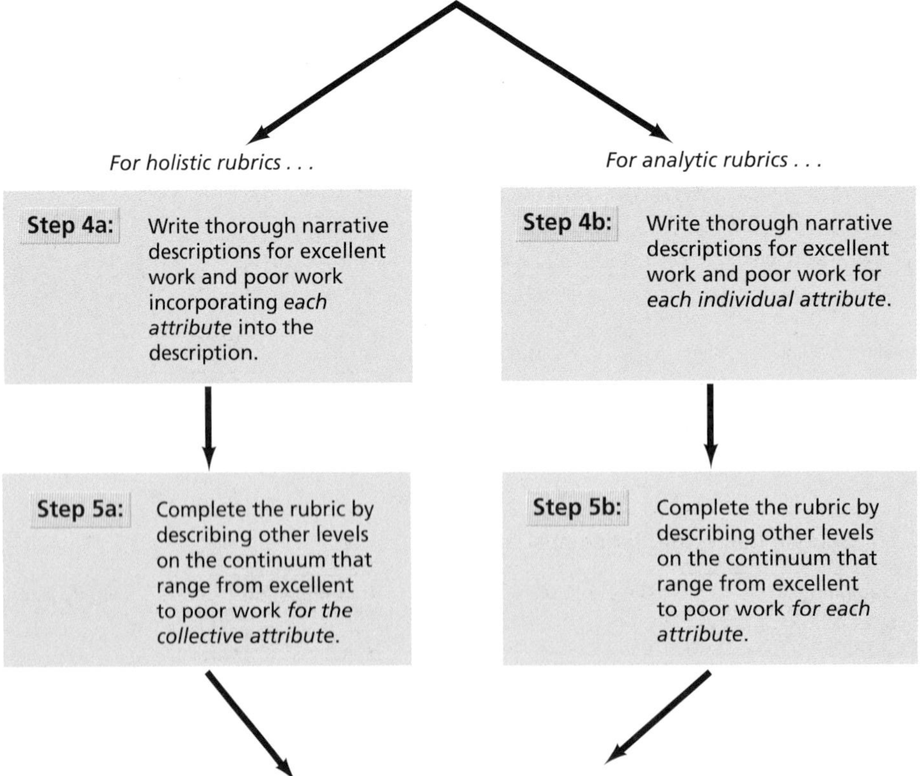

For holistic rubrics . . .
Step 4a: Write thorough narrative descriptions for excellent work and poor work incorporating each attribute into the description.
Step 5a: Complete the rubric by describing other levels on the continuum that range from excellent to poor work for the collective attribute.
For analytic rubrics . . .
Step 4b: Write thorough narrative descriptions for excellent work and poor work for each individual attribute.
Step 5b: Complete the rubric by describing other levels on the continuum that range from excellent to poor work for each attribute.

Step 6: Collect samples of student work that exemplify each level.

Step 7: Revise the rubric, as necessary.

SOURCE: Craig A. Mertler, "Designing Scoring Rubrics for the Classroom," *Practical Assessment, Research & Evaluation*, 2001, *7*(25). Used with permission.

Multiple Measures of Student Learning

There is no single right way to assess student learning. Clearly, it will be important for you to provide your students with multiple opportunities to demonstrate what they know and are able to do. If your students know that they have different ways to demonstrate their success, they will develop more positive views of themselves as learners. They will find learning to be an enjoyable experience.

Students who previously disliked a subject because they associated assessments of learning in that area with failure can develop positive views about a subject if they know they have different ways to demonstrate their learning—in other words, multiple opportunities to be successful. As four assessment experts put it: "Used with skill, assessment can motivate the reluctant, revive the discouraged, and thereby increase, not simply measure, achievement" (Chappuis et al., 2012, p. 1).

Summary

What Do Students Learn from the Curriculum?

- A general definition of curriculum refers to the experiences, both planned and unplanned, that either enhance or impede the education and growth of students.
- Students experience four types of curricula: what teachers intend to teach (the explicit curriculum), the hidden curriculum, the null curriculum, and extracurricular/cocurricular programs.
- Curriculum content reflects the beliefs of society and what the larger society believes young people should learn.
- Curricula are based on the needs and interests of students and also reflect a variety of professional, commercial, local, state, national, and international pressures.
- Three noncognitive factors are receiving more attention in school curricula: grit, tenacity, and perseverance; academic mindset; and mindfulness/meditation.
- Students' strengths in noncognitive areas will increase if their overall curricular experiences are rigorous, supportive, and growth promoting.

How Is the School Curriculum Developed and What Factors Influence It?

- Many school systems develop curricula by addressing the four questions in the Tyler rationale: (1) What educational purposes should the school seek to attain? (2) What educational experiences can be provided that are likely to attain these purposes? (3) How can these educational experiences be organized effectively? (4) How can we determine whether these purposes are being attained?
- Curriculum planning focuses on a continuum between the macro-level and the micro-level, and on a continuum between the present and the future.
- Curricula vary in the degree to which they are student-centered or subject-centered.
- The integrated curriculum draws from several different subject areas and focuses on a theme or concept rather than on a single subject.
- Community pressures, court decisions, students' life situations, testing results, national reports, teachers' professional organizations, textbook publishing, and educational research are among the factors that influence the school curriculum.

What Are Curriculum Standards and What Role Will They Play in Your Classroom?

- Standards at the state and national levels are part of the movement to hold educators and schools more accountable for student learning.
- School administrators, teachers, and students have different perspectives on standards. Administrators are primarily concerned with students' performance on standardized tests of achievement; teachers are primarily concerned with student performance and behavior at the classroom level; and students are primarily concerned with the learning being personally relevant, interesting, and meaningful.
- Developing rigorous academic standards, assessing students' mastery of those standards, and holding students and teachers accountable for meeting those standards are key elements of standards-based education.

- Professional associations have developed standards that reflect the knowledge, skills, and attitudes students should develop in the subject-matter disciplines.
- A good school curriculum is aligned both horizontally and vertically.
- Curriculum frameworks provide guidelines, recommended instructional and assessment strategies, suggested resources, and models for teachers to use as they develop curricula that are aligned with national and state standards.

What Is the Common Core State Standards Initiative, and How Does It Influence Teaching?

- The Council of Chief State School Officers (CCSSO) and the National Governors Association Center for Best Practices (NGA Center) organized the Common Core State Standards Initiative (CCSSI), a set of K–12 standards in English/language arts and mathematics.
- Since the release of the Common Core Standards in 2010, a vigorous debate over the standards has emerged.
- By 2018, seven states officially rejected the Common Core Standards; the remaining states renamed the standards to reflect the state's identity or slightly revised the standards.
- Some critics of the Common Core have mistakenly maintained that the Common Core Standards are a federal "takeover" of education in the United States.
- Proponents of higher standards argue that standards increase student achievement. Opponents argue that higher standards may result in decreased emphasis on subjects not tested.

What Is the Role of Assessment in Teaching?

- Effective schools frequently and systematically assess student learning.
- Classroom assessments of student learning enable teachers to make judgments about the performance of students and about their own performance as teachers.
- Assessment is a process that provides teachers with information about the effectiveness of their teaching and students with information about their learning.
- Classroom assessment provides information that teachers use to (1) determine how well students are learning the material being taught, (2) identify the type of feedback that will enhance student learning, (3) develop strategies for improving their effectiveness as teachers, and (4) determine if students have reached certain levels of performance.
- Standardized assessments (or standardized tests) are pencil-and-paper tests taken by large groups of students and are scored in a uniform manner.
- Norm-referenced assessments compare students' scores with scores of other students who are similar.
- Criterion-referenced assessments compare students' learning with clearly defined criteria or standards.
- State-mandated tests often have high-stakes consequences for students, such as determining eligibility to participate in extracurricular activities or to graduate.
- For teachers, administrators, and schools, test results can be linked to merit rewards, increased funding, or sanctions.
- An unintended consequence of high-stakes tests is that they overemphasize differences in achievement (often termed the "achievement gap") between White students and minority-group students and students from low-income families; the tests can also unfairly highlight achievement differences between students who attend "resource-rich" schools and those who attend "resource-poor" schools.
- High-stakes tests increase the likelihood that minority-group students and students from low-income families will drop out.

How Will You Assess Student Learning and Develop High-Quality Assessments?

- To assess student learning, teachers use informal and formal assessments, quantitative and qualitative assessments, measurement and evaluation techniques, and formative and summative evaluation.
- Among the various types of alternative assessments are authentic assessments, portfolio assessments, peer assessments, self-assessments, performance-based assessments, alternate assessments, and project-based learning.
- Validity and reliability are two qualities of high-quality classroom assessments.
- Scoring rubrics are rating scales that consist of pre-established performance criteria.
- Holistic rubrics are used to evaluate student performance or products related to a performance task.
- Analytic rubrics are used to score separate, individual parts of a performance or product.
- There is no single right way to assess student learning, and students' views of themselves as learners improve if they know that they have different ways to demonstrate their learning.

Professional Reflections and Activities

Teacher's Journal

1. Reflect on the 12,000 or so hours that you have spent as a student in K–12 classrooms. How would you characterize the academic standards you were expected to meet? How were these expectations conveyed to you?
2. Many people believe that high-stakes tests address only a narrow portion of the school curriculum. If a school district decided to "take a break" from high-stakes testing for five years, what data would parents, teachers, and others use to judge whether a school and its students were "successful"?
3. List in order of importance the five factors that you believe have the greatest impact on the curriculum. Then list the five factors that you believe ideally should have the greatest influence. What differences do you notice between your actual and ideal lists? What might be done to reduce the differences between the two lists?
4. Reflect on the hours that you have spent as a student in K–12 classrooms. What did the nonexplicit curricula in the classes teach you about yourself?
5. What are the biggest barriers to student engagement with the curriculum? As a teacher, how might you address these barriers and foster learning for all students?
6. As a K–12 student, what were your experiences with standardized and state-mandated tests? Did you have teachers who "taught to the test"? Did teaching to the test promote (or hinder) your own learning? Explain your answers.
7. Reflect on the many different assessments you experienced when you were a student in K–12 schools. Describe one or two assessments that you felt were accurate assessments of your knowledge and abilities and that motivated you to continue learning. Similarly, describe one or two assessments that you felt were *not* accurate assessments of your knowledge and abilities and that did *not* motivate you to continue learning. What implications do your own experiences have for your future assessment activities as a teacher?
8. In grading group projects, should a teacher give everyone in the group the same grade or assign different grades on the basis of how much each student contributed to the group's effort? Explain your answer.

Teacher's Research

1. Find the professional curriculum standards for your subject area online and compare them to the curriculum standards for that subject area in a state where you plan to teach (most state department of education websites include state-mandated standards). For example, you might download the National Council of Teachers of Mathematics (NCTM) standards and then compare them with the mathematics curriculum in the state where you plan to teach. How are the two sets of standards similar? How are they different? Is one set of standards clearer than the other?
2. Find an online blog by a teacher that discusses his or her experiences related to the Common Core State Standards. Post a thoughtful response to the teacher's blog.
3. On the Internet, review the most recent results of one of the following international assessments: International Assessment of Educational Progress (IAEP), Trends in International Mathematics and Science Study (TIMSS), Progress in International Reading Literacy Study (PIRLS), or Program for International Student Assessment (PISA). How does the achievement of U.S. students compare with the achievement of students from other countries? Based on what you have learned in this chapter's section on international assessments, what cautions should you keep in mind when examining such comparative data?
4. On the Internet, find two examples of project-based learning activities that teachers have posted. How is student learning assessed in these project-based learning activities? How might you adapt or modify these assessment activities when you become a teacher?

Observations and Interviews

1. Spend a half-day at a school at the level you plan to teach, recording your impressions about the degree to which teachers hold students accountable for meeting high academic standards. How do teachers convey their standards or expectations for student learning?
2. As a collaborative project, conduct an informal survey of what people think about retaining elementary, middle, and secondary students at their current grade level as a solution to the dilemma of what to do with students who do not meet standards for promotion. Do you note any differences at the three levels of schooling?
3. Spend a half-day at a school at the level you plan to teach, recording your impressions about the various approaches teachers use to assess students' learning. Which of the assessment approaches discussed in this chapter are used by the teachers?
4. As a collaborative project, conduct an informal survey of what people think about requiring students to pass

an exit exam before they graduate from high school. What conclusions can you draw from the results? Do you agree with those conclusions?

Professional Portfolio

1. Prepare a catalog of interactive multimedia resources and materials in a curricular area of interest. For each entry, include an annotation that briefly describes the resource materials, how teachers might use them, and where they may be obtained. As with the selection of any curriculum materials, try to find evidence of effectiveness, such as results of field tests, published reviews of educational software, awards, or testimonials from educators.

2. Prepare a set of guidelines or strategies for students to follow when they take a standardized test. The strategies might include items such as the following:
    - Survey the test, checking for missing pages.
    - Read directions carefully.
    - Notice use of double negatives.
    - Note use of terms such as *always, never, best*, etc.
    - Read all choices for multiple-choice test items.
    - Check answers.

Chapter 12

Integrating Technology into Teaching

Monkey Business Images/Shutterstock

Learning Outcomes

After reading this chapter, you will be able to do the following:

12.1 Explain how technology is transforming teaching and learning.

12.2 Describe the digital resources that are needed to integrate technology into teaching.

12.3 Summarize key research findings on technology integration and student learning.

12.4 Explain several challenges related to integrating technology into teaching.

READERS' VOICES

How is technology transforming teaching and learning?

Technology is having a huge impact on how, when, and where students learn. With a smartphone or tablet in their hand, students can learn at any hour of the day, wherever they might be.

—KENDRA,
Teacher Education Program, first year

Technology's impact on education is evident in a sampling of session titles from the 2018 International Society for Technology in Education (ISTE) conference attended by more than 18,000 educators and technology leaders from around the world:

- Empowering students to connect globally
- Individually one drop, together an ocean: Students impacting global awareness
- Inspiring the next generation of virtual reality creators
- Technology-based literacy resources and practices with special promise
- Block code to support students in special education with Autism Spectrum Disorder
- STEM Mio: Digital pathways for Latino youth to pursue STEM career futures
- The great debate of virtual reality—A novelty or effective use for learning?
- Closing the equity gap through the use of social media
- 365 days of sharing ideas through a hashtag
- Transforming culture in rural areas by involving younger students in STEM education
- Evaluating learning management systems from online learners' perspectives: Predictors of students' performance
- Why 3D print? The impact of 3D printing on student learning (International Society for Technology in Education [ISTE] Conference Program, 2018)

Technology has transformed how, when, and where students can learn. Generations ago, students came to school with notebooks, pencils, and pens; today, they come to school with smartphones, iPads, Chromebooks, and laptops. Students and teachers are now living and learning in a world of ambient media, a "world of information constantly and pervasively accessible through the various devices we currently use" (Roberts & Koliska, 2014, p. 2). Some schools even allow students to bring their own devices into the classroom, a policy known as "Bring Your Own Technology" (BYOT) or "Bring Your Own Device" (BYOD).

Media Use by Kids Age Zero to Eight (Rideout, 2017) and *Media Use by Tweens and Teens* (Rideout, 2015) reveal that young children (aged 0 to 8 years old) spend an average of 2 hours and 19 minutes with screen media; tweens (aged 8–12 years old) an average of 5 hours and 55 minutes with media; and teenagers (aged 13–18 years old) an average of 8 hours and 56 minutes with media each day. Since these figures do not include educationally based media activities in or out of school, children's total media use is higher than these figures reveal. Figure 12.1 shows how young children spend their screen media time, and Figure 12.2 shows the percentage of time tweens and teens spend on screen media.

To transform teaching and learning with technology requires more than uploading PDF worksheets to a classroom space on the Internet, using PowerPoint slides during lectures, showing videos downloaded from the Internet, or having students take digital quizzes with little or no assessment feedback. Students must become engaged, active learners through hands-on uses of technology in the classroom.

Figure 12.1 Screen media time, by activity, 2017
Among 0- to 8-year-olds, proportion of average daily screen time devoted to:

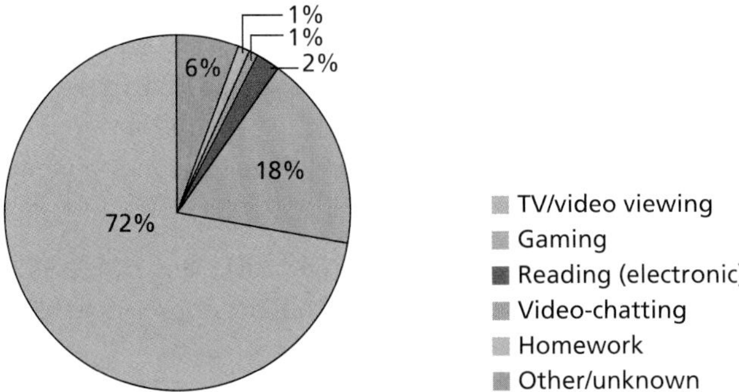

SOURCE: Victoria J. Rideout, *The Common Sense Census: Media Use by Kids Age Zero to Eight*, San Francisco, CA: Common Sense Media, 2017, p. 14.

Figure 12.2 On any given day, proportion of tweens and teens [and time spent] with screen media

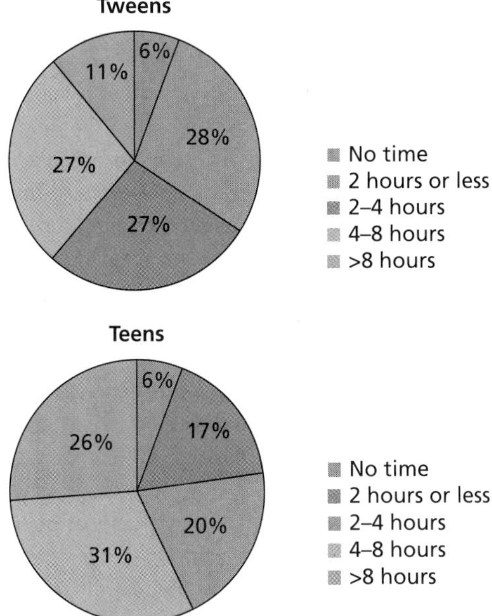

SOURCE: Based on Victoria J. Rideout, *The Common Sense Census: Media Use by Tweens and Teens*, San Francisco, CA: Common Sense Media, 2015, p. 13.

How is Technology Transforming Teaching and Learning?

For today's students, *anywhere, anytime learning* is a reality. Their digital learning options include various forms of **blended learning**—that is, a blending of traditional face-to-face instruction and online learning. Four models of blended learning—Rotation, Flex, A La Carte, and Enriched Virtual—are summarized in the following:

1. **Rotation model:** Students rotate among various learning activities, at least one of which is online learning. Other learning activities might include small- or whole-group instruction, group projects, individual tutoring, and pencil-and-paper assignments.
2. **Flex model:** Students are primarily engaged in online learning in a classroom setting with a teacher present to assist, guide, or lead discussions. Students have an individually customized, fluid schedule and move among learning activities.

3. **A La Carte model:** In addition to their learning at a brick-and-mortar school, students take a course that is entirely online. Students may take an A La Carte course either at school or at an off-campus site.
4. **Enriched Virtual model:** Students have required face-to-face learning sessions with their teacher and then are free to complete remaining online coursework on their own at an off-campus location. The same person is usually the face-to-face and the online teacher. Many Enriched Virtual programs began as full-time online schools and then developed into blended programs to provide students with in-school experiences.

In this chapter's Teachers' Voices: Being an Agent of Change, Melissa Meyers explains how students with learning disabilities benefit from her approach to blended learning.

TEACHERS' VOICES  BEING AN AGENT OF CHANGE

MELISSA MEYERS

Is Blended Learning Worth the Hype?

Yesterday afternoon in my 12th-grade World Literature class, I put my students through Hell, literally. Thanks to a fantastic interactive website called Virtual Inferno, my English class embarked upon a tour of Dante's Hell, from Dante's mysterious awakening in the Dark Wood of Error down, down through nine levels until we reached the Cocytus where Satan himself resides, encased in ice forever.

In the coming weeks, my English students will research and write about the visually stunning *Dante's Inferno* video game, listen to Franz Liszt's *A Symphony to Dante's Divine Comedy* accompanied by Gustave Dore's illustrations on YouTube, and explore Dante-era Florence through the "Firenze-Virtual History" iPad app. They will also read *Inferno* (of course!) and listen to the audio book on their iPads.

As I walked in the front door of my school this morning, one of my students told me that he had spent the long MLK [Martin Luther King] holiday weekend reading the full version of Longfellow's *Inferno* translation online. Another student brought in a graphic novel of it to share with the class. A third asked if he could write an extra-credit short story about the text from the point of view of Virgil, Dante's spiritual guide. I would like to think that my students are just a bunch of gifted, enthusiastic readers, but the truth is that all of them are LD [learning disabled] learners with severe dyslexia, disorder of written expression, and various forms of speech and language difficulties.

Reading is neither pleasurable nor natural for them. Technology isn't a fun extra at my school; it's a voice for dyslexic readers, an essential communication and social device for autistic students, a tool for the dysgraphic, and an organizational must-have for everyone. Is technology in the classroom worth the hype at *my* school? Absolutely.

Occasionally, I come upon a questioning parent who wants to know why students spend so much time using technological do-dads instead of doing good old-fashioned reading and writing. For these naysayers, I rattle off a whole list of reasons why I integrate technology: multi-modal instruction, supplements for remediation or enrichment, 21st-century skill-building, text-to-world connections, collaboration, student buy-in, not to mention marked improvement in essay writing and reading comprehension. And though we study ancient pieces of literature, we view texts through modern eyes, with technology as our lens. This begs the question of why we're not evolving at a faster rate if there are, by Apple's count, 1.5 million iPads in American classrooms and increased funding for 1:1 computer initiatives in all public schools.

The answer is ugly: teachers themselves slow down this evolution when they aren't sufficiently trained to use technology or resist the idea of change altogether. According to a 2009 survey conducted through the National Center for Education Statistics, 99 percent of public school teachers have computer access throughout the day, whereas only 29 percent of them are using computers "often" during instruction. Such a wasted opportunity!

Technology is certainly worth the hype, but it will remain only empty, extravagant claims if teachers aren't trained to use it effectively and aren't as enthusiastic—and evolved—as their students already are. It's time to play catch-up.

PERSONAL REFLECTION

1. Meyers believes that technology integration in teaching is "certainly worth the hype." To what extent do you agree with her?
2. Why do you think some teachers might resist the integration of technology into teaching?

Melissa Meyers teaches at Stanbridge Academy, a small, private K–12 special education school in San Mateo, **CALIFORNIA**.

Source: Used with Permission of Bob Lenz, From the Classroom: What Does Blended Learning Look Like?, Retrieved June 7, 2018, from http://www.edutopia.org/blog/blended-learning-example-classroom-lesson-bob-lenz

Technology has transformed teaching and learning. Each day, students demonstrate their learning by producing podcasts, collaborating with distant experts, and interacting with other students around the block and around the world. They search the web for information about whales, the Brazilian rain forest, or the planet Mars; and then they create podcasts based on what they have learned. They send text messages to students in other countries and collaborate with them on global networking projects. They use technologies to investigate real-world challenges such as local traffic problems, water quality, homelessness, and recycling.

Figure 12.3, based on a survey of pre-K–12 teachers, shows that most "embrace digital resources to propel learning." Approximately three-quarters of the teachers report that technology enables them to reinforce and expand on content (74 percent), to motivate students to learn (74 percent), and to respond to a variety of learning styles (73 percent). More than two-thirds of teachers want more technology in the classroom, and this number is even greater (76 percent) for teachers in low income schools. 7 in 10 teachers (69%) surveyed said educational technology allows them to "do much more than ever before" for their students, and 65 percent of teachers reported that technology allows them to demonstrate something they cannot show in any other way.

Technology enables students to experience events or study phenomena that they could not witness firsthand. By integrating technology into various learning tasks and across subject areas, teachers can provide students with learning experiences that would have been

Video Example 12.1

Authentic Integration with Technology: A preschool teacher shares how technology gives preschoolers unique experiences only possible through the authentic integration of the Internet.

Figure 12.3 Teachers embrace digital resources to propel learning

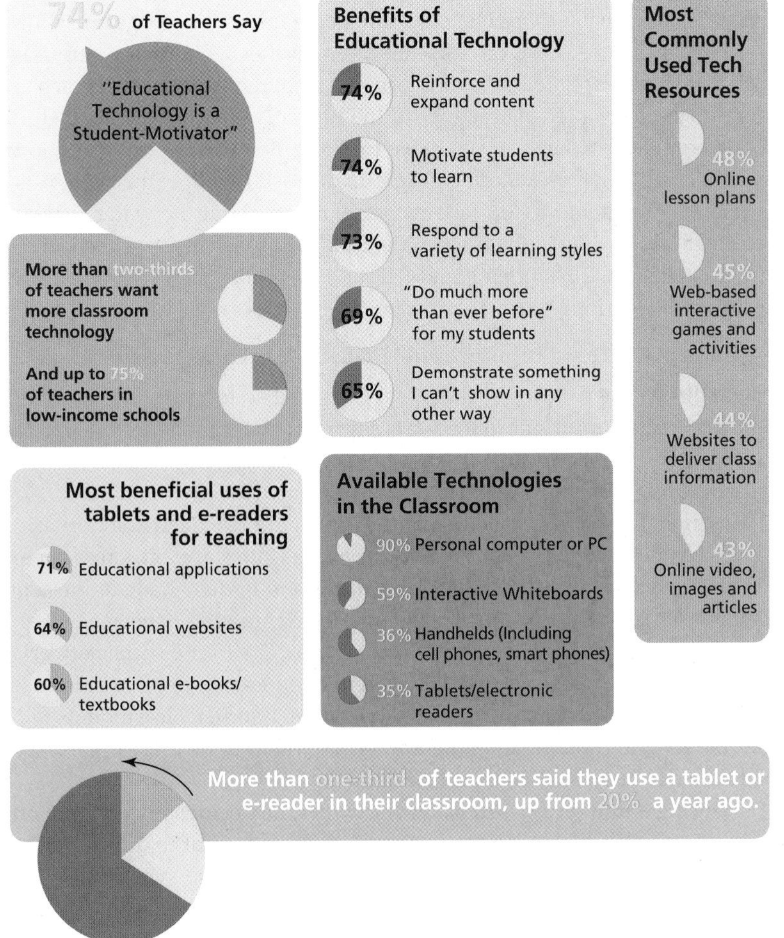

SOURCE: PBS Learning Media. (February 4, 2013). Press Release: PBS Survey Finds Teachers Are Embracing Digital Resources to Propel Student Learning. Used with permission.

impossible a few years ago. Careful and purposeful use of educational technology changes the roles of teachers and students and enhances students' higher-order and problem-solving skills. Read the following three vignettes and consider how the use of educational technology changes the roles of teachers and students.

Vignette 1: The Tech Detectives: Students Take Ownership of Technology

A middle school teacher is struggling to figure out why her SmartBoard is acting up. Typically, she would submit a "tech request" and wait an extended period of time for it to be fixed. One issue, though—she needs the device *now* for a very important math lesson. She suddenly remembers that a group of students called the "Tech Detectives" can come to the rescue and fix the problem. Within minutes, several students arrive, play around with a few wires and buttons, and the malfunction is addressed in no time.

The Tech Detectives Club was created at Black River Middle School in Chester, **NEW JERSEY**, as a way for students to take ownership of the technology they utilize during their various learning experiences. Based on feedback from various school stakeholders who have a passion for technology, it was deemed necessary to start a club that arms students with a strong technological skill set. On a regular basis, students create tutorials, assist teachers, learn about technology trends, collaboratively problem solve issues, and gain exposure to career readiness.

Vignette 2: SOLE Motivates Students to Teach Themselves (and Each Other)

An eighth-grade teacher uses the Self-Organized Learning Environment (SOLE) to teach geography to his students. His students organize themselves into small groups, and each group works at one of four learning centers in the classroom. Each learning center has a computer with Internet access and a few software programs that enable students to acquire geographic knowledge and skills.

As part of the SOLE environment, the teacher gave each group a list of Internet resources related to various topics in geography; then, he let each group choose what it wanted to learn. With their teacher's encouragement, students soon became excited about being able to direct their own learning and to learn from one another. For example, one group decided to follow their interests and to make a movie and a PowerPoint presentation about the water shortage in their state. According to the teacher, the SOLE approach is very effective: "Since I began to use SOLE, students find learning more fun; they are more engaged; and they are learning to collaborate."

Vignette 3: Teaching in a Technology-Rich 1:1 iPad Classroom

An English teacher at a high school that gave an iPad to each student at the start of the school year is eager to integrate several new technologies into his teaching. He agreed to be the English Department's "technology coach" and share with other teachers how to teach in a one-on-one iPad environment.

At first, he was concerned that students might use the iPads primarily for playing games or using social media. Two weeks into a unit on American literature, however, he realizes that his concern was unfounded. Students are actually using the iPads to improve their learning. For example, students make frequent use of a free, online learning management system (LMS) and social network that enables users to create and to share academic content. Students are also using a note-taking and annotation app available on the Internet. His students tell him that the LMS and the note-taking app enable them to be more organized and better able to keep track of their learning.

During a unit on *The Red Badge of Courage*, he decides to use a free online quiz creator that allows him to use a game-show format to quiz students on their reading. In addition, he uses a student response system that allows students to use "clickers" to answer questions. During the unit, he has four game-show quizzes. During each quiz, students are excited and deeply engaged.

During the quizzes, he uses a graph provided at the end of each question to assess and correct immediately students' understanding of the material. After each quiz, he downloads a spreadsheet with each student's answers and then meets individually with students to review the questions they missed.

The three preceding vignettes illustrate how today's students are demonstrating mastery of technology standards developed by the International Society for Technology in Education (ISTE). According to ISTE standards, a "Digital-Age Learner" is a/an Digital Citizen, Knowledge Constructor, Innovative Designer, Computational Thinker, Creative Communicator, and Global Collaborator.

FOCUS ON **DIVERSITY**: CLOSING THE DIGITAL USE DIVIDE

There are two kinds of digital divides: inequitable *access to* technology and inequitable opportunities *to use* technology. "[Closing] the digital divide alone will not transform learning. We must also close the digital use divide" (U.S. Department of Education, 2017).

As Figure 12.5 suggests, students should be active, rather than passive, users of technology. However, students of privileged groups (e.g., high socioeconomic status, dominant demographic groups, high-performing groups, and native English speakers) tend to use technologies in more active ways than lower-income students, students with disabilities, or ELL students (Hohlfeld, Ritzhaupt, Wilson & Dawson, 2016; Rafalow, 2018; Reich & Ito, 2017). Teachers must be vigilant in identifying digital inequities of

Figure 12.5 Digital Use Divide

DIGITAL **USE** DIVIDE

While essential, closing the digital divide alone will not transform learning. We must also close the digital **use** divide by ensuring all students understand how to use technology as a tool to engage in creative, productive, life-long learning rather than simply consuming passive content.

PASSIVE USE

ACTIVE USE

SOURCE: U.S. Department of Education, Office of Educational Technology, *Reimagining the Role of Technology in Education: 2017 National Education Technology Plan Update*, Washington, D.C., 2017, p. 21.

Video Example 12.2

Steps to Close the Digital Use Divide: This English Language Learner (ELL) teacher shares the difference technology has made when her students each were given individual laptops.

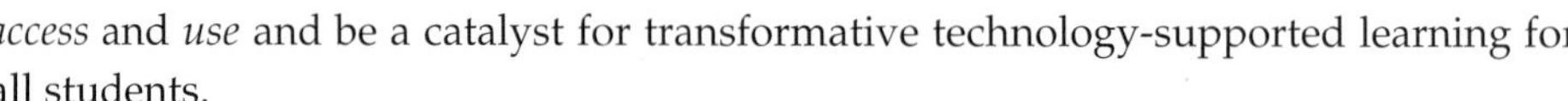

access and *use* and be a catalyst for transformative technology-supported learning for all students.

The following three strategies will help you reduce the **digital use divide** among your students:

- **Communicate and co-develop technology initiatives with multiple stakeholders.** Share your vision for digital learning with others, and seek support for technological resources and expertise.
- **Facilitate intergenerational digital learning experiences.** Include parents and community members in digital learning projects.
- **Align digital learning experiences with the interests, identities, and needs of minority students.** Since software and online communities often reflect the developers' cultural experiences, preview digital materials to ensure that they represent a range of interests, identities, and people (Price-Dennis & Carrion, 2017; Reich & Ito, 2017):

Realizing the Full Transformative Impact of Technology on Learning

Without a doubt, technology can transform teaching and learning. However, a key challenge for teachers is ensuring that all students realize the *full impact* of technology learning. To help teachers meet this challenge, Roblyer and Hughes (2019) developed a "RAT Matrix" so teachers can analyze the degree to which they are integrating technology. The three elements of the RAT Matrix—*Replacement*, *Amplification*, and *Transformation*—are explained in the following.

Replacement—Technology replaces, but does not fundamentally change, instructional practices, student learning, or curriculum goals. Technology is merely a different, technological means to the same instructional end.

- ***Example:*** *Students completed worksheets in class and handed them in to the teacher. Now, students complete PDF worksheets on a tablet and email them to the teacher.*
- ***Example:*** *Teacher encourages students to take notes on their iPads.*

Amplification—Technology increases efficiency or productivity in instructional practices, student learning, or curriculum goals. The focus is on effectiveness rather than change.

- ***Example:*** *Using email to increase teacher-student communication beyond the classroom.*
- ***Example:*** *A teacher uses Google Forms to create and grade quizzes more quickly.*

Video Example 12.3

Amplifying Instruction: A teacher uses tablets as tools for students to record themselves reading a passage with expression. The recording allows students to evaluate themselves and gives the teacher individual student feedback in an efficient manner.

Transformation—Technology shifts, restructures, or reorganizes instructional practices, student learning, or curriculum goals in ways not possible without the inclusion of technology.

- ***Example:*** *Using Project Wild and Aquatic Wild to engage students in physical activity and scientific discussions that go beyond textbook content.*
- ***Example:*** *Students flick the end of a jump-rope and record the waves that move along the rope; they capture a frame that mirrors a sine wave; and they overlay the frame in digital graphic software to calculate the sine equation of the sine wave.*

Figure 12.6 presents a RAT Matrix analysis of how a first-grade teacher used technology during a 5-week unit on animal habitats. The unit included live webcam recordings of animals living in captivity and wild habitats. During the unit, students used iPads for daily observations of animals and online research about habitats.

Figure 12.6 The replacement, amplification, transformation (RAT) matrix applied to a first-grade unit on habitats

	Instruction	Learning	Curriculum
Replacement Technology is different means to same end.		• Read magazines online • Drew habitat in a drawing app • Write report about habitat in writing app	• Met 1st grade science standards—observing and comparing habitals
Amplification Technology increases or intensifies efficiency, productivity, access, and capabilities, etc., but the tasks stay fundamentally the same.	• More efficient everyday access to video streams with iPads vs. computer lab • Increased variety of live habitats	• Customized habitat sorting activity in app	
Transformation Technology redefines restructures, reorganizes, change or creates novel solutions.	• Changed length of time habitats could be observed (5 weeks)	• Created a real-world authentic observational experience for learners	• Lesson became interdisciplinary with science, research, reading, writing, and technology

SOURCE: ROBLYER, M. D.; HUGHES, JOAN E., INTEGRATING EDUCATIONAL TECHNOLOGY INTO TEACHING, 8th Ed., ©2019. Reprinted and Electronically reproduced by permission of Pearson Education, Inc., New York, NY.

Virtual Schools and Online Learning

Westwood Cyber High School, near Detroit, **MICHIGAN** does not have traditional classrooms, academic departments, courses, or tests. Instead, the school is patterned after a British model known as the "Not School." Westwood students do most of their work on the Internet from home, and they report to the school for 2 hours a week to meet with teachers. The rest of the time they work interactively with school personnel and the school's learning management system.

The curriculum at Westwood emphasizes project-based learning that incorporates multiple subject areas. Students create individualized portfolios of creative work tailored to their interests. Teachers certified by the state of Michigan grade students' portfolios with reference to state learning standards.

Westwood is one of a growing number of **virtual schools** in the nation. 34 states had a total of 429 full-time virtual schools in 2018 (Miron, Shank, & Davidson, 2018). Figure 12.7 shows that nearly 300,000 students were enrolled at virtual schools during 2016–2017.

While some early research showed that students at virtual schools outperformed their peers in brick-and-mortar schools (CREDO, 2015; Evergreen Education Group, 2015), recent research suggests the opposite. For example, full-time online school students had lower gains in reading and mathematics—equivalent to 72 fewer days of learning in reading and 180 fewer days in mathematics (Miron, Shank, & Davidson, 2018). Gains were even lower for students of color, low income students, English language learners, and special education students. In addition, online schools had higher student-teacher ratios (45 students per teacher, compared to 16 in public schools) and lower on-time graduation rates (51 percent compared to 83 percent). And only 36 percent of full-time virtual schools received "acceptable" school performance ratings from their state education agencies.

Figure 12.7 Enrollment trends in full-time virtual schools

300,000
250,000
200,000
150,000
100,000
50,000
0

All Virtual Schools
K12 Inc.
Connections

2000 2002 2004 2006 2008 2010 2012 2014 2016/17

SOURCE: Based on Miron, G., Shank, C. & Davidson, C. (2018). *Full-Time Virtual and Blended Schools: Enrollment, Student Characteristics, and Performance*. Boulder, CO: National Education Policy Center, p. 15.

Many districts are creating full-time **blended schools** that combine online and face-to-face instruction. During 2018, nearly 300 blended schools in in 29 states offered **online learning** to nearly 117,000 students (Miron, Shank, & Davidson, 2018). The following programs illustrate a few of the online learning options blended schools offer to students.

- In Chicago, **ILLINOIS**, the Virtual Opportunities Inside a School Environment (VOISE) Academy, a public high school, uses a blended learning approach in which students attend the physical school, but online courses act as the primary source of course content.
- Riverside Virtual School in **CALIFORNIA** offers a blended online learning option to students who want to work remotely. They must communicate with teachers via e-mail throughout the week.
- In **NORTH CAROLINA**, Polk County Early College annually allows up to 20 students to complete high school while earning college credits, leading to early completion of an associate's degree while earning a high school diploma.
- Myron B. Thompson Academy in **HAWAII** is a blended charter school serving about 500 students statewide. Students take some courses face to face at the onsite location and other courses mostly online with some face-to-face requirements. The face-to-face requirements are unique to each island.

Whether in special classes or extracurricular programs, students in today's schools receive a great deal of hands-on involvement with technology. How does this prepare them for postgraduate life?

goodluz/Shutterstock

- In **RHODE ISLAND**, the Village Green Virtual Charter School opened in fall 2013 as the state's first fully blended charter school. Students spend 15 hours in the classroom and 15 hours working online each week (Village Green Virtual Charter School, 2018).

In addition to virtual schools, several hundred public, private, and parochial high schools in the United States offer online learning through Virtual High School (VHS) Inc., a nonprofit foundation. VHS partners with schools to provide "student-centered online education within a high quality, collaborative learning environment. Students learn in cohorts where student exchange and interaction are valued components of the instructional process" (Virtual High School, 2018). Members of the VHS consortium include more than 18,000 students from more than 40 states and territories and 30 countries.

FOCUS ON **STEM**: VHS STUDENTS DEVELOP SCIENTIFIC INQUIRY SKILLS

VHS students can take STEM courses and interact with their peers and experts from around the world. Courses include hands-on, technology-based lab experiences that help students develop a deep understanding of scientific inquiry. STEM-based learning experiences include the following:

- Analyze the microscopic structure of tissues using NIH Image J imaging software in the Anatomy course
- Calculate the rate of seafloor spreading using Google Earth in the Earth and Space Systems Science course
- Investigate Newton's Laws using Vernier Go! Motion probes in the Physics 1 course

During summer 2018, VHS students participated in the Solar Energy Design Challenge. The Challenge was organized by the Concord Consortium (an R&D organization devoted to improving teaching and learning through technology) and STEM-related industries. VHS students modeled or designed solar-powered systems and then submitted their plans for acceptance into the Virtual Solar Grid. The purpose of the Grid is "to figure out how much of humanity's energy need can be realistically met by solar power interconnected through smart grids on a global scale" (Virtual Solar Grid, 2018).

Students participating in the Challenge had unlimited, free use of Energy3D, a computer-aided design simulation tool to model existing solar energy systems or design new ones. Students were able to sketch a realistic-looking structure or import one from an existing CAD file, superimpose it on a map image, and then evaluate its energy performance for any given day and location. To learn about Energy3D and how to use it to build a sustainable, solar energy system, VHS students could enroll in the "Solar Energy Design Summer" course during summer 2018 or the "Solar Energy Design Independent Learning Opportunity (ILO)" available at the VHS website.

A team of experts evaluated the models; those found to be scientifically accurate and environmentally appropriate were admitted into the Virtual Solar Grid.

CONCERNS ABOUT VIRTUAL SCHOOLS AND ONLINE LEARNING With the spread of virtual schools and online learning, some educators, policymakers, and researchers have expressed concern about exaggerated claims for online learning. In addition, they are worried about what is lost when students do not meet face to face with their classmates and teachers.

In *50 Myths and Lies That Threaten America's Public Schools: The Real Crisis in Education*, David Berliner and Gene Glass (2014) make the following points about cyberschooling:

- When the performance of the children who receive their education at cyberschools is assessed, the results are dismal. Dropout rates during the school year are staggering, often exceeding 50%. Graduation rates are abysmal, and achievement lags far behind that of their peers in brick-and-mortar schools. For the 2012–13 school year, Tennessee Virtual Academy—operated by K12 Inc.—scored lower than any of the other 1,300 elementary schools on the state standardized test. (p. 33)
- Legislators are often big proponents of cyberschooling, for which they can pay a fraction of the cost of educating a child in a traditional brick-and-mortar school . . . . The cyberschool industry operates in the grand tradition of crony capitalism, essentially buying the support of politicians through such things as campaign contributions and personal perks like junkets to foreign countries to study other education systems. (p. 34)
- Only about a quarter of online cyberschools meet "adequate yearly progress" as defined by the No Child Left Behind act, as compared with about 50% of traditional schools. In 2011–12, state department of education ratings of virtual schools' academic performance showed that more than 70% were rated academically unacceptable. Students in cyberschools have scored substantially lower than their counterparts in traditional brick-and-mortar schools in math and reading. The on-time graduate rate for students in cyberschools is about two-thirds the rate for traditional schools. (p. 35)

In spite of evidence such as this, the public is generally supportive of virtual schools. According to a Phi Delta Kappan/Gallup Poll (Bushaw & Lopez, 2013, p. 17) public school parents approve, by 63 percent to 36 percent, of allowing high school students to earn high school credits online; and they favor allowing high school students to earn college credits by 80 percent to 19 percent.

The trend toward virtual schools and online learning no doubt will continue. Meanwhile, several questions need to be addressed to ensure that virtual students have high-quality online learning experiences:

Video Example 12.4

Demonstrating Understanding in Online Settings: This video demonstrates how technology can be used to determine student understanding of a math problem in an online or virtual classroom.

- Although online learning may be appropriate for high school students, should online learning be made available to elementary and middle school students?
- Should online courses be aligned with state academic standards?
- Who should provide for students' technological needs while they take an online course?
- Are online teachers trained effectively to teach via the Internet?
- Should parent approval be required before a child enrolls in an online course?
- Should students receive the same credit for an online course as they would for an interactive, face-to-face class?
- How can school officials ensure the quality of online courses, especially those offered by teachers in other states or countries?

FLIPPED CLASSROOMS One form of blended learning is known as a **flipped classroom**. In a flipped classroom, students first learn new content at home by watching online video lectures by the teacher or other online videos related to the subject matter. Then, during time in class, they apply their new knowledge by solving problems or completing "homework," with the teacher providing individual assistance. **Flipped teaching** allows teachers to use their time in class differently. Instead of acting in the well-known role of the "sage on the stage," the teacher is able to be more like the "guide on the side." Teachers can work with individual students or groups of students.

An early innovator of flipped teaching was Clintondale High School in **MICHIGAN**. The principal, who had been posting YouTube videos of baseball skills for his son's team, worked with a social studies teacher to offer two classes with the same material and assignments—one class was flipped, the other traditional. After 20 weeks, students in the flipped class were outperforming traditional students.

Clintondale had been identified as among the state's worst 5 percent of schools. In 2010, more than half of ninth graders had failed science, and almost half had failed math. That same year, the ninth grade flipped. The English failure rate dropped from 52 percent to 19 percent; math, from 44 percent to 13 percent; science, from 41 percent to 19 percent; and social studies, from 28 percent to 9 percent. Following those results, the school decided to flip every class in 2011. After that, the now-flipped school's failure rate dropped from 30 to 10 percent. Graduation rates soared above 90 percent. College attendance went from 63 percent in 2010 to 80 percent in 2012 (Rosenberg, 2013).

Approaches to flipped classrooms and flipped teaching continue to be developed, and their impact on student achievement is being studied. Two high school chemistry teachers in Woodland Park, **COLORADO**, Jonathan Bergmann and Aaron Sams, report impressive results in their book *Flip Your Classroom: Reach Every Student in Every Class Every Day*. In the following, they explain how they developed the flipped model:

> One day, Aaron had an insight that would change our world. It was one simple observation: "The time when students really need me physically present is when they get stuck and need my individual help. They don't need me there in the room with them to yak at them and give them content; they can receive content on their own."
>
> He then asked this question: "What if we prerecorded all of our lectures, students viewed the video as 'homework,' and then we used the entire class period to help students with the concepts they don't understand?" . . .
>
> We implemented the flipped model for one year and we were very pleased with how our students were learning. We had evidence our model worked and was better for kids. (Bergman & Sams, 2012, pp. 4–5)

Recently, Lo and Hew (2017) reviewed 15 studies of flipped teaching in which audio and video content was accessed by K–12 students before formal class sessions. The studies revealed a neutral or positive impact on student achievement and no evidence of a negative impact. Students reported learning gains; they valued being able to view or listen to a lesson repeatedly; and they reported that flipped classes helped them take notes.

At this point, the effects of flipped classrooms on students' learning appear to be limited. In any case, flipped classrooms and flipped teaching provide a model for how technology can be integrated into teaching.

What Digital Resources are Needed to Integrate Technology Into Teaching?

Since "learning, teaching, and assessment enabled by technology require a robust infrastructure" (U.S. Department of Education, Office of Educational Technology, 2017, p. 5), you should become familiar with a school's technological infrastructure when you begin teaching. As shown in Figure 12.8, four key elements of this infrastructure are connectivity, devices, accessibility, and resources.

Figure 12.8 School infrastructure for integrating technology into teaching

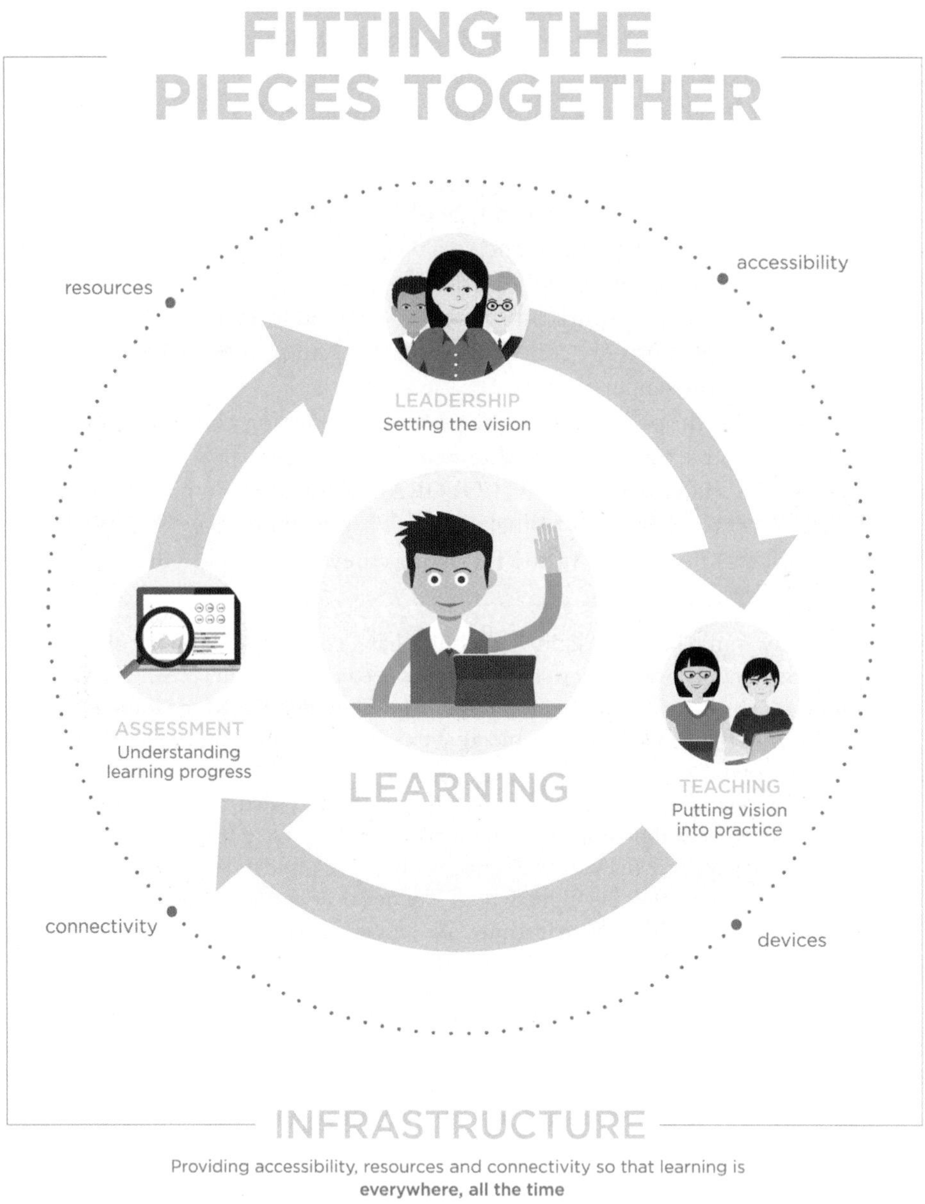

SOURCE: U.S. Department of Education, Office of Educational Technology, *Reimagining the Role of Technology in Education: 2017 National Education Technology Plan Update*, Washington, D.C., 2017, p. 6.

Connectivity

A school should provide high-speed connectivity to the Internet to support the devices at the school, along with secure guest access (e.g., for parents or visitors). The school may have wired or wireless connectivity (or both). Desktop computers may connect to Ethernet wall jacks. Laptops and other handheld devices will require robust wireless connectivity.

Devices

In classrooms, students and teachers may have access to desktop or laptop computers; handheld computing devices (e.g., graphing calculators, tablets, and data collection probes for STEM activities); display and imaging hardware (e.g., interactive white-boards, digital projectors, and scanners); peripheral input or output devices with USB or FireWire connections (e.g., monitors, printers, keyboards, video cameras, and DVD drives); and external storage devices or cloud storage (e.g., hard drives, USB flash "thumb" drives, Google Drive, or Box). Each school arranges access to devices differently, based on the instructional goals and needs of students and teachers. Some common arrangements include the following:

- **Innovation Station:** A moveable or stationary table with a touchscreen control panel for a computer or laptop, a document camera, a mounted projector, and a display screen. The station may also have microphone or speaker inputs/outputs and auxiliary inputs. The innovation station is primarily for technology-supported, whole-class lectures or demonstrations.
- **The One-Computer Classroom:** A teacher may have one computer or tablet in the classroom. A desktop computer is usually situated on the teacher's desk and supports the teacher's work—e.g., recording attendance, grading, creating materials, or showing digital materials on a projector. A tablet or laptop enables the teacher to allow a small group of students, or an individual student, to use the computer.
- **Classroom Computers:** If three or more computers are available, a teacher can set them up as a center so small groups of students, or an individual student, can cycle through teacher-designed activities. To support small group activities, the computers should be far enough apart to allow several students to gather around each computer.
- **Mobile Carts:** Teachers may share a mobile cart of devices such as laptops, tablets, or graphing calculators, possibly with enough for each student to have access to a device. Because the cart is shared, teachers must coordinate with each other to use the cart. Also, the devices need to be charged after prolonged use; typically, a cart has a multi-device charging station that allows charging of all devices simultaneously.
- **Computer Laboratories:** A computer lab may be placed centrally in a school and offer access to desktop computers. Teachers must schedule time to use the lab. A school may designate a lab for special curricular uses—e.g., for computer science (programming, game design, etc.), business or vocational education, music creation, and language learning.
- **Student-Supplied Devices:** Some schools allow students to Bring Your Own Device (BYOD), such as laptops, tablets, phones, or external drives. This approach can supplement school-based devices, but challenges arise such as different software on devices or technical problems with student-owned devices. Also, not all students have access to their own devices.
- **School-Supplied One-to-One Computing:** Some schools are beginning to provide one device, such a laptop or tablet, for each student. One device for each student allows for a wide range of technology integration options—from whole-class simultaneous independent work to small group collaboration.

Accessibility

A school must ensure that its digital infrastructure is accessible—that technological resources have a range of features that enable all students, regardless of disability, learning needs, or geographic location, to engage in technology-supported learning. For example, school and classroom websites should use alternative text for images. "Alt text" explains what images look like in words and can be read by screen readers so that students with visual impairments have the same access to content as sighted students. Links should be made more apparent for students with colorblindness. Videos should be closed-captioned for students with hearing impairments.

Resources

A school should have various resources to support schoolwide technology integration into teaching and learning. Human resources should include an IT specialist who can

Video Example 12.5

Technology Facilitator as a Resource: This technology facilitator talks about her responsibilities as a technology resource for teachers.

fix technical problems such as a virus-infected computer, a jammed printer, or broken tablet screen and a technology integration specialist who can help teachers integrate technology into their teaching. In addition, a school should have **productivity software**, **instructional software**, and easy access to **web-based educational content**. These resources enable teachers and students to become active *communicators, collaborators, designers, creators*, and *makers*. For instance, they can develop multimodal representations of content knowledge; digitally publish stories or make books; create audio or video productions; design game apps or immersive virtual reality (VR) or augmented reality (AR); or develop computer programs.

PRODUCTIVITY SOFTWARE Students and teachers can use productivity software for the following activities: (a) writing and publishing; (b) representing ideas textually, visually, and auditorially; (c) collecting and analyzing data; and (d) planning and organizing. In addition, teachers can use productivity software for assessing student learning. Figure 12.9 presents examples of productivity software currently available.

Figure 12.9: Examples of productivity software

Writing and Publishing	Representing Ideas	Collecting and Analyzing Data	Planning and Organizing	Assessing Learning
• MS Word • Google Docs • Pages • MS Publisher • Canva • iBooks Author	• KidPix • Google Drawings • Photoshop • Freepix • Animation Factory • Picktochart • Canva Infographics • Tableau • MS PowerPoint • google Slides • Prezi • PearDeck	• Google Forms • Survey Monkey • MS Excel • Google Sheets • Numbers • SPSS • R • FileMaker • MS Access • Graphing Calculator • Plotly • Graph Club 2.0	• CorePlanner • Planboard • PlanbookEdu • Google Calender • Calendly • Remind • Doodle • LucidChart • Kidspiration • Inspiration • SmartDraw • Venn Diagram • Bubbl.us • Learning Management Systems(LMS) • Google Classroom • Canvas • Blackboard	• Kahoot! • Socrative • iRespond • Quizlet • Easy TestMaker • RubiStar • iReady • Compass Learning • SeeSaw • Mahara • LiveBinder • Google Sites • eduClipper • PowerSchool • Synergy

Classroom Example: Google Voice Recordings and Mobile Learning for Oral Language Skill Development and Assessment

Mr. Atkins realizes that his middle school beginning Spanish students are not developing sufficient oral language skills. He wants to create ways to support authentic oral language practice and assessment. Mr. Atkins's school supports mobile learning (often termed *m-learning*)—that is, students use mobile technologies to enhance their learning. Since all his students have mobile phones, Mr. Atkins sets up a Google Voice phone number and asks his students to call it to record Spanish-language passages they read aloud. Mr. Atkins then downloads the recordings, syncs them with a digital tablet, and listens to them after school hours to assess students' skill development. He also conducts a monthly, mobile phone-based scavenger hunt with his students. He divides each class into teams of four students and sends them oral clues (via phone) in Spanish.

Classroom Example: Digital Portfolios for Creative Work

Ms. Vacarro, a high school art teacher, has students submit their work to her for assessment. However, she believes they would be more motivated if they had portfolios for their artwork, like professional artists. Ms. Vacarro shares her thoughts with other art teachers, as well as a few English teachers, and they agree. Together, they work with the technology specialist and select a web-based portfolio service that will accommodate students' creative work in image, video, audio, and document formats.

INSTRUCTIONAL SOFTWARE Instructional software commonly includes drill and practice, tutorials, simulations, games or gamification (using video game design and game elements to motivate students), problem solving, and personalized learning. Figure 12.10 presents examples of instructional software currently available.

Figure 12.10: Examples of instructional software

Drill and Practice	Tutorials	Simulations	Games and Gamification	Problem-Solving	Personalized Learning
• BrainPop • Chemistry Formulas • Name the Note (Music) • Typing • Buzz Math • All About Ratios (Cynthia Lanius website)	• Typesy • Edgeunity • Cognitive Tutor • Trigonometry Challenge • Laws of Motion • MathSpring Math Tutor • PLATO • Edmentum • The Constitution • Practica Musica	• BeeSmart (NetLogo Models Library) • SimAnimals • SimCity • BioLab Fly • Digital Frog 2 • Vfrog • Stock Market Simulation • Motion Math: Pizza! • SimCalc • Crisis at Fort Sumter	• First in Math • Illuminations • Lure of the Labyrinth • Minecraft • Satisfraction • Dig-IT! Games • Quest Atlantis • River City • Alien Rescue • My Spanish Coach • Oregon Trail • Crystals of Kador • iCivics • PBS Kids	• Math Explorer • Crazy Machines • Memory challenge • Geometer's Sketchpad • Cognitive Tutor • Flossville Town Park (Thinkport) • Cogmed RoboMemo • Sequences	• ALEKS • Dreambox • iStation • edmemtum • Amplify • Knewton • ThinkCERCA • Lexia Learning Core5 • Renaissance Learning • Edgeunity • Read 180 • Scientific Learning Reading Assistant • Achieve 3000 • iReady

Classroom Example: Using Mathematical Simulations to Examine the Distributive Property

Ms. McGarry, a third-grade teacher, knows that her students have little interest in understanding mathematical principles. They usually complete worksheets correctly, but they are unable to explain the mathematical principles that enable them to arrive at correct answers. Ms. McGarry decides to design a lesson using the PhET interactive simulations from the University of Colorado. Her lesson enables students to use the Area Builder simulation to visualize the distributive property in mathematical reasoning. The simulation allows students to build rectangles and see how a rectangle with sides a and $b + c$ is the sum of a x b and a x c, which was a problem on an earlier worksheet. (McGarry & Perkins, 2018)

Classroom Example: Becoming Lawyers to Apply the Constitution and Bill of Rights to Everyday Issues

Mr. Sanchez just finished teaching the U.S. Constitution and the Bill of Rights in his bilingual class; however, he believes students may not understand that, at times, the Constitution must be consulted to ensure the people's rights. To give his students experience with contemporary interpretations of the law, he groups students into dyads and has each group play the "Do I Have a Right?" game on the iCivics website. Students can choose if they want to play the game in Spanish or English.

In the game, the student teams are lawyers who take cases from people who have issues with their rights. If the lawyers win their cases, their law firm can grow.

To help you evaluate instructional software resources, Figure 12.11 presents criteria for evaluating software programs.

Figure 12.11 Criteria for evaluating software programs

	Poor	Fair	Excellent
User Friendliness			
How easy is it to start the program?	☐	☐	☐
Is there an overview or site map for the program?	☐	☐	☐
Can students easily control the pace of the program?	☐	☐	☐
Can students exit the program easily?	☐	☐	☐
Can students create their own paths through the program and develop their own links among elements?	☐	☐	☐
After first-time use, can students bypass introductory or orientation material?	☐	☐	☐
Does the program include useful hotlinks to Internet sites?	☐	☐	☐
Inclusiveness			
Can students with hearing or visual impairments make full use of the program?	☐	☐	☐
Can students navigate the program by making simple keystrokes with one hand?	☐	☐	☐
Does the material avoid stereotypes and reflect sensitivity to racial, cultural, and gender differences?	☐	☐	☐
Textual Material			
How accurate and thorough is the content?	☐	☐	☐
Is the content well organized and clearly presented?	☐	☐	☐
Is the textual content searchable?	☐	☐	☐
Can the content be integrated into the curriculum?	☐	☐	☐
Images			
Is the image resolution high quality?	☐	☐	☐
Is the layout attractive, user friendly, and uncluttered?	☐	☐	☐
Do the graphics and colors enhance instruction?	☐	☐	☐
How true are the colors of the images?	☐	☐	☐
Are the images large enough?	☐	☐	☐
Does the program have a zoom feature that indicates the power of magnification?	☐	☐	☐
Does the program make effective use of video and animation?	☐	☐	☐
Audio			
Are the audio clips high quality?	☐	☐	☐
Does the audio enhance instruction?	☐	☐	☐
Technical			
Is installation of the program easy and trouble-free?	☐	☐	☐
Are instructions clear and easy to follow?	☐	☐	☐
Is user-friendly online help available?	☐	☐	☐
Are technical support people easy to reach, helpful, and courteous?	☐	☐	☐
Motivational			
Does the program capture and hold students' interest?	☐	☐	☐
Are students eager to use the program again?	☐	☐	☐
Does the program give appropriate, motivational feedback?	☐	☐	☐
Does the program provide prompts or cues to promote students' learning?	☐	☐	☐

WEB-BASED EDUCATIONAL CONTENT Teachers can draw from a vast storehouse of web-based educational content to enrich their teaching. They can access live web content that allows students to learn from experts. They can use interactive or immersive web-based content such as simulations; virtual field trip; and virtual, augmented, or mixed-reality environments.

One form of web-based content is **open educational resources** (OER)—free digital resources that are in the public domain. OER content includes videos, e-textbooks, images, graphics, photographs, assessments and tests, infographics, games, lectures, lesson plans, podcasts or vodcasts (video podcasts), and courses. Some states, like **WISCONSIN**, sponsor the WISELearn educator portal for OER content.

Figure 12.12 presents examples of currently available web-based content that is archived, interactive or immersive, and live.

Figure 12.12: Examples of web-based content

Archived Content	Interactive or Immersive Content	Live Content
• Library of Congress Digital Colletions • HippoCampus-Homework and Study Help • WISELearn Poetal • Wikimedia Commons • CK-12 • NASA PubSpace • PBS • Curriki • Khan Academy • Wikiveresity • YouTube • SchoolTube • TeacherTube • Vimeo • TED Talks • Utah's Open Textbook Projects • National Science Digital Library (NSF) • STEM Education Resource Center (PBS) • Multimedia Educational Resource for Learning and Online Teaching (MERLOT)	• PhET Simulations • National Gallery of Art-NGAkids Art Zone • Web-based Inquiry Science Environment (WISE) • Falstad.com Simulations • Google Expeditions • Visit the Moon • U.S. White House Virtual Tour • Smithsonian Museum Virtual Tours • EcoMUVE • Google Earth VR • New Yark Times VR • YouTube 360 videos • SpaceCraft 3D • National Center for Virtual Manipulatives	• Skype • Google Hangouts • Zoom • Webinato • Adobe Connect • ePals • Adventure Learning • AL@[local variations] • Rocks Around the World • iNaturalist • Webcam feeds

Classroom Example: Using Live Video to Examine Animal Habitats

Ms. Conn, a first-grade teacher, wanted her students to observe animal habitats, but their school was located in a dense urban setting and it was difficult to find sustained evidence of animal habitats. She investigated web-based resources and found several live webcams on explore.org. Using a mobile set of tablets, her students were able to research an animal of their choice by viewing a live feed for a few minutes each day for several weeks to identify and track animal behavior and note habitat characteristics. Her students used writing and drawing apps and additional research to create a final report. (Conn, 2013)

Classroom Example: Adopting and Teaching a Course Using Open Curriculum

Mrs. Banari is, by all accounts, obsessed with computers. She wanted her high school students to become passionate about computers and STEM. She offered elective computer science and advanced mathematics courses for several years, but more high-ability students became interested, and she needed to expand her course offerings to satisfy the demand for advanced STEM coursework. After visiting the MIT OpenCourseWare site, she decided to offer one of the MIT courses, Mathematics for Computer Science, as an elective. Students who signed up for the course knew about MIT's highly ranked programs and were eager to test their abilities at this advanced level. She was able to use the syllabus, some recorded lectures, and the activities to guide her class.

Figure 12.13 presents several areas to consider when evaluating content on websites.

Figure 12.13 Criteria for evaluating content on websites

	Poor	Fair	Excellent
Authoritativeness			
The author(s) are respected authorities in the field.	☐	☐	☐
The author(s) are knowledgeable.	☐	☐	☐
The author(s) provide a list of credentials and/or educational background.	☐	☐	☐
The author(s) represent respected, credible institutions or organizations.	☐	☐	☐
Complete information on references (or sources) is provided.	☐	☐	☐
Information for contacting the author(s) and webmaster is provided.	☐	☐	☐
Comprehensiveness			
All facets of the subject are covered.	☐	☐	☐
Sufficient detail is provided at the site.	☐	☐	☐
Information provided is accurate.	☐	☐	☐
Political, ideological, and other biases are not evident.	☐	☐	☐
Presentation			
Graphics serve an educational, rather than decorative, purpose.	☐	☐	☐
Links are provided to related sites.	☐	☐	☐
What icons stand for is clear and unambiguous.	☐	☐	☐
The website loads quickly.	☐	☐	☐
The website is stable and seldom, if ever, nonfunctional.	☐	☐	☐
Timeliness			
The original website was produced recently.	☐	☐	☐
The website is updated and/or revised regularly.	☐	☐	☐
Links given at the website are up to date and reliable.	☐	☐	☐

RESOURCES FOR COMMUNICATION, COLLABORATION, DESIGN, CREATION, AND MAKING Web-based resources have emerged that open up opportunities for young learners to participate and to create content that can be shared publicly on the web, as appropriate. Teachers have used web-based resources in the classroom to provide the following opportunities for communication, collaboration, design, creation, and making:

- Connect with students and/or parents by using communication technologies.
- Create a classroom blog that allows students to publish their writing for authentic, external audiences
- Share learning activities (without photos of students) with a class hashtag (#) on Twitter.
- Learn from experts and peers around the globe.
- Create student portfolios.
- Support multimodal expression by students through digital presentations, publishing, storytelling, and filmmaking.
- Use a design process to develop game apps.
- Build computational thinking skills through computer programming, robotics, or building virtual or augmented reality.
- Tinker, experiment, and build physical things in a makerspace.

Figure 12.14 lists various resources for web-based communication, collaboration, creation, design, and making.

Figure 12.14 Resources for web-based communication, collaboration, creation, design, and making

Communication	Collaboration	Creation, Design, and Making
• Email	• Blogs	• GoAnimate
• Listservs	• Microblogs	• Prezi
• Instant messaging	• Twitter	• VoiceThread
• Text messaging	• Instagram	• NearPod
• Videoconferences	• Tumblr	• Explain Everything
	• FlipBoard	• StoryKit app
	• Pinterest	• KidPup
	• Wikis	• iBooks Author
	• Wikispaces	• BookCreator
	• FaceBook	• iMovie
	• Ning	• GarageBand
	• Edmodo	• Audacity
		• HP Reveal
		• Computer programming
		• Scratch
		• Robotics

Classroom Example: Leveraging Digital Literacies for Social Justice

Ms. Carrion wanted to design multimodal learning activities linked to local and global social issues that her fifth-grade students hear about in the news and in their communities. Ultimately, she wanted students to care about the wider world, learn from others, and become change agents for themselves and their community. When the topic of police brutality touched their Bronx, **NEW YORK** community, she had students explore the topic by gathering local news stories and posting them on Flipboard and designing interactive glogs (i.e., graphic images similar to posters) using Glogster to share information with their community. (Price-Dennis & Carrion, 2017)

Classroom Example: Podcasting for Review of Content

Mr. Pendergrass realized that many students asked him repeated questions about the content he presented during his lectures and demonstrations in his advanced-placement (AP) chemistry class. He believed his time might be better spent if he provided students with individual guidance during hands-on chemistry experiments, rather than merely repeating the same content. So, he began podcasting his lectures. He clipped a small wireless microphone onto his lapel at the beginning of each class period. The microphone was connected to his computer, allowing the audio to be recorded into Audacity. His lectures and responses to students' questions were recorded into a digital audio file. After each class, Mr. Pendergrass listened to the audio and edited out any long periods of silence. He then published each file to his podcasting site. Students could then listen to the material he presented during each class session or download it and listen later.

Digital Resources for Subject Areas

As the previous classroom examples suggest, the Internet contains a vast array of free, high-quality learning materials to use in your teaching. The following sections provide a brief sampling of the myriad ways these materials can be used in different subject areas.

THE FINE ARTS The fine arts—art, music, theater, and dance—offer numerous opportunities to integrate technology into the classroom. Teachers have used technology in the fine arts classroom to provide students with opportunities to:

- view famous pieces of art in museums around the world.
- create and share compilations of art, music, theater, and dance.
- view legendary performances by various fine artists.
- experience diverse cultural styles of the fine arts.
- express themselves artistically.
- share ideas and thoughts about the fine arts with others.

Classroom Example: Sectional or Individual Practice with Musical Accompaniment

In music, the opportunity to practice one's part with accompaniment can be limited, especially in smaller schools with fewer musicians. Technology, however, can be used to facilitate sectional or individual practice without the need for human accompaniment. For example, notation software, such as Sibelius and Finale, make it possible for musicians to perform while parts of the score are silenced.

Video Example 12.6

Point of View with Voki: A teacher has asked students to create an online character using a web-based tool, Voki. Students will create a character from a book they are reading and put words in the character's mouth to demonstrate that they understand the story from that character's perspective. The students are engaged in sharing what they have been working on with their peers.

LANGUAGE ARTS Language arts—reading, writing, oral communication—offer many opportunities for teachers to integrate technology. Language arts teachers have used technology in the classroom to:

- access great works of literature from special or rare book digital collections.
- show students videos of famous speeches.
- improve student writing by using online writing labs.
- combat plagiarism by using online plagiarism detection programs.
- access hard-to-find journals.
- improve students' word recognition and pronunciation by using animation and audio.
- increase students' reading comprehension by using audio textbooks or e-books.
- facilitate multimodal literacy by engaging students in digital storytelling or video game design.

Classroom Example: Developing a Class Movie to Emphasize Good Reading Strategies

Ms. Landeros wanted her students to identify themselves as readers by examining their own good practices. She facilitated the creation of *Good Readers*, a movie produced by a first-grade class at Highland Ranch Elementary School in San Diego, **CALIFORNIA**. It is a powerful example of technology integration in the language arts classroom. The teacher divided students into teams, each of which included a cinematographer, a director, and a spokesperson. Each student was given an opportunity to try out each role. During the week, each team wrote a script that highlighted the six strategies of "good readers." Then, students learned to speak their lines loudly and clearly while being filmed. After filming, students edited the raw footage using a video editing program. Making the film about "good readers" enabled students to "see" good reading strategies in action; as a result, they became better readers themselves (Poway Unified School District, 2008).

MATHEMATICS Technology has been a part of mathematics for centuries—from the abacus to the supercomputer. Mathematicians have long relied on technology to help solve complex problems. Similarly, mathematics teachers have integrated technology into their teaching to:

- help students understand numerical relationships.
- do math calculations such as addition, subtraction, multiplication, and division; find the square root; and solve trigonometry functions and linear equations.

- help students estimate and measure.
- help students deal with the symbolic manipulations needed in algebra and calculus.
- reduce student anxiety about memorizing complex formulas in geometry and trigonometry.
- help students understand more complex mathematical concepts and ideas.
- allow for the application of mathematical solutions to real-world problems.

Classroom Example: Organizing Mathematics Learning Materials in Google Classroom

Ms. Stone teaches solid geometry at the local high school, and over the years students would lose handouts and materials, leading to numerous questions and inquiries. With their new iPads, her students have 24/7 access to the class website on Google Classroom. The site includes links to podcasts and notes from her in-class lectures, video clips on related topics, and information about assignments and exams. Ms. Stone also gives multiple-choice quizzes on iPads, which automatically calculate scores and give students immediate feedback on their knowledge of content.

SCIENCE Science teachers from the elementary through high school levels have made extensive use of technology in the classroom. Technology integration has enabled them to:

- tour the solar system with students.
- become miniaturized and travel throughout the human body.
- visit the ocean floor.
- experience an earthquake.
- see the schematics of a human cell.
- collect local data using data loggers, analyze it, and submit it to global "citizen science" projects.

Classroom Example: Jet Propulsion Lab SpaceCraft 3D app and Robotics Design

Ms. Gonzales has been teaching her science students a unit on designing and developing robots. Since her students seem puzzled for design ideas, she decides to expose them to real spacecraft rovers that have explored our universe. Borrowing a mobile cart of iPads, she has the SpaceCraft 3D app, created by the Jet Propulsion Lab, installed. The app uses augmented reality and allows students to examine closely the robotic explorers and better understand their engineering design features. This close examination enables students to generate ideas for their own robots.

SOCIAL STUDIES Social studies teachers have used technology to explore economics, geography, political science, psychology, and sociology. For example, social studies teachers have used technology to:

- allow students to be floor traders on the Wall Street stock market.
- enable students to become a leader of a state and understand how their political decisions affect the countries they lead.
- cope with the poverty, hunger, and political corruption that characterize the lives of people in many developing countries.
- examine important primary source documents from different historical periods.
- help students experience how crime and violence affect the lives of victims.

Classroom Example: Experiencing the Israeli-Palestinian Conflict through a Video Game

Mrs. Muralia's students have been studying the Israeli–Palestinian conflict for the past week. They read the textbook, watched a video, listened to historical speeches online, researched articles and current events, and discussed the situation in class.

However, it was not until students experienced a video game that allowed them to role-play various characters in this historical conflict that they understood how complex and difficult the situation is. In the video game, students assumed roles of the Israeli prime minister, local Palestinian political leaders, Israeli settlers, Palestinians working in Gaza, or Israeli soldiers. Each student's role called for an action followed by a reaction, followed by another action, and so on. Allowing students to navigate through this complex political landscape in various roles enabled them to begin to think critically and to understand the various points of view that make up the Israeli–Palestinian situation.

What Does Research Say About Technology Integration And Student Learning?

The integration of technology into teaching and learning has grown enormously since the early 1990s. Now, teachers and other educators want to know if technology integration enhances student learning. Regarding the effects of technology on learning, research results are just now beginning to appear. However, as one observer noted, "Technology integration can be one of the most challenging topics to find quality research on. The term itself is a broad umbrella for numerous practices that may have little in common with each other. In addition, technology tools change rapidly, and outcomes can vary depending on implementation" (Vega, 2013).

Technology's Negative Effects on Students

Some research studies have suggested that technology may have a negative effect on students' ability to focus on learning tasks. For example, the Pew Research Center's Internet & American Life Project (2012) analyzed data from more than 2,400 teachers and concluded:

> Overwhelming majorities . . . agree with the assertions that "today's digital technologies are creating an easily distracted generation with short attention spans" (87%) and "today's students are too 'plugged in' and need more time away from their digital technologies" (86%). Two-thirds (64%) agree with the notion that "today's digital technologies do more to distract students than to help them academically." (p. 7)

An expert in the "psychology of technology," Larry Rosen (2013), makes similar points in his book *iDisorder: Understanding Our Obsession with Technology and Overcoming Its Hold on Us*. According to Rosen, "iDisorder" can change the brain's ability to process information and even lead to psychological disorders, such as stress, sleeplessness, and a compulsive need to monitor technological devices. "What we are looking at is a new disorder, one that combines elements of many psychiatric maladies and is centered on the way we all relate to technology and media: an iDisorder" (p. 4).

Rosen and his research team observed 263 middle school, high school, and university students studying during a 15-minute period in their homes. The researchers wanted to find out if students could maintain focus, and, if not, what distracted them. Rosen and his team found that "these students were only able to stay on task for an average of three to five minutes before losing their focus. Universally, their distractions came from technology, including: (1) having more devices available in their studying environment such as iPods, laptops, and smart phones; (2) texting; and (3) accessing

Facebook." Additionally, the researchers found that "[t]he worst students were those who consumed more media each day and had a preference for switching back and forth between several tasks at the same time." Moreover, the researchers were "stunned" to find that "[i]f the students checked Facebook just once during the 15-minute study period, they had a lower grade-point average. It didn't matter how many times they looked at Facebook; once was enough" (Rosen, 2012).

The American Academy of Pediatrics points out that technology can have other negative effects on today's youth. These effects include weight gain; less sleep; exposure to unsafe information or people; and loss of privacy, security, and confidentiality. The Academy recommends that parents and pediatricians work together to create a Family Media Use Plan (AAP Council on Communications and Media, 2016).

In addition, an article titled "Have Smartphones Destroyed a Generation?" suggests that technology can have a negative effect on teenagers' mental health. The author notes that teenagers are spending more time in their homes, and those who spend more time than average on screen activities are more likely to be unhappy, experience depression, and sleep less. These trends "have affected young people in every corner of the nation and in every type of household. The trends appear among teens poor and rich; of every ethnic background; in cities, suburbs, and small towns" (Twenge, 2017).

Findings from Multiple Research Studies

A powerful way to determine whether certain educational practices actually influence students' learning is to conduct meta-analyses, that is, to "take the findings from single studies and calculate a way to compare them with each other. The goal is to synthesize the findings statistically and determine what the studies reveal when examined all together" (Cuban & Kirkpatrick, 1998). In addition, meta-analyses address the complications and difficulties involved in determining the effects of computers on learning, particularly when much of the research in that area has been shown to be methodologically flawed. For example, research studies of technology integration "are of little use unless they elaborate the children's ages, the subject, the software used, the kinds of outcomes that were sought, and how the study was done."

One of the largest meta-analytic studies of online learning was conducted by the U.S. Department of Education (2009, May). The study, titled *Evaluation of Evidence-Based Practices in Online Learning: A Meta-Analysis and Review of Online Learning Studies*, sought to compare the effectiveness of online learning with face-to-face instruction. Surprisingly, on its first review of research published between 1996 and 2006, the Department of Education team found *no rigorously conducted studies* comparing K–12 online learning with face-to-face instruction. A second review of research, this time through 2008, evaluated more than 1,000 studies of online learning. However, the review identified only five K–12 studies and 44 studies of undergraduate and older learners that met the criteria for quality.

The analysis of these studies found that "on average, students in online learning conditions performed better than those receiving face-to-face instruction" (U.S. Department of Education, 2009, May, p. xiv). However, because the results were based largely on older learners, the research report urged "caution" in applying the results to K–12 settings. In fact, the report stated that "without new random assignment or controlled quasi-experimental studies of the effects of online learning options for K–12 students, policymakers will lack scientific evidence of the effectiveness of these emerging alternatives to face-to-face instruction" (U.S. Department of Education, 2009, May, p. xvii).

The results of several additional meta-analytic studies of integrating technology into education are presented in the following.

- **A Meta-Analysis of the Effects of Computer Technology on School Students Mathematics Learning**—This meta-analytic study found generally positive impacts of technology on K–12 students' math learning. Stronger effects were found for students with special needs and elementary, rather than secondary, students. The greatest effects were found when teachers used constructivist, rather than traditional teaching methods (Li & Ma, 2010).

- **What Forty Years of Research Says About the Impact of Technology on Learning: A Second-Order Meta-Analysis and Validation Study**—This study examined 25 meta-analyses that encompassed more than 1,000 studies. Results indicate that the use of technology has a small to moderate positive effect on student learning. Greater effects were linked to using technology to support knowledge formation rather than using technology to present content. Teacher effectiveness and technology skills may have a greater effect on student learning than the type of technology used (Tamim, Bernard, Borokhovski, Abrami, & Schmid, 2011).
- **The Effectiveness of Educational Technology Applications for Enhancing Reading Achievement in K–12 Classrooms: A Meta-Analysis**—This meta-analysis focused on 84 well-designed studies that included more than 60,000 K–12 students. The largest effects on reading achievement were found for approaches that integrated computer and noncomputer instruction (for example, *READ 180*, *Voyager Passport*, and *Writing to Read*) and included extensive professional development for teachers. For example, in *READ 180* classrooms, "Each period begins with a 20-minute shared reading and skills lesson, and then students in groups of five rotate among three activities: computer-assisted instruction in reading, modeled or independent reading, and small-group instruction with the teacher" (Cheung & Slavin, 2012, p. 19). This meta-analysis also confirmed previous research and found that supplemental computer-assisted programs to augment regular classroom instruction (for example, *Destination Reading*, *Plato Focus*, *Waterford Early Reading Program*, *Headsprout*, *Academy of Reading*, and *LeapTrack*) did not show meaningful effects on reading achievement for K–12 students (Cheung & Slavin, 2011).
- **What Is Our Current Understanding of One-to-One Computer Projects?: A Systematic Narrative Research Review**—This research focused on research studies of 1:1 computer projects in school settings during a five-year period. Generally, laptops were used for searching and exploration (for example, physics simulations), student expression (student presentations and written reports using PowerPoint and Word), communication (e-mail, discussion boards, and instant messaging [IM], between students and between students and teachers), and organization (for example, OneNote). Studies found that laptops tended to improve student motivation and engagement in learning. The use of laptops "slightly improved" students' writing and technology skills, and "very slightly improved" students' scores on high-stakes tests (Fleischer, 2012).
- **Our Princess Is in Another Castle: A Review of Trends in Serious Gaming for Education**—According to the researchers, digital learning games "target the acquisition of knowledge as its own end, and foster habits of mind and understanding that are generally useful within an academic context." The researchers found "promising but inconclusive" evidence that games promote learning in some K–12 settings. The strongest effects on learning were found for language-learning video games, physical education and tactile video games (for example, *Wii* video games), and history video games (for example, role-playing video games). The review found little support for gaming in science and mathematics (Young et al., 2012).
- **The Effectiveness of Educational Technology Applications for Enhancing Mathematics Achievement in K–12 Classrooms**—This meta-analysis focused on 74 well-designed studies that included more than 56,000 K–12 students. Results revealed that computer applications have a small but positive effect on

math achievement. Math programs (for example, *Jostens*, *PLATO*, *Larson Pre-Algebra*, and *SRA Drill and Practice*) based on individual needs and offered as a supplement to traditional instruction had greater effects on math achievement (at all grade levels) if used for more than 30 minutes a week (Cheung & Slavin, 2013).

- **Learning in One-to-One Laptop Environments: A Meta-Analysis and Research Synthesis**—The researchers found that one-to-one laptop programs had a positive impact across reading, writing, English, math, and science. In addition, students developed more control of their learning, and teachers had more ability to individualize instruction. However, the researchers point out that, in many schools, the positive impact did not begin until at least the second year of program implementation (Zheng, Warschauer, Lin, & Chang, 2016).
- **Advantages and Challenges Associated with Augmented Reality for Education: A Systematic Review of the Literature**—This review of 68 studies found that augmented reality (AR) enhanced students' learning outcomes (e.g., achievement, motivation, and attitudes); increased enjoyment, engagement, and interest; and provided more opportunities for student–student interaction. However, the review also concluded that AR is difficult for students to use and resulted in frequent technical problems (Akçayır & Akçayır, 2017).

Research studies such as the preceding indicate that technology *can have* modest, positive effects on students' learning. As more funds are made available to purchase advanced technologies and software, train teachers, and provide technical support, these effects will, no doubt, become even stronger.

Although research has yet to support the hype that surrounded the integration of technology into teaching during the early 1990s, technology will influence all aspects of education even more in the future. Thus, researchers should pose not just a single question about educational technology—Is it effective? Instead, multiple questions should be posed. Answers to questions such as the following will enable educators to understand how and under what circumstances educational technology can powerfully enhance students' learning: In what educational settings is educational technology most effective? For which students is educational technology most effective? For attaining what educational purposes is educational technology most effective? For teachers with what styles of teaching is educational technology most effective?

What are the Challenges of Integrating Technology Into Teaching?

In 2018, the CEO of the International Society for Technology in Education (ISTE) and former head of the U.S. Department of Education's Office of Educational Technology suggested that U.S. education is at a "tipping point" regarding technology integration. He foresaw two possible futures:

> In one scenario, we'll have technology that essentially duplicates what we've traditionally done: Deliver content in front of the room, now we'll deliver it on an app. We log in online to some LMS [learning management system] tool and

> there's a teacher who controls all the options. [The other] is we use technology in a way that transforms learning . . . . Technology [is] used as a tool to design and build and problem-solve.
>
> Both are very real possibilities. [We are at a] tipping point . . . because this is the first year we've really had ubiquitous connectivity in schools across the country. We finally have a situation where we can use technology at scale (Kash, 2018) (https://edscoop.com/why-technology-is-at-a-tipping-point-in-u-s-schools).

Without a doubt, which future unfolds will depend on the degree to which teachers are up to date and proficient in technology integration skills. Using technology to enhance students' learning requires more than investing in the latest hardware, software, and connectivity to the Internet. Conducting classroom demonstrations augmented with multimedia; using digital resources to address students' varied learning styles; and designing lessons that require students to use technology for inquiry should be second nature for teachers.

Technology Training for Teachers

Many school districts have taken steps to encourage teachers to increase their use of technology in the classroom. An example of a district that fosters technology integration is **WASHINGTON** State's Kent School District. At the district's Technology Integration website, teachers can access a variety of resources to use in the classroom and sign up for professional development activities.

Another example of technology support for teachers is the IBM-funded "Reinventing Education" grant program implemented by the **WEST VIRGINIA** and **VERMONT** Departments of Education. Teachers throughout both states can access the Riverdeep Learning Village (RLV), a suite of online applications that support communication and collaboration among teachers, parents, community members, and students. The applications enable teachers to access curriculum content and to create customized lessons and activities based on individual student needs. Through the RLV, parents and guardians can stay informed about their children's academic progress and activities.

Video Example 12.7

Connected Learning: A teacher emphasizes the importance of professional development and collaboration when trying to sort through all the online resources that are now available.

Recently, teachers have increased their technology integration skills by connecting with other teachers. **Connected learning** is a way for teachers to join online learning communities and to use web-based resources. For example, teachers use social networking to learn about short "unconferences" (i.e., informal exchanges of information among participants, rather than conventionally structured conference programs).

Some teachers participate in **professional learning communities (PLCs)**, school-based, face-to-face groups that facilitate technology learning. Some PLCs use videoconferencing to facilitate off-hour collaboration. Other teachers develop a **personal learning network (PLN)**, a professional based network of people selected by the teacher to help him/her pursue learning needs and share knowledge and experiences. Still others participate in **communities of practice (COPs)** organized by a professional organization, such as the International Society for Technology in Education (ISTE). Some COPs are organized by individual teachers and focus on a common interest or topic. For example, Classroom 2.0 uses the Ning online platform to build a community interested in Web 2.0, social media, and participative technologies in the classroom.

In all of these connected learning experiences, teachers use a range of web-based resources to communicate and collaborate, such as blogs, microblogs, social networks, videoconferencing, discussion boards, and curation tools (software used to sort through web content and develop a list of the most informative and useful content which is then shared with a target audience). The Teaching on Your Feet feature in this chapter describes how one teacher values acquiring proficiency and knowledge of technology integration.

Teaching on Your Feet:

Half of Teaching Is Learning

"You have a screen name?" they query in disbelief. Screen name, podcasts, YouTube, Facebook, Instagram, Snapchat . . . this is the jargon of my seventh-grade students. Their world is filled with technology; they accept it—and expect it. They use it to communicate, connect, and create. And they use it constantly and confidently.

Yes, I tell them. I have a screen name . . . It's mrsheebz. I blog, make podcasts, publish online books, and text message. I visit Facebook and YouTube. I use Garageband, Comic Life, Photoshop, and Keynote. I love the world of technology. Of course, my students think I'm kidding when I tell them I grew up with a rotary phone . . . and a black-and-white TV with three stations of snow. No World Wide Web, no cell phones . . . and certainly no computers. But my family did own a typewriter and a complete set of World Book Encyclopedias. I had all the tools necessary to give me an edge in school—then.

Fast-forward 40 years. The typewriter is long gone. Instead my students possess laptops with access to the Internet. It's a powerful tool that gives my kids—and me—an edge on learning.

There is no tool that has changed my teaching practice as much as the laptop. All seventh and eighth graders in the state of Maine have 24/7 access to their own wireless laptops. In 2001, the Maine Learning and Teaching Initiative (MLTI) was voted and approved; as a result, 1 percent of Maine's educational funds was spent on one-to-one computing—a laptop for every seventh grader in the state. The following year, the eighth grade was added, for a total of 35,000 laptops. This was a lofty goal aimed at evening the digital divide by providing the World Wide Web to all students in our largely rural state. This was a true democratic ideal: equal opportunity regardless of economic status. At this time, this initiative was the only program of its kind in the world . . . . Teachers spouted clichés like a potato sprouts eyes: a mixed blessing, throwing money in the wind, a two-edged sword, Christmas in July, can't teach an old dog new tricks. The program was embraced by some teachers, scorned by others. I chose to embrace. To learn. Or at least try to learn. For to teach "is to learn twice" (Joseph Joubert). And that has made all the difference in who I am as a teacher.

Using technology has transformed my curriculum and my teaching style. In particular, one-on-one computing has made the single biggest impact on my 27 years of teaching. My entire belief system has been tested and strengthened not only by the advent, but also by the intrusion of the laptop into my classroom. I'm no longer the expert, the disseminator of all-that-needs-to-be-known. I'm a learner, growing along with my students and along with my colleagues. We are a true community of explorers compelled by the MLTI motto: "If you know how to do it, teach someone else. If you don't know how, ask someone else." It's an energizing environment in which to learn: It's the environment of the connected generation.

I teach seventh-grade language arts in a coastal town in southern Maine. The majority of my students come from professional families who have the ability to travel widely, vacation often, own lovely homes, and pay for higher education. It's a homogeneous community, with poor and minority students few and far between. Ninety-two percent of the families in my district had access to the Internet at home when the MLTI program began, so the digital divide was never a huge issue for my students. Yet access to computers at school for word processing and research had always been minimal. Prior to the laptop program, I'd been lucky to obtain an hour a week in the computer lab for my students. Laptops have given us a portable writing lab, instant access to research, and assistive technology.

My teaching philosophy is simple. I strive to create a democratic classroom—an energetic community of caring people engaged in learning. The laptop is a tool, a powerful communication device that has increased my ability to enact democratic ideals on a daily basis. Engagement, energy, and caring: these are more important to me than the content I teach.

Analyze

Laptop technology has provided multiple ways to create, discover and explore. Students are using their laptops to create movies about global warming and Civil War enactments. They're using software such as Comic Life to design graphic organizers and Keynote to document learning about famous people and places. They are able to visit online museums and talk with Holocaust survivors via videoconferencing. Field trips and service learning are captured with digital cameras and slide shows. Traditional paper-and-pencil tasks have sprung to life with these various programs that appeal in different ways to students and teachers. Many teachers have specialized in particular programs, thereby becoming the "expert down the hall." Learning communities have become much more democratic, with interdependence on others for assistance in learning."

Reflect

1. What does Herbert mean when she says "half of teaching is learning"? Do you agree?
2. Does the use of technology in schools simplify or complicate teachers' lives? Or both? What examples can you give to support your position?

Merry Herbert teaches seventh-grade language arts at a middle school in **MAINE**.

Source: The preceding is excerpted from her contribution to the National Network for Educational Renewal's Teacher Case Story Collection. The Collection is "dedicated to providing a public forum for teachers to share their stories." National Center for Educational Renewal © 2008. Retrieved and adapted from http://nnerpartnerships.org/stories/herbert.html

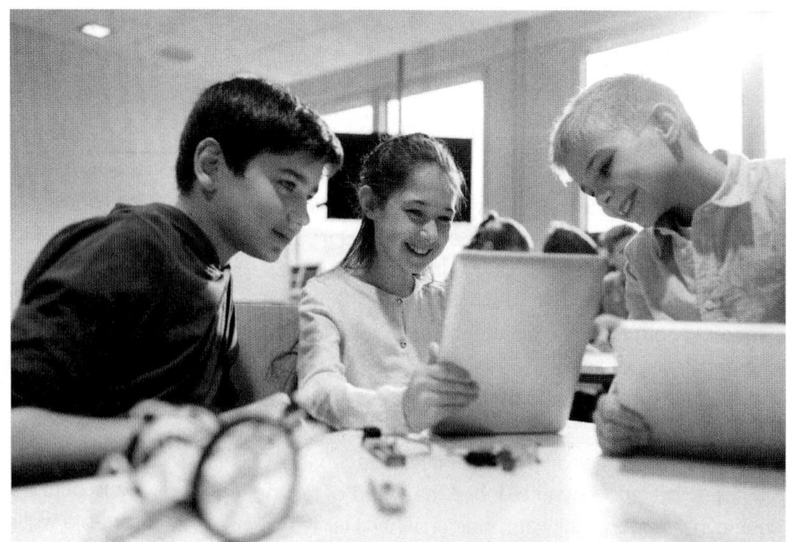
Syda Productions/Shutterstock

These students receive immediate feedback and reinforcement, are more engaged and motivated, and are acquiring important workplace skills by using the latest software programs. Are there any drawbacks to the use of technology in schools?

In response to the uneven quality of professional development and technical support for technology integration, several state departments of education are taking steps to ensure that teachers learn to integrate technology fully into their teaching. About one-third of states require technology training and/or coursework for an initial teacher license, and nine states require a technology test (*Education Week*, 2009).

Also, many teacher education programs have taken innovative steps such as the following to ensure that their graduates possess the ability to integrate technology into the classroom:

- At Washington State University, students develop an online portfolio of literacy strategies that are critiqued by teachers around the state.
- At the University of Virginia, students use the Internet to link with students at 11 other universities to analyze case studies based on commonly occurring problems in classrooms; students also write their own cases and post them on the web.
- At San Diego State University, student teachers, along with classroom teachers and school administrators, participate in a weekly Multimedia Academy taught by university staff and former student teachers.
- At the University of Northern Iowa, students learn from television-mediated observations of "live" classrooms at a pre-K–12 laboratory school and conduct question-and-answer sessions with the laboratory school teachers.
- At Indiana University, students, as well as visitors from around the world, learn about educational technology at the Center for Excellence in Education, a new state-of-the-art facility with 700 computers, an "enhanced technology suite," a building-wide video distribution system, and a two-way video distance-learning classroom.
- At Boise State University, students complete a 15-hour technology fieldwork internship in a public school classroom with a teacher who effectively integrates technology into the curriculum.

Infrastructure for Transformational Learning

In spite of progress in integrating technology into schools, not every school has "a robust and flexible learning infrastructure capable of supporting new types of engagement and providing ubiquitous access to the technology tools that allow students to create, design, and explore" (U.S Department of Education, Office of Educational Technology, 2017, p. 69). The U.S. Department of Education's Office of Educational Technology has identified the following essential components that a school must have to support transformational learning experiences for all students:

- **Ubiquitous connectivity.** Persistent access to high-speed Internet in and out of school
- **Powerful learning devices.** Access to mobile devices that connect learners and educators to the vast resources of the Internet and facilitate communication and collaboration
- **High-quality digital learning content.** Digital learning content and tools that can be used to design and deliver engaging and relevant learning experiences
- **Responsible Use Policies (RUPs).** Guidelines to safeguard students and ensure that the infrastructure is used to support learning

Figure 12.15 illustrates these essential components and points out that Responsible Use Policies (RUPs) address digital citizenship and data privacy and security.

Figure 12.15 Infrastructure to support everywhere, all the time learning

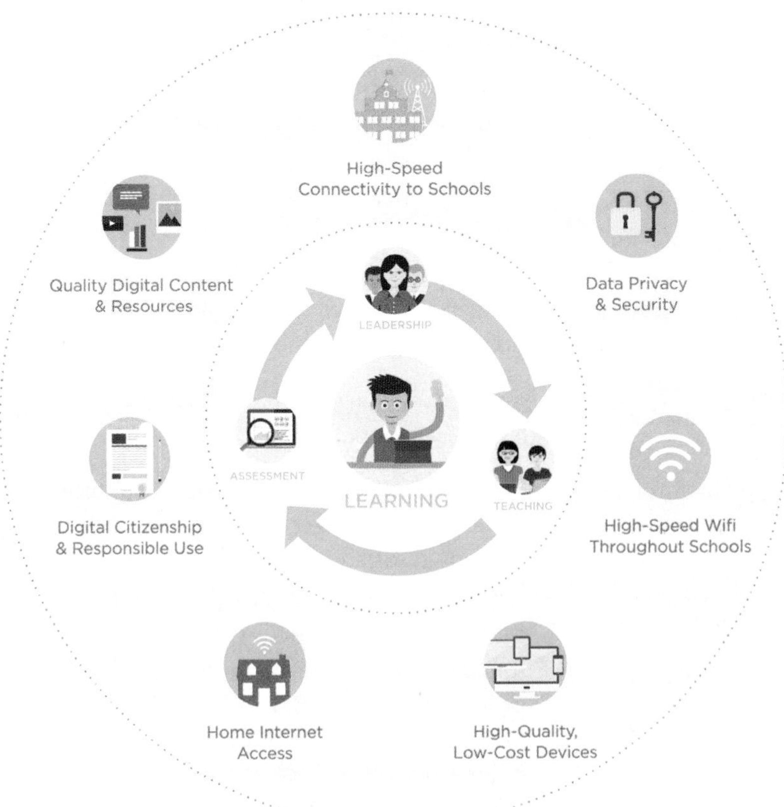

SOURCE: U.S. Department of Education, Office of Educational Technology, *Reimagining the Role of Technology in Education: 2017 National Education Technology Plan Update*, Washington, D.C., 2017, p. 70.

Application 12.2

Determining a District's Infrastructure Status through Focus Questions

Clearly, yet-to-be-invented technologies will impact education during the years to come. As teachers, and others who have an interest in education, prepare for that unknown future, they are becoming more sophisticated in understanding the strengths and limitations of technology as a tool to promote learning. They know full well that, like another educational tool—the book—computers and related digital technologies can be a powerful, almost unlimited medium for instruction and learning, if they carefully reflect on how it will further the attainment of the goals and aspirations they have for their students.

Summary

How Is Technology Transforming Teaching and Learning?

- Today's students have grown up in a technology-rich environment and, with few exceptions, they are more comfortable with technology than their teachers.
- Anywhere, anytime learning is a reality for today's students.
- Many teachers are using blended learning—face-to-face instruction blended with online learning activities.
- Four models of blended learning are Rotation, Flex, A La Carte, and Enriched Virtual.
- Most teachers support the use of digital technologies to promote students' learning and maintain that technology enables them to expand on content, motivate students, and respond to a variety of learning styles.
- The International Society for Technology in Education's (ISTE) Standards for Students call for each student to become a/an Empowered Learner, Digital Citizen, Knowledge Constructor, Innovative Designer, Computational Thinker, Creative Communicator, and Global Collaborator.
- There are two kinds of digital divides: inequitable *access to* technology and inequitable opportunities *to use* technology.
- Students should become active, rather than passive, users of technology.
- Three types or levels of technology integration are *replacement*, *amplification*, and *transformation*.
- Virtual schools and online learning continue to increase.
- Although evidence suggests that virtual schools are not as effective as brick-and-mortar schools, the public is generally supportive of virtual schools.
- In a flipped classroom, students first learn new content at home by watching online videos related to the subject matter, then apply their new knowledge by solving problems or completing "homework" in class, with the teacher providing individual assistance.

What Digital Resources Are Needed to Integrate Technology into Teaching?

- A school's technology infrastructure includes more than hardware; four elements of this infrastructure are connectivity, devices, accessibility, and resources.
- Technology resources include productivity software, instructional software, and web-based educational content.
- Web-based resources can be used for communication, collaboration, design, creation, and making.
- Digital resources for teaching and learning in all academic areas include a vast array of learning objects on the Internet and open-source materials.
- Teachers of students from low income families are more likely to report that their students do not have sufficient access to digital tools both in school and at home.

What Does Research Say About Technology Integration and Student Learning?

- Evidence is beginning to emerge that technology may have a negative effect on students' ability to focus on learning tasks and their mental health.
- A U.S. Department of Education meta-analytic study, *Evaluation of Evidence-Based Practices in Online Learning*, found that students in online learning conditions tend to perform better than those receiving face-to-face instruction—however, most of the studies analyzed were of older learners; thus, the results have limited applicability to K–12 settings.
- Several meta-analytic studies have shown that technology can have modest, positive effects on students' learning.
- Overall, research has yet to support the hype that surrounded the integration of technology into teaching during the early 1990s.

What Are the Challenges of Integrating Technology into Teaching?

- U.S. education is at a "tipping point" regarding technology integration—in one scenario for the future, technology will duplicate what teachers have always done; in the other, technology will transform learning and be used as a tool to design, build, and problem-solve.
- Although classroom Internet access is almost universal, there is evidence that a "digital divide" exists, as low income families are less likely to own and to use advanced technologies.
- Although school district spending on technology training for teachers is often inadequate and the quality of that training uneven, state departments of education, school districts, and individual schools are developing new approaches to providing teachers with support for integrating technology.
- Many teacher education programs have developed innovative approaches to preparing technologically competent teachers. Many teachers, however, still believe they are ill prepared to integrate technology into the curriculum.
- In 2017, the U.S. Department of Education and the Office of Educational Technology released *Reimagining the Role of Technology in Education: 2017 National Education Technology Plan Update* and identified four essential components to support transformational learning experiences for all students: ubiquitous connectivity, powerful learning devices, high-quality digital learning content, and responsible use policies (RUPs).

Professional Reflections and Activities

Teacher's Journal

1. In your opinion, what are the most important benefits of technology for education, and what are its most important drawbacks?
2. A concern voiced by some is that the use of computers and advanced digital technologies in education will lead to a depersonalization of the teacher–student relationship. How valid is this concern?

Teacher's Research

1. With regard to the subject area and grade level for which you are preparing to teach, identify several online resources that you might use in your teaching. Then, in a written narrative, explain how you would use them.
2. Conduct online research on integrating technology into teaching with reference to the grade level and subject area for which you are preparing to teach.

Observations and Interviews

1. Survey teachers at a local school district to determine the educational technologies they use. How and how often are these technologies used for instruction? What is the availability of computers, advanced digital technologies, and software for use by students?
2. Interview two or more teachers at a local elementary, middle, or high school to find out how they integrate technology into their teaching. Ask them to describe their greatest successes at integrating technology. What do they see as the greatest challenges to using technology in the classroom?

Professional Portfolio

Create an e-portfolio that includes at least three resources you developed using three different educational technologies. Include in your e-portfolio a statement that presents two or more principles for effectively integrating these into your teaching.

PART IV
Your Teaching Future

Chapter 13
Becoming a Professional Teacher

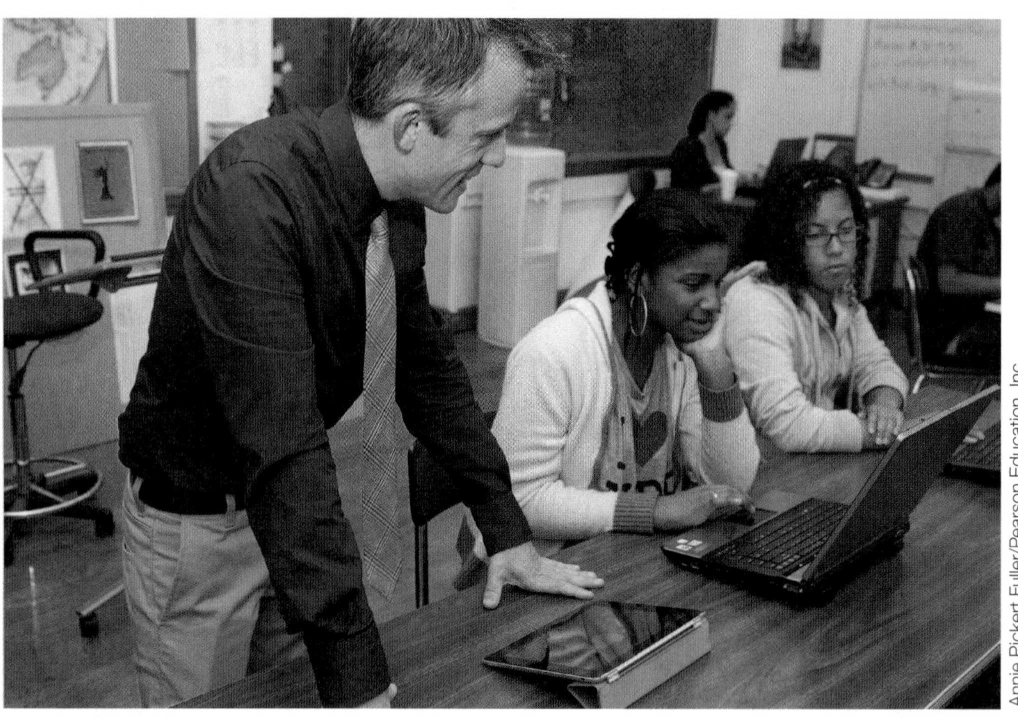

Annie Pickert Fuller/Pearson Education, Inc

Learning Outcomes

After reading this chapter, you will be able to do the following:

13.1 Describe how you can learn from observing in classrooms.

13.2 Explain how you can gain practical experience for becoming a teacher.

13.3 Describe how you can receive support as a beginning teacher.

13.4 Describe the leadership opportunities you will have beyond the classroom.

13.5 Explain how teachers help to build learning communities and participate in teacher collaboration.

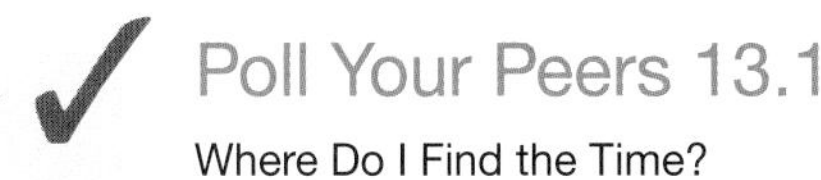

Dear Mentor

Next spring, I will graduate in secondary education with endorsements in biology and basic math. I will look for a teaching position in Seattle, **WASHINGTON**. I plan to substitute or work part-time while obtaining my master's degree in biology. However, I am not sure about the best route to take or how to go about finding the right position. What steps should I take in order for my induction into teaching to be effective?

As I continue through my program, I am finding that things are constantly changing in the teaching profession, and new research findings are always being introduced to teachers. As a teacher, how do you continue to learn and to grow as a professional, as well as continue to connect with your students?

If there is one thing that is consistent in all of my classes, education or otherwise, it is that being a teacher means being a leader and being involved with the community. How does a teacher become a leader and role model to his or her students? How does one become involved not only in teaching, but also in the community?

I appreciate your guidance!

SINCERELY, MONICA HARDING
Used with permission from Monica Harding

Dear Monica

Congratulations on completing your degree in secondary education, and welcome to the most wonderful profession in the world! Being an educator allows you to make a daily difference in the lives of students.

There are several steps you can take to ensure that your induction into teaching is effective. First, surround yourself with positive people at your school. Teaching is difficult and it brings many challenges—thus, you will want to learn from those who look at the glass as "half full," not "half empty." Avoid negative educators. Seek those who are leaders and genuinely love teaching and students. Surround yourself with mentors, administrators, and colleagues who want to grow and learn and are never satisfied with just "getting by."

Growing as a professional is key if you are to become an outstanding educator. At first, you may be overwhelmed as you learn your school's culture, procedures, expectations, and curriculum. Be patient with yourself as you learn about the "real world" of teaching. Ask your colleagues to share articles about new teaching strategies and research about how students learn best. Join an organization that offers professional literature to keep you up-to-date on research and strategies. Join, or start, a book club with your colleagues, and discuss how your new learning can impact your students each day. Remember, graduating from college is not the end of learning; it is truly the beginning.

You are correct, teachers are leaders. All educators should desire to lead their colleagues, their students, and their communities. The foundation of leading comes down to one word: *relationships*. You must begin by building strong relationships with your students, colleagues, and members of your school community. Every student desires a teacher who has a vested interest in who he or she is as an individual. Get to know your students and their families. Know what is important to them and take time to see them excel in things outside school such as sporting events, concerts, and community events. Taking time to get to know students sends a powerful message to them and to their parents. Also, get involved in your community so that you understand the diversity of the cultures you serve. As Dr. James Comer, professor of child psychiatry at Yale and founder of the Comer School Development Program, said: "No significant learning occurs without a significant relationship."

I wish you much success as you begin this new journey. You will grow and change along the way. Embrace the challenges and celebrate the successes.

BEST WISHES, CHRISTI MCCOLLUM
Bookman Road Elementary School
Elgin, **SOUTH CAROLINA**

READERS' VOICES

What are the concerns of a beginning teacher?

Making the transition from student teacher to a teacher of students is challenging. It can result in a kind of reality shock. Students know if a teacher is teaching for the first time, and a few kids may test the teacher's ability to control the classroom. An experienced mentor can help the beginning teacher create a positive learning environment and become comfortable in the classroom.

—THOMAS,
Teacher Education program, first year
Used with permission from Monica Harding

No doubt, you have thought about the day when you will make the transition from being a student to being a teacher of students. It is natural that you feel both excited and a bit fearful when thinking about that transition. As a teacher, you will assume an entirely new role—a role that requires some time before it becomes comfortable.

There are several ways you can prepare for that day. These steps will go a long way toward making your entry into teaching rewarding and personally satisfying. The first two sections of this chapter explain what you can learn from observing in classrooms and how you can gain practical experience for becoming a teacher. Next, the chapter discusses the most critical phase of learning to become a teacher—your induction into the profession and how you can benefit from having a mentor. The final section discusses the leadership opportunities you will have beyond the classroom and your role in building a learning community and collaborating with teachers.

How Can You Learn from Observing in Classrooms?

Classroom observations are an excellent way to develop knowledge about teaching. Most teacher education programs require that students participate in **field experiences** that include classroom observations. Students report that these experiences help them make a final decision about becoming a teacher. Most become more enthusiastic about teaching and more motivated to acquire the essential knowledge and skills; however, a few decide that teaching is not for them.

Recognizing the value of observations, many teacher education programs are increasing the amount of field experiences and placing such fieldwork earlier in students' programs. For example, at **WASHINGTON** State University (WSU), students preparing to become elementary teachers complete one week of classroom observations as part of their first education course. Later in their program, WSU students complete two 45-hour blocks of observations in K–8 classrooms and a 5-week advanced practicum (or field experience) that requires several hours of classroom observation each week.

Video Observations of "Real" Classrooms

In addition to classroom observations during field experiences, many teacher education programs include video observations of "real" classrooms. As illustrated in Figure 13.1, video cameras located in different areas of the classroom enable teacher education students to observe various types of classroom activities.

Figure 13.1 A window into the classroom: What can a camera capture?

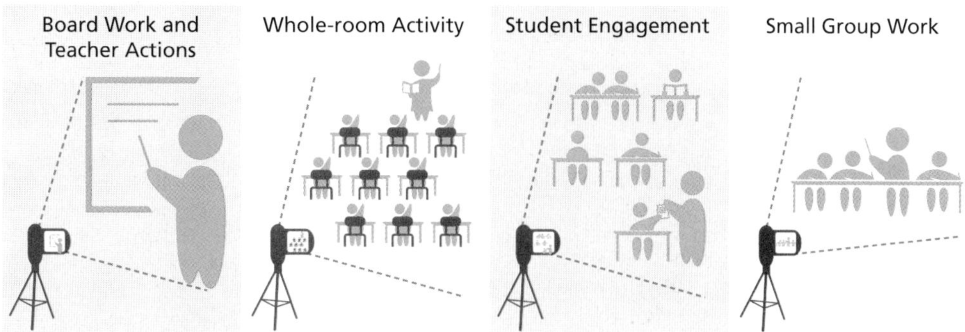

SOURCE: Best Foot Forward: A Toolkit for Fast-Forwarding Classroom Observations Using Video. Center for Education Policy Research, Harvard University, 2015, p. 32.

Students at Central **WASHINGTON** University (CWU), Niagara University (**NEW YORK**), Northwestern State University (**LOUISIANA**), and **CALIFORNIA** State University watch videos of teachers certified by the National Board for Professional Teaching Standards (NBPTS). The universities use ATLAS, an NBPTS-developed library of more than 1,300 videos.

Selected ATLAS video cases are indexed so students can observe how accomplished teachers implement standards such as the Common Core State Standards and Next Generation Science Standards in the classroom. ATLAS cases also include the teachers' own written reflections and analysis. A CWU professor explains how students benefit from the teachers' reflections:

> If [teachers] just observe a classroom they don't get the opportunity to understand the instructional decision-making behind the scenes. They don't get a clear understanding of how that teacher analyzes student data and evidence to inform their instruction or even what the characteristics of the learners were that informed the teacher in their instruction. (National Board for Professional Teaching Standards, 2018, February 23, p. 4)

Teacher education students who view, analyze, and then write about video cases appreciate the ambiguities and complexities of real-life classrooms. They begin to understand that there are no single, simple solutions to complex problems that can arise in the classroom. Viewing authentic video cases enables students to see how "teaching tradeoffs and dilemmas emerge in the video 'text' as do the strategies teachers use, the frustrations they experience, the brilliant and less-brilliant decisions they make" (Grant, Richard, & Parkay, 1996, p. 5).

Focused Observations

Observations are more meaningful when they are focused and conducted with clear purposes. Observers may focus on the students, the teacher, the interactions between the two, the structure of the lesson, or the setting. More specifically, for example, observers may note differences between the ways boys and girls or members of different ethnic groups communicate and behave in the classroom. They may note student interests and ability levels, study student responses to a particular teaching strategy, or analyze the question-and-response patterns in a class discussion.

Observations may also be guided by sets of questions related to specific areas. For instance, since beginning teachers are frequently frustrated by their lack of success in motivating students to learn, asking questions specifically related to motivation can make an observation more meaningful and instructive. Figure 13.2 presents a helpful set of focused questions on motivation. Similar questions can be generated for other focus areas, such as classroom management, student involvement, questioning skills, evaluation, and teacher–student rapport.

Figure 13.2 Guiding questions for observing motivation

Directions: As you observe, note the ways that students are motivated intrinsically (from within) and extrinsically (from factors outside themselves).

Intrinsic Motivation	Extrinsic Motivation
What things seem to interest students at this age?	How do teachers show their approval to students?
Which activities and assignments seem to give them a sense of pride?	What phrases do teachers use in their praise?
When do they seem to be confused? Bored? Frustrated?	What types of rewards do teachers give (e.g., grades, points, tangible rewards)?
What topics do they talk about with enthusiasm?	What reward programs do you notice (e.g., points accumulated toward free time)?
In class discussions, when are they most alert and participating most actively?	What warnings do teachers give?
What seems to please, amuse, entertain, or excite them?	What punishments are given to students?
What do they joke about? What do they find humorous?	How do teachers arouse concern in their students?
What do they report as being their favorite subjects? Favorite assignments?	How do students motivate other students?
What do they report as being their least favorite subjects and assignments?	What forms of peer pressure do you observe?
How do they respond to personalized lessons (e.g., using their names in exercises)?	How do teachers promote enthusiasm for an assignment?
How do they respond to activity-oriented lessons (e.g., fieldwork, project periods)?	How do teachers promote class spirit?
How do they respond to assignments calling for presentations to groups outside the classroom (e.g., parents, another class, the chamber of commerce)?	How do teachers catch their students' interest in the first few minutes of a lesson?
How do they respond to being given a choice in assignments?	Which type of question draws more answers—recall or open-ended?
	How do teachers involve quiet students in class discussions?
	How do teachers involve inactive students in their work?
	In what ways do teachers give recognition to students' accomplishments?

Application Exercise 13.1

Focused Observation – Clear Directions

Observation Instruments

A wide range of methods can be used to conduct classroom observations, ranging from informal, qualitative descriptions to formal, quantitative checklists. With reform efforts to improve education in the United States has come the development of instruments to facilitate the evaluation of teacher performance, a task now widely required of school administrators. Students preparing to teach can benefit by using these evaluative instruments in their observations. An example is the informal "walkthrough" observation instruments that are part of the Ohio Teacher Evaluation System (see Figure 13.3).

In Ohio, principals conduct informal classroom observations ("walkthroughs") that last from 15 to 20 minutes. Principals observe in classrooms as often as their schedules will allow. Since teachers benefit from immediate feedback, principals are expected to give teachers written feedback that same day or the following day, as well as invite teachers to discuss the feedback face to face. During the observations, principals focus on one or two areas, based on the teaching, activities, or discussion that are occurring in the classroom.

Figure 13.3 Classroom walkthroughs and informal observations

a. **Informal Observation: General Form**

Teacher Name:________________ Grade(s)/Subject Area(s): __________ Date: ___________

Evaluator Name: ______________ Time Walkthrough Begins_____ Time Walkthrough Ends_____

Directions: This form serves as a record of an informal walkthrough by the teacher's evaluator. The evaluator will likely not observe all the teaching elements listed below in any one informal observation. This record, along with records of additional informal obeservation, will be used to inform the summative evaluation of the teacher.

EVALUATOR OBSERVATIONS	
☐ Instruction is developmentally appropriate	☐ Lesson content is linked to previous and future learning
☐ Learning outcomes and goals are clearly communicated to students	☐ Classroom learning environment is safe and conducive to learning
☐ Varied instructional tools and strategies reflect student needs and learning objectives	☐ Teacher provides students with timely and responsive feedback
☐ Content presented is accurate and grade appropriate	☐ Instructional time is used effectively
☐ Teacher connects lesson to real-life applications	☐ Routines support learning goals and activities
☐ Instruction and lesson activities are accessible and challenging for students	☐ Multiple methods of assessment of student learning are utilized to guide instruction
☐ Other:	☐ Other:

Evaluator Summary Comments:

Recommendations for Focus of Informal Observations:

b. **Informal Observation: Open-Ended Form**

Teacher Name:________________ Grade(s)/Subject Area(s): __________ Date: ___________

Evaluator Name: ______________ Time Walkthrough Begins_____ Time Walkthrough Ends_____

TIMES	OBSERVATIONS

Evaluator Summary Comments:

SOURCE: Ohio Department of Education. (February 24, 2018). Conducting a Walkthrough. Retrieved from http://education.ohio.gov/

✓ Check Your Understanding 13.1

How Can You Gain Practical Experience for Becoming a Teacher?

Your teacher education program is designed to give you opportunities to experience, to the extent possible, the real world of the teacher. Through practical experiences, you will be given limited exposure to various aspects of teaching, from curriculum development to classroom management.

Classroom Experiences

Opportunities to put theory into practice before student teaching are important. Thus many teacher education programs enable students to participate in microteaching, teaching simulations, field-based practical and clinical experiences, and classroom aide programs.

MICROTEACHING Introduced in the 1960s, microteaching quickly became popular and is widely used today. When **microteaching**, students teach brief, single-concept lessons to a small group of students (i.e., 5 to 10). Microteaching gives students opportunities to practice specific teaching skills, such as positive reinforcement. Often the microteaching is recorded for later study.

As originally developed, microteaching includes the following six steps:

1. Identify a specific teaching skill to learn about and practice.
2. Read about the skill in one of several pamphlets.
3. Observe a master teacher demonstrate the skill in a short video.
4. Prepare a 3- to 5-minute lesson to demonstrate the skill.
5. Teach the lesson, which is recorded, to a small group of peers.
6. Critique, along with the instructor and student peers, the recorded lesson.

SIMULATIONS Simulations can provide opportunities for vicarious practice of a wide range of teaching skills. In **teaching simulations**, students analyze teaching situations that are written or recorded. Typically, students are given background information about a hypothetical school or classroom and the pupils they must prepare to teach. After this orientation, students role-play the student teacher or the teacher who is confronted with the problem situation. Next, students discuss the appropriateness of solutions and work to increase their problem-solving skills and their understanding of the teacher's role as a decision maker in a complex setting.

Some teacher education programs are experimenting with virtual classroom simulations that enable students to hone their classroom planning and decision-making skills (Lynch, 2017; Straub et al., 2015; Dieker et al., 2014a; Dieker, 2014b). One approach to simulations is the TeachLivE (TLE) "mixed reality" classroom developed at the University of Central **FLORIDA**. About 80 teacher education programs around the country are currently using TLE. In the TLE Lab, teacher education students practice skills such as reviewing previous work, presenting new content, or monitoring virtual "students" while they work independently.

The TLE Lab looks like a middle or high school classroom; however, the "students" are avatars that appear on a large screen. Figure 13.4 shows the TLE high school classroom. A trained actor, called an "interactor," controls the movement and speaking of the virtual students from another location. The virtual students move their heads and upper bodies and arms, use gestures, and make eye contact. Most student responses are produced in real time, although the interactor can trigger prerecorded behaviors such as students laughing, excessive pen clicking, or responding to an incoming call on a cell phone. Each avatar has prerecorded behaviors that reflect a unique personality profile and academic profile. For example, here are the profiles for the high school avatar named Sean McGowan:

Personality Profile

- Aggressive dependent
- Looking for teacher approval
- Overparticipates
- Grade sensitive
- Storyteller
- Dramatic

Academic Profile

- Overachiever, but has to work extremely hard
- Average intellect/learner (A/B student with extra credit)
- Genuine enthusiasm and curiosity
- If he doesn't know what the plan is, he gets stressed (e.g., pop quizzes, etc.)
- Performance anxiety
- Testing anxiety
- Procedural learner (Dicker, Hughes, & Hynes, p. 26)

Figure 13.4 High school classroom, TeachLivE Lab

SOURCE: Used with permission from Lisa Dicker, Charles Hughes, & Michael Hynes. Bill & Melinda Gates Foundation Final Report: UCF TLE TeachLivE. August 2016, p. 13. Retrieved from http://teachlive.org/wp-content/uploads/2016/09/Gates-Foundation-Final-Report8_27_2016.pdf.

Researchers examined the effectiveness of the TLE Lab and concluded that "TLE is a promising tool for providing repeated practice and feedback on foundation teaching skills" (Dawson & Lignugaris/Kraft, 2017, p. 45). In addition, education students using the TLE "viewed the TLE students and scenarios as realistic representations of their own classrooms and [believed] that the intervention and assessment procedures were acceptable and valuable to their professional practice" (p. 45).

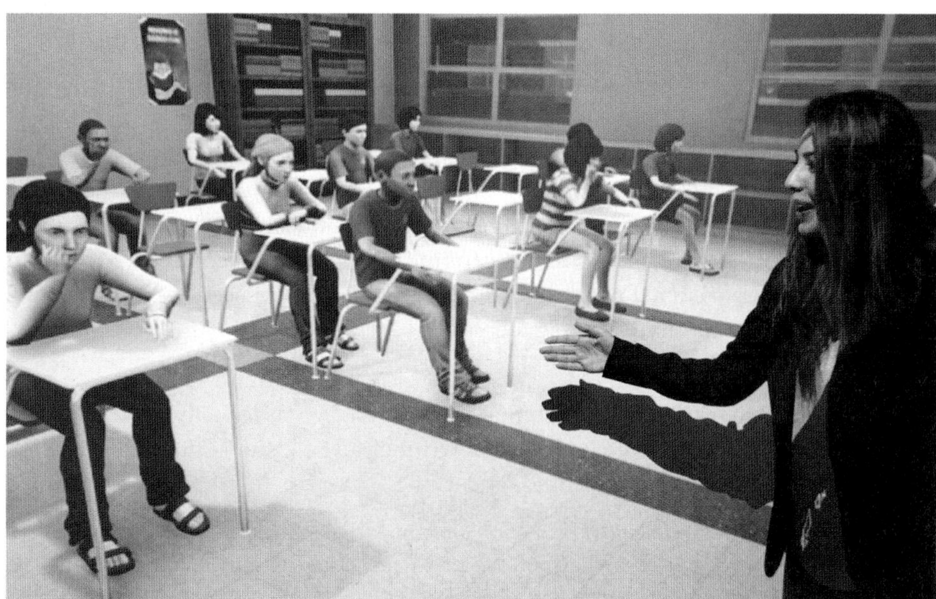

What are some of the benefits of practicing teaching skills with "students" in a virtual classroom?

PRACTICA A **practicum** is a short-term field-based experience (usually about 2 weeks long) that allows teacher education students to spend time observing and assisting in classrooms. Although practica vary in length and purpose, students are often able to begin instructional work with individuals or small groups. For example, a cooperating teacher may allow a practicum student to tutor a small group of students, read a story to the whole class, conduct a spelling lesson, monitor recess, help students with their homework, or teach students a song or game.

CLASSROOM AIDES Serving as a teacher aide is another popular means of providing field experience before student teaching. A teacher aide's role depends primarily on the unique needs of the school and its students. Generally, aides work under the supervision of a certified teacher and perform duties that support the teacher's instruction. Assisting teachers in classrooms familiarizes college students with class schedules, record-keeping procedures, and students' performance levels, as well as providing ample opportunity for observations. In exchange, the classroom teacher receives much-needed assistance.

Student Teaching

The most extensive and memorable field experience in teacher preparation programs is student teaching. Student teaching will provide you with an opportunity to assess your strengths as a future teacher, to identify areas for improvement, and to develop skills in classroom management. Student teaching will be a time of responsibility. As one student teacher told me, "I don't want to mess up [my students'] education!" It will also be an opportunity for growth, a chance to master critical skills.

States require students to have a 5-week to semester-long student teaching experience in the schools before certifying them as teachers. The nature of student teaching varies considerably among teacher education programs. Some programs even pay student teachers during the student teaching experience. Most likely, you will be assigned to a cooperating (or mentor) teacher in the school, and a university supervisor will make periodic visits to observe you.

You will probably have weekly (or even daily) conferences with your mentor teacher. These conferences will focus on what's going well, what needs to be worked on, suggestions for the following day or week, and other dimensions of being a professional teacher. For example, student teachers at **WASHINGTON** State University discuss with their mentors and supervisors the ten "dispositions" presented in the Professional Dispositions Evaluation for Field Experiences (PDEFE) form (see Figure 13.5). By the end of their student teaching experience, WSU students must meet all ten of the dispositions.

During your student teaching assignment, you will probably spend about half of your time teaching, with the remaining time devoted to observing and participating in classroom activities. The amount of time actually spent teaching, however, is not as important as your willingness to reflect carefully on your experiences. Two excellent ways to promote reflection during your student teaching experience are journal writing and maintaining a reflective teaching log.

STUDENT TEACHING JOURNAL Your supervisors may require you to keep a journal of your classroom experiences so that you can engage in reflective teaching. The following two entries illustrate how journal writing can help student teachers develop strategies for dealing with the realities of teaching.

> ***Student Teacher—Rural High School:*** One thing drives me crazy about the kids in my fifth-period class—they don't listen to directions. It's a remedial class, and I know I shouldn't be surprised.
>
> Today, we were working on writing paragraphs that are clear and well organized. All they had to do was rewrite a paragraph—not make corrections,

Figure 13.5 Professional dispositions evaluation for field experiences (PDEFE): Student teaching/internship

Teacher Candidate Name:______________________________ WSU ID#:______________________________

PURPOSE: As an institution that prepares teaches, we owe parents, citizens, and our state's P-12 students our best professional judgement and keenest observations when making assessments that could have profound effects in the future. The identification and evaluation of professional dispositions is part of WSU's professional responsibility.

DISPOSITION STANDARD	EVIDENCE
1. The teacher candidate **centers instruction** on high expectations for student achievement through the **understanding** of individual differences and diverse cultures and communities.	Notes supporting rating: ☐ Met ☐ Not Met
2. The teacher candidate **recognizes** individual student learning needs and **develops** strategies for planning differentiated instruction that supports every student in meeting rigorous learning goals.	Notes supporting rating: ☐ Met ☐ Not Met
3. The teacher candidate **demonstrates** effective teaching practices and knowledge of content that use a variety of instructional strategies and technologies to engage learners in critical thinking, creativity, and collaborative problem solving focused on the learning targets.	Notes supporting rating: ☐ Met ☐ Not Met
4. The teacher candidate **understands** and **uses** both formative and summative methods of assessment, as well as student voice, to engage learners in their own growth, to monitor learner progress, and modify instruction to improve student learning.	Notes supporting rating: ☐ Met ☐ Not Met
5. The teacher candidate **fosters** and **manages** a safe and positive learning environment using a variety of classroom management strategies that take into account the cultural, physical, emotional, and intellectual well-being of students appropriate to their grade level.	Notes supporting rating: ☐ Met ☐ Not Met
6. The teacher candidate **communicates** and **collaborates** with colleagues, parents, and the school community in an ethical and professional manner to promote student learning and growth.	Notes supporting rating: ☐ Met ☐ Not Met
7. The teacher candidate takes the **initiative** to participate and collaborate with learners, families, colleagues, other school professionals, and community members to advance their own professional development and contributions to the broader profession.	Notes supporting rating: ☐ Met ☐ Not Met
8. The teacher candidate respectfully and openly **requests**, **accepts,** and **applies** feedback for improvement.	Notes supporting rating: ☐ Met ☐ Not Met
9. The teacher candidate **reflects** on their own practice and progress to improve instruction for all learners.	Notes supporting rating: ☐ Met ☐ Not Met
10. The teacher candidate **demonstrates** professionalism by attending all field experiences; arriving on time and departing appropriately; preparing to participate and/or teach; dressing professionally; observing confidentiality; and adhering to school and state code of conduct.	Notes supporting rating: ☐ Met ☐ Not Met

Standards adapted from the Teacher Performance Evaluation Program (TPEP) and the Interstate New Teacher Assessment and Support Consortium (INTASC).

______________________________ ______________________________

University Supervisor Signature Mentor Teacher Signature

______________________________ ______________________________

Teacher Candidate Signature Date

SOURCE: Student Teaching Handbook and Resource Guide, Department of Teaching and Learning, Washington State University, College of Education, Spring 2018, p. 31.

just rewrite and make sure their paragraphs had a clear introduction, body, and conclusion. I explained the directions once. Then I even had one of the students read them out loud again. Then I asked for any questions—none. So I thought, "Good, they understand; they know what to do." Then as soon as I said "Begin to rewrite now," the questions started flying. What really got me was that they were questions I had already explained or that were right there on the directions for rewriting paragraphs I gave them. Eventually, I told them they would have to ask their neighbors for answers to any questions they still had. Well, that was a mistake, because the room started to get noisy with all the talking. I had to raise my voice to get them to be quiet and start writing. It was so frustrating.

At the end of the day, Mrs. B. [cooperating teacher] suggested that I tell them next time that I would explain the directions once and ask for questions—then, that would be it. They wouldn't have to ask someone else! Mrs. B. assured me that I would become better at giving directions. Somehow, when she gives directions to students, they usually know what to do. Today, for me, it was the opposite—confusion! I notice that she writes directions on the board and then explains them, step-by-step, to students. Next time, that's what I'll do. Tomorrow, my lesson is on using adjectives to describe the nouns in their writing. If I have a chance before fifth period, I will ask Mrs. B. to look at my directions and let me know if they are clear.

Student Teacher—Urban Middle School: Today I taught a lesson on the solar system, and the kids seemed so bored. I called on my strongest readers to read the material in our science book. One by one, they would read a paragraph or two, and then I would explain it. I was surprised at how much they struggled with the reading. I thought they were strong readers. I guess I was wrong about that. The material was basic—like we have eight planets in our solar system—nine planets until Pluto was "dropped" in 2006. These planets circle around the sun.

Mr. J. [cooperating teacher] told me later that I was spoon-feeding them too much. Tomorrow, I think I will put them into small groups and have each group work on one or two questions rather than give them the answers like I did today. That way, all the students can be involved in talking about the material, not just those who are reading out loud. I hope I don't get those glazed looks on their faces tomorrow. I feel badly if they don't understand and don't seem to be interested.

Mr. J. is great—he is understanding and supportive. He says I'm doing just fine. He had similar problems when he was a student teacher. That's hard to imagine; he seems to communicate so well with the kids. They really pay attention when he's teaching, and they all seem to understand. Actually, I find myself trying to act like Mr. J. while I am teaching. I'm even conscious of moving around the room and trying to build up suspense like he does while he's teaching. He tells the kids things like "What I am going to tell you now you will hardly believe it's true, but it is; so pay close attention." The kids love it when he says things like that.

Unstructured, open-ended journals such as these enable student teachers to reflect on the student teaching experience.

REFLECTIVE TEACHING LOGS To promote more analytical reflections, some supervisors ask student teachers to use a structured form of journal writing, the **reflective teaching log**, in which the student briefly describes the daily classroom activities, selects a single episode to analyze, explains the reason for selecting the episode, and discusses what was learned from the analysis and how that might be applied in the future. To illustrate a reflective teaching log, a partial entry for one episode follows. The entry shows how a college student can disagree with a supervising teacher's response to a classroom situation.

Log for December 1—Erin Tompkins

Sequence of Events

1. Arrival—end of eighth period
2. Ninth period—helped Sharad study science
3. After-school program—worked on science with Ricki, P.K., and Tom
4. Late bus duty with Ms. Soto
5. Departure

Episode

I was helping Ricki and P.K. fill out a table about the location and function of the different cell parts. P.K. asked me a question and two other students laughed at him. I began to answer his question when Ms. Soto came over to the table where we were working and yelled at P.K. She said, "P.K., I don't need you distracting other students who are trying to get their work done." He started to tell her what he asked me and she said, "I don't care. You can leave the room if you don't knock it off. Just do your work and be quiet or you're out!" She then apologized to me and went back to helping another student.

Analysis

I was very frustrated after this episode. This is the first time I've seen Ms. Soto raise her voice with a student and accuse him of causing problems when he was getting his work done and other students were being disruptive. P.K. had asked me a legitimate question; the other students who laughed at him were the problem. I was frustrated because Ricki and P.K. were working hard and asking me good questions. I was annoyed that P.K. was being reprimanded for asking a question that was relevant to the topic we were working on. I also felt helpless because I wanted to tell Ms. Soto that it wasn't P.K. who was the problem. I didn't feel it was my place to correct her in front of her students and kept quiet. I decided that my saying something would only make things worse because it would encourage P.K. to continue arguing with Ms. Soto and he would be in more trouble. (Posner, 2005, p. 122)

Video Example 13.1

Reflecting on a Lesson: Reflecting on your lessons isn't something that you'll only do when you're a student. Good teachers continually analyze, reflect, and tweak their lessons. In this video, a teacher models how she reflects on a social studies lesson and how she might change it in the future.

Although student teaching will be the capstone experience of your teacher education program, the experience should be regarded as an initial rather than a terminal learning opportunity—your first chance to engage in reflection and self-evaluation for a prolonged period. The benefits of reflection are illustrated in the following comment: "teaching can appear deceptively simple; [however], good teaching requires knowledge, awareness . . . and ongoing efforts and reflection to improve" (Good & Lavigne, 2018, p. 2).

Reflecting on your lessons isn't something that you'll only do when you're a student. Good teachers continually analyze, reflect, and tweak their lessons.

Teaching Portfolio

During your journey toward becoming a teacher, you should acquire the habit of assessing your growth in knowledge, skills, and attitudes. Toward this end, you may wish to collect the results of your reflections and self-assessment in a professional portfolio. A **professional portfolio** is a collection of work that documents an individual's accomplishments in an area of professional practice. An artist's portfolio, for example, might consist of a résumé, sketches, paintings, slides and photographs of exhibits, critiques of the artist's work, awards, and other documentation of achievement.

Recently, new approaches to teacher evaluation have included the professional portfolio. The National Board for Professional Teaching Standards, for example, uses portfolios and other evidence of performance prepared by applicants as one way of assessing whether teachers have met the high standards for board certification. Teacher education programs at several universities now use portfolios as one means of assessing the competencies of candidates for teacher certification, and many states have developed specific criteria for teaching portfolios. Many school districts are beginning to ask applicants to submit portfolios that document their effectiveness as teachers.

PORTFOLIO CONTENTS What will your portfolio contain? In addition to the suggestions in the Professional Portfolio activities throughout this book, written materials might include the following: lesson plans and curriculum materials, reflections on your development as a teacher, journal entries, writing assignments given by your instructor, sample tests you have prepared, critiques of textbooks, evaluations of students' work at the level for which you are preparing to teach, sample letters to parents, and a résumé. Non-print materials might include recordings featuring you in simulated teaching and role-playing activities, audiovisual materials (PowerPoint presentations, charts, or other teaching aids), photographs of bulletin boards, charts depicting room arrangements for cooperative learning or other instructional strategies, a sample grade book, certificates of membership in professional organizations, and awards.

Your portfolio should represent your best work and give you an opportunity to become an advocate of who you are as a teacher. Because a primary purpose of the professional portfolio is to stimulate reflection and dialogue, you may wish to discuss what entries to place in your portfolio with your instructor or other teacher education students. In addition, the following questions from *How to Develop a Professional Portfolio: A Manual for Teachers* (Campbell et al., 2014), can help you select appropriate portfolio contents:

> Would I be proud to have my future employer and peer group see this? Is this an example of what my future professional work might look like? Does this represent what I stand for as a professional educator? If not, what can I do to revise or rearrange my artifacts so that they represent my best efforts? (p. 5)

USING A PORTFOLIO In addition to providing teacher education programs with a way to assess their effectiveness, portfolios can be used by students for a variety of purposes. A portfolio may be used as a(n):

- way to establish a record of quantitative and qualitative performance and growth over time.
- tool for reflection and goal setting as well as a way to present evidence of your ability to solve problems and achieve goals.
- way to synthesize many separate experiences; in other words, a way to get the big picture.
- vehicle to help you collaborate with professors and advisers in individualizing instruction.
- vehicle for demonstrating knowledge and skills gained through outside-class experiences, such as volunteer experiences.
- way to share control and responsibility for your own learning.
- alternative assessment measure within the professional education program.
- potential preparation for national, regional, and state accreditation.
- interview tool in the professional hiring process.
- expanded résumé to be used as an introduction during the student-teaching experience.

Substitute Teaching

Upon completion of your teacher education program and prior to securing a full-time teaching assignment, you may choose to gain additional practical experience by **substitute teaching**. If you are unable to locate a full-time position, you may decide to substitute, knowing that many districts prefer to hire from their pool of substitutes when full-time positions become available.

Substitute teachers replace regular teachers who are absent due to illness, family responsibilities, personal reasons, or attendance at professional workshops and conferences. Approximately 500,000 substitutes are employed in schools across the United States, and approximately six months of a student's K–12 education is taught by substitute teachers (U.S. Bureau of Labor Statistics, 2017).

Qualifications for substitutes vary from state to state and district to district. An area with a critical need for subs will often relax its requirements to provide classroom coverage. In many districts, it is possible to substitute-teach without regular certification. Some districts have less stringent qualifications for short-term, day-to-day substitutes and more stringent ones for long-term, full-time substitutes.

Figure 13.6 Advantages and disadvantages of substitute teaching

Advantages	Disadvantages
• Gain teaching experience without spending time grading papers and preparing lessons • Learn about different schools and their environments • Be prepared for interviews by meeting different administrators and teachers • Teach and learn material in different content areas • Get to know educators and network • Learn about job announcements and upcoming vacancies • Further develop your teaching skills • Develop classroom management techniques • Learn about school and district politics • Work on preferred days	• Pays less than full-time teaching • No benefits such as health insurance, retirement plans, or sick days • Lack of organized representation to improve wages or working conditions • May receive a cool reception in some schools • Must adapt quickly to different school cultures • Lack of continuity—may be teaching whole language one day, phonetics the next • Absent teacher may not have left written plans

In many districts, the application process for substitutes is the same as that for full-time applicants; in others, the process may be shorter. Often, substitutes are not limited to working in their area of certification; however, schools try to avoid making out-of-field assignments. If you decide to substitute-teach, contact the schools in your area to learn about the qualifications and procedures for hiring substitutes.

Substitute teaching can be a rewarding, professionally fulfilling experience, as the president of the National Substitute Teachers Alliance (NSTA) explains:

> Substitute teaching can be a rewarding profession for those who love spending time in a learning environment with opportunities for teaching students of diverse ages, backgrounds, and abilities. Moving from school to school and from classroom to classroom provides exciting teaching challenges. For most substitutes, this flexibility is welcome. More importantly, however, the ability to pick one's hours and work days is a great enticement . . . . Substitute teaching provides a dynamic teaching adventure . . . . (Education World, 2018 February 25)
>
>

Figure 13.6 presents several advantages and disadvantages of substitute teaching.

Check Your Understanding 13.2

How Can You Obtain Support as a Teacher?

The retention of public school teachers is a problem in the United States. Each year, scores of beginning teachers enter classrooms with vigor and determination; regrettably, however, many soon leave the profession. The attrition rate among teachers in the U.S. during the first five years is approximately eight percent, with the majority leaving before retirement age (Sutcher, Darling-Hammond, & Carver-Thomas, 2016).

Attrition varies across teaching fields, types of schools, and locations. Attrition is most pronounced in schools that serve students of color and those from low-income families. In addition, high teacher turnover rates in schools negatively impact student achievement for all the students in a school, not just those in a new teacher's classroom (Darling-Hammond, Carver-Thomas, & Sutcher, 2017).

Some beginning teachers eventually give up their chosen profession because their problems and concerns go unattended. Veteran teachers, who recall their own early struggles as beginning teachers, may have a "sink-or-swim" attitude toward the difficulties encountered by those just entering the profession. "Since I learned to cope with the challenges of beginning teaching on my own, today's teachers either have to sink or swim," they reason. In addition, beginning teachers may think they should be as skilled as master teachers with many years of experience.

Feedback from new teachers suggests that they want to talk about the problems they encounter in their work. They want assistance to help them to be successful during the first few years of teaching. Instead, they may experience isolation and have few opportunities to share their experiences with colleagues.

Problems and Concerns of Beginning Teachers

The problems and concerns of beginning teachers can be extensive. The following problems cause some beginning teachers to think about leaving the profession: maintaining classroom discipline, motivating students, responding to individual differences, assessing students' work, maintaining positive relationships with parents, organizing classroom activities, securing adequate teaching materials and supplies, and dealing with the problems of individual students.

In some cases, teachers experience frustration related to lack of preparation time, conflicts with principals, difficulties with student misconduct, and undesirable teaching assignments (for example, larger class sizes than those of experienced teachers). Lack of dialogue with their peers about teaching, minimal involvement in schoolwide decisions about curriculum and instruction, and the absence of a shared technical culture are additional reasons why teachers leave the profession (Glickman, Gordon, & Ross-Gordon, 2017).

Induction into the Profession

One solution to the problem of teacher attrition is to offer beginning teachers **induction programs** that provide them with support during their first years in the profession. Induction program components typically include professional development workshops based on teacher-identified needs, mentoring and peer coaching, small-group meetings to provide support, and observations by and follow-up conferences with individuals not in a supervisory role.

As Figure 13.7 illustrates, induction programs have a direct positive impact on four areas—teacher attitudes, teacher retention, classroom practices, and student achievement. Beginning teachers who do not receive such support leave teaching at about twice the rate of those who receive high-quality induction (Darling-Hammond, Carver-Thomas, & Sutcher, 2017). Induction programs promote the personal and professional well-being of beginning teachers by improving their attitudes toward themselves and the profession. Induction programs also help beginning teachers learn about the culture of the school system within which they work.

Induction programs benefit not only teachers; their students also benefit. Students taught by teachers who receive comprehensive induction support for at least two years demonstrate significantly higher learning gains (New Teacher Center, 2016, 2017; DeCesare McClelland, & Randel, 2017). One study found that students of beginning teachers who participated in a comprehensive induction program achieved up to five additional months of learning in reading and math over the course of a school year, compared to beginning teachers who did not participate in the program (Picucci, 2017).

Figure 13.7 Key components of effective induction programs

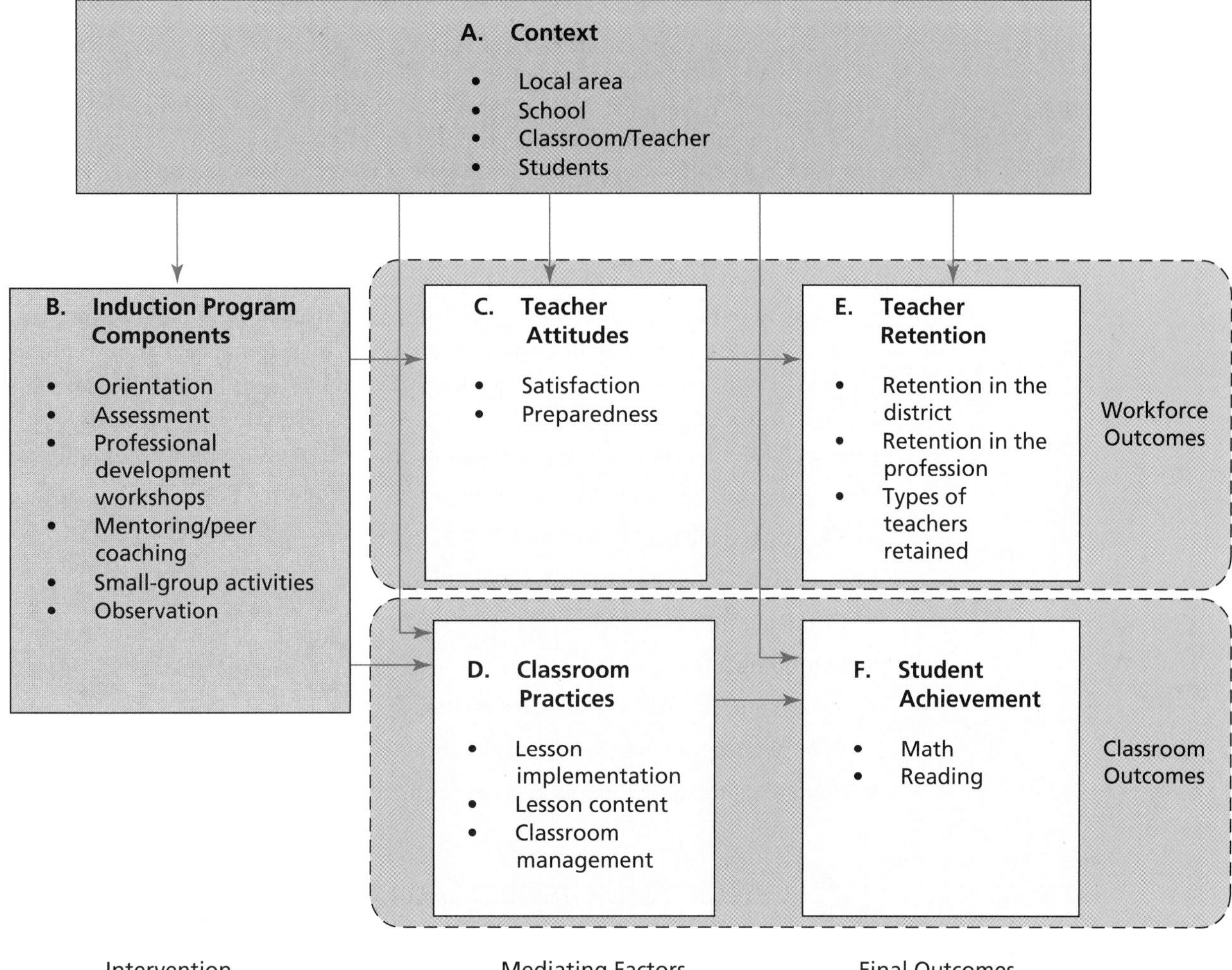

SOURCE: Glazerman, S., E. Isenberg, S. Dolfin, M. Bleeker, A. Johnson, M. Grider, and M. Jacobus. (2010). Impacts of Comprehensive Teacher Induction: Final Results From a Randomized Controlled Study (NCEE 2010-4027). Washington, DC: National Center for Education Evaluation and Regional Assistance, Institute of Education Sciences, U.S. Department of Education, p. 5.

The Benefits of Having a Mentor

A mentor is an experienced teacher who provides a beginning teacher with the support necessary for a successful induction to the school and profession. Several studies have found that teachers who are mentored are less likely to leave the profession, and their students achieve at higher levels (Glazerman et al., 2010; Gray, Taie, & O'Rear, 2015; Ingersoll & Strong, 2011; Smith & Ingersoll, 2004; Strong, 2006).

Many schools have a formal selection process for mentors—"one that not only chooses well-qualified teachers but also conveys to all members of the school community that it is an honor to be chosen as a mentor" (Glickman, Gordon, & Ross-Gordon, 2017, p. 279). The following teacher-mentor explains how she provides help and support for beginning teachers:

> I go into their classrooms frequently to observe them and to give them feedback on what they ask for feedback on, or what they need feedback on. Mostly they will ask, "How am I doing with my questioning strategies?" or something like that. They will give me a focus that they want to look at. I let them know that I am on their side and want to help them. I will do whatever I can to facilitate their professional growth. (Peck, 2008, p. 123)

In reflecting on how my own professional growth was enhanced by my relationship with my mentor, Herbert A. Thelen, I defined **mentoring** as

> an intensive, one-to-one form of teaching in which the wise and experienced mentor inducts the aspiring protégé [one who is mentored] into a particular, usually professional, way of life . . . . [T]he protégé learns from the mentor not only the objective, manifest content of professional knowledge and skills but also a subjective, nondiscursive appreciation for how and when to employ these learnings in the arena of professional practice. In short, the mentor helps the protégé to "learn the ropes," to become socialized into the profession. (Parkay, 1988, p. 196)

Those who have become highly accomplished teachers frequently point out the importance of mentors in their preparation for teaching. A **mentor** can provide moral support, guidance, and feedback to students at various stages of professional preparation. In addition, a mentor can model for the protégé an analytical approach to solving problems in the classroom. For example, an effective mentor might use the following strategies to help a beginning teacher solve classroom-based problems:

- Sharing the mentor's own experiences
- Suggesting strategies for handling situations
- Demonstrating techniques and strategies
- Critiquing lesson plans
- Rehearsing planned classroom activities
- Role-playing various classroom situations with the new teacher
- Reviewing the day's events and exploring alternative approaches

What Leadership Opportunities Will You Have Beyond the Classroom?

The need for teachers to pursue leadership roles became even more evident after the presidential election of 2016. As noted educators Michael Fullan and Andy Hargreaves stated in *Bringing the Profession Back In: Call to Action:*

> There is something different and also disturbing about 2016 and 2017. It is a time of rising global levels of feelings of abandonment, anger, frustration, fear, hatred, violence, inequity, incivility, and distrust . . . Education has never been more important to the future of . . . the U.S. and the world at large. A collaborative and activist teaching profession working jointly with students, families, and communities in the context of state and national policy is perhaps the most powerful instrument we have at our disposal to avoid impending harm and do greater good. (Fullan and Hargreaves, 2016, p. 24)

Fullan and Hargreaves's call for an *activist teaching profession* is timely at this moment in our nation's history. The phrase captures well how professional teachers view their role in society. They willingly respond to the call to leadership, and they become involved at the local, state, and federal levels in the quest to improve our nation's schools. They know that a strong democracy requires teacher leadership to improve education.

Teacher Involvement in Teacher Education, Certification, and Staff Development

Teacher input into key decisions about teacher preparation, certification, and staff development is on the rise. Through their involvement with professional development schools and the National Board for Professional Teaching Standards (NBPTS); state professional standards boards; and scores of local, state, and national education committees, teachers are changing the character of pre- and in-service education.

Since the NBPTS certification program began in 1993, more than 118,000 teachers have earned board certification (National Board for Professional Teaching Standards, 2018 January 7). Teachers who have received National Board Certification are recognized as professionals not only in their schools but also in their districts and beyond. For example, after receiving Board certification, these teachers had the following professional opportunities:

- Helene Alolouf (Early Adolescence/English Language Arts certificate) of Yonkers, **NEW YORK** was invited to teach at the Manhattanville Graduate School of Education as an adjunct professor.
- Sandra Blackman (Early Adolescence/English Language Arts certificate) of San Diego, **CALIFORNIA** was promoted to resource teacher for the humanities departments for 55 schools, where she provides staff development for a standards-based system.
- Edward William Clark Jr. (Early Childhood/Generalist certificate) of Valley, **ALABAMA** helped the State Department of Education and the Alabama Education Association develop National Board Certification training modules to assist Alabama teachers with National Board Certification.
- Linda Lilja (Middle Childhood/Generalist certificate) of Scranton, **KANSAS** was invited to serve as a member of the task force for the National Teachers Hall of Fame.
- Donna W. Parrish (Early Adolescence/Generalist certificate) of Shelby, **NORTH CAROLINA** was appointed curriculum specialist at a middle school.

Teacher Leaders

Throughout the nation, teacher leaders are reshaping the profession and transforming schools. "Teacher leaders fulfill coordinating and managing responsibilities, such as planning events, coordinating schedules, and preparing materials; engage in school- and district-level curriculum work; engage in professional development, including mentoring, peer coaching, and leading workshops; promote organizational change; secure resources and support; nurture supportive collegial relationships; and advocate for children" (Grenda and Hackmann, 2014, p. 56). As dozens of recent books on teacher leadership suggest, the term **teacher leader** has become part of the vocabulary of educational reform. Among those books published in 2018, the titles of four specifically included the term *teacher leader:*

- *Teacher Leadership: New Conceptions for Autonomous Student Learning in the Age of the Internet* (Katyal & Evers, 2018).
- *Teacher Leadership in Professional Development Schools* (Hunzicker, 2018)
- *Creating a Culture of Support for Teacher Leaders: A Vision for Change and Hope* (Gornik & Sanford, 2018)
- *Advocacy for Teacher Leadership: Opportunity, Preparation, Support, and Pathways* (Lovett, 2018)

A brief look at the professional activities of Sandra MacQuinn, a teacher leader who worked with me on a major restructuring effort at Rogers High School in Spokane, **WASHINGTON** illustrates the critical role that a teacher leader can play in school governance. In addition to teaching, here are just a few of MacQuinn's leadership activities while serving as liaison and on-site coordinator of a school–university partnership between Rogers High School and Washington State University's College of Education:

- Writing grant proposals for teacher-developed projects
- Helping other teachers write grant proposals
- Facilitating the development of an integrated school-to-work curriculum
- Preparing newsletters to keep faculty up to date on restructuring
- Organizing and facilitating staff development training
- Developing connections with area businesses and arranging job-shadowing sites for students
- Working with a community college to create an alternative school for Rogers High School students at the college
- Scheduling substitute teachers to provide Rogers High School teachers with release time to work on restructuring
- Making presentations on the Rogers High School restructuring at state and regional conferences
- Arranging for Rogers High School students to visit Washington State University (WSU)
- Meeting with the principal, assistant principals, WSU professors, and others to develop short- and long-range plans for implementing site-based management
- Chairing meetings of the site-based council, the restructuring steering committee, and other restructuring-related committees

To involve teachers in the development and implementation of national education policy, the U.S. Department of Education launched the School Ambassador Fellowship in 2007. The purpose of the fellowship is to:

- Create a community of teachers, principals, and other school staff members who share expertise and collaborate with leaders in the federal government on national education issues.
- Involve educators who work daily with students and teachers in developing policies that affect classrooms and schools.
- Highlight practitioners' voices and expand educators' critical leadership at the national, state, and local levels (U.S. Department of Education, 2018, January 25).

Video Example 13.2

Teacher Leaders: Learn how one district has embraced the teacher leader philosophy through professional development and recognition of the important role they play in student achievement.

During the academic year, Fellows work part-time (about 40 hours a month) at the Department's headquarters in Washington, D.C. Fellows also continue to work at their home schools, also on a part-time basis. The Department pays the teacher's salary during the year and covers all travel and per diem expenses while the teachers are in Washington, D.C. The following three teachers, selected as Fellows for 2017–2018, comment on the importance of the Program:

> The Department of Education values and needs the input of those who interact with students on a daily basis. The [Program] is unique because it gives teachers, counselors, librarians and other school leaders the opportunity to provide input and feedback on policy matters that impact their schools and communities.
> *–Dr. Elmer Harris: Fifth-grade Teacher, Christa McAuliffe Elementary School, Colorado Springs,* **COLORADO**

> I'm really honored and excited to be a part of this, and to be able to help connect and communicate and really try to make an impact on American education. The

Department is very supportive of the School Ambassador Fellows and they really do want our feedback.
–Megan Power: Elementary Teacher/Learning Experience Designer, Poway Unified School District, San Diego, **CALIFORNIA**

The Fellowship has stretched my thinking and taught me so much about policy and the importance of teacher voice,
–Melody Arabo: Third-grade Teacher, Keith Elementary School, West Bloomfield, **MICHIGAN** (U.S. Department of Education Blog, 2018).

Teacher Leadership Beyond the Classroom

Currently, many states have incentives for teachers to assume leadership roles outside the classroom. These incentives are based on a realization that "leadership roles are fluid . . . as a result, teachers—who have the greatest school influence on student achievement—[must be] empowered to engage in leadership roles and transfer their knowledge and skills throughout the school organization" (Grenda and Hackmann, 2014, pp. 55–56).

Figure 13.8 illustrates 11 dimensions of teacher leadership beyond the classroom. The many teachers with whom I have worked on school restructuring projects during the last few years have used these skills to reach an array of educational goals. At schools around the country, teachers and principals are using a "collaborative, emergent" approach to leadership; that is, the person who provides leadership for a particular schoolwide project or activity may or may not be the principal or a member of the administrative team (Parkay, Shindler, & Oaks, 1997). A middle school social studies teacher describes how a collaborative approach to leadership works at her school:

> It's part of [principal's name]'s philosophy . . . . You will hear him say "Many hands make light work," and it is true. Everybody at Blue Trail [Middle School] hears that over and over. It's the expectation in the building. That's the way the administrative team functions, and so does the teaching staff. Everybody has different things they are better at, so they use their strengths and help each other. If you asked the kids, they're not sure who runs the building. Some kids know that [principal's name] is actually the principal, but they're not sure, because everyone runs this building. (Grenda and Hackmann, 2014, p. 63)

Figure 13.8 Eleven dimensions of teacher leadership beyond the classroom

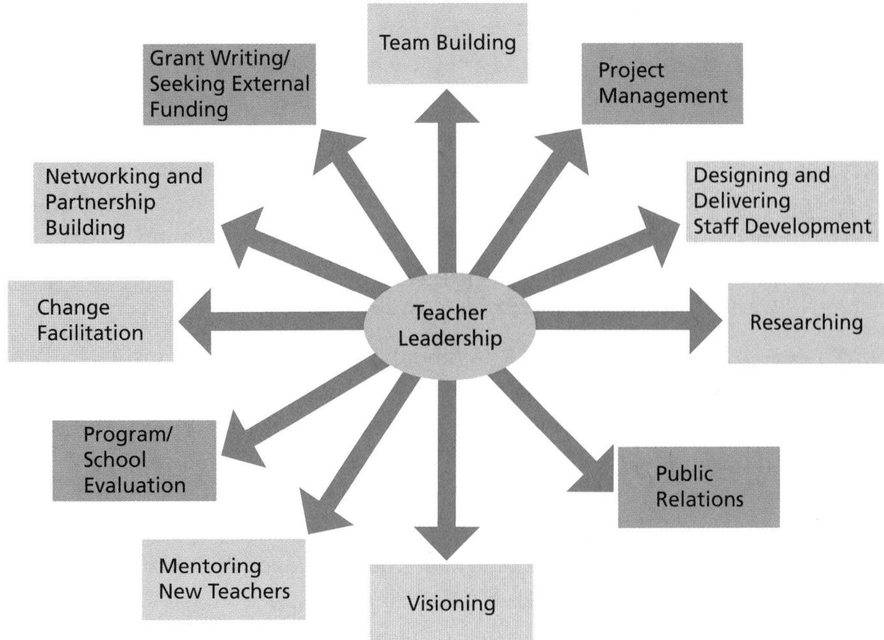

HYBRID TEACHERS AND TEACHERPRENEURS As more teachers assume important leadership roles in their schools and districts, the role of the *hybrid teacher* has emerged. A **hybrid teacher** combines part-time classroom teaching with leadership roles in a school or district. A national survey of 1,000 teachers found that more than half (51 percent) were "interested in a hybrid role that combines classroom teaching with other responsibilities" (Harris Interactive, Inc., 2013, p. 49).

Aware that more teachers are assuming leadership roles beyond the classroom and that many of them are influencing educational policies in entrepreneurial ways, Ariel Sacks, an English teacher in Brooklyn, **NEW YORK**, and a coauthor of *Teaching 2030* (Berry et al., 2011) coined the term *teacherpreneur.* "Growing numbers of classroom experts [have begun] to incubate and execute their own ideas as teacherpreneurs" (Berry, 2017). **Teacherpreneurs** are leading the profession as:

- **co-designers of edugames** and consultants to the exploding tech industry.
- **content curators** to guide teachers as they make decisions about a vast array of curriculum materials.
- **assessment designers** who develop methods for evaluating deep learning by students and other innovative forms of instruction.
- **community organizers** who establish and sustain relationships with health and social service providers in schools that serve high-needs students with wraparound programs.
- **virtual community organizers** who facilitate online communities so teachers can participate in the growing global trade in pedagogy and professional learning (Berry, 2017).

How Will You Help to Build a Learning Community and Collaborate With Teachers?

In addition to the community of learners they develop in the classroom, professional teachers recognize the importance of being part of the learning community beyond the classroom. Success in your first year of teaching will be determined not only by the relationships you develop with students but also the relationships you develop with their families, your colleagues, school administrators, and other members of your school community. Ideally, all of these groups will work together to create a learning community—a school environment "where teachers and principals can continually expand their capacity to create the results they desire, where emergent patterns of thinking are nurtured, where collective aspiration is liberated, and where people are constantly learning how to learn" (Hoy & Hoy, 2013, p. 19).

RELATIONSHIPS WITH STUDENTS Without a doubt, your relationships with students will be the most important (and complex) you will have as a teacher. The quality of your relationships with students will depend in large measure on your knowledge of students and commitment to improving your interactions with them.

Your relationships with students will have many dimensions. Your primary responsibility as a professional teacher will be to see that each student learns as much as possible. You will need to establish relationships with all students based on mutual respect, caring, and concern. Without attention to this personal realm, your effectiveness as a teacher will be limited, as will your ability to have a positive influence on students' attitudes and behaviors.

The importance of teachers' relationships with students was driven home in February 2018 when 14 students and 3 staff members at Marjory Stoneman Douglas High School in Parkland, **FLORIDA** were killed by a former student. In a letter to a local newspaper after the shooting, a school superintendent explained why relationships with students are critical:

> We need to double-down on our relationships with students if we truly want to keep our schools safe and secure. Connecting with students when they arrive at school in the morning, building relationships with students in our classrooms, during passing time in the hallways, at practice or rehearsal, as they leave our schools at the end of the day, during championship games, festivals, and everywhere where our students thrive is our best hope at ensuring the safety and security of our schools. [By] knowing our students well, we will build our own early warning indicator mechanism so that we can provide interventions or make referrals to families as we see changes in student behavior. (Tremblay, 2018)

The following Teaching on Your Feet feature illustrates how a teacher's willingness and ability to establish a positive relationship with a student can have a transformative influence on a student's view of him- or herself as a learner.

Teaching on Your Feet

"I Now Believe I Can Fly!"

It was a hot day in the middle of August and another school year was beginning. Each period, as I greeted the new ninth-grade students coming into my Algebra 1 classes, I couldn't help but wonder what kind of hand I had been dealt for the year. It was a surprise to see a student from the previous year come into one of my classes, and all I could think was, "Is he going to fail—again?"

I liked this young man and I wanted to see him succeed. I knew he was intelligent, but the year before, his immaturity and lack of confidence kept him from passing my class. I told him that, because he failed my class the past year, he should give serious thought to having a different teacher this year. A different teacher with a different approach might be his key to success.

I also made it clear that he was welcome to stay in my class. I told him that my perception of him was that he was an intelligent young man and that I believed he could pass Algebra 1. With his head down, he said, "I just can't understand it."

I said, "I think you can, and I am willing to do whatever it takes to help you pass."

He chose to stay in my class, so I talked with him about some things he needed to do differently this year, but I did not make demands. I wanted him to have the autonomy to choose. My main goal was to help him become successful with a few simple tasks at the beginning. I hoped this would grow into a confidence that he could understand Algebra 1 concepts.

So, as we started the year, I made certain that he understood procedures and meaning. From the very beginning, he started exclaiming, "This stuff is easy, Mr. Quine." He began completing his classwork before anyone else, and his work was exemplary. I encouraged him appropriately every day, hoping to build his confidence and to build a relationship with him. To let him know how interested I was in him, I greeted him every day when he came to class and always made conversation with him about something other than Algebra 1.

Now he was experiencing success, and so he chose to do the things I had suggested. For example, he began sitting at a place in the room where he would not be distracted by others. Whenever I gave an assignment, he worked at it diligently and always asked me questions if he didn't understand something. If he did poorly on an assessment, he would always review the material and take it again. This was my policy for everyone, but not everyone took advantage of the opportunity. It wasn't long before he was the first to class every day. His grades went from C's and D's at the beginning of the year to A's and B's by the second quarter. He was doing so well that he rarely took an assessment over.

By the middle of the third quarter, I started differentiating with him by giving him more challenging problems. I knew he would rise to the occasion, and I wanted to sustain his success. I also encouraged him because of the quality of his new attitude. Near the middle of the fourth quarter, I started having him work in the geometry text to give him a head start for the next year. One day he asked me, "Mr. Quine, can I have you for Geometry next year? I now believe I can fly!"

Used with Permission from **DOUG QUINE**
Ninth-Grade Algebra Teacher, Silverado High School,
Victorville, **CALIFORNIA**

Analyze

Effective teachers like Doug Quine understand how teacher expectations and relationships with students can have a

(*continued*)

powerful, positive influence on student learning. At the beginning of the Algebra 1 class, Quine's student believes that he "just can't understand" algebra; however, his teacher believes otherwise. Buoyed by Quine's belief in his ability to learn, the student gradually experiences success and comes to see himself as a capable learner. In addition, Quine takes responsibility for student learning. In other words, he focuses on what *he* can do as a teacher to increase his student's learning. Furthermore, the student knows that his teacher really cares—that he will do whatever it takes for him to be successful.

Reflect

1. What can a teacher do to motivate a student who has had a pattern of failing and thinks he or she cannot understand a subject?
2. How can a teacher help a student understand abstract concepts?
3. What strategies and approaches can a teacher use to sustain students' growth in achievement so they can progress?

RELATIONSHIPS WITH COLLEAGUES AND STAFF Each working day, you will interact with other teachers and staff members, and they can provide much needed support and guidance. If you have a problem, they can suggest solutions. Often, you will learn that they, too, have experienced the same problem. From the beginning of your first teaching assignment, let your colleagues know that you are willing to learn all you can about your new job and to be a team player. In most schools, it is common practice to give first-time teachers less desirable assignments (classes that have a greater number of lower-ability students, for example), reserving the more desirable assignments (honors or advanced-placement classes, for example) for more experienced teachers. By demonstrating your willingness to take on these assignments with good humor and to give them your best effort, you will do much to establish yourself as a valuable colleague.

It is important that you get along with your colleagues and contribute to a spirit of professional cooperation or collegiality in the school. Some you will enjoy being around; others you may wish to avoid. Some will express obvious enthusiasm for teaching; others may be bitter and pessimistic about their work. Be pleasant and friendly with both types. Accept their advice with a smile, and then act on what you believe is worthwhile.

RELATIONSHIPS WITH ADMINISTRATORS Pay particular attention to the relationships you develop with administrators, department heads, and supervisors. Although your contacts with them will not be as frequent as those with other teachers, they can do much to ensure your initial success.

The principal of your new school will most likely be the one to introduce you to other teachers, members of the administrative team, and staff. He or she should inform you if there are assistant principals or department heads who can help you enforce school rules, keep accurate records, and obtain supplies, for example. The principal may also assign an experienced teacher to serve as a mentor during your first year.

Principals are well aware of the difficulties you might encounter as a first-year teacher, and they are there to help you succeed. Because the demands on their time are intense, however, you should not hesitate to be proactive about meeting with them to discuss issues of concern. They can promote professional development and success by:

1. encouraging various forms of teaming/partnering with colleagues within and outside school (e.g., teaching teams, curriculum teams, technology teams, diversity teams, developing partnerships with other organizations).

2. providing opportunities for teachers to serve in leadership roles (e.g., mentoring graduate student interns, knowledge-based management, technology leaders, sharing decision making, leading accreditation teams).
3. promoting collegial inquiry (e.g., reflection through writing and dialogue).
4. mentoring (Glickman, Gordon, & Ross-Gordon, 2017, p. 74).

RELATIONSHIPS WITH PARENTS OR GUARDIANS Developing positive connections with your students' parents or guardians can contribute significantly to students' learning and to your success as a teacher. In reality, teachers and parents or guardians are partners—both concerned with the learning and growth of the children in their care.

It is important that you become acquainted with parents or guardians at school functions, at meetings of the parent-teacher association (PTA) or parent-teacher organization (PTO), at various community events, and in other social situations. To develop good communication with parents or guardians, you will need to be sensitive to their needs, such as their work schedules and the language spoken at home.

Additionally, you should be aware of the information parents or guardians expect teachers to provide regarding their children's learning at school—for example, if their child is having academic or social problems, homework policies and school procedures, or how parents can help their child succeed.

Table 13.1 shows the percentage of students whose parents participated in school-related activities and during 2015–2016. The most common school-related activity for parents was attending a general school or a parent-teacher organization or association meeting (89 percent). The next most common activities were attending a regularly scheduled parent-teacher conference or a school or class event.

Parents and guardians expect teachers to provide them with important information about their child's performance at school, particularly concerns about factors that might affect a child's success.

Teacher Collaboration

The relationships that build a learning community involve **collaboration**—working together, sharing decision making, and solving problems. As a member of a dynamic, changing profession, your efforts to collaborate will result in an increased understanding

TABLE 13.1 Percentage of students in kindergarten through grade 12 whose parents reported participation in school-related activities and mean number of meetings or activities, by selected school, student, and family characteristics: 2015–16

	Participation in school activities by parent or other household member							
Characteristic	Number of students in kindergarten through grade 12 (thousands)	Attended a general school or PTO/PTA meeting[1]	Attended regularly scheduled parent-teacher conference	Attended a school or class event	Volunteered or served on school committee	Participated in school fundraising	Met with a guidance counselor	Mean number of meetings or activities at child's school
Total	**51,162**	**89**	**78**	**79**	**43**	**59**	**33**	7.5
School type[2]								
Public, assigned	38,730	88	76	78	39	57	33	7.0
Public, chosen	7,282	90	79	78	46	58	33	7.7
Private, religious	3,686	92	85	92	73	80	38	11.6
Private, nonreligious	1,043	97	92	90	67	71	39	10.6
School size[3]								
Under 300	5,800	88	87	85	54	68	33	8.2
300–599	16,953	91	85	82	50	64	30	7.8
600–999	15,126	91	81	78	43	60	29	7.5
1,000 or more	12,990	83	59	74	31	49	42	6.9
Locale of student's household[4]								
City	16,278	86	79	75	42	53	34	7.4
Suburban	22,615	90	78	81	46	62	34	7.4
Town	4,042	87	77	76	35	57	32	7.3
Rural	8,227	90	76	84	44	67	30	8.3
Student's sex								
Male	26,495	87	79	77	42	58	35	7.5
Female	24,667	90	77	82	45	61	31	7.5
Student's race/ethnicity								
White, non-Hispanic	25,703	91	79	86	49	69	32	8.6
Black, non-Hispanic	7,139	87	79	72	34	48	43	6.1
Hispanic	12,281	87	75	71	36	48	33	6.4
Asian or Pacific Islander, non-Hispanic	3,199	80	76	71	42	51	26	5.2
Other, non-Hispanic[5]	2,840	91	79	83	49	60	33	8.3
Student's grade level								
Kindergarten–2nd grade	13,090	91	92	85	56	67	23	7.5
3rd–5th grade	12,040	92	90	84	51	65	27	7.6
6th–8th grade	11,602	90	73	76	35	55	34	6.9
9th–12th grade	14,430	82	58	73	32	51	48	8.0

[1] Parent Teacher Organization (PTO) or Parent Teacher Association (PTA) meeting.
[2] School type classifies the school currently attended as either public or private. Public schools are further classified according to whether the school was chosen or assigned. Private schools are also classified as being religious or nonreligious. School type also excludes 67 cases where the Common Core of Data (CCD) indicated that the school was public but the respondent indicated the student attended a private school.
[3] Excludes 81 cases because of missing data on the Common Core of Data (CCD)/Private School Survey (PSS) data files.
[4] Locale of student's household classifies the residential ZIP code into a set of four major locale categories: city, suburban, town, rural.
[5] "Other, non-Hispanic" includes American Indian and Alaska Native children who are not Hispanic and children reported as a race/ethnicity not listed.

Note: Students who were homeschooled were excluded from the table. Detail may not sum to totals because of rounding. Variables for school characteristics (school type and school size) have a certain number of missing cases owing to school nonreport; therefore, the number of students across the categories for each school variable does not sum to the total number of students.

SOURCE: Adapted from McQuiggan, M. and Megra, M. (2017). Parent and Family Involvement in Education: Results from the National Household Education Surveys Program of 2016 (NCES 2017-102). U.S. Department of C: National Center for Education Statistics, p. 8.

of the teaching–learning process and improved learning for all students. By working with others on school governance, curriculum development, school partnerships, and educational reform, you will play an important role in creating a professional learning environment at your school and increasing collegiality. The following Teachers' Voices: Being An Agent of Change feature profiles a teacher who collaborates with colleagues around the world.

TEACHERS' VOICES  BEING AN AGENT OF CHANGE

CAROLYN FOOTE

A "Techno-Librarian" Shares New Ideas Across the Globe

Providing our students opportunities to be prepared for the future is crucial. Across the nation, thousands of dedicated educators and librarians are leading the charge to help students investigate, create, collaborate and communicate effectively, and to reach beyond the walls of their own schools.

Connected librarians across the nation . . . play a uniquely significant role in assisting teachers as they become comfortable with new technologies, and who link teachers and students with the tools and resources that help them become "connected" learners. While librarians have always been resource mavens and curriculum specialists, our roles have broadened to include the technology tools and strategies that prepare our students for an always connected future. That can mean connecting our ASL (American Sign Language) students via Skype so they can teach a Canadian student sign language, hosting a robotics makerspace in the library, building a list of web resources for our Vietnam memorial project, or discovering new devices that will aid student research.

When tablets entered the commercial marketplace, for example, I was eager to pilot them in the library in order to determine their efficacy for our teachers and students. As an early adopter, I began with just six tablets to gather information on their usefulness for student learning both within the library and the classroom. Three years later, with the dedication of a tribe of people, we are now a one-to-one tablet district K–12 and are entering our third year hosting an annual conference for tablet users across the country.

As a librarian (in concert with technology staff), I supported the initiative in many ways: redesigning the library to include a tech "help desk," building lists of appropriate apps, developing projects with students and teachers, and documenting our initiative on a campus blog. I have networked with librarians around the country as they grapple with similar issues from e-books to library redesign; even when we redesigned our own library six years ago, many of the future-friendly features that make our library a vibrant hub were inspired by other colleagues online.

As a librarian, I play a vital leadership role with my unique expertise about research and literacy. But I and other librarians cannot develop our skills in a vacuum. Wired librarians across the globe have banded together to build resources for one another, like the Teacher Librarian Virtual café. This program, led by volunteers, hosts monthly online programming and supports weekly Twitter chats. I also engage with Texas librarians during the weekly Texas Library Twitter chat and network during national events like the Connected Educator month with [the U.S. Secretary of Education] and the free K12 Online Conference, which gave me the first thrilling taste of connecting with educators globally.

These ongoing connections have imbued my own practice with the most empowering professional learning I have ever been a part of; I can wake up chatting with educators in Australia, connect with colleagues on campus during the day, and go to bed having chatted with colleagues on the West Coast. Rather than work alone, librarians have grown wide networks of colleagues that both support and challenge us, and we, and our schools, are better for it.

We care fiercely about educating our students and about moving our schools forward. And these connections make our work much richer.

PERSONAL REFLECTION

1. Foote calls herself a "techno-librarian." With reference to the grade level and subject area for which you are preparing to teach, describe the curriculum your students would experience if you were a "techno-teacher." For example, as a "techno-elementary teacher," what would you want students to learn? As a "techno-science teacher"? As a "techno-English teacher"? As a "techno-music teacher"?
2. Foote's blog post describes how she "reached beyond the walls" of her school. As a teacher, explain how you will develop a curriculum that "reaches beyond the walls" of your school.

Carolyn Foote is a "techno-librarian" at Westlake High School in Austin, **TEXAS**. She wrote a chapter about her school's iPad program for the book *New Landscapes in Mobile Learning* (Routledge, May 2013).

The preceding is excerpted from her November 26, 2013, blog post written upon being selected by the White House as a Connected Educator Champion of Change. Retrieved from "A 'Techno-Librarian' Shares New Ideas Across the Globe" by Carolyn B. Foote, http://futura.edublogs.org/2014/07/25/librarians-sharing-new-ideas-across-globe/. Used with permission of Dinah McGuire.

The heart of collaboration is meaningful, authentic relationships and trust among professionals. Of course, such relationships do not occur naturally; they require commitment and hard work. Genuine collaboration:

- is voluntary and based on mutual goals;
- requires parity among participants;
- is based on shared responsibility for participation and decision making; and
- requires sharing resources and accountability for outcomes.

In addition, "Cultures of collaborative professionalism build professional judgment in *individuals* as well as in *collectivities*" (Fullan & Hargreaves, 2016, p. 18, italics added). In other words, individuals in a collaborative environment have the autonomy to act differently from the collective, as long as their actions benefit students. "Strong cultures of collaborative professionalism are like strong teams. They thrive on diversity and disagreement, promote good variation of style, strengths, and overall approach, and increase individual as well as collective talent" (Fullan & Hargreaves, 2016, p. 18). Figure 13.9 illustrates how a collaborative community of teachers involves the following individual and collective dimensions:

- Individual Autonomy and Collective Autonomy
- Individual Impact and Collective Impact
- Personal Responsibility and Collective Responsibility
- Individual Inquiry and Collaborative Inquiry
- Self-Efficacy and Collective Efficacy
- Inward Mindset and Outward Mindset

Figure 13.9 Individual and collective dimensions of a collaborative community of teachers

□ **Individual autonomy:** to make on-the-spot judgements in your own classroom as a properly trained and qualified as well as respected professional.	□ **Collective autonomy:** to have more independence from unnecessary and excessive bureaucratic interference but also less independence from one another as colleagues in planning curriculum, improving teaching and learning, and giving as well as receiving feedback.
□ **Individual impact:** being mindful of ensuring that how you teach and the things you do in your classroom are not just interesting and fun for you and the students but have a positive impact on their learning and development—directly or indirectly, short- or long-term.	□ **Collective impact:** awareness of and deliberate attention to how the whole school community of teachers, administrative support staff, community service workers, bus drivers, and volunteers can and does have a positive impact on students.
□ **Personal responsibility:** to work hard, give up other things sometimes, do the best you can, take the first step in helping a colleague or making a change, admit and apologize for mistakes, speak out against the injustices incurred by a poor policy, an uncaring colleague, or climate of racial violence, support a student or colleague who is being bullied, challenge poor leadership, and initiate your own learning.	□ **Collective responsibility:** for all students' success inside and outside one's own school and class; and for other colleagues' success on exactly the same line—in fact, you cannot do one without the other.
□ **Individual inquiry:** into how to improve and innovate in your own teaching, try more authentic tasks and assessments, experiment with different kinds of digital technology tools and applications, and investigate how writing tasks or reading texts impact differently on a culturally diverse student body, for example.	□ **Collaborative inquiry:** into a problem faced by a school or a network of schools and their teachers, such as how to improve the quality and impact of mathematics teaching in an elementary school, how to deal with post-traumatic stresses that many children from refugee families bring into school with them, how to develop programs and procedures for addressing issues of cyberbullying, and so on.
□ **Self-efficacy:** the belief that you can make a difference to your own students even in the face of the very challenging lives that they sometimes have, and the belief that instead of complaining about the students, the parents, yours colleagues, and your leaders, that you can make a difference to their behavior and impact too.	□ **Collective efficacy:** expressed in shared and deliberately bolstered beliefs in the principle that all students can learn a lot more than they and others think they can, and that all of these students can and should experience success.
□ **Inward mindsets:** in terms of learning from one another in shared dialogue, observation, and feedback.	□ **Outward mindsets:** including learning from workshops, keynote addresses, academic research, online resources, and interactions, but in a way that is then cycled back into and through the inside community.

SOURCE: Used with the permission of Learning forward, www.learningforward.org.

The following sections examine four expressions of teacher collaboration: peer coaching, professional development, team teaching, and co-teaching.

FOCUS ON STEM: PBS COLLABORATIVE DISSEMINATES STEM STRATEGIES NATIONWIDE

Science Friday (SciFri), a PBS program that has introduced scientific concepts to listeners since 1991, launched the Educator Collaborative in 2016. The purpose of the Collaborative is to share novel approaches to STEM teaching with a national audience.

Each year, approximately six teachers are selected for the Collaborative. During the year, they work together and develop free, ready-to-use STEM resources for teachers at all levels around the country. *Science Friday* provides guidance and supports the teachers' work by developing professional, high-quality visuals and multimedia that are shared with a national PBS audience. In addition, members of the Collaborative receive a virtual visit to their classrooms from a scientist, engineer, or mathematician affiliated with *Science Friday*. Projects developed by the 2017 Educator Collaborative cohort included the following:

Exploring honeycomb shape using pattern blocks and geometry
Stacy George, STEM teacher, grades 3–5, Mauka Lani Elementary School, Kapolei, **HAWAII**.

Spinning model eggs to gather data on the rotational inertia of raw and hard-boiled eggs
Jose Rivas, physics and engineering teacher, Lennox Mathematics, Science, and Technology Academy, Lennox, **CALIFORNIA**

Investigating how DNA and nutritional experiences influence the longevity of the edible dormouse
Rebecca Brewer, Advanced Placement and ninth-grade biology, Troy High School, Troy, **MICHIGAN** (Garcia & Zych, 2017).

PEER COACHING Experienced teachers traditionally help novice teachers, but more formal peer-coaching programs extend the benefits of collaboration to more teachers. **Peer coaching** is an arrangement whereby teachers grow professionally by observing one another's teaching and providing constructive feedback. The practice encourages teachers to learn together in an emotionally safe environment. According to the authors of *Models of Teaching*, peer coaching is an effective way to create communities of professional educators, and all teachers should be members of coaching teams:

> If we had our way, all school faculties would be divided into coaching teams—that is, teams who regularly observe one another's teaching and learn from watching one another and the students. In short, we recommend the development of a "coaching environment" in which all personnel see themselves as coaches. (Joyce et al., 2015, p. 440)

Ian Wedgewood/Pearson Education Ltd
Opportunities for teachers to collaborate help to create a professional learning environment and lead to improved learning for all students.

Through teacher-to-teacher support and collaboration, peer-coaching programs improve teacher morale and teaching effectiveness.

PROFESSIONAL DEVELOPMENT Today, teachers often contribute to the design of professional development programs that encourage collaboration, risk taking, and experimentation. Some programs, for example, give teachers the opportunity to meet with other teachers at similar grade levels or in similar content areas for the purpose of sharing ideas, strategies, and solutions to problems. A day or part of a day may be devoted to this kind of workshop or idea exchange. Teachers are frequently given released time from regular duties to visit other schools and observe exemplary programs in action.

One example of a collaborative professional development program is being implemented at Hartville Elementary School in Hartville, **MISSOURI**, population 613. The program, called eMINTS (Enhancing Missouri's Instructional Networked Teaching Strategies), trains teachers to use technology to enhance inquiry-based learning in their classrooms. The program consists of 240 hours of professional development over a 2-year period and includes coaching and follow-up training sessions. To date, more than 250,000 students have been taught by eMINTS-trained teachers, and these students consistently outperform their peers on state standardized tests (Meyers, Molefe, Dhillon, & Zhu, 2015).

Hartville Elementary, located in a community hard hit by the nationwide economic slump, had few technology resources and professional development opportunities before eMINT began. As a result of the eMINT professional development program, however, the school's principal made the following comment: "By helping our teachers with training they can apply directly in their classrooms, we not only improved our test results, we changed the entire culture of our school. And our focus has grown from improvement to excellence" (Markus, 2012).

One of the most stimulating ways to pursue professional development is to enroll in a graduate program at a nearby college or university. Most states now require teachers to take some graduate courses to keep their certifications and knowledge up to date.

Graduate-level class schedules are usually developed with teachers in mind, with most courses offered in the evenings, on Saturdays, and during the summer. If you pursue graduate study, not only will you find the professional dialogue with instructors and fellow students stimulating, but you will also acquire theories and practical approaches that you can implement in your classroom the next workday. Also, you might find some other area of education—administration and supervision, guidance and counseling, special education, or curriculum development—that you want to pursue in your long-term career development. The Technology in Action feature in this chapter profiles a teacher who earned an online master's degree.

TECHNOLOGY in ACTION

Teacher Earns Online Master's Degree

Ms. Flick is a second-grade teacher at a small rural elementary school. She has taught there for just over three years. By all accounts, she is doing quite well. Her only complaint is the remote location of the school. She likes the quiet of the small town, but she misses the opportunities of a larger urban setting. One of the opportunities she misses is access to higher education because she wants to pursue a master's degree. The problem is that the nearest university is over 100 miles away. If she planned to pursue her master's at this institution, she would either need to take a leave of absence from her teaching duties and relocate to the city where the university is located, or drive several hundred miles each week and take night and summer courses. With her extracurricular responsibilities and her family and community commitments, neither of these options is appealing.

Last year, a colleague of Ms. Flick took an online course in classroom assessment. He had some very positive things to say about the experience.

After a bit of research into online courses and degrees, Ms. Flick was surprised to find so many options available to her. Through the online medium, she now had the option of "attending" a university anywhere in the world, at nationally and internationally recognized institutions, without ever leaving her community.

She found a university that seemed perfect. It offered a graduate degree in a subject area targeted to her professional interests. The tuition was actually less expensive than her local university. What intrigued her most was that the program was described as highly interactive. In other words, this was not a work-at-your-own-pace, all-by-yourself program. According to the program description, the academic rigor was identical to the on-campus experience.

Although unsure of these claims, Ms. Flick enrolled in the program. She started with just one course the first semester—to measure the accuracy of the program description and determine the level of effort needed for success. At first, it was rough going. This style of learning was quite new to her. The most difficult aspect of online learning was carving out time for the coursework. Ms. Flick realized that she would need to create an individual calendar based on the demands of the course that would allow her to dedicate time for specific assignments.

As she moved through the semester, Ms. Flick found that the description of the program was very accurate. The courses were highly interactive. She connected with classmates, worked in small groups, developed projects, and made presentations. She was already looking forward to the next semester.

Online degrees are one of the fastest growing educational options in the United States. An online degree is an academic degree delivered through an online medium. As with on-campus programs, the student experience depends on the university, the subject matter, and the instructor. Most online degree programs are delivered through a learning management system. In these systems, students interact, submit assignments, make presentations, and follow a guided course experience. Teachers have used online courses and degrees to update their résumés, obtain advanced degrees, and improve their teaching without relocating, traveling long distances, or giving up employment.

VISIT: Numerous online degree options are available to you. You can search for online degrees by level of education, subject matter, or specific institution. Many universities that offer online degree programs provide opportunities for potential students to take a demo course.

FOCUS ON **DIVERSITY**: PROFESSIONAL DEVELOPMENT BY LEARNING ANOTHER LANGUAGE

Increasingly, today's teachers must meet the needs of language-minority students—students whose first language is not English. These needs are best met by teachers who speak their native language as well as English. As a teacher in a multilingual setting, you might consider studying another language if it is the first language for some of your students. Your students will appreciate your efforts to learn their first language, and they will see that you are interested in their culture. In addition, you will model for your students the importance of continuous learning. You will also create important opportunities for them to "teach" you about their first language, and your openness to learning from your students will enhance the teaching and learning process in your classroom.

TEAM TEACHING In team-teaching arrangements, teachers share the responsibility for two or more classes, dividing the subject areas between them, with one preparing lessons in mathematics, science, and health, for instance, while the other plans instruction in reading and language arts. The division of responsibility may also be made in terms of the performance levels of the children, so one teacher may teach the lowest- and highest-ability reading groups and the middle math group, for example, while the other teaches the middle-ability reading groups and the lowest and highest mathematics group.

The practice of **team teaching** is often limited by student enrollments and budget constraints. As integrated curricula and the need for special knowledge and skills increase, however, the use of **collegial support teams** will become more common. A collegial support team (CST) provides teachers with a safe zone for professional growth. The members of a team make wide-ranging decisions about the instruction of students assigned to the team, such as when to use large-group instruction or small-group instruction; how teaching tasks will be divided; and how time, materials, and other resources will be allocated.

CO-TEACHING In co-teaching arrangements, two or more teachers, such as a classroom teacher and a special education teacher or other specialist, teach together in the same classroom. **Co-teaching** builds on the strengths of two teachers and provides increased learning opportunities for all students (Friend & Cook, 2017; Friend & Bursuck, 2015). Typically, co-teaching arrangements occur during a set period of time each day or on certain days of the week. Among the several possible co-teaching variations, Friend and Cook (2017, p. 166) have identified the following six arrangements that are also illustrated in Figure 13.10:

Video Example 13.3

Co-teaching: These two teachers are conducting a math lesson with one teacher leading the lesson and the other assisting. Take note of how each teacher contributes to the instruction.

- **One teaching, one observing** —one teacher teaches the lesson; the other observes.
- **One teaching, one assisting** —one teacher leads the lesson; the other assists.
- **Station teaching** —the lesson is divided into two parts; one teacher teaches one part to half of the students while the other teaches the other part to the rest. The groups then switch and the teachers repeat their part of the lesson. If students can work independently, a third group may be formed, or a volunteer may teach at a third station.
- **Parallel teaching** —a class is divided in half, and each teacher instructs half the class individually.
- **Alternative teaching** —a class is divided into one large group and one small group. For example, one teacher may provide remediation or enrichment to the small group, while the other teacher instructs the large group.
- **Teaming** —teachers fluidly share teaching responsibilities.

Figure 13.10 Co-teaching approaches

One teaching, one observing

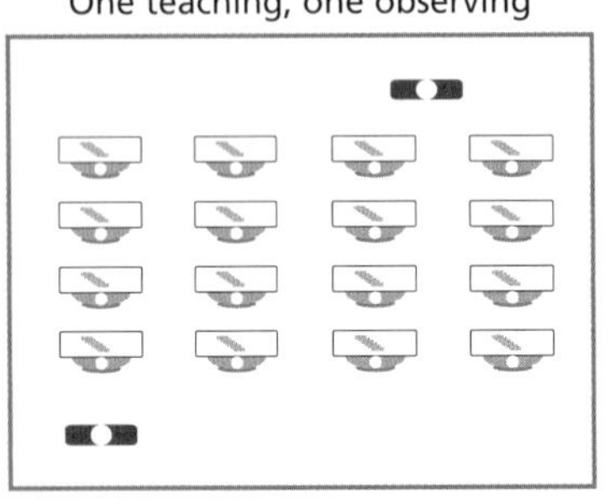

Station teaching

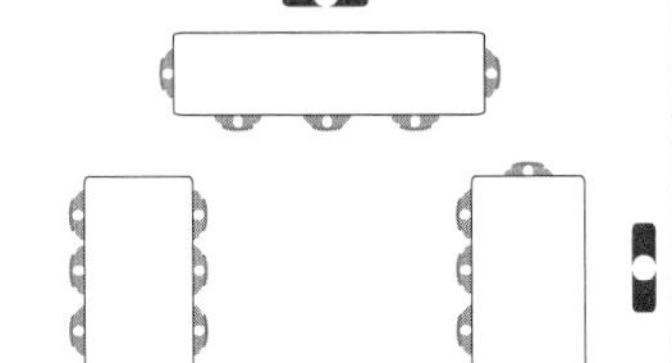

Parallel teaching

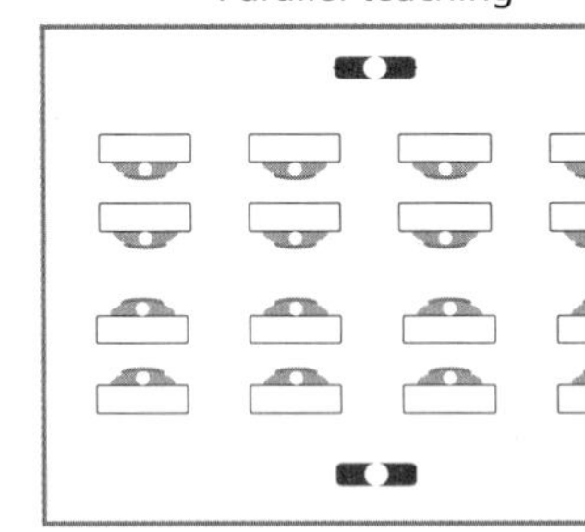

Alternative teaching

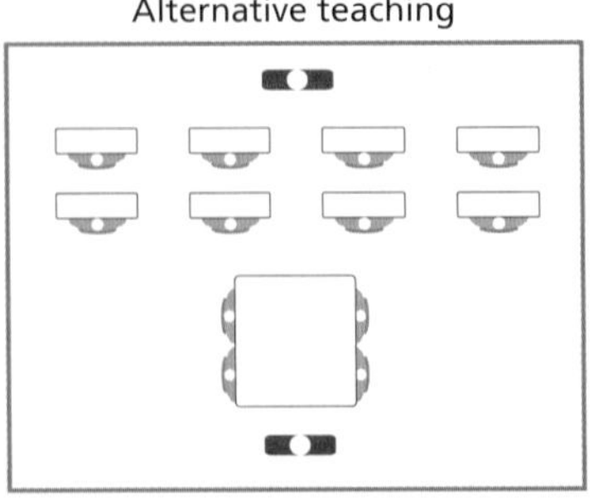

Teaming

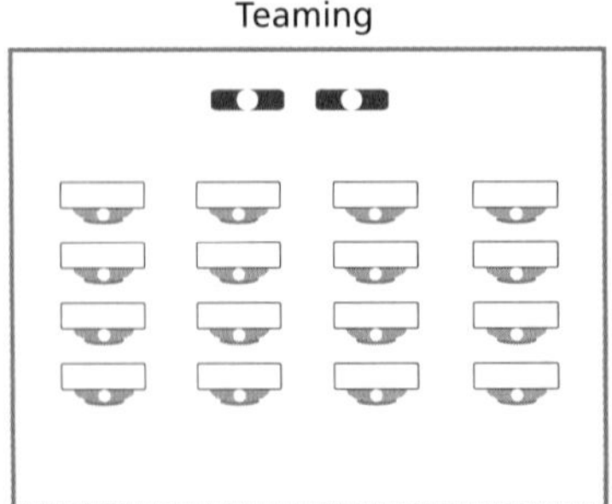

One teaching, one assiting

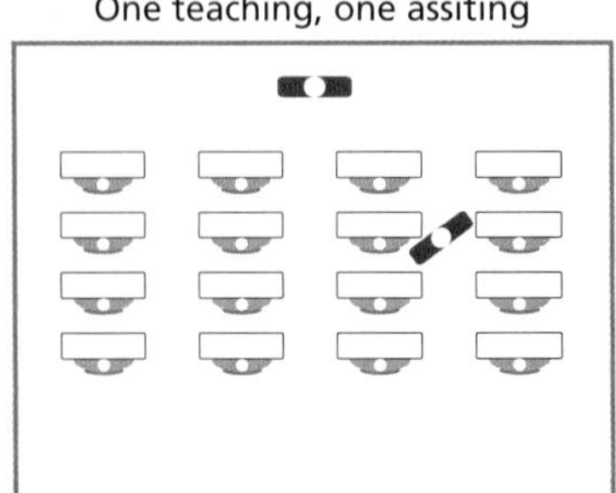

SOURCE: Based on Friend, M., & Cook, L. (2017). Interactions: Collaboration skills for school professionals (8th ed.). Boston, MA: Pearson, p. 166.

Check Your Understanding 13.5

Summary

How Can You Learn from Observing in Classrooms?

- You can develop knowledge about teaching through video observations and analysis of "real" classrooms, focused classroom observations, and the use of various observation instruments.
- Observation instruments range from informal, qualitative descriptions to formal, quantitative checklists.

How Can You Gain Practical Experience for Becoming a Teacher?

- Microteaching, teaching simulations, field-based practica and clinical experiences, classroom aide programs, student teaching, developing a professional portfolio, and substitute teaching are among the ways teacher education students can gain practical experience and prepare for their first teaching position.

How Can You Obtain Support as a Teacher?

- In response to the problem of teacher attrition, many states and school districts provide beginning teachers with induction programs that offer support during their first years in the profession.
- Induction programs offer beginning teachers various types of support, including workshops based on teacher-identified needs, observations and feedback from experienced teachers, mentoring, and support group meetings.
- Mentoring can be a source of professional growth for experienced teachers and enables the protégé to learn about the profession.
- A mentor can model for the protégé an analytical approach to solving problems in the classroom.

What Leadership Opportunities Will You Have Beyond the Classroom?

- Teachers have many opportunities to provide leadership for the profession, including 11 dimensions of leadership beyond the classroom.

How Will You Help to Build a Learning Community and Collaborate with Teachers?

- Effective teachers recognize the importance of being part of the learning community beyond the classroom.
- The learning community includes students, families, colleagues, and members of the community.
- Teachers and parents generally agree on the importance of what teachers can do for parents.
- Teachers collaborate though participation in school governance, curriculum development, school-community partnerships, and educational reform.
- Four approaches to teacher collaboration are peer coaching, professional development, team teaching, and co-teaching.

Professional Reflections and Activities

Teacher's Journal

1. Complete the following sentences as a way to help determine conditions that would be ideal for your first teaching position.

   Ideally, my first position would be teaching students who had the following backgrounds and characteristics: ______________.

   For me, an ideal work setting would be a school that ______________.

   My fellow teachers would help me during my first year at teaching by ______________.

   When not in school, my colleagues and I would enjoy ______________.

   My principal and/or supervisor would appreciate the way I ______________.

   In his or her feedback on my teaching, my principal and/or supervisor would be most impressed with ______________.

   During my first year at the school, I would volunteer to ______________.

   Five years after I begin teaching, I would like to be ______________.

2. Imagine your first day as a teacher. Describe what you see.
3. Do you think there are any limitations regarding the extent to which a teacher should become involved in the 11 dimensions of leadership beyond the classroom that was presented in Figure 13.8 on page 465? Explain your answer. As a teacher, which leadership activities might you become involved in?

Teacher's Research

1. Use your favorite browser to gather online information and resources about teacher networking and mentoring. How might online networking provide you with mentoring support and resources during your induction into teaching?
2. With classmates, join an online discussion on one or more of the following topics discussed in this chapter.
   - Mentoring
   - National Board for Professional Teaching Standards (NBPTS)
   - Teacher leadership
   - Substitute teaching
   - Teacher induction

Observations and Interviews

1. Interview two or more experienced teachers about the triumphs and defeats they experienced as beginning teachers. What lessons are evident in their responses? Are there common themes that characterize the triumphs? The defeats?
2. Interview two or more teachers about their involvement in leadership activities outside the classroom. With which of the 11 dimensions of teacher leadership presented in Figure 13.8 are they involved? What benefits do they obtain from their leadership activities?

Professional Portfolio

With reference to the grade level for which you are preparing to teach, compile a set of rules related to classroom conduct and academic work that you would want to present to students on the first day of class. Classroom conduct rules might address areas such as seat assignments; food, drinks, and gum in class; passes to use the washroom; and talking during class. Rules related to academic work might address areas such as materials required for each class, homework, incomplete work, missed quizzes or examinations, assignments turned in late, and makeup work.

Glossary

A

academic freedom: the right of teachers to teach, free from external constraint, censorship, or interference.

academic learning time: the amount of time students spend working on academic tasks with a high level of success (80 percent or higher).

academic mindset: a positive view of oneself as a learner and an understanding that effort is required to develop ability and competence related to academic work.

academies: early secondary schools with broader and more practical curricula than those found in grammar schools of the previous century.

acceleration: the process of providing academically enriched programs to meet the needs of intellectually advanced students; for example, early entrance, grade skipping, rigorous curricula, credit by examination, and early entrance to college.

accountability: the practice of holding teachers responsible for adhering to high professional and moral standards and creating effective learning environments for all students.

achievement gap: the continuing gap in academic achievement between White students and Hispanic, African American, and American Indian/Alaska Native students.

adequate yearly progress (AYP): a provision of the No Child Left Behind Act of 2001 requiring that schools provide evidence each year that students are making adequate yearly progress.

Adverse Childhood Experiences (ACE) Study: an ongoing national study regarding the prevalence of 10 categories of traumatic experiences people can have during childhood; adverse childhood experiences (ACEs) increase the risk of health and social problems throughout the lifespan.

aesthetics: the branch of axiology concerned with values related to beauty and art.

Afrocentric schools: schools that focus on African American history and cultures for African American students.

allocated time: the amount of time teachers allocate for instruction in various areas of the curriculum.

alternate assessments: alternative ways of measuring the performance of students who are unable to participate in traditional approaches to assessment.

alternative assessments: approaches that assess students' ability to complete real-life tasks rather than merely regurgitate facts.

alternative school: a small, highly individualized school separate from a regular school; designed to meet the needs of students at risk.

alternative teacher certification: a provision allowing people who have completed college to become certified teachers (not a teacher education program).

Amendments to the Individuals with Disabilities Education Act (IDEA 97): amendments to IDEA that emphasize educational outcomes for students with disabilities and provide greater access through changes in eligibility requirements, IEP guidelines, public and private placements, student discipline guidelines, and procedural safeguards.

American Federation of Teachers (AFT): a national professional association for teachers, affiliated with the AFL-CIO.

analytic rubric: a rating scale, or scoring guide, for evaluating part of a student's product or performance.

ASCD: a professional organization for educators interested in school improvement at all levels (formerly, the Association for Supervision and Curriculum Development [ASCD]).

assertive discipline: an approach to classroom discipline requiring that teachers establish firm, clear guidelines for student behavior and follow through with consequences for misbehavior.

assessment: the process of gathering information related to how much students have learned.

assistive technology: technological advances (usually computer based) that help exceptional students learn and communicate.

attention deficit disorder (ADD): a learning disability characterized by difficulty in concentrating on learning.

attention deficit hyperactivity disorder (ADHD): a learning disability characterized by difficulty in remaining still so that one can concentrate on learning.

authentic assessment: an approach to assessing students' learning that requires them to solve problems or work on tasks that approximate as much as possible those they will encounter beyond the classroom.

authentic learning tasks: learning activities that enable students to see the connections between classroom learning and the world beyond the classroom.

axiology: the study of values, including the identification of criteria for determining what is valuable.

B

back-to-basics: a movement begun in the mid-1970s to establish the basic skills of reading, writing, speaking, and computation as the core of the school curriculum.

behaviorism: based on behavioristic psychology, this philosophical orientation maintains that environmental factors shape people's behavior.

benchmarks: statements of what students should understand and be able to do at specific grade levels or developmental stages.

between-class ability grouping: the practice of grouping students at the middle and high school levels for instruction on the basis of ability or achievement, often called tracking.

bicultural: the ability to function effectively in two or more linguistic and cultural groups.

bilingual education programs: curricula for non-English-speaking students in which English and a student's native language are used for instruction.

blended learning: a blending of online and face-to-face instruction.

blended schools: schools that provide a combination of traditional, face-to-face instruction and online learning.

block grants: a form of federal aid given directly to the states, which a state or local education agency may spend as it wishes with few limitations.

block scheduling: a high school scheduling arrangement that provides longer blocks of time each class period, with fewer periods each day.

A Blueprint for Reform: The Reauthorization of the Elementary and Secondary Education Act: the Obama administration's plan for revising the No Child Left Behind Act (NCLB) and reauthorizing the Elementary and Secondary Education Act; released in 2010, the Blueprint supports state and local efforts to ensure that all students graduate prepared for college and a career.

***Brown v. Board of Education of Topeka, 1954*:** a landmark U.S. Supreme Court case rejecting the separate but equal doctrine used to prevent African Americans from attending schools with Whites.

Buckley Amendment: a 1974 law, the Family Educational Rights and Privacy Act, granting parents of students under 18 and students over 18 the right to examine their school records.

C

caring classroom: a classroom in which the teacher communicates clearly an attitude of caring about students' learning and their overall well-being.

categorical aid: state-appropriated funds to cover the costs of educating students with special needs.

censorship: the act of removing from circulation printed material judged to be libelous, vulgar, or obscene.

character education: an approach to education that emphasizes the teaching of values, moral reasoning, and the development of good character.

charter: an agreement between a charter school's founders and its sponsors specifying how the school will operate and what learning outcomes students will master.

charter schools: independent schools, often founded by teachers, that are given a charter to operate by a school district, state, or national government with the provision that students must demonstrate mastery of predetermined outcomes.

chief state school officer: the chief administrator of a state department of education and head of the state board of education, often called the commissioner of education or superintendent of public instruction.

choice theory: an approach to classroom management, developed by psychiatrist William Glasser, based on a belief that students will usually make good choices (i.e., behave in an acceptable manner) if they experience success in the classroom and know that teachers care about them.

classroom climate: the atmosphere or quality of life in a classroom, determined by how individuals interact with one another.

classroom culture: the way of life characteristic of a classroom group; determined by the social dimensions of the group and the physical characteristics of the setting.

classroom management: day-to-day teacher control of student behavior and learning, including discipline.

classroom organization: how teachers and students in a school are grouped for instruction and how time is allocated in classrooms.

code of ethics: a set of guidelines that defines appropriate behavior for professionals.

cognitive development: the process of acquiring the intellectual ability to learn from interaction with one's environment.

cognitive science: the study of the learning process that focuses on how individuals manipulate symbols and process information.

collaboration: the practice of working together, sharing decision making, and solving problems among professionals.

collaborative consultation: an approach in which a classroom teacher meets with one or more other professionals (such as a special educator, school psychologist, or resource teacher) to focus on the learning needs of one or more students.

collective bargaining: a process followed by employers and employees in negotiating salaries, hours, and working conditions; in most states, school boards must negotiate contracts with teacher organizations.

collegial support team (CST): a team of teachers created according to subject area, grade level, or teacher interests and expertise who support one another's professional development.

Commission on the Reorganization of Secondary Education: an NEA committee that called for a high school curriculum designed to accommodate individual differences in scholastic ability and based on seven educational goals, or "cardinal principles" (1913).

Committee of Fifteen: an NEA committee that recommended an academically rigorous curriculum for elementary students (1895).

Committee of Ten: an NEA committee that recommended an academically rigorous curriculum for high school students (1893).

Common Core State Standards Initiative (CCSSI): a set of voluntary K–12 curriculum standards developed and endorsed by 48 of the 50 states.

common schools: free state-supported schools that provide education for all students.

communities of practice (COP): groups of educators who share professional expertise related to an area of common interest—for example, teaching with technology, teaching English language learners (ELLs), or teaching STEM (science, technology, engineering, and mathematics) at the high school level.

community schools: schools that provide students and their families with medical, social, and human services, in addition to their regular educational programs.

compensatory education programs: federally funded educational programs designed to meet the needs of low-ability students from low-income families.

complex trauma: repeated traumatic experiences from which a child cannot escape; over time, this chronic stress produces neurobiological changes in the brain that are linked to poor physical health and to poor cognitive performance.

concrete operations stage: the stage of cognitive development (7 to 11 years of age) proposed by Jean Piaget in which the individual develops the ability to use logical thought to solve concrete problems.

connected learning: professional development activities teachers pursue (often online) by connecting with other teachers; activities are collaboratively developed and led by teachers themselves.

constructive assertiveness: an approach to classroom management that calls for the teacher to communicate to misbehaving student(s) a direct, clear statement of the problem; maintain direct eye contact with the student(s); and insist on correct behavior.

constructivism: a psychological orientation that views learning as an active process in which learners construct understanding of the material they learn in contrast to the view that teachers transmit academic content to students in small segments.

constructivist teaching: a method of teaching based on students' prior knowledge of the topic and the processes they use to construct meaning.

content standards: the content or knowledge and skills students should acquire in various academic disciplines.

cooperative learning: an approach to education in which students work in small groups, or teams, sharing the work and helping one another complete assignments.

copyright laws: laws limiting the use of photocopies, videotapes, and computer software programs.

corporal punishment: physical punishment applied to a student by a school employee as a disciplinary measure.

co-teaching: an arrangement whereby two or more teachers teach together in the same classroom.

Council for the Accreditation of Educator Preparation (CAEP): an accrediting agency formed in 2010 by the merger of the National Council for Accreditation of Teacher Education (NCATE) and the Teacher Education Accreditation Council (TEAC).

criterion-referenced assessments: assessments of achievement that compare students' performance with clearly defined criteria or standards.

critical pedagogy: an educational orientation that emphasizes education as a way to promote social justice and equity for those who do not enjoy positions of power and influence in society.

cross-age tutoring: a tutoring arrangement in which older students tutor younger students; evidence indicates that cross-age tutoring has positive effects on the attitudes and achievement of tutee and tutor.

cultural capital: the knowledge, behaviors, and skills that enable people to be successful in their own cultures.

cultural identity: an overall sense of oneself, derived from the extent of one's participation in various subcultures within the national macroculture.

cultural pluralism: the preservation of cultural differences among groups of people within one society. This view is in contrast to the melting-pot theory that says that ethnic cultures should melt into one.

culturally responsive teaching: teaching that uses instructional strategies and curriculum materials that reflect and value students' cultural backgrounds.

culture: the way of life common to a group of people; includes knowledge deemed important, shared meanings, norms, values, attitudes, ideals, and view of the world.

curriculum: the school experiences, both planned and unplanned, that enhance (and sometimes impede) the education and growth of students.

curriculum alignment: the process of ensuring that the content of curricula and textbooks reflects desired learning outcomes, or academic standards, for students.

curriculum framework: a document that provides guidelines, instructional and assessment strategies, resources, and models for teachers to use as they develop curricula aligned with academic standards.

cyberbullying: using information and/or communication technologies to harass or threaten an individual or group.

D

dame schools: colonial schools, usually held in the homes of widows or housewives, for teaching children basic reading, writing, and mathematical skills.

deficit thinking: personal beliefs that can lead a teacher to have lower expectations for students from cultural backgrounds that differ from the more affluent dominant culture.

democratic classroom: a classroom in which the teacher's leadership style encourages students to take more power and responsibility for their learning.

departmentalization: an organizational arrangement for schools in which students move from classroom to classroom for instruction in different subject areas.

desegregation: the process of eliminating schooling practices based on the separation of racial groups.

Digital Millennium Copyright Act (DMCA): an amendment to the Copyright Act of 1998, making it illegal to reproduce copyrighted material in digital format.

digital use divide: the gap between people at different socioeconomic levels and their use of digital technologies and the Internet.

direct instruction: a systematic instructional method focusing on the transmission of knowledge and skills from the teacher to the students.

discovery learning: an approach to teaching that gives students opportunities to inquire into subjects so that they discover knowledge for themselves.

dismissal: the involuntary termination of a teacher's employment; termination must be made for a legally defensible reason with the protection of due process.

diversity: differences among people in regard to gender, race, ethnicity, culture, and socioeconomic status.

due process: a set of specific guidelines that must be followed to protect individuals from arbitrary, capricious treatment by those in authority.

E

early childhood education: educational programs for children from birth to age 8, also termed pre-K education.

educational malpractice: liability for injury that results from the failure of a teacher, school, or school district to provide a student with adequate instruction, guidance, counseling, and/or supervision.

educational philosophy: a set of ideas and beliefs about education that guide the professional behavior of educators.

educational politics: how people use power, influence, and authority to affect instructional and curricular practices within a school or school system.

educational reform movement: a comprehensive effort made during the 1980s and into the 1990s to improve schools and the preparation of teachers.

Education Consolidation and Improvement Act (ECIA): a 1981 federal law giving the states a broad range of choices for spending federal aid on education.

Education for All Handicapped Children Act (Public Law 94-142): a 1975 federal act that guarantees a free and appropriate education to all children with handicaps (often referred to as the mainstreaming law or Public Law 94–142).

Elementary and Secondary Education Act: part of President Lyndon B. Johnson's Great Society programs, this act allocated federal funds on the basis of the number of poor children in school districts (1965).

emergency certification: temporary, substandard certification requirements set by a state in response to a shortage of teachers.

emotional intelligence: the capacity to be aware of and to manage one's feelings.

English as a second language (ESL): the development of English language skills of students whose first language is not English.

English language learners (ELLs): students not currently proficient in English and in the process of developing their English language skills.

entitlements: federal programs to meet the educational needs of special populations.

epistemology: a branch of philosophy concerned with the nature of knowledge and what it means to know something.

essentialism: formulated in part as a response to progressivism, this philosophical orientation holds that a core of common knowledge about the real world should be transmitted to students in a systematic, disciplined way.

ethical dilemmas: problem situations in which an ethical response is difficult to determine; that is, no single response can be called right or wrong.

ethics: a branch of philosophy concerned with principles of conduct and determining what is good and evil, right and wrong, in human behavior.

ethnic group: individuals within a larger culture who share a racial or cultural identity and a set of beliefs, values, and attitudes and who consider themselves members of a distinct group or subculture.

ethnicity: a shared feeling of common identity that derives, in part, from a common ancestry, common values, and common experiences.

evaluation: making judgments about, or assigning a value to, measurements of students' learning.

Every Student Succeeds Act (ESSA): a K–12 education law that reauthorized the Elementary and Secondary Education Act (ESEA) and replaced the No Child Left Behind Act (NCLB); fully implemented in 2017–2018, ESSA requires that states set high curriculum standards in reading or language arts, math and science, and any other subject(s) identified by the state.

exceptional learners: students whose growth and development deviate from the norm to the extent that their educational needs can be met more effectively through a modification of regular school programs.

existentialism: a philosophical orientation that emphasizes the individual's experiences and maintains that each individual must determine his or her own meaning of existence.

expanded learning time (ELT) schools: schools that add time to the school day as a way to increase student achievement, provide opportunities for enrichment, and partner with community organizations.

explicit curriculum: the behavior, attitudes, and knowledge that a school intends to teach students.

extracurricular/cocurricular programs: activities perceived as additions to the academic curriculum.

F

fair use: the right of an individual to use copyrighted material in a reasonable manner without the copyright holder's consent, provided that use meets certain criteria.

female seminaries: schools established in the early 19th century to train women for higher education and public service outside the home.

feminist pedagogy: a philosophical orientation that emphasizes caring, respect for individual differences, and collaboration to achieve the aims of a democratic and just society.

field experiences: opportunities for teachers-in-training to experience firsthand the world of the teacher by observing, tutoring, and instructing small groups.

flipped classroom: a classroom in which students learn new content at home by watching online video lectures by the teacher or other online videos related to the subject matter. During in-class sessions, students apply their new knowledge by solving problems or completing "homework," with the teacher providing individual assistance.

flipped teaching: an approach to teaching in which teachers prepare online video lectures that students watch at home; during in-class sessions, teachers then help students apply their new knowledge to solving problems or completing "homework."

formal assessments: systematic, pre-planned assessments of student learning – tests, quizzes, homework, and critques of performance.

formal operations stage: the stage of cognitive development (11 to 15 years of age) proposed by Jean Piaget in which cognitive abilities reach their highest level of development.

formative evaluation: an assessment, or diagnosis, of students' learning for the purpose of planning instruction.

for-profit schools: schools that are operated, for profit, by private educational corporations.

Freedmen's Bureau: a U.S. government agency to provide assistance to former slaves after the Civil War.

freedom of expression: freedom, granted by the First Amendment to the Constitution, to express one's beliefs.

fringe benefits: benefits (i.e., medical insurance, retirement, and tax-deferred investment opportunities) that are given to teachers in addition to base salary.

full-funding programs: state programs to ensure statewide financial equity by setting the same per-pupil expenditure level for all schools and districts.

full inclusion: the policy and process of including exceptional learners in general education classrooms.

funds of knowledge: historically accumulated and culturally developed bodies of knowledge and skills essential for an individual to function well in a given culture.

G

gender bias: subtle bias or discrimination on the basis of gender; reduces the likelihood that the target of the bias will develop to the full extent of his or her capabilities.

gender-fair classroom: education that is free of bias or discrimination on the basis of gender.

G.I. Bill of Rights: a 1944 federal law that provides veterans with payments for tuition and room and board at colleges and universities and special schools; formally known as the Servicemen's Readjustment Act.

gifted and talented: exceptional learners who demonstrate high intelligence, high creativity, high achievement, or special talents.

grievance: a formal complaint filed by an employee against his or her employer or supervisor.

group investigation: an approach to teaching in which the teacher facilitates learning by creating an environment that allows students to determine what they will study and how.

H

Head Start: a federal program that promotes the school readiness of children ages birth to 5 years from low income families by enhancing their cognitive, social, and emotional development.

hidden curriculum: the behaviors, attitudes, and knowledge that the school culture unintentionally teaches students.

hierarchy of needs: a set of seven needs, from the basic needs for survival and safety to the need for self-actualization, that motivate human behavior as identified by Abraham Maslow.

highly qualified teachers (HQTs): teachers who have the following qualifications as contained in No Child Left Behind legislation: bachelor's degree, full state certification, and knowledge of the subject(s) they teach.

High School: A Report on Secondary Education in America: a book by Ernest Boyer calling for a strengthened academic core curriculum in high schools (1983).

high-stakes tests: achievement tests that have high-stakes consequences for students, teachers, and administrators; for example, a test that determines if a student is eligible to graduate or whether educators receive merit pay increases for their students' improved scores.

holistic rubric: a rating scale, or scoring guide, for evaluating a student's overall product or performance.

hornbook: a copy of the alphabet covered by a thin transparent sheet made from a cow's horn.

humanism: a philosophy based on the belief that individuals control their own destinies through the application of their intelligence and learning.

humanistic psychology: an orientation to human behavior that emphasizes personal freedom, choice, awareness, and personal responsibility.

hybrid teacher: a teacher who combines part-time classroom teaching with leadership roles in a school or district.

I

inclusion: the practice of integrating all students with disabilities into general education classes.

Indian Education Act of 1972 and 1974 Amendment: a federal law and subsequent amendment designed to provide direct educational assistance to Native American tribes and nations.

individualized education program (IEP): a plan for meeting an exceptional learner's educational needs, specifying goals, objectives, services, and procedures for evaluating progress.

individual racism: the prejudicial belief that one's ethnic or racial group is superior to others.

Individuals with Disabilities Education Act (IDEA): a 1990 federal act providing a free, appropriate education to disabled youth between 3 and 21 years of age. IDEA superseded the earlier Education for All Handicapped Children Act (Public Law 94–142).

induction programs: programs of support for beginning teachers, usually during their first year of teaching.

informal assessments: spontaneous assessments of student learning that teachers make while teaching—noting students' facial expressions; asking questions to gauge students' understanding; and listening to students' explanations of how they solved problems, for example.

information processing: a branch of cognitive science concerned with how individuals use long- and short-term memory to acquire information and solve problems.

inquiry learning: an approach to teaching that gives students opportunities to explore or inquire into subjects so that they develop their own answers to problem situations.

institutional racism: institutional policies and practices, intentional or not, that result in racial inequities.

instructional software: software teachers use to develop learning activities such as the following for students: drill and practice, tutorials, simulations, games or gamification (using video game design and game elements to motivate students), problem solving, and personalized learning.

integrated curriculum: a school curriculum that draws from two or more subject areas and focuses on a theme or concept rather than on a single subject.

intelligence: the ability to learn; the cognitive capacity for thinking.

Interstate Teacher Assessment and Support Consortium (InTASC): a consortium of states that has developed performance-based standards for what beginning teachers should know and be able to do and professional practice standards that apply throughout the developmental stages of a teacher's career.

K

Kentucky Education Reform Act (KERA): comprehensive school-reform legislation requiring all Kentucky schools to form school-based management councils with authority to set policies in eight areas (1990).

kindergarten: a school for children before they begin formal schooling at the elementary level; based on the ideas of German educator Friedrich Froebel, kindergarten means "garden where children grow."

L

Lanham Act: a U.S. government program during World War II that provided funding for training workers in war plants, construction of schools, and child care for working parents.

latchkey children: children who, because of family circumstances, must spend part of each day unsupervised by a parent or guardian.

Latin grammar school: colonial schools established to provide male students with a pre-college education; comparable to today's high schools.

learning disability (LD): a limitation in one's ability to take in, organize, remember, and express information.

learning style preferences: cognitive, affective, and physiological behaviors through which an individual learns most effectively; determined by a combination of hereditary and environmental influences.

least restrictive environment: an educational program that meets a disabled student's special needs in a manner that is identical, to the extent possible, to that provided to students in general education classrooms.

Lemon test: a three-part test, based on *Lemon v. Kurtzman*, to determine whether a state has violated the principle of separation of church and state.

lesbian, gay, bisexual, and transgender (LGBT) students: students whose sexual orientation may subject them to discrimination and/or harassment in school settings.

local school districts: agencies at the local level that have the authority to operate schools in a district.

logic: a branch of philosophy concerned with the processes of reasoning and the identification of rules that will enable thinkers to reach valid conclusions.

M

magnet school: a school offering a curriculum that focuses on a specific area such as the performing arts, mathematics, science, international studies, or technology. Magnet schools, which often draw students from a larger attendance area than regular schools, are frequently developed to promote voluntary desegregation.

mainstreaming: the policy and process of integrating disabled or otherwise exceptional learners into regular classrooms with nonexceptional students.

Massachusetts Act of 1642: a law requiring each town to determine whether its young people could read and write.

Massachusetts Act of 1647: a law mandating the establishment and support of schools; often referred to as the Old Deluder Satan Act because education was seen as the best protection against the wiles of the devil.

mastery learning: an approach to instruction based on the assumptions that (1) nearly all students can learn material if given enough time and taught appropriately, and (2) learning is enhanced if students can progress in small, sequenced steps.

McGuffey readers: an immensely popular series of reading books for students in grades 1 through 6, written in the 1830s by Reverend William Holmes McGuffey.

McKinney-Vento Homeless Assistance Act: the nation's first law to provide assistance to homeless persons, including free public education for children (1987).

measurement: the gathering of data that indicate how much students have learned.

mentor: a wise, knowledgeable individual who provides guidance and encouragement to someone.

mentoring: an intensive form of teaching in which a wise and experienced teacher (the mentor) inducts a student (the protégé) into a professional way of life.

metaphysics: a branch of philosophy concerned with the nature of reality.

microteaching: a brief, single-concept lesson taught by a teacher education student to a small group of students; usually designed to give the education student an opportunity to practice a specific teaching skill.

modeling: the process of thinking out loud that teachers use to make students aware of the reasoning involved in learning new material.

monitorial system: an instructional method whereby a teacher instructs hundreds of pupils through the use of student monitors—older students selected for their academic abilities; developed by Joseph Lancaster (1778–1838).

Montessori method: a method of teaching, developed by Maria Montessori, based on a prescribed set of materials and physical exercises to develop children's independence, knowledge, and skills.

moral reasoning: the reasoning process people follow to decide what is right or wrong.

Morrill Land-Grant Act: an 1862 act that provided federal land that states could sell or rent to raise funds to establish colleges of agriculture and mechanical arts.

multiage classrooms: elementary classrooms with students from different grade levels.

multicultural curriculum: a school curriculum that addresses the needs and backgrounds of all students regardless of their cultural identity and includes the cultural perspectives, or voices, of people who have previously been silent or marginalized.

multicultural education: education that provides equal educational opportunities to all students regardless of socioeconomic status; gender; or ethnic, racial, or cultural backgrounds and is dedicated to reducing prejudice and celebrating the rich diversity of U.S. life.

multiculturalism: a set of beliefs based on the importance of seeing the world from different cultural frames of reference and valuing the diversity of cultures in the global community.

multiple intelligences: a perspective on intellectual ability, proposed by Howard Gardner, suggesting that there are at least eight, and maybe as many as 10, types of human intelligence.

N

National Association of State Directors of Teacher Education and Certifications (NASDTEC) Interstate Agreement: a reciprocity agreement among approximately 47 states and the District of Columbia whereby a teaching certificate obtained in one state will be honored in another.

National Board for Professional Teaching Standards (NBPTS): a board established in 1987 that began issuing professional certificates in 1994–95 to teachers who possess extensive professional knowledge and the ability to perform at a high level.

National Defense Education Act: a 1958 federally sponsored program to promote research and innovation in science, mathematics, modern foreign languages, and guidance.

National Education Association (NEA): the oldest and largest professional association for teachers and administrators.

National Governors Association (NGA): an association of state governors that influences policies in several areas, including teacher education and school reform.

A Nation at Risk: The Imperative for Educational Reform: a 1983 national report critical of U.S. education.

negligence: failure to exercise reasonable, prudent care in providing for the safety of others.

No Child Left Behind (NCLB) Act of 2001: a federal law that mandates statewide testing in reading and mathematics each year in grades 3–8 and holds schools accountable for students' performance on state proficiency tests.

nondiscrimination: conditions characterized by the absence of discrimination; for example, employees receive compensation, privileges, and opportunities for advancement without regard for race, color, religion, sex, or national origin.

normal school: a school that focuses on the preparation of teachers.

norm-referenced assessments: achievement tests that compare students scores with scores of other students who are similar.

null curriculum: the intellectual processes and subject content that schools do not teach.

O

observations: field experiences wherein a teacher education student observes a specific aspect of classroom life such as the students, the teacher, the interactions between the two, the structure of the lesson, or the setting.

online learning: education that is delivered via the Internet.

open educational resources (OER): software, learning materials, and other digital resources that are available for free on the Internet.

open-space schools: schools that have large instructional areas with movable walls and furniture that can be rearranged easily.

opportunity to learn (OTL): the time during which a teacher provides students with challenging content and appropriate instructional strategies to learn that content.

out-of-school time (OST) activities: growth-oriented activities for students that take place beyond the school day; often called extracurricular activities.

P

Paideia Proposal: a book by philosopher Mortimer Adler calling for a perennialist core curriculum based on the Great Books (1982).

parochial schools: schools founded on religious beliefs.

pedagogical expertise: the knowledge accomplished teachers possess regarding how to present subject matter to students through the use of analogies, metaphors, experiments, demonstrations, illustrations, and other instructional strategies.

peer assessment: the practice of having students assess one another's work; usually done informally and during a class session.

peer coaching: an arrangement whereby teachers grow professionally by observing one another's teaching and providing constructive feedback.

peer-counseling programs: an arrangement whereby students, monitored by a school counselor or teacher, counsel one another in areas such as low achievement, interpersonal problems, substance abuse, and career planning.

peer-mediated instruction: approaches to teaching, such as cooperative learning and group investigation, that use the social relationships among students to promote their learning.

peer mediation: experiential activities, such as role-playing and simulations, that encourage students to be more accepting of differences and to develop empathy, social skills, and awareness of prejudice.

peer-mentoring programs: an arrangement whereby students, monitored by a school counselor or teacher, mentor one another in areas such as low achievement, interpersonal problems, substance abuse, and career planning.

peer tutoring: an arrangement whereby students tutor other students in the same classroom or at the same grade level.

perennialism: a philosophical orientation that emphasizes the ideas contained in the Great Books and maintains that the true purpose of education is the discovery of the universal, or perennial, truths of life.

performance-based assessment: the process of determining students' ability to apply knowledge, skills, and work habits to the performance of specific learning tasks; determining what students can do as well as what they know.

performance expectations: established levels of achievement, quality of performance, or level of proficiency.

performance standard: academic standards that reflect levels of proficiency; for example, 1-outstanding, 2-exemplary, 3-proficient, 4-progressing, and 5-standard not met.

per-pupil expenditure: the amount of money spent on each student in a school, school district, state, or nation; usually computed according to average daily attendance.

personal learning network (PLN): a network of professionals developed by a teacher to promote his or her professional learning and to share knowledge and experiences.

Phi Delta Kappa (PDK): a professional and honorary fraternity of educators with 650 chapters and 130,000 members.

philosophy: the use of logical reasoning to inquire into the basic truths about being, knowledge, and conduct.

portfolio assessment: the process of determining how much students have learned by examining collections of work that document their learning over time.

postmodernism: a philosophical orientation that maintains there are no absolute truths; instead, there are many truths and many voices that need to be heard.

practicum: a short field-based experience during which teacher education students spend time observing and assisting in classrooms.

Praxis Series: Professional Assessments for Beginning Teachers: a battery of tests available to states for the initial certification of teachers. Consists of assessments in three areas: academic skills, knowledge of subject, and classroom performance.

pre-K education: educational programs for children from birth to age 5; also termed early childhood education.

preoperational stage: the stage of cognitive development (2 to 7 years of age) proposed by Jean Piaget in which the individual begins to use language and symbols to think of objects and people outside the immediate environment.

privatization movement: umbrella term for reform initiatives that seek to run public schools as private enterprises.

problem-solving orientation: an approach to teaching that places primary emphasis on the teacher's role as a decision maker and problem solver.

productivity software: software that teachers and students use for the following educational activities: (a) writing and publishing, (b) representing ideas textually, visually, and auditorily, (c) collecting and analyzing data, and (d) planning and organizing; in addition, teachers can use productivity software for assessing student learning.

profession: an occupation that requires a high level of expertise, including advanced study in a specialized field, adherence to a code of ethics, and the ability to work without close supervision.

professional learning communities (PLCs): school-based, face-to-face groups of teachers that design and facilitate their own professional development.

professional malpractice: an action or continuing conduct of a professional that fails to meet standards for professional practice, resulting in preventable damage to the professional's client. Malpractice may be the result of negligence, lack of knowledge and/or skills, or intentional wrongdoing.

professional portfolio: a collection of work that documents an individual's accomplishments in an area of professional practice.

professionalization of teaching: the steadily increasing political influence and status of teaching as a profession; increased political influence and status reflect changes such as expanding leadership opportunities for teachers, national board certification, peer review, shared decision making, and teacher-mentor programs.

Program for International Student Assessment (PISA): an international assessment of students' reading, mathematics, and science literacy skills in 34 nations.

Progress in International Reading Literacy Study (PIRLS): an international assessment of students' reading and literacy skills in 44 nations.

progressive movement: a movement during the 1920s and 1930s to create schools that emphasized democracy, children's interests and needs, and closer connections between school and community.

progressivism: a philosophical orientation based on the belief that life is evolving in a positive direction, that people may be trusted to act in their own best interests, and that education should focus on the needs and interests of students.

project-based learning (PBL): an approach to learning in which students work in teams on complex, real-world projects that allow them to develop and apply skills and knowledge.

property taxes: local taxes assessed against real estate and, in some areas, against personal property in the form of cars, household furniture and appliances, and stocks and bonds.

prosocial values: values such as honesty, patriotism, fairness, and civility that promote the well-being of a society.

psychosocial crisis: a life crisis at one of eight different stages of growth and development. According to psychologist Erik Erikson, individuals must resolve each crisis to reach the next stage.

psychosocial development: the progression of an individual through various stages of psychological and social development.

Q

qualitative assessments: subjective assessments of student learning; for example, formal and informal observations of students' performance on learning tasks and/or the manner in which they approach those tasks.

quantitative assessments: assessments of student learning that yield numerical scores that teachers use to evaluate student learning as well as the effectiveness of their teaching.

R

race: a concept of human variation used to distinguish people on the basis of biological traits and characteristics.

reading and writing schools: colonial schools, supported by public funds and fees paid by parents, that used a religiously oriented curriculum to teach boys reading and writing skills and, to a lesser degree, mathematics.

recertification: the practice in some states of requiring experienced teachers to undergo periodic testing to maintain their teaching certificates.

redistricting: the practice of redrawing district boundaries to equalize educational funding by reducing the range of variation in the ability of school districts to finance education.

reflection: the process of thinking carefully and deliberately about the outcomes of one's teaching.

reflective teaching log: a journal of classroom observations in which the teacher education student systematically analyzes specific episodes of teaching.

regional educational service agency (RESA): a state educational agency that provides supportive services to two or more school districts; known in some states as education service centers, intermediate school districts, multicounty education service units, boards of cooperative educational services, or educational service regions.

reliability: the degree to which an assessment provides results that are consistent over time.

response to intervention (RTI) model: to determine if a student has a learning disability, increasingly intensive instruction is provided; if the student is not responsive to the instruction, the student receives appropriate special education services.

restorative justice: an approach that enables students—in small, peer-mediated groups—to hear the concerns of those involved in a conflict and then decide how to resolve the conflict; resolution might involve a student making amends to another or providing restitution.

restructuring: reorganizing how schools are controlled at the local level so that teachers, principals, parents, and community members have greater authority.

S

scaffolding: an approach to teaching based on the students' current level of understanding and ability; the teacher varies the amount of help given (for example, clues, encouragement, or suggestions) to students based on their moment-to-moment understanding of the material being learned.

school-based management (SBM): various approaches to school improvement in which teachers, principals, students, parents, and community members manage individual schools and share in the decision-making processes.

school board: the primary governing body of a local school district.

school choice: various proposals that would allow parents to choose the schools their children attend.

school culture: the collective way of life characteristic of a school; a set of beliefs, values, traditions, and ways of thinking and behaving that distinguish it from other schools.

school improvement research: research studies that identify the characteristics of schools that improve over time.

school traditions: those elements of a school's culture that are handed down from year to year.

school-within-a-school: an alternative school (within a regular school) designed to meet the needs of students at risk.

scientific management: the application of management principles and techniques to the operation of big business and large school districts.

scoring rubrics: rating scales that consist of preestablished criteria for evaluating student performance on learning tasks.

search and seizure: the process of searching an individual and/or his or her property if that person is suspected of an illegal act; reasonable or probable cause to suspect the individual must be present.

self-assessment: the process of measuring one's growth in regard to the knowledge, skills, and attitudes possessed by professional teachers.

self-contained classroom: an organizational structure for schools in which one teacher instructs a group of students (typically, 20 to 30) in a single classroom.

service learning: an approach to teaching in which students participate in community-based service activities and then reflect on the meaning of those experiences.

sex role socialization: socially expected behavior patterns conveyed to individuals on the basis of gender.

sex role stereotyping: beliefs that subtly encourage males and females to conform to certain behavioral norms regardless of abilities and interests.

sexual harassment: unwanted and unwelcome sexual behavior directed toward another person, whether of the same or opposite sex.

social justice: a philosophical orientation that emphasizes equity and equal social benefits for all individuals and groups.

social reconstructionism: a philosophical orientation based on the belief that social problems can be solved by changing, or reconstructing, society.

Socratic questioning: a method of questioning designed to lead students to see errors and inconsistencies in their thinking, based on questioning strategies used by Socrates.

special education: a teaching specialty for meeting the special educational needs of exceptional learners.

stages of development: predictable stages through which individuals pass as they progress through life.

standardized assessments: pencil-and-paper achievement tests taken by large groups of students and scored in a uniform manner; some examples are the Iowa Test of Basic Skills, California Achievement Test, and the Scholastic Aptitude Test.

standards: statements that reflect what students should know and be able to do within a particular discipline or at a particular grade level.

standards-based education (SBE): basing curricula, teaching, and assessment of student learning on rigorous academic standards.

state aid: money given by a state to its cities and towns to provide essential services, including the operation of public schools.

state board of education: the highest educational agency in a state; charged with regulating the state's system of education.

state department of education: the branch of state government, headed by the chief state school officer, charged with implementing the states educational policies.

state takeover: takeover of a chronically low-achieving school or district by the state.

STEM education: student learning in the broad areas of science, technology, engineering, and math (STEM).

stereotyping: the process of attributing behavioral characteristics to all members of a group; formulated on the basis of limited experiences with and information about the group, coupled with an unwillingness to examine prejudices.

student-centered curriculum: curriculum that is organized around students' needs and interests.

student diversity: differences among students in regard to gender, race, ethnicity, culture, and socioeconomic status.

students at risk: students whose living conditions and backgrounds place them at risk for dropping out of school.

students with disabilities: students who need special education services because they possess one or more of the following disabilities: learning disabilities, speech or language impairments, intellectual disability, serious emotional disturbance, hearing impairments, orthopedic impairments, visual impairments, or other health impairments.

student variability: differences among students in regard to their developmental needs, interests, abilities, and disabilities.

subject-centered curriculum: a curriculum that emphasizes learning an academic discipline.

substitute teaching: instruction provided by temporary teachers who replace regular teachers absent due to illness, family responsibilities, personal reasons, or attendance at professional workshops and conferences.

summative evaluation: an assessment of student learning made for the purpose of assigning grades at the end of a unit, semester, or year and deciding whether students are ready to proceed to the next phase of their education.

superintendent: the chief administrator of a school district.

T

teacher leader: a teacher who assumes a key leadership role in the improvement and/or day-to-day operation of a school.

teacherpreneur: a teacher leader who influences educational policies in entrepreneurial ways.

teachers' craft knowledge: the knowledge teachers develop about teaching that derives from their experiences in the classroom, particularly the actions they have taken to solve specific problems of practice.

teachers' thought processes: the thoughts that guide teachers' actions in the classroom; for example, thoughts about how to transition to a new activity, how to increase students' interest in subject matter, or how to divide students into groups for work on small-group projects.

teacher supply and demand: the number of school-age students compared to the number of available teachers; may also be projected on the basis of estimated numbers of students and teachers.

teaching certificate: a license to teach issued by a state or, in a few cases, a large city.

teaching contract: an agreement between a teacher and a board of education that the teacher will provide specific services in return for a certain salary, benefits, and privileges.

teaching simulations: an activity in which teacher education students participate in role-plays designed to create situations comparable to those actually encountered by teachers.

team teaching: an arrangement whereby a team of teachers teaches a group of students equal in number to the combined enrollment of their individual, self-contained classrooms.

tenure: an employment policy in which teachers, after serving a probationary period, retain their positions indefinitely and can be dismissed only on legally defensible grounds.

time on task: the amount of time students are actively and directly engaged in learning tasks.

Title IX: a provision of the 1972 Education Amendments Act prohibiting sex discrimination in educational programs.

tort liability: conditions that would permit the filing of legal charges against a professional for breach of duty and/or behaving in a negligent manner.

trauma-sensitive schools: schools guided by an understanding that students' negative behavior is often the direct or indirect result of physical, emotional, or social maltreatment they have experienced; such schools emphasize safety, empowerment, and collaboration between children and adults.

Trends in International Mathematics and Science Study (TIMSS): an international assessment of mathematics and science achievement among 4th-, 8th-, and 12th-grade students in 41 nations.

Tyler rationale: a four-step model for curriculum development in which teachers identify purposes, select learning experiences, organize experiences, and evaluate.

V

validity: the degree to which assessments measure what they are supposed to measure.

value-added modeling: a method of teacher evaluation that compares test scores of a teacher's current students with their scores during previous school years and with the scores of other students in the same grade; in this way, the "value added" by a teacher is determined, and this "value" can be compared to the "value added" by other teachers.

vertical equity: an effort to provide equal educational opportunity within a state by providing different levels of funding based on economic needs within school districts.

virtual labs: computerized, online simulations of scientific laboratories that enable students to conduct scientific inquiry in a virtual environment.

virtual schools: schools at which students complete all or most of their coursework online.

voucher system: funds allocated to parents that they may use to purchase education for their children from public or private schools in the area.

W

web-based educational content: web-based resources teachers can use in the classroom—for example: videos, e-textbooks, images, graphics, photographs, assessments and tests, infographics, games, lectures, lesson plans, podcasts or vodcasts (video podcasts), and online courses.

within-class ability grouping: the practice of creating small, homogeneous groups of students within a single classroom for the purpose of instruction, usually in reading or mathematics, at the elementary level.

Women's Educational Equity Act (WEEA): a 1974 federal law that guarantees equal educational opportunity for females.

work habits: dispositions important for effective thinking and learning—for example, reading with curiosity and willingness to work hard.

Z

zero tolerance policies: school policies related to discipline and safety that provide for automatic, severe consequences for certain types of misbehavior that involves drugs, violence, sexual harassment, or bullying, for example.

References, 11th Edition

AAP Council on Communications and Media. (2016). Media use in school-aged children and adolescents. *Pediatrics, 138*(5). Retrieved from http://pediatrics.aappublications.org/content/138/5/e20162592

Acton v. Vernonia School District, 1995

Adesope, O. O., Lavin, T., Thompson, T., & Ungerleider, C. (2010, June). A systematic review and meta-analysis of the cognitive correlates of bilingualism. *Review of Educational Research, 80*(2), 207–245.

Adler, M. (1982). *The paideia proposal: An educational manifesto.* New York: Macmillan.

Africatown Center for Education and Innovation. (2014, Spring). The Young Geniuses Academy. Retrieved from http://www.africatowncenter.org/programs/

Afterschool Alliance. (2010, September 22). *Afterschool in Hawaii.* Retrieved from http://www.afterschoolalliance.org/states_docs/pdfs/2010/Hawaii_Fact_Sheet.pdf

Ahmed-Ullah, N. S. (2013, February 27). CPS cracks down on underperforming charters. *Chicago Tribune.* Retrieved from http://articles.chicagotribune.com/2013-02-27/news/ct-met-cps-board-meeting-0228-20130228_1_charter-schools-beth-purvis-schools-ceo-barbara-byrd-bennett

Akçayır, M., & Akçayır, G. (2017). Advantages and challenges associated with augmented reality for education: A systematic review of the literature. *Educational Research Review, 20*, 1–11.

Alaska Native Cultural Charter School. (2018, January). Newsletter. Retrieved from https://mailchimp/1f2725f76007/december-newsletter-268059

Albert, M., Rui, P., & Ashman, J. J. (2017). *Physician office visits for attention-deficit/hyperactivity disorder in children and adolescents aged 4-17 years: United States, 2012–2013.* NCHS data brief, no 269. Hyattsville, MD: National Center for Health Statistics.

Albert Shanker Institute. (2011). A call for common content. *American Educator, 35*(1), 41–45.

Alexander, K., & Alexander, M. D. (2012). *American public school law* (8th ed.). Belmont, CA: Wadsworth, Cengage Learning.

Alfonso v. Fernandez, 606 N.Y.S.2d 259 (N.Y. App. Div. 1993).

Allen, M. (February 21, 2013, February 13). Testimony before the U.S. House of Representatives. Retrieved from http://www.nea.org/assets/docs/Testimony_of_Megan_Allen_2-21-13.pdf

Allix, N. M. (2000). The theory of multiple intelligences: A case of missing cognitive matter. *Australian Journal of Education, 44*, 272–288.

Alvin Independent School District v. Cooper, 404 S.W.2d 76 (Tex. Civ. App. 1966).

American Association of University Women (AAUW). (2002). *Harassment-free hallways: How to stop sexual harassment in schools: A guide for students, parents, and teachers, Section III for schools.* Washington, DC: Author.

American Association of University Women (AAUW). (2008, May). *Where the girls are: The facts about gender equity in education.* Washington, DC: Author.

American Federation of Teachers. (2016). *Becoming a Teacher.* Washington, DC: Author.

American Federation of Teachers. (2017). *About AFT.* Retrieved August 29, 2017, from https://www.aft.org/about

American Immigration Council. (2016, October 24). *Public Education for Immigrant Students: Understanding Plyler v. Doe.* Retrieved from https://www.americanimmigrationcouncil.org/research/plyler-v-doe-public-education-immigrant-students

American Institutes of Research. (2003). *Effects of the implementation of Proposition 227 on the education of English learners, K–12, year 3 report.* Submitted to the California Department of Education, October 29, 2003.

American Library Association. (2017, September 19). *Nation celebrates the power of words during Banned Books Week, Sept. 24 – 30, 2017.* Retrieved from http://www.ala.org/news/member-news/2017/09/nation-celebrates-power-words-during-banned-books-week-sept-24-30-2017

Anderson, C., Hildreth, J. A. D., & Howland, L. (2015). Is the desire for status a fundamental human motive? A review of the empirical literature. *Psychological Bulletin, 141*(3), 574–601. Retrieved from http://dx.doi.org/10.1037/a0038781

Ansari, Z. (2011, February). Advancing our common interests. *American Teacher, 95*(4), 14.

Ansary, T. (2010). The muddle machine: Confessions of a textbook editor. In F. W. Parkay, E. J. Anctil, & G. Hass (Eds.), *Curriculum leadership: Readings for developing quality educational programs* (9th ed., pp. 298–303). Upper Saddle River, NJ: Allyn & Bacon/Pearson.

Anyon, J. (1996). Social class and the hidden curriculum of work. In E. Hollins (Ed.), *Transforming curriculum for a culturally diverse society* (pp. 179–203). Mahwah, NJ: Lawrence Erlbaum.

ArborBridge. (2018). *Your Guide to 2017 State Testing.* Retrieved from https://www.arborbridge.com/us-state-testing-2017/

Ariza, E. N. W. (2006). *Not for ESOL teachers: What every classroom teacher needs to know about the linguistically, culturally, and ethnically diverse student.* Upper Saddle River, NJ: Pearson.

Armitage, L. (2017, July 23). Rural teachers speak out. *University of Wisconsin: Wisconsin Center for Education Research.* Retrieved from https://wcer.wisc.edu/news/detail/rural-teachers-speak-out

Armstrong, P. A. (2008). *What teachers expect in reform: Making their voices heard.* Lanham, MD: Rowman & Littlefield Education.

Ashley, J. & Burke, K., A comparison of punitive and restorative justice responses in schools, (October, 2009). Implementing restorative justice: A guide for schools. Chicago: Illinois Criminal Justice Information Authority, p. 7. Retrieved from http:/www.icjia.state.il.us/publications/implementing-restorative-justice-a-guide-for-schools. Used with Permission from Illinois Criminal Justice Information Authority

Asian Americans/Pacific Islanders in Philanthropy. (1997). *An invisible crisis: The educational needs of Asian Pacific American youth.* New York, NY: Author.

Association of Mindfulness in Education. (2018, January 30). What is mindfulness? Retrieved from http://www.mindfuleducation.org/what-is-mindfulness/

Aud, S., Fox, M., & KewalRamani, A. (2010). *Status and trends in the education of racial and ethnic groups.* Washington, DC: U.S. Department of Education.

Aud, S., Wilkinson-Flicker, S., Kristapovich, P., Rathbun, A., Wang, X., and Zhang, J. (2013). *The Condition of Education 2013* (NCES 2013-037). U.S. Department of Education, National Center for Education Statistics. Washington, DC.

Avramidis, E., Bayliss, P., & Burden, R. (2000). A survey into mainstream teachers' attitudes towards the inclusion of children with special educational needs in the ordinary school in one local education authority. *Educational Psychology, 20*(2), 191–211.

Ayers, W. C., & Miller, J. L. (Eds.). (1998). *A light in dark times: Maxine Greene and the unfinished conversation.* New York, NY: Teachers College Press.

Baker, O., and Lang, K. (2013, June). *The effect of high school exit exams on graduation, employment, wages and incarceration.* National Bureau of Economic Research Working Paper No. 19182.

Baldas, T. (2007, December 10). As "cyber-bullying" grows, so do lawsuits. *National Law Journal.* Retrieved from http://www.law.com/jsp/article.jsp?id=1197281074941

Ballantine, J. H., Hammack, F. M., & Stuber, J. (2017). *The sociology of education: A systematic analysis* (8th ed.). New York: Routledge.

Banks, J. A. (2006). *Cultural diversity and education: Foundations, curriculum and teaching* (5th ed.). Boston: Allyn & Bacon/Pearson.

Banks, J. A. (2009). *Teaching strategies for ethnic studies* (8th ed.). Boston, MA: Allyn & Bacon/Pearson.

Banks, J. A. (2014). *An introduction to multicultural education* (5th ed.). Boston, MA: Pearson.

Banks, J. A., An introduction to multicultural education (Fourth Edition). Upper Saddle River, NJ: Allyn & Bacon. Reprinted with the permission of James A. Banks.

Banks, J. A. (2016). *Cultural diversity and education: Foundations, curriculum and teaching* (6th ed.). Boston, MA: Pearson.

Barnes, S. (2017, June 28). Know my name: know me. HuffPost blog. Retrieved from http://www.huffingtonpost.com/teach-plus/know-my-name-know-me_b_10698750.html

Based on United States: What makes an effective teacher? 2016, Pearson Education, Inc., pp. 3, 30

Battles v. Anne Arundel County Board of Education, 904 F. Supp. 471 (D. Md. 1995), *aff'd*, 95 F.3d 41 (4th Cir. 1996).

Baugh, J. (2012). African American vernacular English (Ebonics). In James A. Banks (Ed.), *Encyclopedia of diversity in education* (pp. 49–54). Thousand Oaks, CA: Sage Publications.

Bell, T. (1986, March). Education policy development in the Reagan administration. *Phi Delta Kappan*, 492.

Bennett, C. I. (2003). *Comprehensive multicultural education: Theory and practice* (5th ed.). Boston: Allyn & Bacon.

Bennett, C. I. (2015). *Comprehensive multicultural education: Theory and practice* (8th ed.). Upper Saddle River, NJ: Pearson.

Bennett, K., & Dorjee, D. (2016). The impact of a mindfulness-based stress reduction course (MBSR) on well-being and academic attainment of sixth-form students. *Mindfulness*, *7*, 105–114.

Bergmann, J., & Sams, A. (2012). Flip your classroom: Reach every student in every class every day. International Society for Technology in Education https://www.liceopalmieri.gov.it/wp-content/uploads/2016/11/Flip-Your-Classroom.pdf.

Berliner, D. C., & Glass, G. V. (2014). *50 myths and lies that threaten America's public schools: The real crisis in education*. New York: Teachers College Press.

Bernstein, B. B. (2000). *Pedagogy, symbolic control and identity: Theory, research, critique (critical perspectives on literacy and education, revised edition)*. New York: Rowman & Littlefield Publishers.

Berry, B., et al. (2011). *Teaching 2030: What we must do for our students and our public schools—now and in the future.* New York, NY: Teachers College Press and Washington, DC: National Education Association.

Berry, B. (2017, August 15). The future leadership of teachers. Retrieved from https://www.teachingquality.org/the-future-leadership-of-teachers/

Bertocci, P. A. (1960). *Education and the vision of excellence.* Boston, MA: Boston University Press.

Betty Shabazz International Charter School. (2014, May 14). *African centered education*. Retrieved from http://www.bsics.net/apps/pages/index.jsp?uREC_ID=179005&type=d

Bissonette, A. M. (2009). *Cyber law: Maximizing safety and minimizing risk in classrooms*. Thousand Oaks, CA: Corwin.

Black, P., Harrison, C., Lee, C., Marshall, B., & Wiliam, D. (2004, September). Working inside the black box: Assessment for learning in the classroom. *Phi Delta Kappan*, 9–21.

Blackwell, L. S., Trzesniewski, K. H., & Dweck, C.S. (2007). Implicit theories of intelligence predict achievement across an adolescent transition: A longitudinal study and an intervention. *Child Development*, *78*(1), 246–263.

Blitzer, J. (2017, March 23). After an immigration raid, a city's students vanish. *The New Yorker.* Retrieved from https://www.newyorker.com/news/news-desk/after-an-immigration-raid-a-citys-students-vanish

Bloom, B. S. (1981). *All our children learning: A primer for parents, teachers, and other educators*. New York, NY: McGraw-Hill.

Board of Education of Oklahoma City Public Schools v. Dowell, 498 U.S. 237, 249–250 (1991).

Board of Education, Sacramento City Unified School District v. Holland, 786 F. Supp. 874 (E.D. Cal. 1992).

Bobbitt, J. F. (1924). *How to make a curriculum*. New York: Houghton Mifflin.

Bond, N. (Ed.). (2014). *The power of teacher leaders: Their roles, influence, and impact*. New York: Routledge.

Borich, G. D. (2017). *Effective teaching methods: Research-based practice* (9th ed.). Boston: Pearson Education.

Bowden, S. (2016, March 13). *A day in the life of an alternative high school teacher*. Retrieved from https://www.cultofpedagogy.com/alternative-school-teacher/

Boyer, E. (1995). *The basic school: A community for learning*. Princeton, NJ: Carnegie Foundation for the Advancement of Teaching.

Brameld, T. (1956). *Toward a reconstructed philosophy of education*. New York, NY: Holt, Rinehart and Winston.

Brimley, V. R., Verstegen, D. A., & Garfield, R. R. (2012). *Financing education in a climate of change* (11th ed.). Boston Pearson.

Brookhart, S.M., & Nitko, A.J. (2015). *Educational assessment of students* (7th ed.). Boston: Pearson.

Brody, N. (1992). *Intelligence* (2nd ed.). San Diego, CA: Academic Press.

Brophy, J. (2010). *Motivating students to learn* (3rd ed.). New York: Routledge.

Broudy, H. S. (1979). Arts education: Necessary or just nice? *Phi Delta Kappan, 60*, 347–350.

Broughman, S.P., and Swaim, N.L. (2016). *Characteristics of private schools in the United States: Results from the 2013–14 Private School Universe Survey* (NCES 2016-243). U.S. Department of Education. Washington, DC: National Center for Education Statistics.

Brown v. Board of Education of Topeka, Kansas, 347 U.S. 483 (1954).

Brown v. Hot, Sexy and Safer Productions, Inc., 68 F.3d 525 (1st Cir. 1995), *cert. denied*, 516 U.S. 1159 (1996).

Brown v. Unified School District No. 501, 56 F. Supp. 2d 1212 (D. Kan. 1999).

Bruecker, E. (2017, October). *Assessing the fiscal impact of Wisconsin's statewide voucher program*. Boulder, CO: National Education Policy Center.

Brunelle v. Lynn Public Schools, 702 N.E.2d 1182 (Mass. 1998).

Bucky, P. A. (1992). *The private Albert Einstein*. Kansas City: Andrews and McMeel.

Buffins, M. (2017, July 24). *Mansur's manifesto: How an aspiring black male teacher plans to turn teaching into activism*. Retrieved from https://edtrust.org/the-equity-line/mansurs-manifesto-aspiring-black-male-teacher-plans-turn-teaching-activism/

Burch v. Barker, 651 F. Supp. 1149 (W.D. Wash. 1987).

Burch v. Barker, 861 F.2d 1149 (9th Cir. 1988).

Bureau of Labor Statistics. (2017). U.S. Department of Labor, *Occupational outlook handbook, 2016-17 edition*, Special Education Teachers. Retrieved August 27, 2017, from https://www.bls.gov/ooh/education-training-and-library/special-education-teachers.htm

Burney, D. (2004). Craft knowledge: The road to transforming schools. *Phi Delta Kappan*, *85*(7), 526–531.

Burton v. Cascade School District Union High School No. 5, 512 F.2d 850 (9th Cir. 1975).

Bush v. Holmes, 767 So. 2d 668, 675 (2006).

Bushaw, W. J., & Lopez, S. J. (2013). Which way do we go? The 45th annual Phi Delta Kappa/Gallup Poll of the public's attitudes toward the public schools. *Phi Delta Kappan*, *95*(1), 9–25.

Button, H. W., & Provenzo, E. F. (1989). *History of education and culture in America* (2nd ed.). Upper Saddle River, NJ: Prentice Hall.

California Alliance of Researchers for Equity in Education. (2016). *Common Core State Standards assessments in California: Concerns and recommendations. Research Brief #1*. Retrieved from www.CARE-ED.org

Campbell, D. M., Melenyzer, B. J., Nettles, D. H., & Wyman, R. M. (2014). *How to develop a professional portfolio: A manual for teachers*. Boston: Pearson.

Canter, L. (1989). Assertive discipline—more than names on the board and marbles in a jar. *Phi Delta Kappan, 71*(1), 57–61.

Carroll, J. (1963). A model of school learning. *Teachers College Record, 64*.

Center on Education Policy. (May 2016). Used with permission from *Listen to Us: Teacher Views and Voices*. Courtesy of the George Washington University © The George Washington University. All rights reserved. Used with Permission.

Centers for Disease Control and Prevention. (2009, Summer). *Suicide: Facts at a glance.* Atlanta, GA: Author.

Centers for Disease Control and Prevention, Kaiser Permanente (2016). The ACE Study Survey Data. *Atlanta, GA: U.S. Department of Health and Human Services*. Retrieved from https://www.cdc.gov/violenceprevention/acestudy/about.html

Centers for Disease Control and Prevention. (2016, July 19). *National suicide statistics*. Atlanta, GA: Author. Retrieved from https://www.cdc.gov/violenceprevention/suicide/statistics/index.html

Center for Education Reform. (2014). *School choice today: Voucher laws across the states*. Washington, DC: Center for Education Reform.

Center for Research on Education Outcomes, Stanford University. (2013). *National charter school study* 2013. http://credo.stanford.edu/documents/NCSS%202013%20Final%20Draft.pdf

Chambers, J. (2016, September 13). Suit: Detroit schoolchildren denied right to literacy, *The Detroit News*. Retrieved from http://www.detroitnews.com/story/news/local/detroit-city/2016/09/13/lawsuit-detroit-schoolchildren-literacy/90298836/

Chapman, C. B. (2017, May 24). *$2.5M NSF grant focuses on indigenous STEM education.* Retrieved from https://news.wsu.edu/2017/05/24/2-5m-nsf-grant-for-indigenous-stem- education/?utm_source=WSU+College+of+Education+email+list&utm_campaign=8b8895cb60-EMAIL_CAMPAIGN_2017_12_06&utm_medium=email&utm_term=0_c5164ae185-8b8895cb60-191835381

Chappuis, J., & Stiggins, R. J. (2017). *An introduction to student-involved assessment for learning* (7th ed.). New York: Pearson.

Chappuis, J., Stiggins, R. J., Chappuis, S., & Arter, J. A. (2012). *Classroom assessment for student learning: Doing it right—using it well* (2nd ed.). Boston: Pearson.

Chen, C. (February 9, 2016). How special needs students can benefit from STEM education. *The Christian Science Monitor*. Retrieved from https://www.csmonitor.com/USA/Education/2016/0209/How-special-needs-students-can-benefit-from-STEM-education

Cheung, A., & Slavin, R. E. (2011). *The effectiveness of educational technology applications for enhancing reading achievement in K-12 classrooms: A meta-analysis.* Baltimore, MD: Johns Hopkins University, Center for Research and Reform in Education.

Cheung, A., & Slavin, R. E. (2013, June). The effectiveness of educational technology applications for enhancing mathematics achievement in K–12 classrooms: A meta-analysis. *Educational Research Review*, Vol. 9, 88-113.

Chiaramonte, P., & Gonen, Y. (2010, October 18). *Teachers fired for flirting on Facebook with students.* Retrieved from http://www.nypost.com/p/news/local/teachers_friending_spree_JVfEO8TmN7XCnWpX5s5hnO

Chicago Public Schools. (2017). *Guidelines: Service learning*. Retrieved from http://cps.edu/ServiceLearning/Pages/Guidelines.aspx

Chiles, N. (2017, August 7). Can Black English help Black children learn better? One educator believes so. *The Hechinger Report.* Retrieved from http://hechingerreport.org/can-black-english-help-black-children-learn-better-one-educator-believes-so/

Coalition for Community Schools. (2017). *Community schools results*. Retrieved from http://www.communityschools.org/assets/1/AssetManager/Community%20School%20Results%202013.pdf

Coalition of Essential Schools. (2017). *Student-centered teaching & learning*. Retrieved from http://essentialschools.org/benchmarks/student-centered-teaching-and-learning/

Cohen, D., & Purkey, J. (2014, November 8). Portland high school STEM design violates students' civil rights: Guest opinion. *Oregon Live*. Retrieved from http://www.oregonlive.com/opinion/index.ssf/2014/11/portland_high_school_stem_desi.html

Cohen, S. (Ed.). (1974). *Massachusetts school law of 1648. Education in the United States*. New York, NY: Random House.

Coleman, J. S., Campbell, E. Q., Hobson, C. J., McPartland, J., Mood, A. L., Weinfeld, F. D., et al. (1966). *Equality of educational opportunity*. Washington, DC: U.S. Government Printing Office.

College Board and Phi Delta Kappa. (2009). *Teachers are the center of education: Profiles of eight teachers.* New York and Bloomington, IN: Authors.

Collier-Thomas, B. (1982, Summer). Guest editorial: The impact of black women in education: An historical overview. *The Journal of Negro Education 51*(3), 173–180.

Colucci, K. (2000). Negative pedagogy. In J. L. Paul & K. Colucci (Eds.), *Stories out of school: Memories and reflections on care and cruelty in the classroom* (pp. 27–44). Stamford, CT: Ablex.

Commager, H. S. (1962). *Noah Webster's American spelling book.* New York, NY: Teachers College Press.

Conaboy, C. (2018, January 1). *A prescription for . . . resiliency?* Retrieved from https://www.politico.com/agenda/story/2018/01/10/childhood-resiliency-health-000610

Concerned Black Men. (2017, September 11). *Our vision*. Retrieved from http://cbmnational.org/our-vision/

Conn, C. (2013). Get deeper learning with tablets. *Learning & Leading with Technology, 41*(2), 35–37.

Connell, G. (2017, March 16). Rethinking homework: How much is too much? *Scholastic top teaching blog*. Retrieved from https://www.scholastic.com/teachers/blog-posts/genia-connell/2017/Rethinking-Homework-How-Much-is-Too-Much/

Cook-Harvey, C. M., Darling-Hammond, L., Lam, L., Mercer, C., & Roc, M. (2016). *Equity and ESSA: Leveraging Educational Opportunity Through the Every Student Succeeds Act*. Palo Alto, CA: Learning Policy Institute.

Cossentino, J., & Whitcomb, J. A. (2007). In D. T. Hansen (Ed.), *Ethical visions of education: Philosophies in practice.* New York, NY: Teachers College Press.

Costello, E., & Lawler, M. (2014). An exploratory study of the effects of mindfulness on perceived levels of stress among school children from lower socioeconomic backgrounds. *The International Journal of Emotional Education*, *6*, 21–29.

Council of the Great City Schools. (2014). *Urban school superintendents: Characteristics, tenure, and salary—Eighth survey and report.* Retrieved from https://www.cgcs.org/cms/lib/DC00001581/Centricity/Domain/87/Urban%20Indicator_Superintendent%20Summary%2011514.pdf

Craig, S. E. (2016). *Trauma-sensitive schools: Learning communities transforming children's lives, K-5*. New York: Teachers College Press.

Craig, S. E. (2016, September). The trauma-sensitive teacher. *Educational Leadership*, 28–32.

Crawford, J. (2004). *Education of English learners: Language diversity in the classroom* (5th ed.). Los Angeles: Bilingual Education Services.

Crawford, J. (2007). The decline of bilingual education: How to reverse a troubling trend. *International Multilingual Research Journal*, *1*(1), 33–37.

Credé, M., Tynan, M. C., & Harms, P. D. (2017). Much ado about grit: A meta-analytic synthesis of the grit literature. *Journal of Personality and Social Psychology*, *113*(3), 492–511.

CREDO. (2015). *Online charter school study 2015*. Stanford, CA: CREDO Center for Research on Education Outcomes. Retrieved from https://credo.stanford.edu/pdfs/OnlineCharterStudyFinal2015.pdf

Cremin, L. A. (1961). *The transformation of the school: Progressivism in American education, 1876–1957*. New York: Alfred A. Knopf.

Cuban, L. (2013, October 2). *Making money in K–12 schools is hard to do. . . for some companies*. Retrieved from http://larrycuban.wordpress.com/2013/10/02/making-money-in-k-12-schools-is-hard-to-do-for-some-companies/

Cuban, L., & Kirkpatrick, H. (1998). Computers make kids smarter—right? *TECHNOS Quarterly*, *7*(2), 26–31.

Curtis v. School Committee of Falmouth, 652 N.E.2d 580 (Mass. 1995), *cert. denied*, 516 U.S. 1067 (1996).

Dailey, R. (2017, June 12). LCS FSA test scores top state averages. *Tallahassee Democrat.* Retrieved from http://www.tallahassee.com/story/news/2017/06/12/lcs-fsa-test-scores-top-state-averages/390058001/

Danilova, M. (May 22, 2017). Betsy DeVos pushes school choice in speech to advocacy group, gives no specifics. *Denver Post*. Retrieved from http://www.denverpost.com/2017/05/22/devos-pushes-school-choice-gives-no-specifics/

Darling-Hammond, L., Carver-Thomas, D., & Sutcher, L. (2017, November 8). Teacher Turnover Debate: Linda Darling-Hammond, Colleagues Respond to Critiques of Their Latest Study. *The 74 Million*. Retrieved from https://www.the74million.org/article/teacher-turnover-debate-linda-darling-hammond-colleagues-respond-to-critiques-of-their-latest-study/

Davis v. Meek, 344 F. Supp. 298 (N.D. Ohio 1972).

Dawson, M. R., & Lignugaris/Kraft, B. (2017). Meaningful practice: Generalizing foundation teaching skills from TLE TeachLivE to the classroom. *Teacher Education and Special Education*, *40*(1), 26–50.

Deal, T. E., & Peterson, K. D. (2009). *Shaping school culture: Pitfalls, paradox, & promises* (2nd ed.). San Francisco, CA: Jossey-Bass.

DeCesare, D., McClelland, A., & Randel, B. (2017). *Impacts of the Retired Mentors for New Teachers program* (REL 2017–225). Washington, DC: U.S. Department of Education, Institute of Education Sciences, National Center for Education Evaluation and Regional Assistance, Regional Educational Laboratory Central.

Dell'Olio, J. M., & Donk, T. (2007). *Models of teaching: Connecting student learning with standards.* Thousand Oaks, CA: Sage.

Democratic Party, 2016 Democratic Party Platform, July 21, 2016.

DePasquale, J. (2017, September 3). *Scholastic top teaching blog*. Retrieved from https://www.scholastic.com/teachers/contributors/bloggers/john-depasquale/

Deskbook encyclopedia of American school law 2013. Malvern, PA: Center for Education & Employment Law.

DeVos, B. (2017, May 22). *Prepared remarks by U.S. Secretary of Education Betsy DeVos to the American Federation for Children's National Policy Summit*. Retrieved August 26, 2017, from https://www.ed.gov/news/speeches/prepared-remarks-us-secretary-education-betsy-devos-american-federation-childrens-national-policy-summit

Dewey, J. (1900). *The school and society*. Chicago: University of Chicago Press.

Dewey, J. (1902). *The child and the curriculum*. Chicago: University of Chicago Press.

Dewey, J. (1904). The relation of theory to practice in education. In Third *Yearbook for the National Society for the Scientific Study of Education*, Part 1. Bloomington, IN: Public School Publishing Co.

Dewey, J. (1955). Quoted in *Organizing the teaching profession: The story of the American Federation of Teachers*. Glencoe, IL: Commission on Educational Reconstruction.

Dicker, L., Hughes, C. & Hynes, M. (2016, August). *Bill & Melinda Gates Foundation Final Report: UCF TLE TeachLivE*. August 2016, p. 13. Retrieved from http://teachlive.org/wp-content/uploads/2016/09/Gates-Foundation-Final-Report8_27_2016.pdf

Dichosa, Julius, Eighth-Grade Physical Science, Department Chair, Las Palmas Middle School Covina, California, Used with permission.

Dieker, L. A., Rodriquez, J. A., Lignugaris/Kraft, B., Hynes, M. C., & Hughes, C. E. (2014a). The potential of simulated environments in teacher education: Current and future possibilities. *Teacher Education and Special Education*, *37*, 21–33.

Dieker, L. A., Straub, C. L., Hughes, C. E., Hynes, M. C., & Hardin, S. (2014b). Learning from virtual students. *Educational Leadership*, *71*(8), 54–58.

Disability Rights Education & Defense Fund. (2017, May 2). *Students with reading disorders sue Berkeley Unified School District (BUSD) for failing to educate them*. Retrieved from https://dredf.org/2017/05/02/students-with-reading-disorders-sue-berkeley-unified-school-district/

Doe v. Renfrow, 631 F.2d 91, *reh'g denied*, 635 F.2d 582 (7th Cir. 1980), *cert. denied*, 451 U.S. 1022 (1981).

Dubuclet v. Home Insurance Co., 660 So. 2d 67 (La. Ct. App. 1995).

Duckworth, A. L., Peterson, C., Matthews, M. D., & Kelly, D. R. (2007). Grit: Perseverance and passion for long-term goals. *Journal of Personality and Social Psychology*, *92*(6), 1087–1101.

Duckworth, A. L., Kirby, T., Tsukayama, E., Berstein, H., & Ericsson, K. (2010). Deliberate practice spells success: Why grittier competitors triumph at the National Spelling Bee. *Social Psychological and Personality Science*, *2*, 174–181.

Duckworth, A. L., & Allred, K. M. (2012). Temperament in the classroom. In R. L. Shiner & M. Zentner (Eds.), *Handbook of temperament* (pp. 627–644). New York, NY: Guilford Press.

Dunklee, D. R., & Shoop, R. J. (2006). *The principal's quick-reference guide to school law: Reducing liability, litigation, and other potential legal tangles* (2nd ed.). Thousand Oaks, CA: Corwin Press.

Dunn, J. M., & West, M. R. (Eds.). (2009). *From schoolhouse to courthouse: The judiciary's role in American education.* Washington, DC: The Brookings Institution.

Durkheim, E. (1956). *Education and sociology* (S. D. Fox, Trans.). Glencoe, IL: Free Press.

Durlak, J. A., Weissberg, R. P., & Pachan, M. (2010). A meta-analysis of after-school programs that seek to promote personal and social skills in children and adolescents. *American Journal of Community Psychology*, *45*, 294–309.

Dweck, C., Walton, G. M., & Cohen, G.L. (2011). Academic tenacity: Mindsets and skills that promote long-term learning. Paper presented at the Gates Foundation, Seattle, WA.

Eamon, M. K. (2001, July). The effects of poverty on children's socio/emotional development: An ecological systems analysis. *Social Work*, *46*(3), 256–266.

EarthEcho International. (2017, April 21). *Lasting ways to spring into action for Earth* Week. Retrieved from http://www.worldwatermonitoringday.org/post/lasting-ways-to-spring-into-action-for-earth-week

Edina Schools. (2017, September 21). *The Highlands Way*. Retrieved from https://www.edinaschools.org/cms/lib07/MN01909547/Centricity/Domain/435/THEHIGHLANDSWAY2013.pdf

Education Commission of the States. (2016, January 25). *50-state comparison: Charter school policies*. Retrieved from https://www.ecs.org/charter-school-policies/

Education Commission of the States. (2016, March). 50-state review: Constitutional obligations for public education. Retrieved from https://www.ecs.org/ec-content/uploads/2016-Constitutional-obligations-for-public-education-1.pdf

Education Commission of the States. (2016, December 15). *Changes in state education leadership*. Retrieved from https://www.ecs.org/changes-in-state-education-leadership/

Education Commission of the States. (2017, March 6). *50-state comparison: Vouchers*. Retrieved from https://www.ecs.org/50-state-comparison-vouchers/

Education Deans for Justice and Equity (2017). *Our Children Deserve Better: A Call to Resist Washington's Dangerous Vision for U.S. Education*. Boulder, CO: National Education Policy Center. Retrieved from http://nepc.colorado.edu/publication/children-deserve-better

Education Week. (2009, March 26). *Technology counts 2005: Breaking away from tradition.*

Education World. (2018, February 25). *Substitute teachers gain national voice*. Retrieved from http://www.educationworld.com/a_issues/chat/chat047.shtml. Copyright Education World, Inc. All Rights Reserved.

Edwards v. Aguillard, 482 U.S. 578 (1987).

Eggen, P., & Kauchak, D. (2016). *Educational psychology: Windows on classrooms* (10th ed.). Boston: Pearson.

Eisner, E. W. (1998). *The kind of schools we need: Personal essays.* Portsmouth, NH: Heinemann.

Eisner, E. (2002). *The educational imagination: On the design and evaluation of school programs* (3rd ed.). New York, NY: Macmillan College.

Eisner, E. (2006, March). The satisfactions of teaching: How we teach is ultimately a reflection of why we teach. *Educational Leadership*, 44–46.

Emdin, C. (2017). *For White folks who teach in the hood . . . and the rest of y'all too: Reality pedagogy and urban education.* Boston: Beacon Press.

Emmer, E. T., & Evertson, C. M. (2017). *Classroom management for middle and high school teachers* (10th ed.). Boston, MA: Pearson Education.

Engel v. Vitale, 370 U.S. 421 (1962).

English, F. W. (2010). *Deciding what to teach & test: Developing, aligning, and leading the curriculum* (3rd ed.). Thousand Oaks, CA: Corwin.

Erikson, E. H. (1963). *Childhood and society* (2nd ed.). New York: Norton.

Essex, Nathan L., School Law and the Public Schools: A Practical Guide For Educational Leaders, 5th Ed., ©2012. Boston: Pearson, pp. 87, 90. Reprinted and Electronically reproduced by permission of Pearson Education, Inc., New York, NY.

Etzioni, A. (1999, June 9). The truths we must face to curb youth violence. *Education Week on the Web*.

Evergreen Education Group. (2015). *Keeping pace with K-12 digital learning, 12th edition: An annual review of policy and practice*. Retrieved from http://www.inacol.org/resource/keeping-pace-with-k-12-digital-learning-12th-edition/

Evers, B., Greene, J. P., Forster, G., Stotsky, S., & Wurman, Z. (2011, May 2). *Closing the door on innovation: Why one national curriculum is bad for America*. Retrieved from http://educationnext.org/closing-the-door-on-innovation/

Evertson, C. M., & Emmer, E. T. (2017). *Classroom management for elementary teachers* (10th ed.). Boston: Pearson Education.

Fagen v. Summers, 498 P.2d 1227 (Wyo. 1972).

FairTest: National Center for Fair and Open Testing. (2017, September). *Time to abolish high school graduation tests*. Jamaica Plain, MA: FairTest: National Center for Fair and Open Testing.

Falvo v. Owasso Independent School District, 233 F.3d 1203 (10th Cir. 2000).

Farbman, D. (2016). *Kuss Middle School: Expanding time to accelerate school improvement.* Retrieved from https://issuu.com/nationalcenterontimelearning/docs/kuss_case_study

Farrington, C. A., Roderick, M., Allensworth, E., Nagaoka, J., Keyes, T. S., Johnson, D. W., & Beechum, N. O. (2012). *Teaching adolescents to become learners. The role of noncognitive factors in shaping school performance: A critical literature review.* Chicago: University of Chicago Consortium on Chicago School Research.

Fein, R., Vossekuil, B., Pollack, W., Borum, R., Modzeleski, W., & Reddy, M. (2004). *Threat assessment in schools: A guide to managing threatening situations and to creating safe school climates.* U.S. Department of Education, Office of Elementary and Secondary Education, Safe and Drug-Free Schools Program and U.S. Secret Service, National Threat Assessment Center, Washington, D.C.

Feistritzer, C. E., & Haar, C. K. (2008). *Alternate routes to teaching.* Upper Saddle River, NJ: Pearson Education.

Ferguson, C. (2003, August 30). *Gay high school draws criticism from conservatives and civil libertarians.* Associated Press.

Ferrari, T. M., Arnett, N., & Cochran, G. (2007). *Preparing teens for success: Building 21st century skills through a 4-H work-based learning program.* Columbus, OH: Ohio State University Extension. Retrieved from www.ohio4h.org/workforceprep/documents/2007JournalofYouthDevelopment_JET.pdf

Ferroni, N. (2014). What my students think makes a great teacher. *Huffington Post* Blog. Retrieved from http://www.huffingtonpost.com/nicholas-ferroni/what-my-students-think-teacher_b_4882495.html

Fetler, M. (2001). Student mathematics achievement test scores, dropout rates, and teacher characteristics. *Teacher Education Quarterly*, *28*(1), 151–168.

Firestone, D. (2008). Alternative schools: When teachers unite to run school. *New York Times.* Retrieved from http://query.nytimes.com/gst/fullpage.html?res=990CE1DF1039F937A15756C0A963958260

Fleischer, H. (2012). What is our current understanding of one-to-one computer projects: A systematic narrative research review. *Educational Research Review*, *7*, 107–122.

Fletcher, J., Denton, C., & Francis, D. (2005). Validity of alternative approaches for the identification of learning disabilities: Operationalizing unexpected underachievement. *Journal of Learning Disabilities*, *38*(6), 545–552.

Flores vs. Morgan Hill Unified School District, 324 F.3d 1130 (9th Cir. 2003).

Florida Department of Education. (2018). Florida school recognition program. Retrieved fromhttp://www.fldoe.org/accountability/accountability-reporting/fl-school-recognition-program/.

Fogleman, J., McNeill, K. L., and Krajcik, J. (2011). Examining the effect of teachers' adaptations of a middle school science inquiry oriented curriculum unit on student learning. *Journal of Research in Science Teaching*, *48*(2), 149–169.

Fong, T. P. (2007). *The contemporary Asian American experience: Beyond the model minority* (3rd ed.). Upper Saddle River, NJ: Prentice Hall.

Franklin, B. (1931). Proposals relating to the education of youth in Pennsylvania. In T. Woody (Ed.), *Educational views of Benjamin Franklin*. New York, NY: McGraw-Hill.

Franklin, J. H. (1947). *From slavery to freedom: A history of Negro Americans* (3rd ed.). New York, NY: Vintage Books.

Franklin v. Gwinnett County Public Schools, 503 U.S. 60 (1992).

Freeman v. Pitts, 503 U.S. 467 (1992).

Freire, P. (2000). *Pedagogy of the oppressed.* 30th anniversary edition. New York: Bloomsbury Academic.

Friedman, M. (2003, March 24). *Milton Friedman interview on CNBC: Friedman on school vouchers.*

Friend, M. (2018). *Special education: contemporary perspectives for school professionals* (5th ed.). New York: Pearson.

Friend, M., & Bursuck, W. D. (2015). *Including students with special needs: A practical guide for classroom teachers* (7th ed.). Boston, MA: Pearson.

Friend, M., & Cook, L. (2017). *Interactions: Collaboration skills for school professionals* (8th ed.). Boston, MA: Pearson.

Fullan, M. & Hargreaves, A. (2016). *Bringing the profession back in: Call to action.* Oxford, OH: Learning Forward.

Future City. (2017). *Future City competition: Program handbook, 2017-2018.* Alexandria, VA: Future City Competition. Retrieved from https://futurecity.org/form/resources?download=/sites/default/files/resources/files/2017_fcc_handbook_fin_hr.pdf

Gagné, R. M. (1974). *Essentials of learning for instruction*. Hinsdale, IL: Dryden.

Gagné, R. M. (1977). *The conditions of learning* (3rd ed.). New York, NY: Holt, Rinehart and Winston.

Gallup. (2017, January 11). *In U.S., More Adults Identifying as LGBT.* Retrieved from http://news.gallup.com/poll/201731/lgbt-identification-rises.aspx

Garan, E. M. (2004). *In defense of our children: When politics, profit, and education collide.* Portsmouth, NH: Heinemann.

Garbarino, J. (1999). *Lost boys: Why our sons turn violent and how we can save them.* New York, NY: Free Press.

Garbarino, J. (2010, December 19). *How a boy becomes a killer.* Retrieved from http://www.cnn.com/2012/12/19/opinion/garbarino-violence-boys/

Garcia, P. (April 29, 2016). Why teachers choose charter schools. Washington, DC: National Alliance for Public Charter Schools. Retrieved from http://blog.publiccharters.org/why-teachers-choose-charter-schools

Garcia, X., & Zych, A. (2017, September 1). *2017 Science Friday Educator Collaborative.* Retrieved from https://www.sciencefriday.com/educational-resources/2017-science-friday-educator-collaborative/

Gardner, H. (1983). *Frames of mind*. New York: Basic Books.

Gardner, H. (2013, October 16). "Multiple intelligences" are not "learning styles." *Washington Post*. Retrieved from http://www.washingtonpost.com/blogs/answer-sheet/

wp/2013/10/16/howard-gardner-multiple-intelligences-are-not-learning-styles/

Gardner, H., & Connell, M. (2000). Response to Nicholas Allix. *Australian Journal of Education, 44*, 288–293.

Gargiulo, R.M., & Gouck, E. C. (2018). *Special education in contemporary society: An introduction to exceptionality* (6th ed.). Thousand Oaks, CA: Sage.

Garringer, M., and MacRae, P. (2008, September). *Building effective peer mentoring programs in schools: An introductory guide.* The Mentoring Resource Center, U.S. Department of Education, Office of Safe and Drug-Free Schools. Washington, DC: Author.

Gaylord v. Tacoma School District No. 10, 599 P.2d 1340 (Wash. 1977).

GE Foundation. (2014, March 10). *Developing futures.* Retrieved August 28, 2014, from http://www.gefoundation.com/education/developing-futures/

Gebser v. Lago Vista Independent School District, 524 U.S. 274 (1998).

Geier, R., Blumenfeld, P. C., Marx, R. W., Krajcik, J. S., Fishman, B., Soloway, E., & Chambers, J. C. (2008). Standardized test outcomes for students engaged in inquiry-based science curricula in the context of urban reform. *Journal of Research in Science Teaching, 45*(8), 922–939.

George Lucas Educational Foundation. (2010, April). *Learning the lingo*. Retrieved from http://www.edutopia.org/global-language-education-schools-online

Gill, B., Zimmer, R., Christman, J., & Blanc, S. (2007). *State takeover, school restructuring, private management, and student achievement in Philadelphia.* Santa Monica, CA: Rand Corporation.

Gilligan, C. (1993). *In a different voice: Psychological theory and women's development*. Cambridge, MA: Harvard University Press.

Gipp, G. (1979, August–September). Help for Dana Fast Horse and friends. *American Education*, p. 15.

Glander, M. (2016). *Selected statistics from the public elementary and secondary education universe: School year 2014–15* (NCES 2016-076). U.S. Department of Education. Washington, DC: National Center for Education Statistics.

Glasser, W. R. (1997, April). A new look at school failure and school success. *Phi Delta Kappan*, 596–602.

Glasser, W. R. (1998a). *Quality school* (3rd ed.). New York, NY: Harper Perennial.

Glasser, W. R. (1998b). *The quality school teacher: Specific suggestions for teachers who are trying to implement the lead-management ideas of the quality school*. New York, NY: Harper Perennial.

Glasser, W. R. (1998c). *Choice theory: A new psychology of personal freedom*. New York, NY: HarperCollins.

Glasser, W. R., & Dotson, K. L. (1998). *Choice theory in the classroom*. New York, NY: Harper Perennial.

Glazerman, S. A. Protik, B. Teh, J. Bruch, N. Seftor, N. (2012). Based on *Moving High-Performing Teachers: Implementation of Transfer Incentives in Seven Districts (NCEE 2012-4051)*. Washington, DC: National Center for Education Evaluation and Regional Assistance, Institute of Education Sciences, U.S. Department of Education, p. 39.

Glazerman, S., Isenberg, E., Dolfin, S., Bleeker, M., Johnson, A., Grider, M., et al. (2010). *Impacts of comprehensive teacher induction: Final results from a randomized controlled study*. Princeton, NJ: Mathematica Policy Research.

Glickman, C., Gordon, S. P., & Ross-Gordon, J. (2017). *Supervision and instructional leadership: A developmental approach* (10th ed.). Boston: Pearson.

Goldhaber, D., & Anthony, E. (2003, May). Teacher quality and student achievement, *ERIC Clearinghouse on Urban Education, Urban Diversity Series, 115*(1).

Gollnick, D. M., & Chinn, P. C. (2009). *Multicultural education in a pluralistic society* (8th ed.). Upper Saddle River, NJ: Merrill/Pearson.

Gollnick, D. M., & Chinn, P. C. (2017). *Multicultural education in a pluralistic society* (10th ed.). Boston: Pearson.

Good, T. E., & Grouws, D. (1979). The Missouri mathematics effectiveness project: An experimental study in fourth-grade classrooms. *Journal of Educational Psychology, 71*, 355–362.

Good, T.E., & Lavigne, A. L. (2018). *Looking in classrooms* (11th ed). London: Routledge.

Gornik, R, & Samford, W. L. (2018). *Creating a culture of support for teacher leaders: A vision for change and hope.* Lanham, MD: Rowman & Littlefield Publishers.

Goss v. Lopez, 419 U.S. 565 (1975).

Government Accountability Office. (2016, April). *K-12 education: Better use of information could help agencies identify disparities and address racial discrimination*. Washington, DC: Author.

Graham, P. A. (1967). *Progressive education: From Arcady to academe: A history of the Progressive Education Association, 1919–1955.* New York, NY: Teachers College Press.

Grant, P. G., Richard, K. J., & Parkay, F. W. (1996, April). *Using video cases to promote reflection among preservice teachers: A qualitative inquiry*. Paper presented at the annual meeting of the American Educational Research Association, New York.

Graves, Laurie, NBCT (National Board Certified Teacher) Middle Childhood Generalist, 2011 Wyoming Teacher of the Year. Used with permission.

Gray, L., Taie, S., & O'Rear, I. (2015). *Public school teacher attrition and mobility in the first five years: Results from the first through fifth waves of the 2007–08 Beginning Teacher Longitudinal Study*. Washington, DC: National Center for Education Statistics, U.S. Department of Education.

Gray, P. (2008). *Council of Chief State School Officers Teacher of the Year video*. Retrieved from http://www.pearsonfoundation.org/ccsso-toy/2008/vid-Arkansas.html

Green, T. D., Brown, A., & Robinson, L. (2008). *Making the most of the Web in your classroom: A teacher's guide to blogs, podcasts, wikis, pages, and sites*. Thousand Oaks, CA: Corwin Press.

Greene, M. (1995a). *Releasing the imagination*. San Francisco, CA: Jossey-Bass.

Greene, M. (1995b). What counts as philosophy of education? In W. Kohli (Ed.), *Critical conversations in philosophy of education* (pp. 3–23). New York, NY: Routledge.

Grenda, P., & Hackmann, D. G. (2014). Advantages and challenges of distributing leadership in middle-level schools. *NASSP Bulletin, 98*(1), 53–74.

Gross, M. U. M. (2008). Highly gifted children and adolescents. In J. A. Plucker & C. M. Callahan (Eds.), *Critical issues and practices in gifted education: What the research says* (pp. 241–251). Waco, TX: Prufrock Press.

Gubbins, Elizabeth, Las Palmas Middle School, Covina, California. Used with permission.

Gurian, M., & Stevens, K. (2007). *The minds of boys: Saving our sons from falling behind in school and life*. San Francisco: Jossey-Bass.

Gutierrez, R. (2008). A "gap-gazing" fetish in mathematics education? Problematizing research on the achievement gap. *Journal for Research in Mathematics Education, 39*(4), 357–364.

GW Community School. (2017). *About GWCS*. Retrieved from http://www.gwcommunityschool.com/what-we-do/

Hakuta, K. (2001a). *Follow-up on Oceanside: Communications with Ron Unz*. Retrieved from http://www.stanford/edu/~hakuta/SAT9/Silence%20from%20Oceanside%202.htm

Hakuta, K. (2001b). *Silence from Oceanside and the future of bilingual education*. Retrieved from http://faculty.ucmerced.edu/khakuta/research/SAT9/silence1.html

Hallahan, D. P., Kauffman, J. M., & Pullen, P.D. (2015). *Exceptional learners: An introduction to special education* (13th ed.) Boston: Pearson Education.

Halvorsen, A-L., Duke, N. K., Brugar, K. A., Block, M. K., Strachan, S. L., Berka, M. B., and Brown, J. M. (2012). Narrowing the achievement gap in second-grade social studies and content area literacy: The promise of a project-based approach. *Theory and Research in Social Education, 40*, 198–229.

Hansen, D. T. (Ed.). (2007). *Ethical visions of education: Philosophies in practice*. New York, NY: Teachers College Press.

Harding, Monica, Used with permission.

Hardman, M. L., Egan, M. W., & Drew, C. J. (2017). *Human exceptionality: Society, school, and family* (11th ed.). South-Western, a part of Cengage Learning, Inc. Reproduced by permission. www.cengage.com/permissions.

Harpin, S. B., Rossi, A., Kim, A. K., & Swanson, L. (2016). Behavioral impacts of a mindfulness pilot intervention for elementary school students. *Education 137*, 149–156.

Harris, C. J., Penuel, W. R., DeBarger, A. H., D'Angelo, C., and Gallagher, L. P. (2014). *Curriculum materials make a difference for next generation science learning: Results from Year 1 of a randomized controlled trial.* Menlo Park, CA: SRI International.

Harris Interactive, Inc. (2013, February). *The MetLife survey of the American teacher—Challenges for school leadership.* New York, NY: Author.

The Harris Poll. Based on Honesty/Ethics in Professions telephone interviews of U.S. adults conducted 2013-2016. Retrieved August 29, 2017, from http://www.gallup.com/poll/1654/honesty-ethics-professions.aspx#1

Harris Poll. (2015). *National survey explores the rewards and challenges of the profession at a critical time in U.S. education and how teachers want parents involved in the classroom.* Harris Poll conducted for the University of Phoenix. Retrieved from http://www.phoenix.edu/news/releases/2015/05/top-reasons-to-join-the-education-profession.html

Harry A. v. Duncan, 351 F.Supp 2d 1060 (Mont. 2005).

Hartigan, J. (Ed.) (2013). *Anthropology of race: Genes, biology, and culture.* Santa Fe, NM: School for Advanced Research Press.

Haselton, B., & Davis, M. (2004). Resources do produce results. *Foresight: A Publication of the Kentucky Long-Term Policy Research Center, II*(1), 7–9.

Hawking, S. W. (1988). *A brief history of time: From the big bang to black holes.* New York, NY: Bantam Books.

Hawkins, B. (2010, July 1). Teacher gets to tout St. Paul's Avalon co-op school to nation's top education officials. *MinnPost.com.* Retrieved from http://www.minnpost.com/stories/2010/07/01/19375/teacher_gets_to_tout_st_pauls_avalon_co-op_school_to_nations_top_education_officials

Heath, S. B. (1983). *Ways with words.* Cambridge, UK: Cambridge University Press.

Hedges, L. V. (1996). Quoted in Hedges finds boys and girls both disadvantaged in school. *Education News.* University of Chicago, Department of Education.

Hennick, C. (September 2, 2017). Get kids moving. *Scholastic teacher.* Retrieved from https://www.scholastic.com/teachers/articles/17-18/get-kids-moving/

Henriques, M. E. (1997, May). Increasing literacy among kindergartners through cross-age training. *Young Children*, pp. 42–47.

Henry, E., Huntley, J., McKamey, C., & Harper, L. (1995). *To be a teacher: Voices from the classroom.* Thousand Oaks, CA: Corwin Press.

Herrell, A. L., & Jordon, M. L. (2016). *50 Strategies for Teaching English Language Learners.* p. 2, Boston: Pearson.

Hess, F., & Meeks, O. (2010). *School boards circa 2010: Governance in the accountability area.* National School Boards Association, The Thomas Fordham Institute, and The Iowa School Boards Foundation.

Hicks, B. (2011). *Letter in support of Michelle Shearer's application for National Teacher of the Year.* Retrieved from http://www.ccsso.org/Documents/2011/news/2011_NTOY_Press.pdf

Hiebert, J., Gallimore, R., & Stigler, J. W. (2002). A knowledge base for the teaching profession: What would it look like and how can we get one? *Educational Researcher, 31*(5), 3–15.

Hirsch, E.D. (1987). *Cultural literacy: What every American needs to know.* Boston, MA: Houghton Mifflin.

Hirschfelder, A. B. (1986). *Happily may I walk: American Indians and Alaska Natives today.* New York, NY: Scribner.

Hohlfeld, T. N., Ritzhaupt, A. D., Wilson, M., & Dawson, K. (2016, April). *A longitudinal study of the Digital Divide in Florida schools: Beyond access.* Paper presented at the American Educational Research Association, Washington, DC.

Holmes, M., & Weiss, B. J. (1995). *Lives of women public schoolteachers: Scenes from American educational history.* New York, NY: Garland.

Holt-Reynolds, D. (1999). Good readers, good teachers? Subject matter expertise as a challenge in learning to teach. *Harvard Educational Review, 69*(1), 29–50.

Holt v. Shelton, 341 F. Supp. 821 (M.D. Tenn. 1972).

hooks, b. (1989). *Talking back: Thinking feminist, thinking black.* Toronto: Between the Lines.

hooks, b. (1994). *Teaching to transgress: Education as the practice of freedom.* New York, NY: Routledge.

hooks, b. (2003) *Teaching community. A pedagogy of hope.* New York, NY: Routledge.

Hopkins, G. (2017). What qualities do principals look for in a new teacher? Education World. Retrieved from http://www.educationworld.com/a_admin/admin/admin071.shtml. Copyright Education World, Inc. All rights reserved. Used with Permission.

Horne v. Flores, 557 U.S. 433. 2009.

Horn, M. B., & Staker, H. (2014). *Blended: Using disruptive innovation to improve schools.* San Francisco: Jossey-Bass.

Hortonville Joint School District No. 1 v. Hortonville Education Association, 426 U.S. 482 (1976).

Howard, V. F., Williams, B. F., Port, P. D., & Lepper, C. (2001). *Very young children with special needs.* Upper Saddle River, NJ: Merrill/Pearson.

"How many assets do young people have?" Minneapolis, MN: Author. Retrieved october 31, 2010, from http://www.search-institute.org/research/assets/asset-levels. Author: Search Institute,© 2010. Reprinted with permission from search Institute, Minneapolis, MN. For more information about the Developmental Assets, Please visit www.searchinstitute.org.

Hoy, A. W., & Hoy, W. K. (2013). *Instructional leadership: A research-based guide to learning in schools* (4th ed.). Boston, MA: Allyn & Bacon.

Human Rights Campaign. (2017). *State maps of laws & policies.* Retrieved from https://www.hrc.org/state-maps/employment

Hunzicker, J. (2018). *Teacher leadership in professional development schools.* Somerville, MA: Emerald Publishing.

Hussar, W. J., & Bailey, T. M. (2016). *Projections of Education Statistics to 2023* (NCES 2015-073). U.S. Department of Education, National Center for Education Statistics. Washington, DC: U.S. Government Printing Office.

Hutchins, R. M., & Adler, M. J. (1963). *Gateway to the Great Books.* Chicago: Encyclopedia Britannica.

Hyde Schools. (2018). About Hyde. Retrieved from http://www.hyde.edu/about/.

Hyslop, A. (2014). *The Case against Exit Exams. New America Education, Policy Brief.* Retrieved from https://www.newamerica.org/downloads/ExitExam_FINAL.pdf

I Am an Educator. (2016, October 16). Blog. Retrieved from https://iamaneducator.com/2016/10/16/blacklivesmatteratschool-faq-answering-why-hundreds-of-seattle-educators-are-wearing-black-lives-matter-shirts-to-school/

IBM MentorPlace. (2017, September 11). IBM MentorPlace. Retrieved from https://www.ibm.com/ibm/responsibility/downloads/initiatives/MentorPlace.pdf

Igoa, C. (1995). *The inner world of the immigrant child.* New York, NY: Lawrence Erlbaum.

Imber, M., & van Geel, T. (2010). *A teacher's guide to education law* (4th ed.). New York, NY: Routledge.

Imber, M., van Geel, T., Blokhuis, J. C., & Feldman, J. (2014). *A teacher's guide to education law* (5th ed.). New York, NY: Routledge.

Ingersoll, R., & Strong, M. (2011). The impact of induction and mentoring programs for beginning teachers: A critical review of the research. *Review of Educational Research, 81*(2), 201–233.

Ingraham v. Wright, 430 U.S. 651 (1977).

Innes, R. G. (2010). *KERA (1990-2010): What have we learned?"* Lexington, KY: Bluegrass Institute.

Inspired Teaching School. (2017, September 14). Our philosophy. Retrieved from http://www.inspiredteachingschool.org/wp-content/uploads/2011/02/Inspired_Teaching_Philosophy.pdf

Institute for Educational Leadership. (2017). *Community schools: A whole-child framework for school improvement.* Washington, DC: Author. Retrieved from http://www.communityschools.org/assets/1/AssetManager/Community-Schools-A-Whole-Child-Approach-to-School-Improvement.pdf

International Society for Technology in Education (ISTE) conference program. (June 24-27). Chicago, IL. Retrieved from https://conference.iste.org/2018/program/search/

J. C. v. Beverly Hills Unified School District. United States District Court for the Central District of California. (CV 08-03824 SVW, 2009). Retrieved from http://lawyersusaonline.com/wp-files/pdfs/jc-v-beverly-hills-a.pdf

Jackson, P. (1965). The way teaching is. *NEA Journal*.

Jackson, P. (1990). *Life in classrooms*. New York, NY: Teachers College Press.

James, W. (1890). *Principles of psychology*. Cambridge, MA: Harvard University Press.

Jeglin v. San Jacinto Unified School District, 827 F. Supp. 1459 (C.D. Cal. 1993).

Jefferson Area High School, Jefferson, OH. Retrieved January 19, 2018, from https://sites.google.com/a/jalsd.org/michaelbarney/language-arts/resources. Used with permission from Janet Grout.

Jencks, C., et al. (1972). *Inequality: A reassessment of the effect of family and schooling in America*. New York, NY: Basic Books.

Jencks, C., & Phillips, M. (Eds.). (1998). *The black-white test score gap*. Washington, DC: Brookings Institution Press.

Job Experience and Training (JET) Program. (2010, September 8). *Job Experience and Training (JET) Program*. Retrieved from http://www.national4-hheadquarters.gov/about/pod-leadership/JET09.pdf

Johanningmeier, E. V. (1980). *Americans and their schools*. Chicago: Rand McNally.

Johnson, D. W., & Johnson, F. P. (2017). *Joining together: Group theory and group skills* (12th ed.). New York, NY: Pearson.

Johnson, L. D. (2010). Reason, purpose & triumph. *Teaching tolerance*, *37*, 9.

Johnson, D. W., Johnson, R. T., & Holubec, E. J. (2008). *Cooperation in the classroom*, 8th Ed. Edina, MN: Interaction Book Company.

Joyce, B., Weil, M., & Calhoun, E. (2015). *Models of teaching* (9th ed.). Upper Saddle River, NJ: Allyn & Bacon/Pearson.

Kamenetz, A. (2017, September 8). Houston students are heading back—what they find could change schools nationwide. Northwest Public Radio blog. Retrieved from http://www.npr.org/sections/ed/2017/09/08/548648307/houston-students-are-heading-back-what-they-find-could-change-schools-nationwide

Kann, L, Olsen, E. O., McManus. T., et al. (2016, August 12). Sexual identity, sex of sexual contacts, and health-related behaviors among students in grades 9–12 — United States and selected sites, 2015. *Morbidity and mortality weekly report, surveillance summaries*, *65*(No. SS-9),1–202. Retrieved from http://dx.doi.org/10.15585/mmwr.ss6509a1.

Karr v. Schmidt, 401 U.S. 1201 (1972).

Kash, W. (2018, March 9). *Why technology is at a tipping point in U.S. schools*. Retrieved from https://edscoop.com/why-technology-is-at-a-tipping-point-in-u-s-schools

Katyal, K. R., & Evers, C. W. (2018). *Teacher leadership: New conceptions for autonomous student learning in the age of the Internet* (2nd ed.). New York, NY: Routledge.

Kauchak, D., & Eggen, P. (2012). *Learning & teaching: Research-based methods* (6th ed.). Upper Saddle River, NJ: Pearson.

Kauffman, G. (2017, January 22). Philadelphia teachers plan "Black Lives Matter week": Does BLM belong in the classroom? *The Christian Science Monitor*. Retrieved from https://www.csmonitor.com/USA/Education/2017/0122/Philadelphia-teachers-plan-Black-Lives-Matter-week-Does-BLM-belong-in-the-classroom

Kaye, E. A. (Ed.). (2016). *Requirements for certification of teachers, counselors, librarians, administrators for elementary and secondary schools—eighty-first edition, 2016-2017*. Chicago: University of Chicago Press.

Keith, T. (2015, September 20). Arkansas teacher of the year finalist reflects. *Arkansas Democrat-Gazette*, Inc. Retrieved from http://www.arkansasonline.com/news/2015/sep/20/arkansas-teacher-year-finalist-reflects/

Kellner, D. (2000). Multiple literacies and critical pedagogies. In P. P. Trifonas (Ed.), *Revolutionary pedagogies—cultural politics, instituting education, and the discourse of theory* (pp. 196–221). New York, NY: Routledge.

Kelly, M. (2000, September 8). *Indian Affairs head makes apology*. Associated Press.

Kennedy Middle School. (2014). P.R.I.D.E. information. Retrieved May 19, 2014, from http://schools.4j.lane.edu/kennedy/documents/kms_pride.pdf.

Kennedy, M. (1999). Ed schools and the problem of knowledge. In J. D. Raths & A. C. McAninch (Eds.), *Advances in teacher education: Vol. 5. What counts as knowledge in teacher education?* (pp. 29–45). Stamford, CT: Ablex.

Kent School District. (2018, March 21). *Welcome to the Kent School District Information Technology Department webpage*. Retrieved from https://www.kent.k12.wa.us/KSD/IT

Kids Count Data Book, 2017: State Trends in Child Well-Being. Baltimore: Annie E. Casey Foundation, 2017, p. 16. Used with Permission

King, M. (2008, February 3). Tribes confront painful legacy of Indian boarding schools. *Seattle Times*. Retrieved from http://seattletimes.nwsource.com/html/localnews/2004161238_boardingschool03m.html

King, M. (2017, July 21). Social media posts as exemplars. George Lucas Educational Foundation, *Edutopia* Blog. Retrieved from https://www.edutopia.org/blog/social-media-posts-exemplars-marissa-king

Kinross, L. (2009). *School board backs adaptive software for all students*. Toronto: Bloorview.

Kitzmiller v. Dover Area School District, 400 F. Supp. 2d 707 (2005).

Kleinfeld, J. (1998). *The myth that schools shortchange girls: Social science in the service of deception*. Washington, DC: Women's Freedom Network.

Knight, D. (December 6, 2013). Teaching courage in a postmodern world. *Teaching Tolerance*. Retrieved from https://www.tolerance.org/magazine/teaching-courage-in-a-postmodern-world

Kohlberg, H. (2014). The cognitive-developmental approach to moral education. In F. W. Parkay, E. J. Anctil, & G. Hass, *Curriculum leadership: Readings for developing quality educational programs* (10th ed.), pp. 181–193. Boston: Pearson.

Kosciw, J. G., & Diaz, E. M. (2006). *The 2005 national school climate survey: The experiences of lesbian, gay, bisexual, and transgender youth in our nation's schools*. New York, NY: Gay, Lesbian and Straight Education Network.

Kostelnik, M. J., Onaga, E., Rohde, B., & Whiren, A. (2002). *Children with special needs: Lessons for early childhood professionals*. New York, NY: Teachers College Press.

Kounin, J. (1970). *Discipline and group management in classrooms*. New York, NY: Holt, Rinehart and Winston.

Kozol, J. (1991). *Savage inequalities: Children in America's schools*. New York, NY: Crown.

Kozol, J. (2005). *The shame of the nation: The restoration of apartheid schooling in America*. New York, NY: Three Rivers Press.

Krashen, S., & McField, G. (2005). What works? Reviewing the latest evidence on bilingual education. *Language Learner*, *1*(2), 7–10.

Kraus, K., Sherratt, E., & Calegari, N. 2017. *Tackling the challenge of raising teacher pay, state by state*. San Francisco: Teacher Salary Project.

Krizek v. Cicero-Stickney Township High School District No. 201, 713 F. Supp. 1131 (N.D. Ill. 1989).

Krough, S. L., & Morehouse, P. (2014). *The early childhood curriculum: inquiry learning through integration* (2nd ed.). New York: Routledge.

Kulik, J. A. (2004). Meta-analytic studies of acceleration. In N. Colangelo, S. G. Assouline, & M. U. M. Gross (Eds.), *A nation deceived: How schools hold back America's brightest students* (Vol. 2, pp. 13–22). Iowa City, IA: The Connie Belin and Jacqueline N. Blank International Center for Gifted Education and Talent Development.

Lahey, J. (2016, October 18). The failing first line of defense. *The Atlantic*. Retrieved from https://www.theatlantic.com/education/archive/2016/10/the-failing-first-line-of-defense/504485/

LaMorte, M. W. (2008). *School law: Cases and concepts* (9th ed.). Upper Saddle River, NJ: Allyn & Bacon/Pearson.

LaMorte, M. W. (2012). *School law: Cases and concepts* (10th ed.). Upper Saddle River, NJ: Pearson.

Lange, C. M., & Sletten, S. J. (2002). *Alternative education: A brief history and research synthesis.* Alexandria, VA: Project Forum at National Association of State Directors of Special Education. Retrieved from http://www.nasdse.org/forum.htm

Larry P. v. Riles, 793 F.2d 969 (9th Cir. 1984).

Larson, R. (2000). Toward a psychology of positive youth development. *The American Psychologist*, *55*, 170–183.

Lau v. Nichols, 414 U.S. 563 (1974).

Laurence, D. (2000). *NEA: The grab for power: A chronology of the National Education Association.* Oklahoma City, OK: Hearthstone.

Layton, L. and Brown, E. (2012, November 17). Quality controls lacking for D.C. schools accepting federal vouchers. *Washington Post*. Retrieved from http://www.washingtonpost.com/local/education/quality-controls-lacking-for-dc-schools-accepting-federal-vouchers/2012/11/17/062bf97a-1e0d-11e2-b647-bb1668e64058_story.html

Leahey, T. H., & Harris, R. J. (2001). *Learning and cognition* (5th ed.). Upper Saddle River, NJ: Merrill/Pearson.

Leahy, R. (2009). *Authentic educating: Solutions for a world at risk.* Lanham, MD: University Press of America, Inc.

Learning in Deed. (2004). *Learning in deed: Service learning in action.* New York, NY: National Service-Learning Partnership, Academy for Educational Development. Retrieved from http://www.learningindeed.org/tools/examples.html

Lee County School District. (2017). *Social media guidelines: The school district of Lee County, FL.* Retrieved from http://lcapst.org/2015-2016/Social%20Media%20Guidelines-UPDATED.pdf

Lee, V. E., Chen, X., & Smerdon, B. A. (1996). *The influence of school climate on gender differences in the achievement and engagement of young adolescents.* Washington, DC: American Association of University Women.

Leinhardt, G. (1990). Capturing craft knowledge in teaching. *Educational Researcher*, *19*(2), 18–25.

Lemon v. Kurtzman, 403 U.S. 602 (1971).

Lenz, Bob, From the Classroom: What Does Blended Learning Look Like?, Retrieved June 7, 2018, from http://www.edutopia.org/blog/blended-learning-example-classroom-lesson-bob-lenz. Used with permission.

Lesley University Center for Special Education and Trauma and Learning Policy Initiative of Massachusetts Advocates for Children and the Harvard Law School. (2012). Used with Permission.

Lewis, C. (2003, August 13). Is it time for cameras in classrooms? *Philadelphia Inquirer*. Retrieved from http://www.philly.com

Lewis, R. B., & Doorlag, D. H. (2006). *Teaching special students in general education classrooms* (7th ed.). Upper Saddle River, NJ: Merrill/Pearson Education.

Li, Q., & Ma, X. (2010). A meta-analysis of the effects of computer technology on school students' mathematics learning. *Educational Psychology Review*, *22*(3), 215–243.

Li, W., & Vandell, D. L. (2013). *Relating type, intensity, and quality of after-school activities to later academic and behavioral outcomes.* Manuscript in preparation.

Lickona, Thomas. (2014) Center for the 4th and 5th Rs. Cortland, NY: SUNY School of Education. Retrieved from http://www2.cortland.edu/centers/characters/12-pt-comprehensive-approach.dot. Used with permission.

Lightfoot, S. L. (1978). *Worlds apart: Relationships between families and schools.* New York, NY: Basic Books.

Lindjord, D. (2000). Families at the century's turn: The troubling economic trends. *Family Review*, *7*(3), 5–6.

Lindsay, D. (1996, March 13). N.Y. bills give teachers power to oust pupils. *Education Week.*

Lipsman v. New York City Board of Education, 1999 WL 498230 (N.Y.).

Littky, D. (2004). *The big picture: Education is everyone's business.* Alexandria, VA: Association for Supervision and Curriculum Development.

Little, P. M. D., & Harris, E. (2003, July). *A review of out-of-school time program quasi-experimental and experimental evaluation results.* Cambridge, MA: Harvard University, Harvard Family Research Project.

Lo, C. K., & Hew, K. F. (2017). A critical review of flipped classroom challenges in K-12 education: Possible solutions and recommendations for future research. *Research and Practice in Technology Enhanced Learning*, *12*(1). https://doi.org/10.1186/s41039-016-0044-2

Lomawaima, K. T. (2012). Education of American Indians. In James A. Banks (Ed). *Encyclopedia of diversity in education* (pp. 104–109). Thousand Oaks, CA: Sage Publications.

Lortie, D. (1975). *School teacher: A sociological study.* Chicago: University of Chicago Press.

Losinski, M., Katsiyannis, A., Ryan, J., & Baughan, C. (2014). Weapons in schools and zero-tolerance policies. *NASSP Bulletin*, *98*(2), 126–141.

Lovett, S. (2018). *Advocacy for teacher leadership: Opportunity, preparation, support, and pathways.* New York, NY: Springer.

Lynch, M. (2017). Virtual classrooms are the future of teacher education. *The Tech Edvocate.* Retrieved from http://www.thetechedvocate.org/virtual-classrooms-future-teacher-education/

Mackinnon, C. (1989). *Toward a feminist theory of the state.* Cambridge, Massachusetts: Harvard University Press.

MacLeod, J. (2008). *Ain't no makin' it: Aspirations & attainment in a low-income neighborhood* (3rd ed.). Boulder, CO: Westview Press.

MacNaughton, R. H., & Johns, F. A. (1991, September). Developing a successful schoolwide discipline program. *NASSP Bulletin*, pp. 47–57.

Magnet Schools of America. (2013, May 7). *Press release: Magnet schools of America announces 2013 national award winners.* Retrieved from http://www.magnet.edu/files/press-releases/2013-award-winners-press-release.pdf

Magnet Schools of America. (2017). *Facts about magnet schools.* Washington, DC: Author. Retrieved August 27, 2017, from http://www.magnet.edu/files/2015-conferences/2015-ptc/2015-ptc-materials/magnet-school-fact-sheet.pdf

Mailloux v. Kiley, 323 F. Supp. 1387, 1393 (D. Mass.), *aff'd*, 448 F.2d 1242 (1st Cir. 1971).

Mann, H. (1868). Annual reports on education. In M. Mann (Ed.), *The life and works of Horace Mann* (Vol. 3). Boston, MA: Horace B. Fuller.

Mann, H. (1957). Twelfth annual report. In L. A. Cremin (Ed.), *The republic and the school: Horace Mann on the education of free men.* New York, NY: Teachers College Press.

Mann, T. (2015, January 9). *An intimate education. Inside Higher Education.* Retrieved from https://www.insidehighered.com/views/2015/01/09/essay-teaching-great-books-low-income-high-school-students

Marcus v. Rowley, 695 F.2d 1171 (9th Cir. 1983).

Markus, D. (2012, July 25). *Blog: High-impact professional development for rural schools.* Retrieved from http://www.edutopia.org/blog/stw-tech-integration-professional-development

Marzano, R. J. (1997). *Eight questions you should ask before implementing standards-based education at the local* level. Aurora, CO: Mid-Continent Research for Education and Learning.

Maslow, A. (1954). *Motivation and personality.* New York: Basic Books.

Maslow, A. (1962). *Toward a psychology of being.* New York: Basic Books.

Massachusetts Department of Elementary & Secondary Education. (2017, September 9). *School redesign: MA Expanded learning time (ELT).* Retrieved from http://www.doe.mass.edu/redesign/elt/

Mastropieri, M. A., & Scruggs, T. E. (2010). *The inclusive classroom: Strategies for effective instruction* (4th ed.). Upper Saddle River, NJ: Merrill/Pearson.

Matthews, L. E. (2008). Illuminating urban excellence: A movement of change within mathematics education. *Journal of Urban Mathematics Education*, *1*(1), 1–4.

Maul, A., & McClelland, A. (2013, July). *Review of national charter school study 2013.* National Education Policy Center, University of Colorado.

Mayer, F. (1973). *A history of educational thought*. Columbus, OH: Merrill.

McCall, A. (2017, May 15). Why I teach where I teach: Representation matters. *The Education Trust blog*. Retrieved from https://edtrust.org/the-equity-line/teach-teach-representation-matters/

McCarthy, B. (2015, January 22). Et tu, Mrs. McCarthy? *Core Knowledge Foundation*. Retrieved from https://www.coreknowledge.org/blog/et-tu-mrs-mccarthy/

McCourt, F. (2005). *Teacher man: A memoir.* New York, NY: Simon & Schuster.

McFarland, J., Hussar, B., de Brey, C., Snyder, T., Wang, X., Wilkinson-Flicker, S., Gebrekristos, S., Zhang, J., Rathbun, A., Barmer, A., Bullock Mann, F., & Hinz, S. (2017). *The Condition of Education 2017* (NCES 2017-144). U.S. Department of Education. Washington, DC: National Center for Education Statistics.

McGarry, A., & Perkins, K. (2018, June). *Implement effective math teacher practices using interactive simulations*. Presented at the ISTE, Chicago, IL. Retrieved from https://conference.iste.org/2018/program/search/detail_session.php?id=110812735

McLeskey, J., Rosenberg, M. S., & Westling, D. L. (2010). *Inclusion: Effective practices for all students*. Upper Saddle River, NJ: Pearson.

McQuiggan, M., & Megra, M. (2017). Parent and family involvement in education: Results from the National Household Education Surveys Program of 2016 (NCES 2017-102). *U.S. Department of Education*. Washington, DC: National Center for Education Statistics.

Meek, C. (2003, April). Classroom crisis: It's about time. *Phi Delta Kappan*, 592–595.

Meyers, C., Molefe, A., Dhillon, S., & Zhu, B. (2015, April). *The Impact of eMINTS Professional Development on Middle School Teacher Instruction and Student Achievement: Year 3 Report*. American Institutes for Research.

MFAS (Metropolitan Federation of Alternative Schools). (2010, September 21). *About us*. Retrieved from http://www.mfas.org/about.html

Miami-Dade County Public Schools. (2013, May 10). *Press release: M-DCPS educator named 2013 national teacher-of-the-year by Magnet Schools of America*. Retrieved from http://news.dadeschools.net/releases/rls13/105_magnet.html

Miech, R. A., Johnston, L. D., O'Malley, P. M., Bachman, J. G., Schulenberg, J. E., & Patrick, M. E. (2017). *Monitoring the future: National survey results on drug use, 1975–2016: Volume I, secondary school students.* Ann Arbor: Institute for Social Research, University of Michigan.

Miller, C., & Doering, A. (2014). *The new landscape of mobile learning: Redesigning education in an app-based world.* New York, NY: Routledge.

Miron, G., & Gulosino, C. (2013, November). *Profiles of for-profit and nonprofit education management organizations: Fourteenth edition—2011–2012*. Boulder, CO: National Education Policy Center. Retrieved from http://nepc.colorado.edu/publication/EMOprofiles-11-12

Miron, G., Shank, C., & Davidson, C. (2018). *Full-time virtual and blended schools: Enrollment, student characteristics, and performance*. Boulder, CO: National Education Policy Center. Retrieved from http://nepc.colorado.edu/publication/virtual-schools-annual-2018

Missouri v. Jenkins, 515 U.S. 70 (1995).

Mohammed ex rel. Mohammed, v. School District of Philadelphia, 355 F. Supp. 2d 779 (Pa. 2005).

Moll, L., Amanti, C., Neff, D., & Gonzalez, N. (2001). Funds of knowledge for teaching: Using a qualitative approach to connect homes and classrooms. *Theory Into Practice*, *31*(2): 132–141.

Molnar A. & Boninger, F. (2018). Why We're Glad that the National *Education Policy Center Deleted Its Facebook Account. Boulder,* CO: National Education Policy Center. Retrieved from http://nepc.colorado.edu/publication/facebook-student-privacy, pp. 3, 6.

Montagu, A. (1974). *Man's most dangerous myth: The fallacy of race* (5th ed.). New York, NY: Oxford University Press.

Moran v. School District No. 7, Yellowstone County, 350 F. Supp. 1180 (D. Mont. *1972*).

Morris, J. E., & Curtis, K. E. (1983, March/April). Legal issues relating to field-based experiences in teacher education. *Journal of Teacher Education*, 2–6.

Morris, V. C., & Pai, Y. (1994). *Philosophy and the American school: An introduction to the philosophy of education*. Lanham, MD: University Press of America.

Morrison, B., & Ahmed, E. (2006). Restorative justice and civil society: Emerging practice, theory, and evidence. *Journal of Social Issues*, *62*(2), 209–215.

Morrison v. State Board of Education, 461 P.2d 375 (Cal. 1969).

Moyers, B.D. (1989). *A world of ideas: Conversations with thoughtful men and women*. New York: Doubleday.

Mozert v. Hawkins County Board of Education, 827 F.2d 1058 (6th Cir. 1987), cert. denied, 484 U.S. 1066 (1988).

Murphy, S. (2010, August 20). Teachers asked to "unfriend" students on Facebook. *TechNewsDaily*. Retrieved from http://www.tech-newsdaily.com/teachers-asked-to-unfriend-students-on-facebook-1075/

Murray v. Pittsburgh Board of Public Education, 919 F. Supp. 838 (W.D. Pa. 1996).

Musu-Gillette, L., Zhang, A., Wang, K., Zhang, J., and Oudekerk, B.A. (2017). *Indicators of School Crime and Safety: 2016* (NCES 2017-064/NCJ 250650). National Center for Education Statistics, U.S. Department of Education, and Bureau of Justice Statistics, Office of Justice Programs, U.S. Department of Justice. Washington, DC.

Nagoaka, J., Farrington, C. A., Ehrlich, S. B., & Heath, R. D. (2015). *Foundations for young adult success: A developmental framework.* Chicago: University of Chicago Consortium on Chicago School Research.

National Alliance of Public Charter Schools. (2016). *2016 annual report*. Washington, DC: Author.

National Alliance of Public Charter Schools. (2017). *Estimated public charter school enrollment, 2016-17*. Washington, DC: Author.

National Association of School Boards. (2017, September). *Busting the myth of "one-size-fits all" public education*. Alexandria, VA: National Association of School Boards.

National Association of School Psychologists. (2008). *Zero tolerance and alternative strategies: A fact sheet for educators and policymakers.* Bethesda, MD: Author. Retrieved from http://www.nasponline.org/educators/zero_alternative.pdf

National Board for Professional Teaching Standards (NBPTS). (2016). *What teachers should know and be able to do*. Arlington, VA: Author.

National Board for Professional Teaching Standards (NBPTS). (2017, August 29). *National Board certification overview.* Retrieved August 29, 2017, from http://www.nbpts.org/national-board-certification/overview/

National Board for Professional Teaching Standards. (2018, January 7). *More than 5,400 Teachers Achieve National Board Certification, Increasing Total to More than 118,000 Board-Certified Teachers Nationwide.* Retrieved from http://www.nbpts.org/newsroom/more-than-5400-teachers-achieve-national-board-certification/

National Board for Professional Teaching Standards. (2018, February 23,). *Welcome to ATLAS*. Arlington, VA: Author. Retrieved from http://www.nbpts.org/atlas/

National Catholic Education Association. (2017). *Catholic school data.* Retrieved July 26, 2017, from http://www.ncea.org/NCEA/Proclaim/Catholic_School_Data/Catholic_School_Data.aspx

National Center for Education Statistics. (1980). *High school and beyond study*. Washington, DC: U.S. Department of Education: Author.

National Center for Education Statistics. (2008, March 25). *Digest of education statistics, 2007*. Washington, DC: Author.

National Center for Education Statistics. (2012). *Schools and Staffing Survey (SASS) 2012*. Washington, DC: Author.

National Center for Education Statistics. (2017a). *Condition of education, 2017*. Washington, DC: Author.

National Center for Education Statistics. (2017b). *Digest of Education Statistics 2016*. National Center for Education Statistics, Institute of Education Sciences, U.S. Department of Education.

National Coalition for the Homeless. (2013a). *Geography of homelessness*. Retrieved from http://nationalhomeless.org/about-homelessness/

National Coalition for the Homeless. (2013b). *Youth and homelessness*. Retrieved from http://nationalhomeless.org/issues/youth/

National Commission on Excellence in Education. (1983). *A nation at risk: The imperative for educational reform*. Washington, DC: U.S. Government Printing Office.

National Council of State Legislatures. (2016, April 29). *Teen pregnancy prevention*. Retrieved from http://www.ncsl.org/research/health/teen-pregnancy-prevention.aspx

National Education Association. (2017a). *About NEA*. Retrieved August 29, 2017, from https://www.nea.org/home/2580.htm

National Education Association. (2017b). *About NEA*. Retrieved August 29, 2017, from https://www.nea.org/home/2580.htm

National Center for Education Statistics. (2012, July). *Characteristics of the 100 largest public elementary and secondary school districts in the United States: 2009–10*. Washington, DC: Author.

National Education Association. (2010, December). *Status of the American public school teacher 2005–2006*. Washington, DC: Author.

National Education Association. (2017). *Code of ethics*. Washington, DC: Author. Retrieved August 29, 2017, from http://www.nea.org/home/30442.htm

National Education Association. (2018). *Rankings of the States 2017 and Estimates of School Statistics 2018*. Washington, DC: National Education Association, April 2018.

National School Boards Association & Center for Public Education. (2011). *Eight characteristics of effective school boards: full report*. Alexandria, VA. Retrieved from http://www.centerforpubliceducation.org/Main-Menu/Public-education/Eight-characteristics-of-effective-school-boards/Eight-characteristics-of-effective-school-boards.html

National School Safety Center, Excerpted from the School Safety Check Book, Dr. Ronald, D. Stephens, 141 Duesenberg Dr., Suite 11, Westlake Village, CA, 91362, http://www.nssc1.org. Used with Permission.

National trade and professional associations of the United States 2017. New York, NY: Columbia Books and Information Service.

Native American Community Academy. (2018, March 8). *Who we are*. Retrieved from http://nacaschool.org/about/

NBC News, Education Nation. (2013, June 10). *NBC News to host 2013 Education Nation Summit from Oct. 6-8 at the New York Public Library*. Retrieved from http://www.educationnation.com/files/dmfile/2013Summit.pdf

National School Boards Association. (2017). *State association services: Who are our members and what do they do?* Retrieved from https://www.nsba.org/services/state-association-services

Navarro, M. (2008, March 31). New dialogue on mixed race: Many of mixed parentage feel Obama's path similar to theirs. *New York Times*. Retrieved from http://www.msnbc.msn.com/id/23875822/

NEA Today. (2003, May). New federal rule supports school prayer, p. 13.

Nelson, J. L., Carlson, K., & Palonsky, S. B. (2000). *Critical issues in education: A dialectic approach* (4th ed.). New York, NY: McGraw-Hill.

New Jersey v. Massa, 231 A.2d 252 (N.J. Sup. Ct. 1967).

New Jersey v. T.L.O., 469 U.S. 325 (1985).

New Teacher Center. (2016). *The Big Picture: Comprehensive Systems of Teacher Induction*. Santa Cruz, CA: New Teacher Center.

New Teacher Center. (2017). *Students gain up to five months of additional learning when new teachers receive high-quality mentoring*. Retrieved from https://newteachercenter.org/blog/2017/06/22/students-gain-five-months-additional-learning-new-teachers-receive-high-quality-mentoring/.

New York City Department of Education. (2017). *About us*. Retrieved from http://schools.nyc.gov/AboutUs/default.htm

Newmann, F. M., & Wehlage, G. G. (1995). *Successful school restructuring: A report to the public and educators by the Center on Organization and Restructuring of Schools*. Madison, WI: University of Wisconsin, Center on Organization and Restructuring of Schools.

Newmann, F. M., et al. (Eds.). (1996). *Authentic achievement: Restructuring schools for intellectual quality*. San Francisco, CA: Jossey-Bass.

NICHE. (2016). *Schools without summer break: An in-depth look at year-round schooling*. Pittsburgh, PA. Retrieved from https://articles.niche.com/schools-without-summer-break-an-in-depth-look-at-year-round-schooling/rlbaum

Nieto, S. (2002). *Language, culture, and teaching: Critical perspectives for a new century*. Mahwah, NJ: Lawrence Erlbaum.

Noddings, N. (2002). *Educating moral people: A caring alternative to character education*. New York, NY: Teachers College Press.

Noddings, N. (2007). *When school reform goes wrong*. New York, NY: Teachers College Press.

Nucaro, A. (2017, August 15). Teaching kids to think for themselves. *HuffPost blog*. Retrieved from http://www.huffingtonpost.com/entry/59931289e4b063e2ae058312

Null v. Board of Education, 815 F. Supp. 937 (D. W. Va. 1993).

Nussbaum, M. (2009). Tagore, Dewey, and the imminent demise of liberal education. In Siegel, H. (Ed.). *The Oxford handbook of philosophy of education*. New York, NY: Oxford University Press.

Oakes, J., & Lipton, M. (2007). *Teaching to change the world* (3rd ed.). Boston, MA: McGraw-Hill.

Oakes, J., Lipton, M., Anderson, L., and Stilman, J. (2013). *Teaching to change the world* (4th ed.). New York: Routledge.

Ohman v. Board of Education, 93 N.E.2d 927 (N.Y. 1950).

Oberti v. Board of Education of the Borough of Clementon School District, 789 F. Supp. 1322 (D.N.J. 1992).

O'Connell, P. M. (2017, January 2). Can in-school meditation help curb youth violence? *Chicago Tribune*. Retrieved from http://www.chicagotribune.com/news/ct-classroom-meditation-disadvantaged-students-met-20161231-story.html

O'Connor, E. E., Dearing, E., & Collins, B. A. (2011). Teacher-child relationship and behavior problem trajectories in elementary school. *American Educational Research Journal*, *48*(1), 120–162.

Ohman v. Board of Education, 93 N.E.2d 927 (N.Y. 1950).

O'Neill, B. (2017, November 2). *8 STEM summer programs that are just for high school girls*. Boston: TeenLife Media. Retrieved from https://www.teenlife.com/blogs/8-stem-summer-programs-are-just-high-school-girls

Orfield, G., & Ee, J. (2017, September). *Patterns of resegregation in Florida's schools*. University of California, Civil Rights Project.

Orfield, G., & Yun, J. T. (1999). *Re-segregation in American schools*. Cambridge, MA: Harvard University, Civil Rights Project.

Organization for Economic Cooperation and Development (OECD). (2016), Adapted from PISA 2015 Results in Focus, Paris: OECD, p. 5. Used with permission.

Ormrod, J. E., & McGuire, D. J. (2007). *Case studies: Applying educational psychology*. Upper Saddle River, NJ: Pearson Education.

Ormrod, J. E., Anderman, E. M., & Anderman, L. (2017). *Educational psychology: Developing learners* (9th ed.) Boston: Pearson.

Owasso Independent School District v. Falvo, 233 F.3d 1203 (10th Cir. 2002).

Ozmon, H. W., & Craver, S. M. (2007). *Philosophical foundations of education* (8th ed.). Upper Saddle River: NJ: Prentice Hall.

Ozmon, H. W., & Craver, S. M. (2012). *Philosophical foundations of education* (9th ed.). Boston: Pearson.

Paige, R., & Witty, E. (2010). *The black-white achievement gap: Why closing it is the greatest civil rights issue of our time*. New York, NY: Amacom Press.

Papay, J. P., Murnane, R. J., and Willet, J. B. 2010. The consequences of high school exit examinations for low-performing urban students: Evidence from Massachusetts. *Educational Evaluation and Policy Analysis*, March (32): 5–23.

Parkay, F. W. (1983). *White teacher, black school: The professional growth of a ghetto teacher*. New York, NY: Praeger.

Parkay, F. W. (1988, Summer). Reflections of a protégé. *Theory into Practice*, pp. 195–200.

Parkay, F. W., Shindler, J., & Oaks, M. M. (1997, January). Creating a climate for collaborative, emergent leadership at an urban high school: Exploring the stressors, role changes, and paradoxes of restructuring. *International Journal of Educational Reform*, 64–74.

Parkay, F. W., Anctil, E., & Hass, G. (2014). *Curriculum leadership: Readings for developing quality educational programs* (10th ed.). Upper Saddle River, NJ: Pearson.

Parker, L., & Shapiro, J. P. (1993). The context of educational administration and social class. In C. A. Capper (Ed.), *Educational administration in a pluralistic society* (pp. 36–65). Albany, NY: State University of New York Press.

PASE (Parents in Action on Special Education) v. Hannon, 506 F. Supp. 831 (E.D. Ill. 1980).

Pashler, H., & Carrier, M. (1996). Structures, processes, and the flow of information. In E. Bjork & R. Bjork (Eds.), *Memory* (pp. 3–29). San Diego, CA: Academic Press.

Pashler, H., McDaniel, M., Rohrer, D., & Bjork, R. (2008). Learning styles: Concepts and evidence. *Psychological Science in the Public Interest*, *7*(3), 105–119.

Patchin, J. W., & Hinduja, S. (August 9, 2017). Cyberbullying facts. *Cyberbullying Research Center.* Retrieved from https://cyberbullying.org/facts

Patchogue-Medford Congress of Teachers v. Board of Education of Patchogue-Medford Union Free School District (1987)

Patterson, Richard, used with permission.

Paul, J. L., Christensen, L., & Falk, G. (2000). Accessing the intimate spaces of life in the classroom through letters to former teachers: A protocol for uncovering hidden stories. In J. L. Paul & T. J. Smith (Eds.), *Stories out of school: Memories and reflections on care and cruelty in the classroom* (pp. 15–26). Stamford, CT: Ablex.

Paul, J. L., & Colucci, K. (2000). Caring pedagogy. In J. L. Paul & T. J. Smith (Eds.), *Stories out of school: Memories and reflections on care and cruelty in the classroom* (pp. 45–63). Stamford, CT: Ablex.

PBS Learning Media. (February 4, 2013). Press Release: PBS Survey Finds Teachers Are Embracing Digital Resources to Propel Student Learning. Used with permission.

PBS NewsHour. (2014, February 20). *To curb conflict, a Colorado high school replaces punishment with conversation.* Retrieved from https://www.pbs.org/newshour/amp/show/new-approach-discipline-school

Peck, D. R. (2008). *New teacher experiences in two rural Washington school districts: A phenomenological study.* Unpublished Ed.D. dissertation, Washington State University.

Peter Doe v. San Francisco Unified School District, 131 Cal. Rptr. 854 (Ct. App. 1976).

Pew Charitable Trust. (2016, January 14). *Governing urban schools in the future: What's facing Philadelphia and Pennsylvania.* Retrieved from http://www.pewtrusts.org/en/research-and-analysis/issue-briefs/2016/01/governing-urban-schools-in-the-future-whats-facing-philadelphia-and-pennsylvania

Pew Research Center. (2012, November 1*). How teens do research in the digital world*. Washington, DC: Author.

Pew Research Center. (2015, May 12). *America's changing religious landscape.*

Pew Research Center. (2015, June). *Multiracial in America: Proud, diverse and growing in numbers.* Washington, D.C.

Pew Research Center. (2016, September 8). *Hispanic trends.* Retrieved from http://www.pewhispanic.org/2016/09/08/4-ranking-the-latino-population-in-the-states/

Pew Research Center. (2016, November 17). *Children of unauthorized immigrants represent rising share of K-12 students.* Retrieved from http://www.pewresearch.org/fact-tank/2016/11/17/children-of-unauthorized-immigrants-represent-rising-share-of-k-12-students/

Pew Research Center. (2017, September 8). *Key facts about Asian Americans, a diverse and growing population.* Retrieved from http://www.pewresearch.org/fact-tank/2017/09/08/key-facts-about-asian-americans/

Pew Research Center. (2017, December 19). *Most Americans say Trump's election has led to worse race relations in the U.S.* Retrieved from http://www.people-press.org/2017/12/19/most-americans-say-trumps-election-has-led-to-worse-race-relations-in-the-u-s/

Phi Delta Kappa. (2017). The 49th annual PDK poll of the public's attitudes toward the public schools. *Phi Delta Kappan*, Vol. 99, No. 1, K1–K32.

Phi Delta Kappa. (2016). The 48th annual PDK poll of the public's attitudes toward the public schools. *Phi Delta Kappan*, Vol. 98, No. 1, K1-K32.

Philips, V., & Wong, C. (2010). Tying together the Common Core of standards, instruction, and assessments. *Phi Delta Kappan*, *91*(5), 37–41.

Picarella v. Terrizzi, 893 F. Supp. 1292 (M.D. Pa. 1995).

Picucci, A.C. (June 28, 2017). *How NTC's teacher mentor program increases student learning.* Santa Cruz, CA: New Teacher Center. Retrieved from https://newteachercenter.org/blog/2017/06/28/i3-final-validation-results/

Pierre, C. E. (1916, October). The work of the Society for the Propagation of the Gospel in Foreign Parts among the Negroes in the Colonies. *Journal of Negro History* 1, 349–360.

Placek, C. (2016, August 12). *Iroquois in Des Plaines, oldest year-round school in suburbs, celebrates 20 years.* *Daily Herald*. Retrieved from http://www.dailyherald.com/article/20160812/news/160819563/

Poe v. Hamilton, 56 Ohio App.3d 137 (1990).

Portner, J. (1999, May 12). Schools ratchet up the rules on student clothing, threats. *Education Week on the Web.*

Posner, George J., *Field Experience: A Guide to Reflective Teaching,* 6th Ed., (C) 2005, p. 122. Reprinted and electronically reproduced by permission of Pearson Education, Inc., Upper Saddle River, NJ.

Poway Unified School District. (2008). *Ed tech central.* Retrieved from http://powayusd.sdcoe.k12.ca.us/projects/edtechcentral/DigitalStorytelling/default.htm

Power, E. J. (1982). *Philosophy of education: Studies in philosophies, schooling, and educational policies.* Upper Saddle River, NJ: Prentice Hall.

Power, F. C., et al. (Eds.). (2008). *Moral education: A handbook* (Vol. 1). Westport, CT: Praeger.

Price-Dennis, D., & Carrion, S. (2017). Leveraging digital literacies for equity and social justice. *Language Arts*, *94*(3), 190–195.

ProEnglish. (2017). *About us.* Retrieved from https://proenglish.org/about-us/

Provenzano, N. (2013, September 26). *If you're not reflecting, you're not trying.* Retrieved from http://www.thenerdyteacher.com/2013/09/if-youre-not-reflecting-youre-not-trying.html

QS World University Rankings. (2018). *QS World University Rankings.* London: QS Quacquarelli Symonds Limited. Retrieved from https://www.topuniversities.com/university-rankings/world-university-rankings/2018

QuestBridge. (2016). *QuestBridge: Mission & vision.* Retrieved from http://www.questbridge.org/about-questbridge/mission-a-vision

Rafalow, M. H. 2018. Disciplining play: Digital youth culture as capital at school. *American Journal of Sociology*, *123*(5), 1416–1452.

Rahman, T., Fox, M.A., Ikoma, S., & Gray, L. (2017). *Certification status and experience of U.S. public school teachers: Variations across student subgroups* (NCES 2017-056). U.S. Department of Education, National Center for Education Statistics. Washington, DC: U.S. Government Printing Office.

Randall, V. R. (2001). *Institutional racism.* Dayton, OH: University of Dayton School of Law.

Ray v. School District of DeSoto County, 666 F. Supp. 1524 (M.D. Fla. 1987).

Recovery School District. (2014, March 3). *About RSD: Empowerment.* Retrieved from http://www.rsdla.net/apps/pages/index.jsp?uREC_ID=205342&type=d&pREC_ID=406074

Reich, J., & Ito, M. (2017.) *From Good Intentions to Real Outcomes: Equity by Design in Learning Technologies.* Irvine, CA: Digital Media and Learning Research Hub.

Renner, Susie, Teaching Tolerance, Fall 2010, p. 15. Used with Permission

Republican Party, Republican Platform, 2016.

Reuters. (2014, February 13). *Law Offices of Howard G. Smith files class action lawsuit against K12 Inc.* Retrieved from http://www.reuters.com/finance/stocks/LRN/key-developments/article/2921866

Richard, A. (2002, May 15). Memphis school board wants uniforms for all. *Education Week on the Web.*

Rickover, H. G. (1959). *Education and freedom.* New York: E. P. Dutton.

Rideout, V. (2015). *The Common Sense census: Media use by tweens and teens.* San Francisco, CA: Common Sense Media, Inc. Retrieved from https://www.commonsensemedia.org/research/the-common-sense-census-media-use-by-tweens-and-teens

Rideout, V. (2017). *The Common Sense census: Media use by kids age zero to eight.* San Francisco, CA: Common Sense Media, Inc. Retrieved from https://www.commonsensemedia.org/research/the-common-sense-census-media-use-by-kids-age-zero-to-eight-2017

Rippa, S. A. (1984). *Education in a free society.* New York, NY: Longman.

Rippa, S. A. (1997). *Education in a free society: An American history* (8th ed.). New York, NY: Longman.

Ripple, R. E., & Rockcastle, V. E. (Eds.). (1964). *Piaget rediscovered: A report of the conference on cognitive studies and curriculum development.* Ithaca, NY: Cornell University, School of Education.

Reprinted with permission from Childabuse.com . (2017). Anchorage, AK. Retrieved from http://www.childabuse.com/help.htm.

Robers, S., Kemp, J., & Truman, J. (2013). *Indicators of school crime and safety: 2012* (NCES 2013-036/NCJ 241446). National Center for Education Statistics, U.S. Department of Education, and Bureau of Justice Statistics, Office of Justice Programs, U.S. Department of Justice. Washington, DC: U.S. Government Printing Office.

Roberts, J., & Koliska, M. (2014). The effects of ambient media: What unplugging reveals about being plugged in. *First Monday, 19*(8).

Roberts, R. D., & Lipnevich, A. A. (2012). From general intelligence to multiple intelligences: Meanings, models, and measures. In K. R. Harris, S. Graham, & T. Urdan (Eds.), *APA educational psychology handbook, Vol 2: Individual differences and cultural and contextual factors* (pp. 33–57). Washington, DC: American Psychological Association.

Roberts v. City of Boston, 59 Mass. (5 Cush.) 198 (1850).

Robinson, M. W. (2008, February/March). Scared not to be straight. *Edutopia: The New World of Learning, 4*(1), 56–58.

Roblyer, M. D., & Hughes, J. E. (2019). *Integrating educational technology into teaching: Transforming learning across disciplines* (8th ed.). Boston, MA: Pearson.

Rodriguez, A. J. (2001). From gap gazing to promising cases: Moving toward equity in urban systemic reform. *Journal of Research in Science Teaching, 38*, 1115–1129.

Rogers, C. (1961). *On becoming a person.* Boston, MA: Houghton Mifflin.

Rogers, J., Franke, M. Yun, J.E., Ishimoto, M., Diera, C., Geller, R., Berryman, A., Brenes, T. (2017). *Teaching and learning in the age of Trump: Increasing stress and hostility in America's high schools.* Los Angeles, CA: UCLA's Institute for Democracy, Education, and Access.

Romans v. Crenshaw, 354 F. Supp. 868 (S.D. Tex. 1972).

Rosen, L. (2012, November 13). Driven to distraction: How to help wired students learn to focus. *eSchool News.* Retrieved August 8, 2014, from http://www.eschoolnews.com/2012/11/13/driven-to-distraction-how-to-help-wired-students-learn-to-focus/

Rosen, L. D. (2013). *iDisorder: Understanding our obsession with technology and overcoming its hold on us.* New York, NY: Palgrave Macmillan.

Rosenberg, T. (2013, October 9). Turning education upside down. *New York Times.* Retrieved July 5, 2014, from http://opinionator.blogs.nytimes.com/2013/10/09/turning-education-upside-down/?_php=true&_type=blogs&_r=1&

Rosenfield, M. (2014, April 7). NH teacher fired for refusing to "unfriend" students on Facebook. Boston, *WBZ.* Retrieved from http://boston.cbslocal.com/2014/04/07/nh-teacher-fired-for-refusing-to-unfriend-students-on-facebook/

Rosenshine, B. (1988). Explicit teaching. In D. Berliner & B. Rosenshine (Eds.), *Talks to teachers* (pp. 75–92). New York, NY: Random House.

Rosenshine, B., & Stevens, R. (1986). Teaching functions. In M. C. Wittrock (Ed.), *Handbook of research on teaching* (3rd ed.) (pp. 376–391). New York, NY: Macmillan.

Ross, M. (March 7, 2016). School-based peer mentoring builds relationships, creates caring communities. *Character.org.* Retrieved from http://info.character.org/blog/school-based-peer-mentoring-builds-relationships

Salovey, P., & Feldman-Barrett, L. (Eds.). (2002). *The wisdom of feelings: Psychological processes in emotional intelligence.* New York: Guilford Press.

Salovey, P., & Sluyter, D. J. (Eds.). (1997). *Emotional development and emotional intelligence: Educational implications.* New York, NY: Basic Books.

Salovey, P., Mayer, J. D., & Caruso, D. (2002). The positive psychology of emotional intelligence. In C. R. Snyder & S. J. Lopez (Eds.), *The handbook of positive psychology* (pp. 159–171). New York, NY: Oxford University Press.

Samsa, A.L. (May 13, 2015). Girls in stem fields. *Teaching Tolerance blog.* Retrieved from https://www.tolerance.org/magazine/girls-in-stem-fields

San Antonio Independent School District v. Rodriguez, 411 U.S. 1 (1973).

Sarah Brown Wessling teaches high school English in the Johnston Community School Dis-trict in Johnston, IOWA. She was the 2010 National Teacher of the Year. The preceding is adapted and excerpted from Sarah Brown Wessling's application for the 2010 National Teacher of the Year award at http://www.ccsso.org/Documents/NTOY/Applications/2010NTOYAPP.pdf.

Scering, G. E. S. (1997, January–February). Theme of a critical/feminist pedagogy: Teacher education for democracy. *Journal of Teacher Education, 48*(1), 62–68.

Schaill v. Tippecanoe School Corp., 864 F.2d 1309 (7th Cir. 1988).

School District of Abington Township v. Schempp, 374 U.S. 203 (1963).

School for Science and Math at Vanderbilt. (2018). *About the SSMV.* Retrieved from https://www.vanderbilt.edu/cso/ssmv/about.php.

Schneider, R. B., & Barone, D. (1997, Spring). Cross-age tutoring. *Childhood Education*, 136–143.

Schubert, W. (1986). *Curriculum: Perspective, paradigm, and possibility.* New York: Macmillan.

Schunk, D. (2012). *Learning theories: An educational perspective* (6th ed.). Upper Saddle River, NJ: Pearson.

Scopes, J. (1966). *Center of the storm.* New York, NY: Holt, Rinehart and Winston.

Scoville v. Board of Education of Joliet Township High School District 204, 425 F.2d 10 (7th Cir.), *cert. denied*, 400 U.S. 826 (1970).

Search Institute. (2010). *How many assets do young people have?* Minneapolis, MN: Author. Retrieved from http://www.search-institute.org/research/assets/asset-levels

Semega, J. L., Fontenot, K.R., & Kollar, M.A. (2017). U.S. Census Bureau, Current Population Reports, P60–259. *Income and Poverty in the United States: 2016.* Washington, DC: U.S. Government Printing Office.

Seth, G., Hart, C. M. D., Lindsay, C. C., & Papageorge, N. W. (2017). *The long-run impacts of same-race teachers.* Discussion Paper. Bonn, Germany: Institute of Labor Economics.

Shanley v. Northeast Independent School District, 462 F.2d 960 (5th Cir. 1972).

Sharan, Y., & Sharan, S. (1989/90, December/January). Group investigation expands cooperative learning. *Educational Leadership*, 17–21.

Shearer, M. (2011). *Application for National Teacher of the Year Award.* Retrieved June 24, 2014, from http://www.ccsso.org/Documents/2011/news/2011_NTOY_Press.pdf

Shechtman, N., DeBarger, A. H., Dornsife, C., Rosier, S., & Yarnall, L. (2013). *Promoting grit, tenacity, and perseverance: Critical factors for success in the 21st century.* U.S. Department of Education, Office of Educational Technology.

Shernoff, D. J., & Vandell, D. L. (2008). Youth engagement and quality of experience in afterschool programs. *Afterschool Matters, Occasional Papers Series*, (9), 1–11.

Showalter, D., Klein, R., Johnson, J., & Hartman, S. L. (June 2017). *Why rural matters 2015-2016: Understanding the changing landscape.* Rural School and Community Trust.

Shulman, L. (1987, August). *Teaching alone, learning together: Needed agendas for the new reform.* Paper presented at the Conference on Restructuring Schooling for Quality Education, San Antonio.

Sibinga, E. M. S., Perry-Parrish, C., Chung, S., Johnson, S. B., Smith, M., & Ellen, J. M. (2013). School-based mindfulness instruction for urban male youth: A small randomized controlled trial. *Preventative Medicine*, *57*, 799–801.

Silvas.T. (2018). Releasing the Mind of Childhood trauma through writing. Newark DE: International literacy Association. Reprinted with the Permission of International literacy Association

Simonetti v. School District of Philadelphia, 454 A.2d 1038 (Pa. Super. 1982).

Simpkins, S. (2003, Spring). Does youth participation in out-of-school time activities make a difference? *The Evaluation Exchange*, *IX*(1). Harvard Graduate School of Education, Harvard Family Research Project (HFRP).

Singh, S., Soamya, & Ramnath. (2016). Effects of mindfulness therapy in managing aggression and conduct problems of adolescents with ADHD symptoms. *Indian Journal of Health & Wellbeing*, *7*, 483–487.

Skinner, B. F. (1972). Utopia through the control of human behavior. In J. M. Rich (Ed.), *Readings in the philosophy of education*. Belmont, CA: Wadsworth.

Slavin, R. E. (2015). *Educational psychology: Theory and practice* (11th ed.). Upper Saddle River, NJ: Pearson.

Smith, D. D. (2007). *Introduction to special education: Making a difference* (6th ed.). Upper Saddle River, NJ: Pearson.

Smith, L. G., & Smith, J. K. (1994). *Lives in education: A narrative of people and ideas* (2nd ed.). New York, NY: St. Martin's Press.

Smith, T., & Ingersoll, R. (2004). What are the effects of induction and mentoring on beginning teacher turnover? *American Educational Research Journal*, *41*(3), 681–714.

Smith v. Board of School Commissioners of Mobile County, 655 F. Supp. 939 (S.D. Ala.), rev'd, 827 F.2d 684 (11th Cir. 1987).

Snipes, J., Soga, K., & Uro, G. (2007). *Improving teaching and learning for English language learners in urban schools.* Council of the Great City Schools, Research Brief. Washington, DC: Author.

Snyder, T. D., & Dillow, S. A. (2010). *Digest of education statistics 2009.* National Center for Education Statistics, Institute of Education Sciences, U.S. Department of Education. Washington, DC: U.S. Government Printing Office.

Snyder, T. D., & Dillow, S. A. (2014). *Digest of education statistics 2013.* National Center for Education Statistics, Institute of Education Sciences, U.S. Department of Education. Washington, DC: U.S. Government Printing Office.

Snyder, T. D., de Brey, C., and Dillow, S.A. (2016). *Digest of Education Statistics 2015* (NCES 2016-014). National Center for Education Statistics, Institute of Education Sciences, U.S. Department of Education. Washington, DC: U.S. Government Printing Office.

Sommers, C. H. (1996, June 12). Where the boys are. *Education Week on the Web.*

Sommers, C. H. (2000). *The war against boys: How misguided feminism is harming our young men.* New York: Simon & Schuster.

Sommers, C. H. (1994). *Who stole feminism? How women have betrayed women.* New York, NY: Simon & Schuster.

Spring, J. (2008). *The American school: From the Puritans to No Child Left Behind.* Boston, MA: McGraw-Hill.

Spring, J. (2013). *The American school, a global context: From the Puritans to the Obama administration* (9th ed.). Boston, MA: McGraw-Hill.

Spring, J. (2018). *American education* (18th ed.). New York: Routledge.

State Policy Report Card. (2014). *Objective: Establish state and mayoral control.* Retrieved June 28, 2014, from http://reportcard.studentsfirst.org/policy/spend_wisely_govern_well/promote_governance_structures_that_streamline_accountability/establish_state_and_mayoral_control/state_by_state

State v. Rivera, 497 N.W.2d 878 (Iowa 1993).

Station v. Travelers Insurance Co., 292 So. 2d 289 (La. Ct. App. 1974).

Statistic Brain Research Institute. (2017, September 9). Year-round school statistics. Retrieved from http://www.statisticbrain.com/year-round-school-statistics/

Stecher, B., & Hamilton, L. (2002, February 20). Test-based accountability: Making it work better. *Education Week on the Web.* Retrieved from http://www.edweek.org/ew/newstory.cfm?slug=23Stecher.h21

STEM to STEAM. (2017, October 15). *What is STEAM?* Retrieved from http://stemtosteam.org/

Sternberg, L., Dornbusch, S., & Brown, B. (1996). *Beyond the classroom: Why school reform has failed and what parents need to do.* New York, NY: Simon & Schuster.

Sternberg, R. J. (2002). Beyond g: The theory of successful intelligence. In R. J. Sternberg & E. L. Grigorenko (Eds.), *The general factor of intelligence: How general is it?* (pp. 447–479). Mahwah, NJ: Lawrence Erlbaum.

Stevens, J. E. (2017, May 2). Addiction doc says: It's not the drugs. It's the ACEs…adverse childhood experiences. *ACEs Too High News.* Retrieved from https://acestoohigh.com/2017/05/02/addiction-doc-says-stop-chasing-the-drug-focus-on-aces-people-can-recover/

Stewart, K. (2017, July 31). What the "government schools" critics really mean. *New York Times.* Retrieved from https://www.nytimes.com/2017/07/31/opinion/donald-trump-school-choice-criticism.html?mcubz=0

Stewart, R. (2016, January 15). Tackling the winter blues. *Scholastic top teaching blog.* Retrieved from https://www.scholastic.com/teachers/blog-posts/rhonda-stewart/tackling-winter-blues/

Stiggins, R. and Chappuis, J. (2012). *An introduction to student-involved assessment for learning* (6th ed.). Boston: Pearson.

Straub, C., Dieker, L., Hynes, M., & Hughes, C. (2015). *Using virtual rehearsal in TLE TeachLivE mixed reality classroom simulator to determine the effects of the performance of science teachers: A follow-up study (year 2).* 2015 TeachLivE National Research Project: Year 2 Findings. Orlando, FL: University of Central Florida.

Strike, K. A., & Soltis, J. F. (1985). *The ethics of teaching.* New York, NY: Teachers College Press.

Strike, K. A. (2007). *Ethical leadership in schools: Creating community in an environment of accountability.* Thousand Oaks, CA: Corwin Press.

Strong, M. (2006). *Does new teacher support affect student achievement?* Santa Cruz, CA: The New Teacher Center.

Student A et al v. Berkeley Unified School District et al, No. 3:2017cv02510 - Document 75 (N.D. Cal. 2017).

Sullivan, B. (2010, October 22). *Blogpost, teachers, students and Facebook, a toxic mix.* Retrieved from http://redtape.msnbc.com/2010/10/the-headlines-conjure-up-every-parents-nightmare-teachers-fired-for-flirting-on-facebook-with-students-the-new-york-post-r.html

Sullivan v. Houston Independent School District, 475 F.2d 1071 (5th Cir.), *cert. denied*, 414 U.S. 1032 (1969).

Sutcher, L., Darling-Hammond, L., & Carver-Thomas, D. (2016). *A coming crisis in teaching? Teacher supply, demand, and shortages in the U.S.* Palo Alto, CA: Learning Policy Institute.

Swanson v. Guthrie Independent School District No. 1, 135 F.3d 694 (10th Cir. 1998).

Tamim, R. M., Bernard, R. M., Borokhovski, E., Abrami, P. C., & Schmid, R. F. (2011). What forty years of research says about the impact of technology on learning: A second-order meta-analysis and validation study. *Review of Educational Research*, *81*(1), 4–28.

Tarasuik, T. J. (2010). Combining traditional and contemporary texts: Moving my English class to the computer lab. *Journal of Adolescent & Adult Literacy*, 57(7), 543–552.

TEP (The Equity Project Charter School). (2017). *The Equity Project Charter School.* New York, NY: Author. Retrieved from http://www.tepcharter.org/

Terman, L. M., & Oden, M. H. (1959). The gifted group in mid-life. In L. M. Terman (Ed.), *Genetic studies of genius* (Vol. 5). Stanford, CA: Stanford University Press.

Terrasi, S. & De Galarce, P. C. (2017). Trauma and learning in America's classrooms. *Phi Delta Kappan, 98*(6), 35–41.

Texas Education Agency. (2017, April 11). 2017–2018 optional flexible year program (OFYP). Retrieved from http://tea.texas.gov/Finance_and_Grants/State_Funding/Additional_Finance_Resources/Optional__Flexible_Year_Program/

The Education Trust. (2017, February 2). *Press Release: John B. King Jr. to Serve as President and CEO of The Ed- cation Trust.* Retrieved from https://edtrust.org/press_release/john-b-king-jr-serve-president-ceo-education-trust/

The New Teacher Project (2013). *Perspectives of irreplaceable teachers: What America's best teachers think about teaching.* Brooklyn, NY.

Thelen, H. A. (1960). *Education and the human quest.* New York, NY: Harper & Row.

Thompson, G. L. (2004). *Through ebony eyes: What teachers need to know but are afraid to ask about African American students.* San Francisco, CA: Jossey Bass.

Tileston, D. W. (2004). *What every teacher should know about student assessment.* Thousand Oaks, CA: Corwin Press.

Times Higher Education World University Rankings. (2018). *The world university rankings.* Retrieved from https://www.timeshighereducation.com/world-university-rankings

Tinker v. Des Moines Independent Community School District, 393 U.S. 503 (1969).

Torres, C. A. (1994). Paulo Freire as Secretary of Education in the municipality of Sao Paulo. *Comparative Education Review, 38*(2), 181–214.

Tremblay, R. (2018, February 16). We need to "reinvest ourselves in our relationships with students and colleagues." *Framingham Source.* Retrieved from http://framinghamsource.com/index.php/2018/02/16/framingham-superintendent-we-need-to-reinvest-ourselves-in-our-relationships-with-students-and-colleagues/

Twenge, J. M. (2017, September). Have smartphones destroyed a generation? *The Atlantic.* Retrieved from https://www.theatlantic.com/magazine/archive/2017/09/has-the-smartphone-destroyed-a-generation/534198/

Tyler, R. (1949). *Basic principles of curriculum and instruction.* Chicago: University of Chicago.

Ulich, R. (1950). *History of educational thought.* New York, NY: American Book Company.

Unified School District No. 241 v. Swanson, 717 P.2d 526 (Kan. Ct. App. 1986).

Union Alternative School. (2017, September 8). Alternative profile. Retrieved from http://www.unionps.org/alternative-profile/

United States District Court, Eastern District of Michigan, Southern Division; Civil Action No: 16-CV-13292, September 13, 2016.

United States Government Accountability Office. (2018). K-12 education: Discipline disparities for Black students, boys, and students with disabilities. Washington, DC: Author. Retrieved from https://www.gao.gov/assets/700/690828.pdf.

Urban, W. J., & Wagoner, J. L. (2009). *American education: A history* (4th ed.). New York, NY: Routledge.

Urban, W. J., & Wagoner, J. L. (2013). *American education: A history* (5th ed.). New York, NY: Routledge.

Uribe, V., & Harbeck, K. M. (1991). Addressing the needs of lesbian, gay and bisexual youth. *Journal of Homosexuality*, 22.

U.S. Bureau of Labor Statistics. (2015, November). *BLS reports: Labor force characteristics by race and ethnicity, 2014.* Washington, DC: Author.

U.S. Bureau of Labor Statistics. (2017). *Occupational Employment Statistics: Substitute Teachers.* Retrieved from https://www.bls.gov/oes/current/oes253098.htm

U.S. Census Bureau. (2010). *2010 population estimates.* Washington, DC: Author.

U.S. Census Bureau. (2013, August). *Language use in the United States: 2011—American community survey reports.* Washington, DC: Author. Retrieved from http://www.census.gov/prod/2013pubs/acs-22.pdf

U.S. Census Bureau. (2013, December). *Percent of people 25 years and over who have completed high school or college, by race, Hispanic origin and sex: Selected years 1940 to 2012.* Washington, DC: U.S. Government Printing Office. Retrieved from http://www.census.gov/hhes/socdemo/education/data/cps/historical/index.html

U.S. Census Bureau. (2014, January 16). *Profile America facts for features: Black (African-American) History Month: February 2014.* Retrieved from https://www.census.gov/newsroom/releases/archives/facts_for_features_special_editions/cb14-ff03.html

U.S. Census Bureau. (2015, March). *Projections of the size and composition of the U.S. population: 2014 to 2060.* Washington, DC: Author.

U.S. Census Bureau. (2016, November 2). American Indian and Alaska Native Heritage Month: November 2016. Retrieved from https://www.census.gov/content/dam/Census/newsroom/facts-for-features/2016/cb26-ff22_aian.pdf

U.S. Census Bureau. (2018). *American community survey 2016.* Washington, DC: Author. Retrieved from https://www.census.gov/programs-surveys/acs/

U.S. Copyright Office (December 1998). The Digital Millennium Copyright Act of 1998: U.S. Copyright Office Summary. Washington, DC: Author, p. 5.

U.S. Department of Education. (2009, January). *Title I implementation—Update on recent evaluation findings.* Washington, DC: Author.

U.S. Department of Education. (2009, May). *Evaluation of evidence-based practices in online learning: A meta-analysis and review of online learning studies.* Washington, DC: Author.

U.S. Department of Education. (2012, February 15). *Obama administration seeks to elevate teaching profession, Duncan to launch RESPECT Project: Teacher-led national conversation.* Retrieved from http://www.ed.gov/news/press-releases/obama-administration-seeks-elevate-teaching-profession-duncan-launch-respect-pro

U.S. Department of Education. (2009, May). *Evaluation of evidence-based practices in online learning: A meta-analysis and review of online learning studies.* Washington, DC: Author.

U.S. Department of Education. (2013, April). *Blueprint for Recognizing Educational Success, Professional Excellence and Collaborative Teaching (RESPECT).* Washington, DC: Author.

U.S. Department of Education. (2013, June 25). *Duncan pushes back on attacks on Common Core Standards.* Press release. Washington, DC: Author.

U.S. Department of Education. (2013, July 2). *Education Secretary's statement on Philadelphia school district.* Washington, DC: Author.

U.S. Department of Education. (2013, December 3). *My child's academic success: Values—Helping your child through early adolescence.* Retrieved from http://www2.ed.gov/parents/academic/help/adolescence/partx5.html

U.S. Department of Education. (2016). *21st Century Community Learning Centers (21st CCLC) overview of the 21st CCLC performance data: 2014–2015* (11th report). Washington, DC.

U.S. Department of Education. (2017, February 10). *U.S. Education Secretary DeVos issues letter to chief state school officers.* Retrieved from https://www.ed.gov/news/press-releases/us-education-secretary-devos-issues-letter-chief-state-school-officers

U.S. Department of Education. (2017, April 27). *Prepared Remarks by U.S. Secretary of Education Betsy DeVos to the Council of Chief State School Officers' National Teacher of the Year Gala.* Retrieved from https://www.ed.gov/news/speeches/

prepared-remarks-us-secretary-education-betsy-devos-council-chief-state-school-officers-national-teacher-year-gala

U.S. Department of Education. (2017, August 31). *About ED.* Retrieved from https://www2.ed.gov/about/landing.jhtml

U.S. Department of Education. (2017, October 7). *President's FY 2018 budget request for the U.S. Department of Education.* Retrieved from https://www2.ed.gov/about/overview/budget/budget18/index.html

U.S. Department of Education. (2018, January 25). *School ambassador fellowship: Purpose.* Retrieved from https://www2.ed.gov/programs/schoolfellowship/index.html

U.S. Department of Education Blog. (2018, February 27). *Homeroom: The Official Blog of the U.S. Department of Education.* Retrieved from https://blog.ed.gov/

U.S. Department of Education & Department of Justice. (2014, May 8). *Dear colleague.* Retrieved from https://www.justice.gov/sites/default/files/crt/legacy/2014/05/08/plylerletter.pdf

U.S. Department of Education, Office of Educational Technology. (2017). *Reimagining the role of technology in education: 2017 national education technology plan update.* Washington, DC: Author.

U.S. Department of Education. Office of Elementary and Secondary Education. (2015). http://www.ed.gov/programs/titleiparta/index.html*Improving basic programs operated by local educational agencies (Title I, Part A).*

U.S. Department of Education, Office of Special Education and Rehabilitative Services. (2013, August 20). *"Dear colleague" letter.* Retrieved from https://www2.ed.gov/policy/speced/guid/idea/memosdcltrs/bullyingdcl-8-20-13.pdf

U.S. Department of Health & Human Services, Administration for Children and Families, Administration on Children, Youth and Families, Children's Bureau. (2017). *Child Maltreatment 2015.* Retrieved from http://www.acf.hhs.gov/programs/cb/research-data-technology/statistics-research/child-maltreatment

U.S. Department of Homeland Security. (2016). *Yearbook of immigration statistics: 2015.* Washington, DC: U.S. Department of Homeland Security, Office of Immigration Statistics. Retrieved from https://www.dhs.gov/sites/default/files/publications/Yearbook_Immigration_Statistics_2015.pdf

U.S. Department of Labor. (2017). *Occupational outlook handbook 2017–18 edition. Teachers—preschool, kindergarten, elementary, middle, and secondary.* Washington, DC: Author.

U.S. English. (2018). *About U.S. English: History.* Retrieved from https://www.usenglish.org/history/

U.S. Equal Employment Opportunity Commission. (1964). *Title VII of the Civil Rights Act of 1964.* Retrieved from https://www.eeoc.gov/laws/statutes/titlevii.cfm

U.S. Equal Opportunity Employment Commission. (1964). *Title VII of the Civil Rights Act of 1964.* Retrieved from https://www.eeoc.gov/laws/statutes/titlevii.cfm

Utay, C., & Utay, J. (1997). Peer-assisted learning: The effects of cooperative learning and cross-age peer tutoring with word processing on writing skills of students with learning disabilities. *Journal of Computing in Childhood Education, 8,* 1043–1055.

Valli, L., & Buese, D. (2007, September). The changing roles of teachers in an era of high-stakes accountability. *American Educational Research Journal, 44*(3), 519–558.

Van Reusen, A. K., Shoho, A. R., & Barker, K. S. (2000). High school teacher attitudes toward inclusion. *High School Journal, 84*(2), 7–20.

Vandell, D. L., Reisner, E. R., & Pierce, K. M. (2007). *Outcomes linked to high-quality afterschool programs: Longitudinal findings from the study of promising afterschool programs.* Report to the Charles Stewart Mott Foundation, Flint, MI.

Vandell, D. L., Pierce, K. M., & Karsh, A. (2011). *Study of promising after-school programs: Follow-up report to participating school districts.* Irvine, CA: University of California–Irvine.

Vandell, D.L. (2013). Afterschool program quality and student outcomes: Reflections on positive key findings on learning and development from recent research. In T.K. Peterson (Ed.). *Expanding minds and opportunities: Leveraging the power of afterschool and summer learning for student success.* Washington, DC: Collaborative Communications Group.

Vaughn, S., Bos, C. S., & Schumm, J. S. (1997). *Teaching mainstreamed, diverse, and at-risk students in the general education classroom.* Boston, MA: Allyn & Bacon.

Vedder, R. K. (2003). *Can teachers own their own schools? New strategies for educational excellence.* Chicago: Paul & Co.

Vega, V. (2013, February 5). Technology Integration Research Review. Edutopia. Retrieved August 7, 2014, from http://www.edutopia.org/technology-integration-research-learning-outcomes

Viafora, D. P. Mathiesen & Unsworth, S. J. (2015). Teaching mindfulness to middle school students and homeless youth in school classrooms. *Journal of Child and Family Studies, 24,* 1179–1191.

Village Green Virtual Charter School. (2018). *About our school.* Retrieved from http://vgonline.org/we-are-public-charter-schools/about/

Virtual High School. (2018). *About us.* Retrieved from http://vhslearning.org/about-u

Virtual High School. (2018, June 18). *High school students invited to compete in new solar energy design challenge.* Retrieved from http://vhslearning.org/node/324

Virtual Solar Grid. (2018, June 18). Retrieved from http://energy.concord.org/energy3d/vsg/syw.html

Vossekuil, B., Fein, R., Reddy, M., Borum, R., & Modzeleski, W. (2002, May). *The final report and findings of the Safe School Initiative: Implications for the prevention of school attacks in the United States.* Washington, DC: U.S. Department of Education, Office of Elementary and Secondary Education, Safe and Drug-Free Schools Program and U.S. Secret Service, National Threat Assessment Center.

Vygotsky, L. S. (1978). *Mind in society: The development of higher mental process.* Cambridge, MA: Harvard University Press.

Vygotsky, L. S. (1986). *Thought and language.* Cambridge, MA: MIT Press.

Walberg, H. J., & Greenberg, R. C. (1997, May). Using the learning environment inventory. *Educational Leadership,* pp. 45–47.

Walker, K.L. (2011). Deficit thinking and the effective teacher. *Education and Urban Society, 43*(5), 576–597.

Waller, W. (1932). *The sociology of teaching.* New York: John Wiley.

Washington, Romaine, English Teacher, Los Osos High School, Alta Loma, California. Used with permission.

Waterhouse, L. (2006). Multiple intelligences, the Mozart effect, and emotional intelligence: A critical review. *Educational Psychologist, 41*(4), 207, 208.

Watson, J. B. (1925). *Behaviorism* (2nd ed.). New York, NY: People's Institute.

We Are Teachers. (2016, June 30). *Why I won't apologize (much) for teaching in a charter school.* Retrieved August 26, 2017, from https://www.weareteachers.com/why-i-wont-apologize-much-for-teaching-in-a-charter-school/

Webb, L. D., & Metha, A. (2017). *Foundations of American education* (8th ed.). Boston: Pearson.

Wechsler, D. (1958). *The measurement and appraisal of adult intelligence* (4th ed.). Baltimore: Williams and Wilkins.

Wei, X., Yu, J. W., Shattuck, P., McCracken, M., & Blackorby, J. (2013, July). Science, technology, engineering, and mathematics (STEM) participation among college students with an autism spectrum disorder. *Journal of Autism and Developmental Disorders, 43*(7), 1539–1546.

Weinbaum, article that appeared in Teaching Tolerance, "At Risk of Greatness," Spring 2007. Retrieved Febru-ary 20, 2011, from http://www.tolerance.org/magazine/number-31-spring-2007/risk-greatness. Reprinted with Permission.

Weingarten, R. (2014, Spring). Teaching and learning over testing. *American Educator,* 1.

Weingarten R. (2017, Summer). Understanding history to fight tyranny. *American Educator,* 1.

Weinstein, C. S., & Romano, M. *Elementary classroom management: Lessons from research and practice* (6th ed.). New York, NY: McGraw-Hill.

Wells, A. S. (2014, March). *Seeking past the "colorblind" myth of education policy: Addressing racial and ethnic inequality and supporting culturally diverse schools*. University of Colorado. Boulder, CO: National Education Policy Center.

West v. Board of Education of City of New York, 8 A.D.2d 291 (N.Y. App. 1959).

West Virginia Department of Education. (2017, September 26). *2017 innovation in education awarded.* Retrieved from https://wvde.state.wv.us/innovationzones/

Weston, S. P., & Sexton, R. F. (2009, December). Substantial and yet not sufficient: Kentucky's effort to build proficiency for each and every child. *Education, Equity, and the Law, 2*. Teachers College, Columbia University.

Westport Public Schools. (2017, September 20). *Mission statement.* Retrieved from https://www.westportps.org/district/about-us

White House. (2018, January 30). *President Donald J. Trump's State of the Union Address.* Retrieved February 3, 2018 from https://www.whitehouse.gov/briefings-statements/president-donald-j-trumps-state-union-address/

White House Press Release. (2009, March 10). *President Obama's speech at the United States Hispanic Chamber of Commerce.* Retrieved from https://obamawhitehouse.archives.gov/blog/2009/03/10/taking-education

White House Press Release. (2010, March 1). *President Obama announces steps to reduce dropout rate and prepare students for college and careers.* Retrieved from http://www.whitehouse.gov/the-press-office/president-obama-announces-steps-reduce-dropout-rate-and-prepare-students-college-an

White House Press Release. (2010, October 8). *Remarks by the president at the signing of the 21st Century Communications and Video Accessibility Act of 2010.* Retrieved from http://www.whitehouse.gov/the-press-office/2010/10/08/remarks-president-signing-21st-century-communications-and-video-accessib

White House Press Release. (2017, April 4). *Remarks by President Trump and Vice President Pence at CEO Town Hall on Unleashing American Business.* Retrieved from https://www.whitehouse.gov/briefings-statements/remarks-president-trump-vice-president-pence-ceo-town-hall-unleashing-american-business/

Willard, N. (2011). Educator's Guide to Cyberbullying, Cyberthreat and Sexting. Center for Safe and Responsible Use of the Internet. Retrieved February 9, 2011, from http://www.scriu.org/documents.documents.educatorsguide.pdf

Willard, N. (2010, August 2). *School response to cyberbullying and sexting: The legal challenges.* Eugene, OR: Center for Safe and Responsible Internet Use. Retrieved from http://www.cyberbully.org/documents/documents/cyberbullyingsextinglegal_000.pdf

Wilson, B. L., & Corbett, H. D. (2001). *Listening to urban kids: School reform and the teachers they want*. Albany, NY: State University of New York Press.

Wirt, F. M., & Kirst, M. W. (2009). *The political dynamics of American education* (4th ed.). Berkeley, CA: McCutchan.

Wolf, P., Gutmann, B., Puma, M., Kisida, B., Rizzo, L., Eissa, N., & Carr, M. (2010, June). *Evaluation of the DC Opportunity Scholarship Program: Final report executive summary* (NCEE 2010-4019). Washington, DC: National Center for Education Evaluation and Regional Assistance, Institute of Education Sciences, U.S. Department of Education.

Woolfolk, A. E. (2016). *Educational psychology* (13th ed.). Boston: Pearson.

Wolpert-Gawron, H. (2009, March 24). What I love about teaching. *Eutopia blog*., March 24, 2009. Retrieved from https://www.edutopia.org/teacher-lifelong-learner. Used with permission from Heather Wolpert-Gawron

Wright, R. J. (2008). *Educational assessment: Tests and measurements in the age of accountability*. Los Angeles, CA: Sage.

Yamamoto, K., Davis, Jr., O. L., Dylak, S., Whittaker, J., Marsh, C., & van der Westhuizen, P. C. (1996, Spring). Across six nations: Stressful events in the lives of children. *Child Psychiatry and Human Development*, pp. 139–150.

Yap v. Oceanside Union Free School District, 303 F. Supp 2d 284 (N.Y. 2004).

Young, C. (1999). *Ceasefire! Why women and men must join forces to achieve true equality*. New York, NY: The Free Press.

Young, M. F., Slota, S., Cutter, A. B., Jalette, G., Mullin, G., Lai, B., & Yukhymenko, M. (2012). Our princess is in another castle: A review of trends in serious gaming for education. *Review of Educational Research*, *82*(1), 61–89.

Zelman v. Simmons-Harris, 536 U.S. 639 (2002).

Zheng, B., Warschauer, M., Lin, C.-H., & Chang, C. (2016). Learning in one-to-one laptop environments: A meta-analysis and research synthesis. *Review of Educational Research*, *86*(4), 1052–1084.

Zirkel, P. A., & Karanxha, Z. (2009). *Student teaching and the law*. Lanham, MD: Rowman & Littlefield Education.

Zubrzycki, J. (2014, January 3). Rival strategies for running schools put Memphis in hot seat: A variety of approaches to running and improving the system challenge local control. *Education Week*. Retrieved from http://www.edweek.org/ew/articles/2014/01/09/16hotseat.h33.html

Zucker v. Panitz, 299 F. Supp. 102 (S.D.N.Y. 1969).

Zukowski, V. (1997, Fall). Teeter-totters and tandem bikes: A glimpse into the world of cross-age tutors. *Teaching and Change*, 71–91.

Name Index

Page numbers in *italics* refer to figures, illustrations, or tables.

A

AAP Council on Communications and Media, 437
Abrami, P.C., 438
Acton v. Vernonia School District, 243
Adams, Alex, 370
Addams, Jane, 155
Adesope, O. O., 286
Adler, Mortimer, 114–115, 140, 164
Africatown Center for Education and Innovation, 277
AFT (American Federation of Teachers), 9, 58
Afterschool Alliance, 93
Ahmed, E., 352
Ahmed-Ullah, N. S., 276
Akçayır, G., 439
Akçayır, M., 439
Alaska Native Cultural Charter School, 282
Albert, M., 312
Alexander, K., 241, 247, 250, 251
Alexander, M. D., 241, 247, 249, 250, 251
Alexander, Ramerra, 127–128
Alfonso v. Fernandez, 246
Allen, Megan, 91
Allix, N. M., 307
Allred, K. M., 370
Alolouf, Helene, 463
Alvin Independent School District v. Cooper, 246
Amanti, C., 105
American Association of University Women, 248, 272
American Federation of Teachers (AFT), 9, 58
American Immigration Council, 236
American Institutes of Research, 284
American Library Association, 182
Anctil, E., 358, 365
Anda, R. F., 79, *80*
Anderman, E. M., 306, 308
Anderman, L., 306, 308
Anderson, C., 50
Anderson, L., 352
Andrews, Roosevelt, 247
Ansari, Zakiyah, 182
Ansary, T., 377
Anthony, E., 11
Anyon, Jean, 69–70
Arabo, Melody, 177–178, 465
ArborBridge, 388
Aristotle, 140
Armitage, L., 33
Armstrong, P. A., 68
Arnett, N., 93
Ashman, J. J., 312
Asian Americans/Pacific Islanders in Philanthropy, 278
Association of Mindfulness in Education, 371
Aud, S., 37, 38
Avramidis, E., 323

B

Bagley, William C., 116
Bailey, T. M., 18, 20, *196*
Baker, O., 393
Bakken, Carrie, 211
Baldas, T., 250
Baldwin, 310
Baldwin, Anna E., 60
Ballantine, J. H., 181
Banks, J. A., 67, 265, 276, 279, 281, 282, 288, 291, 343
Barker, K. S., 323
Barmer, A., *18*, *197*
Barone, D., 361
Barylski, Jessica, 401
Battles v. Anne Arundel County Board of Education, 255
Baugh, J., 264
Baughan, C., 351
Bayliss, P., 323
Beecher, Catherine, 151
Bell, Terrel H., 195
Benezet, Anthony, 149
Bennett, C. I., 276, 277, 278, 279, 280, 281, 284
Bennett, K., 372
Bennett, William, 164
Bergmann, Jonathan, 425
Berliner, David, 388–391, 424
Bernard, R. M., 438
Bernstein, B. B., 69
Berry, B., 8, 466
Berstein, H., 370
Bertocci, P. A., 108
Bethune, Mary McLeod, 159
Betty Shabazz International Charter School, 276
Binet, Alfred, 306
Bissonette, A. M., 249, 250
Bitterman, A., *29*
Bjork, R., 308
Black, Hugo L., 239, 251
Black, P., 402
Blackman, Sandra, 463
Blackwell, L. S., 371
Blanc, S., 190
Bleeker, M., 461
Blitzer, J., 237
Bloom, B. S., 357
Bloomberg, Michael, 185
Blow, Susan, 153
Board of Education, Sacramento City Unified School District v. Holland, 321
Bobbitt, Franklin, 373
Borich, G. D., 332, 335, 348, 399
Borokhovski, E., 438
Borum, R., 83
Bos, C. S., 323
Bowden, Shanna, 92
Boyer, Ernest, 94, 164
Brameld, Theodore, 122–123
Brewer, Rebecca, 473
Brimley, V. R., 33
Brody, N., 307
Bronson, 310
Brookhart, S. M., 385, 407
Brophy, J., 308
Broudy, Harry, 111
Broughman, S. P., 34, 35
Brown, B., 360
Brown, E., 206
Brown v. Board of Education of Topeka, 161, 253, 275
Brown v. Hot, Sexy and Safer Productions, Inc., 251
Bruch, N., *54*
Bruecker, E., 206
Brunelle v. Lynn Public Schools, 254
Bucky, P. A., 6
Buese, D., 38
Buffins, Mansur, 124
Bullock Mann, F., *18*, *197*
Burch v. Barker, 238
Burden, R., 323
Bureau of Labor Statistics, 18, 36, *117*
Burney, D., 47
Bursuck, W. D., 326, 476
Burton v. Cascade School District Union High School No. 5, 221
Bush, George W., 13, 194
Bush, H. W., 194
Bush v. Holmes, 205
Bushaw, W. J., 424
Butterfield, Yvonne, 33
Button, H. W., 147, 148, 149, 150, 153

C

Cadigan, Cathleen, 106
Calegari, N., 11
Calhoun, E., 356, 357, 360, 361, 386
Campbell, D. M., 458
Canter, Lee, 352
Carlson, K., 110
Carnegie Council on Adolescent Development, 164
Carrion, S., 420, 433
Carroll, J., 357

Carter, Jimmy, 195
Caruso, D., 308
Carver-Thomas, D., 459, 460
Center for Education Policy Research, *449*
Center for Education Reform, 205
Center for Research on Education Outcomes, 209
Center on Education Policy, *4*, *6*, 14
Centers for Disease Control and Prevention, 79, 86
Chadwick, D. L., *80*
Chang, C., 439
Chang, Lin, 323
Chapman, C. B., 282
Chappuis, J., 397, 401, 402, 406, 407, 409
Chen, C., 314
Chen, Xianglei, 272
Cheung, A., 438, 439
Chiaramonte, P., 235
Chicago Public Schools, 66
Chiles, N., 264
Chinn, P. C., 263, 265, 284, 287
Christensen, L., 366
Christman, J., 190
Chung, S., 373
Clark, Edward William, Jr., 463
Clifford, Joe, 322
Clinton, Bill, 194
Coalition for Community Schools, 90
Coalition of Essential Schools, 396
Cochran, G., 93
Cohen, D., 237
Cohen, G. I., 370
Cohen, S., 145
Cohn, D., *262*
Coleman, J. S., 268
College Board, 106
Collier-Thomas, B., 159
Collins, B. A., 335
Colucci, K., 336, 366
Commager, H. S., 149
Conaboy, C., 303
Concerned Black Men, 95
Conn, C., 431
Connell, M., 307
Cook, L., 476
Cook-Harvey, C.M., 67
Corbett, H. D., 40, 73, 366
Cossentino, J., 157
Costello, E., 373
Counts, George, 123
Craig, S. E., 87
Craver, S. M., 101, 120
Crawford, J., 284
Crawford, Steven, 106
Credé, M., 370
CREDO, 421
Cremin, Lawrence, 156
Cronbach, Lee, 47
Cuban, Larry, 437
Curtis, K. E., 225
Curtis v. School Committee of Falmouth, 247, 252

D

Danilova, M., 170
Daring, Desiree, 47
Darling-Hammond, L., 67, 459, 460
Davidson, C., 421, 422
Davis, M., 189
Davis v. Meek, 246
Dawson, K., 419
Dawson, M. R., 453
Day, Ramona, 129
de Brey, C., *18*, 25, 33, *166*, *197*
De Galarce, P. C., 79
Deal, T. E., 72, 73
Dearing, E., 335
DeCesare, D., 460
Dell'Olio, J. M., 358
Denton, C., 318
Deskbook Encyclopedia of American School Law, 249
DeVos, Betsy, 17, 35, 170, 194
Dewey, John, 6, 58, 102, 118, 142, 155–156
Dhillon, S., 474
Diaz, E. M., 248
Diaz, Jennifer Michele, 6–7
Dichosa, Julius, 216–217
Dieker, L. A., 452, *453*
Dillow, S. A., 25, 33, 152, 153, 179
Disability Rights Education & Defense Fund, 254
Doe v. Renfrow, 242
Dolfin, S., 461
Donk, T., 358
Doorlag, D. H., 323
Dorjee, D., 372
Dornbusch, S., 360
Drew, C. J., *318*, 319, 322
Dubuclet v. Home Insurance Company, 220
Duckworth, A. L., 370
Dunklee, D. R., 226, 248
Dunn, J. M., 215
Durkheim, Emile, 64
Durlak, J. A., 368
Dweck, C., 370
Dweck, C. S., 371

E

Eamon, M. K., 267
EarthEcho International, 123
Eckert, Audrey, 401
Edina Schools, 89
Education Commission of the States, 192, 204, 205, 208, 236
Education Deans for Justice and Equity, 55
Education Trust, 4
Education Week, 442
Education World, 459
Edwards v. Aguillard, 224
Ee, J., 275
Egan, M. W., *318*, 319, 322
Eggen, P., 308, 349, *359*, 398
Eidam, Robyn, 401
Einstein, Albert, 6, 386
Eisner, E., 40
Eisner, E. W., 47
Eisner, Elliot, 364–365, 366
Elder, Linda L., *112*
Ellen, J. M., 373
Emdin, C., 264
Emmer, E. T., 348, 351, 355
Engel v. Vitale, 251
English, F. W., 394
Equity Project. *See* TEP (The Equity Project Charter School)
Ericsson, K., 370
Erikson, Erik, 297–298, 303
Essex, Nathan L., *228*, *241*
Etzioni, Amitai, 299
Everett, Arthur, 60
Evergreen Education Group, 421
Evers, B., 382
Evers, C. W., 463
Evertson, 351
Evertson, C. M., 348, 355

F

Fagen v. Summers, 228
FairTest, 187, 393
Falk, G., 366
Falvo v. Owasso Independent School District, 245
Farbman, D., 94
Farrington, Camille A., 371
Fein, R., 83
Feistritzer, C. E., 25
Feldman-Barrett, L., 308
Felitti, V. J., 79, *80*
Fenty, Adrian, 185
Ferguson, C., 274
Ferrari, T. M., 93
Fetler, M., 394
Firestone, D., 35
Fleischer, H., 438
Fletcher, J., 318
Flores v. Morgan Hill Unified School District, 248
Florida Department of Education, 392
Fogleman, J., 403
Fong, T. P., 279
Fontenot, K. R., 265, *266*
Foote, Carolyn, 471
Forster, G., 382
Fox, M., 38
Fox, M. A., 51
Francis, D., 318
Franklin, Benjamin, 147
Franklin, J. H., 153
Franklin v. Gwinnett County Public Schools, 248
Freire, Paulo, 104, 124–125
Friedman, Milton, 204
Friend, M., 317, 319, 321, 322, 326, 476
Froebel, Friedrich, 152–153

Fullan, M., 462, 472
Future City, 399

G

Gagné, R. M., 357
Gallimore, R., 47
Gallup, 274
Gandhi, Mahatma, 51
Garbarino, James, 74
Garcia, P., 34
Garcia, X., 473
Gardner, H., 307
Garfield, R. R., 33
Gargiulo, R. M., 322
Garringer, M., 88–89
Gary B. v. Snyder, 253–254
Gates, Algernon, 122
Gaylord v. Tacoma School District No. 10, 221
GE Foundation, 207
Gebrekristos, S., *18*, *197*
Gebser v. Lago Vista Independent School District, 248
Geier, R., 403
George, Stacy, 473
George Lucas Educational Foundation, 15
Gibson, Cynthia, 75–76
Gill, B., 190
Gipp, G., 281
Glander, M., 92
Glass, Gene, 388–391, 424
Glasser, William, 347, 355
Glazerman, S. A., *54*, 461
Glickman, C., 460, 461, 469
Goggin, Catherine, 155
Goldhaber, D., 11
Goldring, R., *29*
Gollnick, D. M., 263, 265, 284, 287
Gonen, Y., 235
Gonzalez, N., 105
Gonzalez, Octavio, 323
Good, T. E., 332, 341, 345, 346, 348, 457
Goodyear, Marcus, 270–271
Gordon S. P., 460, 461, 469
Gore, Leslie U., 400
Gornik, R., 463
Goss v. Lopez, 240
Gouck, E. C., 322
Government Accountability Office, 276
Graham, P. A., 157
Grant, P. G., 449
Graves, Laurie, 260
Gray, L., *29*, 51, 461
Gray, Paul, 103
Greenberg, R. C., 338, *339*
Greene, J. P., 382
Greene, Maxine, 120
Grenda, P., 463, 465
Grider, M., 461
Grimes, Tonia, 313
Gross, M. U. M., 316
Gubbins, Elizabeth, 146
Gulosino, C., 208, 210
Gurian, M., 272
Gutierrez, R., 394
GW Community School, 211

H

Haar, C. K., 25
Hackmann, D. G., 463, 465
Hakuta, K., 284
Haley, Margaret, 155
Hallahan, D. P., 315, 319, 322, 325
Halvorsen, A.-L., 403
Hamilton, L., 384
Hammack, F. M., 181
Hansen, D. T., 102
Harbeck, K. M., 274
Hardman, M. L., *318*, 319, 322
Hargreaves, A., 462, 472
Harms, P. D., 370
Harpin, S. B., 372
Harris, C. J., 403
Harris, E., 93
Harris, Elmer, 464
Harris Interactive, Inc., 466
Harris Poll, 3, *56*
Harrison, C., 402
Harry A. v. Duncan, 248
Hart, C., 41
Hartigan, John, 265
Hartman, S. L., 32, 33
Haselton, B., 189
Hass, G., 358, 365
Hawking, Stephen W., 309
Hawkins, B., 211
Hazelwood School District v. Kuhlmeier, 238
Heath, S. B., 69
Hedges, Larry, 272
Hennick, C., 47
Henriques, M. E., 361
Henry, E., 45
Herbart, Johann Friedrich, 142
Herbert, Merry, 441
Hernandez, Martha, 123–124
Herrell, A. L., 286
Hess, F., 180, 181
Hew, K. F., 425
Hicks, B., 323
Hiebert, J., 47
Hildreth, J. A. D., 50
Hinduja, S., 83, *85*
Hines, Lynn, 100
Hinz, S., *18*, *197*
Hirsch, E.D., 116
Hirschfelder, Arlene, 280
Hohlfeld, T. N., 419
Holmes, M., 151
Holt v. Sheldon, 246
Holt-Reynolds, D., 46
Holubec, E. J., 334
hooks, bell, 125–126
Hopkins, G., *5*
Horne v. Flores, 284
Hortonville Joint School District No. 1 v. Hortonville Education Association, 223
Howard, V. F., 327
Howland, L., 50
Hoy, A. W., 54, 466
Hoy, W. K., 54, 466
Hucaro, Alyssa, 112
Hudson, Carla, 21
Hufstedler, Shirley, 195
Hughes, C., *453*
Hughes, J. E., 420, *421*
Human Rights Campaign, 219
Hunzicker, J., 463
Hussar, B., *18*, *197*
Hussar, W. J., 18, 20, *166*, *196*
Hutchins, Robert Maynard, 114–115
Hyde Schools, 301
Hynes, M., *453*
Hyslop, A., 393

I

I Am an Educator, 367
IBM MentorPlace, 96
iDisorder (Rosen), 436
Igoa, C., 280
Ikoma, S., 51
Imber, M., 227, 251
Ingersoll, R., *36*, 461
Ingraham, James, 247
Ingraham v. Wright, 247
Innes, R. G., 189
Institute for Educational Leadership, 89–90
Isenberg, E, 461
Ito, M., 419, 420

J

Jackson, D. M., *350*
Jackson, Philip, 6, 40
Jacobus, M., 461
James, Amy, 397
James, William, 372
*J.C. v. Beverly Hills Unified School Distric*t, 250
Jefferson, Thomas, 148
Jeglin v. San Jacinto Unified School District, 239
Jencks, C., 268
Job Experience and Training Program, 93
Johanningmeier, 149
Johnson, A., 461
Johnson, D. W., 334, 335, 352, 353
Johnson, F. P., 334, 335, 352, 353
Johnson, J., 32, 33
Johnson, L. D., 33
Johnson, Lyndon, 90, 162
Johnson, R. T., 334
Johnson, S. B., 373
Jordan, M. L., 286
Joyce, B., 356, 357, 360, 361, 386, 473

K

Kaiser Permanente, 79
Kamenetz, A., 90
Kann, L., 86
Karanxha, Z., 225
Karr v. Schmidt, 239
Karsh, A., 368
Kash, W., 440
Katsiyannis, A., 351
Katyal, K. R., 463
Kauchak, D., 308, 349, *359*, 398
Kauffman, G., 367
Kauffman, J. M., 315, 319, 322, 325
Kaye, E. A., 24
Kellner, D., 124
Kelly, D. R., 370
Kelly, M., 281
Kemp, J., 240, *350*
Kennedy, M., 47
Kennedy Middle School, 301
KewalRamani, A., 38
Kim, A. K., 372
King, John, 4
King, M., 158
Kirby, T., 370
Kirkpatrick, H., 437
Kirst, M. W., 182
Kitzmiller v. Dover Area School District, 252
Klein, R., 32, 33
Kleinfeld, Judith, 272
Knight, David, 121
Kohlberg, Lawrence, 298–299
Koliska, M., 414
Kollar, M. A., 265, *266*
Kosciw, J. G., 248
Kostelnik, M.J., 326
Kounin, Jacob, 348
Kozol, Jonathan, 70–71, 202, 384
Krashen, S., 284
Kraus, K., 11
Kristapovich, P., 37
Krizek v. Cicero-Stickney Township High School District No. 201, 224
Krogh, Suzanne, 375
Kulik, J. A., 316

L

Lam, L., 67
LaMorte, M. W., 222, 223, 228, 229, 239, 241, 243, 246, 247, 251, 254
Lancaster, Joseph, 142
Lang, K., 393
Lange, C. M., 35
Larry P. v. Riles, 306
Larson, R., 368
Laurence, D., 57
Lavigne, A. L., 332, 341, 345, 346, 348, 457
Lavin, T., 286
Lawler, M., 373
Layton, L., 206
Leahy, R., 113, 119, 120, *134*
Learning forward, *472*
Learning in Deed, 89
Lee, C., 402
Lee, Valerie, 272
Lee County School District, 234
Lehman, Adrienne, 2
Leinhardt, G., 47
Lemon v. Kurtzman, 251
Lepper, C., 327
Lesley University Center for Special Education, *88*
Lewis, C., 245
Lewis, R. B., 323
Li, Q., 438
Li, W., 368
Liang, Qiu, 280
Lightfoot, S. L, 143
Lignugaris/Kraft, B., 453
Lilja, Linda, 463
Lin, C. -H., 439
Lindjord, D., 394
Lindsay, C. C., 41
Lindsay, D., 242
Lipnevich, A. A., 307
Lipsman v. New York City Board of Education, 240
Lipton, M., 273, 352
Littky, D., 39
Little, P. D. M., 93
Lo, C. K., 425
Lomawaima, K. T., 281
Lopez, S. J., 424
Lortie, Dan, 143
Losinski, M., 351
Lovett, S., 463
Lynch, M., 452

M

Ma, X, 438
MacKinnon, Catharine, 126
MacLeod, J., 69
MacQuinn, Sandra, 464
MacRae, P., 88–89
Magnet Schools of America, 35
Mailloux v. Kiley, 225
Mann, Horace, 150–151, 387
Mann, Tamara, 115
Marcus v. Rowley, 231
Markus, D., 474
Marshall, B., 402
Marzano, R. J., 385
Maslow, A., 127, 301–302
Massachusetts Department of Elementary & Secondary Education, 93
Mastropieri, M. A., 326
Mathiesen, S. G., 373
Matthews, L. E., 394
Matthews, M. D., 370
Maul, A., 209
Mayer, F., 142
Mayer, J. D., 308
McAuliffe, Christa, 464
McCall, Ashley, 101
McCarthy, Bridgit, 116
McClelland, A., 209, 460
McCollum, Christi, 448
McComb, Sean, 60
McCourt, Frank, 12
McDaniel, M., 308
McFarland, J., *18*, 66, *166*, *197*, 260, 263, 282, 368
McField, G., 284
McGuffey, William Holmes, 151
McGuire, D. J., 334
McHugh, Kourtni, 2
McLeskey, J., 322
McQuiggan, M., 254, *470*
Meek, Claudia, 345
Meeks, O., 180, 181
Megra, M., 254, *470*
Mercer, C., 67
Merrill, L., *36*
Mertler, Craig A., *408*
Metha, A., 157
Metropolitan Federation of Alternative Schools (MFAS), 96
Meyers, C., 474
Meyers, Melissa, 416
MFAS (Metropolitan Federation of Alternative Schools), 96
Miami-Dade County Public Schools, 35
Miech, R. A., 81
Migano, 345
Miron, G., 208, 210, 421, 422
Missouri v. Jenkins, 276
Modzeleski, W., 83
Mohammed ex rel. Mohammed v. School District of Philadelphia, 248
Molefe, A., 474
Moll, L., 105
Montagu, Ashley, 265
Montessori, Maria, 157
Mora, Sergio, 43
Moran v. School District No. 7, 246
Morehouse, Pamela, 375
Morrill, Justin S., 152
Morris, J. E., 225
Morris, V. C., 108
Morrison, B., 352
Morrison v. State Board of Education, 219
Moyers, B. D., 57
Mozert v. Hawkins County Board of Education, 224
Murnane, R. J., 393
Murphy, S., 234
Murray v. Pittsburgh Board of Public Education, 223
Musu-Gillette, L., 82, *166*, 267

N

National Alliance of Public Charter Schools, 35, 208
National Association of School Boards, 204
National Association of School Psychologists, 351

National Board for Professional Teaching Standards, 449
National Board for Professional Teaching Standards (NBPTS), 24, 46, 55, 463
National Catholic Education Association, 34
National Center for Education Statistics, 18, 19, 25, *29*, *36*, *75*, 162, 178, *179*, 197, *198*, 260, 268, 309, 315, 318, 324
National Coalition for the Homeless, 78
National Commission on Excellence in Education, 164
National Council of State Legislatures, 84, 85
National Education Association (NEA), 9, *11*, 12, 29, 55, 57, 253
National Education Policy Center, 244
National School Boards Association, 179
National School Safety Center, *84*
Native American Community Academy, 282
Navarro, M., 265
NBC News, 53
NBPTS (National Board for Professional Teaching Standards), 24, 46, 55, 463
NEA (National Education Association), 9, *11*, 12, 29, 55, 57, 253
Neau, Elias, 145
Neff, C., 105
Nelson, J. L., 110
New Jersey v. Massa, 254
New Jersey v. T.L.O., 242
New Teacher Center, 460
New Teacher Project, 5
New York City Department of Education, 179
Newmann, F. M., 345
NICHE, 9
Nieto, S., 284
Nitko, A. J., 385, 407
Noddings, Nel, 338
Nowell, Amy, 272
Nucaro, A., 112
Null v. Board of Education, 255
Nussbaum, M., 111

O

Oakes, J., 273, 352
Oaks, M. M., 465
Obama, Barack, 11, 90, 93, 194, 265, 309
Oberti v. Board of Education of the Borough of Clementon School District, 321
O'Connell, P. M., 372
O'Connor, E. E., 335
Oden, M. H., 310
Office of Elementary and Secondary Education, 90
Office of Planning, Evaluation and Policy Development, *20*
Office of Special Education and Rehabilitative Services, 250
Ohio Department of Education, *451*
Ohman v. Board of Education, 228
Onaga, E., 326
O'Rear, I., 461
Orfield, G., 275
Organization for Economic Cooperation and Development, 390
Ormrod, J. E., 306, 308, 334
Oudekerk, B. A., 82
Owasso Independent School District v. Falvo, 245
Ozmon, H. W., 101, 120

P

Pai, Y., 108
Paige, Rod, 166
Palonsky, S. B., 110
Papageorge, N. W., 41
Papay, J. P., 393
Parkay, F. W., 78–79, 105, 358, 365, 449, 462, 465
Parker, L., 55
Parrish, Donna W., 463
PASE v. Hannon, 306
Pashler, H., 308
Passel, J. S., *262*
Patchin, J. W., 83, *85*
Patchogue- Medford Congress of Teachers v. Board of Education of Patchogue-Medford Union Free School District, 243
Patterson, Richard, 259
Paul, J. L., 336, 366
Paul, Richard, *112*
Pavlov, Ivan, 128
PBS NewsHour, 354
Peabody, Elizabeth Palmer, 153
Peck, D. R., 461
Perry-Parrish, C., 373
Pestalozzi, Johann Heinrich, 142
Peter Doe v. San Francisco Unified School District, 253
Peterson, C., 370
Peterson, K. D., 72, 73
Pew Charitable Trust, 190
Pew Research Center, *262*, 268, *269*, 277, 279
Phi Delta Kappa, 9, 16–17, 86, *87*, 106, 197, 204, *369*
Philips, V., 382
Phillips, M., 268
Piaget, Jean, 295–297
Picarella v. Terrizzi, 229
Picucci, A. C., 460
Pierce, K. M., 368
Pierce, Sarah, 147
Pierre, C. E., 145
Placek, C., 93
Plato, 51, 140
Plyler v. Doe, 236
Poe v. Hamilton, 229
Port, P. D., 327
Portner, J., 240
Posner, George J., 457
Poway Unified School District, 434
Power, E. J., 128
Power, F. C., 299
Power, Megan, 465
Price-Dennis, D., 420, 433
ProEnglish, 277
Protik, B., *54*
Provenzano, Nicholas, 44
Provenzo, E. F., 147, 148, 149, 150, 153
Pujol-Burns, Tere, 35
Pullen, P. D., 315, 319, 322
Purkey, J., 237

Q

QS World University Rankings, 391
QuestBridge, 316
Quine, Doug, 467

R

Rafalow, M. H., 419
Rahman, T., 51
Ramnath, 373
Randall, V. R., 263
Randel, B., 460
Rathbun, A., *18*, *37*, *197*
Ray v. School District of DeSoto County, 246
Reagan, Ronald, 194, 195
Recovery School District, 185
Reddy, M., 83
Reich, J., 419, 420
Renner, Susie, 245–246
Richard, A., 240
Richard, K. J., 449
Rickover, H. G., 160
Rideout, V., 14, 414
Rippa, S. A., 145, 146, 147, 148, 150, 155, 156
Ripple, R. E., 297
Ritzhaupt, A. D., 419
Rivas, Jose, 473
Robers, S., 240
Roberts, J., 414
Roberts, R. D., 307
Roberts v. City of Boston, 152
Robinson, M. W., 248, 315
Roblyer, M. D., 420, *421*
Roc, M., 67
Rockcastle, V. E., 297
Rodriguez, A. J., 394
Rogers, Carl, 127
Rogers, J., 261, 305
Rohde, B., 326
Rohrer, D., 308
Romans v. Crenshaw, 246
Romer, Roy, 190
Roosevelt, Franklin D., 159, 193

Roosevelt, Theodore, 118
Rosen, Larry, 436–437
Rosenberg, T., 425
Rosenfield, M., 235
Rosenshine, B., 357
Ross, M., 89
Ross-Gordon, J., 460, 461, 469
Rossi, A., 372
Rousseau, Jean-Jacques, 142
Rui, P., 312
Russell, Mary, 386
Ryan, J., 351

S

Sacks, Ariel, 466
Salazar, Frank, 371
Salovey, P., 308
Sams, Aaron, 425
Samsa, Ashley Lauren, 125
San Antonio Independent School District v. Rodriguez, 203, 236
Sanchez, Lisa, 130
Sanford, W. L., 463
Sartre, Jean-Paul, 120
Scering, G. E. S., 125
Schaill v. Tippecanoe School Corp., 243
Schmid, R. F., 438
Schneider, R. B., 361
School District of Abington Township v. Schempp, 251
Schubert, W., 142
Schumm, J. S., 323
Schurz, Margarethe, 153
Scopes, John, 223
Scoville v. Board of Education of Joliet Township High School District, 238
Scruggs, T. E., 326
Search Institute, 304
Seftor, N., *54*
Semega, J. L., 265, *266*
Serrano v. Priest, 203
Seth, G., 41
Sexton, R. F., 189
Shank, C., 421, 422
Shanker Institute, 382
Shanley v. Northeast Independent School District, 238
Shapiro, J. P., 55
Sharan, S., 361
Sharan, Y., 361
Shearer, Michelle, 323, 324, 386–387
Shechtman, N., 370
Shernoff, D. J., 368
Sherratt, E., 11
Shindler, J., 465
Shoho, A. R., 323
Shoop, R. J., 226, 248
Shotley, Kristine, 158
Showalter, D., 32, 33
Shulman, Lee, 163
Sibinga, E. M. S., 373
Silvas, Tiana, 81
Simon, Theodore, 306
Simonetti v. School District of Philadelphia, 228
Simpkins, S., 93
Singh, S., 373
Skinner, B. F., 128–129
Slavin, R. E., 247, 308, 310, 438, 439
Sletten, S. J., 35
Sluyter, D. J., 308
Smerdon, Becky A., 272
Smith, D. D., 309
Smith, J. K., 124–125
Smith, L. G., 124–125
Smith, M., 373
Smith, T., 461
Smith v. Board of School Commissioners of Mobile County, 224
Snipes, J., 284
Snyder, T., *18*, *197*
Snyder, T. D., 25, 33, 152, 153, 179
Soamya, 373
Socrates, 140
Soga, K., 284
Soltis, J. F., 111
Sommers, C. H., 272
Sonnenberg, W., *166*
Spring, J., 66, 110, 147, 155, 156, 181
State Policy Report Card, 394
State v. Rivera, 255
Station v. Travelers Insurance Co., 227
Stecher, B., 384
Stemm-Calderon, Andre, 338
Stephens, Ronald D., *84*
Sternberg, L., 360
Sternberg, R. J., 307
Stevens, J. E., 303
Stevens, K., 272
Stevens, R., 357
Stewart, K., 169
Stewart, Rhonda, 45
Stiggins, R. J., 397, 401, 402, 406, 407
Stigler, J. W., 47
Stilman, J., 352
Stotsky, S., 382
Straub, C., 452
Strike, K. A., 111
Strike, Kenneth A., 218
Strong, M., 461
Stuber, J., 181
Student A et al v. Berkeley Unified School District et al., 254
Sullivan, B., 234, 235, 239
Sullivan v. Houston Independent School District, 238
Sutcher, L., 459, 460
Swaim, N. L., 34, 35
Swanson, L., 372
Swanson v. Guthrie Independent School District No. 1, 255

T

Tagore, Rabindranath, 40
Taie, S., 461
Tamim, R. M., 438
Tarasuik, Tracy J., 47–48
Taylor, Frederick W., 152
Teh, J., *54*
TEP (The Equity Project Charter School), 9, 11
Terman, L. M., 306, 310
Terrasi, S., 79
Texas Education Agency, 93
Thelen, H. A., 360
Thompson, Alison, 100
Thompson, Gail, 264
Thompson, T., 286
Tileston, D. W., 401
Times Higher Education World University Rankings, 391
Tinker v. Des Moines Independent Community School District, 237
Toavs, Karen, 109
Torres, C. A., 125
Tremblay, R., 467
Trogdon, Jim, 123
Truman, J., 240
Trump, Donald, 169–170, 194–195, 236–237, 265, 378, 383
Trzesniewski, K. H., 371
Tsukayama, E., 370
Twenge, J. M., 437
Tyler, Ralph, 374
Tynan, M. C., 370

U

Ulich, R., 142
Ungerleider, C., 286
Unified School District No. 241 v. Swanson, 221
Union Alternative School, 92
United States Government Accountability Office, 351
Unsworth, S. J., 373
Urban, W. J., 145, 148, 149, 151, 153
Uribe, V., 274
Uro, G., 284
U.S. Bureau of Labor Statistics, 275, 458
U.S. Census Bureau, 37, 76, *199*, 260, 261, 275, 277, 278, 280
U.S. Department of Education, 8, *29*, 52–53, 55, 59, 64, 90, 91, 96, 190, 194, 236, 250, *273*, 383, 419, 425, 437, 443, 464
U.S. Department of Homeland Security, 261
U.S. Department of Justice, 236
U.S. Department of Labor, 18, 29, *34*, 38
U.S. English, 376
Utay, C., 361
Utay, J., 361

V

Valli, L., 38
Valquez, Maria, 16
van Geel, T., 251
Van Reusen, A. K., 323
Vandell, D. L., 368

Vaughn, S., 323
Vedder, Richard K., 210–211
Vega, V., 436
Verstegen, D. A., 33
Viafora, D. P., 373
Virtual High School, 423
Virtual Solar Grid, 423
Vossekuil, B., 83
Vydra, Joan, 73
Vygotsky, L. S., 358

W

Wagoner, J. L., 145, 148, 149, 151, 153
Walberg, H. J., 338, *339*
Walker, K. L., 105
Waller, Willard, 154–155
Walton, Electa Lincoln, 151
Walton, G. M., 370
Wang, K., 82
Wang, X., *18*, 37, *197*
Warren, Earl, 161
Warschauer, M., 439
Washington, Booker T., 153
Washington, Romaine, 291
Waterhouse, L., 307
Watson, George, 41–42
Watson, John B., 128
Webb, L. D., 157
Webster, Noah, 149
Wechsler, David, 306
Wehlage, G. G., 345
Wei, X., 314
Weil, M., 356, 357, 360, 361, 386
Weinbaum, Lisa M., 185–186
Weingarten, R., 138, 386
Weinstein, 345
Weiss, B. J., 151
Wells, A. S., 268
Wessling, Sarah Brown, 337
West, M. R., 215
West v. Board of Education of City of New York, 228
West Virginia Department of Education, 167
Weston, S. P., 189
Westport Public Schools, 65
Whiren, A., 326
Whitcomb, J. A., 157
White, Byron, 238
White House, 378
White House Press Release, 75, 93, 309, 383
Wiliam, D., 402
Wilkinson-Flicker, S., *18*, 37, *166*, *197*
Willard, Emma, 148
Willard, N., 239, *249*
Willet, J. B., 393
Williams, B. F., 327
Willis, Matthew, 354
Wilson, B. L., 40, 73, 366
Wilson, M., 419
Wirt, F. M., 182
Witty, Elaine, 166
Wolf, P., 206
Wolpert-Gawron, Heather, 53
Wong, 254
Wong, C., 382
Woolfolk, 359
Wright, R. J., 385
Wurman, Z., 382

Y

Yamamoto, K., 302
Yap v. Oceanside Union Free School District, 248
Yoong, Dung, 280
Young, Cathy, 272
Young, Ella Flagg, 155
Young, M. F., 438
Yun, J. T., 275

Z

Zeichner, Noah, 8
Zelman v. Simmons-Harris, 205
Zhang, A., 82
Zhang, J., *18*, 37, *197*
Zheng, B., 439
Zhu, B., 474
Zimmer, R., 190
Zirkel, P. A., 225
Zubrzycki, J., 185
Zucker v. Panitz, 238
Zukowski, V., 361
Zych, A., 473

Subject Index

Page numbers in *italics* refer to figures, illustrations, or tables.

A

AAVE (African American Vernacular English), 264
ability grouping, 341
A Blueprint for Reform (2010), 194
academic achievement
 cooperative learning and, 343
 socioeconomic status and, 268
 technology and, 438–439
 in virtual schools, 421, 424, 425
academic freedom, 223–225
academic learning time, 345
academic mindset, 370–371
academies, 147
accelerated programs, 316
accessibility, of technology, 427
accountability
 achievement gap and, 268, 394–395
 in educational politics, 177, *177*
 of educators, 393–394
 high-stakes testing and, 12–14, 393–394
 in history of education, 162–163
 societal expectations, 17
 in standards-based education, 392
 as 21st century priority, 169
accreditation, of teacher education, 24
ACE (Adverse Childhood Experiences) Study, 79–81, *80*, 302–303, *303*
achievement gap, 166, *166*, 267–268, *267*, 394–395
ACT (American College Test), 387, 398
action zone, 340
ADD (attention deficit disorder), 312
adequate yearly progress (AYP), 13
ADHD (attention deficit hyperactivity disorder), 312
administrators
 political influence of, 176
 teacher relationships with, 468–469
Adverse Childhood Experiences (ACE) Study, 79–81, *80*, 302–303, *303*
Advocacy for Teacher Leadership (Lovett), 463
aesthetics, 111
affluent professional school, 70
African Americans
 discipline disparities in, 351
 equal educational opportunity and, 275–277
 median income, 266
 role models for students, 40–41, *41*
African American schools
 colonial, 145
 early advocate of, 159
 post-Civil War, 153
 racial segregation of, 152, 275–276
 Revolutionary period, 149
African American Vernacular English (AAVE), 264
Afrocentric schools, 276–277
AFT (American Federation of Teachers), 58, 154
After-School Plus (A+) Program, 93
Age of Enlightenment, 141–142
A Grammatical Institute of the English Language (Webster), 149
Alabama, 95
a la carte model, of blended learning, 416
Alaska Native Cultural Charter School, 282
Alaskan Natives, 280–282
allocated time, 345
alternate assessments, 403
alternative (authentic) assessments, 398
alternative curricula, 92
alternative schools, 35, 91–92, 316
alternative teacher certification, 25
alternative teaching, 476
Amendments to the Individuals with Disabilities Education Act (IDEA 97), 318, 321
American College Test (ACT), 387, 398
American Federation of Teachers (AFT), 58, 154
American Revolution, 147
American Spelling Book (Webster), 149
analytic rubric, 407, *407*
Arkansas, 181
art teachers, 38
ASCD, 59
Asian Americans
 equal educational opportunity for, 278–280
 median income, 266
 population, 260, *261*, 278
assertive discipline, 352, *353*
assessments
 authentic (alternative), 398
 challenges of, 386–387
 classroom assessment, 385
 defined, 385
 development of, 404–406
 effective classroom, *395*
 evaluation in, 397
 formal and informal, 395–396
 formative evaluation, 397
 measurement in, 396–397
 quantitative and qualitative, 396
 scoring rubrics for, 406–408
 standardized, 387–392
 in successful schools, 68
 summative evaluation, 397
 trends in, 397–404
assets, external vs. internal, 304
assistive technology, for special needs students, 327–328
ATLAS video library, 449
at-risk students
 drop-out rates, 75, *75*
 identifying, 74–76
 intervention programs for, 86–94
 mindset of, 75–76
 social problems affecting, 77–86, *80*, *81*, *82*, *85*
attention deficit disorder (ADD), 312
attention deficit hyperactivity disorder (ADHD), 312
authentic (alternative) assessments, 398
authentic learning tasks, 344–345, *344*
authority, as knowledge base, 110
autism, 311, *311*
autograded quizzes, 405
autonomy criteria, for professional status, 51–52
Avalon (St. Paul, Minnesota), 211
axiology, 110
AYP (adequate yearly progress), 13

B

back-to-basics movement, 163
beginning teachers. *See also* teachers
 attrition in, 459–460
 induction programs, 460, *461*
 mentors for, 461–462
 problems and concerns of, 460
behaviorism, 128–129, *131*
behaviorist approach, to classroom management, 355
behavior modification, *356*
benchmarks (indicators), 378
Betty Shabazz International Charter School (Chicago), 275
between-class ability grouping, 341
BIA (Bureau of Indian Affairs), 281
biculturalism, 283
Bilingual Education Act (Title VII), 162, 283
bilingual education programs. *See also* English as a second language
 pros and cons, 284
 types of, 283, *283*
Bill and Melinda Gates Foundation, 207
Black academies, 276–277

Black Lives Matter, 367
black students. *See* African Americans
The Black-White Achievement Gap (Paige, Witty), 166
blended learning, 415–416
blended schools, 422–423
block grants, 201
block scheduling, 345
A Blueprint for Reform (2010), 168
Boarding School Healing Project, 158
Boston Latin School, 145
A Brief History of Time (Hawking), 309
Bringing the Profession Back In (Fullan, Hargreaves), 462
Bring Your Own Device (BYOD), 414
Buckley Amendment, 244–245
bullying, 83–84, *85*, 249–250, *249*
Bureau of Indian Affairs (BIA), 281
business–education partnerships, 206–207
Business Roundtable, 206
BYOD (Bring Your Own Device), 414

C

CAEP (Council for the Accreditation of Educator Preparation), 22
California
  accountability initiatives, 169
  Ebonics, 264
  ELL students, 263
  incentive programs, 393
  teacher needs in, 18
California Achievement Test, 387
A Call for Common Content (Shanker Institute), 382
Can Teachers Own Their Own Schools (Vedder), 210–211
Cardinal Principles of Secondary Education (1918), 154
career ladder for teaching, 52–53, *52*
caring classroom, 336–338
categorical aid, 203
CBM (Concerned Black Men), 95
CCLCs (21st Century Community Learning Centers), 96
CCSSI (Common Core State Standards Initiative), 168, 207, 381–385
Ceasefire! (Young), 272
censorship, 238
Center of the Storm (Scopes), 223
certification and licensure
  alternative, 25
  emergency, 51
  legal rights to, 219
  NBPTS, 55
  overview of, 22
  state requirements, 24–25
  teacher involvement in, 463
character education, 299, *300*
charter schools, 34–35, 170, *170*, 208–209
Chicago Public Schools, 66
Chicanos, 277. *See also* Hispanic Americans
chief state school officer, 192
child abuse or neglect
  effects of, 79–81
  Fourth Amendment and, 229
  reporting requirements, 229–230
  signs of, *230–231*
The Child and the Curriculum (Dewey), 156
Childhood and Society (Erickson), 298
Chinese immigrants, 278–279
choice theory, 347, 354, 355
civic organization partnerships, 95
Civil Rights Act of 1964, 219
civil rights complaints, 237
CKT (Praxis Content Knowledge for Teaching Assessments), 24
classical (type S) conditioning, 128
classroom aides, 454
classroom assessment, 385
classroom climate, 332–334
classroom culture, 73–74, 332–336
classroom dynamics, 334–336
classroom management
  approaches to, 355
  in democratic classrooms, 347
  vs. discipline, 346
  discipline problems reported (2015-16), *350*
  preventive planning in, 347–349
  respect in classroom, 216–217
  responses to student behavior, 349–355
  strategies for, 346–347
classroom management approach, 355
classroom observation
  in field experiences, 448
  focused, 449
  guided by questions, 449, *450*
  instruments for, 450, *451*
  video, 448–449, *449*
classroom organization
  defined, 340
  grouping students, 341, 343
  instruction delivery, 343–345
  time usage, 345
classrooms
  caring, 336–338
  culture within, 73–74, 332–336
  democratic, 347
  flipped, 424–425
  gender-fair, 272–273
  inclusive, 325–328
  multiage or multigrade, 31
  physical environments, 72–73, 339–340, *340*
  rules and procedures for, 348
  video cameras in, 245
Clintondale High School (Michigan), 425
"Closing the Door on Innovation," 382
code of ethics, 55
cognitive development, 295–297, *296*, *297*
cognitive science, 129
collaboration
  for building learning community, 469–473
  collaborative consultation, 326
  co-teaching, 476, *476*
  dimensions of, 472, *472*
  PBS Educator Collaborative, 473
  peer coaching, 473–474
  professional development, 474
  team teaching, 475–476
  web-based, 432–433, *433*
collective bargaining, 222
collegiality
  for building learning community, 468
  in successful schools, 68
collegial support team (CST), 475–476
colonial education, 138–139, *139*, 142–146
Colorado, 378
Columbine High School shootings, 240, 299
Commission on the Reorganization of Secondary Education, 154
Committee of Fifteen, 154
Committee of Ten, 154
Common Core State Standards Initiative (CCSSI), 168, 207, 381–385
common schools, 150–152
communication skills, 335
communication technology, 432–433, *433*
communities of practice (COPs), 440
community-based partnerships, 94–95
community schools, 89–90
compensatory education programs, 90–91
complex trauma, 79
compulsory education, 145, 152–155
computers, computer labs, 426–427
Concerned Black Men (CBM), 95
concrete operations stage, *296*
condom-distribution programs, 246–247
confidentiality of records, 321
connected learning, 440
Connecticut, 400
constructive assertiveness, 351–352, 355
constructivism, 103–104, *104*, 129–130, *131*
constructivist teaching, 358
consulting teachers, 326
content integration, in multicultural education, 288, *288*
content standards, 378
cooperative learning, 341, 343, *356*
COPs (communities of practice), 440

copyright laws, 231–234
Core Knowledge Foundation, 116
corporal punishment, 247–248
corporate-education partnerships, 95–96
corporate sector political influence, 176
co-teaching, 476, *476*
Council for the Accreditation of Educator Preparation (CAEP), 22
craft knowledge, teachers', 47
Creating a Culture of Support for Teacher Leaders (Gornik, Sanford), 463
crime, in schools, 82–84
criterion-referenced assessments, 391–392
critical pedagogy, 124–125
cross-age tutoring, 361
cross-cultural competence, modeling, 41–42
CST (collegial support team), 475–476
Cuban, Larry, 210
cultural capital, 105
cultural diversity
  in caring classroom, 336–338
  cultural identity and, 262, 263–268
  increase in, 260–261, *261*
  modeling cross-cultural competence, 41–42
  religious pluralism and, 268, *269*
  stereotyping and racism, 263
  in students vs. teachers, 19, *19*
Cultural Literacy (Hirsch), 116
culturally responsive teaching, 289, *290*
cultural pluralism, 262
cultural preservation, 282
culture, defined, 262. *See also* classroom culture; school culture
curricula
  to address racism, 367
  alternative, 91–92
  curriculum alignment, 380
  curriculum framework, 380–381, *381*
  defined, 364
  development of, 373–375
  in educational politics, 176–177, *177*
  Great Books curriculum, 115
  influences on, 375–377, *376*
  multicultural, 289–292
  Native American identity in, 158
  noncognitive skills in, *369*, 370–373
  standards and, 377–381
  student success and, 368
  teacher's beliefs about, 106–107
  types of, 364–368, *365*
cyberbullying, 83–84, *85*, 249–250, *249*

D

DACA (Deferred Action for Childhood Arrivals), 237
dame schools, 144
DC Opportunity Scholarship Program (OSP), 205–206
deaf-blindness, 311
Deferred Action for Childhood Arrivals (DACA), 237
deficit thinking, 105
democratic classrooms, 347
departmentalization, 73
departments of education
  federal, 195
  state, 191–192
desegregation, 161, 275
Developing Futures in Education program, 207
development, defined, 295. *See also* stages of development
differentiation, 21
Different Voice (Gilligan), 299
digital devices, 426–427
Digital Millennium Copyright Act (DMCA), 231
digital portfolios, 429
digital use divide, 419–420, *419*
direct instruction, 357
disabled (term), 309
discipline
  vs. classroom management, 346
  disparities in, 351
  problems reported (2015–16), *350*
discovery learning, 360
dismissal of teachers, 221–223
District of Columbia School Choice Incentive Act, 205
diversity. *See* cultural diversity; equal educational opportunity; *specific groups*
divine revelation, as knowledge base, 110
DMCA (Digital Millennium Copyright Act), 231
dress codes, 239–240
drop-out prevention, 274
drop-out rates, 75, *75*, 78
drug abuse, in students, 81–82, *81*, *82*
drug testing, 243
DuBois, W. E. B., 154
due process
  corporal punishment, 247
  IEPs or ability evaluations, 321
  search and seizure, 242–243
  suspension and expulsion, 240–242, *241*
  tenure and dismissal, 221–223
Duncan, Arnie, 8
DuSable High School (Illinois), 71–72
dyscalculia, 313
dyslexia, 313

E

early childhood education, 30
Early Head Start, 201
EarthEcho Water Challenge, 123
Ebonics, 264
ECIA (Education Consolidation and Improvement Act), 201
educational malpractice, 253
educational philosophy
  development of, 131
  eclectic, 131, *132*
  educational beliefs in, 103–107, *103*, *104*
  importance to teachers, 101–102
  orientations to teaching in, 113–126, *113*, *126*
  philosophical branches and, 108–112
  philosophic inventory, *132–134*
  psychological orientations in, 127–130, *131*
  school statement of, 102
educational politics
  defined, 176
  dimensions of, 176–177, *177*
  in inequitable funding, 202–203
  influences on schools, *175*
educational reform movement, 164, *164*
educational theory and research
  political influence of, 176
  teacher knowledge of, 46–47
Education Amendments Act Title IX, 163, 271
Education and Freedom (Rickover), 160
Education and Sociology (Durkheim), 64
education–business coalitions, 206–207
Education Consolidation and Improvement Act (ECIA), 201
Education for All Handicapped Children Act, 163, 317
Education Nation Summit, 53
EEOA (Equal Educational Opportunity Act), 283
Elementary and Secondary Education Act (ESEA), 90, 162
elementary school teachers, 30–31
Elementary Spelling Book (Webster), 149
ELLs. *See* English language learners
ELT (expanded learning time) schools, 93–94
email, and copyright law, 232
emergency certification, 51
eMINTS (Enhancing Missouri's Instructional Networked Teaching Strategies), 474
emotional intelligence, 308
empiricism, as knowledge base, 110
Employment Non-Discrimination Act (ENDA), 220
English as a second language (ESL)
  bilingual programs, 283, *283*, 284
  increase in, 36
  language learning vs. acquisition in, 286
  monolingual teachers of, 284–286
  program types, 283
  training in, 38
English language learners (ELLs)
  cultural identity in, 263–264, *264*
  meeting needs of, 283–286

Spanish-speaking students, 277–278
teaching, 37–38
English Language Unity Act, 277
English-only laws, 277
Enhancing Missouri's Instructional Networked Teaching Strategies (eMINTS), 474
enriched virtual model, of blended learning, 416
entitlements, 201
epistemology, 109–110
e-portfolios, 48
equal educational opportunity
African Americans, 275–277
Alaskan Natives, 280–282
Asian Americans, 278–280
exceptional learners, 325–326
gender differences and, 271–274
goal of, 66–67
Hispanic Americans, 277–278
legislation for, 66–67, 163
LGBTQ students, 274
most discriminated groups, 270
multicultural education and, 288–289
Native Americans, 280–282
Equal Educational Opportunity Act (EEOA), 283
Equal Protection Clause, 236
equity pedagogy, in multicultural education, 288, *288*
equity plans, 11
ESEA (Elementary and Secondary Education Act), 90, 162
ESL. *See* English as a second language
ESSA. *See* Every Student Succeeds Act
essentialism, 116–118, *126*
essential service criteria, for professional status, 53
ethics
dilemmas in, 217–218
legal responsibilities and, 215–216
NEA code of ethics, 55, 215
philosophy branch concerned with, 110–111
as professional status criteria, 55, *56*
ethnicity, defined, 265. *See also* racial and ethnic groups
Evaluation of Evidence-Based Practices in Online Learning (U.S. Dept. of Education), 437
Every Student Succeeds Act (ESSA)
accountability in, 169
effect on IDEA, 321
equal opportunity education and, 66–67
vs. NCLB, 13–14, 169
provisions of, 11, 51, 194, 202, 283, 377
Title I entitlements, 90, 201
as 21st century priority, 169
evolution vs. creationism
academic freedom and, 223–224
religious expression and, 251
excellence in education, as 21st century priority, 166–167
exceptional learners. *See* gifted and talented students; special needs students
executive elite schools, 70
existentialism, 120–122, *126*
exit exams, 393
expanded learning time (ELT) schools, 93–94
expenditures, public schools, 196, *196, 197, 199*
experience criteria, for professional status, 52–53
explicit curriculum, 365
expulsion, 240–242, *241*
external assets, 304
extracurricular/cocurricular programs, 92–93, 367–368

F

Facebook, 244
fair-use doctrine, 231, 233
Family Educational Rights and Privacy Act (FERPA), 244–245
federal government
in educational politics, 176
education funding by, 201
role in education, 193–196
female seminaries, 148
feminist pedagogy, 125–126
FERPA (Family Educational Rights and Privacy Act), 244–245
field experiences, 448
Fifth Report (Mann), 150
50 Myths and Lies That Threaten America's Public Schools (Berliner, Glass), 388–391, 424
50 Strategies for Teaching English Language Learners (Herrell, Jordan), 286
Filipino immigrants, 279
finances of schools
equity reforms, 203
expenditures, 196, *196, 197, 199*
Great Recession effects on, 196
inequitable funding, 197, 201–203
private sector funds, 206–207
public sector funds, 197–201, *198*
revenues by source, *200*
school buildings and, 207–208
school choice and, 204
vertical equity in, 203–204
voucher systems, 204–206
fine arts resources, 434
flex model, of blended learning, 415
flipped classrooms, 424–425
Flip Your Classroom (Bergmann, Sams), 425
Florida
accountability of schools, 392
community support in, 94
high-stakes tests, 13
social networking guidelines, 234
teacher needs in, 18
formal assessments, 395–396
formal operations stage, *296*
formative evaluation, 397
for-profit schools, 209–210
Fourth Amendment, 229, 242
Frames of Mind (Gardner), 307
Freedmen's Bureau, 153
freedom of expression, 237–240
fringe benefits, 12
full-funding programs, 203
full inclusion, 322–323
funding. *See* finances of schools
funds of knowledge, 105
Future City competition, 398–399

G

Gage Park High School (Chicago), 372
gang activity, 82, *82*
gay and lesbian students. *See* LGBTQ issues
GE Foundation, 207
gender bias, 271–274
gender differences
discipline disparities, 351
equal educational opportunity and, 271–274
moral reasoning, 299
technology and engineering literacy, 273–274, *273*
gender-fair classrooms, 272–273
gender identity
employment and, 219, 220
student discrimination and, 274
General Mills Foundation, 95
GFE (Grantmakers for Education), 206
G.I. Bill of Rights, 159, 193
gifted and talented students
equal educational opportunity for, 325–326
labeling of, 309–310
meeting needs of, 315–317
Gilligan, Carol, 299
Good Readers (film), 434
governance of schools. *See* school governance
governments, 176. *See* federal government; state governments
governors, 190
graduation rates, in virtual schools, 424, 425
A Grammatical Institute of the English Language (Webster), *134*
Grantmakers for Education (GFE), 206
Great Books curriculum, 115
Great Society program, 162
Greco-Roman education, 139–140
grievances, 222–223

grit, 370
group development, 335, *335*
grouping methods, in classroom organization, 341
group investigation, 360–361
group IQ tests, 306
GW Community School (Springfield, Virginia), 211

H

handicapped (term), 309
Hartville Elementary School (Missouri), 474
Harvey Milk School (New York), 274
"Have Smartphones Destroyed a Generation?" (Twenge), 437
Hawaii
- After-School Plus (A+) Program, 93
- portfolio requirements, 400

Head Start, 201
hearing impairments, 310, *311*
heterogeneous (mixed-ability) grouping, 341
hidden (implicit) curriculum, 365–366
hierarchy of needs (Maslow), 301–302, *301*
highly qualified teachers (HQTs), 20
High School (Boyer), 164
high school teachers, 32
high-stakes testing, 12–14, *14*, 392–395
Hinkley High School (Colorado), 353–354
Hispanic Americans
- equal educational opportunity for, 277–278
- median income, 266
- population, 260, *261*

history of education
- Age of Enlightenment, 141–142
- ancient Greece, 139–140
- ancient Rome, 140
- colonial America, 142–146
- common schools, 150–152
- compulsory education, 152–155
- educational reform movement, 164, *164*
- European influences, 138–139, *139*
- importance of, 138
- Middle Ages to Renaissance, 140–141
- modern postwar era, 160–164, *160*
- progressive era, 155–159
- Revolutionary period, 147–150
- timeline, *165*
- World War II impact, 159

HIV/AIDS, 246
holistic rubrics, 407, *407*
homelessness, 78, 185–186
homeschooling, 254–255
hornbooks, 144
How Gertrude Teaches Her Children (Pestalozzi), 142
How Schools Shortchange Girls (AAUW), 272
How to Make a Curriculum (Bobbitt), 373
HQTs (highly qualified teachers), 20
humanism, 127
humanist approach, to classroom management, 355
humanistic psychology, 127–128, *131*
hybrid teachers, 466
Hyde Schools (Woodstock, Connecticut), 299–300

I

IBM MentorPlace, 96
IDEA (Individuals with Disabilities Education Act), 310–311, *311*, 317–318, 321
IDEA 97 (Amendments to the Individuals with Disabilities Education Act), 318, 321
IEP (individualized education program), 36, 316, 320–321, *320*
Illinois, 70–71
immigrants
- Asian, 278–280
- demographics, 260–261, *261*, 278–279
- in history of education, 157–158
- migrant farm workers, 277
- undocumented parents, 236–237, 261–262, *262*

implicit (hidden) curriculum, 365–366
incentive programs, and high-stakes tests, 393
inclusion, of special needs students, 163, 318, 321–324
income, by race, 266, *266*
income taxes, as funding source, 199
independent study, 316
Indiana, 242
Indian Education Act (1972, 1974), 281
Indian schools, 149–150
indicators (benchmarks), 378
Indicators of School Crime and Safety (Musu-Gillette), 82
individualized education program (IEP), 36, 316, 320–321, *320*
individual racism, 263
Individuals with Disabilities Education Act (IDEA), 310–311, *311*, 317–318, 321
induction programs, 460, *461*
informal assessments, 395–396
information processing, 358–359
inquiry learning, 360
institutional racism, 202, 263
instruction
- child development based, 357–358
- delivery of, 343–345
- direct instruction, 357
- models of, *356*
- peer-mediated, 360–361
- planning and organizing, 348–349
- software resources, 429–430, *429*
- thinking process based, 358–360, *359*

instructional software, 429–430, *429*
InTASC (Interstate Teacher Assessment and Support Consortium), 22
integrated curriculum, 375
intellectual disability, 310, *311*
intelligence
- defined, 306
- learning styles and, 308
- multiple, 307–308, *307*
- testing, 306

intelligent design (ID), 252
internal assets, 304
international assessments, 388–391
Internet connectivity, 426, 443
Internet use, and copyright law, 232–235
Interstate Teacher Assessment and Support Consortium (InTASC), 22
intuition, as knowledge base, 110
Iowa standards, 378–379
Iowa Test of Basic Skills, 387, 398
ISTEM project, 282
IT support, 427–428

J

James Madison High School (Bennett), 164
Japanese immigrants, 279
job outlook, 17–20, 117, *117*
Joplin Plan, 341
journal writing, in student teaching, 454–456
joy of teaching, 5–6

K

K[12] Inc., 210
Kennedy Middle School (Eugene, Oregon), 301
Kent School District (Washington), 440
Kentucky Education Reform Act (KERA), 189
Kentucky school inadequacy ruling, 188–189
KERA (Kentucky Education Reform Act), 189
kindergarten, 152–153
King, Marissa, 15
knowledge
- as criteria for professional status, 54–55
- philosophy branch concerned with, 109–110

knowledge construction, in multicultural education, 288, *288*

L

Lancasterian system, 142
language. *See also* English as a second language; English language learners
- in cultural identity, 263–264, *264*
- Native American, 281
- in professional development, 475
- Spanish-speaking students, 277–278
- in special education, 309

language arts resources, 434
Lanham Act (1941), 159, 193
Latin grammar school, 145
Latinos, 277. *See also* Hispanic Americans
LD (learning disabilities), 310, 311–313, *311*
leadership
in successful schools, 67
in teachers, 462–466, *465*
learning community
relationships in, 466–469
teacher collaboration in, 469–476
learning disabilities (LD), 310, 311–313, *311*
learning environment
caring classroom, 336–338, *339*
classroom organization, 341–345
physical environment, 339–340, *340*
learning style preferences, 308
least restrictive environment, 318
legal rights and responsibilities
changing nature of, 255
ethics and, 215–216
immigrant students, 236–237
of parents, 244–245, 251–252
of school districts, 247–255
of students, 235–247, *235*
of student teachers, 225–226, *226*
teachers' responsibilities, 226–235, *227*
teachers' rights, 218–225, *218*
Lemon test, 251
LGBTQ issues
employment discrimination, 219
equal educational opportunity, 274
sexual harassment, 248
liberal arts, of Renaissance period, 141, *141*
Life in Classrooms (Jackson), 6
Listening to Urban Kids (Wilson), 40
Litchfield Female Academy, 147–148
literacy rights, 253–254
local political influence, 176
local school boards, 179–181
local school districts, 179, *179, 180*
logic, 111–112
logical analysis, as knowledge base, 110
long-term memory, 359
Lost Boys (Garbarino), 74
Louisiana
innovative school governance, 185
social media law, 234

M

magnet schools, 35, 316
mainstreaming law, 163, 318, 321–323
making, web-based content for, 432–433, *433*
malpractice, 229, 253
Man's Most Dangerous Myth (Montagu), 265
Marjory Stoneman Douglas High School (Florida), 467
Massachusetts
anti-discrimination policy, 274
expanded learning time program, 93–94
Massachusetts Act (1642), 145–146
mastery learning, 357
mathematics resources, 434–435
mayoral control, in school governance, 185
McGuffey readers, 151
McKinney-Vento Homeless Assistance Act, 78
meditation skills, 371–373
memoriter, 145
mentorship programs
for beginning teachers, 461–462
community-based volunteer, 95
student peer-mentoring, 88–89
metaphysics, 108
Metropolitan Achievement Tests, 387
Metropolitan Federation of Alternative Schools (MFAS), 95–96
microteaching, 452
Middle Ages, 140
middle-class schools, 69–70
middle school teachers, 31–32
Migrant and Seasonal Head Start, 201
migrant farm workers, 277
mindfulness skills, 371–373
Minnesota
charter school legislation, 208
corporate-education partnerships, 95–96
mixed-ability (heterogeneous) grouping, 341
mobile learning, 428–429
modeling, in instruction, 357–358
Models of Teaching (Joyce, Weil, & Calhoun), 356, 473
monitorial system, 142
monopoly of services criteria, for professional status, 50–51
Montessori method, 157
moral development, 298–301, *300*
Morrill Land-Grant Act, 152
Mott Hall School (New York City), 404
Mountlake Terrace High School (Washington State), 404
multiage classrooms, 31
multicultural education
culturally responsive teaching in, 289, *290*
curricula, 289–292
defined, 287
dimensions of, 288, *288*
multiculturalism, 287
multigrade classrooms, 31
multiple disabilities, 310, *311*
multiple intelligences, 307–308, *307*
music teachers, 38
Myron B. Thompson Academy (Hawaii), 422
The Myth That Schools Shortchange Girls (Kleinfeld), 272

N

NAEP (National Assessment of Educational Progress), 166, *166*, 388
NASSMC (National Alliance of State Science and Mathematics Coalitions), 206
National Alliance of State Science and Mathematics Coalitions (NASSMC), 206
National Assessment of Educational Progress (NAEP), 166, *166*, 388
National Association of State Directors of Teacher Education and Certification's (NASDTEC), 25
National Board for Professional Teaching Standards (NBPTS), 22, 55, 463
National Center for Education Statistics, *267*
National Charter School Study 2013 (Stanford University), 209
National Defense Education Act of 1958, 160–161
National Education Association (NEA), 55, 57–58, 154, 215
National Governors' Association (NGA), 190
A Nation at Risk, 164, 195
Native American Community Academy, 282
Native Americans
educational history, 145, 149–150, 158
equal educational opportunity, 280–282
teachers and curricula, 158
NBPTS (National Board for Professional Teaching Standards), 22, 55, 463
NCLB. *See* No Child Left Behind
NEA (National Education Association), 55, 57–58, 154, 215
needs theory, 301–302, *301*
negligence, 228–229
New England Primer, 144–145
New Jersey, 69–70
Newsome Park Elementary School (Virginia), 404
New York
accountability initiatives, 169
suspensions, 242
New York City school system
incentive programs, 394
innovative school governance, 185
size of, 179
NGA (National Governors' Association), 190

No Child Left Behind (NCLB) Act, 13, 51, 183–184, 194
noncognitive skills, *369*
nondirective teaching, *356*
nondiscrimination
students' rights, 245–246
teachers' rights, 219–220
nonteaching tasks, 12
normal schools, 151
norm-referenced assessments, 391
North Carolina, 191
North Dakota, 378
Northwest Ordinance (1785), 146
Not School model, 421
null curriculum, 366–367
nursery school education, 30

O

observation. *See* classroom observation
occupational therapists, 326
OER (open educational resources), 431
off-air recordings, 232
Ohio, 399
Old Deluder Satan Act, 146
online learning
master's degree programs, 474–475
for students, 421–424
open educational resources (OER), 431
open-space schools, 72–73
operant conditioning, 128–129
opportunity to learn (OTL), 345
orderly environment, 67
orthopedic impairments, 310, *311*
OSP (DC Opportunity Scholarship Program), 205–206
OTL (opportunity to learn), 345
out-of-school-time (OST) activities, 92–93

P

Paideia Proposal (Adler), 164
parallel teaching, 476
PARCC (Partnership for Assessment of Readiness for College and Careers), 387–388
parents
legal rights, 244–245, 246–247, 251–252
participation in school-related activities, *470*
partnerships with, 326–327
political influence of, 176
role in school governance, 182
teacher relationships with, 469
undocumented immigrants, 236–237, 261–262, *262*
parochial schools, 34, 144
Partnership for Assessment of Readiness for College and Careers (PARCC), 387–388
partnerships
community-based, 94–95
corporate-education, 95–96, 206–207
with parents, 326–327
passion, for teaching profession, 5–6
PBL (project-based learning), 386, 403–404
PBS Educator Collaborative, 473
PDEFE (Professional Dispositions Evaluation for Field Experiences), 454, *455*
pedagogical expertise, 46
Pedagogy of the Oppressed (Freire), 125
peer assessments, 400–401
peer coaching, 473–474
peer-counseling programs, 88–89
Peer Group Connection (PGC), 89
peer-mediated instruction, 360
peer mediation, 89
peer-mentoring programs, 88–89
peer tutoring, 361
Pennsylvania
community support in, 95
state takeover of schools in, 190
perennialism, 113–116, *126*
performance-based assessments, 402–403
performance expectations, 379
performance standards, 379
per-pupil expenditures, 196, *197, 199*
perseverance, 370
personal injury, 227–229, *228*
personal learning network (PLN), 440
Pew Research Center, 265
PGC (Peer Group Connection), 89
Phi Delta Kappa, 58
Philadelphia Academy, 147
philosophy. *See also* educational philosophy
defined, 102
major branches of, 108–112
photocopies, 231–232
physical education teachers, 38–39
physical environment of schools, 72–73, 339–340, *340*
physical therapists, 326
PISA (Program for International Student Assessment), 388, *389–390*
planning, in classroom management, 347–349
PLCs (professional learning communities), 440
PLN (personal learning network), 440
podcasting, 342, 433
political climate. *See also* educational politics
effects on students, 237, 304
race relations and, 265
Polk County Early College (North Carolina), 422
portfolio assessments, 399–400
portfolios
professional, 457–458
student assessments, 399–400
postmodernism, 121
poverty
in at-risk students, 76, 77–78, *77*
overcoming effects of, 71–72
rates of, 265–267, *266*
in rural schools, 33
War on Poverty, 162
practica, 453–454
Praxis Series
Praxis Content Knowledge for Teaching Assessments, 24
Praxis Core, 23
Praxis Subject Assessments, 23–24
professional standards, 22
prejudice reduction, in multicultural education, 288, *288*
pre-K education, 30
preoperational thought stage, *296*
presidential policies, 194–195
prestige criteria, for professional status, 55
PRIDE program, 301
principals
roles of, 468–469
walkthroughs, 450, *451*
privacy rights, 244–245
private schools, 34, *34*
privatization movement, 208–211
The Problem of Indian Administration (1928), 158
problem solving, spontaneous, 42–43
problem-solving conferences, 354–355
problem-solving orientation, 48–49, *49*
procedures, in classroom, 348
productivity software, 428–429, *428*
profession, teaching as, *50*, 50–57
professional autonomy, 51–52
professional development, 474–475
Professional Dispositions Evaluation for Field Experiences (PDEFE), 454, *455*
professionalization of teaching, 59–60
professional learning communities (PLCs), 440
professional malpractice, 229
professional organizations
curriculum standards set by, 379–380, *380*
described, 57–59
empowerment through, 56–57
professional portfolios, 457–458
professional standards, 22, *23*
Program for International Student Assessment (PISA), 388, *389–390*
progressive movement, 155–159
progressivism, 118–120, *126*, 155
Project 10, 274
project-based learning (PBL), 386, 403–404
Promoting Grit, Tenacity, and Perseverance (Shechtman), 370
property taxes, as funding source, 198–199, 201–202, 203

Proposals Relating to the Education of Youth in Pennsylvania (Franklin), 147
prosocial values, 64
psychosocial crisis, 297
psychosocial development, 297–298, *298*
public school districts, 179, *179*
public school support, 169–170, *170*
purpose of schools, 64–66, 68

Q

qualitative assessments, 396
quantitative assessments, 396
QuestBridge, 316
Quiet Time (QT), 372
quiz-making websites, 405

R

race, defined, 265
race relations, and public perceptions, 265
Race to the Top program, 168
racial and ethnic groups
  achievement gap in, 267–268, *267*
  cultural identity, 262, 265
  demographics, 260–261
  political influence of, 176
  religious affiliations, 268, *269*
  socioeconomic status, 265–267, *266*
  stereotyping of and racism, 263
racial segregation, 152, 275–276
racism
  addressing in curricula, 367
  individual, 263
  institutional, 202, 263
RAT matrix, 420–421, *421*
reading
  Great Books curriculum, 115
  motivating reluctant readers, 114
reading and writing schools, 144–145
reason, as knowledge base, 110
recertification, 24
Recovery School District, 185
redistricting, 203
reflective teaching logs, 456–457
reflective thinking, 43–44
regional educational service agency (RESA), 192
"Reinventing Education" grant, 440
related services, for special needs students, 321
relationships. *See also* collaboration
  with administrators, 468–469
  with colleagues and staff, 468
  with parents, 469
  with students, 466–468
reliability, in classroom assessments, 406
religious expression, 250–253, *252*
religiously-affiliated schools, 34, 144
religious pluralism, 268, *269*
Renaissance, 140–141
RESA (regional educational service agency), 192
resegregation, 275–276
resource allocation, in educational politics, 176, 177, *177*
resource-room teachers, 326
response to intervention (RTI) model, 37, 318–319, *319*
restorative justice, 352–354, *354*
restructuring, 183–184
Reuters, 210
Rhode Island, 399
ripple effect, 348
Riverdeep Learning Village (RLV), 440
Riverside Virtual School (California), 422
role models, for students, 40–41, *41*
Rosa's Law, 309
rotation model, of blended learning, 415
RTI (response to intervention) model, 37, 318–319, *319*
rules, in classroom, 348
rural schools, 32–33, 70

S

salaries, 9–12, *10–11*, *34*, 55
sales taxes, as funding source, 199
SAT (Scholastic Assessment Test), 387, 398
Savage Inequalities (Kozol), 71, 384
SBAC (Smarter Balanced Assessment Consortium), 388
SBM (school-based management), 184–185
scaffolding, 358
Scholastic Assessment Test (SAT), 387, 398
School Ambassador Fellowship, 464
The School and Society (Dewey), 156
school-based management (SBM), 184–185
school boards
  local, 179–181
  state, 191
school buildings, 207–208
school choice, 204
School Choice Today (Center for Education Reform), 205
school culture
  dimensions of, 72–74
  in multicultural education, 288, *288*
school districts
  largest U.S. public, 179, *179*
  legal rights, 247–255
  organizational structure of, *180*
School for Science and Math at Vanderbilt (SSMV), 316–317
school governance
  federal government role, 193–195
  local community role, 178–185
  regional units in, 192
  state government role, 187–192
school improvement research, 68
school psychologists, 326
schools
  Afrocentric (Black academies), 276–277
  alternative, 91–92
  characteristics of successful, 67–68
  in colonial America, 144–145
  community schools, 89–90
  community settings, 32–33, 70–71
  culture within, 72–74, 288, *288*
  describing, 68
  desegregation of, 161
  enrollment projections, *18*
  funding (*See* finances of schools)
  grade-level designations, *30*, 30–32
  nontraditional settings, 34
  philosophy statements, 102
  physical environment of, 72–73, 339–340, *340*
  political influences on, *175*, *176*
  purpose and roles of, 64–66
  resegregation of, 275–276
  restructuring of, 183–184
  segregation of, 152
  social problems in, 77–86, *77*, *80*, *81*, *82*, *85*
  socioeconomic classification of, 69–70
  state takeover of, 190
School Safety Checklist, 83, *84*
school shootings
  dress codes and, 240
  patterns in, 83
  prevention of, 299, 467
school traditions, 73
school-within-a-school, 92
Science Friday, 473
science resources, 435
scientific management, 152
Scopes trial, 223–224
scoring rubrics, 406–408, *407*, *408*
screen media time, 14–15, 414, *415*
screen-recorder software, 167–168
search and seizure, 242–243
secular humanism, 127
SED (serious emotional disturbance), 310
segregation, racial, 152, 275–276
self-assessments, 401–402
self-contained classroom, 72
self-directed study, 316
self-governance criteria, for professional status, 53–54, *54*
self-knowledge, 45, 106
sensorimotor intelligence, *296*
sensory memory, 359
separation of church and state, 251
serious emotional disturbance (SED), 310
service, as teacher motivation, 8
service learning, 66

Seventh Report (Mann), 151
sex role socialization, 271
sex role stereotyping, 271
sexual discrimination, 163
sexual harassment, 248–249
sexual orientation, and employment, 219, 220
Shabazz School (Chicago), 276
The Shame of the Nation (Kozol), 70–71, 202, 384
Shortchanging Girls, Shortchanging America (AAUW), 272
Smarter Balanced Assessment Consortium (SBAC), 388
social change, school role in, 66
socialization, as school role, 64–65
social justice
  in critical pedagogy, 124
  teaching, 185–186, 245–246
social networking
  by students, 238–239
  by teachers, 234–235
social problems
  in at-risk students, 77–86, *77, 80, 81, 82, 85*
  influence on curricula, 376–377
  intervention strategies, 86–94
  partnership interventions, 94–96
social reconstructionism, 122–124, *126*
social studies resources, 435–436
socioeconomic status
  in cultural identity, 265–267, *266*
  of migrant farm workers, 277
  school classifications by, 69–70
The Sociology of Teaching (Waller), 154–155
Socrates, 111
Socratic questioning, 111–112, *112*, 140
software
  copyright and fair use of, 232
  evaluation criteria, *430*
  instructional, 429–430, *429*
  productivity, 428–429, *428*
  screen-recorder, 167–168
  word-prediction, 314–315
The Souls of Black Folks (Dubois), 154
South Carolina, 392
South Dakota, 400
Spanish-speaking students, 277–278. *See also* Hispanic Americans
special education
  defined, 317
  inclusion requirements, 163, 318, 321–324
  laws related to, 317–321
  response to intervention model, 37
special education teachers, 36–37
special-interest groups, political influence of, 176
special needs students
  assistive technology for, 327–328
  behavioral characteristics, 312
  classifications of, 309–310, *311*
  discipline disparities in, 351
  equal educational opportunity for, 325–326
  labeling of, 309
  learning disabilities in, 311–313
  in STEM education, 314
specific learning disabilities (LD), 310, 311–313, *311*
speech and language specialists, 326
speech or language impairments, 310, *311*
SSMV (School for Science and Math at Vanderbilt), 316–317
staff development, 463
staff relationships, 468
stages of development
  adolescent stress and, 303–304
  childhood stress and, 302–303
  cognitive, 295–297, *296, 297*
  moral, 298–301, *300*
  needs theory and, 301–302, *301*
  psychosocial, 297–298, *298*
  teacher's role in, *304*
standardized tests
  high-stakes testing, 12–14, *14*, 392–395
  types of, 387–392
standards-based education (SBE), 377–381
Stanford Achievement Test, 387
state aid, 199
state governments
  board of education, 191
  chief state school officer, 192
  courts, 188–190
  departments of education, 191–192
  in educational politics, 176
  education funding by, 199
  education improvement initiatives, 187
  governors, 190
  legislatures, 187–188
  school system organization, *188*
  state takeover of schools, 190
states rights, 178, 187, 224–225
state standards, 378
station teaching, 476
STEM education
  in Afrocentric school, 277
  cooperative learning for girls in, 343
  as essentialist example, 117, *117*
  Future City competition, 398–399
  for gifted and talented students, 316–317
  Indigenous learning, 282
  PBS Educator Collaborative, 473
  for special needs students, 314
  Trump memorandum on, 194–195
  in Virtual High School, 423
stereotyping
  gender, 271
  racial and ethnic, 263
stimulus–response model, 128
stress, in students
  adolescent, 303–304
  childhood, 78–81, 302–303
  political rhetoric and, 305, *305*
student-centered curriculum, 374–375
student diversity, defined, 4. *See also* cultural diversity
students
  at-risk, 74–76
  discouraged or withdrawn, 146
  diversity in (*See* cultural diversity)
  empowering, 6–7
  gifted and talented, 309–310, 315–317
  interactions in classroom, 4, 335–336, *335*
  legal rights, 235–247, *235*
  political influence of, 176
  reluctant readers, 114
  screen media time, 14–15, 414, *415*
  social problems in, 77–86, *77, 85*
  special needs, 309–314, *311*, 325–328, 351
  teacher relationships with, 466–468
  teacher's beliefs about, 105–106
  teacher's knowledge of, 45
student teachers
  journal writing, 454–456
  legal rights of, 225–226, *226*
  multicultural immersion programs, 287
  reflective teaching logs, 456–457
  requirements of, 454, *455*
student variability, 4
subcultures, 262
subject-centered curriculum, 374–375
subject matter
  digital resources, 433–436
  subject-specialty teachers, 35–39, *36*
  teacher knowledge of, 46
  teacher passion for, 5
substance abuse, in students, 81–82, *82*
substitute teaching, 458–459, *459*
suburban schools, 33, 70–71
suicide, 86
summative evaluation, 397
superintendents, 181–182
suspension, 240–242, *241*

T

taxpayers, political influence of, 176
tax reform, 203. *See also* property taxes, as funding source
teacher education programs
  classroom experiences in, 452–454
  classroom observation in, 448–451, *450, 451*
  graduate-level, 474–475
  for licensure, 24
  normal schools, 151
  online degree programs, 474–475

professional portfolios, 457–458
as professional status criteria, 52–53, *52*
teacher involvement in, 463
technology training in, 442
teacher expectations, in successful schools, 67
teacher leaders, 59–60, 463–464
Teacher Leadership (Katyal, Evers), 463
Teacher Leadership in Professional Development Schools (Hunzicker), 463
teacher-owned schools, 210–211
teacherpreneur, 466
teachers. *See also* beginning teachers
administrator relationships, 468–469
attrition rate, 459
autonomy of, 51–52
certification and licensure, 22, 24–25, 51, 55, 219
in collaborative consultation, 326
collegiality in, 68, 468
in colonial America, 143
diversity in, 19, *19–20*
elementary school, 30–31
high school, 32
influence in hiring process, 54
influence on students, 3–5, 7–8
knowledge and skills needed, 45–49
leadership roles, 59–60, 462–466, *465*
legal responsibilities, 226–235, *227*
legal rights, 218–225, *218*
middle school, 31–32
Native American, 158
in nontraditional schools, 34–35
number in U.S. public schools, 29, *29*
parent relationships, 469
political influence of, 176
preferred qualities in hiring, 5
pre-K, 30
professional standards, 22, *23*
in public school settings, 32–33
qualities in effective, *333*
as role models, 40–41
as spontaneous problem solvers, 42–43
student interactions, 4, 335–336, *335*
student relationships, 466–468
subject-specialty, 35–39, *36*
substitutes, 458–459, *459*
technology acceptance, 417, *417*
technology support for, 440–442
thought processes, 43–44, *44*
teacher's aides, 454
teachers' craft knowledge, 47
teacher strikes, 223
teacher supply and demand, 17
Teaching 2030 (Berry), 466
Teaching Ambassador Fellows, 60
teaching and teaching methods
collaboration in, 469–473
co-teaching, 476, *476*
culturally responsive, 289, *290*
dimensions of, 39–44
ELL students, 283–286
flipped teaching, 424–425
gifted and talented students, 315–317
instructional methods, 357–361
instructional models, *356*
instruction delivery, 343–345
peer coaching, 473–474
reluctant readers, 114
team teaching, 475–476
time usage, 345
transmission vs. constructivist view, 103–104, *104*
teaching certificates, 22. *See also* certification and licensure
teaching contracts, 220–221
teaching profession
benefits of, 9–12
challenges of, 12–15
induction into, 460, *461*
job outlook, 17–20, 117, *117*
professionalization of, 59–60, 154
professional organizations of, 57–59
professional status of, *50*, 50–57
reasons for choosing, 3–9, *4*, *9*
societal expectations of, 16–17
teaching simulations, 452–453
Teaching to Transgress (hooks), 125–126
TeachLivE (TLE), 452–453
teaming, 476
team teaching, 475–476
TechMatrix, 327–328
techno-librarian, 471
technology and engineering literacy (TEL), 273–274, *273*
technology integration
accessibility of, 427
blended learning, 415–416
blended schools, 422–423
as challenge, 14–15
connectivity for, 426
devices for, 426–427
digital use divide, 419–420, *419*
effects on students and learning, 436–439
future of, 439–440
infrastructure for, 425, *426*, 442–443, *443*
IT support for, 427–428
RAT matrix, 420–421, *421*
as required teacher knowledge, 47–48
software and content, 428–433
subject area resources, 433–436
teacher and student roles and, 418
teachers' acceptance of, 417, *417*
teacher training in, 440–442
virtual schools, 421–424, *422*
technology tools
autograded quizzes, 405
digital portfolios, 429
e-protfolios, 48
mobile learning, 428–429
online degree programs, 474–475
podcasting, 342, 433
screen-recorder software, 167–168
as teaching challenge, 14–15
text-to-speech programs, 285–286
Twitter, 177–178
video editing, 65
virtual labs, 233
virtual worlds, 183–184
web conferencing, 107–108
wikis, 16
word-prediction software, 314–315
teen pregnancy, 84–85, 246
TEL (technology and engineering literacy), 273–274, *273*
tenacity, 370
Tennessee, 185
Tennessee Virtual Academy, 424
tenure, 221–222
TEP (The Equity Project Charter School), 9
Texas
expanded learning time program, 93
high-stakes tests, 13
textbooks
in history of education, 149
influence on curricula, 376–377
state adoption systems, 191
text-to-speech (TTS) programs, 285–286
Theisen, Toni, 15
theory into practice, *356*
Threat Assessment in Schools (Fein), 83
Through Ebony Eyes (Thompson), 264
time on task, 345
Title I programs, 90–91, 201
Title VII (Bilingual Education Act), 162
Title IX of the Education Amendments Act, 163, 271
TLE (TeachLivE), 452–453
tort liability, 227–229, *228*
tracking (grouping method), 341
traditions, in school culture, 73
transgender students. *See* LGBTQ issues
transmission perspective, 103–104, *104*
trauma, childhood, 78–81, *80*
trauma-sensitive schools, 87–88, *88*
Troy Seminary, 148
Turning Points (Carnegie Council on Adolescent Development), 164
Tuskegee Institute, 153
tutoring, peer and cross-age, 361
21st Century Community Learning Centers (CCLCs), 96
21st-century education, 165–171
Twitter, 177–178

Tyler rationale, 374
type S (classical) conditioning, 128

U

unexpected underachievement, 318
Up from Slavery (Washington), 153
urban schools, 33, 70–71

V

validity, in classroom assessments, 405–406
value-added modeling, 13
values
  influence on curricula, 375–376
  philosophy branch concerned with, 110
  teaching, 64, 149
Vermont, 440
vertical equity, 203–204
VHS (Virtual High School) Inc., 423
video cameras, in classrooms, 245
video editing, 65
video observation, 448–449, *449*
Village Green Virtual Charter School (Rhode Island), 423
violence, in schools, 82–84
Virtual High School (VHS) Inc., 423
virtual labs, 232, 233
Virtual Opportunities Inside a School Environment (VOISE) Academy (Chicago), 422
virtual schools, 421–424, *422*
virtual worlds, 183–184
visual impairments, 310
visual mapping, 109
vocational education teachers, 38
VOISE (Virtual Opportunities Inside a School Environment) Academy (Chicago), 422
voucher systems, 170, *170*, 204–206

W

walkthroughs, 450, *451*
War on Poverty, 162
Washington, D.C.
  community support in, 95
  innovative school governance, 185
Washington State
  community support in, 94
  high-stakes tests, 12–13
  teacher technology support, 440
web-based educational content, 430–431, *431*
web conferencing, 107–108
WEEA (Women's Educational Equity Act), 271
West Virginia
  excellence initiative, 166–167
  school board training, 181
  teacher technology support, 440
Westwood Cyber High School (Detroit), 421
Where the Girls Are (AAUW), 272
Who Stole Feminism (Sommers), 272
wikis, 16
within-class ability grouping, 341
with-it-ness, 348
women. *See also* gender bias; gender differences
  anti-discrimination legislation, 163, 271
  education history of, 147–148, 151
  equal educational opportunity for, 271–274
  role in history of education, 154–155
Women's Educational Equity Act (WEEA), 271
word-prediction software, 314–315
work habits, 396
working-class schools, 69
working hours, as challenge, 12
working memory, 359
World War II, 159
wraparound services, 86, *87*
Write On magazine, 78–79
writing, as coping device, 78–79
Wyoming, 378

Y

year-round schooling, 94
Young Geniuses Academy (Seattle), 277

Z

zero tolerance policies, 351
zone of proximal development, 358